WEST ACADEMIC PUBLISHING'S LAW SCHOOL ADVISORY BOARD

WHITE COLLAR CRIME

LAW AND PRACTICE

Fourth Edition

■ ■ ■

by

Jerold H. Israel

Alene and Allan F. Smith Professor of Law Emeritus,
University of Michigan Law School
Ed Rood Eminent Scholar Emeritus,
University of Florida, Levin College of Law

Ellen S. Podgor

Gary R. Trombley Family White-Collar Crime Research Professor
Professor of Law
Stetson University College of Law

Paul D. Borman

Judge, United States District Court for the
Eastern District of Michigan

Peter J. Henning

Professor of Law
Wayne State University Law School

AMERICAN CASEBOOK SERIES®

WEST ACADEMIC PUBLISHING

444 Cedar Street, Suite 700
St. Paul, MN 55101
1-877-888-1330

Printed in the United States of America

ISBN: 978-0-314-28358-0

Dedicated To:

Florence & Harry Israel

Joel R. Podgor

Sarah & Tom Borman

Karen M. Henning

Preface

This course grew out of materials originally prepared for a seminar jointly taught by Paul Borman and Jerry Israel at the University of Michigan Law School. The objective of that seminar was to take a narrow slice of criminal justice practice - the investigation and prosecution of white collar crime in the federal system - and apply to it what is commonly described as a "transactional" analysis. We wanted the students to appreciate how the practice was impacted by the interaction of legal doctrines that traditionally were taught in a wide range of separate law school courses. In the field of white collar crime, they would see how the legal transactions involved in a single case often required consideration of substantive criminal law, criminal procedure, administrative procedure, corporate law, evidence, civil procedure, sentencing law, and even highly specialized regulatory law. We also wanted students to appreciate the influence of administrative policies (in particular, the Department of Justice's internal guidelines) and the influence of the basic "culture" of white collar criminal practice.

Since these materials are designed for a course on White Collar Crime, they are more comprehensive than the Michigan seminar materials, but in large part, the basic objectives remain the same. Accordingly, we utilize a combination of traditional materials (cases and statutes) and not-so-traditional materials (e.g., newspaper articles, forms, and practice manuals). We have sought to keep to a minimum our own shaping of the discussion of these materials. Our "Notes and Questions" contain many more notes than questions, and most of the questions are designed simply to suggest the relevance of additional material.

The conversion of the original Michigan seminar materials into a full fledged set of course materials came about with the addition of Ellen S. Podgor to this project, who added several chapters and filled in gaps in others. In writing the Second Edition we were fortunate to have Peter Henning joining us to add new materials and reshape some of the older material. Now in the Fourth Edition we again offer a statutory and document supplement that accompanies this casebook. There is also a website that provides classroom and other resource materials. It can be found at http://whitecollarcriminallawbook.com/. Prior to this edition a *Hornbook on White Collar Crime* was written. Throughout this casebook we cite to this hornbook as WCH.

Notwithstanding the editorial efforts of all of us, we are sure that there are flaws here and there, and hope that the reader will call them to our attention so that they can be corrected in future editions.

Far too many people assisted us in this venture to list them all. The product was enhanced by discussions with many colleagues. We would like to thank, in particular, Nancy King of Vanderbilt Law School, who used an earlier version of those materials and pointed us in the direction of some needed cuts and additions. We also thank Eli Lederman of Tel Aviv University Faculty of Law, who provided a much needed encouragement in initially bringing about this project. We also appreciated the response of faculty, such as Lance Cole, Lucian Dervan and students who used portions of these materials in courses we taught at the University of Alabama, University of Florida, Georgia State University, the University of Michigan, Kansas University, Stetson University, and Wayne State University.

We also thank Jessica M. Fehr, Olive Hyman, Dianne M. Oeste, Shannon Mullins, Louise Petren, Sue Stinson, and Janice Strawn. We would also like to thank research assistants Jonathan M. Adelman, Ricardo O. Gordillo, Rebecca Guinn, Robert J. Kiser, Wendy N. Kurtzer, and Sean McIlhinney and Librarians Rhea Ballard-Thrower and Joe Morris who assisted with various editions of this book.

Professors Podgor and Henning and Judge Borman add a special thank you "yet again" to Professor Jerold H. Israel for his wonderful suggestions throughout this project. He has been a teacher to all in the process of writing and editing a casebook.

J.H.I.
E.S.P.
P.D.B.
P.J.H.

June, 2015

Acknowledgments

Excerpts from the following books and articles appear with the kind permission of the copyright holders.[a]

Baxter, Andrew T., Federal Discretion in the Prosecution of Local Political Corruption, 10 Pepperdine L. Rev. 321 (1983). Reprinted from Pepperdine Law Review, Volume 10, Number 2, 1983. Copyright © 1983 by the Pepperdine University School of Law. Reprinted by permission.

Beale, Sara Sun, Bryson, William C., Felman, James E., Elston, Michael J., Grand Jury Law and Practice (2d ed.) §§ 5.11; 6.21; 9.21; 9.31 (1997). Copyright © 1997 West Group. Reprinted with permission.

Henry J. Bemporad, An Introduction to Federal Sentencing (13th Ed. 2011). Reprinted with permission.

Bradley, Craig M., Foreward: Mail Fraud After McNally and Carpenter: The Essence of Fraud, 79 J. of Crim. L. & Crim. 573 (1988). Reprinted by special permission of Northwestern University School of Law, Journal of Criminal Law and Criminology, Vol. 79, Issue 3, pp. 573, 586-89, 592, 593, 595, 602-603, (1989).

Brickey, Kathleen F., Criminal Mischief: The Federalization of American Criminal Law, 46 Hastings L. J. 1135, 1172 (1995). Copyright © 1995 by the University of California, Hastings College of Law. Reprinted by permission of University of California, Hastings College of Law and Kathleen F. Brickey.

Bucy, Pamela H., Corporate Ethos: A Standard for Imposing Corporate Criminal Liability, 75 Minn. L. Rev. 1099 (1991). Copyright © 1991 by the University of Minnesota Law School. Reprinted by permission.

Coffee, John C., Jr., From Tort to Crime: Some Reflections on the Criminalization of Fiduciary Breaches and the Problematic Line Between Law and Ethics, 19 Amer. Crim. L. Rev. 117 (1981). Copyright © 1981 American Bar Association. Reprinted by permission.

[a]Case citations in the text, the footnotes of judicial opinions, and in the writings of commentators have been omitted without so specifying. Footnotes in judicial opinions and articles are also omitted without specifying. Numbered footnotes are from the original source; lettered footnotes are written by the authors of this casebook. Asterisks and brackets are used to designate omissions from the original materials. References to Hornbook on White Collar Crime are designated as WCH.

Coffee, John C., Jr., "Corporate Criminal Responsibility," Excerpted with permission of Macmillan Library Reference USA, a Division of Simon & Shuster, from Encyclopedia of Crime and Justice, Sanford H. Kadish, Editor in Chief, Vol. 1, pp. 253-264. Copyright © 1983 by The Free Press.

Coffee, John C., Jr., Hush!: The Criminal Status of Confidential Information After McNally and Carpenter and the Enduring Problem of Overcriminalization, 26 Amer. Crim. L. Rev. 121 (1988). Copyright © 1988 by John C. Coffee, Jr. Reprinted by permission.

Cole, Lance, Revoking Our Privileges: Federal Law Enforcement's Multi-Front Assault on The Attorney-Client Privilege (and Why It Is Misguided), 48 Vil. L. Rev. 469 (2003). Copyright © 2003 by Villanova University and Lance Cole. Reprinted by permission.

The Criminal Justice Newsletter, Volume 19, No. 6 at 4-5 (March 15, 1988). Copyright © 1988 by Pace Publications. Reprinted by permission.

Curriden, Mark, Selective Prosecution: Are Black Officials Investigative Targets, 78 A.B.A. J. 54 (Feb. 1992). Copyright © 1992. Printed in the U.S.A. American Bar Association. Reprinted by permission of the ABA Journal.

Daly, Kathleen, Gender and Varieties of White-Collar Crime, 27 Crim. 769 (1989). Copyright © 1989 by the American Society of Criminology. Reprinted by permission of American Society of Criminology and Kathleen Daly.

Deputy Attorney General Testifies on Fight Against White Collar Crime, 38 Crim.L. Rep. 2486 (1986). Reprinted with permission from Criminal Law Reporter, Vol. 38, p. 2485 (March 26, 1986). Copyright © 1986 by The Bureau of National Affairs, Inc. (800-372-1033).

Edelhertz, Herbert, The Nature, Impact, and Prosecution of White-Collar Crime (1970). Project funded by a grant from the National Institute of Justice. Reprinted by permission.

Excerpts: Regulators and Lawyers, 14 Nat. L.J., April 13, 1992, at 10. Copyright © 1992 by The Association of the Bar of the City of New York. Reprinted with permission.

FBI's White Collar Crime Program, Expanding Rapidly, 8 Corp. Crime Rep. 4 (October 17, 1994). Copyright © 1994 by the American Communications and Publishing Company, Inc. Reprinted by permission.

Fee Forfeiture - Federal Preemption, 9 Crim. Prac. Manual 120 (1995). Copyright © 1995. Reprinted with permission of Pike and Fischer.

Friedenthal, Jack; Kane, Mary Kay; Miller, Arthur R., Civil Procedure 387 (4th ed. 2005). Reprinted from Civil Procedure, Jack Friedenthal, Mary Kay Kane, Arthur Miller, 4th ed., Copyright © 2005, with permission of the West Publishing Corporation.

Garrett, Brandon L., Corporate Confessions, 30 CARDOZO L. REV. 917 (2009). Copyright © 2009. Reprinted by permission.

Geis, Gilbert, White-Collar Crime - What is It?, From White-Collar Crime Reconsidered edited by Kip Schlegel and David Weisburd. Copyright © 1992 by Kip Schlegel and David Weisburd. Reprinted with the permission of Northeastern University Press.

Genego, William J., The New Adversary, 54 Brooklyn L.Rev. 781 (1988). Copyright © 1988 by the Brooklyn Law Review. Reprinted by permission.

Gershman, Bennett L., The New Prosecutors, 53 U. Pitt. L. Rev. 393 (1993). Copyright © 1993 University of Pittsburgh Law Review. Reprinted by permission of University of Pittsburgh Law Review and Bennett Gersham.

Goldsmith, Michael, RICO and Enterprise Liability: A Response to Gerald E. Lynch, 88 Col. L. Rev. 774 (1988). This article originally appeared at 88 Columbia Law Review 774 (1988). Reprinted by permission of the Columbia Law Review and Michael Goldsmith.

Gorelick, Jamie, Litman, Harry, Keynote Address, Prosecutorial Discretion and the Federalization Debate, 46 Hastings L. J. 978 (1995). Copyright © 1995 by the University of California, Hastings College of Law. Reprinted by permission.

Green, Stuart P., Lying, Misleading, and Falsely Denying: How Moral Concepts Inform the Law of Perjury, Fraud, and False Statements, 53 Hastings L.J. 157 (2001). Copyright © 2001 by University of California, Hastings College of the Law and Stuart Green. Reprinted from HASTINGS LAW JOURNAL, Volume 53, Number 1, November 2001, 157-212, by permission.

Gruner, Richard, Towards an Organizational Jurisprudence: Transforming Corporate Criminal Law Through Federal Sentencing Reform, 36 Arizona L. Rev. 407 (1994). Copyright © 1994 by the Arizona Board of Regents. Reprinted by permission.

Hartmus, Diane M., Inspection and Oversight in the Federal Courts: Creating an Office of Inspector General, 35 Calif. West. L. Rev. 243 (1999). Copyright © 1999 by California Western School of Law and Diane Hartmus. Reprinted by permission.

Henning, Peter J., Finding What Was Lost: Sorting Out the Custodian's Privilege Against Self-Incrimination from the Compelled Production of Records, 77 Neb. L. Rev. 34 (1998). Copyright © 1998 Peter J. Henning. Reprinted by permission.

Henning, Peter J., Testing the Limits of Investigating and Prosecuting White-Collar Crime: How Far Will the Courts Allow Prosecutors to Go?, 54 U. Pitt. L. Rev. 405 (1993). Copyright © 1993 University of Pittsburgh Law Review. Reprinted with permission of University of Pittsburgh Law Review and Peter Henning.

Hirschi, Travis; Gottfredson, Michael, Causes of White-Collar Crime, 25 Crim. 949 (1987). Copyright © 1987 by the American Society of Criminology. Reprinted by permission of American Society of Criminology , Travis Hirschi, and Michael Gottfredson.

Hughes, Graham, Administrative Subpoenas and the Grand Jury: Converging Streams of Criminal and Civil Compulsory Process, 47 Vand. L. Rev. 573 (1994). Copyright © 1994 by the Vanderbilt Law Review. Reprinted by permission of Vanderbilt Law Review and Graham Hughes.

Kellman, Barry, Criminal Law and Environmental Protection, International Review of Penal Law-Crimes Against the Environment 885 (1994). Copyright © 1994 by the Revué Internationale de Droit Penal. Reprinted by permission.

Knight, Ray A. & Knight, Lee G., Criminal Tax Fraud: An Analytical Review, 57 Mo. L. Rev. 175 (1992). Copyright © 1992 by the Curators of the University of Missouri, Ray A. Knight, and Lee G. Knight. Reprinted by permission

LaFave, Wayne R., Israel, Jerold H., King, Nancy J., Kerr, Orin S. Criminal Procedure 3d (2007). Copyright © 2007 by Thomson Reuters/West. Reprinted with permission of Thomson Reuters/West Publishing Corporation.

Laufer, William S., Corporate Prosecution, Cooperation, and the Trading of Favors, 87 Iowa L. Rev. 643 (2002). Copyright © 2002 by the Iowa Law Review and William S. Laufer. Reprinted by permission.

Leipold, Andrew D., Why Grand Juries Do Not (and Cannot) Protect the Accused, 80 Cornell L. Rev. 260 (1995). Copyright © 1995 by Cornell University and Andrew Leipold. Reprinted by permission.

Mann, Kenneth, Defending White-Collar Crime (1985). Copyright © 1985 by Yale University Press. Reprinted by permission.

Maus, Donna M., Comment, License Procurement and the Federal Mail Fraud Statute, 58 U. Chi. L. Rev. 1125 (1991). Copyright © 1991 by the University of Chicago Law Review. Reprinted by permission.

Model Penal Code, Section 2.07. Copyright by the American Law Institute. Reprinted with the permission of The American Law Institute.

Model Rules of Professional Conduct, Rules 1.13, 3.8, and 4.2. Copyright © 2002 American Bar Association. All rights reserved. Reprinted by permission of the American Bar Association.

Mokhiber, Russell, Voices: Viewpoint; Don't Hinder Pollution Police, The New York Times, October 15, 1995, § 3, at 11, col. 4. Copyright © 1995 by The New York Times Company. Reprinted by permission.

Mosteller, Robert P., Simplifying Subpoena Law: Taking the Fifth Amendment Seriously, 73 Va. L. Rev. 1 (1987). Copyright © 1987 by the Virginia Law Review Association and Robert P. Mosteller. Reprinted by permission.

Mulroy, Thomas R. & Munoz, Eric J., The Internal Corporate Investigation, 1 DePaul Bus. & Com. L.J. 49 (2002). Copyright © 2002 by DePaul Business & Commercial Law Journal, Thomas R. Mulroy, and Eric J. Munoz. Reprinted by permission.

Palm, Craig W., RICO Forfeiture and the Eighth Amendment: When Is Everything Too Much? 53, U. Pitt. L. Rev. 1, 37 (1991). Copyright © 1991 by the University of Pittsburgh School of Law. Reprinted by permission of University of Pittsburgh Law Review and Craig Palm.

Raab, Selwyn, New York Investigators Searched Tons of Records, The New York Times, March 6, 1986, at Y16. Copyright © 1986 by The New York Times Company. Reprinted by permission.

Richman, Daniel C., Cooperating Clients, 56 Ohio St. L.J. 69 (1995). Copyright © 1995 by The Ohio State University. Reprinted by permission.

Shabecoff, Philip, Federal Statutes Cited in Indictment of Exxon, The New York Times, Mar. 1, 1990, A14. Copyright © 1990 by The New York Times Company. Reprinted by permission.

Shapiro, Susan, Thinking About White-Collar Crime: Matters of Conceptualization and Research (1980). Copyright © 1980 by Susan Shapiro. Reprinted by permission.

Simons, Michael A., Vicarious Snitching: Crime, Cooperation, and "Good Corporate Citizenship," 76 St. John's L. Rev. 979 (2002). Copyright © 2002 by the St. John's Law Review Association and Michael A. Simons. Reprinted by permission.

Spaulding, Karla R., "Hit Them Where It Hurts": RICO Criminal Forfeitures and White-Collar Crime, 80 J. of Crim. L. and Criminology 197 (1989). Copyright © (1989) by Karla R. Spaulding. Reprinted by permission.

Sutherland, Edwin H., White Collar Crime: The Uncut Version (1983). Copyright © 1983 by the Yale University Press. Reprinted by permission.

Tarlow, Barry, RICO: The New Darling of the Prosecutor's Nursery, 49 Fordham L. Rev. 165 (1980). Copyright © 1980 by the Fordham University Law Review. Reprinted by permission.

Underwood, Richard H., Perjury! The Charges and the Defenses, 36 Duq. L. Rev. 715 (1998). Copyright © 1998 by Duquesne University and Richard H. Underwood. Reprinted by permission.

Wheeler, Stanton; Weisbund, David; Warning, Elin, White-Collar Crime and Criminals, 25 Amer. Crim. L. Rev. 351 (1988). Reprinted with the permission of the publisher, © (1988) and Georgetown University.

Whitley, Joe D., White-Collar Crime: A Real Priority, Legal Times page 19, cont. page 22, September 27, 1993. Reprinted with permission of the Legal Times. Copyright © 1993.

Whitley, Joe D., Garber, Marc N., McCarty, Mark A., and Henry, Steven D., The Case for Reevaluating DOJ Policies on Prosecuting White Collar Crime, Washington Legal Foundation, Working Paper Series No. 108, May 2002. Copyright © 2002 by Washington Legal Foundation, Joe D. Whitley, Marc N. Garber,Mark A. McCarty, and Steven D. Henry. Reprinted by permission.

Winter, Ralph K., Paying Lawyers, Empowering Prosecutors, and Protecting Managers: Raising the Cost of Capital in America, 42 Duke L. J. 945 (1993). Copyright © 1993 by the Duke University School of Law. Reprinted by permission.

Wizard of ID, Cartoon, August 13, 1979. Copyright © 1979. Reprinted by permission of Johnny Hart and Creators Syndicate, Inc.

Zabel, Richard B. & Benjamin, James J., "Queen for a Day" or "Courtesan for a Day": The Sixth Amendment Limits to Proffer Agreements, 15 White-Collar Crime Rep. 1 (Oct. 2001). Copyright © 2001 by the Andrews Publications, Richard B. Zabel, and James J. Benjamin. Reprinted by permission.

Summary of Contents

Table of Contents

PART THREE
PROCEDURAL ISSUES

PART FOUR
PUNISHMENT

Table of Cases

Principal cases are in bold type. Cases cited or discussed in the text are in roman type. References are to the pages where the case appears in the text. References to principal cases are not repeated within the principal case.

Table of Statutes, Standards, and Court Rules

References are to the pages where statutes, standards, or court rules appear in the text. References, however, within principal cases are cited to the first time that they appear within the principal case and are not repeated throughout the principal case.

FEDERAL RULES OF EVIDENCE

GEORGIA ANNOTATED CODE

LOUISIANA REV. STATUTES ANN.

MISSOURI RULES OF PROFESSIONAL CONDUCT

MODEL PENAL CODE

MODEL RULES OF PROFESSIONAL CONDUCT

PENNSYLVANIA RULES OF PROFESSIONAL RESPONSIBILITY

STATUTES-POPULAR NAMES

UNITED STATES ATTORNEYS MANUAL (U.S.A.M.)

UNITED STATES CODE ANNOTATED (U.S.C.A.)

WEST VIRGINIA CODE

WHITE COLLAR CRIME

LAW AND PRACTICE

Fourth Edition

CHAPTER ONE
INTRODUCTION

* * * An examination of the various definitions of "white-collar crime" and their actual usage in the literature yields fundamental inconsistencies and incompatibilities. It is unclear whether the term characterizes acts or actors, types of offenses or types of offenders; or whether it refers to the social location of deviant behavior, the social role or social status of the actor, the *modus operandi* of the behavior, or the social relationship of victim and offender. There are frequent disputes over whether the phenomenon is necessarily "white collar," and even more serious disagreement over whether the behavior is criminal. * * *

These fundamental confusions result from the fact that "white collar crime" has always been a catch-all category for social theorists, policy analysts, and law enforcement officials. It has referred to that group of offenders (wealthy, respectable persons, corporations, etc.) for whom traditional explanations of criminal behavior are not appropriate or to that group of offenses to which the criminal justice system responds differently—if at all. The category—white collar crime— generally has been used to demonstrate the incompleteness of our knowledge, the inadequacy of our theory, or the injustice of our social control responses. * * *

Susan Shapiro, THINKING ABOUT WHITE-COLLAR CRIME: MATTERS OF CONCEPTUALIZATION AND RESEARCH 1 (1980).

Edwin Sutherland, a sociologist, coined the term "white collar crime" in a speech given to the American Sociological Society in 1939. In the years following this lecture, the nonlegal origins of this term evolved with varying sociological perspectives. The adaptation of this term by the legal community has resulted in ambiguity as to what is encompassed within the term "white collar crime" and what impact the term should play in grading offenses, lawyer specialization, and prosecutorial priorities.

In examining the various definitions of "white collar crime," consider the following two questions: (1) Is there a useful categorization of something called "white collar crime" (a category that could be employed, for example, in establishing a special investigative or prosecutorial unit, in a defense counsel's designation of his or her special area of expertise, or in assessing appropriate levels of punishment for different groupings of crime), and (2) if so, what characteristics would be useful in establishing a white collar category for the particular purpose?

A. DEFINITIONS OF CRIMINOLOGISTS AND SOCIOLOGISTS

1. Social Status, Occupation, and Organization

In his speech to the American Sociological Society, Edwin Sutherland concentrated on "crime in relation to business." He criticized those who claimed that crime was "concentrated in the lower classes." The thesis of his speech was that the explanation of crime as being "closely correlated with poverty or with the psychopathic and sociopathic conditions associated with poverty" was "misleading and incorrect." He claimed that "conventional explanations [were] invalid principally because they [were] derived from biased samples." He focused in his talk on a "neglected" area of crime, that being "the criminal behavior of business and professional men." *Reprinted in* Edwin H. Sutherland, *White-Collar Criminality*, 5 AM. SOC. REV. 1 (1940).

In his later book, Sutherland defined "white-collar crime" in terms of social status and occupation. He stated:

> * * * This concept is not intended to be definitive, but merely to call attention to crimes which are not ordinarily included within the scope of criminology. White collar crime may be defined approximately as a crime committed by a person of respectability and high social status in the course of his occupation. * * * (emphasis added).

Edwin H. Sutherland, WHITE COLLAR CRIME: THE UNCUT VERSION 7 (1983). For a summary of white-collar crime theory as it developed from Sutherland's work, see James William Coleman, *The Theory of White-Collar Crime: From Sutherland to the 1990s*, WHITE-COLLAR CRIME RECONSIDERED 53 (KIP SCHLEGEL & DAVID WEISBURD, EDS.) (1992); see also David T. Johnson & Richard A. Leo, *The Yale White-Collar Crime Project: A Review and Critique*, LAW AND SOCIAL INQUIRY 63 (1993) (review of varying definitions of white collar crime).

NOTES AND QUESTIONS

1. ***Social Status***. Does a definition of "white collar crime" premised upon the class or social status of the individual provide a biased methodology for examining criminal behavior? Consider the following questions raised by Susan Shapiro, supra at 3:

> * * * Does one want to definitionally discriminate, for example, between medicaid fraud by doctors and that engaged in by patients; between the business executive who does not disclose perks in his tax return and the waitress who fails to disclose tips on her return? Does one take a single illegal activity reflecting the conspiracy of assorted individuals and label the activities of the wealthier participants white collar crime and those of the less wealthy traditional crime? * * *

2. ***Occupation***. What limitations result from Sutherland's prerequisite that the crime occur in the ***course of one's occupation***? Does this requirement focus on the use of occupation as an aspect of the offense or on the position of the particular actor? "Is the motorist who pays a bribe to a traffic policeman or meter maid a traditional criminal and the bribe recipient a white collar criminal?" Susan Shapiro, supra at 6. Does it draw an artificial distinction even as to the character of the offense? Consider the following comments by Susan Shapiro, supra at 17:

> Similarly, the behavior of individuals may not differ in kind when they move from non-business to business contexts. * * * Individuals both in and out of business often assert their eligibility for particular benefits, and do so by misrepresenting their status. The employee pads his or her expense account or falsifies the number of hours worked; the individual lies on his or her tax return, application for welfare, food stamps, or insurance compensation. * * *

3. ***Organization***. Although Sutherland spoke in terms of social status and occupation, "his book was devoted * * * to the crimes of organizations, not of persons: seventy large corporations and fifteen public utilities. * * * Those following Sutherland sometimes focused on persons of high status, sometimes on occupation, and sometimes on corporate bodies." Stanton Wheeler, *White-Collar Crime: History of an Idea*, 4 ENCYCLOPEDIA OF CRIME AND JUSTICE 1652, 1653 (1983). Does concentrating on the organization provide a more comprehensive definition of white collar crime? Consider the following excerpt from Susan Shapiro, supra at 11, on adding an organizational component to the definition of white collar crime:

> It includes business and non-business settings. Violations that pertain to government, non-profit organizations, associations, educational institutions, religious groups, and the like, would be included in this definition. Futhermore, the stipulation does not require that the violation be made by an organization or occur in an organizational role—only that organizations be involved in the violative activity. Thus, the case of the insurance company that defrauds consumers by promising non-existent benefits reflects white collar illegality. So too does the case of the policy holder who defrauds the insurance company by submitting false claims for benefit. * * *

> Perhaps the only events commonly thought of as white collar crimes that would be excluded by this standard are abuses that occur in face-to-face interactions between individuals—very simply con games, "consumer" type frauds in the sale of personal property or illicit goods or services. * * *

What problems arise in employing a definition that focuses on the organization? Consider the following excerpt from Susan Shapiro, supra at 16-17:

> In order to determine whether illicit behavior is organizational, then, one must possess considerable information about organizational norms, organizational socialization, and the extent of knowledge about the behavior across the organizational leadership hierarchy. * * * But this is the very problem. The boundaries of organizational norms are incredibly unclear. * * *
>
> More troubling is the fact that the categories sometimes differentiate identical behavior. For example, both individuals and organizations engage in tax violations or in misrepresentations in the application for credit and insurance or the qualification for benefits and services, and presumably for the same reasons.

2. Behavior Characteristics

Eventually, there was a shift from concentrating on the offender to focusing on the offense in defining white collar crime. A chief proponent of this approach was Herbert Edelhertz, former chief of the Fraud Section-Criminal Division of the Department of Justice, who defined "white-collar crime" as "an illegal act or series of illegal acts committed by nonphysical means and by concealment or guile, to obtain money or property, to avoid the payment or loss of money or property, or to obtain business or personal advantage." See Herbert Edelhertz, THE NATURE, IMPACT AND PROSECUTION OF WHITE-COLLAR CRIME 3, 12 (1970). He noted:

> In any white-collar crime, we will find the following elements:
>
> (a) Intent to commit a wrongful act or to achieve a purpose inconsistent with law or public policy.
>
> (b) Disguise of purpose or intent.
>
> (c) Reliance by perpetrator on ignorance or carelessness of victim.
>
> (d) Acquiescence by victim in what he believes to be the true nature and content of the transaction.
>
> (e) Concealment of crime by—
>
> (1) Preventing the victim from realizing that he has been victimized, or

(2) Relying on the fact that only a small percentage of victims will react to what has happened, and making provisions for restitution to or other handling of the disgruntled victim, or

(3) Creation of a deceptive paper, organizational, or transactional facade to disguise the true nature of what has occurred.

As with other definitions of white-collar crime, the approach taken by Edelhertz also met with criticism. Consider the following excerpt from Gilbert Geis, *White-Collar Crime—What Is It?,* WHITE-COLLAR CRIME RECONSIDERED 31, 39 (Kip Schlegel & David Weisburd, eds.) (1992):

> Criticism of the Edelhertz position predictably came from sociologists who regretted his slighting of the idea of abuse of power as the key aspect of white-collar offenses and his expansive extension of the term to such a variegated range of behaviors. They were puzzled by the excision of violence from the realm of white-collar crime, noting that crimes such as unnecessary surgical operations, the manufacture of unsafe automobiles, and the failure to label poisonous substances at the workplace could be regarded as white-collar crimes with a strong component of violence. * * * Later, the American Bar Association would adopt the term "economic offense" for behaviors within the white-collar crime realm set forth by Edelhertz, and would modify the term "nonviolent" with the footnoted observation that this referred to "the means by which crime is committed" even though "the harm to society can frequently be described as violent."

Professor Stuart P. Green in his book LYING, CHEATING, AND STEALING: A MORAL THEORY OF WHITE-COLLAR CRIME (2006) notes the disagreement in how to define the term "white-collar crime." He concludes that "in the absence of any viable alternative, and in light of its powerful cultural resonances—the term 'white-collar crime' is worth preserving, provided that certain features are understood, and various caveats observed." He states that "[w]e would do better to think of the term 'white-collar crime' as referring to a set of offenses connected by a series of what philosophers call 'family resemblances,' rather than as susceptible to definition through a precise set of necessary and sufficient conditions."

B. LAW ENFORCEMENT DEFINITIONS

Department of Justice, Attorney General's Report (1983)

White collar crimes are illegal acts that use deceit and concealment—rather than the application or threat of physical force or violence—to obtain money, property, or service; to avoid the payment or loss of money; or to secure a business or personal advantage. White-collar criminals occupy positions of responsibility and trust in government, industry, the professions, and civic organizations.

Bureau of Justice Statistics, U.S. Department of Justice, Dictionary of Criminal Justice Data Terminology 215 (2d Ed. 1981)

White-collar crime: Definition. Nonviolent crime for financial gain committed by means of deception by persons whose occupational status is entrepreneurial, professional or semi-professional and utilizing their special occupational skills and opportunities; also, nonviolent crime for financial gain utilizing deception and committed by anyone having special technical and professional knowledge of business and government, irrespective of the person's occupation.

Annotation. * * * The term reflects a traditional classification of occupations into white-collar: those utilizing technical knowledge and skills in the manipulation of numbers and concepts, and blue-collar: those utilizing skill in the manipulation of objects. It originally referred to nonviolent crime committed by persons in the upper socio-economic class in their occupational roles, and defined a social class of interest to social scientists. In current criminal justice usage of the term, the focus of the meaning has shifted to the nature of the crime instead of the persons or occupations. The categorization of "white-collar" crime as crime having a particular modus operandi (committed in a manner that utilizes deception and special knowledge of business practices and committed in a particular kind of economic environment) is of use in coordinating the resources of the appropriate agencies for purposes of investigation and prosecution. * * *

Federal Bureau of Investigation (Cynthia Barnett, The Measurement of White Collar Crime Using Uniform Crime Reporting (UCR) Data) (2002)

* * * The Federal Bureau of Investigation has opted to approach white collar crime in terms of the offense. The Bureau has defined white-collar crime as "... those illegal acts which are characterized by deceit, concealment, or violation of trust and which are not dependent upon the application or threat of physical force or violence. Individuals and organizations commit these acts to obtain money, property, or services; to avoid the payment or loss of money or services; or to secure personal or business advantage." Some experts have criticized defining white-collar in terms or type of offense because this definition emphasizes the nature of the acts rather than the background of the offender. Within the FBI definition, there is no mention of the type of occupation or the socioeconomic position of the "white-collar" offender. * * *

NOTES AND QUESTIONS

1. ***Prosecutorial Selection/Enforcement Priorities.*** How does the definition adopted by the Department of Justice (DOJ) impact on the prosecutorial selection of cases? Does the definition given to white collar crime impact the enforcement priorities, resources provided to these priorities, and statistical reporting of cases in this area? See *FBI'S White Collar Crime Program Expanding Rapidly*, 8 CORP. CRIME REP. 4 (Oct. 17, 1994) ("The [FBI] spokesperson could not answer why there is not a public FBI generated database for corporate and white-collar crime that mirrors the FBI's annual Crime in the United States report on street crime.").

2. ***Gender Considerations.*** Does a definition that focuses on the offense, as opposed to the offender, fail to account for gender distinctions in white-collar crime? Consider the following excerpt from Kathleen Daly, *Gender and Varieties of White-Collar Crime*, 27 CRIM. 769, 770-771, 789-791 (1989):

> The disagreement in defining white-collar crime revolves around whether characteristics of the offense or the offender should be primary. An offense-related approach focuses on how a crime is committed, while an offender-related approach focuses on a particular group of people—those in high-status or "respected" occupations or in positions of power. If one takes an offender-related approach, a Medicaid fraud is considered a white-collar crime if it is carried out by a doctor or nursing home owner, but not if it is carried out by a clerical worker or poor person. If one uses an offense-related approach, that distinction is not important.
>
> The different definitions affect how scholars conceptualize gender and white-collar crime. * * * The offense-based approach suggests a rising tide of "new" female white-collar criminals; the offender-based approach suggests that white-collar crime is a male-only domain. * * *
>
> In this group of white-collar offenders, some men are "big fish," but most are "little fish" and do not comport with images of highly placed or powerful white-collar criminals. Men's white-collar crimes were both petty and major, but almost all the women's were petty. Although half or more of the employed men were managerial or professional workers, most employed women were clerical workers. * * *
>
> Finally, in building theories of white-collar crime, scholars should be cognizant of the points of gender difference found in this study. * * * Men's white-collar crime, though more frequent than women's and exacting more social injury or harm, should not be used as the "norm"

> from which women's white-collar crime is thought to deviate. Women's illegalities should be explored on their own terms. The multiple influences of gender, class, and race relations, both within and outside work organizations and occupations, should also be investigated. These relations not only generate many varieties of white-collar crime, they also undoubtedly play a role in who is caught and prosecuted for white-collar crime.

Compare Ellen S. Podgor, *Corporate and White Collar Crime: Simplifying The Ambiguous*, 31 AM. CRIM. L. REV. 391, 393-394 (1994) (rejects a definition that encompasses gender, class, or race of a person and suggests "[a]n approach that looks to the activity involved and classifies that activity based upon its attributes as opposed to the socio-economic status of the individuals who engage in the acts.[20]"). According to the National Incident-Based Reporting System (NIBRS) data for 1997 through 1999:

> * * * white collar offenders are, on average, in their late-twenties to early-thirties, which is only slightly older than most other offenders captured in NIBRS. The majority of white-collar crime offenders are white-males, except for those who committed embezzlement. However, in comparison to offenders committing property crimes, there is a higher proportion of females committing these white-collar offenses.

Cynthia Barnett, *The Measurement of White-Collar Crime Using Uniform Crime Reporting (UCR) Data*, NIBRS Publications Series 5 (2002).

3. ***Quantifying White Collar Crime.*** In an attempt to quantify the amount of white collar crime, the FBI issued a report using offense categories as the basis for determining the level of white collar crime using Uniform Crime Reporting Data. The report designated the following offenses as white collar crimes: "fraud, bribery, counterfeiting/forgery, embezzlement (all of which are Group A offenses), and bad checks (a Group B offense)." The report found:

> In 1997 through 1999, white-collar crime accounted for approximately 3.8 percent of the incidents reported to the FBI. The majority of those offenses are frauds and counterfeiting/forgery. Additionally, the Group B offense of *bad checks* accounted for approximately 4 percent of the arrests during 1997-1999.

Cynthia Barnett, *The Measurement of White-Collar Crime Using Uniform Crime Reporting (UCR) Data*, NIBRS Publications Series 2 (2002). Recent

---

[20] These factors, however, may warrant consideration in sentencing an individual. See generally Myrna Raeder, Gender and Sentencing: Single Moms, Battered Women, and Other Sex-Based Anomalies in the Gender-Free World of the Federal Sentencing Guidelines, 20 PEPP. L. REV. 905 (1993).See also Laura Mansnerus, *Sometimes, the Punishment Fits the Gender*, N.Y.Times, Nov. 16, 1997, at Sec. 4, p. 1.

data can be found on TRAC Reports, Inc., with tracking in a variety of categories of white collar crime. For example, reports are now issued on criminal mortgage fraud cases. See http://trac.syr.edu/tracreports/crim/200/.

4. ***Specific White Collar Offenses.*** Even though a specific crime may be thought of as white collar crime, the conduct may fall into the category of both white collar and street crime depending upon the specific conduct involved in the crime. For example, one can use a computer to commit both a white collar or non-white collar offense. According to a recent FBI Report, supra Note 3, "[o]f the offense committed using computer equipment, 42 percent are white-collar offenses. The largest proportion of those offense[s] are larceny-thefts." Id. at 4.

5. ***White Collar Statutes.*** There can also be a question of whether a particular statute is white collar. Some crimes are typically charged with offenses that apply only to white collar conduct, such as insider trading. Other crimes may use generic statutes that apply to both white collar and non-white collar conduct. For example, it is common to have white collar conduct charged with mail fraud, obstruction of justice, or perjury statutes. The Racketeer Influenced and Corrupt Organization Act (RICO) includes predicate acts that are both federal and state crimes, some of which may be considered street crimes, while others are more closely associated white collar criminality. ELLEN S. PODGOR, PETER J. HENNING, JEROLD H. ISRAEL, & NANCY J. KING, WHITE COLLAR CRIME HORNBOOK 4-5 (2013)(hereinafter WCH).

C. THE WHITE COLLAR CRIMINAL LAWYER

By Permission of Johnny L. Hart FLP and Creators Syndicate, Inc.

NOTES

1. ***White Collar Crime/Street Crime.*** Professor Kenneth Mann, in Defending White Collar Crime (1985), describes several characteristics of white collar defense practice that distinguish it from criminal defense in "street crime" cases. He notes that defense attorneys handling street crime

typically come onto the scene after the police have investigated the offense and arrested counsel's client. Accordingly, the defense attorney "usually assumes when he takes the case that the government has sufficient evidence to convict his client," and focuses his energy on achieving a satisfactory plea-bargain. The white collar crime defense attorney, in contrast, enters the picture substantially before the government has completed its investigation and sometimes before the investigation has even started. The "white-collar defense attorney does not assume that the government has the evidence to convict his client" but assumes instead that, even if "his client is guilty, he may be able to keep the government from knowing this or from concluding that it has a strong enough case to prove it." Counsel's first line of defense accordingly is "information control," which "entails keeping documents away from and preventing clients and witnesses from talking to government investigators, prosecutors, and judges."

Information control, Professor Mann notes, is practiced in two different ways. First, counsel "oppose their [government] adversaries in quasi-judicial and court settings," challenging subpoenas and seeking to suppress evidence already obtained by the government. Second, counsel uses a strategy that "focuses on the potential sources of inculpatory information," and seeks to ensure that such sources will not make that information available to the government apart from its use of the legal process. Success here depends on a variety of factors, including: (1) the influence that the client has over the information sources; (2) how broadly damaging evidence and information is dispersed among third-party sources (the greater the number of sources, the more likely that the government will locate and gain the cooperation of at least one); and (3) whether the crime is one that, in effect, manufactures and exposes its own sources of incriminating evidence, or is one that is reflected only in evidence that remains hidden in particular artifacts and persons not readily distinguishable from all others that relate to the client.[a]

White collar defense attorneys also are said to have a "distinctive role," separating them from the attorney handling street crime, in their presenta-

---

[a] "Certain crimes create sources of information—witnesses and artifacts—which are exposed as potential evidence of sources of evidence. One example is the victim of crime who knows that he has been victimized * * *. Other crimes do not expose information as evidence to the same extent. * * * [The] crimes do not alert the victim * * *. The artifacts used for the commission of [the] crimes are not readily identifiable as evidence, for instance, individual documents in a complex filing system. And witnesses * * *are not readily exposed because the location of the occurrence of the crime is not apparent, as in a bankruptcy of a multistate company. * * * When inculpatory information is embedded in normal social life, that is, when it is not easily identifiable as potential evidence, there is a higher probability that the government will not identify it. Thus even where the client has no influence over the source and the information is concentrated in one third-party source (not dispersed)—conditions that work against the success of an information control defense—the defense attorney may conclude that he can rely on the government not discovering the information because it is embedded." Mann, supra at 233-34.

tion of "substantive defenses" (i.e., a defense claiming that the client has not violated the law). "Rather than waiting until trial or until the immediate pretrial period when plea negotiations usually take place, these defense attorneys [have] an opportunity to make a substantive defense before a charge is made," as white collar cases "typically [present a] series of institutionalized settings for conducting precharge adversarial proceedings on questions of substantive criminal responsibility." Defense counsel in white collar cases also have a further advantage in this regard because of the character of the substantive offense. White collar offenses are more likely to have ambiguity in their definition (although that is hardly true of all white collar offenses), and "ambiguity of definition leads to increased substantive legal arguments about the scope of prohibited behavior."

Client resources also tend to shape the practice of the defense attorney handling a white collar case. "In contrast to the attorney handling street crime, his time is not a scarce resource, and each case is individually cultivated with great care. * * * The defense attorney employs his own investigators, who are experts in accounting and finance, as well as a staff of legal researchers." Of equal significance, client resources are often accompanied by client sophistication that leads the client to call upon the lawyer at an early stage, which will enable the lawyer to employ strategies that would not be available if the government was farther along in its investigation.

2. ***Prosecutorial Practices.*** Margaret Cronin Fisk, *White Collar Boom*, 14 Nat. L.J., No. 13, Dec, 2, 1991, reports that prosecutors are seeking to offset what they see as potential adversarial advantages of the white collar defense bar. In particular, they are coming to treat suspected white collar offenders in much the same manner as persons suspected of committing other crimes. For example, they are making more frequent use of arrest and search authority rather than utilizing alternatives (summons and subpoena) that are less disruptive to the individual. The end result, it is noted, is "more pressure on the lawyers who defend accused white-collar offenders." Consider also William J. Genego, *The New Adversary*, 54 BROOK. L. REV. 781, 782-84 (1988):

> In recent years federal prosecutors have adopted practices which respond to the special investigative and prosecutorial needs associated with drug and white collar offenses. Many of these practices directly affect criminal defense attorneys and, in turn, the representation received by criminal defendants. Examples of third party enforcement practices utilized by the government include grand jury and trial subpoenas directed to defense counsel, summonses from the Internal Revenue Service (IRS), forfeiture of attorneys' fees, law office searches, tapping of attorneys' telephones, use of undisclosed informants at defense meetings, and efforts to disqualify attorneys. Criminal defense lawyers have been the subject of criminal investigations and prosecutions in which it is alleged that they participated in or supported criminal activity in their professional capacities. While many of the practices were previously available to prosecutors, they were used infrequently. Recently, however, prosecutors have begun

to increase the use of such practices. In addition, the government has sought and obtained legislation and judicial decisions which enable prosecutors to affect the manner in which defense attorneys investigate and prepare cases and which, in turn, affect defense attorneys' willingness to represent certain defendants. The legislative changes mandate special fee reporting requirements, and in some cases limit attorneys' ability to obtain fees for their services.

A heated debate has emerged in the legal community over claims that federal prosecutors regularly engage in aggressive practices hostile to criminal defense attorneys with the purpose of restricting defendants' right to counsel. Criminal defense attorneys charge that federal prosecutors employ these third party enforcement practices not to fulfill legitimate prosecutorial needs, but to discourage zealous representation by defense attorneys and to prevent particular attorneys from representing specific clients. For example, defense attorneys claim that prosecutors direct grand jury subpoenas and IRS summonses to attorneys to seek information about past or present clients, even though the information is available from other sources. Such practices place the attorney in the position of providing information which can be used against the client, thus creating a potential conflict and possibly preventing the attorney from further representation of the client. The defense bar maintains that these practices are part of a general prosecutorial program which targets vigorous and successful attorneys for government harassment. Defense attorneys also charge that prosecutors are using these practices in a calculated effort to affect the representation received by criminal defendants.

Government attorneys respond that the challenged practices are used only for legitimate investigatory and prosecutorial reasons; that the peculiar needs and demands of white collar and drug offense prosecutions, as well as the role that lawyers occasionally play in the perpetration of such crimes, warrant and require such practices. Prosecutors deny that they target criminal defense lawyers or attempt to interfere with defendants' constitutional rights to representation. Further, prosecutors insist that such practices are not widespread but are used selectively in appropriate circumstances. Commentators reach different conclusions as to the constitutionality of these practices. * * *"[b]

---

[b] For a discussion of government practices against criminal defense attorneys, see Chapter 16.

CHAPTER TWO
THE FEDERAL ROLE

A. LIMITS OF THE FEDERAL CRIMINAL JUSTICE SYSTEM

The Numbers. In many fields in which both federal and state governments have the authority to legislate, the federal law has come to dominate. It is the primary source of regulation and the vast majority of all litigation deals with that law. A similar dominance is not found in the field of criminal law. Here the vast majority of all prosecutions are brought under state law in state courts, and the applicable process is governed, apart from federal constitutional law, by the law of the particular state. Indeed, measured by the number of prosecutions alone, the federal criminal justice system is just another player among the fifty-two criminal justice systems found in this country (i.e., the fifty state systems, the District of Columbia, and the federal system) and far less significant than a good many of the state systems.

Congressional Policy. The Supreme Court has noted on numerous occasions that "the States under our federal system have the principal responsibility for defining and prosecuting crimes." At one time it was thought that the federal constitutional structure prevented the federal government from assuming any such responsibility for itself, for that structure was seen as allowing federal legislation to reach only a narrow slice of all criminal activity. Today, however, that structure generally is considered to impose only a fairly modest restriction upon the reach of federal criminal law. While it places on federal legislative authority limitations that do not apply to the states, the key to the limited reach of current federal substantive law is the refusal of Congress to exercise that legislative authority to its fullest extent and the role of the Supreme Court in limiting federal jurisdiction.

Unlike the states, which have an inherent power to legislate in the interest of the general welfare (i.e., a general "police power"), federal legislative authority is limited to the enumerated powers granted to Congress in the United States Constitution. Thus, while the state may reach in its criminal code all behavior within its jurisdiction that threatens the health, safety, welfare or morals of the public, Congress can criminalize behavior only where doing so is "necessary and proper" to the implementation of one of the powers specifically given to it by the Constitution. The offense must relate to an operational function (e.g., to operate a postal system or coin money) or to a regulatory authority (e.g., to "regulate commerce . . . among the several states") that the Constitution specifically confers upon the federal government. Over the years, however, the Supreme Court has adopted an exceptionally broad interpretation of what may be necessary and proper in the exercise of these enumerated powers and has allowed Congress considerable leeway in reaching what might be viewed as "local" activities, particularly under the Commerce Clause. Thus, Congress presumably could make it a federal offense to engage in various "local" activities currently punished under state law, such as robberies committed with a firearm (typically shipped in interstate commerce). Of course, even the flexible Commerce Clause authority has its limits. Congressional authority could not readily be stretched to reach many other commonplace local crimes (e.g., assaults or petty thefts) which are punished by the states.

Congress over the years has extended federal legislative authority into more and more areas traditionally viewed as the primary responsibility of the states. To some extent, that tendency has also been reflected in the field of criminal law, but as compared to fields such as labor relations and environmental protection, here the congressional movement toward nationalization has been much more restrained. Initially, the federal criminal code was limited basically to prohibiting acts directly injurious to the federal government itself. It was not until after the Civil War that the nation was launched upon a course of employing the federal criminal law to protect private individuals from invasions of their rights by other private individuals—a traditional function of state criminal law. That first step was confined to civil rights legislation, but shortly thereafter Congress turned to other sources of federal legislative authority as the springboard for a steady growth in what came to be known as "federal auxiliary criminal jurisdiction." These were offenses, primarily relying on the commerce power, reaching activities as to which there was no special federal interest or federal responsibility, with the offense designed primarily to supplement state laws that also encompassed the same basic criminality. Those early auxiliary offenses included the mail fraud statute enacted in 1872 and the Dyer Act enacted in 1919 (prohibiting interstate transportation of stolen vehicles). The enactment of such offenses was commonly a response to a particular problem of the moment, as Congress failed to develop a general blueprint as to what types of basic criminal prohibitions should be "nationalized" through their inclusion in the federal criminal code. Thus, *a cause celebre*, the Lindberg kidnapping, led to a federal statute reaching most kidnappings; the progressive era focus upon major social problems produced anti-vice provisions like the Mann Act (prohibiting transporting a woman across state lines for illicit purposes); and the threat of "gangsterism" contributed to the adoption of a series of federal offenses relating to dealings in firearms, robbery of federally insured banks, and racketeering extortion.

The one common justification offered for all such legislation was that the social problem presented was serious and that state law enforcement lacked the capacity (or willingness) to answer it. In the latter half of this century, the nationalization movement gained considerable impetus through a wholesale expansion of federal auxiliary offenses. As a result, the federal criminal code today substantially overlaps with many strands of state criminal law. It reaches the vast bulk of narcotics offenses, almost all offenses involving the use of fraud to obtain property, and a much smaller but still significant and ever growing slice of various "street crimes" (e.g., carjackings, drug related crimes, drive-by shootings, and gang violence).

The Supreme Court has occasionally restricted the expansion of federal statutes into areas that are exclusive to state law. In **United States v. Lopez**, 514 U.S. 549 (1995), the Court held that the Gun-Free School Zones Act exceeded Congress' Commerce Clause authority in that it involved intrastate activity that was not involved in commerce and was not an economic activity. Chief Justice Rehnquist, writing for the majority, stated:

> Consistent with this structure, we have identified three broad categories of activity that Congress may regulate under its commerce power. * * * First, Congress may regulate the use of the channels of interstate commerce. Second, Congress is empowered to regulate and protect the instrumentalities of interstate commerce, or persons or things in interstate commerce, even though the threat may come only from intrastate activities. * * * Finally, Congress' commerce authority includes the power to regulate those activities having a substantial relation to interstate commerce, i.e., those activities that substantially affect interstate commerce.
>
> Within this final category, admittedly, our case law has not been clear whether an activity must "affect" or "substantially affect" interstate commerce in order to be within Congress' power to regulate it under the Commerce Clause.* * * We conclude, consistent with the great weight of our case law, that the proper test requires an analysis of whether the regulated activity "substantially affects" interstate commerce.

In **United States v. Morrison**, 529 U.S. 598 (2000), the Court held that "like [the] Gun-Free School Zones Act at issue in *Lopez,* § 13981 [provision of the Violence Against Women Act of 1994] contains no jurisdictional element establishing that the federal cause of action is in pursuance of Congress' power to regulate interstate commerce." The Court stated, "[t]he regulation and punishment of intrastate violence that is not directed at the instrumentalities, channels, or goods involved in interstate commerce has always been the province of the States." *Lopez* and *Morrison*, however, do not apply when the activities regulated by Congress are "quintessentially economic." See Gonzales v. Raich, 545 U.S. 1 (2005).

Though Congress has continuously expanded the federal code to include more and more offenses that substantially overlap with state offenses, it also has continuously noted its adherence to the view that the states must carry the primary responsibility for protecting the public against criminal activity.

Thus, the Omnibus Crime Control and Safe Streets Act of 1968, while including a series of federal firearms provisions that supplemented state criminal prohibitions, also provided substantial federal financial assistance to state enforcement agencies and set forth in support of that aid the following congressional finding: "Congress finds further that crime is essentially a local problem that must be dealt with by State and local governments if it is to be controlled effectively."

Congressional recognition of the primacy of the states' role is reflected only in part by Congress' refusal to extend the federal criminal code to fully encompass all harmful acts subject to federal legislative authority (which would provide an even greater overlap with state law than currently exists). The major impact of that policy, however, is found in Congress' refusal to expand the federal law enforcement apparatus commensurate with the expanded reach of the federal criminal law. The four basic components of the federal system are: a substantial number of agencies (F.B.I., Homeland Security) that may have personnel with arrest and investigative authority, the offices of the United States Attorneys and the Criminal Division of the Department of Justice, the federal courts, and the United States Bureau of Prisons.[a]

Congressional expansion can be seen in some areas, with the passage of legislation such as the Patriot Act and the Sarbanes-Oxley Act of 2002. Although the number of criminal prosecutions in federal district courts rose significantly in the last twenty-five years, state dockets also increased, and the ratio of state-federal prosecutions has not been significantly altered.

NOTES AND QUESTIONS

1. ***Federal Crimes.*** Should federal criminal jurisdiction be limited to specific categories of crime and "only in instances in which state court prosecution is not appropriate or where federal interests are paramount"? Commenting on such a proposed plan of the Committee on Long Range Planning of the Federal Judicial Conference, Former Deputy Attorney General Jamie Gorelick and Deputy Assistant Attorney General Harry Litman stated:

> * * * First, we believe that Congress should not be foreclosed from enacting legislation in areas that are also appropriate for state regulation; rather, where there are aspects of a criminal law problem that states cannot adequately address, and where the

[a] To view the structural organization of the Department of Justice see <http://www.usdoj. gov/dojorg.htm>.

> federal government would be positioned to make a qualitative difference, it is appropriate for Congress to act. Once Congress has acted, the federalization issue becomes a question of prosecutorial discretion. It falls to the Department, in cooperation with state and local counterparts, to target for prosecution only those few cases in which federal prosecution is the most effective way to bring criminal justice resources to bear on our nation's law enforcement problems.
> * * *

Jamie Gorelick & Harry Litman, Keynote Address, *Prosecutorial Discretion and the Federalization Debate*, 46 HASTINGS L.J. 967, 978 (1995). See also G. Robert Blakey, *Federal Criminal Law: The Need, Not for Revised Constitutional Theory or New Congressional Statutes, But the Exercise of Responsible Prosecutive Discretion*, 46 HASTINGS L. J. 1175 (1995).

2. ***Overfederalization/Overcriminalization.*** An American Bar Association Task Force that studied the federalization of criminal law, documented the increase in federal cases and federal crimes. The Preface to the Report states that "[a]lthough it may be impossible to determine exactly how many federal crimes could be prosecuted today, it is clear that of all federal crimes enacted since 1865, over forty percent have been created since 1970." Preface, *Report of the Task Force on the Federalization of Criminal Law*, ABA Criminal Justice Section 2 (1998). Are the concerns about increased federalization being "overstated"? For a discussion of the "myths" of the federalization debate see Rory K. Little, *Myths and Principles of Federalization*, 46 HASTINGS L.J. 1029 (1995); see also Susan Klein & Ingrid B. Grobey, *Debunking Claims of Over-Federalization of Criminal Law*, 62 EMORY L. J. 1 (2012). Recently, there has been a strong movement called "Smart on Crime" to respond to overcriminalization. See Roger Fairfax, From *"Overcriminalization" to "Smart on Crime": American Criminal Justice Reform - Legacy and Prospects*, 7 J. L. ECON. & POL'Y 597 (2011).

B. FEDERAL PRIORITIES

Should white collar crime be a Justice Department priority? Consider the following excerpt from Joe D. Whitley, *White Collar-Crime: A Real Priority*, Legal Times, Sept. 27, 1993, at 19, cont. on 22.

> Increased demand on federal prosecutors also comes from the expanding list of agencies referring matters for criminal prosecution. Although federal prosecutors receive a substantial percentage of their white-collar crime cases from such well-known agencies as the Federal Bureau of Investigation, the Internal Revenue Service, and Secret Service, numerous other agencies now investigate and refer such cases. As a result of the Inspectors General Act, virtually every federal agency has an inspector general whose mission is to ferret out fraud, waste, and abuse in their respective agencies' programs.

Federal prosecutors also receive referrals in white-collar crime cases from the Defense Criminal Investigative Service and individual branches of the military. There are also criminal investigators who investigate willful regulatory criminal violations at the Department of Agriculture, the Environmental Protection Agency, the Food and Drug Administration, the Fish and Wildlife Service, among others.

Government agencies that do not have criminal investigators are encouraged to coordinate with U.S. attorneys' offices on potential white-collar criminal matters. Accordingly, bank regulatory agencies like the Federal Reserve, the Federal Deposit Insurance Corp., the Office of Thrift Supervision, the Office of the Comptroller of the Currency, and the Resolution Trust Corp., are part of bank-fraud working groups around the country that meet periodically to discuss cases with federal prosecutors. Likewise, the Office of the U.S. Bankruptcy Trustee and the Securities Exchange Commission coordinate with, and refer cases, to U.S. attorneys.

Furthermore, state regulators and investigators now look almost exclusively to the federal government for prosecution of criminal activities involving state programs that receive federal funds. These state regulators and investigators refer these cases to federal prosecutors because they are confronted with an unwillingness or inability on the part of many state and local prosecutors to devote significant resources to white-collar crime. * * *

Finally, federal prosecutors now do not simply prosecute but, as a result of laws passed in the 1980s, have responsibilities for such matters as asset forfeiture, fine collection, restitution, and notification to victims and witnesses * * *

With respect to white-collar crime, the federal government has a unique role to play, with only a minimum of overlap with state prosecutors. The reality is that cases of criminal tax violations, fraud, and corruption in such federal programs as health care, multi-victim interstate consumer frauds, large-scale interstate business frauds, including insurance frauds, securities fraud, environmental crime, corruption by public officials, civil-rights prosecutions and money laundering, would go unprosecuted in most states if they were not handled by federal prosecutors. Even assuming that state district attorneys had the financial resources to tackle these cases, they would be severely hindered by lack of applicable statutes and the complications of securing witnesses and other evidence in other states and foreign countries. * * *

NOTES AND QUESTIONS

1. ***Drugs, Violent Crimes, & Immigration Offenses.*** The three fastest growing areas of the federal docket have been drug offenses, immigration offenses, and firearms offenses. WAYNE R. LAFAVE, JEROLD H. ISRAEL, NANCY J. KING, & ORIN S. KERR, CRIMINAL PROCEDURE 3D § 1.2(d)(2007) at 71. The Department of Justice has stressed the prosecution of drug offenses over the last few decades. Violent crimes received national attention in the late 1990s, with some arguing that this area should become a top priority of the Department of Justice. See, e.g., Senator Arlen Specter (former Philadelphia D.A.) and Paul Michel (former Associate Deputy Atty. Gen.), *The Need For A New Federalism In Criminal Justice*, July 1982, Annals of the AAPSS. This increased federal emphasis on violent crimes was met with criticism by those who believed that the prosecution of white collar offenses would suffer. "[S]ome defense lawyers fear that the Justice Department, responding to political perceptions rather than reality, is shrinking its white-collar caseload and trumpeting a $30-billion crime bill with little to say on office-suite crime." Benjamin Wittes, *Defense Bar Sees Dip in White-Collar Crime Cases*, 17 Legal Times, Oct. 24, 1994, at 2. The DOJ, however, continued to see white collar crime as a growing area of concentration, although one in which priorities must be drawn to accommodate limited resources. Consider the following excerpt from *FBI'S White Collar Crime Program Expanding Rapidly*, 8 Corp. Crime Rep. 4 (Oct. 17, 1994):

> The Federal Bureau of Investigation's (FBI) white collar crime program has been expanding rapidly in recent years, with the program consuming 27 percent of the FBI's Direct Agent Work years in FY 1993, federal officials said last week. The number of white-collar crime cases the FBI investigates has been increasing steadily over the years, with the FBI reporting 4,596 convictions and pre-trial diversions and $1 billion in fines imposed in FY 1993. The FBI's white-collar crime program covers a broad range of activities which include financial institution fraud, government fraud, including health care fraud and environmental crimes, public corruption and economic crimes. An FBI spokesperson told Corporate Crime Reporter that "because limited resources make it impossible for the FBI to address all white-collar cases that come to our attention, we are constantly analyzing trends and evaluating priorities to ensure maximum efficiency."

2. ***Terrorism.*** The tragic events of September 11th had a profound effect on the priorities of the Justice Department. On November 8, 2001, Attorney General Ashcroft and Deputy Attorney General Thompson announced a "reorganization and mobilization" of the Department of Justice. The following is an excerpt from Attorney General Ashcroft's speech:

> * * * The attacks of September 11th have redefined the mission of the Department of Justice. Defending our nation and defending

> the citizens of America against terrorist attacks is now our first and overriding priority. To fulfill this mission, we are devoting all the resources necessary to eliminate terrorist networks, to prevent terrorist attacks, and to bring to justice those who kill Americans in the name of murderous ideologies.

Following September 11, 2001 the FBI shifted "nearly one-third of all agents in criminal programs, to terrorism and intelligence duties." Eric Lichtblau, David Johnston & Ron Nixon, *F.B.I. Struggles to Handle Financial Fraud Cases*, N.Y.Times, Oct. 19, 2008, at A1.

3. ***Corporate Criminality.*** Did white collar crime become a top priority as a result of a "general social movement" in which people are "concerned about white-collar crime, and more specifically, about corporate criminality?" Is this a reflection of "a shift in cultural values about corporate misbehavior, and, at the same time, a strong commitment to equal justice as the ideological underpinnings of the legal order"? Francis T. Cullen, William J. Maakestad & Gray Cavender, CORPORATE CRIME UNDER ATTACK 27 (1987); see also Stephen Labaton, *Downturn and Shift in Population Feed Boom in White-Collar Crime,* The N.Y. Times, June 2, 2002, at A1 ("The bursting of the stock market bubble, combined with the changing face of the American Population, has led to a surge in business fraud and corruption prosecutions and investigations."). Consider the following excerpt from Ralph K. Winter, *Paying Lawyers, Empowering Prosecutors, and Protecting Managers: Raising the Cost of Capital in America*, 42 DUKE L.J. 945, 953 (1993):

> One can no longer teach or practice in the area of corporate or securities law without being attentive to the possible exposure of the corporation or its managers to criminal liability. This liability has become important for a number of reasons, including: new attitudes on the part of prosecutors, the substantial penalties that now may be levied on corporations under the Federal Sentencing Guidelines, the extraordinary breadth the federal courts accord the definition of fraud in the mail and wire fraud statutes, and the use of forfeiture as an adjunct to criminal RICO and money laundering prosecutions.

Perhaps the most significant impact on corporate criminal prosecution came in the wake of the Enron debacle. On September 27, 2002, Attorney General John Ashcroft stated the following at a Corporate Fraud/Responsibility Conference:

> * * * The past months have revealed a series of allegations of deception, fraud and malfeasance among a few individuals in whom we have placed our trust, and who have in turn assumed a fiduciary obligation to us. These are allegations of criminal conduct spanning years and, as their numbers have mounted, they have eroded confidence in the integrity of U.S. markets. Some investors both at

> home and overseas have done what was previously unthinkable: questioned the security, stability, and honesty of American markets.
>
> The malignancy of corporate corruption threatens more than the future of a few companies - it destroys workers' incomes, decimates families' savings and casts a shadow on the health, integrity and good name of American business itself. The success of the free market depends on a marketplace of integrity - a marketplace that operates on information of integrity. Reliable, truthful information is the unseen force that drives the economy. * * *
>
> Under the leadership of our Corporate Fraud Task Force, created earlier this summer by President Bush and headed by Deputy Attorney General Larry Thompson, the Department of Justice is taking a tough, new, cooperative approach to the real time enforcement of our corporate fraud statutes. The result is a lengthening list of both individuals and corporations that have become the targets of Department of Justice investigations and prosecutions * * *

http://www.justice.gov/archive/ag/speeches/2002/092702agremarkscorporatefraudconference.htm. See also Chapter 3.

4. ***Financial Fraud***. Under Attorney General Holder, the Obama Administration had as one of its policy initiatives, "targeting financial fraud." A Department of Justice Progress Report stated that:

> the Department has devoted significant attention to preventing, investigating, and prosecuting mortgage fraud. The Federal Bureau of Investigation is currently investigating more than 2,100 mortgage fraud cases, up almost 400 percent from five years ago. The Bureau also has more than doubled the number of agents investigating mortgage scams, has created a National Mortgage Fraud Team at headquarters in Washington, and is working hand-in-hand with our partners at other agencies. The Department also has brought indictments and obtained convictions against perpetrators of rescue schemes in the past months. In one case, the Department recently indicted 24 individuals for alleged activity related to an extensive mortgage fraud scheme based in San Diego, which involved 220 properties with a total sales price of more than $100 million dollars.

Progress Report, Department of Justice, available at http://www.justice.gov/sites/default/files/ag/legacy/2009/04/29/progress-report.pdf (April 2009). President Obama also renamed the Corporate Fraud Task Force as the Financial Fraud Enforcement Task Force. See http://www.stopfraud.gov/.

C. FEDERAL INFLUENCE AND LOCAL CORRUPTION

In the early 1970's, federal prosecutors began to target local political corruption as a major federal law enforcement priority. Federal prosecutors believed that "corrupt schemes at the state and local level . . . [were] at least as corrosive of the governmental process as corruption at the federal level." They determined that vigorous federal enforcement efforts were "required to fill a vacuum created by the inability or unwillingness of state and local law enforcement agencies to deal adequately with the task of ferreting out corruption."

Faced with an inadequate statutory basis for prosecuting corrupt local officials, federal enforcement officials began to apply four federal statutes which traditionally had been applied to other forms of criminal activity: the Hobbs Act, the Mail Fraud Act, the Travel Act, and most significantly, the Racketeer Influenced and Corrupt Organizations Act (RICO). The interpretations of the general language of the four statutes advanced by federal prosecutors have been described by many Justice Department officials as "creative" and by others as inconsistent with the legislative intent. Nonetheless, the federal courts generally validated the application of these statutes to local corruption. Encouraged by continuing judicial acquiescence, federal prosecutors dramatically escalated their efforts to police local corruption in the following decade. * * *

Assuming that Congress *had* clearly granted federal jurisdiction over local corruption, there are admittedly instances in which a substantial federal interest in the exercise of that jurisdiction does exist. However, federal discretion under RICO and the other federal statutes is so broad that prosecutions which fail to serve a substantial federal interest can and do result.

If state and local corruption causes the breakdown of local law enforcement, the case for federal intervention is strong. Corruption in enforcement of state laws often encourages offenses that are also federal crimes. * * *

Federal prosecutions of corrupt local officials who are not involved in law enforcement are often justified by the argument that local enforcement officials are unwilling to prosecute such defendants themselves. When local officials request federal intervention or when there is evidence of systematic or improper failure to prosecute at the local level, federal intervention is, * * * perhaps justified. * * *

Federal prosecution of local offenses such as political corruption is justified in cases where local enforcement officials are incapable of successfully prosecuting serious offenses. For example, federal intervention may be necessary to police complex multistate criminal ventures that involve corruption of state and local government units. It is inefficient and impractical for local authorities to investigate multistate crime because they are limited to prosecution of the local aspects of the criminal activity. Moreover, the states lack the legal mechanisms possessed by federal officials to bring scattered defendants to a single trial and compel the appearance of distant witnesses. Finally, it seems inequitable to saddle one jurisdiction with the entire cost of investigation and prosecution of criminal conduct that transcends that jurisdiction.

Federal exercise of criminal jurisdiction in political corruption cases may also be appropriate when organized crime is involved, since the adverse social consequences of allowing such activity to escape enforcement are substantial. "Corruption of public officials is one of the standard techniques of organized crime." A study by the Senate indicated that attorneys general in many states lack the authority to prosecute, successfully, complex organized crime activities.

Efficient prosecution of local corruption frequently requires the use of highly specialized investigatory techniques which the Federal Bureau of Investigation and United States Attorneys (USA's) are better equipped to employ. * * * However, "if efficiency were the sole criterion for federal participation, many traditional state functions might be usurped by a more efficient federal bureaucracy. . . . Federalism, rather than efficient administration, is the issue." Given a "state's special interest in policing its own political process," a federal interest greater than relative efficiency seems necessary to justify federal intervention. * * *

Prosecution may serve a substantial federal interest when the applicable state or local charges are less serious than the applicable federal charges. If the federal offense covering particular conduct is more grave than the relevant state offense, local prosecution will not vindicate those federal interests that Congress contemplated in enacting the provision.

A sufficient federal interest in intervention may also exist where the jurisdictional base is closely related to the offense involved. For example, an offense which substantially threatens the integrity of the United States mails or imposes a direct burden on interstate commerce would seem appropriate for federal prosecution. A substantial federal interest in the prosecution of local political corruption may also arise from resulting interference with federal programs or the improper use of federal funds.

There are many examples, however, of federal prosecutions lacking any of the federal interests discussed above. The increasing

> occurrence of federal prosecutions of local corruption, when there is no substantial federal interest, indicates that prosecutorial discretion is too broad and that its exercise is inconsistent with constitutional notions of federalism. * * *

Andrew T. Baxter, *Federal Discretion in the Prosecution of Local Political Corruption,* 10 PEPPERDINE L. REV. 321 (1983).

NOTES AND QUESTIONS

1. ***Federal/State Prosecution of Corruption.*** Should federal prosecutors take a backseat to local prosecutors in the prosecution of local corruption? Should priority be granted to the prosecutor who initiated the investigation? Should the controlling considerations be expertise and resources? What happens when there is a conflict between the federal and local prosecutor? Who has the authority to take the lead, and who resolves the conflict? See Arnold H. Lubasch, *Lindenhauer Pleads Not Guilty as Officials Debate Subpoena,* The New York Times, Mar. 1, 1986, at A29 (describing a conflict between then federal prosecutor Rudolph W. Guiliani and Robert M. Morgenthau. the Manhattan District Attorney).

2. ***Federalism Challenges.*** In **Sabri v. United States**, 541 U.S. 600 (2004), the Supreme Court rejected a federalism challenge to § 666, a federal anti-corruption statute that targets, among others, officials of state and local governments. The defendant was a real estate developer who offered bribes to a member of the Board of Commissioners of the Minneapolis Community Development Agency. He was charged with a violation of § 666(a)(2). Sabri argued that the statute is facially unconstitutional because it does not require a nexus between the local corruption and the federal funds received by the organization or agency, and therefore violated the limitations imposed by federalism on congressional power to punish local crimes. The Court upheld the constitutionality of § 666, stating:

> We can readily dispose of th[e] position that, to qualify as a valid exercise of Article I power, the statute must require proof of connection with federal money as an element of the offense. We simply do not presume the unconstitutionality of federal criminal statutes lacking explicit provision of a jurisdictional hook, and there is no occasion even to consider the need for such a requirement where there is no reason to suspect that enforcement of a criminal statute would extend beyond a legitimate interest cognizable under Article I, § 8.
>
> Congress has authority under the Spending Clause to appropriate federal monies to promote the general welfare, Art. I, § 8, cl. 1, and it has corresponding authority under the Necessary and Proper Clause, Art. I, § 8, cl. 18, to see to it that taxpayer dollars

appropriated under that power are in fact spent for the general welfare, and not frittered away in graft or on projects undermined when funds are siphoned off or corrupt public officers are derelict about demanding value for dollars. See generally M'Culloch v. Maryland, 4 Wheat. 316 (1819) (establishing review for means-ends rationality under the Necessary and Proper Clause). Congress does not have to sit by and accept the risk of operations thwarted by local and state improbity. See, e.g., M'Culloch, (power to " 'establish post-offices and post- roads' " entails authority to "punish those who steal letters"). Section 666(a)(2) addresses the problem at the sources of bribes, by rational means, to safeguard the integrity of the state, local, and tribal recipients of federal dollars.

It is true, just as Sabri says, that not every bribe or kickback offered or paid to agents of governments covered by § 666(b) will be traceably skimmed from specific federal payments, or show up in the guise of a quid pro quo for some dereliction in spending a federal grant. But this possibility portends no enforcement beyond the scope of federal interest, for the reason that corruption does not have to be that limited to affect the federal interest. Money is fungible, bribed officials are untrustworthy stewards of federal funds, and corrupt contractors do not deliver dollar-for-dollar value. Liquidity is not a financial term for nothing; money can be drained off here because a federal grant is pouring in there. And officials are not any the less threatening to the objects behind federal spending just because they may accept general retainers. See Westfall v. United States, 274 U.S. 256 (1927) (majority opinion by Holmes, J.) (upholding federal law criminalizing fraud on a state bank member of federal system, even where federal funds not directly implicated). It is certainly enough that the statutes condition the offense on a threshold amount of federal dollars defining the federal interest, such as that provided here, and on a bribe that goes well beyond liquor and cigars.

3. ***Prosecutorial Guidelines.*** Would guidelines assist in resolving potential state-federal conflicts? The United States Attorneys' Manual provides that prosecution should be declined when "1. No substantial federal interest would be served by prosecution; 2. The person is subject to effective prosecution in another jurisdiction; or 3. There exists an adequate non-criminal alternative to prosecution." U.S.A.M. § 9-27.220. The Manual further notes that:

A. In determining whether prosecution should be declined because the person is subject to effective prosecution in another jurisdiction, the attorney for the government should weigh all relevant considerations, including:

1. The strength of the other jurisdiction's interest in prosecution;

2. The other jurisdiction's ability and willingness to prosecute effectively; and

3. The probable sentence or other consequences if the person is convicted in the other jurisdiction.

U.S.A.M. § 9-27.240. See also Charles F. C. Ruff, *Federal Prosecution of Local Corruption: A Case Study in the Making of Law Enforcement Policy*, 65 GEO. L.J. 1171 (1977). Professor Sara Sun Beale states that "[g]enerally, the decision to bring charges in federal rather than state court is made on an ad hoc basis. The United States Attorney's Manual (the Manual) does contain some general standards for the exercise of prosecutorial discretion, but they are written so broadly that they provide little guidance." Sara Sun Beale, *Too Many and Yet Too Few: New Principles to Define the Proper Limits for Federal Criminal Jurisdiction*, 46 HASTINGS L.J. 979, 999 (1995).

4. ***Benefits of State/Federal Prosecution.*** Are there beneficial aspects to having both state and federal prosecutors pursue the same alleged local or state corruption? "Many Federal and local prosecutors maintain that competition between their offices is healthy and prevents possible cover-ups and oversights." Selwyn Raab, *Why Federal Attorneys Are the Gang-Busters Nowadays*, The New York Times, Mar. 8, 1987, at D6.

5. ***Dual Sovereignty Rule.*** Neither the double jeopardy bar of the federal constitution nor its due process requirement preclude federal and state entities from both prosecuting the same defendant for the same criminal conduct. "In the case of *United States v. Lanza,* [260 U.S. 377 (1922)], the Supreme Court promulgated what is customarily referred to as the 'dual sovereignty' doctrine: 'an act denounced as a crime by both national and state sovereignties is an offense against the peace and dignity of both and may be punished by each.' That the dual sovereignty doctrine allows a federal prosecution notwithstanding a prior state prosecution for the same conduct was thereafter affirmed in *Abbate v. United States,* [359 U.S. 187 (1959)]." WAYNE R. LAFAVE, JEROLD H. ISRAEL, & NANCY J. KING, ORIN S. KERR, CRIMINAL PROCEDURE, § 25.5 (a) (3d Ed. 2007). The Department of Justice, however, has a policy on dual prosecution and successive federal prosecution that:

> * * * precludes the initiation or continuation of a federal prosecution, following a prior state or federal prosecution based on substantially the same act(s) or transaction(s), unless three substantive prerequisites are satisfied: first, the matter must involve a substantial federal interest; second, the prior prosecution must have left that interest demonstrably unvindicated; and third, applying the same test applicable to all federal prosecutions, the

> government must believe that the defendant's conduct constitutes a federal offense, and that the admissible evidence probably will be sufficient to obtain and sustain a conviction by an unbiased trier of fact. In addition, there is a procedural prerequisite to be satisfied, that is, the prosecution must be approved by the appropriate Assistant Attorney General.
>
> Satisfaction of the three substantive prerequisites does not mean that a proposed prosecution must be approved or brought. The traditional elements of federal prosecutorial discretion continue to apply. See Principles of Federal Prosecution, U.S.A.M. 9-27.110.

U.S.A.M. § 9-2.031. This policy is known as the Petite policy, based on its recognition by the Supreme Court in Petite v. United States, 361 U.S. 529 (1960). The most prominent federal authorizations of criminal prosecutions following state prosecutions have come in civil rights cases. See Symposium, The Rodney King Trials: Civil Rights Prosecutions and Double Jeopardy, 41 U.C.L.A. L. REV. 509-720 (1994).

6. ***Political or Racial Motivations.*** Will the federal emphasis on prosecution of local corruption invariably open the door to discriminatory decision-making (or at least allegations of discriminatory decision-making)? Consider the following excerpts from Mark Curriden, *Selective Prosecution: Are Black Officials Investigative Targets*, 78 A.B.A. J. 54 (Feb. 1992):

> Kansas City, Mo., Mayor Emanuel Cleaver admits he is paranoid. The rookie chief executive of one of the largest cities in the Midwest fears that he will be investigated by the federal government.
>
> "I've done nothing wrong," Cleaver asserts. "But from what I've heard and seen, that really doesn't matter. Some of my colleagues say I can expect to be investigated at least once during my term in office, even if there is no probable cause. It appears that selective prosecution is the order of the day at the Department of Justice."
>
> Mayor Cleaver, who is black, is no radical. Nor does he subscribe to the conspiracy theory that envisions a secret plot master-minded by members of the Justice Department, the Federal Bureau of Investigation and the Internal Revenue Service against elected and appointed black officials in the United States. But he is concerned about the possibility, suggested by extensive anecdotal evidence, that black officials are subject to selective investigation and prosecution. * * * Mayor Cleaver is not alone in his thinking. A growing number of politicians, lawyers and researchers say selective prosecution exists, although their explanations for its causes vary widely.
>
> Some, like New York City attorney William Kunstler, who has represented political radicals throughout his career, believe that

there is an organized effort to destroy the country's black leadership, which even includes the use of an alleged FBI "hit squad" that travels across the country setting up black officials just to disgrace their race. "The proof that these guys exist is impossible to come up with," acknowledges Kunstler, "but the pure number of black officials being investigated tells me there's a conspiracy and a belief at [the Justice Department] that blacks are not qualified to be in positions of leadership." Others, like Kenneth O'Reilly, a political science professor at the University of Alaska, maintain that there are a few renegade prosecutors and agents remaining from the days of J. Edgar Hoover, the late FBI director. * * *

A more mainstream view is that the issue intertwines politics and race. According to this view, black officials, who by and large are Democrats, find themselves on the receiving end of a very political criminal justice system controlled, at least at the federal level, by prosecutors and investigators with largely Republican backgrounds. As Democratic officials who happen to be black, they find themselves likely targets for investigation.

"Whatever the case," says Julius Chambers, director of the NAACP's Legal Defense Fund in New York City, "it appears that black leaders are being investigated more frequently than their white counterparts simply because of their race, and that's not fair, and it's certainly not constitutional." Officials at the Justice Department and the FBI deny engaging in selective prosecutions, but otherwise refused to comment on the issue to the ABA Journal. * * *

A 1990 study by the National Council of Churches shows that more than 14 percent of the public corruption cases over the past five years targeted black officials, who make up less than two percent of the country's elected officials. In the South, where three percent of all elected officials are black, the study found that 40 percent of public corruption cases were pursued against blacks. More than half of the 24 members of the Congressional Black Caucus report being targeted for investigation or subjected to harassment by federal investigators. Since 1980, 21 black elected officials have been prosecuted in Alabama alone. Of those, 16 were found not guilty, two pleaded guilty, and three were convicted. Though less than one-half of one percent of the federal judiciary is black, three of the five U.S. District Court judges indicted in the past decade were black. * * *

In 1990, 77 percent of black respondents to a poll conducted by the New York Times said they believed that 'the government deliberately singles out and investigates black elected and appointed officials in order to discredit them in a way it doesn't do with white officials. "Thirty-four percent of the whites responding also believed that such selective prosecution 'could be going on."

D. FEDERAL INFLUENCE IN INTERNATIONAL PROSECUTIONS

UNITED STATES v. CASTLE
925 F.2d 831 (5th Cir. 1991)

PER CURIAM:

In this case, we are called upon to consider the Foreign Corrupt Practices Act of 1977 (hereinafter "FCPA"), 15 U.S.C. §§ 78dd-1, 78dd-2, and determine whether "foreign officials," who are excluded from prosecution under the FCPA itself, may nevertheless be prosecuted under the general conspiracy statute, 18 U.S.C. § 371, for conspiring to violate the FCPA.

We hold that foreign officials may not be prosecuted under 18 U.S.C. § 371 for conspiring to violate the FCPA. The scope of our holding, as well as the rationale that undergirds it, is fully set out in Judge Sanders's memorandum opinion of June 4, 1990, 741 F.Supp. 116, which we adopt and attach as an appendix hereto. * * *

APPENDIX

* * * Defendants Castle and Lowry have moved to dismiss the indictment against them on the grounds that as Canadian officials, they cannot be convicted of the offense charged against them. The two other defendants, Blondek and Tull, are U.S. private citizens, and they do not challenge their indictment on this ground. * * *

The indictment charges all four defendants with conspiring to bribe foreign officials in violation of the FCPA. Blondek and Tull were employees of Eagle Bus Company, a U.S. concern as defined in the FCPA. According to the indictment, they paid a $50,000 bribe to Defendants Castle and Lowry to ensure that their bid to provide buses to the Saskatchewan provincial government would be accepted.

There is no question that the payment of the bribe by Defendants Blondek and Tull is illegal under the FCPA, and that they may be prosecuted for conspiring to violate the Act. Nor is it disputed that Defendants Castle and Lowry could not be charged with violating the FCPA itself, since the Act does not criminalize the receipt of a bribe by a foreign official. The issue here is whether the Government may prosecute Castle and Lowry under the general conspiracy statute, 18 U.S.C. § 371, for conspiring to violate the FCPA. Put more simply, the question is whether foreign officials, whom the Government concedes it cannot prosecute under the FCPA itself, may be prosecuted under the general conspiracy statute for conspiring to violate the Act. * * *

The principle enunciated by the Supreme Court in *Gebardi* [v. United States, 287 U.S. 112 (1932)], squarely applies to the case before this Court. Congress intended in both the FCPA and the Mann Act to deter and punish certain activities which necessarily involved the agreement of at least two people, but Congress chose in both statutes to punish only one party to the agreement. In *Gebardi* the Supreme Court refused to disregard Congress' intention to exempt one party by allowing the Executive to prosecute that party under the general conspiracy statute for precisely the same conduct. Congress made the same choice in drafting the FCPA, and by the same analysis, this Court may not allow the Executive to override the Congressional intent not to prosecute foreign officials for their participation in the prohibited acts.

* * * [T]he exclusive focus [of Congress in passing the FCPA] was on the U.S. companies and the effects of their conduct within and on the United States.

First, Congress was concerned about the domestic effects of such payments. In the early 1970's, the Watergate affair and resulting investigations revealed that the payment of bribes to foreign officials was a widespread practice among U.S. companies. In the House Report accompanying an earlier version of the Act, it was noted that more than 400 companies had admitted making such payments, distributing well over 300 million dollars in corporate funds to foreign officials. Such massive payments had many negative domestic effects, not the least of which was the distortion of, and resulting lack of confidence in, the free market system within the United States.

> The payment of bribes to influence the acts or decision of foreign officials . . . is unethical. It is counter to the moral expectations and values of the American public. But not only is it unethical, it is bad business as well. It erodes public confidence in the integrity of the free market system . . . . In short, it rewards corruption instead of efficiency and puts pressure on ethical enterprises to lower their standards or risk losing business.

The House Committee further noted that many of the payments were made not to compete with foreign companies, but rather to gain an edge over a competitor in the United States.

Congress' second motivation was the effect of such payments by U.S. companies on the United States' foreign relations. The legislative history repeatedly cited the negative effects the revelations of such bribes had wrought upon friendly foreign governments and officials. Yet the drafters acknowledged, and the final law reflects this, that some payments that would be unethical or even illegal within the United States might not be perceived similarly in foreign countries, and those payments should not be criminalized. For example, grease payments, those payments made "to assure or to speed the proper performance of a foreign official's duties," are not illegal under the

Act since they were often a part of the custom of doing business in foreign countries. Additionally, the Act was later amended to permit an affirmative defense on the grounds that the payment was legal in the country in which it was made. 15 U.S.C. § 78dd-2(c)(1). These exclusions reinforce the proposition that Congress had absolutely no intention of prosecuting the foreign officials involved, but was concerned solely with regulating the conduct of U.S. entities and citizens.[1]

[The government argued that a statement in a House Report showed congressional intent to allow conspiracy prosecutions of foreign officials.] * * *

This language [in the House Report] does not refute the overwhelming evidence of a Congressional intent to exempt foreign officials from prosecution for receiving bribes, especially since Congress knew it had the power to reach foreign officials in many cases, and yet declined to exercise that power. (United States has power to reach conduct of noncitizens under international law). Congress' awareness of the extent of its own power reveals the fallacy in the Government's position that only those classes of persons deemed by Congress to need protection are exempted from prosecution under the conspiracy statute. The question is not whether Congress could have included foreign officials within the Act's proscriptions, but rather whether Congress intended to do so, or more specifically, whether Congress intended the general conspiracy statute, passed many years before the FCPA, to reach foreign officials.

The drafters of the statute knew that they could, consistently with international law, reach foreign officials in certain circumstances. But they were equally well aware of, and actively considered, the "inherent jurisdictional, enforcement, and diplomatic difficulties" raised by the application of the bill to non-citizens of the United States. In the conference report, the conferees indicated that the bill would reach as far as possible, and listed all the persons or entities who could be prosecuted. The list includes virtually every person or entity involved, including foreign nationals

---

[1] Congress considered, and rejected, the idea that a demand for a payment by a foreign official would be a valid defense to a criminal prosecution under the Act, because

> at some point the U.S. company would make a conscious decision whether or not to pay a bribe. That the payment may have been first proposed by the recipient rather than the U.S. company does not alter the corrupt purpose on the part of the person paying the bribe.

The very fact that Congress considered this issue underscores Congress' exclusive focus on the U.S. companies in making the payment. If the drafters were concerned that a demand by a foreign official might be considered a defense to a prosecution, they clearly were expecting that only the payors of the bribes, and not the foreign officials demanding and/or receiving the bribes, would be prosecuted.

who participated in the payment of the bribe when the U.S. courts had jurisdiction over them. But foreign officials were not included.

It is important to remember that Congress intended that these persons would be covered by the Act itself, without resort to the conspiracy statute. Yet the very individuals whose participation was required in every case--the foreign officials accepting the bribe--were excluded from prosecution for the substantive offense. Given that Congress included virtually every possible person connected to the payments except foreign officials, it is only logical to conclude that Congress affirmatively chose to exempt this small class of persons from prosecution.

Most likely Congress made this choice because U.S. businesses were perceived to be the aggressors, and the efforts expended in resolving the diplomatic, jurisdictional, and enforcement difficulties that would arise upon the prosecution of foreign officials was not worth the minimal deterrent value of such prosecutions. Further minimizing the deterrent value of a U.S. prosecution was the fact that many foreign nations already prohibited the receipt of a bribe by an official. * * * In fact, whenever a nation permitted such payments, Congress allowed them as well. *See* 15 U.S.C. § 78dd-2(c)(1).

Based upon the language of the statute and the legislative history, this Court finds in the FCPA what the Supreme Court in *Gebardi* found in the Mann Act: an affirmative legislative policy to leave unpunished a well-defined group of persons who were necessary parties to the acts constituting a violation of the substantive law. The Government has presented no reason why the prosecution of Defendants Castle and Lowry should go forward in the face of the congressional intent not to prosecute foreign officials. If anything, the facts of this case support Congress' decision to forego such prosecutions since foreign nations could and should prosecute their own officials for accepting bribes. * * *

NOTES AND QUESTIONS

1. ***International Bribery.*** At the time of the *Castle* case, the United States was the only country with a Foreign Corrupt Practices Act. The International Anti-Bribery and Fair Competition Act of 1998, signed into law on November 18, 1998, serves to strengthen the prohibitions on international bribery. See also FCPA- *A Resource Guide to the U.S. Foreign Corrupt Practices Act*, http://www.justice.gov/criminal/fraud/fcpa/guidance/guide.pdf.

2. ***Coordinated Enforcement Actions.*** Siemens Aktiengesellschaft (Siemens AG), a German corporation, and three of its subsidiaries plead guilty to violations of the Foreign Corrupt Practices Act (FCPA), and "Siemens AG agreed to pay a $448.5 million fine; and Siemens Argentina, Bangladesh, and Venezuela each agreed to pay a $500,000 fine, for a combined total criminal fine of $450 million." "Siemens AG also reached a

settlement of a related civil complaint filed by the Securities and Exchange Commission (SEC), charging Siemens AG with violating the FCPA's anti-bribery, books and records, and internal controls provisions in connection with many of its international operations including those discussed in the criminal charges. Siemens AG agreed to pay $350 million in disgorgement of profits relating to those violations. "Also at this same time, "Siemens AG agreed to a disposition resolving an ongoing investigation by the Munich Public Prosecutor's Office of Siemens AG's operating groups other than the Telecommunications group. The charges were based on corporate failure to supervise its officers and employees, and in connection with those charges Siemens AG agreed to pay €395 million or approximately $569 million, including a €250,000 corporate fine and €394.75 million in disgorgement of profits.'" The coordinated efforts of U.S. and German law enforcement authorities in this case set the standard for multi-national cooperation in the fight against corrupt business practices,' said U.S. Attorney for the District of Columbia Jeffrey A. Taylor." DOJ Press Release, December 15, 2008, available at www.justice.gov/opa/pr/2008/December/08-crm-1105.html.

3. ***Scope of FCPA.*** In addition to limiting who can be charged with a violation of the Foreign Corrupt Practices Act, the statute also limits the conduct subject to prosecution and it offers exceptions to accommodate necessary business practices in foreign countries. Consider the following case:

UNITED STATES v. KAY
359 F.3d 738 (5th Cir. 2004)

Weiner, Circuit Judge:

In 2001, a grand jury charged Kay with violating the FCPA and subsequently returned the indictment, which charges both Kay and Murphy with 12 counts of FCPA violations. * * * The indictment * * * spells out in detail how Kay and Murphy allegedly orchestrated the bribing of Haitian customs officials to accept false bills of lading and other documentation that intentionally understated by one-third the quantity of rice shipped to Haiti, thereby significantly reducing ARI's customs duties and sales taxes. * * *

Because an offense under the FCPA requires that the alleged bribery be committed for the purpose of inducing foreign officials to commit unlawful acts, the results of which will assist in obtaining or retaining business in their country, the questions before us in this appeal are (1) whether bribes to obtain illegal but favorable tax and customs treatment can ever come within the scope of the statute, and (2) if so, whether, in combination, there are minimally sufficient facts alleged in the indictment to inform the defendants regarding the nexus between, on the one hand, Haitian taxes avoided through bribery, and, on the other hand, assistance in getting or keeping some business or business opportunity in Haiti. * * *

None contend that the FCPA criminalizes every payment to a foreign official: It criminalizes only those payments that are intended to (1) influence a foreign official to act or make a decision in his official capacity, or (2) induce such an official to perform or refrain from performing some act in violation of his duty, or (3) secure some wrongful advantage to the payor. And even then, the FCPA criminalizes these kinds of payments only if the result they are intended to produce–their quid pro quo–will assist (or is intended to assist) the payor in efforts to get or keep some business for or with "any person." Thus, the first question of statutory interpretation presented in this appeal is whether payments made to foreign officials to obtain unlawfully reduced customs duties or sales tax liabilities can ever fall within the scope of the FCPA, i.e., whether the illicit payments made to obtain a reduction of revenue liabilities can ever constitute the kind of bribery that is proscribed by the FCPA. The district court answered this question in the negative * * *

The principal thrust of the defendants' argument is that the business nexus element, i.e., the "assist . . . in obtaining or retaining business" element, narrowly limits the statute's applicability to those payments that are intended to obtain a foreign official's approval of a bid for a new government contract or the renewal of an existing government contract. In contrast, the government insists that, in addition to payments to officials that lead directly to getting or renewing business contracts, the statute covers payments that indirectly advance ("assist") the payor's goal of obtaining or retaining foreign business with or for some person. The government reasons that paying reduced customs duties and sales taxes on imports, as is purported to have occurred in this case, is the type of "improper advantage" that always will assist in obtaining or retaining business in a foreign country, and thus is always covered by the FCPA. * * *

Congress enacted the FCPA in 1977, in response to recently discovered but widespread bribery of foreign officials by United States business interests. Congress resolved to interdict such bribery, not just because it is morally and economically suspect, but also because it was causing foreign policy problems for the United States. In particular, these concerns arose from revelations that United States defense contractors and oil companies had made large payments to high government officials in Japan, the Netherlands, and Italy. Congress also discovered that more than 400 corporations had made questionable or illegal payments in excess of $300 million to foreign officials for a wide range of favorable actions on behalf of the companies.

In deciding to criminalize this type of commercial bribery, the House and Senate each proposed similarly far-reaching, but non-identical, legislation. In its bill, the House intended "broadly [to] prohibit[ ] transactions that are corruptly intended to induce the recipient to use his or her influence to affect any act or decision of a foreign official . . . ." Thus, the House bill contained no limiting "business nexus" element. Reflecting a somewhat narrower purpose, the Senate expressed its desire to ban payments made for the purpose of inducing foreign officials to act "so as to direct business to any person, maintain an established business opportunity with any person, divert any business opportunity from any person or influence the enactment or promulgation of legislation or regulations of that government or instrumentality."

At conference, compromise language "clarified the scope of the prohibition by requiring that the purpose of the payment must be to influence any act or decision of a foreign official ... so as to assist an issuer in obtaining, retaining or directing business to any person." In the end, then, Congress adopted the Senate's proposal to prohibit only those payments designed to induce a foreign official to act in a way that is intended to facilitate ("assist") in obtaining or retaining of business.

Congress expressly emphasized that it did not intend to prohibit "so-called grease or facilitating payments," such as "payments for expediting shipments through customs or placing a transatlantic telephone call, securing required permits, or obtaining adequate police protection, transactions which may involve even the proper performance of duties." Instead of making an express textual exception for these types of non-covered payments, the respective committees of the two chambers sought to distinguish permissible grease payments from prohibited bribery by only prohibiting payments that induce an official to act "corruptly," i.e., actions requiring him "to misuse his official position" and his discretionary authority, not those "essentially ministerial" actions that "merely move a particular matter toward an eventual act or decision or which do not involve any discretionary action."

In short, Congress sought to prohibit the type of bribery that (1) prompts officials to misuse their discretionary authority and (2) disrupts market efficiency and United States foreign relations, at the same time recognizing that smaller payments intended to expedite ministerial actions should remain outside of the scope of the statute. The Conference Report explanation, on which the district court relied to find a narrow statutory scope, truly offers little insight into the FCPA's precise scope, however; it merely parrots the statutory language itself by stating that the purpose of a payment must be to induce official action "so as to assist an issuer in obtaining, retaining or directing business to any person."

To divine the categories of bribery Congress did and did not intend to prohibit, we must look to the Senate's proposal, because the final statutory language was drawn from it, and from the SEC Report on which the Senate's legislative proposal was based. In distinguishing among the types of illegal payments that United States entities were making at the time, the SEC Report identified four principal categories: (1) payments "made in an effort to procure special and unjustified favors or advantages in the enactment or administration of the tax or other laws" of a foreign country; (2) payments "made with the intent to assist the company in obtaining or retaining government contracts"; (3) payments "to persuade low-level government officials to perform functions or services which they are obliged to perform as part of their governmental responsibilities, but which they may refuse or delay unless compensated" ("grease"), and (4) political contributions. The SEC thus exhibited concern about a wide range of questionable payments (explicitly including the kind at issue here) that were resulting in millions of dollars being recorded falsely in corporate books and records.

As noted, the Senate Report explained that the statute should apply to payments intended "to direct business to any person, maintain an established business opportunity with any person, divert any business opportunity from any person or influence the enactment or promulgation of legislation or regulations of that government or instrumentality." * * * It is clear, however, that even though the Senate was particularly concerned with bribery intended to secure new business, it was also mindful of bribes that influence legislative or regulatory actions, and those that maintain established business opportunities, a category of economic activity separate from, and much more capacious than, simply "directing business" to someone.

The statute's ultimate language of "obtaining or retaining" mirrors identical language in the SEC Report. But, whereas the SEC Report highlights payments that go toward "obtaining or retaining government contracts," the FCPA, incorporating the Senate Report's language, prohibits payments that assist in obtaining or retaining business, not just government contracts. Had the Senate and ultimately Congress wanted to carry over the exact, narrower scope of the SEC Report, they would have adopted the same language. We surmise that, in using the word "business" when it easily could have used the phraseology of SEC Report, Congress intended for the statute to apply to bribes beyond the narrow band of payments sufficient only to "obtain or retain government contracts." The Senate's express intention that the statute apply to corrupt payments that maintain business opportunities also supports this conclusion.

For purposes of deciding the instant appeal, the question nevertheless remains whether the Senate, and concomitantly Congress, intended this broader statutory scope to encompass the administration of tax, customs, and other laws and regulations affecting the revenue of foreign states. To reach this conclusion, we must ask whether Congress's remaining expressed desire to prohibit bribery aimed at getting assistance in retaining business or maintaining business opportunities was sufficiently broad to include bribes meant to affect the administration of revenue laws. When we do so, we conclude that the legislative intent was so broad. Congress was obviously distraught not only about high profile bribes to high-ranking foreign officials, but also by the pervasiveness of foreign bribery by United States businesses and businessmen. Congress thus made the decision to clamp down on bribes intended to prompt foreign officials to misuse their discretionary authority for the benefit of a domestic entity's business in that country. This observation is not diminished by Congress's understanding and accepting that relatively small facilitating payments were, at the time, among the accepted costs of doing business in many foreign countries. * * *

After the FCPA's enactment, United States business entities and executives experienced difficulty in discerning a clear line between prohibited bribes and permissible facilitating payments. As a result, Congress amended the FCPA in 1988, expressly to clarify its original intent in enacting the statute. Both houses insisted that their proposed amendments only clarified ambiguities "without changing the basic intent or effectiveness of the law."

In this effort to crystallize the scope of the FCPA's prohibitions on bribery, Congress chose to identify carefully two types of payments that are not proscribed by the statute. It expressly excepted payments made to procure "routine governmental action" (again, the grease exception), and it incorporated an affirmative defense for payments that are legal in the country in which they are offered or that constitute bona fide expenditures directly relating to promotion of products or services, or to the execution or performance of a contract with a foreign government or agency.

We agree with the position of the government that these 1988 amendments illustrate an intention by Congress to identify very limited exceptions to the kinds of bribes to which the FCPA does not apply. A brief review of the types of routine governmental actions enumerated by Congress shows how limited Congress wanted to make the grease exceptions. Routine governmental action, for instance, includes "obtaining permits, licenses, or other official documents to qualify a person to do business in a foreign country," and "scheduling inspections associated with contract performance or inspections related to transit of goods across country." Therefore, routine governmental action does not include the issuance of every official document or every inspection, but only (1) documentation that qualifies a party to do business and (2) scheduling an inspection–very narrow categories of largely non-discretionary, ministerial activities performed by mid- or low-level foreign functionaries. In contrast, the FCPA uses broad, general language in prohibiting payments to procure assistance for the payor in obtaining or retaining business, instead of employing similarly detailed language, such as applying the statute only to payments that attempt to secure or renew particular government contracts. Indeed, Congress had the opportunity to adopt narrower language in 1977 from the SEC Report, but chose not to do so. * * *

As we have demonstrated, the 1977 and 1988 legislative history already make clear that the business nexus requirement is not to be interpreted unduly narrowly. We therefore agree with the government that there really was no need for Congress to add "or other improper advantage" to the requirement. In fact, such an amendment might have inadvertently swept grease payments into the statutory ambit–or at least created new confusion as to whether these types of payments were prohibited–even though this category of payments was excluded by Congress in 1977 and remained excluded in 1988; and even though Congress showed no intention of adding this category when adopting its 1998 amendments. That the Convention, which the Senate ratified without reservation and Congress implemented, would also appear to prohibit the types of payments at issue in this case only bolsters our conclusion that the kind of conduct allegedly engaged in by defendants can be violative of the statute.

Given the foregoing analysis of the statute's legislative history, we cannot hold as a matter of law that Congress meant to limit the FCPA's applicability to cover only bribes that lead directly to the award or renewal of contracts. Instead, we hold that Congress intended for the FCPA to apply broadly to payments intended to assist the payor, either directly or indirectly, in obtaining or retaining business for some person, and that bribes paid to foreign tax officials to secure illegally reduced customs and tax liability constitute a type of payment that can fall within this broad coverage. * * *

NOTES

1. ***Statutory Authority for Extraterritoriality.*** Should the United States use federal statutes to prosecute conduct occurring outside its boundaries? In some cases the federal statute is enacted with the purpose of reaching extraterritorial activities. For example, in the case of the Foreign Corrupt Practices Act, Congress wrote the statute with a clear intent that the statute have an international application. This is also true with respect to export control legislation.

Some statutes have a specific extraterritorial provision to indicate the extraterritorial application. For example, 18 U.S.C. § 1621, a perjury statute, provides that "[t]his section is applicable whether the statement or subscription is made within or without the United States." Although the statute itself has a national focus, it is clear that Congress intended for either the specific provision or the entire statute to be used both for acts occurring within its borders and for acts occurring extraterritorially.

In Morrison v. National Australia Bank LTD., 561 U.S. 247 (2010), the Court looked at whether § 10(b) of the Securities Exchange Act should apply to conduct outside the United States. In this civil matter, the Court held that "longstanding principle of American law 'that legislation of Congress, unless a contrary intent appears, is meant to apply only within the territorial jurisdiction of the United States.'" See also Kiobel v. Royal Dutch Petroleum Co., 133 S.Ct. 1659 (2013)(looking at extraterritoriality under the Alien Tort Claims Act).

2. ***International Norms.*** In deciding whether a statute should have an extraterritorial application, courts examine the issue from a national perspective and/or an international perspective. When approaching the issue nationally, courts are trying to discern whether Congress intended for the statute to have an international application. When approaching the question internationally, courts are looking to see if under international law the United States has jurisdiction.

In international law there are five principles commonly used to determine whether a criminal statute should have extraterritorial application. These five general principles are:

> (1) territorial, wherein jurisdiction is based on the place where the offense is committed; (2) national, wherein jurisdiction is based on the nationality or national character of the offender; (3) protective, wherein jurisdiction is based on whether the national interest is injured; (4) universal, which amounts to physical custody of the offender; and (5) passive personality, wherein jurisdiction is based on the nationality or national character of the victim.

Chua Han Mow v. United States, 730 F.2d 1308 (9th Cir. 1984). See also *Harvard Research in International Law, Jurisdiction With Respect to Crime*, 28 AM. J. INT'L. 437 (1935). Consider the First Circuit's resolution of extraterritoriality with regard to an antitrust prosecution:

UNITED STATES v. NIPPON PAPER INDUSTRIES CO., LTD.
109 F.3d 1 (1st Cir. 1997)

SELYA, Circuit Judge.

This case raises an important, hitherto unanswered question. In it, the United States attempts to convict a foreign corporation under the Sherman Act, a federal antitrust statute, alleging that price-fixing activities which took place entirely in Japan are prosecutable because they were intended to have, and did in fact have, substantial effects in this country. The district court, declaring that a criminal antitrust prosecution could not be based on wholly extraterritorial conduct, dismissed the indictment. * * * We reverse. * * *

In 1995, a federal grand jury handed up an indictment naming as a defendant Nippon Paper Industries Co., Ltd. (NPI), a Japanese manufacturer of facsimile paper. The indictment alleges that in 1990 NPI and certain unnamed coconspirators held a number of meetings in Japan which culminated in an agreement to fix the price of thermal fax paper throughout North America. NPI and other manufacturers who were privy to the scheme purportedly accomplished their objective by selling the paper in Japan to unaffiliated trading houses on condition that the latter charge specified (inflated) prices for the paper when they resold it in North America. The trading houses then shipped and sold the paper to their subsidiaries in the United States who in turn sold it to American consumers at swollen prices. The indictment further relates that, in 1990 alone, NPI sold thermal fax paper worth approximately $6,100,000 for eventual import into the United States; and that in order to ensure the success of the venture, NPI monitored the paper trail and confirmed that the prices charged to end users were those that it had arranged. These activities, the indictment posits, had a substantial adverse effect on commerce in the United States and unreasonably restrained trade in violation of Section One of the Sherman Act, 15 U.S.C. § 1 (1994).

NPI moved to dismiss because, inter alia, if the conduct attributed to NPI occurred at all, it took place entirely in Japan, and, thus, the indictment failed to limn an offense under Section One of the Sherman Act. The government opposed this initiative on two grounds. First, it claimed that the law deserved a less grudging reading and that, properly read, Section One of the Sherman Act applied criminally to wholly foreign conduct as long as that conduct produced substantial and intended effects within the United States. Second, it claimed that the indictment, too, deserved a less grudging reading and that, properly read, the bill alleged a vertical conspiracy in restraint of trade that involved overt acts by certain coconspirators within the United States. Accepting a restrictive reading of both the statute and the indictment, the district court dismissed the case. ***

Our law has long presumed that "legislation of Congress, unless a contrary intent appears, is meant to apply only within the territorial jurisdiction of the United States." EEOC v. Arabian American Oil Co., 499 U.S. 244, 248, S.Ct. 1227, 1230, 113 L.Ed.2d 274 (1991). In this context, the Supreme Court has charged inquiring courts with determining whether Congress has clearly expressed an affirmative desire to apply particular laws to conduct that occurs beyond the borders of the United States.

The earliest Supreme Court case which undertook a comparable task in respect to Section One of the Sherman Act determined that the presumption against extraterritoriality had not been overcome. In American Banana Co. v. United Fruit Co., 213 U.S. 347, 29 S.Ct. 511, 53 L.Ed. 826 (1909), the Court considered the application of the Sherman Act in a civil action concerning conduct which occurred entirely in Central America and which had no discernible effect on imports to the United States. Starting with what Justice Holmes termed "the general and almost universal rule" holding "that the character of an act as lawful or unlawful must be determined wholly by the law of the country where the act is done," and the ancillary proposition that, in cases of doubt, a statute should be "confined in its operation and effect to the territorial limits over which the lawmaker has general and legitimate power," the Court held that the defendant's actions abroad were not proscribed by the Sherman Act.

Our jurisprudence is precedent-based, but it is not static. By 1945, a different court saw a very similar problem in a somewhat softer light. In United States v. Aluminum Co. of Am., 148 F.2d 416 (2d Cir.1945) (Alcoa), the Second Circuit, sitting as a court of last resort, mulled a civil action brought under Section One against a Canadian corporation for acts committed entirely abroad which, the government averred, had produced substantial anticompetitive effects within the United States. The *Alcoa* court read *American Banana* narrowly; that case, Judge Learned Hand wrote, stood only for the principle that "[w]e should not impute to Congress an intent to punish all whom its courts can catch, for conduct which has no consequences within the United States." But a sovereign ordinarily can impose liability for conduct outside its borders that produces consequences within them, and while considerations of comity argue against applying Section One to situations in which no effect within the United States has been shown--the *American Banana* scenario--the statute, properly interpreted, does proscribe extraterritorial acts which were "intended to affect imports [to the United States] and did affect them." On the facts of *Alcoa*, therefore, the presumption against extraterritoriality had been overcome, and the Sherman Act had been violated.

Any perceived tension between *American Banana* and *Alcoa* was eased by the Supreme Court's most recent exploration of the Sherman Act's extraterritorial reach. In Hartford Fire Ins. Co. v. California, 509 U.S. 764, 113 S.Ct. 2891, 125 L.Ed.2d 612 (1993), the Justices endorsed Alcoa 's core holding, permitting civil antitrust claims under Section One to go forward despite the fact that the actions which allegedly violated Section One occurred entirely on British soil. While noting *American Banana*'s initial disagreement with this proposition, the *Hartford Fire* Court deemed it "well established by now that the Sherman Act applies to foreign conduct that was meant to produce and did in fact produce some substantial effect in the United States." The conduct alleged, a London-based conspiracy to alter the American insurance market, met that benchmark.

To sum up, the case law now conclusively establishes that civil antitrust actions predicated on wholly foreign conduct which has an intended and substantial effect in the United States come within Section One's jurisdictional reach. * * *

Were this a civil case, our journey would be complete. But here the United States essays a criminal prosecution for solely extraterritorial conduct rather than a civil action. This is largely uncharted terrain; we are aware of no authority directly on point, and the parties have cited none.

Be that as it may, one datum sticks out like a sore thumb: in both criminal and civil cases, the claim that Section One applies extraterritorially is based on the same language in the same section of the same statute: "Every contract, combination in the form of trust or otherwise, or conspiracy, in restraint of trade or commerce among the several States, or with foreign nations, is declared to be illegal." 15 U.S.C. § 1. Words may sometimes be chameleons, possessing different shades of meaning in different contexts, but common sense suggests that courts should interpret the same language in the same section of the same statute uniformly, regardless of whether the impetus for interpretation is criminal or civil. * * *

NPI and its amicus, the Government of Japan, urge that special reasons exist for measuring Section One's reach differently in a criminal context. We have reviewed their exhortations and found them hollow. We discuss the five most promising theses below. The rest do not require comment.

1. *Lack of Precedent.* NPI and its amicus make much of the fact that this appears to be the first criminal case in which the United States endeavors to extend Section One to wholly foreign conduct. We are not impressed. There is a first time for everything, and the absence of earlier criminal actions is probably more a demonstration of the increasingly global nature of our economy than proof that Section One cannot cover wholly foreign conduct in the criminal milieu.

Moreover, this argument overstates the lack of precedent. There is, for example, solid authority for applying a state's criminal statute to conduct occurring entirely outside the state's borders. * * *

2. *Difference in Strength of Presumption.* The lower court and NPI both cite United States v. Bowman, 260 U.S. 94, 43 S.Ct. 39, 67 L.Ed. 149 (1922), for the proposition that the presumption against extraterritoriality operates with greater force in the criminal arena than in civil litigation. This misreads the opinion. To be sure, the *Bowman* Court, dealing with a charged conspiracy to defraud, warned that if the criminal law "is to be extended to include those [crimes] committed outside of the strict territorial jurisdiction, it is natural for Congress to say so in the statute, and failure to do so will negative the purpose of Congress in this regard." But this pronouncement merely restated the presumption against extraterritoriality previously established in civil cases like *American Banana.* The *Bowman* Court nowhere suggested that a different, more resilient presumption arises in criminal cases. * * *

3. *The Restatement.* NPI and the district court, both sing the praises of the Restatement (Third) of Foreign Relations Law (1987), claiming that it supports a distinction between civil and criminal cases on the issue of extraterritoriality. The passage to which they pin their hopes states:

> [I]n the case of regulatory statutes that may give rise to both civil and criminal liability, such as the United States antitrust and securities laws, the presence of substantial foreign elements will ordinarily weigh against application of criminal law. In such cases, legislative intent to subject conduct outside the state's territory to its criminal law should be found only on the basis of express statement or clear implication.

Id. at § 403 cmt. f. We believe that this statement merely reaffirms the classic presumption against extraterritoriality--no more, no less. After all, nothing in the text of the Restatement proper contradicts the government's interpretation of Section One. * * * What is more, other comments indicate that a country's decision to prosecute wholly foreign conduct is discretionary. * * *

4. *The Rule of Lenity.* The next arrow which NPI yanks from its quiver is the rule of lenity. The rule itself is venerable; it provides that, in the

course of interpreting statutes in criminal cases, a reviewing court should resolve ambiguities affecting a statute's scope in the defendant's favor. * * * But the rule of lenity is inapposite unless a statutory ambiguity looms, and a statute is not ambiguous for this purpose simply because some courts or commentators have questioned its proper interpretation. * * * Put bluntly, the rule of lenity cannot be used to create ambiguity when the meaning of a law, even if not readily apparent, is, upon inquiry, reasonably clear. * * * In view of the fact that the Supreme Court deems it "well established" that Section One of the Sherman Act applies to wholly foreign conduct, *Hartford Fire*, we effectively are foreclosed from trying to tease an ambiguity out of Section One relative to its extraterritorial application. Accordingly, the rule of lenity plays no part in the instant case.

5. *Comity*. International comity is a doctrine that counsels voluntary forbearance when a sovereign which has a legitimate claim to jurisdiction concludes that a second sovereign also has a legitimate claim to jurisdiction under principles of international law. * * * Comity is more an aspiration than a fixed rule, more a matter of grace than a matter of obligation. * * *

In this case the defendant's comity-based argument is even more attenuated. The conduct with which NPI is charged is illegal under both Japanese and American laws, thereby alleviating any founded concern about NPI being whipsawed between separate sovereigns. And, moreover, to the extent that comity is informed by general principles of reasonableness, see Restatement (Third) of Foreign Relations Law § 403, the indictment lodged against NPI is well within the pale. In it, the government charges that the defendant orchestrated a conspiracy with the object of rigging prices in the United States. If the government can prove these charges, we see no tenable reason why principles of comity should shield NPI from prosecution. We live in an age of international commerce, where decisions reached in one corner of the world can reverberate around the globe in less time than it takes to tell the tale. Thus, a ruling in NPI's favor would create perverse incentives for those who would use nefarious means to influence markets in the United States, rewarding them for erecting as many territorial firewalls as possible between cause and effect.

We need go no further. *Hartford Fire* definitively establishes that Section One of the Sherman Act applies to wholly foreign conduct which has an intended and substantial effect in the United States. We are bound to accept that holding. Under settled principles of statutory construction, we also are bound to apply it by interpreting Section One the same way in a criminal case. The combined force of these commitments requires that we accept the government's cardinal argument, reverse the order of the district court, reinstate the indictment, and remand for further proceedings. * * *

Reversed and remanded.

LYNCH, Circuit Judge (concurring).

* * * While courts, including this one, speak of determining congressional intent when interpreting statutes, the meaning of the antitrust laws has emerged through the relationship among all three branches of government. In this criminal case, it is our responsibility to ensure that the executive's interpretation of the Sherman Act does not conflict with other legal principles, including principles of international law.

That question requires examination beyond the language of Section One of the Sherman Act. It is, of course, generally true that, as a principle of statutory interpretation, the same language should be read the same way in all contexts to which the language applies. But this is not invariably true. New content is sometimes ascribed to statutory terms depending upon context. * * * Where Congress intends that our laws conform with international law, and where international law suggests that criminal enforcement and civil enforcement be viewed differently, it is at least conceivable that different content could be ascribed to the same language depending on whether the context is civil or criminal. * * *

NOTES AND QUESTIONS

1. ***Using Civil Law for Extraterritoriality.*** Considering the different standards of proof applicable to civil and criminal matters, should a substantive holding in a civil case be authority for a criminal action? Do criminal and civil matters use the same standard of causation? Does the fact that the statute involves antitrust, a business crime that crosses into both civil and criminal actions, provide a basis for using civil law cases as authority? The United States is not the only country scrutinizing price-fixing. See Stephen Labaton, *The World Gets Tough on Price Fixers*, N.Y.Times, June 3, 2001, at Sec.3. ("Taking the lead from the United States, governments in Europe and Asia are beginning to take price-fixing more seriously.").

2. ***Extraterritoriality and the Revenue Rule.*** In **Pasquantino v. United States**, 544 U.S. 349 (2005), the Court considered an extraterritorial application of the wire fraud statute, and whether the revenue rule precludes a prosecution of a scheme involving the smuggling of "large quantities of liquor into Canada from the United States." "[T]he Pasquantinos, while in New York, ordered liquor over the telephone from discount package stores in Maryland." They employed individuals "to drive the liquor over the Canadian border, without paying the required excise taxes." "Uncontested evidence at trial showed that Canadian taxes then due on alcohol purchased in the United States and transported to Canada were approximately double the liquor's purchase price." Justice Thomas writing the opinion for the majority stated:

* * * We granted certiorari to resolve a conflict in the Courts of Appeals over whether a scheme to defraud a foreign government of tax revenue violates the wire fraud statute. * * *

Neither the antismuggling statute, 18 U.S.C. § 546, nor U.S. tax treaties convince us that petitioners' scheme falls outside the terms of the wire fraud statute. Unlike the treaties and the antismuggling statute, the wire fraud statute punishes fraudulent use of domestic wires, whether or not such conduct constitutes smuggling, occurs aboard a vessel, or evades foreign taxes. Petitioners would be equally liable if they had used interstate wires to defraud Canada not of taxes due, but of money from the Canadian treasury. * * *

[T]his prosecution poses little risk of causing the principal evil against which the revenue rule was traditionally thought to guard: judicial evaluation of the policy-laden enactments of other sovereigns. See, e.g., Moore v. Mitchell, 30 F.2d 600 (2d Cir. 1929) (L.Hand, J., concurring). As Judge Hand put it, allowing courts to enforce another country's revenue laws was thought to be a delicate inquiry

> when it concerns the relations between the foreign state and its own citizens .... To pass upon the provisions for the public order of another state is, or at any rate should be, beyond the powers of a court; it involves the relations between the states themselves, with which courts are incompetent to deal, and which are intrusted to other authorities.

The present prosecution creates little risk of causing international friction through judicial evaluation of the policies of foreign sovereigns. This action was brought by the Executive to enforce a statute passed by Congress. In our system of government, the Executive is "the sole organ of the federal government in the field of international relations," United States v. Curtiss-Wright Export Corp., 299 U.S. 304 (1936), and has ample authority and competence to manage "the relations between the foreign state and its own citizens" and to avoid "embarass[ing] its neighbor[s]," *Moore* (L.Hand, J., concurring). True, a prosecution like this one requires a court to recognize foreign law to determine whether the defendant violated U.S. law. But we may assume that by electing to bring this prosecution, the Executive has assessed this prosecution's impact on this Nation's relationship with Canada, and concluded that it poses little danger of causing international friction. We know of no common-law court that has applied the revenue rule to bar an action accompanied by such a safeguard, and neither petitioners nor the dissent directs us to any. The greater danger, in fact, would lie in our judging this prosecution barred based on the foreign policy

> concerns animating the revenue rule, concerns that we have "neither aptitude, facilities nor responsibility" to evaluate.
>
> More broadly, petitioners argue that the revenue rule avoids giving domestic effect to politically sensitive and controversial policy decisions embodied in foreign revenue laws, regardless of whether courts need pass judgment on such laws. This worries us little here. The present prosecution, if authorized by the wire fraud statute, embodies the policy choice of the two political branches of our Government — Congress and the Executive — to free the interstate wires from fraudulent use, irrespective of the object of the fraud. Such a reading of the wire fraud statute gives effect to that considered policy choice. It therefore poses no risk of advancing the policies of Canada illegitimately.
>
> Still a final revenue rule rationale petitioners urge is the concern that courts lack the competence to examine the validity of unfamiliar foreign tax schemes. Foreign law, of course, posed no unmanageable complexity in this case. The District Court had before it uncontroverted testimony of a Government witness that petitioners' scheme aimed at violating Canadian tax law.
>
> Nevertheless, Federal Rule of Criminal Procedure 26.1 addresses petitioners' concern by setting forth a procedure for interpreting foreign law that improves on those available at common law. Specifically, it permits a court, in deciding issues of foreign law, to consider "any relevant material or source — including testimony — without regard to the Federal Rules of Evidence." By contrast, common-law procedures for dealing with foreign law — those available to the courts that formulated the revenue rule--were more cumbersome. Rule 26.1 gives federal courts sufficient means to resolve the incidental foreign law issues they may encounter in wire fraud prosecutions.
>
> Finally, our interpretation of the wire fraud statute does not give it "extraterritorial effect." Petitioners used U.S. interstate wires to execute a scheme to defraud a foreign sovereign of tax revenue. * * * It may seem an odd use of the Federal Government's resources to prosecute a U.S. citizen for smuggling cheap liquor into Canada. But the broad language of the wire fraud statute authorizes it to do so and no canon of statutory construction permits us to read the statute more narrowly. * * *

Justice Ginsburg, in her dissent, advocated that the wire fraud statute should not extend to schemes to evade foreign tax and customs laws. She stated in part:

> * * * Today's novel decision is all the more troubling for its failure to take account of Canada's primary interest in the matter at stake.

United States citizens who have committed criminal violations of Canadian tax law can be extradited to stand trial in Canada. Canadian courts are best positioned to decide "whether, and to what extent, the defendants have defrauded the governments of Canada and Ontario out of tax revenues owed pursuant to their own, sovereign, excise laws."

* * * Expansively interpreting the text of the wire fraud statute, which prohibits "any scheme or artifice to defraud, or for obtaining money or property by means of . . . fraudulent pretenses," the Court today upholds the Government's deployment of § 1343 essentially to enforce foreign tax law. * * * Construing § 1343 to encompass violations of foreign revenue laws, the Court ignores the absence of anything signaling Congress' intent to give the statute such an extraordinary extraterritorial effect. "It is a longstanding principle of American law," *Aramco*, that Congress, in most of its legislative endeavors, "is primarily concerned with domestic conditions."

Section 1343, which contains no reference to foreign law as an element of the domestic crime of wire fraud, contrasts with federal criminal statutes that chart the courts' course in this regard. See, e.g., 18 U.S.C. § 1956(c)(1) (defendant must know that transaction involved the proceeds of activity "that constitutes a felony under State, Federal, or foreign law"); 16 U.S.C. § 3372(a)(2)(A) (banning importation of wildlife that has been "taken, possessed, transported, or sold in violation of any . . . foreign law"). These statutes indicate that Congress, which has the sole authority to determine the extraterritorial reach of domestic laws, is fully capable of conveying its policy choice to the Executive and the courts. I would not assume from legislative silence that Congress left the matter to Executive discretion.

The presumption against extraterritoriality, which guides courts in the absence of congressional direction, provides ample cause to conclude that § 1343 does not extend to the instant scheme. Moreover, as to foreign customs and tax laws, there is scant room for doubt about Congress' general perspective: Congress has actively indicated, through both domestic legislation and treaties, that it intends "strictly [to] limit the parameters of any assistance given" to foreign nations. * * *

Complementing the principle that courts ordinarily should await congressional instruction before giving our laws extraterritorial thrust, the common-law revenue rule holds that one nation generally does not enforce another's tax laws. The Government argues, and the Court accepts, that domestic wire fraud prosecutions premised on violations of foreign tax law do not implicate the revenue rule because the court, while it must "recognize foreign [revenue] law to determine whether the defendant violated U.S.

> law," need only "enforce" foreign law "in an attenuated sense." As discussed above, however, the defendants' conduct arguably fell within the scope of § 1343 only because of their purpose to evade Canadian customs and tax laws; shorn of that purpose, no other aspect of their conduct was criminal in this country. It seems to me unavoidably obvious, therefore, that this prosecution directly implicates the revenue rule. It is equally plain that Congress did not endeavor, by enacting § 1343, to displace that rule. * * *

3. ***Foreign Commerce.*** In **United States v. Tarkoff**, 242 F.3d 991 (11th Cir. 2001), the court considered "whether a defendant may be convicted for conspiring to violate and violating the money laundering statute, 18 U.S.C. § 1956(h) and (a)(1)(B)(i), where the indictment charged and the government proved that the two monetary transactions at issue occurred wholly outside the United States." On appeal, Michael Tarkoff, a criminal defense attorney, contended that "that he was entitled to [a] judgment of acquittal because the transactions in which he took part occurred wholly outside the United States, and therefore did not affect interstate or foreign commerce, which is a necessary component of an element of the money laundering statute under which he was convicted." In affirming the conviction, Circuit Judge Kravitch writes:

> Tarkoff's convictions are based on his participation in two transactions: (1) the wire transfer of $400,000 from Curacao to Fernandez's bank account in Israel, and (2) the transfer of $50,000 of those funds to Tarkoff's Israeli bank account. * * * Because the evidence is sufficient to prove that Tarkoff correctly believed that the funds involved in the Israeli transactions were the proceeds of Arnaiz's Medicare fraud, and that Tarkoff participated in conducting the transactions knowing that they were designed in whole or in part to conceal or disguise the nature, location, source, ownership, or control of the proceeds of the Medicare fraud, we address only the first element of a section 1956(a)(1)(B)(i) offense-that is, whether the Israeli transactions satisfy the statutory definition of 'financial transaction.'
>
> The statute defines "financial transaction" as "(A) a transaction which in any way or degree affects interstate or foreign commerce (i) involving the movement of funds by wire or other means or (ii) involving one or more monetary instruments ..., or (B) a transaction involving the use of a financial institution which is engaged in, or the activities of which affect, interstate or foreign commerce in any way or degree." 18 U.S.C. § 1956(c)(4). Tarkoff argues that because the two transactions with the Israeli bank occurred wholly outside the United States, they were not "financial transactions" under 18 U.S.C. § 1956(c)(4). In support of this proposition, Tarkoff relies

primarily on United States v. Kramer, 73 F.3d 1067 (11th Cir.1996), in which this Court reversed a money laundering conviction under 18 U.S.C. § 1956(a)(2)(B)(i) because the defendant participated only in a transfer of money from Switzerland to Luxembourg, and not a transfer of money to or from the United States, as required to violate section 1956(a)(2)(B)(i). * * * *Kramer* does not control in this case, however, because Tarkoff was convicted under a different subsection of the money laundering statute (§ 1956(a)(1)(B)(i)) than the one at issue in *Kramer*. The difference between the two subsections is that violation of the subsection at issue in *Kramer* specifically requires a transfer of funds to or from the United States, whereas a violation of the subsection under which Tarkoff was convicted can occur so long as the defendant was involved in a "financial transaction."

There are two ways to establish that a defendant conducted a "financial transaction" under 18 U.S.C. § 1956(a)(1)(B)(i). To satisfy its burden, the government had to prove either (1) that Tarkoff participated in a transaction that *in any way or degree* affected interstate or foreign commerce and involved the transfer of funds or the use of one or more monetary instruments, that Tarkoff participated in a transaction that involved the use of a financial institution that was engaged in, or the activities of which affected, interstate or foreign commerce *in any way or degree.*

The government argues that it proved Tarkoff participated in a 'financial transaction' as defined in section 1956(c)(4)(A) by virtue of the evidence that Tarkoff and Fernandez, two U.S. citizens, traveled from the United States to Israel to transact business with a bank there, and that the Israeli bank transactions required telephone communication between Israel and Miami, and between Miami and Curacao, to arrange for the funds transfer from Curacao to Israel. We agree that these facts support a finding that Tarkoff participated in a "financial transaction" as that term is defined in 18 U.S.C. § 1956(c)(4)(A) because the international travel and communication required to execute the wire transactions affected foreign commerce "in any way or degree." The evidence also supports a finding that Tarkoff participated in a "financial transaction" as that term is defined in 18 U.S.C. § 1956(c)(4)(B) because the transactions involved the use of the Israeli bank-a financial institution which, by communicating with parties in the United States and providing banking services to United States citizens, was a "financial institution that was engaged in, or the activities of which affected, foreign commerce in any way or degree." * * *

Because Tarkoff knowingly participated in a financial transaction designed in whole or in part to conceal or disguise the nature, the location, the source, the ownership, or the control of the proceeds of specified unlawful activity, we affirm his conviction for violating and conspiring to violate 18 U.S.C. § 1956(a)(1)(B)(i).

CHAPTER THREE
CORPORATE AND INDIVIDUAL RESPONSIBILITY

A. CORPORATE LIABILITY

1. Introduction

NEW YORK CENTRAL & HUDSON RIVER RAILROAD COMPANY v. UNITED STATES
212 U.S. 481 (1909)

Justice DAY delivered the opinion of the Court.

* * * The principal attack in this court is upon the constitutional validity of certain features of the Elkins act. That act, among other things, provides:

> (1) That anything done or omitted to be done by a corporation common carrier subject to the act to regulate commerce, and the acts amendatory thereof, which, if done or omitted to be done by any director or officer thereof, or any receiver, trustee, lessee, agent, or person acting for or employed by such corporation, would constitute a misdemeanor under said acts, or under this act, shall also be held to be a misdemeanor committed by such corporation; and, upon conviction thereof, it shall be subject to like penalties as are prescribed in said acts, or by this act, with reference to such persons, except as such penalties are herein changed. * * *
>
> In construing and enforcing the provisions of this section, the act, omission, or failure of any officer, agent, or other person acting for or employed by any common carrier, acting within the scope of his employment, shall, in every case, be also deemed to be the act, omission, or failure of such carrier, as well as that of the person.

It is contended that these provisions of the law are unconstitutional because Congress has no authority to impute to a corporation the commission of criminal offenses, or to subject a corporation to a criminal prosecution by reason of the things charged. The argument is that to thus punish the corporation is in reality to punish the innocent stockholders, and to deprive them of their property without opportunity to be heard, consequently without due process of law. And it is further contended that these provisions of the statute deprive the corporation of the presumption of innocence—a presumption which is part of due process in criminal prosecutions. It is urged that, as there is no authority shown by the board of directors or the stockholders for the criminal acts of the agents of the company, in contracting for and giving rebates, they could not be lawfully charged against the corporation. As no action of the board of directors could legally authorize a crime, and as, indeed, the stockholders could not do so, the arguments come to this: that, owing to the nature and character of its organization and the extent of its power and authority, a corporation cannot commit a crime of the nature charged in this case.

Some of the earlier writers on common law held the law to be that a corporation could not commit a crime. It is said to have been held by Lord Chief Justice Holt that "a corporation is not indictable, although the particular members of it are." In Blackstone's Commentaries, we find it stated: "A corporation cannot commit treason, or felony, or other crime in its corporate capacity, though its members may, in their distinct individual capacities." The modern authority, universally, so far as we know, is the other way. In considering the subject, Bishop's New Criminal Law, § 417, devotes a chapter to the capacity of corporations to commit crime, and states the law to be: "Since a corporation acts by its officers and agents, their purposes, motives, and intent are just as much those of the corporation as are the things done. If, for example, the invisible, intangible essence or air which we term a corporation can level mountains, fill up valleys, lay down iron tracks, and run railroad cars on them, it can intend to do it, and can act therein as well viciously as virtuously." Without citing the state cases holding the same view, we may note Telegram Newspaper Co. v. Commonwealth, 172 Mass. 294, 52 N.E. 445, in which it was held that a corporation was subject to punishment for criminal contempt; and the court, speaking by Mr. Chief Justice Field, said: "We think that a corporation may be liable criminally for certain offenses of which a specific intent may be a necessary element. There is no more difficulty in imputing to a corporation a specific intent in criminal proceedings than in civil. A corporation cannot be arrested and imprisoned in either civil or criminal proceedings, but its property may be taken either as compensation for a private wrong or as punishment for a public wrong." * * *

It is now well established that, in actions for tort, the corporation may be held responsible for damages for the acts of its agent within the scope of his employment. * * * And this is the rule when the act is done by the agent in the course of his employment, although done wantonly or recklessly or against the express orders of the principal. In such cases the liability is not imputed because the principal actually participates in the malice or fraud, but because the act is done for the benefit of the principal, while the agent is acting within the scope of his employment in the business of the principal, and justice requires that the latter shall be held responsible for damages to the individual who has suffered by such conduct.

A corporation is held responsible for acts not within the agent's corporate powers strictly construed, but which the agent has assumed to perform for the corporation when employing the corporate powers actually authorized, and in such cases there need be no written authority under seal or vote of the corporation in order to constitute the agency or to authorize the act.

In this case we are to consider the criminal responsibility of a corporation for an act done while an authorized agent of the company is exercising the authority conferred upon him. It was admitted by the defendant at the trial that, at the time mentioned in the indictment, the general freight traffic manager and the assistant freight traffic manager were authorized to establish rates at which freight should be carried over the line of the New York Central & Hudson River Company, and were authorized to unite with other companies in the establishing, filing, and publishing of through rates, including the through rate or rates between New York and Detroit referred to in the indictment. Thus, the subject-matter of making and fixing rates was within the scope of the authority and employment of the agents of the company, whose acts in this connection are sought to be charged upon the company. Thus clothed with authority, the agents were bound to respect the regulation of interstate commerce enacted by Congress, requiring the filing and publication of rates and punishing departures therefrom. Applying the principle governing civil liability, we go only a step farther in holding that the act of the agent, while exercising the authority delegated to him to make rates for transportation, may be controlled, in the interest of public policy, by imputing his act to his employer and imposing penalties upon the corporation for which he is acting in the premises.

It is true that there are some crimes which, in their nature, cannot be committed by corporations. But there is a large class of offenses, of which rebating under the Federal statutes is one, wherein the crime consists in purposely doing the things prohibited by statute. In that class of crimes we see no good reason why corporations may not be held responsible for and charged with the knowledge and purposes of their agents, acting within the authority conferred upon them. If it were not so, many offenses might go unpunished and acts be committed in violation of law where, as in the present case, the statute requires all persons, corporate or private, to refrain from certain practices, forbidden in the interest of public policy. * * *

We see no valid objection in law, and every reason in public policy, why the corporation, which profits by the transaction, and can only act through its agents and officers, shall be held punishable by fine because of the knowledge and intent of its agents to whom it has intrusted authority to act in the subject-matter of making and fixing rates of transportation, and whose knowledge and purposes may well be attributed to the corporation for which the agents act. While the law should have regard to the rights of all, and to those of corporations no less than to those of individuals, it cannot shut its eyes to the fact that the great majority of business transactions in modern times are conducted through these bodies, and particularly that interstate commerce is almost entirely in their hands, and to give them immunity from all punishment because of the old and exploded doctrine that a corporation cannot commit a crime would virtually take away the only means of effectually controlling the subject-matter and correcting the abuses aimed at.

There can be no question of the power of Congress to regulate interstate commerce, to prevent favoritism, and to secure equal rights to all engaged in interstate trade. It would be a distinct step backward to hold that Congress cannot control those who are conducting this interstate commerce by holding them responsible for the intent and purposes of the agents to whom they have delegated the power to act in the premises. * * *

NOTES AND QUESTIONS

1. ***Development of Corporate Criminal Liability.*** At common law, corporations were not subject to criminal liability. "[I]t had no mind, and thus was incapable of the criminal intent then required for all crimes; it had no body, and thus could not be imprisoned." WAYNE R. LAFAVE & AUSTIN W. SCOTT, JR., CRIMINAL LAW 2D ED. 257 (1986). The development of corporate criminal liability initially occurred in regulatory offenses involving acts of omission. This extension was consistent with the arguments that a corporation could not form intent and could not be imprisoned. Since these offenses involved strict liability crimes, requiring no *mens rea*, and assessed a penalty of merely a fine, a corporation could legitimately be subject to criminal liability. Ellen S. Podgor, *Corporate and White Collar Crime: Simplifying the Ambiguous*, 31 AM. CRIM. L. REV. 391, 394 (1994). To what extent does *New York Central* extend corporate criminal liability beyond the strict liability realm?

2. ***Corporate Sentencing.*** At the time of *New York Central,* a finding of corporate criminal liability meant that fines could be imposed against the corporation. Today the consequences to the corporation include a range of sanctions beyond those imposed at the time of *New York Central.* The Organizational Sentencing Guidelines increase fines and also provide for sanctions such as restitution and court-ordered compliance programs. Consideration is given to organizational culpability. [Chapter 17, pt. E].

3. ***Pros/Cons of Corporate Criminal Liability.*** As a matter of legislative policy, does it make sense to have corporate criminal liability? Does corporate criminal liability in fact impose punishment on innocent shareholders, as argued in *New York Central?* Will the real effect of corporate criminal liability be to punish the consumer by increasing the cost of products in the market? Does competition within the market balance these concerns? See FRANCIS T. CULLEN, WILLIAM J. MAAKESTAD, GRAY CAVENDER, CORPORATE CRIME UNDER ATTACK: THE FORD PINTO CASE AND BEYOND 352-53 (1987) (rejects the argument that corporate criminal fines will just result in increased prices to consumers). See also Jennifer Arlen, *Rewarding Whistleblowers: The Costs and Benefits of an Incentive-Based Compliance Strategy*, *in* CORPORATE DECISION-MAKING IN CANADA (Ronald Daniels &

RANDALL MORCK EDS., 1995); Jennifer Arlen, *The Potentially Perverse Effects of Corporate Criminal Liability,* 23 J. OF LEGAL STUD. 833 (1994).

4. ***Deterrence.*** Does the imposition of corporate criminal liability truly serve as a deterrent of future criminality? "Corporations are largely undeterrable; fines are ineffective, and only the imprisonment of guilty individuals achieves real deterrence." John S. Coffee, Jr., *Corporate Criminal Responsibility,*1 ENCYCLOPEDIA OF CRIME AND JUSTICE 257 (1983). Could deterrence be better accomplished by using civil remedies? See Eliezer Lederman, *Criminal Law, Perpetrator and Corporation: Rethinking a Complex Triangle,* 76 J. CRIM. L. & CRIMINOLOGY 285, 315-16 (1985); V.S. Khanna, *Corporate Criminal Liability: What Purpose Does It Serve?*, 109 HARV. L. REV. 1477 (1996). Consider the following from Joe D. Whitley, Marc N. Garber, Mark A. McCarty, and Steven D. Henry, *The Case for Reevaluating DOJ Policies on Prosecuting White Collar Crime*, Washington Legal Foundation, Working Paper Series No. 108, May 2002, at 14-15:

> In the case of a corporate conviction, a wide variety of individuals are punished, including the corporation's shareholders and its innocent employees. Such shareholders and innocent employees will have had no involvement in the wrongful conduct and may not have benefitted from it. As a result, no just retribution is dispensed when they are punished along with the truly culpable parties. Moreover, because these individuals most likely lacked the ability to prevent the wrongful conduct, punishing such individuals does not provide any deterrent effect on other, similarly situated shareholders and innocent employees who may, likewise, be unable to stop wrongful conduct in their own organization.

5. ***Government Position on Corporate Criminal Liability.*** On July 25, 2002, in a speech to the Citizens' Crime Commission in New York, Deputy Attorney General Larry D. Thompson, who also served as Chair of the Corporate Fraud Task Force, ad interagency group, stated:

> Although it should be done sparingly, we should never hesitate to prosecute corporations themselves when the circumstances warrant it. * * * [T]he reasons why I believe that it is imperative to continue to prosecute business organizations where appropriate:
>
> First, corporations are economic and cultural facts in our society. Employees act on the corporation's behalf and take on the corporation's identity. Large corporations, develop their own methods and culture that guide employees' thoughts and actions. That culture is a web of attitudes and practices that tends to replicate and perpetuate itself beyond the tenure of any individual manager. That culture may instill respect for the law or breed contempt and malfeasance. The organization itself must be held accountable for the culture and the conduct it promotes. Without this tool, the public would have no adequate deterrent to corporate

> criminal conduct because the culture that condoned, or at least acquiesced in, that behavior would be beyond the criminal law's power to correct. Only by clearly preserving the possibility of prosecuting the corporation itself can we ensure systemic reform.
>
> Second, the corporations that are prosecuted have generally transgressed before and proven themselves immune to civil persuasion. The Justice Department has long recognized the principle that an employee's criminal wrongdoing does not mean that the employing organization should automatically be charged with a crime, especially where it would not serve a substantial federal interest to prosecute and adequate non-criminal alternatives exist. In reality, the corporations that are criminally prosecuted - that is, for which the enforcement authorities choose to subject their case to the criminal standard of proof beyond a reasonable doubt - are ones in which the company has flagrantly crossed the line in one or more ways that demonstrate that the guilty mind of individual actors was borne out of the guilty culture of the organization itself.
>
> Third, civil regulatory regimes may do a good job sorting out the normal range of problems in an industry, but it takes criminal sanctions to deal with extreme cases of serious or repeated wrongdoing. Traditional civil remedies have proven ineffective against recidivist companies that are the primary targets of criminal prosecution. Civil sanctions simply do not have the power of criminal penalties to concentrate the corporate mind and change corporate culture. Large business organizations, particularly public companies that are already regulated in myriad ways, sometimes have the disappointing tendency to view civil sanctions as merely the "cost of doing business" - a cost that can be passed on to customers and shareholders without lingering effect in the management suite and the board room. Civil sanctions are particularly impotent in combating crimes against society at large, such as regulatory reporting violations or obstruction of justice, that may undermine the legal system, but do not create easily quantifiable harm. The severe potential collateral consequences to a corporation resulting from a criminal conviction is sometime the best and most effective way to punish a corporation.
>
> Without corporate criminal liability, there would be no effective deterrent to a corporate culture that—expressly or tacitly—condones criminal conduct. * * *

6. ***Good Faith Defense.*** Should a corporation that acts in good faith be entitled to a defense when a rogue employee within the corporation fails to abide by a corporate compliance program that has been properly administered? A good faith defense is offered to companies in civil actions when facing respondeat superior in tort. See Burlington Industries v. Ellerth, 524 U.S. 742 (1998)(providing an affirmative defense for corporations

in sexual harassment cases). Amici, in the case of **United States v. Ionia Management S.A.,** 555 F.3d 303 (2d Cir. 2009), suggested that the court consider such an affirmative defense, but the Second Circuit stated that "regardless of asserted new Supreme Court cases in other areas of the law," there was no precedent for an affirmative defense for corporate criminal liability. The court stated that "a corporate compliance program may be relevant to whether an employee was acting in the scope of his employment, but it is not a separate element." See Andrew Weissmann & David Newman, *Rethinking Criminal Corporate Liability*, 82 IND. L.J. 411 (2007). Good faith may be considered by the court in imposing a sentence on the corporation. See Chapter 17.

7. ***Corporations as "Persons"***. 1 U.S.C. § 1 provides that "the words 'person' and 'whoever' as used throughout the federal code, include corporations, companies, associations, firms, partnerships, societies, and joint stock companies, as well as individuals." In Citizens United v. Federal Election Commission, 558 U.S. 310 (2010), the Court held that "political speech does not lose First Amendment protection 'simply because its source is a corporation.'" See also Joan MacLeod Heminway, *Thoughts on the Corporation as a Person for Purposes of Corporate Criminal Liability*, 41 STETSON L. REV. 137 (2011).

2. "For the Benefit"

STANDARD OIL COMPANY OF TEXAS v. UNITED STATES
307 F.2d 120 (5th Cir. 1962)

BROWN, Circuit Judge.

This appeal by two corporate defendants [Standard and its wholly-owned subsidiary Pasotex], from fines imposed on judgments of conviction under the Connally Hot Oil Act, raises this basic question. May a corporate employer be held liable for a crime committed by employees who, although ostensibly acting in the performance of their duties, were really cooperating with a third person in the accomplishment of a criminal purpose for the benefit of that third person, and whose acts not only did not benefit the employer, but in some instances, at least, result in a theft of its property? * * *

* * * Standard's interest [here] was limited to that of a purchaser having a statutory duty of buying oil tendered to it by Thompson and other producers in the field.

* * * Thompson has nine wells. Some were capable of producing their daily allowable under rules of the Texas Railroad Commission. Some of them could not. But under the Texas Conservation Laws and Regulations, the underage from one lease may not be made up from other commonly owned leases which have a capacity in excess of their assigned allowables. Oil swapped in this fashion is most certainly hot oil under the Connally Act

which, forbidding "the transportation in interstate commerce * * * of contraband oil * * *," 15 U.S.C.A. § 715b, defines this as "petroleum which, * * * was produced * * * or withdrawn * * * in excess of the amounts permitted to be produced * * * or withdrawn * * * under the laws of a State * * *," 15 U.S.C.A. § 715a(1).

Over a period of approximately twelve months, Morgan (or Hart as his relief) issued false run tickets covering oil supposedly received at Pumping Station No. 2 from or produced by specified Thompson wells. Some of these purported to show that the oil actually received (and receipted for) was produced by a given well rather than the one from which it was known by Morgan (or Hart) to have come. But in numerous other instances, a false run ticket was used showing receipt of Thompson oil which had never been produced or received at all. For rendering this vital and knowing participation in these two schemes which benefited Thompson, these two Pasotex employees were paid or received substantial sums in cash or merchandise from Thompson.

In those instances where, though receipted for, no oil was actually received at Pumping Station No. 2, a new problem came up. Oil received at Station No. 2 moved to Station No. 1 where Purcell was in charge. But since Station No. 2 had less oil than it had receipted for, the shortage continued at Station No. 1 when No. 2 "moved" all of its oil to No. 1. This was an actual shortage of oil in contrast to mere swapping of oil among leases. This shortage had to be made up or the whole scheme would collapse.

* * * As operator of Segment 1 of SACROC, [Standard] operated all of the wells * * *. It therefore had control over the movement of the oil from the leases. More than that, by reason of the unitizing agreement Standard was an owner of a substantial undivided interest (approximately 19%) in all such oil. Purcell, aware of the continuing shortages from Station No. 2, gave instructions to pumpers to increase production from Segment 1 sufficient to make up the shortage. This amounted to 6,000 or so barrels every month for a considerable period. Records, of course, had to be falsified so that this "excess" oil moving through Station No. 1 to make up Station No. 2 "shortages" would be concealed. Standard had still another role. It was the purchaser of the oil. Since this make-up of Station No. 2 shortage was the only way Standard was getting oil ostensibly purchased earlier by it from Thompson at Station No. 2, Standard was, in effect, paying Thompson for oil which belonged to Standard (and the other Unit co-owners).

How Standard or Pasotex may be held criminally liable for "knowingly violating" the statute by transportation of oil " * * * produced * * * in excess of the amounts permitted to be produced * * * under the laws of (the) state" of Texas when all of such oil came into the custody of each corporation solely as a result of a deliberate purpose by unfaithful employees to cheat or steal is the legal question for our determination. Adding irony to what some might regard as amazement is the fact that the very first moment knowledge of this activity came to light, Pasotex, after preliminary verification of its suspicions, reported the matter immediately to the Texas Railroad Commission. Thereafter followed this prosecution.

We start with the proposition that what is involved is statutory construction. We may assume that Congress can subject corporations to criminal accountability for acts of this kind committed by unfaithful servants. But the question is whether any such purpose was intended with regard to the Connally Hot Oil Act.

Since the record is absolutely barren of even the most remote whisper of suspicion that this was the case of corporations winking at dereliction by energetic, zealous employees, the Government stresses, for both a legal and psychological purpose, the contention that the two corporations received some benefit. But as we point out later, no benefit was either intended or obtained.

We have some difficulty in understanding the contentions which the Government makes in its effort to support the District Court's finding of guilt which, in turn, was based almost wholly on the idea that what these unfaithful agents were doing was their usual function for the corporation. * * *

As this statute prescribes a mental state as an element of the crime, usual principles must be applied in order to impute to the lifeless legal entity the requisite knowledge. So far as this case is concerned, we do not have to deal with the difficult and troublesome problem of determining whether the "knowledge" required is merely of the actions which constitute the crime as is true of some offenses, or whether it requires the so called "evil intent," that is a consciousness that the actions taken violate a known law. We may assume that the standard is the less exacting one and is satisfied if the evidence shows beyond a reasonable doubt that the acts were done "* * * deliberately and with knowledge * * *" and were "* * * not * * * merely careless or negligent or inadvertent. * * *" Browder v. United States, 312 U.S. 335, 341(1941).

The corporations can be found guilty, therefore, only if the evidence shows that each, acting through its human agents, deliberately did these acts, that is, with the corporation "knowing" that they were being done for it. Inquiry along this line brings us face-to-face with the everyday problem of imputing knowledge to a corporation.

* * * [T]he Court, in recognizing that Congress has the power to "personify the company" and thereby charge a partnership entity with criminal liability, spelled out that it was "through the doctrine of respondeat superior" that "corporations and other * * * impersonal entities can be guilty of 'knowing' or 'willful' violations of regulatory statutes * * *." United States v. A. & P. Trucking Co., 358 U.S. 121 (1958). And again the rationale is couched in the familiar concepts of civil tort law of (1) a purpose to benefit the corporation and (2) an act by an agent in line of his duties. "The treasury of

the business may not with impunity obtain the fruits of violations which are committed knowingly by agents of the entity in the scope of their employment."

Of course the defendants do not contend, nor could they, that criminal accountability and actual benefit are equated. There have been many cases, and there may well be others in the future, in which the corporation is criminally liable even though no benefit has been received in fact. But while benefit is not essential in terms of result, the purpose to benefit the corporation is decisive in terms of equating the agent's action with that of the corporation. For it is an elementary principle of agency that "an act of a servant is not within the scope of employment if it is done with no intention to perform it as a part of or incident to a service on account of which he is employed." Restatement of the Law of Agency (2d) § 235.

It is for this reason that the simple "function" test applied by the District Court—while obviously a factor of relevance—is alone insufficient upon which to rest convictions here. Thus the taking in or paying out of money by a bank teller, while certainly one of his regular functions, would hardly cast the corporation for criminal liability if in such "handling" the faithless employee was pocketing the funds as an embezzler or handing them over to a confederate under some ruse. * * *

On the facts of this record, only the most hypercritical, artificial view would find any benefit intended by the actions of Morgan, Hart or Purcell. * * * Standard's oil was either stolen from it or it was, through these faithless agents, compelled to pay twice for oil supposedly purchased by it from Thompson. While the matter is not a spectacular theft as to Pasotex, it is equally positive that no benefit was conferred, nor, as the critical thing, was one intended by the actions taken at Pumping Station No. 2 by Hart and Morgan. * * * As ostensible employees of Pasotex, they were each in the secret pay of Thompson for the purpose of assisting him in violating Texas (and hence federal) law through the movement and sale of oil produced in violation of applicable Texas statutes and regulations. Their purpose was to aid Thompson in his criminal enterprise. Of course it could not succeed for Thompson unless, through these false run tickets, the oil could be channeled into legitimate commercial transportation facilities. Without Pasotex and its pipeline transportation, and without Standard's purchase of such "hot" or non-existent oil, Thompson could not succeed. But Hart and Morgan were doing their usual tasks in handling run tickets not to advance or further the interest of Pasotex. This was done to further the criminal enterprise of which they were an indispensable part.

Hart and Morgan and Purcell each knew what he did and what he was doing. But to say that acts done by servants actuated by such evil and specifically unlawful motives were the acts of the very corporations thus sought to be cheated or implicated in practices known to be in serious violation of law and, moreover, to impute not only accountability but "knowledge" of such acts to the corporations, would be to disregard every accepted notion of respondeat superior. For these corporations to be found guilty of violating the Connally Hot Oil Act we may assume that it is not necessary to prove that through imputation each corporation consciously knew that the acts being done were in violation of the law. But to subject these corporations to criminal accountability it was necessary on accepted principles of imputation for each to know that these acts of Morgan, Hart and Purcell were being done. Under a statute requiring that there be "a specific wrongful intent," and the "presence of culpable intent as a necessary element of the offense * * *," the corporation does not acquire that knowledge or possess the requisite "state of mind essential for responsibility," through the activities of unfaithful servants whose conduct was undertaken to advance the interests of parties other than their corporate employer. * * *

As to all counts, therefore, the judgments of conviction as to the corporate defendants must be reversed and rendered in favor of the appellants.

UNITED STATES v. HILTON HOTELS CORP.

467 F.2d 1000 (9th Cir. 1972)

BROWNING, Circuit Judge.

This is an appeal from a conviction under an indictment charging a violation of section 1 of the Sherman Act, 15 U.S.C. § 1.

Operators of hotels, restaurants, hotel and restaurant supply companies, and other businesses in Portland, Oregon, organized an association to attract conventions to their city. To finance the association, members were asked to make contributions in predetermined amounts. Companies selling supplies to hotels were asked to contribute an amount equal to one per cent of their sales to hotel members. To aid collections, hotel members, including appellant, agreed to give preferential treatment to suppliers who paid their assessments, and to curtail purchases from those who did not.

I

The jury was instructed that such an agreement by the hotel members, if proven, would be a per se violation of the Sherman Act. [The court rejected a challenge to that charge.] * * *

II

Appellant's president testified that it would be contrary to the policy of the corporation for the manager of one of its hotels to condition purchases upon payment of a contribution to a local association by the supplier. The manager of appellant's Portland hotel and his assistant testified that it was the hotel's policy to purchase supplies solely on the basis of price, quality, and service. They also testified that on two occasions they told the hotel's purchasing agent that he was to take no part in the boycott. The purchasing agent confirmed the receipt of these instructions, but admitted that, despite them, he had threatened a supplier with loss of the hotel's business unless the supplier paid the association assessment. He testified that he violated his instructions because of anger and personal pique toward the individual representing the supplier.

Based upon this testimony, appellant requested certain instructions bearing upon the criminal liability of a corporation for the unauthorized acts of its agents. These requests were rejected by the trial court. The court instructed the jury that a corporation is liable for the acts and statements of its agents "within the scope of their employment," defined to mean "in the corporation's behalf in performance of the agent's general line of work," including "not only that which has been authorized by the corporation, but also that which outsiders could reasonably assume the agent would have authority to do." The court added:

> "A corporation is responsible for acts and statements of its agents, done or made within the scope of their employment, even though their conduct may be contrary to their actual instructions or contrary to the corporation's stated policies."

Appellant objects only to the court's concluding statement. * * * The breadth and critical character of the public interests protected by the Sherman Act, and the gravity of the threat to those interests that led to the enactment of the statute, support a construction holding business organizations accountable, as a general rule, for violations of the Act by their employees in the course of their businesses. In enacting the Sherman Act, "Congress was passing drastic legislation to remedy a threatening danger to the public welfare. . . ." United Mine Workers v. Coronado Coal Co., 259 U.S. 344 (1922). The statute "was designed to be a comprehensive charter of economic liberty aimed at preserving free and unfettered competition as the rule of trade. It rests on the premise that the unrestrained interaction of competitive forces will yield the best allocation of our economic resources, the lowest prices, the highest quality and the greatest material progress, while at the same time providing an environment conducive to the preservation of our democratic political and social institutions." Northern Pacific Ry. v. United States.

With such important public interests at stake, it is reasonable to assume that Congress intended to impose liability upon business entities for the acts of those to whom they choose to delegate the conduct of their affairs, thus stimulating a maximum effort by owners and managers to assure adherence by such agents to the requirements of the Act. * * *

Because of the nature of Sherman Act offenses and the context in which they normally occur, the factors that militate against allowing a corporation to disown the criminal acts of its agents apply with special force to Sherman Act violations.

Sherman Act violations are commercial offenses. They are usually motivated by a desire to enhance profits. They commonly involve large, complex, and highly decentralized corporate business enterprises, and intricate business processes, practices, and arrangements. More often than not they also involve basic policy decisions, and must be implemented over an extended period of time.

Complex business structures, characterized by decentralization and delegation of authority, commonly adopted by corporations for business purposes, make it difficult to identify the particular corporate agents responsible for Sherman Act violations. At the same time, it is generally true that high management officials, for whose conduct the corporate directors and stockholders are the most clearly responsible, are likely to have participated in the policy decisions underlying Sherman Act violations, or at least to have become aware of them.

Violations of the Sherman Act are a likely consequence of the pressure to maximize profits that is commonly imposed by corporate owners upon managing agents and, in turn, upon lesser employees. In the face of that pressure, generalized directions to obey the Sherman Act, with the probable effect of foregoing profits, are the least likely to be taken seriously. And if a violation of the Sherman Act occurs, the corporation, and not the individual agents, will have realized the profits from the illegal activity.

In sum, identification of the particular agents responsible for a Sherman Act violation is especially difficult, and their conviction and punishment is peculiarly ineffective as a deterrent. At the same time, conviction and punishment of the business entity itself is likely to be both appropriate and effective.

For these reasons we conclude that as a general rule a corporation is liable under the Sherman Act for the acts of its agents in the scope of their employment, even though contrary to general corporate policy and express instructions to the agent.

Thus the general policy statements of appellant's president were no defense. Nor was it enough that appellant's manager told the purchasing agent that he was not to participate in the boycott. The purchasing agent was authorized to buy all of appellant's supplies. Purchases were made on the basis of specifications, but the purchasing agent exercised complete authority as to source. He was in a unique position to add the corporation's buying power to the force of the boycott. Appellant could not gain exculpation by issuing general instructions without undertaking to enforce those instructions by means commensurate with the obvious risks. * * *Affirmed.

NOTES AND QUESTIONS

1. ***Statutory Basis for Corporate Liability.*** To what extent is the imposition of corporate criminal liability contingent upon the statute the defendant is alleged to have violated? (E.g., Connolly Act, Sherman Act.) How does the statute's *mens rea*, or lack thereof, impact a finding of corporate criminal liability? Consider also Sea Horse Ranch v. Superior Court, 30 Cal. Rptr. 2d 681 (Ct. App. 1994) (court considers, in the context of a probable cause determination, whether a president of a corporation and the corporation can be held criminally liable for involuntary manslaughter).

2. ***Determining "For the Benefit".*** Should the benefit incurred to the corporation be used only to determine whether an agency relationship exists, or should it also serve as a basis for imposing criminal liability? Should a commercial focus of a statute be conclusive for finding that an agent's acts benefit the corporation? Can market supply and demand play a factor in determining whether acts of an agent are for the benefit of the corporation?

3. ***Jury Unanimity.*** What happens when the jury concurs that actors on behalf of the corporation violated the law, but the jury does not concur on the same actors? Are the acts of different officers separate "violations" or do they supply different "means"? In United States v. Andersen [p. 342], the jury asked whether it was necessary for them to agree on the individual employee who violated the law that served as the basis for a charge of obstruction of justice. The judge ruled that it was not necessary for the jurors to agree on which Andersen employee "had the intent to commit the crime," as they all agreed that someone from the a corporation intended to obstruct justice by impeding the investigation. See Kurt Eichenwald, *Judges Ruling on Andersen Hurts Defense,* June 15, 2002, at C1. But see Richardson v. United States, 526 U.S. 813, 815 (1999) (finding that "a jury in a federal criminal case brought under § 848 must unanimously agree not only that the defendant committed some 'continuing series of violations' but also that the defendant committed each of the individual 'violations' necessary to make up that continuing series.").

3. Restricting Corporate Criminal Liability

Corporate criminal liability has continually been the subject of criticism. The focus of much of this criticism has been on the disadvantages inherent in using a *respondeat superior* and vicarious liability approach in criminal law. It has been claimed that:

> 1. Vicarious liability is appropriate only as a principle of tort law since its justification lies in its allocation of the loss to the party more able to bear it (or at least more deserving of the burden), but it is unrelated to the purposes of retribution, deterrence, prevention, and rehabilitation that underlie the criminal law.

2. Vicarious liability is unjust because its burden falls on the innocent rather than the guilty—that is, the penalty is borne by stockholders and others having an interest in the corporation, rather than by the guilty individual.

3. Vicarious liability results in a disparity between businesses conducted in the corporate form and those run as a proprietorship, since the individual proprietor will not be criminally liable for independent acts of his employees.

4. Vicarious liability for the corporation may in the future open the door to expanded vicarious criminal liability for individuals as well.

John C. Coffee, Jr., *Corporate Criminal Responsibility,* 1 ENCYCLOPEDIA OF CRIME AND JUSTICE 257 (1983).

MODEL PENAL CODE

Section 2.07. Liability of Corporations, Unincorporated Associations and Persons Acting, or Under a Duty to Act, in Their Behalf.

(1) A corporation may be convicted of the commission of an offense if:

(a) the offense is a violation or the offense is defined by a statute other than the Code in which a legislative purpose to impose liability on corporations plainly appears and the conduct is performed by an agent of the corporation acting in behalf of the corporation within the scope of his office or employment, except that if the law defining the offense designates the agents for whose conduct the corporation is accountable, such provisions shall apply; or

(b) the offense consists of an omission to discharge a specific duty of affirmative performance imposed on corporations by law; or

(c) the commission of the offense was authorized, requested, commanded, performed or recklessly tolerated by the board of directors or by a high managerial agent acting in behalf of the corporation within the scope of his office or employment.

(2) When absolute liability is imposed for the commission of an offense, a legislative purpose to impose liability on a corporation shall be assumed, unless the contrary plainly appears.

* * *

(4) As used in this Section:

* * *

> (c) "high managerial agent" means an officer of a corporation * * *, or any other agent of a corporation * * * having duties of such responsibility that his conduct may fairly be assumed to represent the policy of the corporation * * * .

(5) In any prosecution of a corporation * * * for the commission of an offense included within the terms of Subsection (1)(a) or Subsection (3)(a) of this Section, other than an offense for which absolute liability has been imposed, it shall be a defense if the defendant proves by a preponderance of evidence that the high managerial agent having supervisory responsibility over the subject matter of the offense employed due diligence to prevent its commission. This paragraph shall not apply if it is plainly inconsistent with the legislative purpose in defining the particular offense.

* * *

NOTES AND QUESTIONS

1. ***Federal/Model Penal Code Distinction.*** Federal courts and many state courts use the common law *respondeat superior* approach in assessing whether to impute the acts of an agent to the corporation for the purposes of criminal liability. These courts examine whether the agent acted within the scope of their employment and whether it was on behalf of the corporation. In contrast, the Model Penal Code focuses on whether the individual who committed the act was a "high managerial agent." Does the requirement of a "high managerial agent" unduly restrict corporate criminal liability? How difficult is it to discern whether an agent is a "high managerial agent?"

2. ***Deficiencies of Model Penal Code Approach.*** Do the acts of a high managerial agent truly have a connection with the blameworthiness of the corporation? See Brent Fisse, *Reconstructing Corporate Criminal Law: Deterrence, Retribution, Fault, and Sanctions*, 56 S. CAL. L. REV. 1141, 1186 (1983). In rejecting a Model Penal Code approach for imposing corporate criminal liability, the court in **Commonwealth v. Beneficial Finance Co.**, 275 N.E. 2d 33, 83 (Mass. 1971), stated:

> * * * [T]he title or position of an individual in a corporation should not be conclusively determinative in ascribing criminal responsibility. In a large corporation, with many numerous and distinct departments, a high ranking corporate officer or agent may have no authority or involvement in a particular sphere of corporate activity, whereas a lower ranking corporate executive might have much broader power in dealing with a matter peculiarly within the scope of his authority. Employees who are in the lower echelon of

> the corporate hierarchy often exercise more responsibility in the everyday operations of the corporation than the directors or officers. Assuredly, the title or office that the person holds may be considered, but it should not be the decisive criterion upon which to predicate corporate responsibility.

There has also been scholarly criticism of the Model Penal Code approach. See Michael E. Tigar, *Corporations' Liability for Criminal Acts*, National L.J., Vol. 8, No. 27, March 17, 1986, p. 15, cont. on p. 17.

3. ***Corporate Dissolution.*** Does criminal liability survive a corporate dissolution? See Melrose Distillers, Inc. v. United States, 359 U.S. 271 (1959) (Supreme Court permitted a criminal action against a corporation that had dissolved); see also United States v. Alamo Bank of Texas, 880 F.2d 828 (5th Cir. 1989). Does criminal liability transfer to successor corporations? See H. Lowell Brown, *Successor Corporate Criminal Liability: The Emerging Federal Common Law*, 49 ARK. L. REV. 469 (1996).

4. ***Procedural Considerations.*** The creation of corporate criminal liability does not have a bearing on the privilege against self-incrimination [p. 417], as the corporation has none. Thus corporate criminal liability does not expand the procedural protections with respect to investigations. Lawyer-client privileges and Fourth Amendment rights exist [p. 697], whether there is corporate liability or not.

4. Collective Knowledge

UNITED STATES v. BANK OF NEW ENGLAND

821 F.2d 844 (1st Cir. 1987)

BOWNES, Circuit Judge.

The Bank of New England appeals a jury verdict convicting it of thirty-one violations of the Currency Transaction Reporting Act (the Act). Department of Treasury regulations promulgated under the Act require banks to file Currency Transaction Reports (CTRs) within fifteen days of customer currency transactions exceeding $10,000. 31 C.F.R. § 103.22 (1986). The Act imposes felony liability when a bank willfully fails to file such reports "as part of a pattern of illegal activity involving transactions of more than $100,000 in a twelve-month period . . . ." 31 U.S.C. § 5322(b).

I. THE ISSUES

The Bank was found guilty of having failed to file CTRs on cash withdrawals made by James McDonough. It is undisputed that on thirty-one separate occasions between May 1983 and July 1984, McDonough withdrew from the Prudential Branch of the Bank more than $10,000 in cash by using multiple checks—each one individually under $10,000—presented simultaneously to a single bank teller. The Bank contends that such conduct did not trigger the Act's reporting requirements. * * * The Bank also argues that the trial judge's instructions on willfulness were fatally flawed, and that, in any event, the evidence did not suffice to show that it willfully failed to file CTRs on McDonough's transactions. * * *

The Bank had been named in a federal grand jury indictment which was returned on October 15, 1985. Count One of the indictment alleged that between May 1983 and May 1985, James McDonough, the Bank, and Carol Orlandella and Patricia Murphy—both of whom were former head tellers with the Bank's Prudential Branch—unlawfully conspired to conceal from the IRS thirty-six of McDonough's currency transactions. The trial court directed a verdict of acquittal on this count. Defendants Murphy and Orlandella were found not guilty of charges that they individually aided and abetted the failure to file CTRs on McDonough's transactions.

The bulk of the indictment alleged that the Bank, as principal, and McDonough, as an aider and abettor, willfully failed to file CTRs on thirty-six occasions between May 1983 and July 1984. Five counts were dismissed because, on those occasions, McDonough received cashier's checks from the Bank, rather than currency. McDonough was acquitted of all charges against him. The Bank was found guilty on the thirty-one remaining counts. We affirm.

II. THE REPORTABILITY OF McDONOUGH'S TRANSACTIONS

* * * On thirty-one occasions, James McDonough visited the same branch of the same bank at one time in a single day. He presented between two and four checks totalling more than $10,000 to one bank teller and received from the teller a single sum of cash in excess of $10,000. Since the regulations define transaction in currency to mean "the physical transfer of currency from one person to another," we hold that the Bank had adequate warning that a single, lump-sum transfer of cash exceeding $10,000 was reportable, regardless of the number of checks the customer uses to obtain the money. * * *

IV. WILLFULNESS OF THE BANK'S CONDUCT

A. The Trial Court's Instruction on Willfulness

Criminal liability under 31 U.S.C. § 5322 only attaches when a financial institution "willfully" violates the CTR filing requirement. A finding of willfulness under the Reporting Act must be supported by "proof of the defendant's knowledge of the reporting requirements and his specific intent to commit the crime." Willfulness can rarely be proven by direct evidence, since it is a state of mind; it is usually established by drawing reasonable inferences from the available facts.

The Bank contends that the trial court's instructions on knowledge and specific intent effectively relieved the government of its responsibility to prove that the Bank acted willfully. The trial judge began her instructions on this element by outlining generally the concepts of knowledge and willfulness:

> Knowingly simply means voluntarily and intentionally. It's designed to exclude a failure that is done by mistake or accident, or for some other innocent reason. Willfully means voluntarily, intentionally, and with a specific intent to disregard, to disobey the law, with a bad purpose to violate the law.

The trial judge properly instructed the jury that it could infer knowledge if a defendant consciously avoided learning about the reporting requirements. The court then focused on the kind of proof that would establish the Bank's knowledge of its filing obligations. The judge instructed that the knowledge of individual employees acting within the scope of their employment is imputed to the Bank. She told the jury that "if any employee knew that multiple checks would require the filing of reports, the bank knew it, provided the employee knew it within the scope of his employment, ..."

The trial judge then focused on the issue of "collective knowledge":

> In addition, however, you have to look at the bank as an institution. As such, its knowledge is the sum of the knowledge of all of the employees. That is, the bank's knowledge is the totality of what all of the employees know within the scope of their employment. So, if Employee A knows one facet of the currency reporting requirement, B knows another facet of it, and C a third facet of it, the bank knows them all. So if you find that an employee within the scope of his employment knew that CTRs had to be filed, even if multiple checks are used, the bank is deemed to know it. The bank is also deemed to know it if each of several employees knew a part of that requirement and the sum of what the separate employees knew amounted to knowledge that such a requirement existed.

After discussing the two modes of establishing knowledge—via either knowledge of one of its individual employees or the aggregate knowledge of all its employees—the trial judge turned to the issue of specific intent:

> There is a similar double business with respect to the concept of willfulness with respect to the bank. In deciding whether the bank acted willfully, again you have to look first at the conduct of all employees and officers, and, second, at what the bank did or did not do as an institution. The bank is deemed to have acted willfully if one of its employees in the scope of his employment acted willfully. So, if you find that an employee willfully failed to do what was necessary to file these reports, then that is deemed to be the act of

> the bank, and the bank is deemed to have willfully failed to file. * * *
>
> Alternatively, the bank as an institution has certain responsibilities; as an organization, it has certain responsibilities. And you will have to determine whether the bank as an organization consciously avoided learning about and observing CTR requirements. The Government to prove the bank guilty on this theory, has to show that its failure to file was the result of some flagrant organizational indifference. In this connection, you should look at the evidence as to the bank's effort, if any, to inform its employees of the law; its effort to check on their compliance; its response to various bits of information that it got in August and September of '84 and February of '85; its policies, and how it carried out its stated policies. * * *
>
> If you find that the Government has proven with respect to any transaction either that an employee within the scope of his employment willfully failed to file a required report or that the bank was flagrantly indifferent to its obligations, then you may find that the bank has willfully failed to file the required reports.

The Bank contends that the trial court's instructions regarding knowledge were defective because they eliminated the requirement that it be proven that the Bank violated a known legal duty. It avers that the knowledge instruction invited the jury to convict the Bank for negligently maintaining a poor communications network that prevented the consolidation of the information held by its various employees. The Bank argues that it is error to find that a corporation possesses a particular item of knowledge if one part of the corporation has half the information making up the item, and another part of the entity has the other half.

A collective knowledge instruction is entirely appropriate in the context of corporate criminal liability. The acts of a corporation are, after all, simply the acts of all of its employees operating within the scope of their employment. The law on corporate criminal liability reflects this. Similarly, the knowledge obtained by corporate employees acting within the scope of their employment is imputed to the corporation. * * * Corporations compartmentalize knowledge, subdividing the elements of specific duties and operations into smaller components. The aggregate of those components constitutes the corporation's knowledge of a particular operation. It is irrelevant whether employees administering one component of an operation know the specific activities of employees administering another aspect of the operation * * *: ["]Rather the corporation is considered to have acquired the collective knowledge of its employees and is held responsible for their failure to act accordingly.["] United States v. T.I.M.E.-D.C., Inc., 381 F.Supp. [730, 738 W.D. Va. 1974]. Since the Bank had the compartmentalized structure common to all large corporations, the court's collective knowledge instruction was not only proper but necessary.

Nor do we find any defects in the trial court's instructions on specific intent. The court told the jury that the concept of willfulness entails a voluntary, intentional, and bad purpose to disobey the law. Her instructions on this element, when viewed as a whole, directed the jury not to convict for accidental, mistaken or inadvertent acts or omissions. It is urged that the court erroneously charged that willfulness could be found via flagrant indifference by the Bank toward its reporting obligations. With respect to federal regulatory statutes, the Supreme Court has endorsed defining willfulness, in both civil and criminal contexts, as "a disregard for the governing statute and an indifference to its requirements." Trans World Airlines, Inc. v. Thurston, 469 U.S. 111, 127 & n. 20 (1985). Accordingly, we find no error in the court's instruction on willfulness.

B. Evidence of Willfulness

The Bank asserts that the evidence did not suffice to show that it had willfully failed to comply with the Act's reporting requirements. We review the evidence in the light most favorable to the government.

* * * [T]he language of the Treasury regulations itself gave notice that cash withdrawals over $10,000 were reportable, regardless of the number of checks used. Primary responsibility for CTR compliance in the Bank's branch offices was assigned to head tellers and branch managers. Head tellers Orlandella and Murphy, who knew of the nature of McDonough's transactions, also knew of the CTR filing obligations imposed by the Bank. The jury heard testimony from former bank teller Simona Wong, who stated that she knew McDonough's transactions were reportable, and that the source of her knowledge was head teller Murphy.

Even if some Bank personnel mistakenly regarded McDonough as engaging in multiple transactions, there was convincing evidence that the Bank knew that his withdrawals were reportable. An internal memo sent * * * to all branch managers and head tellers stated that "'[r]eportable transactions are expanded to include multiple transactions which aggregate more than $10,000 in any *one day*.' This includes deposits or withdrawals by a customer to or from more than one account." (Emphasis in original.) The Prudential Branch Manual instructed that if Bank personnel know that a customer has engaged in multiple transactions totalling $10,000 or more, then such transactions should be regarded as a single transaction. In addition, since 1980, the instructions on the back of CTR forms have directed that reports be filed on multiple transactions which aggregate to over $10,000. Finally, a Bank auditor discussed with Orlandella and Murphy, the Bank's obligation to report a customer's multiple transactions in a single day which amount to more than $10,000. We do not suggest that these evidentiary items in themselves legally bound the Bank to report McDonough's transactions; it is the language of the regulations that impose such a duty. This evidence, however, proved that the Bank had ample knowledge that transactions like McDonough's came within the purview of the Act.

Regarding the Bank's specific intent to violate the reporting obligation, Simona Wong testified that head teller Patricia Murphy knew that McDonough's transactions were reportable, but, on one occasion, deliberately chose not to file a CTR on him because he was "a good customer." In addition, the jury heard testimony that bank employees regarded McDonough's transactions as unusual, speculated that he was a bookie, and suspected that he was structuring his transactions to avoid the Act's reporting requirements. An internal Bank memo, written after an investigation of the McDonough transactions, concluded that a "person managing the branch would have to have known that something strange was going on." Given the suspicions aroused by McDonough's banking practices and the abundance of information indicating that his transactions were reportable, the jury could have concluded that the failure by Bank personnel to, at least, inquire about the reportability of McDonough's transactions constituted flagrant indifference to the obligations imposed by the Act.

We hold that the evidence was sufficient for a finding of willfulness. * * * Affirmed.

NOTES AND QUESTIONS

1. ***Collective Knowledge.*** Does holding a corporation liable based upon the "collective knowledge" of its employees add a new dimension to corporate criminal liability? Is "it better than designating a corporate officer as the 'Vice President in Charge of Going to Jail' or allowing wrongdoers to go unpunished"? Martin J. Weinstein & Patricia Bennett Ball, *Criminal Law's Greatest Mystery Thriller: Corporate Guilt Through Collective Knowledge,* 29 N. ENG. L. REV. 65 (1994). How does this case impact information systems within corporations? Is this decision a recognition of the availability to corporations of technological advancements?

2. ***"Corporate Ethos."*** Professor Pamela H. Bucy, in her article *Corporate Ethos: A Standard for Imposing Corporate Criminal Liability*, 75 MINN. L. REV. 1095, 1099 (1991), "proposes a standard of corporate criminal liability that uses a new conceptual paradigm for identifying and proving corporate intent." She states:

> * * * [E]ach corporate entity has a distinct and identifiable personality or "ethos." The government can convict a corporation under this standard only if it proves that the corporate ethos encouraged agents of the corporation to commit the criminal act. Central to this approach is the assumption that organizations possess an identity that is independent of specific individuals who control or work for the organization. This corporate identity, or "ethos," results from the dynamic of many individuals working together toward corporate goals. The living cell provides an apt analogy: Just as a living cell has an identity separate from the

activities of its constituent molecules, a corporation has an identity separate from its individual agents.

3. ***Corporate Self-Identity.*** A new model of corporate criminal liability has been developing in legal literature. This new model, premised upon "self-identity," "resembles the theory of corporate organs." Eli Lederman, *Models for Imposing Corporate Criminal Liability: From Adaptation and Imitation Toward Aggregation and the Search for Self-Identity*, 4 BUFF. CRIM. L. REV. 641, 678 (2000). "The chief assumption underlying the self-identity model of corporations is that a large organization is not only a collection of people who shape it and activate it, but also a set of attributes and positions, which influence, constrain, and at times even define the modes of thinking and behavior of the people who populate it..." Id. at 686.

5. Government Responses to Corporate Misconduct

In the past few years, the government has proceeded against several major corporations with civil or criminal charges, although few actually proceed to trial. Many companies enter into deferred (DPA) and non-prosecution (NPA) agreements with the government. The difference between these two is that an NPA occurs pre-indictment and a DPA occurs after indictment. See WCH § 2.4. A variety of different terms and conditions can be found in these agreements. Some terms within these agreements, such as the nonpayment of employee attorney's fees [p. 763] and the waiver of attorney-client privilege, have been extremely controversial. Other less controversial terms within these agreements typically provide for effective compliance programs and monitors. [See Chap. 17 (E)]. In January 2010, the Securities Exchange Commission instituted "new cooperation tools" which include deferred and non-prosecution agreements with the SEC. Consider the following different approaches taken by the government in resolving corporate criminal activity:

a. Faro Technologies. Faro Technologies entered into a non-prosecution agreement with the government and agreed to pay a $1.1 million dollar criminal fine "in connection with corrupt payments to Chinese government officials in violation of the Foreign Corrupt Practices Act (FCPA)." The Department of Justice Press Release (available at http://www.justice.gov/archive/opa/pr/2008/ June/08-crm-505.html) states:

> In recognition of Faro's voluntary disclosure and thorough review of the improper payments, its cooperation with the Department's investigation, the company's implementation of and commitment to implement in the future enhanced compliance policies and procedures, and the company's agreement to engage an independent corporate monitor, the Department has agreed to enter into a non-prosecution agreement with a term of two years. If Faro abides by the terms of that agreement, the Department will not prosecute Faro for the conduct admitted in the statement of facts.

In a related matter, Faro agreed to the entry of a cease and desist order with the Securities and Exchange Commission and "to pay approximately $1.85 million in disgorgement and prejudgment interest in connection" with conduct similar to what was alleged by the Department of Justice.

b. UBS. UBS AG, Switzerland's largest bank entered into a deferred prosecution agreement on "charges of conspiring to defraud the United States by impeding the Internal Revenue Service (IRS)." The DOJ Press Release announcing the agreement states that the company "agreed to immediately provide the United States government with the identities of, and account information for, certain United States customers of UBS's cross-border business." They also "agreed to expeditiously exit the business of providing banking services to United States clients with undeclared accounts," and they agreed to pay $780 million in fines, penalties, interest and restitution." See Press Release, *UBS Enters into Deferred Prosecution Agreement*, available at http://www.justice.gov/archive/opa/pr/ubs-enters-deferred-prosecution-agreement.

c. Archer Daniels. Archer Daniels-Midland agreed to plead guilty to "conspiring with competitors to fix the prices of two agricultural products and pay $100 million in fines." "The settlement's most burdensome aspect for company employees may well be the cooperation agreement." "Archer Daniels will be required to dismiss employees [who have been granted immunity], who still fail to cooperate." Kurt Eichenwald, *Archer Daniels Agrees to Big Fine for Price Fixing*, N.Y. Times, Oct. 15, 1996, at A1; see also *Justice Department Hits ADM With $100 Million Criminal Fine. Shareholders, Victims Cry Foul,* 10 Corp. Crime Rep., No. 40, Oct. 21, 1996; Marilyn Geewax, *Punish White-Collar Criminals, Not Stockholders*, Atl. J./Const., Oct. 20, 1996, at H3; KURT EICHEHWALD, THE INFORMANT (2000); United States v. Andreas, 216 F.3d 645 (7th Cir. 2000).

d. Andersen. The government charged Arthur Andersen LLP, the auditor for Enron Corp., with obstruction of justice (18 U.S.C. § 1512(b)) for the alleged destruction of documents related to the Enron investigation. Anderson pled not guilty and proceeded to trial. After ten days of deliberation, the jury reached a verdict of guilty. The court sentenced Andersen to five years probation and a fine of $500,000. See Thereas M. Church, *Arthur Andersen Receives Probation, Fine*, Aberdeen Am. News, Oct. 17, 2002, at 7 (2002 WL 101098535) ("Probation seems like a hollow threat for a firm that shuttered its audit practice and closed offices across the country after its conviction in June."). A consequence of conviction can be exclusion as an auditor under SEC rules. Many clients left the partnership following indictment, but not all. See Ken Y. Chen & Jian Zhou, *Audit Committee, Board Characteristics and Auditor Switch Decisions by Andersen's Clients*, forthcoming *Contemporary Accounting Research*, available at http://papers.ssrn.com/sol3/papers.cfm?abstract_id=980938 (examining auditor switch decisions "where the auditor's reputation is clearly tarnished). Although the Supreme Court reversed the conviction, the partnership did not survive.

NOTES AND QUESTIONS

1. ***Rationale for Different Approaches.*** Do the different approaches taken by the government in Faro, UBS, Archer Daniels, and Andersen produce different results? Which, if any, is most likely to deter future corporate criminal conduct? Should the government have the discretion to chose a different approach for different types of conduct?

2. ***Corporate Dilemma.*** Are corporations placed in the position of having to accept a deferred prosecution agreement, and does the type of industry make a difference in this decision? Is the stigma to the company more significant than the criminal penalty? In deciding on liability under a plea agreement, should the United States Attorney take into account potential civil liability that may accrue to the corporation as a result of the corporation pleading guilty or that collateral consequences may be more severe for certain companies? BRANDON L. GARRETT, TOO BIG TO JAIL: HOW PROSECUTORS COMPROMISE WITH CORPORATIONS (2014).

3. ***Corporation Versus Individual.*** Does the prosecution of both the corporation and the individual increase the likelihood of a plea by one of these parties in return for their testimony against the other? What are the potential ramifications of pitting the corporation and the individuals working within the corporation against each other? See Ellen S. Podgor, Essay, *White Collar Cooperators: The Government in Employer-Employee Relationships,* 23 CARDOZO L. REV. 795 (2002). [See Chapter 15, pt. 3 & 4; Chapter 16].

4. ***Corporate Internal Investigations.*** Corporations typically will conduct an internal investigation to determine if there is corporate misconduct. Does the corporation become an arm of the prosecutor in turning over misconduct to the government? See Harry First, *Branch Office of the Prosecutor: The New Role of the Corporation in Business Crime Prosecutions*, 89 N.C. L. REV. 23 (2010). Can there be problems with unregulated internal investigations? See Bruce A. Green & Ellen S. Podgor, *Unregulated Internal Investigations: Achieving Fairness for Corporate Constituents*, 54 B.C. L. REV. 73 (2013).

5. ***Government Policy.*** The Department of Justice provides policy as to when it is appropriate to charge a corporation, although the policy has fluctuated under different Attorney Generals' administration. What does the government consider in deciding whether to prosecute a corporation? The Department of Justice Guidelines provide some general and specific guidance. Some of these guidelines are considered below:

9 - 28.200 - General Considerations of Corporate Liability

A. General Principle: Corporations should not be treated leniently because of their artificial nature nor should they be subject to harsher treatment. Vigorous enforcement of the criminal laws against corporate wrongdoers, where appropriate, results in great benefits for law enforcement and the public, particularly in the area of white collar crime. Indicting corporations for wrongdoing enables the government to address and be a force for positive change of corporate culture, and a force to prevent, discover, and punish serious crimes. * * *

9 - 28.300 - Factors to Be Considered

A. General Principle: Generally, prosecutors should apply the same factors in determining whether to charge a corporation as they do with respect to individuals.* * * Thus, the prosecutor should weigh all of the factors normally considered in the sound exercise of prosecutorial judgment: the sufficiency of the evidence, the likelihood of success at trial, the probable deterrent, rehabilitative, and other consequences of conviction, and the adequacy of non-criminal approaches. However, due to the nature of the corporate "person," some additional factors are present. In conducting an investigation, determining whether to bring charges, and negotiating plea or other agreements, prosecutors should consider the following factors in reaching a decision as to the proper treatment of a corporate target:

1. The nature and seriousness of the offense, including the risk of harm to the public, and applicable policies and priorities, if any, governing the prosecution of corporations for particular categories of crime * * *

2. The pervasiveness of wrongdoing within the corporation, including the complicity in, or the condoning of, the wrongdoing by corporate management * * *

3. The corporation's history of similar conduct, including prior criminal, civil, and regulatory enforcement actions against it * * *

4. The corporation's timely and voluntary disclosure of wrongdoing and its willingness to cooperate in the investigation of its agents, * * *

5. The existence and effectiveness of the corporation's existing compliance program * * *

6. The corporation's remedial actions, including any efforts to implement an effective corporate compliance program or to improve an existing one, to replace responsible management, to discipline or terminate wrongdoers, to pay restitution, and to cooperate with the relevant government agencies * * *

7. Collateral consequences, including whether there is disproportionate harm to shareholders, pension holders, employees, and others not proven personally culpable, as well as impact on the public arising from the prosecution * * *

8. The adequacy of the prosecution of individuals responsible for the corporation's malfeasance; and

9. The adequacy of remedies such as civil or regulatory enforcement actions * * *

9-28.400 - Special Policy Concerns

A. General Principle: The nature and seriousness of the crime, including the risk of harm to the public from the criminal conduct, are obviously primary factors in determining whether to charge a corporation. In addition, corporate conduct, particularly that of national and multi-national corporations, necessarily intersects with federal economic, tax, and criminal law enforcement policies. In applying these principles, prosecutors must consider the practices and policies of the appropriate Division of the Department, and must comply with those policies to the extent required. * * *

9-28.500 - Pervasiveness of Wrongdoing Within the Corporation

A. General Principle: A corporation can only act through natural persons, and it is therefore held responsible for the acts of such persons fairly attributable to it. Charging a corporation for even minor misconduct may be appropriate where the wrongdoing was pervasive and was undertaken by a large number of employees or by all the employees in a particular role within the corporation, or was condoned by upper management. On the other hand, it may not be appropriate to impose liability upon a corporation, particularly one with a robust compliance program in place, under a strict *respondeat superior* theory for the single isolated act of a rogue employee. There is, of course, a wide spectrum between these two extremes, and a prosecutor should exercise sound discretion in evaluating the pervasiveness of wrongdoing within a corporation. * * *

9-28.600 - The Corporation's Past History

A. General Principle: Prosecutors may consider a corporation's history of similar conduct, including prior criminal, civil, and regulatory enforcement actions against it, in determining whether to bring criminal charges and how best to resolve cases. * * *

9-29.700 - The Value of Cooperation

A. General Principle: In determining whether to charge a corporation and how to resolve corporate cases, the corporation's timely and voluntary disclosure of wrongdoing and its cooperation with the government's investigation may be relevant factors. In gauging the extent of the corporation's cooperation, the prosecutor may consider among other things, whether the corporation made a voluntary and timely disclosure, and the corporation's willingness to provide relevant information and

> evidence and identify relevant actors within and outside the corporation, including senior executives. * * *

See also chapters 15 & 16. The guidelines also discuss other factors such as the attorney-client privilege (9-28.710), cooperation and disclosing relevant facts (9-28.720), obstructing the investigation (9-28-730), offering cooperation - no entitlement to immunity (9-28.740), qualifying for immunity, amnesty, or reduced sanctions through voluntary disclosure (9-28.750), oversight concerning demands for waivers of attorney-client privilege or work product protection by corporations contrary to this policy (9-28.760), corporate compliance programs (9-28.800), and plea agreements with corporations (9-28.1300). See Statutory and Documentary Supplement.

B. INDIVIDUAL RESPONSIBILITY

UNITED STATES v. PARK
421 U.S. 658 (1975)

Chief Justice BURGER delivered the opinion of the Court.

We granted certiorari to consider whether the jury instructions in the prosecution of a corporate officer under § 301(k) of the Federal Food, Drug, and Cosmetic Act, 52 Stat. 1042, as amended, 21 U.S.C. § 331(k), were appropriate under United States v. Dotterweich, 320 U.S. 277 (1943).

Acme Markets, Inc., is a national retail food chain with approximately 36,000 employees, 874 retail outlets, 12 general warehouses, and four special warehouses. Its headquarters, including the office of the president, respondent Park, who is chief executive officer of the corporation, are located in Philadelphia, Pa. In a five-count information filed in the United States District Court for the District of Maryland, the Government charged Acme and respondent with violations of the Federal Food, Drug and Cosmetic Act. Each count of the information alleged that the defendants had received food that had been shipped in interstate commerce and that, while the food was being held for sale in Acme's Baltimore warehouse following shipment in interstate commerce, they caused it to be held in a building accessible to rodents and to be exposed to contamination by rodents. These acts were alleged to have resulted in the food's being adulterated within the meaning of 21 U.S.C. §§ 342(a)(3) and (4), in violation of 21 U.S.C. § 331(k).

Acme pleaded guilty to each count of the information. Respondent pleaded not guilty. The evidence at trial demonstrated that in April 1970 the Food and Drug Administration (FDA) advised respondent by letter of insanitary conditions in Acme's Philadelphia warehouse. In 1971 the FDA found that similar conditions existed in the firm's Baltimore warehouse. An FDA consumer safety officer testified concerning evidence of rodent infestation and other insanitary conditions discovered during a 12-day inspection of the

Baltimore warehouse in November and December 1971. He also related that a second inspection of the warehouse had been conducted in March 1972. On that occasion the inspectors found that there had been improvement in the sanitary conditions, but that "there was still evidence of rodent activity in the building and in the warehouses and we found some rodent-contaminated lots of food items."

The Government also presented testimony by the Chief of Compliance of the FDA's Baltimore office, who informed respondent by letter of the conditions at the Baltimore warehouse after the first inspection. There was testimony by Acme's Baltimore division vice president, who had responded to the letter on behalf of Acme and respondent and who described the steps taken to remedy the insanitary conditions discovered by both inspections. The Government's final witness, Acme's vice president for legal affairs and assistant secretary, identified respondent as the president and chief executive officer of the company and read a bylaw prescribing the duties of the chief executive officer. He testified that respondent functioned by delegating "normal operating duties," including sanitation, but that he retained "certain things, which are the big, broad, principles of the operation of the company," and had "the responsibility of seeing that they all work together."

At the close of the Government's case in chief, respondent moved for a judgment of acquittal on the ground that "the evidence in chief has shown that Mr. Park is not personally concerned in this Food and Drug violation." The trial judge denied the motion, stating that *Dotterweich* [p. 78] was controlling.

Respondent was the only defense witness. He testified that, although all of Acme's employees were in a sense under his general direction, the company had an "organizational structure for responsibilities for certain functions" according to which different phases of its operation were "assigned to individuals who, in turn, have staff and departments under them." He identified those individuals responsible for sanitation, and related that upon receipt of the January 1972 FDA letter, he had conferred with the vice president for legal affairs, who informed him that the Baltimore division vice president "was investigating the situation immediately and would be taking corrective action and would be preparing a summary of the corrective action to reply to the letter." Respondent stated that he did not "believe there was anything (he) could have done more constructively than what (he) found was being done."

On cross-examination, respondent conceded that providing sanitary conditions for food offered for sale to the public was something that he was "responsible for in the entire operation of the company," and he stated that it was one of many phases of the company that he assigned to "dependable subordinates." Respondent was asked about and, over the objections of his counsel, admitted receiving, the April 1970 letter addressed to him from the FDA regarding insanitary conditions at Acme's Philadelphia warehouse. He acknowledged that, with the exception of the division vice president, the same individuals had responsibility for sanitation in both Baltimore and

Philadelphia. Finally, in response to questions concerning the Philadelphia and Baltimore incidents, respondent admitted that the Baltimore problem indicated the system for handling sanitation "wasn't working perfectly" and that as Acme's chief executive officer he was responsible for "any result which occurs in our company."

At the close of the evidence, respondent's renewed motion for a judgment of acquittal was denied. The relevant portion of the trial judge's instructions to the jury challenged by respondent is set out in the margin.[9] Respondent's counsel objected to the instructions on the ground that they failed fairly to reflect our decision in *Dotterweich,* and to define "responsible relationship." The trial judge overruled the objection. The jury found respondent guilty on all counts of the information, and he was subsequently sentenced to pay a fine of $50 on each count.

The Court of Appeals reversed the conviction and remanded for a new trial. That court viewed the Government as arguing "that the conviction may be predicated solely upon a showing that . . . (respondent) was the President of the offending corporation," and it stated that as "a general proposition, some act of commission or omission is an essential element of every crime." 499 F.2d 839, 841 (CA4 1974). * * *

We granted certiorari because of an apparent conflict among the Courts of Appeals with respect to the standard of liability of corporate officers under the Federal Food, Drug, and Cosmetic Act as construed in *Dotterweich,* and because of the importance of the question to the Government's enforcement program. We reverse.

---

[9] "In order to find the Defendant guilty on any count of the Information, you must find beyond a reasonable doubt on each count . . . " * * *

Thirdly, that John R. Park held a position of authority in the operation of the business of Acme Markets, Incorporated.

"However, you need not concern yourselves with the first two elements of the case. The main issue for your determination is only with the third element, whether the Defendant held a position of authority and responsibility in the business of Acme Markets. * * *

"The statute makes individuals, as well as corporations, liable for violations. An individual is liable if it is clear, beyond a reasonable doubt, that the elements of the adulteration of the food as to travel in interstate commerce are present. As I have instructed you in this case, they are, and that the individual had a responsible relation to the situation, even though he may not have participated personally.

"The individual is or could be liable under the statute, even if he did not consciously do wrong. However, the fact that the Defendant is pres(id)ent and is a chief executive officer of the Acme Markets does not require a finding of guilt. Though, he need not have personally participated in the situation, he must have had a responsible relationship to the issue. The issue is, in this case, whether the Defendant, John R. Park, by virtue of his position in the company, had a position of authority and responsibility in the situation out of which these charges arose."

I

The question presented by the Government's petition for certiorari in *Dotterweich,* and the focus of this Court's opinion, was whether "the manager of a corporation, as well as the corporation itself, may be prosecuted under the Federal Food, Drug, and Cosmetic Act of 1938 for the introduction of misbranded and adulterated articles into interstate commerce." * * *

In reversing the judgment of the Court of Appeals and reinstating Dotterweich's conviction, this Court looked to the purposes of the Act and noted that they "touch phases of the lives and health of the people which, in the circumstances of modern industrialism, are largely beyond self-protection." It observed that the Act is of "a now familiar type" which "dispenses with the conventional requirement for criminal conduct—awareness of some wrongdoing. In the interest of the larger good it puts the burden of acting at hazard upon a person otherwise innocent but standing in responsible relation to a public danger."

Central to the Court's conclusion that individuals other than proprietors are subject to the criminal provisions of the Act was the reality that "the only way in which a corporation can act is through the individuals who act on its behalf."

* * * In this context, the Court concluded, those doctrines dictated that the offense was committed "by all who . . . have . . . a responsible share in the furtherance of the transaction which the statute outlaws."

The Court recognized that, because the Act dispenses with the need to prove "consciousness of wrongdoing," it may result in hardship even as applied to those who share "responsibility in the business process resulting in" a violation. It regarded as "too treacherous" an attempt "to define or even to indicate by way of illustration the class of employees which stands in such a responsible relation." The question of responsibility, the Court said, depends "on the evidence produced at the trial and its submission—assuming the evidence warrants it—to the jury under appropriate guidance." The Court added: "In such matters the good sense of prosecutors, the wise guidance of trial judges, and the ultimate judgment of juries must be trusted."

II

The rule that corporate employees who have "a responsible share in the furtherance of the transaction which the statute outlaws" are subject to the criminal provisions of the Act was not formulated in a vacuum. Cf. Morissette v. United States, 342 U.S. 246 (1952). Cases under the Federal Food and Drugs Act of 1906 reflected the view both that knowledge or intent were not required to be proved in prosecutions under its criminal provisions, and that responsible corporate agents could be subjected to the liability thereby imposed. Moreover, the principle had been recognized that a corporate agent, through whose act, default, or omission the corporation committed a crime, was himself guilty individually of that crime. The principle had been applied whether or not the crime required "consciousness of wrongdoing," and it had been applied not only to those corporate agents who themselves committed the criminal act, but also to those who by virtue of their managerial positions or other similar relation to the actor could be deemed responsible for its commission.

In the latter class of cases, the liability of managerial officers did not depend on their knowledge of, or personal participation in, the act made criminal by the statute. Rather, where the statute under which they were prosecuted dispensed with "consciousness of wrongdoing," an omission or failure to act was deemed a sufficient basis for a responsible corporate agent's liability. It was enough in such cases that, by virtue of the relationship he bore to the corporation, the agent had the power to prevent the act complained of. * * *

Thus *Dotterweich* and the cases which have followed reveal that in providing sanctions which reach and touch the individuals who execute the corporate mission—and this is by no means necessarily confined to a single corporate agent or employee—the Act imposes not only a positive duty to seek out and remedy violations when they occur but also, and primarily, a duty to implement measures that will insure that violations will not occur. The requirements of foresight and vigilance imposed on responsible corporate agents are beyond question demanding, and perhaps onerous, but they are no more stringent than the public has a right to expect of those who voluntarily assume positions of authority in business enterprises whose services and products affect the health and well-being of the public that supports them.

The Act does not, as we observed in *Dotterweich,* make criminal liability turn on "awareness of some wrongdoing" or "conscious fraud." The duty imposed by Congress on responsible corporate agents is, we emphasize, one that requires the highest standard of foresight and vigilance, but the Act, in its criminal aspect, does not require that which is objectively impossible. The theory upon which responsible corporate agents are held criminally accountable for "causing" violations of the Act permits a claim that a defendant was "powerless" to prevent or correct the violation to "be raised defensively at a trial on the merits." United States v. Wiesenfeld Warehouse Co., 376 U.S. 86, 91 (1964). If such a claim is made, the defendant has the burden of coming forward with evidence, but this does not alter the Government's ultimate burden of proving beyond a reasonable doubt the defendant's guilt, including his power, in light of the duty imposed by the Act, to prevent or correct the prohibited condition. Congress has seen fit to enforce the accountability of responsible corporate agents dealing with products which may affect the health of consumers by penal sanctions cast in rigorous terms, and the obligation of the courts is to give them effect so long as they do not violate the Constitution.

III

We cannot agree with the Court of Appeals that it was incumbent upon the District Court to instruct the jury that the Government had the burden of establishing "wrongful action" in the sense in which the Court of Appeals used that phrase. The concept of a "responsible relationship" to, or a "responsible share" in, a violation of the Act indeed imports some measure of blameworthiness; but it is equally clear that the Government establishes a prima facie case when it introduces evidence sufficient to warrant a finding by the trier of the facts that the defendant had, by reason of his position in the corporation, responsibility and authority either to prevent in the first instance, or promptly to correct, the violation complained of, and that he failed to do so. * * *

Reading the entire charge satisfies us that the jury's attention was adequately focused on the issue of respondent's authority with respect to the conditions that formed the basis of the alleged violations. Viewed as a whole, the charge did not permit the jury to find guilt solely on the basis of respondent's position in the corporation; rather, it fairly advised the jury that to find guilt it must find respondent "had a responsible relation to the situation," and "by virtue of his position . . . had authority and responsibility" to deal with the situation. * * *

* * * Finally, we note that there was no request for an instruction that the Government was required to prove beyond a reasonable doubt that respondent was not without the power or capacity to affect the conditions which founded the charges in the information. In light of the evidence adduced at trial, we find no basis to conclude that the failure of the trial court to give such an instruction *sua sponte* was plain error or a defect affecting substantial rights.

IV

Our conclusion that the Court of Appeals erred in its reading of the jury charge suggests as well our disagreement with that court concerning the admissibility of evidence demonstrating that respondent was advised by the FDA in 1970 of insanitary conditions in Acme's Philadelphia warehouse. We are satisfied that the Act imposes the highest standard of care and permits conviction of responsible corporate officials who, in light of this standard of care, have the power to prevent or correct violations of its provisions. Implicit in the Court's admonition that "the ultimate judgment of juries must be trusted," however, is the realization that they may demand more than corporate bylaws to find culpability.

Respondent testified in his defense that he had employed a system in which he relied upon his subordinates, and that he was ultimately responsible for this system. He testified further that he had found these subordinates to be "dependable" and had "great confidence" in them. By this and other testimony respondent evidently sought to persuade the jury that, as the president of a large corporation, he had no choice but to delegate duties to those in whom he reposed confidence, that he had no reason to suspect his subordinates were failing to insure compliance with the Act, and that, once violations were unearthed, acting through those subordinates he did everything possible to correct them.

Although we need not decide whether this testimony would have entitled respondent to an instruction as to his lack of power, had he requested it,[19] the testimony clearly created the "need" for rebuttal evidence. That evidence was not offered to show that respondent had a propensity to commit criminal acts. * * * [I]ts purpose was to demonstrate that respondent was on notice that he could not rely on his system of delegation to subordinates to prevent or correct insanitary conditions at Acme's warehouses, and that he must have been aware of the deficiencies of this system before the Baltimore violations were discovered. The evidence was therefore relevant since it served to rebut respondent's defense that he had justifiably relied upon subordinates to handle sanitation matters. * * *

Reversed.

Mr. Justice STEWART, with whom Mr. Justice MARSHALL and Mr. Justice POWELL join, dissenting.

Although agreeing with much of what is said in the Court's opinion, I dissent from the opinion and judgment, because the jury instructions in this case were not consistent with the law as the Court expounds it.

As I understand the Court's opinion, it holds that in order to sustain a conviction under § 301(k) of the Food, Drug, and Cosmetic Act the prosecution must at least show that by reason of an individual's corporate position and responsibilities, he had a duty to use care to maintain the physical integrity of the corporation's food products. A jury may then draw the inference that when the food is found to be in such condition as to violate the statute's prohibitions, that condition as "caused" by a breach of the standard of care imposed upon the responsible official. This is the language of negligence, and I agree with it.

To affirm this conviction, however, the Court must approve the instructions given to the members of the jury who were entrusted with determining whether the respondent was innocent or guilty. Those instructions did not conform to the standards that the Court itself sets out today.

---

[19] Assuming, *arguendo,* that it would be objectively impossible for a senior corporate agent to control fully day-to-day conditions in 874 retail outlets, it does not follow that such a corporate agent could not prevent or remedy promptly violations of elementary sanitary conditions in 16 regional warehouses.

The trial judge instructed the jury to find Park guilty if it found beyond a reasonable doubt that Park "had a responsible relation to the situation . . . The issue is, in this case, whether the Defendant, John R. Park, by virtue of his position in the company, had a position of authority and responsibility in the situation out of which these charges arose." Requiring, as it did, a verdict of guilty upon a finding of "responsibility," this instruction standing alone could have been construed as a direction to convict if the jury found Park "responsible" for the condition in the sense that his position as chief executive officer gave him formal responsibility within the structure of the corporation. But the trial judge went on specifically to caution the jury not to attach such a meaning to his instruction, saying that "the fact that the Defendant is pres(id)ent and is a chief executive officer of the Acme Markets does not require a finding of guilt." "Responsibility" as used by the trial judge therefore had whatever meaning the jury in its unguided discretion chose to give it.

The instructions, therefore, expressed nothing more than a tautology. They told the jury: "You must find the defendant guilty if you find that he is to be held accountable for this adulterated food." In other words: "You must find the defendant guilty if you conclude that he is guilty." The trial judge recognized the infirmities in these instructions, but he reluctantly concluded that he was required to give such a charge under United States v. Dotterweich, which, he thought, in declining to define "responsible relation" had declined to specify the minimum standard of liability for criminal guilt. * * *

But before a person can be convicted of a criminal violation of this Act, a jury must find—and must be clearly instructed that it must find—evidence beyond a reasonable doubt that he engaged in wrongful conduct amounting at least to common-law negligence. There were no such instructions, and clearly, therefore, no such finding in this case. * * *

NOTES AND QUESTIONS

1. ***Indemnification of Corporate Officers.*** Why is Park appealing a $250 fine all the way to the Supreme Court? Does society truly consider individuals such as Park to be criminals? What ramifications does this decision have on corporate officers? Should the corporation or the corporate executive pay the legal fees and fines assessed? See Pamela H. Bucy, *Indemnification of Corporate Executives Who Have Been Convicted of Crimes: An Assessment and Proposal*, 24 IND. L. REV. 279 (1991); see also United States v. Stein [p. 763], and note 2 at p. 778 (discussing attorney fees). Do directors and officers' insurance policies serve legitimate goals? See Note, *Liability Insurance for Corporate Executives*, 80 HARV. L. REV. 648 (1967). Do these policies mitigate the impact of decisions such as *Park*? See Bennett L. Ross, Note, *Protecting Corporate Directors and Officers: Insurance and Other Alternatives*, 40 VAND. L. REV. 775 (1987).

2. ***Responsible Share.*** Is the "responsible share" doctrine closer to a negligence or strict liability theory? Does the insertion of the concept of "powerlessness" in *Park* move it further from strict liability and closer to requiring some culpability? See Norman Abrams, *Criminal Liability of Corporate Officers for Strict Liability Offenses - A Comment on Dotterweich and Park*, 28 U.C.L.A. L. REV. 463 (1981); Kathleen F. Brickey, *Criminal Liability of Corporate Officers for Strict Liability Offenses - Another View*, 35 Vand. L. Rev. 1337 (1982). [For discussion of the "responsible corporate officer" in environmental cases and statutes, see chapter 7, p. 293].

3. ***Powerlessness of Corporate Officer.*** When is a defendant entitled to an instruction on "objective impossibility" or lack of "power or capacity?" Is this defense available "to anyone, organization or individual, offering to prove inability to prevent or correct in [a] timely fashion a violation despite maintenance of the highest standard of foresight and vigilance?" Or is this defense "available only to the corporate officer and not the corporation itself, and appl[ied] only when the officer was in fact powerless to prevent or correct the violation, even by suspending the corporation's food warehousing activity if necessary." United States v. Y. Hata, 535 F.2d 508, 511 (9th Cir. 1976).

4. ***Corporate Position.*** In a case involving whether individuals should be excluded from participation in future federal health care programs, District Judge Huvelle, stated that a defendant's position within the corporation is relevant, but that "it is simply not the case that a defendant can be convicted of a misdemeanor under the responsible corporate offer doctrine based solely on his position within the corporate hierarchy." Friedman v. Sebelius, 755 F. Supp.2d 98 (D.C. Cir. 2010), rev. on other grounds, rehearing en banc 686 F.3d 813 (D.C. Cir. 2012).

5. ***Recent Prosecutions of Corporate Executives.*** In 2002, President George W. Bush created the Corporate Fraud Task Force. In a 2008 report of the Task Force, it stated that DOJ had "obtained nearly 1,300 corporate fraud convictions." This number included "convictions of more than 200 chief executives and corporate presidents, more than 120 corporate vice presidents, and more than 50 chief financial officers." See Report to the President, Corporate Fraud Task Force (2008). Some of the recent high-level executives convicted include Jeffrey Skilling – the former CEO of Enron; Bernard Ebbers - former CEO of Worldcom; John Rigas – former CEO of Adelphia Communications Corporation. In many cases the sentences given to the executives have been higher than those previously seen in white collar cases (e.g., Bernard Ebbers - 25 years). See Sentencing [p. 819]. In some of these cases, the courts have included jury instructions of willful blindness, when the executive claimed that he or she was unaware of the criminality occurring within the corporation.

6. ***Compliance Programs-Obligations of Corporate Officers.*** Do corporate directors have an obligation to adopt compliance programs that meet the standards of the Organizational Sentencing Guidelines [Chapter 17]? In **In re Caremark International Inc. Derivative Litigation**, 698 A.2d 959, 970

(Ct. Chancery Del. 1996) the court stated, "a director's obligation includes a duty to attempt in good faith to assure that a corporate information and reporting system, which the board concludes is adequate, exists, and that failure to do so under some circumstances may, in theory at least, render a director liable for losses caused by non-compliance with applicable legal standards." In **McCall v. Scott**, 239 F.3d 808 (6th Cir. 2001), the court after referring to the *Caremark* decision, stated that, "[u]nconsidered inaction can be the basis for director liability because, even though most corporate decisions are not subject to director attention, ordinary business decisions of officers and employees deeper in the corporation can significantly injure the corporation and make it subject to criminal sanctions." Amended 250 F.3d 997 (6th Cir. 2001). In **Stone v. Ritter**, 911 A.2d 362 (Del. 2006), the Delaware Supreme Court held:

> We hold that *Caremark* articulates the necessary conditions predicate for director oversight liability: (a) the directors utterly failed to implement any reporting or information system or controls; or (b) having implemented such a system or controls, consciously failed to monitor or oversee its operations thus disabling themselves from being informed of risks or problems requiring their attention. In either case, imposition of liability requires a showing that the directors knew that they were not discharging their fiduciary obligations. Where directors fail to act in the face of a known duty to act, thereby demonstrating a conscious disregard for their responsibilities, they breach their duty of loyalty by failing to discharge that fiduciary obligation in good faith.

7. ***Verdict Consistency (Individual/Corporation).*** Is there any requirement for consistency between a verdict against a corporation and a verdict against an individual defendant who is an employee of the corporation acting on behalf of the corporation? In *Dotterwich*, the corporation was acquitted while the individual was convicted. The Court held that "[w]hether the jury's verdict was a result of carelessness or compromise or a belief that the responsible individual should suffer the penalty instead of merely increasing, as it were, the cost of running the business of the corporation, is immaterial." In **United States v. Hughes Aircraft Co., Inc.,** 20 F.3d 974 (9th Cir. 1994), the court considered this issue stating:

> * * * Hughes contracted with the United States to manufacture microelectronic circuits, known as "hybrids," which are used as components in weapons defense systems. The contracts required Hughes to perform a series of tests on each hybrid. As the hybrids made their way through the testing process, they were accompanied by paperwork indicating what tests had been performed, the results of those tests, and the identity of the operator of the testing equipment.
>
> Hughes's former employee, Donald LaRue ("LaRue"), was a supervisor responsible for ensuring the accuracy of the hybrid testing

process. LaRue arranged for the paperwork to indicate falsely that all tests had been performed and that each hybrid had passed each test. When LaRue's subordinates called his actions to the attention of LaRue's supervisors, the supervisors did nothing about it. Instead, they responded that LaRue's decisions were his own and were not to be questioned by his subordinates.

Hughes and LaRue were charged with one count of conspiracy to defraud and make false statements to the United States in violation of 18 U.S.C. § 371, and two counts of making false statements in furtherance of that conspiracy in violation of 18 U.S.C. § 1001. LaRue was acquitted on all counts. Hughes was convicted of the conspiracy charge, but acquitted of the other two charges. Hughes appeals from both its conviction and fine of $3.5 million.

* * * Hughes first argues that it must be acquitted as a matter of law because the same jury that convicted Hughes acquitted its "indispensable co-conspirator," LaRue, of the identical charges on identical evidence. Hughes bases its argument on three Supreme Court cases from the 1930's and 1940's, arguing that they provide an exception to the general rule that inconsistency of jury verdicts is not a ground for reversal. See Dunn v. United States, 284 U.S. 390, 393, 52 S.Ct. 189, 190, 76 L.Ed. 356 (1932); United States v. Powell, 469 U.S. 57, 64-65, 105 S.Ct. 471, 476, 83 L.Ed.2d 461 (1984). According to Hughes, the post-*Dunn* Supreme Court cases indicate that the inconsistent verdict rule applies only to situations involving inconsistencies in multiple verdicts against a single defendant, not inconsistencies in multiple verdicts against multiple defendants. Controlling Ninth Circuit precedent precludes us from adopting such a rule. * * * The Supreme Court's decision in *Powell* supports this extension of the application of the *Dunn* rule insulating inconsistent jury verdicts from appellate review. "[T]he Government's inability to invoke review, the general reluctance to inquire into the workings of the jury, and the possible exercise of lenity--suggest that the best course to take is simply to insulate jury verdicts from review on [inconsistency] ground." * * * Contrary to Hughes's contentions, this Circuit has not recognized a post-*Powell* exception to the *Dunn* rule. Accordingly, the conviction of one co-conspirator is valid even when all the other co-conspirators are acquitted. * * *

Hughes next argues that it is entitled to a judgment of acquittal because the evidence against it and LaRue was identical, yet one was convicted while the other was acquitted. This argument is predicated on the assumption that LaRue was the sole employee for whose actions Hughes could be found vicariously guilty and that the evidence against each of the two defendants was necessarily identical. However, some of the evidence of conspiracy was offered against Hughes alone. Moreover, as this evidence indicates, the jury could have found Hughes guilty based on the actions or omissions of its supervisors and employees other than LaRue. As Hughes's assumption that the facts against both defendants were identical is erroneous, and no other facts support its argument, we reject this contention.

Hughes's third argument is that the plain language of 18 U.S.C. § 371, which states that if "two or more persons conspire ... each" may be punished, prevents its conviction because it is legally impossible for a party to conspire with itself. Hughes argues that, because it is vicariously liable for each of its employees, a conspiracy between employees would necessitate a finding that Hughes conspired with itself. We reject this creative construction. The statutory language does not exclude criminal liability for a corporation simply because its employees are the actual conspirators. To rule otherwise would effectively insulate all corporations from liability for conspiracies involving only employees acting on behalf of that corporation. We hold that a corporation may be liable under § 371 for conspiracies entered into by its agents and employees. * * *

Hughes also contends that we should extend the reach of the intracorporate conspiracy doctrine in antitrust law, which holds that a conspiracy requires "an agreement among two or more persons or distinct business entities." * * * While this doctrine has been extended by some circuits to civil rights cases, * * * other circuits have declined to do so, * * * and we have reserved the issue.

However, this doctrine has never been applied to criminal cases. As the First Circuit noted, "There is a world of difference between invoking the fiction of corporate personality to subject a corporation to civil liability for acts of its agents and invoking it to shield a corporation or its agents from criminal liability where its agents acted on its behalf." * * * Every other circuit to address the issue has come to the same conclusion. * * *

Hughes argues that public policy requires us to apply the intracorporate conspiracy doctrine to criminal cases. However, a stronger public policy mandates a contrary result. Simply because no other corporation or individual is involved, or there is no joining of previously divergent goals, does not mean there is no conspiracy. If we applied the intracorporate conspiracy doctrine to this case, no corporation acting on its own behalf by and through its employees could be found guilty of conspiracy. This result is illogical. * * * We decline to extend the intracorporate conspiracy doctrine to criminal activity. * * *

Wharton's Rule prevents a conspiracy conviction when an underlying substantive offense requires more than one actor, such as adultery or dueling, and in which "the immediate consequences of the crime rest on the parties themselves rather than on society." Iannelli v. United

States, 420 U.S. 770, 782-83, 95 S.Ct. 1284, 1293, 43 L.Ed.2d 616 (1975). Here we have a conspiracy to defraud the government, a violation of 18 U.S.C. § 1001.

Hughes argues that a corporation could only violate 18 U.S.C. § 1001 through the efforts of at least two of its employees due to the supervisory and reporting structure of a corporation. Of course, that is not true: a corporation could be liable under § 1001 for false statements to the government by just one of its employees. A conspiracy arises when more than one of its employees agree to defraud the government.

Moreover, the consequences of government fraud certainly do not rest on the parties themselves rather than society. Government fraud has an adverse effect on the government treasury, the quality of government projects, and in cases such as this one, the safety of individuals utilizing the government goods purchased. * * * This argument is rejected.* * * Because we find no merit to any of Hughes's arguments on this point, we affirm the conviction. * * *AFFIRMED.

CHAPTER FOUR
PRINCIPLES OF STATUTORY INTERPRETATION

> Certain situations do not readily demonstrate that a crime has occurred. One cannot make a reliable presumption that the elements of a crime are present, as one can when a bank manager finds a vault broken open. In situations of ambiguity, determining whether a crime occurred requires careful examination of fact and law. Many suspected cases of fraud— tax and securities fraud, for instance—leave open basic questions about whether criminal intent was formed by the so-called perpetrator. In the extreme, this phenomenon is exemplified by the potential client who thinks that he has committed a crime—say, he failed to report certain income—but the attorney can demonstrate that it was quite reasonable for the client to believe that an exemption or offset permitted the client's not reporting that income. There are at least two characteristics in potential criminal situations that create ambiguity. First, unclarity about the facts creates ambiguity. When the evidence to prove a crime is dispersed among many sources, the government's access to a limited number of sources may create suspicion but leave doubt. Second, and even where all the facts are known to the government, statutory definitions create ambiguity at their margins about what behavior is criminal and what is not. Certain kinds of statutes create more ambiguity than others. Attorneys interviewed said that white-collar crimes typically are defined in language creating a broad margin of ambiguity.

KENNETH MANN, DEFENDING WHITE-COLLAR CRIME 114-15 (1985).

A. THE MENS REA ELEMENT

RATZLAF v. UNITED STATES
510 U.S. 135 (1994)

Justice GINSBURG delivered the opinion of the Court.

Federal law requires banks and other financial institutions to file reports with the Secretary of the Treasury whenever they are involved in a cash transaction that exceeds $10,000. 31 U.S.C. § 5313; 31 CFR § 103.22(a) (1993). It is illegal to "structure" transactions—i.e., to break up a single transaction above the reporting threshold into two or more separate transactions—for the purpose of evading a financial institution's reporting requirement. 31 U.S.C. § 5324. "A person willfully violating" this antistructuring provision is subject to criminal penalties. § 5322. This case presents a question on which Courts of Appeals have divided: Does a defendant's purpose to circumvent a bank's reporting obligation suffice to sustain a conviction for "willfully violating" the antistructuring provision? We hold that the "willfulness" requirement mandates something more. To establish that a defendant "willfully violat[ed]" the antistructuring law, the Government must prove that the defendant acted with knowledge that his conduct was unlawful.

I.

On the evening of October 20, 1988, defendant-petitioner Waldemar Ratzlaf ran up a debt of $160,000 playing blackjack at the High Sierra Casino in Reno, Nevada. The casino gave him one week to pay. On the due date, Ratzlaf returned to the casino with cash of $100,000 in hand. A casino official informed Ratzlaf that all transactions involving more than $10,000 in cash had to be reported to state and federal authorities. The official added that the casino could accept a cashier's check for the full amount due without triggering any reporting requirement. The casino helpfully placed a limousine at Ratzlaf's disposal, and assigned an employee to accompany him to banks in the vicinity. Informed that banks, too, are required to report cash transactions in excess of $10,000, Ratzlaf purchased cashier's checks, each for less than $10,000 and each from a different bank. He delivered these checks to the High Sierra Casino.

Based on this endeavor, Ratzlaf was charged with "structuring transactions" to evade the banks' obligation to report cash transactions exceeding $10,000; this conduct, the indictment alleged, violated 31 U.S.C. §§ 5322(a) and 5324(3). The trial judge instructed the jury that the Government had to prove defendant's knowledge of the banks' reporting obligation and his attempt to evade that obligation, but did not have to prove defendant knew the structuring was unlawful. Ratzlaf was convicted, fined, and sentenced to prison.[2]

Ratzlaf maintained on appeal that he could not be convicted of "willfully violating" the antistructuring law solely on the basis of his knowledge that a financial institution must report currency transactions in excess of $10,000 and his intention to avoid such reporting. To gain a conviction for "willful" conduct, he asserted, the Government must prove he was aware of the illegality of the "structuring" in which he engaged. The Ninth Circuit upheld the trial court's construction of the legislation and affirmed Ratzlaf's conviction. We granted certiorari, and now conclude that, to give effect to the statutory "willfulness" specification, the Government had to prove Ratzlaf

---

[2] Ratzlaf's wife and the casino employee who escorted Ratzlaf to area banks were codefendants. For convenience, we refer only to Waldemar Ratzlaf in this opinion.

knew the structuring he undertook was unlawful. We therefore reverse the judgment of the Court of Appeals.

II

* * * Congress enacted the Currency and Foreign Transactions Reporting Act (Bank Secrecy Act) in 1970, in response to increasing use of banks and other institutions as financial intermediaries by persons engaged in criminal activity. The Act imposes a variety of reporting requirements on individuals and institutions regarding foreign and domestic financial transactions. The reporting requirement relevant here, § 5313(a), applies to domestic financial transactions. Section 5313(a) reads:

> "When a domestic financial institution is involved in a transaction for the payment, receipt, or transfer of United States coins or currency (or other monetary instruments the Secretary of the Treasury prescribes), in an amount, denomination, or amount and denomination, or under circumstances the Secretary prescribes by regulation, the institution and any other participant in the transaction the Secretary may prescribe shall file a report on the transaction at the time and in the way the Secretary prescribes ..."[3]

To deter circumvention of this reporting requirement, Congress enacted an antistructuring provision, 31 U.S.C. § 5324, as part of the Money Laundering Control Act of 1986,[4] Section 5324, which Ratzlaf is charged with "willfully violating," reads:

> "No person shall for the purpose of evading the reporting requirements of section 5313(a) with respect to such transaction—
>
> * * *
>
> "(3) structure or assist in structuring, or attempt to structure or assist in structuring, any transaction with one or more domestic financial institutions."[6]

---

[3] By regulation, the Secretary ordered reporting of "transaction[s] in currency of more than $10,000." 31 CFR § 103.22(a) (1993). Although the Secretary could have imposed a report-filing requirement on "any . . . participant in the transaction," 31 U.S.C. § 5313(a), the Secretary chose to require reporting by the financial institution but not by the customer. 31 CFR § 103.22(a) (1993).

[4] Other portions of this Act make "money laundering" itself a crime. See 18 U.S.C. § 1956(a)(2)(B) (prohibiting various transactions involving the "proceeds of some form of unlawful activity"). The Government does not assert that Ratzlaf obtained the cash used in any of the transactions relevant here in other than a lawful manner.

[6] Regarding enforcement of § 5324, the Secretary considered, but did not promulgate, a regulation requiring banks to inform currency transaction customers of the section's proscription. * * *

The criminal enforcement provision at issue, 31 U.S.C. § 5322(a), sets out penalties for "[a] person willfully violating," *inter alia*, the antistructuring provision. Section 5322(a) reads:

> "A person willfully violating this subchapter [31 U.S.C. § 5311 et seq.] or a regulation prescribed under this subchapter (except section 5315 of this title or a regulation prescribed under section 5315) shall be fined not more than $250,000, or imprisoned for not more than five years, or both."

* * * Section 5324 forbids structuring transactions with a "purpose of evading the reporting requirements of section 5313(a)." Ratzlaf admits that he structured cash transactions, and that he did so with knowledge of, and a purpose to avoid, the banks' duty to report currency transactions in excess of $10,000. The statutory formulation (§ 5322) under which Ratzlaf was prosecuted, however, calls for proof of "willful[ness]" on the actor's part. The trial judge in Ratzlaf's case, with the Ninth Circuit's approbation, treated § 5322(a)'s "willfulness" requirement essentially as surplusage—as words of no consequence. Judges should hesitate so to treat statutory terms in any setting, and resistance should be heightened when the words describe an element of a criminal offense. * * *

"Willful," this Court has recognized, is a "word of many meanings," and "its construction [is] often ... influenced by its context." Spies v. United States, 317 U.S. 492, 497 (1943). Accordingly, we view §§ 5322(a) and 5324(3) mindful of the complex of provisions in which they are embedded. In this light, we count it significant that § 5322(a)'s omnibus "willfulness" requirement, when applied to other provisions in the same subchapter, consistently has been read by the Courts of Appeals to require both "knowledge of the reporting requirement" and a "specific intent to commit the crime," i.e., "a purpose to disobey the law." * * *

Notable in this regard are 31 U.S.C. § 5314, concerning records and reports on monetary transactions with foreign financial agencies, and § 5316, concerning declaration of the transportation of more than $10,000 into, or out of, the United States. Decisions involving these provisions describe a "willful" actor as one who violates "a known legal duty."[10] * * *

The United States urges, however, that § 5324 violators, by their very conduct, exhibit a purpose to do wrong, which suffices to show "willfulness" * * *. " '[S]tructuring is not the kind of activity that an ordinary person would engage in innocently,' " the United States asserts. It is therefore "reasonable," the Government concludes, "to hold a structurer responsible for

---

[10] "[S]pecific intent to commit the crime[s]" described in 31 U.S.C. §§ 5313, 5314, and 5316 might be negated by, e.g., proof that defendant relied in good faith on advice of counsel. See United States v. Eisenstein [p. 102].

evading the reporting requirements without the need to prove specific knowledge that such evasion is unlawful."

Undoubtedly there are bad men who attempt to elude official reporting requirements in order to hide from Government inspectors such criminal activity as laundering drug money or tax evasion. But currency structuring is not inevitably nefarious. Consider, for example, the small business operator who knows that reports filed under 31 U.S.C. § 5313(a) are available to the Internal Revenue Service. To reduce the risk of an IRS audit, she brings $9,500 in cash to the bank twice each week, in lieu of transporting over $10,000 once each week. That person, if the United States is right, has committed a criminal offense, because she structured cash transactions "for the specific purpose of depriving the Government of the information that Section 5313(a) is designed to obtain." Nor is a person who structures a currency transaction invariably motivated by a desire to keep the Government in the dark. But under the Government's construction an individual would commit a felony against the United States by making cash deposits in small doses, fearful that the bank's reports would increase the likelihood of burglary, or in an endeavor to keep a former spouse unaware of his wealth.

Courts have noted "many occasions" on which persons, without violating any law, may structure transactions "in order to avoid the impact of some regulation or tax." This Court, over a century ago, supplied an illustration:

> "The Stamp Act of 1862 imposed a duty of two cents upon a bank-check, when drawn for an amount not less than 20 dollars. A careful individual, having the amount of twenty dollars to pay, pays the same by handing to his creditor two checks of ten dollars each. He thus draws checks in payment of his debt to the amount of twenty dollars, and yet pays no stamp duty. . . . While his operations deprive the government of the duties it might reasonably expect to receive, it is not perceived that the practice is open to the charge of fraud. He resorts to devices to avoid the payment of duties, but they are not illegal. He has the legal right to split up his evidences of payment, and thus to avoid the tax." United States v. Isham, 84 U.S. (17 Wall.) 496, 506 (1873).

In current days, as an *amicus* noted, countless taxpayers each year give a gift of $10,000 on December 31 and an identical gift the next day, thereby legitimately avoiding the taxable gifts reporting required by 26 U.S.C. § 2503(b).

In light of these examples, we are unpersuaded by the argument that structuring is so obviously "evil" or inherently "bad" that the "willfulness" requirement is satisfied irrespective of the defendant's knowledge of the illegality of structuring. Had Congress wished to dispense with the requirement, it could have furnished the appropriate instruction.[16]

* * * In § 5322, Congress subjected to criminal penalties only those "willfully violating" § 5324, signaling its intent to require for conviction proof that the defendant knew not only of the bank's duty to report cash transactions in excess of $10,000, but also of his duty not to avoid triggering such a report. There are, we recognize, contrary indications in the statute's legislative history.[17] But we do not resort to legislative history to cloud a

---

[16] Congress did provide for civil forfeiture without any "willfulness" requirement in the Money Laundering Control Act of 1986. See 18 U.S.C. § 981(a) (subjecting to forfeiture "[a]ny property, real or personal, involved in a transaction . . . in violation of section 5313(a) or 5324(a) of title 31 . . ."); see also 31 U.S.C. § 5317(a) (subjecting to forfeiture any "monetary instrument . . . being transported [when] a report on the instrument under section 5316 of this title has not been filed or contains a material omission or misstatement").

[17] The United States points to one of the Senate Reports accompanying the Money Laundering Control Act of 1986, which stated that "a person who converts $18,000 in currency to cashier's checks by purchasing two $9,000 cashier's checks at two different banks or on two different days with the specific intent that the participating bank or banks not be required to file Currency Transaction Reports for those transactions, would be subject to potential civil and criminal liability." S.Rep. No. 99-433, p. 22 (1986). The same Report also indicated that § 5324 "would codify [United States v.] *Tobon-Builes* [706 F.2d 1092 (11th Cir. 1983)] and like cases [by] expressly subject[ing] to potential liability a person who causes or attempts to cause a financial institution to fail to file a required report or who causes a financial institution to file a required report that contains material omissions or misstatements of fact." S.Rep. No. 99-433, at 22.

But the legislative history cited by the United States is hardly crystalline. The reference to *Tobon-Builes* is illustrative. In that case, the defendant was charged under 18 U.S.C. § 1001, the False Statements Act, with "conceal[ing] . . . the existence, source, and transfer of approximately $185,200 in cash by purchasing approximately twenty-one cashier's checks in amounts less than $10,000 [and] using a variety of names, including false names . . . ." The defendant's "main contention," rejected by the Eleventh Circuit, was that he "could not have violated the concealment prohibition of § 1001 because he was under no legal duty to report any of his cash transactions." No "ignorance of the law" defense was asserted. Congress may indeed have "codified" that decision in § 5324 by "expressly subject[ing] to potential liability a person who causes or attempts to cause a financial institution to fail to file a required report or who causes a financial institution to file a required report that contains material omissions or misstatements of fact," but it appears that Congress did so in the first and second subsections of § 5324, which track the Senate Report language almost verbatim. See 31 U.S.C. § 5324(1) (no person shall "cause or attempt to cause a domestic financial institution to fail to file a report required under section 5313(a)"); 31 U.S.C. § 5324(2) (no person shall "cause or attempt to cause a domestic financial institution to file a report required under section 5313(a) that contains a material omission or misstatement of fact"). Indeed, the Senate Report stated that "[i]n addition " to codifying *Tobon-Builes* § 5324 would also "create the offense of structuring a transaction to evade the reporting requirements." The

statutory text that is clear. Moreover, were we to find § 5322(a)'s "willfulness" requirement ambiguous as applied to § 5324, we would resolve any doubt in favor of the defendant. Hughey v. United States, 495 U.S. 411, 422 (1990) (lenity principles "demand resolution of ambiguities in criminal statutes in favor of the defendant") * * *.

We do not dishonor the venerable principle that ignorance of the law generally is no defense to a criminal charge. See Cheek v. United States, [p. 102]. In particular contexts, however, Congress may decree otherwise. That, we hold, is what Congress has done with respect to 31 U.S.C. § 5322(a) and the provisions it controls. To convict Ratzlaf of the crime with which he was charged, violation of 31 U.S.C. §§ 5322(a) and 5324(3), the jury had to find he knew the structuring in which he engaged was unlawful.[19] Because the jury was not properly instructed in this regard, we reverse the judgment of the Ninth Circuit and remand this case for further proceedings consistent with this opinion.

Justice BLACKMUN, with whom THE CHIEF JUSTICE, Justice O'CONNOR, and Justice THOMAS join, dissenting.

* * * A jury found beyond a reasonable doubt that Ratzlaf knew of the financial institutions' duty to report cash transactions in excess of $10,000 and that he structured transactions for the specific purpose of evading the reporting requirements.

The Court today, however, concludes that these findings are insufficient for a conviction under 31 U.S.C. §§ 5322(a) and 5324(3), because a defendant also must have known that the structuring in which he engaged was illegal. Because this conclusion lacks support in the text of the statute, conflicts in my view with basic principles governing the interpretation of criminal statutes, and is squarely undermined by the evidence of congressional intent, I dissent.

I

"The general rule that ignorance of the law or a mistake of law is no defense to criminal prosecution is deeply rooted in the American legal

---

relevance of *Tobon-Builes* to the proper construction of § 5324(3), the subsection under which Ratzlaf was convicted, is not evident.

[19] The dissent asserts that our holding "largely nullifies the effect" of § 5324 by "mak[ing] prosecution for structuring difficult or impossible in most cases." Even under the dissent's reading of the statute, proof that the defendant knew of the bank's duty to report is required for conviction; we fail to see why proof that the defendant knew of his duty to refrain from structuring is so qualitatively different that it renders prosecution "impossible." A jury may, of course, find the requisite knowledge on defendant's part by drawing reasonable inferences from the evidence of defendant's conduct, see Spies v. United States, 317 U.S. 492, 499-500 (1943) * * *.

system." Cheek v. United States. The Court has applied this common-law rule "in numerous cases construing criminal statutes."

Thus, the term "willfully" in criminal law generally "refers to consciousness of the act but not to consciousness that the act is unlawful." * * *

* * * The offense of structuring * * * requires (1) knowledge of a financial institution's reporting requirements, and (2) the structuring of a transaction for the purpose of evading those requirements. These elements define a violation that is "willful" as that term is commonly interpreted. The majority's additional requirement that an actor have actual knowledge that structuring is prohibited strays from the statutory text, as well as from our precedents interpreting criminal statutes generally and "willfulness" in particular.

The Court reasons that the interpretation of the Court of Appeals for the Ninth Circuit, and that of nine other circuits, renders § 5322(a)'s willfulness requirement superfluous. This argument ignores the generality of § 5322(a), which sets a single standard—willfulness—for the subchapter's various reporting provisions. Some of those provisions do not themselves define willful conduct, so the willfulness element cannot be deemed surplusage. Moreover, the fact that § 5322(a) requires willfulness for criminal liability to be imposed does not mean that each of the underlying offenses to which it applies must involve something less than willfulness. Thus, the fact that § 5324 does describe a "willful" offense, since it already requires "the purpose of evading the reporting requirements," provides no basis for imposing an artificially heightened scienter requirement.

* * * The Court next concludes that its interpretation of "willfully" is warranted because structuring is not inherently "nefarious." It is true that the Court, on occasion, has imposed a knowledge-of-illegality requirement upon criminal statutes to ensure that the defendant acted with a wrongful purpose. [citing Liparota v. United States, p. 110]. I cannot agree, however, that the imposition of such a requirement is necessary here. First, the conduct at issue—splitting up transactions involving tens of thousands of dollars in cash for the specific purpose of circumventing a bank's reporting duty—is hardly the sort of innocuous activity involved in cases such as *Liparota*, in which the defendant had been convicted of fraud for purchasing food stamps for less than their face value. Further, an individual convicted of structuring is, by definition, aware that cash transactions are regulated, and he cannot seriously argue that he lacked notice of the law's intrusion into the particular sphere of activity. By requiring knowledge of a bank's reporting requirements as well as a "purpose of evading" those requirements, the antistructuring provision targets those who knowingly act to deprive the Government of information to which it is entitled. In my view, that is not so plainly innocent a purpose as to justify reading into the statute the additional element of knowledge of illegality. In any event, Congress has determined that purposefully structuring transactions is not innocent conduct.

In interpreting federal criminal tax statutes, this Court has defined the term "willfully" as requiring the "voluntary, intentional violation of a known legal duty." Cheek v. United States [p. 102]. Our rule in the tax area, however, is an "exception to the traditional rule," applied "largely due to the complexity of the tax laws." The rule is inapplicable here, where, far from being complex, the provisions involved are perhaps among the simplest in the United States Code.

II

Although I believe the statutory language is clear in light of our precedents, the legislative history confirms that Congress intended to require knowledge of (and a purpose to evade) the reporting requirements but not specific knowledge of the illegality of structuring.[9]

Before 1986, the reporting requirements included no provision explicitly prohibiting the structuring of transactions to evade the reporting requirements. The Government attempted to combat purposeful evasion of the reporting requirements through 18 U.S.C. § 1001, which applies to anyone who "knowingly and willfully falsifies, conceals or covers up by any trick, scheme, or device a material fact" within the jurisdiction of a federal agency, and 18 U.S.C. § 2(b), which applies to anyone who "willfully causes an act to be done which if directly performed by him or another would be an offense" under federal law. Some Courts of Appeals upheld application of those criminal statutes where a report would have been filed but for the defendant's purposeful structuring. As the leading case explained, a defendant's willfulness was established if he "knew about the currency reporting requirements and . . . purposely sought to prevent the financial institutions from filing required reports . . . by structuring his transactions as multiple smaller transactions under $10,000." *Tobon-Builes.*

Other courts rejected imposition of criminal liability for structuring under §§ 1001 and 2(b), concluding either that the law did not impose a duty not to structure or that criminal liability was confined to limited forms of structuring. See, e.g., United States v. Varbel, 780 F.2d 758 (9th Cir. 1986); United States v. Denemark, 779 F.2d 1559 (11th Cir. 1986); United States v. Anzalone, 766 F.2d 676 (1st Cir. 1985).

Congress enacted the antistructuring provision in 1986 "to fill a loophole in the Bank Secrecy Act caused by" the latter three decisions, which "refused to apply the sanctions of [the Act] to transactions 'structured' to evade the act's $10,000 cash reporting requirement." As explained by the Report of the Senate Judiciary Committee: "[The antistructuring provision] would codify

---

[9] Because the statutory language unambiguously imposes no requirement of knowledge of the illegality of structuring, I would not apply the rule of lenity. Moreover, I am not persuaded that that rule should be applied to defeat a congressional purpose that is as clear as that evidenced here. See *Liparota*, 471 U.S., at 427.

Tobon-Builes and like cases and would negate the effect of *Anzalone, Varbel* and *Denemark*. * * * " Congress' stated purpose to "codify *Tobon-Builes*" reveals its intent to incorporate *Tobon-Builes'* standard for a willful violation, which required knowledge of the reporting requirements and a purpose to evade them. Nothing in *Tobon-Builes* suggests that knowledge of the illegality of one's conduct is required.[10]

The Senate Report proceeds to explain the intent required under the antistructuring provision:

> "For example, a person who converts $18,000 in currency to cashier's checks by purchasing two $9,000 cashier's checks at two different banks or on two different days *with the specific intent that the participating bank or banks not be required to file Currency Transaction Reports for those transactions,* would be subject to potential civil and criminal liability. A person conducting the same transactions for any other reasons or a person splitting up an amount of currency that would not be reportable if the full amount were involved in a single transaction (for example, splitting $2,000 in currency into four transactions of $500 each), would not be subject to liability under the proposed amendment." (Emphasis added.)

The Committee's specification of the requisite intent as only the intent to prevent a bank from filing reports confirms that Congress did not contemplate a departure from the general rule that knowledge of illegality is not an essential element of a criminal offense.

---

[10] Contrary to the majority's suggestion, Congress did sanction *Tobon-Builes'* scienter standard. In that case, which Congress intended to "codify," the Eleventh Circuit clearly addressed the level of knowledge required for a willful violation. Moreover, Congress was aware of the standard that the court had adopted, explicitly characterizing *Tobon-Builes* as imposing criminal liability upon individuals who structure transactions "to evade the reporting requirements." The majority misreads the Senate Report as stating that § 5324 creates the structuring offense " '[i]n addition' to codifying *Tobon-Builes*." The phrase "in addition" plainly refers to the previous sentence in the Report, which states that § 5324 "would expressly subject to potential liability a person who causes or attempts to cause a financial institution to fail to file a required report or who causes a financial institution to file a required report that contains material omissions or misstatements of fact." The "codification" of *Tobon-Builes* encompasses both sentences, and thus all three subsections of the original § 5324. * * * Even more direct evidence of Congress's intent to incorporate the *Tobon- Builes* scienter standard is found in the response to a question from Senator D'Amato, the Senate sponsor of the antistructuring provision. He asked Deputy Assistant Attorney General Knapp and Assistant United States Attorney Sun: "Assuming that [the antistructuring] provision had been on the books, could you have demonstrated a willful violation in the *Anzalone, Varbel* and *Denemark* cases?" The written response stated: "Assuming that the terms of [the antistructuring provision] were in effect at the time of the conduct described in *Anzalone, Varbel,* and *Denemark,* the result would, or should have been markedly different." * * *

A recent amendment to § 5324 further supports the interpretation of the court below. In 1992, Congress enacted the Annunzio-Wylie Anti-Money Laundering Act, creating a parallel antistructuring provision for the reporting requirements under 31 U.S.C. § 5316, which governs international monetary transportation. Like the provision at issue here, the new provision prohibits structuring "for the purpose of evading the reporting requirements" (in that case, the requirements of § 5316). At the time Congress amended the statute, every court of appeals to consider the issue had held that a willful violation of the antistructuring provision requires knowledge of the bank's reporting requirements and an intent to evade them; none had held that knowledge of the illegality of structuring was required. * * *

* * * [T]he majority's interpretation of § 5324 as a practical matter largely nullifies the effect of that provision. In codifying the currency transaction reporting requirements in 1970, "Congress recognized the importance of reports of large and unusual currency transactions in ferreting out criminal activity." California Bankers Assn. v. Shultz, 416 U.S. 21, 38 (1974). Congress enacted the antistructuring law to close what it perceived as a major loophole in the federal reporting scheme due to easy circumvention. Because requiring proof of actual knowledge of illegality will make prosecution for structuring difficult or impossible in most cases, the Court's decision reopens the loophole that Congress tried to close. * * *

NOTES AND QUESTIONS

1. ***Legislative Response.*** Shortly after the Supreme Court's ruling in *Ratzlaf*, Congress, as part of the Riegle Community Development and Regulatory Improvement Act of 1994, modified § 5324. The statute now provides that, "[w]hoever violates this section shall be fined in accordance with title 18, United States Code, imprisoned not more than five years, or both." A House report states that it was Congress' intent to overrule the *Ratzlaf* decision by this amendment. This section "restores the clear Congressional intent that a defendant need only have the intent to evade the reporting requirment as the sufficient *mens rea* for the offense." See 1994 U.S.C.C.A.N. 1977. Although Congress modified § 5324, other statutes that use the original terminology have been faced with *Ratzlaf* type challenges. See, e.g., Hanlester Network v. Shalala, 51 F.3d 1390 (9th Cir. 1995) (applying *Ratzlaf* in interpreting the terms "knowingly and willfully" in a Medicare/Medicaid anti-kickback statute).

2. ***Wilfulness in Tax Statutes.*** In light of *Ratzlaf,* what should be the *mens rea* of 26 U.S.C.A. § 6050I, which requires trades or businesses receiving more than $10,000 in cash to report the transaction to the Treasury on Form 8300? See United States v. Rogers, 18 F.3d 265 (4th Cir. 1994) (prosecution under '6050I(f), which prohibits various actions taken "for the purpose of evading the return requirements of this section," and '7203, which provides criminal penalty for a "willful violation" of that provision, remanded for new

trial where trial court's instruction, contrary to *Ratzlaf*, stated that "[w]illful means no more than the Defendant charged with the duty knows what he is doing"). [For discussion of the application of ' 6050I to attorneys, see Chapter 16]

3. ***Ignorance of the Law.*** In Lambert v. California, 355 U.S. 225 (1957), the majority reaffirmed the rule that "ignorance of the law will not excuse." The Court, however, excused the defendant's conduct finding a violation of due process when a felony registration ordinance was applied to an individual who had no knowledge of her duty to register. Justice Frankfurter, in his dissent in Lambert v. California, stated that "I feel confident that the present decision will turn out to be an isolated deviation from the strong current of precedents–a derelict on the waters of the law." Does the common law principle that "ignorance of the law will not excuse" remain intact after the *Ratzlaf* decision?

4. ***Good Faith Reliance on Counsel.*** *Ratzlaf*, in footnote 10, suggests that specific intent to commit the crime can be negated by "good faith reliance on the advice of counsel. To what extent should a defendant's reliance on the advice of counsel negate specific intent? See United States v. Eisenstein, 731 F.2d 1540, 1543-44 (11th Cir. 1984). Consider this issue in the context of United States v. Cheek, 3 F.3d 1057 (7th Cir. 1993). Defendant, a commercial airline pilot, was convicted of willfully attempting to evade payment of income taxes and willfully failing to file income tax returns. He failed to file returns after 1979 and increased his withholding allowances on his W-2 form to 60 allowances. In **Cheek v. United States**, 498 U.S. 192 (1991), the Supreme Court overturned his initial conviction, finding that the trial court's jury instruction improperly limited Cheek's claim that he truly believed that the tax code did not treat wages as income. The Court noted that the tax laws had long been held to reflect a congressional purpose of creating an exception to the general principle that ignorance of the law is no excuse. In this area of the law, Congress has required a "willful" violation of tax laws, which has been read to require a "specific intent to violate the law." Accordingly, a good faith belief that one is not violating the law negates willfulness. The Court held that it was error for the trial court to insist that this was only so if the good faith belief was objectively reasonable.

On retrial, Cheek argued that a good faith belief was established here because of his reliance upon the advice of counsel. The trial court refused an instruction on advice of counsel. Affirming Cheek's conviction, the Seventh Circuit noted:

> In order to establish an advice of counsel defense, a defendant must establish that:
>
> > (1) before taking action, (2) he in good faith sought the advice of an attorney whom he considered competent, (3) for the purpose of securing advice of the lawfulness of his possible

> future conduct, (4) and made a full and accurate report to his attorney of all material facts which the defendant knew, (5) and acted strictly in accordance with the advice of his attorney who had been given a full report.
>
> A crucial element of this defense is that "defendant secured the advice on the lawfulness of his *possible future conduct.*"
>
> Cheek testified that he received the advice of at least three different attorneys on the status of the tax laws, but we are not satisfied that he sought or received advice on "possible future conduct." He did not seek any advice until after 1980, when he first failed to file proper tax returns. Furthermore, Cheek had been told by the IRS, American Airlines personnel and by at least one court that his contentions were without merit prior to his discussions with counsel. Reduced to its essence, the record indicates that Cheek merely continued a course of illegal conduct begun prior to contacting counsel. * * *
>
> Nowhere does Mr. Cheek contend either that he made a full and accurate report as to his tax status to any attorney or that he "acted strictly in accordance with the advice of his attorney." * * * None of these attorneys advised him not to file tax returns. To the contrary, each advised him that he might be criminally prosecuted if he failed to file. Accordingly, on the basis of the evidence presented, the district court did not err in refusing to give a jury instruction on the advice of counsel defense.

5. ***Reading in a Mens Rea Element.*** When is it appropriate for the Court to read a *mens rea* requirement into the statute? **United States v. United States Gypsum Company**, 438 U.S. 422 (1978), involved an appeal from convictions for alleged violations of the Sherman Act. The Act prohibits combinations "in restraint of trade," and the government argued that if the effect of the exchange of pricing information among the defendants was "to raise, fix, maintain, and stabilize prices," that was sufficient to establish liability, as the statute prohibited such action "if it has either the purpose or the effect of stabilizing prices." The defense argued that liability did not exist absent a culpable *mens rea.* Thus, the issue was presented as to "whether intent is an element of a criminal antitrust offense." Chief Justice Burger, writing for the court, stated:

> We start with the familiar proposition that "[t]he existence of a mens rea is the rule of, rather than the exception to, the principles of Anglo-American criminal jurisprudence." Dennis v. United States, 341 U.S. 494, 500 (1951). * * *

> This Court, in keeping with the common-law tradition and with the general injunction that "ambiguity concerning the ambit of criminal statutes should be resolved in favor of lenity," Rewis v. United States, 401 U.S. 808, 812 (1971), has on a number of occasions read a state-of-mind component into an offense even when the statutory definition did not in terms so provide. Indeed, the holding in *Morissette* [*v. United States*, 342 U.S. 246 (1952)] can be fairly read as establishing, at least with regard to crimes having their origin in the common law, an interpretative presumption that *mens rea* is required. "[M]ere omission . . . of intent [in the statute] will not be construed as eliminating that element from the crimes denounced"; instead Congress will be presumed to have legislated against the background of our traditional legal concepts which render intent a critical factor, and "absence of contrary direction [will] be taken as satisfaction with widely accepted definitions, not as a departure from them."
>
> While strict-liability offenses are not unknown to the criminal law and do not invariably offend constitutional requirements, the limited circumstances in which Congress has created and this Court has recognized such offenses attest to their generally disfavored status. Certainly far more than the simple omission of the appropriate phrase from the statutory definition is necessary to justify dispensing with an intent requirement. In the context of the Sherman Act, this generally inhospitable attitude to non-*mens rea* offenses is reinforced by an array of considerations arguing against treating antitrust violations as strict-liability crimes.

6. ***Level of Mens Rea.*** Having determined that intent was a necessary element of a criminal antitrust violation, the Court in *Gypsum* next examined what level of *mens rea* would be appropriate:

> * * * [T]he language of the Act provides minimal assistance in determining what standard of intent is appropriate, and the sparse legislative history of the criminal provisions is similarly unhelpful. We must therefore turn to more general sources and traditional understandings of the nature of the element of intent in the criminal law. * * *
>
> The ALI Model Penal Code is one source of guidance upon which the Court has relied to illuminate questions of this type. Recognizing that "mens rea is not a unitary concept," the Code enumerates four possible levels of intent—purpose, knowledge, recklessness, and negligence. In dealing with the kinds of business decisions upon which the antitrust laws focus, the concepts of recklessness and negligence have no place. Our question instead is whether a criminal violation of the antitrust laws requires, in addition to proof of anticompetitive effects, a demonstration that the disputed conduct

> was undertaken with the "conscious object" of producing such effects, or whether it is sufficient that the conduct is shown to have been undertaken with knowledge that the proscribed effects would most likely follow. While the difference between these formulations is a narrow one, we conclude that action undertaken with knowledge of its probable consequences and having the requisite anticompetitive effects can be a sufficient predicate for a finding of criminal liability under the antitrust laws.
>
> Several considerations fortify this conclusion. The element of intent in the criminal law has traditionally been viewed as a bifurcated concept embracing either the specific requirement of purpose or the more general one of knowledge or awareness. * * * Generally this limited distinction between knowledge and purpose has not been considered important since "there is good reason for imposing liability whether the defendant desired or merely knew of the practical certainty of the results." In either circumstance, the defendants are consciously behaving in a way the law prohibits, and such conduct is a fitting object of criminal punishment.
>
> Nothing in our analysis of the Sherman Act persuades us that this general understanding of intent should not be applied to criminal antitrust violations such as charged here. The business behavior which is likely to give rise to criminal antitrust charges is conscious behavior normally undertaken only after a full consideration of the desired results and a weighing of the costs, benefits, and risks. A requirement of proof not only of this knowledge of likely effects, but also of a conscious desire to bring them to fruition or to violate the law would seem, particularly in such a context, both unnecessarily cumulative and unduly burdensome. Where carefully planned and calculated conduct is being scrutinized in the context of a criminal prosecution, the perpetrator's knowledge of the anticipated consequences is a sufficient predicate for a finding of criminal intent.

During the same Term in which *Ratzlaf* was decided, the Court also struggled with the required *mens rea* in two other cases. **Posters 'N' Things Ltd. v. United States**, 511 U.S. 513 (1994), involved a prosecution under a provision of the Mail Order Drug Paraphernalia Control Act, now codified at 21 U.S.C. § 863. "Section 863(a) makes it unlawful for any person '(1) to sell or offer for sale drug paraphernalia; (2) to use the mails or any other facility of interstate commerce to transport drug paraphernalia; or (3) to import or export drug paraphernalia.'" It identifies two categories of drug paraphernalia: items "primarily intended . . . for use" with controlled substances and items "designed for use" with such substances. Justice Blackmun's opinion for the Court concluded that Congress intended to establish "objective standards" for determining what constitutes drug paraphernalia. An item falls within that classification if it is "designed specially" for use with controlled substances (having "no other use besides contrived ones—such as the use of a bong as a flower vase"). Whether an item falls within that classification under the "primarily intended" category requires reference to still other objective factors, also specified in the statutes (e.g., advertising, instructions accompanying the items sold, expert testimony concerning common use, existence and scope of legitimate uses in the community). Thus, whether or not an item was drug paraphernalia did not depend upon whether the seller intended that it be used with drugs.

The Court concluded, however, that the statute did have a *mens rea* requirement as to the seller. Justice Blackmun reasoned:

> As in * * * *United States Gypsum*, we conclude that a defendant must act knowingly in order to be liable under § 857. Requiring that a seller of drug paraphernalia act with the 'purpose' that the items be used with illegal drugs would be inappropriate. The purpose of a seller of drug paraphernalia is to sell his product; the seller is indifferent as to whether that product ultimately is used in connection with illegal drugs, or otherwise. If § 857 required a purpose that the items be used with illegal drugs, individuals could avoid liability for selling bongs and cocaine freebase kits simply by establishing that they lacked the 'conscious object' that the items be used with illegal drugs.
>
> Further, we do not think that the knowledge standard in this context requires knowledge on the defendant's part that a particular customer actually will use an item of drug paraphernalia with illegal drugs. It is sufficient that the defendant be aware that customers in general are likely to use the merchandise with drugs. Therefore, the Government must establish that the defendant knew that the items at issue are likely to be used with illegal drugs. Cf. United States Gypsum (knowledge of "probable consequences" sufficient for conviction). * * *
>
> Finally, although the Government must establish that the defendant knew that the items at issue are likely to be used with illegal drugs, it need not prove specific knowledge that the items are "drug paraphernalia" within the meaning of the statute. * * *

Staples v. United States, 511 U.S. 600 (1994), was decided on the same day as *Posters 'N' Things*. Staples was charged with possessing an unregistered machinegun in violation of § 5861(d) after officers searching his home seized a semiautomatic rifle, i.e., a weapon that normally fires only one shot with each trigger pull, but apparently had been modified for fully automatic firing. The National Firearms Act criminalizes possession of an unregistered "firearm," 26 U.S.C.A. § 5861(d), which includes a "machinegun," defined as a weapon that automatically fires more than one shot with a single pull of the trigger. At trial, Staples testified that the rifle had never fired automatically while he possessed it and that he had been ignorant of any automatic firing capability. He was convicted after the district court rejected his proposed jury instruction under which, to establish a § 5861(d) violation, the Government would have been required to prove beyond a reasonable doubt that Staples knew that the gun would fire automatically. The court of appeals affirmed, concluding that the prosecution need not prove a defendant's knowledge of a weapon's physical properties to obtain a conviction under § 5861(d).

In an opinion by Justice Thomas, the Supreme Court majority reversed, holding that to obtain a § 5861(d) conviction, the government should have been required to prove beyond a reasonable doubt that Staples knew his rifle had the characteristics that brought it within the statutory definition of a machinegun. This was not a "public welfare" or "regulatory" offense.[a] In cases involving public welfare offenses, the Court inferred from silence a congressional intent to dispense with conventional *mens rea* requirements in statutes that regulate potentially harmful or injurious items. Guns, however, do not fall within the category of dangerous devices as developed in public welfare offense cases. The Court reasoned that had Congress intended to make outlaws of such citizens, it would have spoken more clearly to that effect. Moreover, the potentially harsh penalty attached to violation of § 5861(d)—up to 10 years' imprisonment —confirmed this reading of the law.

Justice Stevens, joined by Justice Blackmun, dissented. They argued that, "[t]he Court has substituted its views of sound policy for the judgment Congress made." The dissent stated that "the text of the statute does provide 'explicit guidance in this case.'" "An examination of § 5861(d) in light of our precedent dictates that the crime of possession of an unregistered machinegun is in a category of offenses described as 'public welfare' crimes." The dissent asserted that "[t]he history and interpretation of the National Firearms Act supports the conclusion that Congress did not intend to require knowledge of all the facts that constitute the offense of possession of an unregistered weapon."

In **Bryan v. United States**, 524 U.S. 184 (1998), the Supreme Court held the willfully element for sale of a firearm without a license in violation of § 924(a)(1)(D) did not carve out an exception to the traditional rule that "ignorance of the law is no excuse." The majority stated that "knowledge that the conduct is unlawful" was sufficient without also requiring proof the defendant knew about the actual federal licensing requirement for dealing in firearms. In distinguishing *Ratzlaf* the Court stated:

> Both the tax cases and *Ratzlaf* involved highly technical statutes that presented the danger of ensnaring individuals engaged in apparently innocent conduct. As a result, we held that these statutes "carv[e] out an exception to the traditional rule" that ignorance of the law is no excuse and require that the defendant have knowledge of the law. The danger of convicting individuals

[a] See Chapter 7 for a discussion of regulatory offenses.

> engaged in apparently innocent activity that motivated our decisions in the tax cases and *Ratzlaf* is not present here because the jury found that this petitioner knew that his conduct was unlawful.

See also United States v. Georgopoulos, 149 F.3d 169 (2nd Cir. 1998) (willfulness element of 29 U.S.C. § 186, prohibiting union officials from accepting payments from employers, "requires only a finding of general intent."); United States v. Danielczyk, 917 F. Supp.2d 573 (E.D. Va. 2013)(intent for a violation of the campaign finance law is controlled by *Bryan*).

7. ***Willful Blindness.*** White collar cases can include claims that the accused, such as a corporate executive, did not know of the criminal activities occurring in the entity. In these circumstances, the government may argue that the defendant was willfully blind. In a civil patent infringement case, **Global Tech Appliances, Inc. v. SEB**, 131 S.Ct. 2060 (2011), the Court examined the concept of willful blindness using criminal law finding that mere recklessness or negligence will not suffice. The Court stated:

> While the Courts of Appeals articulate the doctrine of willful blindness in slightly different ways, all appear to agree on two basic requirements: (1) the defendant must subjectively believe that there is a high probability that a fact exists and (2) the defendant must take deliberate actions to avoid learning of that fact. * * * We think these requirements give willful blindness an appropriately limited scope that surpasses recklessness and negligence. Under this formulation, a willfully blind defendant is one who takes deliberate actions to avoid confirming a high probability of wrongdoing and who can almost be said to have actually known the critical facts. See G. Williams, Criminal Law § 57, p. 159 (2d ed. 1961) ("A court can properly find wilful blindness only where it can almost be said that the defendant actually knew"). By contrast, a reckless defendant is one who merely knows of a substantial and unjustified risk of such wrongdoing, see ALI, Model Penal Code § 2.02(2)(c) (1985), and a negligent defendant is one who should have known of a similar risk but, in fact, did not, see § 2.02(2)(d).
>
> The test applied by the Federal Circuit in this case departs from the proper willful blindness standard in two important respects. First, it permits a finding of knowledge when there is merely a "known risk" that the induced acts are infringing. Second, in demanding only "deliberate indifference" to that risk, the Federal Circuit's test does not require active efforts by an inducer to avoid knowing about the infringing nature of the activities.

B. AMBIGUITY

DOWLING v. UNITED STATES
473 U.S. 207 (1985)

Justice BLACKMUN delivered the opinion of the Court.

The National Stolen Property Act provides for the imposition of criminal penalties upon any person who "transports in interstate or foreign commerce any goods, wares, merchandise, securities or money, of the value of $5,000 or more, knowing the same to have been stolen, converted or taken by fraud." 18 U.S.C. § 2314. In this case, we must determine whether the statute reaches the interstate transportation of "bootleg" phonorecords, "stolen, converted or taken by fraud" only in the sense that they were manufactured and distributed without the consent of the copyright owners of the musical compositions performed on the records.

I

After a bench trial in the United States District Court for the Central District of California conducted largely on the basis of a stipulated record, petitioner Paul Edmond Dowling was convicted of one count of conspiracy to transport stolen property in interstate commerce, in violation of 18 U.S.C. § 371; eight counts of interstate transportation of stolen property, in violation of 18 U.S.C. § 2314; nine counts of copyright infringement, in violation of 17 U.S.C. § 506(a); and three counts of mail fraud, in violation of 18 U.S.C. § 1341. The offenses stemmed from an extensive bootleg record operation involving the manufacture and distribution by mail of recordings of vocal performances by Elvis Presley.[2] The evidence demonstrated that sometime around 1976, Dowling, to that time an avid collector of Presley recordings, began in conjunction with codefendant William Samuel Theaker to manufacture phonorecords of unreleased Presley recordings. They used material from a variety of sources, including studio outtakes, acetates, soundtracks from Presley motion pictures, and tapes of Presley concerts and television appearances. Until early 1980, Dowling and Theaker had the

---

[2] A "bootleg" phonorecord is one which contains an unauthorized copy of a commercially unreleased performance. As in this case, the bootleg material may come from various sources. For example, fans may record concert performances, motion picture soundtracks, or television appearances. Outsiders may obtain copies of "outtakes," those portions of the tapes recorded in the studio but not included in the "master," that is, the final edited version slated for release after transcription to phonorecords or commercial tapes. Or bootleggers may gain possession of an "acetate," which is a phonorecord cut with a stylus rather than stamped, capable of being played only a few times before wearing out, and utilized to assess how a performance will likely sound on a phonorecord. Though the terms frequently are used interchangeably, a "bootleg" record is not the same as a "pirated" one, the latter being an unauthorized copy of a performance already commercially released.

records manufactured at a record-pressing company in Burbank, Cal. When that company later refused to take their orders, they sought out other record-pressing companies in Los Angeles and, through codefendant Richard Minor, in Miami, Fla. The bootleg entrepreneurs never obtained authorization from or paid royalties to the owners of the copyrights in the musical compositions. * * *

The eight § 2314 counts on which Dowling was convicted arose out of six shipments of bootleg phonorecords from Los Angeles to Baltimore and two shipments from Los Angeles to Miami. The evidence established that each shipment included thousands of albums, that each album contained performances of copyrighted musical compositions for the use of which no licenses had been obtained nor royalties paid, and that the value of each shipment attributable to copyrighted material exceeded the statutory minimum. * * *

We granted certiorari to resolve an apparent conflict among the Circuits concerning the application of the statute [§ 2314] to interstate shipments of bootleg and pirated sound recordings and motion pictures whose unauthorized distribution infringed valid copyrights.

II

Federal crimes, of course, "are solely creatures of statute." Liparota v. United States, 471 U.S. 419, 424 (1985), citing United States v. Hudson, 7 Cranch 32, 3 L.Ed. 259 (1812). Accordingly, when assessing the reach of a federal criminal statute, we must pay close heed to language, legislative history, and purpose in order strictly to determine the scope of the conduct the enactment forbids. Due respect for the prerogatives of Congress in defining federal crimes prompts restraint in this area, where we typically find a "narrow interpretation" appropriate. Chief Justice Marshall early observed:

> "The rule that penal laws are to be construed strictly, is perhaps not much less old than construction itself. It is founded on the tenderness of the law for the rights of individuals; and on the plain principle that the power of punishment is vested in the legislative, not in the judicial department. It is the legislature, not the Court, which is to define a crime, and ordain its punishment." United States v. Wiltberger, 5 Wheat. 76, 95, 5 L.Ed. 37 (1820).

Thus, the Court has stressed repeatedly that "when choice has to be made between two readings of what conduct Congress has made a crime, it is appropriate, before we choose the harsher alternative, to require that Congress should have spoken in language that is clear and definite." Williams v. United States, 458 U.S., at 290, quoting United States v. Bass, 404 U.S. 336, 347 (1971), which in turn quotes United States v. Universal C.I.T. Credit Corp., 344 U.S. 218, 221-222 (1952). * * *

Applying that prudent rule of construction here, we examine at the outset the statutory language. Section 2314 requires, first, that the defendant have transported "goods, wares, [or] merchandise" in interstate or foreign commerce; second, that those goods have a value of "$5,000 or more"; and, third, that the defendant "kno[w] the same to have been stolen, converted or taken by fraud." Dowling does not contest that he caused the shipment of goods in interstate commerce, or that the shipments had sufficient value to meet the monetary requirement. He argues, instead, that the goods shipped were not "stolen, converted or taken by fraud." In response, the Government does not suggest that Dowling wrongfully came by the phonorecords actually shipped or the physical materials from which they were made; nor does it contend that the objects that Dowling caused to be shipped, the bootleg phonorecords, were "the same" as the copyrights in the musical compositions that he infringed by unauthorized distribution of Presley performances of those compositions. The Government argues, however, that the shipments come within the reach of § 2314 because the phonorecords physically embodied performances of musical compositions that Dowling had no legal right to distribute. According to the Government, the unauthorized use of the musical compositions rendered the phonorecords "stolen, converted or taken by fraud" within the meaning of the statute.[7] We must determine, therefore, whether phonorecords that include the performance of copyrighted musical compositions for the use of which no authorization has been sought nor royalties paid are consequently "stolen, converted or taken by fraud" for purposes of § 2314. We conclude that they are not.

The courts interpreting § 2314 have never required, of course, that the items stolen and transported remain in entirely unaltered form. See, e.g., United States v. Moore, 571 F.2d 154, 158 (3d Cir. 1978) (counterfeit printed Ticketron tickets "the same" as stolen blanks from which they were printed). Nor does it matter that the item owes a major portion of its value to an intangible component. See, e.g., United States v. Seagraves, 265 F.2d 876 (3d Cir. 1959) (geophysical maps identifying possible oil deposits); United States v. Greenwald, 479 F.2d 320 (6th Cir. 1973) (documents bearing secret chemical formulae). But these cases and others prosecuted under § 2314

---

[7] The Government argues in the alternative that even if the unauthorized use of copyrighted musical compositions does not alone render the phonorecords contained in these shipments "stolen, converted or taken by fraud," the record contains evidence amply establishing that the bootleggers obtained the source material through illicit means. The Government points to testimony, for example, that the custodians of the tapes containing the outtakes which found their way onto Dowling's records neither authorized their release nor permitted access to them by unauthorized persons. * * * [W]e decline to consider this alternative basis for upholding Dowling's convictions. The § 2314 counts in the indictment were founded exclusively on the allegations that the shipped phonorecords, which contained "Elvis Presley performances of copyrighted musical compositions," were "stolen, converted and taken by fraud, in that they were manufactured without the consent of the copyright proprietors." * * *

have always involved physical "goods, wares, [or] merchandise" that have themselves been "stolen, converted or taken by fraud." This basic element comports with the common-sense meaning of the statutory language: by requiring that the "goods, wares, [or] merchandise" be "the same" as those "stolen, converted or taken by fraud," the provision seems clearly to contemplate a physical identity between the items unlawfully obtained and those eventually transported, and hence some prior physical taking of the subject goods.

In contrast, the Government's theory here would make theft, conversion, or fraud equivalent to wrongful appropriation of statutorily protected rights in copyright. The copyright owner, however, holds no ordinary chattel. A copyright, like other intellectual property, comprises a series of carefully defined and carefully delimited interests to which the law affords correspondingly exact protections. * * * [T]he property rights of a copyright holder have a character distinct from the possessory interest of the owner of simple "goods, wares, [or] merchandise," for the copyright holder's dominion is subjected to precisely defined limits.

It follows that interference with copyright does not easily equate with theft, conversion, or fraud. The Copyright Act even employs a separate term of art to define one who misappropriates a copyright: " 'Anyone who violates any of the exclusive rights of the copyright owner,' that is, anyone who trespasses into his exclusive domain by using or authorizing the use of the copyrighted work in one of the five ways set forth in the statute, 'is an infringer of the copyright.' [17 U.S.C.] § 501(a)." There is no dispute in this case that Dowling's unauthorized inclusion on his bootleg albums of performances of copyrighted compositions constituted infringement of those copyrights. It is less clear, however, that the taking that occurs when an infringer arrogates the use of another's protected work comfortably fits the terms associated with physical removal employed by § 2314. * * * While one may colloquially like infringement with some general notion of wrongful appropriation, infringement plainly implicates a more complex set of property interests than does run-of-the-mill theft, conversion, or fraud. As a result, it fits but awkwardly with the language Congress chose—"stolen, converted or taken by fraud"—to describe the sorts of goods whose interstate shipment § 2314 makes criminal. "And, when interpreting a criminal statute that does not explicitly reach the conduct in question, we are reluctant to base an expansive reading on inferences drawn from subjective and variable 'understandings.' " Williams v. United States, 458 U.S., at 286. * * *

In light of the ill-fitting language, we turn to consider whether the history and purpose of § 2314 evince a plain congressional intention to reach interstate shipments of goods infringing copyrights. Our examination of the background of the provision makes more acute our reluctance to read § 2314 to encompass merchandise whose contraband character derives from copyright infringement.

Congress enacted § 2314 as an extension of the National Motor Vehicle Theft Act, currently codified at 18 U.S.C. § 2312. Passed in 1919, the earlier Act was an attempt to supplement the efforts of the States to combat automobile thefts. Particularly in areas close to state lines, state law enforcement authorities were seriously hampered by car thieves' ability to transport stolen vehicles beyond the jurisdiction in which the theft occurred. Legislating pursuant to its commerce power, Congress made unlawful the interstate transportation of stolen vehicles, thereby filling in the enforcement gap by "strik[ing] down State lines which serve as barriers to protect [these interstate criminals] from justice." 58 Cong.Rec. 5476 (1919) (statement of Rep. Newton).

Congress acted to fill an identical enforcement gap when in 1934 it "extend [ed] the provisions of the National Motor Vehicle Theft Act to other stolen property" by means of the National Stolen Property Act. Again, Congress acted under its commerce power to assist the States' efforts to foil the "roving criminal," whose movement across state lines stymied local law enforcement officials. As with its progenitor, Congress responded in the National Stolen Property Act to "the need for federal action" in an area that normally would have been left to state law.

No such need for supplemental federal action has ever existed, however, with respect to copyright infringement, for the obvious reason that Congress always has had the bestowed authority to legislate directly in this area. Article I, § 8, cl. 8, of the Constitution provides that Congress shall have the power "[t]o promote the Progress of Science and useful Arts, by securing for limited Times to Authors and Inventors the exclusive Right to their respective Writings and Discoveries." By virtue of the explicit constitutional grant, Congress has the unquestioned authority to penalize directly the distribution of goods that infringe copyright, whether or not those goods affect interstate commerce. Given that power, it is implausible to suppose that Congress intended to combat the problem of copyright infringement by the circuitous route hypothesized by the Government. * * * In sum, the premise of § 2314—the need to fill with federal action an enforcement chasm created by limited state jurisdiction—simply does not apply to the conduct the Government seeks to reach here. * * *

The history of copyright infringement provisions affords additional reason to hesitate before extending § 2314 to cover the interstate shipments in this case. Not only has Congress chiefly relied on an array of civil remedies to provide copyright holders protection against infringement, see 17 U.S.C. §§ 502-505, but in exercising its power to render criminal certain forms of copyright infringement, it has acted with exceeding caution. * * *

* * * [T]he history of the criminal infringement provisions of the Copyright Act reveals a good deal of care on Congress' part before subjecting copyright infringement to serious criminal penalties. First, Congress hesitated long before imposing felony sanctions on copyright infringers.

Second, when it did so, it carefully chose those areas of infringement that required severe response—specifically, sound recordings and motion pictures—and studiously graded penalties even in those areas of heightened concern. This step-by-step, carefully considered approach is consistent with Congress' traditional sensitivity to the special concerns implicated by the copyright laws.

In stark contrast, the Government's theory of this case presupposes a congressional decision to bring the felony provisions of § 2314, which make available the comparatively light fine of not more than $10,000 but the relatively harsh term of imprisonment of up to 10 years, to bear on the distribution of a sufficient quantity of any infringing goods simply because of the presence here of a factor—interstate transportation—not otherwise though relevant to copyright law. The Government thereby presumes congressional adoption of an indirect but blunderbuss solution to a problem treated with precision when considered directly. To the contrary, the discrepancy between the two approaches convinces us that Congress had no intention to reach copyright infringement when it enacted § 2314. * * *

The broad consequences of the Government's theory, both in the field of copyright and in kindred fields of intellectual property law, provide a final and dispositive factor against reading § 2314 in the manner suggested. ***

* * * [T]he field of copyright does not cabin the Government's theory, which would as easily encompass the law of patents and other forms of intellectual property. * * * [I]ts view of the statute would readily permit its application to interstate shipments of patent-infringing goods. Despite its undoubted power to do so, however, Congress has not provided criminal penalties for distribution of goods infringing valid patents. Thus, the rationale supporting application of the statute under the circumstances of this case would equally justify its use in wide expanses of the law which Congress has evidenced no intention to enter by way of criminal sanction. This factor militates strongly against the reading proffered by the Government. Cf. Williams v. United States, 458 U.S., at 287.

III

No more than other legislation do criminal statutes take on straitjackets upon enactment. In sanctioning the use of § 2314 in the manner urged by the Government here, the Courts of Appeals understandably have sought to utilize an existing and readily available tool to combat the increasingly serious problem of bootlegging, piracy, and copyright infringement. Nevertheless, the deliberation with which Congress over the last decade has addressed the problem of copyright infringement for profit, as well as the precision with which it has chosen to apply criminal penalties in this area, demonstrates anew the wisdom of leaving it to the legislature to define crime and prescribe penalties.[21] Here, the language of § 2314 does not "plainly and unmistakably" cover petitioner Dowling's conduct, United States v. Lacher, 134 U.S. 624, 628 (1890); the purpose of the provision to fill gaps in state law enforcement does not couch the problem under attack; and the rationale employed to apply the statute to petitioner's conduct would support its extension to significant bodies of law that Congress gave no indication it intended to touch. In sum, Congress has not spoken with the requisite clarity. Invoking the "time-honored interpretive guideline" that "ambiguity concerning the ambit of criminal statutes should be resolved in favor of lenity,' " Liparota v. United States, 471 U.S., at 427, quoting Rewis v. United States, 401 U.S. 808, 812 (1971), we reverse the judgment of the Court of Appeals.

Justice POWELL, with whom The Chief Justice and Justice WHITE join, dissenting.

The Court holds today that 18 U.S.C. § 2314 does not apply to this case because the rights of a copyright holder are "different" from the rights of owners of other kinds of property. The Court does not explain, however, how the differences it identifies are relevant either under the language of § 2314 or in terms of the purposes of the statute. Because I believe that the language of § 2314 fairly covers the interstate transportation of goods containing unauthorized use of copyrighted material, I dissent.

Section 2314 provides for criminal penalties against any person who "transports in interstate or foreign commerce any goods, wares, merchandise, securities or money, of the value of $5,000 or more, knowing the same to have been stolen, converted or taken by fraud." There is no dispute that the items Dowling transported in interstate commerce—bootleg Elvis Presley records—are goods, wares, or merchandise. Nor is there a dispute that the records contained copyrighted Elvis Presley performances that Dowling had no right to reproduce and distribute. The only issue here is whether the unauthorized use of a copyright may be "equate[d] with theft, conversion, or fraud" for purposes of § 2314. Virtually every court that has considered the

---

[21] Indeed, in opposing the petition for a writ of certiorari in this case, the Government acknowledged that it no longer needs § 2314 to prosecute and punish serious copyright infringement. Adverting to the most recent congressional copyright action, it advised the Court: "[A]pplication of Section 2314 . . . to the sort of conduct involved in this case is of considerably diminished significance since passage, subsequent to the offenses involved in this case, of the Piracy and Counterfeiting Amendments Act of 1982, (17 U.S.C. 506(a) and 18 U.S.C. 2318, 2319). The new statute provides for felony treatment for most serious cases of copyright infringement involving sound recordings and audiovisual materials and trafficking in counterfeit labels, while prior law provided only for misdemeanor treatment for first offenses under the copyright statutes. * * * These observations suggest the conclusion we have reached—that § 2314 was not in the first place the proper means by which to counter the spread of copyright infringement in sound recordings and motion pictures.

question has concluded that § 2314 is broad enough to cover activities such as Dowling's. * * *

The Court focuses on the fact that "[t]he copyright owner . . . holds no ordinary chattel." The Court quite correctly notes that a copyright is "comprise[d] . . . of carefully defined and carefully delimited interests," and that the copyright owner does not enjoy " 'complete control over all possible uses of his work,' ". But among the rights a copyright owner enjoys is the right to publish, copy, and distribute the copyrighted work. Indeed, these rights define virtually the entire scope of an owner's rights in intangible property such as a copyright. Interference with these rights may be "different" from the physical removal of tangible objects, but it is not clear why this difference matters under the terms of § 2314. The statute makes no distinction between tangible and intangible property. The basic goal of the National Stolen Property Act, thwarting the interstate transportation of misappropriated goods, is not served by the judicial imposition of this distinction. Although the rights of copyright owners in their property may be more limited than those of owners of other kinds of property, they are surely "just as deserving of protection . . . ."

The Court concedes that § 2314 has never been interpreted to require that the goods, wares, or merchandise stolen and transported in violation of the statute remain in unaltered form. It likewise recognizes that the statute is applicable even when the misappropriated item "owes a major portion of its value to an intangible component." The difficulty the Court finds with the application of § 2314 here is in finding a theft, conversion, or fraudulent taking, in light of the intangible nature of a copyright. But this difficulty, it seems to me, has more to do with its views on the relative evil of copyright infringement versus other kinds of thievery, than it does with interpretation of the statutory language. * * *

NOTES AND QUESTIONS

1. ***Source of Ambiguity.*** To what extent does the Court employ the methodology used in *Ratzlaf* to interpret this statute? Ambiguity in statutes can in part be attributed to the legislators having to write laws in substantive areas that are constantly developing. In Fischer v. United States, 529 U.S. 667 (2000), the Supreme Court provided an interpretation of the word "benefits" and found health care providers, like hospitals, that received payments for services provided as part of the Medicare program also received "benefits" even though the funds were intended largely as reimbursement for services provided.

2. ***Trade Secrets Under the NSPA.*** The National Stolen Property Act (NSPA) and the Economic Espionage Act (EEA), 18 U.S.C. § 1831 et. seq. are common statutes used to prosecute the theft of trade secrets. In **United States v. Aleynikov**, 676 F.3d 71 (2d Cir. 2012), the Second Circuit overturned the convictions under the NSPA and Economic Espionage Act

(EEA) of a computer programmer employed at Goldman, Sachs & Co., who developed computer source code for the company's proprietary high-frequency trading ("HFT") system. "High frequency trading is a competitive business that depends in large part on the speed with which information can be processed to seize fleeting market opportunities." The defendant downloaded the code that he planned to use at a new job. In reversing the NSPA count, the court stated:

> By uploading Goldman's proprietary source code to a computer server in Germany, Aleynikov stole purely intangible property embodied in a purely intangible format. There was no allegation that he physically seized anything tangible from Goldman, such as a compact disc or thumb drive containing source code, so we need not decide whether that would suffice as a physical theft. Aleynikov later transported portions of the source code to Chicago, on his laptop and flash drive. However, there is no violation of the statute unless the good is transported with knowledge that "the same" has been stolen; the statute therefore presupposes that the thing stolen was a good or ware, etc., *at the time of the theft.* The wording "contemplate[s] a physical identity between the items lawfully obtained and those eventually transported." *Dowling.* The later storage of intangible property on a tangible medium does not transform the intangible property into a stolen good.

The government took a different approach in a case involving computer code important to operating a HFT system in **United States v. Agrawal**, 726 F.3d 235 (2d Cir. 2013). In this case, the defendant printed the code onto thousands of sheets of paper, which he then physically removed from his employer's office in New York, the French bank Société Générale ("SocGen"), to his New Jersey home, where he could use it to replicate the trading systems for a competitor. The Second Circuit affirmed his conviction stating: "while *Dowling*, *Aleynikov*, and *Bottone* instruct that the NSPA's reference to 'goods, wares [or] merchandise,' does not permit a defendant to be prosecuted under that statute for stealing intangible property in a purely intangible form, no such error is present in this case where the defendant stole complex computer code in the tangible form of thousands of sheets of paper."

3. ***Economic Espionage Act.*** Congress passed the Economic Espionage Act (EEA) in 1996 to specifically deal with the theft of trade secrets. In **United States v. Hsu**, 155 F.3d 189, 194-97 (3rd Cir. 1998), the court summarized parts of the Act stating:

> The EEA consists of nine sections which protect proprietary information from misappropriation. * * * The EEA criminalizes two principal categories of corporate espionage, including "economic espionage" as defined by 18 U.S.C. § 1831, and the "theft of trade secrets" as defined by § 1832. The former provision punishes those who knowingly misappropriate, or attempt or conspire to

misappropriate, trade secrets with the intent or knowledge that their offense will benefit a foreign government, foreign instrumentality, or foreign agent. The legislative history indicates that § 1831 is designed to apply only when there is "evidence of foreign government sponsored or coordinated intelligence activity." By contrast, § 1832, the section under which the defendants are charged, is a general criminal trade secrets provision. It applies to anyone who knowingly engages in the theft of trade secrets, or an attempt or conspiracy to do so, "with intent to convert a trade secret, that is related to or included in a product that is produced for or placed in interstate or foreign commerce, to the economic benefit of anyone other than the owner thereof, and intending or knowing that the offense will, injure any owner of that trade secret." Section 1832(a) makes clear that attempt and conspiracy are distinct offenses, and it lists them separately from those acts that constitute completed crimes under the statute.

Section 1832 also contains at least three additional limitations not found in § 1831. First, a defendant charged under § 1832 must intend to convert a trade secret "to the economic benefit of anyone other than the owner thereof," including the defendant himself. This "economic benefit" requirement differs from § 1831, which states merely that the offense "benefit," in any manner, a foreign government, instrumentality, or agent. Therefore, prosecutions under § 1832 uniquely require that the defendant intend to confer an economic benefit on the defendant or another person or entity. Second, § 1832 states that the defendant must intend or know that the offense will injure an owner of the trade secret, a restriction not found in § 1831. The legislative history indicates that this requires "that the actor knew or was aware to a practical certainty that his conduct would cause such a result." Finally, unlike § 1831, § 1832 also requires that the trade secret be "related to or included in a product that is produced for or placed in interstate or foreign commerce."

* * * The EEA defines a "trade secret" to expressly extend protection to the misappropriation of intangible information for the first time under federal law. 18 U.S.C. § 1839(3) provides that a "trade secret" means:

all forms and types of financial, business, scientific, technical, economic, or engineering information, including patterns, plans, compilations, program devices, formulas, designs, prototypes, methods, techniques, processes, procedures, programs, or codes, whether tangible or intangible, and whether or how stored, compiled, or memorialized physically, electronically, graphically, photographically, or in writing if--

(A) the owner thereof has taken reasonable measures to keep such information secret; and

(B) the information derives independent economic value, actual or potential, from not being generally known to, and not being readily ascertainable through proper means by, the public.

See also United States v. Martin, 228 F.3d 1 (1st Cir. 2000) (finding sufficient evidence to sustain conviction for conspiracy to steal trade secrets under the Economic Espionage Act). In *Aleynikov*, supra note 2, the Second Circuit reversed the EEA conviction finding that "[b]ecause the HFT system was not designed to enter or pass in commerce, or to make something that does, Alynikov's theft of source code relating to that system was not an offense under the EEA."

4. ***Supreme Court Interpretation.*** Do some justices on the Supreme Court treat white collar cases differently than cases concerning street crimes? Professor J. Kelly Strader states that "[t]he justices' voting in white collar criminal cases [ ] often appear to be philosophically at odds with their overall criminal justice philosophies, a conclusion" he refers to as the "white collar paradox." J. Kelly Strader, *The Judicial Politics of White Collar Crime*, 50 HASTINGS L.J. 1199 (1999).

C. EXPANDING THE SCOPE OF A STATUTE?

McCORMICK v. UNITED STATES

500 U.S. 257 (1991)

Justice WHITE delivered the opinion of the Court.

This case requires us to consider whether the Court of Appeals properly affirmed the conviction of petitioner, an elected public official, for extorting property under color of official right in violation of the Hobbs Act, 18 U.S.C. § 1951. We also must address the affirmance of petitioner's conviction for filing a false income tax return.

I

Petitioner Robert L. McCormick was a member of the West Virginia House of Delegates in 1984. He represented a district that had long suffered from a shortage of medical doctors. For several years, West Virginia had allowed foreign medical school graduates to practice under temporary permits while studying for the state licensing exams. Under this program, some doctors were allowed to practice under temporary permits for years even though they repeatedly failed the state exams. McCormick was a leading advocate and supporter of this program.

In the early 1980's, following a move in the House of Delegates to end the temporary permit program, several of the temporarily licensed doctors formed an organization to press their interests in Charleston. The organization hired a lobbyist, John Vandergrift, who in 1984 worked for legislation that would extend the expiration date of the temporary permit program. McCormick sponsored the House version of the proposed legislation and a bill was passed extending the program for another year. Shortly thereafter, Vandergrift and McCormick discussed the possibility of introducing legislation during the 1985 session that would grant the doctors a permanent medical license by virtue of their years of experience. McCormick agreed to sponsor such legislation.

During his 1984 reelection campaign, McCormick informed Vandergrift that his campaign was expensive, that he had paid considerable sums out of his own pocket, and that he had not heard anything from the foreign doctors. Vandergrift told McCormick that he would contact the doctors and see what he could do. Vandergrift contacted one of the foreign doctors and later received from the doctors $1,200 in cash. Vandergrift delivered an envelope containing nine $100 bills to McCormick. Later the same day, a second delivery of $2,000 in cash was made to McCormick. During the fall of 1984, McCormick received two more cash payments from the doctors. McCormick did not list any of these payments as campaign contributions[1] nor did he report the money as income on his 1984 federal income tax return. And although the doctors' organization kept detailed books of its expenditures, the cash payments were not listed as campaign contributions. Rather, the entries for the payments were accompanied only by initials or other codes signifying that the money was for McCormick.

In the spring of 1985, McCormick sponsored legislation permitting experienced doctors to be permanently licensed without passing the state licensing exams. McCormick spoke at length in favor of the bill during floor debate and the bill ultimately was enacted into law. Two weeks after the legislation was enacted, McCormick received another cash payment from the foreign doctors.

Following an investigation, a federal grand jury returned an indictment charging McCormick with five counts of violating the Hobbs Act,[2] by

---

[1] West Virginia law prohibits cash contributions in excess of $50 per person. W. Va. Code § 3-8-5d (1990).

[2] The Hobbs Act, 18 U.S.C. § 1951, provides in relevant part as follows:

> "(a) Whoever in any way or degree obstructs, delays, or affects commerce . . . by robbery or extortion . . . in violation of this section shall be fined not more than $10,000 or imprisoned not more than twenty years, or both.
>
> "(b) As used in this section— * * *
>
> "(2) The term 'extortion' means the obtaining of property from

extorting payments under color of official right, and with one count of filing a false income tax return in violation of 26 U.S.C. § 7206(1), by failing to report as income the cash payments he received from the foreign doctors. At the close of a 6-day trial, the jury was instructed that to establish a Hobbs Act violation the Government had to prove that McCormick induced a cash payment and that he did so knowingly and willfully by extortion. * * *

The next day the jury informed the court that it "would like to hear the instructions again with particular emphasis on the definition of extortion under the color of official right and on the law as regards the portion of moneys received that does not have to be reported as income." The court then reread most of the extortion instructions to the jury, but reordered some of the paragraphs and made the following significant addition:

> "Extortion under color of official right means the obtaining of money by a public official when the money obtained was not lawfully due and owing to him or to his office. Of course, extortion does not occur where one who is a public official receives a legitimate gift or a voluntary political contribution even though the political contribution may have been made in cash in violation of local law. Voluntary is that which is freely given without expectation of benefit."

It is also worth noting that with respect to political contributions, the last two paragraphs of the supplemental instructions on the extortion counts were as follows:

> "It would not be illegal, in and of itself, for Mr. McCormick to solicit or accept political contributions from foreign doctors who would benefit from this legislation.
>
> "In order to find Mr. McCormick guilty of extortion, you must be convinced beyond a reasonable doubt that the payment alleged in a given count of the indictment was made by or on behalf of the doctors with the expectation that such payment would influence Mr. McCormick's official conduct, and with knowledge on the part of Mr. McCormick that they were paid to him with that expectation by virtue of the office he held."

The jury convicted McCormick of the first Hobbs Act count (charging him with receiving the initial $900 cash payment) and the income tax violation but could not reach verdicts on the remaining four Hobbs Act counts. The District Court declared a mistrial on those four counts.

---

another, with his consent, induced by wrongful use of actual or threatened force, violence, or fear, or under color of official right."

The Court of Appeals affirmed, observing that nonelected officials may be convicted under the Hobbs Act without proof that they have granted or agreed to grant some benefit or advantage in exchange for money paid to them and that elected officials should be held to the same standard when they receive money other than "legitimate" campaign contributions. * * *

* * * Because of disagreement in the Courts of Appeals regarding the meaning of the phrase "under color of official right" as it is used in the Hobbs Act,[5] we granted certiorari. We reverse and remand for further proceedings.

II

McCormick's challenge to the judgment below affirming his conviction is limited to the Court of Appeals' rejection of his claim that the payments made to him by or on behalf of the doctors were campaign contributions, the receipt of which did not violate the Hobbs Act. Except for a belated claim not properly before us,[6] McCormick does not challenge any rulings of the courts

---

[5] Until the early 1970's, extortion prosecutions under the Hobbs Act rested on allegations that the consent of the transferor of property had been "induced by wrongful use of actual or threatened force, violence, or fear—"; public officials had not been prosecuted under the "color of official right" phrase standing alone. Beginning with the conviction involved in United States v. Kenny, 462 F.2d 1205 (3rd Cir. 1972), however, the federal courts accepted the Government's submission that because of the disjunctive language of § 1951(b)(2), allegations of force, violence or fear were not necessary. Only proof of the obtaining of property under claims of official right was necessary. Furthermore, every Court of Appeals to have construed the phrase held that it did not require a showing that the public official "induced" the payor's consent by some affirmative act such as a demand or solicitation. Although there was some difference in the language of these holdings, the "color of official right" element required no more than proof of the payee's acceptance knowing that the payment was made for the purpose of influencing his official actions. In 1984, however, the Court of Appeals for the Second Circuit, en banc, held that some affirmative act of inducement by the official had to be shown to prove the Government's case. United States v. O'Grady, 742 F.2d 682 (1984). In 1988, the Ninth Circuit, en banc, agreed with the Second Circuit, overruling a prior decision expressing the majority rule. United States v. Aguon, 851 F.2d 1158 (1988). Other courts have been unimpressed with the view expressed in *O'Grady* and *Aguon.*

The conflict on this issue is clear, but this case is not the ocasion to resolve it. * * *

[6] In briefing the merits in this Court, McCormick has argued that the Hobbs Act was never intended to apply to corruption involving local officials and that in any event an official has not acted under color of official right unless he falsely represents that by virtue of his office he has a legal right to the money or property he receives. These arguments were not presented to the courts below. They are not expressly among the questions presented in the petition for certiorari and are only arguably subsumed by the questions presented. Nor in view of the language of the Hobbs Act and the many cases approving the conviction of local officials under the Act can it be said that plain error occurred in the lower courts for failure to recognize that the Act

below with respect to the application of the Hobbs Act to payments made to nonelected officials or to payments made to elected officials that are properly determined not to be campaign contributions. Hence, we do not consider how the "under color of official right" phrase is to be interpreted and applied in those contexts. In two respects, however, we agree with McCormick that the Court of Appeals erred. * * *

First, we are quite sure that the Court of Appeals affirmed the conviction on legal and factual grounds that were never submitted to the jury. Although McCormick challenged the adequacy of the jury instructions to distinguish between campaign contributions and payments that are illegal under the Hobbs Act, the Court of Appeals' opinion did not examine or mention the instructions given by the trial court. The court neither dealt with McCormick's submission that the instructions were too confusing to give adequate guidance to the jury, nor, more specifically, with the argument that although the jury was instructed that voluntary campaign contributions were not vulnerable under the Hobbs Act, the word "voluntary" as used "in several places during the course of these instructions," was defined as "that which is freely given without expectation of benefit." Neither did the Court of Appeals note that the jury was not instructed in accordance with the court's holding that the difference between legitimate and illegitimate campaign contributions was to be determined by the intention of the parties after considering specified factors.[7] Instead, the Court of Appeals, after announcing a rule of law for determining when payments are made under color of official right, went on to find sufficient evidence in the record to support findings that McCormick was extorting money from the doctors for his continued support of the 1985 legislation, and further that the parties never intended any of the payments to be a campaign contribution.

It goes without saying that matters of intent are for the jury to consider. Cheek v. United States [p. 102]. It is also plain that each of the seven factors that the Court of Appeals thought should be considered in determining the parties' intent present an issue of historical fact. Thus even assuming the Court of Appeals was correct on the law, the conviction should not have been

---

was inapplicable to the extortion charges brought against McCormick. * * * [The Court also rejected the false pretenses argument.]

[7] "Some of the circumstances that should be considered in making this determination include, but are not limited to, (1) whether the money was recorded by the payor as a campaign contribution, (2) whether the money was recorded and reported by the official as a campaign contribution, (3) whether the payment was in cash, (4) whether it was delivered to the official personally or to his campaign, (5) whether the official acted in his official capacity at or near the time of the payment for the benefit of the payor or supported legislation that would benefit the payor, (6) whether the official had supported similar legislation before the time of the payment, and (7) whether the official had directly or indirectly solicited the payor individually for the payment."

affirmed on that basis but should have been set aside and a new trial ordered. * * *

We agree with the Court of Appeals that in a case like this it is proper to inquire whether payments made to an elected official are in fact campaign contributions, and we agree that the intention of the parties is a relevant consideration in pursuing this inquiry. But we cannot accept the Court of Appeals' approach to distinguishing between legal and illegal campaign contributions. * * *

* * * Serving constituents and supporting legislation that will benefit the district and individuals and groups therein is the everyday business of a legislator. It is also true that campaigns must be run and financed. Money is constantly being solicited on behalf of candidates, who run on platforms and who claim support on the basis of their views and what they intend to do or have done. Whatever ethical considerations and appearances may indicate, to hold that legislators commit the federal crime of extortion when they act for the benefit of constituents or support legislation furthering the interests of some of their constituents, shortly before or after campaign contributions are solicited and received from those beneficiaries, is an unrealistic assessment of what Congress could have meant by making it a crime to obtain property from another, with his consent, "under color of official right." To hold otherwise would open to prosecution not only conduct that has long been thought to be well within the law but also conduct that in a very real sense is unavoidable so long as election campaigns are financed by private contributions or expenditures, as they have been from the beginning of the Nation. It would require statutory language more explicit than the Hobbs Act contains to justify a contrary conclusion.

This is not to say that it is impossible for an elected official to commit extortion in the course of financing an election campaign. Political contributions are of course vulnerable if induced by the use of force, violence, or fear. The receipt of such contributions is also vulnerable under the Act as having been taken under color of official right, but only if the payments are made in return for an explicit promise or undertaking by the official to perform or not to perform an official act. In such situations the official asserts that his official conduct will be controlled by the terms of the promise or undertaking. This is the receipt of money by an elected official under color of official right within the meaning of the Hobbs Act. * * *

The United States agrees that if the payments to McCormick were campaign contributions, proof of a *quid pro quo* would be essential for an extortion conviction, and quotes the instruction given on this subject in 9 Department of Justice Manual § 9-85A.306: "campaign contributions will not be authorized as the subject of a Hobbs Act prosecution unless they can be proven to have been given in return for the performance of or abstaining from an official act; otherwise any campaign contribution might constitute a violation."

We thus disagree with the Court of Appeals' holding in this case that a quid pro quo is not necessary for conviction under the Hobbs Act when an official receives a campaign contribution.[10] By the same token, we hold, as McCormick urges, that the District Court's instruction to the same effect was error.[11] * * *

Justice SCALIA, concurring.

I agree with the Court's conclusion and, given the assumption on which this case was briefed and argued, with the reasons the Court assigns. If the prohibition of the Hobbs Act, 18 U.S.C. § 1951, against receipt of money "under color of official right" includes receipt of money from a private source for the performance of official duties, that ambiguously described crime assuredly need not, and for the reasons the Court discusses should not, be interpreted to cover campaign contributions with anticipation of favorable future action, as opposed to campaign contributions in exchange for an explicit promise of favorable future action.

I find it unusual and unsettling, however, to make such a distinction without any hint of a justification in the statutory text: § 1951 contains not even a colorable allusion to campaign contributions or *quid pro quos.* I find it doubly unsettling because there is another interpretation of § 1951, contrary to the one that has been the assumption of argument here, that would render the distinction unnecessary. While I do not feel justified in adopting that interpretation without briefing and argument, neither do I feel comfortable giving tacit approval to the assumption that contradicts it. I write, therefore, a few words concerning the text of this statute, and the history that has produced the unexamined assumption underlying our opinion.

[Justice Scalia here discussed the position later taken in the *Evans* dissent, p. 134]

Justice STEVENS, with whom Justice BLACKMUN and Justice O'CONNOR join, dissenting. * * *

As I understand its opinion, the Court would agree that these facts would constitute a violation of the Hobbs Act if the understanding that the money was a personal payment rather than a campaign contribution had been explicit rather than implicit and if the understanding that, in response to the payment, petitioner would endeavor to provide the payers with the

---

[10] As noted previously, McCormick's sole contention in this case is that the payments made to him were campaign contributions. Therefore, we do not decide whether a *quid pro quo* requirement exists in other contexts, such as when an elected official receives gifts, meals, travel expenses, or other items of value.

[11] In so holding, we do not resolve the conflict mentioned * * * with respect to the necessity of proving inducement.

specific benefit they sought had also been explicit rather than implicit. In my opinion there is no statutory requirement that illegal agreements, threats, or promises be in writing, or in any particular form. Subtle extortion is just as wrongful—and probably much more common—than the kind of express understanding that the Court's opinion seems to require.

Nevertheless, to prove a violation of the Hobbs Act, I agree with the Court that it is essential that the payment in question be contingent on a mutual understanding that the motivation for the payment is the payer's desire to avoid a specific threatened harm or to obtain a promised benefit that the defendant has the apparent power to deliver, either through the use of force or the use of public office. In this sense, the crime does require a "*quid pro quo*." * * *

* * * [T]he crime of extortion was complete when petitioner accepted the cash pursuant to an understanding that he would not carry out his earlier threat to withhold official action and instead would go forward with his contingent promise to take favorable action on behalf of the unlicensed physicians. What he did thereafter might have evidentiary significance, but could neither undo a completed crime or complete an uncommitted offense. When petitioner took the money, he was either guilty or not guilty. For that reason, proof of a subsequent *quid pro quo*—his actual support of the legislation—was not necessary for the Government's case. And conversely, evidence that petitioner would have supported the legislation anyway is not a defense to the already completed crime. The thug who extorts protection money cannot defend on the ground that his threat was only a bluff because he would not have smashed the shopkeeper's windows even if the extortion had been unsuccessful. It was in this sense that the District Court correctly advised the jury that the Government did not have to prove the delivery of a postpayment *quid pro quo,* * * *.

* * * Given that the District Court's instructions to the jury largely tracked the instructions requested by petitioner at trial, I can see no legitimate reason for this Court now to find these instructions inadequate. Because I am convinced that the petitioner was fairly tried and convicted by a properly instructed jury, I would affirm the judgment of the Court of Appeals. Of course, an affirmance of the Court of Appeals' judgment would not mean that we necessarily affirm the Court of Appeals' opinion. It is sufficient that an affirmance of McCormick's conviction rest on the legal and factual theories actually presented to the jury, whether or not these theories were the ones relied upon by the Court of Appeals. I respectfully dissent.

EVANS v. UNITED STATES
504 U.S. 255 (1992)

Justice STEVENS delivered the opinion of the Court.

We granted certiorari, to resolve a conflict in the Circuits over the question whether an affirmative act of inducement by a public official, such as a demand, is an element of the offense of extortion "under color of official right" prohibited by the Hobbs Act, 18 U.S.C. § 1951. We agree with the Court of Appeals for the Eleventh Circuit that it is not, and therefore affirm the judgment of the court below.

I

Petitioner was an elected member of the Board of Commissioners of DeKalb County, Georgia. During the period between March 1985 and October 1986, as part of an effort by the Federal Bureau of Investigation (FBI) to investigate allegations of public corruption in the Atlanta area, particularly in the area of rezonings of property, an FBI agent posing as a real estate developer talked on the telephone and met with petitioner on a number of occasions. Virtually all, if not all, of those conversations were initiated by the agent and most were recorded on tape or video. In those conversations, the agent sought petitioner's assistance in an effort to rezone a 25-acre tract of land for high-density residential use. On July 25, 1986, the agent handed petitioner cash totaling $7,000 and a check, payable to petitioner's campaign, for $1,000. Petitioner reported the check, but not the cash, on his state campaign-financing disclosure form; he also did not report the $7,000 on his 1986 federal income tax return. Viewing the evidence in the light most favorable to the Government, as we must in light of the verdict, we assume that the jury found that petitioner accepted the cash knowing that it was intended to ensure that he would vote in favor of the rezoning application and that he would try to persuade his fellow commissioners to do likewise. Thus, although petitioner did not initiate the transaction, his acceptance of the bribe constituted an implicit promise to use his official position to serve the interests of the bribe-giver.

In a two-count indictment, petitioner was charged with extortion in violation of 18 U.S.C. § 1951 and with failure to report income in violation of 26 U.S.C. § 7206(1). He was convicted by a jury on both counts. * * *

In affirming petitioner's conviction, the Court of Appeals noted that the [trial court's] instruction did not require the jury to find that petitioner had demanded or requested the money, or that he had conditioned the performance of any official act upon its receipt. The Court of Appeals held, however, that "passive acceptance of a benefit by a public official *is* sufficient to form the basis of a Hobbs Act violation if the official knows that he is being offered the payment in exchange for a specific requested exercise of his official power. The official need not take any specific action to induce the offering of the benefit." (emphasis in original).

This statement of the law by the Court of Appeals for the Eleventh Circuit is consistent with holdings in eight other Circuits. Two Circuits, however, have held that an affirmative act of inducement by the public official is required to support a conviction of extortion under color of official right. United States v. O'Grady, 742 F.2d 682, 687 (2d Cir. 1984) (en banc) ("Although receipt of benefits by a public official is a necessary element of the crime, there must also be proof that the public official did something, under color of his public office, to cause the giving of benefits"); United States v. Aguon, 851 F.2d 1158, 1166 (9th Cir. 1988) (en banc) ("We find ourselves in accord with the Second Circuit's conclusion that inducement is an element required for conviction under the Hobbs Act"). Because the majority view is consistent with the common-law definition of extortion, which we believe Congress intended to adopt, we endorse that position.

II

It is a familiar "maxim that a statutory term is generally presumed to have its common-law meaning." Taylor v. United States, 495 U.S. 575, 592 (1990). As we have explained, "where Congress borrows terms of art in which are accumulated the legal tradition and meaning of centuries of practice, it presumably knows and adopts the cluster of ideas that were attached to each borrowed word in the body of learning from which it was taken and the meaning its use will convey to the judicial mind unless otherwise instructed. In such case, absence of contrary direction may be taken as satisfaction with widely accepted definitions, not as a departure from them." Morissette v. United States, 342 U.S. 246, 263 (1952).

At common law, extortion was an offense committed by a public official who took "by colour of his office"[4] money that was not due to him for the performance of his official duties.[5] A demand, or request, by the public

---

[4] Blackstone described extortion as "an abuse of public justice, which consists in an officer's unlawfully taking, *by colour of his office,* from any man, any money or thing of value, that is not due to him, or more than is due, or before it is due." 4 W. Blackstone, Commentaries (emphasis added). He used the phrase "by colour of his office," rather than the phrase "under color of official right," which appears in the Hobbs Act. Petitioner does not argue that there is any difference in the phrases. Hawkins' definition of extortion is probably the source for the official right language used in the Hobbs Act. See Lindgren, The Elusive Distinction Between Bribery and Extortion: From the Common Law to the Hobbs Act, 35 UCLA L.Rev. 815, 864 (1988) (hereinafter Lindgren). Hawkins defined extortion as follows:

"[I]t is said, That extortion in a large sense signifies any oppression under colour of right; but that in a strict sense, it signifies the taking of money by any officer, by colour of his office, either where none at all is due, or not so much is due, or where it is not yet due." 1 W. Hawkins, Pleas of the Crown 316 (6th ed. 1787).

[5] See Lindgren 882-889. The dissent says that we assume that "common law extortion encompassed any taking by a public official of something of value that he was not 'due.' " That statement, of course, is incorrect because, as stated in the text

official was not an element of the offense. Extortion by the public official was the rough equivalent of what we would now describe as "taking a bribe." It is clear that petitioner committed that offense. The question is whether the federal statute, insofar as it applies to official extortion, has narrowed the common-law definition.

Congress has unquestionably expanded the common-law definition of extortion to include acts by private individuals pursuant to which property is obtained by means of force, fear, or threats. It did so by implication in the Travel Act, 18 U.S.C. § 1952, and expressly in the Hobbs Act. * * *

* * * Although the present statutory text is much broader than the common-law definition of extortion because it encompasses conduct by a private individual as well as conduct by a public official, the portion of the statute that refers to official misconduct continues to mirror the common-law definition. There is nothing in either the statutory text or the legislative history that could fairly be described as a "contrary direction," from Congress to narrow the scope of the offense.

The legislative history is sparse and unilluminating with respect to the offense of extortion. There is a reference to the fact that the terms "robbery and extortion" had been construed many times by the courts and to the fact that the definitions of those terms were "based on the New York law." In view of the fact that the New York statute applied to a public officer "who asks, or receives, or agrees to receive" unauthorized compensation, N.Y.Penal Code § 557 (1881), the reference to New York law is consistent with an intent to apply the common-law definition. The language of the New York statute quoted above makes clear that extortion could be committed by one who merely received an unauthorized payment. This was the statute that was in force in New York when the Hobbs Act was enacted.

The two courts that have disagreed with the decision to apply the common-law definition have interpreted the word "induced" as requiring a wrongful use of official power that "begins with the public official, not with the gratuitous actions of another." United States v. O'Grady; see United States v. Aguon (" 'inducement' can be in the overt form of a 'demand,' or in a more subtle form such as 'custom' or 'expectation' "). If we had no common-law history to guide our interpretation of the statutory text, that reading would be plausible. For two reasons, however, we are convinced that it is incorrect.

First, we think the word "induced" is a part of the definition of the offense by the private individual, but not the offense by the public official. In the case of the private individual, the victim's consent must be "induced by wrongful use of actual or threatened force, violence or fear." In the case of the public official, however, there is no such requirement. The statute

---

above, the payment must be "for the performance of his official duties."

merely requires of the public official that he obtain "property from another, with his consent, . . . under color of official right." The use of the word "or" before "under color of official right" supports this reading.[15]

Second, even if the statute were parsed so that the word "induced" applied to the public officeholder, we do not believe the word "induced" necessarily indicates that the transaction must be initiated by the recipient of the bribe. Many of the cases applying the majority rule have concluded that the wrongful acceptance of a bribe establishes all the inducement that the statute requires. They conclude that the coercive element is provided by the public office itself. And even the two courts that have adopted an inducement requirement for extortion under color of official right do not require proof that the inducement took the form of a threat or demand.

Petitioner argues that the jury charge with respect to extortion, allowed the jury to convict him on the basis of the "passive acceptance of a contribution."[18] He contends that the instruction did not require the jury to find "an element of duress such as a demand," and it did not properly describe the *quid pro quo* requirement for conviction if the jury found that the payment was a campaign contribution.

We reject petitioner's criticism of the instruction, and conclude that it satisfies the *quid pro quo* requirement of *McCormick,* [p. 119], because the offense is completed at the time when the public official receives a payment in return for his agreement to perform specific official acts; fulfillment of the *quid pro quo* is not an element of the offense. We also reject petitioner's contention that an affirmative step is an element of the offense of extortion "under color of official right" and need be included in the instruction. As we explained above, our construction of the statute is informed by the common-law tradition from which the term of art was drawn and understood. We hold today that the Government need only show that a

---

[15] This meaning would, of course, have been completely clear if Congress had inserted the word "either" before its description of the private offense because the word "or" already precedes the description of the public offense. The definition would then read: "The term 'extortion' means the obtaining of property from another, with his consent, *either* induced by wrongful use of actual or threatened force, violence, or fear, or under color of official right."

[18] Petitioner also makes the point that "[t]he evidence at trial against [petitioner] is more conducive to a charge of bribery than one of extortion." Although the evidence in this case may have supported a charge of bribery, it is not a defense to a charge of extortion under color of official right that the defendant could also have been convicted of bribery. * * * We agree with the Seventh Circuit in United States v. Braasch, 505 F.2d 139, 151, n. 7 (1974), that " 'the modern trend of the federal courts is to hold that bribery and extortion as used in the Hobbs Act are not mutually exclusive.'"

public official has obtained a payment to which he was not entitled, knowing that the payment was made in return for official acts.[20]

Our conclusion is buttressed by the fact that so many other courts that have considered the issue over the last 20 years have interpreted the statute in the same way. Moreover, given the number of appellate court decisions, together with the fact that many of them have involved prosecutions of important officials well known in the political community, it is obvious that Congress is aware of the prevailing view that common-law extortion is proscribed by the Hobbs Act. The silence of the body that is empowered to give us a "contrary direction" if it does not want the common-law rule to survive is consistent with an application of the normal presumption identified in *Taylor* and *Morissette.*

III

An argument not raised by petitioner is now advanced by the dissent. It contends that common-law extortion was limited to wrongful takings under a false pretense of official right. It is perfectly clear, however, that although extortion accomplished by fraud was a well- recognized type of extortion, there were other types as well. As the court explained in Commonwealth v. Wilson, 30 Pa.Super. 26 (1906), an extortion case involving a payment by a would-be brothel owner to a police captain to ensure the opening of her house:

> "The form of extortion most commonly dealt with in the decisions is the corrupt taking by a person in office of a fee for services which should be rendered gratuitously; or when compensation is permissible, of a larger fee than the law justifies, or a fee not yet due; but this is not a complete definition of the offense, by which I mean that it does not include every form of common-law extortion."
> * * *

The dissent's theory notwithstanding, not one of the cases it cites holds that the public official is innocent unless he has deceived the payor by representing that the payment was proper. Indeed, none makes any reference to the state of mind of the payor, and none states that a "false pretense" is an element of the offense. Instead, those cases merely support the proposition that the services for which the fee is paid must be official and that the official must not be entitled to the fee that he collected—both elements of the offense that are clearly satisfied in this case. The complete absence of support for the dissent's thesis presumably explains why it was

---

[20] The dissent states that we have "simply made up," the requirement that the payment must be given in return for official acts. On the contrary, that requirement is derived from the statutory language "under color of official right," which has a well-recognized common-law heritage that distinguished between payments for private services and payments for public services. See, for example, Collier v. State, 55 Ala. 125 (1877), which the dissent describes as a "typical case."

not advanced by petitioner in the District Court or the Court of Appeals, is not recognized by any Court of Appeals, and is not advanced in any scholarly commentary.

The judgment is affirmed. * * *

Justice O'CONNOR, concurring in part and concurring in the judgment.

I join Parts I and II of the Court's opinion, because in my view they correctly answer the question on which the Court granted certiorari—whether or not an act of inducement is an element of the offense of extortion under color of official right. The issue raised by the dissent and discussed in Part III of the Court's opinion is not fairly included in this question, see our Rule 14.1(a), and sound prudential reasons suggest that the Court should not address it. * * *

Justice KENNEDY, concurring in part and concurring in the judgment.

The Court gives a summary of its decision in these words: "We hold today that the Government need only show that a public official has obtained a payment to which he was not entitled, knowing that the payment was made in return for official acts." In my view the dissent is correct to conclude that this language requires a *quid pro quo* as an element of the Government's case in a prosecution under 18 U.S.C. § 1951, and the Court's opinion can be interpreted in a way that is consistent with this rule. Although the Court appears to accept the requirement of a *quid pro quo* as an alternative rationale, in my view this element of the offense is essential to a determination of those acts which are criminal and those which are not in a case in which the official does not pretend that he is entitled by law to the property in question. Here the prosecution did establish a *quid pro quo* that embodied the necessary elements of a statutory violation. I join part III of the Court's opinion and concur in the judgment affirming the conviction. I write this separate opinion to explain my analysis and understanding of the statute.

With regard to the question whether the word "induced" in the statutory definition of extortion applies to the phrase "under color of official right," 18 U.S.C. § 1951(b)(2), I find myself in substantial agreement with the dissent. Scrutiny of the placement of commas will not, in the final analysis, yield a convincing answer, and we are left with two quite plausible interpretations. Under these circumstances, I agree with the dissent that the rule of lenity requires that we avoid the harsher one. We must take as our starting point the assumption that the portion of the statute at issue here defines extortion as "the obtaining of property from another, with his consent, induced . . . under color of official right."

I agree with the Court, on the other hand, that the word "induced" does not "necessarily indicat[e] that the transaction must be *initiated* by the" public official. (emphasis in original). Something beyond the mere acceptance of property from another is required, however, or else the word "induced" would be superfluous. That something, I submit, is the *quid pro quo*. The ability of the official to use or refrain from using authority is the "color of official right" which can be invoked in a corrupt way to induce payment of money or to otherwise obtain property. The inducement generates a quid pro quo, under color of official right, that the statute prohibits. The term "under color of" is used, as I think both the Court and the dissent agree, to sweep within the statute those corrupt exercises of authority that the law forbids but that nevertheless cause damage because the exercise is by a governmental official.

The requirement of a *quid pro quo* means that without pretense of any entitlement to the payment, a public official violates § 1951 if he intends the payor to believe that absent payment the official is likely to abuse his office and his trust to the detriment and injury of the prospective payor or to give the prospective payor less favorable treatment if the *quid pro quo* is not satisfied. The official and the payor need not state the *quid pro quo* in express terms, for otherwise the law's effect could be frustrated by knowing winks and nods. The inducement from the official is criminal if it is express or if it is implied from his words and actions, so long as he intends it to be so and the payor so interprets it.

* * * [I] agree with the Court, that the *quid pro quo* requirement is not simply made up, as the dissent asserts. Instead, this essential element of the offense is derived from the statutory requirement that the official receive payment under color of official right, as well as the inducement requirement. And there are additional principles of construction which justify this interpretation. First is the principle that statutes are to be construed so that they are constitutional. * * *

Moreover, the mechanism which controls and limits the scope of official right extortion is a familiar one: a state of mind requirement. See Morissette v. United States, 342 U.S. 246 (1952) (refusing to impute to Congress the intent to create a strict liability crime despite the absence of any explicit mens rea requirement in the statute). Hence, even if the *quid pro quo* requirement did not have firm roots in the statutory language, it would constitute no abuse of judicial power for us to find it by implication. * * *

The requirement of a *quid pro quo* in a § 1951 prosecution such as the one before us, in which it is alleged that money was given to the public official in the form of a campaign contribution, was established by our decision last term in McCormick v. United States, [p. 119]. Readers of today's opinion should have little difficulty in understanding that the rationale underlying the Court's holding applies not only in campaign contribution cases, but all § 1951 prosecutions. That is as it should be, for, given a corrupt motive, the *quid pro quo,* as I have said, is the essence of the offense.

Because I agree that the jury instruction in this case complied with the quid pro quo requirement, I concur in the judgment of the Court.

Justice THOMAS, with whom THE CHIEF JUSTICE and Justice SCALIA join, dissenting.

* * * The "under color of office" element of extortion, however, had a definite and well-established meaning at common law. "At common law it was essential that the money or property be obtained under color of office, *that is, under the pretense that the officer was entitled thereto by virtue of his office.* The money or thing received must have been claimed or accepted in right of office, and the person paying must have yielded to official authority." 3 R. Anderson, Wharton's Criminal Law and Procedure § 1393, pp. 790-791 (1957) (emphasis added). Thus, although the Court purports to define official extortion under the Hobbs Act by reference to the common law, its definition bears scant resemblance to the common-law crime Congress presumably codified in 1946. * * *

* * * *Regardless* of whether extortion contains an "inducement" requirement, bribery and extortion are different crimes. An official who solicits or takes a bribe does *not* do so "under color of office"; i.e., under any pretense of official entitlement. "The distinction between bribery and extortion seems to be that the former offense consists in offering a present or receiving one, the latter in *demanding* a fee or present *by color of office."* State v. Pritchard, 107 N.C. 921, 929 (1890) (emphasis added). Where extortion is at issue, the public official is the sole wrongdoer; because he acts "under color of office," the law regards the payor as an innocent victim and not an accomplice. With bribery, in contrast, the payor knows the recipient official is not entitled to the payment; he, as well as official, may be punished for the offense. Congress is well aware of the distinction between the crimes; it has always treated them separately. * * * By stretching the bounds of extortion to make it encompass bribery, the Court today blurs the traditional distinction between the crimes. * * *

Perhaps because the common-law crime—as the Court defines it—is so expansive, the Court, at the very end of its opinion, appends a qualification: "We hold today that the Government need only show that a public official has obtained a payment to which he was not entitled, *knowing that the payment was made in return for official acts."* (emphasis added). This *quid pro quo* requirement is simply made up. The Court does not suggest that it has any basis in the common law or the language of the Hobbs Act, and I have found no treatise or dictionary that refers to any such requirement in defining "extortion." * * * Its only conceivable source, in fact, is our opinion last Term in McCormick v. United States, [p. 119]. * * *

Because the common-law history of extortion was neither properly briefed nor argued in *McCormick,* the *quid pro quo* limitation imposed there represented a reasonable first step in the right direction. Now that we squarely consider that history, however, it is apparent that that limitation was in fact overly modest: at common law, McCormick was innocent of extortion not because he failed to offer a *quid pro quo* in return for campaign contributions, but because he did not take the contributions under color of official right. Today's extension of *McCormick's* reasonable (but textually and historically artificial) *quid pro quo* limitation to all cases of official extortion is both unexplained and inexplicable—except insofar as it may serve to rescue the Court's definition of extortion from substantial overbreadth.

* * * [A]ccording to the Court, the statute should read: " 'The term "extortion" means the obtaining of property from another, with his consent, *either* [1] induced by wrongful use of actual or threatened force, violence, or fear, or [2] under color of official right.' " That is, I concede, a *conceivable* construction of the words. But it is—at the very least—forced, for it sets up an unnatural and ungrammatical parallel between the *verb* "induced" and the *preposition* "under."

The more natural construction is that the verb "induced" applies to *both* types of extortion described in the statute. Thus, the unstated "either" belongs *after* "induced": "The term 'extortion' means the obtaining of property from another, with his consent, induced *either* [1] by wrongful use of actual or threatened force, violence, or fear, or [2] under color of official right." This construction comports with correct grammar and standard usage by setting up a parallel between two prepositional phrases, the first beginning with "by"; the second with "under."

Our duty in construing this criminal statute, then, is clear: "The Court has often stated that when there are two rational readings of a criminal statute, one harsher than the other, we are to choose the harsher only when Congress has spoken in clear and definite language." Because the Court's expansive interpretation of the statute is not the only plausible one, the rule of lenity compels adoption of the narrower interpretation. * * * Given the text of the statute and the rule of lenity, I believe that inducement is an element of official extortion under the Hobbs Act.

Perhaps sensing the weakness of its position, the Court suggests an alternative interpretation: even if the statute *does* set forth an "inducement" requirement for official extortion, that requirement is always satisfied, because "the coercive element is provided by the public office itself." I disagree. A particular public official, to be sure, may wield his power in such a way as to coerce unlawful payments, even in the absence of any explicit demand or threat. But it ignores reality to assert that *every* public official, in *every* context, automatically exerts coercive influence on others by virtue of his office. If the Chairman of General Motors meets with a local court clerk, for example, whatever implicit coercive pressures exist will surely not emanate from the clerk. * * *

The Court's construction of the Hobbs Act is repugnant not only to the basic tenets of criminal justice reflected in the rule of lenity, but also to basic tenets of federalism. Over the past 20 years, the Hobbs Act has served as the engine for a stunning expansion of federal criminal jurisdiction into a field traditionally policed by state and local laws—acts of public corruption by state and local officials. See generally Ruff, Federal Prosecution of Local Corruption: A Case Study in the Making of Law Enforcement Policy, 65 Geo.L.J. 1171 (1977). * * * [C]oncerns of federalism require us to give a *narrow* construction to federal legislation in such sensitive areas unless Congress' contrary intent is "unmistakably clear in the language of the statute." Gregory v. Ashcroft, 111 S.Ct. 2395, 2401 (1991). * * * Similarly, in McNally v. United States, [p. 147]—a case closely analogous to this one—we rejected the Government's contention that the federal mail fraud statute, 18 U.S.C. § 1341, protected the citizenry's "intangible right" to good government, and hence could be applied to all instances of state and local corruption. * * *

I have no doubt that today's opinion is motivated by noble aims. Political corruption at any level of government is a serious evil, and, from a policy perspective, perhaps one well suited for federal law enforcement. But federal judges are not free to devise new crimes to meet the occasion. Chief Justice Marshall's warning is as timely today as ever: "It would be dangerous, indeed, to carry the principle that a case which is within the reason or mischief of a statute, is within its provisions, so far as to punish a crime not enumerated in the statute, because it is of equal atrocity, or of kindred character, with those which are enumerated." United States v. Wiltberger, 5 Wheat. 76, 96, 5 L.Ed. 37 (1820). * * *

NOTES AND QUESTIONS

1. ***Interpreting Statutes.*** How has the Court in *McCormick* and *Evans* dealt with the ambiguity in the Hobbs Act statute about the meaning of "under color of official right"? Has the Court, as a result of an inartfully drawn statute, created new doctrine that cannot be found in the statutory language? Is it necessary for courts to use federal statutes as "stopgap devices" [C.J. Burger, *Maze*, p. 145] until Congress can create particularized legislation "to deal directly with the evil?" For a discussion of the rule of lenity, see Dan M. Kahan, *Lenity and Federal Common Law Crimes*, 1994 SUP. CT. REV. 345 (1994).

2. ***Bribery/Extortion.*** Can all acts of simple bribery involving a public official be presented as extortion? Has the court "blurred" the distinction between bribery and extortion? See James Lindgren, *The Theory, History, and Practice of the Bribery-Extortion Distinction*, 141 U. PA. L. REV. 1695 (1993).

3. ***Quid Pro Quo.*** After *Evans*, how explicit does the *quid pro quo* have to be for a case in which the payment does not have the appearance of a campaign contribution? For a discussion of the varying views taken by lower

courts, see Ilissa B. Gold, Note, *Explicit, Express, and Everything in Between: The Quid Pro Quo Requirement for Bribery and Hobbs Act Prosecutions in the 2000s*, 36 WASH. U. J.L. & POL'Y 261 (2011) ("Since *Evans*, three Circuits – the Second, Sixth, and Ninth – have determined that *McCormick* and *Evans* established different standards, with *McCormick* governing campaign contribution cases and *Evans* governing any other instances of public officials receiving bribes. Two other Circuits – the Third and Seventh – have indicated that they will hold *McCormick* to be the sole standard for campaign contribution cases in the future. The Eleventh Circuit stands alone in trying to reconcile *McCormick* and *Evans* in the campaign context in *United States v. Siegelman*."). In **United States v. Giles**, 246 F.3d 966, 972 (7th Cir. 2001), the court stated:

> We are not convinced that *Evans* clearly settles the question. And we recognize a policy concern which might justify distinguishing campaign contributions from other payments. After all, campaign contributions often are made with the hope that the recipient, if elected, will further interests with which the contributor agrees; there is nothing illegal about such contributions. To distinguish legal from illegal campaign contributions, it makes sense to require the government to prove that a particular contribution was made in exchange for an explicit promise or undertaking by the official. Other payments to officials are not clothed with the same degree of respectability as ordinary campaign contributions. For that reason, perhaps it should be easier to prove that those payments are in violation of the law.

4. ***Gifts Under the Gratuities Statute.*** How does the receipt of gifts by public officials differ in the context of the gratuities statute? Consider the issue in the context of the following case:

UNITED STATES v. SUN-DIAMOND GROWERS OF CALIFORNIA

526 U.S. 398 (1999)

Justice SCALIA delivered the opinion of the Court.

Talmudic sages believed that judges who accepted bribes would be punished by eventually losing all knowledge of the divine law. The Federal Government, dealing with many public officials who are not judges, and with at least some judges for whom this sanction holds no terror, has constructed a framework of human laws and regulations defining various sorts of impermissible gifts, and punishing those who give or receive them with administrative sanctions, fines, and incarceration. One element of that framework is 18 U.S.C. § 201(c)(1)(A), the "illegal gratuity statute," which prohibits giving "anything of value" to a present, past, or future public official "for or because of any official act performed or to be performed by such public official." In this case, we consider whether conviction under the illegal gratuity statute requires any showing beyond the fact that a gratuity was given because of the recipient's official position.

Respondent is a trade association that engaged in marketing and lobbying activities on behalf of its member cooperatives, which were owned by approximately 5,000 individual growers of raisins, figs, walnuts, prunes, and hazelnuts. Petitioner United States is represented by Independent Counsel Donald Smaltz, who, as a consequence of his investigation of former Secretary of Agriculture Michael Espy, charged respondent with, inter alia, making illegal gifts to Espy in violation of § 201(c)(1)(A). That statute provides, in relevant part, that anyone who

> "otherwise than as provided by law for the proper discharge of official duty ... directly or indirectly gives, offers, or promises anything of value to any public official, former public official, or person selected to be a public official, for or because of any official act performed or to be performed by such public official, former public official, or person selected to be a public official ... shall be fined under this title or imprisoned for not more than two years, or both."

Count One of the indictment charged Sun-Diamond with giving Espy approximately $5,900 in illegal gratuities: tickets to the 1993 U.S. Open Tennis Tournament (worth $2,295), luggage ($2,427), meals ($665), and a framed print and crystal bowl ($524). The indictment alluded to two matters in which respondent had an interest in favorable treatment from the Secretary at the time it bestowed the gratuities. First, respondent's member cooperatives participated in the Market Promotion Plan (MPP), a grant program administered by the Department of Agriculture to promote the sale of U.S. farm commodities in foreign countries. The cooperatives belonged to trade organizations, such as the California Prune Board and the Raisin Administrative Committee, which submitted overseas marketing plans for their respective commodities. If their plans were approved by the Secretary of Agriculture, the trade organizations received funds to be used in defraying the foreign marketing expenses of their constituents. Each of respondent's member cooperatives was the largest member of its respective trade organization, and each received significant MPP funding. Respondent was understandably concerned, then, when Congress in 1993 instructed the Secretary to promulgate regulations giving small-sized entities preference in obtaining MPP funds. If the Secretary did not deem respondent's member cooperatives to be small-sized entities, there was a good chance they would no longer receive MPP grants. Thus, respondent had an interest in persuading the Secretary to adopt a regulatory definition of "small-sized entity" that would include its member cooperatives.

Second, respondent had an interest in the Federal Government's regulation of methyl bromide, a low-cost pesticide used by many individual growers in respondent's member cooperatives. In 1992, the Environmental Protection Agency announced plans to promulgate a rule to phase out the use of methyl bromide in the United States. The indictment alleged that respondent sought the Department of Agriculture's assistance in persuading EPA to abandon its proposed rule altogether, or at least to mitigate its impact. In the latter event, respondent wanted the Department to fund research efforts to develop reliable alternatives to methyl bromide.

Although describing these two matters before the Secretary in which respondent had an interest, the indictment did not allege a specific connection between either of them--or between any other action of the Secretary--and the gratuities conferred. The District Court denied respondent's motion to dismiss Count One because of this omission. The court stated:

> "[T]o sustain a charge under the gratuity statute, it is not necessary for the indictment to allege a direct nexus between the value conferred to Secretary Espy by Sun-Diamond and an official act performed or to be performed by Secretary Espy. It is sufficient for the indictment to allege that Sun- Diamond provided things of value to Secretary Espy because of his position."

At trial, the District Court instructed the jury along these same lines. It read § 201(c)(1)(A) to the jury twice (along with the definition of "official act" from § 201(a)(3)), but then placed an expansive gloss on that statutory language, saying, among other things, that "[i]t is sufficient if Sun-Diamond provided Espy with unauthorized compensation simply because he held public office," and that "[t]he government need not prove that the alleged gratuity was linked to a specific or identifiable official act or any act at all." The jury convicted respondent on, inter alia, Count One (the only subject of this appeal), and the District Court sentenced respondent on this count to pay a fine of $400,000. * * *

The Court of Appeals reversed the conviction on Count One and remanded for a new trial, stating:

> "Given that the 'for or because of any official act' language in ' 201(c)(1)(A) means what it says, the jury instructions invited the jury to convict on materially less evidence than the statute demands--evidence of gifts driven simply by Espy's official position."

In rejecting respondent's attack on the indictment, however, the court stated that the Government need not show that a gratuity was given "for or because of" any particular act or acts: "That an official has an abundance of relevant matters on his plate should not insulate him or his benefactors from the gratuity statute--as long as the jury is required to find the requisite intent to reward past favorable acts or to make future ones more likely." We granted certiorari.

Initially, it will be helpful to place § 201(c)(1)(A) within the context of the statutory scheme. Subsection (a) of § 201 sets forth definitions applicable to the section–including a definition of "official act," § 201(a)(3). Subsections (b) and (c) then set forth, respectively, two separate crimes–or two pairs of crimes, if one counts the giving and receiving of unlawful gifts as separate crimes–with two different sets of elements and authorized punishments. The first crime, described in § 201(b)(1) as to the giver, and § 201(b)(2) as to the recipient, is bribery, which requires a showing that something of value was corruptly given, offered, or promised to a public official (as to the giver) or corruptly demanded, sought, received, accepted, or agreed to be received or accepted by a public official (as to the recipient) with intent, inter alia, "to influence any official act" (giver) or in return for "being influenced in the performance of any official act" (recipient). The second crime, defined in § 201(c)(1)(A) as to the giver, and § 201(c)(1)(B) as to the recipient, is illegal gratuity, which requires a showing that something of value was given, offered, or promised to a public official (as to the giver), or demanded, sought, received, accepted, or agreed to be received or accepted by a public official (as to the recipient), "for or because of any official act performed or to be performed by such public official."

The distinguishing feature of each crime is its intent element. Bribery requires intent "to influence" an official act or "to be influenced" in an official act, while illegal gratuity requires only that the gratuity be given or accepted "for or because of" an official act. In other words, for bribery there must be a quid pro quo–a specific intent to give or receive something of value in exchange for an official act. An illegal gratuity, on the other hand, may constitute merely a reward for some future act that the public official will take (and may already have determined to take), or for a past act that he has already taken. The punishments prescribed for the two offenses reflect their relative seriousness: Bribery may be punished by up to 15 years' imprisonment, a fine of $250,000 ($500,000 for organizations) or triple the value of the bribe, whichever is greater, and disqualification from holding government office. See 18 U.S.C. §§ 201(b) and 3571. Violation of the illegal gratuity statute, on the other hand, may be punished by up to two years' imprisonment and a fine of $250,000 ($500,000 for organizations).

The District Court's instructions in this case, in differentiating between a bribe and an illegal gratuity, correctly noted that only a bribe requires proof of a quid pro quo. The point in controversy here is that the instructions went on to suggest that § 201(c)(1)(A), unlike the bribery statute, did not require any connection between respondent's intent and a specific official act. It would be satisfied, according to the instructions, merely by a showing that respondent gave Secretary Espy a gratuity because of his official position–perhaps, for example, to build a reservoir of goodwill that might ultimately affect one or more of a multitude of unspecified acts, now and in the future. The United States, represented by the Independent Counsel, and the Solicitor General as amicus curiae, contend that this instruction was correct. The Independent Counsel asserts that "section 201(c)(1)(A) reaches any effort to buy favor or generalized goodwill from an official who either has been, is, or may at some unknown, unspecified later time, be in a position to act favorably to the giver's interests." The Solicitor General contends that § 201(c)(1)(A) requires only a showing that a "gift was motivated, at least in part, by the recipient's capacity to exercise governmental power or influence in the donor's favor" without necessarily showing that it was connected to a particular official act.

In our view, this interpretation does not fit comfortably with the statutory text, which prohibits only gratuities given or received "for or because of any official act performed or to be performed". It seems to us that this means "for or because of some particular official act of whatever identity"–just as the question "Do you like any composer?" normally means "Do you like some particular composer?" It is linguistically possible, of course, for the phrase to mean "for or because of official acts in general, without specification as to which one"–just as the question "Do you like any composer?" could mean "Do you like all composers, no matter what their names or music?" But the former seems to us the more natural meaning, especially given the complex structure of the provision before us here. Why go through the trouble of requiring that the gift be made "for or because of any official act performed or to be performed by such public official," and then defining "official act" (in § 201(a)(3)) to mean "any decision or action on any question, matter, cause, suit, proceeding or controversy, which may at any time be pending, or which may by law be brought before any public official, in such official's official capacity," when, if the Government's interpretation were correct, it would have sufficed to say "for or because of such official's ability to favor the donor in executing the functions of his office"? The insistence upon an "official act," carefully defined, seems pregnant with the requirement that some particular official act be identified and proved.

Besides thinking that this is the more natural meaning of § 201(c)(1)(A), we are inclined to believe it correct because of the peculiar results that the Government's alternative reading would produce. It would criminalize, for example, token gifts to the President based on his official position and not linked to any identifiable act–such as the replica jerseys given by championship sports teams each year during ceremonial White House visits, see, e.g., Gail Gibson, Masters of the Game, Lexington Herald- Leader, Nov. 10, 1998, p. A1. Similarly, it would criminalize a high school principal's gift of a school baseball cap to the Secretary of Education, by reason of his office, on the occasion of the latter's visit to the school. That these examples are not fanciful is demonstrated by the fact that counsel for the United States maintained at oral argument that a group of farmers would violate § 201(c)(1)(A) by providing a complimentary lunch for the Secretary of Agriculture in conjunction with his speech to the farmers concerning various matters of USDA policy–so long as the Secretary had before him, or had in prospect, matters affecting the farmers. Of course the Secretary of Agriculture always has before him or in prospect matters that affect farmers, just as the President always has before him or in prospect matters that affect college and professional sports, and the Secretary of Education matters that affect high schools.

It might be said in reply to this that the more narrow interpretation of the statute can also produce some peculiar results. In fact, in the above-given examples, the gifts could easily be regarded as having been conferred, not only because of the official's position as President or Secretary, but also (and perhaps principally) "for or because of" the official acts of receiving the sports teams at the White House, visiting the high school, and speaking to the farmers about USDA policy, respectively. The answer to this objection is that those actions–while they are assuredly "official acts" in some sense–are not "official acts" within the meaning of the statute, which, as we have noted, defines "official act" to mean "any decision or action on any question, matter, cause, suit, proceeding or controversy, which may at any time be pending, or which may by law be brought before any public official, in such official's official capacity, or in such official's place of trust or profit." Thus, when the violation is linked to a particular "official act," it is possible to eliminate the absurdities through the definition of that term. When, however, no particular "official act" need be identified, and the giving of gifts by reason of the recipient's mere tenure in office constitutes a violation, nothing but the Government's discretion prevents the foregoing examples from being prosecuted. * * *

Our refusal to read § 201(c)(1)(A) as a prohibition of gifts given by reason of the donee's office is supported by the fact that when Congress has wanted to adopt such a broadly prophylactic criminal prohibition upon gift giving, it has done so in a more precise and more administrable fashion. For example, another provision of Chapter 11 of Title 18, the chapter entitled "Bribery, Graft, and Conflicts of Interest," criminalizes the giving or receiving of any "supplementation" of an Executive official's salary, without regard to the purpose of the payment. Other provisions of the same chapter make it a crime for a bank employee to give a bank examiner, and for a bank examiner to receive from a bank employee, "any loan or gratuity," again without regard to the purpose for which it is given. A provision of the Labor Management Relations Act makes it a felony for an employer to give to a union representative, and for a union representative to receive from an employer, anything of value. With clearly framed and easily administrable provisions such as these on the books imposing gift-giving and gift-receiving prohibitions specifically based upon the holding of office, it seems to us most implausible that Congress intended the language of the gratuity statute–"for or because of any official act performed or to be performed"–to pertain to the office rather than (as the language more naturally suggests) to particular official acts. * * *

We hold that, in order to establish a violation of 18 U.S.C. § 201(c)(1)(A), the Government must prove a link between a thing of value conferred upon a public official and a specific "official act" for or because of which it was given. We affirm the judgment of the Court of Appeals, which remanded the case to the District Court for a new trial on Count One. Our decision today casts doubt upon the lower courts' resolution of respondent's challenge to the sufficiency of the indictment on Count One--an issue on which certiorari was neither sought nor granted. We leave it to the District Court to determine whether that issue should be reopened on remand. * * * It is so ordered.

NOTES AND QUESTIONS

1. ***Aftermath.*** On December 2, 1998, a federal jury found former Agriculture Secretary Mike Espy not guilty of the thirty counts brought against him as a result of an investigation conducted by an Independent Counsel. Following this acquittal, Archibald R. Schaffer III, who was convicted of bribing Secretary Espy, sought a new trial premised on the "newly-found and arguably exculpatory testimony of former Secretary of the Department of Agriculture, Alphonso Michael Espy, which had become available following Espy's own acquittal in a related prosecution." On December 22, 2000, President Clinton granted a full and unconditional pardon to Schaffer, and his appeal of the bribery conviction was dismissed as moot. See United States v. Schaffer, 240 F.3d 35 (D.C. Cir. 2001).

2. ***Unlawful Gratuities Under 18 U.S.C. § 666.*** Another federal statute used to prosecute corruption in state and local government, along with organizations that receive federal funding, is 18 U.S.C. § 666. Congress enacted the statute in 1984 to "augment the ability of the United States to vindicate significant acts of theft, fraud, and bribery involving Federal monies which are disbursed to private organizations or State and local governments pursuant to a Federal program." S.Rep. No. 98-225 (1984). It ensures that federal prosecutors had a tool similar to § 201 to reach bribery involving lower levels of government that would not have the limitation of the Hobbs Act, which only reaches the recipient of the corrupt *quid pro quo*. The statute covers the offer or solicitation of anything of value "intending to be influenced or rewarded in connection with any business, transaction, or series of transactions of such organization, government, or agency involving any thing of value of $5,000 or more." In addition, the prosecution must prove "the organization, government, or agency receives, in any one year period, benefits in excess of $10,000 under a Federal program involving a grant, contract, subsidy, loan, guarantee, insurance, or other form of Federal assistance."

There is a split in the circuit courts about whether § 666 covers gifts as well as bribes paid to an official. Most courts interpret the reference to an intent to be "rewarded" to mean that Congress wanted the statute to be coextensive with § 201(c)'s prohibition on unlawful gratuities. See United States v. Ganim, 510 F.3d 134 (2d Cir.2007) ("[A] payment made to 'influence' connotes bribery, whereas a payment made to 'reward' connotes an illegal gratuity."); United States v. Anderson, 517 F.3d 953 (7th Cir.2008); United States v. Zimmermann, 509 F.3d 920 (8th Cir.2007). The First Circuit, in United States v. Fernandez, 722 F.3d 1 (1st Cir. 2013) rejected application of the statute to unlawful gratuities, finding that it is limited to only bribes, whether paid before or after the official action. The circuit court stated:

Other than the ambiguous use of the word "rewarded," the text of § 666, as well as its legislative history and purpose, do not support the argument that Congress intended the statute to reach gratuities. The statute was amended in a way that brought its language closer to § 201's bribery provision, and further from § 201's gratuity provision, suggesting the true targets of § 666 are bribes, not gratuities. Critically, accepting that § 666 criminalizes gratuities would expose defendants convicted of gratuities violations under § 666 to penalties far greater than those faced by individuals convicted of gratuities violations under § 201—a strange outcome that we doubt Congress intended. We therefore hold that gratuities are not criminalized under § 666.

CHAPTER FIVE
MAIL AND WIRE FRAUD

A. INTRODUCTION

The crime of mail fraud emanates from an 1872 recodification of the Postal Act. At its inception, the crux of the offense was on the misuse of the postal system by way of a counterfeit scheme. The emphasis of the offense has now shifted to the "scheme to defraud" element of the statute. A mail fraud prosecution requires the government to prove 1) a scheme devised or intending to defraud or for obtaining money or property by fraudulent means; and 2) use or causing the use of the mails (or private courier) in furtherance of the fraudulent scheme. Materiality is essential to proving mail fraud.

The mail fraud statute's enormous breadth allows federal prosecutors to use this offense to combat many different types of fraudulent conduct. Jed Rakoff called mail fraud the prosecutor's "Stradivarius" or "Colt 45." Jed S. Rakoff, *The Federal Mail Fraud Statute* (pt. 1), 18 DUQ. L. REV. 771, 784 (1980). Chief Justice Burger termed it the "stopgap" provision. United States v. Maze, below. Professor Ellen S. Podgor maintains that it is the prosecutor's "Uzi." Ellen S. Podgor, *Mail Fraud: Opening Letters,* 43 S.C. L. REV. 223, 224 (1992). Judge Ralph K. Winter notes that "[w]ith regard to the statutory weapons available to prosecutors, they rank by analogy with hydrogen bombs on stealth aircraft. Foremost among them are the various federal fraud statutes—in particular, the mail and wire fraud statutes * * *." Ralph K. Winter, *Paying Lawyers, Empowering Prosecutors and Protecting Managers: the Cost of Capital in America*, 42 DUKE L.J. 945, 954 (1993). The statute is used by prosecutors to criminalize fraudulent conduct that might not be covered in other legislation. See Peter Henning, *Maybe It Should Just Be Called Federal Fraud: The Changing Nature of the Mail Fraud Statute,* 36 B.C. L. REV. 435 (1995).

B. SCHEME TO DEFRAUD

In **United States v. Maze**, 414 U.S. 395 (1974), the United States Supreme Court rejected the use of the mail fraud statute where the mailing in furtherance of the scheme to defraud was premised on an alleged use of a stolen credit card and the subsequent mailing to collect on the bills. The Court rejected the government's argument that these collection mailings were necessary to the scheme's success. Dissenting, Chief Justice Burger, joined by Justice White, stated:

> * * * Section 1341 of Title 18 U.S.C. has traditionally been used against fraudulent activity as a first line of defense. When a "new" fraud develops—as constantly happens—the mail fraud statute becomes a stopgap device to deal on a temporary basis with the new phenomenon, until particularized legislation can be developed and passed to deal directly with the evil. "Prior to the passage of the 1933 (Securities) Act, most criminal prosecutions for fraudulent securities transactions were brought under the Federal Mail Fraud Statute." * * * Loan sharks were brought to justice by means of 18 U.S.C. § 1341, * * * before Congress, in 1968, recognized the interstate character of loansharking and the need to provide federal protection against this organized crime activity, and enacted 18 U.S.C. § 891 et seq., outlawing extortionate extensions of credit. Although inadequate to protect the buying and investing public fully, the mail fraud statute stood in the breach against frauds connected with the burgeoning sale of undeveloped real estate, until Congress could examine the problems of the land sales industry and pass into law the Interstate Land Sales Full Disclosure Act, 82 Stat. 590, 15 U.S.C. § 1701 et seq. * * * Similarly, the mail fraud statute was used to stop credit card fraud, before Congress moved to provide particular protection by passing 15 U.S.C. § 1644.
>
> The mail fraud statute continues to remain an important tool in prosecuting frauds in those areas where legislation has been passed more directly addressing the fraudulent conduct. Mail fraud counts fill pages of securities fraud indictments even today. * * * Despite the prevasive Government regulation of the drug industry, postal fraud statutes still play an important role in controlling the solicitation of mail-order purchases by drug distributors based upon fraudulent misrepresentations. * * *
>
> The criminal mail fraud statute must remain strong to be able to cope with the new varieties of fraud that the ever-inventive American "con artist" is sure to develop. Abuses in franchising and the growing scandals from pyramid sales schemes are but some of the threats to the financial security of our citizenry that the Federal Government must be ever alert to combat. * * *

NOTES AND QUESTIONS

1. ***Schemes to Defraud.*** Courts have found that the "scheme to defraud" element of this statute encompasses an endless array of frauds. See, e.g., Carpenter v. United States, 484 U.S. 19 (1987) (securities fraud); United States v. Serlin, 538 F.2d 737 (7th Cir. 1976) (franchise fraud); United States v. Cavalier, 17 F.3d 90 (5th Cir. 1994) (insurance fraud); United States v. Edwards, 458 F.2d 875 (5th Cir. 1972) ("divorce mill" fraud); United States v. Hayes, 231 F.3d 663 (9th Cir. 2000) (scheme to sell grades for classes that foreign students did not attend).

2. ***Limitations.*** Are there any limits as to what fraudulent conduct can be prosecuted under the mail fraud statute? In Fasulo v. United States, 272 U.S. 620, 625 (1926), the Supreme Court found that a "use of the mails for the purpose of obtaining money by means of threats of murder or bodily harm" was not a scheme to defraud for the purposes of mail fraud. "Mere 'puffing' or 'sellers' talk' is not a crime under federal fraud statutes." United States v. Rodriguez, 732 F.3d 1299 (11th Cir. 2013).

3. ***Tax Fraud/ Mail Fraud.*** Can the mailing of a fraudulent tax return be charged as mail fraud? Compare the majority view as expressed in United States v. Miller, 545 F.2d 1204, 1216 (9th Cir. 1976) (mail fraud can be a cumulative and alternative charge to tax fraud) with the minority view expressed in United States v. Henderson, 386 F. Supp. 1048 (S.D.N.Y. 1974) (mail fraud improper for alleged income tax evasion due to existence of "particularized legislation"). The Department of Justice has issued a guideline that places limits on when the Tax Division will approve mail, wire or bank fraud charges in tax-related cases involving schemes to defraud the Government or other persons. They look at whether "there was a large fraud loss or a substantial pattern of conduct and [if] there is a significant benefit to bringing the charges instead of or in addition to" tax charges. The guideline states that "[a]bsent unusual circumstances, however, the Tax Division will not approve mail or wire fraud charges if a case involves only one person's tax liability or when submissions to the IRS were truthful." U.S.A.M. § 6-4.210(A) (2010).

4. ***Particularized Legislation.*** Once Congress provides the particularized legislation to combat the new fraud, can prosecutors still use the mail fraud statute? Compare the majority view expressed in United States v. Simon, 510 F. Supp. 232 (E.D. Pa. 1981) (permitted mail fraud despite the enactment of a specific Medicaid fraud statute) with the minority view expressed in United States v. Gallant, 570 F. Supp. 303, 310 (S.D. N.Y. 1983) (mail fraud improper where particularized legislation existed within the Copyright Act), but see United States v. Dowling, 739 F.2d 1445, 1450 (9th Cir. 1984), reversed on other grounds, [p. 109]. Particularized legislation was passed to address health care fraud. See 18 U.S.C. § 1347 (1996) (health care fraud statute has penalties of up to 10 years imprisonment, 20 years if the violation results in serious bodily injury, and any term of years or life if the violation results in death).

McNALLY v. UNITED STATES

483 U.S. 350 (1987)

Justice WHITE delivered the opinion of the Court.

This action involves the prosecution of petitioner Gray, a former public official of the Commonwealth of Kentucky, and petitioner McNally, a private individual, for alleged violation of the federal mail fraud statute, 18 U.S.C. § 1341. The prosecution's principal theory of the case, which was accepted by the courts below, was that petitioners' participation in a self-dealing patronage scheme defrauded the citizens and government of Kentucky of certain "intangible rights," such as the right to have the Commonwealth's affairs conducted honestly. We must consider whether the jury charge permitted a conviction for conduct not within the scope of the mail fraud statute.

We accept for the sake of argument the Government's view of the evidence, as follows. Petitioners and a third individual, Howard P. "Sonny" Hunt, were politically active in the Democratic Party in the Commonwealth of Kentucky during the 1970's. After Democrat Julian Carroll was elected Governor of Kentucky in 1974, Hunt was made chairman of the state Democratic Party and given *de facto* control over selecting the insurance agencies from which the Commonwealth would purchase its policies. In 1975, the Wombwell Insurance Company of Lexington, Kentucky (Wombwell), which since 1971 had acted as the Commonwealth's agent for securing a workmen's compensation policy, agreed with Hunt that in exchange for a continued agency relationship it would share any resulting commissions in excess of $50,000 a year with other insurance agencies specified by him. The commissions in question were paid to Wombwell by the large insurance companies from which it secured coverage for the Commonwealth.

From 1975 to 1979, Wombwell funneled $851,000 in commissions to 21 separate insurance agencies designated by Hunt. Among the recipients of these payments was Seton Investments, Inc. (Seton), a company controlled by Hunt and petitioner Gray and nominally owned and operated by petitioner McNally.

Gray served as Secretary of Public Protection and Regulation from 1976 to 1978 and also as Secretary of the Governor's Cabinet from 1977 to 1979. Prior to his 1976 appointment, he and Hunt established Seton for the sole purpose of sharing in the commissions distributed by Wombwell. Wombwell paid some $200,000 to Seton between 1975 and 1979, and the money was used to benefit Gray and Hunt. Pursuant to Hunt's direction, Wombwell also made excess commission payments to the Snodgrass Insurance Agency, which in turn gave the money to McNally.

On account of the foregoing activities, Hunt was charged with and pleaded guilty to mail and tax fraud and was sentenced to three years' imprisonment. Petitioners were charged with one count of conspiracy and seven counts of mail fraud, six of which were dismissed before trial.[2] The

---

[2] The six counts dismissed were based on the mailing of Seton's tax returns. The Court of Appeals held that mailings required by law cannot be made the basis for liability under § 1341 unless the documents are themselves false, see Parr v. United States, 363 U.S. 370 (1960), and that the six counts were properly dismissed since the indictment did not allege that Seton's tax returns were false. The Government

remaining mail fraud count was based on the mailing of a commission check to Wombwell by the insurance company from which it had secured coverage for the State. This count alleged that petitioners had devised a scheme (1) to defraud the citizens and government of Kentucky of their right to have the Commonwealth's affairs conducted honestly, and (2) to obtain, directly and indirectly, money and other things of value by means of false pretenses and the concealment of material facts. * * *

After informing the jury of the charges in the indictment, the District Court instructed that the scheme to defraud the citizens of Kentucky and to obtain money by false pretenses and concealment could be made out by either of two sets of findings: (1) that Hunt had *de facto* control over the award of the workmen's compensation insurance contract to Wombwell from 1975 to 1979; that he directed payments of commissions from this contract to Seton, an entity in which he had an ownership interest, without disclosing that interest to persons in state government whose actions or deliberations could have been affected by the disclosure; and that petitioners, or either of them, aided and abetted Hunt in that scheme; or (2) that Gray, in either of his appointed positions, had supervisory authority regarding the Commonwealth's workmen's compensation insurance at a time when Seton received commissions; that Gray had an ownership interest in Seton and did not disclose that interest to persons in state government whose actions or deliberations could have been affected by that disclosure; and that McNally aided and abetted Gray (the latter finding going only to McNally's guilt).

The jury convicted petitioners on both the mail fraud and conspiracy counts, and the Court of Appeals affirmed the convictions. In affirming the substantive mail fraud conviction, the court relied on a line of decisions from the Courts of Appeals holding that the mail fraud statute proscribes schemes to defraud citizens of their intangible rights to honest and impartial government. * * *

We granted certiorari, and now reverse.

The mail fraud statute clearly protects property rights, but does not refer to the intangible right of the citizenry to good government. As first enacted in 1872, as part of a recodification of the postal laws, the statute contained a general proscription against using the mails to initiate correspondence in furtherance of "any scheme or artifice to defraud." The sponsor of the recodification stated, in apparent reference to the antifraud provision, that measures were needed "to prevent the frauds which are mostly gotten up in the large cities . . . by thieves, forgers, and rapscallions generally, for the purpose of deceiving and fleecing the innocent people in the country." Insofar as the sparse legislative history reveals anything, it indicates that the original impetus behind the mail fraud statute was to protect the people from schemes to deprive them of their money or property.

---

has not sought review of this holding.

Durland v. United States, 161 U.S. 306 (1896), the first case in which this Court construed the meaning of the phrase "any scheme or artifice to defraud," held that the phrase is to be interpreted broadly insofar as property rights are concerned, but did not indicate that the statute had a more extensive reach. The Court rejected the argument that "the statute reaches only such cases as, at common law, would come within the definition of 'false pretences,' in order to make out which there must be a misrepresentation as to some existing fact and not a mere promise as to the future." Instead, it construed the statute to "includ[e] everything designed to defraud by representations as to the past or present, or suggestions and promises as to the future." Accordingly, the defendant's use of the mails to sell bonds which he did not intend to honor was within the statute. The Court explained that "[i]t was with the purpose of protecting the public against all such intentional efforts to despoil, and to prevent the post office from being used to carry them into effect, that this statute was passed . . . ."

Congress codified the holding of *Durland* in 1909, and in doing so gave further indication that the statute's purpose is protecting property rights. The amendment added the words "or for obtaining money or property by means of false or fraudulent pretenses, representations, or promises" after the original phrase "any scheme or artifice to defraud." Act of Mar. 4, 1909, ch. 321, § 215, 35 Stat. 1130. The new language is based on the statement in *Durland* that the statute reaches "everything designed to defraud by representations as to the past or present, or suggestions and promises as to the future." However, instead of the phrase "everything designed to defraud" Congress used the words "[any scheme or artifice] for obtaining money or property."

After 1909, therefore, the mail fraud statute criminalized schemes or artifices "to defraud" or "for obtaining money or property by means of false or fraudulent pretenses, representation, or promises . . . ." Because the two phrases identifying the proscribed schemes appear in the disjunctive, it is arguable that they are to be construed independently and that the money-or-property requirement of the latter phrase does not limit schemes to defraud to those aimed at causing deprivation of money or property. This is the approach that has been taken by each of the Courts of Appeals that has addressed the issue: schemes to defraud include those designed to deprive individuals, the people, or the government of intangible rights, such as the right to have public officials perform their duties honestly. As the Court long ago stated, however, the words "to defraud" commonly refer "to wronging one in his property rights by dishonest methods or schemes," and "usually signify the deprivation of something of value by trick, deceit, chicane or overreaching." Hammerschmidt v. United States, 265 U.S. 182, 188 (1924).[8]

---

[8] *Hammerschmidt* concerned the scope of the predecessor of 18 U.S.C. § 371, which makes criminal any conspiracy "to defraud the United States, or any agency thereof in any manner or for any purpose." Hammerschmidt indicates, in regard to that statute, that while "[t]o conspire to defraud the United States means primarily to

The codification of the holding in *Durland* in 1909 does not indicate that Congress was departing from this common understanding. As we see it, adding the second phrase simply made it unmistakable that the statute reached false promises and misrepresentations as to the future as well as other frauds involving money or property.

We believe that Congress' intent in passing the mail fraud statute was to prevent the use of the mails in furtherance of such schemes. The Court has often stated that when there are two rational readings of a criminal statute, one harsher than the other, we are to choose the harsher only when Congress has spoken in clear and definite language. United States v. Bass, 404 U.S. 336, 347 (1971); United States v. Universal C.I.T. Credit Corp., 344 U.S. 218, 221-222 (1952). See also Rewis v. United States, 401 U.S. 808, 812 (1971). As the Court said in a mail fraud case years ago: "There are no constructive offenses; and before one can be punished, it must be shown that his case is plainly within the statute." Fasulo v. United States, 272 U.S. 620, 629 (1926). Rather than construe the statute in a manner that leaves its outer boundaries ambiguous and involves the Federal Government in setting standards of disclosure and good government for local and state officials, we read § 1341 as limited in scope to the protection of property rights. If Congress desires to go further, it must speak more clearly than it has.

For purposes of this action, we assume that Hunt, as well as Gray, was a state officer. The issue is thus whether a state officer violates the mail fraud statute if he chooses an insurance agent to provide insurance for the State but specifies that the agent must share its commissions with other named insurance agencies, in one of which the officer has an ownership interest and hence profits when his agency receives part of the commissions. We note that as the action comes to us, there was no charge and the jury was not required to find that the Commonwealth itself was defrauded of any money or property. It was not charged that in the absence of the alleged scheme the Commonwealth would have paid a lower premium or secured better insurance. Hunt and Gray received part of the commissions but those commissions were not the Commonwealth's money. Nor was the jury charged that to convict it must find that the Commonwealth was deprived of control over how its money was spent. Indeed, the premium for insurance would have been paid to some agency, and what Hunt and Gray did was to assert

---

cheat the Government out of property or money, . . . it also means to interfere with or obstruct one of its lawful governmental functions by deceit, craft or trickery, or at least by means that are dishonest." 265 U.S., at 188. Other cases have held that § 371 reaches conspiracies other than those directed at property interests. However, we believe that this broad construction of § 371 is based on a consideration not applicable to the mail fraud statute. * * *

Section 371 is a statute aimed at protecting the Federal Government alone; however, the mail fraud statute, as we have indicated, had its origin in the desire to protect individual property rights, and any benefit which the Government derives from the statute must be limited to the Government's interests as property holder.

control that the Commonwealth might not otherwise have made over the commissions paid by the insurance company to its agent. Although the Government now relies in part on the assertion that petitioners obtained property by means of false representations to Wombwell, there was nothing in the jury charge that required such a finding. We hold, therefore, that the jury instruction on the substantive mail fraud count permitted a conviction for conduct not within the reach of § 1341.

The Government concedes that if petitioners' substantive mail fraud convictions are reversed their conspiracy convictions should also be reversed.

The judgment of the Court of Appeals is reversed, and the case is remanded for proceedings consistent with this opinion.

It is so ordered.

Justice STEVENS, with whom Justice O'CONNOR joins as to Parts I, II, and III, dissenting.

* * * The same question of statutory construction has arisen in a variety of contexts over the past few decades. In the public sector, judges, State Governors, chairmen of state political parties, state cabinet officers, city aldermen, Congressmen and many other state and federal officials have been convicted of defrauding citizens of their right to the honest services of their governmental officials. In most of these cases, the officials have secretly made governmental decisions with the objective of benefitting themselves or promoting their own interests, instead of fulfilling their legal commitment to provide the citizens of the State or local government with their loyal service and honest government. Similarly, many elected officials and their campaign workers have been convicted of mail fraud when they have used the mails to falsify votes, thus defrauding the citizenry of its right to an honest election. In the private sector, purchasing agents, brokers, union leaders, and others with clear fiduciary duties to their employers or unions have been found guilty of defrauding their employers or unions by accepting kickbacks or selling confidential information. In other cases, defendants have been found guilty of using the mails to defraud individuals of their rights to privacy and other nonmonetary rights.[4] All of these cases have something in common—they involved what the Court now refers to as "intangible rights." They also share something else in common. The many federal courts that have confronted the question whether these sorts of schemes constitute a "scheme or artifice to defraud" have uniformly and consistently read the statute in the same, sensible way. They have realized that nothing in the

[4] See e.g. United States v. Condolon, 600 F.2d 7 (4th Cir. 1979) (wire fraud conviction related to bogus talent agency designed to seduce women); United States v. Louderman, 576 F.2d 1383 (9th Cir.) (scheme to fraudulently obtain confidential personal information); see also United States v. Castor, 558 F.2d 379, 393 (7th Cir. 1977) (fraudulent information on application for liquor license).

words "any scheme or artifice to defraud," or in the purpose of the statute, justifies limiting its application to schemes intended to deprive victims of money or property.

I

The mail fraud statute sets forth three separate prohibitions. It prohibits the use of the United States mails for the purpose of executing "[1] *any* scheme or artifice to defraud, [2] *or* for obtaining money or property by means of false or fraudulent pretenses, representations, or promises, [3] *or* to sell, dispose of, loan, exchange, alter, give away, distribute, supply, or furnish or procure for unlawful use any counterfeit or spurious coin, obligation, security, or other article, or anything represented to be or intimated or held out to be such counterfeit or spurious article . . . ." 18 U.S.C. § 1341 (emphasis and brackets added).

As the language makes clear, each of these restrictions is independent. One can violate the second clause—obtaining money or property by false pretenses—even though one does not violate the third clause—counterfeiting. Similarly, one can violate the first clause—devising a scheme or artifice to defraud—without violating the counterfeiting provision. Until today it was also obvious that one could violate the first clause by devising a scheme or artifice to defraud, even though one did not violate the second clause by seeking to obtain money or property from his victim through false pretenses. *Cf.* Streep v. United States, 160 U.S. 128, 132-133 (1895). Every court to consider the matter had so held. Yet, today, the Court, for all practical purposes, rejects this longstanding construction of the statute by imposing a requirement that a scheme or artifice to defraud does not violate the statute unless its purpose is to defraud someone of money or property. I am at a loss to understand the source or justification for this holding. Certainly no canon of statutory construction requires us to ignore the plain language of the provision.

In considering the scope of the mail fraud statute it is essential to remember Congress' purpose in enacting it. Congress sought to protect the integrity of the United States mails by not allowing them to be used as "instruments of crime." United States v. Brewer, 528 F.2d 492, 498 (CA4 1975). * * * "The focus of the statute is upon the misuse of the Postal Service, not the regulation of state affairs, and Congress clearly has the authority to regulate such misuse of the mails. See Badders v. United States, 240 U.S. 391 (1916)." United States v. States, 488 F.2d 761, 767 (CA8 1973). Once this purpose is considered, it becomes clear that the construction the Court adopts today is senseless. Can it be that Congress sought to purge the mails of schemes to defraud citizens of money but was willing to tolerate schemes to defraud citizens of their right to an honest government, or to unbiased public officials? Is it at all rational to assume that Congress wanted to ensure that the mails not be used for petty crimes, but did not prohibit election fraud accomplished through mailing fictitious ballots? Given Congress' "broad purpose," I "find it difficult to believe, absent some indication in the statute itself or the legislative history, that Congress would have undercut sharply that purpose by hobbling federal prosecutors in their effort to combat" use of the mails for fraudulent schemes. McElroy v. United States, 455 U.S. 642, 655 (1982). * * *

II

* * * The term "defraud" is not unique to § 1341. Another federal statute, 18 U.S.C. § 371, uses the identical term in prohibiting conspiracies to "defraud the United States," and the construction we have given to that statute should be virtually dispositive here. In Haas v. Henkel, 216 U.S. 462 (1910), the Court, dealing with the predecessor to § 371, rejected the argument that there could be no conspiracy to defraud in the absence of contemplated monetary or property loss. "The statute is broad enough in its terms to include any conspiracy for the purpose of impairing, obstructing or defeating the lawful function of any department of Government." Again, in Hammerschmidt v. United States, the Court described the scope of the statute as prohibiting not only conspiracies to "cheat the Government out of property or money, but it also means to interfere with or obstruct one of its lawful governmental functions by deceit, craft or trickery, or at least by means that are dishonest." It is thus clear that a conspiracy to defraud the United States does not require any evidence that the Government has suffered any property or pecuniary loss. * * *

There is no basis for concluding that the term "defraud" means something different in § 1341 (first enacted in 1872) than what it means in § 371 (first enacted in 1867). Although § 371 includes the words "in any manner or for any purpose," those words only modify the underlying act—fraud, and if that term does not include nonproperty interests then our longstanding interpretation of § 371 is unjustified. In any event, § 1341 itself includes the expansive phrase "any scheme or artifice to defraud."

The Court nonetheless suggests that interpreting the two statutes differently can be justified because § 371 applies exclusively to frauds against the United States, while § 1341 benefits private individuals. This argument is wide of the mark. The purpose of § 1341 is to protect the integrity of the United States Postal Service, and, as I have explained, it is ludicrous to think that a Congress intent on preserving the integrity of the Postal Service would have used the term "defraud" in a narrow sense so as to allow mailings whose purpose was merely to defraud citizens of rights other than money or property. There is, therefore, no reason to believe that Congress used the term "defraud" in a more limited way in § 1341 than it did in § 371. * * *

III

To support its crabbed construction of the Act, the Court makes a straightforward but unpersuasive argument. Since there is no explicit, unambiguous evidence that Congress actually contemplated "intangible rights" when it enacted the mail fraud statute in 1872, the Court explains, any ambiguity in the meaning of the criminal statute should be resolved in favor of lenity. The doctrine of lenity is, of course, sound, for the citizen is entitled to fair notice of what sort of conduct may give rise to punishment. But the Court's reliance on that doctrine in this case is misplaced * * * .

IV

* * * In the long run, it is not clear how grave the ramifications of today's decision will be. Congress can, of course, negate it by amending the statute. Even without congressional action, prosecutions of corrupt officials who use the mails to further their schemes may continue since it will frequently be possible to prove some loss of money or property. But many other types of fraudulent use of the mail will now be immune from prosecution. The possibilities that the decision's impact will be mitigated do not moderate my conviction that the Court has made a serious mistake. Nor do they erase my lingering questions about why a Court that has not been particularly receptive to the rights of criminal defendants in recent years has acted so dramatically to protect the elite class of powerful individuals who will benefit from this decision.

I respectfully dissent.

NOTES AND QUESTIONS

1. ***McNally's Reach.*** Would the result of this case be different if the government had alleged a deprivation of money or property in the indictment and if the jury had been instructed on the necessity of the government proving a loss of money or property? Was *McNally* an extremely limited decision?

2. ***Wording of the Indictment.*** In alleging property rights, how important is the wording of the indictment. For example, will "an alleged scheme to defraud the Educational Testing Service, Inc. ('ETS'), by using imposters to take the Test of English as a Foreign Language ('TOEFL') on behalf of other students, constitute a deprivation of property within the meaning of the mail-fraud statute?" See United States v. Alkaabi, 223 F. Supp.2d 583 (D. N.J. 2002) (finding that the indictment did not allege a scheme to deprive the testing service of property); United States v. Alsugair, 256 F. Supp.2d 306 (D.N.J. 2003) (finding that a "superseding indictment adequately alleges that Alsugair obtained property from ETS.").

3. ***Retroactivity.*** Many of the convictions based upon intangible rights required reversal as a result of *McNally*. See Craig M. Bradley, *Foreword: Mail Fraud After* McNally *and* Carpenter: *The Essence of Fraud,* 79 J. CRIM. L. & CRIMINOLOGY 573 (1988); Peter M. Oxman, Note, *The Federal Mail Fraud Statute After* McNally v. United States, *107 S.Ct. 2875 (1987): The Remains of the Intangible Rights Doctrine and Its Proposed Congressional*

Restoration, 25 AM. CRIM. L. REV. 743 (1988). The decision spurred the use of the *writ of coram nobis* when a defendant was are no longer in custody and there case could not be brought under a *writ of habeas corpus*.

4. ***Conspiracy to Defraud.*** Justice Stevens argues in his dissent that "defraud" as used in § 1341 should be interpreted in the same way that the term has been interpreted in 18 U.S.C.A. § 371. (Conspiracy to Defraud the United States). 18 U.S.C.A. § 371 provides:

> If two or more persons conspire either to commit any offense against the United States, or to defraud the United States, or any agency thereof in any manner or for any purpose, and one or more of such persons do any act to effect the object of the conspiracy, each shall be fined under this title or imprisoned not more than five years, or both.
>
> If, however, the offense, the commission of which is the object of the conspiracy, is a misdemeanor only, the punishment for such conspiracy shall not exceed the maximum punishment provided for such misdemeanor.

This general conspiracy statute criminalizes both conspiracies to commit any offense against the United States as well as conspiracies to defraud the United States or its agencies. In referring to conspiracies to defraud the United States, the Department of Justice Criminal Resource Manual 923 notes that "[t]he general purpose of the statute is to protect governmental functions from frustration and distortion through deceptive practices." * * * those activities which courts have held defraud the United States under 18 U.S.C. § 371 affect the government in at least one of three ways: 1) They cheat the government out of money or property; 2) They interfere or obstruct legitimate Government activity; or 3) They make wrongful use of a governmental instrumentality." See also Abraham S. Goldstein, *Conspiracy to Defraud the United States,* 68 YALE L.J. 405 (1959).

C. WHAT CONSTITUTES "PROPERTY"?

1. Intangible Property

CARPENTER v. UNITED STATES

484 U.S. 19 (1987)

Justice WHITE delivered the opinion of the Court.

Petitioners Kenneth Felis and R. Foster Winans were convicted of violating § 10(b) of the Securities Exchange Act of 1934, 48 Stat. 891, 15

U.S.C. § 78j(b),[1] and Rule 10b-5, 17 CFR § 240.10b-5 (1987).[2] They were also found guilty of violating the federal mail and wire fraud statutes, 18 U.S.C. §§ 1341, 1343, and were convicted for conspiracy under 18 U.S.C. § 371. Petitioner David Carpenter, Winans' roommate, was convicted for aiding and abetting. With a minor exception, the Court of Appeals for the Second Circuit affirmed; we granted certiorari.

I

In 1981, Winans became a reporter for the Wall Street Journal (the Journal) and in the summer of 1982 became one of the two writers of a daily column, "Heard on the Street." That column discussed selected stocks or groups of stocks, giving positive and negative information about those stocks and taking "a point of view with respect to investment in the stocks that it reviews." Winans regularly interviewed corporate executives to put together interesting perspectives on the stocks that would be highlighted in upcoming columns, but, at least for the columns at issue here, none contained corporate inside information or any "hold for release" information. Because of the "Heard" column's perceived quality and integrity, it had the potential of affecting the price of the stocks which it examined. The District Court concluded on the basis of testimony presented at trial that the "Heard" column "does have an impact on the market, difficult though it may be to quantify in any particular case."

The official policy and practice at the Journal was that prior to publication, the contents of the column were the Journal's confidential information. Despite the rule, with which Winans was familiar, he entered into a scheme in October 1983 with Peter Brant and petitioner Felis, both connected with the Kidder Peabody brokerage firm in New York City, to give them advance information as to the timing and contents of the "Heard" column. This permitted Brant and Felis and another conspirator, David

---

[1] Section 10(b) provides: "It shall be unlawful for any person, directly or indirectly, by the use of any means or instrumentality of interstate commerce or of the mails, or of any facility of any national securities exchange— * * *

"(b) To use or employ, in connection with the purchase or sale of any security registered on a national securities exchange or any security not so registered, any manipulative or deceptive device or contrivance in contravention of such rules and regulations as the [Securities and Exchange] Commission may prescribe as necessary or appropriate in the public interest or for the protection of investors."

[2] Rule 10b-5 provides: "It shall be unlawful for any person, directly or indirectly, by the use of any means or instrumentality of interstate commerce, or of the mails or of any national securities exchange, "(a) To employ any device, scheme, or artifice to defraud, "(b) To make any untrue statement of a material fact or to omit to state a material fact necessary in order to make the statements made, in the light of the circumstances under which they were made, not misleading, or "(c) To engage in any act, practice, or course of business which operates or would operate as a fraud or deceit upon any person, "in connection with the purchase or sale of any security."

Clark, a client of Brant, to buy or sell based on the probable impact of the column on the market. Profits were to be shared. The conspirators agreed that the scheme would not affect the journalistic purity of the "Heard" column, and the District Court did not find that the contents of any of the articles were altered to further the profit potential of petitioners' stock-trading scheme. Over a 4-month period, the brokers made prepublication trades on the basis of information given them by Winans about the contents of some 27 "Heard" columns. The net profits from these trades were about $690,000.

In November 1983, correlations between the "Heard" articles and trading in the Clark and Felis accounts were noted at Kidder Peabody and inquiries began. Brant and Felis denied knowing anyone at the Journal and took steps to conceal the trades. Later, the Securities and Exchange Commission began an investigation. Questions were met by denials both by the brokers at Kidder Peabody and by Winans at the Journal. As the investigation progressed, the conspirators quarreled, and on March 29, 1984, Winans and Carpenter went to the SEC and revealed the entire scheme. This indictment and a bench trial followed. Brant, who had pleaded guilty under a plea agreement, was a witness for the Government. * * *

The Court is evenly divided with respect to the convictions under the securities laws and for that reason affirms the judgment below on those counts. For the reasons that follow, we also affirm the judgment with respect to the mail and wire fraud convictions.

II

Petitioners assert that their activities were not a scheme to defraud the Journal within the meaning of the mail and wire fraud statutes;[6] and that in any event, they did not obtain any "money or property" from the Journal, which is a necessary element of the crime under our decision last Term in McNally v. United States [p. 147]. We are unpersuaded by either submission and address the latter first.

We held in *McNally* that the mail fraud statute does not reach "schemes to defraud citizens of their intangible rights to honest and impartial government," and that the statute is "limited in scope to the protection of property rights." Petitioners argue that the Journal's interest in prepublication confidentiality for the "Heard" columns is no more than an intangible consideration outside the reach of § 1341; nor does that law, it is urged, protect against mere injury to reputation. This is not a case like *McNally,* however. The Journal, as Winans' employer, was defrauded of much more than its contractual right to his honest and faithful service, an

---

[6] The mail and wire fraud statutes share the same language in relevant part, and accordingly we apply the same analysis to both sets of offenses here.

interest too ethereal in itself to fall within the protection of the mail fraud statute, which "had its origin in the desire to protect individual property rights." Here, the object of the scheme was to take the Journal's confidential business information—the publication schedule and contents of the "Heard" column—and its intangible nature does not make it any less "property" protected by the mail and wire fraud statutes. *McNally* did not limit the scope of § 1341 to tangible as distinguished from intangible property rights.

Both courts below expressly referred to the Journal's interest in the confidentiality of the contents and timing of the "Heard" column as a property right, and we agree with that conclusion. Confidential business information has long been recognized as property. See Ruckelshaus v. Monsanto Co., 467 U.S. 986, 1001-1004 (1984); Dirks v. SEC, 463 U.S. 646, 653, n. 10 (1983); Board of Trade of Chicago v. Christie Grain & Stock Co., 198 U.S. 236, 250-251 (1905); cf. 5 U.S.C. § 552(b)(4). "Confidential information acquired or compiled by a corporation in the course and conduct of its business is a species of property to which the corporation has the exclusive right and benefit, and which a court of equity will protect through the injunctive process or other appropriate remedy." 3 W. Fletcher, Cyclopedia of Law of Private Corporations § 857.1, p. 260 (rev. ed. 1986) (footnote omitted). The Journal had a property right in keeping confidential and making exclusive use, prior to publication, of the schedule and contents of the "Heard" column. Christie Grain, supra. As the Court has observed before: "[N]ews matter, however little susceptible of ownership or dominion in the absolute sense, is stock in trade, to be gathered at the cost of enterprise, organization, skill, labor, and money, and to be distributed and sold to those who will pay money for it, as for any other merchandise." International News Service v. Associated Press, 248 U.S. 215, 236 (1918).

Petitioners' arguments that they did not interfere with the Journal's use of the information or did not publicize it and deprive the Journal of the first public use of it miss the point. The confidential information was generated from the business, and the business had a right to decide how to use it prior to disclosing it to the public. Petitioners cannot successfully contend based on *Associated Press* that a scheme to defraud requires a monetary loss, such as giving the information to a competitor; it is sufficient that the Journal has been deprived of its right to exclusive use of the information, for exclusivity is an important aspect of confidential business information and most private property for that matter.

We cannot accept petitioners' further argument that Winans' conduct in revealing prepublication information was no more than a violation of workplace rules and did not amount to fraudulent activity that is proscribed by the mail fraud statute. Sections 1341 and 1343 reach any scheme to deprive another of money or property by means of false or fraudulent pretenses, representations, or promises. As we observed last Term in *McNally*, the words "to defraud" in the mail fraud statute have the "common understanding" of "'wronging one in his property rights by dishonest methods or schemes,' and 'usually signify the deprivation of something of value by trick, deceit, chicane or overreaching.'" 483 U.S., at 358 (quoting Hammerschmidt v. United States). The concept of "fraud" includes the act of embezzlement, which is " 'the fraudulent appropriation to one's own use of the money or goods entrusted to one's care by another.' " Grin v. Shine, 187 U.S. 181, 189 (1902).

The District Court found that Winans' undertaking at the Journal was not to reveal prepublication information about his column, a promise that became a sham when in violation of his duty he passed along to his co-conspirators confidential information belonging to the Journal, pursuant to an ongoing scheme to share profits from trading in anticipation of the "Heard" column's impact on the stock market. * * * As the New York courts have recognized: "It is well established, as a general proposition, that a person who acquires special knowledge or information by virtue of a confidential or fiduciary relationship with another is not free to exploit that knowledge or information for his own personal benefit but must account to his principal for any profits derived therefrom." Diamond v. Oreamuno, 24 N.Y.2d 494, 497, 301 N.Y.S.2d 78, 80, 248 N.E.2d 910, 912 (1969); see also Restatement (Second) of Agency §§ 388, Comment c, 396(c) (1958).

We have little trouble in holding that the conspiracy here to trade on the Journal's confidential information is not outside the reach of the mail and wire fraud statutes, provided the other elements of the offenses are satisfied. The Journal's business information that it intended to be kept confidential was its property; the declaration to that effect in the employee manual merely removed any doubts on that score and made the finding of specific intent to defraud that much easier. Winans continued in the employ of the Journal, appropriating its confidential business information for his own use, all the while pretending to perform his duty of safeguarding it. In fact, he told his editors twice about leaks of confidential information not related to the stock-trading scheme, demonstrating both his knowledge that the Journal viewed information concerning the "Heard" column as confidential and his deceit as he played the role of a loyal employee. Furthermore, the District Court's conclusion that each of the petitioners acted with the required specific intent to defraud is strongly supported by the evidence.

Lastly, we reject the submission that using the wires and the mail to print and send the Journal to its customers did not satisfy the requirement that those mediums be used to execute the scheme at issue. The courts below were quite right in observing that circulation of the "Heard" column was not only anticipated but an essential part of the scheme. Had the column not been made available to Journal customers, there would have been no effect on stock prices and no likelihood of profiting from the information leaked by Winans. * * *

Affirmed.

NOTES AND QUESTIONS

1. ***Securities Fraud.*** The Court was equally divided and therefore affirmed the securities fraud convictions. The lower court had accepted a misappropriation theory as the basis for finding a breach of section 10(b) and Rule 10b-5. See United States v. Carpenter, 791 F.2d 1024 (2d Cir. 1986). In *United States v. O'Hagan*, 561 U.S. 642 (1997), the Supreme Court endorsed the use of the misappropriation theory. The Court held that the "the misappropriation theory outlaws trading on the basis of nonpublic information by a corporate 'outsider' in breach of a duty owed not to a trading party, but to the source of the information. The misappropriation theory is thus designed to protec[t] the integrity of the securities markets against abuses by 'outsiders' to a corporation who have access to confidential information that will affect th[e] corporation's security price when revealed, but who owe no fiduciary or other duty to that corporation's shareholders." See also Jennifer H. Arlen & William J. Carney, *Vicarious Liability for Fraud on Securities Markets: Theory and Evidence*, 1992 U. OF ILL. L. REV. 691 (1992).

2. ***Conspiracy to Commit Insider Trading.*** When one adds a charge of conspiracy to commit insider trading, proof of the conspiracy is required. This can require an agreement to pass on the insider information. In *United States v. McDermott*, 245 F.3d 133, 138 (2d Cir. 2001), a Second Circuit court stated "[w]e decline to hold as a matter of law that a cheating heart must foresee a cheating heart."

COMMENTS ON CARPENTER

Excerpts from John C. Coffee, Jr., *Hush!: The Criminal Status of Confidential Information After* McNally *and* Carpenter *and the Enduring Problem of Overcriminalization*, 26 Am. Crim. L. Rev. 121 (1988).

> In *Carpenter*, the Court took two important doctrinal steps. First, it recognized that there can be intangible forms of property, of which a victim may be defrauded. This seems an obvious conclusion, as one can imagine many valuable forms of intangible property: for example, patents, copyrights, contract rights, etc. Second, it found that one form of intangible property, confidential business information, is embezzled whenever an employee reveals it to others so as to deprive the employer of exclusive possession.
>
> In contrast to this remarkable first step, the second step is extraordinary, because it eliminates any need for a showing of actual or intended economic injury to the employer. * * *
>
> The *Carpenter* decision is also a marked departure from prior law in its casual assertion that depriving the owner of exclusive possession of information amounts to an embezzlement. The history of

embezzlement and the law of theft is long and tortuous, but one historical fact is clear beyond serious argument: intangibles could not be stolen or embezzled. * * *

Excerpts from Craig M. Bradley, *Foreword: Mail Fraud After* McNally *and* Carpenter: *The Essence of Fraud,* 79 J. Crim. L. & Criminology 573 (1988).

* * * [I]t is not clear how the Journal was deprived of "property" here. As the case was originally tried by the government, the fraudulent behavior was the failure to disclose the breach and the harm to the victim was the loss of the Journal's intangible right to the honest and faithful services of its employee. After *McNally,* the government filed a supplemental brief urging that the fraudulent behavior was the embezzlement of confidential information and the harm was the loss of the exclusive use of that information. The Court adopted this latter theory, endeavoring to conform to the 'property' limitation of *McNally.*

By holding that "the concept of fraud includes the act of embezzlement" the Court ignored the very history of fraud that it had relied on in *McNally*. On the contrary, the crime of fraud had always been understood by both Congress and the Supreme Court as proscribing only the fraud of false pretenses, rather than any crime that involved "fraudulent" behavior, which crimes included larceny, embezzlement, forgery, and larceny by trick as well as false pretenses. According to the Court's holding in *Carpenter,* any employee who helps himself to money or property which his or her employer has entrusted to him or her is now guilty of the federal offense of wire or mail fraud if only the mails or wires are used or caused to be used in some way. The Congress that enacted this statute would surely have been surprised at this declaration.

But while it was an overstatement by the Court to suggest that any embezzlement is a "fraud," it is fair to say that Winans' acts constituted "fraud," whether they are characterized as "embezzlement" or "false pretenses." [Professor Bradley had previously noted that there had been a "breach of fiduciary duty not to disclose confidential information, and a further duty to disclose such breaches to his employer," that created a potential for harm to the employer, and "this had long been recognized as satisfying the 'deceit' element of fraud."] The difficulty arises because neither of these traditional crimes were defined in terms of intangible property.

* * * Contrary to *Carpenter,* the legislative history as well as the general understanding of "fraud" at the time of the enactment of the mail fraud statute suggests that "fraud" was limited to money or tangible property, * * *.

> [O]nce it is recognized that the term "defraud" implied a deprivation of tangible property, the fact, as the Court observed in *Carpenter,* that "confidential business information has long been recognized as property" in other contexts is irrelevant. Whether or not confidential information had long been regarded as "property," it and other intangibles, such as a business' reputation, had not long been recognized, and certainly were not recognized in 1872 and 1909, as covered by a statute prohibiting "fraud."
>
> The Court put itself in a box in *McNally* from which it could only escape, in *Carpenter,* by a gross distortion of the historical evidence on which *McNally* had been based. A far better approach would have been to have recognized the problem in *McNally* as being the lack of an identifiable victim who suffered economic harm, rather than holding that a traditional view of "property" was an essential element of fraud. Then, in *Carpenter,* it could have noted the presence of a specific victim and a potential economic loss to that victim as satisfying the *McNally* requirement. In response to the argument that "fraud" traditionally required a deprivation of tangible property, the Court in *Carpenter,* not constrained by a contrary reliance on history in *McNally,* could simply have agreed with this point but held, forthrightly, that, in this information age much that is intangible is just as valuable as tangible property. The key question is not what kind of property was involved but whether there was an economic loss to an identifiable victim as well as an unjust gain to the defendant. As will be argued, while this is not precisely what the Court said, this line of reasoning is the only way to explain what it did in *McNally* and Carpenter. * * *
>
> *McNally* and *Carpenter,* read together, require an economic gain to the defendant and loss to the victim (or the prospect of same) but do not require that this gain and loss be of "property" as that term had been understood by Congress. * * *

2. Licenses

CLEVELAND v. UNITED STATES
531 U.S. 12 (2000)

Justice GINSBURG delivered the opinion of the Court.

This case presents the question whether the federal mail fraud statute, 18 U.S.C. § 1341, reaches false statements made in an application for a state license. Section 1341 proscribes use of the mails in furtherance of "any scheme or artifice to defraud, or for obtaining money or property by means of false or fraudulent pretenses, representations, or promises." Petitioner Carl W. Cleveland and others were prosecuted under this federal measure for making false statements in applying to the Louisiana State Police for permission to operate video poker machines. We conclude that permits or licenses of this order do not qualify as "property" within § 1341's compass. It does not suffice, we clarify, that the object of the fraud may become property in the recipient's hands; for purposes of the mail fraud statute, the thing obtained must be property in the hands of the victim. State and municipal licenses in general, and Louisiana's video poker licenses in particular, we hold, do not rank as "property," for purposes of § 1341, in the hands of the official licensor. * * *

Louisiana law allows certain businesses to operate video poker machines. La.Rev.Stat. Ann. §§ 27:301 to 27:324 (West Supp.2000). The State itself, however, does not run such machinery. The law requires prospective owners of video poker machines to apply for a license from the State. § 27:306. The licenses are not transferable, § 27:311(G), and must be renewed annually, La. Admin.Code, tit. 42, § 2405(B)(3) (2000). To qualify for a license, an applicant must meet suitability requirements designed to ensure that licensees have good character and fiscal integrity. La.Rev.Stat. Ann. § 27:310 (West Supp.2000).

In 1992, Fred Goodson and his family formed a limited partnership, Truck Stop Gaming, Ltd. (TSG), in order to participate in the video poker business at their truck stop in Slidell, Louisiana. Cleveland, a New Orleans lawyer, assisted Goodson in preparing TSG's application for a video poker license. The application required TSG to identify its partners and to submit personal financial statements for all partners. It also required TSG to affirm that the listed partners were the sole beneficial owners of the business and that no partner held an interest in the partnership merely as an agent or nominee, or intended to transfer the interest in the future.

TSG's application identified Goodson's adult children, Alex and Maria, as the sole beneficial owners of the partnership. It also showed that Goodson and Cleveland's law firm had loaned Alex and Maria all initial capital for the partnership and that Goodson was TSG's general manager. In May 1992, the State approved the application and issued a license. TSG successfully renewed the license in 1993, 1994, and 1995 pursuant to La. Admin. Code, tit. 42, § 2405(B)(3) (2000). Each renewal application identified no ownership interests other than those of Alex and Maria.

In 1996, the FBI discovered evidence that Cleveland and Goodson had participated in a scheme to bribe state legislators to vote in a manner favorable to the video poker industry. The Government charged Cleveland and Goodson with multiple counts of money laundering under 18 U.S.C. § 1957, as well as racketeering and conspiracy under § 1962. Among the predicate acts supporting these charges were four counts of mail fraud under § 1341. The indictment alleged that Cleveland and Goodson had violated § 1341 by fraudulently concealing that they were the true owners of TSG in the initial license application and three renewal applications mailed to the State. They concealed their ownership interests, according to the Government, because they had tax and financial problems that could have undermined their suitability to receive a video poker license. * * *

Before trial, Cleveland moved to dismiss the mail fraud counts on the ground that the alleged fraud did not deprive the State of "property" under § 1341. The District Court denied the motion, concluding that "licenses constitute property even before they are issued." 951 F.Supp. 1249, 1261 (E.D.La.1997). A jury found Cleveland guilty on two counts of mail fraud (based on the 1994 and 1995 license renewals) and on money laundering, racketeering, and conspiracy counts predicated on the mail fraud. The District Court sentenced Cleveland to 121 months in prison.

On appeal, Cleveland again argued that Louisiana had no property interest in video poker licenses, relying on several Court of Appeals decisions holding that the government does not relinquish "property" for purposes of § 1341 when it issues a permit or license. See United States v. Shotts, 145 F.3d 1289, 1296 (C.A.11 1998) (license to operate a bail bonds business); United States v. Schwartz, 924 F.2d 410, 418 (C.A.2 1991) (arms export license); United States v. Granberry, 908 F.2d 278, 280 (C.A.8 1990) (school bus operator's permit); Toulabi v. United States, 875 F.2d 122, 125 (C.A.7 1989) (chauffeur's license); United States v. Dadanian, 856 F.2d 1391, 1392 (C.A.9 1988) (gambling license); United States v. Murphy, 836 F.2d 248, 254 (C.A.6 1988) (license to conduct charitable bingo games).

The Court of Appeals for the Fifth Circuit nevertheless affirmed Cleveland's conviction and sentence, United States v. Bankston, 182 F.3d 296, 309 (1999), considering itself bound by its holding in United States v. Salvatore, 110 F.3d 1131, 1138 (1997), that Louisiana video poker licenses constitute "property" in the hands of the State. Two other Circuits have concluded that the issuing authority has a property interest in unissued licenses under § 1341. United States v. Bucuvalas, 970 F.2d 937, 945 (C.A.1 1992) (entertainment and liquor license); United States v. Martinez, 905 F.2d 709, 715 (C.A.3 1990) (medical license).

We granted certiorari to resolve the conflict among the Courts of Appeals, 529 U.S. 1017, 120 S.Ct. 1416, 146 L.Ed.2d 309 (2000), and now reverse the Fifth Circuit's judgment. * * *

In McNally v. United States, [p. 147], this Court held that the federal mail fraud statute is "limited in scope to the protection of property rights." *McNally* reversed the mail fraud convictions of two individuals charged with participating in "a self-dealing patronage scheme" that defrauded Kentucky citizens of "the right to have the Commonwealth's affairs conducted honestly." At the time *McNally* was decided, federal prosecutors had been using § 1341 to attack various forms of corruption that deprived victims of "intangible rights" unrelated to money or property. Reviewing the history of § 1341, we concluded that "the original impetus behind the mail fraud statute was to protect the people from schemes to deprive them of their money or property." * * *

Soon after *McNally,* in Carpenter v. United States, [p. 156], we again stated that § 1341 protects property rights only. *Carpenter* upheld convictions under § 1341 and the federal wire fraud statute, 18 U.S.C. § 1343, of defendants who had defrauded the Wall Street Journal of confidential business information. Citing decisions of this Court as well as a corporate lawtreatise, we observed that "[c]onfidential business information has long been recognized as property."

The following year, Congress amended the law specifically to cover one of the "intangible rights" that lower courts had protected under § 1341 prior to *McNally:* "the intangible right of honest services." Anti-Drug Abuse Act of 1988, § 7603(a), 18 U.S.C. § 1346. Significantly, Congress covered only the intangible right of honest services even though federal courts, relying on *McNally,* had dismissed, for want of monetary loss to any victim, prosecutions under § 1341 for diverse forms of public corruption, including licensing fraud.

In this case, there is no assertion that Louisiana's video poker licensing scheme implicates the intangible right of honest services. The question presented is whether, for purposes of the federal mail fraud statute, a government regulator parts with "property" when it issues a license. For the reasons we now set out, we hold that § 1341 does not reach fraud in obtaining a state or municipal license of the kind here involved, for such a license is not "property" in the government regulator's hands. Again, as we said in *McNally,* "[i]f Congress desires to go further, it must speak more clearly than it has."

To begin with, we think it beyond genuine dispute that whatever interests Louisiana might be said to have in its video poker licenses, the State's core concern is *regulatory.* Louisiana recognizes the importance of "public confidence and trust that gaming activities ... are conducted honestly and are free from criminal and corruptive elements." * * * The video poker licensing statute accordingly asserts the State's "legitimate interest in providing strict regulation of all persons, practices, associations, and activities related to the operation of ... establishments licensed to offer video draw poker devices." The statute assigns the Office of State Police, a part of the Department of Public Safety and Corrections, the responsibility to promulgate rules and regulations concerning the licensing process. It also authorizes the State Police to deny, condition, suspend, or revoke licenses, to levy fines of up to $1,000 per violation of any rule, and to inspect all premises where video poker devices are offered for play. In addition, the statute defines criminal penalties for unauthorized use of video poker devices, and prescribes detailed suitability requirements for licensees.

In short, the statute establishes a typical regulatory program. It licenses, subject to certain conditions, engagement in pursuits that private actors may not undertake without official authorization. In this regard, it resembles other licensing schemes long characterized by this Court as exercises of state police powers. * * *

Acknowledging Louisiana's regulatory interests, the Government offers two reasons why the State also has a property interest in its video poker licenses. First, the State receives a substantial sum of money in exchange for each license and continues to receive payments from the licensee as long as the license remains in effect. Second, the State has significant control over the issuance, renewal, suspension, and revocation of licenses.

Without doubt, Louisiana has a substantial economic stake in the video poker industry. The State collects an upfront "processing fee" for each new license application, * * * a separate "processing fee" for each renewal application, * * * an "annual fee" from each device owner, * * * an additional "device operation" fee, * * * and, most importantly, a fixed percentage of net revenue from each video poker device. It is hardly evident, however, why these tolls should make video poker licenses "property" in the hands of the State. The State receives the lion's share of its expected revenue not while the licenses remain in its own hands, but only *after* they have been issued to licensees. Licenses pre-issuance do not generate an ongoing stream of revenue. At most, they entitle the State to collect a processing fee from applicants for new licenses. Were an entitlement of this order sufficient to establish a state property right, one could scarcely avoid the conclusion that States have property rights in any license or permit requiring an upfront fee, including drivers' licenses, medical licenses, and fishing and hunting licenses. Such licenses, as the Government itself concedes, are "purely regulatory." * * *

Tellingly, as to the character of Louisiana's stake in its video poker licenses, the Government nowhere alleges that Cleveland defrauded the State of any money to which the State was entitled by law. Indeed, there is no dispute that TSG paid the State of Louisiana its proper share of revenue, which totaled more than $1.2 million, between 1993 and 1995. If Cleveland defrauded the State of "property," the nature of that property cannot be economic.

Addressing this concern, the Government argues that Cleveland frustrated the State's right to control the issuance, renewal, and revocation of video poker licenses under La.Rev.Stat. Ann. §§ 27:306, 27:308 (West Supp.2000). The Fifth Circuit has characterized the protected interest as "Louisiana's right to choose the persons to whom it issues video poker licenses." * * * But far from composing an interest that "has long been recognized as property," these intangible rights of allocation, exclusion, and control amount to no more and no less than Louisiana's sovereign power to regulate. Notably, the Government overlooks the fact that these rights include the distinctively sovereign authority to impose criminal penalties for violations of the licensing scheme, La.Rev.Stat. Ann. § 27:309 (West Supp.2000), including making false statements in a license application, § 27:309(A). Even when tied to an expected stream of revenue, the State's right of control does not create a property interest any more than a law licensing liquor sales in a State that levies a sales tax on liquor. Such regulations are paradigmatic exercises of the States' traditional police powers. * * *

We reject the Government's theories of property rights not simply because they stray from traditional concepts of property. We resist the Government's reading of § 1341 as well because it invites us to approve a sweeping expansion of federal criminal jurisdiction in the absence of a clear statement by Congress. Equating issuance of licenses or permits with deprivation of property would subject to federal mail fraud prosecution a wide range of conduct traditionally regulated by state and local authorities. We note in this regard that Louisiana's video poker statute typically and unambiguously imposes criminal penalties for making false statements on license applications. * * * Moreover, to the extent that the word "property" is ambiguous as placed in § 1341, we have instructed that "ambiguity concerning the ambit of criminal statutes should be resolved in favor of lenity." Rewis v. United States, 401 U.S. 808, 812, 91 S.Ct. 1056, 28 L.Ed.2d 493 (1971). This interpretive guide is especially appropriate in construing § 1341 because, as this case demonstrates, mail fraud is a predicate offense under RICO, 18 U.S.C. § 1961(1) (1994 ed., Supp. IV), and the money laundering statute, § 1956(c)(7)(A). In deciding what is "property" under § 1341, we think "it is appropriate, before we choose the harsher alternative, to require that Congress should have spoken in language that is clear and definite." * * *

Although we do not here question that video poker licensees may have property interests in their licenses, we nevertheless disagree with the Government's reading of § 1341. In *McNally,* we recognized that "[b]ecause the two phrases identifying the proscribed schemes appear in the disjunctive, it is arguable that they are to be construed independently." But we rejected that construction of the statute, instead concluding that the second phrase simply modifies the first by "ma[king] it unmistakable that the statute reached false promises and misrepresentations as to the future as well as other frauds involving money or property." Indeed, directly contradicting the Government's view, we said that "the mail fraud statute ... had its origin in the desire to protect individual property rights, and any benefit which the Government derives from the statute must be limited to *the Government's interests as property holder*." * * * For reasons already stated, * * * we decline to attribute to § 1341 a purpose so encompassing where Congress has not made such a design clear.

We conclude that § 1341 requires the object of the fraud to be "property" in the victim's hands and that a Louisiana video poker license in the State's hands is not "property" under § 1341. Absent clear statement by Congress, we will not read the mail fraud statute to place under federal superintendence a vast array of conduct traditionally policed by the States. Our holding means that Cleveland's § 1341 conviction must be vacated. Accordingly, the judgment of the United States Court of Appeals for the Fifth Circuit is reversed, and the case is remanded for further proceedings consistent with this opinion. * * *

D. INTANGIBLE RIGHT TO HONEST SERVICES

CONGRESSIONAL OVERRULING OF *MCNALLY*

As part of the Anti-Drug Abuse Act of 1988, Congress enacted 18 U.S.C.A. § 1346 which provides:

> For the purposes of this chapter, the term "scheme or artifice to defraud" includes a scheme or artifice to deprive another of the intangible right of honest services.

UNITED STATES v. SKILLING
561 U.S. 358 (2010)

Justice GINSBURG delivered the opinion of the Court.

In 2001, Enron Corporation, then the seventh highest-revenue-grossing company in America, crashed into bankruptcy. We consider in this opinion two questions arising from the prosecution of Jeffrey Skilling, a longtime Enron executive, for crimes committed before the corporation's collapse. First, did pretrial publicity and community prejudice prevent Skilling from obtaining a fair trial? Second, did the jury improperly convict Skilling of conspiracy to commit "honest-services" wire fraud, 18 U.S.C. §§ 371, 1343, 1346?

Answering no to both questions, the Fifth Circuit affirmed Skilling's convictions. We conclude, in common with the Court of Appeals, that Skilling's fair-trial argument fails; Skilling, we hold, did not establish that a presumption of juror prejudice arose or that actual bias infected the jury that tried him. But we disagree with the Fifth Circuit's honest-services ruling. In proscribing fraudulent deprivations of "the intangible right of honest services," § 1346, Congress intended at least to reach schemes to defraud involving bribes and kickbacks. Construing the honest-services statute to extend beyond that core meaning, we conclude, would encounter a vagueness shoal. We therefore hold that § 1346 covers only bribery and kickback schemes. Because Skilling's alleged misconduct entailed no bribe or kickback, it does not fall within § 1346's proscription. We therefore affirm in part and vacate in part.

I

Founded in 1985, Enron Corporation grew from its headquarters in Houston, Texas, into one of the world's leading energy companies. Skilling launched his career there in 1990 when Kenneth Lay, the company's founder, hired him to head an Enron subsidiary. Skilling steadily rose through the corporation's ranks, serving as president and chief operating officer, and then, beginning in February 2001, as chief executive officer. Six months later, on August 14, 2001, Skilling resigned from Enron.

Less than four months after Skilling's departure, Enron spiraled into bankruptcy. The company's stock, which had traded at $90 per share in August 2000, plummeted to pennies per share in late 2001. Attempting to comprehend what caused the corporation's collapse, the U.S. Department of Justice formed an Enron Task Force, comprising prosecutors and FBI agents from around the Nation. The Government's investigation uncovered an elaborate conspiracy to prop up Enron's short-run stock prices by overstating the company's financial well-being. In the years following Enron's bankruptcy, the Government prosecuted dozens of Enron employees who participated in the scheme. In time, the Government worked its way up the corporation's chain of command: On July 7, 2004, a grand jury indicted Skilling, Lay, and Richard Causey, Enron's former chief accounting officer.

These three defendants, the indictment alleged,

> "engaged in a wide-ranging scheme to deceive the investing public, including Enron's shareholders, ... about the true performance of Enron's businesses by: (a) manipulating Enron's publicly reported financial results; and (b) making public statements and representations about Enron's financial performance and results that were false and misleading." * * *

Skilling and his co-conspirators, the indictment continued, "enriched themselves as a result of the scheme through salary, bonuses, grants of stock and stock options, other profits, and prestige." * * *

Count 1 of the indictment charged Skilling with conspiracy to commit securities and wire fraud; in particular, it alleged that Skilling had sought to "depriv[e] Enron and its shareholders of the intangible right of [his] honest services." * * * The indictment further charged Skilling with more than 25 substantive counts of securities fraud, wire fraud, making false representations to Enron's auditors, and insider trading. * * *

On December 28, 2005, three weeks before the date scheduled for the commencement of trial, Causey pleaded guilty. * * * Following a 4-month trial and nearly five days of deliberation, the jury found Skilling guilty of 19 counts, including the honest-services-fraud conspiracy charge, and not guilty of 9 insider-trading counts. The District Court sentenced Skilling to 292 months' imprisonment, 3 years' supervised release, and $45 million in restitution.

II

In sum, Skilling failed to establish that a presumption of prejudice arose or that actual bias infected the jury that tried him. Jurors, the trial court correctly comprehended, need not enter the box with empty heads in order to determine the facts impartially. "It is sufficient if the juror[s] can lay aside [their] impression[s] or opinion[s] and render a verdict based on the evidence presented in court." * * * Taking account of the full record, rather than incomplete exchanges selectively culled from it, we find no cause to upset the lower courts' judgment that Skilling's jury met that measure. We therefore affirm the Fifth Circuit's ruling that Skilling received a fair trial.

III

We next consider whether Skilling's conspiracy conviction was premised on an improper theory of honest-services wire fraud. The honest-services statute, § 1346, Skilling maintains, is unconstitutionally vague. Alternatively, he contends that his conduct does not fall within the statute's compass.

A

To place Skilling's constitutional challenge in context, we first review the origin and subsequent application of the honest-services doctrine.

1

Enacted in 1872, the original mail-fraud provision, the predecessor of the modern-day mail-and wire-fraud laws, proscribed, without further elaboration, use of the mails to advance "any scheme or artifice to defraud." See McNally v. United States, [p. 147]. In 1909, Congress amended the statute to prohibit, as it does today, "any scheme or artifice to defraud, or for obtaining money or property by means of false or fraudulent pretenses, representations, or promises." § 1341 (emphasis added); * * * Emphasizing Congress' disjunctive phrasing, the Courts of Appeals, one after the other, interpreted the term "scheme or artifice to defraud" to include deprivations not only of money or property, but also of intangible rights.

In an opinion credited with first presenting the intangible-rights theory, Shushan v. United States, 117 F.2d 110 (1941), the Fifth Circuit reviewed the mail-fraud prosecution of a public official who allegedly accepted bribes from entrepreneurs in exchange for urging city action beneficial to the bribe payers. "It is not true that because the [city] was to make and did make a saving by the operations there could not have been an intent to defraud," the Court of Appeals maintained. * * * "A scheme to get a public contract on more favorable terms than would likely be got otherwise by bribing a public official," the court observed, "would not only be a plan to commit the crime of bribery, but would also be a scheme to defraud the public." * * *

The Fifth Circuit's opinion in Shushan stimulated the development of an "honest-services" doctrine. Unlike fraud in which the victim's loss of money or property supplied the defendant's gain, with one the mirror image of the other, * * *, the honest-services theory targeted corruption that lacked similar symmetry. While the offender profited, the betrayed party suffered no deprivation of money or property; instead, a third party, who had not been deceived, provided the enrichment. For example, if a city mayor (the offender) accepted a bribe from a third party in exchange for awarding that party a city contract, yet the contract terms were the same as any that could have been negotiated at arm's length, the city (the betrayed party) would suffer no tangible loss. * * * Even if the scheme occasioned a money or property gain for the betrayed party, courts reasoned, actionable harm lay in the denial of that party's right to the offender's "honest services." * * *

"Most often these cases ... involved bribery of public officials," * * *, but courts also recognized private-sector honest-services fraud. * * *Over time, "[a]n increasing number of courts" recognized that "a recreant employee"-public or private-"c[ould] be prosecuted under [the mail-fraud statute] if he breache[d] his allegiance to his employer by accepting bribes or kickbacks in the course of his employment," * * *; by 1982, all Courts of Appeals had embraced the honest-services theory of fraud, Hurson, Limiting the Federal Mail Fraud Statute-A Legislative Approach, 20 Am.Crim. L.Rev. 423, 456 (1983). * * *

2

In 1987, this Court, in McNally v. United States, stopped the development of the intangible-rights doctrine in its tracks. McNally involved a state officer who, in selecting Kentucky's insurance agent, arranged to procure a share of the agent's commissions via kickbacks paid to companies the official partially controlled. * * * The prosecutor did not charge that, "in the absence of the alleged scheme[,] the Commonwealth would have paid a lower premium or secured better insurance." * * * Instead, the prosecutor maintained that the kickback scheme "defraud [ed] the citizens and government of Kentucky of their right to have the Commonwealth's affairs conducted honestly." * * *

We held that the scheme did not qualify as mail fraud. "Rather than constru[ing] the statute in a manner that leaves its outer boundaries ambiguous and involves the Federal Government in setting standards of disclosure and good government for local and state officials," we read the statute "as limited in scope to the protection of property rights." * * * "If Congress desires to go further," we stated, "it must speak more clearly." * * *

3

Congress responded swiftly. The following year, it enacted a new statute "specifically to cover one of the 'ntangible rights' that lower courts had protected ... prior to McNally: 'the intangible right of honest services.'" * * * In full, the honest-services statute stated:

> "For the purposes of th[e] chapter [of the United States Code that prohibits, inter alia, mail fraud, § 1341, and wire fraud, § 1343], the term 'scheme or artifice to defraud' includes a scheme or artifice to deprive another of the intangible right of honest services." § 1346.

B

Congress, Skilling charges, reacted quickly but not clearly: He asserts that § 1346 is unconstitutionally vague. To satisfy due process, "a penal statute [must] define the criminal offense [1] with sufficient definiteness that ordinary people can understand what conduct is prohibited and [2] in a manner that does not encourage arbitrary and discriminatory enforcement." Kolender v. Lawson, 461 U.S. 352, 357, 103 S.Ct. 1855, 75 L.Ed.2d 903 (1983). The void-for-vagueness doctrine embraces these requirements.

According to Skilling, § 1346 meets neither of the two due process essentials. First, the phrase "the intangible right of honest services," he contends, does not adequately define what behavior it bars. * * * Second, he alleges, § 1346's "standardless sweep allows policemen, prosecutors, and juries to pursue their personal predilections," thereby "facilitat[ing] opportunistic and arbitrary prosecutions." * * *

In urging invalidation of § 1346, Skilling swims against our case law's current, which requires us, if we can, to construe, not condemn, Congress' enactments. * * *. Alert to § 1346's potential breadth, the Courts of Appeals have divided on how best to interpret the statute.[37] Uniformly, however, they have declined to throw out the statute as irremediably vague.

We agree that § 1346 should be construed rather than invalidated. First, we look to the doctrine developed in pre-McNally cases in an endeavor to ascertain the meaning of the phrase "the intangible right of honest services." Second, to preserve what Congress certainly intended the statute to cover, we pare that body of precedent down to its core: In the main, the pre-McNally cases involved fraudulent schemes to deprive another of honest services through bribes or kickbacks supplied by a third party who had not been deceived. Confined to these paramount applications, § 1346 presents no vagueness problem.

1

There is no doubt that Congress intended § 1346 to refer to and incorporate the honest-services doctrine recognized in Court of Appeals' decisions before *McNally* derailed the intangible-rights theory of fraud. * * * Congress enacted § 1346 on the heels of *McNally* and drafted the statute using that decision's terminology. * * *

---

[37] Courts have disagreed about whether § 1346 prosecutions must be based on a violation of state law, compare, * * *; whether a defendant must contemplate that the victim suffer economic harm, * * *; and whether the defendant must act in pursuit of private gain, * * *.

2

* * * In parsing the Courts of Appeals decisions, we acknowledge that Skilling's vagueness challenge has force, for honest-services decisions preceding *McNally* were not models of clarity or consistency. * * * While the honest-services cases preceding *McNally* dominantly and consistently applied the fraud statute to bribery and kickback schemes-schemes that were the basis of most honest-services prosecutions-there was considerable disarray over the statute's application to conduct outside that core category. In light of this disarray, Skilling urges us, as he urged the Fifth Circuit, to invalidate the statute *in toto*. * * *

It has long been our practice, however, before striking a federal statute as impermissibly vague, to consider whether the prescription is amenable to a limiting construction. * * * Arguing against any limiting construction, Skilling contends that it is impossible to identify a salvageable honest-services core; "the pre-*McNally* caselaw," he asserts, "is a hodgepodge of oft-conflicting holdings" that are "hopelessly unclear." * * * We have rejected an argument of the same tenor before. In Civil Service Comm'n v. Letter Carriers, federal employees challenged a provision of the Hatch Act that incorporated earlier decisions of the United States Civil Service Commission enforcing a similar law. "[T]he several thousand adjudications of the Civil Service Commission," the employees maintained, were "an impenetrable jungle"–"undiscoverable, inconsistent, [and] incapable of yielding any meaningful rules to govern present or future conduct." * * * Mindful that "our task [wa]s not to destroy the Act if we c[ould], but to construe it," we held that "the rules that had evolved over the years from repeated adjudications were subject to sufficiently clear and summary statement." * * *

A similar observation may be made here. Although some applications of the pre-*McNally* honest-services doctrine occasioned disagreement among the Courts of Appeals, these cases do not cloud the doctrine's solid core: The "vast majority" of the honest-services cases involved offenders who, in violation of a fiduciary duty, participated in bribery or kickback schemes. * * * Indeed, the *McNally* case itself, which spurred Congress to enact § 1346, presented a paradigmatic kickback fact pattern. * * * Congress' reversal of *McNally* and reinstatement of the honest-services doctrine, we conclude, can and should be salvaged by confining its scope to the core pre-*McNally* applications. * * *

* * * Both before *McNally* and after § 1346's enactment, Courts of Appeals described schemes involving bribes or kickbacks as "core ... honest services fraud precedents," * * * "paradigm case[s]," * * *; "[t]he most obvious form of honest services fraud," * * *; "core misconduct covered by the statute," * * * "most [of the] honest services cases," * * "typical," * * * "clear-cut," * * *; and "uniformly ... cover[ed],* * *.

In view of this history, there is no doubt that Congress intended § 1346 to reach *at least* bribes and kickbacks. Reading the statute to proscribe a wider range of offensive conduct, we acknowledge, would raise the due process concerns underlying the vagueness doctrine.[43] To preserve the statute without transgressing constitutional limitations, we now hold that § 1346 criminalizes *only* the bribe-and-kickback core of the pre-*McNally* case law.* * *

3

The Government urges us to go further by locating within § 1346's compass another category of proscribed conduct: "undisclosed self-dealing by a public official or private employee-*i.e.,* the taking of official action by the employee that furthers his own undisclosed financial interests while purporting to act in the interests of those to whom he owes a fiduciary duty." * * * "[T]he theory of liability in *McNally* itself was nondisclosure of a conflicting financial interest," the Government observes, and "Congress clearly intended to revive th[at] nondisclosure theory." * * * Moreover, "[a]lthough not as numerous as the bribery and kickback cases," the Government asserts, "the pre-*McNally* cases involving undisclosed self-dealing were abundant." * * *

Neither of these contentions withstands close inspection. *McNally,* as we have already observed, * * * involved a classic kickback scheme: A public official, in exchange for routing Kentucky's insurance business through a middleman company, arranged for that company to share its commissions with entities in which the official held an interest. * * * This was no mere failure to disclose a conflict of interest; rather, the official conspired with a third party so that both would profit from wealth generated by public contracts. * * * Reading § 1346 to proscribe bribes and kickbacks-and nothing more-satisfies Congress' undoubted aim to reverse *McNally* on its facts.

Nor are we persuaded that the pre-*McNally* conflict-of-interest cases constitute core applications of the honest-services doctrine. Although the Courts of Appeals upheld honest-services convictions for "some schemes of non-disclosure and concealment of material information," * * * they reached no consensus on which schemes qualified. In light of the relative infrequency of conflict-of-interest prosecutions in comparison to bribery and kickback charges, and the intercircuit inconsistencies they produced, we conclude that a reasonable limiting construction of § 1346 must exclude this amorphous category of cases.

Further dispelling doubt on this point is the familiar principle that "ambiguity concerning the ambit of criminal statutes should be resolved in favor of lenity." Cleveland, 531 U.S., at 25, 121 S.Ct. 365 (quoting Rewis v.

---

[43] Apprised that a broader reading of § 1346 could render the statute impermissibly vague, Congress, we believe, would have drawn the honest-services line, as we do now, at bribery and kickback schemes. * * *.

United States, 401 U.S. 808, 812, 91 S.Ct. 1056, 28 L.Ed.2d 493 (1971)). "This interpretive guide is especially appropriate in construing [§ 1346] because ... mail [and wire] fraud [are] predicate offense[s] under [the Racketeer Influenced and Corrupt Organizations Act], 18 U.S.C. § 1961(1) * * *, and the money laundering statute, § 1956(c)(7)(A)." * * * Holding that honest-services fraud does not encompass conduct more wide-ranging than the paradigmatic cases of bribes and kickbacks, we resist the Government's less constrained construction absent Congress' clear instruction otherwise. * * *

In sum, our construction of § 1346 "establish[es] a uniform national standard, define[s] honest services with clarity, reach[es] only seriously culpable conduct, and accomplish[es] Congress's goal of 'overruling' *McNally*." Brief for Albert W. Alschuler as Amicus Curiae in Weyhrauch v. United States, * * * "If Congress desires to go further," we reiterate, "it must speak more clearly than it has."[45] * * *

4

Interpreted to encompass only bribery and kickback schemes, § 1346 is not unconstitutionally vague. Recall that the void-for-vagueness doctrine addresses concerns about (1) fair notice and (2) arbitrary and discriminatory prosecutions. * * * A prohibition on fraudulently depriving another of one's honest services by accepting bribes or kickbacks does not present a problem on either score.

As to fair notice, "whatever the school of thought concerning the scope and meaning of § 1346, it has always been 'as plain as a pikestaff that' bribes and kickbacks constitute honest-services fraud," Williams v. United States, 341 U.S. 97, 101 (1951), and the statute's *mens rea* requirement further blunts any notice concern, * * *Today's decision clarifies that no other misconduct falls within § 1346's province. * * *

As to arbitrary prosecutions, we perceive no significant risk that the honest-services statute, as we interpret it today, will be stretched out of shape. Its prohibition on bribes and kickbacks draws content not only from the pre-*McNally* case law, but also from federal statutes proscribing-and

[45] If Congress were to take up the enterprise of criminalizing "undisclosed self-dealing by a public official or private employee," * * * it would have to employ standards of sufficient definiteness and specificity to overcome due process concerns. The Government proposes a standard that prohibits the "taking of official action by the employee that furthers his own undisclosed financial interests while purporting to act in the interests of those to whom he owes a fiduciary duty," so long as the employee acts with a specific intent to deceive and the undisclosed conduct could influence the victim to change its behavior. * * * That formulation, however, leaves many questions unanswered. How direct or significant does the conflicting financial interest have to be? To what extent does the official action have to further that interest in order to amount to fraud? To whom should the disclosure be made and what information should it convey? These questions and others call for particular care in attempting to formulate an adequate criminal prohibition in this context.

defining-similar crimes. See, *e.g.*, 18 U.S.C. §§ 201(b), 666(a)(2); 41 U.S.C. § 52(2) ("The term 'kickback' means any money, fee, commission, credit, gift, gratuity, thing of value, or compensation of any kind which is provided, directly or indirectly, to [enumerated persons] for the purpose of improperly obtaining or rewarding favorable treatment in connection with [enumerated circumstances].").[46] See also, e.g., United States v. Ganim, 510 F.3d 134, 147-149 (C.A.2 2007) (Sotomayor, J.) (reviewing honest-services conviction involving bribery in light of elements of bribery under other federal statutes); United States v. Whitfield, 590 F.3d 325, 352-353 (C.A.5 2009); United States v. Kemp, 500 F.3d 257, 281-286 (C.A.3 2007). A criminal defendant who participated in a bribery or kickback scheme, in short, cannot tenably complain about prosecution under § 1346 on vagueness grounds.

C

It remains to determine whether Skilling's conduct violated § 1346. Skilling's honest-services prosecution, the Government concedes, was not "prototypical." * * * The Government charged Skilling with conspiring to defraud Enron's shareholders by misrepresenting the company's fiscal health, thereby artificially inflating its stock price. It was the Government's theory at trial that Skilling "profited from the fraudulent scheme ... through the receipt of salary and bonuses, ... and through the sale of approximately $200 million in Enron stock, which netted him $89 million." * * *

The Government did not, at any time, allege that Skilling solicited or accepted side payments from a third party in exchange for making these misrepresentations. * * * ("[T]he indictment does not allege, and the government's evidence did not show, that [Skilling] engaged in bribery."). It is therefore clear that, as we read § 1346, Skilling did not commit honest-services fraud.

Because the indictment alleged three objects of the conspiracy-honest-services wire fraud, money-or-property wire fraud, and securities fraud-Skilling's conviction is flawed. See Yates v. United States, 354 U.S. 298 (1957) (constitutional error occurs when a jury is instructed on alternative theories of guilt and returns a general verdict that may rest on a legally invalid theory). This determination, however, does not necessarily require reversal of the conspiracy conviction; we recently confirmed, in Hedgpeth v. Pulido, 129 S.Ct. 530 (2008), that errors of the *Yates* variety are subject to harmless-error analysis. The parties vigorously dispute whether the error was harmless. Compare Brief for United States ("[A]ny juror who voted for conviction based on [the honest-services theory] also would have

[46] Overlap with other federal statutes does not render § 1346 superfluous. The principal federal bribery statute, § 201, for example, generally applies only to federal public officials, so § 1346's application to state and local corruption and to private-sector fraud reaches misconduct that might otherwise go unpunished.

found [Skilling] guilty of conspiring to commit securities fraud.") with Reply Brief (The Government "cannot show that the conspiracy conviction rested *only* on the securities-fraud theory, rather than the distinct, legally-flawed honest-services theory."). We leave this dispute for resolution on remand.[47]

Whether potential reversal on the conspiracy count touches any of Skilling's other convictions is also an open question. All of his convictions, Skilling contends, hinged on the conspiracy count and, like dominoes, must fall if it falls. The District Court, deciding Skilling's motion for bail pending appeal, found this argument dubious, * * *, but the Fifth Circuit had no occasion to rule on it. That court may do so on remand.

* * *

For the foregoing reasons, we affirm the Fifth Circuit's ruling on Skilling's fair-trial argument, vacate its ruling on his conspiracy conviction, and remand the case for proceedings consistent with this opinion. * * *

Justice SCALIA, with whom Justice THOMAS joins, and with whom Justice KENNEDY joins except as to Part III, concurring in part and concurring in the judgment.

I agree with the Court that petitioner Jeffrey Skilling's challenge to the impartiality of his jury and to the District Court's conduct of the *voir dire* fails. I therefore join Parts I and II of the Court's opinion. I also agree that the decision upholding Skilling's conviction for so-called "honest-services fraud" must be reversed, but for a different reason. In my view, the specification in 18 U.S.C. § 1346 (2006 ed., Supp. II) that "scheme or artifice to defraud" in the mail-fraud and wire-fraud statutes, §§ 1341 and 1343 (2006 ed.), includes "a scheme or artifice to deprive another of the intangible right of honest services," is vague, and therefore violates the Due Process Clause of the Fifth Amendment. The Court strikes a pose of judicial humility in proclaiming that our task is "not to destroy the Act ... but to construe it, * * * . But in transforming the prohibition of "honest-services fraud" into a prohibition of "bribery and kick-backs" it is wielding a power we long ago abjured: the power to define new federal crimes. * * *

* * * In short, the first step in the Court's analysis-holding that "the intangible right of honest services" refers to "the honest-services doctrine recognized in Court of Appeals' decisions before *McNally*," * * *is a step out of the frying pan into the fire. The pre-*McNally* cases provide no clear

[47] The Fifth Circuit appeared to prejudge this issue, noting that, "if any of the three objects of Skilling's conspiracy offers a legally insufficient theory," it "must set aside his conviction." * * * That reasoning relied on the mistaken premise that Hedgpeth v. Pulido, * * *, governs only cases on collateral review. * * * Harmless-error analysis, we clarify, applies equally to cases on direct appeal. Accordingly, the Fifth Circuit, on remand, should take a fresh look at the parties' harmless-error arguments.

indication of what constitutes a denial of the right of honest services. The possibilities range from any action that is contrary to public policy or otherwise immoral, to only the disloyalty of a public official or employee to his principal, to only the secret use of a perpetrator's position of trust in order to harm whomever he is beholden to. The duty probably did not have to be rooted in state law, but maybe it did. It might have been more demanding in the case of public officials, but perhaps not. At the time § 1346 was enacted there was no settled criterion for choosing among these options, for conclusively settling what was in and what was out. * * *

The Court is aware of all this. It knows that adopting by reference "the pre-*McNally* honest-services doctrine," * * *, is adopting by reference nothing more precise than the referring term itself ("the intangible right of honest services"). Hence the *deus ex machina:* "[W]e pare that body of precedent down to its core," * * *. Since the honest-services doctrine "had its genesis" in bribery prosecutions, and since several cases and counsel for Skilling referred to bribery and kickback schemes as "core" or "paradigm" or "typical" examples, or "[t]he most obvious form," of honest-services fraud, * * *, and since two cases and counsel for the Government say that they formed the "vast majority," or "most" or at least "[t]he bulk" of honest-services cases, * * *, THEREFORE it must be the case that they are *all* Congress meant by its reference to the honest-services doctrine.

Even if that conclusion followed from its premises, it would not suffice to eliminate the vagueness of the statute. It would solve (perhaps) the indeterminacy of what acts constitute a breach of the "honest services" obligation under the pre-*McNally* law. But it would not solve the most fundamental indeterminacy: the character of the "fiduciary capacity" to which the bribery and kickback restriction applies. Does it apply only to public officials? Or in addition to private individuals who contract with the public? Or to everyone, including the corporate officer here? The pre-*McNally* case law does not provide an answer. Thus, even with the bribery and kickback limitation the statute does not answer the question "What is the criterion of guilt?" * * *

Thus, the Court's claim to "respec[t] the legislature," * * * , is false. It is entirely clear (as the Court and I agree) that Congress meant to reinstate the body of pre-*McNally* honest-services law; and entirely clear that that prohibited much more (though precisely what more is uncertain) than bribery and kickbacks. Perhaps it is true that "Congress intended § 1346 to reach *at least* bribes and kickbacks," * * * That simply does not mean, as the Court now holds, that "§ 1346 criminalizes *only* " bribery and kickbacks, * * *

Arriving at that conclusion requires not interpretation but invention. * * * I certainly agree with the Court that we must, "if we can," uphold, rather than "condemn," Congress's enactments, * * * But I do not believe we have the power, in order to uphold an enactment, to rewrite it. Congress enacted the entirety of the pre-*McNally* honest-services law, the content of which is (to put it mildly) unclear. In prior vagueness cases, we have resisted the temptation to make all things right with the stroke of our pen. * * * I would show the same restraint today, and reverse Skilling's conviction on the basis that § 1346 provides no "ascertainable standard" for the conduct it condemns, * * * . Instead, the Court today adds to our functions the prescription of criminal law. * * *

Justice ALITO, concurring in part and concurring in the judgment.

I join the judgment of the Court and all but Part II of the Court's opinion. * * * I write separately to address petitioner's jury-trial argument. The Sixth Amendment guarantees criminal defendants a trial before "an impartial jury." In my view, this requirement is satisfied so long as no biased juror is actually seated at trial. * * *

Justice SOTOMAYOR, with whom Justice STEVENS and Justice BREYER join, concurring in part and dissenting in part.

I concur in the Court's resolution of the honest-services fraud question and join Part III of its opinion. I respectfully dissent, however, from the Court's conclusion that Jeffrey Skilling received a fair trial before an impartial jury. * * * In this case, passions ran extremely high. The sudden collapse of Enron directly affected thousands of people in the Houston area and shocked the entire community. The accompanying barrage of local media coverage was massive in volume and often caustic in tone. As Enron's one-time CEO, Skilling was at the center of the storm. Even if these extraordinary circumstances did not constitutionally compel a change of venue, they required the District Court to conduct a thorough *voir dire* in which prospective jurors' attitudes about the case were closely scrutinized. The District Court's inquiry lacked the necessary thoroughness and left serious doubts about whether the jury empaneled to decide Skilling's case was capable of rendering an impartial decision based solely on the evidence presented in the courtroom. Accordingly, I would grant Skilling relief on his fair-trial claim. * * *

NOTES AND QUESTIONS

1. **Skilling *Remand*.** The Court noted that in Skilling's case there were "three objects of the conspiracy-honest-services wire fraud, money-or-property wire fraud, and securities fraud" and found that because of this his "conviction is flawed." But the Court remanded the case to determine if the error was harmless. [p. 178 n.47]. See WAYNE R. LAFAVE, JEROLD H. ISRAEL, NANCY KING, AND ORIN S. KERR, *Harmless Error or Automatic Reversal*, CRIMINAL PROCEDURE § 27.6 (2009)(discussing what constitutes harmless error). On remand the Fifth Circuit found any errors to be harmless errors and affirmed Skilling's convictions. United States v. Skilling, 638 F.3d 480 (5th Cir. 2011). The court did, however, vacate the sentence. Thereafter, Skilling entered in a sentencing agreement with the government to reduce his sentence of 292 months to a guidelines range of 168

to 210 months. The district court eventually re-sentenced Skilling to 168 months in prison. See DOJ Press Release http://www.justice.gov/opa/pr/former-enron-ceo-jeffrey-skilling-resentenced-168-months-fraud-conspiracy-charges.

2. ***Bribery and Kickbacks***. Courts wrestled with cases of whether convictions should be overturned in light of *Skilling*, often looking at whether there were references to honest services fraud in the indictment or instructions used at trial. Issues were also raised as to what conduct is encompassed within the terms "bribery and kickbacks." For example, in United States v. DeMizio, 741 F.3d 373 (2d Cir. 2014), the Second Circuit examined the term "kickbacks" with regard to "payments in a private sector scheme." The court rejected defendant's argument that "a payment in a private-sector scheme does not qualify as a kickback unless the defendant employee himself or herself receives the payoff." The court stated that "[t]he evidence overwhelmingly established that DeMizio directed Morgan Stanley stock-loan business to companies that agreed to pay commissions to his father and/or brother, in whom DeMizio plainly had an interest." See also PETER J. HENNING AND LEE S. RADEK, THE PROSECUTION AND DEFENSE OF PUBLIC CORRUPTION: THE LAW AND LEGAL STRATEGIES (2010).

3. ***Self-dealing/Conflicts of Interests.*** In some cases the lower courts reversed counts, such as when they were premised on self-dealing or conflicts of interest. Thus, in United States v. Siegelman, 640 F.3d 1159 (11th Cir. 2011), the former governor of Alabama had two counts of his conviction reversed that were based upon self-dealing, while other counts premised on bribery remained. Likewise, in United States v. Riley, 621 F.3d 312 (3d Cir. 2010), the Third Circuit reversed one count premised on *Skilling*, stating where the fraudulent act is the non-disclosure of a conflict of interest, it would demean the judicial process to attempt to put the genie back in the bottle by essentially rewriting the charge to the jury on Count 5 and assuming the jury made distinctions the Government did not bring out in its summation.

4. ***Congressional Response***. Justice Scalia contends that the Court engaged in "invention," as opposed to "interpretation." What arguments can be made for and against this position? In looking at footnote 45 [p. 176], is it possible for Congress to write a statute that criminalizes self-dealing that will not be struck down by the Court as vague?

5. ***Weyhrauch and Black***. On the same day *Skilling* was decided, the Court also ruled on two other cases involving issues related to § 1346. In *Weyhrauch v. United States*, 561 U.S. 476 (2010), the Court was asked to consider whether § 1346 required that the accused violate a duty imposed by state law. The Court vacated the judgment and remanded this case in light of *Skilling*. The Court also vacated the judgment and remanded the case of **Black v. United States**, 561 U.S. 465 (2010), but resolved one matter in the defendant's favor. The Court stated:

At trial, the Government pursued alternative theories: (1) money-or-property fraud; and (2) honest-services fraud. To pinpoint whether the jury based its verdict on money-or-property fraud, or honest-services fraud, or both, the Government proposed special interrogatories to accompany the verdict. The defendants resisted, preferring an unelaborated general verdict, and the Government ultimately acquiesced in that standard form of submission.

The Court of Appeals held that the defendants, by opposing the Government-suggested special interrogatories, forfeited their objection to the honest-services-fraud instructions given to the jury. 530 F.3d 596, 603 (C.A.7 2008). We reverse that ruling. A criminal defendant, we hold, need not request special interrogatories, nor need he acquiesce in the Government's request for discrete findings by the jury, in order to preserve in full a timely raised objection to jury instructions on an alternative theory of guilt.[a]

E. INTENT

UNITED STATES v. D'AMATO

39 F.3d 1249 (2d Cir. 1994)

WINTER, Circuit Judge.

* * * [Armand P.] D'Amato was convicted of seven counts of mail fraud in violation of 18 U.S.C. § 1341 and sentenced principally to a term of five months imprisonment, two years of supervised release including five months of home detention, and payment of $7,500 restitution. D'Amato's conviction arises from services he provided to the Unisys Corporation ("Unisys"). The government claimed at trial that D'Amato was hired by a "rogue" Unisys employee, Charles Gardner, and that D'Amato, with Gardner's aid, defrauded Unisys in two ways. First, the government maintained that D'Amato committed mail fraud by structuring his billings to conceal from those in control of corporate funds the nature of his relationship with Unisys and the fact that his actual services involved lobbying his brother, a United States Senator and member of the Senate Appropriations Committee. We will style this theory the "right to control theory." The government maintained, second, that D'Amato committed mail fraud by contracting with Unisys to provide written reports on Senate proceedings while never intending to provide those reports. We will style this theory the "false pretenses theory."

[a] In *Black*, the Court stated that "[a]lthough not dispositive, the absence of a Criminal Rule authorizing special verdicts counsels caution." In footnote 11 of this opinion, the Court stated, "By calling for caution, we do not mean to suggest that special verdicts in criminal cases are never appropriate. * * * "

Because the evidence of criminal intent was insufficient on either theory, we reverse the judgment of conviction and order the indictment dismissed. * * *

D'Amato, an attorney, started a law partnership with Jeffrey Forchelli in 1976. By 1988, the two were practicing as partners of D'Amato, Forchelli, Libert, Schwartz, Mineo & Carlino ("D'Amato Forchelli"), a firm of roughly twenty lawyers based in Mineola, New York. D'Amato's brother, Alfonse D'Amato, was a United States Senator from the State of New York throughout the period of relevant events. Senator D'Amato was a member of the Senate Appropriations Committee, the Senate committee charged with oversight of defense procurement programs.

Unisys, a Fortune 100 company, maintained a Surveillance and Fire Control Systems Division ("S & FCS") in Great Neck, New York. This division manufactured radar missile control systems that were sold to the United States government. Charles Gardner served as a Unisys vice president in charge of marketing for S & FCS from the early 1980's until March 1988. Throughout the pertinent period, Gardner bribed Navy officials, made illegal campaign contributions to Congressmen, and personally profited through kickbacks. The government has stipulated, however, that none of these illegal activities involved D'Amato or Senator D'Amato, and there was no evidence that D'Amato was aware of any of Gardner's illegal activities. * * *

In fall 1987, Unisys began an internal investigation of alleged unethical behavior by Unisys employees. The investigation was headed by Lawrence Cresce, * * * In November 1987, Cresce questioned Gardner about his activities. Gardner acknowledged that the reports mentioned in the purchase orders "just weren't worth the money," and that the "reports were window dressing, and simply paper so that the consultants can get paid." * * * Cresce eventually prepared a report dated May 1988 that concluded that Gardner had, among other activities, used D'Amato Forchelli to gain access to Senator D'Amato. * * *

In connection with the sentencing, the district court found that D'Amato spent approximately 100 hours performing lobbying services for Unisys. The court further found that D'Amato travelled three times to Washington, D.C., at least in part on behalf of Unisys. In addition, D'Amato met with Unisys employee Lynch around ten times in his office, where Lynch briefed D'Amato on Unisys's programs and needs. D'Amato also helped cause two letters by Senator D'Amato and one by Congressman Norman Lent to be sent to Navy and Commerce Department officials concerning defense contracts. * * *

The mail fraud statute criminalizes use of the mails in furtherance of a "scheme or artifice to defraud, or for obtaining money or property by means of false or fraudulent pretenses . . . ." 18 U.S.C. § 1341. Therefore, an essential element of any mail fraud prosecution is proof of a "scheme or artifice to defraud." Id.; see also United States v. Starr, 816 F.2d 94, 98 (2d Cir.1987). Essential to a scheme to defraud is fraudulent intent. Durland v. United States, [p. 150]. ("The significant fact is the intent and purpose."); *Starr,* 816 F.2d at 98 (fraudulent intent "critical" to a scheme to defraud); United States v. Regent Office Supply Co., 421 F.2d 1174, 1180 (2d Cir.1970) (same).

The scheme to defraud need not have been successful or complete. Therefore, the victims of the scheme need not have been injured. United States v. Andreadis, 366 F.2d 423, 431-32 (2d Cir.1966). However, the government must show "that some actual harm or injury was contemplated by the schemer."

Because the defendant must intend to harm the fraud's victims, "[m]isrepresentations amounting only to a deceit are insufficient to maintain a mail or wire fraud prosecution. Instead, the deceit must be coupled with a contemplated harm to the victim." In many cases, this requirement poses no additional obstacle for the government. Actors are presumed to intend the natural and probable consequences of their actions. So when the "necessary result" of the actor's scheme is to injure others, fraudulent intent may be inferred from the scheme itself. Where the scheme does not cause injury to the alleged victim as its necessary result, the government must produce evidence independent of the alleged scheme to show the defendant's fraudulent intent.

1. The Right to Control Theory

a) The Elements.

We first address the right to control theory. That "theory is predicated on a showing that some person or entity has been deprived of potentially valuable economic information." *Wallach,* 935 F.2d at 462-63. Thus, "the withholding or inaccurate reporting of information that could impact on economic decisions can provide the basis for a mail fraud prosecution." A person charged with mail fraud under the right to control theory must intend to injure the person or entity misled—here Unisys, its management, and/or its shareholders—and the person or entity must thus be a specific target of the inaccurate or concealed information. Mail fraud cannot be charged against a corporate agent who in good faith believes that his or her (otherwise legal) misleading or inaccurate conduct is in the corporation's best interests.

Where no rule otherwise provides, persons acting on behalf of a corporation may well find it necessary to disguise or conceal certain matters in the interests of that corporation. For example, failure to disclose the nature of a service provided or the identity of the entity performing such a service may minimize the risk of disclosure of information that would enable competitors to learn of a corporation's future activities or plans. Mining companies may thus conceal the hiring of geologists and the site of their work. Such measures may be necessary also to protect company assets. A company may thus disguise the hiring of forensic accountants in order to avoid giving warning to an undetected embezzler. The preservation of a positive public relations image is a proper corporate goal and may be pursued by a policy of concealment. Such a policy may be necessary also to prevent insider trading. Firms planning a takeover may thus wish to conceal relationships with law firms, accountants, or banks until required to disclose under the Williams Act. 15 U.S.C. §§ 78m(d),(e) & 78n(d)-(f) (1988).

The critical elements are: (i) whether corporate management has made an otherwise lawful decision that concealment or a failure to disclose is in the corporation's best interests and (ii) whether management acted in good faith in making, and did not personally profit from, the decision. As we noted in *Wallach,* the principle that directors and officers may act on behalf of a corporation does not extend to acts of self-enrichment. However, a good faith, unconflicted decision may not be second-guessed by the government or by the courts. See *Miller,* 507 F.2d at 762 ("The sound business judgment rule . . . expresses the unanimous decision of American courts to eschew intervention in corporate decision-making if the judgment of directors and officers i[s] uninfluenced by personal considerations and is exercised in good faith.").

In the instant matter, of course, the defendant is not someone in corporate management but a person hired to perform services for the corporation. Such a person cannot be found to intend to harm a corporation or its shareholders through otherwise lawful misleading conduct if he or she follows the instructions of an appropriate corporate agent who appears to be unconflicted and acting in good faith. So far as the duty of a party contracting to provide ordinary business or professional services to the corporation is concerned, therefore, that party may rely upon instructions from a corporate agent with apparent authority and no ostensible conflict of interest to determine the contracting party's obligations and appropriate billing practices.

Additional considerations apply to a claim that shareholders have been deprived of their right to control. Unlike management, shareholders have no right to manage the business. Nevertheless, they do have property rights of which they may not be fraudulently deprived by "the withholding or inaccurate reporting of information that could impact on economic decisions."
* * *

The otherwise lawful "withholding or inaccurate reporting of information" must thus relate to: (i) information available to shareholders as provided by the state of incorporation's laws providing access to corporate books and records, see *Wallach,* 935 F.2d at 463 (maintenance of accurate books and records is of "central importance" to preservation of shareholders' property interest); (ii) information that, if withheld or inaccurate would result in rendering information that is public materially misleading, see id. (right to public information, required to be disclosed by law, is important component of shareholders' property rights), and (iii) information that would materially aid shareholders in enforcing management's fiduciary obligations under state law, see id. ("complete information" enables a stockholder to take "steps" to prevent corporate actions of which he or she disapproves). Where a third party acting upon instructions from a corporate agent is charged with depriving shareholders of their right to control, the government must prove that the third party knew that the concealment would involve (i), (ii), or (iii).

b) Sufficiency of the Evidence.

The government's claim that D'Amato intended to injure Unisys by depriving its management or its shareholders of their right to control was not based on legally sufficient evidence. The jury could have found that D'Amato knew that his services on behalf of Unisys were disguised. However, the government concedes that the payments to D'Amato for the purpose of gaining "access" to his brother were not illegal. From D'Amato's point of view, if such access resulted in political support from the Senator that helped Unisys's sales, Unisys and its shareholders would benefit. Also from D'Amato's point of view, it was evident that Unisys might desire to keep its source of access to the Senator confidential because the means of access could easily become controversial and self-defeating if disclosed. D'Amato thus could have intended to deprive Unisys management (or shareholders) of "valuable" information that "could impact" on economic decisions only if (i) Gardner had no authority to instruct D'Amato to disguise his services in billing Unisys and D'Amato knew it, (ii) the payments to D'Amato were otherwise unlawful and D'Amato knew it, or (iii) Gardner was personally profiting from the concealed arrangement with D'Amato and D'Amato knew it. None of these conditions has been met in the instant matter. * * *

Our conclusion is in no way inconsistent with *Wallach*. In *Wallach,* false bills were submitted in order to perpetuate, in conjunction with Wedtech officers, securities fraud on Wedtech shareholders. Two of the defendants, London and Chinn, submitted false invoices in order to disguise the fact that they had been paid for assisting in a stock parking scheme. The third defendant, Wallach, performed lobbying services for Wedtech yet submitted bills that attributed his services to assistance with a public offering and various capital acquisitions. Wallach's misstatements enabled Wedtech to capitalize the cost of his services rather than to expense them in the current accounting period. This artificially inflated Wedtech's current earnings and caused misleading reports, which were available to shareholders, to be filed with the Securities and Exchange Commission. There was evidence, moreover, that Wallach was aware of, and was to share in, the diversion of Wedtech funds to London and Chinn. He was thus not an innocent provider of services to Wedtech unaware of the effect of his actions.

2. The False Pretenses Theory

The false pretenses theory, simply stated, is a claim that D'Amato represented to Unisys that he would prepare reports in exchange for the fees he received, and took the money but prepared no reports. The government's false pretenses theory thus rests on the allegation that D'Amato did not perform the services that he contracted to perform for Unisys and for which he was paid.

* * * The government's theory was and is that D'Amato was paid for lobbying his Senator brother, concededly lawful conduct. There is no evidence that he did not perform such services. It is inconceivable on this record that Unisys could survive a motion for summary judgment in a civil suit to recover fees from D'Amato based on a false pretenses theory, even under the lower burden of proof applicable to civil cases.

Finally, the government argues that D'Amato's services were not worth what Unisys paid for them. This argument is seriously misguided. The mail fraud statute does not criminalize the charging of an allegedly excessive fee, where, as here, a corporate agent with at least apparent authority to do so agreed to the fee, received no personal benefit from the fee, and was not deceived by the payee. Retainer agreements that keep providers of services available are commonplace, and sometimes those services are not needed. We decline the government's invitation to infer fraudulent intent on the part of an attorney who accepts a retainer arrangement and is subsequently not called upon to perform services that the government or trier of fact deems worth the fee paid. Moreover, the government offered no evidence that access to the Senator was not worth the fees paid.

We vacate the conviction, and order dismissal of the indictment.

NOTES AND QUESTIONS

1. ***Political Prosecution?.*** Prior to the second circuit's ruling, the propriety of the D'Amato prosecution was hotly debated in the New York and national press. See, e.g., Richard W. Painter, The Wall Street Journal, May 4, 1994, at A15 (questioning whether the decision to prosecute was related to "the fact that Mr. D'Amato's brother is a U.S. senator").

2. ***Attorney Billing.*** Can the mailing of a bill by a lawyer to a client ever be the basis for a mail fraud prosecution? Would a misleading bill constitute mail fraud? In United States v. Myerson, 18 F.3d 153, 156 (2d Cir. 1994), Myerson was convicted and sentenced to 60 months imprisonment after being charged with "defrauding six clients and his own law firm while he was a partner at the New York law firm he founded * * *. This fraud was based on Myerson's submitting a legal fee that overbilled his clients by millions of dollars and by his fraudulent claims that personal charges were legitimate business expenses."

F. MATERIALITY

NEDER v. UNITED STATES
527 U.S. 1 (1999)

CHIEF JUSTICE REHNQUIST delivered the opinion of the Court.

* * * In the mid-1980's, petitioner Ellis E. Neder, Jr., an attorney and real estate developer in Jacksonville, Florida, engaged in a number of real estate transactions financed by fraudulently obtained bank loans. Between 1984 and 1986, Neder purchased 12 parcels of land using shell corporations set up by his attorneys and then immediately resold the land at much higher prices to limited partnerships that he controlled. Using inflated appraisals, Neder secured bank loans that typically amounted to 70 to 75% of the inflated resale price of the land. In so doing, he concealed from lenders that he controlled the shell corporations, that he had purchased the land at prices substantially lower than the inflated resale prices, and that the limited partnerships had not made substantial down payments as represented. In several cases, Neder agreed to sign affidavits falsely stating that he had no relationship to the shell corporations and that he was not sharing in the profits from the inflated land sales. By keeping for himself the amount by which the loan proceeds exceeded the original purchase price of the land, Neder was able to obtain more than $7 million. He failed to report nearly all of this money on his personal income-tax returns. He eventually defaulted on the loans.

Neder also engaged in a number of schemes involving land development fraud. In 1985, he obtained a $4,150,000 construction loan to build condominiums on a project known as Cedar Creek. To obtain the loan, he falsely represented to the lender that he had satisfied a condition of the loan by making advance sales of 20 condominium units. In fact, he had been unable to meet the condition, so he secured additional buyers by making their down payments himself. He then had the down payments transferred back to him from the escrow accounts into which they had been placed. Neder later defaulted on the loan without repaying any of the principal. He employed a similar scheme to obtain a second construction loan of $5,400,000, and unsuccessfully attempted to obtain an additional loan in the same manner.

Neder also obtained a consolidated $14 million land acquisition and development loan for a project known as Reddie Point. Pursuant to the loan, Neder could request funds for work actually performed on the project. Between September 1987 and March 1988, he submitted numerous requests based on false invoices, the lender approved the requests, and he obtained almost $3 million unrelated to any work actually performed.

Neder was indicted on, among other things, 9 counts of mail fraud, in violation of 18 U.S.C. § 1341; 9 counts of wire fraud, in violation of § 1343; 12 counts of bank fraud, in violation of § 1344; and 2 counts of filing a false income tax return, in violation of 26 U.S.C. § 7206(1). The fraud counts charged Neder with devising and executing various schemes to defraud lenders in connection with the land acquisition and development loans, totaling over $40 million. The tax counts charged Neder with filing false statements of income on his tax returns. According to the Government, Neder failed to report more than $1 million in income for 1985 and more than $4 million in income for 1986, both amounts reflecting profits Neder obtained from the fraudulent real estate loans.

In accordance with then-extant Circuit precedent and over Neder's objection, the District Court instructed the jury that, to convict on the tax offenses, it "need not consider" the materiality of any false statements "even though that language is used in the indictment." The question of materiality, the court instructed, "is not a question for the jury to decide." The court gave a similar instruction on bank fraud, and subsequently found, outside the presence of the jury, that the evidence established the materiality of all the false statements at issue. In instructing the jury on mail fraud and wire fraud, the District Court did not include materiality as an element of either offense. Neder again objected to the instruction. The jury convicted Neder of the fraud and tax offenses, and he was sentenced to 147 months' imprisonment, 5 years' supervised release, and $25 million in restitution.

The Court of Appeals for the Eleventh Circuit affirmed the conviction. It held that the District Court erred under our intervening decision in United States v. Gaudin, 515 U.S. 506, 115 S.Ct. 2310, 132 L.Ed.2d 444 (1995), in failing to submit the materiality element of the tax offense to the jury. It concluded, however, that the error was subject to harmless-error analysis and, further, that the error was harmless because "materiality was not in dispute," and thus the error " 'did not contribute to the verdict obtained,' " * * *. The Court of Appeals also held that materiality is not an element of the mail fraud, wire fraud, and bank fraud statutes, and thus the District Court did not err in failing to submit the question of materiality to the jury.

We granted certiorari, to resolve a conflict in the Courts of Appeals on two questions: (1) whether, and under what circumstances, the omission of an element from the judge's charge to the jury can be harmless error, and (2) whether materiality is an element of the federal mail fraud, wire fraud, and bank fraud statutes.

[The Court found the failure to submit materiality as an issue for the jury on the tax charges was harmless error.]

* * * We also granted certiorari in this case to decide whether materiality is an element of a "scheme or artifice to defraud" under the federal mail fraud (18 U.S.C. § 1341), wire fraud (§ 1343), and bank fraud (§ 1344) statutes. The Court of Appeals concluded that the failure to submit materiality to the jury was not error because the fraud statutes do not require that a "scheme to defraud" employ material falsehoods. We disagree.

Under the framework set forth in United States v. Wells, 519 U.S. 482, 117 S.Ct. 921, 137 L.Ed.2d 107 (1997), we first look to the text of the statutes at issue to discern whether they require a showing of materiality. In this case, we need not dwell long on the text because, as the parties agree, none of the fraud statutes defines the phrase "scheme or artifice to defraud," or even mentions materiality. Although the mail fraud and wire fraud statutes contain different jurisdictional elements (§ 1341 requires use of the mails while § 1343 requires use of interstate wire facilities), they both prohibit, in pertinent part, "any scheme or artifice to defraud" or to obtain money or property "by means of false or fraudulent pretenses, representations, or promises." The bank fraud statute, which was modeled on the mail and wire fraud statutes, similarly prohibits any "scheme or artifice to defraud a financial institution" or to obtain any property of a financial institution "by false or fraudulent pretenses, representations, or promises." Thus, based solely on a "natural reading of the full text," materiality would not be an element of the fraud statutes.

That does not end our inquiry, however, because in interpreting statutory language there is a necessary second step. It is a well-established rule of construction that "'[w]here Congress uses terms that have accumulated settled meaning under ... the common law, a court must infer, unless the statute otherwise dictates, that Congress means to incorporate the established meaning of these terms.' " * * * Neder contends that "defraud" is just such a term, and that Congress implicitly incorporated its common-law meaning, including its requirement of materiality, into the statutes at issue.

The Government does not dispute that both at the time of the mail fraud statute's original enactment in 1872, and later when Congress enacted the wire fraud and bank fraud statutes, actionable "fraud" had a well-settled meaning at common law. Nor does it dispute that the well-settled meaning of "fraud" required a misrepresentation or concealment of material fact. Indeed, as the sources we are aware of demonstrate, the common law could not have conceived of "fraud" without proof of materiality. * * * Thus, under the rule that Congress intends to incorporate the well-settled meaning of the common-law terms it uses, we cannot infer from the absence of an express reference to materiality that Congress intended to drop that element from the fraud statutes. On the contrary, we must presume that Congress intended to incorporate materiality " 'unless the statute otherwise dictates.'"

The Government attempts to rebut this presumption by arguing that the term "defraud" would bear its common-law meaning only if the fraud statutes "indicated that Congress had codified the crime of false pretenses or one of the common-law torts sounding in fraud." Instead, the Government argues, Congress chose to unmoor the mail fraud statute from its common-law analogs by punishing, not the completed fraud, but rather any person "having devised or intending to devise a scheme or artifice to defraud." Read in this light, the Government contends, there is no basis to infer that Congress intended to limit criminal liability to conduct that would constitute "fraud" at common law, and in particular, to material misrepresentations or omissions. Rather, criminal liability would exist so long as the defendant intended to deceive the victim, even if the particular means chosen turn out to be immaterial, i.e., incapable of influencing the intended victim.

The Government relies heavily on Durland v. United States, [p. 150], our first decision construing the mail fraud statute, to support its argument that the fraud statutes sweep more broadly than common-law fraud. But Durland was different from this case. * * * Although Durland held that the mail fraud statute reaches conduct that would not have constituted "false pretenses" at common law, it did not hold, as the Government argues, that the statute encompasses more than common-law fraud.

In one sense, the Government is correct that the fraud statutes did not incorporate all the elements of common-law fraud. The common-law requirements of "justifiable reliance" and "damages," for example, plainly have no place in the federal fraud statutes. * * * By prohibiting the "scheme to defraud," rather than the completed fraud, the elements of reliance and damage would clearly be inconsistent with the statutes Congress enacted. But while the language of the fraud statutes is incompatible with these requirements, the Government has failed to show that this language is inconsistent with a materiality requirement.

Accordingly, we hold that materiality of falsehood is an element of the federal mail fraud, wire fraud, and bank fraud statutes. Consistent with our normal practice where the court below has not yet passed on the harmlessness of any error, we remand this case to the Court of Appeals for it to consider in the first instance whether the jury- instruction error was harmless. * * *

The judgment of the Court of Appeals respecting the tax fraud counts is affirmed. The judgment of the Court of Appeals on the remaining counts is reversed, and the case is remanded for further proceedings consistent with this opinion. * * *

JUSTICE STEVENS, concurring in part and concurring in the judgment.

[Disagreeing “with the Court's analysis of the harmless-error issue” in another part of its opinion.]

* * * The Court's conclusion that materiality is an element of the offenses defined in 18 U.S.C. §§ 1341, 1343, and 1344 is obviously correct. In my dissent in United States v. Wells, 519 U.S. 482, 510, 117 S.Ct. 921, 137 L.Ed.2d 107 (1997), I pointed out that the vast majority of judges who had confronted the question had placed the same construction on the federal statute criminalizing false statements to federally insured banks, 18 U.S.C. § 1014. I repeat this point to remind the Congress that an amendment to §

1014 would both harmonize these sections and avoid the potential injustice created by the Court's decision in Wells.

JUSTICE SCALIA, with whom JUSTICE SOUTER and JUSTICE GINSBURG join, concurring in part and dissenting in part.

* * * I dissent from the judgment of the Court, because I believe that depriving a criminal defendant of the right to have the jury determine his guilt of the crime charged--which necessarily means his commission of every element of the crime charged--can never be harmless. * * *

NOTE

On remand the Eleventh Circuit Court of Appeals found that "the failure to instruct on materiality was harmless error." United States v. Neder, 197 F.3d 1122 (11th Cir. 1999).

G. MAILING

The government must prove a mailing by the defendant or that the mailing was caused to be mailed by the defendant. Circumstantial evidence of office custom and procedure have been used to prove a mailing. See United States v. Flaxman, 495 F.2d 344, 349 (7th Cir. 1974). "[R]eliance upon inferences drawn from evidence of standard business practice without specific reference to the mailing in question is insufficient." United States v. Burks, 867 F.2d 795, 797 (3rd Cir. 1989).

Section 1341 was amended as part of the Violent Crime Control and Law Enforcement Act of 1994, inserting the language, "or deposits or causes to be deposited any matter or thing whatever to be sent or delivered by any private or commercial interstate carrier." Violent Crime Control and Law Enforcement Act of 1994 § 250006. Mailings using Federal Express or UPS may now be subject to prosecution under the mail fraud statute. Who is a private interstate carrier? Is this new provision using Congress' postal powers, the Commerce Clause, or both? See Ellen S. Podgor, *Mail Fraud: Limiting the Limitless,* 18 Champion 4 (Dec. 1994); see also Peter J. Henning, *Maybe It Should Just Be Called Federal Fraud: The Changing Nature of the Mail Fraud Statute*, 36 BOSTON COL. L. REV. 435 (1995).

H. IN FURTHERANCE

SCHMUCK v. UNITED STATES
489 U.S. 705 (1989)

Justice BLACKMUN delivered the opinion of the Court.

I

In August 1983, petitioner Wayne T. Schmuck, a used-car distributor, was indicted in the United States District Court for the Western District of Wisconsin on 12 counts of mail fraud, in violation of 18 U.S.C. §§ 1341 and 1342.

The alleged fraud was a common and straightforward one. Schmuck purchased used cars, rolled back their odometers, and then sold the automobiles to Wisconsin retail dealers for prices artificially inflated because of the low-mileage readings. These unwitting car dealers, relying on the altered odometer figures, then resold the cars to customers, who in turn paid prices reflecting Schmuck's fraud. To complete the resale of each automobile, the dealer who purchased it from Schmuck would submit a title-application form to the Wisconsin Department of Transportation on behalf of his retail customer. The receipt of a Wisconsin title was a prerequisite for completing the resale; without it, the dealer could not transfer title to the customer and the customer could not obtain Wisconsin tags. The submission of the title-application form supplied the mailing element of each of the alleged mail frauds.

Before trial, Schmuck moved to dismiss the indictment on the ground that the mailings at issue—the submissions of the title-application forms by the automobile dealers—were not in furtherance of the fraudulent scheme and, thus, did not satisfy the mailing element of the crime of mail fraud. Schmuck also moved under Federal Rule of Criminal Procedure 31(c)[1] for a jury instruction on the then misdemeanor offense of tampering with an odometer, 15 U.S.C. §§ 1984 and 1990c(a) (1982 ed.).[2] The District Court denied both motions. After trial, the jury returned guilty verdicts on all 12 counts.

A divided panel of the United States Court of Appeals for the Seventh Circuit reversed and remanded the case for a new trial. Although the panel rejected Schmuck's claim that he was entitled to a judgment of acquittal because the mailings were not made in furtherance of his scheme, it ruled

---

[1] Rule 31(c) provides in relevant part: "The defendant may be found guilty of an offense necessarily included in the offense charged."

[2] In 1986, Congress made odometer tampering a felony. Pub.L. 99-579, § 3(b), 100 Stat. 3311, 15 U.S.C. § 1990c(a) (1982 ed., Supp. V).

that under Rule 31(c) the District Court should have instructed the jury on the lesser offense of odometer tampering. The panel applied the so- called "inherent relationship" test for determining what constitutes a lesser included offense for the purpose of Rule 31(c). * * * The Court of Appeals vacated the panel decision and ordered the case to be reheard en banc. * * * On rehearing, by a divided vote * * *, the en banc court rejected the "inherent relationship" test for defining lesser included offenses, and adopted instead the "elements test" whereby one offense is necessarily included within another only when the elements of the lesser offense form a subset of the offense charged. * * * Applying the elements test, the Court of Appeals held that Schmuck was not entitled to a jury instruction on the offense of odometer tampering * * * [s]ince the elements of odometer tampering are not a subset of the elements of mail fraud * * *

We granted certiorari to define further the scope of the mail fraud statute and to resolve a conflict among the Circuits over which test to apply in determining what constitutes a lesser included offense for the purposes of Rule 31(c).

II

"The federal mail fraud statute does not purport to reach all frauds, but only those limited instances in which the use of the mails is a part of the execution of the fraud, leaving all other cases to be dealt with by appropriate state law." Kann v. United States, 323 U.S. 88, 95 (1944). To be part of the execution of the fraud, however, the use of the mails need not be an essential element of the scheme. Pereira v. United States, 347 U.S. 1, 8 (1954). It is sufficient for the mailing to be "incident to an essential part of the scheme," ibid., or "a step in [the] plot," Badders v. United States, 240 U.S. 391, 394 (1916).

Schmuck, relying principally on this Court's decisions in *Kann,* supra, Parr v. United States, 363 U.S. 370 (1960), and United States v. Maze, 414 U.S. 395 (1974), argues that mail fraud can be predicated only on a mailing that affirmatively assists the perpetrator in carrying out his fraudulent scheme. The mailing element of the offense, he contends, cannot be satisfied by a mailing, such as those at issue here, that is routine and innocent in and of itself, and that, far from furthering the execution of the fraud, occurs after the fraud has come to fruition, is merely tangentially related to the fraud, and is counterproductive in that it creates a "paper trail" from which the fraud may be discovered. We disagree both with this characterization of the mailings in the present case and with this description of the applicable law.

We begin by considering the scope of Schmuck's fraudulent scheme. Schmuck was charged with devising and executing a scheme to defraud Wisconsin retail automobile customers who based their decisions to purchase certain automobiles at least in part on the low-mileage readings provided by the tampered odometers. This was a fairly large-scale operation. Evidence at trial indicated that Schmuck had employed a man known only as "Fred" to turn back the odometers on about 150 different cars. Schmuck then marketed these cars to a number of dealers, several of whom he dealt with on a consistent basis over a period of about 15 years. Indeed, of the 12 automobiles that are the subject of the counts of the indictment, 5 were sold to "P and A Sales," and 4 to "Southside Auto." Thus, Schmuck's was not a "one-shot" operation in which he sold a single car to an isolated dealer. His was an ongoing fraudulent venture. A rational jury could have concluded that the success of Schmuck's venture depended upon his continued harmonious relations with, and good reputation among, retail dealers, which in turn required the smooth flow of cars from the dealers to their Wisconsin customers.

Under these circumstances, we believe that a rational jury could have found that the title-registration mailings were part of the execution of the fraudulent scheme, a scheme which did not reach fruition until the retail dealers resold the cars and effected transfers of title. Schmuck's scheme would have come to an abrupt halt if the dealers either had lost faith in Schmuck or had not been able to resell the cars obtained from him. These resales and Schmuck's relationships with the retail dealers naturally depended on the successful passage of title among the various parties. Thus, although the registration-form mailings may not have contributed directly to the duping of either the retail dealers or the customers, they were necessary to the passage of title, which in turn was essential to the perpetuation of Schmuck's scheme. As noted earlier, a mailing that is "incident to an essential part of the scheme," satisfies the mailing element of the mail fraud offense. The mailings here fit this description. * * *

Once the full flavor of Schmuck's scheme is appreciated, the critical distinctions between this case and the three cases in which this Court has delimited the reach of the mail fraud statute—*Kann, Parr,* and *Maze*—are readily apparent. The defendants in *Kann* were corporate officers and directors accused of setting up a dummy corporation through which to divert profits into their own pockets. As part of this fraudulent scheme, the defendants caused the corporation to issue two checks payable to them. The defendants cashed these checks at local banks, which then mailed the checks to the drawee banks for collection. This Court held that the mailing of the cashed checks to the drawee banks could not supply the mailing element of the mail fraud charges. The defendants' fraudulent scheme had reached fruition. "It was immaterial to them, or to any consummation of the scheme, how the bank which paid or credited the check would collect from the drawee bank."

In *Parr,* several defendants were charged, inter alia, with having fraudulently obtained gasoline and a variety of other products and services through the unauthorized use of a credit card issued to the school district which employed them. The mailing element of the mail fraud charges in Parr was purportedly satisfied when the oil company which issued the credit card mailed invoices to the school district for payment, and when the district mailed payment in the form of a check. Relying on *Kann,* this Court held that these mailings were not in execution of the scheme as required by the statute because it was immaterial to the defendants how the oil company went about collecting its payment.[7]

Later, in *Maze,* the defendant allegedly stole his roommate's credit card, headed south on a winter jaunt, and obtained food and lodging at motels along the route by placing the charges on the stolen card. The mailing element of the mail fraud charge was supplied by the fact that the defendant knew that each motel proprietor would mail an invoice to the bank that had issued the credit card, which in turn would mail a bill to the card owner for payment. The Court found that these mailings could not support mail fraud charges because the defendant's scheme had reached fruition when he checked out of each motel. The success of his scheme in no way depended on the mailings; they merely determined which of his victims would ultimately bear the loss. 414 U.S., at 402.

The title-registration mailings at issue here served a function different from the mailings in *Kann, Parr,* and *Maze.* The intrabank mailings in *Kann* and the credit card invoice mailings in *Parr* and *Maze* involved little more than post-fraud accounting among the potential victims of the various schemes, and the long-term success of the fraud did not turn on which of the potential victims bore the ultimate loss. Here, in contrast, a jury rationally could have found that Schmuck by no means was indifferent to the fact of who bore the loss. The mailing of the title-registration forms was an essential step in the successful passage of title to the retail purchasers. Moreover, a failure of this passage of title would have jeopardized Schmuck's relationship of trust and goodwill with the retail dealers upon whose unwitting cooperation his scheme depended. Schmuck's reliance on our prior cases limiting the reach of the mail fraud statute is simply misplaced.

To the extent that Schmuck would draw from these previous cases a general rule that routine mailings that are innocent in themselves cannot supply the mailing element of the mail fraud offense, he misapprehends this Court's precedents. In *Parr* the Court specifically acknowledged that "innocent" mailings—ones that contain no false information—may supply the mailing element. In other cases, the Court has found the elements of mail fraud to be satisfied where the mailings have been routine. See, e.g., Carpenter v. United States, [p.156].

---

[7] *Parr* also involved a second fraudulent scheme through which the defendant school board members misappropriated school district tax revenues. The Government argued that the mailing element of the mail fraud charges was supplied by the mailing of tax statements, checks, and receipts. This Court held, however, that in the absence of any evidence that the tax levy was increased as part of the fraud, the mailing element of the offense could not be supplied by mailings "made or caused to be made under the imperative command of duty imposed by state law." 363 U.S., at 391. No such legal duty is at issue here. * * *

We also reject Schmuck's contention that mailings that someday may contribute to the uncovering of a fraudulent scheme cannot supply the mailing element of the mail fraud offense. The relevant question at all times is whether the mailing is part of the execution of the scheme as conceived by the perpetrator at the time, regardless of whether the mailing later, through hindsight, may prove to have been counterproductive and return to haunt the perpetrator of the fraud. The mail fraud statute includes no guarantee that the use of the mails for the purpose of executing a fraudulent scheme will be risk free. Those who use the mails to defraud proceed at their peril.

For these reasons, we agree with the Court of Appeals that the mailings in this case satisfy the mailing element of the mail fraud offenses. * * *

V

We conclude that Schmuck's conviction was consistent with the statutory definition of mail fraud and that he was not entitled to a lesser included offense instruction on odometer tampering. The judgment of the Court of Appeals, accordingly, is affirmed. It is so ordered.

Justice SCALIA, with whom Justice BRENNAN, Justice MARSHALL, and Justice O'CONNOR join, dissenting.

* * * The purpose of the mail fraud statute is "to prevent the post office from being used to carry [fraudulent schemes] into effect." Durland v. United States, [p. 150]; Parr v. United States. The law does not establish a general federal remedy against fraudulent conduct, with use of the mails as the jurisdictional hook, but reaches only "those limited instances in which the use of the mails is a part of the execution of the fraud, leaving all other cases to be dealt with by appropriate state law." In other words, it is mail fraud, not mail and fraud, that incurs liability. This federal statute is not violated by a fraudulent scheme in which, at some point, a mailing happens to occur—nor even by one in which a mailing predictably and necessarily occurs. The mailing must be in furtherance of the fraud. * * *

What Justice Frankfurter observed almost three decades ago remains true: "The adequate degree of relationship between a mailing which occurs during the life of a scheme and the scheme is . . . not a matter susceptible of geometric determination." Parr v. United States, (dissenting opinion). All the more reason to adhere as closely as possible to past cases. I think we have not done that today, and thus create problems for tomorrow.

NOTES AND QUESTIONS

1. ***Limitations to "In Furtherance".*** Prior to *Schmuck* the cases reflected four types of limitations to a mailing being "in furtherance" of a scheme to

defraud. See Ellen S. Podgor, *Mail Fraud: Opening Letters,* 43 S.C. L. REV. 223, 242-254 (1992).

a. Mailings that conflicted with the scheme to defraud, that aided in detection, or that were diametrically opposed to the defendant acting with an evil mens rea, were not in furtherance of the scheme to defraud. See United States v. Maze, [p. 194].

b. Mailings that were part of an imperative duty to the state were not considered to be in furtherance of the scheme to defraud. See Parr v. United States, [p.194].

c. Mailing that were prior to the commencement of the scheme to defraud were not in furtherance of the scheme. See United States v. Beall, 126 F. Supp. 363 (N. Cal. 1954).

d. Mailings after fruition of the scheme to defraud were not considered to be in furtherance of the scheme. See Kann v. United States, [p. 194]; Parr v. United States, [p. 194]; United States v. Maze, [p. 194].

Do these legal limitations to "in furtherance" exist after *Schmuck?*

2. ***Non-Misleading Compelled Mailings.*** In **United States v. Lake**, 472 F.3d 1247 (10th Cir. 2007), the court held that "[m]ost circuits to address the issue have interpreted *Parr* to hold that mailings of documents which are required by law to be mailed, and which are not themselves false and fraudulent, cannot be regarded as mailed for the purpose of executing a fraudulent scheme."

3. ***Lulling.*** Prior to *Schmuck* there were two Supreme Court cases that allowed mail fraud charges that were after the scheme to defraud. These cases involved mailings that were used to "lull" the victims into the defendant's scheme. See United States v. Sampson, 371 U.S. 75 (1962); United States v. Lane, 474 U.S. 438 (1986). Why did the Supreme Court ignore the cases of *Lane* and *Sampson* in deciding the *Schmuck* case?

I. WIRE FRAUD AND OTHER FRAUDS

UNITED STATES v. BRYANT
766 F.2d 370 (8th Cir. 1985)

ARNOLD, Circuit Judge.

Henry Paul Bryant and Melissa Dalton appeal their convictions on three counts of mail fraud and two counts of wire fraud involving a scheme to bribe Emeric Martin, then Director of the Cervantes Convention Center in St.

Louis, for favorable treatment of their convention-booking business, known as Showboard. * * *

II

Dalton and Bryant argue that their convictions under 18 U.S.C. § 1343 (1982) for wire fraud must be vacated because the government has failed to prove that they knew or could reasonably foresee that the telegrams were being sent interstate. Both of the telegrams at issue were sent from Kansas City, Missouri, to Bridgeton, Missouri, but were routed through Middletown, Virginia.[4]

In response, the United States contends that there is no requirement under § 1343 that the accused know or foresee that the telegram is being sent interstate. The legislative history of § 1343 sheds no light on this question, but we agree with the government that the words of the statute, the general purpose of interstate requirements, and the decisions of other courts support the conclusion that the accused need not know or foresee that the communication was interstate.

We start with the language of Section 1343. It reads as follows:

> Whoever, having devised or intending to devise any scheme or artifice to defraud, or for obtaining money or property by means of false or fraudulent pretenses, representations, or promises, transmits or causes to be transmitted by means of wire, radio, or television communication in interstate or foreign commerce, any writings, signs, signals, pictures, or sounds for the purpose of executing such scheme or artifice, shall be fined not more than $1,000 or imprisoned not more than five years, or both.

Certainly the statute requires that defendant be a party to some kind of scheme to defraud, a requirement that includes a high degree of scienter and moral culpability. It also requires that the defendant intend that a communication by wire be sent in furtherance of the scheme, or at least that the use of wire communication be reasonably foreseeable. But the words themselves, read literally, require only that the wire communication be interstate, not that defendants know that it is to be interstate. The literal meaning of the statute should control, unless it is contrary to the manifest purpose of Congress or inconsistent with binding case law.

Section 1343 was intended to proscribe the use of certain interstate communication media to perpetrate or facilitate a fraudulent scheme. The

---

[4] Appellants do not dispute that these communications are "interstate" within the terms of § 1343. Their argument is that they did not know that Western Union would route the telegrams in question through another State.

requirement of an interstate nexus arises from constitutional limitations on congressional power over intrastate activities under the Commerce Clause. Its inclusion in criminal and civil statutes is most often solely for the purpose of conferring federal jurisdiction rather than of defining substantive elements of an offense. * * * Here, likewise, the requirement seems clearly to be only jurisdictional. The interstate nature of the communication does not make the fraud more culpable. Thus, whether or not a defendant knows or can foresee that a communication is interstate, the offense is still every bit as grave in the moral sense. * * *

The government, however, admits that there is an exception to the general rule that knowledge or foreseeability of the interstate character of the communication is not required under § 1343. The government must show that the accused knew or could have foreseen that a communication in furtherance of a fraudulent scheme was interstate, if the conduct giving rise to the scheme would not be a violation of state law and was not itself morally wrongful. See United States v. Feola, 420 U.S. 671, 685 (1975). In other words, if what happened was not a violation of state law or wrongful in nature, but is a violation of federal law, an innocent defendant could be ensnared in a federal prosecution if, unknown to him, the communication is in fact interstate. [The court rejected appellants' argument that their conduct was "lawful under state law and morally blameless."] * * * The convictions of the appellants are affirmed.

NOTES AND QUESTIONS

1. ***Wire Fraud.*** Congress added the wire fraud statute (18 U.S.C.A. § 1343) in 1952. Wire fraud operates parallel to the mail fraud statute with the differing element being the method used in the transmission. Wire fraud requires the transmission to be "by means of wire, radio, or television communication." According to *Bryant* the accused may not be required to have knowledge of the jurisdiction element of this offense. There may, however, be a venue requirement imposed on the government, limiting venue only where there is a direct of causal connection to the misuse of wires." United States v. Pace, 301 F.3d 1034 (9th Cir. 2002).

2. ***Bank Fraud.*** Not all fraud statutes modeled after the mail fraud statute are interpreted exactly the same as the mail fraud statute. For example, in **Loughrin v. United States**, 134 S.Ct. 2384 (2014), the Court resolved a circuit split regarding § 2 of the bank fraud statute. The defendant stole checks from mailboxes, altered them, and then "posing as the accountholder, present[ed] an altered check to a cashier to purchase merchandise." In holding that the government does not need to prove that the defendant charged with violating 18 U.S.C. § 1344(2) intended to defraud a bank, the Court noted that unlike the mail fraud statute, this statute had separate clauses with distinct meanings. The Court also rejected the defendant's argument that such an interpretation would permit prosecution of garden-variety frauds. The Court stated:

> Under that clause, it is not enough that a fraudster scheme to obtain money from a bank and that he make a false statement. The provision as well includes a relational component: The criminal must acquire (or attempt to acquire) bank property "by means of" the misrepresentation. That phrase typically indicates that the given result (the "end") is achieved, at least in part, *through* the specified action, instrument, or method (the "means"), such that the connection between the two is something more than oblique, indirect, and incidental. * * * In other words, not every but-for cause will do.

3. ***Other "Scheme to Defraud" Statutes.*** In addition to mail and wire fraud, Congress has added other fraud statutes that require a similar "scheme to defraud" as an element of the offense. See, e.g., bankruptcy fraud (18 U.S.C. § 157); health care fraud (18 U.S.C. § 1347); travel fraud (18 U.S.C. § 2314); major fraud act (18 U.S.C. § 1031). Many of the cases emanating from these statutes use the precedent found in mail and wire fraud cases. See Ellen S. Podgor, *Criminal Fraud*, 48 Am. U. L. Rev. 729 (1999). As with many white collar crime cases, the intent of the accused is often an issue. For example, **United States v. Gellene**, 182 F.3d 578 (7th Cir. 1999), affirmed convictions, stating:

> John G. Gellene, a partner at the law firm of Milbank Tweed Hadley & McCloy ("Milbank") in New York, represented the Bucyrus-Erie Company ("Bucyrus") in its Chapter 11 bankruptcy. Mr. Gellene filed in the bankruptcy court a sworn declaration that was to include all of his firm's connections to the debtor, creditors, and any other parties in interest. The declaration failed to list the senior secured creditor and related parties. Mr. Gellene was charged with two counts of knowingly and fraudulently making a false material declaration in the Bucyrus bankruptcy case, in violation of 18 U.S.C. § 152, and one count of using a document while under oath, knowing that it contained a false material declaration, in violation of 18 U.S.C. § 1623. Although Mr. Gellene admitted that he had used bad judgment in concluding that the representations did not need to be disclosed, he asserted that he had no fraudulent intent. After a six-day trial, on March 3, 1998, the jury returned guilty verdicts against Mr. Gellene on all three counts. Mr. Gellene was sentenced to 15 months of imprisonment on each count, to run concurrently, and was fined $15,000. * * *
>
> Mr. Gellene submits that the court's definition of "fraudulent" as "with intent to deceive" is erroneous. In his view, the statute requires that the statement be made not simply with the intent to deceive but with the intent to defraud. He further claims that, because the government misapprehended the statutory requirement, it failed to present evidence that he made his declarations with an intent to defraud because it believed it needed to prove merely an intent to deceive. He submits that the distinction between the two terms is significant: To deceive is to cause to believe the false or to

> mislead; to defraud is to deprive of some right, interest or property by deceit. Therefore, under § 152 of the Bankruptcy Code, he contends, the defendant must have a specific intent to alter or to impact the distribution of a debtor's assets and not merely to impact the integrity of the legal system, as the government argued. * * *
>
> We cannot accept Mr. Gellene's narrowly circumscribed definition of "intent to defraud" or "fraudulently." Mr. Gellene would limit exclusively the statute's scope to false statements that deprive the debtor of his property or the bankruptcy estate of its assets. In our view, such a parsimonious interpretation was not intended by Congress. * * *
>
> We agree that § 152 requires that materiality be an element of the crime of bankruptcy fraud and, indeed, we have incorporated such a requirement in our analysis of § 152 fraud. * * * The statute is therefore construed to require that the false oath be in relation to some material matter. * * * We conclude that the materiality element does not require proof of the potential impact on the disposition of assets. * * *

4. ***False Claims***. The criminal false claims statute, 18 U.S.C. § 287, was initially combined with the false statement statute (see chap. 8(B)). There are also civil false claims statutes that permit the government to proceed against individuals in civil cases involving fraudulent false claims to the government. WCH § 9.8. Some of the civil false claims cases arise from whistleblower or *qui tam* actions. In 2014, the Department of Justice recovered nearly six billion dollars from false claims act cases, many involving frauds in the financial and health care sector. See DOJ Press Release, Justice Department Recovers Nearly $6 Billion From False Claims Act Cases in Fiscal Year 2014, http://www.justice.gov/opa/pr/justice-department-recovers-nearly-6-billion-false-claims-act-cases-fiscal-year-2014.

5. ***Specific Fraud Statutes.*** In some instances, Congress has provided a fraud statute that is not premised upon a "scheme to defraud," but is premised on specific types of fraudulent conduct. For example, the marriage fraud statute does not require proof of a "scheme or artifice to defraud." See 8 U.S.C. § 1325(c). Likewise, the computer fraud statute limits the possible schemes to defraud by listing specific activities that can be subject to prosecution. See 18 U.S.C. § 1030. But this specificity may not be needed when the government pursues conduct that falls outside the boundaries of both the general (wire fraud) and specific (computer fraud) statute. Consider the application of the computer fraud statute and wire fraud statute in the following case:

UNITED STATES v. CZUBINSKI

106 F.3d 1069 (1st Cir. 1997)

TORRUELLA, Chief Judge.

Defendant-appellant Richard Czubinski ("Czubinski") appeals his jury conviction on nine counts of wire fraud, 18 U.S.C. §§ 1343, 1346, and four counts of computer fraud, 18 U.S.C. § 1030(a)(4). * * *

For all periods relevant to the acts giving rise to his conviction, the defendant Czubinski was employed as a Contact Representative in the Boston office of the Taxpayer Services Division of the Internal Revenue Service ("IRS"). To perform his official duties, which mainly involved answering questions from taxpayers regarding their returns, Czubinski routinely accessed information from one of the IRS's computer systems known as the Integrated Data Retrieval System ("IDRS"). Using a valid password given to Contact Representatives, certain search codes, and taxpayer social security numbers, Czubinski was able to retrieve, to his terminal screen in Boston, income tax return information regarding virtually any taxpayer -information that is permanently stored in the IDRS "master file" located in Martinsburg, West Virginia. In the period of Czubinski's employ, IRS rules plainly stated that employees with passwords and access codes were not permitted to access files on IDRS outside of the course of their official duties.

In 1992, Czubinski carried out numerous unauthorized searches of IDRS files. He knowingly disregarded IRS rules by looking at confidential information obtained by performing computer searches that were outside of the scope of his duties as a Contact Representative, including, but not limited to, the searches listed in the indictment. Audit trails performed by internal IRS auditors establish that Czubinski frequently made unauthorized accesses on IDRS in 1992. For example, Czubinski accessed information regarding: the tax returns of two individuals involved in the David Duke presidential campaign; the joint tax return of an assistant district attorney (who had been prosecuting Czubinski's father on an unrelated felony offense) and his wife; the tax return of Boston City Counselor Jim Kelly's Campaign Committee (Kelly had defeated Czubinski in the previous election for the Counselor seat for District 2); the tax return of one of his brothers' instructors; the joint tax return of a Boston Housing Authority police officer, who was involved in a community organization with one of Czubinski's brothers, and the officer's wife; and the tax return of a woman Czubinski had dated a few times. Czubinski also accessed the files of various other social acquaintances by performing unauthorized searches.

Nothing in the record indicates that Czubinski did anything more than knowingly disregard IRS rules by observing the confidential information he accessed. No evidence suggests, nor does the government contend, that Czubinski disclosed the confidential information he accessed to any third parties. The government's only evidence demonstrating any intent to use the confidential information for nefarious ends was the trial testimony of William A. Murray, an acquaintance of Czubinski who briefly participated in Czubinski's local Invisible Knights of the Ku Klux Klan ("KKK") chapter and worked with him on the David Duke campaign. Murray testified that Czubinski had once stated at a social gathering in "early 1992" that "he intended to use some of that information to build dossiers on people" involved in "the white supremacist movement." There is, however, no evidence that Czubinski created dossiers, took steps toward making dossiers (such as by printing out or recording the information he browsed), or shared any of the information he accessed in the years following the single comment to Murray. No other witness testified to having any knowledge of Czubinski's alleged intent to create "dossiers" on KKK members.

The record shows that Czubinski did not perform any unauthorized searches after 1992. He continued to be employed as a Contact Representative until June 1995, when a grand jury returned an indictment against him on ten counts of federal wire fraud under 18 U.S.C. §§ 1343, 1346, and four counts of federal interest computer fraud under 18 U.S.C. § 1030(a)(4).

The portion of the indictment alleging wire fraud states that Czubinski defrauded the IRS of confidential property and defrauded the IRS and the public of his honest services by using his valid password to acquire confidential taxpayer information as part of a scheme to: 1) build "dossiers" on associates in the KKK; 2) seek information regarding an assistant district attorney who was then prosecuting Czubinski's father on an unrelated criminal charge; and 3) perform opposition research by inspecting the records of a political opponent in the race for a Boston City Councilor seat. The wire fraud indictment, therefore, articulated particular personal ends to which the unauthorized access to confidential information through interstate wires was allegedly a means. * * *

* * * To support a conviction for wire fraud, the government must prove two elements beyond a reasonable doubt: (1) the defendant's knowing and willing participation in a scheme or artifice to defraud with the specific intent to defraud, and (2) the use of interstate wire communications in furtherance of the scheme. * * * The government pursued two theories of wire fraud in this prosecution: first, that Czubinski defrauded the IRS of its property, under section 1343, by acquiring confidential information for certain intended personal uses; second, that he defrauded the IRS and the public of their intangible right to his honest services, under sections 1343 and 1346. We consider the evidence with regard to each theory, in turn.

* * * The government correctly notes that confidential information may constitute intangible "property" and that its unauthorized dissemination or other use may deprive the owner of its property rights. See Carpenter v. United States [p. 158] Where such deprivation is effected through dishonest or deceitful means, a "scheme to defraud," within the meaning of the wire fraud statute, is shown. Thus, a necessary step toward satisfying the

"scheme to defraud" element in this context is showing that the defendant intended to "deprive" another of their protected right.

The government, however, provides no case in support of its contention here that merely accessing confidential information, without doing, or clearly intending to do, more, is tantamount to a deprivation of IRS property under the wire fraud statute. In *Carpenter*, for example, the confidential information regarding the contents of a newspaper column was converted to the defendants's use to their substantial benefit. * * * We do not think that Czubinski's unauthorized browsing, even if done with the intent to deceive the IRS into thinking he was performing only authorized searches, constitutes a "deprivation" within the meaning of the federal fraud statutes.

Binding precedents, and good sense, support the conclusion that to "deprive" a person of their intangible property interest in confidential information under section 1343, either some articulable harm must befall the holder of the information as a result of the defendant's activities, or some gainful use must be intended by the person accessing the information, whether or not this use is profitable in the economic sense. Here, neither the taking of the IRS' right to "exclusive use" of the confidential information, nor Czubinski's gain from access to the information, can be shown absent evidence of his "use" of the information. Accordingly, without evidence that Czubinski used or intended to use the taxpayer information (beyond mere browsing), an intent to deprive cannot be proven, and, a fortiori, a scheme to defraud is not shown. * * *

The fatal flaw in the government's case is that it has not shown beyond a reasonable doubt that Czubinski intended to carry out a scheme to deprive the IRS of its property interest in confidential information. Had there been sufficient proof that Czubinski intended either to create dossiers for the sake of advancing personal causes or to disseminate confidential information to third parties, then his actions in searching files could arguably be said to be a step in furtherance of a scheme to deprive the IRS of its property interest in confidential information. The government's case regarding Czubinski's intent to make any use of the information he browsed rests on the testimony of one witness at trial who stated that Czubinski once remarked at a social gathering that he intended to build dossiers on potential KKK informants. We must assume, on this appeal, that Czubinski did indeed make such a comment. Nevertheless, the fact that during the months following this remark—that is, during the period in which Czubinski made his unauthorized searches—he did not create dossiers (there was no evidence that he created dossiers either during or after the period of his unauthorized searches); given the fact that he did not even take steps toward creating dossiers, such as recording or printing out the information; given the fact that no other person testifying as to Czubinski's involvement in white supremacist organizations had any knowledge of Czubinski's alleged intent to create dossiers or use confidential information; and given the fact that not a single piece of evidence suggests that Czubinski ever shared taxpayer information with others, no rational jury could have found beyond a reasonable doubt that, when Czubinski was browsing taxpayer files, he was doing so in furtherance of a scheme to use the information he browsed for private purposes, be they nefarious or otherwise. In addition, there was no evidence that Czubinski disclosed, or used to his advantage, any information regarding political opponents or regarding the person prosecuting his father.

Mere browsing of the records of people about whom one might have a particular interest, although reprehensible, is not enough to sustain a wire fraud conviction on a "deprivation of intangible property" theory. Curiosity on the part of an IRS officer may lead to dismissal, but curiosity alone will not sustain a finding of participation in a felonious criminal scheme to deprive the IRS of its property. * * *

[The court then discussed 18 U.S.C. § 1346]

* * * First, this case falls outside of the core of honest services fraud precedents. Czubinski was not bribed or otherwise influenced in any public decisionmaking capacity. Nor did he embezzle funds. He did not receive, nor can it be found that he intended to receive, any tangible benefit. His official duty was to respond to informational requests from taxpayers regarding their returns, a relatively straightforward task that simply does not raise the specter of secretive, self-interested action, as does a discretionary, decision-making role. * * *

Second, we believe that the cautionary language of *Sawyer* is particularly appropriate here, given the evidence amassed by the defendant at trial indicating that during his span of employment at IRS, he received no indication from his employer that this workplace violation--the performance of unauthorized searches--would be punishable by anything more than dismissal. "To allow every transgression of state governmental obligations to amount to mail fraud would effectively turn every such violation into a federal felony; this cannot be countenanced." Here, the threat is one of transforming governmental workplace violations into felonies. We find no evidence that Congress intended to create what amounts to a draconian personnel regulation. We hesitate to imply such an unusual result in the absence of the clearest legislative mandate.

These general considerations, although serious, are not conclusive: they raise doubts as to the propriety of this conviction that can be outweighed by sufficient evidence of a scheme to defraud. The third principle identified in Sawyer, instructing us as to the basic requirements of a scheme to defraud in this context, settles any remaining doubts. The conclusive consideration is that the government simply did not prove that Czubinski deprived, or intended to deprive, the public or his employer of their right to his honest services. Although he clearly committed wrongdoing in searching confidential information, there is no suggestion that he failed to carry out his official tasks adequately, or intended to do so.

The government alleges that, in addition to defrauding the public of his honest services, Czubinski has defrauded the IRS as well. The IRS is a public entity, rendering this contention sufficiently answered by our holding above that Czubinski did not defraud the public of his honest services. Even if the IRS were a private employer, however, the pre-*McNally* honest services convictions involving private fraud victims indicate that there must be a breach of a fiduciary duty to an employer that involves self-dealing of an order significantly more serious than the misconduct at issue here. * * * Once again, the government has failed to prove that Czubinski intended to use the IRS files he browsed for any private purposes, and hence his actions, however reprehensible, do not rise to the level of a scheme to defraud his employer of his honest services. * * *

* * * For the same reasons we deemed the trial evidence could not support a finding that Czubinski deprived the IRS of its property, see discussion of wire fraud under section 1343 supra, we find that Czubinski has not obtained valuable information in furtherance of a fraudulent scheme for the purposes of section 1030(a)(4). * * *

We add a cautionary note. The broad language of the mail and wire fraud statutes are both their blessing and their curse. They can address new forms of serious crime that fail to fall within more specific legislation. * * * On the other hand, they might be used to prosecute kinds of behavior that, albeit offensive to the morals or aesthetics of federal prosecutors, cannot reasonably be expected by the instigators to form the basis of a federal felony. The case at bar falls within the latter category. Also discomforting is the prosecution's insistence, before trial, on the admission of inflammatory evidence regarding the defendant's membership in white supremacist groups purportedly as a means to prove a scheme to defraud, when, on appeal, it argues that unauthorized access in itself is a sufficient ground for conviction on all counts. Finally, we caution that the wire fraud statute must not serve as a vehicle for prosecuting only those citizens whose views run against the tide, no matter how incorrect or uncivilized such views are.

For the reasons stated in this opinion, we hold the district court's denial of defendant's motion for judgment of acquittal on counts 1, 2, and 4 through 14, to be in error. The defendant's conviction is thus reversed on all counts.

J. MONEY LAUNDERING

UNITED STATES v. WARSHAK

631 F.3d 266 (6th Cir. 2010)

BOGGS, Circuit Judge.

Berkeley Premium Nutraceuticals, Inc. ("Berkeley"), was an incredibly profitable company that served as the distributor of Enzyte, an herbal supplement purported to enhance male sexual performance. In this appeal, defendant Steven Warshak [and his mother challenge their convictions] stemming from a massive scheme to defraud Berkeley's customers. * * *

In the latter half of 2001, Berkeley launched Enzyte, its flagship product. At the time of its launch, Enzyte was purported to increase the size of a man's erection. The product proved tremendously popular, and business rose sharply. By 2004, demand for Berkeley's products had grown so dramatically that the company employed 1500 people, and the call center remained open throughout the night, taking orders at breakneck speed. Berkeley's line of supplements also expanded, ballooning from approximately four products to around thirteen. By year's end, Berkeley's annual sales topped out at around $250 million, largely on the strength of Enzyte.

The popularity of Enzyte appears to have been due in large part to Berkeley's aggressive advertising campaigns. The vast majority of the advertising—approximately 98%—was conducted through television spots. Around 2004, network television was saturated with Enzyte advertisements featuring a character called "Smilin' Bob," whose trademark exaggerated smile was presumably the result of Enzyte's efficacy. The "Smilin' Bob" commercials were rife with innuendo and implied that users of Enzyte would become the envy of the neighborhood.

In addition to the television commercials, however, there were also advertisements in other media, such as print and radio. In 2001, just after Enzyte's premiere, advertisements appeared in a number of men's interest magazines. At Warshak's direction, those advertisements cited a 2001 independent customer study, which purported to show that, over a three-month period, 100 English-speaking men who took Enzyte experienced a 12 to 31% increase in the size of their penises. The 2001 study was also referenced in radio advertisements and appeared on the company's website, as well as in brochures and sales calls. * * * [Berkeley's Chief Operating Officer] later testified that the survey was bogus [and] * * * that he plucked the numbers out of the air and generated the spreadsheet over a twenty-four hour period. * * *

[Warshak and Berkeley adopted an "auto-pay" program under which a customer who signed up for a free sample was automatically billed for additional shipments until the person opted out. When calling the company to cancel the shipments, a number of such requests were not filled until after multiple calls. Warshak also misled banks that processed Berkeley's credit card payments to mask the number of customer chargebacks because of disputes about the amount of products ordered to keep from having his accounts cancelled. These formed the basis for the mail, wire, and bank fraud convictions that supported the money laundering charges.]

Warshak argues that the government failed to present sufficient evidence that he committed various acts of so-called promotional money laundering.

Promotional money laundering is defined in 18 U.S.C. § 1956(a)(1)(A)(i), which states:

> Whoever, knowing that the property involved in a financial transaction represents the proceeds of some form of unlawful activity, conducts or attempts to conduct such a financial transaction which in fact involves the proceeds of specified unlawful activity ... with the intent to promote the carrying on of specified unlawful activity ... shall be [subject to criminal penalties].

To prove a defendant guilty of promotional money laundering, the government must demonstrate that he: (1) conducted a financial transaction that involved the proceeds of unlawful activity; (2) knew the property involved was proceeds of unlawful activity; and (3) intended to promote that unlawful activity. The paradigmatic example of this crime is a drug dealer using the proceeds of a drug transaction to purchase additional drugs and consummate future sales.

In the present case, Warshak was charged with six counts of promotional money laundering * * * made to his sisters * * *, both of whom worked for Berkeley. Count 79 dealt with a third million-dollar payment Warshak made to * * *, another Berkeley employee and a longtime friend of Warshak's mother. Count 80 described a payment of $100,000 to Strong Foundations, Inc., "a purported non-profit charitable entity by which [Berkeley] would provide homes to single-parent households." Count 82 involved a transfer of $180,000 to Hallmark Homes, LLC, a Kentucky corporation owned by one of Warshak's brothers-in-law. Finally, Count 98 pertained to a transfer of $1 million to * * * Warshak's mother.

Arguing that he should not have been convicted of any of these counts, Warshak claims that there was not enough evidence to establish the first element of the crime, namely, that the charged transactions involved the proceeds of an unlawful activity. Warshak renews his argument that the government failed to prove that he committed mail, wire, or bank fraud. He argues that, without the underlying convictions, there are no illegal activities from which proceeds could have been derived. He also argues that, even if his convictions were proper, the transactions at issue occurred in 2004 or later, by which time the company was "gross[ing] hundreds of millions of dollars in legitimate sales." He contends that "[t]he fact that the monies at issue originated at Berkeley . . . does not, therefore, suffice to prove that the transactions at issue involved the proceeds of mail or wire fraud."

Warshak's argument fails. As an initial matter, a reasonable juror could easily conclude that Berkeley's sales operation was, for the entire duration of its existence, little more than a colossal fraud. * * * Furthermore, even allowing that some of the sales were legitimate, the evidence nonetheless indicates that many of Berkeley's sales during the relevant time period were generated through deceptive practices rising to the level of mail fraud. Because the proceeds from fraudulent sales were mixed with the proceeds of any arguably above-board sales, any transaction involving Berkeley's revenues can be said to involve the proceeds of an illegal activity.

Warshak also argues that the evidence was insufficient to establish that the transactions at issue were undertaken for the purpose of promoting a specified unlawful activity. He notes that most of the charged transactions involved gifts to family and friends. * * *

This argument presents a fairly close question. It is true that the transactions charged in these counts were payments to Berkeley employees, and it is also true that a number of cases support the proposition that payments to employees may constitute sufficient evidence of an intent to promote an unlawful activity. See United States v. Alerre, 430 F.3d 681 (4th Cir.2005) ("[T]he promotion element [was] satisfied when a defendant paid his subordinate employee for being involved in an unlawful scheme, because such payments compensated the employee for his illegal activities and encouraged his continued participation."). However, in this case, the employees to whom the payments were made had close personal relationships with Warshak; two of the payments went to Warshak's sisters, one went to his mother, and one went to his mother's close friend. The payments could therefore be seen as resulting from the magnanimity of a dutiful brother, son, and friend. Moreover, there is no direct evidence that the payments were intended as compensation for services performed on the company's behalf—i.e., the payments were not listed as salary. As a result, the circumstances of the present case differ from those of a run-of-the-mill case involving direct remuneration of a mere worker.

Nonetheless, the evidence was sufficient to permit a reasonable juror to conclude that the payments were intended to promote a specified unlawful activity. The fact remains that every one of the individuals to whom a payment was made was a Berkeley employee. A juror could look at this fact and conclude that the payments were intended to reward faithful service and encourage future commitment to the criminal endeavor. Ironically, such a conclusion might actually garner support from Warshak's letters, in which he thanked his relatives for their "loyalty and support." Consequently, it cannot be said that the government failed to carry its evidentiary burden with respect to the million-dollar payments.

Additionally, there was sufficient evidence to permit the conclusion that the payments to Strong Foundations, Inc., and Hallmark Homes, LLC, were made with an intent to promote the fraudulent scheme. At trial, there was testimony that Strong Foundations was a charity that funded homes for single-parent households, and there was also testimony that Hallmark Homes, LLC, was a company that built houses. A reasonable juror could conclude that the payments to these entities were intended to raise Berkeley's philanthropic profile and create an "aura of legitimacy." Thus, a rational finder of fact could infer that the intent element was satisfied, and Warshak's challenge to the sufficiency of the evidence fails.

Like promotional money laundering, concealment money laundering is defined in 18 U.S.C. § 1956(a), which states, in relevant part:

> Whoever, knowing that the property involved in a financial transaction represents the proceeds of some form of unlawful activity, conducts or attempts to conduct such a financial transaction which in fact involves the proceeds of specified unlawful activity ... knowing that the transaction is designed in whole or in part ... to conceal or disguise the nature, the location, the source, the ownership, or the control of the proceeds of specified unlawful activity ... shall be [subject to criminal penalties].

To make out a violation of this provision, the government must prove three elements: (1) use of funds that are proceeds of unlawful activity; (2) knowledge that the funds are proceeds of unlawful activity; and (3) knowledge that the transaction is designed in whole or in part to disguise the source, ownership or control of the proceeds.

Warshak was charged with approximately sixty-five counts of concealment money. * * * The transactions on which the counts were based involved an assortment of business accounts, personal accounts, investments, and purchases.

Warshak argues that the government failed to prove that the transactions were made with the intent "to conceal or disguise the nature, the location, the source, the ownership, or the control of the proceeds." 18 U.S.C. § 1956(a)(1)(B)(i). He notes that "[m]ost of the charged transactions were completely open transfers of funds to Warshak personally, into accounts bearing his name, or to family members with the surname Warshak, or to corporations of which Warshak was the owner and 100% shareholder and with which he was openly and publicly affiliated." The defendant also notes that many of the charged transactions were simply transfers to and from "companies and accounts openly associated with Warshak." In addition, the defendant observes that some of the "charged transactions involved purchases of investment products such as life insurance policies and annuities in Warshak's own name, the simple and visible spending of money that falls outside the ambit of § 1956." In sum, the defendant contends that the transactions were all benign and transparent and that their convictions for concealment money laundering were simply not supported by the evidence.

While superficially attractive, the defendant's position overlooks several key points. It is certainly true that a number of the transactions were made under relatively open circumstances. However, that does not foreclose the possibility that the transactions were designed to conceal some characteristic of the funds involved. * * *

In this case, there was other evidence that the defendant intended to conceal the exact source of the proceeds. Specifically, the government introduced the testimony of [an FBI agent who] * * * testified that "[t]he transactions [involved in the case] were very complex, some of the most complex and lengthy transactions that I have ever had the occasion to examine." * * * This evidence was sufficient to support a finding of intent to conceal. When a sequence of transactions is "sufficiently complex," a reasonable juror may infer that the transactions were made for the purpose of concealment. * * *

Nor is that conclusion undermined by the fact that some of the charged transactions involved the purchase of an annuity or an insurance policy. While it is true that § 1956(a)(1)(B)(i) does not criminalize the simple spending of illegally obtained money, the purchases at issue here occurred at the end of a chain of transactions, allowing the inference that the expenditures were made with an intent to conceal as well as an intent to purchase.

In addition to being convicted of the foregoing charges, Warshak was found guilty of concealment money laundering in connection with 49 cash shipments made to his home in San Diego, California. Between 2002 and 2004, Warshak repeatedly instructed Berkeley employees to cash $5,000 checks drawn on Berkeley accounts and ship him the cash via FedEx.

Warshak argues that the evidence was insufficient to demonstrate that these transactions were intended to conceal the nature, source, location, ownership, or control of the funds. In making this argument, he relies on Cuellar v. United States, in which the Supreme Court stated: "how one moves the money is distinct from why one moves the money. Evidence of the former, standing alone, is not sufficient to prove the latter." 553 U.S. 550 (2008).

But the facts of this case are readily distinguishable from those confronted in *Cuellar*. There, the Supreme Court encountered a situation in which an individual was apprehended while crossing the United States–Mexico border in a Volkswagen Beetle with a secret compartment containing $81,000 in cash. Ultimately, the Supreme Court found that "[t]he evidence suggested that the secretive aspects of the transportation were employed to facilitate the transportation . . . but not necessarily that secrecy was the purpose of the transportation."

In the present case, the facts are different. The method of transportation does not suggest that the money was only concealed for the purposes of getting it from Point A to Point B. Indeed, placing stacks of money in FedEx envelopes is not the most prudent way to keep them hidden. Furthermore, the manner in which the funds were transported is not the only relevant evidence in the record. There is also testimony that the funds were removed from Berkeley's business accounts and shipped directly to Warshak's personal address. That testimony suggests that the transactions themselves were designed to conceal where the money came from, not where it was at a given moment. Consequently, *Cuellar* does not mandate reversal of Warshak's conviction.

[The court, however, reversed the mother's convictions of concealment money laundering. She argued that "the government failed to prove that she knew these transactions were designed to conceal an attribute of the transferred funds. She contends that she simply received a large monetary gift from her son and then used it." The court accepted this argument stating that "she must have had knowledge that the transactions were designed to conceal some aspect of the money at issue." The court said that there here was no evidence that she "knew the gift from her son was intended to conceal the source of the funds."][65]

NOTES AND QUESTIONS

1. ***Money Laundering As White Collar Crime.*** Money laundering has become a significant tool used by prosecutors in white collar cases. One finds 18 U.S.C. § 1956 and § 1957 included as counts in many recent white collar indictments. See Note, Teresa E. Adams, *Tacking on Money Laundering Charges to White Collar Crimes: What Did Congress Intend, And What Are The Courts Doing?*, 17 GA. ST. L. REV. 531 (2000). The charges appear in a wide array of different contexts including mail fraud. See also United States v. Butler, 211 F.3d 826 (4th Cir. 2000) (bankruptcy fraud). "Money laundering, [however,] must be a crime distinct from the crime by which the money is obtained. The money laundering statute is not simply the addition of a further penalty to a criminal deed; it is a prohibition of processing the fruits of a crime or of a completed phase of an ongoing offense." United States v. Abuhouran, 162 F.3d 230 (3rd Cir. 1998); see also United States v. Seward, 272 F.3d 831 (7th Cir. 2001) ("Although it is true that the defendant must have control of the proceeds of a fraudulent transaction before he can engage in money laundering with those proceeds, there is no requirement that the entire fraudulent scheme be complete before the defendant starts laundering the proceeds from early portions of the scheme.").

2. ***Sentencing Ramifications.*** The addition of money laundering can increase a defendant's sentence. Under the Federal Sentencing Guidelines, a conviction for money laundering increases the offense level used to calculate the sentence, usually resulting in a longer term of imprisonment than would be the case if mail fraud were the sole charge. See Chapter 18 for a discussion of the Federal Sentencing Guidelines. Thus, the suggestion that prosecutors add money laundering to an indictment that includes mail fraud increases the pressure on the defendant to enter a plea agreement to avoid a longer sentence.

---

[65] Granted, the fact that a given transfer is large or conspicuous does not preclude the finding that the transfer violated 18 U.S.C. § 1956. However, the size of the transfers is a proper consideration when determining whether the context supports a finding of intent to conceal. Here, given the relative simplicity of the transfers, the fact that large amounts were involved becomes more probative of the lack of intent.

3. ***Proceeds of Specified Unlawful Activity.*** Courts have struggled over when is the money "proceeds." In **United States v. Yusuf**, 536 F.3d 178 (3rd Cir. 2008), the Third Circuit looked at "whether unpaid taxes, which were unlawfully disguised and retained by means of the filing of false tax returns through the U.S. mail, are 'proceeds' of mail fraud for purposes of sufficiently stating a money laundering offense under the federal, international money laundering statute, 18 U.S.C. § 1956(a)(2)." The court held:

> Although the federal money laundering statute does not define what constitutes "proceeds" of a specified unlawful activity, see United States v. Santos, [553 U.S. 507] (2008), it specifically identifies which criminal offenses constitute "specified unlawful activities." 18 U.S.C. § 1956(c)(7). The term "specified unlawful activity" covers a broad array of offenses. For example, the fraudulent *concealment* of a bankruptcy estate's assets is categorized as a "specified unlawful activity." * * * Moreover, simply because funds are *originally* procured through *lawful* activity does not mean that one cannot thereafter convert those same funds into the "proceeds" of an unlawful activity.* * * See United States v. Ladum, 141 F.3d 1328, 1340 (9th Cir.1998) (sustaining money laundering conviction where the defendant concealed rental income derived from lawfully operated retail stores); United States v. Levine, 970 F.2d 681, 686 (10th Cir.1992) (sustaining money laundering conviction where the defendant concealed corporate tax refund checks deposited in a hidden bank account). Accordingly, we reject the suggestion that to qualify as "proceeds" under the federal money laundering statute, funds must have been *directly* produced by or through a specified unlawful activity, and we agree that funds *retained* as a result of the unlawful activity can be treated as the "proceeds" of such crime.
>
> Furthermore, the Supreme Court, in United States v. Santos, recently clarified that the term "proceeds," as that term is used in the federal money laundering statute, applies to criminal profits, not criminal receipts, derived from a specified unlawful activity. * * * The Supreme Court affirmed the trial court's decision to vacate the money laundering convictions because the transactions on which such convictions were based involved the gross receipts, as opposed to the profits, of the specified unlawful activity-the operation of an illegal lottery. The Supreme Court reasoned that the transactions upon which the money laundering charges were based could not be considered to have involved "proceeds" of the illegal lottery's operation because such transactions involved the mere payment of the illegal operation's *expenses* rather than the operation's *profits*.* * * Moreover, we have previously determined that "proceeds are derived from an already completed offense, or a completed phase of an ongoing offense, before they can be laundered." United States v. Conley, 37 F.3d 970, 980 (3d Cir.1994). * * * Based upon the Supreme Court's decisions in *Santos, Schmuck*, and *Kann,* and our decision in *Morelli,* we hold that unpaid taxes, which are unlawfully disguised and retained by means

> of the filing of false tax returns through the U.S. mail, constitute "proceeds" of mail fraud for purposes of supporting a charge of federal money laundering. * * * Furthermore, the mailings of the fraudulent tax returns resulted in "proceeds" of mail fraud based on the nature of the *entire ongoing fraudulent scheme* because the unpaid taxes unlawfully retained by defendants represented the "proceeds" of a fraud that was also furthered by previous mailings. * * * Accordingly, it logically follows that the unpaid taxes, unlawfully disguised and retained through the mailing of the tax forms, were "proceeds" of defendants' overall scheme to defraud the government. * * *

4. ***Patriot Act.*** Title III of the "Uniting and Strengthening America by Providing Appropriate Tools Required to Intercept and Obstruct Terrorism (USA Patriot Act) Act of 2001" is called the "International Money Laundering Abatement and Anti-Terrorist Funding Act of 2001." This act provides for expanded obligations on the part of financial institutions. See Gary Fields, *Antiterrorism Law Used to Seize Cash From Fraud Ring*, The Wall St. Jrl., Jan. 29, 2003, at B10.

CHAPTER SIX
THE RACKETEER INFLUENCED AND CORRUPT ORGANIZATION ACT (RICO)

A. INTRODUCTION

1. Statutes

The Racketeer Influenced and Corrupt Organization Act (RICO) was enacted by Congress as Title IX of the Organized Crime Control Act of 1970. In its early years, prosecutors seldom used RICO provisions. Today RICO is a charge used not only by federal prosecutors, but also by plaintiffs seeking civil relief. Although prosecutors initially focused on "organized crime," they later took the Act far beyond any such limitation. This was in part a product of an inability to define who and what is encompassed within the term "organized crime," and in part a product of the expanded prosecutorial authority made available through RICO. With RICO, federal prosecutors could: (1) reach certain activity that otherwise would not violate either federal or state criminal law; (2) reach activity (particularly violent activity) that otherwise would violate only state law; (3) gain enhanced penalties (including asset forfeiture) for activity that violated other provisions of the federal criminal law; and (4) gain broader joinder and more flexible venue than was available in prosecutions under other federal code provisions.

18 U.S.C.A. § 1962 enumerates the four types of prohibited conduct under this Act. RICO actions can, and often do, include more than one type of prohibited conduct. In essence, RICO requires that the defendant have invested in, maintained an interest in, participated in the affairs of an enterprise, or conspired to engage in conduct constituting a pattern of racketeering activity or collection of an unlawful debt. Case law provides interpretations of the word "enterprise," a term defined in 18 U.S.C.A. § 1961.

Each of the provisions in § 1962 allow prosecutions to be premised upon either a "pattern of racketeering" or the collection of an "unlawful debt," terms whose definitions are also outlined in RICO's definitional provision, 18 U.S.C.A. § 1961. The vast majority of RICO actions employ a pattern of racketeering as the focus of the unlawful conduct. A pattern of racketeering activity encompasses at least two acts of racketeering activity. Nine possible state offenses and over thirty federal offenses can serve as predicate acts for a RICO prosecution.

18 U.S.C.A. § 1963 provides the criminal penalties available in a RICO prosecution. These include incarceration, fines, and the forfeiture of property. Section 1963 also authorizes prosecutors to seek restraining orders

to prevent the dissipation of assets that may be subject to forfeiture. Extensive procedural rules regarding forfeiture of property and the protection of third party interests in the property are specified in this section.

18 U.S.C.A. § 1964 extends RICO outside the criminal context, allowing its use in civil proceedings. This latter provision has been the subject of significant controversy in its allowance of "garden variety" frauds to be subject to treble damages and attorney fees. Proposals have been suggested and rejected to limit RICO's application in civil actions. For example, one House Bill provided that a criminal conviction of racketeering activity or a violation under § 1962 was necessary for bringing a civil RICO action. [See H.R. 2943, 99th Cong., 1st Sess. (1985)].

2. Civil RICO

RICO actions brought by the government require prior approval from the Criminal Division. Private civil RICO cases, however, are not subject to any governmental review or restrictions. Courts have generally been hostile to private RICO claims, but the broad language of the statute makes direct restrictions on filing such actions difficult to impose. In **Sedima v. Imrex Co.**, 473 U.S. 479 (1985), a case involving a civil action brought under § 1964(c), the Court held that there is no requirement in a private civil RICO action that the defendant previously have been criminally convicted of the predicate offenses that constitute the pattern of racketeering or of the RICO violation itself. Justice White, writing for the majority, stated:

> RICO was an aggressive initiative to supplement old remedies and develop new methods for fighting crime. See generally Russello v. United States, 464 U.S. 16, 26-29 (1983). While few of the legislative statements about novel remedies and attacking crime on all fronts were made with direct reference to § 1964(c), it is in this spirit that all of the Act's provisions should be read. The specific references to § 1964(c) are consistent with this overall approach. Those supporting § 1964(c) hoped it would "enhance the effectiveness of title IX's prohibitions" and provide "a major new tool." Its opponents, also recognizing the provision's scope, complained that it provided too easy a weapon against 'innocent businessmen' and would be prone to abuse. * * *

In his dissent, Justice Marshall noted:

> * * * The Court's interpretation of the civil RICO statute quite simply revolutionizes private litigation; it validates the federalization of broad areas of state common law of frauds, and it approves the displacement of well-established federal remedial provisions. We do not lightly infer a congressional intent to effect such fundamental changes. To infer such intent here would be

untenable, for there is no indication that Congress even considered, much less approved, the scheme that the Court today defines.

The single most significant reason for the expansive use of civil RICO has been the presence in the statute, as predicate acts, of mail and wire fraud violations. Prior to RICO, no federal statute had expressly provided a private damages remedy based upon a violation of the mail or wire fraud statutes, which make it a federal crime to use the mail or wires in furtherance of a scheme to defraud. * * *

The responsible use of prosecutorial discretion is particularly important with respect to criminal RICO prosecutions—which often rely on mail and wire fraud as predicate acts—given the extremely severe penalties authorized by RICO's criminal provisions. * * * [Justice Marshall here describes the limits set forth in the Justice Department's guidelines.] In the context of civil RICO, however, the restraining influence of prosecutors is completely absent. Unlike the Government, private litigants have no reason to avoid displacing state common-law remedies. Quite to the contrary, such litigants, lured by the prospect of treble damages and attorney's fees, have a strong incentive to invoke RICO's provisions whenever they can allege in good faith two instances of mail or wire fraud. Then the defendant, facing a tremendous financial exposure in addition to the threat of being labeled a "racketeer," will have a strong interest in settling the dispute. * * * The civil RICO provision consequently stretches the mail and wire fraud statutes to their absolute limits and federalizes important areas of civil litigation that until now were solely within the domain of the States.

B. THE ENTERPRISE

1. Nature of an "Enterprise"

UNITED STATES v. TURKETTE
452 U.S. 576 (1981)

Justice WHITE delivered the opinion of the Court.

* * * Count Nine of a nine-count indictment charged respondent and 12 others with conspiracy to conduct and participate in the affairs of an enterprise engaged in interstate commerce through a pattern of racketeering activities, in violation of 18 U.S.C. § 1962(d). The indictment described the enterprise as "a group of individuals associated in fact for the purpose of illegally trafficking in narcotics and other dangerous drugs, committing arsons, utilizing the United States mails to defraud insurance companies, bribing and attempting to bribe local police officers, and corruptly influencing and attempting to corruptly influence the outcome of state court proceedings

. . . ." The other eight counts of the indictment charged the commission of various substantive criminal acts by those engaged in and associated with the criminal enterprise, including possession with intent to distribute and distribution of controlled substances, and several counts of insurance fraud by arson and other means. The common thread to all counts was respondent's alleged leadership of this criminal organization through which he orchestrated and participated in the commission of the various crimes delineated in the RICO count or charged in the eight preceding counts.

After a 6-week jury trial, in which the evidence focused upon both the professional nature of this organization and the execution of a number of distinct criminal acts, respondent was convicted on all nine counts. He was sentenced to a term of 20 years on the substantive counts, as well as a 2-year special parole term on the drug count. On the RICO conspiracy count he was sentenced to a 20-year concurrent term and fined $20,000.

On appeal, respondent argued that RICO was intended solely to protect legitimate business enterprises from infiltration by racketeers and that RICO does not make criminal the participation in an association which performs only illegal acts and which has not infiltrated or attempted to infiltrate a legitimate enterprise. The Court of Appeals agreed. We reverse. * * *

Section 1961(4) describes two categories of associations that come within the purview of the "enterprise" definition. The first encompasses organizations such as corporations and partnerships, and other "legal entities." The second covers "any union or group of individuals associated in fact although not a legal entity." The Court of Appeals assumed that the second category was merely a more general description of the first. * * * But that assumption is untenable. Each category describes a separate type of enterprise to be covered by the statute—those that are recognized as legal entities and those that are not. The latter is not a more general description of the former. The second category itself not containing any specific enumeration that is followed by a general description, *ejusdem generis* has no bearing on the meaning to be attributed to that part of § 1961(4).

A second reason offered by the Court of Appeals in support of its judgment was that giving the definition of "enterprise" its ordinary meaning would create several internal inconsistencies in the Act. With respect to § 1962(c), it was said:

> "If 'a pattern of racketeering' can itself be an 'enterprise' for purposes of section 1962(c), then the two phrases 'employed by or associated with any enterprise' and 'the conduct of such enterprise's affairs through [a pattern of racketeering activity]' add nothing to the meaning of the section. The words of the statute are coherent and logical only if they are read as applying to legitimate enterprises."

This conclusion is based on a faulty premise. That a wholly criminal enterprise comes within the ambit of the statute does not mean that a "pattern of racketeering activity" is an "enterprise." In order to secure a conviction under RICO, the Government must prove both the existence of an "enterprise" and the connected "pattern of racketeering activity." The enterprise is an entity, for present purposes a group of persons associated together for a common purpose of engaging in a course of conduct. The pattern of racketeering activity is, on the other hand, a series of criminal acts as defined by the statute. 18 U.S.C. § 1961(1). The former is proved by evidence of an ongoing organization, formal or informal, and by evidence that the various associates function as a continuing unit. The latter is proved by evidence of the requisite number of acts of racketeering committed by the participants in the enterprise. While the proof used to establish these separate elements may in particular cases coalesce, proof of one does not necessarily establish the other. The "enterprise" is not the "pattern of racketeering activity"; it is an entity separate and apart from the pattern of activity in which it engages. The existence of an enterprise at all times remains a separate element which must be proved by the Government.[5]

Apart from § 1962(c)'s proscription against participating in an enterprise through a pattern of racketeering activities, RICO also proscribes the investment of income derived from racketeering activity in an enterprise engaged in or which affects interstate commerce as well as the acquisition of an interest in or control of any such enterprise through a pattern of racketeering activity. 18 U.S.C. §§ 1962(a) and (b). The Court of Appeals concluded that these provisions of RICO should be interpreted so as to apply only to legitimate enterprises. If these two sections are so limited, the Court of Appeals held that the proscription in § 1962(c), at issue here, must be similarly limited. Again, we do not accept the premise from which the Court of Appeals derived its conclusion. It is obvious that § 1962(a) and (b) address the infiltration by organized crime of legitimate businesses, but we cannot agree that these sections were not also aimed at preventing racketeers from investing or reinvesting in wholly illegal enterprises and from acquiring through a pattern of racketeering activity wholly illegitimate enterprises such as an illegal gambling business or a loan-sharking operation. There is no inconsistency or anomaly in recognizing that § 1962 applies to both legitimate and illegitimate enterprises. Certainly the language of the statute does not warrant the Court of Appeals' conclusion to the contrary.

Similarly, the Court of Appeals noted that various civil remedies were provided by § 1964, including divestiture, dissolution, reorganization, restrictions on future activities by violators of RICO, and treble damages.

---

[5] The Government takes the position that proof of a pattern of racketeering activity in itself would not be sufficient to establish the existence of an enterprise: "We do not suggest that any two sporadic and isolated offenses by the same actor or actors *ipso facto* constitute an 'illegitimate' enterprise; rather, the existence of the enterprise as an independent entity must also be shown." * * *

These remedies it thought would have utility only with respect to legitimate enterprises. As a general proposition, however, the civil remedies could be useful in eradicating organized crime from the social fabric, whether the enterprise be ostensibly legitimate or admittedly criminal. The aim is to divest the association of the fruits of its ill-gotten gains. Even if one or more of the civil remedies might be inapplicable to a particular illegitimate enterprise, this fact would not serve to limit the enterprise concept. Congress has provided civil remedies for use when the circumstances so warrant. It is untenable to argue that their existence limits the scope of the criminal provisions.

Finally, it is urged that the interpretation of RICO to include both legitimate and illegitimate enterprises will substantially alter the balance between federal and state enforcement of criminal law. This is particularly true, so the argument goes, since included within the definition of racketeering activity are a significant number of acts made criminal under state law. 18 U.S.C. § 1961(1). But even assuming that the more inclusive definition of enterprise will have the effect suggested, the language of the statute and its legislative history indicate that Congress was well aware that it was entering a new domain of federal involvement through the enactment of this measure. Indeed, the very purpose of the Organized Crime Control Act of 1970 was to enable the Federal Government to address a large and seemingly neglected problem. * * *

Contrary to the judgment below, neither the language nor structure of RICO limits its application to legitimate "enterprises." Applying it also to criminal organizations does not render any portion of the statute superfluous nor does it create any structural incongruities within the framework of the Act. The result is neither absurd nor surprising. On the contrary, insulating the wholly criminal enterprise from prosecution under RICO is the more incongruous position.

Section 904(a) of RICO, directs that "[t]he provisions of this Title shall be liberally construed to effectuate its remedial purposes." With or without this admonition, we could not agree with the Court of Appeals that illegitimate enterprises should be excluded from coverage. We are also quite sure that nothing in the legislative history of RICO requires a contrary conclusion. * * *

The statement of findings that prefaces the Organized Crime Control Act of 1970 reveals the pervasiveness of the problem that Congress was addressing by this enactment:

"The Congress finds that (1) organized crime in the United States is a highly sophisticated, diversified, and widespread activity that annually drains billions of dollars from America's economy by unlawful conduct and the illegal use of force, fraud, and corruption; (2) organized crime derives a major portion of its power through money obtained from such illegal endeavors as syndicated gambling, loan sharking, the theft and fencing of property, the importation and distribution of narcotics and other dangerous drugs, and other forms of social exploitation; (3) this money and power are increasingly used to infiltrate and corrupt legitimate business and labor unions and to subvert and corrupt our democratic processes; (4) organized crime activities in the United States weaken the stability of the Nation's economic system, harm innocent investors and competing organizations, interfere with free competition, seriously burden interstate and foreign commerce, threaten the domestic security, and undermine the general welfare of the Nation and its citizens; and (5) organized crime continues to grow because of defects in the evidence-gathering process of the law inhibiting the development of the legally admissible evidence necessary to bring criminal and other sanctions or remedies to bear on the unlawful activities of those engaged in organized crime and because the sanctions and remedies available to the Government are unnecessarily limited in scope and impact."

In light of the above findings, it was the declared purpose of Congress "to seek the eradication of organized crime in the United States by strengthening the legal tools in the evidence-gathering process, by establishing new penal prohibitions, and by providing enhanced sanctions and new remedies to deal with the unlawful activities of those engaged in organized crime." * * *

Considering this statement of the Act's broad purposes, the construction of RICO suggested by respondent and the court below is unacceptable. Whole areas of organized criminal activity would be placed beyond the substantive reach of the enactment. * * *

Accepting that the primary purpose of RICO is to cope with the infiltration of legitimate businesses, applying the statute in accordance with its terms, so as to reach criminal enterprises, would seek to deal with the problem at its very source. Supporters of the bill recognized that organized crime uses its primary sources of revenue and power—illegal gambling, loan sharking and illicit drug distribution—as a springboard into the sphere of legitimate enterprise. * * *

As a measure to deal with the infiltration of legitimate businesses by organized crime, RICO was both preventive and remedial. Respondent's view would ignore the preventive function of the statute. If Congress had intended the more circumscribed approach espoused by the Court of Appeals, there would have been some positive sign that the law was not to reach organized criminal activities that give rise to the concerns about infiltration. The language of the statute, however—the most reliable evidence of its intent—reveals that Congress opted for a far broader definition of the word "enterprise," and we are unconvinced by anything in the legislative history that this definition should be given less than its full effect.

The judgment of the Court of Appeals is accordingly reversed.

Justice STEWART agrees with the reasoning and conclusion of the Court of Appeals as to the meaning of the term "enterprise" in this statute. See 632 F.2d 896. Accordingly, he respectfully dissents.

NOTE

Courts have permitted state and local government offices to be the enterprise in a RICO case. See United States v. Ganim, 225 F.Supp.2d 145 (D.Conn. 2002) (Office of the Mayor of Bridgeport); United States v. Cianci, 210 F.Supp.2d 71 (D.R.I. 2002) (City of Providence, Rhode Island); United States v. Genova, 187 F.Supp.2d 1015 (N.D. Ill. 2002) (Calumet City, Illinois). Although the court allowed "The Office of Governor of Tennessee" to be an enterprise in United States v. Thompson, 685 F.2d 993, 1000 (6th Cir.1982), dicta noted that it "is disruptive of comity in federal-state relations" and "may also needlessly cast unfair reflection upon innocent individuals." The court stated that preferably the indictment should be premised upon a "group of individual[s] associated in fact although not a legal entity which made use of the Office of Governor of the State of Tennessee." In United States v. Warner, 498 F.3d 666 (7th Cir. 2007), the Seventh Circuit allowed a RICO charge identifying the State of Illinois as the enterprise. The court stated, "We endorse the Sixth Circuit's call for caution. We also agree with the Sixth Circuit's ultimate conclusion that the prosecution's approach to this issue in cases such as *Thompson* and the case at hand may often not be absolutely necessary under RICO, but it is not forbidden. Some cases, however, are exceptional, and ours is one of them. In such a case, the prosecution may have no real alternative to naming the state as the RICO enterprise."

2. Association-in-Fact Enterprise

BOYLE v. UNITED STATES
556 U.S. 938 (2009)

Justice ALITO delivered the opinion of the Court.

* * * In instructing the jury on the meaning of a RICO "enterprise," the District Court relied largely on language in *United States v. Turkette,* [p. 218]. The court told the jurors that, in order to establish the existence of such an enterprise, the Government had to prove that: "(1) There [was] an ongoing organization with some sort of framework, formal or informal, for carrying out its objectives; and (2) the various members and associates of the association function[ed] as a continuing unit to achieve a common purpose." * * * Over petitioner's objection, the court also told the jury that it could "find an enterprise where an association of individuals, without structural hierarchy, form[ed] solely for the purpose of carrying out a pattern of racketeering acts" and that "[c]ommon sense suggests that the existence of an association-in-fact is oftentimes more readily proven by what it does, rather than by abstract analysis of its structure." * * *

Petitioner requested an instruction that the Government was required to prove that the enterprise "had an ongoing organization, a core membership that functioned as a continuing unit, and an ascertainable structural hierarchy distinct from the charged predicate acts." * * * The District Court refused to give that instruction.

Petitioner was convicted on 11 of the 12 counts against him, including the RICO counts, * * * we granted certiorari, 129 S.Ct. 29 (2008), to resolve conflicts among the Courts of Appeals concerning the meaning of a RICO enterprise. * * *

RICO makes it "unlawful for any person employed by or *associated with any enterprise* engaged in, or the activities of which affect, interstate or foreign commerce, to conduct or participate, directly or indirectly, in the conduct of such enterprise's affairs through a pattern of racketeering activity or collection of unlawful debt."18 U.S.C. § 1962(c) (emphasis added).

The statute does not specifically define the outer boundaries of the "enterprise" concept but states that the term "includes any individual, partnership, corporation, association, or other legal entity, and any union or group of individuals associated in fact although not a legal entity."§ 1961(4). This enumeration of included enterprises is obviously broad, encompassing "*any*... group of individuals associated in fact." * * * The term "any" ensures that the definition has a wide reach, * * * and the very concept of an association in fact is expansive. In addition, the RICO statute provides that its terms are to be "liberally construed to effectuate its remedial purposes." * * *

In light of these statutory features, we explained in *Turkette* that "an enterprise includes any union or group of individuals associated in fact" and that RICO reaches "a group of persons associated together for a common purpose of engaging in a course of conduct." * * * Such an enterprise, we said, "is proved by evidence of an ongoing organization, formal or informal, and by evidence that the various associates function as a continuing unit." * * *

As noted, the specific question on which we granted certiorari is whether an association-in-fact enterprise must have "an ascertainable structure beyond that inherent in the pattern of racketeering activity in which it engages." * * * We will break this question into three parts. First, must an association-in-fact enterprise have a "structure"? Second, must the structure be "ascertainable"? Third, must the "structure" go "beyond that inherent in the pattern of racketeering activity" in which its members engage?

"Structure." We agree with petitioner that an association-in-fact enterprise must have a structure. In the sense relevant here, the term "structure" means "[t]he way in which parts are arranged or put together to form a whole" and "[t]he interrelation or arrangement of parts in a complex entity." * * *

From the terms of RICO, it is apparent that an association-in-fact enterprise must have at least three structural features: a purpose, relationships among those associated with the enterprise, and longevity sufficient to permit these associates to pursue the enterprise's purpose. As we succinctly put it in *Turkette,* an association-in-fact enterprise is "a group of persons associated together for a common purpose of engaging in a course of conduct." * * *

That an "enterprise" must have a purpose is apparent from meaning of the term in ordinary usage, *i.e.,* a "venture," "undertaking," or "project." Webster's Third New International Dictionary 757 (1976). The concept of "associat[ion]" requires both interpersonal relationships and a common interest. * * *

Although an association-in-fact enterprise must have these structural features, it does not follow that a district court must use the term "structure" in its jury instructions. A trial judge has considerable discretion in choosing the language of an instruction so long as the substance of the relevant point is adequately expressed.

"*Ascertainable.*" Whenever a jury is told that it must find the existence of an element beyond a reasonable doubt, that element must be "ascertainable" or else the jury could not find that it was proved. Therefore, telling the members of the jury that they had to ascertain the existence of an "ascertainable structure" would have been redundant and potentially misleading.

"*Beyond that inherent in the pattern of racketeering activity.*" This phrase may be interpreted in least two different ways, and its correctness depends on the particular sense in which the phrase is used. If the phrase is interpreted to mean that the existence of an enterprise is a separate element that must be proved, it is of course correct. As we explained in *Turkette,* the existence of an enterprise is an element distinct from the pattern of racketeering activity and "proof of one does not necessarily establish the other." [4] * * *

On the other hand, if the phrase is used to mean that the existence of an enterprise may never be inferred from the evidence showing that persons associated with the enterprise engaged in a pattern of racketeering activity, it is incorrect. We recognized in *Turkette* that the evidence used to prove the

---

[4] It is easy to envision situations in which proof that individuals engaged in a pattern of racketeering activity would not establish the existence of an enterprise. For example, suppose that several individuals, independently and without coordination, engaged in a pattern of crimes listed as RICO predicates-for example, bribery or extortion. Proof of these patterns would not be enough to show that the individuals were members of an enterprise.

pattern of racketeering activity and the evidence establishing an enterprise "may in particular cases coalesce." * * *

The crux of petitioner's argument is that a RICO enterprise must have structural features in addition to those that we think can be fairly inferred from the language of the statute. Although petitioner concedes that an association-in-fact enterprise may be an "'informal'" group and that "not 'much'" structure is needed, * * *, he contends that such an enterprise must have at least some additional structural attributes, such as a structural "hierarchy," "role differentiation," a "unique *modus operandi,*" a "chain of command," "professionalism and sophistication of organization," "diversity and complexity of crimes," "membership dues, rules and regulations," "uncharged or additional crimes aside from predicate acts," an "internal discipline mechanism," "regular meetings regarding enterprise affairs," an "enterprise 'name,'" and "induction or initiation ceremonies and rituals." * * *

We see no basis in the language of RICO for the structural requirements that petitioner asks us to recognize. As we said in *Turkette,* an association-in-fact enterprise is simply a continuing unit that functions with a common purpose. Such a group need not have a hierarchical structure or a "chain of command"; decisions may be made on an ad hoc basis and by any number of methods-by majority vote, consensus, a show of strength, etc. Members of the group need not have fixed roles; different members may perform different roles at different times. The group need not have a name, regular meetings, dues, established rules and regulations, disciplinary procedures, or induction or initiation ceremonies. While the group must function as a continuing unit and remain in existence long enough to pursue a course of conduct, nothing in RICO exempts an enterprise whose associates engage in spurts of activity punctuated by periods of quiescence. Nor is the statute limited to groups whose crimes are sophisticated, diverse, complex, or unique; for example, a group that does nothing but engage in extortion through old-fashioned, unsophisticated, and brutal means may fall squarely within the statute's reach. * * *

The instructions the District Court judge gave to the jury in this case were correct and adequate. These instructions explicitly told the jurors that they could not convict on the RICO charges unless they found that the Government had proved the existence of an enterprise. * * * The instructions made clear that this was a separate element from the pattern of racketeering activity. We therefore affirm the judgment of the Court of Appeals.

Justice STEVENS, with whom Justice BREYER joins, dissenting.

In my view, Congress intended the term "enterprise" as it is used in the Racketeer Influenced and Corrupt Organizations Act (RICO), 18 U.S.C. § 1961 *et seq.,* to refer only to business-like entities that have an existence apart from the predicate acts committed by their employees or associates.

NOTE

In the context of white collar crime cases, the "association-in-fact" enterprise has come in a variety of forms. For example, in **United States v. Console**, 13 F.3d 641 (3d Cir. 1993), the "government alleged that the RICO enterprise was an association-in-fact composed of [a] law firm and * * * medical practice [that was] designed 'to enrich its members through the pursuit of personal injury business.' " Appellants in *Console* argued that there was insufficient evidence of a RICO enterprise to support their convictions. "[A]ccording to appellants, '[a]ll that was shown was that the medical practice and the lawyer's office combined to commit mail fraud on an ad hoc basis.' " In rejecting appellants' arguments, the court noted that an association-in-fact can "be composed of legal as well as non-legal entities," and that the association-in-fact between a law firm and medical practice constituted a RICO enterprise under § 1961(4). See also G-I Holding, Inc. v. Baron & Budd, 238 F.Supp.2d 521, 547 (S.D.N.Y. 2002) (considering the agency relationship).

3. Distinctiveness of the Enterprise and the Defendant

CEDRIC KUSHNER PROMOTIONS, LTD. v. KING

533 U.S. 158 (2001)

Justice BREYER delivered the opinion of the Court.

The Racketeer Influenced and Corrupt Organizations Act (RICO or Act), 18 U.S.C. § 1961 et seq., makes it "unlawful for any person employed by or associated with any enterprise ... to conduct or participate ... in the conduct of such enterprise's affairs" through the commission of two or more statutorily defined crimes--which RICO calls "a pattern of racketeering activity." § 1962(c). The language suggests, and lower courts have held, that this provision foresees two separate entities, a "person" and a distinct "enterprise."

This case focuses upon a person who is the president and sole shareholder of a closely held corporation. The plaintiff claims that the president has conducted the corporation's affairs through the forbidden "pattern," though for present purposes it is conceded that, in doing so, he acted within the scope of his authority as the corporation's employee. In these circumstances, are there two entities, a "person" and a separate "enterprise"? Assuming, as we must given the posture of this case, that the allegations in the complaint are true, we conclude that the "person" and "enterprise" here are distinct and that the RICO provision applies.

Petitioner, Cedric Kushner Promotions, Ltd., is a corporation that promotes boxing matches. Petitioner sued Don King, the president and sole shareholder of Don King Productions, a corporation, claiming that King had conducted the boxing-related affairs of Don King Productions in part through a RICO "pattern," i.e., through the alleged commission of at least two instances of fraud and other RICO predicate crimes. The District Court, citing Court of Appeals precedent, dismissed the complaint.* * * And the Court of Appeals affirmed that dismissal. * * * In the appellate court's view, § 1962(c) applies only where a plaintiff shows the existence of two separate entities, a "person" and a distinct "enterprise," the affairs of which that "person" improperly conducts. In this instance, "it is undisputed that King was an employee" of the corporation Don King Productions and also "acting within the scope of his authority." Under the Court of Appeals' analysis, King, in a legal sense, was part of, not separate from, the corporation. There was no "person," distinct from the "enterprise," who improperly conducted the "enterprise's affairs." And thus § 1962(c) did not apply.

Other Circuits, applying § 1962(c) in roughly similar circumstances, have reached a contrary conclusion. * * * We granted certiorari to resolve the conflict. We now agree with these Circuits and hold that the Second Circuit's interpretation of § 1962(c) is erroneous.

We do not quarrel with the basic principle that to establish liability under § 1962(c) one must allege and prove the existence of two distinct entities: (1) a "person"; and (2) an "enterprise" that is not simply the same "person" referred to by a different name. The statute's language, read as ordinary English, suggests that principle. The Act says that it applies to "person[s]" who are "employed by or associated with" the "enterprise." § 1962(c). In ordinary English one speaks of employing, being employed by, or associating with others, not oneself. See Webster's Third New International Dictionary 132 (1993) * * * In addition, the Act's purposes are consistent with that principle. Whether the Act seeks to prevent a person from victimizing, say, a small business, * * * or to prevent a person from using a corporation for criminal purposes, National Organization for Women, Inc. v. Scheidler, 510 U.S. 249, 259, 114 S.Ct. 798, 127 L.Ed.2d 99 (1994), the person and the victim, or the person and the tool, are different entities, not the same.

The Government reads § 1962(c) "to require some distinctness between the RICO defendant and the RICO enterprise." * * * And it says that this requirement is "legally sound and workable." We agree with its assessment, particularly in light of the fact that 12 Courts of Appeals have interpreted the statute as embodying some such distinctness requirement without creating discernible mischief in the administration of RICO. * * * Indeed, this Court previously has said that liability "depends on showing that the defendants conducted or participated in the conduct of the 'enterprise's affairs,' not just their own affairs." Reves v. Ernst & Young [p. 245].

While accepting the "distinctness" principle, we nonetheless disagree with the appellate court's application of that principle to the present circumstances--circumstances in which a corporate employee, "acting within the scope of his authority," * * * allegedly conducts the corporation's affairs in a RICO-forbidden way. The corporate owner/employee, a natural person, is distinct from the corporation itself, a legally different entity with different rights and responsibilities due to its different legal status. And we can find nothing in the statute that requires more "separateness" than that. Cf. McCullough v. Suter, 757 F.2d 142, 144 (7th Cir.1985) (finding either formal or practical separateness sufficient to be distinct under § 1962(c)).

Linguistically speaking, an employee who conducts the affairs of a corporation through illegal acts comes within the terms of a statute that forbids any "person" unlawfully to conduct an "enterprise," particularly when the statute explicitly defines "person" to include "any individual ... capable of holding a legal or beneficial interest in property," and defines "enterprise" to include a "corporation." 18 U.S.C. §§ 1961(3), (4). And, linguistically speaking, the employee and the corporation are different "persons," even where the employee is the corporation's sole owner. After all, incorporation's basic purpose is to create a distinct legal entity, with legal rights, obligations, powers, and privileges different from those of the natural individuals who created it, who own it, or whom it employs. * * *

* * * Further, to apply the RICO statute in present circumstances is consistent with the statute's basic purposes as this Court has defined them. The Court has held that RICO both protects a legitimate "enterprise" from those who would use unlawful acts to victimize it, United States v. Turkette, [p. 216] and also protects the public from those who would unlawfully use an "enterprise" (whether legitimate or illegitimate) as a "vehicle" through which "unlawful ... activity is committed," * * * A corporate employee who conducts the corporation's affairs through an unlawful RICO "pattern ... of activity," § 1962(c), uses that corporation as a "vehicle" whether he is, or is not, its sole owner.

Conversely, the appellate court's critical legal distinction--between employees acting within the scope of corporate authority and those acting outside that authority – is inconsistent with a basic statutory purpose. * * * It would immunize from RICO liability many of those at whom this Court has said RICO directly aims – e.g., high-ranking individuals in an illegitimate criminal enterprise, who, seeking to further the purposes of that enterprise, act within the scope of their authority. * * *

Finally, we have found nothing in the statute's history that significantly favors an alternative interpretation. That history not only refers frequently to the importance of undermining organized crime's influence upon legitimate businesses but also refers to the need to protect the public from those who would run "organization[s] in a manner detrimental to the public interest." S.Rep. No. 91-617, at 82. This latter purpose, as we have said, invites the legal principle we endorse, namely, that in present circumstances the statute requires no more than the formal legal distinction between "person" and "enterprise" (namely, incorporation) that is present here.

In reply, King argues that the lower court's rule is consistent with (1) the principle that a corporation acts only through its directors, officers, and agents,* * * (2) the principle that a corporation should not be liable for the criminal acts of its employees where Congress so intends, * * * and (3) the Sherman Act principle limiting liability under 15 U.S.C. § 1 by excluding "from unlawful combinations or conspiracies the activities of a single firm," Copperweld Corp. v. Independence Tube Corp., 467 U.S. 752, 769-770, n. 15, 104 S.Ct. 2731, 81 L.Ed.2d 628 (1984). The alternative that we endorse, however, is no less consistent with these principles. It does not deny that a corporation acts through its employees; it says only that the corporation and its employees are not legally identical. It does not assert that ordinary respondeat superior principles make a corporation legally liable under RICO for the criminal acts of its employees; that is a matter of congressional intent not before us. * * * Neither is it inconsistent with antitrust law's intracorporate conspiracy doctrine; that doctrine turns on specific antitrust objectives. * * * Rather, we hold simply that the need for two distinct entities is satisfied; hence, the RICO provision before us applies when a corporate employee unlawfully conducts the affairs of the corporation of which he is the sole owner – whether he conducts those affairs within the scope, or beyond the scope, of corporate authority.

For these reasons, the Court of Appeals' judgment is reversed, and the case is remanded for further proceedings consistent with this opinion.

4. Interstate Commerce

1. ***"Engaged In Interstate Commerce."*** The different types of RICO violations in § 1962 apply to "any enterprise which is engaged in, or the activities of which affect, interstate or foreign commerce . . . ." In **United States v. Roberston**, 514 U.S. 669 (1995), the Supreme Court overturned a lower court decision finding that a claimed violation of § 1962(a) involving a gold mining operation in Alaska did not meet the interstate commerce element. The Court summarized the defendant's interstate activities related to the mine:

> Robertson, who resided in Arizona, made a cash payment of $125,000 for placer gold mining claims near Fairbanks. He paid approximately $100,000 (in cash) for mining equipment and supplies, some of which were purchased in Los Angeles and transported to Alaska for use in the mine. Robertson also hired and paid the expenses for seven out- of-state employees to travel to Alaska to work in the mine. The partnership dissolved during the first mining season, but Robertson continued to operate the mine through 1987 as a sole proprietorship. He again hired a number of employees from outside Alaska to work in the mine. During its operating life, the mine produced between $200,000 and $290,000 worth of gold, most of which was sold to refiners within Alaska, although Robertson personally transported approximately $30,000 worth of gold out of the State.

The Court did not need to consider whether the enterprise "affected" interstate commerce, holding instead that "[w]hether or not these activities met (and whether or not, to bring the gold mine within the "affecting commerce" provision of RICO, they would have to meet) the requirement of substantially affecting interstate commerce, they assuredly brought the gold mine within § 1962(a)'s alternative criterion of 'any enterprise . . . engaged in . . . interstate or foreign commerce.'"

2. ***Affecting Commerce.*** If the Court had used the "affecting interstate commerce" alternative of the statute in *Robertson*, as opposed to finding the enterprise engaged in interstate commerce, what level of proof would be necessary to show that the enterprise affects interstate commerce? See United States v. Lopez [p. 15] and United States v. Morrison [p. 15]. In the past, courts have found a sufficient nexus with interstate commerce when there is some minimal connection with interstate commerce. For example, in United States v. Joseph, 510 F. Supp. 1001 (E.D. Pa. 1981), the defendant, the Clerk of Courts of Lehigh County, Pennsylvania, was alleged to have violated RICO "by soliciting and accepting various amounts of cash from a bailbondsman in consideration for defendant's favorable recommendations and exercise of discretion in his official decisions." In rejecting defendant's motion to dismiss premised upon the indictment failing to show an affect upon interstate commerce, the court noted that "most courts do have an effect upon interstate commerce, as do sheriff's departments and the offices of prosecuting attorneys, all of which place interstate telephone calls, purchase supplies and materials through interstate commerce and involve non-citizens of the forum state in litigation." See also Waucaush v. United States, 380 F.3d 251 (6th Cir. 2004)(finding that when there is no economic activity present, a minimal effect on commerce is insufficient.) WCH § 8.3.

3. ***Affecting Commerce: Predicate Acts or Enterprise.*** In a RICO prosecution, should a court look to whether the predicate acts or the enterprise is affecting (or is engaged in) interstate commerce? See United States v. Rone, 598 F.2d 564, 573 (9th Cir. 1979) ("The statute requires that the activity of the 'enterprise,' not each predicate act of racketeering, have an effect on interstate commerce."); see also United States v. Bagnariol, 665 F.2d 877, 893 (9th Cir. 1981) ("The interstate commerce nexus must result from the enterprise. It is permissible to find that nexus from acts also charged as predicate acts when those constitute the activities of the enterprise.").

4. Extraterritoriality. The RICO statutes do not have an extraterritorial provision. When confronted with the question of whether the statute applies to conduct outside the United States, most courts have rejected an extraterritorial application. Some courts have premised the decision upon the enterprise while others have focused on the location of the racketeering activity. WCH § 8.1(G). See also Melvin L. Otey, *Why RICO's Extraterritorial Reach is Properly Coextensive with the Reach of its Predicates*, 14 J. OF INT'L BUS. L. 33 (2015).

5. Economic Motive

NATIONAL ORGANIZATION FOR WOMEN v. SCHEIDLER
510 U.S. 249 (1994)

Chief Justice REHNQUIST delivered the opinion of the Court.

* * * Section 1962(c) prohibits any person associated with an enterprise from conducting its affairs through a pattern of racketeering activity. We granted certiorari to determine whether RICO requires proof that either the racketeering enterprise or the predicate acts of racketeering were motivated by an economic purpose. We hold that RICO requires no such economic motive. * * *

Petitioner National Organization For Women, Inc. (NOW), is a national nonprofit organization that supports the legal availability of abortion; petitioners Delaware Women's Health Organization, Inc. (DWHO), and Summit Women's Health Organization, Inc. (SWHO), are health care centers that perform abortions and other medical procedures. Respondents are a coalition of antiabortion groups called the Pro-Life Action Network (PLAN), Joseph Scheidler and other individuals and organizations that oppose legal abortion, and a medical laboratory that formerly provided services to the two petitioner health care centers.

Petitioners sued respondents in the United States District Court for the Northern District of Illinois, alleging violations of the Sherman Act, 15 U.S.C. § 1 et seq., and RICO's §§ 1962(a), (c), and (d), as well as several pendent state-law claims stemming from the activities of antiabortion protesters at the clinics. * * *

The amended complaint alleged that respondents were members of a nationwide conspiracy to shut down abortion clinics through a pattern of racketeering activity including extortion in violation of the Hobbs Act, 18 U.S.C. § 1951. * * *

The District Court dismissed the case pursuant to Federal Rule of Civil Procedure 12(b)(6). Citing Eastern Railroad Presidents Conference v. Noerr Motor Freight, Inc., 365 U.S. 127 (1961), it held that since the activities alleged "involve[d] political opponents, not commercial competitors, and political objectives, not marketplace goals," the Sherman Act did not apply. It dismissed petitioners' RICO claims under § 1962(a) because the "income" alleged by petitioners consisted of voluntary donations from persons opposed to abortion which "in no way were derived from the pattern of racketeering alleged in the complaint." The District Court then concluded that petitioners failed to state a claim under § 1962(c) since "an economic motive requirement exists to the extent that some profit-generating purpose must be alleged in order to state a RICO claim." Finally, it dismissed petitioners' RICO conspiracy claim under § 1962(d) since petitioners' other RICO claims could not stand.

The Court of Appeals affirmed. 968 F.2d 612 (CA7 1992).

* * * Nowhere in either § 1962(c), or in the RICO definitions in § 1961, is there any indication that an economic motive is required. * * *

We do not believe that the usage of the term "enterprise" in subsections (a) and (b) leads to the inference that an economic motive is required in subsection (c). The term "enterprise" in subsections (a) and (b) plays a different role in the structure of those subsections than it does in subsection (c). Section 1962(a) provides that it "shall be unlawful for any person who has received any income derived, directly or indirectly, from a pattern of racketeering activity . . . to use or invest, directly or indirectly, any part of such income, or the proceeds of such income, in acquisition of any interest in, or the establishment or operation of, any enterprise which is engaged in, or the activities of which affect, interstate or foreign commerce." Correspondingly, § 1962(b) states that it "shall be unlawful for any person through a pattern of racketeering activity or through collection of an unlawful debt to acquire or maintain, directly or indirectly, any interest in or control of any enterprise which is engaged in, or the activities of which affect, interstate or foreign commerce." The "enterprise" referred to in subsections (a) and (b) is thus something acquired through the use of illegal activities or by money obtained from illegal activities. The enterprise in these subsections is the victim of unlawful activity and may very well be a "profit-seeking" entity that represents a property interest and may be acquired. But the statutory language in subsections (a) and (b) does not mandate that the enterprise be a "profit-seeking" entity; it simply requires that the enterprise be an entity that was acquired through illegal activity or the money generated from illegal activity.

By contrast, the "enterprise" in subsection (c) connotes generally the vehicle through which the unlawful pattern of racketeering activity is committed, rather than the victim of that activity. Subsection (c) makes it unlawful for "any person employed by or associated with any enterprise ... to conduct or participate ... in the conduct of such enterprise's affairs through a pattern of racketeering activity...." Consequently, since the enterprise in subsection (c) is not being acquired, it need not have a property interest that can be acquired nor an economic motive for engaging in illegal activity; it need only be an association in fact that engages in a pattern of racketeering activity. Nothing in subsections (a) and (b) directs us to a contrary conclusion. * * *

We therefore hold that petitioners may maintain this action if respondents conducted the enterprise through a pattern of racketeering activity. The questions of whether the respondents committed the requisite predicate acts, and whether the commission of these acts fell into a pattern, are not before us. We hold only that RICO contains no economic motive requirement.

The judgment of the Court of Appeals is accordingly reversed.

Justice SOUTER, with whom Justice KENNEDY joins, concurring.

I join the Court's opinion and write separately to explain why the First Amendment does not require reading an economic-motive requirement into the RICO, and to stress that the Court's opinion does not bar First Amendment challenges to RICO's application in particular cases. * * *

NOTE

Following the above decision, the case proceeded to a seven-week trial.

> [A] six-member jury concluded that petitioners violated the civil provisions of RICO. By answering a series of special interrogatory questions, the jury found, inter alia, that petitioners' alleged "pattern of racketeering activity" included 21 violations of the Hobbs Act, 18 U.S.C. § 1951; 25 violations of state extortion law; 25 instances of attempting or conspiring to commit either federal or state extortion; 23 violations of the Travel Act, 18 U.S.C. § 1952; and 23 instances of attempting to violate the Travel Act. The jury awarded $31,455.64 to respondent, the National Women's Health Organization of Delaware, Inc., and $54,471.28 to the National Women's Health Organization of Summit, Inc. These damages were trebled pursuant to § 1964(c). Additionally, the District Court entered a permanent nationwide injunction prohibiting petitioners from obstructing access to the clinics, trespassing on clinic property, damaging clinic property, or using violence or threats of violence against the clinics, their employees, or their patients. * * *

The Supreme Court reviewed this decision to determine "whether petitioners committed extortion within the meaning of the Hobbs Act, 18 U.S.C. § 1951." The decision, written by Chief Justice Rehnquist found that "[b]ecause all of the predicate acts supporting the jury's finding of a RICO violation must be reversed, the judgment that petitioners violated RICO must also be reversed. Without an underlying RICO violation, the injunction issued by the District Court must necessarily be vacated." Scheidler v. National Organization for Women, Inc., 537 U.S.393 (2003).

The case returned to the Supreme Court a third time when the Seventh Circuit determined that it need not direct the district court to dissolve the injunction because the alleged acts of violence could be the basis for a Hobbs Act violation. **Scheidler v. National Organization for Women, Inc.**, 547 U.S. 9 (2006). The Court rejected that reading of the Hobbs Act:

> The question, as we have said, concerns the meaning of the phrase that modifies the term "physical violence," namely, the words "in furtherance of a plan or purpose to do anything in violation of this section." Do those words refer to violence (1) that furthers a plan or purpose to "affec[t] commerce ... by robbery or extortion," or to violence (2) that furthers a plan or purpose simply to "affec[t] commerce"? We believe the former, more restrictive, reading of the text–the reading that ties the violence to robbery or extortion–is correct.
>
> For one thing, the language of the statute makes the more restrictive reading the more natural one. The text that precedes the physical violence clause does not forbid obstructing, delaying, or affecting commerce (or the movement of any article or commodity in commerce); rather, it forbids obstructing, delaying, or affecting commerce " by robbery or extortion." Ibid. * * * This language means that behavior that obstructs, delays, or affects commerce is a "violation" of the statute only if that behavior also involves robbery or extortion (or related attempts or conspiracies). Consequently, the reference in the physical violence clause to actions or threats of violence "in furtherance of a plan or purpose to do anything in violation of this section" * * * would seem to mean acts or threats of violence in furtherance of a plan or purpose to engage in robbery or extortion, for that is the only kind of behavior that the section otherwise makes a violation.

The Court directed entry of a judgment in favor of the defendants because of the failure to allege a RICO violation through the Hobbs Act.

6. RICO Injury

Courts have also examined the causation between the alleged violation and the RICO injury. In **Anza v. Ideal Steel Supply Corp.**, 547 U.S. 451 (2006), the Court stated:

> In Holmes v. Securities Investor Protection Corporation [SIPC], 503 U.S. 258 (1992), this Court held that a plaintiff may sue under § 1964(c) only if the alleged RICO violation was the proximate cause of the plaintiff's injury. The instant case requires us to apply the principles discussed in *Holmes* to a dispute between two competing businesses. * * *
>
> The *Holmes* Court turned to the common-law foundations of the proximate-cause requirement, and specifically the "demand for some direct relation between the injury asserted and the injurious conduct alleged." It concluded that even if SIPC were subrogated to the rights of certain aggrieved customers, the RICO claims could not satisfy this requirement of directness. The deficiency, the Court explained, was

that "the link is too remote between the stock manipulation alleged and the customers' harm, being purely contingent on the harm suffered by the broker-dealers."

Applying the principles of *Holmes* to the present case, we conclude Ideal cannot maintain its claim based on § 1962(c). * * * Ideal's theory is that Joseph and Vincent Anza harmed it by defrauding the New York tax authority and using the proceeds from the fraud to offer lower prices designed to attract more customers. The RICO violation alleged by Ideal is that the Anzas conducted National's affairs through a pattern of mail fraud and wire fraud. The direct victim of this conduct was the State of New York, not Ideal. It was the State that was being defrauded and the State that lost tax revenue as a result.

The Court of Appeals reached a contrary conclusion, apparently reasoning that because the Anzas allegedly sought to gain a competitive advantage over Ideal, it is immaterial whether they took an indirect route to accomplish their goal. This rationale does not accord with *Holmes*. A RICO plaintiff cannot circumvent the proximate-cause requirement simply by claiming that the defendant's aim was to increase market share at a competitor's expense. When a court evaluates a RICO claim for proximate causation, the central question it must ask is whether the alleged violation led directly to the plaintiff's injuries. In the instant case, the answer is no. We hold that Ideal's § 1962(c) claim does not satisfy the requirement of proximate causation. * * *

C. PATTERN OF RACKETEERING

H.J. INC. v. NORTHWESTERN BELL TELEPHONE CO.
492 U.S. 229 (1989)

Justice BRENNAN delivered the opinion of the Court.

* * * Petitioners, customers of respondent Northwestern Bell Telephone Co., filed this putative class action in 1986 in the District Court for the District of Minnesota. Petitioners alleged violations of §§ 1962(a), (b), (c), and (d) by Northwestern Bell and the other respondents—some of the telephone company's officers and employees, various members of the Minnesota Public Utilities Commission (MPUC), and other unnamed individuals and corporations—and sought an injunction and treble damages under RICO's civil liability provisions, §§ 1964(a) and (c).

The MPUC is the state body responsible for determining the rates that Northwestern Bell may charge. Petitioners' five-count complaint alleged that between 1980 and 1986 Northwestern Bell sought to influence members of the MPUC in the performance of their duties—and in fact caused them to approve rates for the company in excess of a fair and reasonable amount—by making cash payments to commissioners, negotiating with them regarding future employment, and paying for parties and meals, for tickets to sporting events and the like, and for airline tickets. Based upon these factual allegations, petitioners alleged in their first count a pendent state-law claim, asserting that Northwestern Bell violated the Minnesota bribery statute, Minn.Stat. § 609.42 (1988), as well as state common law prohibiting bribery. They also raised four separate claims under § 1962 of RICO. Count II alleged that, in violation of § 1962(a), Northwestern Bell derived income from a pattern of racketeering activity involving predicate acts of bribery and used this income to engage in its business as an interstate "enterprise." Count III claimed a violation of § 1962(b), in that, through this same pattern of racketeering activity, respondents acquired an interest in or control of the MPUC, which was also an interstate "enterprise." In Count IV, petitioners asserted that respondents participated in the conduct and affairs of the MPUC through this pattern of racketeering activity, contrary to § 1962(c). Finally, Count V alleged that respondents conspired together to violate §§ 1962(a), (b), and (c), thereby contravening § 1962(d).

The District Court granted respondents' Federal Rule of Civil Procedure 12(b)(6) motion, dismissing the complaint for failure to state a claim upon which relief could be granted. 648 F.Supp. 419 (Minn.1986). The court found that "[e]ach of the fraudulent acts alleged by [petitioners] was committed in furtherance of a single scheme to influence MPUC commissioners to the detriment of Northwestern Bell's ratepayers." * * * The Court of Appeals for the Eighth Circuit affirmed the dismissal of petitioners' complaint, confirming that under Eighth Circuit precedent "[a] single fraudulent effort or scheme is insufficient" to establish a pattern of racketeering activity, 829 F.2d 648, 650 (1987), and agreeing with the District Court that petitioners' complaint alleged only a single scheme. Two members of the panel suggested in separate concurrences, however, that the Court of Appeals should reconsider its test for a RICO pattern. Most Courts of Appeals have rejected the Eighth Circuit's interpretation of RICO's pattern concept to require an allegation and proof of multiple schemes, and we granted certiorari to resolve this conflict. We now reverse. * * *

In Sedima, [p.217] this Court rejected a restrictive interpretation of § 1964(c) that would have made it a condition for maintaining a civil RICO action both that the defendant had already been convicted of a predicate racketeering act or of a RICO violation, and that plaintiff show a special racketeering injury. * * * [W]e suggested that RICO's expansive uses "appear to be primarily the result of the breadth of the predicate offenses, in particular the inclusion of wire, mail, and securities fraud, and the failure of Congress and the courts to develop a meaningful concept of 'pattern' "—both factors that apply to criminal as well as civil applications of the Act. Congress has done nothing in the interim further to illuminate RICO's key requirement of a pattern of racketeering; and as the plethora of different views expressed by the Courts of Appeals since Sedima demonstrates, developing a meaningful concept of "pattern" within the existing statutory framework has proved to be no easy task. * * *

We begin, of course, with RICO's text, in which Congress followed a "pattern [of] utilizing terms and concepts of breadth." Russello v. United States, 464 U.S. 16, 21 (1983). As we remarked in Sedima, the section of the statute headed "definitions," 18 U.S.C. § 1961, does not so much define a pattern of racketeering activity as state a minimum necessary condition for the existence of such a pattern. Unlike other provisions in § 1961 that tell us what various concepts used in the Act "mean," 18 U.S.C. § 1961(5) says of the phrase "pattern of racketeering activity" only that it "requires at least two acts of racketeering activity, one of which occurred after [October 15, 1970,] and the last of which occurred within ten years (excluding any period of imprisonment) after the commission of a prior act of racketeering activity." It thus places an outer limit on the concept of a pattern of racketeering activity that is broad indeed.

Section 1961(5) does indicate that Congress envisioned circumstances in which no more than two predicates would be necessary to establish a pattern of racketeering—otherwise it would have drawn a narrower boundary to RICO liability, requiring proof of a greater number of predicates. But, at the same time, the statement that a pattern "requires at least" two predicates implies "that while two acts are necessary, they may not be sufficient." Section 1961(5) concerns only the minimum number of predicates necessary to establish a pattern; and it assumes that there is something to a RICO pattern beyond simply the number of predicate acts involved. The legislative history bears out this interpretation, for the principal sponsor of the Senate bill expressly indicated that "proof of two acts of racketeering activity, without more, does not establish a pattern." 116 Cong.Rec. 18940 (1970) (statement of Sen. McClellan). Section § 1961(5) does not identify, though, these additional prerequisites for establishing the existence of a RICO pattern.

In addition to § 1961(5), there is the key phrase "pattern of racketeering activity" itself, from § 1962, and we must "start with the assumption that the legislative purpose is expressed by the ordinary meaning of the words used." In normal usage, the word "pattern" here would be taken to require more than just a multiplicity of racketeering predicates. A "pattern" is an "arrangement or order of things or activity," 11 Oxford English Dictionary 357 (2d ed. 1989), and the mere fact that there are a number of predicates is no guarantee that they fall into any arrangement or order. It is not the number of predicates but the relationship that they bear to each other or to some external organizing principle that renders them "ordered" or "arranged." The text of RICO conspicuously fails anywhere to identify, however, forms of relationship or external principles to be used in determining whether racketeering activity falls into a pattern for purposes of the Act.

It is reasonable to infer, from this absence of any textual identification of sorts of pattern that would satisfy § 1962's requirement, in combination with the very relaxed limits to the pattern concept fixed in § 1961(5), that Congress intended to take a flexible approach, and envisaged that a pattern might be demonstrated by reference to a range of different ordering principles or relationships between predicates, within the expansive bounds set. * * *

The legislative history, which we discussed in Sedima, shows that Congress indeed had a fairly flexible concept of a pattern in mind. A pattern is not formed by "sporadic activity," and a person cannot "be subjected to the sanctions of title IX simply for committing two widely separated and isolated criminal offenses." Instead, "[t]he term 'pattern' itself requires the showing of a relationship" between the predicates, and of "'the threat of continuing activity.'" "It is this factor of continuity plus relationship which combines to produce a pattern." * * * RICO's legislative history reveals Congress' intent that to prove a pattern of racketeering activity a plaintiff or prosecutor must show that the racketeering predicates are related, and that they amount to or pose a threat of continued criminal activity.

For analytic purposes these two constituents of RICO's pattern requirement must be stated separately, though in practice their proof will often overlap. The element of relatedness is the easier to define, for we may take guidance from a provision elsewhere in the Organized Crime Control Act of 1970 (OCCA), of which RICO formed Title IX. * * * As we noted in Sedima, Congress defined Title X's pattern requirement solely in terms of the relationship of the defendant's criminal acts one to another: "[C]riminal conduct forms a pattern if it embraces criminal acts that have the same or similar purposes, results, participants, victims, or methods of commission, or otherwise are interrelated by distinguishing characteristics and are not isolated events." § 3575(e). We have no reason to suppose that Congress had in mind for RICO's pattern of racketeering component any more constrained a notion of the relationships between predicates that would suffice.

RICO's legislative history tells us, however, that the relatedness of racketeering activities is not alone enough to satisfy § 1962's pattern element. To establish a RICO pattern it must also be shown that the predicates themselves amount to, or that they otherwise constitute a threat of, continuing racketeering activity. As to this continuity requirement, § 3575(e) is of no assistance. * * *

"Continuity" is both a closed- and open-ended concept, referring either to a closed period of repeated conduct, or to past conduct that by its nature projects into the future with a threat of repetition. It is, in either case, centrally a temporal concept—and particularly so in the RICO context, where what must be continuous, RICO's predicate acts or offenses, and the relationship these predicates must bear one to another, are distinct requirements. A party alleging a RICO violation may demonstrate continuity over a closed period by proving a series of related predicates extending over a substantial period of time. Predicate acts extending over a few weeks or months and threatening no future criminal conduct do not satisfy this requirement: Congress was concerned in RICO with long-term criminal conduct. Often a RICO action will be brought before continuity can be established in this way. In such cases, liability depends on whether the threat of continuity is demonstrated. * * *

The limits of the relationship and continuity concepts that combine to define a RICO pattern, and the precise methods by which relatedness and continuity or its threat may be proved, cannot be fixed in advance with such clarity that it will always be apparent whether in a particular case a "pattern of racketeering activity" exists. The development of these concepts must await future cases, absent a decision by Congress to revisit RICO to provide clearer guidance as to the Act's intended scope. * * *

Under the analysis we have set forth above, and consistent with the allegations in their complaint, petitioners may be able to prove that the multiple predicates alleged constitute "a pattern of racketeering activity," in that they satisfy the requirements of relationship and continuity. The acts of bribery alleged are said to be related by a common purpose, to influence commissioners in carrying out their duties in order to win approval of unfairly and unreasonably high rates for Northwestern Bell. Furthermore, petitioners claim that the racketeering predicates occurred with some frequency over at least a 6-year period, which may be sufficient to satisfy the continuity requirement. Alternatively, a threat of continuity of racketeering activity might be established at trial by showing that the alleged bribes were a regular way of conducting Northwestern Bell's ongoing business, or a regular way of conducting or participating in the conduct of the alleged and ongoing RICO enterprise, the MPUC.

The Court of Appeals thus erred in affirming the District Court's dismissal of petitioners' complaint for failure to plead "a pattern of racketeering activity." The judgment is reversed, and the case is remanded for further proceedings consistent with this opinion.

It is so ordered.

Justice SCALIA, with whom THE CHIEF JUSTICE, Justice O'CONNOR, and Justice KENNEDY join, concurring in the judgment.

* * * Elevating to the level of statutory text a phrase taken from the legislative history, the Court counsels the lower courts: " 'continuity plus relationship.' " This seems to me about as helpful to the conduct of their affairs as "life is a fountain." Of the two parts of this talismanic phrase, the relatedness requirement is said to be the "easier to define," yet here is the Court's definition, in toto: " '[C]riminal conduct forms a pattern if it embraces criminal acts that have the same or similar purposes, results, participants, victims, or methods of commission, or otherwise are interrelated by distinguishing characteristics and are not isolated events.' " This definition

has the feel of being solidly rooted in law, since it is a direct quotation of 18 U.S.C. § 3575(e). Unfortunately, if normal (and sensible) rules of statutory construction were followed, the existence of § 3575(e)—which is the definition contained in another title of the Act that was explicitly not rendered applicable to RICO—suggests that whatever "pattern" might mean in RICO, it assuredly does not mean that. "[W]here Congress includes particular language in one section of a statute but omits it in another section of the same Act, it is generally presumed that Congress acts intentionally and purposely in the disparate inclusion or exclusion." But that does not really matter, since § 3575(e) is utterly uninformative anyway. It hardly closes in on the target to know that "relatedness" refers to acts that are related by "purposes, results, participants, victims, . . . methods of commission, or [just in case that is not vague enough] otherwise." Is the fact that the victims of both predicate acts were women enough? Or that both acts had the purpose of enriching the defendant? Or that the different coparticipants of the defendant in both acts were his coemployees? I doubt that the lower courts will find the Court's instructions much more helpful than telling them to look for a "pattern"— which is what the statute already says.

The Court finds "continuity" more difficult to define precisely. "Continuity," it says, "is both a closed- and open-ended concept, referring either to a closed period of repeated conduct, or to past conduct that by its nature projects into the future with a threat of repetition." I have no idea what this concept of a "closed period of repeated conduct" means. Virtually all allegations of racketeering activity, in both civil and criminal suits, will relate to past periods that are "closed" (unless one expects plaintiff or the prosecutor to establish that the defendant not only committed the crimes he did, but is still committing them), and all of them must relate to conduct that is "repeated," because of RICO's multiple-act requirement. * * *

It is, however, unfair to be so critical of the Court's effort, because I would be unable to provide an interpretation of RICO that gives significantly more guidance concerning its application. It is clear to me from the prologue of the statute, which describes a relatively narrow focus upon "organized crime," that the word "pattern" in the phrase "pattern of racketeering activity" was meant to import some requirement beyond the mere existence of multiple predicate acts. Thus, when § 1961(5) says that a pattern "requires at least two acts of racketeering activity" it is describing what is needful but not sufficient. * * * But what that something more is, is beyond me. As I have suggested, it is also beyond the Court. Today's opinion has added nothing to improve our prior guidance, which has created a kaleidoscope of Circuit positions, except to clarify that RICO may in addition be violated when there is a "threat of continuity." It seems to me this increases rather than removes the vagueness. There is no reason to believe that the Courts of Appeals will be any more unified in the future, than they have in the past, regarding the content of this law.

That situation is bad enough with respect to any statute, but it is intolerable with respect to RICO. For it is not only true, as Justice Marshall [dissenting opinion] commented in Sedima, that our interpretation of RICO has "quite simply revolutionize[d] private litigation" and "validate[d] the federalization of broad areas of state common law of frauds," so that clarity and predictability in RICO's civil applications are particularly important; but it is also true that RICO, since it has criminal applications as well, must, even in its civil applications, possess the degree of certainty required for criminal laws. No constitutional challenge to this law has been raised in the present case, and so that issue is not before us. That the highest Court in the land has been unable to derive from this statute anything more than today's meager guidance bodes ill for the day when that challenge is presented. * * *

NOTES AND QUESTIONS

1. ***Pattern***. In **Apparel Art Int'l Inc. v. Jacobson**, 967 F.2d 720 (1st Cir. 1992), the First Circuit considered how to define what constitutes the requisite continuity for a pattern:

> We can begin with the Supreme Court's statement that, to prove a "pattern of racketeering activity," one must show separate predicate acts that 1) are "related," and 2) "amount to or pose a threat of continued criminal activity." We can be reasonably certain that this definition does not encompass a single criminal event, a single criminal episode, a single "crime" (in the ordinary, nontechnical sense of that word). (We deliberately employ a vague term like "episode," for we do not want to use a word such as "scheme," which might have a technical meaning.) For example, a single (interstate) bank robbery consists of several different parts (say, using a gun, threatening a teller, stealing a getaway car, perhaps abducting the teller as well, and eventually lying about participation). Some of those separate parts may themselves constitute separate criminal acts or "crimes" (in the technical sense that each, separately, violates a specific statute). Yet, those several separate criminal parts, taken together, do not generally make out a "pattern." To hold otherwise would mean that many individual bank robberies, frauds, drug sales, embezzlements, and other crimes as well would automatically fall within the scope of the RICO statute, a result contrary to RICO's basic purpose. One might express the fact that a single criminal episode, or event, is not a "pattern" by stating that its parts, taken together, do not "amount to or pose a threat of continued criminal activity." Or, one might risk circularity and simply state that those parts do not bear to each other the relevant ("pattern of racketeering") relationship. But, however courts express the point, they have consistently held that a single episode does not constitute a "pattern," even if that single episode involves behavior that amounts to several crimes (for example, several unlawful mailings).

> Moving now to the opposite extreme, we can also be reasonably certain that, to show a "pattern," one must do more than simply show several different but totally "separate" instances of criminal conduct taking place over time. One 1982 securities fraud and one 1987 drug importation, for example, presumably constitute two separate instances of "racketeering activity." But, if the two separate securities fraud and drug episodes take place several years apart and involve different victims, methods, purposes, and (almost all) participants, they may well lack the requisite "racketeering" relationship to each other. Thus, they would not constitute a "pattern of racketeering activity."

In **Jackson v. BellSouth Telecommunications**, 372 F.3d 1250 (11th Cir. 2004), the Eleventh Circuit found that the closed-end pattern that lasted only nine months was insufficient to establish the continuity aspect of the pattern of racketeering activity. The court stated:

> While the plaintiffs generally alleged that the defendants committed mail and wire fraud violations that extended "over a substantial period of time," the specific incidents they actually charged began only on April 22, 1997, and ended, at the very latest, sometime in January 1998. The plaintiffs maintain that no bright-line rule has been established definitively stating that nine months is too short a period to establish a "substantial period of time," for the purposes of closed-ended continuity. While the plaintiffs are correct that no court has unequivocally declared a minimum period of time that can be considered "substantial," the great weight of authority suggests that nine months is a wholly insufficient interlude. * * *
>
> The overwhelming weight of case authority suggests that nine months is not an adequately substantial period of time. Moreover, the alleged racketeering activity was related to the settlement of a single lawsuit, and, notably, was not designed to perpetrate racketeering with respect to a series of cases. Indeed, in cases like this one, where the RICO allegations concern only a single scheme with a discrete goal, the courts have refused to find a closed-ended pattern of racketeering even when the scheme took place over longer periods of time.

2. ***Relationship***. In **United States v. Indelicato**, 865 F.2d 1370 (2d Cir. 1989), the Second Circuit explained that the issue of relationship is based on the "interrelationship between acts, suggesting the existence of a pattern, [that] may be established in a number of ways. These include proof of their temporal proximity, or common goals, or similarity of methods, or repetitions. The degree to which these factors establish a pattern may depend on the degree of proximity, or any similarities in goals or methodology, or the number of repetitions." The court distinguished between proof of the pattern element and whether there was an enterprise through an association-in-fact, asserting that "relationship and continuity are necessary characteristics of

a RICO enterprise. Neither the statutory definition of enterprise nor the legislative history suggests that those concepts pertain to the notion of enterprise . . . We conclude that relatedness and continuity are essentially characteristics of activity rather than of enterprise."

3. ***Predicate Acts***. Both state and federal offenses can serve as predicate acts to form a pattern of racketeering. When using a state predicate offense, it is necessary that the offense be chargeable under state law and that it have a punishment of more than one year imprisonment. The label used by the state legislature to describe the offense is not crucial to it being included under RICO. For example, violations of the Illinois official misconduct statute, which prohibits "a public official or employee" from "solicit[ing] or knowingly accept[ing] for the performance of any act a fee or reward which he knows is not authorized by law," fall under bribery in § 1961(1). See United States v. Garner, 837 F.2d 1404 (7th Cir. 1987), where the court stated, "The labels placed on a state statute do not determine whether that statute proscribes bribery for purposes of the RICO statute. Congress intended for 'bribery' to be defined generically when it included bribery as a predicate act. * * * Thus any statute that proscribes conduct which could be generically defined as bribery can be the basis for a predicate act."

4. ***Pleading Mail and Wire Fraud as Predicate Acts***. The two most commonly alleged predicate acts for the RICO pattern of racketeering activity are violations of the mail fraud (§ 1341) and wire fraud (§ 1343) statutes. These two provisions cover a wide array of dishonest and questionable business practices, so they can be alleged for many business practices, such as breach of contract, overcharges, and submission of false information. Some lower courts had imposed an actual reliance requirement for civil RICO claims based on the two fraud statutes, importing this element from common law fraud even though it is not required to prove a violation of §§ 1341 and 1343. In **Bridge v. Phoenix Bond & Indemnity Co.**, 553 U.S. 639 (2008), the Supreme Court rejected the actual reliance limitation on RICO in a case in which the false statements were made to a city government to obtain a greater share of properties being sold at a tax auction. While the plaintiffs did not directly receive the alleged false statements mailed by the defendants to the city, they were the victims of them, and the Court held:

> If petitioners' proposed requirement of first-party reliance seems to come out of nowhere, there is a reason: Nothing on the face of the relevant statutory provisions imposes such a requirement. Using the mail to execute or attempt to execute a scheme to defraud is indictable as mail fraud, and hence a predicate act of racketeering under RICO, even if no one relied on any misrepresentation. See Neder v. United States, 527 U.S. 1 (1999) ("The common-law requiremen[t] of 'justifiable reliance' . . . plainly ha[s] no place in the [mail, wire, or bank] fraud statutes"). And one can conduct the affairs of a qualifying enterprise through a pattern of such acts without anyone relying on a fraudulent misrepresentation.

D. THE NEXUS REQUIREMENT

REVES v. ERNST & YOUNG
507 U.S.170 (1993)

Justice BLACKMUN delivered the opinion of the Court.[1]

* * * The question presented is whether one must participate in the operation or management of the enterprise itself to be subject to liability under [§ 1962 (c)]. * * *

The Farmer's Cooperative of Arkansas and Oklahoma, Inc. (the Co-op), began operating in western Arkansas and eastern Oklahoma in 1946. To raise money for operating expenses, the Co-op sold promissory notes payable to the holder on demand. * * * In 1952, the board appointed Jack White as general manager.

In January 1980, White began taking loans from the Co-op to finance the construction of a gasohol plant by his company, White Flame Fuels, Inc. By the end of 1980, White's debts to the Co-op totalled approximately $4 million. * * * At a board meeting on November 12, 1980, White proposed that the Co-op purchase White Flame. The board agreed. One month later, however, the Co-op filed a declaratory action against White and White Flame in Arkansas state court alleging that White actually had sold White Flame to the Co-op in February 1980. The complaint was drafted by White's attorneys and led to a consent decree relieving White of his debts and providing that the Co-op had owned White Flame since February 15, 1980.

White and Kuykendall [who served as both accountant for the Co-op and White Flame] were convicted of tax fraud in January 1981. Harry Erwin, the managing partner of Russell Brown and Company, an Arkansas accounting firm, testified for White, and shortly thereafter the Co-op retained Russell Brown to perform its 1981 financial audit. Joe Drozal, a partner in the Brown firm, was put in charge of the audit and Joe Cabaniss was selected to assist him. On January 2, 1982, Russell Brown and Company merged with Arthur Young and Company, which later became respondent Ernst & Young.

One of Drozal's first tasks in the audit was to determine White Flame's fixed-asset value. * * * Drozal concluded that the Co-op had owned White Flame from the start and that the plant should be valued at $4.5 million on its books.

---

[1] Justice SCALIA and Justice THOMAS do not join Part IV-A of this opinion. [Part IV-A discussed how the legislative history of § 1962 supported the Court's holding.]

On April 22, 1982, Arthur Young presented its 1981 audit report to the Co-op's board. In that audit's Note 9, Arthur Young expressed doubt whether the investment in White Flame could ever be recovered. Note 9 also observed that White Flame was sustaining operating losses averaging $100,000 per month. Arthur Young did not tell the board of its conclusion that the Co-op always had owned White Flame or that without that conclusion the Co-op was insolvent.

On May 27, the Co-op held its 1982 annual meeting. At that meeting, the Co-op, through Harry C. Erwin, a partner in Arthur Young, distributed to the members condensed financial statements. These included White Flame's $4.5 million asset value among its total assets but omitted the information contained in the audit's Note 9. * * * In response to questions, Erwin explained that the Co-op owned White Flame and that the plant had incurred approximately $1.2 million in losses but he revealed no other information relevant to the Co-op's true financial health.

The Co-op hired Arthur Young also to perform its 1982 audit. The 1982 report, presented to the board on March 7, 1983, was similar to the 1981 report and restated (this time in its Note 8) Arthur Young's doubt whether the investment in White Flame was recoverable. The gasohol plant again was valued at approximately $4.5 million and was responsible for the Co-op's showing a positive net worth. * * *

In February 1984, the Co-op experienced a slight run on its demand notes. On February 23, when it was unable to secure further financing, the Co-op filed for bankruptcy. As a result, the demand notes were frozen in the bankruptcy estate and were no longer redeemable at will by the noteholders. * * *

On February 14, 1985, the trustee in bankruptcy filed suit against 40 individuals and entities, including Arthur Young, on behalf of the Co-op and certain noteholders.[a] The District Court certified a class of noteholders, petitioners here, consisting of persons who had purchased demand notes between February 15, 1980, and February 23, 1984. Petitioners settled with all defendants except Arthur Young. * * * The District Court applied the test established by the Eighth Circuit in Bennett v. Berg, 710 F.2d 1361, 1364 (en banc) (1983), that § 1962(c) requires "some participation in the operation or management of the enterprise itself." The court ruled: "Plaintiffs have failed to show anything more than that the accountants reviewed a series of completed transactions, and certified the Co-op's records as fairly portraying its financial status as of a date three or four months preceding the meetings of the directors and the shareholders at which they presented their

[a] "The class alleged in its complaint that Erwin, Drozal, and Cabaniss conducted or participated in the affairs of the co-op, committing both mail fraud and securities fraud, in violation of 18 U.S.C. § 1962(c), * * *." Arthur Young & Co. v. Reves, 937 F.2d 1310 (8th Cir. 1991).

reports. We do not hesitate to declare that such activities fail to satisfy the degree of management required by Bennett v. Berg." * * *

The narrow question in this case is the meaning of the phrase "to conduct or participate, directly or indirectly, in the conduct of such enterprise's affairs." The word "conduct" is used twice, and it seems reasonable to give each use a similar construction. As a verb, "conduct" means to lead, run, manage, or direct. Webster's Third New International Dictionary 474 (1976). Petitioners urge us to read "conduct" as "carry on," so that almost any involvement in the affairs of an enterprise would satisfy the "conduct or participate" requirement. But context is important, and in the context of the phrase "to conduct . . . [an] enterprise's affairs," the word indicates some degree of direction.

The dissent agrees that, when "conduct" is used as a verb, "it is plausible to find in it a suggestion of control." The dissent prefers to focus on "conduct" as a noun, as in the phrase "participate, directly or indirectly, in the conduct of [an] enterprise's affairs." But unless one reads "conduct" to include an element of direction when used as a noun in this phrase, the word becomes superfluous. Congress could easily have written "participate, directly or indirectly, in [an] enterprise's affairs," but it chose to repeat the word "conduct." We conclude, therefore, that as both a noun and a verb in this subsection "conduct" requires an element of direction.

The more difficult question is what to make of the word "participate." This Court previously has characterized this word as a "ter[m] . . . of breadth." Petitioners argue that Congress used "participate" as a synonym for "aid and abet." That would be a term of breadth indeed, for "aid and abet" "comprehends all assistance rendered by words, acts, encouragement, support, or presence." Black's Law Dictionary 68 (6th ed. 1990). But within the context of § 1962(c), "participate" appears to have a narrower meaning. We may mark the limits of what the term might mean by looking again at what Congress did not say. On the one hand, "to participate . . . in the conduct of . . . affairs" must be broader than "to conduct affairs" or the "participate" phrase would be superfluous. On the other hand, as we already have noted, "to participate . . . in the conduct of . . . affairs" must be narrower than "to participate in affairs" or Congress' repetition of the word "conduct" would serve no purpose. It seems that Congress chose a middle ground, consistent with a common understanding of the word "participate"—"to take part in." Webster's Third New International Dictionary 1646 (1976).

Once we understand the word "conduct" to require some degree of direction and the word "participate" to require some part in that direction, the meaning of § 1962(c) comes into focus. In order to "participate, directly or indirectly, in the conduct of such enterprise's affairs," one must have some part in directing those affairs. Of course, the word "participate" makes clear that RICO liability is not limited to those with primary responsibility for the enterprise's affairs, just as the phrase "directly or indirectly" makes clear that RICO liability is not limited to those with a formal position in the enterprise, but some part in directing the enterprise's affairs is required. The "operation or management" test expresses this requirement in a formulation that is easy to apply. * * *

[The Court then discussed the legislative history of § 1962 and concluded that] the legislative history confirms what we have already deduced from the language of § 1962(c)—that one is not liable under that provision unless one has participated in the operation or management of the enterprise itself. * * *

RICO's "liberal construction" clause does not require rejection of the "operation or management" test. Congress directed, by § 904(a) of Pub.L. 91-452, that the "provisions of this title shall be liberally construed to effectuate its remedial purposes." This clause obviously seeks to ensure that Congress' intent is not frustrated by an overly narrow reading of the statute, but it is not an invitation to apply RICO to new purposes that Congress never intended. Nor does the clause help us to determine what purposes Congress had in mind. Those must be gleaned from the statute through the normal means of interpretation. The clause " 'only serves as an aid for resolving an ambiguity; it is not to be used to beget one.' " In this case it is clear that Congress did not intend to extend RICO liability under § 1962(c) beyond those who participate in the operation or management of an enterprise through a pattern of racketeering activity.[8] * * *

Petitioners argue that the "operation or management" test is flawed because liability under § 1962(c) is not limited to upper management but may extend to "any person employed by or associated with [the] enterprise." We agree that liability under § 1962(c) is not limited to upper management, but we disagree that the "operation or management" test is inconsistent with this proposition. An enterprise is "operated" not just by upper management but also by lower-rung participants in the enterprise who are under the direction of upper management.[9] An enterprise also might be "operated" or "managed" by others "associated with" the enterprise who exert control over it as, for example, by bribery.

The United States also argues that the "operation or management" test is not consistent with § 1962(c) because it limits the liability of "outsiders" who have no official position within the enterprise. The United States correctly points out that RICO's major purpose was to attack the "infiltration

---

[8] Because the meaning of the statute is clear from its language and legislative history, we have no occasion to consider the application of the rule of lenity. We note, however, that the rule of lenity would also favor the narrower "operation or management" test that we adopt.

[9] * * * We need not decide in this case how far § 1962(c) extends down the ladder of operation because it is clear that Arthur Young was not acting under the direction of the Co-ops officers or board.

of organized crime and racketeering into legitimate organizations," but its argument fails on several counts. First, it ignores the fact that § 1962 has four subsections. Infiltration of legitimate organizations by "outsiders" is clearly addressed in subsections (a) and (b), and the "operation or management" test that applies under subsection (c) in no way limits the application of subsections (a) and (b) to "outsiders." Second, § 1962(c) is limited to persons "employed by or associated with" an enterprise, suggesting a more limited reach than subsections (a) and (b), which do not contain such a restriction. Third, § 1962(c) cannot be interpreted to reach complete "outsiders" because liability depends on showing that the defendants conducted or participated in the conduct of the "enterprise's affairs," not just their own affairs. Of course, "outsiders" may be liable under § 1962(c) if they are "associated with" an enterprise and participate in the conduct of its affairs—that is, participate in the operation or management of the enterprise itself—but it would be consistent with neither the language nor the legislative history of § 1962(c) to interpret it as broadly as petitioners and the United States urge.

In sum, we hold that "to conduct or participate, directly or indirectly, in the conduct of such enterprise's affairs," § 1962(c), one must participate in the operation or management of the enterprise itself. * * *

Both the District Court and the Court of Appeals applied the standard we adopt today to the facts of this case, and both found that respondent was entitled to summary judgment. Neither petitioners nor the United States have argued that these courts misapplied the "operation or management" test. The dissent argues that by creating the Co-op's financial statements Arthur Young participated in the management of the Co-op because "'financial statements are management's responsibility.'" Although the professional standards adopted by the accounting profession may be relevant, they do not define what constitutes management of an enterprise for the purposes of § 1962(c).

In this case, it is undisputed that Arthur Young relied upon existing Co-op records in preparing the 1981 and 1982 audit reports. The AICPA's professional standards state that an auditor may draft financial statements in whole or in part based on information from management's accounting system. It is also undisputed that Arthur Young's audit reports revealed to the Co-op's board that the value of the gasohol plant had been calculated based on the Co-op's investment in the plant. Thus, we only could conclude that Arthur Young participated in the operation or management of the Co-op itself if Arthur Young's failure to tell the Co-op's board that the plant should have been given its fair market value constituted such participation. We think that Arthur Young's failure in this respect is not sufficient to give rise to liability under § 1962(c).

The judgment of the Court of Appeals is affirmed.

Justice SOUTER, with whom Justice WHITE joins, dissenting.

In the word "conduct," the Court today finds a clear congressional mandate to limit RICO liability under 18 U.S.C. § 1962(c) to participants in the "operation or management" of a RICO enterprise. What strikes the Court as clear, however, looks at the very least hazy to me, and I accordingly find the statute's "liberal construction" provision not irrelevant, but dispositive. But even if I were to assume, with the majority, that the word "conduct" clearly imports some degree of direction or control into § 1962(c), I would have to say that the majority misapplies its own "operation or management" test to the facts presented here. I therefore respectfully dissent.

The word "conduct" occurs twice in § 1962(c), first as a verb, then as a noun.

> "It shall be unlawful for any person employed by or associated with any enterprise engaged in, or the activities of which affect, interstate or foreign commerce, to conduct or participate, directly or indirectly, in the conduct of such enterprise's affairs through a pattern of racketeering activity or collection of unlawful debt." 18 U.S.C. § 1962(c).

Although the Court is surely correct that the cognates should receive consistent readings, and correct again that "context is important" in coming to understand the sense of the terms intended by Congress, the majority goes astray in quoting only the verb form of "conduct" in its statement of the context for divining a meaning that must fit the noun usage as well. Thus, the majority reaches its pivotal conclusion that "in the context of the phrase 'to conduct ... [an] enterprise's affairs,' the word indicates some degree of direction." To be sure, if the statutory setting is so abbreviated as to limit consideration to the word as a verb, it is plausible to find in it a suggestion of control, as in the phrase "to conduct an orchestra." * * *

In any event, the context is not so limited, and several features of the full subsection at issue support a more inclusive construction of "conduct." The term, when used as a noun, is defined by the majority's chosen dictionary as, for example, "carrying forward" or "carrying out," Webster's Third New International Dictionary 473 (1976), phrases without any implication of direction or control. The suggestion of control is diminished further by the fact that § 1962(c) covers not just those "employed by" an enterprise, but those merely "associated with" it, as well. And associates (like employees) are prohibited not merely from conducting the affairs of an enterprise through a pattern of racketeering, not merely from participating directly in such unlawful conduct, but even from indirect participation in the conduct of an enterprise's affairs in such a manner. The very breadth of this prohibition renders the majority's reading of "conduct" rather awkward, for it is hard to imagine how the "operation or management" test would leave the statute with the capacity to reach the indirect participation of someone merely associated with an enterprise. I think, then, that this contextual examination shows "conduct" to have a long arm, unlimited by any requirement to prove that the activity includes an element of direction. But at the very least, the full context is enough to defeat the majority's conviction that the more restrictive interpretation of the word "conduct" is clearly the one intended.

What, then, if we call it a tie on the contextual analysis? The answer is that Congress has given courts faced with uncertain meaning a clear tie-breaker in RICO's "liberal construction" clause, which directs that the "provisions of this title shall be liberally construed to effectuate its remedial purposes." We have relied before on this "express admonition" to read RICO provisions broadly, and in this instance, the "liberal construction" clause plays its intended part, directing us to recognize the more inclusive definition of the word "conduct," free of any restricting element of direction or control. Because the Court of Appeals employed a narrower reading, I would reverse.

Even if I were to adopt the majority's view of § 1962(c), however, I still could not join the judgment, which seems to me unsupportable under the very "operation or management" test the Court announces. If Arthur Young had confined itself in this case to the role traditionally performed by an outside auditor, I could agree with the majority that Arthur Young took no part in the management or operation of the Co-op. But the record on summary judgment, viewed most favorably to Reves, shows that Arthur Young created the very financial statements it was hired, and purported, to audit. Most importantly, Reves adduced evidence that Arthur Young took on management responsibilities by deciding, in the first instance, what value to assign to the Co-op's most important fixed asset, the White Flame gasohol plant, and Arthur Young itself conceded below that the alleged activity went beyond traditional auditing. Because I find, then, that even under the majority's "operation or management" test the Court of Appeals erroneously affirmed the summary judgment for Arthur Young, I would (again) reverse.
* * *

NOTES AND QUESTIONS

1. "***Operation or Management***". Are mere employees within the "operation or management" of an enterprise? The majority in *Reves* notes that "operation" is not limited to upper management. Footnote 9 of this decision leaves lower courts to wrestle with the question of how far down the ladder of operation § 1962(c) will extend. In United States v. Shifman, 124 F.3d 31 (1st Cir. 1997), the First Circuit noted that the concerns in *Reves* for the liability of outside advisers was different than the issue of how far down the organizational chart RICO liability could extend. "Special care is required in translating *Reves*' concern with 'horizontal' connections-focusing on the liability of an outside adviser-into the 'vertical' question of how far RICO liability may extend within the enterprise but down the organizational ladder. In our view, the reason the accountants were not liable in Reves is that, while they were undeniably involved in the enterprise's decisions, they

neither made those decisions nor carried them out; in other words, the accountants were outside the chain of command through which the enterprise's affairs were conducted. We have held, post-*Reves*, however, that a defendant who is 'plainly integral to carrying out' the enterprise's activities may be held criminally liable under RICO."

In **United States v. Cummings**, 395 F.3d 392 (7th Cir. 2005), the Seventh Circuit reversed the conviction of the defendants for RICO conspiracy based on the payment of bribes to low-level workers in the Illinois Department of Employment Security (IDES). Morris, a former worker at IDES, operated a "skip tracing" business to track down debtors for collection agencies. The database maintained by IDES contained information that would be very valuable to a skip tracer, and he paid bribes to former co-workers to obtain addresses of debtors for clients of his business. The court found the defendants did not meet the "operation or management" test:

> The charged racketeering activity was bribery – Morris paid Cummings and the others in exchange for the confidential information contained in the IDES database. The defendants candidly concede that their scheme likely violated state bribery and official misconduct laws as well as IDES policies. But defendants argue that the government failed to show that any of the scheme's participants directed or managed the enterprise as Reves requires, and thus the evidence cannot support their convictions on the RICO count.
>
> We agree. Regardless of which standard of review applies, the record is devoid of evidence that the defendants conspired knowingly to facilitate the activities of anyone to whom § 1962(c) would apply–namely, an operator or manager of the IDES, the charged RICO enterprise. In this regard, none of Morris's accomplices fits the bill. True, Duniver and Harris held customer service "supervisor" positions at the IDES, but nothing in the record explains the scope of their duties or the relevance of their duty titles to the RICO conspiracy with which Morris and Cummings were charged. Likewise, Cummings held a minor position in the IDES's purchasing department, and no evidence indicates that she held any position by which it may be said that she operated or managed the IDES. No evidence indicates that any of these defendants was an operator or manager of the IDES, whether by official duty position or by means of some de facto control over the agency's affairs. Certainly, nothing in the record provides any basis for the jury to have concluded that Morris's associates met the Reves operation or management test or that Morris and Cummings conspired to facilitate the activities of anyone else who might meet that test.
>
> Notwithstanding this evidentiary shortcoming, the government also tries to characterize Morris–an outsider–as the enterprise's operator or manager. After all, *Reves* envisioned that an enterprise may be

> operated or managed by an outsider who "exert[s] control over it as, for example, by bribery." Moreover, a lower level defendant "may conspire to violate § 1962(c) even if that defendant could not be characterized as an operator or manager of a RICO enterprise under Reves." MCM Partners, Inc. v. Andrews-Bartlett & Assocs., Inc., 62 F.3d 967, 979 (7th Cir.1995). Thus, the government contends that Morris's bribery of the IDES employees satisfies Reves because the employees' acceptance of bribes amounted to their agreement to facilitate Morris's control of the enterprise. Even though there is no evidence that Morris exercised control over the IDES, the government explains that "an outsider who bribes a public official rarely, if ever, obtains full control of the government agency in question; rather, the purpose of the bribe is to affect the exercise of a particular function of the agency in a particular situation."
>
> While we cannot fault this proposition as it applies to bribery generally, the government's argument is inapplicable in the RICO context. No evidence adduced at trial reveals that Morris conspired to operate or manage the affairs of the IDES through the bribery of his IDES associates. The undisputed purpose of Morris's bribes reinforces this conclusion. Morris bribed his friends at the IDES in return for confidential information to be used in his skip tracing business. He did not pay bribes in order to exert control over the IDES's core functions of collecting insurance premiums and paying of unemployment benefits. This would be an entirely different ball game if, for example, Morris had bribed his accomplices to make payments of unemployment benefits to unqualified recipients or to falsify payment of premiums by employers. In these hypothetical situations, the bribery schemes at issue would look more like a prototypical RICO conspiracy, in which low-level government employees are bribed to facilitate an outsider's illegal control over the enterprise.

2. ***"Operation or Management" & Aiding and Abetting***. After *Reves,* does "aiding and abetting" play any factor in determining if an individual participated in the "operation or management" of the enterprise? In **United States v. Viola**, 35 F.3d 37 (2d Cir. 1994), the court reversed defendants' convictions, finding an improper jury instruction in light of *Reves*. In discussing the relation of "aiding and abetting" to the "operation or management" test of *Reves*, the court noted:

> In *Reves*, the Court adopted an "operation or management" test to gauge whether a defendant had a sufficient connection to the enterprise to warrant imposing liability under § 1962(c). Under the Court's interpretation, simply aiding and abetting a violation is not sufficient to trigger liability even though § 1962(c) punishes those who participate "directly or indirectly" in the enterprise's affairs. This is so because "aiding and abetting liability extends beyond persons who engage, even indirectly, in a proscribed activity; aiding

> and abetting liability reaches persons who do not engage in the proscribed activity at all, but who give a degree of aid to those who do." Central Bank of Denver, N.A. v. First Interstate Bank of Denver, N.A., 114 S.Ct. 1439, 1447 (1994). The Court did not determine "how far § 1962 extends down the ladder of operation," though it indicated that "[a]n enterprise is 'operated' not just by upper management but also by lower-rung participants in the enterprise who are under the direction of upper management." Some insight into the scope of the operation or management test can be discerned from the Court's intimation that while the operation or management test is more restrictive than aiding and abetting liability, it requires less than "significant" control over the enterprise.

3. ***Professionals***. Do professionals, such as accountants or lawyers, who usually operate outside the "operation or management" of an organization, receive immunity from RICO actions as a result of the *Reves* decision? While the answer to that question is certainly "No," *Reves*' "operation or management" test makes it very difficult to pursue a RICO case against outside professionals based on their conduct that assists a pattern or racketeering activity so long as it is just their professional activities that is at issue. In **Department of Economic Development v. Arthur Andersen & Co.**, 924 F.Supp. 449 (S.D.N.Y. 1996), a British government agency sued an auto manufacturers outside accounting firm and three partners under RICO. In dismissing the suit, the district court emphasized that after *Reves,* courts must recognize

> the difference between actual control over an enterprise and association with an enterprise in ways that do not involve control; only the former is sufficient under *Reves* because "the test is not involvement but control . . . ." The importance of control is illustrated by the one example specifically cited by the *Reves* majority to demonstrate control over a RICO enterprise by a person outside the enterprise: bribery. Bribery is qualitatively different from mere influence or assistance because the outsider paying the bribes buys actual control over the actions of a person within the enterprise. Giving a bribe can be tantamount to gaining a management position within the enterprise, because the insider taking the bribes acts under the direction of the outsider giving them in conducting the affairs of the RICO enterprise. The Court's choice of bribery as an example of an act that might qualify as "operation or management" emphasizes how difficult it is to hold an outsider liable under § 1962(c) after *Reves*.
>
> An outsider who merely enjoys "substantial persuasive power to induce management to take certain actions," unlike an outsider who bribes, does not exercise control over the enterprise within the meaning of *Reves*. Similarly, it is not enough to control even

fraudulent activity that is ancillary to the fraud carried out by the RICO enterprise.

E. CONSPIRACY AND RICO

BECK v. PRUPIS
529 U.S. 494 (2000)

Justice THOMAS delivered the opinion of the Court.

The Racketeer Influenced and Corrupt Organizations Act (RICO) creates a civil cause of action for "[a]ny person injured in his business or property by reason of a violation of section 1962." 18 U.S.C. § 1964(c). Subsection (d) of § 1962 in turn provides that "[i]t shall be unlawful for any person to conspire to violate any of the provisions of subsection (a), (b), or (c) of [§ 1962]." The question before us is whether a person injured by an overt act done in furtherance of a RICO conspiracy has a cause of action under § 1964(c), even if the overt act is not an act of racketeering. We conclude that such a person does not have a cause of action under § 1964(c). * * *

Petitioner, Robert A. Beck II, is a former president, CEO, director, and shareholder of Southeastern Insurance Group (SIG). Respondents, Ronald M. Prupis, Leonard Bellezza, William Paulus, Jr., Ernest S. Sabato, Harry Olstein, Frederick C. Mezey, and Joseph S. Littenberg, are former senior officers and directors of SIG. Until 1990, when it declared bankruptcy, SIG was a Florida insurance holding company with three operating subsidiaries, each of which was engaged in the business of writing surety bonds for construction contractors.

Beginning in or around 1987, certain directors and officers of SIG, including respondents, began engaging in acts of racketeering. They created an entity called Construction Performance Corporation, which demanded fees from contractors in exchange for qualifying them for SIG surety bonds. Respondents also diverted corporate funds to personal uses and submitted false financial statements to regulators, shareholders, and creditors. During most of the time he was employed at SIG, petitioner was unaware of these activities. In early 1988, however, petitioner discovered respondents' unlawful conduct and contacted regulators concerning the financial statements. Respondents then orchestrated a scheme to remove petitioner from the company. They hired an insurance consultant to write a false report suggesting that petitioner had failed to perform his material duties. The day after this report was presented to the SIG board of directors, the board fired petitioner, relying on a clause in his contract providing for termination in the event of an "inability or substantial failure to perform [his] material duties." Petitioner sued respondents, asserting, among other things, a civil cause of action under § 1964(c). In particular, petitioner claimed that respondents used or invested income derived from a pattern of racketeering activity to establish and operate an enterprise, in violation of § 1962(a); acquired and maintained an interest in and control of their enterprise through a pattern of racketeering activity, in violation of § 1962(b); engaged in the conduct of the enterprise's affairs through a pattern of racketeering activity, in violation of § 1962(c); and, most importantly for present purposes, conspired to commit the aforementioned acts, in violation of § 1962(d). With respect to this last claim, petitioner's theory was that his injury was proximately caused by an overt act – namely, the termination of his employment-done in furtherance of respondents' conspiracy, and that § 1964(c) therefore provided a cause of action. Respondents filed a motion for summary judgment, arguing * * * that employees who are terminated for refusing to participate in RICO activities, or who threaten to report RICO activities, do not have standing to sue under RICO for damages from their loss of employment. The District Court agreed and dismissed petitioner's RICO conspiracy claim. The Court of Appeals affirmed, holding that a cause of action under § 1964(c) for a violation of § 1962(d) is not available to a person injured by an overt act in furtherance of a RICO conspiracy unless the overt act is an act of racketeering. Since the overt act that allegedly caused petitioner's injury was not an act of racketeering, see § 1961(1), it could not support a civil cause of action. The court held, "RICO was enacted with an express target –racketeering activity – and only those injuries that are proximately caused by racketeering activity should be actionable under the statute." [The petitioner did not challenge the dismissal of the § 1962(a), (b), and (c) claims.]

This case turns on the combined effect of two provisions of RICO that, read in conjunction, provide a civil cause of action for conspiracy. Section 1964(c) states that a cause of action is available to anyone "injured . . . by reason of a violation of section 1962." Section 1962(d) makes it unlawful for a person "to conspire to violate any of the provisions of subsection (a), (b), or (c) of this section." To determine what it means to be "injured . . . by reason of" a "conspir[acy]," we turn to the well-established common law of civil conspiracy. As we have said, when Congress uses language with a settled meaning at common law, Congress "presumably knows and adopts the cluster of ideas that were attached to each borrowed word in the body of learning from which it was taken and the meaning its use will convey to the judicial mind unless otherwise instructed. In such case, absence of contrary direction may be taken as satisfaction with widely accepted definitions, not as a departure from them." Morissette v. United States, 342 U.S. 246 (1952).

By the time of RICO's enactment in 1970, it was widely accepted that a plaintiff could bring suit for civil conspiracy only if he had been injured by an act that was itself tortious. See, e.g., 4 Restatement (Second) of Torts § 876, Comment b (1977) ("The mere common plan, design or even express agreement is not enough for liability in itself, and there must be acts of a tortious character in carrying it into execution"); W. Prosser, Law of Torts § 46, p. 293 (4th ed. 1971) ("It is only where means are employed, or purposes are accomplished, which are themselves tortious, that the conspirators who have not acted but have promoted the act will be held liable" (footnotes omitted)) * * *.

Consistent with this principle, it was sometimes said that a conspiracy claim was not an independent cause of action, but was only the mechanism for subjecting co-conspirators to liability when one of their member committed a tortious act.

The principle that a civil conspiracy plaintiff must claim injury from an act of a tortious character was so widely accepted at the time of RICO's adoption as to be incorporated in the common understanding of "civil conspiracy." See Ballentine's Law Dictionary 252 (3d ed. 1969) ("It is the civil wrong resulting in damage, and not the conspiracy which constitutes the cause of action"); Black's Law Dictionary 383 (4th ed. 1968) ("[W]here, in carrying out the design of the conspirators, overt acts are done causing *legal* damage, the person injured has a right of action" (emphasis added)). We presume, therefore, that when Congress established in RICO a civil cause of action for a person "injured . . . by reason of" a "conspir[acy]," it meant to adopt these well-established common-law civil conspiracy principles.

Justice STEVENS does not challenge our view that Congress meant to incorporate common-law principles when it adopted RICO. Nor does he attempt to make an affirmative case from the common law for his reading of the statute by pointing to a case in which there was (a) an illegal agreement; (b) injury proximately caused to the plaintiff by a nontortious overt act in furtherance of the agreement; and (c) recovery by the plaintiff. Instead, he argues only that courts, authoritative commentators, and even dictionaries repeatedly articulated a rule with no meaning or application. We find this argument to be implausible and, accordingly, understand RICO to adopt the common-law principles we have cited. Interpreting the statute in a way that is most consistent with these principles, we conclude that injury caused by an overt act that is not an act of racketeering or otherwise wrongful under RICO, is not sufficient to give rise to a cause of action under § 1964(c) for a violation of § 1962(d). As at common law, a civil conspiracy plaintiff cannot bring suit under RICO based on injury caused by any act in furtherance of a conspiracy that might have caused the plaintiff injury. Rather, consistency with the common law requires that a RICO conspiracy plaintiff allege injury from an act that is analogous to an "ac[t] of a tortious character," see 4 Restatement (Second) of Torts § 876, Comment b, meaning an act that is independently wrongful under RICO. The specific type of act that is analogous to an act of a tortious character may depend on the underlying substantive violation the defendant is alleged to have committed. However, respondents' alleged overt act in furtherance of their conspiracy is not independently wrongful under any substantive provision of the statute. Injury caused by such an act is not, therefore, sufficient to give rise to a cause of action under § 1964(c).

Petitioner challenges this view of the statute under the longstanding canon of statutory construction that terms in a statute should not be construed so as to render any provision of that statute meaningless or superfluous. He asserts that under our view of the statute, any person who had a claim for a violation of § 1962(d) would necessarily have a claim for a violation of § 1962(a), (b), or (c). However, contrary to petitioner's assertions, our interpretation of § 1962(d) does not render it mere surplusage. Under our interpretation, a plaintiff could, through a § 1964(c) suit for a violation of § 1962(d), sue co-conspirators who might not themselves have violated one of the substantive provisions of § 1962.

We conclude, therefore, that a person may not bring suit under § 1964(c) predicated on a violation of § 1962(d) for injuries caused by an overt act that is not an act of racketeering or otherwise unlawful under the statute.
Justice STEVENS, with whom Justice SOUTER joins, dissenting.

For the purpose of decision, I assume – as I think the Court does – that petitioner has alleged an injury proximately caused by an overt act in furtherance of a conspiracy that violated 18 U.S.C. § 1962(d). In my judgment, the plain language of the Racketeer Influenced and Corrupt Organizations Act (RICO) makes it clear that petitioner therefore has a cause of action under § 1964(c), whether or not the overt act is a racketeering activity listed in § 1961(1). The common-law civil conspiracy cases relied upon by the Court prove nothing to the contrary.

A "conspiracy" is an illegal agreement. There is, of course, a difference between the question whether an agreement is illegal and the question whether an admittedly illegal agreement gives rise to a cause of action for damages. Section 1962(d), which makes RICO conspiracies unlawful, addresses the former question; § 1964(c), which imposes civil liability, concerns the latter. Section 1964(c) requires a person to be "injured in his business or property" by a violation before bringing an action for damages. And because that kind of injury only results from some form of overt act in furtherance of the conspiracy, liability under § 1964(c) naturally requires injury via an overt act. But there is nothing in either § 1962(d) or § 1964(c) requiring the overt act to be a racketeering activity as defined in § 1961(1).
* * *

[B]ased on its understanding of the common law, the Court concludes that "a RICO conspiracy plaintiff [must] allege injury from an act that is analogous to an 'ac[t] of a tortious character.'" Even assuming that statement is correct, though, it is not at all clear to me why an overt act that "injure[s]" a person "in his business or property" (as § 1964(c) requires) would not be "analogous to an 'ac[t] of a tortious character'" simply because the overt act is not listed in § 1961(1). Nor do I understand why the only qualifying "tortious act" must be "an act that is independently wrongful under RICO."

And if one assumes further that the Court is correct to say that the only qualifying "'ac[t] of a tortious character'" is "an act that is independently wrongful under RICO," the analogy does not actually support what the Court has held. The majority holds that § 1964(c) liability could be imposed if the overt acts injuring the plaintiff are among those racketeering activities listed in § 1961(1) – such as murder, bribery, arson, and extortion. Racketeering activities, however, are not "independently wrongful under RICO." They are, of course, independently wrongful under other provisions of state and federal criminal law, but RICO does not make racketeering activity itself wrongful under the Act. The only acts that are "independently wrongful under RICO" are violations of the provisions of § 1962. Thus, even accepting the Court's own analogy, if petitioner were harmed by predicate acts defined in § 1961(1), that still would not, by itself, give rise to a cause of action under § 1964(c). Only if those racketeering activities also constituted a violation of § 1962(a), (b), or (c) would petitioner be harmed by "an act that is independently wrongful under RICO." And, of course, if petitioner were already harmed by conduct covered by one of those provisions, he would hardly need to use § 1962(d)'s conspiracy provision to establish a cause of action.

The plain language of RICO makes it clear that petitioner's civil cause of action under § 1964(c) for a violation of § 1962(d) does not require that he be injured in his business or property by any particular kind of overt act in furtherance of the conspiracy. * * *

NOTE

Overt Act Not Required. The Supreme Court, in **Salinas v. United States**, 522 U.S. 52 (1997), held that, "[t]here is no requirement of some overt act or specific in the statute before us, unlike the general conspiracy provision applicable to federal crimes, which requires that at least one of the conspirators have committed an 'act to effect the object of the conspiracy.' § 371. The RICO conspiracy offense in § 371." The Court also stated that, "[i]t makes no difference that the substantive offense under subsection (c) requires two or more predicate acts. The interplay between subsections (c) and (d) does not permit us to excuse from the reach of the conspiracy provision an actor who does not himself commit or agree to commit the two or more predicate acts requisite to the underlying offense."

F. FORFEITURE

1. Overview of Forfeiture

Crucial to RICO is its forfeiture provisions, allowing the government to use economic sanctions to attack the alleged criminality. RICO forfeiture is controlled by § 1963, with subsection (a) providing enormous breadth as to what property will be subject to forfeiture. For example, a union officer's positions in a union were found to be subject to forfeiture as included within § 1963(a)'s language of "any interest, security, claim, or property or contract right." This does not, however, mean that one is permanently banned from reaquiring that office. United States v. Rubin, 559 F.2d 975 (5th Cir. 1977).

"The present RICO forfeiture statute has three basic categories of forfeitable property: (a)(1) interests acquired or maintained through racketeering; (a)(2) interests in or providing a source of influence over the racketeering enterprise; and (a)(3) proceeds of racketeering activity." Karla

R. Spaulding, *"Hit Them Where It Hurts": RICO Criminal Forfeitures and White Collar Crime*, 80 J. CRIM. L. & CRIMINOLOGY 197 (1989). It is sometimes difficult to discern the distinctions between subsections (a)(1) and (a)(2) of § 1963. Professor Craig W. Palm noted that:

> The causal connection between the racketeering activity and forfeitable property need be present only if forfeiture is sought pursuant to subsection 1963(a)(1); it is not required under subsection 1963(a)(2). Since property may be forfeitable if it falls within any of the subsections, property that lacks a causal connection to the racketeering activity may still be forfeitable under subsection 1963(a)(2) because of the property's connection with the enterprise. While subsection (a)(1) focuses on the relationship between the racketeering activity and the interests acquired or maintained by virtue of that activity, subsection (a)(2) focuses on the connection between the charged RICO enterprise and the defendant's interests in that enterprise. Subsection 1963(a)(2) does not, on its face, require that the government establish any connection between the activity and the interests in the enterprise; a mere showing of the link between the enterprise and the interests fulfills the requirements of the section.

Craig W. Palm, *RICO Forfeiture and the Eighth Amendment: When Is Everything Too Much?*, 53 U. PITT. L. REV. 1 (1991).

In the third subsection, providing forfeiture of the "proceeds" of "racketeering activity," Congress codified the Court's holding in Russello v. United States, 464 U.S. 16 (1983). The Court held in *Russello* that "interest" as used in the statute in § 1963(a)(1) includes "profits and proceeds."

Subsection (b) of § 1963 extends the scope of property subject to forfeiture by including intangible property. Subsection (c) codifies the "relation-back" doctrine in providing that the property vests in the government at the time that § 1962 is violated. Property transferred is subject to forfeiture unless the recipient is a bona fide purchaser for value who "was reasonably without cause to believe that the property was subject to forfeiture." Temporary restraining orders or injunctions may be obtained by the government to preserve the assets subject to forfeiture. [§ 1963(d)]. Substitute assets can also be subject to forfeiture where, as a result of defendant's act or omission, the property "cannot be located," "has been transferred," "has been placed beyond the jurisdiction of the court," "has been substantially diminished in value, or has been commingled with other property which cannot be divided without difficulty." [§ 1963(m)]. There is an *Asset Forfeiture Policy of the Department of Justice* that guides prosecutors on forfeiture matters. See http://www.justice.gov/criminal/foia/docs/2008policy-manual.pdf.

2. The Relation-Back Principle

In **United States v. Angiulo**, 897 F.2d 1169 (1st Cir. 1990), the court remanded a forfeiture order for modification. In discussing the "relation-back" doctrine as applied in RICO, the court stated:

> As part of its overall verdict, the jury returned a special verdict form finding various assets of defendants to be subject to forfeiture pursuant to 18 U.S.C. § 1963. Section 1963 sets forth criminal penalties to be applied to those who have been found guilty, as defendants were, of engaging in racketeering activities in violation of 18 U.S.C. § 1962. The specific forfeiture provisions applied by the jury in this case were § 1963(a)(1) and (a)(2). * * * Determining that some assets had been acquired or maintained in violation of (a)(1) and that others had afforded a source of influence under (a)(2), the jury found that several pieces of real estate, a substantial amount of cash, six Chrysler bonds, and a yacht all were subject to forfeiture. * * *
>
> Defendants first contend that the trial court erred in failing to instruct the jury that, before forfeiting an asset on the ground that it provided a source of influence under § 1963(a)(2), the jury had to find initially that the defendant owned the property at issue at the time of indictment. The government responds that its interest in forfeitable property vests at the time of the unlawful activity and cannot be extinguished by a subsequent transfer of the property prior to the indictment.
>
> The government's position clearly is the accepted view with respect to forfeitures under § 1963(a)(1). Courts that have considered RICO forfeitures in this context have held that RICO forfeiture, unlike forfeiture under other statutes, "is a sanction against the individual rather than a judgment against the property itself." United States v. Ginsburg, 773 F.2d 798, 801 (7th Cir.1985). Because RICO forfeiture is an in personam action, rather than an in rem action, it has been held that the government's interest in the forfeitable property vests at the time of the unlawful activity and cannot be defeated by the defendants' subsequent transfer of the property.
>
> Defendants acknowledge the holdings of these cases but argue that (a)(2) forfeiture should be treated differently from (a)(1) forfeiture. They, however, have cited nothing in the legislative history of RICO or anywhere else to support the proposition that RICO forfeiture under § 1963(a)(2) should be treated as an in rem action, in contrast to forfeiture under (a)(1), which is universally treated as an in personam action. The cases that we have reviewed in the (a)(1) context make no mention of such a distinction, and do not suggest that their in personam reasoning is limited only to (a)(1) forfeiture.

Rather, they state that RICO forfeiture, presumably in general, is an in personam sanction.

We, therefore, reject defendants' contention that (a)(2) forfeiture can only occur when the property was owned at the time of the indictment. Due to the in personam nature of RICO forfeiture, we find that under (a)(2) as well as under (a)(1), the government's interest in the forfeitable property vests at the time of the unlawful activity and cannot be defeated by the defendants' subsequent transfer of the property.[24]

NOTES AND QUESTIONS

1. ***In personam/In rem.*** The government has the option of proceeding with criminal (*in personam*) or civil forfeiture (*in rem*). "In the civil context, the forfeiture action focuses on whether the property itself was used during the commission of a crime or whether the property constituted proceeds from a crime. In this context, the government may seek to proceed against the *res* administratively or by way of a civil suit." Arthur W. Leach & John G. Malcolm, Criminal Forfeiture: An Appropriate Solution to the Civil Forfeiture, 10 GA. ST. U. L. REV. 241 (1994). A civil forfeiture does not require that the defendant first be convicted. "Because an *in rem* action is a proceeding against the property itself, a separate civil action must be filed in each district in which the property is located. In contrast, criminal forfeiture is not limited to property within the district of the criminal prosecution." U.S.A.M. § 9-110A.100. Criminal forfeiture is a statutory creation found in statutes such as RICO, the Currency and Foreign Transactions Act, and the Continuing Criminal Enterprise statute. Criminal forfeiture provisions can also be found in statutes related to financial institutions and are clearly prevalent in drug related offenses. Since RICO forfeitures are limited to interests acquired, maintained, or used in violation of § 1962, is the effect of the forfeiture really a forfeiture *in rem*? See United States v. Grande, 620 F.2d 1026 (4th Cir. 1980) ("forfeiture under § 1963 is the functional equivalent of a forfeiture *in rem*").

2. ***RICO Forfeiture.*** Is there a broader reach to the forfeiture provisions in RICO than in other statutes that have forfeiture provisions? In United States v. A Parcel of Land Buildings, Appurtenances and Improvements, Known as 92 Buena Vista Avenue, Rumson, New Jersey, 507 U.S. 111 (1993), the Court found that "an owner's lack of knowledge of the fact that her home had been purchased with proceeds of illegal drug transactions" provided a

---

[24] We note that the 1984 amendments to RICO make it explicitly clear that the government's interest vests at the time of the unlawful activity. While it can be disputed whether the actions of a later Congress provide a valid basis for discerning the intent of an earlier Congress, the 1984 amendments have been interpreted as merely confirming 'the already clearly-established legislative intent behind RICO's forfeiture provision.'

defense to a forfeiture proceeding brought under the Comprehensive Drug Abuse Prevention and Control Act of 1970 (21 U.S.C.A. § 881(a)(6)). The Court noted that "the protection afforded to innocent owners is not limited to bona fide purchasers." Further, the Court held that both an amendment to the statute and the common law relation-back doctrine did not make "the Government an owner of property before forfeiture has been decreed." *Buena Vista* involved a civil *in rem* action brought by the government against a parcel of land of which there was a homeowner. "The new manual [U.S.A.M.] concedes that because of the decision, the 'relation back' doctrine can no longer stop any innocent owner, including a donee, from claiming his/her property in a civil forfeiture. But it reminds prosecutors they still should use the relation back doctrine to block similar innocent owners in criminal forfeitures unless they are 'bona fide purchasers for value.' " *Forfeiture Manual Signals Help for Victims*, 3 DOJ Alert, No.11, at 2 (1993).

RICO specifically precludes parties claiming an interest in property from "interven[ing] in a trial or appeal of a criminal case involving the forfeiture of such property." [18 U.S.C.A. § 1963(i)(1)]. Following the entry of an order of forfeiture, individuals asserting an interest in the property can "petition the court for a hearing to adjudicate the validity of the alleged interest in the property." [18 U.S.C.A. § 1963(l)(2)].

3. Forfeiture of Attorney's Fees

UNITED STATES v. SACCOCCIA

354 F.3d 9 (1st Cir. 2003)

CYR, Senior Circuit Judge.

Three attorneys who represented Stephen A. Saccoccia–a convicted drug dealer and money launderer–appeal from a district court order directing that they forfeit some of their attorney fees to the government.

[The grand jury indicted Saccoccia in November 1991, charging him with one count of RICO conspiracy under 18 U.S.C. § 1963(d) and several counts of laundering proceeds from an illegal drug trafficking operation. The government also sought the forfeiture of all the business and personal property directly or indirectly derived from Saccoccia's racketeering activities, explicitly including almost $137,000,000 in currency, and, in the alternative, sought the surrender of all non-tainted property of equivalent value (if any) should Saccoccia's tainted property have become unavailable. The district court enjoined the transfer of the forfeitable property designated in the indictment.]

Saccoccia retained Jack Hill, Esquire, and Kenneth O'Donnell, Esquire, to defend him in the RICO prosecution; he retained Stephen Finta, Esquire, to defend him against money laundering charges pending in California. * * *

Beginning in March 1992, under rather suspicious circumstances, Saccoccia caused $504,985 to be delivered to Hill, $410,000 to O'Donnell, and $469,200 to Finta, all for legal fees. Approximately one year later, Saccoccia was convicted and ordered to forfeit the $137,000,000 in currency specified in the indictment. We subsequently affirmed both the conviction and the forfeiture. Once the government discovered that Saccoccia had paid large legal fees to Hill, O'Donnell, and Finta, it submitted a motion to compel them to turn over the fees as property subject to forfeiture.

The district court granted the motion to compel, holding that (i) the government established that the legal fees paid to the appellants must have derived from Saccoccia's racketeering activity, given that Saccoccia had no legitimate sources of income, and the legal fees were paid "under especially suspicious circumstances" (viz., by "covert deliveries of large quantities of cash, made by anonymous intermediaries"); (ii) appellants met their burden of proving that they had no reasonable cause to believe that the monies Saccoccia used to pay their fees, prior to Saccoccia's conviction, were subject to forfeiture, given that an Assistant United States Attorney's pre-conviction assurances to appellants–that the government would not seek forfeiture of their legal fees–implied some government uncertainty regarding whether Saccoccia might possess sufficient non-tainted assets with which to pay his attorneys; (iii) following the trial at which Saccoccia was convicted, appellants could not have held a reasonable belief that Saccoccia's assets were not subject to forfeiture, given that the trial record made it clear that virtually all of Saccoccia's assets had been derived through illegitimate means; (iv) appellants were ordered to turn over only the portion of their legal fees received following Saccoccia's conviction; and (v) the government could not reach their pre-conviction legal fees by means of the district court's contempt power due to the fact that the government had initiated no such proceeding and the district court had already determined that appellants lacked reasonable cause to believe that the pre-conviction legal fees were subject to forfeiture, hence appellants could not have violated the post-indictment injunction willfully.

Appellants now challenge the district court order which determined that their post-conviction legal fees are subject to forfeiture.

Appellants Hill and O'Donnell contend, as they did in opposing the government's motion to compel below, that the forfeiture statute does not permit the government to reach the legal fees they received from Saccoccia, due to the fact that those fees have been expended.

The operative statutory language requires that a defendant forfeit "tainted" property, viz., property (i) acquired by committing the offense, and (ii) "constituting, or derived from, any proceeds . . . obtained, directly or indirectly" from its commission. 18 U.S.C. § 1963(a)(1), (3). Once an indictment issues, the district court may enjoin the transfer of all property "subject to forfeiture under [section 1963]." Id. § 1963(d)(1). In the event that tainted property is unavailable for forfeiture (as when it has been transferred to a third party), the government may recover "substitute" property, viz., defendant's other untainted property of equivalent value. See id. § 1963(m); United States v. Lester, 85 F.3d 1409 (9th Cir.1996) (" '[S]ubstitute property,' ... by its very nature is 'not connected to the underlying *13 crime.' ").

The operative statute enables the government to recover from the defendant "tainted" or "substitute" property in a defendant's possession, or "tainted" property held by a third party by virtue of a voidable fraudulent transfer. Id. § 1963(c). A third party may petition the court for a hearing to determine the validity of its legal interest in tainted property, id. § 1963 (l)-(2), and may defeat a forfeiture petition by establishing, inter alia, that it is a bona fide purchaser for value, "reasonably without cause to believe" that the property was subject to forfeiture at the time it was purchased, id. § 1963(l)(6)(B).

Nonetheless, the "substitute property" provision is exclusively applicable to "any other property of the defendant." Id. § 1963(m). The statutory language plainly does not afford an avenue through which the government may reach a third party's untainted assets as a substitute for tainted assets which the third party had already transferred prior to the date of forfeiture.

The government does not contend that it can recover the "tainted" property already transferred to Hill and O'Donnell by Saccoccia (i.e., the in-cash legal fees), nor does it maintain that either Hill or O'Donnell presently holds any property fairly traceable to, or acquired with the proceeds of, their legal fees. Rather, it argues that its right to recover derives from the knowing violations, by Hill and O'Donnell, of the post-indictment injunction entered pursuant to § 1963(d)(1), which constrained Saccoccia and his counsel from transferring any funds subject to forfeiture under subsection 1963(a).

The absence of language in subsection 1963(m), relating to the forfeitability vel non of a third party's substitute assets, simply forecloses one form of remedy, not all. Relief from a willful violation of a subsection 1963(d)(1) injunction may be obtained in a contempt proceeding. On the other hand, the government's initiation of contempt proceedings would significantly alter its burden in litigation. Whereas subsections 1963(c) and (l)(6) require the third party to establish that it was without reasonable cause to believe that the transferred property was subject to forfeiture under subsection 1963(a), in a criminal or civil contempt proceeding the government would bear the burden of persuasion on that issue. In a criminal contempt proceeding, moreover, the government's burden of proof would be beyond-a-reasonable-doubt, see Fed.R.Crim.P. 42; and in a civil contempt proceeding, clear and convincing evidence would be required. The district court noted, however, that "the government is not seeking to hold the attorneys in contempt."

Additionally, subsection 1963(m) would not preempt various remedies otherwise available to the government outside the forfeiture statute, which would maximize its monetary recovery from the substitute assets of culpable third parties. See United States v. Moffitt, Zwerling & Kemler, 83 F.3d 660 (4th Cir.1996) (holding that § 1963(m) does not preempt state common-law claims that enable the government to reach a third-party transferee's substitute assets). For instance, since the government's right, title, and interest in all tainted property "relates back" to the date Saccoccia committed the relevant acts, see 18 U.S.C. § 1963(c) ("All right, title, and interest in property described in subsection (a) vests in the United States upon the commission of the act giving rise to the forfeiture."), presumably it could initiate a state-law proceeding against Hill and O'Donnell for conversion of such property, and recover compensatory damages from their non-tainted assets. However, had the government brought such a tort claim in the district court, the claim presumably would be adjudicated under substantially different standards than a claim under subsection 1963(a) or (m), since the government would bear the burden of proof, and appellants might be entitled to additional procedural safeguards under state law, such as a right to jury trial.

At first blush, the present holding may appear to diverge from the stated legislative intent to accord the government extremely aggressive forfeiture remedies so as to preclude criminals from realizing the monetary benefits of their crimes. See Caplin & Drysdale, Chartered v. United States, 491 U.S. 617 (1989). On the other hand, the very potency of the forfeiture power demands that it be reasonably contained within ascertainable limits. Thus, for example, Congress provided that a non-defendant third party with rights in forfeitable property may redeem its interest by establishing either (i) that it predated the defendant's crime, or (ii) that it subsequently acquired a non-forfeitable interest under a bona fide purchase for value, see 18 U.S.C. § 1963(l)(6).

The implicit limitation in § 1963(m) – the "substitute assets" provision – that the government may reach only the defendant's substitute assets and not those of a third party–is similar in nature. Forfeiture is an in personam criminal remedy, targeted primarily at the defendant who committed the criminal offense.

Finally, the implicit limitation in § 1963(m) does not trammel the basic statutory policy by foreclosing all other remedies available to the government, nor does it enable culpable attorneys to dissipate tainted fees with impunity. Rather, the government may utilize its enforcement powers under subsection 1963(k) to "trace" tainted funds, thereby disproving the contention that appellants' cash-on-hand is neither the tainted fees, nor other property directly or indirectly derived from the tainted fees. Furthermore, absent such evidence, the government may reach other non-tainted cash of the attorneys by sustaining the somewhat weightier, though not insurmountable, burden of establishing the elements of either contempt or conversion.

As our construction of the language utilized in the forfeiture statute is one of first impression, the forfeiture award against Hill and O'Donnell must be vacated and the case must be remanded to the district court for further proceedings consistent with this opinion. Upon remand, the government is to be accorded a reasonable opportunity to determine whether it intends to institute contempt proceedings or submit conversion claims against appellants. * * *

4. Excessiveness

In **Alexander v. United States**, 509 U.S. 544 (1993), the Supreme Court considered possible Eighth Amendment limitations on forfeiture under the Excessive Fines Clause. After a conviction for RICO violations based on selling obscene material, the defendant received a six-year prison term and $100,000 fine. In addition, the district court ordered Alexander to forfeit his wholesale and retail businesses (including all the assets of those businesses) and almost $9 million in moneys acquired through racketeering activity. In remanding the case for the lower court to consider whether the forfeiture constituted an excessive fine, the Court stated:

> The personam criminal forfeiture at issue here is clearly a form of monetary punishment no different, for Eighth Amendment purposes, from a traditional "fine." Accordingly, the forfeiture in this case should be analyzed under the Excessive Fines Clause.
>
> Petitioner contends that forfeiture of his entire business was an "excessive" penalty for the Government to exact "[o]n the basis of a few materials the jury ultimately decided were obscene." It is somewhat misleading, we think, to characterize the racketeering crimes for which petitioner was convicted as involving just a few materials ultimately found to be obscene. Petitioner was convicted of creating and managing what the District Court described as "an enormous racketeering enterprise." It is in the light of the extensive criminal activities which petitioner apparently conducted through this racketeering enterprise over a substantial period of time that the question of whether or not the forfeiture was "excessive" must be considered. We think it preferable that this question be addressed by the Court of Appeals in the first instance.

In **United States v. Bajakajian**, 524 U.S. 321 (1998) the Court held forfeiture "of the entire $357,144 that respondent failed to declare" on a customs currency reporting form to "be grossly disproportional to the gravity of his offense." The Court stated that "a punitive forfeiture violates the Excessive Fines Clause if it is grossly disproportional to the gravity of a defendant's offense." The Court further stated:

> The harm that respondent caused was also minimal. Failure to report his currency affected only one party, the Government, and in

> a relatively minor way. There was no fraud on the United States, and respondent caused no public loss to the public fisc. Had his crime gone undetected, the Government would have been deprived only of the information that $357,144 had left the country.

Congress, in the "Uniting and Strengthening America by Providing Appropriate Tools Required to Intercept and Obstruct Terrorism Act of 2001" (USA Patriot Act), created a bulk cash smuggling offense with new penalties for the undeclared movement of more than $10,000 across U.S. borders.

CHAPTER SEVEN
REGULATORY OFFENSES

A. INTRODUCTION

Regulatory offenses are crimes involving a violation of government regulation. The regulation will often provide specific procedures, including licensing, for maintaining activities that the government considers "a special threat to the community at large." Edmund W. Kitch, Kevin A. Russell, & Steven Duke, *Economic Crime,* 2 ENCYCLOPEDIA OF CRIMINAL JUSTICE 670, 672-73 (1983). Regulatory crimes can also be a product of a failure to comply with a regulation's reporting requirements. Id. For a discussion of the enforcement of economic regulations through criminal sanctions, see Sanford H. Kadish, *Some Observations on the Use of Criminal Sanctions in Enforcing Economic Regulations,* 30 U. CHI. L. REV. 423 (1962).

Regulatory statutes are found throughout state and federal codes. It is evident in examining recent legislation that government regulation has increased in recent years. For example, crimes relating to the environment have now received priority status by the Department of Justice. Also apparent are an increased number of prosecutions for OSHA (Occupational Health and Safety Act) violations and health offenses.

An investigation for an alleged regulatory violation usually commences with the agency overseeing the administration of the regulation. This agency will often make an initial determination as to whether the enforcement of the regulation will be through an administrative, civil, or criminal action. Parallel civil and criminal proceeding are common occurrences in the enforcement of regulatory statutes. (See Chapter 14). Cases to be pursued criminally are turned over to the Department of Justice for prosecution.

NOTES AND QUESTIONS

1. ***Prosecutorial Charging Discretion.*** Prosecutors have the discretion of whether to proceed with criminal charges and what charges to use against the accused. The prosecution of regulatory offenses is not always limited to criminal statutes contained within one environmental act (e.g., Clean Water Act). Indictments often include charges such as conspiracy (18 U.S.C. § 371), false statements (18 U.S.C. § 1001), mail fraud (18 U.S.C. § 1341), and obstruction of justice (18 U.S.C. § 1503). The U.S.A.M. provides a list of statutes for consideration when charging an environmental crime. See U.S.A.M. § 5-11.102. Although environmental offenses are not specifically

listed as predicate acts for a RICO prosecution, mail and wire fraud have served as the predicates for RICO prosecutions involving environmental offenses. See United States v. Paccione, 738 F. Supp. 691, 699 (S.D. N.Y. 1990) ("Nothing in the decisions of this Circuit suggests that mail and wire fraud, properly alleged, in the conduct of an enterprise cannot be included as racketeering activity because the enterprise is alleged to have engaged in violations of regulatory schemes which do not constitute racketeering activity on their own.") Consider the following excerpts from Philip Shabecoff, *Federal Statutes Cited In Indictment of Exxon*, N.Y.Times, Mar. 1, 1990, A14, noting how statutes from several different Acts were used in the indictment of Exxon.

> A Federal grand jury in Alaska invoked five Federal statutes on Tuesday when it indicted the Exxon Corporation and the Exxon Shipping Company on felony and misdemeanor charges in the Exxon Valdez oil spill.
>
> Following are the applicable laws and the ways the indictment charges that Exxon violated them:
>
> ***The Clean Water Act*** makes it illegal to discharge pollutants or hazardous substances negligently into United States waters without a permit. The indictment charges that Exxon and Exxon Shipping negligently caused pollutants, "namely 10 million gallons of crude oil,' to be discharged from the tanker Exxon Valdez into Prince William Sound, 'a navigable water of the United States," without a permit.
>
> ***The Refuse Act*** makes it unlawful to discharge refuse, including oil, from a ship. The indictment says the corporation and its subsidiary caused refuse matter, "namely 10 million gallons of crude oil," to be "thrown, discharged and deposited in Prince William Sound."
>
> ***The Migratory Bird Treaty Act*** prohibits the killing of any migratory bird without a permit. The indictment did not list the number of birds killed by the Exxon Valdez spill, but a Justice Department document noted that as of last September more than 36,000 dead birds had been collected and that they were believed to be only a fraction of the actual number killed.
>
> ***The Ports and Waterways Act*** requires that the master or anyone else in charge of a vessel insure that the wheelhouse is manned by competent people. The indictment charges that the corporation and the company, as well as the master of the tanker, Capt. Joseph J. Hazelwood, failed to assure that the vessel was in the hands of those competent to perform their duty.
>
> ***The Dangerous Cargo Act*** makes it a felony to violate a regulation that bars from tanker crews any person known by an employer to be

> physically or mentally incapable of performing assigned duties. The indictment contends that Exxon "willfully and knowingly" employed people incapable of performing the duties assigned to them. * * *

2. ***Pleas and Settlements.*** Plea agreements account for 94.4% of the resolutions in corporate environmental cases. WCH § 14.1(D). For example, following the 2010 Deepwater Horizon disaster, BP Exploration and Production Inc. (BP) entered into a plea agreement with the government in which they would pay "$4 billion dollars in criminal fines and penalties." DOJ Press Release, BP Exploration and Production Inc. Agrees to Plead Guilty to Felony Manslaughter, Environmental Crimes and Obstruction of Congress Surrounding Deepwater Horizon Incident, available at http://www.justice.gov/opa/pr/bp-exploration-and-production-inc-agrees-plead-guilty-felony-manslaughter-environmental. Many cases are resolved through non-prosecution and deferred prosecution agreements. See Chap. 3. Prosecutors are often looking at whether there was a voluntary disclosure and whether the company had an effective compliance program. See Chap. 17.

3. ***International.*** The Lacey Act,(16 U.S.C. § 3372(a)(2)(A)), criminalizes the unlawful importation into the United States of "fish or wildlife [that has been] taken, possessed, transported, or sold in violation of ...any foreign law." Determining what is the foreign law, however, may be difficult. In **United States v. McNabb**, 331 F.3d 1228 (11th Cir. 2003), the defendants challenged the validity of the Honduran laws used in their Lacey Act prosecution. The court noted that "[t]hroughout the investigation and trial, Honduran officials offered support and assistance to the United States government, and both the government and the district court relied upon the Honduran officials' verification of the Honduran laws." After the trial had concluded, the Honduran government took a different position and the Eleventh Circuit needed to determine whether it should consider the original interpretation of the Honduran government, or its new interpretation of its laws. In a 2-1 decision, the court affirmed the convictions holding:

> The reference to foreign law in the Lacey Act is there to define what constitutes illegal conduct. Thus, the subsequent invalidation of the underlying foreign laws does not make the defendants any less culpable for their actions. If the laws were valid in Honduras during the time period covered by the indictment, the defendants violated the Lacey Act by importing the lobsters in violation of those laws. Whatever changes in the laws occurred after the lobsters were imported into the United States illegally have no effect on the defendants' convictions.

The dissent, however, did not see this case as one in which the Honduran government had "shifted" its position. Rather, Circuit Judge Fay maintained that "there was never unanimity nor agreement concerning the validity" of the resolution used as the Honduran law basis for the Lacey Act violation.

B. THE MENS REA *ELEMENT*

There is no consistent mental state required for all of the regulatory offenses. In some cases courts have interpreted regulatory statutes to be strict liability crimes. In other instances the statutes have required a mens rea of willfulness or knowledge. In examining the mental state used in different regulatory offenses, consider whether the principles of statutory interpretation discussed in Chapter Four should differ here. Should regulatory crimes have a higher or lesser *mens rea* than traditional crimes? See Chapter 17 for a discussion of how the United States Sentencing Commission treats regulatory offenses.

1. Strict Liability

UNITED STATES v. WHITE FUEL CORPORATION
498 F.2d 619 (1st Cir. 1974)

CAMPBELL, Circuit Judge.

White Fuel Corporation was convicted after a jury-waived trial of violating Section 13 of the Rivers and Harbors Act of 1899, 33 U.S.C. § 407 (the Refuse Act).[1] White Fuel operates a tank farm abutting a small cove off the Reserved Channel, part of Boston harbor. Both the cove and the channel are navigable waters of the United States. On May 3, 1972, the Coast Guard found oil in the water of the cove. White Fuel, which in January 1972 had been alerted by state authorities to possible oil spoilage problems, immediately undertook to clean up the oil and to trace its source. Although at first an oil-water separator and later a leaky pipe were suspected, experts called in by White Fuel finally determined that the oil was seeping from an immense accumulation (approximately half a million gallons) which had gathered under White Fuel's property. White Fuel concedes, and the court found, that it owned the oil, which continued to seep into the cove throughout the summer of 1972 even though White Fuel worked diligently to drain or divert the accumulation. By September it was successful and seepage had ceased. As part of its clean-up efforts, and to prevent the oil from spreading, White Fuel had installed booms across the mouth of the cove. There was testimony that on occasion these booms were tended improperly, so that some of the oil drifted out into the channel.

---

[1] "It shall not be lawful to throw, discharge, or deposit, or cause, suffer, or procure to be thrown, discharged, or deposited either from or out of . . . the shore [or] . . . manufacturing establishment . . . any refuse matter of any kind or description . . . into any navigable water of the United States, . . ."

The district court found that the seepage was a violation of the Refuse Act and imposed a $1,000 fine.[3] The court denied White Fuel's motion for judgment of acquittal and, ruling that intent or scienter is irrelevant to guilt, also denied White Fuel's offer to present evidence that it had not known of the underground deposit, had not appreciated its hazards, and had acted diligently when the deposit became known. The court held that White Fuel's only defense would be to show that third parties caused the oil seepage—that "this oil escaped from a source other than that under the control of the defendant". White Fuel contends that the government was required to prove scienter or at least negligence as part of its case, and that the court erred by precluding the proffered defense. * * *

* * * [T]he sole question for us to decide is whether the conviction is supported by the undisputed fact that oil owned by White Fuel leached from its property into adjacent navigable waters. White Fuel first insists that this sort of seepage is not even covered by the Refuse Act because it did not "throw, discharge, or deposit" oil, and that since it did not know the oil was entering the cove it did not "suffer" the discharge. But a defendant which allows its own oil to be discharged, even unwittingly, seems to us in everyday language to "suffer" the discharge. That this discharge was more of an indirect percolation than a direct flow is, of course, immaterial.

There is no greater merit in White Fuel's next argument, that common law *mens rea* had to be alleged or proven. * * * In the seventy-five years since enactment, no court to our knowledge has held that there must be proof of scienter; to the contrary, the Refuse Act has commonly been termed a strict liability statute. The offense falls within the category of public welfare offenses which

> "are not in the nature of positive aggressions or invasions, with which the common law so often dealt, but are in the nature of neglect where the law requires care, or inaction where it imposes a duty .... The accused, if he does not will the violation, usually is in a position to prevent it with no more care than society might reasonably expect and no more exertion than it might reasonably exact from one who assumed his responsibilities." Morissette v. United States, 342 U.S. 246, 255-56 (1952).

We do not accept White Fuel's further argument that if the government need not prove scienter it must at least prove negligence. Actually, merely by showing that White Fuel's oil escaped into public waters, the government presented facts from which negligence could be inferred. See Restatement (Second) of Torts § 328D. The real issue is not the government's prima facie case, which was sufficient by any standard, but whether due care—lack of negligence—is available as a defense. In the Federal Water Pollution Control

---

[3] The offense, a misdemeanor, allows a maximum fine of $2,500 and a year's imprisonment.

Act Amendments of 1972, 33 U.S.C. § 1251 et seq., Congress imposed criminal penalties only upon any person who "willfully or negligently" violates its prohibitions, 33 U.S.C. § 1319(c)(1), but provided civil penalties for all violations. 33 U.S.C. § 1319(d). In the Refuse Act, on the other hand, Congress made no such distinction, and we have been told to read the latter "charitably in light of the purpose to be served," United States v. Republic Steel Corp., 362 U.S. 482, 491 (1960). The dominant purpose is to require people to exercise whatever diligence they must to keep refuse out of public waters. Given this aim, we are disinclined to invent defenses beyond those necessary to ensure a defendant constitutional due process. Specifically we reject the existence of any generalized "due care" defense that would allow a polluter to avoid conviction on the ground that he took precautions conforming to industry-wide or commonly accepted standards.

Merely to attempt to formulate, let alone apply, such standards, would be to risk crippling the Refuse Act as an enforcement tool. The defendant, if a substantial business enterprise, would usually have exclusive control of both the expertise and the relevant facts; it would be difficult indeed, and to no purpose, for the government to have to take issue with elaborate factual and theoretical arguments concerning who, why and what went wrong. A municipality may require dog owners to keep their dogs off the public streets, and the court may enforce the ordinance by criminal sanctions without paying attention, except in mitigation, to the owner's tales concerning his difficulty in getting Fido to stay home. In the present circumstances we see no unfairness in predicating liability on actual non-compliance rather than either intentions or best efforts. See O. W. Holmes, The Common Law 49 (1881). Whatever occasional harshness this could entail is offset by the moderateness of the permitted fine, the fact that the statute's command—to keep refuse out of the public waters—scarcely imposes an impossible burden, and the benefit to society of having an easily defined, enforcible standard which inspires performance rather than excuses. The President Coolidge, 101 F.2d 638 (9th Cir. 1939). As a corporate defendant like White Fuel cannot be imprisoned, we need not consider to what extent absolute liability would carry over to cases where incarceration is a real possibility.

Although there is no generalized "due care" defense, a defendant may always, of course, show that someone other than himself was responsible for the discharge. White Fuel might, for example, undertake to prove that oil had percolated through its soil from the supply of an adjacent landowner. If a plane crashed into one of its tanks causing a spill, White Fuel would not be liable. If thieves overpowered its watchmen and somehow caused a pipe to overflow, White Fuel would not be liable. Acts of God would be another legitimate defense. It might be a defense that the spill was caused by an independent contractor who was entirely outside the defendant's control. * * *

As the above instances illustrate, the law recognizes some defenses even where liability generally is predicated on the sole fact of non-compliance. One is not expected to take all conceivable measures to erect a fail-safe system which would be impregnable to sabotage, thievery, accidental intrusions, the negligence of third parties, and extreme natural disasters. Even if perfect protection could be insured, such is not the "some other course open" of which the law speaks. But, with this caveat concerning human frailty, it remains true that the standard of proof of exculpatory facts is of a much more rigorous and exceptional nature than that of reasonable care. Particularly is this true of an enterprise such as that we deal with here—an oil tank farm, with its inherent risk of spills, leaks, and seepage, abutting navigable waters. Such a high risk enterprise carries with it, even under conventional tort law, a high burden of responsibility.

Against such a requirement for exculpation, White Fuel's proffered defenses, even if proven, were inadequate. White Fuel offered to prove that its personnel did not know of the existence of the oil prior to May 3, 1972 and could not, in any event, have predicted that such oil would seep into the cove. It also wished to show its diligence in cleaning up and checking the seepage once it was discovered. But it was conceded that White Fuel owned the offending oil, that it had occupied the property continuously for years, that the accumulation was vast, and that its property bordered the cove. Given such facts, we do not think that the excluded evidence, even if true, could have demonstrated that it was so far beyond White Fuel's power to have avoided the accumulation and consequent seepage as to render the conviction and fine improper.

Affirmed.

NOTE AND QUESTION

Has the court in *White Fuel* ruled consistently with how the Supreme Court ruled in *Posters 'N' Things, Ltd*, [p.105], and *Staples*, [p.106]? Recall how Justice Thomas, in *Staples*, distinguished the National Firearms Act from "public welfare" or "regulatory offenses." Should a higher *mens rea* be required for offenses committed under the National Firearms Act than for offenses under the Refuse Act?

2. Willfulness

UNITED STATES v. DYE CONSTRUCTION COMPANY
510 F.2d 78 (10th Cir. 1975)

DOYLE, Circuit Judge.

Following the death of a workman in a trench cave-in, the appellant was charged with willfully failing to shore, sheet, brace, slope and otherwise support by means of sufficient strength sides of trenches in unstable or soft material sufficient to protect employees working within the trenches, five feet or more in depth. The cause which arose under the Occupational Safety and Health Act of 1970, 29 U.S.C. § 651 et seq.[1] was tried to a jury. * * *

The entire thrust of the Dye argument here is that the jury should have been instructed that willfulness in terms of intent to do the act knowingly and purposefully is not enough; that an evil motive is an essential element. The instruction given reads as follows:

> The failure to comply with a safety standard under the Occupational Safety and Health Act is willful if done knowingly and purposely by an employer who, having a free will or choice, either intentionally disregards the standard or is plainly indifferent to its requirement. An omission or failure to act is willfully done if done voluntarily and intentionally.

The Supreme Court and our court have recognized that willfulness has different meanings when used in different contexts. The distinction which is usually drawn in defining willfulness is between crimes in which moral turpitude is required and those which do not demand a moral taint. * * *

> In statutes denouncing offenses involving turpitude, "willfully" is generally used to mean with evil purpose, criminal intent or the like. But in those denouncing acts not in themselves wrong, the word is often used without any such implication.

Perhaps a very clear example of this distinction appears in Spies v. United States, [317 U.S. 492 (1943)], wherein the Court considered the difference between failure to file an income tax return and tax fraud which involves moral turpitude. In the tax fraud case the Court said "willfulness" includes evil motive, but in the charge of failure to file no such element is necessary. * * *

At bar neither the statute nor the regulation requires that there be moral turpitude. The object of these provisions is prevention of injury or death and its

---

[1] Section 655 of the Act authorizes the Secretary of Labor to promulgate regulations to insure that employees covered by the Act are provided with a place of employment that is free from recognized hazards that are likely to cause death or serious bodily harm.

Section 666(e) states:

> Any employer who willfully violates any standard, rule, or order promulgated pursuant to section 655 of this title, or of any regulations prescribed pursuant to this chapter, and that violation caused death to any employee, shall, upon conviction, be punished by a fine of not more than $10,000 or by imprisonment for not more than six months, or by both; . . . * * *

application is not limited to the situation in which the employer entertained a specific intent to harm the employee. * * *

The judgment of the district court is affirmed.

NOTES

1. ***No Knowledge Proviso.*** A violation of the Securities Exchange Act of 1934 can become a criminal felony offense when the defendant acts willfully. The Act, however, specifically provides that "no person shall be subject to imprisonment under this section for the violation of any rule or regulation if he proves that he had no knowledge of such rule or regulation." The "no knowledge" proviso does not negate the criminal conviction, but does offer a limitation of punishment to those included within 15 U.S.C.A. § 78ff(a). This section does not serve as a defense for one who claims "no knowledge" of the "standards prescribed in the securities acts themselves." In United States v. Lilley, 291 F. Supp. 989 (S.D. Tex. 1968), the court found the "no knowledge" proviso inapplicable to defendants who pled guilty. The court stated, "These admissions by each defendant preclude him from discharging his burden of showing 'no knowledge' of Rule 10b-5."

2. ***Mens Rea Determined By Misdemeanor or Felony.*** The mens rea for acts under the Food, Drug, and Cosmetic Act may depend upon the level of the offense. In **United States v. Watkins**, 278 F.3d 961 (9th Cir. 2002) the court stated:

> The FDCA provides two tiers of liability for misbranding violations under § 331(a). The misdemeanor provision imposes criminal liability in the form of imprisonment, fines, or both. *See* 21 U.S.C. § 333(a)(1) ("Any person who violates [§ 331(a)(1)] shall be imprisoned for not more than one year or fined not more than $1,000, or both."). An article may be misbranded pursuant to the misdemeanor provision "without any conscious fraud at all," thus creating a form of strict criminal liability. * * * Felony misbranding, on the other hand, requires a showing that the defendant acted "with intent to defraud or mislead" * * * Thus, felony liability for misbranding requires an additional mens rea element that is absent from the broader-reaching misdemeanor provision.* * *

The court in *Watkins* also found that "felony liability for misbranding requires proof of materiality."

3. Knowingly

UNITED STATES v. BRONX REPTILES, INC.
217 F.3d 82 (2d Cir. 2000)

SACK, Circuit Judge:

* * * When a criminal statute renders unlawful an act "knowingly" undertaken by the defendant, what must the extent of the defendant's knowledge be to permit conviction?

The defendant, Bronx Reptiles, Inc., was convicted following a bench trial in the United States District Court for the Eastern District of New York * * *of violating that portion of the Lacey Act, codified as amended at 18 U.S.C. § 42(c), that makes it a misdemeanor "for any person, including any importer, knowingly to cause or permit any wild animal or bird to be transported to the United States, or any Territory or district thereof, under inhumane or unhealthful conditions or in violation of such requirements" as the Secretary of the Interior may prescribe. * * * The defendant argues on appeal that under § 42(c), the government was required to prove not only that the defendant knowingly caused the transportation to the United States of a wild animal or bird, but also that the defendant knew the conditions under which the animal or bird was transported were "inhumane or unhealthful." * * *

First, § 42(c) is a provision of a criminal statute describing behavior that it declares to be "unlawful." The reader therefore expects the sentence to tell him or her what it is that a person must do "knowingly" to perform a criminally punishable act. Reading knowingly to apply (1) to the language "to cause or permit any wild animal or bird to be transported" and (2) to the phrase "to the United States," but not to (3) the requirement that such transportation be "under inhumane or unhealthful conditions," leads to a highly unlikely result: A vast range of remarkably innocuous behavior is rendered criminal. Not only the importer but the pet store owner or the casual purchaser of pets may well become guilty of a crime by purchasing a once-wild animal or bird–* * *–knowing only that the direct or indirect result of the purchase is that a "wild animal or bird [will] be transported to the United States." To avoid this extraordinary and unlikely result, the reader is bound to read the requirement of knowledge to apply to the provision that the animal or bird be transported "under inhumane or unhealthful conditions" so that the "unlawful" act prohibited involves wrongdoing.

Second, there is nothing in the structure or punctuation of § 42(c) that signals the reader that "knowingly" does *not* apply to the phrase "under inhumane or unhealthful conditions." The statute could have been written, for example, to render it "unlawful for any person knowingly to cause or permit any wild animal or bird to be transported to the United States, *the conditions of which transportation* are inhumane or unhealthful," or "knowingly to cause or permit any wild animal or bird to be transported to the United States (*insofar as the conditions of transporting* the animal are inhumane or unhealthful)." In the former case, the comma and the word "which," and in the latter, the parentheses and the words "insofar as," indicate that "knowingly" might have been intended to apply only to causing or permitting a wild animal to be transported to the United States. But § 42(c) as written contains no punctuation or phrasing--no comma, no "which," no parentheses, no "insofar as"--to undermine the most obvious reading of § 42(c): that "knowingly" extends to the phrase "inhumane or unhealthful."

If a simple review of the language of § 42(c) does not establish that "knowingly" refers to "inhumane or unhealthful," however, the legal principle that criminal statutes are presumed to contain a *mens rea* requirement does. * * * There is, moreover, neither statutory language nor legislative history to overcome the *mens rea* presumption. We would expect that if Congress meant, contrary to the presumption, to impose liability absent a "guilty mind," it would have said so. * * * In sum, to permit the defendant to be convicted of a crime under 18 U.S.C. § 42(c) without knowledge of the "inhumane or unhealthful" conditions under which the frogs were transported to the United States would be to impose upon them guilt absent a *mens rea*. This is contrary to the fundamental presumption that *mens rea,* a "guilty mind," is a prerequisite to conviction for a crime.* * *

The government points out that in cases involving "public welfare offenses," courts have declined to read into statutes a *mens rea* requirement, concluding that Congress intended to impose a form of strict criminal liability instead. * * *

"[P]ublic welfare offenses have been created by Congress, and recognized" by courts "in limited circumstances." * * * Although the Supreme Court has explicitly declined to define this category of offenses precisely, * * * it has noted that cases recognizing such offenses "[t]ypically ... involve statutes that regulate potentially harmful or injurious items." * * * Frogs are not "potentially harmful or injurious items," * * * and there is in our view nothing about transporting them that would "place[ ] [a defendant] in responsible relation to a public danger, ... alert[ing it] to the probability of strict regulation." * * * We thus decline to recognize a violation of § 42(c) as a "public welfare offense."

The government also argues that a *mens rea* requirement need not be inferred where the penalties for violating a statute are relatively small. That is simply wrong. While "a severe penalty is a further factor tending to suggest that Congress did not intend to eliminate a *mens rea* requirement," * * * it does not follow that whenever a penalty is not "severe," we may dispense with the need to prove *mens rea* as to a critical element of a crime. This is especially so where, as here, dispensing with such a requirement would "criminalize a broad range of apparently innocent conduct." * * * Because the government failed to satisfy its burden under 18 U.S.C. § 42(c), we reverse the judgment of the district court and remand with instructions to enter a judgment of not guilty.

OAKES, Senior Circuit Judge:

I respectfully dissent. * * *Bronx Reptiles imports live animals, including reptiles, into the country approximately twice a week. Since at least 1993, it has been well aware of the IATA guidelines used by the industry to determine how a specific species is to be shipped and of the container requirements listed in the guidelines. Indeed, a special agent of the U.S. Fish and Wildlife Service, Division of Law Enforcement, who spoke with Bruce Edelman, the owner of Bronx Reptiles, testified that Mr. Edelman knew of the IATA guidelines and knew that as an importer he was liable for the conditions under which wildlife entered the United States.

Despite its knowledge of IATA guidelines, Bronx Reptiles has arranged for a number of shipments that involved inadequately packed and ventilated shipments. In 1993, Bronx Reptiles arranged for an importation of iguanas and boa constrictors from Colombia that resulted in a substantial number of dead reptiles due to improper ventilation and improper labeling. Based on the two shipments from Colombia, notices of violation were issued to Bronx Reptiles and civil fines were subsequently paid. A similar incident occurred in March of 1994, involving small mammals and reptiles from Egypt in which a number of dead animals were discovered and as well a number of weaning mothers with young were improperly packaged. In March of 1995, Bronx Reptiles was cited for yet another importation of chameleons, skinks, geckos and other lizards and frogs in inhumane fashion.

There was no doubt whatsoever that the shipment of frogs from the Solomon Islands, at the center of this case, was improper. The container was shallow and the frogs were not separated. Furthermore, no damp materials or water trays were included to keep the frogs properly hydrated. This was highly improper since, as should be obvious to anyone, frogs have to have sufficient water to keep their skin from dehydrating. The former superintendent of reptiles and amphibians at the Bronx Zoo testified to the wide knowledge in the importation business of the IATA guidelines. These, of course, were violated by the shipment. He also testified to the customary practice of those in the importing business to check out the shipper, seek out references, and call the shipper to be certain that the shipper was aware of and understood the shipping requirements, including the IATA standards. Despite its vast experience in shipping and its prior violations, Bronx Reptiles did not fulfill its obligations under the guidelines.

No evidence was introduced by Bronx Reptiles to contradict any of the foregoing.

The majority holds that a violation of § 42(c) is not a public welfare offense and further holds that for a conviction under § 42(c) to stand, Bronx Reptiles had to know specifically that the frogs were improperly packed. In my view § 42(c), under the law of this Circuit, is properly treated as a public welfare statute. * * * The majority here has determined that § 42(c) is not a public welfare law, reasoning that there is nothing about transporting frogs that would "place a defendant in responsible relation to a public danger, ... [thus] alerting it to the probability of strict regulation." * * * I disagree.

The provision against inhumane transportation, which is the subject of this prosecution, has been in the law since 1948. The legislative history makes it clear that Congress knew that it could not hold foreign shippers liable for the conditions in which animals were shipped, and that it was necessary to hold the United States importer responsible for ensuring, by contract or otherwise, that the transportation would be done in a humane fashion. * * * Thus, Congress plainly contemplated that United States importers would be in a position where they could be responsible for ensuring safe transport of live animals.

The IATA guidelines themselves illustrate that the transport of live animals, including live reptiles and amphibians, is a delicate and risky business. As Congress clearly found, it is the United States importer who is in a position to take responsibility for ensuring the safe and humane transport for foreign animals. The fact that it is arranging for the transport of animals that are *alive* puts it on notice of the "probability of strict regulation." The United States importer can arrange by contract to ensure the safety of the animals. Thus, the United States importer is in responsible relation to the public danger of harm to the wildlife that it caused to be shipped to this country and should be strictly regulated. * * * I would affirm the conviction.

NOTES AND QUESTIONS

1. ***Mistake of Fact.*** In **United States v. Quarrell,** 310 F.3d 664 (10th Cir. 2002), the court first examined whether the Archaeological Resources Protection Act (ARPA) required the accused to know they were excavating on public land and then decided whether a mistake was allowed. In finding that the statute did not require knowledge the court stated:

> * * * Neither the legislative history nor the purpose behind the statute directly answers the issue of whether the government must prove that the defendant knew he or she was on public land in order to establish a § 470ee(a) violation. However, extending the *mens rea* requirement to the "located on public lands" element would frustrate the purpose of the Act. For example, it would often be difficult for the government to prove that a defendant knew he was on public land unless signs were posted at or near the archaeological site. Placing signs near sites, however, would draw the attention of potential looters. Archaeological sites in the Gila National Forest are kept confidential to protect the sites from vandalism, especially since, at the time of the offenses, there were only two law enforcement officers patrolling approximately three million acres of public land. Congress' desire that land managers inform the public

> of the Act's requirements does not indicate that Congress intended to convict only those offenders who knew they were on public land. A public information campaign simply furthers the purpose of the Act by informing the public of ARPA's prohibitions. * * *

In deciding whether the accused should be allowed to present a mistake of fact under this statute, the court stated:

> The Quarrells argue the district court erred in not allowing them to present a defense based on their belief that they were excavating on private, not public, land. ARPA is silent as to the defenses available. * * * ARPA superseded the Antiquities Act of 1906. Therefore, we may look to this prior statute to determine whether a mistake of fact defense is available. Although the Antiquities Act is silent on this issue, its case law provides some insight.
>
> We * * * hold that a defendant charged with violating ARPA may present a mistake of fact defense. After the government establishes an ARPA violation, the defendant should be allowed to argue a mistake of fact defense based on his reasonable belief that he was excavating on private land *with permission*. The defendant must establish that he reasonably believed he was *lawfully* excavating on private land because such "an honest mistake of fact would not be consistent with criminal intent." * * * However, if a defendant merely argues that he thought he was excavating on private land, such a mistake of fact would not negate criminal intent because such conduct is unlawful. In addition, a defendant, * * * must present evidence that his mistake of fact was "honestly and conscientiously made."

2. ***Mistake of Law.*** In **United States v. Whiteside**, 285 F.3d 1345 (11th Cir. 2002), the court reversed criminal convictions and sentences for making false statements in Medicare/Medicaid and CHAMPUS reimbursement cost reports and for conspiracy to defraud the government by making false statements in those cost reports. The court stated:

> In a case where the truth or falsity of a statement centers on an interpretive question of law, the government bears the burden of proving beyond a reasonable doubt that the defendant's statement is not true under a reasonable interpretation of the law. * * * The government cannot meet its burden in this case because, despite its contention to the contrary, no Medicare regulation, administrative ruling, or judicial decision exists that clearly requires interest expense to be reported in accordance with the original use of the loan. * * * The government's position that the regulation is pellucid on this point is refuted by the relevant text of the regulation. * * * Neither the regulations nor administrative authority clearly answer the dilemma the defendants faced here. * * * The testimony indicates that the experts disagreed as to the validity of the theory

of capital reimbursement suggested by the government. This contradictory evidence lends credence to defendants' argument that their interpretation was not unreasonable. * * *

3. ***Knowing Endangerment.*** "Knowing endangerment" provisions are found in both the Resource Conservation and Recovery Act, 42 U.S.C.A. § 6928(e), and the Clean Water Act, 33 U.S.C.A. § 1319(c)(3)(A). In **United States v. Protex Industries, Inc.**, 874 F.2d 740 (10th Cir. 1989), the court, in affirming a criminal conviction under the "knowing endangerment" provision in RCRA, stated:

> Counts 17 through 19 of that indictment charged Protex with knowingly placing three of its employees in imminent danger of death or serious bodily injury as a result of its other alleged violations of the RCRA. The evidence showed that safety provisions for the employees in the drum recycling facility were woefully inadequate to protect the employees against the dangers of the toxic chemicals. Government experts testified that without these proper safety precautions, the employees were at an increased risk of suffering solvent poisoning. * * *
>
> Title 42, United States Code, Section 6928(e) provides that: "Any person who knowingly transports, treats, stores, disposes of, or exports any hazardous waste identified or listed under [the RCRA] in violation of [the criminal provisions of the RCRA] who knows at that time that he thereby places another person in imminent danger of death or serious bodily injury, shall [be guilty of an offense against the United States.]" Title 42, United States Code, Section 6928(f)(6) defines "serious bodily injury" as: (A) bodily injury which involves a substantial risk of death; (B) unconsciousness; (C) extreme physical pain; (D) protracted and obvious disfigurement; or (E) protracted loss or impairment of the function of a bodily member, organ, or mental faculty. Protex contends that the trial court rendered section 6928(e) unconstitutionally vague by expanding the definition of "serious bodily injury" beyond that set out in section 6928(f)(6). Protex states that if the employees were placed in any "danger" at all, it was a danger of developing Type 2-A psychoorganic syndrome, a condition which does not come within the scope of subparagraphs (A)-(E) of section 6928(f)(6). Protex also argues that the enhanced "risk" of contracting some indeterminate type of cancer at some unspecified time in the future is not sufficient to constitute "serious bodily injury."
>
> Appellant's position demonstrates a callousness toward the severe physical effect the prolonged exposure to toxic chemicals may cause or has caused to the three former employees. * * *
>
> * * * The gist of the "knowing endangerment" provision of the RCRA is that a party will be criminally liable if, in violating other

provisions of the RCRA, it places others in danger of great harm and it has knowledge of that danger. The district court conveyed this same idea to the jury in its instructions. The court rejects appellant's argument that it could not be aware that its behavior was prohibited by the "knowing endangerment" provision of the RCRA.

4. Willful Blindness

UNITED STATES v. YI

704 F.3d 800 (9th Cir. 2013)

GOODWIN, Circuit Judge:

Yi was the CEO of Millennium Pacific Icon Group, a real estate development company. In April 2004, Millennium purchased Forest Glen, a 204–unit condominium complex, after Yi and some of his Millennium associates did a walk-through of the property.

[One witness testified that during the walk-through Yi made the comment] that he was certain the ceilings contained asbestos because of the age of the building. Yi's sister, * * *, was also present at the walk-through [and] she discussed the ceilings with Yi and the two decided not to touch the ceilings because they assumed the ceilings contained asbestos, which would be costly to remove.

Yi signed a purchase offer for Forest Glen that included a due diligence clause allowing time to review environmental materials and to conduct an environmental review. The seller provided a due diligence binder that included two Phase I environmental reports and an "Operations and Maintenance Plan for Asbestos–Containing Materials" ("The O & M Plan"). The reports contained test results showing the presence of asbestos in the ceilings. * * *

[A witness also testified that Yi had instructed him to secure a bid for removing the asbestos from the Forest Glen ceilings, but after receiving the bids, he "said asbestos abatement would be too expensive."]

After Millennium purchased Forest Glen, an agent for Millennium's insurance carrier visited the property, observed ceiling material on the ground, and took a sample to test for asbestos. The agent later emailed [a] Millennium employee * * *, stating that the test showed 1% asbestos. Yi testified that he was told the sample came back "negative," * * * .

In September 2005, unit sales at Forest Glen began to slow and evidence showed Yi became concerned about the slowdown in November 2005. * * *on January 16, 2006, Millennium contracted to have the ceilings scraped. The agreed-upon price broke down to $1,500 per unit for the first ten—less per unit than either the previously rejected bid for asbestos abatement or for installing drywall over the ceilings. The contractor, * * *, testified that no one informed him that the ceilings contained asbestos. * * *They wore no special clothing to protect against asbestos exposure and only "white masks." He also stated that powdery ceiling material was simply placed into bags and wheelbarrows before being thrown into dumpsters.

A state inspector, * * *, testified that the work site was one of the worst he had ever seen and that ceiling material was blowing everywhere: public walkways, sidewalks, driveways, and around the dumpsters.

Yi testified that he did not remember being shown the due diligence binder; he never read either environmental report; and he did not believe Forest Glen's ceilings contained asbestos because one of the Millennium managers had told him that the insurance agent's asbestos test "came [back] negative" for asbestos. According to Yi, he was not shown the actual test results; he simply trusted the manager. As to the abatement work, Yi testified that he was not involved in choosing the ceiling-scraping crew, and did not know who made the choice or how it was made. * * * Yi also offered testimony about the closing documents, claiming he did not read the due diligence paragraph and its reference to environmental review. * * *

Yi argues that the district court erred in giving a jury instruction on deliberate ignorance, asserting that it was not warranted because the facts shown at trial did not support a finding of deliberate ignorance. The district court instructed the jury using the Ninth Circuit model instruction:

> You may find that the defendant acted knowingly if you find beyond a reasonable doubt that the defendant:
>
> 1. was aware of a high probability that there was asbestos in the ceilings at Forest Glen Condominiums, and
>
> 2. deliberately avoided learning the truth.
>
> You may not find such knowledge, however, if you find that the defendant actually believed that there was no asbestos in the ceilings at the Forest Glen Condominiums, or if you find that the defendant was simply careless.

"Willful blindness" is inconsistent with actual knowledge, and thus a deliberate ignorance instruction is appropriate only where "the jury could rationally find willful blindness even though it has rejected the government's evidence of actual knowledge." * * * Deliberate ignorance contains two prongs: (1) a subjective belief that there is a high probability a fact exists; and (2) deliberate actions taken to avoid learning the truth. Global–Tech Appliances, Inc. v. SEB S.A., ––– U.S. ––––, 131 S.Ct. 2060, 2070, (2011).

Regarding the first *Global–Tech* prong, testimony from [two witnesses], and Yi himself supports an inference that Yi was aware of a high probability that the Forest Glen ceilings contained asbestos. * * * Yi's 16–year experience in property management bolsters the evidence that he suspected the ceilings contained asbestos, as the age of the Forest Glen building and the ceiling's physical appearance would, * * *, have put a person experienced in property management on notice of the likelihood that it contained asbestos. While he argues that the insurance company's supposedly negative test allayed his suspicions, that inference need not be drawn when viewing the evidence in the government's favor. Thus, there was sufficient evidentiary support for the first *Global–Tech* prong.

Turning to the second *Global–Tech* prong, if the jury could infer that Yi was aware of a high probability that the ceilings contained asbestos, it also could infer that Yi engaged in a deliberate pattern of failing to read documents that might clarify whether asbestos was in fact present. The jury would not be required to believe Yi's argument that he was very busy, that he trusted all of his subordinates to read everything for him, or even that he was told the insurance company's test had come back "negative" for asbestos. The evidence regarding Yi's real estate experience and pattern of failing to read documents common to real estate transactions supports a finding that Yi deliberately avoided learning the truth about whether the Forest Glen ceilings contained asbestos. * * *

Yi also argues that the instruction itself was legally flawed. He primarily takes issue with the term "simply careless." Yi argues that instructing a jury that it may not find knowledge where a defendant is "simply" careless leaves the door open for some other level of carelessness. But [United States v.] *Heredia* [,483 F.3d 913] makes clear that the Ninth Circuit model instruction is appropriate "and there is little reason to suspect that juries will import [recklessness or negligence] concepts, as to which they are not instructed, into their deliberations." * * * The district court did not err in giving or formulating the deliberate ignorance instruction. AFFIRMED.

5. Negligently

UNITED STATES v. HANOUSEK

176 F.3d 1116 (9th Cir. 1999)

THOMPSON, Circuit Judge.

Edward Hanousek, Jr., appeals his conviction and sentence for negligently discharging a harmful quantity of oil into a navigable water of the United States, in violation of the Clean Water Act, 33 U.S.C. §§ 1319(c)(1)(A) & 1321(b)(3). Hanousek contends that the district court erred: (1) by failing to instruct the jury that the government must prove that he acted with criminal negligence as opposed to ordinary negligence, * * *

Hanousek also argues that section 1319(c)(1)(A) violates due process if it permits a criminal conviction for ordinary negligence and that, in any event, the evidence was insufficient to support his conviction. We have jurisdiction under 28 U.S.C. § 1291 and we affirm. * * *

Hanousek was employed by the Pacific & Arctic Railway and Navigation Company (Pacific & Arctic) as roadmaster of the White Pass & Yukon Railroad, which runs between Skagway, Alaska, and Whitehorse, Yukon Territory, Canada. As roadmaster, Hanousek was responsible under his contract "for every detail of the safe and efficient maintenance and construction of track, structures and marine facilities of the entire railroad ... and [was to] assume similar duties with special projects."

One of the special projects under Hanousek's supervision was a rock-quarrying project at a site alongside the railroad referred to as "6-mile," located on an embankment 200 feet above the Skagway River. * * * Pacific & Arctic hired Hunz & Hunz, a contracting company, to provide the equipment and labor for the project. * * * On the evening of October 1, 1994, Shane Thoe, a Hunz & Hunz backhoe operator, used the backhoe on the work platform to load a train with rocks. After the train departed, Thoe noticed that some fallen rocks had caught the plow of the train as it departed and were located just off the tracks in the vicinity of the unprotected pipeline. At this location, the site had been graded to finish grade and the pipeline was covered with a few inches of soil. Thoe moved the backhoe off the work platform and drove it down alongside the tracks between 50 to 100 yards from the work platform. While using the backhoe bucket to sweep the rocks from the tracks, Thoe struck the pipeline causing a rupture. The pipeline was carrying heating oil, and an estimated 1,000 to 5,000 gallons of oil were discharged over the course of many days into the adjacent Skagway River, a navigable water of the United States.

Following an investigation, Hanousek was charged with one count of negligently discharging a harmful quantity of oil into a navigable water of the United States, in violation of the Clean Water Act, 33 U.S.C. §§ 1319(c)(1)(A) & 1321(b)(3). Hanousek was also charged with one count of conspiring to provide false information to United States Coast Guard officials who investigated the accident, in violation of 18 U.S.C. §§ 371, 1001.

After a twenty-day trial, the jury convicted Hanousek of negligently discharging a harmful quantity of oil into a navigable water of the United States, but acquitted him on the charge of conspiring to provide false information. The district court imposed a sentence of six months of imprisonment, six months in a halfway house and six months of supervised release, as well as a fine of $5,000. This appeal followed.

* * * Hanousek contends the district court erred by failing to instruct the jury that, to establish a violation under 33 U.S.C. § 1319(c)(1)(A), the government had to prove that Hanousek acted with criminal negligence, as opposed to ordinary negligence, in discharging a harmful quantity of oil into

the Skagway River. In his proposed jury instruction, Hanousek defined criminal negligence as "a gross deviation from the standard of care that a reasonable person would observe in the situation." See American Law Institute, Model Penal Code § 2.02(2)(d) (1985). Over Hanousek's objection, the district court instructed the jury that the government was required to prove only that Hanousek acted negligently, which the district court defined as "the failure to use reasonable care." * * *

Statutory interpretation begins with the plain language of the statute. If the language of the statute is clear, we need look no further than that language in determining the statute's meaning. "Particular phrases must be construed in light of the overall purpose and structure of the whole statutory scheme." "When we look to the plain language of a statute in order to interpret its meaning, we do more than view words or sub-sections in isolation. We derive meaning from context, and this requires reading the relevant statutory provisions as a whole."

Codified sections 1319(c)(1)(A) & 1321(b)(3) of the Clean Water Act work in tandem to criminalize the conduct of which Hanousek was convicted. Section 1319(c)(1)(A) provides that any person who negligently violates 33 U.S.C. § 1321(b)(3) shall be punished by fine or imprisonment, or both. Section 1321(b)(3) proscribes the actual discharge of oil in harmful quantities into navigable waters of the United States, adjoining shore lines or waters of a contiguous zone, as well as other specified activity.

Neither section defines the term "negligently," nor is that term defined elsewhere in the CWA.[b] In this circumstance, we "start with the assumption that the legislative purpose is expressed by the ordinary meaning of the words used." The ordinary meaning of "negligently" is a failure to use such care as a reasonably prudent and careful person would use under similar circumstances. See Black's Law Dictionary 1032 (6th ed.1990); The Random House College Dictionary 891 (Rev. ed.1980).

If Congress intended to prescribe a heightened negligence standard, it could have done so explicitly, as it did in 33 U.S.C. § 1321(b)(7)(D). This section of the CWA provides for increased civil penalties "[i]n any case in which a violation of [33 U.S.C. § 1321(b)(3)] was the result of gross negligence or willful misconduct." 33 U.S.C. § 1321(b)(7)(D). This is significant. "[W]here Congress includes particular language in one section of a statute but omits it in another section of the same Act, it is generally

---

[b] For a statistical analysis of criminal negligence prosecutions brought under the Clean Water Act see Steven P. Solow & Ronald A. Sarachan, *Criminal Negligence Prosecutions Under the Federal Clean Water Act: A Statistical Analysis and the Evaluation of the Impact of* Hanousek *and* Hong, 32 ENVIR. L. RPTR. 11153 (2002).

presumed that Congress acts intentionally and purposely in the disparate inclusion or exclusion." * * *

Hanousek argues that Congress could not have intended to distinguish "negligently" in 33 U.S.C. § 1319(c)(1)(A) from "gross negligence" in 33 U.S.C. § 1321(b)(7)(D) because the phrase "gross negligence" was only recently added to the statute in 1990. See Oil Pollution Control Act of 1990, Pub.L. No. 101-380, 104 Stat. 484 (1990). We reject this argument because Congress is presumed to have known of its former legislation and to have passed new laws in view of the provisions of the legislation already enacted. * * *

We conclude from the plain language of 33 U.S.C. § 1319(c)(1)(A) that Congress intended that a person who acts with ordinary negligence in violating 33 U.S.C. § 1321(b)(3) may be subject to criminal penalties. We next consider Hanousek's argument that, by imposing an ordinary negligence standard for a criminal violation, section 1319(c)(1)(A) violates the due process clause of the Constitution.

* * * The criminal provisions of the CWA constitute public welfare legislation. * * * It is well established that a public welfare statute may subject a person to criminal liability for his or her ordinary negligence without violating due process. * * * Recognizing that our holding in *Weitzenhoff* [35 F.3d 1275 (9th Cir. 1994)] would defeat his due process argument, Hanousek attempts to distinguish *Weitzenhoff.* The attempt fails. In *Weitzenhoff,* two managers of a sewage treatment plant operating under a National Pollution Discharge Elimination System permit were convicted of knowingly discharging pollutants into a navigable water of the United States, in violation of 33 U.S.C. §§ 1311(a) & 1319(c)(2). * * * In rejecting the defendants' contention that the district court erred by failing to instruct the jury that the government had to prove that the defendants knew their acts violated the permit or the CWA, we held that the criminal provisions of the CWA constitute public welfare legislation and that the government was not required to prove that the defendants knew their conduct violated the law. We explained that, "[w]here ... dangerous or deleterious devices or products or obnoxious waste materials are involved, the probability of regulation is so great that anyone who is aware that he is in possession of them or dealing with them must be presumed to be aware of the regulation." * * *

Hanousek argues that, unlike the defendants in *Weitzenhoff* who were permittees under the CWA, he was simply the roadmaster of the White Pass & Yukon railroad charged with overseeing a rock-quarrying project and was not in a position to know what the law required under the CWA. This is a distinction without a difference. In the context of a public welfare statute, "as long as a defendant knows he is dealing with a dangerous device of a character that places him 'in responsible relation to a public danger,' he should be alerted to the probability of strict regulation."* * * Although Hanousek was not a permittee under the CWA, he does not dispute that he was aware that a high-pressure petroleum products pipeline owned by Pacific & Arctic's sister company ran close to the surface next to the railroad tracks at 6-mile, and does not argue that he was unaware of the dangers a break or puncture of the pipeline by a piece of heavy machinery would pose. Therefore, Hanousek should have been alerted to the probability of strict regulation.

In light of our holding in Weitzenhoff that the criminal provisions of the CWA constitute public welfare legislation, and the fact that a public welfare statute may impose criminal penalties for ordinary negligent conduct without offending due process, we conclude that section 1319(c)(1)(A) does not violate due process by permitting criminal penalties for ordinary negligent conduct. * * *

In light of the plain language of 33 U.S.C. § 1319(c)(1)(A), we conclude Congress intended that a person who acts with ordinary negligence in violating 33 U.S.C. § 1321(b)(3) may be subjected to criminal penalties. These sections, as so construed, do not violate due process. Accordingly, the district court properly instructed the jury on ordinary negligence. * * * AFFIRMED

C. INDIVIDUALS LIABLE

1. Persons In Charge

APEX OIL COMPANY v. UNITED STATES

530 F.2d 1291 (8th Cir. 1976)

HEANEY, Circuit Judge.

Apex Oil Company, a Missouri corporation whose business includes the transportation and storage of various types of fuel oil, appeals from a final judgment of conviction on two counts of a three-count indictment for failing to notify an appropriate agency of the United States government of a known oil spill in violation of the Water Pollution Control Act, 33 U.S.C. § 1321(b)(5). It was fined a total of $20,000 and placed on probation for three years. The execution of $15,000 of the fine was stayed on the condition that the corporation not violate any law relating to pollution during the probationary period. Two issues are raised on appeal: (1) whether the corporation is a "person in charge" within the meaning of 33 U.S.C. § 1321(b)(5), and (2) whether the evidence was sufficient to support the conviction. We affirm.

Section 1321(b)(5) of Title 33 of the United States Code, upon which the convictions are based, states in relevant part: Any person in charge of * * * an onshore facility * * * shall, as soon as he has knowledge of any discharge of oil * * * from such * * * facility in violation of paragraph (3) of this subsection, immediately notify the appropriate agency of the United States Government of such discharge. Any such person who fails to notify immediately such agency of such discharge shall, upon conviction, be fined not more than $10,000, or imprisoned for not more than one year, or both. Notification received pursuant to this paragraph or information obtained by the exploitation of such notifications shall not be used against any such person in any criminal case, except a prosecution for perjury or for giving a false statement. The appellant argues that only an individual, or natural person, and not a corporation, can be a "person in charge" within the meaning of the statute and, hence, it cannot be prosecuted.

A "person," as defined by the Act, "includes an individual, firm, corporation, association, and a partnership(.)" 33 U.S.C. § 1321(a)(7) (Emphasis supplied.) Apex Oil, thus, raises a distinction between the meaning of "person" when used alone and its meaning when used in conjunction with the words "in charge." It is a distinction which the Act does not itself make. It is, moreover, a distinction that cannot be supported by the purposes of the Act.

Section 1321(b)(5) prompts the timely reporting and discovery of oil discharges into or upon the navigable waters of the United States to facilitate the mitigation of pollution damage. It is designed to insure, so far as possible, that small discharges will not go undetected and that the possibility of effective abatement will not be lost. The purpose is best served by holding the corporation responsible under the provision of the statute. * * *

[The court rejected arguments that inclusion of the corporation within the meaning of the term "person in charge" would be inconsistent with civil penalty provisions of the Act and Coast Guard regulations.] * * * [T]he appellant argues that the government failed to prove that it was "in charge" at the time of the spills and that it had knowledge of their occurrence. * * * Each argument is meritless. The corporation is no less "in charge" of the oil facility than is its employee.

Further, the knowledge of the employees is the knowledge of the corporation. * * * The judgment of conviction on Counts two and three is affirmed.

NOTES AND QUESTIONS

1. ***Corporate Liability.*** What effect will the court's finding a corporation as a "person in charge" have on future corporations reporting discharges? Can there be problems in finding employees high enough in the corporation to be "in charge" who also have sufficient knowledge?

2. ***Reporting Requirements.*** Reporting requirements are found in other environmental statutes as well. (e.g., CERCLA, 42 U.S.C.A. § 9603(a)). Who within an organization has the burden of reporting the discharge of a

hazardous substance? In **United States v. Carr**, 880 F.2d 1550 (2d Cir. 1989), the court discussed who is a person "in charge" under CERCLA's reporting requirement:

> * * * Under section 103, only those who are "in charge" of a facility must report a hazardous release. There is, however, no definition of the term "in charge" within CERCLA. Appellant argues that the district court's instruction was erroneous because Congress never intended to extend the statute's reporting requirement to those, like Carr, who are relatively low in an organization's chain of command.
>
> * * * The language of the statute itself sheds little light on the meaning of the term "in charge." Section 103 of CERCLA states only that: Any person in charge of a vessel or an offshore or an onshore facility shall, as soon as he has knowledge of any release (other than a federally permitted release) of a hazardous substance from such vessel or facility in quantities equal to or greater than those determined pursuant to [42 U.S.C.A. § 9602], immediately notify the National Response Center established under the Clean Water Act [33 U.S.C.A. § 1251 et seq.] of such release. The National Response Center shall convey the notification expeditiously to all appropriate Government agencies, including the Governor of any affected State. The regulations implementing the statute fail to define the term "in charge." See 40 C.F.R. § 302 (1988) (EPA regulations). * * * The legislative history of CERCLA makes clear that Congress modeled the reporting requirements of section 103 on section 311 of the Clean Water Act, 33 U.S.C. § 1321(b)(5). Like CERCLA's section 103, the reporting requirements of section 311 of the Clean Water Act require any person "in charge" of a facility to report a release of hazardous substances. * * *
>
> Since CERCLA's use of the term "in charge" was borrowed from section 311 of the Clean Water Act, and the two sections share the same purpose, the parallel provisions can, as a matter of general statutory construction, be interpreted to be in pari materia. * * *
>
> The legislative history of section 311 bears out appellant's argument that CERCLA's reporting requirements should not be extended to all employees involved in a release. 'The term "person in charge" [was] deliberately designed to cover only supervisory personnel who have the responsibility for the particular vessel or facility and not to include other employees. "Indeed, as the Fifth Circuit has stated, to the extent that legislative history does shed light on the meaning of 'persons in charge,' it suggests at the very most that Congress intended the provisions of [section 311] to extend, not to every person who might have knowledge of [a release] (mere employees, for example), but only to persons who occupy positions of responsibility and power."

That is not to say, however, that section 311 of the Clean Water Act—and section 103 of CERCLA—do not reach lower-level supervisory employees. The reporting requirements of the two statutes do not apply only to owners and operators, but instead extend to any person who is "responsible for the operation" of a facility from which there is a release, * * *

2. Responsible Corporate Officer

UNITED STATES v. MacDONALD & WATSON WASTE OIL COMPANY

933 F.2d 35 (1st Cir. 1991)

CAMPBELL, Circuit Judge.

This appeal concerns the criminal liability of individuals and corporations under hazardous waste disposal laws.

Following a jury trial in the district court, appellants were convicted, inter alia, of having violated criminal provisions of the Resource Conservation and Recovery Act ("RCRA"), 42 U.S.C. § 6901 et seq. and the Comprehensive Environmental Response, Compensation and Liability Act ("CERCLA"), 42 U.S.C. § 9603(b). * * *D'Allesandro, the President and owner of MacDonald & Watson, contends that his conviction under RCRA, § 3008(d)(1), 42 U.S.C. § 6928(d)(1), must be vacated because the district court incorrectly charged the jury regarding the element of knowledge in the case of a corporate officer. Section 3008(d)(1) penalizes "Any person who. . . . (1) knowingly transports or causes to be transported any hazardous waste identified or listed under this subchapter . . . . to a facility which does not have a permit . . . .". (Emphasis supplied.) In his closing, the prosecutor conceded that the government had "no direct evidence that Eugene D'Allesandro actually knew that the Master Chemical shipments were coming in," i.e., were being transported to the Poe Street Lot under contract with his company. The prosecution did present evidence, however, that D'Allesandro was not only the President and owner of MacDonald & Watson but was a "hands-on" manager of that relatively small firm. There was also proof that that firm leased the Poe Street Lot from NIC, and managed it, and that D'Allesandro's subordinates had contracted for and transported the Master Chemical waste for disposal at that site. The government argued that D'Allesandro was guilty of violating § 3008(d)(1) because, as the responsible corporate officer, he was in a position to ensure compliance with RCRA and had failed to do so even after being warned by a consultant on two earlier occasions that other shipments of toluene-contaminated soil had been received from other customers, and that such material violated NIC's permit. In the government's view, any failure to prove D'Allesandro's actual knowledge of the Master Chemical contract and shipments was irrelevant to his criminal responsibility under § 3008(d)(1) for those shipments.

The court apparently accepted the government's theory. It instructed the jury as follows: When an individual Defendant is also a corporate officer, the Government may prove that individual's knowledge in either of two ways. The first way is to demonstrate that the Defendant had actual knowledge of the act in question. The second way is to establish that the defendant was what is called a responsible officer of the corporation committing the act. In order to prove that a person is a responsible corporate officer three things must be shown. First, it must be shown that the person is an officer of the corporation, not merely an employee. Second, it must be shown that the officer had direct responsibility for the activities that are alleged to be illegal. Simply being an officer or even the president of a corporation is not enough. The Government must prove that the person had a responsibility to supervise the activities in question. And the third requirement is that the officer must have known or believed that the illegal activity of the type alleged occurred. The court's phrasing of the third element at first glance seems ambiguous: it could be read to require actual knowledge of the Master Chemical shipments themselves. We are satisfied, however, that the court meant only what it literally said: D'Allesandro must have known or believed that illegal shipments of the type alleged had previously occurred. This tied into evidence that D'Allesandro had been advised of two earlier shipments of toluene-contaminated waste, and was told that such waste could not legally be received. For the court to require a finding that D'Allesandro knew of the alleged shipments themselves (i.e., the Master Chemical shipments), would have duplicated the court's earlier instruction on actual knowledge, and was not in accord with the government's theory.

D'Allesandro challenges this instruction, contending that the use of the "responsible corporate officer" doctrine is improper under § 3008(d)(1) which expressly calls for proof of knowledge, i.e., requires scienter. The government responds that the district court properly adapted the responsible corporate officer doctrine traditionally applied to strict liability offenses to this case, instructing the jury to find knowledge "that the illegal activity of the type alleged occurred,"—a finding that, together with the first two, made it reasonable to infer knowledge of the particular violation. We agree with D'Allesandro that the jury instructions improperly allowed the jury to find him guilty without finding he had actual knowledge of the alleged transportation of hazardous waste on July 30 and 31, 1986, from Master Chemical Company, Boston, Massachusetts, to NIC's site, knowledge being an element the statute requires. We must, therefore, vacate his conviction.

The seminal cases regarding the responsible corporate officer doctrine are United States v. Dotterweich, 320 U.S. 277 (1943), and United States v. Park, [p.78]. These cases concerned misdemeanor charges under the Federal Food, Drug, and Cosmetic Act, 21 U.S.C. §§ 301-392, as amended, relating to the handling or shipping of adulterated or misbranded drugs or food. The offenses alleged in the informations failed to state a knowledge element, and the Court found that they, in fact, dispensed with a scienter requirement, placing "the burden of acting at hazard upon a person otherwise innocent but standing in responsible relation to a public danger." The Court in *Park* clarified that corporate officer liability in that situation requires only a finding that the officer had "authority with respect to the conditions that formed the basis of the alleged violations." But while *Dotterweich* and *Park* thus reflect what is now clear and well-established law in respect to public welfare statutes and regulations lacking an express knowledge or other scienter requirement, we know of no precedent for failing to give effect to a knowledge requirement that Congress has expressly included in a criminal statute. Especially is that so where, as here, the crime is a felony carrying possible imprisonment of five years and, for a second offense, ten.

The district court, nonetheless, applied here a form of the responsible corporate officer doctrine established in *Dotterweich* and *Park* for strict liability misdemeanors, as a substitute means for proving the explicit knowledge element of this RCRA felony, 42 U.S.C. § 6928(d)(1). As an alternative to finding actual knowledge, the district court permitted the prosecution to constructively establish defendant's knowledge if the jury found the following: (1) that the defendant was a corporate officer; (2) with responsibility to supervise the allegedly illegal activities; and (3) knew or believed "that the illegal activity of the type alleged occurred." As previously stated, the third element did not necessitate proof of knowledge of the Master Chemical shipments charged in the indictment, but simply proof of earlier occasions when D'Allesandro was told his firm had improperly accepted toluene-contaminated soil.

Contrary to the government's assertions, this instruction did more than simply permit the jury, if it wished, to infer knowledge of the Master Chemical shipments from relevant circumstantial evidence including D'Allesandro's responsibilities and activities as a corporate executive. With respect to circumstantial evidence, the district court properly instructed elsewhere that knowledge did not have to be proven by direct evidence but could be inferred from the defendant's conduct and other facts and circumstances. The court also instructed that the element of knowledge could be satisfied by proof of willful blindness. These instructions allowed the jury to consider whether relevant circumstantial evidence established that D'Allesandro actually knew of the charged Master Chemical shipments. These would have sufficed had it merely been the court's purpose to point out that knowledge could be established by circumstantial evidence, although the court could, had it wished, have elaborated on the extent to which D'Allesandro's responsibilities and duties might lead to a reasonable inference that he knew of the Master Chemical transaction.

Instead, the district court charged, in effect, that proof that D'Allesandro was a responsible corporate officer would conclusively prove the element of his knowledge of the Master Chemical shipments. The jury was told that knowledge could be proven "in either of two ways." Besides demonstrating actual knowledge, the government could simply establish the defendant was a responsible corporate officer—the latter by showing three things, none of which, individually or collectively, necessarily established his actual knowledge of the illegal transportation charged. Under the district court's instruction, the jury's belief that the responsible corporate officer lacked actual knowledge of, and had not willfully blinded himself to, the criminal transportation alleged would be insufficient for acquittal so long as the officer knew or even erroneously believed that illegal activity of the same type had occurred on another occasion.

We have found no case, and the government cites none, where a jury was instructed that the defendant could be convicted of a federal crime expressly requiring knowledge as an element, solely by reason of a conclusive, or "mandatory" presumption of knowledge of the facts constituting the offense. The government's primary reliance on the Third Circuit's more limited decision in Johnson & Towers, 741 F.2d 662 (3d Cir. 1984), is misplaced. There, the court of appeals concluded that "knowingly" applies to all elements of the offense, including permit status, in RCRA § 3008(d)(2)(A). The court of appeals advised that proof of knowledge of the permit requirement and the nonexistence of the permit did not impose a great burden because such knowledge might, in a proper case, be inferred. Relying on the Supreme Court's decision in United States v. International Minerals & Chemical Corp., 402 U.S. 558, 563 (1971), the court of appeals emphasized "that under certain regulatory statutes requiring 'knowing' conduct, the government need prove only knowledge of the actions taken and not of the statute forbidding them." Thus, this case supports only the position that knowledge of the law may be inferred, and does not address knowledge of acts. * * *

We agree with the decisions discussed above that knowledge may be inferred from circumstantial evidence, including position and responsibility of defendants such as corporate officers, as well as information provided to those defendants on prior occasions. Further, willful blindness to the facts constituting the offense may be sufficient to establish knowledge. However, the district court erred by instructing the jury that proof that a defendant was a responsible corporate officer, as described, would suffice to conclusively establish the element of knowledge expressly required under § 3008(d)(1). Simply because a responsible corporate officer believed that on a prior occasion illegal transportation occurred, he did not necessarily possess knowledge of the violation charged. In a crime having knowledge as an express element, a mere showing of official responsibility under *Dotterweich* and *Park* is not an adequate substitute for direct or circumstantial proof of knowledge. * * *

NOTES AND QUESTIONS

1. ***Clean Water/Clean Air Acts.*** Both the Clean Water Act (33 U.S.C.A. § 1319 (c)(6)) and the Clean Air Act (42 U.S.C.A. § 7413(c)(6)) have

incorporated the "responsible corporate officer" within the definition of "person." Does including the responsible corporate officer as a "person" into the statute serve to make the statute a strict liability offense when a responsible corporate officer is involved? In **United States v. Brittain**, 931 F.2d 1413, 1419 (10th Cir. 1991), the court stated:

> * * * We interpret the addition of "responsible corporate officers" as an expansion of liability under the Act rather than, as defendant would have it, an implicit limitation. The plain language of the statute, after all, states that "responsible corporate officers" are liable "in addition to the definition [of persons] contained in section 1362(5) . . . ." § 1319(c)(3) (emphasis supplied). Under this interpretation, a "responsible corporate officer," to be held criminally liable, would not have to "willfully or negligently" cause a permit violation. Instead, the willfulness or negligence of the actor would be imputed to him by virtue of his position of responsibility. * * *

Should the term "responsible corporate officer" be interpreted differently, dependant upon the statute involved? For example, should a court in an action involving an environmental crime, as opposed to an FDA violation, refuse to impute liability merely on the basis of an individual being a responsible corporate officer? See Barry M. Hartman & Charles A. De Monaco, *The Present Use of the Responsible Corporate Officer Doctrine in the Criminal Enforcement of Environmental Laws*, 23 ENVIRONMENTAL L. RPTR. 10145, 10153 (1993) ["While (the responsible corporate officer doctrine) renders corporate officials criminally liable for acts of their subordinates, it does not eliminate the knowledge requirement set forth in the applicable statute."].

2. ***Attributes of a Responsible Corporate Officer.*** What makes a person a responsible corporate officer? Consider the following case:

UNITED STATES v. IVERSON

162 F.3d 1015 (9th Cir. 1998)

GRABER, Circuit Judge:

A jury convicted defendant of four counts of violating federal water pollution law, as embodied in the Clean Water Act (CWA), the Washington Administrative Code (WAC), and the City of Olympia's Municipal Code (Olympia code). The jury also convicted defendant of one count of conspiring to violate the WAC or the CWA. Defendant appeals, arguing that: (1) the district court misinterpreted the CWA, the WAC, and the Olympia code; (2) those provisions are unconstitutionally vague; (3) the district court erred in formulating its "responsible corporate officer" jury instruction; and (4) the district court erred by admitting evidence of defendant's prior discharges of industrial waste. We are not persuaded by any of defendant's arguments and, thus, we affirm his convictions. * * *

Defendant was a founder of CH2O, Inc., and served as the company's President and Chairman of the Board. CH2O blends chemicals to create numerous products, including acid cleaners and heavy-duty alkaline compounds. The company ships the blended chemicals to its customers in drums.

CH2O asked its customers to return the drums so that it could reuse them. Although customers returned the drums, they often did not clean them sufficiently. Thus, the drums still contained chemical residue. Before CH2O could reuse the drums, it had to remove that residue.

To remove the residue, CH2O instituted a drum-cleaning operation, which in turn generated wastewater. In the early to mid-1980s, defendant approached the manager of the local sewer authority to see whether the sewer authority would accept the company's wastewater. The sewer authority refused, because the wastewater "did not meet the parameters we had set for accepting industrial waste. It had too high of a metal content." Thereafter, defendant and the general manager of CH2O made two other attempts to convince the sewer authority to accept the wastewater. Both times, it refused.

Beginning in about 1985, defendant personally discharged the wastewater and ordered employees of CH2O to discharge the wastewater in three places: (1) on the plant's property, (2) through a sewer drain at an apartment complex that defendant owned, and (3) through a sewer drain at defendant's home. (The plant did not have sewer access.) Those discharges continued until about 1988, when CH2O hired Bill Brady.

Brady initially paid a waste disposal company to dispose of the wastewater. Those efforts cost the company thousands of dollars each month. Beginning in late 1991, CH2O stopped its drum-cleaning operation and, instead, shipped the drums to a professional outside contractor for cleaning.

In April 1992, CH2O fired Brady. Around that same time, defendant bought a warehouse in Olympia. Unlike the CH2O plant, the warehouse had sewer access. After the purchase, CH2O restarted its drum-cleaning operation at the warehouse and disposed of its wastewater through the sewer. CH2O obtained neither a permit nor permission to make these discharges. The drum-cleaning operation continued until the summer of 1995, when CH2O learned that it was under investigation for discharging pollutants into the sewer.

A few months before CH2O restarted its drum-cleaning operation, defendant announced his "official" retirement from CH2O. Thereafter, he continued to receive money from CH2O, to conduct business at the company's facilities, and to give orders to employees. Moreover, the company continued to list him as the president in documents that it filed with the state, and the employee who was responsible for running the day-to-day aspects of the drum-cleaning operation testified that he reported to defendant.

During the four years of the operation at the warehouse, defendant was sometimes present when drums were cleaned. During those occasions, defendant was close enough to see and smell the waste.

In some instances, defendant informed employees that he had obtained a permit for the drum-cleaning operation and that the operation was on the "up and up." At other times, however, defendant told employees that, if they got caught, the company would receive only a slap on the wrist. * * *

After an eight-day trial, the jury found defendant guilty on all counts. Thereafter, the district court sentenced defendant to one year in custody, three years of supervised release, and a $75,000 fine. This timely appeal ensued. * * *

The district court instructed the jury that it could find defendant liable under the CWA as a "responsible corporate officer" if it found, beyond a reasonable doubt:

1. That the defendant had knowledge of the fact that pollutants were being discharged to the sewer system by employees of CH2O, Inc.;

2. That the defendant had the authority and capacity to prevent the discharge of pollutants to the sewer system; and

3. That the defendant failed to prevent the on-going discharge of pollutants to the sewer system.

Defendant argues that the district court misinterpreted the scope of "responsible corporate officer" liability. Specifically, defendant suggests that a corporate officer is "responsible" only when the officer in fact exercises control over the activity causing the discharge or has an express corporate duty to oversee the activity. We have not previously interpreted the scope of "responsible corporate officer" liability under the CWA. We do so now and reject defendant's narrow interpretation.

* * * The CWA defines the term "person" to include "any responsible corporate officer." See 33 U.S.C. § 1319(c)(6) ("For the purpose of this subsection, the term 'person' means, in addition to the definition contained in section 1362(5) of this title, any responsible corporate officer."). However, the CWA does not define the term "responsible corporate officer." * * * When a statute does not define a term, we generally interpret that term by employing the ordinary, contemporary, and common meaning of the words that Congress used. * * * As pertinent here, the word "responsible" means "answerable" or "involving a degree of accountability." Webster's Third New Int'l Dictionary 1935 (unabridged ed.1993). Using that meaning, "any

corporate officer" who is "answerable" or "accountable" for the unlawful discharge is liable under the CWA.

The history of "responsible corporate officer" liability supports the foregoing construction. The "responsible corporate officer" doctrine originated in a Supreme Court case interpreting the Federal Food, Drug, and Cosmetic Act (FFDCA), United States v. Dotterweich, 320 U.S. 277, 64 S.Ct. 134, 88 L.Ed. 48 (1943). * * * Because Congress used a similar definition of the term "person" in the CWA, we can presume that Congress intended that the principles of *Dotterweich* apply under the CWA. * * * Under *Dotterweich*, whether defendant had sufficient "responsibility" over the discharges to be criminally liable would be a question for the jury.

After Congress initially enacted the CWA in 1972, the Supreme Court further defined the scope of the "responsible corporate officer" doctrine under the FFDCA. In United States v. Park [p. 78], a corporate president argued that he could not be "responsible" under *Dotterweich*, because he had delegated decision- making control over the activity in question to a subordinate. The Court rejected that argument, holding that

> the Government establishes a prima facie case when it introduces evidence sufficient to warrant a finding by the trier of the facts that the defendant had, by reasons of his position in the corporation, responsibility and authority either to prevent in the first instance or promptly to correct, the violation complained of, and that he failed to do so.

Stated another way, the question for the jury is whether the corporate officer had "authority with respect to the conditions that formed the basis of the alleged violations." The Court did not, however, require the corporate officer actually to exercise any authority over the activity.

In 1987, after the Supreme Court decided *Park*, Congress revised and replaced the criminal provisions of the CWA. (Most importantly, Congress made a violation of the CWA a felony, rather than a misdemeanor.) In replacing the criminal provisions of the CWA, Congress made no changes to its "responsible corporate officer" provision. That being so, we can presume that Congress intended for Park's refinement of the "responsible corporate officer" doctrine to apply under the CWA.

Moreover, this court has interpreted similar terms in other statutes consistently with the Court's decision in *Park*. For example, the Internal Revenue Code (IRC) holds liable any "person required to collect, truthfully account for, and pay over any tax" under the IRC. 26 U.S.C. § 6672(a). The IRC defines "person" to include any "officer ... under a duty to perform the act in respect of which the violation occurs." 26 U.S.C. § 6671(b). This court consistently has interpreted the term "person" to include corporate officers with authority to pay taxes, whether or not they exercise that authority. * * *

Taken together, the wording of the CWA, the Supreme Court's interpretations of the "responsible corporate officer" doctrine, and this court's interpretation of similar statutory requirements establish the contours of the "responsible corporate officer" doctrine under the CWA. Under the CWA, a person is a "responsible corporate officer" if the person has authority to exercise control over the corporation's activity that is causing the discharges. There is no requirement that the officer in fact exercise such authority or that the corporation expressly vest a duty in the officer to oversee the activity. * * * AFFIRMED.

3. Aiding and Abetting

UNITED STATES v. DOIG

950 F.2d 411 (7th Cir. 1991)

BAUER, Chief Judge.

In this case of first impression, we must determine whether an employee may be charged with aiding and abetting his corporate employer in a criminal violation of The Occupational Health and Safety Act of 1970, 29 U.S.C. § 666(e) (1988) ("OSHA" or "the Act"). We find that Congress did not intend to subject employees to such liability under OSHA, and, therefore, affirm the district court's dismissal of criminal charges against Defendant-Appellee, Patrick J. Doig.

The S.A. Healy Company ("Healy") and Patrick J. Doig ("Doig") were charged with twelve counts of criminal OSHA violations under 29 U.S.C. § 666(e). The section imposes criminal liability on "[a]ny employer" whose willful violation of an OSHA regulation causes the death of any employee. The alleged violations occured while Healy was building a tunnel as part of the Milwaukee Metropolitan Sewerage District's water pollution abatement program. Doig was the manager of the tunnel project. An explosion in the tunnel on November 10, 1988, killed three of Healy's employees.

Healy was charged with willful violations of various safety regulations under the Act resulting in the death of the three employees. Doig was charged with aiding and abetting Healy in those violations. Specifically, the government claimed that Healy violated four OSHA regulations covering ventilation, safety training, the use of explosion-proof electrical equipment, and electrical power shutoff during a gas encounter. The government also asserted that Doig aided and abetted Healy's failure to comply with the electrical power shutoff and explosion-proof equipment regulations.

Doig moved to dismiss, asserting that because he is not an employer, he cannot be held criminally liable under § 666(e) as either a principal or an aider and abettor. The district court granted Doig's motion to dismiss. On February 20, 1991, a jury convicted Healy of all counts under the indictment. While Healy's trial was proceeding, the government appealed the district court's order dismissing Doig.

OSHA's stated purpose is "to assure so far as possible every working man and woman in the Nation safe and healthful working conditions . . . by providing that employers and employees have separate but dependent responsibilities and rights with respect to achieving safe and healthful working conditions . . . ." 29 U.S.C. § 651 (1988). In this case, the government argues that an employee may be subjected to criminal liability under § 666(e). The section provides: Any employer who willfully violates any standard, rule, or order promulgated pursuant to section 655 of this title, or of any regulations prescribed pursuant to this chapter, and that violation caused death to any employee, shall, upon conviction, be punished by a fine of not more than $10,000 or by imprisonment for not more than six months, or by both . . . . 29 U.S.C. § 666(e). The government does not argue that Doig is an employer. It maintains, however, that he may be sanctioned under § 666(e) pursuant to the provisions of 18 U.S.C.A. § 2(a) (1991). Under § 2(a), "[w]hoever commits an offense against the United States or aids, abets, counsels, commands, induces or procures its commission, is punishable as a principal."

Generally, the provisions of § 2(a) apply automatically to every criminal offense. In Pino-Perez, [870 F.2d 1230, 1233 (7th Cir.1989)], this court revisited the question of aider and abettor liability and reaffirmed its position that there must be " 'an affirmative legislative policy' to create an exemption from the ordinary rules of accessorial liability." In this case, we believe that the affirmative legislative policy placing the onus of workplace safety upon employers precludes finding that an employee may aid and abet his employer's criminal OSHA violation.

Although we have found no authority directly on point, the Third Circuit has considered whether the Occupational Safety and Health Review Commission may penalize employees who refuse to comply with OSHA regulations. It concluded that OSHA gives neither the Commission nor the Secretary of Labor the power to sanction employees. Atlantic & Gulf Stevedores v. Occupational Safety & Health Review Comm'n, 534 F.2d 541 (3d Cir.1976). * * *

* * * We agree with the Third Circuit's conclusion that sanctioning employees for OSHA violations is not part of the detailed scheme of enforcement Congress established in the statute.

One district court has considered whether a corporate officer could be liable for aiding and abetting his corporate employer's criminal violation of OSHA. United States v. Pinkston-Hollar, Inc., 4 O.S.H. Cas. (BNA) 1697, 1699 (D.Kan. Aug. 16, 1976). The Pinkston-Hollar court stated that "responsible corporate officials who have the power to prevent or correction [sic] violations of the Occupational Safety and Health Act may be prosecuted in the same sense as they may be under the Federal Food, Drug, & Cosmetic

Act of 1938." Nevertheless, the court explained, it would still be necessary to find that the corporate official was an employer before applying the criminal sanctions of § 666(e).

Based upon our examination of OSHA and its legislative history, we disagree with the conclusion that any corporate employee may be found liable for aiding and abetting an employer's violation of OSHA. A corporate officer or director acting as a corporation's agent could be sanctioned under § 666(e) as a principal, because, arguably an officer or director would be an employer. Of course, the corporation would also be responsible for its officer's actions. We hold that an employee who is not a corporate officer, and thus not an employer, cannot be sanctioned under § 666(e). This does not bar state law liability for an employee whose recklessness or criminal negligence causes the death of a co- worker. OSHA's stated purpose is to force employers to ensure that employees have safe working conditions. It is not to punish employees whose reckless or willful actions injure their co-workers. State law remains the appropriate means of sanctioning such conduct.

The government asserts that our interpretation of OSHA will deprive § 666(e) of its bite. Because only employers who are sole proprietorships or partnerships will be threatened with jail terms, it argues, the section's deterrent effect will be emasculated. We disagree. First, this problem does not seem terribly significant given the small number of criminal prosecutions brought under OSHA. Second, incarceration is still a potential sanction for corporate officers. As the Supreme Court has held on numerous occasions, responsible corporate officers may be liable for a corporation's violation of a criminal law. Third, if the inability to prosecute employees under § 666(e) hampers the government's efforts to enforce OSHA, the remedy for this difficulty lies with Congress, not with the courts. "If Congress desires to go further, it must speak more clearly than it has."* * *

Our conclusion is bolstered by the particular facts in this case. The government asserts that Healy is criminally liable for the violations it allegedly committed through its agent, Doig. At the same time, it argues that Doig is criminally liable for aiding and abetting Healy's violation under 18 U.S.C. § 2(a). Thus, the government seeks to "double-count" Doig's actions. "Simply put, '[a]iding and abetting means to assist the perpetrator of the crime.' " Under the government's theory, then, Doig would have had to assist himself in violating the relevant OSHA standards, because no other individual or natural person was indicted for the offense. "[I]nherent in the evolution of the concept of accessory is the idea that the accessory and the principal are ordinarily different persons." Thus, we agree with the district court's conclusion that it is logically inconsistent to hold a corporation criminally liable because of the acts of its agent, and, at the same time to hold the agent liable for aiding and abetting the corporation.

For the foregoing reasons, we hold that an employee may not be subjected to liability as an aider and abettor under 29 U.S.C. § 666(e) and 18 U.S.C. § 2. The judgment of the district court is AFFIRMED.

NOTES AND QUESTIONS

1. ***Employers Only.*** In **United States v. Shear**, 962 F.2d 488 (5th Cir. 1992), the court noted that Section 666 was intended to cover employers and not employees. The court held:

> The terms "employer" and "employee" are defined in the statute. The duties of employers and employees are also carefully delineated. See 29 U.S.C. § 654. Section 654(a) requires "[e]ach employer" to "furnish to each of his employees employment and a place of employment which are free from recognized hazards that are causing or are likely to cause death or serious physical harm to his employees" and to "comply with occupational safety and health standards promulgated under this chapter." Section 654(b) requires "[e]ach employee" to "comply with occupational safety and health standards and all rules, regulations, and orders issued pursuant to this chapter which are applicable to his own actions and conduct." Section 666, entitled "Civil and Criminal Penalties," establishes the civil and criminal penalties for violating OSHA. It distinguishes between employers and broader classes of individuals in imposing liability. For example, subsection (f) imposes liability upon "[a]ny person" who gives advance notice of an inspection, and section (g) imposes liability on "[w]hoever" makes false statements or representations. In contrast, subsections (a)-(e) and (i) penalize "any employer." "[W]here Congress includes particular language in one section of a statute but omits it in another section of the same Act, it is generally presumed that Congress acts intentionally and purposely in the disparate inclusion or exclusion." This juxtaposition indicates that Congress intended to subject employers, but not employees, to criminal liability under section 666(e). * * *

2. ***Third Parties.*** Can a third party be held liable as an employer, for an OSHA violation, under a theory of aiding and abetting? *Shear,* supra ("We are not presented with, and do not address, the situation where a third party, or even an employee acting in some other capacity, is charged with aiding and abetting an employer's violation of section 666(e).").

3. ***RCRA - Employees.*** Employees have, however, been found liable under the RCRA Act. In **United States v. Dean**, 969 F.2d 187 (6th Cir. 1992) the defendant argued that subsection 6928(d)(2)(A) was not intended to reach employees who were not "owners" or "operators" of facilities. In rejecting this argument, the court noted:

* * *"Person" is a defined term meaning "an individual, trust, firm, joint stock company, corporation (including a government corporation), partnership, association, State, municipality, commission, political subdivision of a State, or any interstate body." 42 U.S.C. § 6903(15).

Defendant would be hard pressed to convince the court that he is not an "individual." He argues, however, that because only owners and operators of facilities are required to obtain permits, the penalty imposed for hazardous waste handling without a permit by subsection 6928(d)(2)(A) must apply only to owners and operators.

This contention is unpersuasive for numerous reasons. Of primary importance is the fact that it is contrary to the unambiguous language of the statute. We agree with the Third Circuit that "[h]ad Congress meant in § 6928(d)(2)(A) to take aim more narrowly, it could have used more narrow language." United States v. Johnson & Towers, Inc., 741 F.2d 662 (3d Cir.1984). Second, while defendant's argument at first glance has logical appeal in relation to subsection 6928(d)(2)(A), the relevant language "any person" prefaces § 6928(d) generally. A number of separate crimes are set out in § 6928(d), several of them having nothing to do with the permit requirement (e.g., failure to maintain requisite documentation or to comply with regulations). Defendant's argument would accordingly impose a limitation on all of the crimes set out in § 6928(d) on a ground relevant to few of them. Third, even the logical appeal of the assertion does not withstand scrutiny. The fact that Congress chose to impose the permit requirement upon owners and operators does not undercut the value of further assuring permit compliance by enacting criminal penalties which would lead others to make inquiry into the permit status of facilities. Given that "[s]uch wastes typically have no value, yet can only be safely disposed of at considerable cost," facilities generating hazardous waste have a strong incentive to evade the law. Moreover, clean-up of the resulting environmental damage almost always involves far greater cost than proper disposal would have, and may be limited to containing the spread of the harm. Defendant argues that employees are the least likely persons to know facilities' permit status. However, employees of a facility are more able to ascertain the relevant facts than the general public, which the statute is intended to protect. In light of these factors, it was entirely reasonable for Congress to have created broad criminal liability. Fourth, it is far from clear that defendant is in fact not an "operator" of GMF, a term defined in the regulations to mean "the person responsible for the overall operation of a facility." 40 C.F.R. § 260.10 (1991). Finally, we agree with the Court of Appeals for the Third Circuit that this result is also supported by the decision of the Supreme Court in *Dotterweich* [p.78], and by the legislative history.

We conclude that employees may be criminally liable under § 6928(d).

4. ***RCRA - Government Employees.*** Government employees have been found criminally liable under RCRA. In **United States v. Dee**, 912 F.2d 741 (4th Cir. 1990), defendant engineers were civilian employees of the United States Army. They claimed immunity from the criminal provisions of RCRA because of their status as federal employees working at a federal facility. Circuit Judge Sprouse, in rejecting this argument stated:

> * * * The Act defines "person" as an individual, trust, firm, joint stock company, corporation (including a government corporation), partnership, association, State, municipality, commission, political subdivision of a State, or any interstate body. 42 U.S.C. § 6903(15). The definition begins with an inclusion of "an individual" as a person. The defendants, of course, were indicted, tried, and convicted as individuals, not as agents of the government. Suffice it to say that sovereign immunity does not attach to individual government employees so as to immunize them from prosecution for their criminal acts. * * * Even where certain federal officers enjoy a degree of immunity for a particular sphere of official actions, there is no general immunity from criminal prosecution for actions taken while serving their office. * * *

D. JUDICIAL REVIEW

ADAMO WRECKING CO. v. UNITED STATES
434 U.S. 275 (1978)

Justice REHNQUIST delivered the opinion of the Court.

The Clean Air Act authorizes the Administrator of the Environmental Protection Agency to promulgate "emission standards" for hazardous air pollutants "at the level which in his judgment provides an ample margin of safety to protect the public health." The emission of an air pollutant in violation of an applicable emission standard is prohibited by § 112(c)(1)(B) of the Act, 42 U.S.C. § 1857c-7(c)(1)(B). The knowing violation of the latter section, in turn, subjects the violator to fine and imprisonment under the provisions of § 113(c)(1)(C) of the Act, 42 U.S.C. § 1857c-8(c)(1)(C). The final piece in this statutory puzzle is § 307(b) of the Act, 42 U.S.C. § 1857h-5(b), which provides in pertinent part:

> "(1) A petition for review of action of the Administrator in promulgating . . . any emission standard under section 112 . . . may be filed only in the United States Court of Appeals for the District of Columbia. . . . Any such petition shall be filed within 30 days from the date of such promulgation, or approval, or after

> such date if such petition is based solely on grounds arising after such 30th day. (2) Action of the Administrator with respect to which review could have been obtained under paragraph (1) shall not be subject to judicial review in civil or criminal proceedings for enforcement."

It is within this legislative matrix that the present criminal prosecution arose.

Petitioner was indicted in the United States District Court for the Eastern District of Michigan for violation of § 112(c)(1)(B). The indictment alleged that petitioner, while engaged in the demolition of a building in Detroit, failed to comply with 40 CFR § 61.22(d)(2)(i) (1975). That regulation, described in its caption as a "National Emission Standard for Asbestos," specifies procedures to be followed in connection with building demolitions, but does not by its terms limit emissions of asbestos which occur during the course of a demolition. The District Court granted petitioner's motion to dismiss the indictment on the ground that no violation of § 112(c)(1)(B), necessary to establish criminal liability under § 113(c)(1)(C), had been alleged, because the cited regulation was not an "emission standard" within the meaning of § 112(c). The United States Court of Appeals for the Sixth Circuit reversed, holding that Congress had in § 307(b) precluded petitioner from questioning in a criminal proceeding whether a regulation ostensibly promulgated under § 112(b)(1)(B) was in fact an emission standard. We granted certiorari, and we now reverse.

We do not intend to make light of a difficult question of statutory interpretation when we say that the basic question in this case may be phrased: "When is an emission standard not an emission standard?" Petitioner contends, and the District Court agreed, that while the preclusion and exclusivity provisions of § 307(b) of the Act prevented his obtaining "judicial review" of an emission standard in this criminal proceeding, he was nonetheless entitled to claim that the administrative regulation cited in the indictment was actually not an emission standard at all. The Court of Appeals took the contrary view. It held that a regulation designated by the Administrator as an "emission standard," however different in content it might be from what Congress had contemplated when it authorized the promulgation of emission standards, was sufficient to support a criminal charge based upon § 112(c), unless it had been set aside in an appropriate proceeding commenced in the United States Court of Appeals for the District of Columbia Circuit pursuant to § 307(b).

The Court of Appeals in its opinion relied heavily on Yakus v. United States, 321 U.S. 414 (1944), in which this Court held that Congress in the context of criminal proceedings could require that the validity of regulatory action be challenged in a particular court at a particular time, or not at all. That case, however, does not decide this one. Because § 307(b) expressly applies only to "emission standards," we must still inquire as to the validity of the Government's underlying assumption that the Administrator's mere designation of a regulation as an "emission standard" is sufficient to foreclose any further inquiry in a criminal prosecution under § 113(c)(1)(C) of the Act. For the reasons hereafter stated, we hold that one such as respondent who is charged with a criminal violation under the Act may defend on the ground that the "emission standard" which he is charged with having violated was not an "emission standard" within the contemplation of Congress when it employed that term, even though the "emission standard" in question has not been previously reviewed under the provisions of § 307(b) of the Act.

In resolving this question, we think the statutory provisions of the Clean Air Act are far less favorable to the Government's position than were the provisions of the Emergency Price Control Act considered in *Yakus*. The broad language of that statute gave clear evidence of congressional intent that any actions taken by the Price Administrator under the purported authority of the designated sections of the Act should be challenged only in the Emergency Court of Appeals. * * *

This relatively simple statutory scheme contrasts with the Clean Air Act's far more complex interrelationship between the imposition of criminal sanctions and judicial review of the Administrator's actions. * * *

The conclusion we draw from this excursion into the complexities of the criminal sanctions provided by the Act are several. First, Congress has not chosen to prescribe either civil or criminal sanctions for violations of every rule, regulation, or order issued by the Administrator. Second, Congress, as might be expected, has imposed civil liability for a wider range of violations of the orders of the Administrator than those for which it has imposed criminal liability. Third, even where Congress has imposed criminal liability for the violation of an order of the Administrator, it has not uniformly precluded judicial challenge to the order as a defense in the criminal proceeding. Fourth, although Congress has applied the preclusion provisions of § 307(b)(2) to implementation plans approved by the Administrator, and it has in § 113(c)(1)(A) provided criminal penalties for violations of those plans, it has nonetheless required, under normal circumstances, that a violation continue for a period of 30 days after receipt of notice of the violation from the Administrator before the criminal sanction may be imposed.

These conclusions in no way detract from the fact that Congress has precluded judicial review of an "emission standard" in the court in which the criminal proceeding for the violation of the standard is brought. Indeed, the conclusions heighten the importance of determining what it was that Congress meant by an "emission standard," since a violation of that standard is subject to the most stringent criminal liability imposed by § 113(c)(1) of the Act: Not only is the Administrator's promulgation of the standard not subject to judicial review in the criminal proceeding, but no prior notice of violation from the Administrator is required as a condition for criminal liability. Since Congress chose to attach these stringent sanctions to the violation of an emission standard, in contrast to the violation of various other kinds of orders that might be issued by the Administrator, it is crucial to determine whether the Administrator's mere designation of a regulation as an "emission standard" is conclusive as to its character.

The stringency of the penalty imposed by Congress lends substance to petitioner's contention that Congress envisioned a particular type of regulation when it spoke of an "emission standard." The fact that Congress dealt more leniently, either in terms of liability, of notice, or of available defenses, with other infractions of the Administrator's orders suggests that it attached a peculiar importance to compliance with "emission standards." Unlike the situation in *Yakus,* Congress in the Clean Air Act singled out violators of this generic form of regulation, imposed criminal penalties upon them which would not be imposed upon violators of other orders of the Administrator, and precluded them from asserting defenses which might be asserted by violators of other orders of the Administrator. All of this leads us to conclude that Congress intended, within broad limits, that "emission standards" be regulations of a certain type, and that it did not empower the Administrator, after the manner of Humpty Dumpty in Through the Looking-Glass, to make a regulation an "emission standard" by his mere designation.

The statutory scheme supports the conclusion that § 307(b)(2), in precluding judicial review of the validity of emission standards, does not relieve the Government of the duty of proving, in a prosecution under § 113(c)(1)(C), that the regulation allegedly violated is an emission standard. * * *

In sum, a survey of the totality of the statutory scheme does not compel agreement with the Government's contention that Congress intended that the Administrator's designation of a regulation as an emission standard should be conclusive in a criminal prosecution. At the very least, it may be said that the issue is subject to some doubt. Under these circumstances, we adhere to the familiar rule that, "where there is ambiguity in a criminal statute, doubts are resolved in favor of the defendant." * * * The narrow inquiry to be addressed by the court in a criminal prosecution is not whether the Administrator has complied with appropriate procedures in promulgating the regulation in question, or whether the particular regulation is arbitrary, capricious, or supported by the administrative record. Nor is the court to pursue any of the other familiar inquiries which arise in the course of an administrative review proceeding. The question is only whether the regulation which the defendant is alleged to have violated is on its face an "emission standard" within the broad limits of the congressional meaning of that term. * * *

Most clearly supportive of petitioner's position that a standard was intended to be a quantitative limit on emissions is this provision of § 112(b)(1)(B): "The Administrator shall establish any such standard at the level which in his judgment provides an ample margin of safety to protect the public health from such hazardous air pollutant." (Emphasis added.) All these provisions lend force to the conclusion that a standard is an quantitative "level" to be attained by use of "techniques," "controls," and "technology." This conclusion is fortified by recent amendments to the Act, by which Congress authorized the Administrator to promulgate a "design, equipment, work practice, or operational standard" when "it is not feasible to prescribe or enforce an emission standard."

This distinction, now endorsed by Congress, between "work practice standards" and "emission standards" first appears in the Administrator's own account of the development of this regulation. Although the Administrator has contended that a "work practice standard" is just another type of emission standard, the history of this regulation demonstrates that he chose to regulate work practices only when it became clear he could not regulate emissions. The regulation as originally proposed would have prohibited all visible emissions of asbestos during the course of demolitions. In adopting the final form of the regulation, the Administrator concluded "that the no visible emission requirement would prohibit repair or demolition in many situations, since it would be impracticable, if not impossible, to do such work without creating visible emissions." Therefore the Administrator chose to "specif[y] certain work practices" instead.

The Government concedes that, prior to the 1977 Amendments, the statute was ambiguous with regard to whether a work-practice standard was properly classified as an emission standard, but argues that this Court should defer to the Administrator's construction of the Act.[5] While such deference is entirely appropriate under ordinary circumstances, in this case the 1977 Amendments to the Clean Air Act tend to undercut the administrative construction. * * * The clear distinction drawn in § 112(e) between work-practice standards and emission standards practically forecloses any such inference. * * *

[W]e conclude that the work-practice standard involved here was not an emission standard. The District Court's order dismissing the indictment was therefore proper, and the judgment of the Court of Appeals is Reversed.

---

[5] Our Brother Stevens quite correctly points out, that an administrative "'contemporaneous construction'" of a statute is entitled to considerable weight, and it is true that the originally proposed regulations contain, with respect to some uses of asbestos, the sort of provisions which the Administrator and the Congress later designated as "work practice standards." It bears noting, however, that these regulations can only be said to define by implication the meaning of the term "emission standard." The Administrator promulgated both of them; both were denominated "emission standards"; and it is undoubtedly a fair inference that the Administrator thought each to be an "emission standard." But neither the regulations themselves nor the comments accompanying them give any indication of the Administrator's reasons for concluding that Congress, in authorizing him to promulgate "emission standards," intended to include "work practice standards" within the meaning of that term. * * *

Justice POWELL, concurring.

If the constitutional validity of § 307(b) of the Clean Air Act had been raised by petitioner, I think it would have merited serious consideration. This section limits judicial review to the filing of a petition in the United States Court of Appeals for the District of Columbia Circuit within 30 days from the date of the promulgation by the Administrator of an emission standard. No notice is afforded a party who may be subject to criminal prosecution other than publication of the Administrator's action in the Federal Register. The Act in this respect is similar to the preclusion provisions of the Emergency Price Control Act before the Court in *Yakus*, and petitioner may have thought the decision in that case effectively foreclosed a due process challenge in the present case.

Although I express no considered judgment, I think *Yakus* is at least arguably distinguishable. The statute there came before the Court during World War II, and it can be viewed as a valid exercise of the war powers of Congress under Art. I, § 8, of the Constitution. * * *

The 30-day limitation on judicial review imposed by the Clean Air Act would afford precariously little time for many affected persons even if some adequate method of notice were afforded. It also is totally unrealistic to assume that more than a fraction of the persons and entities affected by a regulation— especially small contractors scattered across the country—would have knowledge of its promulgation or familiarity with or access to the Federal Register. Indeed, following *Yakus*, and apparently concerned by Mr. Justice Rutledge's eloquent dissent. Congress amended the most onerous features of the Emergency Price Control Act.

I join the Court's opinion with the understanding that it implies no view as to the constitutional validity of the preclusion provisions of § 307(b) in the context of a criminal prosecution.

Justice STEWART, with whom Justice BRENNAN and Justice BLACKMUN join, dissenting.

Section 307(b)(1) of the Clean Air Act provides that a "petition for review of action of the Administrator in promulgating . . . any emission standard under section 112" may be filed only in the United States Court of Appeals for the District of Columbia Circuit within 30 days of promulgation. Section 307(b)(2) of the Act provides that an "[a]ction of the Administrator with respect to which review could have been obtained under paragraph (1) shall not be subject to judicial review in civil or criminal proceedings for enforcement." Despite these unambiguous provisions, the Court holds in this case that such an action of the Administrator shall be subject to judicial review in a criminal proceeding for enforcement of the Act, at least sometimes. Because this tampering with the plain statutory language threatens to destroy the effectiveness of the unified and expedited judicial review procedure established by Congress in the Clean Air Act, I respectfully dissent.

The inquiry that the Court today allows a trial court to make—whether the asbestos regulation at issue is an emission standard of the type envisioned by Congress—is nothing more than an inquiry into whether the Administrator has acted beyond his statutory authority. But such an inquiry is a normal part of judicial review of agency action. And it is precisely such "judicial review" of an "[a]ction of the Administrator" that Congress has, in § 307(b)(2), expressly forbidden a trial court to undertake. There is not the slightest indication in the Act or in its legislative history that Congress, in providing for review of the Administrator's actions only in the Court of Appeals for the District of Columbia Circuit, meant nonetheless to allow some kinds of review to be available in other courts. To the contrary, Congress clearly ordained that "any review of such actions" be controlled by the provisions of § 307.

The Court's interpretation of § 307(b)(2) also conspicuously frustrates the intent of Congress to establish a speedy and unified system of judicial review under the Act. * * *

Finally, the Court provides no real guidance as to which aspects of an emission standard are so critical that they fall outside the scope of the exclusive judicial review procedure provided by Congress. * * * The Court today has allowed the camel's nose into the tent, and I fear that the rest of the camel is almost certain to follow.

Since I believe that the Administrator's action in promulgating this regulation could have been reviewed in the Court of Appeals for the District of Columbia Circuit under § 307(b)(1), and that such review could have included the petitioner's claim that the Administrator's action was beyond his authority under the Act, I would hold that the petitioner was barred by the express language of § 307(b)(2) from raising that issue in the present case.

Justice STEVENS, dissenting.

The reason Congress attached "the most stringent criminal liability," to the violation of an emission standard for a "hazardous air pollutant" is that substances within that narrow category pose an especially grave threat to human health. That is also a reason why the Court should avoid a construction of the statute that would deny the Administrator the authority to regulate these poisonous substances effectively.

The reason the Administrator did not frame the emission standard for asbestos in numerical terms is that asbestos emissions cannot be measured numerically. For that reason, if Congress simultaneously commanded him (a) to regulate asbestos emissions by establishing and enforcing emission standards and (b) never to use any kind of standard except one framed in numerical terms, it commanded an impossible task.

Nothing in the language of the 1970 statute, or in its history, compels so crippling an interpretation of the Administrator's authority. On the contrary, I am persuaded (1) that the Administrator's regulation of asbestos emissions was entirely legitimate; (2) that if this conclusion were doubtful, we would nevertheless be required to respect his reasonable interpretation of the governing statute; (3) that the 1977 Amendments, fairly read, merely clarified his pre-existing authority; and (4) that the Court's reading of the statute in its current form leads to the anomalous conclusion that work-practice rules, even though properly promulgated, are entirely unenforceable. * * *

CHAPTER EIGHT
PERJURY, FALSE STATEMENTS & OBSTRUCTION

A. PERJURY

UNITED STATES v. BRONSTON
409 U.S. 352 (1973)

Chief Justice BURGER delivered the opinion of the Court.

* * * Petitioner is the sole owner of Samuel Bronston Productions, Inc., a company that between 1958 and 1964, produced motion pictures in various European locations. For these enterprises, Bronston Productions, opened bank accounts in a number of foreign countries; in 1962, for example, it had 37 accounts in five countries. As president of Bronston Productions, petitioner supervised transactions involving the foreign bank accounts.

In June 1964, Bronston Productions, petitioned for an arrangement with creditors under Chapter XI of the Bankruptcy Act. On June 10, 1966, a referee in bankruptcy held a § 21(a) hearing to determine, for the benefit of creditors, the extent and location of the company's assets. Petitioner's perjury conviction was founded on the answers given by him as a witness at that bankruptcy hearing, and in particular on the following colloquy with a lawyer for a creditor of Bronston Productions:

Q. Do you have any bank accounts in Swiss banks, Mr. Bronston?

A. No, sir.

Q. Have you ever?

A. The company had an account there for about six months, in Zurich. [Emphasis added]

Q. Have you any nominees who have bank accounts in Swiss banks?

A. No, sir.

Q. Have you ever?
A. No, sir.

It is undisputed that for a period of nearly five years, between October 1959 and June 1964, petitioner had a personal bank account at the International Credit Bank in Geneva, Switzerland, into which he made deposits and upon which he drew checks totaling more than $180,000. It is likewise undisputed that petitioner's answers were literally truthful. (a) Petitioner did not at the time of questioning have a Swiss bank account. (b) Bronston Productions, Inc., did have the account in Zurich described by petitioner. (c) Neither at the time of questioning nor before did petitioner have nominees who had Swiss accounts. The Government's prosecution for perjury went forward on the theory that in order to mislead his questioner, petitioner answered the second question with literal truthfulness but unresponsively addressed his answer to the company's assets and not to his own–thereby implying that he had no personal Swiss bank account at the relevant time.

At petitioner's trial, the District Court instructed the jury that the "basic issue" was whether petitioner "spoke his true belief." Perjury, the court stated, "necessarily involves the state of mind of the accused" and "essentially consists of wilfully testifying to the truth of a fact which the defendant does not believe to be true"; petitioner's testimony could not be found "wilfully" false unless at the time his testimony was given petitioner "fully understood the questions put to him but nevertheless gave false answers knowing the same to be false." The court further instructed the jury that if petitioner did not understand the question put to him and for that reason gave an unresponsive answer, he could not be convicted of perjury. Petitioner could, however, be convicted if he gave an answer "not literally false but when considered in the context in which it was given, nevertheless constitute(d) a false statement." [3] * * *

In the Court of Appeals, petitioner contended, as he had in post-trial motions before the District Court, that the key question was imprecise and

---

[3] The District Court gave the following example "as an illustration only":

> [I]f it is material to ascertain how many times a person has entered a store on a given day and that person responds to such a question by saying five times when in fact he knows that he entered the store 50 times that day, that person may be guilty of perjury even though it is technically true that he entered the store five times.

The illustration given by the District Court is hardly comparable to petitioner's answer, the answer "five times" is responsive to the hypothetical question and contains nothing to alert the questioner that he may be sidetracked. Moreover, it is very doubtful that an answer which, in response to a specific quantitative inquiry, baldly understates a numerical fact can be described as even "technically true." Whether an answer is true must be determined with reference to the question it purports to answer not in isolation. An unresponsive answer is unique in this respect because its unresponsiveness by definition prevents its truthfulness from being tested in the context of the question–unless there is to be speculation as to what the unresponsive answer "implies."

suggestive of various interpretations. In addition, petitioner contended that he could not be convicted of perjury on the basis of testimony that was concededly truthful, however unresponsive. A divided Court of Appeals held that the question was readily susceptible of a responsive reply and that it adequately tested the defendant's belief in the veracity of his answer. The Court of Appeals further held that, "(f)or the purposes of 18 U.S.C. § 1621, an answer containing half of the truth which also constitutes a lie by negative implication, when the answer is intentionally given in place of the responsive answer called for by a proper question, is perjury." In this Court, petitioner renews his attack on the specificity of the question asked him and the legal sufficiency of his answer to support a conviction for perjury. The problem of the ambiguity of the question is not free from doubt, but we need not reach that issue. Even assuming, as we do, that the question asked petitioner specifically focused on petitioner's personal bank accounts, we conclude that the federal perjury statute cannot be construed to sustain a conviction based on petitioner's answer.

The statute, 18 U.S.C. § 1621, substantially identical in its relevant language to its predecessors for nearly a century, is "a federal statute enacted in an effort to keep the course of justice free from the pollution of perjury." * * * The need for truthful testimony in a § 21(a) bankruptcy proceeding is great, since the proceeding is "a searching inquiry into the condition of the estate of the bankrupt, to assist in discovering and collecting the assets, and to develop facts and circumstances which bear upon the question of discharge." Here, as elsewhere, the perpetration of perjury "well may affect the dearest concerns of the parties before a tribunal. . . ." United States v. Norris, 300 U.S. 564 (1937).

There is, at the outset, a serious literal problem in applying § 1621 to petitioner's answer. The words of the statute confine the offense to the witness who "willfully . . . states . . . any material matter which he does not believe to be true." Beyond question, petitioner's answer to the crucial question was not responsive if we assume, as we do, that the first question was directed at personal bank accounts. There is, indeed, an implication in the answer to the second question that there was never a personal bank account; in casual conversation this interpretation might reasonably be drawn. But we are not dealing with casual conversation and the statute does not make it a criminal act for a witness to willfully state any material matter that implies any material matter that he does not believe to be true.[4]

---

[4] Petitioner's answer is not to be measured by the same standards applicable to criminally fraudulent or extortionate statements. In that context, the law goes "rather far in punishing intentional creation of false impressions by a selection of literally true representations, because the actor himself generally selects and arranges the representations." In contrast, "under our system of adversary questioning and cross-examination the scope of disclosure is largely in the hands of counsel and presiding officer." A.L.I. Model Penal Code § 208.20, Comment (Tent.Draft No. 6, 1957, p. 124).

The Government urges that the perjury statute be construed broadly to reach petitioner's answer and thereby fulfill its historic purpose of reinforcing our adversary factfinding process. We might go beyond the precise words of the statute if we thought they did not adequately express the intention of Congress, but we perceive no reason why Congress would intend the drastic sanction of a perjury prosecution to cure a testimonial mishap that could readily have been reached with a single additional question by counsel alert--as every examiner ought to be–to the incongruity of petitioner's unresponsive answer. Under the pressures and tensions of interrogation, it is not uncommon for the most earnest witnesses to give answers that are not entirely responsive. Sometimes the witness does not understand the question, or may in an excess of caution or apprehension read too much or too little into it. It should come as no surprise that a participant in a bankruptcy proceeding may have something to conceal and consciously tries to do so, or that a debtor may be embarrassed at his plight and yield information reluctantly. It is the responsibility of the lawyer to probe; testimonial interrogation, and cross-examination in particular, is a probing, prying, pressing form of inquiry. If a witness evades, it is the lawyer's responsibility to recognize the evasion and to bring the witness back to the mark, to flush out the whole truth with the tools of adversary examination.

It is no answer to say that here the jury found that petitioner intended to mislead his examiner. A jury should not be permitted to engage in conjecture whether an unresponsive answer, true and complete on its face, was intended to mislead or divert the examiner; the state of mind of the witness is relevant only to the extent that it bears on whether "he does not believe (his answer) to be true." To hold otherwise would be to inject a new and confusing element into the adversary testimonial system we know. Witnesses would be unsure of the extent of their responsibility for the misunderstandings and inadequacies of examiners, and might well fear having that responsibility tested by a jury under the vague rubric of "intent to mislead" or "perjury by implication." The seminal modern treatment of the history of the offense concludes that one consideration of policy overshadowed all others during the years when perjury first emerged as a common-law offense: "that the measures taken against the offense must not be so severe as to discourage witnesses from appearing or testifying." Study of Perjury, reprinted in Report of New York Law Revision Commission, Legis.Doc.No.60, p. 249 (1935). A leading 19th century commentator, quoted by Dean Wigmore, noted that the English law "throws every fence round a person accused of perjury," for

> the obligation of protecting witnesses from oppression, or annoyance, by charges, or threats of charges, of having borne false testimony, is far paramount to that of giving even perjury its deserts. To repress that crime, prevention is better than cure: and the law of England relies, for this purpose, on the means provided for detecting and exposing the crime at the moment of commission,–such as publicity, cross-examination, the aid of a jury, etc.; and on the infliction of a severe, though not excessive punishment, wherever the commission

> of the crime has been clearly proved." W. Best, Principles of the Law of Evidence § 606 (C. Chamberlayne ed. 1883).

See J. Wigmore, *Evidence* 275-276 (3d ed. 1940). * * *

Thus, we must read § 1621 in light of our own and the traditional Anglo-American judgment that a prosecution for perjury is not the sole, or even the primary, safeguard against errant testimony. While "the lower federal courts have not dealt with the question often,' and while their expressions do not deal with unresponsive testimony and are not precisely in point, 'it may be said that they preponderate against the respondent's contention." *United States v. Norris*. The cases support petitioner's position that the perjury statute is not to be loosely construed, nor the statute invoked simply because a wily witness succeeds in derailing the questioner–so long as the witness speaks the literal truth. The burden is on the questioner to pin the witness down to the specific object to the questioner's inquiry. * * *

It may well be that petitioner's answers were not guileless but were shrewdly calculated to evade. Nevertheless, we are constrained to agree with Judge Lumbard, who dissented from the judgment of the Court of Appeals, that any special problems arising from the literally true but unresponsive answer are to be remedied through the "questioner's acuity" and not by a federal perjury prosecution.

NOTES AND QUESTIONS

1. ***Elements of Perjury.*** Section 1621, the perjury statute, makes it a crime for someone (1) "having taken an oath before a competent tribunal, officer, or person," (2) "willfully and contrary to such oath" (3) "states or subscribes any material matter" (4) "that he does not believe to be true."

2. ***Telling the Whole Truth***. Professors Bierschbach and Stein argue that the statute should be interpreted narrowly to protect an individual's right to privacy:

> [E]vasive as opposed to affirmatively misleading testimony raises normatively difficult questions about the extent to which an individual's moral entitlement to privacy and nonexposure should limit her truthtelling obligations to society. From a moral (as opposed to formal legal) point of view, it is one thing to actively bring about an injustice, and it is quite another thing to withdraw one's testimonial assistance from a justice-making proceeding. From the moral perspective, only outright liars who actively mislead the court can properly be identified and condemned as perjurers.

Richard A. Bierschbach & Alex Stein, *Overenforcement*, 93 GEO. L.J. 1743 (2005).

3. ***High Profile Prosecutions***. While *Bronston* makes it more difficult to win a conviction for perjury, prosecutors have been more willing to charge the offense in white collar crime cases, sometimes not filing charges related to the underlying transactions or conduct that triggered the testimony. Recent prosecutions for perjury have included I. Lewis (Scooter) Libby, former chief of staff for Vice President Cheney, and a number of prominent athletes who testified falsely about receiving steroids from Balco (Bay Area Laboratory Co-operative), including former Olympic gold medalist Marion Jones and former NFL player Dana Stubblefield.

4. ***Materiality.*** Perjury requires that the statement be material. See United States v. Gremillion, 464 F.2d 901 (5th Cir. 1972) ("The test of materiality is whether the false testimony was capable of influencing the tribunal on the issue, or whether the false testimony would have the natural effect or tendency to influence, impede, or dissuade the Grand Jury from pursuing its investigation."). The impeachment of President Clinton largely involved allegations that he committed perjury in a civil deposition. In addition to questions as to what constitutes a "false" statement that permits the government to prosecute the declarant, there were also questions raised regarding the materiality of the statements. See Alan Heinrich, Note, *Clinton's Little White Lies: The Materiality Requirement for Perjury in Civil Discovery*, 33 LOY. L.A. L. REV. 1303 (1999).

5. ***Two-Witness Rule.*** Courts in assessing the sufficiency of the evidence in a perjury case use a two-witness rule. The policy rationale for this rule is to assure that a perjury conviction is not premised upon one person's oath against another. Although at common law the rule required two witnesses, today it is a more relaxed permitting "the testimony of two witnesses or the testimony of one witness, plus corroborating evidence." United States v. Davis, 548 F.2d 840 (9th Cir. 1977). Courts are not always in agreement on what constitutes corroborating evidence. In **United States v. Diggs**, 560 F.2d 266 (7th Cir. 1977), the court stated:

> As currently applied the two-witness rule does not literally require the direct testimony of two separate witnesses, but rather may be satisfied by the direct testimony of one witness and sufficient corroborative evidence. * * * While this interpretation is not seriously questioned, there is an apparent division among the circuits over the precise wording of the rule to be applied in determining the sufficiency of the corroborative evidence. In analyzing the various expressions of the rule and their application, we agree with the Second Circuit that "(t)he division in the Circuits, judged by its results, appears to be a matter of semantics and a slight difference in emphasis."* * * No wording of the rule requires the corroborative evidence to be sufficient for conviction; nor does any phrasing permit conviction where the corroboration consists of

> merely peripheral testimony not tending to show the falsity of the accused's statements while under oath.
>
> The two-witness rule is thus satisfied when there is direct testimony from one witness and additional independent evidence so corroborative of the direct testimony that the two when considered together are sufficient to establish the falsity of the accused's statements under oath beyond a reasonable doubt. "Independent" evidence in this context means evidence coming from a source other than that of the direct testimony. * * * This independent corroborating evidence must be trustworthy enough to convince the jury that what the principal witness said was correct, the ultimate determination of its credibility being an exclusive function of the jury.

But see United States v. Forrest, 639 F.2d 1224, 1226 (5th Cir. 1981) (holding that "the corroborative evidence must be inconsistent with the innocence of the accused and must tend to show the perjury independently of the testimony which it is intended to corroborate.").

6. ***Literal Truth.*** In **United States v. Shotts**, 145 F.3d 1289 (11th Cir. 1998), the Eleventh Circuit reversed a perjury conviction where the defendant, an attorney, provided an answer that was "literally" true. Shotts testified before the grand jury as follows:

> "Q: Do you own a bail bonds business?
>
> A: No, sir.
>
> Q: Have you been associated in some fashion with a bail bonds business?
>
> A: I would at this time invoke my right of self-incrimination, Your Honor.
>
> Q: All right.
>
> A: I have a client that is a bail bonds company.
>
> Q: Well, have you in the past either been an officer in or had an interest in a bail bonds company, any time prior to today?
>
> A: I would respectfully decline to answer the question on the ground it might tend to incriminate me."

In reversing the conviction under *Bronston,* the Eleventh Circuit noted that "[u]nder Alabama law, a corporation is 'owned' by its shareholders." The court stated:

> The government's argument is that Shotts ignores the "context" of his testimony. He was, "in fact", the owner even if he didn't own the stock. He had told others he "owned" the business. When asked before the grand jury if he owned a bail bond business, "he knew ... what was meant by the question." * * *
>
> A perjury conviction must rest on the utterance by the accused of a false statement; it may not stand on a particular interpretation that the questioner places upon an answer. The government cannot require Shotts to interpret its question in a way that is contrary to the law of Alabama, and he may not be convicted of perjury if he does not. *Bronston* expressly places on the questioner the burden of pinning the witness down to the specific object of the inquiry.

7. ***Contextual Setting*: United States v. DeZarn.** In *Schotts*, the court rejected any reference to the context of the question or external evidence. Does the court in **United States v. DeZarn**, 157 F.3d 1042 (6th Cir. 1998), take an opposite position? In *DeZarn*, a government investigator questioned the defendant under oath about campaign contributions being made at a "Preakness Party" in 1991. During the examination, the investigator asked whether the "1991 Preakness Party" "was a political fundraising activity." The defendant answered "Absolutely not." The response was literally true because the party had occurred in 1990, but the Sixth Circuit held that the context of the question made it clear that the defendant knew the investigator was asking about the 1990 party and had misspoken when using the wrong date. In distinguishing *Bronston*, the Sixth Circuit stated:

> The question presented here, then, is whether in a perjury case in which a mistaken premise exists in one of the questions asked of the testifier, the Government is entitled to present, and the jury to consider, evidence of the context of the questioning which would establish that the Defendant – despite the false premise of the question – knew exactly what the questions meant and exactly what they were referring to. We hold that the law of perjury not only permits this, but in cases such as this, requires it.
>
> First, perjury must be shown to be willful, and it must be shown that the testifier did not believe his responses to be true. * * * Thus, by its very nature, perjury requires an inquiry into the Defendant's state of mind and his intent to deceive at the time the testimony was given. Indeed, the entire focus of a perjury inquiry centers upon what the testifier knew and when he knew it because in order to make a determination as to whether that person intended to testify falsely, it must be established beyond a reasonable doubt that he knew his testimony to be false when he gave it. In order to prove this, the Government, of necessity, must present evidence of the extent of a Defendant's knowledge of the subject matter of the questioning and the circumstances surrounding how he came to that knowledge. This, of course, requires the Government to show the

> full context of the Defendant's activities as well as other information of which he may have had knowledge and which may have influenced him.
>
> Thus, a perjury inquiry which focuses only upon the precision of the question and ignores what the Defendant knew about the subject matter of the question at the time it was asked, misses the very point of perjury: that is, the Defendant's intent to testify falsely and, thereby, mislead his interrogators. Such a limited inquiry would not only undermine the perjury laws, it would undermine the rule of law as a whole, as truthseeking is the critical component which allows us to determine if the laws are being followed, and it is only through the requirement that a witness testify truthfully that a determination may be made as to whether the laws are being followed. Indeed, that is the entire purpose of the sworn oath: To impress upon the testifier the need – under penalty of punishment – to testify truthfully.
>
> This is not to say that the question to which the answer is made is not an important part of a perjury inquiry. Of course it is. A question that is truly ambiguous or which affirmatively misleads the testifier can never provide a basis for a finding of perjury, as it could never be said that one intended to answer such a question untruthfully. But, where it can be shown from the context of the question and the state of the testifier's knowledge at the time that the testifier clearly knew what the question meant, the Government must be permitted to present, and the fact-finder to consider, those contextual facts. * * *
>
> * * * [T]he *Bronston* "literal truth" defense applies in cases where a perjury defendant responds to a question with an *unresponsive* answer. As noted, "[a]n unresponsive answer is unique . . . because its unresponsiveness ... prevents it from being tested in the context of the question – unless there is speculation as to what the unresponsive answer 'implies '." * * * [I]n this case, Defendant DeZarn gave unequivocal and directly and fully responsive answers to the questions asked * * *. Furthermore, * * * there is more than ample context and evidence to test the meaning and falsity of DeZarn's answers.

8. ***Parsing the Questions***. *Bronston* teaches that the question is as important as the answer in a perjury prosecution. Courts will often parse a series of questions very carefully to determine the exact meaning of the particular question that the government alleges formed the predicate for the defendant's perjury. Just as the Sixth Circuit did in *DeZarn*, context is of paramount importance because it is rare that a defendant will have given a wholly untruthful answer that is easily determinable to be false. Is the level of clarity required for a question that can trigger a perjury prosecution so

high that an attorney examining a witness in a grand jury investigation, deposition, or other sworn testimony cannot reasonably be expected to meet it at all times? Even if the courts examine every question as closely as *Bronston* requires, should the system expect any less from a prosecutor when a criminal violation can result simply from one's response, which may be made when the person is nervous or intimidated by the surroundings? See United States v. Serafini, 167 F.3d 812 (3rd Cir. 1999) (demonstrating the court going to great lengths to determine the meaning of the prosecutors questions and the defendant's response, refusing to look solely at a single question and answer).

9. ***Leading Questions.*** If an individual is charged with perjury premised upon statements made in a grand jury or during cross-examination, what arguments can the defense make to have the jury understand the context of the statements? Consider the following analysis by Professor Underwood:

> In prosecutions predicated upon false statements made before a grand jury, it must be remembered that the witness will not have had counsel's advice in the grand jury room. It's the prosecutor's turf. The prosecutor's questioning may consist entirely of leading questions, and the prosecution may be founded upon the witness' guarded responses to these questions. "This kind of interrogation always creates a great risk that the witness will misunderstand the questions or that the prosecutor will put words in the witness' mouth." * * * The same caveat may be in order when a witness is charged with committing perjury in his or her responses to leading questions in cross-examination. Indeed, one noted defense counsel has asserted that 'any witness will lie under repeated cross-examination.' ***

Richard H. Underwood: *Perjury! The Charges and the Defenses*, 36 DUQ. L. REV. 715 (1998).

10. ***False Declarations.*** In addition to the general perjury statute found in 18 U.S.C. § 1621, there is also a false declarations statute, found in section 1623. Section 1623 makes it a crime for someone (1) "under oath... in any proceeding before or ancillary to any court or grand jury"(2) "knowingly makes" (3) "any false" (4) "material declaration." Section 1621 applies in a wide variety of circumstances, including civil depositions, while § 1623 is limited to judicial or grand jury proceedings. Sections 1621 and 1623 require that the statement or declaration be actually false, and use the same test for materiality. Only the perjury statute, § 1621, includes the "two witness rule." Unlike the perjury statute, section § 1623 provides an affirmative defense of retraction. This requires the defendant to admit that the previous statement was false, the admission of falsity must be made in the same court or grand jury proceeding, and the false declaration must not already have "substantially affected the proceeding" and it must not have "become manifest that such falsity has been or will be exposed."

11. ***Other Perjury Statutes.*** Specific offense related perjury statutes exist throughout the United States Code. See, e.g., 26 U.S.C. § 7206 (filing of a perjurious tax return). Is there a correlation between crimes of fraud and crimes of perjury? See Stuart P. Green, *Lying, Misleading, and Falsely Denying: How Moral Concepts Inform the Law of Perjury, Fraud, and False Statements*, 53 HASTINGS L.J. 157 (2001) ("[T]he moral concepts of lying, misleading, and falsely denying correspond, respectively, to the legal concepts of perjury, fraud, and 'exculpatory noes.'").

B. FALSE STATEMENTS

UNITED STATES v. HIXON
987 F.2d 1261 (6th Cir. 1993)

KENNEDY, Circuit Judge.

Defendant Wesley E. Hixon appeals his jury conviction and sentence for making a false and material statement and representation on claims he submitted for continuing disability compensation.

In 1974, the defendant began working for the Tennessee Valley Authority (TVA). On February 21, 1989, in an accident occurring during the performance of his assigned duties, defendant sustained a strained right knee. As a result of this injury, defendant underwent four surgical procedures. He claimed he was unable to work because his job required him to walk on rough terrain. Between the time defendant was injured and the time he returned to work in October of 1990, defendant was considered partially or totally disabled. * * * [Defendant filed two forms with the Department of Labor (DOL), Office of Workers' Compensation Programs (OWCP), to receive temporary workers compensation for work-related injuries. Defendant wrote "not applicable" after the line on the form stating "Commission and Self-Employment. Show all activities, whether or not income resulted from your efforts." Defendant was found eligible to receive long-term benefits, and filed a different form with the OWCP that contained the following quesiton:]

> 2. *Self-Employment.* Earnings from self-employment (such as farming, sales, service, operating a store, business, etc.) must be reported. Report any such enterprise in which you worked, and from which you received revenue, even if it operated at a loss or if profits were reinvested. You must show as "rate of pay" what it would have cost you to have hired someone to perform the work you did.
>
> a) Were you self-employed during any time covered by this form?

Defendant filled out two of these forms, one dated November 15, 1989 and the other dated April 27, 1990. On these two forms, defendant answered "No" to both questions.

In March of 1991, the TVA Office of Inspector General, fraud division, received three phone calls regarding defendant. Thereafter, an agent, Duane Broome, began an investigation to determine whether defendant was misusing or abusing the worker's compensation program. In March, Agent Broome saw the defendant, with several of his associates, working a booth at the Dixie Deer Classic, an outdoor show where booking or travel agents display their wares in an effort to persuade potential customers to use their services. TVA agents observed the defendant carrying and setting up a portable booth with various stuffed animal heads used for wall mounts. They also saw him carrying his work table, supplies, brochures, and paraphernalia to promote his business. Subsequent investigation of defendant's business records revealed that defendant had worked numerous other shows and took several (business and) hunting trips for Woods and Water Outdoor Consultants while on disability.

Agent Broome discovered that Woods and Water Outdoor Consultants was a Georgia (Subchapter S) corporation that provided, planned, and booked fishing, hunting and outdoor vacations. Defendant was the sole stockholder (100% owner) of the corporation, as well as the President, Treasurer, registered agent, and sole member of the Board of Directors. Defendant did not receive a salary from the corporation, but allegedly earned income on commissions received from those who utilized his "travel agent type" services.

In August, 1991, Agents Broome and Derryberry went to defendant's home to interview him. In front of the house was a large red trailer bearing the name "Woods and Water Outdoor Consultants." Defendant explained to the agents that Woods and Water was a business he had started six years previously. However, defendant initially told the agents the company was his wife's business, that she attended all the shows, and that his personal involvement was nothing more than staying home and answering the phone and taking one business related trip in a year's time.

Agent Broome then confronted defendant with the information he had gathered during the course of his investigation, *e.g.*, he had read the company brochures and paperwork and the wife's name appeared nowhere; he had attended and videotaped several shows, but never saw the defendant's wife. According to Agent Broome's testimony, defendant "looked at me with a blank stare, looked back out the window and looked back at me and he said you got me." Defendant then told the agents "I've been employed since day one." Finally, defendant broke down, cried, and asked what he had to do to get this behind him as quickly as possible. On August 30, 1991, defendant's employment at TVA was terminated due to his failure to report his activities to OWCP. [Defendant was charged with four counts of violating § 1001 for "falsely indicating that he was not self-employed and concealing his self-employment and ownership of Woods and Water Outdoor Consultants, Inc.," on the four forms he filed for workers compensation.]

Defendant * * * contends that the District Court erred in denying his motion for judgment of acquittal because he is not guilty as a matter of law. Defendant argues that the only work he performed was for Woods and Water Outdoor Consultants Corporation. He maintains that under Georgia law (and federal law) as a corporate officer he was an employee of the corporation, and as such could not, as a matter of law, be self-employed. Consequently, he did not make a false material statement or representation on his disability claim forms when he answered that he was not self-employed. This statement simply was not false.

The District Court held that whether the defendant was self-employed was a question of fact for the jury to decide. The statute, 18 U.S.C. § 1001, speaks in terms of knowingly and willfully making false material statements and representations, or concealing a material fact. It is clear that the material *fact* alleged by the indictment to have been concealed was defendant's self- employment. He was not indicted for his answer to the questions regarding employment other than self-employment. The District Court instructed the jury that whether the fact of self-employment was material was a question of law for it to decide, but it was for the jury to decide whether the defendant knowingly and willfully concealed his self-employment status or falsely stated he was not self-employed. The court instructed the jury that if it concluded beyond a reasonable doubt that because of defendant's stock ownership, his position as the corporation's president, and the actions he took on the corporation's behalf, the defendant was, in effect, the corporation, "you may disregard the existence of the corporation in your determination of whether the defendant was self-employed." We now turn to the issue whether there was sufficient evidence for the jury to convict the defendant for falsely stating he was not self-employed.

A violation of 18 U.S.C. § 1001 for the making of a false statement or representation requires: (1) the making of a statement; (2) the falsity of such statement; (3) knowledge of the falsity of such statement; (4) relevance of such statement to the functioning of a federal department or agency; and (5) that the false statement was material. Thus, a violation of section 1001 requires a determination of whether Hixon's response on his claims for continuing disability that he was not self-employed was a false representation.

The only evidence of defendant's self-employment was his presidency of Woods and Water, a Georgia Corporation, and his services to that corporation. The Official Code of Georgia Annotated Section 14-2-140(8) reads:

> "Employee" includes an officer but not a director. A director may accept duties that make him also an employee.

Defendant's expert witness, an Atlanta lawyer and CPA, testified that, "in my opinion, by definition, an officer of the corporation is an employee of the corporation." It is undisputed that defendant was an officer of Woods and Water. As such, he was an employee of the corporation. The government has presented no evidence that defendant personally kept any commissions for trips sold (rather than turning them over to the corporation). Admittedly, some persons may refer to themselves as self-employed when they are sole owners of a corporation. That does not make them self-employed. We see no basis for permitting the jury to conclude that defendant was self-employed simply because he owned all the stock in the corporation and was its president. Payments by a corporation for the president's services require withholding and W-2's, as with all wages. Other questions on the form asked for information regarding salaried employment and employment other than self-employment, as well as whether defendant was employed in any manner. However, defendant was not indicted for giving false answers to those questions. The indictment here simply failed to charge the making of false answers to the questions which were falsely answered but instead charged the making of false answers to the questions where the answers were not false.

The government relies on the dictionary definition of self-employed as "making a living working for oneself rather than others." Webster II New Riverside Dictionary (1988). However, where one works for a corporation, he or she works for another, namely the corporation, a distinct legal entity which must file its own separate reports to the state of incorporation and its own income tax. The corporate income tax returns of Woods and Water showed substantial receipts. There was no evidence here that the corporation was not in good standing or the corporate structure otherwise ignored so that the jury could pierce the corporate veil. The government also relies on Morgan v. Finch, 423 F.2d 551, 553 (6th Cir.1970), a social security benefits case. The wage earner, an insurance salesman, continued to work while receiving social security benefits. He reported his commissions from policies sold during the year but not on renewal commissions for policies. If he were self-employed, these commissions were required to be included under a prior administrative ruling. If he were an employee, renewal premiums would be considered as earned the year the policy was sold. The court held that whether claimant was an employee or self-employed was a question of fact to be reviewed on a substantial evidence basis. The case does not involve the officer of a corporation. We are unable to find any evidence here that defendant, as opposed to the corporation, received any commissions. It is impossible to tell from the *Morgan* opinion just what evidence there was that Morgan was an employee.

* * * The Eighth Circuit reached an analogous conclusion when it reversed a section 1001 false statement conviction in United States v. Vesaas, 586 F.2d 101 (8th Cir.1978). In that case, the defendant was convicted for

falsely reporting that he had no knowledge of property owned by his deceased mother and himself in joint tenancy. The Eighth Circuit held that defendant's denial of such ownership "cannot constitute a false statement since it is legally impossible to be a joint tenant with a decedent."

> [A] prosecution for a false statement under § 1001 ... cannot be based on an ambiguous question where the response *may* be literally and factually correct.... An indictment premised on a statement which on its face is not false cannot survive.

Here, Hixon's representation that he was not self-employed was, on its face, not a false representation.

The indictment further charges the defendant with "concealing his self-employment and ownership of Woods and Water Outdoor Consultants, Inc." A violation of section 1001 for concealment requires "knowing and willful concealment 'by any trick, scheme, or device' of a material fact." With regard to concealment, therefore, we must determine whether Hixon's self-employment was a "fact" the concealment of which was sufficient to sustain the conviction. Because we have already determined that Hixon was an employee of Woods and Water and therefore not self-employed, Hixon could not be guilty of concealing his self-employment. Nowhere was he asked if he was the owner of any corporation.[5]

Accordingly, we REVERSE Hixon's conviction for violating 18 U.S.C. § 1001.

BATCHELDER, Circuit Judge, concurring.

I concur in this case, but I write separately because my analysis of the issue in regard to the motion for acquittal differs from that of the majority.

The majority has accurately set forth what the indictment did and did not charge in this case, and what the evidence did and did not demonstrate. It is undisputed that the defendant was an officer of his corporation, Woods and Water. It is undisputed that the law applicable to this defendant's employment status is Georgia law, and that under Georgia law an officer of a corporation is an employee of that corporation. Accordingly, it seems to me that because this defendant was an employee of the corporation, he was not, as a matter of law, self-employed. Thus his statement that he was not self-

[5] Similarly, Hixon cannot be convicted for concealing his ownership of Woods and Water. All of Hixon's allegedly fraudulent answers pertained to questions about his employment activity. Nowhere was Hixon asked about any corporate ownership. It was Hixon's status as a corporate officer that made him a corporate employee, not his status as a corporate owner. The questions asking Hixon whether he was employed, self-employed or unemployed, did not require him to reveal his corporate ownership. Consequently, while Hixon might have been guilty of concealing his position as a corporate officer, he was only indicted for concealing his corporate ownership.

employed was not, as a matter of law, false, and therefore he was entitled to a judgment of acquittal unless the evidence permitted a finding that the corporate veil could be pierced. Here, as the majority opinion makes clear, the government simply did not present any evidence that the defendant had done any of the things with regard to the corporation which would permit such a finding. Because the actual falsity of the statement is an element of the offense, a failure of proof on that issue is fatal to a conviction. Therefore, since the evidence presented did not warrant an instruction to the jury on piercing the corporate veil, even if the instruction which the district court gave the jury had been adequate to explain what the jury must consider in determining whether to disregard the existence of the corporation, the district court erred in sending this matter to the jury at all.

It is clear that this defendant intended to make and indeed, did make a false statement to the government. However, he was not indicted for the false statement which he actually made, but for the statement which could only have been false if the government adequately established the identity between the defendant and his corporation. This the government did not do.

NOTES AND QUESTIONS

1. ***Legislative History.*** One of the broadest criminal statutes in the federal criminal code is 18 U.S.C. § 1001, which prohibits material false or fraudulent statements to an officer or agency of the federal government. Professor Stuart Green states:

> The statutory progenitor of Section 1001 was enacted in 1863. Entitled "An Act to Prevent and Punish Frauds Upon the Government of the United States," it prohibited the filing of "false, fictitious, or fraudulent" claims against the government. Passed in the midst of the Civil War, the statute was a response to a "spate of frauds"–particularly, procurement frauds–being committed on the U.S. Government. In 1918, this time at the end of the First World War, the statute was broadened slightly, to cover false statements made "for the purpose and with the intent of cheating and swindling or defrauding the Government of the United States."

Stuart P. Green, *Lying, Misleading, and Falsely Denying: How Moral Concepts Inform the Law of Perjury, Fraud, and False Statements*, 53 HASTINGS L.J. 157 (2001).

Prior to 1996, the statute prohibited false statements to departments and agencies of the federal government. Congress amended § 1001 to apply to any false statement made within the jurisdiction of the executive, legislative, or judicial branch. The amendment largely overruled the Supreme Court's decision in **Hubbard v. United States**, 514 U.S. 695 (1995), which interpreted the statute to exclude statements made to federal courts because it would chill advocacy on behalf of clients. The statute now explicitly covers false statements to all three branches, except that the submission to the legislative branch must be for administrative purposes or in connection with an investigation, and the prohibition "does not apply to a party to a judicial proceeding, or that party's counsel, for statements, representations, writings or documents submitted by such party or counsel to a judge or magistrate in that proceeding." Section 1001 has been used in a wide variety of areas, including false statements to regulatory agencies, to law enforcement agents, and on loan and aid applications.

The key issue in a § 1001 prosecution is whether the statement was "false." The statute covers more than just false statements because the prohibition reaches fraudulent misstatements or omissions.

2. ***"Exculpatory No" Doctrine***. At one time, a defense to a § 1001 charge was fashioned by the lower courts known as the "exculpatory no" doctrine. Under the doctrine, a false response to a question that was limited to a denial of involvement in criminal activity was viewed as not constituting a "false" statement. The rationale of the "exculpatory no" defense was based in part on the Fifth Amendment privilege against self-incrimination, that a person should not be compelled to respond to an agent's question, so a limited denial of involvement in criminal conduct did not otherwise pervert a government function. The Supreme Court rejected the "exculpatory no" defense in **Brogan v. United States**, 522 U.S. 398 (1998), stating that "[w]hether or not the predicament of the wrongdoer run to ground tugs at the heartstrings, neither the text nor the spirit of the Fifth Amendment confers a privilege to lie."

3. ***Concealment***. In addition to affirmative misstatements, § 1001 also makes it a crime to conceal information. In order to be guilty of concealment, the person must have a legal obligation to disclose the information to the government. In **United States v. Safavian**, 528 F.3d 957 (D.C.Cir. 2008), the defendant, a former deputy director of the General Services Administration (GSA), was convicted of concealing information about a golfing trip he planned to take that would be paid for by a lobbyist. The charge arose from his failure to disclose information about the lobbyist's intention to do business with the GSA to an ethics officer in connection with receiving an opinion about the propriety of taking the trip. In overturning the conviction, the D.C. Circuit noted that there was no obligation to make full disclosure to the ethics officer, and therefore no concealment under § 1001:

> [Safavian] points out that officers and employees of the executive, judicial, and legislative branches regularly seek advice from their respective ethics committees. They are encouraged to do so. The value of the advice they receive depends upon the accuracy and fullness of the information they provide. At GSA, as elsewhere in the federal government, the officer or employee making the inquiry may or may not follow the advice of the ethics committee. That he did not

> follow that advice does not in itself constitute an ethical transgression. The prosecutors in this case are mistaken when they write that the GSA "ethics opinion . . . permitted [Safavian] to engage in behavior that would be prohibited if he had disclosed all relevant information." The ethics opinion did no such thing. It was not up to the GSA ethics officers to permit or forbid; their function was to offer advice. It is not apparent how this voluntary system, replicated throughout the government, imposes a duty on those seeking ethical advice to disclose-in the government's words–"all relevant information" upon pain of prosecution for violating § 1001(a)(1). As Safavian argues and as the government agrees, there must be a legal duty to disclose in order for there to be a concealment offense in violation of § 1001(a)(1), yet the government failed to identify a legal disclosure duty except by reference to vague standards of conduct for government employees.

4. ***Fundamental Ambiguity***. Perjury and § 1001 prosecutions often arise from responses to questions posed by the government, which can be in person (e.g., in a grand jury) or on government forms (e.g., a benefits application). The questions are often a problem because of their breadth or ambiguity, that can permit a defendant to argue that an answer was literally true, at least in some sense, thereby precluding a conviction. In **United States v. Strohm**, 671 F.3d 1173 (10th Cir. 2011), the Tenth Circuit distinguished between questions that are "fundamentally" or "arguably" ambiguous. It stated:

> A question is fundamentally ambiguous in narrow circumstances. To qualify, the question must lack a meaning about which men of ordinary intellect could agree, nor one which could be used with mutual understanding by a questioner and answerer unless it were defined at the time it were sought and offered as testimony. That is, the question itself is excessively vague, making it impossible to know—without guessing—the meaning of the question and whether a witness intended to make a false response. The "rule of fundamental ambiguity" serves to: (1) preclude convictions grounded on surmise or conjecture; (2) prevent witnesses from unfairly bearing the risks of inadequate examination; and (3) encourage witnesses to testify (or at least not discourage them from doing so).

A claim of arguable ambiguity is a challenge to the sufficiency of the evidence that the defendant intended to provide a false answer. The circuit court stated, "A question is arguably ambiguous where more than one reasonable interpretation of a question exists. But even so, a witness can still intend, and in fact give, a response that was literally false. The meaning of a prosecutor's question and the truthfulness of a defendant's answer are best left to the jury. To mitigate the ambiguity, the government must present evidence of the examiner's interpretation of the question as well as what the defendant understood it to mean."

A compound question presents a similar problem of ambiguity. Consider **United States v. Rendon-Marquez**, 79 F.Supp.2d 1361 (N.D. Ga. 1999), involving an immigration form that asked the following question: "Have you knowingly committed any crime or offense, for which you have not been arrested; or have you been arrested, cited, charged, indicted, convicted, fined, or imprisoned for breaking or violating any law or ordinance, including traffic violations?" The prescribed form asked for only a "yes" or "no" answer, and the defendant responded in the negative even though he had once been arrested. The District Court granted a judgment of acquittal to a § 1001 charge for the following reason:

> * * * [T]he question that formed the basis of the indictment asked two separate and distinct questions. The form, however, provided space for only one 'yes' or "no" answer. Consequently, either way the defendant answered the question, he was answering truthfully as to one question and falsely as to the other. * * * It follows that the issue in this case could have been easily avoided had the question at issue been drafted to provide for two separate answers. The issue could have further been avoided had the question been written as one complete question which called for one distinct answer. As it now reads it is a compound question that is confusing and ambiguous. Because the defendant Rendon-Marquez's "no" response is literally and factually correct as to the first part of question three, the court finds that the government failed to provide sufficient evidence to establish the element of falsity as required under the statute. Thus, the evidence presented is insufficient to support a conclusion of defendant's guilt.

5. ***Literal Truth for § 1001.*** Much like a perjury prosecution, a false statement charge requires that the statement actually be false, at least when the government does not charge the statement was intended to defraud. In **United States v. Fontenot**, 665 F.3d 640 (5th Cir. 2011), the Fifth Circuit upheld the dismissal of a § 1001 charge against a Louisiana state senator for making a false statement to federally insured banks to obtain mortgage refinancing loans. His loan application did not list a debt he owed to two businessmen who secretly lent him $100,000 in cash for his campaign, which was illegal under Louisiana's campaign finance laws. The circuit court explained why there was no false statement:

> According to the indictment itself, he requested that the loan be in cash and assured the two businessmen that "he would take other steps to conceal the cash loan since it would be a violation of Louisiana's campaign finance law." The superseding indictment further alleges that, true to his word, Fontenot destroyed the two bags that were used in the exchange of the cash between Fontenot and Businessman #1 the next day. Moreover, all parties agree, as the superseding indictment specifically alleges, that the loan violated Louisiana law and public policy. Thus, under the principles of

> Louisiana * * *, we conclude that the cause of the obligation, or the reason the parties obligated themselves, was to circumvent Louisiana's campaign finance law through the covert financing of Fontenot's state senate campaign. As such, the entire agreement, i.e., the contract—such as it may have been—is absolutely null and the "loan agreement," therefore, is deemed never to have existed. If the loan is deemed absolutely null, then there exists no debt under the laws of Louisiana. Or to use the words of the loan application, there is no liability nor any "outstanding debt." We thus hold that, because the money Fontenot received from the two businessmen did not create a "debt," Fontenot did not make false statements on the loan applications when he failed to list the $100,000 as an "outstanding debt."

C. OBSTRUCTION OF JUSTICE

UNITED STATES v. BONDS
784 F.3d F.3d (9th Cir. 2015)

PER CURIAM:

During a grand jury proceeding, defendant gave a rambling, non-responsive answer to a simple question. Because there is insufficient evidence that Statement C was material, defendant's conviction for obstruction of justice in violation of 18 U.S.C. § 1503 is not supported by the record. Whatever section 1503's scope may be in other circumstances, defendant's conviction here must be reversed.

A reversal for insufficient evidence implicates defendant's right under the Double Jeopardy Clause. His conviction and sentence must therefore be vacated, and he may not be tried again on that count. REVERSED.

KOZINSKI, Circuit Judge, with whom Circuit Judges O'SCANNLAIN, GRABER, CALLAHAN and NGUYEN join, concurring:

Can a single non-responsive answer by a grand jury witness support a conviction for obstruction of justice under 18 U.S.C. § 1503?

Defendant, who was then a professional baseball player, was summoned before a grand jury and questioned for nearly three hours about his suspected use of steroids. He was subsequently charged with four counts of making false statements and one count of obstruction of justice, all based on his grand jury testimony. The jury convicted him on the obstruction count and was otherwise unable to reach a verdict.

The jury instructions identified seven of defendant's statements that the government alleged obstructed justice. The jury, however, found only one statement obstructive. That statement was referred to as Statement C at trial * * *:

> Q: Did Greg[, your trainer,] ever give you anything that required a syringe to inject yourself with?
>
> A: I've only had one doctor touch me. And that's my only personal doctor. Greg, like I said, we don't get into each others' personal lives. We're friends, but I don't—we don't sit around and talk baseball, because he knows I don't want—don't come to my house talking baseball. If you want to come to my house and talk about fishing, some other stuff, we'll be good friends. You come around talking about baseball, you go on. I don't talk about his business. You know what I mean?
>
> Q: Right.
>
> A: That's what keeps our friendship. You know, I am sorry, but that—you know, that—I was a celebrity child, not just in baseball by my own instincts. I became a celebrity child with a famous father. I just don't get into other people's business because of my father's situation, you see.

Defendant was again asked about injectable steroids immediately following this exchange and a few other times during his testimony. He provided direct responses to the follow-up questions. For example, he was asked whether he ever "injected [him]self with anything that Greg . . . gave [him]." He responded "I'm not that talented, no." The government believed that those answers were false but, as noted, the jury failed to convict defendant on the false statement counts.

Title 18 U.S.C. § 1503(a), which defendant was convicted of violating, provides in relevant part as follows: "Whoever . . . corruptly or by threats or force, or by any threatening letter or communication, influences, obstructs, or impedes, or endeavors to influence, obstruct, or impede, the due administration of justice, shall be punished as provided in subsection (b)." Known as the omnibus clause, this language was designed to proscribe all manner of corrupt methods of obstructing justice. We have held that a defendant "corruptly" obstructs justice if he acts "with the purpose of obstructing justice."

As should be apparent, section 1503's coverage is vast. By its literal terms, it applies to all stages of the criminal and civil justice process, not just to conduct in the courtroom but also to trial preparation, discovery and pretrial motions. Indeed, it arguably covers conduct taken in anticipation that a civil or criminal case might be filed, such as tax planning, hiding assets or talking to police. And the text of the omnibus clause, in concert with our definition of corruptly, encompasses any act that a jury might infer was intended to "influence, obstruct, or impede . . . the due administration of justice." That's true even if no actual obstruction occurs, because the clause's use of "endeavors" makes success irrelevant.

Stretched to its limits, section 1503 poses a significant hazard for everyone involved in our system of justice, because so much of what the adversary process calls for could be construed as obstruction. Did a tort plaintiff file a complaint seeking damages far in excess of what the jury ultimately awards? That could be viewed as corruptly endeavoring to "influence . . . the due administration of justice" by seeking to recover more than the claim deserves. So could any of the following behaviors that make up the bread and butter of litigation: filing an answer that denies liability for conduct that is ultimately adjudged wrongful or malicious; unsuccessfully filing (or opposing) a motion to dismiss or for summary judgment; seeking a continuance in order to inflict delay on the opposing party; frivolously taking an appeal or petitioning for certiorari—the list is endless. Witnesses would be particularly vulnerable because, as the Supreme Court has noted, "[u]nder the pressures and tensions of interrogation, it is not uncommon for the most earnest witnesses to give answers that are not entirely responsive." Bronston v. United States, [p. 314].

Lawyers face the most pervasive threat under such a regime. Zealous advocacy sometimes calls for pushing back against an adversary's just case and casting a despicable client in a favorable light, yet such conduct could be described as "endeavor[ing] to . . . impede . . . the due administration of justice." Even routine advocacy provides ample occasion for stumbling into the heartland of the omnibus clause's sweeping coverage. Oral arguments provide a ready example. One need not spend much time in one of our courtrooms to hear lawyers dancing around questions from the bench rather than giving pithy, direct answers. There is, for instance, the ever popular "but that is not this case" retort to a hypothetical, which could be construed as an effort to divert the court and thereby "influence . . . the due administration of justice."

It is true that any such maneuver would violate section 1503 only if it were done "corruptly." But it is equally true that we have given "corruptly" such a broad construction that it does not meaningfully cabin the kind of conduct that is subject to prosecution. As noted, we have held that a defendant acts "corruptly," as that term is used in section 1503, if he does so with the purpose of obstructing justice. In the examples above, a prosecutor could argue that a complaint was filed corruptly because it was designed to extort a nuisance settlement, or an answer was filed corruptly because its principal purpose was to pressure a needy plaintiff into an unjust settlement, or that the lawyer who parried a judicial hypothetical with "but that is not this case" was endeavoring to distract the court so it would reach a wrong result. That a jury or a judge might not buy such an argument is neither here nor there; a criminal prosecution, even one that results in an acquittal, is a life-wrenching event. Nor does an acquittal wipe clean the suspicion that a guilty defendant got off on a technicality.

We have no doubt that United States Attorneys and their Assistants would use the power to prosecute for such crimes judiciously, but that is not the point. Making everyone who participates in our justice system a potential criminal defendant for conduct that is nothing more than the ordinary tug and pull of litigation risks chilling zealous advocacy. It also gives prosecutors the immense and unreviewable power to reward friends and punish enemies by prosecuting the latter and giving the former a pass. The perception that prosecutors have such a potent weapon in their arsenal, even if never used, may well dampen the fervor with which lawyers, particularly those representing criminal defendants, will discharge their duties. The amorphous nature of the statute is also at odds with the constitutional requirement that individuals have fair notice as to what conduct may be criminal.

Because the statute sweeps so broadly, due process calls for prudential limitations on the government's power to prosecute under it. Such a limitation already exists in our case law interpreting section 1503: the requirement of materiality. Materiality screens out many of the statute's troubling applications by limiting convictions to those situations where an act "has a natural tendency to influence, or was capable of influencing, the decision of the decisionmaking body." See Kungys v. United States, 485 U.S. 759 (1988). Put another way, the government must prove beyond a reasonable doubt that the charged conduct was capable of influencing a decisionmaking person or entity – for example, by causing it to cease its investigation, pursue different avenues of inquiry or reach a different outcome. * * *

We start with the self-evident proposition that Statement C, standing alone, did not have the capacity to divert the government from its investigation or influence the grand jury's decision whether to indict anyone. * * * Statement C communicates nothing of value or detriment to the investigation. * * *The most one can say about this statement is that it was non-responsive and thereby impeded the investigation to a small degree by wasting the grand jury's time and trying the prosecutors' patience. But real-life witness examinations, unlike those in movies and on television, invariably are littered with non-responsive and irrelevant answers. This happens when the speaker doesn't understand the question, begins to talk before thinking (lawyers do this with surprising frequency), wants to avoid giving a direct answer (ditto), or is temporizing. Courtrooms are pressure-laden environments and a certain number of non-responsive or irrelevant statements can be expected as part of the give-and-take of courtroom discourse. Because some non-responsive answers are among the road hazards of witness examination, any one such statement is not, standing alone, capable of influencing the decision of a decisionmaking body. * * *

Statement C does not, however, stand alone. It was a small portion of a much longer examination, and we must look at the record as a whole to determine whether a rational trier of fact could have found the statement capable of influencing the grand jury's investigation, in light of defendant's entire grand jury testimony. If, for example, a witness engages in a pattern of irrelevant statements, or launches into lengthy disquisitions that are clearly designed to waste time and preclude the questioner from continuing his examination, the jury could find that the witness's behavior was capable of having some sway. * * *

The government charged a total of seven statements, only one of which the jury found to be obstructive. Two of these statements (including Statement C) appear to be wholly irrelevant—verbal detours with no bearing on the proceedings. One statement is "I don't know," followed by a brief explanation for the lack of knowledge. The rest are direct answers that the government claimed were false, all concerning whether defendant's trainer had provided or injected him with steroids. In the context of three hours of grand jury testimony, these six additional statements are insufficient to render the otherwise innocuous Statement C material. If this were enough to establish materiality, few witnesses or lawyers would be safe from prosecution.

N.R. SMITH, Circuit Judge, with whom Circuit Judges WARDLAW, CALLAHAN, and FRIEDLAND join, concurring:

* * * Our conclusion that Statement C could not have "the natural and probable effect" of impeding the grand jury's investigative function stems from two sources: (1) the Government's duty to clarify merely misleading or evasive testimony and (2) relevant precedent indicating that the Government must show that truthful but misleading or evasive testimony must amount to a refusal to testify before it is material. Taken together, these two sources lead to the conclusion that a single truthful but evasive or misleading statement cannot satisfy § 1503's materiality requirement * * *.[3]

The Supreme Court's decision in Bronston v. United States [p. 314], requires the conclusion that Statement C does not violate § 1503. Although *Bronston* dealt with a conviction for perjury, the Supreme Court's language regarding the government's duty to conduct competent and thorough questioning is illuminating. In short, "[t]he burden is on the questioner to pin the witness down to the specific object of the questioner's inquiry." Extending § 1503's reach to transient evasive or misleading statements would obviate the prosecutor's duty to thoroughly examine the witness. It would be contrary to the statute's purpose to allow the government to permit an evasive or

---

[3]In coming to this conclusion, I do not mean to suggest that the materiality of Statement C turns on whether it was truthful. Because Statement C was obviously non-responsive, it could not have constituted obstruction even if it had been false. A witness who is asked about the location of key documents and responds "I am surprised it is raining" is not liable for obstruction regardless of whether it is raining. But if the same witness knows where the documents are and yet claims never to have heard of them, that potentially could be material and so could amount to obstruction. The truthfulness or falsity of a statement alone is not dispositive: the relevant inquiry will be whether the statement was material * * *.

misleading statement to go unchallenged, in the hopes of obtaining an obstruction of justice conviction later. The government is obligated to do all it can to obtain a direct statement in response to its questioning. The truth-seeking function of the grand jury may be impaired by lax questioning as much, if not more than, an inarticulate or wandering answer. * * *

The Supreme Court's materiality standard reinforces *Bronston*'s core holding: we should not find liability for a single statement that is merely misleading or evasive. The judicially-created materiality requirement is a primary objective limitation on § 1503's expansive reach. This materiality standard necessarily takes into account the context of the charged conduct, evaluating whether the misleading or evasive statement could have the natural and probable effect of interfering with the due administrative of justice given the entirety of a witness's examination The Government may not isolate a single statement, prove it misleading or evasive, and argue that the statement is material based solely on that fact.

Evasive or misleading statements are different from false statements. Instead of providing the tribunal with bad information, information that can be evaluated for its capability to influence, a misleading or evasive statement is meant to divert or slow the truth-seeking function in the first instance; it does not so much influence an investigation as divert it by depriving the question of its force. In this sense, offering evasive or misleading testimony is closely analogous to the destruction of evidence. We should evaluate the materiality of evasive or misleading testimony the same way: for its capability to impede the investigative function of the grand jury. * * *

[T]he "natural and probable effect" of a single true but evasive response to the government's questioning is not to impede the grand jury but, rather, to prompt follow-up questioning. A statement that "goes off into the cosmos" merely triggers the prosecutor's duty to pin the witness down and elicit a clear response. Indeed, that is exactly what happened in this case. Faced with a rambling response, the prosecutor restated the same question and elicited a direct, unambiguous answer from Bonds: "No." No rational juror could conclude that Bonds refused to answer the question; it is plain in the record that Bonds gave his testimony to the grand jury. Further, this is thus not a situation in which a witness testified evasively for so long and with such persistence that the grand jury's investigation would likely have been thwarted, as would be required for the testimony to be material. Statement C was therefore not material, and Bonds's conviction must be reversed.

[The concurring opinions of Circuit Judges Reinhardt and Fletcher have been deleted.]

RAWLINSON, Circuit Judge, dissenting:

There is no joy in this dissenting judge. The per curiam and concurring opinions have struck out.[1]

Strike One–The per curiam and concurring opinions second-guess the jury's verdict rather than deferring to it.

I join the principal concurring opinion [of Judge Kozinski] in its view that context matters in determining whether sufficient evidence supports the conviction in this case A vital part of that context is the evidence before the jury. After all, it is that evidence we examine to determine whether any reasonable juror could have convicted the defendant. In doing so, we view the evidence in the light most favorable to the prosecution. * * *

At the trial of this matter, the jurors were informed that the charges against Bonds stemmed from his appearance before a grand jury investigating steroid use by athletes. * * * Prior to his grand jury testimony, Bonds was granted immunity from prosecution if he complied with the immunity order. * * * The purpose of immunizing a witness in exchange for his testimony is to ensure that the witness, freed from the specter of prosecution, will provide complete and truthful testimony. Giving evasive testimony is inconsistent with the obligation to provide complete and truthful testimony. * * *

At trial, Special Agent Novitsky described the BALCO Laboratories investigation primarily involving the distribution of anabolic steroids. One of the principal targets of the criminal investigation was Greg Anderson, Bonds' fitness trainer. According to Agent Novitsky, execution of search warrants at BALCO Laboratories produced a "treasure [trove] of drugs and documents indicating usage and distribution [of anabolic steroids] to elite professional athletes." * * *

It was against this backdrop that Bonds was immunized and brought before the grand jury to testify, with the grand jury process considered a continuation of the investigation. Bonds was not a target of the grand jury. Rather, he and other athletes were expected to testify candidly and truthfully to further the investigation into those who were the targets of the grand jury.

Agent Novitsky testified that the inconsistencies between Bonds' testimony and other evidence before the grand jury regarding the relationship between the athletes and the steroid distributors, including the evasions, required the investigators to conduct additional inquiries that would not have been necessary had Bonds given non-evasive testimony. ***

As the principal concurring opinion acknowledges, § 1503 sweeps broadly. Applying that broad statute to the facts of this case, we must

---

[1]Apologies to Ernest Lawrence Thayer, Casey at the Bat (1888) ("But there is no joy in Mudville – Mighty Casey has struck out.").

determine whether there was sufficient evidence before the jury that Bonds sought to corruptly impede the work of the grand jury. We are not called upon to determine how far § 1503 can be prudentially applied. Nor need we decide whether attorneys at oral argument could be prosecuted for giving evasive answers to questions from members of the oral argument panel. Such a discussion is more akin to resolving a claim that a statute is overbroad, an issue that is not before us in this appeal. In any event, a hypothetical overreach of the statute cannot affect Bonds' conviction for conduct that falls squarely within the statute.

The jury necessarily found that Bonds' evasive testimony was material because it was instructed that it had to make that finding before Bonds could be convicted of violating § 1503. Nevertheless, the principal concurring opinion relies upon the "self-evident" proposition that Bonds' evasive statement "did not have the capacity to divert the government from its investigation . . ." But this conclusion ignores Agent Novitzky's testimony and the jury's finding of fact. At a minimum, the jury's finding is supported by Agent Novitsky's testimony that Bonds' evasive responses diverted and impeded the investigation by requiring the investigators to determine whether Bonds was being injected with steroids unknowingly, and whether Bonds' inconsistent testimony compromised the testimony of the other witnesses. The jury chose among reasonable constructions of the evidence, and we must respect that choice rather than second-guess it as the concurring opinions do.

Strike Two–The per curiam and concurring opinions disregard precedent that supports upholding the jury's verdict.

This is not the first time we have considered whether evasive testimony may serve as the basis for an obstruction of justice charge. It may be the first time we have considered the statute as applied to a famous athlete. But that should not be the deciding factor, and there is no other reason to interpret the statute differently in this case. * * *

Once Bonds acted with the intent to evade giving the testimony that was compelled by the immunity order, the obstruction of justice offense was complete. Even if Bonds eventually ceased his evasive efforts, his prior intent to obstruct was not negated. Bonds' evasive testimony could and did interfere with the continued BALCO investigation as reflected in the testimony of Agent Novitsky. * * *

Strike Three–The concurring opinions rely on precedent more applicable to perjury than to obstruction of justice.

* * * In *Bronston*, the United States Supreme Court addressed the perjury statute, 18 U.S.C. § 1621 (not the obstruction of justice statute, 18 U.S.C. § 1503), and decided the issue of whether a witness may be convicted of perjury for giving an answer that is literally true, but non-responsive to

the question asked. There was absolutely no discussion of evasive testimony or obstruction of justice. * * *

Application of *Bronston*'s literal truth analysis guts the obstruction of justice provision prohibiting any attempt to "corruptly ... endeavor to influence ... or impede any grand or petit juror ..." 18 U.S.C. § 1503(a). Equating obstruction of justice with perjury actually superimposes the heightened knowledge requirement contained in the perjury statute upon the "endeavor to influence or impede" provisions of the obstruction statute. 18 U.S.C. § 1503(a); cf. 18 U.S.C. § 1621(1). Specifically, *Bronston*'s requirement that an attorney must ask clarifying questions in order to cure potentially perjurious testimony should not be extended to a witness afforded immunity who attempts to obstruct a grand jury investigation through misleading and evasive answers. Bonds was liable for obstruction of justice at the moment he endeavored to influence or impede the grand jury's investigation with his misleading and evasive answer to the government's direct and unambiguous question. * * *

Final Pitch

Barry Bonds received a grant of immunity in exchange for his truthful and candid testimony before the grand jury. Rather than aiding the grand jury in its investigatory quest, Bonds elected to obstruct the grand jury process by giving evasive testimony. There is sufficient evidence to support his conviction because the jury was instructed that it must find his evasive testimony to be material before rendering a guilty verdict. In my view, the per curiam and concurring opinions impermissibly second-guess the jury verdict, disregard our precedent, create an unwarranted circuit split and import inapplicable principles from *Bronston* into the obstruction of justice analysis. I cry foul.

NOTES AND QUESTIONS

1.***Nexus Requirment.*** In **United States v. Aguilar**, 515 U.S. 593 (1995), the Supreme Court discussed the scope of the Omnibus Clause in §1503, which it described as a "catch-all" provision:

> The action taken by the accused must be with an intent to influence judicial or grand jury proceedings; it is not enough that there be an intent to influence some ancillary proceeding, such as an investigation independent of the court's or grand jury's authority. Some courts have phrased this showing as a "nexus" requirement–that the act must have a relationship in time, causation, or logic with the judicial proceedings. In other words, the endeavor must have the "natural and probable effect" of interfering with the due administration of justice. This is not to say that the defendant's actions need be successful; an "endeavor" suffices. But * * * if the defendant lacks knowledge that his actions are likely to

affect the judicial proceeding, he lacks the requisite intent to obstruct.

2. ***Agency Proceedings.*** Section 1505 reaches any person who "corruptly . . . endeavors to influence, obstruct, or impede the due and proper administration of the law under which any *pending proceeding* is being had before any department or agency of the United States" or congressional investigation. While § 1503 applies to judicial proceedings, including civil actions, § 1505 applies to proceedings before administrative agencies in the Executive Branch and inquiries undertaken by the Legislative Branch. For example, in **United States v. Stewart**, 433 F.3d 273 (2d Cir. 2006), Martha Stewart and Peter Bacanovic were charged with offenses including a conspiracy to violate § 1505. The charges arose from "their answers to questions to government investigators who were probing trading activity of ImClone Systems, Inc. ("ImClone") stock ahead of the company's public announcement that its lead pharmaceutical product [the cancer-treating drug Erbitux] would not receive government approval." "In connection with the investigation, Stewart was interviewed twice," by the Securities and Exchange Commission ("SEC"), and other government agencies. Although Stewart nor Bacanovic received sentences that included five months' incarceration, neither were charged with insider trading.

3. ***The Demise of Arthur Andersen.*** In 2002, as Enron Corporation was engulfed in an accounting scandal that eventually led to its bankruptcy, the company's outside auditor, Arthur Andersen LLP, instructed employees to destroy documents pursuant to its "document retention policy." It was charged with obstruction of justice in violation of 18 U.S.C. § 1512, which made it a crime to "knowingly . . . corruptly" persuade another person to alter a document in connection with an official proceeding. A jury convicted Arthur Andersen after deliberating for 7 days, and the firm then gave up its licenses and ceased doing business as an accounting and auditing firm. In **Arthur Andersen LLP v. United States**, 544 U.S. 696 (2005), the Court reversed this conviction finding that the jury instructions were flawed because they did not properly instruct on the elements of a "corrup[t] persuas[ion]" under § 1512(b). The Court focused on the failure to distinguish between "knowingly" and "corruptly." The Court stated:

> In this case, our attention is focused on what it means to "knowingly . . . corruptly persuad[e]" another person "with intent to . . . cause" that person to "withhold" documents from, or "alter" documents for use in, an "official proceeding."
>
> "We have traditionally exercised restraint in assessing the reach of a federal criminal statute, both out of deference to the prerogatives of Congress, Dowling v. United States, 473 U.S. 207, (1985), and out of concern that 'a fair warning should be given to the world in language that the common world will understand, of what the law intends to do if a certain line is passed,' * * *

Such restraint is particularly appropriate here, where the act underlying the conviction — "persua[sion]" — is by itself innocuous. Indeed, "persuad[ing]" a person "with intent to . . . cause" that person to "withhold" testimony or documents from a Government proceeding or Government official is not inherently malign. Consider, for instance, a mother who suggests to her son that he invoke his right against compelled self-incrimination, see U.S. CONST., AMDT. 5, or a wife who persuades her husband not to disclose marital confidences, * * * Nor is it necessarily corrupt for an attorney to "persuad[e]" a client "with intent to . . . cause" that client to "withhold" documents from the Government.

"Document retention policies," which are created in part to keep certain information from getting into the hands of others, including the Government, are common in business. It is, of course, not wrongful for a manager to instruct his employees to comply with a valid document retention policy under ordinary circumstances.

Acknowledging this point, the parties have largely focused their attention on the word "corruptly" as the key to what may or may not lawfully be done in the situation presented here. Section 1512(b) punishes not just "corruptly persuad[ing]" another, but "knowingly (3)27 corruptly persuad[ing]" another. (Emphasis added.) The Government suggests that "knowingly" does not modify "corruptly persuades," but that is not how the statute most naturally reads. It provides the mens rea – "knowingly" – and then a list of acts – "uses intimidation or physical force, threatens, or corruptly persuades." We have recognized with regard to similar statutory language that the mens rea at least applies to the acts that immediately follow, if not to other elements down the statutory chain. * * *

The parties have not pointed us to another interpretation of "knowingly . . . corruptly" to guide us here. In any event, the natural meaning of these terms provides a clear answer. "[K]nowledge" and "knowingly" are normally associated with awareness, understanding, or consciousness. See BLACK'S LAW DICTIONARY 888 (8th ed.2004); WEBSTER'S THIRD NEW INTERNATIONAL DICTIONARY 1252-1253 (1993); AMERICAN HERITAGE DICTIONARY OF THE ENGLISH LANGUAGE 725 (1981). "Corrupt" and "corruptly" are normally associated with wrongful, immoral, depraved, or evil. Joining these meanings together here makes sense both linguistically and in the statutory scheme. Only persons conscious of wrongdoing can be said to "knowingly . . . corruptly persuad[e]." And limiting criminality to persuaders conscious of their wrongdoing sensibly allows § 1512(b) to reach only those with the level of "culpability . . . we usually require in order to impose criminal liability." * * *

The outer limits of this element need not be explored here because the jury instructions at issue simply failed to convey the requisite consciousness of wrongdoing. Indeed, it is striking how little culpability the instructions required. For example, the jury was told that, "even if [petitioner] honestly and sincerely believed that its conduct was lawful, you may find [petitioner] guilty." The instructions also diluted the meaning of "corruptly" so that it covered innocent conduct.

4. ***Legislative Response to Andersen***. In response to a perceived gap in the statutory coverage in connection with the document destruction by Arthur Andersen, Congress expanded the scope of § 1512 as part of the Sarbanes-Oxley Act of 2002. The new provision now reaches any person who "corruptly . . . (1) alters, destroys, mutilates, or conceals a record, document, or other object, or attempts to do so, with the intent to impair the object's integrity or availability for use in an *official proceeding*; or (2) otherwise obstructs, influences, or impedes any official proceeding, or attempts to do so." Unlike § 1503, which only covers judicial and grand jury proceedings, § 1512(c) is now much broader because the statute states that "an official proceeding need not be pending or about to be instituted at the time of the offense." The Sarbanes-Oxley Act also added two additional obstruction statutes: §§ 1519 and 1520. Section 1520 requires auditors of a publicly traded company to "maintain all audit or review workpapers for a period of 5 years from the end of the fiscal period in which the audit or review was concluded," and any destruction of such records is a separate criminal offense. The Court examined the reach of § 1519 below:

YATES v. UNITED STATES

135 S.Ct. 1074 (2015)

Justice GINSBURG announced the judgment of the Court and delivered an opinion, in which THE CHIEF JUSTICE, Justice BREYER, and Justice SOTOMAYOR join.

John Yates, a commercial fisherman, caught undersized red grouper in federal waters in the Gulf of Mexico. To prevent federal authorities from confirming that he had harvested undersized fish, Yates ordered a crew member to toss the suspect catch into the sea. For this offense, he was charged with, and convicted of, violating 18 U.S.C. § 1519, which provides:

> Whoever knowingly alters, destroys, mutilates, conceals, covers up, falsifies, or makes a false entry in any record, document, or tangible object with the intent to impede, obstruct, or influence the investigation or proper administration of any matter within the jurisdiction of any department or agency of the United States or any case filed under title 11, or in relation to or contemplation of any such matter or case, shall be fined under this title, imprisoned not more than 20 years, or both.

Yates was also indicted and convicted under § [18 U.S.C. §] 2232(a),*** Yates does not contest his conviction for violating § 2232(a) * * *

On August 23, 2007, the *Miss Katie,* a commercial fishing boat, was six days into an expedition in the Gulf of Mexico. * * * Engaged in a routine offshore patrol to inspect both recreational and commercial vessels, Officer John Jones of the Florida Fish and Wildlife Conservation Commission decided to board the *Miss Katie* to check on the vessel's compliance with fishing rules. * * * Because he had been deputized as a federal agent by the National Marine Fisheries Service, Officer Jones had authority to enforce federal, as well as state, fishing laws.

Upon boarding the *Miss Katie,* Officer Jones noticed three red grouper that appeared to be undersized hanging from a hook on the deck. At the time, federal conservation regulations required immediate release of red grouper less than 20 inches long. * * * Violation of those regulations is a civil offense punishable by a fine or fishing license suspension. * * *

Suspecting that other undersized fish might be on board, Officer Jones proceeded to inspect the ship's catch, setting aside and measuring only fish that appeared to him to be shorter than 20 inches. Officer Jones ultimately determined that 72 fish fell short of the 20–inch mark. * * * With few exceptions, the measured fish were between 19 and 20 inches; three were less than 19 inches; none were less than 18.75 inches. After separating the fish measuring below 20 inches from the rest of the catch by placing them in wooden crates, Officer Jones directed Yates to leave the fish, thus segregated, in the crates until the *Miss Katie* returned to port. Before departing, Officer Jones issued Yates a citation for possession of undersized fish.

Four days later, after the *Miss Katie* had docked in Cortez, Florida, Officer Jones measured the fish contained in the wooden crates. This time, however, the measured fish, although still less than 20 inches, slightly exceeded the lengths recorded on board. * * * Under questioning, one of the crew members admitted that, at Yates's direction, he had thrown overboard the fish Officer Jones had measured at sea, and that he and Yates had replaced the tossed grouper with fish from the rest of the catch.

For reasons not disclosed in the record before us, more than 32 months passed before criminal charges were lodged against Yates. On May 5, 2010, he was indicted for destroying property to prevent a federal seizure, in violation of § 2232(a), and for destroying, concealing, and covering up undersized fish to impede a federal investigation, in violation of § 1519.[2] By

[2] Yates was also charged with making a false statement to federal law enforcement officers, in violation of 18 U.S.C. § 1001(a)(2). That charge, on which Yates was acquitted, is not relevant to our analysis.

the time of the indictment, the minimum legal length for Gulf red grouper had been lowered from 20 inches to 18 inches. * * * No measured fish in Yates's catch fell below that limit. * * *

Yates was tried on the criminal charges in August 2011. * * * For violating § 1519 and § 2232(a), the court sentenced Yates to imprisonment for 30 days, followed by supervised release for three years. * * * For life, he will bear the stigma of having a federal felony conviction. We * * * now reverse the Eleventh Circuit's judgment.

The Sarbanes–Oxley Act, all agree, was prompted by the exposure of Enron's massive accounting fraud and revelations that the company's outside auditor, Arthur Andersen LLP, had systematically destroyed potentially incriminating documents. The Government acknowledges that § 1519 was intended to prohibit, in particular, corporate document-shredding to hide evidence of financial wrongdoing. * * * In the Government's view, § 1519 extends beyond the principal evil motivating its passage. The words of § 1519, the Government argues, support reading the provision as a general ban on the spoliation of evidence, covering all physical items that might be relevant to any matter under federal investigation.

Yates urges a contextual reading of § 1519, tying "tangible object" to the surrounding words, the placement of the provision within the Sarbanes–Oxley Act, * * *. Section 1519, he maintains, targets not all manner of evidence, but records, documents, and tangible objects used to preserve them, *e.g.*, computers, servers, and other media on which information is stored. * * *

The ordinary meaning of an "object" that is "tangible," as stated in dictionary definitions, is "a discrete ... thing," Webster's Third New International Dictionary 1555 (2002), that "possess[es] physical form," Black's Law Dictionary 1683 (10th ed. 2014). From this premise, the Government concludes that "tangible object," as that term appears in § 1519, covers the waterfront, including fish from the sea.

Whether a statutory term is unambiguous, however, does not turn solely on dictionary definitions of its component words. Rather, "[t]he plainness or ambiguity of statutory language is determined [not only] by reference to the language itself, [but as well by] the specific context in which that language is used, and the broader context of the statute as a whole." * * * In law as in life, however, the same words, placed in different contexts, sometimes mean different things. * * * Familiar interpretive guides aid our construction of the words "tangible object" as they appear in § 1519.

We note first § 1519's caption: "Destruction, alteration, or falsification of records in Federal investigations and bankruptcy." That heading conveys no suggestion that the section prohibits spoliation of any and all physical evidence, however remote from records. Neither does the title of the section of the Sarbanes–Oxley Act in which § 1519 was placed, § 802: "Criminal penalties for altering documents." * * * Furthermore, § 1520, the only other provision passed as part of § 802, is titled "Destruction of corporate audit records" and addresses only that specific subset of records and documents. While these headings are not commanding, they supply cues that Congress did not intend "tangible object" in § 1519 to sweep within its reach physical objects of every kind, including things no one would describe as records, documents, or devices closely associated with them. * * *

Section 1519's position within Chapter 73 of Title 18 further signals that § 1519 was not intended to serve as a cross-the-board ban on the destruction of physical evidence of every kind. Congress placed § 1519 (and its companion provision § 1520) at the end of the chapter, following immediately after the pre-existing § 1516, § 1517, and § 1518, each of them prohibiting obstructive acts in specific contexts. See § 1516 (audits of recipients of federal funds); § 1517 (federal examinations of financial institutions); § 1518 (criminal investigations of federal health care offenses). * * *

The words immediately surrounding "tangible object" in § 1519—"falsifies, or makes a false entry in any record [or] document"—also cabin the contextual meaning of that term. * * * we rely on the principle of *noscitur a sociis*—a word is known by the company it keeps—to "avoid ascribing to one word a meaning so broad that it is inconsistent with its accompanying words, thus giving unintended breadth to the Acts of Congress." * * * The *noscitur a sociis* canon operates in a similar manner here. "Tangible object" is the last in a list of terms that begins "any record [or] document." The term is therefore appropriately read to refer, not to any tangible object, but specifically to the subset of tangible objects involving records and documents, *i.e.,* objects used to record or preserve information. * * *

This moderate interpretation of "tangible object" accords with the list of actions § 1519 proscribes. The section applies to anyone who "alters, destroys, mutilates, conceals, covers up, *falsifies,* or *makes a false entry in* any record, document, or tangible object" with the requisite obstructive intent. (Emphasis added.) * * *

A canon related to *noscitur a sociis, ejusdem generis,* counsels: "Where general words follow specific words in a statutory enumeration, the general words are [usually] construed to embrace only objects similar in nature to those objects enumerated by the preceding specific words." * * * Had Congress intended "tangible object" in § 1519 to be interpreted so generically as to capture physical objects as dissimilar as documents and fish, Congress would have had no reason to refer specifically to "record" or "document." The Government's unbounded reading of "tangible object" would render those words misleading surplusage.

Having used traditional tools of statutory interpretation to examine markers of congressional intent within the Sarbanes–Oxley Act and § 1519 itself, we are persuaded that an aggressive interpretation of "tangible object" must be rejected. It is highly improbable that Congress would have buried a general spoliation statute covering objects of any and every kind in a provision targeting fraud in financial record-keeping. * * *

Finally, if our recourse to traditional tools of statutory construction leaves any doubt about the meaning of "tangible object," as that term is used in § 1519, we would invoke the rule that "ambiguity concerning the ambit of criminal statutes should be resolved in favor of lenity." * * *

For the reasons stated, we resist reading § 1519 expansively to create a coverall spoliation of evidence statute, advisable as such a measure might be. Leaving that important decision to Congress, we hold that a "tangible object" within § 1519's compass is one used to record or preserve information. The judgment of the U.S. Court of Appeals for the Eleventh Circuit is therefore reversed, and the case is remanded for further proceedings.

Justice ALITO, concurring in the judgment.

This case can and should be resolved on narrow grounds. And though the question is close, traditional tools of statutory construction confirm that John Yates has the better of the argument. Three features of 18 U.S.C. § 1519 stand out to me: the statute's list of nouns, its list of verbs, and its title. Although perhaps none of these features by itself would tip the case in favor of Yates, the three combined do so.

Start with the nouns. Section 1519 refers to "any record, document, or tangible object." The *noscitur a sociis* canon instructs that when a statute contains a list, each word in that list presumptively has a "similar" meaning. * * * A related canon, *ejusdem generis* teaches that general words following a list of specific words should usually be read in light of those specific words to mean something "similar." * * * Applying these canons to § 1519's list of nouns, the term "tangible object" should refer to something similar to records or documents. A fish does not spring to mind—nor does an antelope, a colonial farmhouse, a hydrofoil, or an oil derrick. All are "objects" that are "tangible." But who wouldn't raise an eyebrow if a neighbor, when asked to identify something similar to a "record" or "document," said "crocodile"? ***

Next, consider § 1519's list of verbs: "alters, destroys, mutilates, conceals, covers up, falsifies, or makes a false entry in." Although many of those verbs could apply to nouns as far-flung as salamanders, satellites, or sand dunes, the last phrase in the list—"makes a false entry in"—makes no sense outside of filekeeping. How does one make a false entry in a fish? "Alters" and especially "falsifies" are also closely associated with filekeeping. Not one of the verbs, moreover, *cannot* be applied to filekeeping—certainly not in the way that "makes a false entry in" is always inconsistent with the aquatic. * * *

Finally, my analysis is influenced by § 1519's title: "Destruction, alteration, or falsification of *records* in Federal investigations and bankruptcy." (Emphasis added.) This too points toward filekeeping, not fish. Titles can be useful devices to resolve "'doubt about the meaning of a statute.' "* * * Titles, of course, are also not dispositive. Here, if the list of nouns did not already suggest that "tangible object" should mean something similar to records or documents, especially when read in conjunction with § 1519's peculiar list of verbs with their focus on filekeeping, then the title would not be enough on its own. In conjunction with those other two textual features, however, the Government's argument, though colorable, becomes too implausible to accept. * * *

Justice KAGAN, with whom Justice SCALIA, Justice KENNEDY, and Justice THOMAS join, dissenting.

A criminal law, 18 U.S.C. § 1519, prohibits tampering with "any record, document, or tangible object" in an attempt to obstruct a federal investigation. This case raises the question whether the term "tangible object" means the same thing in § 1519 as it means in everyday language—any object capable of being touched. The answer should be easy: Yes. The term "tangible object" is broad, but clear. Throughout the U.S. Code and many States' laws, it invariably covers physical objects of all kinds. And in § 1519, context confirms what bare text says: All the words surrounding "tangible object" show that Congress meant the term to have a wide range. That fits with Congress's evident purpose in enacting § 1519: to punish those who alter or destroy physical evidence—*any* physical evidence—with the intent of thwarting federal law enforcement.

The plurality instead interprets "tangible object" to cover "only objects one can use to record or preserve information." * * *The concurring opinion similarly, if more vaguely, contends that "tangible object" should refer to "something similar to records or documents"—and shouldn't include colonial farmhouses, crocodiles, or fish. * * * In my view, conventional tools of statutory construction all lead to a more conventional result: A "tangible object" is an object that's tangible. I would apply the statute that Congress enacted and affirm the judgment below.

While the plurality starts its analysis with § 1519's heading, * * *, I would begin with § 1519's text. When Congress has not supplied a definition, we generally give a statutory term its ordinary meaning. * * * As the plurality must acknowledge, the ordinary meaning of "tangible object" is "a discrete thing that possesses physical form." * * * A fish is, of course, a discrete thing that possesses physical form. See generally Dr. Seuss, One Fish Two Fish Red Fish Blue Fish (1960). So the ordinary meaning of the term "tangible object" in § 1519, as no one here disputes, covers fish (including too-small red grouper).

That interpretation accords with endless uses of the term in statute and rule books as construed by courts. Dozens of federal laws and rules of procedure (and hundreds of state enactments) include the term "tangible object" or its first cousin "tangible thing"—some in association with documents, others not. * * * To my knowledge, no court has ever read any such provision to exclude things that don't record or preserve data; rather, all courts have adhered to the statutory language's ordinary (*i.e.,* expansive) meaning. * * *

And legislative history, for those who care about it, puts extra icing on a cake already frosted. Section 1519, as the plurality notes, * * * was enacted after the Enron Corporation's collapse, as part of the Sarbanes–Oxley Act of 2002, * * *. But the provision began its life in a separate bill, and the drafters emphasized that Enron was "only a case study exposing the shortcomings in our current laws" relating to both "corporate and criminal" fraud.* * *

As Congress recognized in using a broad term, giving immunity to those who destroy non-documentary evidence has no sensible basis in penal policy. A person who hides a murder victim's body is no less culpable than one who burns the victim's diary. A fisherman, like John Yates, who dumps undersized fish to avoid a fine is no less blameworthy than one who shreds his vessel's catch log for the same reason. Congress thus treated both offenders in the same way. It understood, in enacting § 1519, that destroying evidence is destroying evidence, whether or not that evidence takes documentary form. * * *

The plurality searches far and wide for anything—*anything*—to support its interpretation of § 1519. But its fishing expedition comes up empty.

The plurality's analysis starts with § 1519's title: "Destruction, alteration, or falsification of records in Federal investigations and bankruptcy." * * * That's already a sign something is amiss. I know of no other case in which we have *begun* our interpretation of a statute with the title, or relied on a title to override the law's clear terms. Instead, we have followed "the wise rule that the title of a statute and the heading of a section cannot limit the plain meaning of the text." * * * The reason for that "wise rule" is easy to see: A title is, almost necessarily, an abridgment. Attempting to mention every term in a statute "would often be ungainly as well as useless"; accordingly, "matters in the text ... are frequently unreflected in the headings."* * *

As an initial matter, this Court uses *noscitur a sociis* and *ejusdem generis* to resolve ambiguity, not create it. Those principles are "useful rule[s] of construction where words are of obscure or doubtful meaning." * * * But when words have a clear definition, and all other contextual clues support that meaning, the canons cannot properly defeat Congress's decision to draft broad legislation. * * *

Finally, when all else fails, the plurality invokes the rule of lenity. * * * But even in its most robust form, that rule only kicks in when, "after all legitimate tools of interpretation have been exhausted, 'a reasonable doubt persists' regarding whether Congress has made the defendant's conduct a federal crime." * * *

The concurring opinion is a shorter, vaguer version of the plurality's. It relies primarily on the *noscitur a sociis* and *ejusdem generis* canons, tries to bolster them with § 1519's "list of verbs," and concludes with the section's title. * * * Courts sometimes say, when explaining the Latin maxims, that the "words of a statute should be interpreted consistent with their neighbors." * * * But § 1519's meaning should not hinge on the odd game of Mad Libs the concurrence proposes. No one reading § 1519 needs to fill in a blank after the words "records" and "documents." That is because Congress, quite helpfully, already did so—adding the term "tangible object." The issue in this case is what that term means. So if the concurrence wishes to ask its neighbor a question, I'd recommend a more pertinent one: Do you think a fish (or, if the concurrence prefers, a crocodile) is a "tangible object"? As to that query, "who wouldn't raise an eyebrow" if the neighbor said "no"?

In insisting on its different question, the concurrence neglects the proper function of catchall phrases like "or tangible object." The reason Congress uses such terms is precisely to reach things that, in the concurrence's words, "do[ ] not spring to mind"—to my mind, to my neighbor's, or (most important) to Congress's. * * * But the sum total of three mistaken arguments is ... three mistaken arguments. They do not get better in the combining. And so the concurrence ends up right where the plurality does, except that the concurrence, eschewing the rule of lenity, has nothing to fall back on. * * *

If none of the traditional tools of statutory interpretation can produce today's result, then what accounts for it? The plurality offers a clue when it emphasizes the disproportionate penalties § 1519 imposes if the law is read broadly. * * * Section 1519, the plurality objects, would then "expose[ ] individuals to 20–year prison sentences for tampering with *any* physical object that *might* have evidentiary value in *any* federal investigation into *any* offense." * * * That brings to the surface the real issue: overcriminalization and excessive punishment in the U.S. Code.

* * * But whatever the wisdom or folly of § 1519, this Court does not get to rewrite the law. "Resolution of the pros and cons of whether a statute should sweep broadly or narrowly is for Congress." * * * If judges disagree with Congress's choice, we are perfectly entitled to say so—in lectures, in law review articles, and even in dicta. But we are not entitled to replace the statute Congress enacted with an alternative of our own design. * * *

CHAPTER NINE
GRAND JURY INVESTIGATIONS

A. *THE FEDERAL GRAND JURY AS AN INVESTIGATIVE BODY*

At the time of the adoption of the United States Constitution, the grand jury was renowned as "the people's panel," serving as both the "shield" and "sword" of the criminal justice process that the colonists had brought with them from England. The grand jury served as a shield against unfounded and oppressive initiation of prosecution by refusing to issue an indictment when it viewed the Crown's evidence as insufficient or the prosecution simply appeared unjust. Exercising that screening authority, colonial grand juries had shown their independence in refusing to indict various persons who had spoken or acted in opposition to Royalist power (including twice refusing to indict Peter Zenger for seditious libel, although the Crown then proceeded against Zenger by prosecutor's information). The grand jury served as a sword when it investigated on its own initiative and brought criminal charges, even over the opposition of the Crown, by issuing a presentment (an authority colonial grand juries had exercised even against appointed Royal officials and British soldiers). Thus, it was not surprising that the grand jury's powers were given constitutional recognition in the Fifth Amendment, through the provision that no person "be held to answer for a capital or otherwise infamous crime, unless on a presentment or indictment of a Grand Jury."

During the nineteenth century, the grand jury, in many quarters, lost much of its luster. Its value as a shield was questioned by critics who contended that the grand jury was unrepresentative and inefficient, inferior to the magistrate in screening the sufficiency of the prosecution's evidence. A substantial group of states (eventually to become a majority) abolished the requirement that all felony prosecutions be initiated by indictment, thereby allowing prosecutors to proceed by information (ordinarily, only if supported by a magistrate's finding of probable cause at a preliminary hearing). In the federal system, where a constitutional amendment was not a realistic prospect, the only modification achievable by the critics was to authorize the prosecution to proceed by information in noncapital felony cases if defendant waived his right to indictment. See Fed. R. Crim. P. 7(b).

During the twentieth century, in many states the grand jury's investigative role was substantially reduced, though not abolished. With the growing urbanization of communities, grand jurors could no longer be expected to be familiar with the full range of local criminal activity by virtue of their ties to the community. Moreover, with the development of enforcement agencies staffed by full time professionals, investigation of most crimes was now handled more efficiently and effectively by those agencies. In the states that no longer needed the grand jury for screening (i.e., those allowing all felony prosecutions to be brought by information), many communities found that there remained so little need for the grand jury in investigations that grand juries were no longer regularly empaneled. In states where grand juries were continuously sitting for the purpose of screening, prosecutors often utilized the grand jury's subpoena authority to complement police investigations, but reliance upon the grand jury as a primary vehicle for investigation was limited to a narrow range of cases. One area of criminality that continued to be investigated through the grand jury was governmental graft and malfeasance, and it was here that grand juries on rare occasions became "runaways" and instigated investigations on their own initiative, thereby reinforcing the public image of the grand jury as the "people's watchdog against public corruption".

Professor Andrew D. Leipold described the general operation of a federal grand jury:

> The operation of a typical federal grand jury is straightforward. A pool of citizens is summoned at random from the judicial district where the jury will sit. From the group of qualified people who appear, twenty-three are chosen to serve on the jury. The jurors sit for an indefinite period not to exceed eighteen months; the number of days per month when they must actually appear depends on the prosecutor's case load. A district court judge administers the oath and gives the jurors general instructions about their duties. This marks the end of the judge's formal involvement in the process. From that point forward, the prosecutor dictates the course of the proceedings. The most striking feature of grand jury hearings is their secrecy. The press and public are barred from the proceedings, as are suspects and their counsel. Even judges are not allowed in the grand jury room; attendance is limited to the prosecutor, the jurors, the court reporter, and the single witness being questioned. Those who participate in the hearing [except for the witness] are sworn to secrecy, and the court may use its contempt powers to ensure that this silence is maintained even after the case is resolved. Once in session, the grand jury's primary task is to review the cases presented to it by the government. The prosecutor calls and questions witnesses, and presents documentary evidence related to the crime in question. Unlike trial jurors, grand jurors may ask questions of the witness and may discuss the case with the prosecutor as evidence is submitted. After the case is presented, the prosecutor asks the jurors to vote to return an indictment accusing the defendant of a specific crime that the prosecutor believes is supported by the evidence. The jurors then deliberate in private. If at least twelve agree that there is probable cause to believe that the suspect committed the crime, the grand jury returns a "true bill" that, when signed by the prosecutor, becomes the indictment. If the

> grand jury concludes that the evidence is insufficient, it returns a "no bill" (or "no true bill"), and any preliminary charges filed against the suspect are dismissed.

Andrew D. Leipold, *Why Grand Juries Do Not (and Cannot) Protect the Accused*, 80 CORNELL L. REV. 260 (1995). The investigative aspect of the grand jury is often much more important than the adjudicative role, but the individual grand jurors have no real role in conducting the investigation, which is done by the prosecutor.

NOTES AND QUESTIONS

1. ***Investigative Advantages***. Compared to police investigations, grand jury investigations are usually much more expensive, time consuming, and logistically cumbersome. There are certain types of cases, however, in which prosecutors are likely to view the grand jury's investigatory assistance as either essential or highly desirable, and therefore worth the extra costs of the grand jury process. These are primarily cases in which investigators face one or more of the following tasks: unraveling a complex criminal structure, dealing with victims or witnesses reluctant to cooperate, obtaining incriminating information buried in extensive business records, controlling the information revealed about the investigation while it is ongoing and countering the likely claims of the target that the investigation is being used for the purpose of harassment or political manipulation. Criminal activities likely to present such investigative problems include almost the entire range of white collar crime.

The cornerstone of the grand jury's investigative power is its ability to use the subpoena authority of the court that impaneled it. In **Branzburg v. Hayes**, 408 U.S. 665 (1972), the Supreme Court described the broad authority of the grand jury to compel the production of information to aid its investigations:

> Although the powers of the grand jury are not unlimited and are subject to the supervision of a judge, the longstanding principle that 'the public . . . has a right to every man's evidence,' except for those persons protected by a constitutional, common-law, or statutory privilege, is particularly applicable to grand jury proceedings.

The grand jury may utilize the subpoena "duces tecum" to obtain tangible evidence and the subpoena "ad testificandum" to obtain testimony. These are not mere requests for assistance (as in the case of a police officer who asks a witness or suspect to make a statement). Both subpoenas are supported by the court's authority to hold in contempt any person who willfully refuses, without legal justification, to comply with a subpoena's directive. See Fed. R. Crim. P. 17(g) (The court "may hold in contempt a witness who, without adequate excuse, disobeys a subpoena issued by a federal court in that district."). This contempt authority includes both civil and criminal contempt, although Shillitani v. United States, 384 U.S. 364 (1966), directs district courts ordinarily to look first to civil contempt. Under the civil contempt process, the recalcitrant witness is sentenced initially to imprisonment or to a fine (which may increase daily), but the recalcitrant witness may be purged of the contempt by complying with the subpoena. It is said that the recalcitrant witness held in civil contempt "carries the keys of the prison in his own pockets." Civil contemnors who refuse to purge themselves will remain under sentence until the grand jury completes its term and is discharged, although the Recalcitrant Witness Act, 28 U.S.C. § 1826, limits the term to a maximum of 18 months, less than the 36 month maximum term for an extended special grand jury. Moreover, if the information that the contemnor possesses is still needed, the contemnor may be subpoenaed by a successor grand jury and again held in contempt if there is a continual refusal to supply that information. See United States v. Bonds, 608 F.3d 495 (9th Cir. 2010) ("The government tried to prove the source of the samples with the indisputably admissible testimony of a trainer, Greg Anderson, that Barry Bonds identified the samples as his own before giving them to Anderson, who took them to BALCO for testing. Anderson refused to testify, however, and has been jailed for contempt of court."). Courts have held that if imprisonment of a contemnor becomes punitive rather than coercive then the confinement must end. There is no bright line indicating when the nature of the confinement changes. The Recalcitrant Witness Act places an outer limit of eighteen months on the amount of time a grand jury witness can be held, which is the usual term of a grand jury.

2. ***Obtaining Testimony From Reluctant Witnesses***. The grand jury subpoena is especially useful in obtaining information from persons who will not voluntarily furnish information to federal investigative agents (including both those who refuse to provide any information and those who will only give the agent-so-much time or so much information). Faced with compulsory process, which is backed up by a possible jail sentence for contempt, many such individuals not only will testify before the grand jury, but will do so fully (and for such period) as the prosecutor desires. Of course, if the information sought could be incriminating, the witness (unless granted immunity) may still refuse to cooperate by relying on a privilege against self-incrimination. Many persons, however, though unwilling to furnish information voluntarily, will testify before the grand jury without even considering reliance upon the privilege, as incrimination was not their primary reason for previously refusing to cooperate. Thus, a victim of a fraud may refuse to discuss the matter with investigators out of embarrassment over the victim's gullibility or greedy objectives, yet be willing to testify before the grand jury when faced with the threat of contempt. Similarly, an employee may wish to avoid the appearance of voluntarily assisting a federal agency investigating her employer, yet testify freely when the employee can tell the employer that she was forced to do so under the compulsion of a subpoena.

The secrecy requirements of the grand jury process pursuant to Federal Rule of Criminal Procedure 6(e)(2) also may encourage the witness to be more forthcoming. The witness knows that he is in control of who will learn of what has been told to the grand jury (at least until charges are brought[a]). The witness generally is free to inform others of the testimony the witness has given, but the prosecutor's staff (including the agents from federal agencies–such as the FBI–that are assisting the prosecutors in the grand jury investigation), the grand jurors, and all grand jury personnel (e.g., stenographers) are sworn to secrecy. An employee/witness need not inform an employer of being called to testify, or if the witness desires, inform the employer that he or she testified, but not fully reveal what was said in this testimony. Since the witness testifies out of the presence of counsel (who may be receiving his or her fee from the employer), the witness need not even tell counsel exactly what was said before the grand jury.

3. ***"Fishing" For Documents.*** The grand jury subpoena duces tecum offers several advantages over the primary device available to law enforcement agents to obtain records and physical evidence—the search pursuant to a warrant. Unlike the search warrant, the subpoena duces tecum can issue without a showing of probable cause. Indeed, as will be seen in the later sections of this chapter, no showing at all is required as to the likelihood that a particular crime was committed and, at most, a quite lenient standard need be met to connect the records sought to possible criminal activity. Courts recognize that the "paper trail" establishing the presence of white collar offenses is often buried in the offender's everyday business records and therefore "some exploration or fishing necessarily is inherent" in the use of the grand jury subpoena duces tecum to investigate the possible commission of those offenses.

Moreover, even where probable cause could be established, and a search warrant could be obtained, the grand jury subpoena duces tecum often will be preferred for its administrative advantages. For example, there may be a need to obtain so many different types of records from so many different locations that law enforcement officers would find a search highly burdensome if not absolutely impractical. With a subpoena duces tecum, the party served is required to undertake the extensive task of bringing together records from several different locations and sorting through them to collect those covered by the subpoena. At other times, there may be a need to obtain records from uninvolved third parties (e.g., a bank) and a subpoena will be preferred over a search because it will be far less disruptive to the third party's operations. Subpoenas to certain types of businesses, such as banks or internet service providers, are subject to separate restrictions on the grand jury's right to obtain evidence without notifying the account owner. On the other hand, the search warrant offers the advantage of a direct seizure of the

---

[a] If a prosecution is brought and if the grand jury witness is called to testify as a prosecution witness at the trial, then the defendant will have a right to discover at that point the witness' prior grand jury testimony. See 18 U.S.C. § 3500(e) (including grand jury testimony within the Jencks Act provision governing a trial witness' prior recorded statements).

records, in contrast to a subpoena that provides the recipient with time to respond and, possibly, to destroy records. See Chapter 12 for a discussion of the advantages and disadvantages of search warrants.

B. THE GRAND JURY SUBPOENA

1. ***Federal Rule of Criminal Procedure 17.*** Grand jury subpoenas are governed by Federal Rule of Criminal Procedure 17, which deals with subpoenas utilized for proceedings of all types in the federal district court.[b] Subsection (a) of that Rule sets forth the basic requirements for the issuance and form of the subpoena. It provides that "[t]he clerk must issue a blank subpoena–signed and sealed–to the party requesting it," and that party must fill in the blanks by providing "the court's name and the title of the proceeding, include the seal of the court, and command the witness to attend and testify at the time and place the subpoena specifies." Because a grand jury proceeding has no title, unlike a filed case, the direction on the subpoena is simply is to give testimony "before the grand jury").[c] Ordinarily, the grand jury is not informed before the issuance of a subpoena, although in some districts the custom is to notify the grand jurors shortly afterwards.

Rule 17(c)(1) deals with the subpoena duces tecum by providing that it may require the recipient "may order the witness to produce any books, papers, documents, data, or other objects the subpoena designates." Very often the subpoena duces tecum and subpoena ad testificandum are combined in a single document, which then directs the subpoenaed person to appear on the specified date to give testimony before the grand jury and to bring the specified documents or tangible item. Because there is limited space to list items on the subpoena itself, typically the subpoena duces tecum will direct the party to produce such items as are specified in an "attachment" to the subpoena.

The grand jury subpoena is a deceptively simple document that informs recipients when and where they must appear, what documents or other tangible items to bring, and the name of the federal prosecutor responsible

---

[b] In special situations, other provisions also will bear upon the use of the grand jury subpoena. Thus, a subpoena directed to telephone companies and internet service providers for account holder information also is subject to the notice requirements of 18 U.S.C. § 2703; a subpoena directed to a financial institution for a customer's financial records is subject to the additional requirements of 12 U.S.C. §§ 3401 et seq.; a subpoena to a consumer reporting agency must meet the requirements of 15 U.S.C. §§ 1681 et seq.; and a subpoena directed to a foreign government is subject to the limitations imposed by 28 U.S.C. §§ 1602-1611.

[c] Ordinarily, the grand jury need not be consulted prior to the issuance of the subpoena. In some districts, it is the custom to inform the grand jury shortly afterwards of the subpoenas that have been issued on its behalf, and in some, the foreperson will be notified in advance and asked to initial the subpoena. See also pp. 594-95 as to special settings in which grand jury authorization prior to issuance may be required.

for the issuance of the subpoena. In addition the United States Attorney's Manual prescribes the content of an "Advice of Rights" form that must be attached to a subpoena directed to a "target" or "subject" of an investigation. USAM § 9-11.150. As a matter of practice, that form is usually attached to all subpoenas, with an additional attachment added to the subpoena duces tecum. The Advice of Rights form deals primarily with advice regarding the witness' privilege against self-incrimination and opportunity to consult with counsel. However, it also includes a brief description of the "general subject matter of the inquiry," such as the following: "The grand jury is conducting an investigation of possible violations of Federal criminal laws involving: (State here the general subject matter of inquiry, e.g., conducting an illegal gambling business in violation of 18 U.S.C. §§ 1955)." It is common practice also to send to a subpoenaed witness a letter that explains the basics of testifying before the grand jury: that the witness will testify under oath, that the only persons present will be the witness, the grand jurors, the stenographer, and the government attorneys, and that the grand jury will be composed of 16-23 persons drawn from the community. This letter also will refer to the subject of the investigation, but typically will describe it in the same language as the "Advice of Rights" attachment.

2. ***The Attachment to the Subpoena Duces Tecum***. The attachment to a subpoena duces tecum provides the critical content of the subpoena. The specific documents requested will vary with the subject matter of the investigation. Federal prosecutors draft the subpoenas broadly to ensure that all relevant documents are covered. The government does not need to know specifically of the existence of a particular document, although enforcement of a subpoena to an individual–as opposed to a corporation or other organization–may hinge on whether the subpoena recipient can assert the Fifth Amendment privilege against self-incrimination [see Chapter 13]. The subpoena attachment below was reprinted in an appendix to the Supreme Court's opinion in United States v. Hubbell, 530 U.S. 27 (2000) [p. 400]. A grand jury investigating President Clinton's involvement in the Whitewater transactions subpoenaed personal records of Webster Hubbell, a former partner of First Lady Hillary Clinton and later the Associate Attorney General before pleading guilty to mail fraud charges. The investigation sought to determine whether he violated the requirement of his plea agreement to cooperate in the investigation. In the attachment, note especially paragraphs A, B, I, J, and K, which are good examples of the breadth of the documents a grand jury subpoena duces tecum can compel a recipient to produce:

> A. Any and all documents reflecting, referring, or relating to any direct or indirect sources of money or other things of value received by or provided to Webster Hubbell, his wife, or children from January 1, 1993 to the present, including but not limited to the identity of employers or clients of legal or any other type of work.
>
> B. Any and all documents reflecting, referring, or relating to any direct or indirect sources of money of other things of value received

by or provided to Webster Hubbell, his wife, or children from January 1, 1993 to the present, including but not limited to billing memoranda, draft statements, bills, final statements, and/or bills for work performed or time billed from January 1, 1993 to the present.

C. Copies of all bank records of Webster Hubbell, his wife, or children for all accounts from January 1, 1993 to the present, including but not limited to all statements, registers and ledgers, cancelled checks, deposit items, and wire transfers.

D. Any and all documents reflecting, referring, or relating to time worked or billed by Webster Hubbell from January 1, 1993 to the present, including but not limited to original time sheets, books, notes, papers, and/or computer records.

E. Any and all documents reflecting, referring, or relating to expenses incurred by and/or disbursements of money by Webster Hubbell during the course of any work performed or to be performed by Mr. Hubbell from January 1, 1993 to the present.

F. Any and all documents reflecting, referring, or relating to Webster Hubbell's schedule of activities, including but not limited to any and all calendars, day-timers, time books, appointment books, diaries, records of reverse telephone toll calls, credit card calls, telephone message slips, logs, other telephone records, minutes, databases, electronic mail messages, travel records, itineraries, tickets for transportation of any kind, payments, bills, expense backup documentation, schedules, and/or any other document or database that would disclose Webster Hubbell's activities from January 1, 1993 to the present.

G. Any and all documents reflecting, referring, or relating to any retainer agreements or contracts for employment of Webster Hubbell, his wife, or his children from January 1, 1993 to the present.

H. Any and all tax returns and tax return information, including but not limited to all W-2s, form 1099s, schedules, draft returns, work papers, and backup documents filed, created or held by or on behalf of Webster Hubbell, his wife, his children, and/or any business in which he, his wife, or his children holds or has held an interest, for the tax years 1993 to the present.

I. Any and all documents reflecting, referring, or relating to work performed or to be performed or on behalf of the City of Los Angeles, California, the Los Angeles Department of Airports or any other Los Angeles municipal Governmental entity, Mary Leslie, and/or Alan S. Arkatov, including but not limited to correspondence, retainer agreements, contracts, time sheets, appointment calendars, activity calendars, diaries, billing statements, billing memoranda, telephone records, telephone message slips, telephone credit card statements, itineraries, tickets for transportation, payment records, expense receipts, ledgers, check registers, notes, memoranda, electronic mail, bank deposit items, cashier's checks, traveler's checks, wire transfer records and/or other records of financial transactions.

J. Any and all documents reflecting, referring, or relating to work performed or to be performed by Webster Hubbell, his wife, or his children on the recommendation, counsel or other influence of Mary Leslie and/or Alan S. Arkatov, including but not limited to correspondence, retainer agreements, contracts, time sheets, appointment calendars, activity calendars, diaries, billing statements, billing memoranda, telephone records, telephone message slips, telephone credit card statements, itineraries, tickets for transportation, payment records, expense receipts, ledgers, check registers, notes, memoranda, electronic mail, bank deposit items, cashier's checks, traveler's checks, wire transfer records and/or other records of financial transactions.

K. Any and all documents related to work performed or to be performed for or on behalf of Lippo Ltd. (formerly Public Finance (H.K.) Ltd.), the Lippo Group, the Lippo Bank, Mochtar Riady, James Riady, Stephen Riady, John Luen Wai Lee, John Huang, Mark W. Grobmyer, C. Joseph Giroir, Jr., or any affiliate, subsidiary, or corporation owned or controlled by or related to the aforementioned entities or individuals, including but not limited to correspondence, retainer agreements, contracts, time sheets, appointment calendars, activity calendars, diaries, billing statements, billing memoranda, telephone records, telephone message slips, telephone credit card statements, itineraries, tickets for transportation, payment records, expense receipts, ledgers, check registers, notes, memoranda, electronic mail, bank deposit items, cashier's checks, traveler's checks, wire transfer records and/or other records of financial transactions.

3. ***Subpoena Challenges***. The most common ground for refusing to comply with a grand jury subpoena is the assertion of a common law, statutory, or constitutional privilege. The full range of privileges applicable in federal courts apply to grand jury proceedings. See Fed. R. Evid. 1101(d) (noting that the Federal Rules of Evidence "other than with respect to privileges" do not apply in grand jury proceedings). The most prominent of the privileges, at least in the context of grand jury investigations, are discussed in Chapter 15. Ordinarily, claims of privilege do not challenge the subpoena in its entirety. They usually are directed at specific questions asked of the witness testifying pursuant to a subpoena ad testificandum or at specific items demanded under a subpoena duces tecum.

In determining whether to move to quash, the subpoenaed party will weigh various considerations in addition to the legal strength of its objection. In some instances, a successful objection will only result in a narrower government subpoena that will lead the prosecutors directly to what they seek. Where the government has asked for immense quantities of documents, "information control" may best be practiced by giving the government everything that could possibly fall within its demands and then counting on the lack of resources in the prosecutor's office to sort out potentially damaging material. The advent of electronically stored information largely obviates problems caused by a large volume of paper records because investigators can put the files in a searchable format that allows for much more efficient review. On the other side, even when the motion to quash is not likely to be successful, making the motion may force the government to disclose information not otherwise available to the subpoenaed party, and that information may be helpful in later tactical decisions. Also, where the same judge will rule on later issues, including post-indictment objections should the subpoenaed party be prosecuted, there may be value in making a motion–even though likely to fail–where it will familiarize the judge with the questionable character of the investigation.

If the objection is made and rejected, that often ends the matter for the subpoenaed party. The denial of a motion to quash generally is not viewed as a final order, and therefore is not appealable under 28 U.S.C. § 1291, which limits appellate review to the "final decisions" of the district court. In contrast, the grant of a motion to quash is appealable by the government under 18 U.S.C. § 3731. The Supreme Court has consistently rejected the contention that a denial of a witness' motion to quash should be treated as a collateral order, separate from the ongoing proceeding and therefore a final order within § 1291. It has held that a subpoenaed party does not face such a final order unless the party continues to refuse to comply with the subpoena, notwithstanding the rejection of the motion, and the party subsequently is held in contempt. The justification for this requirement was succinctly stated in United States v. Ryan, 402 U.S. 530 (1971): "[W]e have consistently held that the necessity for expedition in the administration of the criminal law justifies putting one who seeks to resist the production of desired information to a choice between compliance with a trial court's order to produce prior to any review of that order, and resistance to that order with the concomitant possibility of an adjudication of contempt if his claims are rejected on appeal." This justification has been held equally applicable to the grand jury setting, for "it is no less important to safeguard against undue interruption of the inquiry instituted by a grand jury than to protect from delay the progress of the trial after an indictment has been found." Cobbledick v. United States, 309 U.S. 323 (1940).

The only exception recognized is for that limited class of cases where the subpoenaed party possesses documents belonging to another, has no substantial interest in challenging the subpoena, and therefore would not stand in contempt. Under Perlman v. United States, 247 U.S. 7 (1918), a party is generally permitted to pursue an interlocutory appeal of a disclosure order if it is directed at a disinterested third party lacking a sufficient stake in the proceeding to risk contempt by refusing compliance. In In re Grand Jury, 705 F.3d 133 (3d Cir. 2012), however, the Third Circuit refused to find *Perlman* applicable to a defunct corporation whose documents were held by a law firm that wanted to appeal the district court's finding that certain records were not protected by the attorney-client privilege or work product protection. The corporation has not been held in contempt because it did not possess the records, and the circuit court held that the district court could order the documents transferred to a designated agent who would then suffer the necessary contempt to provide jurisdiction for the appeal.

The subpoenaed party who stands in contempt after the motion to quash is denied in order to pursue an appeal ordinarily faces civil rather than criminal contempt. Thus, should the party lose on appeal, subsequent compliance with the grand jury subpoena will relieve the person of any further sanctions. However, the party has no assurance that the imposition of contempt sanctions will be stayed pending the appeal. The Recalcitrant Witness Act, 28 U.S.C. § 1826(a), provides: "Whenever a witness in any proceeding before * * * any grand jury of the United States refuses without just cause to comply with an order of the court * * *, the court * * * may summarily order his confinement." Courts do impose the sanction of immediate confinement on occasion, so it presents a real danger for a subpoena recipient. Furthermore, § 1826(b) prescribes that "no person confined pursuant to subsection (a) of this section shall be admitted to bail pending the determination of an appeal taken by him from the order of confinement if it appears that the appeal is frivolous or taken for delay." Where the contemnor is held in confinement pending appeal, § 1826(b) requires that the appeal be expedited, with its disposition coming "no later than thirty days from the filing of such appeal." Hence, the price for pursuing an appeal may be incarceration for thirty days. Note that a lawyer may be required to assert a claim on behalf of a client, including the Fifth Amendment and the attorney-client privilege, and could be forced to suffer the contempt in order to preserve the right to appeal the lower court's decision. Subpoenas to lawyers for information relating to their clients is a growing trend. Therefore, a lawyer representing a client in an investigation runs the risk of being compelled to provide documents and testimony, and may risk his or her livelihood to vindicate the client's rights by going to jail for a substantial period of time. See also Chapter 16.

C. RULE 17(c) OBJECTIONS TO THE SUBPOENA

Rule 17(c) of the Federal Rules of Criminal Procedure permit a subpoena recipient to quash or modify a subpoena on the grounds that it is "unreasonable or oppressive." The Rule does not define that standard, and does not distinguish between subpoenas issued by a grand jury in the course of an investigation and a trial subpoena. The Supreme Court determined the standard for quashing a grand jury subpoena in the following.

UNITED STATES v. R. ENTERPRISES, INC.

498 U.S. 292 (1991)

Justice O'CONNOR delivered the opinion of the Court.

This case requires the Court to decide what standards apply when a party seeks to avoid compliance with a subpoena *duces tecum* issued in connection with a grand jury investigation. * * *

Since 1986, a federal grand jury sitting in the Eastern District of Virginia has been investigating allegations of interstate transportation of obscene materials. In early 1988, the grand jury issued a series of subpoenas to three companies—Model Magazine Distributors, Inc. (Model), R. Enterprises, Inc., and MFR Court Street Books, Inc. (MFR). Model is a New York distributor of sexually oriented paperback books, magazines, and videotapes. R. Enterprises, which distributes adult materials, and MFR, which sells books, magazines, and videotapes, are also based in New York. All three companies are wholly owned by Martin Rothstein. The grand jury subpoenas sought a variety of corporate books and records and, in Model's case, copies of 193 videotapes that Model had shipped to retailers in the Eastern District of Virginia. All three companies moved to quash the subpoenas, arguing that the subpoenas called for production of materials irrelevant to the grand jury's investigation and that the enforcement of the subpoenas would likely infringe their First Amendment rights.

The District Court, after extensive hearings, denied the motions to quash. As to Model, the court found that the subpoenas for business records were sufficiently specific and that production of the videotapes would not constitute a prior restraint. As to R. Enterprises, the court found a "sufficient connection with Virginia for further investigation by the grand jury." The court relied in large part on the statement attributed to Rothstein that the three companies were "all the same thing, I'm president of all three." Additionally, the court explained in denying MFR's motion to quash that it was "inclined to agree" with "the majority of the jurisdictions," which do not require the Government to make a "threshold showing" before a grand jury subpoena will be enforced. Even assuming that a preliminary showing of relevance was required, the court determined that the Government had made such a showing. It found sufficient evidence that the companies were "related entities," at least one of which "certainly did ship sexually explicit material into the Commonwealth of Virginia." * * * Notwithstanding these findings, the companies refused to comply with the subpoenas. The District Court found each in contempt and fined them $500 per day, but stayed imposition of the fine pending appeal.

The Court of Appeals for the Fourth Circuit upheld the business records subpoenas issued to Model, but remanded the motion to quash the subpoena for Model's videotapes. Of particular relevance here, the Court of Appeals quashed the business records subpoenas issued to R. Enterprises and MFR. In doing so, it applied the standards set out by this Court in United States v. Nixon, 418 U.S. 683 (1974). The court recognized that *Nixon* dealt with a trial subpoena, not a grand jury subpoena, but determined that the rule was "equally applicable" in the grand jury context. Accordingly, it required the Government to clear the three hurdles that *Nixon* established in the trial context—relevancy, admissibility, and specificity—in order to enforce the grand jury subpoenas. The court concluded that the challenged subpoenas did not satisfy the *Nixon* standards, finding no evidence in the record that either company had ever shipped materials into, or otherwise conducted business in, the Eastern District of Virginia. The Court of Appeals specifically criticized the District Court for drawing an inference that, because Rothstein owned all three businesses and one of them had undoubtedly shipped sexually explicit materials into the Eastern District of Virginia, there might be some link between the Eastern District of Virginia and R. Enterprises or MFR. It then noted that "any evidence concerning Mr. Rothstein's alleged business activities outside of Virginia, or his ownership of companies which distribute allegedly obscene materials outside of Virginia, would most likely be inadmissible on relevancy grounds at any trial that might occur," and that the subpoenas therefore failed "to meet the requirements [sic] that any documents subpoenaed under [Federal] Rule [of Criminal Procedure] 17(c) must be admissible as evidence at trial." The Court of Appeals did not consider whether enforcement of the subpoenas *duces tecum* issued to respondents implicated the First Amendment.

We granted certiorari to determine whether the Court of Appeals applied the proper standard in evaluating the grand jury subpoenas issued to respondents. We now reverse. * * *

The grand jury occupies a unique role in our criminal justice system. * * * [It] "can investigate merely on suspicion that the law is being violated, or even just because it wants assurance that it is not." * * * As a necessary consequence of its investigatory function, the grand jury paints with a broad brush. * * * A grand jury subpoena is thus much different from a subpoena issued in the context of a prospective criminal trial, where a specific offense has been identified and a particular defendant charged. * * *

This Court has emphasized on numerous occasions that many of the rules and restrictions that apply at a trial do not apply in grand jury proceedings. This is especially true of evidentiary restrictions. The same rules that, in an adversary hearing on the merits, may increase the likelihood of accurate determinations of guilt or innocence do not necessarily advance the mission of a grand jury, whose task is to conduct an *ex parte* investigation to determine whether or not there is probable cause to prosecute a particular defendant. * * * The teaching of the Court's decisions is clear: A grand jury "may compel the production of evidence or the testimony of witnesses as it considers appropriate, and its operation generally is unrestrained by the technical procedural and evidentiary rules governing the conduct of criminal trials." United States v. Calandra, 414 U.S. 338 (1974).

This guiding principle renders suspect the Court of Appeals' holding that the standards announced in *Nixon* as to subpoenas issued in anticipation of trial apply equally in the grand jury context. The multifactor test announced in *Nixon* would invite procedural delays and detours while courts evaluate the relevancy and admissibility of documents sought by a particular subpoena. We have expressly stated that grand jury proceedings should be free of such delays. * * * United States v. Dionisio, 410 U.S. 1 (1973). Additionally, application of the *Nixon* test in this context ignores that grand jury proceedings are subject to strict secrecy requirements. See Fed.Rule Crim.Proc. 6(e). Requiring the Government to explain in too much detail the particular reasons underlying a subpoena threatens to compromise "the indispensable secrecy of grand jury proceedings." Broad disclosure also affords the targets of investigation far more information about the grand jury's internal workings than the Federal Rules of Criminal Procedure appear to contemplate. * * *

The investigatory powers of the grand jury are nevertheless not unlimited. Grand juries are not licensed to engage in arbitrary fishing expeditions, nor may they select targets of investigation out of malice or an intent to harass. In this case, the focus of our inquiry is the limit imposed on a grand jury by Federal Rule of Criminal Procedure 17(c), which governs the issuance of subpoenas duces tecum in federal criminal proceedings. The Rule provides that "[t]he court on motion made promptly may quash or modify the subpoena if compliance would be unreasonable or oppressive."

This standard is not self-explanatory. As we have observed, "what is reasonable depends on the context." In *Nixon*, this Court defined what is reasonable in the context of a jury trial. We determined that, in order to require production of information prior to trial, a party must make a reasonably specific request for information that would be both relevant and admissible at trial. But, for the reasons we have explained above, the *Nixon* standard does not apply in the context of grand jury proceedings. In the grand jury context, the decision as to what offense will be charged is routinely not made until after the grand jury has concluded its investigation. One simply cannot know in advance whether information sought during the investigation will be relevant and admissible in a prosecution for a particular offense.

To the extent that Rule 17(c) imposes some reasonableness limitation on grand jury subpoenas, however, our task is to define it. In doing so, we recognize that a party to whom a grand jury subpoena is issued faces a difficult situation. As a rule, grand juries do not announce publicly the subjects of their investigations. A party who desires to challenge a grand jury subpoena thus may have no conception of the Government's purpose in seeking production of the requested information. Indeed, the party will often not know whether he or she is a primary target of the investigation or merely a peripheral witness. Absent even minimal information, the subpoena recipient is likely to find it exceedingly difficult to persuade a court that "compliance would be unreasonable." As one pair of commentators has summarized it, the challenging party's "unenviable task is to seek to persuade the court that the subpoena that has been served on [him or her] could not possibly serve any investigative purpose that the grand jury could legitimately be pursuing." Sara Sun Beale, William C. Bryson, James E. Felman, and Michael J. Elston, Grand Jury Law and Practice § 6:21 (2nd ed.).

Our task is to fashion an appropriate standard of reasonableness, one that gives due weight to the difficult position of subpoena recipients but does not impair the strong governmental interests in affording grand juries wide latitude, avoiding minitrials on peripheral matters, and preserving a necessary level of secrecy. We begin by reiterating that the law presumes, absent a strong showing to the contrary, that a grand jury acts within the legitimate scope of its authority. * * * Consequently, a grand jury subpoena issued through normal channels is presumed to be reasonable, and the burden of showing unreasonableness must be on the recipient who seeks to avoid compliance. Indeed, this result is indicated by the language of Rule 17(c), which permits a subpoena to be quashed only "on motion" and "if *compliance* would be unreasonable" (emphasis added). To the extent that the Court of Appeals placed an initial burden on the Government, it committed error. Drawing on the principles articulated above, we conclude that where, as here, a subpoena is challenged on relevancy grounds, the motion to quash must be denied unless the district court determines that there is no reasonable possibility that the category of materials the Government seeks will produce information relevant to the general subject of the grand jury's investigation. Respondents did not challenge the subpoenas as being too indefinite nor did they claim that compliance would be overly burdensome. The Court of Appeals accordingly did not consider these aspects of the subpoenas, nor do we. * * *

It seems unlikely, of course, that a challenging party who does not know the general subject matter of the grand jury's investigation, no matter how valid that party's claim, will be able to make the necessary showing that compliance would be unreasonable. After all, a subpoena recipient "cannot put his whole life before the court in order to show that there is no crime to be investigated." Consequently, a court may be justified in a case where unreasonableness is alleged in requiring the Government to reveal the general subject of the grand jury's investigation before requiring the challenging party to carry its burden of persuasion. We need not resolve this question in the present case, however, as there is no doubt that respondents knew the subject of the grand jury investigation pursuant to which the business records subpoenas were issued. In cases where the recipient of the subpoena does not know the nature of the investigation, we are confident that district courts will be able to craft appropriate procedures that balance the interests of the subpoena recipient against the strong governmental interests in maintaining secrecy, preserving investigatory flexibility, and avoiding procedural delays. For example, to ensure that subpoenas are not routinely challenged as a form of discovery, a district court may require that the Government reveal the subject of the investigation to the trial court *in camera*, so that the court may determine whether the motion to quash has a reasonable prospect for success before it discloses the subject matter to the challenging party. * * *

Applying these principles in this case demonstrates that the District Court correctly denied respondents' motions to quash. It is undisputed that all three companies—Model, R. Enterprises, and MFR—are owned by the same person, that all do business in the same area, and that one of the three, Model, has shipped sexually explicit materials into the Eastern District of Virginia. The District Court could have concluded from these facts that there was a reasonable possibility that the business records of R. Enterprises and MFR would produce information relevant to the grand jury's investigation into the interstate transportation of obscene materials. Respondents' blanket denial of any connection to Virginia did not suffice to render the District Court's conclusion invalid. A grand jury need not accept on faith the self-serving assertions of those who may have committed criminal acts. Rather, it is entitled to determine for itself whether a crime has been committed.

Both in the District Court and in the Court of Appeals, respondents contended that these subpoenas sought records relating to First Amendment activities, and that this required the Government to demonstrate that the records were particularly relevant to its investigation. The Court of Appeals determined that the subpoenas did not satisfy Rule 17(c) and thus did not pass on the First Amendment issue. We express no view on this issue and leave it to be resolved by the Court of Appeals. * * *

Justice STEVENS, with whom Justice MARSHALL and Justice BLACKMUN join, concurring in part and concurring in the judgment.

Federal Rule of Criminal Procedure 17(c) * * * requires the district court to balance the burden of compliance, on the one hand, against the governmental interest in obtaining the documents on the other. A more burdensome subpoena should be justified by a somewhat higher degree of probable relevance than a subpoena that imposes a minimal or nonexistent burden. Against the procedural history of this case, the Court has attempted to define the term "reasonable" in the abstract, looking only at the relevance side of the balance. Because I believe that this truncated approach to the Rule will neither provide adequate guidance to the district court nor place any meaningful constraint on the overzealous prosecutor, I add these comments. * * *

The moving party has the initial task of demonstrating to the Court that he has some valid objection to compliance. This showing might be made in various ways. Depending on the volume and location of the requested materials, the mere cost in terms of time, money, and effort of responding to a dragnet subpoena could satisfy the initial hurdle. Similarly, if a witness showed that compliance with the subpoena would intrude significantly on his privacy interests, or call for the disclosure of trade secrets or other confidential information, further inquiry would be required. Or, as in this case, the movant might demonstrate that compliance would have First Amendment implications.

The trial court need inquire into the relevance of subpoenaed materials only after the moving party has made this initial showing. And, as is true in the parallel context of pretrial civil discovery, a matter also committed to the sound discretion of the trial judge, the degree of need sufficient to justify denial of the motion to quash will vary to some extent with the burden of producing the requested information. For the reasons stated by the Court, in the grand jury context the law enforcement interest will almost always prevail, and the documents must be produced. I stress, however, that the Court's opinion should not be read to suggest that the deferential relevance standard the Court has formulated will govern decision in every case, no matter how intrusive or burdensome the request. * * *

NOTE

The Aftermath of R. Enterprises. The Court's analysis makes it almost impossible to win a Rule 17(c) motion to quash, although as noted at pp. 352-53, there may be strategic reasons for bringing the motion, especially if the goal is to convince the government to limit the scope of a subpoena. How much control do the courts have over the issuance of grand jury subpoenas? Grand jury subpoenas are not self-executing, in the sense that a recipient may simply ignore the subpoena and wait to see if the government will seek to compel the person to comply with it. To enforce a subpoena, the federal prosecutor must call on the district court to hold the recipient in contempt, at which point the person can challenge the propriety of the subpoena.

The import of *R. Enterprises* is to limit the scope of review a court can undertake to assess whether a subpoena is enforceable. In **In re Grand Jury Proceedings**, 616 F.3d 1186 (10th Cir. 2010), the Tenth Circuit rejected the district court's review of a grand jury subpoena challenged on relevancy grounds that resulted in the judge redefining the categories of material required to be produced and then engaging in a document-by-document and even a line-by-line assessment to determine whether the material was relevant. The court stated that the reference in *R. Enterprises* to a "category of materials" means the district court

> will assess relevancy based on the broad types of material sought by the Government. This broad analysis forecloses the document-by-document or line-by-line approach to assessing relevancy that the district court took in this case. The district court's approach entails a much more exacting assessment of relevancy than the relaxed, categorical approach articulated by *R. Enterprises* . . . In accord with Rule 17(c)(2), we conclude that the district court may modify the subpoena by quashing entire categories or sub-categories of material as irrelevant, but, under *R. Enterprises*, the district court cannot go further and quash the subpoena as to specific documents within

> those sub-categories (or specific lines within relevant documents). Thus, the district court may consider the relevancy of each category or sub category contained in the subpoena.

The Tenth Circuit went on to state, "[w]e can sympathize with the district court's desire to prevent the grand jury from subpoenaing wholly irrelevant information. Incidental production of irrelevant documents, however, is simply a necessary consequence of the grand jury's broad investigative powers and the categorical approach to relevancy adopted in *R. Enterprises.*"

D. UNREASONABLE OR OPPRESSIVE

In addition to the Fourth Amendment's reasonableness requirement for searches, Rule 17(c) permits a subpoena recipient to challenge the demand for documents on the ground that it is unreasonable or oppressive. Is the test of what is "reasonable" different? Can a defendant challenge a subpoena under both the Constitution and Rule 17(c)? What factors should a district court consider in determining whether the grand jury subpoena is "unreasonable or oppressive"?

IN RE GRAND JURY, JOHN DOE NO. G.J. 2005-2
478 F.3d 581 (4th Cir. 2007)

WILKINSON, Circuit Judge.

This appeal arises from an order by the district court quashing a subpoena duces tecum. The subpoena was issued by a federal grand jury to a City Police Department ("the Department") to obtain the records of the Department's internal investigation into a complaint filed against an officer.
* * *

An individual arrested by the City Police Department filed a complaint with the Department, alleging that a particular officer used excessive force against him in the course of arrest. The complaint resulted in an investigation by the Department's internal affairs office. During the internal investigation, Department officials interviewed various officers, including the officer identified in the arrested individual's complaint. It is Department policy that officers are required to comply fully with internal investigations as a condition of their employment. False testimony or other failure to comply may result in disciplinary action or dismissal. Officers who are questioned as part of an internal investigation are notified in writing that their responses may not be used against them in criminal proceedings. The Department's general written policy on internal investigations reiterates this guarantee and further states that material relating to internal investigations will be treated as confidential. The policy goes on to state, "This is not to imply that such files are not discoverable in legal proceedings."

The United States Attorney's Office and the Criminal Section of the Civil Rights Division of the United States Department of Justice undertook an investigation of the same incident to determine whether it constituted a civil rights violation under 18 U.S.C. § 242 (2000)(deprivation of rights under color of law). In connection with this investigation and at the United States' behest, a federal grand jury issued a subpoena duces tecum requiring the production of documents relating to the Department's internal investigation.

The City moved to quash the subpoena, claiming that compliance would be "unreasonable" pursuant to Federal Rule of Criminal Procedure 17(c) for two reasons. First, the City argued that compliance would destroy the confidentiality of the internal investigation and would thus severely undermine the Department's ability to conduct such investigations effectively. Second, the City contended that compliance would be inconsistent with the interviewed officers' Fifth Amendment rights against self-incrimination. * * *

The United States * * * asserted its own interest in obtaining the information and the grand jury''s power to subpoena it. At the hearing on the City's motion to quash, the government noted that any false statements by officers in the course of the internal investigation might form the basis of an independent charge of obstruction of justice. The government also asserted that it required the internal investigation materials in order to "close . . . the file" on the complaint. Counsel for the United States stated there was "no expectation that [the case] will turn into a prosecutable offense" and that it was "99.9 percent certain" that the civil rights complaint was "a bunch of baloney."

The district court granted the City's motion to quash the subpoena. The court found that both the City and the United States asserted highly significant law enforcement interests with respect to the "'policing' of the police." The court found that the City established that compliance would pose substantial risks for confidentiality and Fifth Amendment interests, while the United States for its part could easily obtain the desired information by subpoenaing the interviewed officers directly, thus avoiding the risks of self-incrimination, * * * and the potential destruction of the Department's ability to investigate itself. While noting that the interests of the grand jury would as a general matter prevail, the court held that, in this particular instance, the City's asserted interests outweighed those of the United States, and thus compliance with the subpoena would be unreasonable under Rule 17(c). ***

Although the grand jury operates with great independence, "the powers of the grand jury are not unlimited and are subject to the supervision of a judge." Branzburg v. Hayes, 408 U.S. 665 (1972). One such judicial limitation arises from Federal Rule of Criminal Procedure 17(c)(2), which provides that a district judge may quash or modify a subpoena duces tecum "if compliance would be unreasonable or oppressive."

Courts have recognized various ways in which a subpoena may be unreasonable or oppressive under Rule 17(c). Rule 17(c) offers a vehicle for a subpoenaed party to assert a constitutional, statutory, or common-law privilege. In the absence of such a privilege, a subpoena may still be unreasonable or oppressive under Rule 17(c) if it is irrelevant; abusive or harassing; overly vague; or excessively broad. Additionally, some courts have recognized that Rule 17(c) enables district courts to quash a subpoena that intrudes gravely on significant interests outside of the scope of a recognized privilege, if compliance is likely to "entail consequences more serious than even severe inconveniences occasioned by irrelevant or overbroad requests for records." In re Grand Jury Matters, 751 F.2d 13 (1st Cir.1984).

In this case, the City argued that compliance was unreasonable because it would burden the City's significant interests in preserving the confidentiality of its investigations and forestalling the potential violation of officers' Fifth Amendment rights. As the party seeking to avoid compliance with the subpoena under Rule 17(c), the City bore the burden of demonstrating unreasonableness.

To determine whether the City met this burden, the district court balanced its asserted interests against the United States' interests in enforcing the subpoena. This balancing took place with an explicit recognition that a presumption of regularity attaches to grand jury subpoenas; in fact, the district court acknowledged that in most cases the interests in favor of enforcing the subpoena would prevail. Thus the balancing undertaken by the district court did not constitute an abuse of discretion.

Nor did the district court abuse its discretion in concluding that, in this instance, the City's interests outweighed those asserted by the United States. As the Supreme Court has stated with regard to Rule 17(c), "what is reasonable depends on the context." *R. Enterprises.* The factors the district court must consider under Rule 17(c)(2) cannot sensibly be converted into a mechanical rule enabling an escape from case-by-case judgment. We have explicitly left such case-by-case analysis to the district court's considered discretion. The district court acted within its discretion in assessing the factors at issue here.

We address the City's interests initially. First, the district court permissibly took cognizance of the City's very real concern that the Police Department preserve its ability to police itself by maintaining the confidentiality of its investigations. The internal investigation mechanism serves the same purpose as a criminal investigation by the United States Attorney's Office or Department of Justice: to uncover, and ultimately to deter, civil rights violations and other abuses. In many instances, internal investigations may offer the most effective way to pursue those goals. A police department is able to respond to a complaint quickly, while witnesses are still available and memories are still fresh. Perhaps most importantly, a strong and visible internal investigations office is in a unique position to deter misconduct in the first place.

Yet such investigations face an uphill battle due to the so-called "blue wall," the tendency of law enforcement officers to place solidarity above all else and to be less than fully cooperative with investigations of fellow officers. "Officers who report misconduct are ostracized and harassed; become targets of complaints and even physical threats; and are made to fear that they will be left alone on the streets in a time of crisis." Report of the Commission to Investigate Allegations of Police Corruption and the Anti–Corruption Procedures of the Police Department 53 (1994). In such a setting, the confidentiality of internal investigations may be not only desirable but essential. The district court was permitted to recognize that handing the statements over to an outside party or agency, including one involved in criminal investigations, would be perceived by cooperating officers as a serious compromise of confidentiality, notwithstanding the provisions of Federal Rule of Criminal Procedure 6(e).

The United States contends that the subpoena does not disrupt an expectation of confidentiality, because Departmental policy states that its confidentiality safeguards are "not to imply that [internal investigation materials] are not discoverable in legal proceedings." This disclaimer does not change the fact that the policy as a whole reflects the Department's interest in maintaining confidentiality to the fullest extent possible, an understandable concern given the policy's importance to the lawful functioning of law enforcement. The disclaimer certainly does not foreclose any recognition of the importance of confidentiality by the district court.

Moreover, in this case, where the ultimate interests of both federal and local law enforcement are in exposing and deterring police misconduct; where compliance with the subpoena arguably inflicts a lasting harm on the local entity's ability to pursue that goal; and where the federal grand jury has other means to achieve this goal without co-opting the work of the local entity, it is not unreasonable to conclude that principles of federalism require some modest recognition of a local government's efforts which the record leaves no reason to believe were pursued in other than good faith. For these reasons, the district court did not err in recognizing the City's interest in fostering the efficacy of internal investigations by protecting their confidentiality.

Second, the district court recognized the City's concern about the potential for self-incrimination involved in releasing the internal investigation materials. [The district court found that the need to protect the statements made by the officers could be damaged substantially by disclosure to the grand jury.] We note moreover that the district court took the City's two interests—in preserving confidentiality and forestalling possible self-incrimination problems—together, and weighed those interests as a whole against those of the United States. * * * In the absence of the City's assertion of an interest in the confidentiality of its own investigative procedures, this may well have been a different case.

On the other side of the ledger, the district court found the United States' interest in obtaining this particular information, by the specific method of a subpoena *duces tecum*, to be less substantial. The court noted that the federal grand jury could obtain the information by subpoenaing the interviewed officers directly. The district court went too far in this respect, because the existence of an alternative means of obtaining information is insufficient to render a subpoena unreasonable or subpoenaed material irrelevant to a grand jury investigation.

The district court, however, was not required to ignore the fact that counsel for the United States repeatedly suggested that the information sought was of negligible value to the government. Counsel stated that the government merely required the internal investigation materials in order to "close . . . the file," as the government attorneys were "99.9 percent certain" that the complaint was "a bunch of baloney" and there was "no expectation that it [would] turn into a prosecutable offense."

We recognize, of course, that the government has an interest in ascertaining whether a crime has been committed and that in many instances it will be unable to do so until the grand jury has undertaken its own investigation. This interest remains valid, even where, as here, the subpoena is not directed against an individual but against a local entity with an identical interest in investigating whether misconduct has occurred. This being the case, we do not think that the district court was in any sense compelled to quash this subpoena, only that it did not abuse its discretion by taking into account the government's representations.

The United States now argues that the court should ignore its "extremely frank" statements regarding the subpoena and the underlying investigation. But the court is under no such obligation. The government obviously made these statements in the hope that they would influence the district court in its favor, and thus it is in a precarious position to complain that the opposite occurred. The district court was within its discretion to take cognizance of the government's own assessment of its interest in the information.

The court also did not abuse its discretion in crediting these repeated statements over the government's suggestion that the subpoena might uncover evidence that officers lied during the internal investigation and thus provide a basis for an obstruction of justice charge. We certainly recognize that cover-ups and otherwise inadequate procedures on the part of state and local law enforcement entities are a real danger, and that the Department of Justice or the United States Attorney's Office may at times need to investigate not only officer misconduct, but the very procedures by which such misconduct is dealt with at the state and local level. But while fully recognizing these concerns as a general matter, we are confident that the district court properly assessed the government's interest in this case in accordance with the government's own characterization.

We thus conclude on these facts that the district court did not abuse its discretion in finding that the City had established that compliance with the subpoena would be unreasonable under Rule 17(c). A reversal on this record would be a declaration that state and local investigations of possible police misconduct were seldom worthy of federal respect.

NOTES AND QUESTIONS

1. ***Burdensomeness***. Subpoena recipients often claim that a demand for a large volume of documents would be "oppressive or unreasonable" in violation of Rule 17(c) because it is unduly burdensome. See **United States v. Vilar**, 2007 WL 1075041 (S.D.N.Y. Apr. 4, 2007), in which the district court modified a subpoena because of the large volume of records sought from an investment advisory firm. The district court explained:

> A subpoena also may be quashed or modified pursuant to Federal Rule of Criminal Procedure 17(c)(2) if compliance therewith would be overly burdensome. The burden of compliance often derives from the time period covered in the subpoena. With respect to the burdensomeness inquiry, before a movant may seek to quash a subpoena on this basis, courts may require the movant to first seek reasonable conditions from the government to ameliorate the subpoena's breadth.
>
> The Government argues that because no such application was made here, "Defendants' motion to quash must fail." However, the requirement that a movant first seek to modify the subpoena before moving to quash is applied at the discretion of court. And strict application of this requirement would be inappropriate here, where: (1) the movants were not themselves the subpoenaed party and were therefore not directly in a position to seek modification of the subpoena; and (2) Amerindo had already shut its doors and thus faced no further threat that compliance with the Subpoena would be so burdensome as to "put a stop to the business," a consideration that the Supreme Court has stressed.
>
> This is not to say, however, that Amerindo's initial failure to object to the breadth of the subpoena, let alone the Defendants' six-month delay before moving to quash, is irrelevant to this inquiry. Rather, the failure to object is some evidence that counsel for Amerindo U.S. did not in fact find the subpoena burdensome. Nevertheless, looking at the totality of the circumstances, the Court finds that the Subpoena here, in its entirety, was unduly burdensome. As noted, the Subpoena called for the production of every business record possessed by Amerindo, a company that managed $1.2 billion in assets, and nowhere does the Subpoena contain any restrictions based on time frame. In fact, the Subpoena's broadest paragraphs

> make no restrictions even as to content. While it cannot be said that the Subpoena sought wholly irrelevant documents, given the relatively well-defined focus of the Government's investigation and the resulting indictments, a number of paragraphs in the Subpoena were nevertheless excessive. Under the circumstances, however, it is more appropriate to modify the Subpoena than to quash it. See In re Grand Jury Subpoena Duces Tecum Addressed to Corrado Bros., Inc., 367 F.Supp. 1126 (D.Del.1973) ("Only in the most extreme case of a clear showing of unreasonableness, of Government abuse of power, will the Court be induced to quash an otherwise valid grand jury subpoena on the basis that it was overly burdensome."). It must be remembered that the grand jury's investigation included financial fraud and misuse of client funds involving long-time clients over several years. Accordingly, the grand jury is properly given some leeway to seek documents pre-dating the earliest known fraud, as well as documents that may enlighten the grand jury about other potential fraud victims.

2. ***Burden of Proof.*** Why is the burden on the subpoena recipient to accommodate the government when the subpoena is so extensive that it may cripple the defendant's business? Fourth Amendment challenges place the burden on the government to establish there will be no constitutional violation, but in the context of a grand jury subpoena the burden is on the recipient. Is this because the claim is not really based on an alleged violation of the Fourth Amendment claim, but instead a challenge to the reasonableness of the subpoena under Rule 17(c)? If it is really a Rule 17(c) challenge, then the presumption of regularity discussed in *R. Enterprises* may be sufficient to overcome almost any overbreadth claim. What incentive, then, does the government have to write its grand jury subpoenas more narrowly?

3. ***First Amendment.*** In In re Grand Jury Subpoena No. 11116275, 846 F. Supp. 2d 1 (D.D.C. 2012), the district court held that there was a First Amendment right to post anonymously to the internet, so that the government could not subpoena the internet service provider for information about the poster's identity absent a "compelling interest." In that case, the judge found such an interest when the posting to Twitter included a threat against a presidential candidate.

4. ***The Expense of Complying.*** With the availability of photocopying and with many records already stored digitally, claims that document production will substantially impede the continuing operations of a subpoenaed enterprise usually focus on the cost of collecting the records rather than — as in *Hale v. Henkel* — the lost use of the records. The government generally refuses to reimburse parties for their costs in complying with subpoenas, except where the subpoena is governed by the Financial Privacy Act, 12 U.S.C. § 3415, or the Electronic Communications Privacy Act, 18 U.S.C. § 2706, which require reimbursement of subpoena recipients who produce records of their account holders. A few courts have suggested that Rule 17(c)

gives the court sufficient authority to order reimbursement in cases not falling within those statutes. See In re Grand Jury Investigation, 459 F.Supp. 1335 (E.D. Pa. 1978). At the same time, those courts recognize that any such authority is to be utilized only in the most exceptional situation.

The courts note that the prevailing principle is that there is a public obligation to provide evidence and that this obligation persists no matter how financially burdensome it may be. Thus, on a subpoena requiring testimony before a grand jury, the witness cannot gain reimbursement for the true cost of testifying (such as loss of wages or income, etc.), but simply receives a standard attendance fee, plus costs of transportation. Accordingly, it is reasoned, the case for reimbursement must rest on a showing not merely that compliance will be expensive, but that it is essentially beyond the means of the subpoenaed party. See Matter of Midland Asphalt Corp., 616 F.Supp. 223 (W.D.N.Y. 1985) (showing that cost to corporations of complying with grand jury subpoena duces tecum would constitute 41% of their net operating income, but less than 2% of their operating expenses, was insufficient to establish unreasonable or oppressiveness such as to warrant government advancement or reimbursement of such costs).

5. ***Subpoenas As "Seizures."*** Are there any circumstances under which a grand jury subpoena might be viewed as producing a "seizure" triggering the protections of the Fourth Amendment? In United States v. Dionisio, 410 U.S. 1 (1973), the Supreme Court held, "It is clear that a subpoena to appear before a grand jury is not a 'seizure' in the Fourth Amendment sense." The Court quoted the distinctions described by Judge Henry Friendly in United States v. Doe, 457 F.2d 895 (2d Cir. 1972) between a subpoena and an arrest or even an investigative stop: "The latter is abrupt, is effected with force or the threat of it and often in demeaning circumstances, and, in the case of arrest, results in a record involving social stigma. A subpoena is served in the same manner as other legal process; it involves no stigma whatever; if the time for appearance is inconvenient, this can generally be altered; and it remains at all times under the control and supervision of a court."

6. ***The Exclusionary Rule in the Grand Jury.*** In **United States v. Calandra**, 414 U.S. 338 (1974), grand jury witness Calandra was asked questions about certain records (evidencing "loan-sharking" activities) that had been seized by federal agents in connection with a search of Calandra's office. Calandra initially invoked his privilege against self-incrimination, but subsequently was granted immunity. He then requested and received a postponement of the grand jury proceedings so that he could present a pre-charge motion for return and suppression of the seized evidence under what is now Federal Rule of Criminal Procedure 41(g). The district court granted the motion, holding that the search was unconstitutional. The district court also held that "Calandra need not answer any of the grand jury's questions based on suppressed evidence," since such questions would constitute the fruit of the poisonous tree. The Supreme Court reversed:

In deciding whether to extend the exclusionary rule to grand jury proceedings, we must weigh the potential injury to the historic role and functions of the grand jury against the potential benefits of the rule as applied in this context. It is evident that this extension of the exclusionary rule would seriously impede the grand jury. Because the grand jury does not finally adjudicate guilt or innocence, it has traditionally been allowed to pursue its investigative and accusatorial functions unimpeded by the evidentiary and procedural restrictions applicable to a criminal trial. Permitting witnesses to invoke the exclusionary rule before a grand jury would precipitate adjudication of issues hitherto reserved for the trial on the merits and would delay and disrupt grand jury proceedings. Suppression hearings would halt the orderly progress of an investigation and might necessitate extended litigation of issues only tangentially related to the grand jury's primary objective. The probable result would be "protracted interruptions of grand jury proceedings," effectively transforming them into preliminary trials on the merits. In some cases the delay might be fatal to the enforcement of the criminal law. Just last Term we reaffirmed our disinclination to allow litigious interference with grand jury proceedings. United States v. Dionisio, [p. 365].

Against this potential damage to the role and functions of the grand jury, we must weigh the benefits to be derived from this proposed extension of the exclusionary rule. * * * [The Court here considered the "incremental deterrent effect which might be achieved by extending the exclusionary rule to grand jury proceedings," and found "unrealistic" the assumption that such an extension would significantly further deterrence of illegal searches.] We therefore decline to embrace a view that would achieve a speculative and undoubtedly minimal advance in the deterrence of police misconduct at the expense of substantially impeding the role of the grand jury.

7. ***Grand Jury Session.*** Civil enforcement of a grand jury subpoena is limited to the life of the grand jury. Once the grand jury has expired, and the matter has been turned over to a new grand jury, the original grand jury cannot enforce the subpoena. In In re Grand Jury Proceedings, 744 F.3d 211 (1st Cir. 2014), the court stated, "the government's proposed alternative–allowing reiterative civil contempt sanctions before future grand juries based on noncompliance with an old subpoena–would render the grand jury subpoena process all but meaningless."

E. CIVIL PROTECTIVE ORDERS AND GRAND JURY SUBPOENAS

White collar crime investigations frequently include or spring from related civil litigation brought by private parties and regulatory agencies. Federal Rule of Civil Procedure 26(c)(1) provides that "[a] party or any person from whom discovery is sought may move for a protective order in the court where the action is pending." Courts grant such orders almost as a matter of routine, unless there are First Amendment prior restraint issues involved. The information gathered during discovery in a civil action may be relevant to a grand jury investigation, so prosecutors can subpoena the parties or their counsel to produce the records to the grand jury. A protective order in the civil case prohibits any disclosure of discovery materials outside the litigation, so the interplay can be very difficult to navigate for the criminal defense lawyer who may also be subject to the protective order.

As an initial matter, there is an issue about whether the authority of the grand jury to obtain evidence supersedes a protective order issued by a judge sealing documents and prohibiting the parties from disclosing information. Whose has greater authority in this circumstance: the court hearing the civil matter or the federal grand jury? This can be very important in situations in which a party to civil litigation testified in a deposition or responded to interrogatories without considering the possibility that a criminal investigation might develop. Had that possibility been known, counsel could have sought a stay of the civil case or advised the client to assert the Fifth Amendment privilege against self-incrimination to avoid making potentially incriminating statements. Should a defense lawyer ever permit a client to testify or create documents in relation to a civil case if there is a reasonable chance of a criminal investigation? It is sometimes difficult to assess the likelihood of a criminal investigation, and not every civil case with potential criminal ramifications results in a federal grand jury investigation or state prosecution. The possibility of refusing to testify by asserting the Fifth Amendment privilege against self-incrimination is discussed infra in Chapter 13. Note that there may be collateral consequences from asserting the Fifth Amendment in civil litigation, including an adverse inference drawn against the party asserting the constitutional privilege discussed infra in Chapter 14.

There is a split in the circuit courts on the issue of whether the grand jury subpoena or the civil protective order is paramount, with three different approaches taken, although two are very close and usually reach the same result.

(1) The Civil Protective Order Controls: The Second Circuit, in Martindell v. International Telephone and Telegraph Corp., 594 F.2d 291 (2d Cir. 1979), held that "absent a showing of improvidence in the grant of a Rule 26(c) protective order or some extraordinary circumstance or compelling need, * * * a witness should be entitled to rely upon the enforceability of a protective order against any third parties, including the Government, and that such an order should not be vacated or modified merely to accommodate the Government's desire to inspect protected testimony for possible use in a criminal investigation, either as evidence or as the subject of a possible perjury charge." In S.E.C. v. TheStreet.Com, 273 F.3d 222 (2d Cir. 2001), the circuit court explained the rationale for enforcing a protective order over a grand jury subpoena: "If protective orders

were easily modified, moreover, parties would be less forthcoming in giving testimony and less willing to settle their disputes."

(2) Per Se Rule Enforcing the Grand Jury Subpoena: The Fourth, Ninth, and Eleventh Circuits adopted a per se rule requiring enforcement of the grand jury subpoena without regard to the scope or propriety of the protective order, a position diametrically opposed to the Second Circuit's position. See In re Grand Jury Subpoena, 836 F.2d 1468 (4th Cir. 1988); In re Grand Jury Subpoena Served on Meserve, Mumper & Hughes, 62 F.3d 1222 (9th Cir. 1995); In re Grand Jury Proceedings, 995 F.2d 1013 (11th Cir. 1993). In In re Grand Jury Subpoenas, 627 F.3d 1143 (9th Cir. 2010), the Ninth Circuit enforced a grand jury subpoena issued to a company to produce documents it received from a foreign affiliate in connection with pending civil litigation. The records would not have otherwise been available to the grand jury had they remained outside the United States, and the company argued that it relied on the civil protective order to bring the records from abroad. The circuit court turned a deaf ear to that argument, explaining that "[b]y a chance of litigation, the documents have been moved from outside the grasp of the grand jury to within its grasp. No authority forbids the government from closing its grip on what lies within the jurisdiction of the grand jury." The Fourth Circuit took the same position in a factually similar case in In re Grand Jury Subpoena, 646 F.3d 159 (4th Cir. 2011).

(3) Rebuttable Presumption in Favor of Enforcing the Grand Jury Subpoena: The First and Third Circuits reject the per se approach but instead apply a balancing test that strongly favors enforcement of the grand jury subpoena by adopting a rebuttable presumption in favor of requiring disclosure of materials subject to a civil protective order. This is not all that different from the per se approach because, as the Third Circuit explained in In re: Grand Jury, 286 F.3d 153 (3d Cir. 2002), "absent exceptional circumstances, protective orders should not serve to interfere with the unique and essential mechanism of a grand jury investigation." See In re Grand Jury Subpoena (Roach), 138 F.3d 442 (1st Cir. 1998). The circuit court noted how difficult it would be to succeed on a claim that a civil protective order should stand in the face of a grand jury subpoena: "In the vast majority of cases, a protective order should yield to a grand jury subpoena. On the other hand, we also understand that on very rare occasions, the public interest in speedy resolution of private civil litigation could outweigh the strong public interest in favor of prosecution of criminal wrongdoing."

An interesting question is whether the Supreme Court will ever resolve the split by deciding which approach applies? Does the presumption in favor of the grand jury subpoena expressed in *R. Enterprises* affect the analysis, and how much does the Court want to see federal judges injected into deciding how a grand jury investigation should be conducted?

CHAPTER TEN
THE PRODUCTION OF DOCUMENTS

The grand jury is entitled to "every man's evidence," so it has the authority to compel the production of documents absent a valid claim of privilege. The Fifth Amendment privilege against self-incrimination has been a means by which an individual can resist a subpoena to testify before the grand jury, a topic discussed in Chapter 13. The Supreme Court admonished that while "the powers of the grand jury are not unlimited and are subject to the supervision of a judge, the longstanding principle that 'the public . . . has a right to every man's evidence,' except for those persons protected by a constitutional, common-law, or statutory privilege, is particularly applicable to grand jury proceedings." Branzburg v. Hayes, 408 U.S. 665 (1972). The grand jury's investigative power had to give way to a Fifth Amendment claim, but the Court had been leery about extending the self-incrimination privilege to the point that investigations can be effectively thwarted. Thus, the Court had taken radically different approaches to a privilege claim under the Fifth Amendment depending on whether the demand to produce documents was made on an individual or a corporation. While the Fifth Amendment affords a measure of protection to the individual, a business or other organization was precluded from asserting the constitutional protection to resist a subpoena for records. How the Court has analyzed these issues of document production is the subject of this Chapter.

A. THE FOURTH AMENDMENT OVERBREADTH DOCTRINE

1. ***Boyd v. United States***. The Fourth Amendment provides: "The right of the people to be secure in their persons, houses, papers, and effects, against unreasonable searches and seizures, shall not be violated, and no Warrants shall issue, but upon probable cause, supported by Oath or affirmation, and particularly describing the place to be searched, and the persons or things to be seized." The second clause—starting with "and no Warrants shall issue" commonly is described as the "warrant" clause, while the first is sometimes described as the "reasonableness" clause. Although Boyd v. United States, 116 U.S. 616 (1886), was the foundational ruling on the application of the Fourth Amendment to the required production of documents by subpoena, and has been widely celebrated as a "case that will be remembered as long as civil liberties live in the United States" [Brandeis, J., dissenting in Olmstead v. United States, 277 U.S. 438, 474 (1928)], the *Boyd* decision today has a quite limited precedential impact. Its holding would not be followed under currently applicable precedent, and its doctrinal foundation has been largely reshaped, where not entirely discarded. Still, *Boyd* remains a case commonly cited and discussed in connection with the application of both the Fourth

Amendment requirement that searches be "reasonable" and the Fifth Amendment privilege against self-incrimination related to the subpoena of documents.

Boyd itself did not involve a traditional subpoena. At issue was a customs forfeiture proceeding in which the government sought to utilize an 1847 statutory provision allowing it to obtain documentary evidence from the importer of the property to be forfeit. The provision authorized the trial judge, on motion of the government describing a particular document and indicating what it might prove, to issue a notice directing the importer to produce that document. The petitioners in *Boyd* challenged such a notice directing them to produce the invoices for thirty-five cases of plate glass allegedly imported by their partnership without payment of customs duties. The Supreme Court sustained their challenge, holding that the notice and the statute authorizing it violated both the Fourth Amendment and the self-incrimination clause of the Fifth Amendment.

Justice Bradley's opinion for the *Boyd* Court first established that the trial judge's order to produce was subject to the Fourth Amendment. Justice Bradley noted:

> [I]n regard to Fourth Amendment, it is contended that * * * [the Act of 1874], under which the order in the present case was made, is free from constitutional objection, because it does not authorize the search and seizure of books and papers, but only requires the defendant or claimant to produce them. That is so; but it declares that if he does not produce them, the allegations which it is affirmed they will prove shall be taken as confessed. This is tantamount to compelling their production; for the prosecuting attorney will always be sure to state the evidence expected to be derived from them as strongly as the case will admit of. It is true that certain aggravating incidents of actual search and seizure, such as forcible entry into a man's house and searching amongst his papers, are wanting, and to this extent the proceeding under the act of 1874 is a mitigation of that which was authorized by the former acts; but it accomplishes the substantial object of those acts in forcing from a party evidence against himself. It is our opinion, therefore, that a compulsory production of a man's private papers to establish a criminal charge against him, or to forfeit his property, is within the scope of the Fourth Amendment to the Constitution, in all cases in which a search and seizure would be; because it is a material ingredient, and effects the sole object and purpose of search and seizure.

Justice Bradley then explained that "it is not the breaking of * * * doors, and the rummaging of * * * drawers, that constitutes the essence of the offence, but * * * the invasion of [the] indefeasible right of personal security, personal liberty, and private property." Accordingly, he reasoned that "any forcible and compulsory extortion of a man's * * * private papers to be used as evidence to convict him" brings into play the Fourth as well as the Fifth Amendment, which here "almost run into each other." For the "Fifth Amendment throws light on what is an 'unreasonable search and seizure' within the meaning of the Fourth Amendment," and the seizure of a man's books and papers to be used in evidence "against him" is not "substantially different from compelling him to be a witness against himself."

> The Court concluded that it therefore was "of the opinion that a compulsory production of the private books and papers of the owners of goods sought to be forfeited in such a suit is compelling him to be a witness against himself within the meaning of the Fifth Amendment to the Constitution and is the equivalent of a search and seizure–and an unreasonable search and seizure–within the meaning of the Fourth Amendment."

2. **The Demise of *Boyd*.** Insofar as *Boyd* suggested that the Fourth Amendment prohibited searches for property the defendant was entitled to possess (i.e., property other than the fruits or instrumentalities of crime), it spawned a reading of the Fourth Amendment that received considerable support in later years but was eventually limited and then flatly rejected in Warden v. Hayden, 387 U.S. 294 (1967). To the extend *Boyd* read the Fourth Amendment as prohibiting a search for documents, that interpretation was finally rejected in Andresen v. Maryland, 427 U.S. 463 (1976). But long before either of these developments, the Court completely restructured *Boyd*'s view of the bearing of the Fourth Amendment upon a subpoena duces tecum. That came in **Hale v. Henkel**, 201 U.S. 43 (1906), a case decided twenty years after *Boyd*.

The *Hale* Court had before it a challenge to a subpoena directing the petitioner, a corporate official, to produce various corporate documents to a grand jury investigating possible violations of the antitrust laws. Petitioner's challenge, relying on *Boyd*, sought to use the combined impact of the Fourth and Fifth Amendments to quash the subpoena, but the Court initially separated those claims. Cases subsequent to *Boyd*, it noted, had "treated the Fourth and Fifth Amendments as quite distinct, having different histories, and performing separate functions." Turning first to the petitioner's self-incrimination claim, the Court found that claim clearly unsupportable since the statute authorizing the subpoena granted petitioner immunity from prosecution (thereby eliminating his grounding for relying on the Fifth Amendment privilege against self-incrimination [see pp. 557-630], and the corporation itself had no privilege claim as an artificial entity [see p. 393]). The Fourth Amendment claim did have merit, but for reasons other than what might have been assumed from *Boyd*. The Court stated:

> Although * * * we are of the opinion that an officer of a corporation * * * cannot refuse to produce the books and papers of such corporation, we do not wish to be understood as holding that a corporation is not entitled to immunity, under the Fourth Amendment, against unreasonable searches and seizures. A

corporation is, after all, but an association of individuals under an assumed name and with a distinct legal entity. In organizing itself as a collective body it waives no constitutional immunities appropriate to such body. * * * We are also of opinion that an order for the production of books and papers may constitute an unreasonable search and seizure within the Fourth Amendment. While a search ordinarily implies a quest by an officer of the law, and a seizure contemplates a forcible dispossession of the owner, still, as was held in the *Boyd* case, the substance of the offense is the compulsory production of private papers, whether under a search warrant or a subpoena duces tecum, against which the person, be he individual or corporation, is entitled to protection. Applying the test of reasonableness to the present case, we think the subpoena duces tecum is far too sweeping in its terms to be regarded as reasonable. It does not require the production of a single contract, or of contracts with a particular corporation, or a limited number of documents, but all understandings, contracts, or correspondence between the MacAndrews & Forbes Company, and no less than six different companies, as well as all reports made, and accounts rendered by such companies from the date of the organization of the MacAndrews & Forbes Company, as well as all letters received by that company since its organization from more than a dozen different companies, situated in seven different States in the Union.

If the writ had required the production of all the books, papers and documents found in the office of the MacAndrews & Forbes Company, it would scarcely be more universal in its operation, or completely put a stop to the business of that company. Indeed, it is difficult to say how its business could be carried on after it had been denuded of this mass of material, which is not shown to be necessary in the prosecution of this case, and is clearly in violation of the general principle of law with regard to the particularity required in the description of documents necessary to a search warrant or subpoena. Doubtless many, if not all, of these documents may ultimately be required, but some necessity should be shown, either from an examination of the witnesses orally, or from the known transactions of these companies with the other companies implicated, or some evidence of their materiality produced, to justify an order for the production of such a mass of papers. A general subpoena of this description is equally indefensible as a search warrant would be if couched in similar terms.

3. ***Explaining the Overbreadth Doctrine***. Judge Friendly noted in **In re Horowitz**, 482 F.2d 72 (2d Cir. 1973): "The Fourth Amendment portion of the *Boyd* decision was surely not based on the overbreadth of the Government's demand; the Government [there] sought only a single invoice of unquestionable relevance." Although relying on *Boyd*, *Hale v. Henkel* shifted the Court's underlying reasoning and "left the applicability of the Fourth Amendment to subpoena duces tecum in a most confusing state. None

of the Justices seemed to think that such a subpoena could be issued only 'upon probable cause, supported by oath or affirmation,' as would be required for a search warrant. Nevertheless, except for Mr. Justice McKenna, all were of the view that an overbroad subpoena duces tecum against an individual would be an unreasonable search and seizure."

Judge Friendly suggested in *Horowitz* that the *Hale v. Henkel* overbreadth doctrine might find firmer support in the Due Process Clause than in the Fourth Amendment. Although a due process grounding for the doctrine was suggested in Oklahoma Press Publishing Co. v. Walling, 327 U.S. 186 (1946), a leading case on the application of the overbreadth doctrine to an administrative agency subpoena, later decisions applying the overbreadth doctrine have relied on the Fourth Amendment.

Accepting the Court's premise that the Fourth Amendment does apply to a subpoena duces tecum, why should the overbreadth doctrine be the sole Fourth Amendment limitation as to the subpoena duces tecum? Does *Hale* reflect a determination that the requirements of the Fourth Amendment's warrant clause are inapplicable in light of the long history of subpoenas issued without regard to probable cause and the subpoena's lesser intrusion upon privacy (as compared to the traditional search), thereby leaving applicable only the Fourth Amendment's general mandate of reasonableness in its first clause? "The theory here is that the subpoena which is too sweeping, which calls for a mass of documents without regard to what is relevant, necessarily requires a sifting through the documents to obtain those that are needed. Whether that sifting takes place on the premises of the owner or in the offices of the prosecutor assisting the grand jury, it constitutes a search. Thus, *Hale* and other courts have compared the overbroad subpoena to a 'general warrant.'" WAYNE R. LAFAVE, JEROLD H. ISRAEL, NANCY J. KING, & ORIN S. KERR, CRIMINAL PROCEDURE §8.7(a) (3d ed. 2007).

B. THE FIFTH AMENDMENT ACT OF PRODUCTION DOCTRINE

1. Personal Papers

FISHER v. UNITED STATES
425 U.S. 391(1976)

Justice WHITE delivered the opinion of the Court.

In these two cases we are called upon to decide whether a summons directing an attorney to produce documents delivered to him by his client in connection with the attorney-client relationship is enforceable over claims that the documents were constitutionally immune from summons in the hands of the client and retained that immunity in the hands of the attorney.

In each case, an Internal Revenue agent visited the taxpayer or taxpayers and interviewed them in connection with an investigation of possible civil or criminal liability under the federal income tax laws. Shortly after the interviews * * *, the taxpayers obtained from their respective accountants certain documents relating to the preparation by the accountant of their tax returns. Shortly after obtaining the documents * * *, the taxpayers transferred the documents to their lawyers—each of whom was retained to assist the taxpayer in connection with the investigation. Upon learning of the whereabouts of the documents, the Internal Revenue Service served summonses on the attorneys directing them to produce documents listed therein. [Those documents were accountants' work sheets, retained copies of income tax returns, and the accountants' copies of correspondence between the accounting firm and the taxpayer]. * * * In each case, the lawyer declined to comply with the summons directing production of the documents, and enforcement actions were commenced by the Government. * * *

All of the parties in these cases and the Court of Appeals have concurred in the proposition that if the Fifth Amendment would have excused a taxpayer from turning over the accountant's papers had he possessed them, the attorney to whom they are delivered for the purpose of obtaining legal advice should also be immune from subpoena. Although we agree with this proposition for the reasons set forth * * * infra, we are convinced that, under our decision in Couch v. United States, 409 U.S. 322 (1973), it is not the taxpayer's Fifth Amendment privilege that would excuse the attorney from production.

The relevant part of that Amendment provides: "No person . . . shall be compelled in any criminal case to be a witness against himself." (Emphasis added.) The taxpayer's privilege under this Amendment is not violated by enforcement of the summonses involved in these cases because enforcement against a taxpayer's lawyer would not "compel" the taxpayer to do anything—and certainly would not compel him to be a "witness" against himself. The Court has held repeatedly that the Fifth Amendment is limited to prohibiting the use of "physical or moral compulsion" exerted on the person asserting the privilege. In *Couch*, supra, we recently ruled that the Fifth Amendment rights of a taxpayer were not violated by the enforcement of a documentary summons directed to her accountant and requiring production of the taxpayer's own records in the possession of the accountant. We did so on the ground that in such a case "the ingredient of personal compulsion against an accused is lacking." Here, the taxpayers are compelled to do no more than was the taxpayer in *Couch*. The taxpayers' Fifth Amendment privilege is therefore not violated by enforcement of the summonses directed toward their attorneys. This is true whether or not the Amendment would have barred a subpoena directing the taxpayer to produce the documents while they were in his hands.

The fact that the attorneys are agents of the taxpayers does not change this result. Couch held as much, since the accountant there was also the taxpayer's agent, and in this respect reflected a longstanding view. * * * "It is extortion of information from the accused which offends our sense of justice." Couch. Agent or no, the lawyer is not the taxpayer. The taxpayer is the "accused," and nothing is being extorted from him. Nor is this one of those situations, which Couch suggested might exist, where constructive possession is so clear or relinquishment of possession so temporary and insignificant as to leave the personal compulsion upon the taxpayer substantially intact. * * *

The Court of Appeals suggested that because legally and ethically the attorney was required to respect the confidences of his client, the latter had a reasonable expectation of privacy for the records in the hands of the attorney and therefore did not forfeit his Fifth Amendment privilege with respect to the records by transferring them in order to obtain legal advice. It is true that the Court has often stated that one of the several purposes served by the constitutional privilege against compelled testimonial self-incrimination is that of protecting, personal privacy. See, e.g., Murphy v. Waterfront Comm'n, 378 U.S. 52 (1964). But the Court has never suggested that every invasion of privacy violates the privilege. Within the limits imposed by the language of the Fifth Amendment, which we necessarily observe, the privilege truly serves privacy interests; but the Court has never on any ground, personal privacy included, applied the Fifth Amendment to prevent the otherwise proper acquisition or use of evidence which, in the Court's view, did not involve compelled testimonial self-incrimination of some sort.

The proposition that the Fifth Amendment protects private information obtained without compelling self-incriminating testimony is contrary to the clear statements of this Court that under appropriate safeguards private incriminating statements of an accused may be overheard and used in evidence, if they are not compelled at the time they were uttered, Katz v. United States, 389 U.S. 347 (1987); and that disclosure of private information may be compelled if immunity removes the risk of incrimination. Kastigar v. United States [p. 574]. If the Fifth Amendment protected generally against the obtaining of private information from a man's mouth or pen or house, its protections would presumably not be lifted by probable cause and a warrant or by immunity. * * * We cannot cut the Fifth Amendment completely loose from the moorings of its language, and make it serve as a general protector of privacy—a word not mentioned in its text and a concept directly addressed in the Fourth Amendment. We adhere to the view that the Fifth Amendment protects against "compelled self-incrimination, not [the disclosure of] private information." * * * Insofar as private information not obtained through compelled self-incriminating testimony is legally protected, its protection stems from other sources—the Fourth Amendment's protection against seizures without warrant or probable cause and against subpoenas which suffer from "too much indefiniteness or breadth in the things required to be 'particularly described,'" the First Amendment, or evidentiary privileges such as the attorney-client privilege.[7]

* * * [While the] taxpayers have erroneously relied on the Fifth Amendment without urging the attorney-client privilege in so many words, they have nevertheless invoked the relevant body of law and policies that govern the attorney-client privilege. In this posture of the case, we feel obliged to inquire whether the attorney-client privilege applies to documents in the hands of an attorney which would have been privileged in the hands of the client by reason of the Fifth Amendment. * * * This Court and the lower courts have * * * uniformly held that pre-existing documents which could have been obtained by court process from the client when he was in possession may also be obtained from the attorney by similar process following transfer by the client in order to obtain more informed legal advice. * * * It is otherwise if the documents are not obtainable by subpoena duces tecum or summons while in the exclusive possession of the client, for the client will then be reluctant to transfer possession to the lawyer unless the documents are also privileged in the latter's hands. Where the transfer is made for the purpose of obtaining legal advice, the purposes of the attorney-client privilege would be defeated unless the privilege is applicable. * * *

Since each taxpayer [here] transferred possession of the documents in question from himself to his attorney in order to obtain legal assistance in the tax investigations in question, the papers, if unobtainable by summons from the client, are unobtainable by summons directed to the attorney by reason of the attorney-client privilege. We accordingly proceed to the question whether the documents could have been obtained by summons addressed to the taxpayer while the documents were in his possession. The only bar to enforcement of such summons asserted by the parties or the courts below is the Fifth Amendment's privilege against self-incrimination. * * *

The proposition that the Fifth Amendment prevents compelled production of documents over objection that such production might incriminate stems from Boyd v. United States * * *. The invoice in question [there] was held to have been obtained in violation of the Fourth Amendment. The Court went on to hold that the accused in a criminal case or the defendant in a forfeiture action could not be forced to produce evidentiary items without violating the Fifth Amendment as well as the Fourth. More specifically, the Court declared, "a compulsory production of the private books and papers of the owner of goods sought to be forfeited . . . is compelling him

[7] The taxpayers and their attorneys have not raised arguments of a Fourth Amendment nature before this Court and could not be successful if they had. The summonses are narrowly drawn and seek only documents of unquestionable relevance to the tax investigation. Special problems of privacy which might be presented by subpoena of a personal diary, United States v. Bennett, 409 F.2d 888, 897 (CA2 1969) (Friendly, J.), are not involved here. First Amendment values are also plainly not implicated in these cases.

to be a witness against himself, within the meaning of the Fifth Amendment to the Constitution." * * *

Several of *Boyd's* express or implicit declarations have not stood the test of time. The application of the Fourth Amendment to subpoenas was limited by Hale v. Henkel and more recent cases. Purely evidentiary (but "nontestimonial") materials, as well as contraband and fruits and instrumentalities of crime, may now be searched for and seized under proper circumstances, Warden v. Hayden. Also, any notion that "testimonial" evidence may never be seized and used in evidence is inconsistent with [various cases] approving the seizure under appropriate circumstances of conversations of a person suspected of crime. See Katz v. United States, supra. It is also clear that the Fifth Amendment does not independently proscribe the compelled production of every sort of incriminating evidence but applies only when the accused is compelled to make a testimonial communication that is incriminating. * * * Furthermore, despite *Boyd*, neither a partnership nor the individual partners are shielded from compelled production of partnership records on self-incrimination grounds. Bellis v. United States. It would appear that under that case the precise claim sustained in *Boyd* would now be rejected for reasons not there considered.

The pronouncement in *Boyd* that a person may not be forced to produce his private papers has nonetheless often appeared as dictum in later opinions of this Court. * * * To the extent, however, that the rule against compelling production of private papers rested on thc proposition that seizures of or subpoenas for "mere evidence," including documents, violated the Fourth Amendment and therefore also transgressed the Fifth, the foundations for the rule have been washed away. In consequence, the prohibition against forcing the production of private papers has long been a rule searching for a rationale consistent with the proscriptions of the Fifth Amendment against compelling a person to give "testimony" that incriminates him. Accordingly, we turn to the question of what, if any, incriminating testimony within the Fifth Amendment's protection, is compelled by a documentary summons.

A subpoena served on a taxpayer requiring him to produce an accountant's workpapers in his possession without doubt involves substantial compulsion. But it does not compel oral testimony; nor would it ordinarily compel the taxpayer to restate, repeat, or affirm the truth of the contents of the documents sought. Therefore, the Fifth Amendment would not be violated by the fact alone that the papers on their face might incriminate the taxpayer, for the privilege protects a person only against being incriminated by his own compelled testimonial communications. The accountant's workpapers are not the taxpayer's. They were not prepared by the taxpayer, and they contain no testimonial declarations by him. Furthermore, as far as this record demonstrates, the preparation of all of the papers sought in these cases was wholly voluntary, and they cannot be said to contain compelled testimonial evidence, either of the taxpayers or of anyone else. The taxpayer cannot avoid compliance with the subpoena merely by asserting that the item of evidence which he is required to produce contains incriminating writing, whether his own or that of someone else.

The act of producing evidence in response to a subpoena nevertheless has communicative aspects of its own, wholly aside from the contents of the papers produced. Compliance with the subpoena tacitly concedes the existence of the papers demanded and their possession or control by the taxpayer. It also would indicate the taxpayer's belief that the papers are those described in the subpoena. The elements of compulsion are clearly present, but the more difficult issues are whether the tacit averments, of the taxpayer are both "testimonial" and "incriminating" for purposes of applying the Fifth Amendment. These questions perhaps do not lend themselves to categorical answers; their resolution may instead depend on the facts and circumstances of particular cases or classes thereof. In light of the records now before us, we are confident that however incriminating the contents of the accountant's workpapers might be, the act of producing them—the only thing which the taxpayer is compelled to do—would not itself involve testimonial self-incrimination.

It is doubtful that implicitly admitting the existence and possession of the papers rises to the level of testimony within the protection of the Fifth Amendment. The papers belong to the accountant, were prepared by him, and are the kind usually prepared by an accountant working on the tax returns of his client. Surely the Government is in no way relying on the "truthtelling" of the taxpayer to prove the existence of or his access to the documents. The existence and location of the papers are a foregone conclusion and the taxpayer adds little or nothing to the sum total of the Government's information by conceding that he in fact has the papers. Under these circumstances by enforcement of the summons "no constitutional rights are touched. The question is not of testimony but of surrender." * * *

When an accused is required to submit a handwriting exemplar he admits his ability to write and impliedly asserts that the exemplar is his writing. But in common experience, the first would be a near truism and the latter self-evident. In any event, although the exemplar may be incriminating to the accused and although he is compelled to furnish it. his Fifth Amendment privilege is not violated because nothing he has said or done is deemed to be sufficiently testimonial for purposes of the privilege. This Court has also time and again allowed subpoenas against the custodian of corporate documents or those belonging to other collective entities such as unions and partnerships and those of bankrupt businesses over claims that the documents will incriminate the custodian despite the fact that producing the documents tacitly admits their existence and their location in the hands of their possessor. The existence and possession or control of the subpoenaed documents being no more in issue here than in the above cases, the summons is equally enforceable.

Moreover, assuming that these aspects of producing the accountant's papers have some minimal testimonial significance, surely it is not illegal to seek accounting help in connection with one's tax returns or for the accountant to prepare workpapers and deliver them to the taxpayer. At this juncture, we are quite unprepared to hold that either the fact of existence of the papers or of their possession by the taxpayer poses any realistic threat of incrimination to the taxpayer.

As for the possibility that responding to the subpoena would authenticate the workpapers, production would express nothing more than the taxpayer's belief that the papers are those described in the subpoena. The taxpayer would be no more competent to authenticate the accountant's workpapers or reports by producing them than he would be to authenticate them if testifying orally. The taxpayer did not prepare the papers and could not vouch for their accuracy. The documents would not be admissible in evidence against the taxpayer without authenticating testimony. Without more, responding to the subpoena in the circumstances before us would not appear to represent a substantial threat of self-incrimination. * * *

Whether the Fifth Amendment would shield the taxpayer from producing his own tax records in his possession is a question not involved here; for the papers demanded here are not his "private papers," see Boyd, supra. We do hold that compliance with a summons directing the taxpayer to produce the accountant's documents involved in this case would involve no incriminating testimony within the protection of the Fifth Amendment.

Justice BRENNAN, concurring in the judgment.

Given the prior access by accountants retained by the taxpayers to the papers involved in these cases and the wholly business rather than personal nature of the papers, I agree that the privilege against compelled self-incrimination did not in either of these cases protect the papers from production in response to the summonses. See Couch v. United States. I do not join the Court's opinion, however, because of the portent of much of what is said of a serious crippling of the protection secured by the privilege against compelled production of one's private books and papers. * * * [I]t is but another step in the denigration of privacy principles settled nearly 100 years ago in Boyd v. United States. * * *

Expressions are legion in opinions of this Court that the protection of personal privacy is a central purpose of the privilege against compelled self-incrimination. * * * The Court pays lip-service to this bedrock premise of privacy in the statement that "[w]ithin the limits imposed by the language of the Fifth Amendment, which we necessarily observe, the privilege truly serves privacy interests." But this only makes explicit what elsewhere highlights the opinion, namely, the view that protection of personal privacy is merely a byproduct and not, as our precedents and history teach, a factor controlling in part the determination of the scope of the privilege. This cart-before-the-horse approach is fundamentally at odds with the settled principle that the scope of the privilege is not constrained by the limits of the wording of the Fifth Amendment but has the reach necessary to protect the cherished value of privacy which it safeguards. * * * History and principle, not the mechanical application of its wording, have been the life of the amendment. * * *

History and principle teach that the privacy protected by the Fifth Amendment extends not just to the individual's immediate declarations, oral or written, but also to his testimonial materials in the form of books and papers. The common-law and constitutional extension of the privilege to testimonial materials, such as books and papers, was inevitable. An individual's books and papers are generally little more than an extension of his person. They reveal no less than he could reveal upon being questioned directly. Many of the matters within an individual's knowledge may as easily be retained within his head as set down on a scrap of paper. I perceive no principle which does not permit compelling one to disclose the contents of one's mind but does permit compelling the disclosure of the contents of that scrap of paper by compelling its production. Under a contrary view, the constitutional protection would turn on fortuity, and persons would, at their peril, record their thoughts and the events of their lives. The ability to think private thoughts, facilitated as it is by pen and paper, and the ability to preserve intimate memories would be curtailed through fear that those thoughts or the events of those memories would become the subjects of criminal sanctions however invalidly imposed. Indeed, it was the very reality of those fears that helped provide the historical impetus for the privilege. * * *

The Court's treatment in the instant cases of the question whether the evidence involved here is within the protection of the privilege is, with all respect, most inadequate. The gaping hole is in the omission of any reference to the taxpayer's privacy interests and to whether the subpoenas impermissibly invade those interests. * * * For the reasons I have stated at the outset, however, I do not believe that the evidence involved in these cases falls within the scope of privacy protected by the Fifth Amendment. * * *

Justice MARSHALL, concurring in the judgment.

* * * I would have preferred it had the Court found some room in its theory for recognition of the import of the contents of the documents themselves. * * * Nonetheless, I am hopeful that the Court's new theory, properly understood and applied, will provide substantially the same protection as our prior focus on the contents of the documents. * * * Indeed, there would appear to be a precise inverse relationship between the private nature of the document and the permissibility of assuming its existence. Therefore, under the Court's theory, the admission through production that one's diary, letters, prior tax returns, personally maintained financial records, or canceled checks exist would ordinarily provide substantial testimony. The incriminating nature of such an admission is clear, for while it may not be criminal to keep a diary, or write letters or checks, the admission that one does and that those documents are still available may quickly—or simultaneously-lead to incriminating evidence. If there is a "real

danger" of such a result, that is enough under our cases to make such testimony subject to the claim of privilege. Thus, in practice, the Court's approach should still focus upon the private nature of the papers subpoenaed and protect those about which Boyd and its progeny were most concerned. * * *

The Court's theory will also limit the prosecution's ability to use documents secured through a grant of immunity. If authentication that the document produced is the document demanded were the only testimony inherent in production, immunity would be a useful tool for obtaining written evidence. So long as a document obtained under an immunity grant could be authenticated through other sources, as would often be possible, reliance on the immunized testimony–the authentication–and its fruits would not be necessary, and the document could be introduced. The Court's recognition that the act of production also involves testimony about the existence and possession of the subpoenaed documents mandates a different result. Under the Court's recognition that the act of production also involves testimony about the existence and possession of the subpoenaed documents mandates a different result. Under the Court's theory, if the document is to be obtained the immunity grant must extend to the testimony that the document is presently in existence. Such a grant will effectively shield the contents of the document, for the contents are a direct fruit of the immunized testimony–that the document exists–and cannot usually be obtained without reliance on that testimony. Accordingly, the Court's theory offers substantially the same protection against procurement of documents under grant of immunity that our prior cases afford.

NOTES AND QUESTIONS

1. **The Role of Privacy.** Both critics and supporters of the view that the Fifth Amendment is designed to protect a "private enclave" acknowledge that such a privacy rationale remains unpersuasive unless it offers a satisfactory explanation as to why the particular element of privacy that falls within the privilege is given absolute protection, as compared to the relative protection given other privacy interests under the Fourth and First Amendments. The answer usually offered is that the privilege protects the most significant element of individual privacy, the privacy "of the mind"; it "respects a private inner sanctum of individual feeling and thought." Couch v. United States [p. 386]. But this response only raises the further question as to why the privilege, if it is designed to protect mental privacy from state intrusion, affords such protection only as to thoughts, feelings, and beliefs that would furnish a link in the chain of evidence needed to establish criminal liability. One explanation for this limitation is that privilege seeks to protect only a "particular corner of the private enclave" that is especially significant in the development of "moral autonomy"—the "integrity of conscience." See Robert Gerstein, *The Demise of Boyd: Self-Incrimination and Private Papers in the Burger Court*, 27 U.C.L.A. L. REV. 343 (1979). The critical element of the privilege, from this perspective, is that it preserves to the individual alone

the essential right of determining whether and when to acknowledge responsibility for his actions. See also Abe Fortas, *The Fifth Amendment, Nemo Tenetur Prodere Seipsum*, 25 CLEVE. B.A.J. 95 (1954) ("Mea culpa belongs to a man and his God. It is a plea that cannot be extracted from free men by human authority").

Looking back to *Boyd*, can the ruling there be viewed (as suggested by Justices Brennan and Marshall) as resting upon a privacy rationale of the Fifth Amendment? The *Fisher* majority apparently subscribed to the view (held by most commentators) that the *Boyd* ruling rested on a subsequently discarded "property rights" rationale. Boyd, under this view, simply utilized the privilege to characterize as "unreasonable" all "searches" (which included required production) aimed at obtaining a person's personal property for possible use against him in a "criminal case" (which included a forfeiture proceeding). See Robert Heidt, *The Fifth Amendment Privilege and Documents–Cutting Fisher's Tangled Line*, 49 MO. L. REV. 440 (1984). Yet, *Boyd*, particularly because of its reliance on *Entick v. Carrington* and the characterization there of the individual's papers as his "dearest property" has also been viewed as suggesting a broad personal privacy grounding for the self-incrimination privilege. *Entick*, it is suggested, regards a person as being "embodied" in his papers and *Boyd* recognized that it was therefore a violation of the privilege to make his papers "speak" against him. Entick, however, had in mind the individual's personal political writings, while Boyd had before it an invoice written by another firm.

2. ***Sole Proprietorship Records***. In **United States v. Doe**, 465 U.S. 605 (1984), commonly referred to as *Doe I* to distinguish it from the Court's decision in Doe v. United States, 487 U.S. 201 (1988) (*Doe II*), infra p. 398, which also involved the Fifth Amendment and obtaining records, the Court considered a challenge to subpoenas for the business records of a sole proprietorship. Respondent, the owner of several sole proprietorships, objected to a series of five subpoenas directing him to produce a broad range of business records, including billings, ledgers, cancelled checks, telephone records, contracts, and paid bills. The district court sustained the respondent's Fifth Amendment challenge, noting that the act of producing the documents had "communicative aspects" which could prove incriminating since the respondent would thereby be required to "admit that the records exist, that they are in his possession, and that they are authentic." On appeal, the Third Circuit agreed with the district court, but also added another self-incrimination ground justifying the quashing of the subpoenas. Following *Fisher*, that circuit had held, relying on *Boyd*, that an individual's private papers, though created voluntarily, were still privileged under the self-incrimination clause. That analysis, the Third Circuit reasoned, was also applicable to the business records of a sole proprietor.

The Court stated that "[a]s we noted in *Fisher*, the Fifth Amendment only protects the person asserting the privilege only from compelled self-incrimination. Where the preparation of business records is voluntary, no compulsion is present." With regard to whether the sole proprietor could assert the Fifth Amendment for the act of production, the Court held:

> Although the contents of a document may not be privileged, the act of producing the document may be. *Fisher*. A government subpoena compels the holder of the document to perform an act that may have testimonial aspects and an incriminating effect. * * * In *Fisher*, the Court explored the effect that the act of production would have on the taxpayer [there] and determined that the act of production would have only minimal testimonial value and would not operate to incriminate the taxpayer. Unlike the Court in *Fisher*, we have the explicit finding of the District Court that the act of producing the documents would involve testimonial self-incrimination."[11] The Court of Appeals agreed.[12] The District Court's finding essentially rests on its determination of factual issues. Therefore, we will not overturn that finding unless it has no support in the record. Traditionally, we also have been reluctant to disturb findings of fact in which two courts below have concurred. Rogers v. Lodge, 458 U.S. 613 (1982). We therefore decline to overturn the finding of the District Court in this regard, where, as here, it has been affirmed by the Court of Appeals.[13]

---

[11] The District Court stated: "With few exceptions, enforcement of the subpoenas would compel [respondent] to admit that the records exist, that they are in his possession, and that they are authentic. These communications, if made under compulsion of a court decree, would violate [respondent's] Fifth Amendment rights. . . . The government argues that the existence, possession and authenticity of the documents can be proved without [respondent's] testimonial communication, but it cannot satisfy this court as to how that representation can be implemented to protect the witness in subsequent proceedings."

[12] The Court of Appeals stated: "In the matter sub judice, however, we find nothing in the record that would indicate that the United States knows, as a certainty, that each of the myriad documents demanded by the five subpoenas in fact is in the appellee's possession or subject to his control. The most plausible inference to be drawn from the broad-sweeping subpoenas is that the Government, unable to prove that the subpoenaed documents exist—or that the appellee even is somehow connected to the business entities under investigation—is attempting to compensate for its lack of knowledge by requiring the appellee to become, in effect, the primary informant against himself."

[13] The Government concedes that the act of producing the subpoenaed documents might have had some testimonial aspects, but it argues that any incrimination would be so trivial that the Fifth Amendment is not implicated. * * * On the basis of the findings made in this case we think it clear that the risk of incrimination was "substantial and real" and not "trifling or imaginary." Respondent did not concede in the District Court that the records listed in the subpoena actually existed or were in his possession. Respondent argued that by producing the records, he would tacitly admit their existence and his possession. Respondent also pointed out that if the Government obtained the documents from another source, it would have to authenticate them before they would be admissible at trial. See Fed. R. Evid. 901. By

* * * The Government, as it concedes, could have compelled respondent to produce the documents listed in the subpoena. Sections 6002 and 6003 of Title 18 provide for the granting of use immunity with respect to the potentially incriminating evidence. The Court upheld the constitutionality of the use immunity statute in Kastigar v. United States [p. 574]. The Government did state several times before the District Court that it would not use respondent's act of production against him in any way. But counsel for the Government never made a statutory request to the District Court to grant respondent use immunity. We are urged to adopt a doctrine of constructive use immunity. Under this doctrine, the courts would impose a requirement on the Government not to use the incriminatory aspects of the act of production against the person claiming the privilege even though the statutory procedures have not been followed.

We decline to extend the jurisdiction of courts to include prospective grants of use immunity in the absence of the formal request that the statute requires. As we stated in Pillsbury Co. v. Conbody, 459 U.S. 248 (1983), in passing the use immunity statute, "Congress gave certain officials in the Department of Justice exclusive authority to grant immunities." "Congress foresaw the courts as playing only a minor role in the immunizing process . . . ." Id. The decision to seek use immunity necessarily involves a balancing of the Government's interest in obtaining information against the risk that immunity will frustrate the Government's attempts to prosecute the subject of the investigation. Congress expressly left this decision exclusively to the Justice Department. If, on remand, the appropriate official concludes that it is desirable to compel respondent to produce his business records, the statutory procedure for requesting use immunity will be available.[17]

---

producing the documents, respondent would relieve the Government of the need for authentication. These allegations were sufficient to establish a valid claim of the privilege against self-incrimination. This is not to say that the Government was foreclosed from rebutting respondent's claim by producing evidence that possession, existence, and authentication were a "foregone conclusion." *Fisher*. In this case, however, the Government failed to make such a showing.

[17] Respondent argues that any grant of use immunity must cover the contents of the documents as well as the act of production. We find this contention unfounded. To satisfy the requirements of the Fifth Amendment, a grant of immunity need be only as broad as the privilege against self-incrimination. Murphy v. Waterfront Commission. As discussed above, the privilege in this case extends only to the act of production. Therefore, any grant of use immunity need only protect respondent from the self-incrimination that might accompany the act of producing his business records.

> We conclude that the Court of Appeals erred in holding that the contents of the subpoenaed documents were privileged under the Fifth Amendment. The act of producing the documents at issue in this case is privileged and cannot be compelled without a statutory grant of use immunity pursuant to 18 U.S.C. §§ 6002 and 6003. The judgment of the Court of Appeals is, therefore, affirmed in part, reversed in part, and the case is remanded to the District Court for further proceedings in accordance with this decision.

3. ***The Demise of Boyd?*** Justice O'Connor wrote a short concurring opinion in *Doe I*:

> [J]ust to make explicit what is implicit in the analysis of that opinion: that the Fifth Amendment provides absolutely no protection for the contents of private papers of any kind. The notion that the Fifth Amendment protects the privacy of papers originated in Boyd v. United States, but our decision in Fisher v. United States, sounded the death-knell for *Boyd*. "Several of *Boyd's* express or implicit declarations [had] not stood the test of time," *Fisher*, and its privacy of papers concept "had long been a rule searching for a rationale." Today's decision puts a long-overdue end to that fruitless search.

Justice Marshall, joined by Justice Brennan, rejected Justice O'Connor's assertion about the demise of *Boyd*:

> * * * Contrary to what Justice O'Connor contends, I do not view the Court's opinion in this case as having reconsidered whether the Fifth Amendment provides protection for the contents of "private papers of any kind." This case presented nothing remotely close to the question that Justice O'Connor eagerly poses and answers. First, as noted above, the issue whether the Fifth Amendment protects the contents of the documents was obviated by the Court of Appeals' rulings relating to the act of production and statutory use immunity. Second, the documents at stake here are business records which implicate a lesser degree of concern for privacy interests than, for example, personal diaries.
>
> Were it true that the Court's opinion stands for the proposition that "the Fifth Amendment provides absolutely no protection for the contents of private papers of any kind," (O'Connor, J.), I would assuredly dissent. I continue to believe that under the Fifth Amendment "there are certain documents no person ought to be compelled to produce at the Government's request." Fisher v. United States (Justice Marshall, concurring).

Lower courts usually have found it unnecessary to decide whether anything remains of *Boyd's* Fifth Amendment analysis. "If the contents of papers are protected at all," they note, "it is only in rare situations, where compelled disclosure would break the heart of our sense of privacy." In re Steinberg, 837 F.2d 527 (1st Cir. 1988). Relying on *Steinberg*, the district court in In re Grand Jury Subpoena (ABC, Inc.), 668 F. Supp. 2d 307 (D. Mass. 2009), considered a privilege claim to resist a subpoena for a "tally sheet" that was "more akin to a check register or other personal financial record than to an intimately personal document, like a diary." The district court rejected the Fifth Amendment claim based on the content of the document, finding that "[w]hatever vestige of *Boyd* remains good law, Doe has not demonstrated or proffered that the documents at issue evoke the sort of privacy interests necessary to invoke content-based Fifth Amendment protection."

4. ***Non-Testimonial Response***. In **Doe v. United States**, 487 U.S. 201 (1988) ("Doe II"), the Supreme Court relied upon the underlying rationale of the foregone conclusion doctrine in finding that still another form of response to a subpoena was not testimonial in character. The petitioner was the target of a grand jury investigation, and invoked the Fifth Amendment in refusing to provide documents related to bank accounts he had in the Bahamas and Cayman Islands. Branches of the banks located in the United States refused to provide account information because of bank secrecy laws in their home country. The government moved for an order requiring Doe "to sign 12 forms consenting to disclosure of any bank records respectively relating to 12 foreign bank accounts over which the Government knew or suspected that Doe had control. The forms indicated the account numbers and described the documents that the Government wished the banks to produce." According to the government, "The form purported to apply to any and all accounts over which Doe had a right of withdrawal, without acknowledging the existence of any such account."[f]

---

[f] The form the government sought to require Doe to sign stated:

> I, ______, of the State of Texas in the United States of America, do hereby direct any bank or trust company at which I may have a bank account of any kind or at which a corporation has a bank account of any kind upon which I am authorized to draw, and its officers, employees and agents, to disclose all information and deliver copies of all documents of every nature in your possession or control which relate to said bank account to Grand Jury 84-2, empaneled May 7, 1984 and sitting in the Southern District of Texas, or to any attorney of the District of Texas, or to any attorney of the United States Department of Justice assisting said Grand Jury, and to give evidence relevant thereto, in the investigation conducted by Grand Jury 84-2 in the Southern District of Texas, and this shall be irrevocable authority for so doing. This direction has been executed pursuant to that certain order of the United States District Court for the Southern District of Texas issued in connection with the aforesaid investigation, dated ______. This direction is intended to apply to the Confidential Relationships (Preservation) Law of the Cayman Islands, and to any implied contract of confidentiality between Bermuda banks and their customers which may be imposed by Bermuda common law, and shall be construed as consent with respect thereto as the same shall apply to any of the bank accounts for which I may be a relevant principal.

Doe II concluded that even the act of making a verbal statement does not use to the level of a testimonial where the government's objective in forcing the subpoenaed party to make that statement is other than to have that person "relate a factual assertion or disclose information." *Doe II* held that signing the form did not compel "testimony" for Fifth Amendment purposes because "[a]s in *Fisher*, the Government is not relying upon the 'truthtelling' of *Doe's* directive to show the existence of, or his control over, foreign bank account records . . . By signing the form, *Doe* makes no statement, explicit or implicit, regarding the existence of a foreign bank account or his control over any such account. Nor would his execution of the form admit the authenticity of any records produced by the bank." This was so since the government did not seek to use the signed form itself as a factual assertion of the individual, although it intended to use the documents that might be produced by the bank in response to the signed directive as evidence against Doe in a later proceeding.

The *Doe II* Court noted that it had before it an unusual situation in which the verbal statement required of the subpoenaed party was not directed at requiring him to "convey information or assert facts." While it did constitute a communication, the government was directing the petitioner to do an act in a manner analogous to a directive requiring production of a handwriting sample or voice exemplar. Admittedly, the act could result in the production of evidence that would be used against the petitioner, but the directive did not "point the government toward hidden accounts or otherwise provide information that will assist the prosecution in uncovering evidence." It simply allowed the government through the directive, if accepted by the foreign bank, to seek evidence located through the government's own labor. Justice Stevens' dissent argued that the directive was no different than compelling a person to reveal the combination to his safe, but the majority characterized it as more like "requiring the individual to surrender a key to a strong box containing incriminating documents."

2. Foregone Conclusion Doctrine

To determine whether a witness' testimony might be viewed as incriminatory under the "link-in-the-chain" standard for a Fifth Amendment claim, courts do not look to whether the facts conveyed in the witness' testimony might be established by the government through other sources. Does the Fisher/Doe ruling that the privilege does not apply when "possession, existence and authentication" are a "foregone conclusion" require precisely that inquiry in determining the communicative aspects of the act of production? If so, why this special treatment for that act? Consider in this connection, Robert Mosteller, *Simplifying Subpoena Law: Taking the Fifth Amendment Seriously*, 73 VA. L. REV. 1, 32-33 (1987):

> More plausibly, the Court is suggesting [in its "foregone conclusion" analysis] that when an implicit as opposed to an explicit communication is involved, it is necessary to consider whether the

government is really asking a "question" through the subpoena. Granted, the defendant's response to a documentary subpoena always reveals that the item does or does not exist; the government cannot eliminate the implicit question about the document's existence no matter how it phrases the subpoena's demand. But if the government already knows the answer to that question and is truly uninterested in the implicit answer provided by production, the witness' gratuitous communication of it should not violate the fifth amendment. In short, the *Fisher* decision suggests that constitutional rights are not violated by implicit communications that are inherent in a response to a documentary subpoena where those communications are unwanted because, though technically admissible, they are not substantially relevant to the prosecution's case given its other evidence.

UNITED STATES v. HUBBELL

530 U.S. 27 (2000)

Justice STEVENS delivered the opinion of the Court.

The two questions presented concern the scope of a witness' protection against compelled self-incrimination: (1) whether the Fifth Amendment privilege protects a witness from being compelled to disclose the existence of incriminating documents that the Government is unable to describe with reasonable particularity; and (2) if the witness produces such documents pursuant to a grant of immunity, whether 18 U.S.C. § 6002 prevents the Government from using them to prepare criminal charges against him.

This proceeding arises out of the second prosecution of respondent, Webster Hubbell, commenced by the Independent Counsel appointed in August 1994 to investigate possible violations of federal law relating to the Whitewater Development Corporation. The first prosecution was terminated pursuant to a plea bargain. In December 1994, respondent pleaded guilty to charges of mail fraud and tax evasion arising out of his billing practices as a member of an Arkansas law firm from 1989 to 1992, and was sentenced to 21 months in prison. In the plea agreement, respondent promised to provide the Independent Counsel with "full, complete, accurate, and truthful information" about matters relating to the Whitewater investigation.

The second prosecution resulted from the Independent Counsel's attempt to determine whether respondent had violated that promise. In October 1996, while respondent was incarcerated, the Independent Counsel served him with a subpoena duces tecum calling for the production of 11 categories of documents before a grand jury sitting in Little Rock, Arkansas. See

Appendix, infra.[a] On November 19, he appeared before the grand jury and invoked his Fifth Amendment privilege against self-incrimination. In response to questioning by the prosecutor, respondent initially refused "to state whether there are documents within my possession, custody, or control responsive to the Subpoena." Thereafter, the prosecutor produced an order, which had previously been obtained from the District Court pursuant to 18 U.S.C. § 6003(a), directing him to respond to the subpoena and granting him immunity "to the extent allowed by law." Respondent then produced 13,120 pages of documents and records and responded to a series of questions that established that those were all of the documents in his custody or control that were responsive to the commands in the subpoena, with the exception of a few documents he claimed were shielded by the attorney-client and attorney work- product privileges.

The contents of the documents produced by respondent provided the Independent Counsel with the information that led to this second prosecution. On April 30, 1998, a grand jury in the District of Columbia returned a 10-count indictment charging respondent with various tax-related crimes and mail and wire fraud. The District Court dismissed the indictment relying, in part, on the ground that the Independent Counsel's use of the subpoenaed documents violated § 6002 because all of the evidence he would offer against respondent at trial derived either directly or indirectly from the testimonial aspects of respondent's immunized act of producing those documents. Noting that the Independent Counsel had admitted that he was not investigating tax-related issues when he issued the subpoena, and that he had "'learned about the unreported income and other crimes from studying the records' contents,'" the District Court characterized the subpoena as "the quintessential fishing expedition." * * *

The Court of Appeals vacated the judgment and remanded for further proceedings. The majority concluded that the District Court had incorrectly relied on the fact that the Independent Counsel did not have prior knowledge of the contents of the subpoenaed documents. The question the District Court should have addressed was the extent of the Government's independent knowledge of the documents' existence and authenticity, and of respondent's possession or control of them. It explained: "On remand, the district court should hold a hearing in which it seeks to establish the extent and detail of the [G]overnment's knowledge of Hubbell's financial affairs (or of the paperwork documenting it) on the day the subpoena issued. It is only then that the court will be in a position to assess the testimonial value of Hubbell's response to the subpoena. Should the Independent Counsel prove capable of demonstrating with reasonable particularity a prior awareness that the exhaustive litany of documents sought in the subpoena existed and were in Hubbell's possession, then the wide distance evidently traveled from

---

[a] The Appendix to Justice Stevens' opinion set forth verbatim the "subpoena rider," which identified the 11 categories of documents in paragraphs (A)-(K). The rider is reprinted on p. 358.

the subpoena to the substantive allegations contained in the indictment would be based upon legitimate intermediate steps. To the extent that the information conveyed through Hubbell's compelled act of production provides the necessary linkage, however, the indictment deriving therefrom is tainted."

In the opinion of the dissenting judge, the majority failed to give full effect to the distinction between the contents of the documents and the limited testimonial significance of the act of producing them. In his view, as long as the prosecutor could make use of information contained in the documents or derived therefrom without any reference to the fact that respondent had produced them in response to a subpoena, there would be no improper use of the testimonial aspect of the immunized act of production. In other words, the constitutional privilege and the statute conferring use immunity would only shield the witness from the use of any information resulting from his subpoena response "beyond what the prosecutor would receive if the documents appeared in the grand jury room or in his office unsolicited and unmarked, like manna from heaven."

On remand, the Independent Counsel acknowledged that he could not satisfy the "reasonable particularity" standard prescribed by the Court of Appeals and entered into a conditional plea agreement with respondent. In essence, the agreement provides for the dismissal of the charges unless this Court's disposition of the case makes it reasonably likely that respondent's "act of production immunity" would not pose a significant bar to his prosecution. The case is not moot, however, because the agreement also provides for the entry of a guilty plea and a sentence that will not include incarceration if we should reverse and issue an opinion that is sufficiently favorable to the Government to satisfy that condition. Despite that agreement, we granted the Independent Counsel's petition for a writ of certiorari in order to determine the precise scope of a grant of immunity with respect to the production of documents in response to a subpoena. We now affirm.

It is useful to preface our analysis of the constitutional issue with a restatement of certain propositions that are not in dispute. The term "privilege against self-incrimination" is not an entirely accurate description of a person's constitutional protection against being "compelled in any criminal case to be a witness against himself." The word "witness" in the constitutional text limits the relevant category of compelled incriminating communications to those that are "testimonial" in character.[8] As Justice

[8] "It is consistent with the history of and the policies underlying the Self-Incrimination Clause to hold that the privilege may be asserted only to resist compelled explicit or implicit disclosures of incriminating information. Historically, the privilege was intended to prevent the use of legal compulsion to extract from the accused a sworn communication of facts which would incriminate him. Such was the process of the ecclesiastical courts and the Star Chamber—the inquisitorial method of putting the accused upon his oath and compelling him to answer questions

Holmes observed, there is a significant difference between the use of compulsion to extort communications from a defendant and compelling a person to engage in conduct that may be incriminating. Thus, even though the act may provide incriminating evidence, a criminal suspect may be compelled to put on a shirt, to provide a blood sample or handwriting exemplar, or to make a recording of his voice. The act of exhibiting such physical characteristics is not the same as a sworn communication by a witness that relates either express or implied assertions of fact or belief.***

More relevant to this case is the settled proposition that a person may be required to produce specific documents even though they contain incriminating assertions of fact or belief because the creation of those documents was not "compelled" within the meaning of the privilege. [Fisher v. United States, p. 385] * * * It is clear, therefore, that respondent Hubbell could not avoid compliance with the subpoena served on him merely because the demanded documents contained incriminating evidence, whether written by others or voluntarily prepared by himself. * * * On the other hand, we have also made it clear that the act of producing documents in response to a subpoena may have a compelled testimonial aspect. We have held that "the act of production" itself may implicitly communicate "statements of fact" [Doe II]. By "producing documents in compliance with a subpoena, the witness would admit that the papers existed, were in his possession or control, and were authentic." Moreover, as was true in this case, when the custodian of documents responds to a subpoena, he may be compelled to take the witness stand and answer questions designed to determine whether he has produced everything demanded by the subpoena. The answers to those questions, as well as the act of production itself, may certainly communicate information about the existence, custody, and authenticity of the documents. Whether the constitutional privilege protects the answers to such questions, or protects the act of production itself, is a question that is distinct from the question whether the unprotected contents of the documents themselves are incriminating.

Finally, the phrase "in any criminal case" in the text of the Fifth Amendment might have been read to limit its coverage to compelled testimony that is used against the defendant in the trial itself. It has, however, long been settled that its protection encompasses compelled statements that lead to the discovery of incriminating evidence even though the statements themselves are not incriminating and are not introduced into evidence. * * * Compelled testimony that communicates information that may "lead to incriminating evidence" is privileged even if the information itself is not inculpatory. * * * It is the Fifth Amendment's protection against the prosecutor's use of incriminating information derived directly or indirectly from the compelled testimony of the respondent that is of primary relevance in this case.

---

designed to uncover uncharged offenses, without evidence from another source. * * *" *Doe II.*

Acting pursuant to 18 U.S.C. § 6002, the District Court entered an order compelling respondent to produce "any and all documents" described in the grand jury subpoena and granting him "immunity to the extent allowed by law." In Kastigar v. United States [p. 574], we upheld the constitutionality of § 6002 because the scope of the "use and derivative-use" immunity that it provides is coextensive with the scope of the constitutional privilege against self-incrimination. * * * We particularly emphasized the critical importance of protection against a future prosecution "'based on knowledge and sources of information obtained from the compelled testimony.'" * * * [W]e held that the statute imposes an affirmative duty on the prosecution, not merely to show that its evidence is not tainted by the prior testimony, but "to prove that the evidence it proposes to use is derived from a legitimate source wholly independent of the compelled testimony." * * * The "compelled testimony" that is relevant in this case is not to be found in the contents of the documents produced in response to the subpoena. It is, rather, the testimony inherent in the act of producing those documents. The disagreement between the parties focuses entirely on the significance of that testimonial aspect.

The Government correctly emphasizes that the testimonial aspect of a response to a subpoena duces tecum does nothing more than establish the existence, authenticity, and custody of items that are produced. We assume that the Government is also entirely correct in its submission that it would not have to advert to respondent's act of production in order to prove the existence, authenticity, or custody of any documents that it might offer in evidence at a criminal trial; indeed, the Government disclaims any need to introduce any of the documents produced by respondent into evidence in order to prove the charges against him. It follows, according to the Government, that it has no intention of making improper "use" of respondent's compelled testimony. The question, however, is not whether the response to the subpoena may be introduced into evidence at his criminal trial. That would surely be a prohibited "use" of the immunized act of production. But the fact that the Government intends no such use of the act of production leaves open the separate question whether it has already made "derivative use" of the testimonial aspect of that act in obtaining the indictment against respondent and in preparing its case for trial. It clearly has.

It is apparent from the text of the subpoena itself that the prosecutor needed respondent's assistance both to identify potential sources of information and to produce those sources. See Appendix [fn. a supra]. Given the breadth of the description of the 11 categories of documents called for by the subpoena, the collection and production of the materials demanded was tantamount to answering a series of interrogatories asking a witness to disclose the existence and location of particular documents fitting certain broad descriptions. The assembly of literally hundreds of pages of material in response to a request for "any and all documents reflecting, referring, or relating to any direct or indirect sources of money or other things of value received by or provided to" an individual or members of his family during a 3-year period, is the functional equivalent of the preparation of an answer to either a detailed written interrogatory or a series of oral questions at a discovery deposition. Entirely apart from the contents of the 13,120 pages of materials that respondent produced in this case, it is undeniable that providing a catalog of existing documents fitting within any of the 11 broadly worded subpoena categories could provide a prosecutor with a "lead to incriminating evidence," or "a link in the chain of evidence needed to prosecute."

Indeed, the record makes it clear that that is what happened in this case. The documents were produced before a grand jury sitting in the Eastern District of Arkansas in aid of the Independent Counsel's attempt to determine whether respondent had violated a commitment in his first plea agreement. The use of those sources of information eventually led to the return of an indictment by a grand jury sitting in the District of Columbia for offenses that apparently are unrelated to that plea agreement. What the District Court characterized as a "fishing expedition" did produce a fish, but not the one that the Independent Counsel expected to hook. It is abundantly clear that the testimonial aspect of respondent's act of producing subpoenaed documents was the first step in a chain of evidence that led to this prosecution. The documents did not magically appear in the prosecutor's office like "manna from heaven." They arrived there only after respondent asserted his constitutional privilege, received a grant of immunity, and—under the compulsion of the District Court's order—took the mental and physical steps necessary to provide the prosecutor with an accurate inventory of the many sources of potentially incriminating evidence sought by the subpoena. It was only through respondent's truthful reply to the subpoena that the Government received the incriminating documents of which it made "substantial use . . . in the investigation that led to the indictment."

For these reasons, we cannot accept the Government's submission that respondent's immunity did not preclude its derivative use of the produced documents because its "possession of the documents [was] the fruit only of a simple physical act–the act of producing the documents." It was unquestionably necessary for respondent to make extensive use of "the contents of his own mind" in identifying the hundreds of documents responsive to the requests in the subpoena. The assembly of those documents was like telling an inquisitor the combination to a wall safe, not like being forced to surrender the key to a strongbox. *Doe II.* The Government's anemic view of respondent's act of production as a mere physical act that is principally non-testimonial in character and can be entirely divorced from its "implicit" testimonial aspect so as to constitute a "legitimate, wholly independent source" (as required by *Kastigar*) for the documents produced simply fails to account for these realities.

In sum, we have no doubt that the constitutional privilege against self-incrimination protects the target of a grand jury investigation from being compelled to answer questions designed to elicit information about the existence of sources of potentially incriminating evidence. That constitutional privilege has the same application to the testimonial aspect of a response to a subpoena seeking discovery of those sources. Before the District Court, the Government arguably conceded that respondent's act of production in this case had a testimonial aspect that entitled him to respond to the subpoena by asserting his privilege against self-incrimination. * * * On appeal and again before this Court, however, the Government has argued that the communicative aspect of respondent's act of producing ordinary business records is insufficiently "testimonial" to support a claim of privilege because the existence and possession of such records by any businessman is a "foregone conclusion" under our decision in Fisher v. United States. This argument both misreads Fisher and ignores our subsequent decision in *Doe I*. * * * Whatever the scope of this "foregone conclusion" rationale, the facts of this case plainly fall outside of it. While in *Fisher* the Government already knew that the documents were in the attorneys' possession and could independently confirm their existence and authenticity through the accountants who created them, here the Government has not shown that it had any prior knowledge of either the existence or the whereabouts of the 13,120 pages of documents ultimately produced by respondent. The Government cannot cure this deficiency through the overbroad argument that a businessman such as respondent will always possess general business and tax records that fall within the broad categories described in this subpoena. The *Doe I* subpoenas also sought several broad categories of general business records, yet we upheld the District Court's finding that the act of producing those records would involve testimonial self-incrimination.

Given our conclusion that respondent's act of production had a testimonial aspect, at least with respect to the existence and location of the documents sought by the Government's subpoena, respondent could not be compelled to produce those documents without first receiving a grant of immunity under § 6003. As we construed § 6002 in *Kastigar*, such immunity is co-extensive with the constitutional privilege. *Kastigar* requires that respondent's motion to dismiss the indictment on immunity grounds be granted unless the Government proves that the evidence it used in obtaining the indictment and proposed to use at trial was derived from legitimate sources "wholly independent" of the testimonial aspect of respondent's immunized conduct in assembling and producing the documents described in the subpoena. The Government, however, does not claim that it could make such a showing. Rather, it contends that its prosecution of respondent must be considered proper unless someone—presumably respondent—shows that "there is some substantial relation between the compelled testimonial communications implicit in the act of production (as opposed to the act of production standing alone) and some aspect of the information used in the investigation or the evidence presented at trial." Brief for United States 9. We could not accept this submission without repudiating the basis for our conclusion in *Kastigar* that the statutory guarantee of use and derivative-use immunity is as broad as the constitutional privilege itself. This we are not prepared to do. Accordingly, the indictment against respondent must be dismissed. The judgment of the Court of Appeals is affirmed. * * *

Chief Justice REHNQUIST dissents and would reverse the judgment of the Court of Appeals in part, for the reasons given by Judge Williams in his dissenting opinion in that court.

Justice THOMAS, with whom Justice SCALIA joins, concurring.

Our decision today involves the application of the act-of-production doctrine, which provides that persons compelled to turn over incriminating papers or other physical evidence pursuant to a subpoena duces tecum or a summons may invoke the Fifth Amendment privilege against self-incrimination as a bar to production only where the act of producing the evidence would contain "testimonial" features. I join the opinion of the Court because it properly applies this doctrine, but I write separately to note that this doctrine may be inconsistent with the original meaning of the Fifth Amendment's Self-Incrimination Clause. A substantial body of evidence suggests that the Fifth Amendment privilege protects against the compelled production not just of incriminating testimony, but of any incriminating evidence. In a future case, I would be willing to reconsider the scope and meaning of the Self-Incrimination Clause.

The Fifth Amendment provides that "[n]o person . . . shall be compelled in any criminal case to be a witness against himself." The key word at issue in this case is "witness." The Court's opinion, relying on prior cases, essentially defines "witness" as a person who provides testimony, and thus restricts the Fifth Amendment's ban to only those communications "that are 'testimonial' in character." None of this Court's cases, however, has undertaken an analysis of the meaning of the term at the time of the founding. A review of that period reveals substantial support for the view that the term "witness" meant a person who gives or furnishes evidence, a broader meaning than that which our case law currently ascribes to the term. If this is so, a person who responds to a subpoena duces tecum would be just as much a "witness" as a person who responds to a subpoena ad testificandum.[1]

This Court has not always taken the approach to the Fifth Amendment that we follow today. The first case interpreting the Self-Incrimination Clause–Boyd v. United States–was decided, though not explicitly, in accordance with the understanding that "witness" means one who gives evidence. In *Boyd*, this Court unanimously held that the Fifth Amendment protects a defendant against compelled production of books and papers. And the Court linked its interpretation of the Fifth Amendment to the

---

[1]Even if the term "witness" in the Fifth Amendment referred to someone who provides testimony, as this Court's recent cases suggest without historical analysis, it may well be that at the time of the founding a person who turned over documents would be described as providing testimony. See Amey v. Long, 9 East. 472, 484, 103 Eng. Rep. 653, 658 (K.B.1808) (referring to documents requested by subpoenas duces tecum as "written ... testimony"). * * *

common-law understanding of the self-incrimination privilege. But this Court's decision in Fisher v. United States, rejected this understanding, permitting the Government to force a person to furnish incriminating physical evidence and protecting only the "testimonial" aspects of that transfer. In so doing, *Fisher* not only failed to examine the historical backdrop to the Fifth Amendment, it also required–as illustrated by extended discussion in the opinions below in this case–a difficult parsing of the act of responding to a subpoena duces tecum. None of the parties in this case has asked us to depart from Fisher, but in light of the historical evidence that the Self-Incrimination Clause may have a broader reach than *Fisher* holds, I remain open to a reconsideration of that decision and its progeny in a proper case.

NOTE

The Effect of Hubbell. The grant of "act of production" immunity effectively prevented the prosecutors from using the content of the records. How far does a grant of immunity extend? In **In re Grand Jury Subpoena Duces Tecum Dated March 25, 2011**, 670 F.3d 1335 (11th Cir. 2012), the Eleventh Circuit considered the effect of a grant of immunity requiring the production of unencrypted laptop hard drives. The subpoena recipient refused to produce the unencrypted records, claiming that immunity for decrypting the files should extend to their contents, which the district court refused to do. The Eleventh Circuit first concluded that the act of decryption was testimonial, and therefore subject to an assertion of the Fifth Amendment privilege against self-incrimination. Regarding the scope of a grant of immunity related to this type of act of production, the circuit court stated:

> The district court still could have compelled Doe to turn over the unencrypted contents—and held him in contempt if he refused to do so—had the Government offered and the district court granted Doe constitutionally sufficient immunity. The district court erred in limiting Doe's immunity under 18 U.S.C. §§ 6002 and 6003 to the Government's use of his act of decryption and production while allowing the Government derivative use of the evidence such act disclosed. Doe's immunity was not coextensive with the protections afforded by the Fifth Amendment; consequently, he could not have been compelled to decrypt and produce the contents of the hard drives.
>
> In evaluating the immunity Doe received, we must look beyond the act-of-production label and ask this question: what conduct was actually immunized and what use would the Government make of the evidence derived from such conduct in a future prosecution? The Government stated in its letter served on Doe on April 7, 2011, and before the district court on April 19, 2011, that it would not use Doe's act of production against him in a future prosecution; but it would

use the contents of the unencrypted drives against him. The district court incorporated the Government's position in its order granting immunity under 18 U.S.C. § 6002. The act-of-production immunity, as the Government and the district court framed it, is not synonymous with use and derivative-use immunity. More to the point, it is not the type of immunity mandated by 18 U.S.C. § 6002. The question thus becomes, is the act-of-production immunity offered here sufficient to compel Doe to testify? We hold that the answer is most certainly, no. * * *

Supreme Court precedent is clear: Use and derivative-use immunity establishes the critical threshold to overcome an individual's invocation of the Fifth Amendment privilege against self-incrimination. No more protection is necessary; no less protection is sufficient.

The Government gave no such immunity in this case. In essence, the Government attempted to immunize the testimony itself, treating everything else as fair game. But for the reasons we just noted, the Government cannot obtain immunity only for the act of production and then seek to introduce the contents of the production, regardless of whether those contents are characterized as nontestimonial evidence, because doing so would allow the use of evidence derived from the original testimonial statement.

The Court in *Hubbell* expressly rejected the "manna from heaven" theory, which contended that if the Government omitted any description of how the documents were obtained, it would be as if they magically appeared on the courthouse steps and the Government could use the documents themselves. The Government, in essence, asks us to revisit the "manna from heaven" theory. The Supreme Court definitively foreclosed such an argument; hence, we must decline to consider it.

To conclude, because Doe's act of production would have testimonial aspects to it, an order to compel him to produce the unencrypted contents of the drives would require immunity coextensive with the Fifth Amendment (and § 6002). Immunity coextensive with the Fifth Amendment requires both use and derivative-use immunity. The Government's offer of act-of-production immunity clearly could not provide the requisite protection because it would allow the Government to use evidence derived from the immunized testimony. Thus, because the immunity offered here was not coextensive with the Fifth Amendment, Doe could not be compelled to decrypt the drives.

3. Proving Existence, Possession, and Authenticity

IN RE GRAND JURY SUBPOENA DATED APRIL 18, 2003
383 F.3d 905 (9th Cir. 2004)

CANBY, Circuit Judge.

Appellant John Doe was held in contempt by the district court and he appeals, challenging the district court's denial of his motion to quash a subpoena duces tecum. * * *

This appeal presents a challenge to one of several subpoenas issued in connection with the government's investigation into antitrust violations in the Dynamic Random Access Memory (DRAM) semiconductor memory chip industry. On June 17, 2002, a grand jury sitting in the Northern District of California issued subpoenas duces tecum to all the major worldwide DRAM manufacturers, including Doe's former employer (the "Corporation"). The subpoena served on the Corporation covered the period from January 1, 1998, through the date of the subpoena and requested, among other things, all documents relating to contacts and communications among competitors regarding the sale of DRAM. The subpoena also asked the Corporation for the names of all its current and former employees who had any responsibility for pricing DRAM, as well as the calendars, appointment books, telephone directories, and travel and entertainment expense records on file for those employees.

The Corporation identified Doe as an employee who was responsible for pricing DRAM. Doe worked for the Corporation from 1991 through 1998. The documents produced by the Corporation in response to the subpoena did not reveal any calendars, appointment books, notebooks, address books, or business diaries for Doe. These types of materials were found in the employee records of other DRAM salesmen, including Doe's successor.

During the government's investigation, a cooperating witness from another DRAM manufacturer provided detailed information regarding meetings and telephone conversations he had with Doe, in which they discussed the price at which the Corporation and its competitors would sell DRAM to computer manufacturers. After the government obtained this information, FBI agents interviewed Doe at his home in April 2003. During the interview, Doe indicated that he had shared DRAM pricing information with competitors, including the government's cooperating witness. Doe further stated that he had memorialized these conversations in e-mails to his supervisors. Doe stated, however, that he did not believe he had any records, notes, or documents related to the government's investigation because he had left such records at the Corporation. At the end of the interview, the agents served Doe with a subpoena duces tecum, which is the subject of this appeal. The subpoena commanded Doe to appear and testify before the grand jury and bring with him all documents in his possession "relating to the production or sale of Dynamic Random Access Memory ('DRAM') components, including but not limited to, handwritten notes, calendars, diaries, daybooks, appointment calendars, or notepads, or any similar documents." * * *

Doe, claiming a Fifth Amendment privilege against self-incrimination, informed the government that he would not testify without immunity and would not produce the subpoenaed documents. The government postponed indefinitely Doe's appearance before the grand jury, but did not relieve him of his obligation to produce the documents described in the subpoena duces tecum, nor did the government offer Doe immunity under 18 U.S.C. § 6003. Instead, the government informed counsel for the Corporation that Doe might have documents responsive to the subpoenas served on the Corporation. The Corporation requested from Doe "any company records or property" that may be in Doe's possession and covered by the Proprietary Information Agreement or the Exit Interview statement that Doe had signed. Without admitting that he had any company records in his possession, Doe declined to produce any such documents to the Corporation.

Doe then moved to quash the subpoena that had been served on him, claiming that the act of producing the documents responsive to the subpoena would violate his Fifth Amendment rights. The district court denied the motion to quash, finding that the existence of Doe's documents was a "foregone conclusion," and therefore the act of producing the documents was not testimonial in nature. Doe again refused to turn over any documents and was held in contempt by the district court pursuant to a Stipulation and Order of Contempt. Doe timely appealed, and enforcement of the contempt order has been stayed pending appeal. * * *

Where the preparation of business records is voluntary, there is no compulsion present, and consequently the contents of those records are not privileged by the Fifth Amendment. It is not contested that the documents in Doe's possession were created voluntarily during the course of his employment with the Corporation. The contents of those documents are therefore not protected by the Fifth Amendment.

Doe's claim of privilege is directed, however, not to the documents themselves but to the act of producing the documents. A witness' production of documents in response to a subpoena may have incriminating testimonial aspects. See United States v. Hubbell, 530 U.S. 27 (2000) (Hubbell II). By producing documents in compliance with a subpoena, the witness admits that the documents exist, are in his possession or control, and are authentic. These types of admissions implicitly communicate statements of fact that may lead to incriminating evidence. Whether the act of production has a testimonial aspect sufficient to attract Fifth Amendment protection is a fact-intensive inquiry.

When the "existence and location" of the documents under subpoena are a "foregone conclusion" and the witness "adds little or nothing to the sum total of the Government's information by conceding that he in fact has the [documents]," then no Fifth Amendment right is touched because the "question is not of testimony but of surrender." Fisher. When deciding whether the government has met its burdens of production and proof, courts should look to the "quantum of information possessed by the government before it issued the relevant subpoena." United States v. Hubbell, 167 F.3d 552 (D.C.Cir. 1999) (Hubbell I).

At the time the government served the subpoena on Doe, the government possessed insufficient information to make the existence or possession of all of Doe's documents relating to the production or sale of DRAM, "including, but not limited to, handwritten notes, calendars, diaries, daybooks, appointment calendars, or notepads, or any similar documents" a foregone conclusion. The government was not required to have actual knowledge of the existence and location of each and every responsive document; the government was required, however, to establish the existence of the documents sought and Doe's possession of them with "reasonable particularity" before the existence and possession of the documents could be considered a foregone conclusion and production therefore would not be testimonial.

Although the government possessed extensive knowledge about Doe's price-fixing activities as a result of interviews with cooperating witnesses and Doe's own incriminating statements made to federal agents on April 26, 2003, it is the government's knowledge of the existence and possession of the actual documents, not the information contained therein, that is central to the foregone conclusion inquiry. The breadth of the subpoena in this case far exceeded the government's knowledge about the actual documents that Doe created or possessed during his former employment and that he retained after he terminated his employment. The government probably could identify with sufficient particularity the existence of e-mails between Doe and some of his competitors, e-mails between Doe and his superiors regarding pricing, phone records corroborating that Doe spoke to his competitors, and records establishing meetings with certain competitors because Doe made substantial admissions to investigators during his living room interview regarding these documents. The government, however, failed to draft the subpoena narrowly to identify the documents that it could establish with reasonable particularity. Thus, on the record before us, the subpoena's breadth far exceeded the reasonably particular knowledge that the government actually possessed when it served the subpoena on Doe.

The Supreme Court has stated on more than one occasion that such broad language contributes to a finding that the response to a subpoena may be testimonial. In *Hubbell*, the Supreme Court noted:

> It is apparent from the text of the subpoena itself that the prosecutor needed respondent's assistance both to identify potential sources of information and to produce those sources .... Given the breadth of the description of the 11 categories of documents called for by the subpoena, the collection and production of the materials demanded

> was tantamount to answering a series of interrogatories asking a witness to disclose the existence and location of particular documents fitting certain broad descriptions.

A subpoena such as this, which seeks all documents within a category but fails to describe those documents with any specificity indicates that the government needs the act of production to build its case against Doe.

This conclusion is supported by the timing of the subpoena in Doe's case. When the government issued its April 26, 2003, subpoena duces tecum to Doe, it had not yet served the May 19, 2003, second document subpoena on Doe's former employer, the response to which subsequently led the government to conclude that Doe possessed business records that were created during his former employment. It is the "quantum of information possessed by the government before it issue[s] the relevant subpoena" that is central to the foregone conclusion inquiry. See Hubbell I. At the time the government served the subpoena duces tecum on Doe, it had no reason to believe that Doe possessed the myriad of documents it sought. The argument that a salesman such as Doe will always possess business records describing or memorializing meetings or prices does not establish the reasonably particular knowledge required. It was therefore improper for the district court to consider evidence of Doe's business records produced by Doe's former employer in response to the May 19, 2003, subpoena to support the foregone conclusion inquiry.

The authenticity prong of the foregone conclusion doctrine requires the government to establish that it can independently verify that the compelled documents "are in fact what they purport to be." Independent verification not only requires the government to show that the documents sought to be compelled would be admissible independent of the witness' production of them, but also inquires into whether the government is compelling the witness to use his discretion in selecting and assembling the responsive documents, and thereby tacitly providing identifying information that is necessary to the government's authentication of the subpoenaed documents.

In this case, the district court simply stated it would "hold the government to its representation that [Doe's] testimony via production of these documents will not be needed for authentication," without explaining why this was an appropriate solution to overcome Doe's Fifth Amendment challenge. The subpoena commanded Doe to produce all documents "relating to the production or sale of Dynamic Random Access Memory ("DRAM") components, including but not limited to, handwritten notes, calendars, diaries, daybooks, appointment calendars, or notepads, or any similar documents." It thus sought many documents that Doe created himself. It further required him to discriminate among the many documents he might possess, requiring him specifically to identify and produce to the grand jury those that related to the production or sale of DRAM.

Although the government could probably authenticate the writing on Doe's handwritten documents through handwriting analysis, it made little effort to demonstrate how anyone beside Doe could sift through his handwritten notes, personal appointment books, and diaries to produce what Doe's attorney estimates may be 4,500 documents related to the production or sale of DRAM. Such a response by Doe would provide the government with the identifying information that it would need to authenticate these documents. Doe's notes to himself would be difficult, if not impossible, to authenticate by anyone besides Doe. * * *

In this case, the government has failed to demonstrate that it can authenticate the documents so broadly described in the subpoena without the identifying information that Doe would provide by using his knowledge and judgment to sift through, select, assemble, and produce the documents.

This case is a far cry from *Fisher*, where the government had prior knowledge that the documents were in the custodian's possession and the government could independently confirm their existence and authenticity through the accountants who created them. The government in *Fisher* did not need to rely on the "'truth-telling' of the taxpayer to prove the existence of or his access to the documents." Here, as in *Hubbell*, the government simply has not shown that it had prior knowledge of the existence of the estimated 4,500 documents.

The district court erred when it determined that the act of producing these documents was not testimonial because their existence, possession, and authenticity was a "foregone conclusion." We accordingly reverse its order denying on that ground Doe's motion to quash the subpoena, and its order holding Doe in contempt. * * *

NOTES

1. ***Potential Incrimination***. Assuming that the government does not establish that possession, authentication, and existence are a foregone conclusion, under what circumstances will the privilege nonetheless not be applicable because the likelihood of incrimination is not "substantial and real" ? Note in this regard *Fisher's* comments on the incriminatory aspects of producing records that were authored by another and clearly could be lawfully possessed. What did the Court mean when it said that "at this juncture," it was unwilling to hold that either the existence of the papers or their possession posed a realistic threat of incrimination? Assuming that the contents of the papers were incriminatory, wouldn't acknowledgment of their existence pose a realistic threat of incrimination as found in *Doe I*? Assuming that the contents were incriminatory, wouldn't possession suggest knowledge of that content and thereby pose a realistic threat? Is the answer that the Court in *Fisher* may not have been willing to conclude, on the record before it in the context of an IRS investigation (rather than a grand jury investigation), that a realistic threat existed that the contents were

incriminatory? In a criminal investigation, unlike a civil IRS investigation, it may be easier for the subpoena recipient to establish the potential incrimination from responding to the demand for records, and so assert the Fifth Amendment privilege.

2. ***How Much Knowledge Is Required***. The need for care in providing immunity to obtain documents pursuant to a subpoena duces tecum was emphasized in **United States v. Ponds**, 454 F.3d 313 (D.C Cir. 2006). The District of Columbia Circuit reversed the conviction of the defendant – a criminal defense lawyer being investigated for his fee arrangements with a client who was a drug dealer – who provided documents to the grand jury only after a grant of immunity. The court stated:

> [T]he government has failed to show with reasonable particularity that it had prior knowledge of the existence and location of many of the subpoenaed documents necessary to render their existence and location a "foregone conclusion." The Supreme Court has not defined the precise amount of cognition on the part of an immunized party necessary to render a subpoena response "testimonial," but it is clear here that, as in Hubbell, the government "needed [Ponds'] assistance both to identify potential sources of information and to produce those sources," and "it is undeniable that providing a catalog of existing documents" rendered this subpoena response "testimony" rather than mere "surrender." So much is evident in the government's admission that it was "surprised" by some of the documents produced.

If the government chooses not to grant immunity to the subpoena recipient, then the failure to establish the requisite level of knowledge for a foregone conclusion means the subpoena will not be enforced. In **United States v. Sabit**, 2014 WL 1317082 (E.D. Mich. 2014), the Department of Justice was investigating possible kickbacks paid by an medical implant manufacturer to a neurosurgeon, and a Civil Investigative Demand sought e-mails between the doctor and the company over five years. The doctor asserted the Fifth Amendment "act of production" privilege, and the government argued the e-mails should be produced under *Fisher*'s foregone conclusion analysis. The district court found the government's knowledge of existence, possession, and authenticity insufficient to enforce the CID:

> As to the request for e-mails, Sabit contends that even this more limited request is overly broad, as it would require him to sort through all of his e-mails and also, to sort out the relationships between various individuals and Reliance. Sabit claims the government has identified only one e-mail between himself and Reliance, and thus, the government's request is not based on "reasonable particularity" but is a fishing expedition. The government responds that it has identified the e-mail account from which Sabit sent and received e-mails, and that it has identified one e-mail. At oral argument, the government stated that it knows of

other e-mails and could identify them to the court for in camera review. At the hearing, the government also stated that it is seeking e-mails for the five-year period beginning in 2009 to the present, and guessed that the number of e-mails in existence would be less than 50. The government provided no basis for such speculation. The government also failed to identify the nature of the communications sought. The government's argument is reminiscent of the argument the Supreme Court rejected in *Hubbell* where the government claimed production of business records was not testimonial because Hubbell, as a businessman, could be expected to maintain business records. The Court held greater particularity is required and the same is true here.

The government could likely identify an e-mail address for anyone; this does not make the production of all e-mails non-testimonial. Sabit would be required to sift through all of his e-mails to respond to the document request which might require him to identify which individuals were affiliated with Reliance. Such an exercise would require Sabit to use the contents of his mind, and is akin to answering written interrogatories or answering oral questions at a discovery deposition would be constitutionally protected by the Fifth Amendment. The government has failed to identify the existence of the e-mails sought with reasonable particularity, and the request appears to be akin to a fishing expedition that was found to be testimonial in *Hubbell.*

3. ***Failing to Assert the Act of Production Privilege.*** In **United States v. Grable**, 98 F.3d 251 (6th Cir. 1996), the Sixth Circuit stated:

> The government * * * contends that because the defendant did not assert his 'act of production' privilege at the enforcement hearing (which he neglected to attend), he was consequently precluded from asserting it at the later contempt hearing. In support of this argument, the government relies on United States v. Rylander, 460 U.S. 752 (1983), in which the Supreme Court prohibited a taxpayer from raising at a civil contempt hearing, for the first time, a defense of lack of possession and control of the corporate documents sought by an IRS summons.
>
> The Courts of Appeals for the Fourth and Ninth Circuits appear to have rejected similar arguments. See United States v. Sharp, 920 F.2d 1167 (4th Cir.1990) (*Rylander* does not require barring a taxpayer from relying on the Fifth Amendment at a contempt hearing because he failed to assert the privilege 'in a technically proper form while unrepresented by counsel.'); United States v. Rendahl, 746 F.2d 553 (9th Cir.1984) (A defendant is not barred from claiming a Fifth Amendment privilege at a contempt hearing because of his failure to raise the claim at an enforcement hearing.).

The government's position is based either on a claim of waiver or res judicata resulting from the taxpayer's failure to claim the privilege at the enforcement hearing. Viewed either way, we cannot resolve the question from the record made in the district court. Upon remand the district court will make a determination, following such proceedings as it finds necessary, as to whether any earlier act (or failure to act) of Grable's barred him from claiming the privilege at the contempt hearing. In this regard, we note that the ruling in Sharp appears to have been based, in part at least, on the fact that the taxpayer was unrepresented by counsel and thus presented the defense in a form that was not technically proper. We agree that this is an important factor in determining whether a party has forfeited a constitutional privilege. It is not clear from the record before us that Grable was not represented by counsel when he failed to appear for the enforcement proceeding or the show cause hearing before the magistrate.

C. ENTITY DOCUMENTS

1. Collective Entity Doctrine

BRASWELL v. UNITED STATES
487 U.S. 99 (1988)

Chief Justice REHNQUIST delivered the opinion of the Court.

This case presents the question whether the custodian of corporate records may resist a subpoena for such records on the ground that the act of production would incriminate him in violation of the Fifth Amendment. We conclude that he may not. * * *

[A federal grand jury issued a subpoena to petitioner Braswell as the president of two corporations, requiring him to produce the books and records of the two corporations, Worldwide Machinery, Inc. and Worldwide Purchasing, Inc. Petitioner had funded Worldwide Purchasing with his 100 percent interest in Worldwide Machinery and was the sole shareholder of Worldwide Purchasing. While both corporations had three directors, petitioner, his wife, and his mother, only petitioner had authority over the business affairs of the corporations. The grand jury subpoena provided that petitioner could deliver the records to the grand jury agent serving the subpoena and did not require petitioner to testify. Petitioner moved to quash the subpoena, arguing that the act or producing the records would continue a violation of his Fifth Amendment privilege against self-incrimination. The district court denied the motion and the Fifth Circuit affirmed.]

There is no question but that the contents of the subpoenaed business records are not privileged. See United States v. Doe; Fisher v. United States. Similarly, petitioner asserts no self-incrimination claim on behalf of the corporations; it is well established that such artificial entities are not protected by the Fifth Amendment. Bellis v. United States, 417 U.S. 85 (1974). Petitioner instead relies solely upon the argument that his act of producing the documents has independent testimonial significance, which would incriminate him individually, and that the Fifth Amendment prohibits government compulsion of that act. The bases for this argument are extrapolated from the decisions of this Court in *Fisher* and *Doe*. * * *

Had petitioner conducted his business as a sole proprietorship, *Doe* would require that he be provided the opportunity to show that his act of production would entail testimonial self-incrimination. But petitioner has operated his business through the corporate form, and we have long recognized that for purposes of the Fifth Amendment, corporations and other collective entities are treated differently from individuals. This doctrine—known as the collective entity rule—has a lengthy and distinguished pedigree.

The rule was first articulated by the Court in the case of Hale v. Henkel [p. 383]. Hale, a corporate officer, had been served with a subpoena ordering him to produce corporate records and to testify concerning certain corporate transactions. Although Hale was protected by personal immunity, he sought to resist the demand for the records by interposing a Fifth Amendment privilege on behalf of the corporation. The Court rejected that argument: "We are of the opinion that there is a clear distinction * * * between an individual and a corporation, and * * * the latter has no right to refuse to submit its books and papers for an examination at the suit of the State." The Court explained that the corporation "is a creature of the State," with powers limited by the State. As such, the State may, in the exercise of its right to oversee the corporation, demand the production of corporate records. * * *

Although *Hale* settled that a corporation has no Fifth Amendment privilege, the Court did not address whether a corporate officer could resist a subpoena for corporate records by invoking his personal privilege–Hale had been protected by immunity. In Wilson v. United States, 221 U.S. 361 (1911), the Court answered that question in the negative. * * * Wilson refused to produce [subpoenaed corporate] books, arguing that the Fifth Amendment prohibited compulsory production of personally incriminating books that he held and controlled. The Court rejected this argument, observing * * *: "[Wilson] held the corporate books subject to the corporate duty. If the corporation were guilty of misconduct, he could not withhold its books to save it; and if he were implicated in the violations of law, he could not withhold the books to protect himself from the effect of their disclosures. The [State's] reserved power of visitation would seriously be embarrassed, if not wholly defeated in its effective exercise, if guilty officers could refuse inspection of the records and papers of the corporation. No personal privilege to which they are entitled requires such a conclusion." * * * In a companion case, Dreier

v. United States, 221 U.S. 394 (1911), the Court applied the holding in Wilson to a Fifth Amendment attack on a subpoena addressed to the corporate custodian. * * *

The next significant step in the development of the collective entity rule occurred in United States v. White, 322 U.S. 694 (1944), in which the Court held that a labor union is a collective entity unprotected by the Fifth Amendment. [We reasoned] that the Fifth Amendment privilege applies only to natural individuals and protects only private papers. Representatives of a "collective group" act as agents "[a]nd the official records and documents of the organization that are held by them in a representative rather than in a personal capacity cannot be the subject of the personal privilege against self-incrimination, even though production of the papers might tend to incriminate them personally." With this principle in mind, the Court turned to whether a union is a collective group:

> The test * * * is whether one can fairly say under all the circumstances that a particular type of organization has a character so impersonal in the scope of its membership and activities that it cannot be said to embody or represent the purely private or personal interests of its constituents, but rather to embody their common or group interests only. If so, the privilege cannot be invoked on behalf of the organization or its representatives in their official capacity. Labor unions–national or local, incorporated or unincorporated–clearly meet that test.

In applying the collective entity rule to unincorporated associations such as unions, the Court jettisoned reliance on the visitatorial powers of the State over corporations owing their existence to the State–one of the bases for earlier decisions.

The frontiers of the collective entity rule were expanded even further in Bellis v. United States, [p. 418], in which the Court ruled that a partner in a small partnership could not properly refuse to produce partnership records. * * * After rehearsing prior precedent involving corporations and unincorporated associations, the Court examined the partnership form and observed that is had many of the incidents found relevant in prior collective entity decisions. The Court suggested that the test articulated in White for determining the applicability of the Fifth Amendment to organizations was "not particularly helpful in the broad range of cases." The Court rejected the notion that the "formulation in White can be reduced to a simple proposition based solely upon the size of the organization. It is well settled that no privilege can be claimed by the custodian of corporate records, regardless of how small the corporation may be." Bellis held the partnership's financial records in a "representative capacity" and therefore "his personal privilege against compulsory self-incrimination is inapplicable."

The plain mandate of these decisions is that without regard to whether the subpoena is addressed to the corporation, or as here, to the individual in his capacity as a custodian, see *Dreier*, Bellis, a corporate custodian such as petitioner may not resist a subpoena for corporate records on Fifth Amendment grounds. Petitioner argues, however, that this rule falls in the wake of *Fisher* and *Doe*. In essence, petitioner's argument is as follows: In response to *Boyd v. United States*, with its privacy rationale shielding personal books and records, the Court developed the collective entity rule, which declares simply that corporate records are not private and therefore are not protected by the Fifth Amendment. The collective entity decisions were concerned with the contents of the documents subpoenaed, however, and not with the act of production. In *Fisher* and *Doe*, the Court moved away from the privacy based collective entity rule, replacing it with a compelled testimony standard under which the contents of business documents are never privileged but the act of producing the documents may be. Under this new regime, the act of production privilege is available without regard to the entity whose records are being sought. * * *

To be sure, the holding in *Fisher*–later reaffirmed in *Doe*–embarked upon a new course of Fifth Amendment analysis. We cannot agree, however, that it rendered the collective entity rule obsolete. The agency rationale undergirding the collective entity decisions, in which custodians asserted that production of entity records would incriminate them personally, survives. From Wilson forward, the Court has consistently recognized that the custodian of corporate or entity records holds those documents in a representative rather than a personal capacity. Artificial entities such as corporations may act only through their agents, and, a custodian's assumption of his representative capacity leads to certain obligations, including the duty to produce corporate records on proper demand by the Government. Under those circumstances, the custodian's act of production is not deemed a personal act, but rather an act of the corporation. Any claim of Fifth Amendment privilege asserted by the agent would be tantamount to a claim of privilege by the corporation-which of course possesses no such privilege. * * *

Indeed, the opinion in *Fisher*–upon which petitioner places primary reliance–indicates that the custodian of corporate records may not interpose a Fifth Amendment objection to the compelled production of corporate records, even though the act of production may prove personally incriminating. The Fisher court cited the collective entity decisions with approval and offered those decisions to support the conclusion that the production of the accountant's workpapers would "not * * * involve testimonial self-incrimination." * * * In a footnote, the Court explained: "In these cases compliance with the subpoena is required even though the books have been kept by the person subpoenaed and his producing them would itself be sufficient authentication to permit their introduction against him." *Fisher*. The Court thus reaffirmed the obligation of a corporate custodian to comply with a subpoena addressed to him.

That point was reiterated by Justice Brennan in his concurrence in *Fisher*. Although Justice Brennan disagreed with the majority as to its use of the collective entity cases to support the proposition that the act of production is not testimonial, he nonetheless acknowledged that a custodian may not resist a subpoena on the ground that the act of production would be incriminating. * * * [For] "one in control of the records of an artificial organization undertakes an obligation with respect to those records foreclosing any exercise of his privilege." Thus, whether one concludes–as did the Court–that a custodian's production of corporate records is deemed not to constitute testimonial self-incrimination, or instead that a custodian waives the right to exercise the privilege, the lesson of *Fisher* is clear: A custodian may not resist a subpoena for corporate records on Fifth Amendment grounds.

Petitioner also attempts to extract support for his contention from Curcio v. United States, 354 U.S. 118 (1957). But rather than bolstering petitioner's argument, we think *Curcio* substantiates the Government's position. Curcio had been served with two subpoenas addressed to him in his capacity as secretary treasurer of a local union. One subpoena required that he produce union records, the other that he testify. Curcio appeared before the grand jury, stated that the books were not in his possession, and refused to answer any questions as to their whereabouts. * * * The *Curcio* Court made clear that with respect to a custodian of a collective entity's records, the line drawn was between [that] oral testimony and other forms of incrimination. "A custodian, by assuming the duties of his office, undertakes the obligation to produce the books of which he is custodian in response to a rightful exercise of the State's visitorial [sic] powers. But he cannot lawfully be compelled, in the absence of a grant of adequate immunity from prosecution, to condemn himself by his own oral testimony." (Emphasis added) In distinguishing those cases in which a corporate officer was required to produce corporate records and merely identify them by oral testimony, the Court showed that it understood the testimonial nature of the act of production: "The custodian's act of producing books or records in response to a subpoena duces tecum is itself a representation that the documents produced are those demanded by the subpoena. Requiring the custodian to identify or authenticate the documents for admission in evidence merely makes explicit what is implicit in the production itself." In the face of this recognition, the Court nonetheless noted: "In this case petitioner might have been proceeded against for his failure to produce the records demanded by the subpoena duces tecum."

We note further that recognizing a Fifth Amendment privilege on behalf of the records custodians of collective entities would have a detrimental impact on the Government's efforts to prosecute "white-collar crime," one of the most serious problems confronting law enforcement authorities. "The greater portion of evidence of wrongdoing by an organization or its representatives is usually found in the official records and documents of that organization. Were the cloak of the privilege to be thrown around these impersonal records and documents, effective enforcement of many federal and state laws would be impossible." White. If custodians could assert a privilege, authorities would be stymied not only in their enforcement efforts against those individuals but also in their prosecutions of organizations. In Bellis, the Court observed: "In view of the inescapable fact that an artificial entity can only act to produce its records through its individual officers or agents, recognition of the individual's claim of privilege with respect to the financial records of the organization would substantially undermine the unchallenged rule that the organization itself is not entitled to claim any Fifth Amendment privilege, and largely frustrate legitimate governmental regulation of such organizations."

Petitioner suggests, however, that these concerns can be minimized by the simple expedient of either granting the custodian statutory immunity as to the act of production, 18 U.S.C. §§ 6002-6003, or addressing the subpoena to the corporation and allowing it to choose an agent to produce the records who can do so without incriminating himself. We think neither proposal satisfactorily addresses these concerns. Taking the last first, it is no doubt true that if a subpoena is addressed to a corporation, the corporation "must find some means by which to comply because no Fifth Amendment defense is available to it." The means most commonly used to comply is the appointment of an alternate custodian. But petitioner insists he cannot be required to aid the appointed custodian in his search for the demanded records, for any statement to the surrogate would itself be testimonial and incriminating. If this is correct, then petitioner's "solution" is a chimera. In situations such as this–where the corporate custodian is likely the only person with knowledge about the demanded documents–the appointment of a surrogate will simply not ensure that the documents sought will ever reach the grand jury room; the appointed custodian will essentially be sent on an unguided search.

This problem is eliminated if the Government grants the subpoenaed custodian statutory immunity for the testimonial aspects of his act of production. But that "solution" also entails a significant drawback. All of the evidence obtained under a grant of immunity to the custodian may of course be used freely against the corporation, but if the Government has any thought of prosecuting the custodian, a grant of act of production immunity can have serious consequences. Testimony obtained pursuant to a grant of statutory use immunity may be used neither directly nor derivatively. 18 U.S.C. § 6002. And "[o]ne raising a claim under [the federal immunity] statute need only show that he testified under a grant of immunity in order to shift to the government the heavy burden of proving that all of the evidence it proposes to use was derived from legitimate independent sources." *Kastigar.* Even in cases where the Government does not employ the immunized testimony for any purpose–direct or derivative–against the witness, the Government's inability to meet the "heavy burden" it bears may result in the preclusion of crucial evidence that was obtained legitimately.[10]

[10] The dissent asserts that recognition of an act of production privilege on behalf of corporate custodians will not seriously undermine law enforcement efforts directed against those custodians because only the custodian's act of production need be

Although a corporate custodian is not entitled to resist a subpoena on the ground that his act of production will be personally incriminating, we do think certain consequences flow from the fact that the custodian's act of production is one in his representative rather than personal capacity. Because the custodian acts as a representative, the act is deemed one of the corporation and not the individual. Therefore, the Government concedes, as it must, that it may make no evidentiary use of the "individual act" against the individual. For example, in a criminal prosecution against the custodian, the Government may not introduce into evidence before the jury the fact that the subpoena was served upon and the corporation's documents were delivered by one particular individual, the custodian. The Government has the right, however, to use the corporation's act of production against the custodian. The Government may offer testimony–for example, from the process server who delivered the subpoena and from the individual who received the records–establishing that the corporation produced the records subpoenaed. The jury may draw from the corporation's act of production the conclusion that the records in question are authentic corporate records, which the corporation possessed, and which it produced in response to the subpoena. And if the defendant held a prominent position within the corporation that produced the records, the jury may, just as it would had someone else produced the documents, reasonably infer that he had possession of the documents or knowledge of their contents. Because the jury is not told that the defendant produced the records, any nexus between the defendant and the documents results solely from the corporation's act of production and other evidence in the case.[11]

Consistent with our precedent, the United States Court of Appeals for the Fifth Circuit ruled that petitioner could not resist the subpoena for corporate documents on the ground that the act of production might tend to incriminate him. The judgment is therefore affirmed.

Justice KENNEDY, with whom Justice BRENNAN, Justice MARSHALL, and Justice SCALIA join, dissenting.

---

immunized. But the burden of proving an independent source that a grant of immunity places on the Government could, in our view, have just such a deleterious effect on law enforcement efforts.

[11]We reject the suggestion that the limitation on the evidentiary use of the custodian's act of production is the equivalent of constructive use immunity barred under our decision in *Doe*. Rather, the limitation is a necessary concomitant of the notion that a corporate custodian acts as an agent and not an individual when he produces corporate records in response to a subpoena addressed to him in his representative capacity.

We leave open the question whether the agency rationale supports compelling a custodian to produce corporate records when the custodian is able to establish, by showing for example that he is the sole employee and officer of the corporation, that the jury would inevitably conclude that he produced the records.

* * * The majority's apparent reasoning is that collective entities have no privilege and so their employees must have none either. The Court holds that a corporate agent must incriminate himself even when he is named in the subpoena and is a target of the investigation, and even when it is conceded that compliance requires compelled, personal, testimonial, incriminating assertions. I disagree with that conclusion; find no precedent for it; maintain that if there is a likelihood of personal self-incrimination the narrow use immunity permitted by statute can be granted without frustrating the investigation of collective entities; and submit that basic Fifth Amendment principles should not be avoided and manipulated, which is the necessary effect of this decision. * * *

The collective entity rule provides no support for the majority's holding. * * * In none of the collective entity cases cited by the majority, and in none that I have found, were we presented with a claim that the custodian would be incriminated by the act of production, in contrast to the contents of the documents.

The distinction is central. * * * Our decision in *Wilson*, and in later collective entity cases reflected, I believe, the Court's understandable unease with drawing too close a connection between an individual and an artificial entity. On a more practical level, the Court was also unwilling to draw too close a connection between the custodian and the contents of business documents over which he had temporary control but which belonged to his employer, often were prepared by others, and in all events were prepared voluntarily. This last factor became the focus of our analysis in *Fisher*, where we made clear that the applicability of the Fifth Amendment privilege depends on compulsion. *Fisher* put to rest the notion that a privilege may be claimed with respect to the contents of business records that were voluntarily prepared.

The act of producing documents stands on an altogether different footing. While a custodian has no necessary relation to the contents of documents within his control, the act of production is inescapably his own. Production is the precise act compelled by the subpoena, and obedience, in some cases, will require the custodian's own testimonial assertions. That was the basis of our recognition of the privilege in *United States v. Doe*. The entity processing the documents in *Doe* was, as the majority points out, a sole proprietorship, not a corporation, partnership, or labor union. But the potential for self-incrimination inheres in the act demanded of the individual, and as a consequence the nature of the entity is irrelevant to determining whether there is ground for the privilege.

* * * Recognition of the privilege here would * * * avoid adoption of the majority's metaphysical progression, which, I respectfully submit, is flawed. Beginning from ordinary principles of agency, the majority proceeds to the conclusion that when a corporate employee, or an employee of a labor union or partnership, complies with a subpoena for production of documents, his act is necessarily and solely the act of the entity. * * * [But] the heart of the

matter, as everyone knows, is that the Government does not see Braswell as a mere agent at all, and the majority's theory is difficult to square with what will often be the Government's actual practice. The subpoena in this case was not directed to Worldwide Machinery Sales, Inc., or Worldwide Purchasing, Inc. It was directed to "Randy Braswell, President, Worldwide Machinery Sales, Inc., Worldwide Purchasing, Inc." and informed him that "[y]ou are hereby commanded" to provide the specified documents. The Government explained at oral argument that it often chooses to designate an individual recipient, rather than the corporation generally, when it serves a subpoena because "[we] want the right to make that individual comply with the subpoena." This is not the language of agency. By issuing a subpoena which the Government insists is "directed to petitioner personally," it has forfeited any claim that it is simply making a demand on a corporation that, in turn, will have to find a physical agent to perform its duty. What the Government seeks instead is the right to choose any corporate agent as a target of its subpoena and compel that individual to disclose certain information by his own actions.

The majority gives the corporate agent fiction a weight it simply cannot bear. In a peculiar attempt to mitigate the force of its own holdings, it impinges upon its own analysis by concluding that, while the Government may compel a named individual to produce records, in any later proceeding against the person it cannot divulge that he performed the act. But if that is so, it is because the Fifth Amendment protects the person without regard to his status as a corporate employee; and once this be admitted, the necessary support for the majority's case has collapsed. * * *

The majority's abiding concern is that if a corporate officer who is the target of a subpoena is allowed to assert the privilege, it will impede the Government's power to investigate corporations, unions. and partnerships, to uncover and prosecute white collar crimes, and otherwise to enforce its visitatorial powers. There are at least two answers to this. The first, and most fundamental, is that the text of the Fifth Amendment does not authorize exceptions premised on such rationales. Second, even if it were proper to invent such exceptions, the dangers prophesied by the majority are overstated.

Recognition of the right to assert a privilege does not mean it will exist in many cases. In many instances, the production of documents may implicate no testimonial assertions at all. In *Fisher*, for example, we held that the specific acts required by the subpoena before us "would not itself involve testimonial self-incrimination" because, in that case, "the existence and location of the papers [were] a foregone conclusion and the taxpayer adds little or nothing to the sum total of the Government's information by conceding that he in fact has the papers." Whether a particular act is testimonial and self-incriminating is largely a factual issue to be decided in each case. In the case before us, the Government has made its submission on the assumption that the subpoena would result in incriminating testimony.

The existence of a privilege in future cases, however, is not an automatic result.

Further, to the extent testimonial assertions are being compelled, use immunity can be granted without impeding the investigation. Where the privilege is applicable, immunity will be needed for only one individual, and solely with respect to evidence derived from the act of production itself. The Government would not be denied access to the records it seeks, it would be free to use the contents of the records against everyone, and it would be free to use any testimonial act implicit in production against all but the custodian it selects. In appropriate cases the Government will be able to establish authenticity, possession, and control by means other than compelling assertions about them from a suspect.

In one sense the case before us may not be a particularly sympathetic one. Braswell was the sole stockholder of the corporation and ran it himself. Perhaps that is why the Court suggests he waived his Fifth Amendment self-incrimination rights by using the corporate form. One does not always, however, have the choice of his or her employer, much less the choice of the business enterprise through which the employer conducts its business. Though the Court here hints at a waiver, nothing in Fifth Amendment jurisprudence indicates that the acceptance of employment should be deemed a waiver of a specific protection that is as basic a part of our constitutional heritage as is the privilege against self-incrimination.

The law is not captive to its own fictions. Yet, in the matter before us the Court employs the fiction that personal incrimination of the employee is neither sought by the Government nor cognizable by the law. That is a regrettable holding, for the conclusion is factually unsound, unnecessary for legitimate regulation, and a violation of the Self-Incrimination Clause of the Fifth Amendment of the Constitution. For these reasons, I dissent.

NOTES AND QUESTIONS

1. ***The Custodian's Obligation***. In **Curcio v. United States**, discussed in *Braswell*, the Court held that the obligation of the entity agent did not extend to explaining the whereabouts of records no longer in his possession. *Curcio* noted that lower court rulings had held that "a corporate officer who has been required by subpoena to produce corporate records may also be required, by oral testimony, to identify them," but those cases were "distinguishable" and the Court had no need "to pass on their validity." Does *Braswell* necessarily affirm those rulings? See In re Custodian of Records of Variety Distributing, 927 F.2d 244 (6th Cir. 1991). Looking to *Braswell's* discussion of *Curcio*, the Sixth Circuit there concluded that the custodian can be required to authenticate the documents for admission in evidence, as that "merely makes explicit what is implicit in the production itself." This duty existed even though the necessary statements (e.g., that the custodian is familiar with the

company's recordkeeping and knows the company has kept the records in the course of regular business activity) may be potentially incriminating in some situations. However, "because the custodian of corporate records is acting in a representative rather than a personal capacity, he is protected against the future evidentiary use of the testimony."

In re Grand Jury Proceedings, 473 F.Supp.2d 201 (D. Mass. 2007), criticized the approach of *Variety Distributing* that would permit a custodian to be required to provide the foundational testimony for admitting documents under the business records exception to the hearsay rule. The District Court stated:

> Rule 803(6) testimony, unlike authentication testimony, is not "implicit" in the act of producing a document. A witness who produces a document and testifies that the document is responsive to the subpoena has implicitly indicated that the document is genuine; it is but a tiny step from there to authentication testimony, which essentially consists of testimony to the same effect. However, to qualify a document as a business record under Rule 803(6), at a minimum there must be testimony concerning the regular record-creation and record-maintaining practices of the corporation at the relevant time. That testimony may or may not be routine, depending on the facts and circumstances, but it is never implicit in the act of producing records.
>
> Finally, there is no logical stopping point to the principle that a corporate custodian can be required to provide an evidentiary foundation for a document. There is no special magic in the business records exception that it should be elevated over the other hearsay exceptions, or for that matter the definition of hearsay itself set forth in Rule 801.

See also Id. at 209 ("[T]estimony sufficient to qualify documents as business records under Rule 803(6) cannot be compelled from a corporate records custodian who asserts a valid Fifth Amendment privilege."); Peter J. Henning, *Finding What Was Lost: Sorting Out the Custodian's Privilege Against Self-Incrimination from the Compelled Production of Records*, 77 NEB. L. REV. 34 (1998) ("*Variety Distributing's* extension of the custodian's duty to testify regarding the recordkeeping practices of the organization is questionable because the Sixth Circuit equated the admissibility of hearsay with authentication of records, failing to recognize the different issues addressed by the two rules of evidence. Proof of one is not necessarily proof of the other, so it is not a fair reading of *Curcio*'s erroneous endorsement of compelling authentication testimony to include statements that furnish evidentiary proof related to the introduction of documents at trial under an exception to the hearsay rule.").

2. ***Personal Documents.*** What characteristics should be considered in ruling on a claim that the subpoenaed records, though kept by a corporate employee, were "personal" and therefore not subject to the entity doctrine? Consider **In re Grand Jury Proceedings**, 55 F.3d 1012 (5th Cir. 1995), in which the court adopted a "multi-factor balancing approach" to determine whether a document constituted a corporate record, and therefore governed by *Braswell*, or a personal record, and therefore subject to a potential act-of-production Fifth Amendment claim under *Fisher*. In determining whether individual "daytimers" were corporate records, the court stated:

> A multi-factor balancing approach attempts to answer the key question: what is the essential nature of the document? It attempts to answer this question in light of the entire context of the ownership, preparation and use of the document. We agree with the Second Circuit that the following nonexhaustive list of criteria is relevant in this inquiry: who prepared the document; the nature of its contents; its purpose or use; who possessed it; who had access to it; whether the corporation required its preparation; and whether its existence was necessary to or in furtherance of corporate business. * * *
>
> We agree that the determination of the essential character of a document does not hinge upon some magical percentage of personal versus corporate entries. However, this does not mean that the ratio of personal to corporate entries is irrelevant. As a general rule, the greater proportion of personal entries, the more likely it is that the trier of fact could reasonably conclude that it was prepared, used, and maintained as a personal document. Conversely, the greater proportion of business-related entries, the more likely it is that the trier of fact could reasonably conclude that the document was prepared, used, and maintained as a corporate document. This is not to say, however, that other evidence regarding the preparation, use, and maintenance of a given document may not tilt the balance in the other direction. A multi-factor approach to the determining the nature of a document requires a court to view all relevant factors in context, giving greater or lesser weight to a given factor as the quality or quantity of evidence demands.

3. ***Effect of* Citizens United *and* Hobby Lobby.** In In re In the Matter of the Grand Jury Empaneled on May 9, 2014 John Doe, ABC Entity, 2015 WL 2262650 (3d Cir. 2014), the Third Circuit affirmed a contempt finding against a professional corporation that failed to produce documents to a grand jury. In a footnote, the court rejected appellants argument that the Supreme Court had "demonstrated an increasing proclivity to extend a greater protection to corporate entities" in Citizens United v. Federal Election Comm'n, 558 U.S. 310 (2010) and Burwell v. Hobby Lobby Stores, 134 S.Ct. 2751 (2014). The court stated, "[w]hatever merit there may be to Appellant's general observation, we discern nothing in Supreme Court jurisprudence that suggests the Court has, in any way, signaled its readiness to depart from its

longstanding precedent regarding corporate custodians' inability to invoke the Fifth Amendment privilege against self-incrimination." See also Peter J. Henning, *The Conundrum of Corporate Criminal Liability: Seeking a Consistent Approach to the Constitutional Right of Corporations in Criminal Procedure*, 63 TENN. L. REV. 793 (1996).

2. Scope of the Collective Entity Doctrine

a. Closely-Held Business

AMATO v. UNITED STATES
450 F.3d 46 (1st Cir. 2006)

BOWMAN, Senior Circuit Judge.

Dr. Steven P. Amato appeals the denial of his motion to quash two administrative subpoenas duces tecum served on him as custodian of records for two corporations in which he was the sole shareholder, director, officer and employee. We affirm.

Amato is a chiropractor in Damariscotta, Maine. He has conducted his chiropractor business as a sole proprietorship and as a corporation. In October 1997, Amato incorporated the business as Dr. Steven Amato, D.C., P.C. ("Amato P.C.") in New York and is Amato P.C.'s sole shareholder, director, officer and employee. In September 2002, Amato incorporated Mainecures.com, Inc. ("Mainecures") in Maine. A year later, Maine dissolved Mainecures for failing to file an annual report. Amato was Mainecures's sole shareholder, director, officer and employee.

In January 2005, law enforcement, acting under the authority of a search warrant, searched Amato's office for evidence of federal health-care crimes. During the search, law enforcement served two administrative subpoenas duces tecum on Amato as the records custodian of Amato P.C. and Mainecures. The subpoenas required the records custodian to appear with the records at the United States Attorney's Office or, in lieu of an appearance, to deliver the records with certificates of authenticity to the United States Attorney's Office.

Amato moved to quash the subpoenas. Amato argued that the act-of-production doctrine protects production of the records because the testimonial aspects of the production would incriminate him. Recognizing the collective-entity doctrine, Amato nevertheless asserted that the act-of-production doctrine controls in his case. For support, Amato invoked a footnote in Braswell v. United States that left open the question of whether the collective-entity doctrine would apply if the custodian of corporate records is "able to establish, by showing for example that he is the sole employee and officer of the corporation, that the jury would inevitably conclude that he produced the records." Because Amato is his corporations' sole shareholder, director, officer and employee, he asserted his personal Fifth Amendment privilege against producing the corporate records. Amato also argued that Mainecures's records are privileged because Mainecures was a dissolved corporation.

In considering the motion to quash, the magistrate judge recognized that the collective-entity doctrine has not provided Fifth Amendment protection to custodians of corporate records because custodians act in their representative, rather than their personal, capacities when complying with a subpoena directed at the corporation. The magistrate judge declined to recognize an exception to the collective-entity doctrine that would fit Amato's situation: he is the target of an investigation, the custodian of records, and the corporation's sole shareholder, director, officer and employee. The judge reasoned that the First Circuit has rejected such an exception, see United States v. Lawn Builders of New Eng., Inc., 856 F.2d 388 (1st Cir.1988); In re Grand Jury Proceedings (The John Doe Co.), 838 F.2d 624 (1st Cir.1988), and concluded that *Braswell*'s footnote does not contradict the First Circuit's holdings. The magistrate judge also rebuffed Amato's argument that Mainecures's records are privileged because the records now belong to Amato's sole proprietorship, Mainecures having been dissolved before the subpoena issued. The judge concluded that Maine law dictates that a dissolved corporation exists for up to three years after dissolution to wind up its business affairs. Thus, the judge held that no Fifth Amendment privilege guards against the subpoena directed at Mainecures's custodian of records.
* * *

It is fair to say that while the collective-entity doctrine focuses on the contents of corporate records or at least the status of the records, i.e., corporate or individual, the act-of-production doctrine focuses on whether an individual's compelled acts in producing records involve testimonial self-incrimination. This case tests Fifth Amendment boundaries when the act-of-production doctrine intersects with the collective-entity doctrine. In the present case, the issue is whether the Fifth Amendment protects Amato's act of producing the subpoenaed records in his capacity as custodian of the corporate records because the act itself would incriminate Amato personally. In other words, we ask whether the Fifth Amendment recognizes an exception to the collective-entity doctrine such that an act-of-production privilege protects a custodian of corporate records from producing those records when the custodian is the corporation's sole shareholder, director, officer and employee.

Our resolution of this issue is controlled by our decision in *John Doe Co.*, in which we decided that the act-of-production doctrine is not an exception to the collective-entity doctrine even when the corporate custodian is the corporation's sole shareholder, officer and employee. In asserting a Fifth Amendment privilege, Amato ignores the holding of *John Doe Co.* Instead, he seeks refuge in the language later used by the Supreme Court in footnote eleven in *Braswell*: "We leave open the question whether the agency rationale [behind the collective-entity doctrine] supports compelling a custodian to produce corporate records when the custodian [can] establish, by showing for example that he is the sole employee and officer of the corporation, that the jury would inevitably conclude that he produced the records." Our reading of Braswell and of our caselaw, however, leads us to conclude that such refuge is unavailable in this circuit.

Although *Braswell* does not directly contradict Amato's argument, the decision contains nothing that would justify our reconsideration of our holding in *John Doe Co.* * * *

Our caselaw rejects Amato's argument suggesting that we should recognize an exception to the collective-entity doctrine where the custodian of records is the corporation's sole shareholder, director, officer and employee. Four months before the Supreme Court decided *Braswell*, this court held "that the sole shareholder of a one-man corporation has no 'act of production privilege' under the fifth amendment to resist turnover of corporate documents." *John Doe Co.* In *John Doe Co.*, which is very similar to Amato's case, a grand jury investigated an individual (referred to by the court as "Owner") who was a corporation's sole shareholder, officer and employee. When the grand jury issued a subpoena to the corporation's "Keeper of the Records," the Owner's attorney provided the government some of the records, but "the corporation refused to authenticate the documents before the grand jury or to provide testimony (through Owner or by designating some other agent) that they were all the records of the corporation." The Owner also "refused to stipulate to these facts or to appoint an agent of the corporation to provide the requested testimony." Id. The government moved to compel the production of the corporate records, while the corporation moved to quash the subpoena. The district court denied the motion to compel and granted the motion to quash "on the basis that the compelled testimony would likely force Owner to incriminate himself in violation of his fifth amendment right not to be a witness against himself." This circuit reversed "on the basis that the subpoena is directed at the corporation which receives no constitutional protection from self-incrimination."

Acknowledging that "the very act of producing the documents may, in some circumstances, be a testimonial act of authentication," we nevertheless concluded that "production, including implied authentication, can be required of a corporation through a corporate officer regardless of the potential for self-incrimination." This court also concluded that a so-called "one-man corporation" fares no better under the collective-entity doctrine: "It was Owner's choice to incorporate. With that choice came all the attendant benefits and responsibilities of being a corporation. One of those responsibilities is to produce and authenticate records of the corporation when they are subpoenaed by a grand jury. How the corporation chooses to fulfill this duty is not the court's concern."

In a case argued eight days after *Braswell* was decided, this court, citing *Braswell*, reaffirmed its application of the collective-entity doctrine to a corporation where the sole shareholder was also the sole officer and employee: "even assuming [the corporation] to be a one-man corporation and [the corporate custodian] to be that one man, the corporate records are not shielded from production, nor may [the corporate custodian] resist a subpoena for those records on the ground that the act of production would impermissibly infringe on his Fifth Amendment right against self-incrimination." *Lawn Builders.* * * *

Finally, we conclude that the district court committed no error in concluding that Mainecures's records remained corporate records after the corporation's dissolution. See Me.Rev.Stat. Ann. tit. 13-C, § 1406(1) ("A dissolved corporation continues corporate existence for a period not exceeding 3 years from the effective date of the articles of dissolution ... to wind up and liquidate its business and affairs...."); 1406(2) ("Dissolution of a corporation does not: A. Transfer title to the corporation's property; ... E. Prevent commencement of a proceeding by or against the corporation in its corporate name; ... or G. Terminate the authority of the clerk of the corporation."). Mainecures was dissolved in late 2003, less than three years before the service of the subpoena in January 2005. And nothing in the record suggests that Mainecures's dissolution effected a transfer of its corporate records to Amato personally. Moreover, the Supreme Court has stated that corporate records receive no Fifth Amendment protection even after dissolution. *Bellis* (recognizing that Supreme Court decisions make "clear that the dissolution of a corporation does not give the custodian of the corporate records any greater claim to the Fifth Amendment privilege").

For the reasons discussed, we decline Amato's invitation to reconsider our prior caselaw on the applicability of the collective-entity doctrine in cases involving a records custodian who is also the corporation's sole shareholder, officer and employee. We also conclude that Mainecures's dissolution did not protect its records from the reach of the subpoena in this case. Therefore, we affirm the district court's order denying Amato's motion to quash.

NOTE

The entity in Amato was a professional corporation, which is treated in the same way under state corporations law as a regular corporation, such as the one used by Randy Braswell. In **United States v. Milligan**, 324 F.Supp.2d 1062 (D. Ariz. 2004), the IRS issued a summons – which is similar to a subpoena – to the president of an S-Corporation. Under the tax laws, an S-Corporation is treated as a pass-through entity, so the corporate form is disregarded for tax purposes and the owner is responsible for the taxes as if the organization did not exist. The recipient argued that this type of entity is more like a sole proprietorship, and therefore he could assert the act-of-production doctrine to resist compliance rather than being treated under the collective entity doctrine. The District Court rejected that argument:

> Milligan asserts in his Supplemental Response that, because the corporation at issue is an S Corporation, which is a "flow-through/conduit" with respect to individuals, the S Corporation should receive personal treatment for purposes of the Fifth Amendment. However, the United States Supreme Court has consistently held that the privilege against self-incrimination should be limited "to its historic function of protecting only the natural individual." Bellis. Milligan has not presented any authority to extend the Fifth Amendment privilege to an S Corporation. The Court finds Milligan is not entitled to assert a Fifth Amendment privilege merely because the corporation at issue is an S Corporation.

Should the same analysis apply to a limited liability company or limited liability partnership, especially if there is only a single member or partner so that it acts largely like a sole proprietorship? Why does the selection of a particular business form determine the availability of the Fifth Amendment?

b. Former Employees

If dissolution of the entity does not change the character of corporate records, then what about documents taken by a former employee from the workplace: are they corporate records, and therefore no Fifth Amendment privilege claim can be made, or are they personal records of the individual now that the person is no longer an agent of the corporation? Consider how the Second Circuit analyzed that situation.

In re THREE GRAND JURY SUBPOENAS DUCES TECUM DATED JANUARY 29, 1999 v. John Doe # 1, John Doe # 2, John Doe # 3

191 F.3d 173 (2nd Cir. 1999)

WALKER, Circuit Judge.

This case presents the question of whether an ex-employee of a corporation may assert a Fifth Amendment privilege to refuse to respond to a grand jury subpoena demanding that he produce documents belonging to his former employer on the ground that the act of producing the documents would be both testimonial and incriminating. Because we conclude that a Fifth Amendment privilege is available to the ex-employee in such circumstances, we affirm the order of the district court denying the government's motion to compel production pursuant to the subpoenas in this case. * * *

The essential facts in this appeal are undisputed. The subpoenas the government seeks to enforce were issued by a grand jury in the Southern District of New York in connection with the government's criminal investigation of a corporation and its employees. The alleged wrongdoing, which included falsification of the corporation's books and records and the misapplication of funds in the corporation's custody, occurred between 1993 and 1996 in one division of the corporation. In the spring of 1999, the corporation pled guilty to making false entries in its books and records, and, pursuant to a plea agreement, agreed to cooperate in the government's ongoing investigation of a number of individuals who may have been involved in the improper corporate activities.

Doe I, Doe II and Doe III were all officers of the corporation during the period in which the illegal activities occurred, and worked in the division where the wrongdoing took place. Before the subpoenas sought to be enforced were issued, the employees resigned from the corporation or their employment was terminated. * * * On appeal, the government contends that the district court erred in refusing to apply *Braswell* to reject a Fifth Amendment act of production privilege claim by former employees holding corporate documents. For the reasons that follow, we disagree. Some legal background is needed.

* * * In Hale v. Henkel [p. 383], the Supreme Court rejected the argument that a corporate officer served with a subpoena for corporate documents (but personally immunized) could assert a Fifth Amendment privilege on behalf of the corporation. The Court held that a corporation was "a creature of the state" with powers limited by the state, and, thus, that the state could, in its oversight of the corporation, demand production of corporate documents. Hale thus "carved an exception out of *Boyd* by establishing that corporate books and records are not 'private papers' protected by the Fifth Amendment." Later, in Wilson v. United States, 221 U.S. 361 (1911), the Court held that a corporate president could not refuse to produce corporate records on the grounds that the books were personally incriminating. * * *

Later, the Court expanded the reach of the collective entity doctrine beyond the corporate circumstances presented in *Hale* and *Wilson*, by holding that entities such as labor unions, see [United States v.] White, 322 U.S. 694 (1944), and partnerships, see Bellis [v. United States], 417 U.S. 85 (1974), were bound by the collective entity rule. In doing so, "the Court jettisoned reliance on the visitorial powers of the State over corporations owing their existence to the State--one of the bases for earlier decisions." * * * Instead, the Court relied on the fact that the individual subpoenaed held the collective entity's records in " 'a representative capacity,' " rendering " 'his personal privilege against compulsory self-incrimination . . . inapplicable.' " * * *

It was against this backdrop that the Supreme Court held in 1976 in Fisher v. United States, [and] in 1984 in United States v. Doe, that the "foundations for the [*Boyd*] rule have been washed away," * * * and that the contents of voluntarily-prepared records are not protected by the Fifth Amendment against compelled production. However, in *Fisher*, the Court recognized that a person, in the act of producing a document, may communicate information apart from its contents, and that the communication may amount to compelled testimony: * * * Accordingly, it is now settled that an individual may claim an act of production privilege to decline to produce documents, the contents of which are not privileged, where the act of production is, itself, (1) compelled, (2) testimonial, and (3) incriminating. * * *

In *Braswell*, the Court addressed the question of whether a current corporate employee could claim a Fifth Amendment act of production privilege to refuse to produce corporate documents. The Court held that the employee–an officer of two closely-held corporations–who had been individually subpoenaed to produce corporate books and records, could not invoke the Fifth Amendment to refuse production even though the documents might provide the government with evidence that could incriminate him. * * * In short, the Court applied the collective entity doctrine, introduced by *Hale* and developed in *Wilson* and its progeny, to preclude the claim of an act of production privilege by a current corporate employee. In doing so, the Court employed something of a fiction–to wit, that a corporate employee acts only as an agent or custodian of the corporation when he produces corporate documents in response to a subpoena, even a subpoena directed to the employee personally. * * *

While a current employee is not entitled to raise the Fifth Amendment as a shield against producing corporate documents under the rule set forth in Braswell, the Braswell Court created a mitigating evidentiary privilege to reduce the risk that the individual will incriminate himself in the course of producing such documents. * * *

We have since had occasion to apply *Braswell* to deny to a current employee of a collective entity a Fifth Amendment privilege to decline to produce documents. In In re Grand Jury Subpoenas Dated October 22, 1991, and November 1, 1991, 959 F.2d 1158 (2d Cir.1992), following Braswell, we held that "the custodian of corporate records has no Fifth Amendment privilege to refuse to produce those records on the ground that the act of production itself would tend to incriminate him." * * *

The question presented by this appeal, however, is different from that presented in Braswell. It is whether former employees of a corporation, who have corporate documents in their possession, may claim an act of production privilege notwithstanding Braswell. To hold, as the government suggests, that Braswell governs this appeal would require an extension of Braswell to the former employee based upon a conception that the former corporate employee who has corporate records holds them solely in a representative capacity, and acts as the corporation's agent when he or she produces them, even though the employment relationship has ended. Such a holding would also require us to overrule our decision in Saxon Industries, which is otherwise on point.

Saxon Industries, 722 F.2d 981 (2d Cir.1983), involved an appeal by a former corporate officer who was held in civil contempt for his refusal to comply with a grand jury subpoena duces tecum commanding production of corporate records retained by him after he left the corporation. Though decided before *Braswell*, the Saxon Industries panel anticipated its holding, stating that "if the witness were still a [corporate] officer or employee he would normally be obligated as a representative of the company to produce its documents, regardless of whether they contained information incriminating him." * * * We held, however, that "[o]nce the officer leaves the company's employ, . . . he no longer acts as a corporate representative but functions in an individual capacity in his possession of corporate records." * * * Thus, in *Saxon Industries*, we remanded the case to the district court to determine "whether appellant's production of the [corporate] documents, regardless of their contents, might have [a] self-incriminatory effect." * * * We further noted that should the district court determine that the production would prove incriminatory, "the government could either by stipulation or by obtaining a grant of immunity pursuant to 18 U.S.C. §§ 6002-6003, immunize the act of production; such immunity would preserve the appellant's Fifth Amendment rights with respect to his conduct in producing the documents, Kastigar v. United States."

* * * The rule in *Braswell* was predicated on the rationale that corporate custodians hold and produce documents only in a representational capacity and that when a corporate custodian produces subpoenaed corporate records, at bottom, "the corporation produce[s] the documents subpoenaed." * * * It follows, as we noted in *Saxon Industries*, that once the agency relationship terminates, the former employee is no longer an agent of the corporation and is not a custodian of the corporate records. When such an individual produces records in his possession he cannot be acting in anything other than his personal capacity. In no sense can it be said, as *Braswell* requires, that "the corporation produced the records subpoenaed." Nothing in *Braswell* convinces us otherwise, and neither the government nor the dissent has directed us to any authority for the proposition that the agency relationship between an employee and an employer somehow continues after the employment relationship ends.

Indeed, this is the crux of our difference with the dissent. In the absence of legal authority to the effect that a former employee remains an agent of the corporation, or any evidence that the corporation and the individual intended to maintain an agency relationship, the foundation upon which *Braswell* rests–that one who is currently employed by the corporation holds documents as an agent in a custodial capacity so that it is actually the corporation that is producing the records–is removed.

The government's reliance on *Bellis* and *Wheeler* is wholly misplaced. In *Bellis*, the Supreme Court held that a law partner of a dissolved partnership could not assert a Fifth Amendment privilege with respect to the contents of certain partnership records, since the partner held the records in a representational capacity. There, the Court recognized that the subpoenaed partner, unlike appellees in this case, was still an agent of the dissolved partnership, since the "dissolution of the partnership does not terminate the entity; rather it continues until the winding up of the partnership affairs is completed." * * *

In any event, it is inherent in the Fifth Amendment's privilege against self-incrimination that a greater burden is placed on law enforcement than would otherwise be the case. If our determination of the Fifth Amendment's reach turned on the policy considerations of the sort advanced by the government, the basic protection against self-incrimination that the Founders prescribed in the Fifth Amendment would be substantially undermined. It is inescapable that, because the privilege protects against self-incrimination, the greater and more varied the criminal conduct, the wider the application of the privilege. For example, in this case the individuals asserting the privilege are likely concerned about being compelled to incriminate themselves not only with respect to the original investigation but also with respect to the subsequent theft of, or failure to return, corporate documents and any resulting obstruction of justice. * * *

The Supreme Court stated long ago that "the basic purposes that lie behind the privilege against self-incrimination do not relate to protecting the innocent from conviction, but rather to preserving the integrity of a judicial system in which even the guilty are not to be convicted unless the prosecution shoulder the entire load." * * * Our recognition of the act of production privilege on the facts presented in this case comports with these purposes.

Other circuits have split on this issue. Two circuit courts have recognized Braswell's inapplicability to former employees. The Third Circuit, in United States v. McLaughlin, 126 F.3d 130 (3d Cir.1997), stated in dicta that "a former employee, for example, who produces purloined corporate documents is obviously not within the scope of the *Braswell* rule." And the Ninth Circuit in In re Grand Jury Proceedings, 71 F.3d 723 (9th Cir.1995), followed Saxon Industries and held "that the collective entity rule . . . does not apply to a former employee of a collective entity who is no longer acting on behalf of [the] collective entity." Two other circuits have held that *Braswell* does apply in such cases. See In re Grand Jury Subpoena Dated November 12, 1991, 957 F.2d 807 (11th Cir.1992) (rejecting the analysis of *Saxon Industries*, and holding that it is the "immutable character of the records as corporate which requires their production and which dictates that they are held in a representative capacity"); In re Sealed Case (Government Records), 950 F.2d 736 (D.C.Cir.1991) ("Just as corporate records belong to the corporation and are held for the entity by the custodian in an agency capacity, so government records do not belong to the custodian, in this case the [former employee], but to the government agency. Their production thus falls outside the Fifth Amendment Privilege."). We are unpersuaded by the analysis in the latter two cases.

* * * Since Doe I, Doe II and Doe III are no longer employed by the corporation whose documents the government seeks, and therefore do not hold the corporate documents in a representational capacity, we conclude

that each may claim a Fifth Amendment act of production privilege with respect to the documents called for in the 1999 subpoenas.

Affirmed.

CABRANES, Circuit Judge, dissenting.

It has been settled for more than a decade that a custodian of corporate records may not "resist a subpoena for such records on the ground that the act of production would incriminate him in violation of the Fifth Amendment." Braswell v. United States. Relying on our pre-*Braswell* decision in In re Grand Jury Subpoenas Duces Tecum Dated June 13, 1983 and June 22, 1983, 722 F.2d 981 (2d Cir.1983) ("Saxon Industries"), the majority today excepts from *Braswell's* reach any former corporate agent who possesses corporate documents that he retained after leaving the corporation's employ. The majority does so despite the fact that all three of the former employees resisting the subpoenas in this case left the corporation after the corporation had been served with its subpoenas, and despite the fact that two of the former employees had signed severance agreements in which they accepted a continuing duty to assist the corporation in any investigation conducted by or involving the corporation.

The majority's exception to the rule of *Braswell* finds no support in Supreme Court precedent and it creates a powerful incentive for corporate employees and other agents to abscond with subpoenaed records in order to avoid judicial process. Accordingly, I dissent. * * *

The majority today insists on limiting *Braswell* to its facts by treating that decision as having established a rule that applies only to current agents of an entity. * * * But *Braswell* itself purports to apply the collective entity rule, in full, to assertions of the "act of production" privilege. * * * And, * * *, the collective entity rule has long applied to current and former agents alike, continuing to treat corporate documents as such, even when they remain in the custody of an erstwhile corporate agent whose employment with the corporation has terminated. * * *

I recognize that our pre-*Braswell* decision in *Saxon Industries* would have drawn precisely the distinction embraced by the majority in this case, and thereby given former (but not current) agents the benefit of the "act of production" privilege. In my view, however, the distinction drawn in *Saxon Industries* runs contrary to the Supreme Court's rule in *Braswell.* Because we obviously must apply Supreme Court precedent, even when it conflicts with our own, earlier authority, I believe we are bound to recognize that *Saxon Industries* is no longer good law.

Even if I believed that *Saxon Industries* retained its vitality, I would disagree with the majority's refusal to distinguish it here. In the instant case, John Doe I, John Doe II, and John Doe III were all in the corporation's employ at the time the initial subpoena was served on the corporation. John

Doe I and John Doe II were still employed by the corporation at the time it was served with two subsequent subpoenas, which were broader in scope. By contrast, in Saxon Industries, it appears that the first subpoena issued in the case was the one issued to the witness-appellant, who had ceased to work for the corporation approximately one year earlier. * * * Thus, unlike the instant case, there was little reason there to fear that the former agent had left the corporation's employ specifically to conceal evidence relating to an ongoing investigation.

Nor is there any indication from the *Saxon Industries* decision that the employee there had signed an agreement under which he assumed any post-employment obligations with respect to investigations. Significantly, in the instant case, John Doe II and John Doe III signed severance agreements requiring them to assist the corporation in any investigation. To be sure, as the majority observes, the severance agreements do not purport to waive the employees' Fifth Amendment rights.

* * * The unintended consequences of the majority opinion are not difficult to imagine: A person who is well-informed on the state of the law, and whose activities within a "collective entity" are under investigation, hereafter will have a clear incentive to leave the organization, take with him–with or without the assistance of the organization–any documents that he knows may contain evidence of wrongdoing, and then resist production of these documents by asserting a claim of privilege against compelled self-incrimination. We should not be surprised if in the future, as a direct result of today's holding, we see more "reported incidents," of this sort of obstructionist behavior. For all of the foregoing reasons, I respectfully dissent.

NOTES AND QUESTIONS

1. ***An "Incentive" to Steal Documents***. Is Judge Cabranes overstating the effect of the majority's ruling? Is it realistic to think that many corporate officers are "well-informed" about the state of the law in the area of the Fifth Amendment privilege with regard to documents to know that they might be able to assert the Act of Production privilege to shield documents? If an officer consulted an attorney, who advised the officer that she could remove corporate records and thereby shield them from production, would that constitute obstruction of justice? Even if an officer removed documents, the government could execute a search warrant for the materials if it has sufficient information regarding the location of the items to satisfy the particularity of location requirement for a valid search warrant.

2. ***Former Employees and Fiduciary Duty***. Even former employees may owe a fiduciary duty to their former employer, including the duty to maintain the secrecy of confidential information. Is there a continuing duty to hold the records of a corporation that was a former employer in a representative capacity? Consider the argument advanced by Alice W. Yao, Comment,

Former Corporate Officers and Employees in the Contest of the Collective Entity and Act of Production Doctrines, 48 U. CHI. L. REV. 1487 (2001):

> [T]he collective entity doctrine should apply to former employees in cases where there is a continuing fiduciary relationship following the termination of employment. For instance, following the dissolution of a corporation, the former business's directors have fiduciary obligations to the corporation until the resolution of all remaining corporate affairs. Consequently, these directors maintain a representative relationship with that corporation, and the collective entity doctrine should govern. However, where there is no such continuing fiduciary or other such obligation, the act of production doctrine should apply in order to protect the individual's fundamental privilege against self-incrimination. Thus, in the context of a continuing fiduciary obligation, as with current employees and officers, the documents requested may be produced, but the act of production may not be attributed to any individual. If there is no continuing obligation on the part of the former employee or officer, then the documents may not be produced by virtue of the potentially incriminating nature of the act of production.

3. ***Criticism of Three Subpoenas***. With a clear split in the circuits, how do you think the Supreme Court would resolve the issue? In **Gloves, Inc. v Berger**, 198 F.R.D. 6 (D. Mass. 2000), the plaintiff sought the production of records under Federal Rule of Civil Procedure 34 from former officers and controlling shareholders whom it accused of engaging in illegal acts prior to selling the corporation to its current owners. The former officers asserted the Fifth Amendment privilege to prevent being compelled to turn over the records, which the plaintiff alleged they had stolen from the company once they learned that they would be sued for their illegal conduct. In rejecting the privilege claim, the magistrate judge said the following about the analysis in Three Subpoenas:

> In my opinion, the reasoning of * * * Judge Cabranes' dissent is more persuasive than that of the majority in the *Three Subpoenas* case. The majority's main premise is that a person who comes into possession of corporate records as an employee holds them in a representative capacity but if the individual leaves the corporation with the records, he holds the very same records not in a representative capacity but in a personal capacity. This distinction makes no sense. The plain fact is that the person, whether a present employee or a former employee, came into possession of the documents because at the time, he or she was an agent of the corporation. The person would not have had the ability to take possession of the corporate records but for the person's status as an agent of the corporation at the time. In these circumstances, there is nothing illogical in the notion that the former employee continues to hold the documents in a representative capacity. This appears to be the rationale of the decision in *In Re Sealed Case* when the

[District of Columbia Circuit] wrote that a former government employee, like a former corporate employee, could not resist producing government (or corporate) records because the records "'belong to the government' and are held for the entity only in an agency capacity . . . ." The same point is made by the Eleventh Circuit which wrote that "[w]e hold that a custodian of corporate records continues to hold them in a representative capacity even after his employment is terminated." In re Grand Jury Subpoena Dated November 12, 1991.

D. REQUIRED RECORDS

IN RE SPECIAL FEBRUARY 2011-1 GRAND JURY SUBPOENA DATED SEPTEMBER 12, 2011

691 F.3d 903 (7th Cir. 2012)

BAUER, Circuit Judge.

In this appeal, we are asked to decide whether compulsory production of foreign bank account records required to be maintained under the Bank Secrecy Act would violate appellee T.W.'s Fifth Amendment privilege against self-incrimination. Because we find that the Required Records Doctrine applicable to this case, we hold that T.W. must produce the subpoenaed records.

Appellee T.W. (T.W. stands for target witness) learned in October 2009 that the IRS had opened a "file" on him, and that two investigators—an IRS special agent and DOJ tax division prosecutor—were assigned to investigate whether he used secret offshore bank accounts to evade his federal income taxes. About two years into the investigation, a grand jury issued T.W. a subpoena requiring that he produce, for the time period of October, 2006 until present,

> Any and all records required to be maintained pursuant to 31 C.F.R. § 103.32 [subsequently relocated to 31 C.F.R. § 1010.420] relating to foreign financial accounts that you had/have a financial interest in, or signature authority over, including records reflecting the name in which each such account is maintained, the number or other designation of such account, the name and address of the foreign bank or other person with whom such account is maintained, the type of such account, and the maximum value of each such account during each specified year.

The records that the Government demands T.W. to produce are records that he is required to keep under the Bank Secrecy Act of 1970. T.W. filed a motion to quash the subpoena on the grounds that producing the demanded records would violate his Fifth Amendment privilege against self-incrimination; complying with the subpoena may, for instance, reveal that T.W. has not reported bank accounts that should have been reported or that he has reported inaccurate information. On the other hand, if T.W. denies having the requested records, he still risks incriminating himself because failure to keep those records is a felony under the Act.

The Government argued that the Required Records Doctrine overrides T.W.'s Fifth Amendment privilege. Under that doctrine, records required to be kept pursuant to a valid regulatory program fall outside the scope of the Fifth Amendment privilege if certain conditions are met. The district court quashed the Grand Jury's subpoena, concluding that the required records doctrine did not apply because the act of producing the required records was testimonial and would compel T.W. to incriminate himself. The Government appeals that order. * * *

The Required Records Doctrine's origin can be traced to Shapiro v. United States, 335 U.S. 1 (1948). In *Shapiro*, a fruit wholesaler invoked his Fifth Amendment privilege in response to an administrative subpoena that sought various business records. The records in question were required to be maintained under the Emergency Price Control Act (EPCA), which was passed immediately following the outbreak of World War II to prevent inflation and price gouging.

The Supreme Court determined that the EPCA represented a valid exercise of Congress' regulatory authority and that the record-keeping provisions of the EPCA were essential to the administration of the statute's objectives. The Court reasoned that "the privilege which exists as to private papers cannot be maintained in relation to records required by law to be kept in order that there may be suitable information of transactions which are the appropriate subjects of governmental regulation, and the enforcement of restrictions validly established."

Critical to its holding, the Court observed that the required records had attained "public aspects," such that they could be considered quasi-public records; it was the quasi-public nature of the records in *Shapiro* that allowed their compulsory production.

The Court revisited its decision in *Shapiro* twenty years later in Marchetti v. United States, 390 U.S. 39 (1968) and Grosso v. United States, 390 U.S. 62 (1968). In holding that the Required Records Doctrine was inapplicable to the circumstances before it in both those cases, the Court articulated three requirements—derived from *Shapiro*'s holding—for determining the applicability of the Required Records Doctrine. As summarized in *Grosso*, those three requirements are: (1) the purposes of the government inquiry must be essentially regulatory; (2) information is to be obtained by requiring the preservation of records of a kind which the regulated party has customarily kept; and (3) the records themselves must have assumed public aspects which render them at least analogous to a public document. When the requirements of the Required Records Doctrine are met, a witness cannot resist a subpoena by invoking the Fifth Amendment privilege against compelled, testimonial self-incrimination.

The criteria for the Required Records Doctrine aside, T.W. argues that the doctrine is not applicable to a case such as his where the act of producing the requested documents is compelled, testimonial, and self-incriminating. That the act of producing documents may be testimonial and incriminating is not a phenomenon unique to this case. The act of production privilege recognizes that, while the contents of the documents may not be privileged, the act of producing them may be. In other words, producing incriminating documents under government compulsion may have testimonial aspects—aside from the contents of the documents—that are protected under the Fifth Amendment. For example, compliance with the subpoena tacitly concedes the existence (or nonexistence) of the records demanded and their possession or control by the witness. The Government does not dispute this, but argues the Required Records Doctrine applies nonetheless, and overrides any act of production privilege that T.W. has.

The Government's position finds support in several cases where the Required Records Doctrine—or its rationale—was applied to negate a witness's act of production privilege.

T.W. makes several arguments to get out from underneath these cases. He first argues that, under *Shapiro*, the Required Records Doctrine is not a stand-alone exception to the privilege against self-incrimination; rather, he argues, it is a threshold inquiry to determine whether there is a privilege in the first place—i.e., whether the witness is being compelled to incriminate himself through some form of testimony. We disagree with that characterization of the Required Records Doctrine.

We note that it makes little difference, practically speaking, whether the Required Records Doctrine is an outright exception to the Fifth Amendment privilege—and by exception we mean that it overrides or supersedes the privilege—or whether it is a threshold inquiry to determine whether the privilege attaches in the first place; under the former, the privilege exists but is superseded and, under the latter, the privilege cannot attach because one or more of its requirements (usually the testimonial aspect) are missing by virtue of the records satisfying the three requirements laid out in *Grosso*; either way, the outcome is the same: the witness is denied the use of the privilege and must produce the potentially incriminating documents. Still, we think the Required Records Doctrine is better regarded as an exception rather than a threshold test to determine whether there is a privilege.

Building on his argument above, T.W. twists *Shapiro* even further by asserting that the Required Records Doctrine, as a mechanism to determine if there is a privilege, is only relevant when challenging the constitutionality of a record-keeping requirement on its face. It is true that *Shapiro* started out primarily as a statutory interpretation case and that it did decide whether a record-keeping and reporting requirement was facially unconstitutional. To that effect, the *Shapiro* Court stated, "It may be assumed at the outset that there are limits which the Government cannot constitutionally exceed in requiring the keeping of records which may be inspected by an administrative agency and may be used in prosecuting statutory violations committed by the record-keeper himself." But *Shapiro* did more than set the constitutional parameters for record-keeping requirements; it determined that the Fifth Amendment is not a barrier to the enforcement of a valid civil regulatory scheme.

Since *Shapiro*, several courts, including this one, have applied the Required Records Doctrine broadly and in situations where the act of production privilege has been invoked. See, e.g., Baltimore City Dep't of Soc. Servs. v. Bouknight, 493 U.S. 549 (1990); Smith v. Richert, 35 F.3d 300 (7th Cir.1994); United States v. Lehman, 887 F.2d 1328 (7th Cir.1989); United States v. Porter, 711 F.2d 1397 (7th Cir.1983); In re Grand Jury Subpoena, 21 F.3d 226 (8th Cir.1994); In re Grand Jury Subpoena Duces Tecum Served Upon Underhill, 781 F.2d 64 (6th Cir.1986).

To get around these cases, T.W. argues that in each of them one or more of the requirements of the Fifth Amendment privilege (testimonial, incriminating, and compelled) were missing. Again, T.W. is wrong. In each of those cases, a valid Fifth Amendment privilege existed, or was assumed, and any such assumption naturally presupposes that all the requirement of the privilege have been met.

That is perhaps best illustrated in *Bouknight*, which was not a required records case, but nonetheless, applied its underlying principles. In *Bouknight*, the Court held that the Fifth Amendment did not shield a mother from complying with a juvenile court order directing her to produce her infant son. In coming to that conclusion, the Court assumed that an act of production privilege existed: "Even assuming that this limited testimonial assertion is sufficiently incriminating and sufficiently testimonial for purposes of the privilege . . . *Bouknight* may not invoke the privilege to resist the production order because ... production is required as part of a noncriminal regulatory regime."

In United States v. Lehman, the petitioner—like T.W.—argued that by "producing the records he would be testifying as to their existence and to his control over them in a way that is protected by his Fifth Amendment privilege against self-incrimination." We rejected that argument and accepted the Sixth Circuit's reasoning that the required records exception must apply to the act of production. To get around our holding in *Lehman*, T.W. argues that, in that case, the witness's act of production was neither testimonial nor incriminating. But even assuming that were true, it proves nothing; in *Lehman*, we said that *Fisher* and its progeny "might be applicable . . . were it not for the required records exception." Thus in *Lehman* we held that, to whatever extent the petitioner might have had an act of production privilege under *Doe* and *Fisher*, the Required Records Doctrine superseded it.

In Smith v. Richert, 35 F.3d 300 (7th Cir.1994), we provided a thumbnail sketch of the evolution of the Required Records Doctrine, and in doing so, recapitulated *Lehman*'s holding. There, we said that if the documents being sought were required records, "the person could not resist the subpoena" on the ground that producing the records was testimonial and incriminating, "for the only acknowledgment conveyed by compliance would be of the existence and applicability of the regulatory program that required him to maintain the records." The district court incorrectly interpreted this to mean that the Required Records Doctrine is not applicable when the "compelled production of the subpoenaed records causes [an individual] to admit any incriminating fact beyond the mere existence and applicability of the regulatory program." But we never held that a witness's acknowledgment of the existence and application of a regulatory scheme could not be incriminating. In fact, we said that is precisely the context in which the Required Records Doctrine is particularly useful:

> The only time the government needed the required records doctrine anymore was when the act of production was itself testimonial, that is, when it communicated knowledge possessed by the person making the production and was, therefore—but for the doctrine—protected by the Fifth Amendment from being compelled by the government.

One of the rationales, if not the main rationale, behind the Required Records Doctrine is that the government or a regulatory agency should have the means, over an assertion of the Fifth Amendment Privilege, to inspect the records it requires an individual to keep as a condition of voluntarily participating in that regulated activity. That goal would be easily frustrated if the Required Records Doctrine were inapplicable whenever the act of production privilege was invoked.

The voluntary choice to engage in an activity that imposes record-keeping requirements under a valid civil regulatory scheme carries consequences, perhaps the most significant of which, is the possibility that those records might have to be turned over upon demand, notwithstanding any Fifth Amendment privilege. That is true whether the privilege arises by virtue of the contents of the documents or the by act of producing them. The district court erred to the extent that it held that the Required Records Doctrine was not applicable because T.W.'s compelled production was incriminating and thus protected under the Fifth Amendment.

Having determined that T.W.'s act of production privilege is not an obstacle to the Required Records Doctrine, we must decide whether the records sought under the subpoena fall within the Required Records Doctrine. * * *

Recently, in a case nearly identical to this one, the Ninth Circuit held that records required under the Bank Secrecy Act fell within the Required Record Doctrine. In re M.H., 648 F.3d 1067 (9th Cir.2011). In the Ninth

Circuit's case, the court held that the witness could not resist a subpoena—identical to the one in this case—on Fifth Amendment grounds because the records demanded met the three requirements of the Required Records Doctrine. Id. We need not repeat the Ninth Circuit's thorough analysis, determining that records under the Bank Secrecy Act fall within the exception. It is enough that we find—and we do—that all three requirements of the Required Records Doctrine are met in this case.

Because the Required Records Doctrine is applicable, and the records sought in the subpoena fall within the doctrine, T.W. must comply with the subpoena.

NOTE

"Essentially Regulatory." In **In re M.H.**, 648 F.3d 1067 (9th Cir. 2011), the Ninth Circuit explained why the foreign account information reporting requirement under the Bank Secrecy Act was "essentially regulatory" even though a violation carries with it a potential criminal penalty:

> There is nothing inherently illegal about having or being a beneficiary of an offshore foreign banking account. According to the Government, § 1010.420 applies to "hundreds of thousands of foreign bank accounts—over half a million in 2009." Nothing about having a foreign bank account on its own suggests a person is engaged in illegal activity. That fact distinguishes this case from *Marchetti* and *Grosso*, where the activity being regulated—gambling—was almost universally illegal, so that paying a tax on gambling wagers necessarily implicated a person in criminal activity. Admitting to having a foreign bank account carries no such risk. That the information contained in the required record may ultimately lead to criminal charges does not convert an essentially regulatory regulation into a criminal one.

The circuit court's language about an overseas bank account is reminiscent of the Supreme Court's analysis in Ratzlaff v. United States [p. 91] finding that transactions designed to avoid the currency transaction reporting requirement under the Bank Secrecy Act were not "inevitably nefarious." Even though both might be suspicious, and are often the subject of criminal prosecution, that does not make them sufficiently wrongful to make either reporting requirement effectively an extension of the criminal law.

CHAPTER ELEVEN
CHALLENGES TO THE GRAND JURY PROCESS

The Fifth Amendment requires that "No person shall be held to answer for a capital, or otherwise infamous crime, unless on a presentment or indictment of a Grand Jury." In Wood v. Georgia, 370 U.S. 375 (1962), the Supreme Court stated that the grand jury "has been regarded as a primary security to the innocent against hasty, malicious and oppressive persecution." The grand jury has both an investigatory and an accusatory function. The authority of the body is used by the prosecutor to compel the production of documents and testimony. After the investigation is complete, a prosecutor will seek to have the grand jury issue an indictment. The prosecutor drafts the charges and advises the grand jury on the applicable legal standards. It is then up to the grand jury to decide, in secret, whether or not the evidence establishes probable cause for the charges. If so, it will approve the indictment by returning a "true bill" and, once the prosecutor signs the indictment, the criminal prosecution has been initiated. If the grand jury determines that there is not probable cause, then it issues a "no true bill." Even after a "no true bill," however, the prosecutor can present the case to a second grand jury for an independent determination of probable cause, and it can issue a valid indictment despite the decision of the prior grand jury.

The Supreme Court has been highly protective of the grand jury's screening function by rejecting challenges of defendants to the probable cause determination. **United States v. Costello**, 350 U.S. 359 (1956), rejected a defendant's request to overturn a conviction on the ground that the grand jury did not have sufficient admissible evidence to charge him with a crime. The Court stated that "neither the Fifth Amendment nor any other constitutional provision prescribes the kind of evidence upon which grand juries must act. * * * An indictment returned by a legally constituted and unbiased grand jury * * * if valid on its face, is enough to call for trial of the charge on the merits."

Costello effectively rules out challenges to the evidentiary basis for an indictment, and requires a defendant to go to trial to test the government's case. The Supreme Court relied on *Costello*'s analysis in *United States v. Williams*, [p. 448], to limit the authority of lower courts to impose rules on the prosecutor's conduct before the grand jury because any challenge would call into question the evidence the grand jury considered in making its probable cause assessment.

The effectiveness of the grand jury as a screen on the prosecutor has been strongly criticized because they rarely, if ever, reject the prosecutor's request to return an indictment. Professor Andrew D. Leipold analyzed the problem in this way:

> The barriers to a grand jury's ability to screen are not obvious, because its task seems so simple. Jurors listen to the prosecutor's case and then are asked to answer a single question: is there probable cause to believe that the suspect committed the specified crime? Stated simply, grand jurors are not qualified to answer this question. Whether probable cause exists is ultimately a legal determination about the sufficiency of the evidence: whether the prosecutor put forth enough information to surpass the legal threshold established by the probable cause standard. In submitting a case to the grand jury we are asking nonlawyers with no experience in weighing evidence to decide whether a legal test is satisfied, and to do so after the only lawyer in the room, the prosecutor, has concluded that it has. Because jurors lack any experience or expertise in deciding whether probable cause exists, it becomes not only predictable but also logical that the jurors will return a true bill. This is not because they are a rubber stamp, but because they have no benchmark against which to weigh the evidence, and thus no rational basis for rejecting the prosecutor's recommendation to indict.

Andrew D. Leipold, *Why Grand Juries Do Not (and Cannot) Protect the Accused*, 80 CORNELL L. REV. 260 (1995).

Why is the Supreme Court so protective of the grand jury? Should the process be reformed? Section A reviews challenges to the prosecutor's use of the grand jury in the pre-indictment phase of a case, and Section B reviews challenges to misuse of the grand jury after it has returned an indictment. Note that the grand jury's authority pre-indictment is much less constrained by judicial review than when it is used post-indictment to gather information. Section C reviews the strict rule of grand jury secrecy, and Section D considers a new law–the Hyde Amendment–that permits exonerated defendants to seek attorneys fees for prosecutorial misconduct.

A. SUPERVISORY POWER OVER THE CONDUCT OF THE GRAND JURY

UNITED STATES v. WILLIAMS
504 U.S. 36 (1992)

Justice SCALIA delivered the opinion of the Court.

The question presented in this case is whether a district court may dismiss an otherwise valid indictment because the Government failed to disclose to the grand jury "substantial exculpatory evidence" in its possession. * * * On May 4, 1988, respondent John H. Williams, Jr., a Tulsa, Oklahoma, investor, was indicted by a federal grand jury on seven counts of "knowingly mak[ing] [a] false statement or report . . . for the purpose of influencing . . . the action [of a federally insured financial institution]," in violation of 18 U.S.C. § 1014 (1988 ed., Supp. II). According to the indictment, between September 1984 and November 1985 Williams supplied four Oklahoma banks with "materially false" statements that variously overstated the value of his current assets and interest income in order to influence the banks' actions on his loan requests.

Williams' misrepresentation was allegedly effected through two financial statements provided to the banks, a "Market Value Balance Sheet" and a "Statement of Projected Income and Expense." The former included as "current assets" approximately $6 million in notes receivable from three venture capital companies. Though it contained a disclaimer that these assets were carried at cost rather than at market value, the Government asserted that listing them as "current assets"—i.e., assets quickly reducible to cash—was misleading, since Williams knew that none of the venture capital companies could afford to satisfy the notes in the short term. The second document—the Statement of Projected Income and Expense—allegedly misrepresented Williams' interest income, since it failed to reflect that the interest payments received on the notes of the venture capital companies were funded entirely by Williams' own loans to those companies. The Statement thus falsely implied, according to the Government, that Williams was deriving interest income from "an independent outside source." Brief of the United States 3.

Shortly after arraignment, the District Court granted Williams' motion for disclosure of all exculpatory portions of the grand jury transcripts, see Brady v. Maryland, 373 U.S. 83 (1963). Upon reviewing this material, Williams demanded that the District Court dismiss the indictment, alleging that the Government had failed to fulfill its obligation under the Tenth Circuit's prior decision in United States v. Page, 808 F.2d 723, 728 (1987), to present "substantial exculpatory evidence" to the grand jury (emphasis omitted). His contention was that evidence which the Government had chosen not to present to the grand jury—in particular, Williams' general ledgers and tax returns, and Williams' testimony in his contemporaneous Chapter 11 bankruptcy proceeding—disclosed that, for tax purposes and otherwise, he had regularly accounted for the "notes receivable" (and the interest on them) in a manner consistent with the Balance Sheet and the Income Statement. This, he contended, belied an intent to mislead the banks, and thus directly negated an essential element of the charged offense.

The District Court initially denied Williams' motion, but upon reconsideration ordered the indictment dismissed without prejudice. It found, after a hearing, that the withheld evidence was "relevant to an essential element of the crime charged," created " 'a reasonable doubt about [respondent's] guilt,' " and thus "render[ed] the grand jury's decision to indict gravely suspect." Upon the Government's appeal, the Court of Appeals affirmed the District Court's order, following its earlier decision in *Page*. It first sustained as not "clearly erroneous" the District Court's determination that the Government had withheld "substantial exculpatory evidence" from the grand jury. It then found that the Government's behavior " 'substantially influence[d]' " the grand jury's decision to indict, or at the very least raised a " 'grave doubt that the decision to indict was free from such substantial influence,' " (quoting Bank of Nova Scotia v. United States, 487 U.S. 250, 263 (1988)). Under these circumstances, the Tenth Circuit concluded, it was not an abuse of discretion for the District Court to require the Government to begin anew before the grand jury. We granted certiorari. * * *

Respondent does not contend that the Fifth Amendment itself obliges the prosecutor to disclose substantial exculpatory evidence in his possession to the grand jury. Instead, building on our statement that the federal courts "may, within limits, formulate procedural rules not specifically required by the Constitution or the Congress," United States v. Hasting, 461 U.S. 499, 505 (1983), he argues that imposition of the Tenth Circuit's disclosure rule is supported by the courts' "supervisory power." We think not. Hasting, and the cases that rely upon the principle it expresses, deal strictly with the courts' power to control their own procedures. That power has been applied not only to improve the truth-finding process of the trial, but also to prevent parties from reaping benefit or incurring harm from violations of substantive or procedural rules (imposed by the Constitution or laws) governing matters apart from the trial itself, see, e.g., Weeks v. United States, 232 U.S. 383 (1914). Thus, Bank of Nova Scotia v. United States makes clear that the supervisory power can be used to dismiss an indictment because of misconduct before the grand jury, at least where that misconduct amounts to a violation of one of those "few, clear rules which were carefully drafted and approved by this Court and by Congress to ensure the integrity of the grand jury's functions," United States v. Mechanik, 475 U.S. 66 (1986) (O'Connor, J., concurring in judgment).[6]

---

[6] Rule 6 of the Federal Rules of Criminal Procedure contains a number of such rules, providing, for example, that "no person other than the jurors may be present while the grand jury is deliberating or voting," Rule 6(d)(2), and placing strict controls on disclosure of "matters occurring before the grand jury," Rule 6(e)(2)(B). Additional standards of behavior for prosecutors (and others) are set forth in the United States Code. See 18 U.S.C. §§ 6002, 6003 (setting forth procedures for granting a witness immunity from prosecution); § 1623 (criminalizing false declarations before grand jury); § 2515 (prohibiting grand jury use of unlawfully intercepted wire or oral communications); § 1622 (criminalizing subornation of perjury). That some of the misconduct alleged in Bank of Nova Scotia v. United States was not specifically proscribed by Rule, statute, or the Constitution does not make the case stand for a judicially prescribable grand jury code, as the dissent suggests. All of the allegations of violation were dismissed by the Court—without considering their validity in law—for failure to meet *Nova Scotia 's* dismissal standard.

We did not hold in *Bank of Nova Scotia*, however, that the courts' supervisory power could be used, not merely as a means of enforcing or vindicating legally compelled standards of prosecutorial conduct before the grand jury, but as a means of prescribing those standards of prosecutorial conduct in the first instance–just as it may be used as a means of establishing standards of prosecutorial conduct before the courts themselves. It is this latter exercise that respondent demands. Because the grand jury is an institution separate from the courts, over whose functioning the courts do not preside, we think it clear that, as a general matter at least, no such "supervisory" judicial authority exists, and that the disclosure rule applied here exceeded the Tenth Circuit's authority. * * *

"[R]ooted in long centuries of Anglo-American history," the grand jury is mentioned in the Bill of Rights, but not in the body of the Constitution. It has not been textually assigned, therefore, to any of the branches described in the first three Articles. It "'is a constitutional fixture in its own right.' " United States v. Chanen, 549 F.2d 1306 (9th Cir. 1977). In fact the whole theory of its function is that it belongs to no branch of the institutional government, serving as a kind of buffer or referee between the Government and the people. Although the grand jury normally operates, of course, in the courthouse and under judicial auspices, its institutional relationship with the judicial branch has traditionally been, so to speak, at arm's length. Judges' direct involvement in the functioning of the grand jury has generally been confined to the constitutive one of calling the grand jurors together and administering their oaths of office.

The grand jury's functional independence from the judicial branch is evident both in the scope of its power to investigate criminal wrongdoing, and in the manner in which that power is exercised. "Unlike [a] [c]ourt, whose jurisdiction is predicated upon a specific case or controversy, the grand jury 'can investigate merely on suspicion that the law is being violated, or even because it wants assurance that it is not.' " United States v. R. Enterprises, [p. 363]. It need not identify the offender it suspects, or even "the precise nature of the offense" it is investigating. Blair v. United States, 250 U.S. 273 (1919). The grand jury requires no authorization from its constituting court to initiate an investigation, nor does the prosecutor require leave of court to seek a grand jury indictment. And in its day-to-day functioning, the grand jury generally operates without the interference of a presiding judge. It swears in its own witnesses, Fed. Rule Crim. Proc. 6(c), and deliberates in total secrecy.

True, the grand jury cannot compel the appearance of witnesses and the production of evidence, and must appeal to the court when such compulsion is required. And the court will refuse to lend its assistance when the compulsion the grand jury seeks would override rights accorded by the Constitution, see, e.g., Gravel v. United States, 408 U.S. 606 (1972) (grand jury subpoena effectively qualified by order limiting questioning so as to preserve Speech or Debate Clause immunity), or even testimonial privileges recognized by the common law, see In re Grand Jury Investigation of Hugle,

754 F.2d 863 (9th Cir. 1985) (same with respect to privilege for confidential marital communications) (opinion of Kennedy, J.). Even in this setting, however, we have insisted that the grand jury remain "free to pursue its investigations unhindered by external influence or supervision so long as it does not trench upon the legitimate rights of any witness called before it." United States v. Dionisio. Recognizing this tradition of independence, we have said that the Fifth Amendment's "constitutional guarantee presupposes an investigative body 'acting independently of either prosecuting attorney or judge '. . . ." *Dionisio* (emphasis added).

No doubt in view of the grand jury proceeding's status as other than a constituent element of a "criminal prosecutio[n]," U.S. Const., Amdt. VI, we have said that certain constitutional protections afforded defendants in criminal proceedings have no application before that body. The Double Jeopardy Clause of the Fifth Amendment does not bar a grand jury from returning an indictment when a prior grand jury has refused to do so. We have twice suggested, though not held, that the Sixth Amendment right to counsel does not attach when an individual is summoned to appear before a grand jury, even if he is the subject of the investigation. See United States v. Mandujano [p. 567]. And although "the grand jury may not force a witness to answer questions in violation of [the Fifth Amendment's] constitutional guarantee" against self-incrimination, our cases suggest that an indictment obtained through the use of evidence previously obtained in violation of the privilege against self-incrimination "is nevertheless valid." *Calandra.*

Given the grand jury's operational separateness from its constituting court, it should come as no surprise that we have been reluctant to invoke the judicial supervisory power as a basis for prescribing modes of grand jury procedure. Over the years, we have received many requests to exercise supervision over the grand jury's evidence-taking process, but we have refused them all, including some more appealing than the one presented today. In *Calandra*, a grand jury witness faced questions that were allegedly based upon physical evidence the Government had obtained through a violation of the Fourth Amendment; we rejected the proposal that the exclusionary rule be extended to grand jury proceedings, because of "the potential injury to the historic role and functions of the grand jury." In Costello v. United States, 350 U.S. 359 (1956), we declined to enforce the hearsay rule in grand jury proceedings, since that "would run counter to the whole history of the grand jury institution, in which laymen conduct their inquiries unfettered by technical rules."

These authorities suggest that any power federal courts may have to fashion, on their own initiative, rules of grand jury procedure is a very limited one, not remotely comparable to the power they maintain over their own proceedings. It certainly would not permit judicial reshaping of the grand jury institution, substantially altering the traditional relationships between the prosecutor, the constituting court, and the grand jury itself. * * * As we proceed to discuss, that would be the consequence of the proposed rule here. * * *

Respondent argues that the Court of Appeals' rule can be justified as a sort of Fifth Amendment "common law," a necessary means of assuring the constitutional right to the judgment "of an independent and informed grand jury," Wood v. Georgia, 370 U.S. 375, 390 (1962). Respondent makes a generalized appeal to functional notions: Judicial supervision of the quantity and quality of the evidence relied upon by the grand jury plainly facilitates, he says, the grand jury's performance of its twin historical responsibilities, i.e., bringing to trial those who may be justly accused and shielding the innocent from unfounded accusation and prosecution. We do not agree. The rule would neither preserve nor enhance the traditional functioning of the institution that the Fifth Amendment demands. To the contrary, requiring the prosecutor to present exculpatory as well as inculpatory evidence would alter the grand jury's historical role, transforming it from an accusatory to an adjudicatory body.

It is axiomatic that the grand jury sits not to determine guilt or innocence, but to assess whether there is adequate basis for bringing a criminal charge. That has always been so; and to make the assessment it has always been thought sufficient to hear only the prosecutor's side. As Blackstone described the prevailing practice in 18th-century England, the grand jury was "only to hear evidence on behalf of the prosecution[,] for the finding of an indictment is only in the nature of an enquiry or accusation, which is afterwards to be tried and determined." 4 W. Blackstone, Commentaries 300 (1769). So also in the United States. According to the description of an early American court, three years before the Fifth Amendment was ratified, it is the grand jury's function not "to enquire . . . upon what foundation [the charge may be] denied," or otherwise to try the suspect's defenses, but only to examine "upon what foundation [the charge] is made" by the prosecutor. Respublica v. Shaffer, 1 U.S. (1 Dall.) 236 (Philadelphia Oyer and Terminer 1788); see also F. Wharton, Criminal Pleading and Practice § 360, pp. 248-249 (8th ed. 1880). As a consequence, neither in this country nor in England has the suspect under investigation by the grand jury ever been thought to have a right to testify, or to have exculpatory evidence presented.

Imposing upon the prosecutor a legal obligation to present exculpatory evidence in his possession would be incompatible with this system. If a "balanced" assessment of the entire matter is the objective, surely the first thing to be done—rather than requiring the prosecutor to say what he knows in defense of the target of the investigation—is to entitle the target to tender his own defense. To require the former while denying (as we do) the latter would be quite absurd. It would also be quite pointless, since it would merely invite the target to circumnavigate the system by delivering his exculpatory evidence to the prosecutor, whereupon it would have to be passed on to the grand jury—unless the prosecutor is willing to take the chance that a court will not deem the evidence important enough to qualify for mandatory disclosure. * * *

Respondent acknowledges (as he must) that the "common law" of the grand jury is not violated if the grand jury itself chooses to hear no more evidence than that which suffices to convince it an indictment is proper. Thus, had the Government offered to familiarize the grand jury in this case with the five boxes of financial statements and deposition testimony alleged to contain exculpatory information, and had the grand jury rejected the offer as pointless, respondent would presumably agree that the resulting indictment would have been valid. Respondent insists, however, that courts must require the modern prosecutor to alert the grand jury to the nature and extent of the available exculpatory evidence, because otherwise the grand jury "merely functions as an arm of the prosecution." We reject the attempt to convert a nonexistent duty of the grand jury itself into an obligation of the prosecutor. The authority of the prosecutor to seek an indictment has long been understood to be "coterminous with the authority of the grand jury to entertain [the prosecutor's] charges." United States v. Thompson, 251 U.S. 407 (1920). If the grand jury has no obligation to consider all "substantial exculpatory" evidence, we do not understand how the prosecutor can be said to have a binding obligation to present it.

There is yet another respect in which respondent's proposal not only fails to comport with, but positively contradicts, the "common law" of the Fifth Amendment grand jury. Motions to quash indictments based upon the sufficiency of the evidence relied upon by the grand jury were unheard of at common law in England. And the traditional American practice was described by Justice Nelson, riding circuit in 1852, as follows:

> "No case has been cited, nor have we been able to find any, furnishing an authority for looking into and revising the judgment of the grand jury upon the evidence, for the purpose of determining whether or not the finding was founded upon sufficient proof, or whether there was a deficiency in respect to any part of the complaint . . . ." United States v. Reed, 27 Fed. Cas. 727, 738 (No. 16,134) (C.C. N.D.N.Y. 1852).

We accepted Justice Nelson's description in Costello, where we held that "it would run counter to the whole history of the grand jury institution" to permit an indictment to be challenged "on the ground that there was incompetent or inadequate evidence before the grand jury." And we reaffirmed this principle recently in *Bank of Nova Scotia*, where we held that "the mere fact that evidence itself is unreliable is not sufficient to require a dismissal of the indictment," and that "a challenge to the reliability or competence of the evidence presented to the grand jury" will not be heard. It would make little sense, we think, to abstain from reviewing the evidentiary support for the grand jury's judgment while scrutinizing the sufficiency of the prosecutor's presentation. A complaint about the quality or adequacy of the evidence can always be recast as a complaint that the prosecutor's presentation was "incomplete" or "misleading."[8] Our words in Costello bear repeating: Review of facially valid indictments on such grounds "would run counter to the whole history of the grand jury institution[,] [and] [n]either justice nor the concept of a fair trial requires [it]." * * *

Echoing the reasoning of the Tenth Circuit in United States v. Page, respondent argues that a rule requiring the prosecutor to disclose exculpatory evidence to the grand jury would, by removing from the docket unjustified prosecutions, save valuable judicial time. That depends, we suppose, upon what the ratio would turn out to be between unjustified prosecutions eliminated and grand jury indictments challenged–for the latter as well as the former consume "valuable judicial time." We need not pursue the matter; if there is an advantage to the proposal, Congress is free to prescribe it. For the reasons set forth above, however, we conclude that courts have no authority to prescribe such a duty pursuant to their inherent supervisory authority over their own proceedings. The judgment of the Court of Appeals is accordingly reversed and the cause remanded for further proceedings consistent with this opinion. * * *

Justice STEVENS, with whom Justice BLACKMUN and Justice O'CONNOR join, and with whom Justice THOMAS joins as to Parts II and III, dissenting.[b]

* * * Like the Hydra slain by Hercules, prosecutorial misconduct has many heads. * * * [It has not] been limited to judicial proceedings: the reported cases indicate that it has sometimes infected grand jury proceedings as well. The cases contain examples of prosecutors presenting perjured testimony, questioning a witness outside the presence of the grand jury and then failing to inform the grand jury that the testimony was exculpatory, failing to inform the grand jury of its authority to subpoena witnesses, operating under a conflict of interest, misstating the law, and misstating the facts on cross-examination of a witness.

---

[8] In *Costello,* for example, instead of complaining about the grand jury's *reliance* upon hearsay evidence the petitioner could have complained about the prosecutor's *introduction* of it. See, e.g., United States v. Estepa, 471 F.2d 1132 (2d Cir. 1972) (prosecutor should not introduce hearsay evidence before grand jury when direct evidence is available); see also Arenella, *Reforming the Federal Grand Jury and the State Preliminary Hearing to Prevent Conviction Without Adjudication,* 78 MICH.L.REV. 463, 540 (1980) ("[S]ome federal courts have cautiously begun to . . . us[e] a revitalized prosecutorial misconduct doctrine to circumvent *Costello 's* prohibition against directly evaluating the sufficiency of the evidence presented to the grand jury").

[b] Part I of Justice Stevens' opinion, deleted here, argued that certiorari was improvidently granted. That portion of the majority's opinion responding to this argument also has been deleted.

* * * [T]he prosecutor's duty to protect the fundamental fairness of judicial proceedings assumes special importance when he is presenting evidence to a grand jury. As the Court of Appeals for the Third Circuit recognized, "the costs of continued unchecked prosecutorial misconduct" before the grand jury are particularly substantial because there

> "the prosecutor operates without the check of a judge or a trained legal adversary, and virtually immune from public scrutiny. The prosecutor's abuse of his special relationship to the grand jury poses an enormous risk to defendants as well. For while in theory a trial provides the defendant with a full opportunity to contest and disprove the charges against him, in practice, the handing up of an indictment will often have a devastating personal and professional impact that a later dismissal or acquittal can never undo. Where the potential for abuse is so great, and the consequences of a mistaken indictment so serious, the ethical responsibilities of the prosecutor, and the obligation of the judiciary to protect against even the appearance of unfairness, are correspondingly heightened." United States v. Serubo, 604 F.2d 807, 817 (3d Cir. 1979). * * *

The standard for judging the consequences of prosecutorial misconduct during grand jury proceedings is essentially the same as the standard applicable to trials. In *Mechanik*, [p. 462] we held that there was "no reason not to apply [the harmless error rule] to 'errors, defects, irregularities, or variances' occurring before a grand jury just as we have applied it to such error occurring in the criminal trial itself." We repeated that holding in *Bank of Nova Scotia*, when we rejected a defendant's argument that an indictment should be dismissed because of prosecutorial misconduct and irregularities in proceedings before the grand jury. Referring to the prosecutor's misconduct before the grand jury, we "concluded that our customary harmless-error inquiry is applicable where, as in the cases before us, a court is asked to dismiss an indictment prior to the conclusion of the trial." Moreover, in reviewing the instances of misconduct in that case, we applied precisely the same standard to the prosecutor's violations of Rule 6 of the Federal Rules of Criminal Procedure and to his violations of the general duty of fairness that applies to all judicial proceedings. * * * Unquestionably, the plain implication of that discussion is that if the misconduct, even though not expressly forbidden by any written rule, had played a critical role in persuading the jury to return the indictment, dismissal would have been required.

In an opinion that I find difficult to comprehend, the Court today repudiates the assumptions underlying these cases and seems to suggest that the court has no authority to supervise the conduct of the prosecutor in grand jury proceedings so long as he follows the dictates of the Constitution, applicable statutes, and Rule 6 of the Federal Rules of Criminal Procedure. The Court purports to support this conclusion by invoking the doctrine of separation of powers and citing a string of cases in which we have declined to impose categorical restraints on the grand jury. Needless to say, the Court's reasoning is unpersuasive.

Although the grand jury has not been "textually assigned" to "any of the branches described in the first three Articles" of the Constitution, it is not an autonomous body completely beyond the reach of the other branches. Throughout its life, from the moment it is convened until it is discharged, the grand jury is subject to the control of the court. As Judge Learned Hand recognized over sixty years ago, "a grand jury is neither an officer nor an agent of the United States, but a part of the court." Falter v. United States, 23 F.2d 420, 425 (2d Cir. 1928). This Court has similarly characterized the grand jury: * * * "A grand jury is clothed with great independence in many areas, but it remains an appendage of the court, powerless to perform its investigative function without the court's aid, because powerless itself to compel the testimony of witnesses. It is the court's process which summons the witness to attend and give testimony, and it is the court which must compel a witness to testify if, after appearing, he refuses to do so." Brown v. United States.

* * * [T]he Court has recognized that it has the authority to create and enforce limited rules applicable in grand jury proceedings. Thus, for example, the Court has said that the grand jury "may not itself violate a valid privilege, whether established by the Constitution, statutes, or the common law." And the Court may prevent a grand jury from violating such a privilege by quashing or modifying a subpoena, or issuing a protective order forbidding questions in violation of the privilege. Moreover, there are, as the Court notes, a series of cases in which we declined to impose categorical restraints on the grand jury. In none of those cases, however, did we question our power to reach a contrary result.

Although the Court recognizes that it may invoke its supervisory authority to fashion and enforce privilege rules applicable in grand jury proceedings, and suggests that it may also invoke its supervisory authority to fashion other limited rules of grand jury procedure, it concludes that it has no authority to "prescrib[e] standards of prosecutorial conduct before the grand jury," because that would alter the grand jury's historic role as an independent, inquisitorial institution. I disagree.

We do not protect the integrity and independence of the grand jury by closing our eyes to the countless forms of prosecutorial misconduct that may occur inside the secrecy of the grand jury room. After all, the grand jury is not merely an investigatory body; it also serves as a "protector of citizens against arbitrary and oppressive governmental action." *Calandra.* * * * It blinks reality to say that the grand jury can adequately perform this important historic role if it is intentionally misled by the prosecutor—on whose knowledge of the law and facts of the underlying criminal investigation the jurors will, of necessity, rely.

Unlike the Court, I am unwilling to hold that countless forms of prosecutorial misconduct must be tolerated—no matter how prejudicial they may be, or how seriously they may distort the legitimate function of the grand jury—simply because they are not proscribed by Rule 6 of the Federal Rules of Criminal Procedure or a statute that is applicable in grand jury proceedings. Such a sharp break with the traditional role of the federal judiciary is unprecedented, unwarranted, and unwise. Unrestrained prosecutorial misconduct in grand jury proceedings is inconsistent with the administration of justice in the federal courts and should be redressed in appropriate cases by the dismissal of indictments obtained by improper methods. * * *

What, then, is the proper disposition of this case? I agree with the Government that the prosecutor is not required to place all exculpatory evidence before the grand jury. A grand jury proceeding is an ex parte investigatory proceeding to determine whether there is probable cause to believe a violation of the criminal laws has occurred, not a trial. Requiring the prosecutor to ferret out and present all evidence that could be used at trial to create a reasonable doubt as to the defendant's guilt would be inconsistent with the purpose of the grand jury proceeding and would place significant burdens on the investigation. But that does not mean that the prosecutor may mislead the grand jury into believing that there is probable cause to indict by withholding clear evidence to the contrary. I thus agree with the Department of Justice that "when a prosecutor conducting a grand jury inquiry is personally aware of substantial evidence which directly negates the guilt of a subject of the investigation, the prosecutor must present or otherwise disclose such evidence to the grand jury before seeking an indictment against such a person." U.S. Dept. of Justice, United States Attorneys' Manual, Title 9, ch. 11, § 9-11.233, 88 (1988).

Although I question whether the evidence withheld in this case directly negates respondent's guilt, I need not resolve my doubts because the Solicitor General did not ask the Court to review the nature of the evidence withheld. Instead, he asked us to decide the legal question whether an indictment may be dismissed because the prosecutor failed to present exculpatory evidence. Unlike the Court and the Solicitor General, I believe the answer to that question is yes, if the withheld evidence would plainly preclude a finding of probable cause. I therefore cannot endorse the Court's opinion. * * *

NOTES AND QUESTIONS

1. ***The Effect of* Williams.** Prior to *Williams*, federal lower courts had characterized a broad range of prosecutorial actions and inactions as "misconduct" that would lead to dismissal of an indictment unless that misconduct constituted harmless error. Lower courts have recognized that *Williams* cuts deeply into the prior precedent on other types of misconduct

claims. See United States v. Gillespie, 974 F.2d 796 (7th Cir. 1992) ("after Williams, then, nothing short of a violation of laws or procedural rules regulating grand jury matters will permit a court to exercise its supervisory authority in the grand jury area"). Based on *Williams*, the Fifth Circuit overturned the district court's dismissal of an indictment when the government allegedly used perjured testimony to obtain it: "[W]e are persuaded that perjury before the grand jury that was not knowingly sponsored by the government may not form the basis for a district court's dismissal of an indictment under its supervisory power." United States v. Strouse, 286 F.3d 767 (5th Cir. 2002). In United States v. Breslin, 916 F.Supp. 438 (E.D. Pa. 1996), however, the court dismissed an indictment without prejudice under its supervisory power for the "cumulative effect of the many instances of misconduct" before the grand jury. One of the concerns with the prosecutor's presentation to the grand jury included his attempt to bond with the grand jury by providing donuts at one of the meetings. The court found "that it is inappropriate for the prosecutor to provide snacks to a grand jury, and that his suggestion that the donuts were provided because the task they were about to start was unpleasant made the situation worse." Did the district court miss the implications of *Williams* in using its supervisory power to dismiss an indictment even though no single violation supported such a remedy? A different grand jury later reindicted the defendant on the same charges, and the district court refused to dismiss the indictment because of the earlier misconduct. United States v. Breslin, 1997 WL 50422 (E.D. Pa. 1997).

The Department of Justice maintains a policy that its prosecutors should provide the grand jury with any exculpatory evidence, as Justice Stevens noted in his dissent in *Williams*. The U.S. Attorney's Manual now provides:

> In *United States v. Williams*, the Supreme Court held that the Federal courts' supervisory powers over the grand jury did not include the power to make a rule allowing the dismissal of an otherwise valid indictment where the prosecutor failed to introduce substantial exculpatory evidence to a grand jury. It is the policy of the Department of Justice, however, that when a prosecutor conducting a grand jury inquiry is personally aware of substantial evidence that directly negates the guilt of a subject of the investigation, the prosecutor must present or otherwise disclose such evidence to the grand jury before seeking an indictment against such a person. While a failure to follow the Department's policy should not result in dismissal of an indictment, appellate courts may refer violations of the policy to the Office of Professional Responsibility for review.

U.S.A.M. § 9-11.233.

2. ***The Fifth Amendment Grand Jury Right.*** As the Court noted in *Williams*, there was no claim that the alleged prosecutorial misconduct amounted to a constitutional violation. The Supreme Court has said very

little about what prosecutorial action before a grand jury would constitute a violation of the Fifth Amendment right to a grand jury indictment that would justify dismissing an indictment. In *Bank of Nova Scotia*, [p. 462], the defendant claimed that the prosecutor had "violated the Fifth Amendment by calling a number of witnesses [associated with the target] for having them assert their privilege against self-incrimination," but the Court found no need to rule explicitly on whether the target's constitutional rights would be violated by such action if aimed at having the grand jury draw adverse inferences against the target based on the witnesses' assertion of the privilege. It agreed with the Court of Appeals that there had been "no error" in the handling of these particular witnesses. The government "was not required to take at face value" the witnesses earlier assertions that they would invoke the privilege if called to testify, the questioning before the grand jury ceased as soon as the witnesses asserted the privilege, and "throughout the proceedings, the prosecution repeated the caution to the grand jury that it was not to draw an adverse inference from a witness' invocation of the Fifth Amendment." Lower court rulings have dealt more extensively with the question of what prosecutorial misconduct reaches the level of a constitutional violation. The intentional prosecutorial introduction of perjured testimony on a critical issue has been characterized by several courts as a constitutional violation. Consider also SARA SUN BEALE, WILLIAM C. BRYSON, JAMES E. FELMAN, & MICHAEL J. ELSTON , GRAND JURY LAW AND PRACTICE § 9.31 (2nd ed.):

> As several courts have explicitly recognized, the goal of constitutional or supervisory power analysis is generally the same: to protect the integrity of the judicial process from unfair or improper prosecutorial conduct. Supervisory power may be exercised if the prosecutor's conduct threatens the impartiality or independence of the grand jury's processes. The requirement of an impartial and independent grand jury is ultimately derived from the grand jury clause of the Fifth Amendment. Supervisory power cases not infrequently recognize this point implicitly, citing constitutional decisions such as *Costello v. United States* and *Stirone v. United States* to explain that the grand jury's function requires it to act independently of either the prosecutor or judge. Thus supervisory power cases can be seen as simply enforcing the requirements of the grand jury clause, rather than as defining new nonconstitutional standards for prosecutorial conduct. This interpretation of the function of supervisory power in grand jury cases would be consistent with its use in other contexts.

In United States v. Storey, 2 F.3d 1037 (10th Cir. 1993), the court rejected the defendant's appeal of a district court's denial of a motion to dismiss charges because the prosecutorial misconduct amounted to a denial of the Fifth Amendment right to a grand jury indictment. The court stated that the "alleged Rule 6(e)(2) violations do not raise a right not to be tried, and we disagree with Appellants that the other alleged misconduct either made the grand jury not a grand jury, or the indictment not an indictment.

The district court expressed dissatisfaction with the conduct of the Government, but evinced no concern with the conduct, independence, or product of the grand jury."

3. ***State Court Rejection of*** **Williams**. While *Williams* is the rule for federal courts, the states interpret their own constitutions, or apply their own supervisory authority, to impose a rule similar to the one rejected by the Supreme Court. In State v. Hogan, 676 A.2d 533 (N.J. 1996), the New Jersey Supreme Court rejected *Williams* and used its supervisory power over the lower courts to require prosecutors to present exculpatory evidence to a grand jury. The New Jersey Supreme Court extended the rule in a later case involving a different defendant with the same last name, State v. Hogan, 764 A.2d 1012 (N.J. 2001), to recognize "a prosecutor's obligation to instruct the grand jury on possible defenses is a corollary to his responsibility to present exculpatory evidence. The extent of the prosecutor's duty must be defined with reference to the role of the grand jury–to protect the innocent, and bring to trial those who may be guilty. Viewed from this perspective, the question of whether a particular defense need be charged depends upon its potential for eliminating a needless or unfounded prosecution. The appropriate distinction for this purpose is between exculpatory and mitigating defenses. An exculpatory defense is one that would, if believed, result in a finding of no criminal liability, i.e., a complete exoneration." Other states that require prosecutors to disclose exculpatory evidence to the grand jury include California (Johnson v. Superior Court, 539 P.2d 792 (1975) (requiring production of any evidence that reasonably tends to negate guilt), and Massachusetts (Commonwealth v. LaVelle, 605 N.E.2d 852 (1993) (evidence that would greatly undermine credibility of evidence likely to affect grand jury's decision to indict).

4. ***Grand Jury Independence***. The grand jury is independent of both the judiciary and the prosecutor, but the prosecutor plays a key role in providing legal advice and drafting the indictment that the grand jury may consider. How much involvement can a prosecutor have in the process before the grand jury's independence is undermined? If there is prosecutorial misconduct in the grand jury's consideration of whether probable cause exists to indict, does that violate a defendant's Fifth Amendment right to a grand jury indictment? In United States v. Navarro-Vargas, 408 F.3d 1184 (9th Cir. 2005), the Ninth Circuit, sitting en banc, rejected the claim that the grand jury instructions provided at the start of the term of service must include a specific statement that it need not return an indictment even if they found probable cause that the defendant committed the offense. The majority stated that the "instruction does not violate the grand jury's independence. The language of the model charge does not state that the jury 'must' or 'shall' indict, but merely that it 'should' indict if it finds probable cause. As a matter of pure semantics, it does not eliminate discretion on the part of the grand jurors, leaving room for the grand jury to dismiss even if it finds probable cause." A dissenting opinion by Judge Hawkins argued against "the essential hypocrisy of the government's position. Standing firmly in the defense of its exercise of discretion (amounting at times to nullification), it just as firmly argues that

grand jurors are without authority to make similar judgments about which laws deserve vigorous enforcement and which ones do not, in deciding whom to indict, and on what charges. In the government's eye, the grand jury is a mere instrument of prosecutorial will, a probable cause screening device obligated to act at the direction of the prosecutor and then only when the prosecutor has decided whom and how much to charge."

5. ***The Dismissal Remedy*: Mechanik *and* Bank of Nova Scotia**. In **United States v. Mechanik**, 475 U.S. 66 (1986), the defense learned during its cross-examination of a government agent that the agent had appeared together with another agent before the grand jury, where they had testified in tandem. The defense then moved for dismissal of the indictment on the ground that this practice violated Rule 6(d), which specifies those persons who may be present at grand jury proceedings and refers only to "the witness under examination" (emphasis added). Although Rule 12(b)(2) requires that such motions to dismiss ordinarily be raised before trial, an exception is made where there is "good cause" for the late objection. The trial judge took the motion under advisement until after the trial. It was then considered, after the jury had returned its verdict of guilty, with the trial judge ruling that Rule 6(d) had been violated but the violation was harmless because it had no impact upon the grand jury's decision to indict. The Court of Appeals reversed, holding that a Rule 6(d) violation should require automatic reversal. That ruling was then reversed by the Supreme Court, and the conviction reinstated.

Three different approaches were advanced in the three opinions in *Mechanik*. Justice Marshall, in dissent, adopted the analysis of the Court of Appeals. Three concurring judges (in an opinion by Justice O'Connor) agreed with the trial judge's conclusion that the critical question was whether the violation was harmless as it impacted upon the grand jury's decision to indict. The opinion for the Court (per Rehnquist, C.J.) argued that the impact of the Rule 6(d) violation should be evaluated in light of the supervening jury verdict. It reasoned:

> Both the District Court and the Court of Appeals observed that Rule 6(d) was designed, in part, "to ensure that grand jurors, sitting without the direct supervision of a judge, are not subject to undue influence that may come with the presence of an unauthorized person." The Rule protects against the danger that a defendant will be required to defend against a charge for which there is no probable cause to believe him guilty. The error involving Rule 6(d) in these cases had the theoretical potential to affect the grand jury's determination whether to indict these particular defendants for the offenses for which they were charged. But the petit jury's subsequent guilty verdict not only means that there was probable cause to believe that the defendants were guilty as charged, but that they are in fact guilty as charged beyond a reasonable doubt. Measured by the petit jury's verdict, then, any error in the grand

jury proceeding connected with the charging decision was harmless beyond a reasonable doubt.

It might be argued in some literal sense that because the Rule was designed to protect against an erroneous charging decision by the grand jury, the indictment should not be compared to the evidence produced by the Government at trial, but to the evidence produced before the grand jury. But even if this argument was accepted, there is no simple way after the verdict to restore the defendant to the position in which he would have been had the indictment been dismissed before trial. He will already have suffered whatever inconvenience, expense, and opprobrium that a proper indictment may have spared him. In courtroom proceedings as elsewhere, "the moving finger writes, and having writ moves on." Thus reversal of a conviction after a trial free from reversible error cannot restore to the defendant whatever benefit might have accrued to him from a trial on an indictment returned in conformity with Rule 6(d). * * *

We express no opinion as to what remedy may be appropriate for a violation of Rule 6(d) that has affected the grand jury's charging decision and is brought to the attention of the trial court before the commencement of trial. We hold only that however diligent the defendants may have been in seeking to discover the basis for the claimed violation of Rule 6(d), the petit jury's verdict rendered harmless any conceivable error in the charging decision that might have flowed from the violation. In such a case, the societal costs of retrial after a jury verdict of guilty are far too substantial to justify setting aside the verdict simply because of an error in the earlier grand jury proceedings. * * * [d]

---

[d] As to those costs, the Court noted:

The reversal of a conviction entails substantial social costs: it forces jurors, witnesses, courts, the prosecution, and the defendants to expend further time, energy, and other resources to repeat a trial that has already once taken place; victims may be asked to relive their disturbing experiences. The "[p]assage of time, erosion of memory, and dispersion of witnesses may render retrial difficult, even impossible." * * *. Thus, while reversal "may, in theory, entitle the defendant only to retrial, in practice it may reward the accused with complete freedom from prosecution," and thereby "cost society the right to punish admitted offenders." * * * Even if a defendant is convicted in a second trial, the intervening delay may compromise society's "interest in the prompt administration of justice," * * * and impede accomplishment of the objectives of deterrence and rehabilitation. These societal costs of reversal and retrial are an acceptable and often necessary consequence when an error in the first proceeding has deprived a defendant of a fair determination of the issue of guilt or innocence. But the balance of interest tips decidedly the other way when an error has had no effect on the outcome of the trial.

In **Bank of Nova Scotia v. United States**, 487 U.S. 250 (1988), the Supreme Court spelled out the governing standard for the dismissal of an indictment prior to conviction. *Bank of Nova Scotia* was decided prior to *Williams* and dealt with some prosecutorial actions that would not constitute cognizable misconduct under *Williams* [see p. 448]. *Bank of Nova Scotia* applied the same standard to actions that would be subject to a supervisory-authority dismissal under *Williams*, and *Williams* itself assumed the applicability of the *Bank of Nova Scotia* standard to such misconduct.

The trial court in *Bank of Nova Scotia* had dismissed the indictment pretrial on the basis of numerous prosecutorial actions characterized as misconduct, including The district court in the Bank of Nova Scotia case had based its dismissal order on several instances of alleged misconduct that included: (1) various violations of Rule 6(e) secrecy provisions through disclosures of grand jury materials to government agents and potential witnesses and through instructions to witnesses not to disclose their testimony to the target; (2) violations of Rule 6(d) in allowing joint appearances by IRS agents reading transcripts to the grand jury; (3) alleged violation of 18 U.S.C. § 6002 in the use of "pocket immunity"; (4) causing government agents to mischaracterize prior testimony that they summarized for the grand jury; (5) calling witnesses associated with the target for the sole purpose of having them assert their privilege against self-incrimination before the grand jury; and (6) administering unauthorized oaths to IRS agents, characterizing them as agents of the grand jury, in violation of Rule 6(e). The district court found that dismissal was appropriate to declare "with unmistakable intention" that "such conduct * * * will not be tolerated." A divided Court of Appeals reversed the dismissal order. It concluded that the prosecutorial actions had not "significantly infringe[d] on the grand jury's ability to exercise independent judgment" and that "without a showing of such infringement," federal supervisory authority could not be used to dismiss an indictment. A dissenting judge disagreed with "the view of the majority that prejudice to the defendant must be shown before a court can exercise its supervisory power to dismiss an indictment on the basis of egregious prosecutorial misconduct." The Supreme Court, with only Justice Marshall dissenting, held in an opinion by Justice Kennedy that the Court of Appeals majority had been correct in insisting upon a prejudicial impact and in finding no such impact here. Speaking first to the requisite showing of prejudice, Justice Kennedy articulated a standard somewhat differently than the Court of Appeals. He noted:

> We hold that, as a general matter, a District Court may not dismiss an indictment for errors in grand jury proceedings unless such errors prejudiced the defendants. * * * In the exercise of its supervisory authority, a federal court "may, within limits, formulate procedural rules not specifically required by the Constitution or the Congress." United States v. Hasting, 461 U.S. 499 (1983). Nevertheless, it is well established that "[e]ven a sensible and efficient use of the supervisory power . . . is invalid if it conflicts with constitutional or statutory provisions." * * * . Our previous cases

have not addressed explicitly whether this rationale bars exercise of a supervisory authority where, as here, dismissal of the indictment would conflict with the harmless error inquiry mandated by the Federal Rules of Criminal Procedure. * * * We now hold that a federal court may not invoke supervisory power to circumvent the harmless error inquiry prescribed by Federal Rule of Criminal Procedure 52(a). Rule 52(a) provides that "[a]ny error, defect, irregularity or variance which does not affect substantial rights shall be disregarded." * * * Rule 52 is, in every pertinent respect, as binding as any statute duly enacted by Congress, and federal courts have no more discretion to disregard the Rule's mandate than they do to disregard constitutional or statutory provisions. * * *

Having concluded that our customary harmless-error inquiry is applicable where, as in the case before us, a court is asked to dismiss an indictment prior to the conclusion of the trial, we turn to the standard of prejudice that courts should apply in assessing such claims. We adopt for this purpose, at least where dismissal is sought for nonconstitutional error, the standard articulated by Justice O'Connor in her concurring opinion in United States v. Mechanik. Under this standard, dismissal of the indictment is appropriate only "if it is established that the violation substantially influenced the grand jury's decision to indict," or if there is "grave doubt" that the decision to indict was free from the substantial influence of such violations. This standard is based on our decision in Kotteakos v. United States, 328 U.S. 750 (1946), where, in construing a statute later incorporated into Rule 52(a), we held that a conviction should not be overturned unless, after examining the record as a whole, a court concludes that an error may have had "substantial influence" on the outcome of the proceeding.

To be distinguished from the cases before us are a class of cases in which indictments are dismissed, without a particular assessment of the prejudicial impact of the errors in each case, because the errors are deemed fundamental. These cases may be explained as isolated exceptions to the harmless error rule. We think, however, that an alternative and more clear explanation is that these cases are ones in which the structural protections of the grand jury have been so compromised as to render the proceedings fundamentally unfair, allowing the presumption of prejudice. * * *

In the cases before us we do not inquire whether the grand jury's independence was infringed. Such an infringement may result in grave doubt as to a violation's effect on the grand jury's decision to indict, but we did not grant certiorari to review this conclusion. We note that the Court of Appeals found that the prosecution's conduct was not "a significant infringement on the grand jury's ability to exercise independent judgment," and we accept that conclusion here. Finally, we note that we are not faced with a history of prosecutorial

> misconduct, spanning several cases, that is so systematic and pervasive as to raise a substantial and serious question about the fundamental fairness of the process which resulted in the indictment.

The Court concluded that there was no factual basis for some of the alleged violations, that the alleged Rule 6(e) violations clearly "could not have affected the charging decision," and that as to those that could conceivably have had an impact, the circumstances under which they occurred did not pose the requisite likelihood of prejudicial effect to escape being characterized as "harmless error."

6. ***The Scope of* Mechanik.** Federal lower courts have disagreed as to how broadly *Mechanik* should be read. The Tenth Circuit has reasoned that *Mechanik* was "carefully crafted along very narrow lines" and involved misconduct that "at worst, was [a] technical [violation]." It would hold postconviction review available for allegations of misconduct suggesting the prosecutor "attempted to unfairly sway the grand jury or to otherwise affect the accusatory process" or misconduct that "transgressed the defendant's right to fundamental fairness." United States v. Taylor, 798 F.2d 1337 (10th Cir. 1986) (finding reviewable a pre-*Williams* "totality of the circumstances" challenge that cited the prosecutor's failure to present exculpatory evidence, use of inadmissible and inflammatory evidence, violation of the attorney-client privilege, and unauthorized use of state officers in the grand jury's investigation). In United States v. Colon-Munoz, 192 F.3d 210 (1st Cir. 1999), the defendant sought to overturn his conviction because the appointment of an interim United States Attorney by the district court violated the Appointments Clause, and therefore the grand jury indictment was invalid. The First Circuit stated, "As a matter of law, any error in the charging decision of the grand jury was rendered harmless by the verdict and Colon cannot claim that Gil's presence before the grand jury entitles him to a dismissal of the indictment. We caution, however, that this conclusion implies no judgment about the importance of the issues raised by Colon or the Association in their challenge to the constitutionality of the lengthy interim judicial appointment of the United States Attorney."

7. ***Interlocutory Appeal.*** Justice Marshall, in his dissent in *Mechanik*, complained that the majority was leaving the enforcement of Rule 6(d) to the "unreviewable largesse of the district courts." He noted that if a judge should rule against a defendant on a pretrial motion to dismiss, that ruling might not be subject to appeal until after the trial, where a conviction would then preclude any relief under the majority's view. He offered the possibility of viewing the denial of the pretrial motion as a collateral order, so that it would be immediately appealable. The Court rejected that position in Midland Asphalt Corp. v. United States, 489 U.S. 794 (1989), holding that the trial court's refusal to dismiss an indictment because of the improper disclosure of grand jury material in violation of Federal Rule of Criminal Procedure 6(e) was not appealable under the collateral order doctrine.

Justice Marshall also suggested that the district court might simply defer ruling on a motion until after trial, thereby basically avoiding the need for a ruling on the merits of the motion, since an acquittal would render the motion moot and a conviction would render the error per se harmless. While the trial judge did defer ruling on the motion made in *Mechanik*, that motion was made during trial, and it generally is assumed that deferral is inappropriate where motions are made pretrial. This has led to increased efforts by defense counsel to gain pretrial disclosure of possible grand jury misconduct, so that challenges can be presented pretrial. However, as discussed below, that is not easily done.

8. ***Establishing Misconduct***. How does a defendant first discover, and then establish, that there was prosecutorial misconduct? The best source for determining what happened before the grand jury usually is the transcript of the grand jury proceedings. Under Federal Rule 6(e)(3)(C)(ii), that transcript can be obtained "when permitted by the court at the request of the defendant, upon a showing that grounds may exist for a motion to dismiss the indictment because of matters occurring before the grand jury." Federal courts generally hold that disclosure will not be permitted under this provision unless the defense first makes a preliminary showing, from the sources available to it, of likely misconduct that might justify dismissal. See, e.g., Beatrice Foods Co. v. United States, 312 F.2d 29 (8th Cir. 1963). But see United States v. Singer, 660 F.2d 1295 (8th Cir. 1981) (district court has discretion to examine the transcript *in camera* even if the requisite showing is not made). Courts have generally been unwilling to grant defense requests to review grand jury transcripts for only potential misconduct claims.. See BEALE ET AL., GRAND JURY LAW AND PRACTICE § 5.11 ("In order to make the preliminary showing that is a prerequisite to obtaining disclosure under Rule 6(e)(3)(C)(ii), the defendant must point to more than 'mere speculation' that improprieties may have occurred before the grand jury. Defendants have not succeeded in obtaining disclosure under this rule when they have argued that the grand jury materials, if disclosed, might reveal improprieties. Courts denying motions for disclosure have been unsympathetic to claims that it is impossible to determine whether grand jury abuses might have occurred without first having access to the grand jury record.").

The preliminary-showing requirement is most likely to be met where the misconduct occurred while a witness was present. A friendly witness, not being sworn to secrecy, may call the misconduct to the attention of the defense, and provide the testimony needed to make the preliminary showing. Even if the witness is not friendly, should the grand jury witness later testify at trial, the defense will be given access at the trial to the witness' recorded grand jury testimony, which may suggest (in the prosecutor's comments and questions) the likely misconduct. Of course, at this point, the trial judge may put off the misconduct inquiry, as was done in *Mechanik*. If only the jurors and the prosecutor were present when the misconduct occurred, the defense counsel faces what may be an insurmountable task in ever making a preliminary showing.[e]

B. CHALLENGES TO USE OF THE GRAND JURY

UNITED STATES v. ARTHUR ANDERSEN, L.L.P.

Crim. Action No. H-02-0121 (S.D. Texas April 9, 2002)

Unpublished Order

[HARMON, District Judge.]

Pending before the Court in the above referenced action is Defendant Arthur Andersen L.L.P.'s motion to quash subpoenas and limit grand jury proceedings.

Defendant contends that once an indictment has been returned, the government is prohibited from using the grand jury to conduct discovery or otherwise prepare its case for trial. United States v. Beasley, 550 F.2d 261 (5th Cir. 1977) ("prosecutorial agents many not use the Grand Jury for the primary purpose of strengthening [their] case on a pending indictment or as a substitute for discovery"); In re Grand Jury Subpoena Duces Tecum Dated January 2, 1985 ("Simels"), 767 F.2d 26 (2nd Cir. 1985) (the government may not use the grand jury to prepare "an already pending indictment for trial"). Defendant charges that the government is abusing the grand jury process by seeking to use the grand jury to assist in its trial preparation and to conduct discovery and "freeze" testimony. Defendant complains that only now, after obtaining the indictment on March 7, 2002, charging it with obstruction of justice in violation of 18 U.S.C. § 1512(b)(2), and after Defendant refused to plead guilty, is the government impermissibly subpoenaing Arthur Andersen personnel as fact witnesses to testify under oath about evidence relating to the obstruction of justice charge to strengthen its case, to "lock in–for trial purposes–those witnesses previously furnished through their voluntary interviews." Defendant argues that not only the timing of these delayed subpoenas, but also the implausibility of the government's claim that it is now seeking to investigate whether to indict individuals in addition to the accounting institution, its subpoenas for Arthur Andersen witnesses whose

---

[e] *Bank of Nova Scotia* presented an unusual situation in this regard, as explained in James Stewart, *The Prosecutors* 361 (1987):

> [O]ne of the witnesses, * * * a lawyer who advised Kilpatrick on one of the tax shelter programs, was left alone by [the prosecutors] * * * in the office where secret exhibits and transcripts related to the investigation were stored * * * [and] he took the opportunity to read through much of the material. As a result, defense lawyers were able to mount an unusually detailed assault on the prosecutors handling of the grand jury investigation.

testimony might constitute admissions attributable to their employer at trial support Defendant's charge of abuse by the government. Moreover, urges Defendant, the imminence of the trial setting eliminates any need to place witnesses before the grand jury now. Finally, Defendant asserts that "the government . . . made this bed; having rushed to indict on an extraordinarily expedited schedule, the Justice Department is in no position to complain if temporary restrictions on the grand jury are necessary to prevent the government from obtaining an unfair and improper advantage at trial."

In its memorandum in opposition, the government reiterates a point made in open court, *i.e.*, that Andersen urged the Department of Justice to expedite a decision about whether to indict the firm for obstruction of justice based on document destruction; then after Defendant was indicted, Andersen reversed its position and asked the government to delay investigating individual employees, including those that Andersen has publicly blamed for the destruction of documents. The government further complains that in light of Andersen's campaign to enlist public sympathy by slanted statements and demonstrations, to influence the potential jury pool, and to signal its desired factual stance to current and former employees, including potential targets, subjects or witnesses in the grand jury investigation, expeditious investigation by the grand jury of current and former employees is necessary.

Emphasizing that the grand jury, charged with determining whether a crime has been committed and, if so, uncovering its perpetrators, is a separate entity from the courts, which have only a "very limited" supervisory power over grand jury proceedings. *United States v. Williams* * * * also underscores that grand jury proceedings are entitled to a presumption of regularity. The government points to the long settled principle that "where the primary purpose of the investigation is to determine whether others not indicted were involved in the same criminal activity, or whether the indicted party committed still other crimes, the government may go forward with the inquiry even though one result may be the production of evidence that could then be used at the trial of the pending indictment." Wayne R. LaFave, Jerold H. Israel & Nancy J. King. 3 *Criminal Procedure* § 8.8 (f) at 173 (2d ed. 1999). Thus a grand jury subpoena may issue to assist the grand jury in its investigation even where the incidental effect might be that the prosecutor will use any information obtained for purposes other than that grand jury's investigation. See also Port v. Heard, 594 F. Supp. 1212 (S.D. Tex. 1984) (fact that "some pretrial discovery" may follow from proper grand jury investigation provides no basis for court intervention). Furthermore, the government highlights the fact that it is Defendant's burden to prove that the government's primary purpose for proceeding before the grand jury is to collect evidence relating to the pending indictment against Arthur Andersen L.L.P. *R. Enterprises, Inc.* The government contends that Defendant has failed to meet that burden.

In support of its response, the government submits its two declarations from attorneys working with the Enron Task Force, investigating all criminal matters associated with the collapse of Enron Corporation. The first, filed ex parte and under seal, was made by an Assistant United States Attorney ("AUSA") and explains in detail that the challenged subpoenas were issued by a different grand jury than the one that indicted Defendant and were properly issued to investigate uncharged criminal conduct by individuals and entities. A second, unsealed declaration by AUSA Leslie Caldwell delineating the procedural steps and negotiations between the government and Defendant up to the unsealing of the indictment for the instant case on March 14, 2002.

The Court has reviewed the applicable law and the record before it. A court should not intervene in the grand jury process absent a compelling reason. The existence of a pending indictment does not per se bar the government from using the grand jury to make a good faith, continuing inquiry into charges not included in that pending indictment. Abuse of the grand jury process occurs only when the government's sole or dominant purpose in convening a grand jury is to gather evidence for an already pending litigation. This sole or dominant purpose rule serves obvious purposes. It allows grand juries to continue investigations without having to wait to indict individuals or entities against which sufficient information to indict has already been uncovered, as well as to investigate additional individuals or entities who become suspects only after the indictment has been returned.

The government has explained with particularity and with documentary support that the government's expedited indictment was due to Arthur Andersen's urging. Thus the timing of the subpoenas is not a factor bolstering Defendant's argument, as it was in *Simels*. Other than conclusory statements, Defendant has failed to show that the government's investigation in subpoenaing the Defendant's employees as witnesses is for the sole and dominant purpose of developing evidence for trial on its pending destruction-of-documents obstruction charge against Arthur Andersen L.L.P. The Court finds that the government's affidavits have that shown it is acting in good faith to investigate unindicted charges against individuals and entities. As anyone following the news is fully aware, the collapse of Enron has spawned a complex and seemingly ever expanding investigation involving a wide range of parties and potential causes of action. The Court finds that there has been no abuse of grand jury process here. For these reasons the Court ORDERS that Defendant's motion to quash subpoenas and limit grand jury proceedings is DENIED.

NOTES AND QUESTIONS

1. ***Scope***. The misuse objection alleged in *Arthur Andersen*–that the prosecution's primary purpose in utilizing the grand jury's investigative authority was helping it prepare for trial on indictments already brought–is one member of a family of objections centering on use of the grand jury's investigative powers for purposes other than determining whether to issue

an indictment. Other objections in the same family include the use of the grand jury (1) to gather evidence for use in a pending or future civil action (note 2, infra); (2) to gather evidence to further independent investigations by law enforcement agencies (note 3, infra); and, (3) to "harass" witnesses by forcing an unneeded personal appearance or placing a witness in a situation where he or she is likely to commit perjury (note 4, infra).

2. ***Use for Civil Discovery***. In **United States v. Procter & Gamble**, 356 U.S. 677 (1958), the district court had granted broad disclosure of grand jury testimony to defendants in a civil antitrust action brought by the government. That ruling was apparently influenced in large part by the district court's belief that the government had used the grand jury investigation at which the testimony was given "to elicit evidence" for its subsequent civil action. The Supreme Court rejected the district court's disclosure order as not supported by a showing of particularized need, but it also acknowledged that the alleged government use of the grand jury process to prepare a civil case would have been improper. If the grand jury had been employed in that fashion, the Court noted, the government clearly would have been guilty of "flouting the policy of the law," both in using the grand jury for a purpose other than criminal investigation and in circumventing limits that would be placed upon a plaintiff in civil discovery. The Court added, however, that if the grand jury investigation was aimed at developing evidence for the possible issuance of an indictment, then there was no need to deny the government the incidental benefit of civil use of properly acquired evidence.

Lower courts applying the civil misuse standard of *Procter & Gamble* agree that whether or not an abuse exists depends upon the government's purpose in using the grand jury process, rather than the relevancy of the requested information to possible civil litigation. They recognize that a proper criminal investigation may readily encompass elements that also relate to civil cases, and that in some areas of the law (e.g., antitrust), the overlap between the criminal and civil investigation will be substantial. Some disagreement appears to exist, however, as to exactly how "pure" the government's purpose must be. Several courts have suggested that the *Procter & Gamble* standard is violated only when the investigation was aimed "primarily" at civil discovery. The issue, as they see it, is whether the grand jury proceedings are simply a "cover" or "subterfuge" for a civil investigation. Under this view, an investigation directed at concurrent criminal and civil uses is acceptable, provided the criminal use is at least equal in significance. In In re Grand Jury Subpoena Under Seal, 175 F.3d 332 (4th Cir. 1999), the Fourth Circuit stated that when "a showing of relevance [to a criminal investigation] can be made, a subpoena will issue even if the subpoena is also being sought for another, illegitimate purpose."

3. ***Harassment***. Opinions upholding broad investigatory powers of the grand jury frequently add that, "of course," any use of those powers for the purpose of "harassment" will be subject to judicial remedy. See e.g., Branzburg v. Hayes, 408 U.S. 665 (1972). Such statements usually do not indicate precisely

what is meant by "harassment," but the reference apparently is to something more than simply using the grand jury process for some unauthorized purpose, such as civil discovery. Courts that have offered illustrations of harassment tend to stress a vindictive element in the use of the grand jury, usually a use designed to intimidate the witness. Thus, one court cited the "bad faith harassment of a political dissident" by imposing the burdens (political and otherwise) of a grand jury appearance with "no expectation that any testimony concerning a crime would be forthcoming." In re Maury Santiago, 533 F.2d 727 (1st Cir. 1976). Similarly, repeated subpoenas to appear before one grand jury after another, without any additional investigative need, would constitute harassment. See In re Grand Jury (Schmidt), 619 F.2d 1022 (3d Cir. 1988). So too would purposeful leaks to the press designed to create adverse publicity. See In re Grand Jury Investigation (Lance), 610 F.2d 202 (5th Cir. 1980). It has also been argued that calling a witness before the grand jury solely to trap him into committing perjury constitutes a form of harassment. United States v. Howard, 867 F.2d 548 (9th Cir. 1989). In large part, courts recognizing that such uses would constitute harassment have also found that the objecting party has failed to establish that the subpoena authority was being used in that fashion. An objecting party here bears an especially heavy burden.

C. GRAND JURY SECRECY

1. ***Preventing Disclosure of Grand Jury Information***. Federal Rule of Criminal Procedure 6(e) imposes a strict secrecy requirement related to a "matter occurring before the grand jury" on all participants in the grand jury process, which includes the grand jurors, an interpreter, court reporter, operator of a recording device, person who transcribes recorded testimony, and attorneys for the government. An important exception to the secrecy requirement is the testifying witness who is not bound by the secrecy requirement. Rule 6(e)(2)(A) provides that "[n]o obligation of secrecy may be imposed on any person except in accordance with Rule 6(e)(2)(B)." Under Rule 6(e)(3)(A)(ii), grand jury material may be disclosed without a court order to "any government personnel–including those of a state, state subdivision, Indian tribe, or foreign government–that an attorney for the government considers necessary to assist in performing that attorney's duty to enforce federal criminal law." "Government personnel" for this purpose includes not only federal criminal investigators, such as FBI agents, but also employees from administrative agencies or other executive departments who are on loan to the Department of Justice for the purpose of assisting in the grand jury investigation. The decision as to which personnel is needed for this purpose lies within the discretion of the prosecutor and need not be justified to the court. In re Perlin, 589 F.2d 260, 268 (7th Cir. 1978). However, under 6(e)(3)(B), the prosecutor must furnish to the supervising judge a listing of the personnel to whom grand jury matter will be disclosed and must also certify that those persons have been advised of their secrecy obligation. In 2000, Congress amended Rule 6(e) in the Civil Asset Forfeiture Reform Act

to allow disclosure of grand jury material to government attorneys "in connection with any civil forfeiture provision of Federal law." 18 U.S.C. § 3322.

Since agency personnel receiving grand jury information under Rule 6(e)(3)(A)(i) are restricted to using that information only in the assistance of the government attorney's "duty to enforce federal criminal law," they may not disclose that information to their administrative agency absent a Rule 6(e)(3)(C)(i) court order. This limitation is stressed in USAM, § 9-11.251, which provides: "Strict precautions should be taken when employing personnel from agencies which have a civil function, such as the Securities and Exchange Commission, the Environmental Protection Agency, or the Internal Revenue Service, to ensure that knowledge of the grand jury investigation or documents subpoenaed by the grand jury are not used improperly for civil purposes by the agency. Grand jury documents should be segregated and personnel assisting the grand jury investigation should not work on a civil matter involving the same subjects unless a court order has been obtained authorizing such use."

2. ***Grand Jury Leaks.*** Most grand jury secrecy issues do not involve the imposition of secrecy in the grand jury process, but challenging improper disclosure of information in violation of Federal Rule of Criminal Procedure 6(e) The Rule provides that, *inter alia*, prosecutors "must not disclose a matter occurring before the grand jury," and Rule 6(e)(7) provides "A knowing violation of Rule 6 * * * may be punished as a contempt of court." What constitutes a "matter occurring before the grand jury" is a "term of art" that is by no means clear (infra., p. 477). Disclosures of grand jury information tend to fall into two categories. First, there are disclosures openly made by government personnel in the belief that their disclosures do not violate Rule 6(e). These are usually cases in which the government contends that the information disclosed did not fit within the Rule 6(e)(2) secrecy requirement because it did not reveal a "matter occurring before the grand jury," or that disclosure is of grand jury matter but is authorized under one of the "exceptions" in Rule 6(e)(3) permitting disclosure without a court order. The central issue is the legal question of whether the disclosure did or did not violate Rule 6(e). Ordinarily, the remedy for a violation is to order cessation of any further improper disclosure, although courts have noted that an exclusionary remedy may also be appropriate when the disclosure was to a party who now desires to use the improperly revealed information in a civil proceeding against the subject of the disclosure. See United States v. Couhlan, 842 F.2d 737 (4th Cir. 1988) (material given to government's civil attorney without the required Rule 6(e)(3)(c) order).

The second group of challenged disclosures are of a quite different order, and potentially more serious for those being investigated by the grand jury. They involve the alleged "leaking" of grand jury material to the press. Here, the disclosure would clearly violate Rule 6(e), and the central issue is whether there was in fact a leak by government personnel subject to the secrecy requirement. These types of disclosure can have significant effects on those named as being the target or subject of a grand jury investigation because there is often an assumption that the person is guilty of a crime. Moreover, there is often no way to rebut the leaked information beyond a denial of any involvement in any misconduct, which is often viewed skeptically by the public. There is a split in the circuit courts about whether there is any redress in the courts for a violation of grand jury secrecy requirement.

In **Finn v. Schiller**, 72 F.3d 1182 (4th Cir. 1996), the Fourth Circuit held that Rule 6(e)(2) "does not establish a private cause of action, but a person claiming damage as a result of a violation of the rule has the right to call such violation to the court's attention, and the court shall take action as hereinafter directed. Notice to the court may be by way of petition or by letter to the district judge." Finn filed suit against Assistant United States Attorney Schiller for "an ongoing pattern of prosecutorial misconduct" and sought injunctive relief to prevent any further disclosure of grand jury material. Finn had served on the Virginia Retirement System ("VRS") Board of Trustees, and Schiller filed a charge against another person for mail fraud related to transactions by VRS. Schiller also filed a separate 83-page document in the case containing a "statement of the case" in which only six pages dealt with the defendant's guilty plea while the reset alleged that Finn and other VRS officials conspired to commit mail, wire, and securities fraud in VRS transactions; "Finn was mentioned by name over 370 times in the Statement." A filing the statement, a number of newspapers, including the *Richmond Times-Dispatch* and *Washington Post* ran front-page articles with Finn's picture claiming that he was involved in fraudulent transactions at VRS. A magazine article a few months later stated that Finn had pleaded guilty to mail fraud charges. In fact, no charges were ever filed against Finn or anyone else connected to VRS. The Fourth Circuit held:

> Although we find that the language of the rule provides both civil and criminal contempt, it does not follow that the rule creates a private cause of action. A claimant may notify the court of a violation of the rule or may petition the court to investigate an alleged violation, but such complainant may not proceed by way of a civil action against the alleged violator.

The person who is the subject of a leak of grand jury material is not without any protection. The circuit court explained that "upon a prima facie showing to the district court of an alleged Rule 6(e) violation, the court *must* take appropriate steps to determine whether a violation has occurred." If there is evidence of a violation, then "the court should take appropriate action to prevent further violations and to sanction the violator as provided by the Rule." The problem with this approach is that any investigation of the leak may take months, while the damage to the person's reputation is immediate.

In re U.S., 441 F.3d 44 (1st Cir. 2006), refused to adopt any specific test for triggering an investigation of pre-indictment leaks of grand jury material. The First Circuit stated:

> [T]here must be some reasonable basis for a district court to launch an inquiry into claims that the prosecutor has engaged in grand jury misconduct. Some courts have adopted a rule that a prima facie case must be shown first. We are reluctant to use such a test. The "prima facie case" test is used in many different ways and means many different things. Further, a formulaic approach helps little: the varieties of possible misconduct and the factual variations are myriad. Depending on context, mere suspicion may be enough to cause further inquiry into violation of a well-established rule, particularly where infringement of a defendant's constitutional rights is potentially involved.

While the district court's initial investigation of leaks was justified, its later order halting trial a year after the leaks ended was not justified under Rule 6(e)(2). The First Circuit found that "the court's actions in launching an investigation of the government as a source of the pre-indictment leaks, more than a year after the leaks had stopped and after a decision had been made de facto not to investigate leaks further, were unjustified in this context."

Unlike the Fourth Circuit, the Fifth and District of Columbia Circuits recognize that an individual who is the subject of a grand jury leak can pursue a civil cause of action for relief under Rule 6(e). **In re Grand Jury Investigation (Lance)**, 610 F.2d 202 (5th Cir. 1980), involved a claim by Bert Lance, a former senior official in the Carter administration, who sought relief, including dismissal of the grand jury and termination of the investigation, because of information published about the grand jury's investigation of his conduct in connection with a national bank. The court set out a five factor test to determine is the claimant established a prima facie violation of Rule 6(e), which would require the district court to hold an evidentiary hearing to determine whether there was a violation: (1) the court must have before it news reports that "clearly indicate * * * [disclosure of] information about matters occurring before the grand jury"; (2) the reports must also indicate that the source of such information was "one of those [persons] proscribed from disclosing such matter" by Rule 6(e)(2) (i.e., government personnel, jurors, or jury personnel); (3) in "assessing the what and who of disclosure at the prima facie case stage, the court must assume that all statements in the news reports are correct"; (4) the "court must consider the nature of the relief requested and the extent to which it interferes with the grand jury process," requiring a "lesser showing for a prima facie case" on a request for contempt sanctions than on a request to dismiss the grand jury; and (5) "the court must weigh any evidence presented by the government to rebut the assumed truthfulness of reports which otherwise make a prima facie case of misconduct."

In **Barry v. United States**, 865 F.2d 1317 (D.C. Cir. 1989), former District of Columbia Mayor Marion Barry filed a complaint for equitable relief and contempt sanctions against the Attorney General of the United States, the United States Attorney for the District of Columbia, and other federal officials, claiming that they had unlawfully disclosed matters occurring before the grand jury that was investigating allegations of governmental corruption. The District of Columbia Circuit found that one newspaper article disclosed information about matters occurring before the grand jury and indicated that the sources of the information included attorneys and agents of the government. It ordered the district court to conduct an evidentiary hearing on the claim, "which, if proven, would justify civil contempt sanctions and/or injunctive relief under Rule 6(e)(2)." In **In re Sealed Case**, 151 F.3d 1059 (D.C. Cir. 1998), the court explained the process for pursuing a Rule 6(e) complaint:

> *Barry* thus envisions that a two-step analysis will be employed to determine whether a violation of Rule 6(e)(2) has occurred. First, the district court must determine whether the plaintiff has established a prima facie case. This determination will typically be based solely on an assessment of news articles submitted by the plaintiff; indeed, we acknowledged in *Barry* that a Rule 6(e)(2) plaintiff could not be "expected to do more at this juncture of the litigation" given that he or she would "almost never have access to anything beyond the words of the [news] report." Second, if the court determines that a prima facie case has been established, the burden shifts to the government to "attempt to explain its actions" in a show cause hearing. If the government fails to rebut the prima facie case, a violation of Rule 6(e)(2) is deemed to have occurred. The court then determines what remedy will be sufficient to deter further leaks. The remedy may be the imposition of civil contempt sanctions or equitable relief or both, "depending upon the nature of the violation and what the trial court deems necessary to prevent further unlawful disclosures of matters before the grand jury." Significantly, in establishing this two-step framework, *Barry* said nothing about the burden shifting back to the plaintiff after the government's presentation or about the plaintiff retaining the burden of persuasion after a prima facie case has been established. Under *Barry*, then, the plaintiff's burden is minimal; the responsibility of coming forward with evidence to rebut the accusation of unauthorized disclosure lies squarely with the government, the party in "the best position to know whether [it is] responsible for a violation of the Rule." If, of course, the government convinces the trial judge that no violation of Rule 6(e)(2) has occurred, that is the end of the proceeding.

The Rule 6(e) challenges to alleged disclosure of secret grand jury information are very difficult to prove, if the courts in that circuit can even hear the case. Are their strategic reasons for raising the issue, even if it is unlikely to succeed? The claim that the grand jury's strict rule of secrecy has been violated will likely result in an end to leaks, if they came from the prosecutor's office or the criminal investigators. If the Rule 6(e) claim will be heard by the same judge who would also be responsible for a subsequent prosecution, then bringing potential violations to the court's attention can alert the judge to possible governmental misconduct. Moreover, as discussed below in Section D, a defendant who is acquitted may be able to bring a suit against the government for attorney's fees if the government's conduct in prosecuting the case can be shown to be "vexatious, frivolous, or in bad faith." Proof of a Rule 6(e) violation would help to establish that the government's conduct warrants such an award.

3. ***"Matters Occurring Before the Grand Jury."*** Rule 6(e)(2)(B) does not define what constitutes a "matters occurring before the grand jury," and the phrase can be interpreted broadly–anything related to the grand jury investigation or obtained pursuant to its authority, or narrowly–only those things that actually take place in the presence of the grand jury. The District of Columbia Circuit considered the threshold question in relation to a claim by President Clinton that the Office of Independent Counsel (OIC) had improperly leaked information to the *New York Times* that involved "matters occurring before the grand jury," specifically whether the OIC planned to indict the President.

In re: SEALED CASE NO. 99-3091
(Office of Independent Counsel Contempt Proceeding)
192 F.3d 995 (D.C. Cir. 1999)

PER CURIAM.

On January 31, 1999, while the Senate was trying President William J. Clinton on articles of impeachment, the New York Times published a front page article captioned "Starr is Weighing Whether to Indict Sitting President." * * * The next day, the Office of the President (the White House) and Mr. Clinton jointly filed in district court a motion for an order to show cause why OIC, or the individuals therein, should not be held in contempt for disclosing grand jury material in violation of Federal Rule of Criminal Procedure 6(e). The White House and Mr. Clinton pointed to several excerpts from the article as evidence of OIC's violations of the grand jury secrecy rule. * * * OIC responded that the matters disclosed in the article merely rehashed old news reports and, in any event, did not fall within Rule 6(e)'s definition of "matters occurring before the grand jury." * * *

A prima facie violation based on a news report is established by showing that the report discloses "matters occurring before the grand jury" and indicates that sources of the information include government attorneys. See Barry v. United States, [p. 476]. Because OIC has withdrawn its argument that none of its attorneys was the source of the disclosures in the New York Times article at issue here, the only remaining issue is whether those disclosures qualify as "matters occurring before the grand jury." Fed.R.Crim.P. 6(e)(2).

The district court concluded that only one excerpt from the New York Times article constituted a prima facie violation of Rule 6(e). That excerpt, * * * disclosed the desire of some OIC prosecutors to seek, not long after the conclusion of the Senate trial, an indictment of Mr. Clinton on perjury and obstruction of justice charges, including lying under oath in his deposition in the Paula Jones matter and in his grand jury testimony. These statements, according to the district court, reveal a specific time frame for seeking an indictment, the details of a likely indictment, and the direction a group of prosecutors within OIC believes the grand jury investigation should take. Not surprisingly, Mr. Clinton and the White House agree with the district court's expansive reading of Rule 6(e). OIC takes a narrow view of the Rule's coverage, arguing that matters occurring outside the physical presence of the grand jury are covered only if they reveal grand jury matters. DOJ generally supports OIC with respect to the Rule's coverage, but emphasizes the importance of the context and concreteness of disclosures.

The key to the district court's reasoning is its reliance on this court's definition of "matters occurring before the grand jury." In In re Motions of Dow Jones & Co., 142 F.3d 496, 500 (D.C.Cir. 1998), we noted that this phrase encompasses "not only what has occurred and what is occurring, but also what is likely to occur," including "the identities of witnesses or jurors, the substance of testimony as well as actual transcripts, the strategy or direction of the investigation, the deliberations or questions of jurors, and the like." In the earlier contempt proceeding against Independent Counsel Starr, however, we cautioned the district court about "the problematic nature of applying so broad a definition, especially as it relates to the 'strategy or direction of the investigation,' to the inquiry as to whether a government attorney has made unauthorized disclosures." In re Sealed Case No. 98-3077, 151 F.3d at 1071 n. 12. Despite the seemingly broad nature of the statements in Dow Jones, we have never read Rule 6(e) to require that a "veil of secrecy be drawn over all matters occurring in the world that happen to be investigated by a grand jury." * * * Indeed, we have said that "[t]he disclosure of information 'coincidentally before the grand jury [which can] be revealed in such a manner that its revelation would not elucidate the inner workings of the grand jury' is not prohibited." * * * Thus, the phrases "likely to occur" and "strategy and direction" must be read in light of the text of Rule 6(e)–which limits the Rule's coverage to "matters occurring before the grand jury"–as well as the purposes of the Rule.

As we have recited on many occasions,

> Rule 6(e) . . . protects several interests of the criminal justice system: "First, if preindictment proceedings were made public, many prospective witnesses would be hesitant to come forward voluntarily, knowing that those against whom they testify would be aware of that testimony. Moreover, witnesses who appeared before the grand jury would be less likely to testify fully and frankly, as they would be open to retribution as well as to inducements. There also would be the risk that those about to be indicted would flee, or would try to influence individual grand jurors to vote against indictment. Finally, by preserving the secrecy of the proceedings, we assure that

> persons who are accused but exonerated by the grand jury will not be held up to public ridicule."

In re Sealed Case No. 98-3077, 151 F.3d 1059 (D.C.Cir.1998) (quoting Douglas Oil Co. v. Petrol Stops Northwest, 441 U.S. 211 (1979)). These purposes, as well as the text of the Rule itself, reflect the need to preserve the secrecy of the grand jury proceedings themselves. It is therefore necessary to differentiate between statements by a prosecutor's office with respect to its own investigation, and statements by a prosecutor's office with respect to a grand jury's investigation, a distinction of the utmost significance upon which several circuits have already remarked. * * *

Information actually presented to the grand jury is core Rule 6(e) material that is afforded the broadest protection from disclosure. Prosecutors' statements about their investigations, however, implicate the Rule only when they directly reveal grand jury matters. To be sure, we have recognized that Rule 6(e) would be easily evaded if a prosecutor could with impunity discuss with the press testimony about to be presented to a grand jury, so long as it had not yet occurred. Accordingly, we have read Rule 6(e) to cover matters "likely to occur." And even a discussion of "strategy and direction of the investigation" could include references to not yet delivered but clearly anticipated testimony. * * * But that does not mean that any discussion of an investigation is violative of Rule 6(e). Indeed, the district court's Local Rule 308(b)(2), which governs attorney conduct in grand jury matters, recognizes that prosecutors often have a legitimate interest in revealing aspects of their investigations "to inform the public that the investigation is underway, to describe the general scope of the investigation, to obtain assistance in the apprehension of a suspect, to warn the public of any dangers, or otherwise aid in the investigation."

It may often be the case, however, that disclosures by the prosecution referencing its own investigation should not be made for tactical reasons, or are in fact prohibited by other Rules or ethical guidelines. For instance, prosecutors may be prohibited by internal guidelines, see, e.g., United States Attorney Manual § 1-7.530, from discussing the strategy or direction of their investigation before an indictment is sought. This would serve one of the same purposes as Rule 6(e): protecting the reputation of innocent suspects. But a court may not use Rule 6(e) to generally regulate prosecutorial statements to the press. The purpose of the Rule is only to protect the secrecy of grand jury proceedings.

Thus, internal deliberations of prosecutors that do not directly reveal grand jury proceedings are not Rule 6(e) material. * * * It may be thought that when such deliberations include a discussion of whether an indictment should be sought, or whether a particular individual is potentially criminally liable, the deliberations have crossed into the realm of Rule 6(e) material. This ignores, however, the requirement that the matter occur before the grand jury. Where the reported deliberations do not reveal that an indictment has been sought or will be sought, ordinarily they will not reveal anything definite enough to come within the scope of Rule 6(e).

For these reasons, the disclosure that a group of OIC prosecutors "believe" that an indictment should be brought at the end of the impeachment proceedings does not on its face, or in the context of the article as a whole, violate Rule 6(e). We acknowledge, as did OIC, that such statements are troubling, for they have the potential to damage the reputation of innocent suspects. But bare statements that some assistant prosecutors in OIC wish to seek an indictment do not implicate the grand jury; the prosecutors may not even be basing their opinion on information presented to a grand jury.

The fact that the disclosure also reveals a time period for seeking the indictment of "not long after the Senate trial concludes" does not in any way indicate what is "likely to occur" before the grand jury within the meaning of Rule 6(e). That disclosure reflects nothing more than a desire on the part of some OIC prosecutors to seek an indictment at that time, not a decision to do so. The general uncertainty as to whether an indictment would in fact be sought (according to the article, only some prosecutors in OIC thought one should be) leads us to conclude that this portion of the article did not reveal anything that was "occurring before the grand jury."

Nor does it violate the Rule to state the general grounds for such an indictment–here, lying under oath in a deposition and before the grand jury–where no secret grand jury material is revealed. In ordinary circumstances, Rule 6(e) covers the disclosure of the names of grand jury witnesses. Therefore, the statement that members of OIC wished to seek an indictment based on Mr. Clinton's alleged perjury before a grand jury would ordinarily be Rule 6(e) material. In this case, however, we take judicial notice that the President's status as a witness before the grand jury was a matter of widespread public knowledge well before the New York Times article at issue in this case was written; the President himself went on national television the day of his testimony to reveal this fact. * * * Where the general public is already aware of the information contained in the prosecutor's statement, there is no additional harm in the prosecutor referring to such information. * * * Therefore, it cannot be said that OIC "disclosed" the name of a grand jury witness, in violation of Rule 6(e), by referring to the President's grand jury testimony.

Similarly, it would ordinarily be a violation of Rule 6(e) to disclose that a grand jury is investigating a particular person. Thus, the statement that a grand jury is "hearing the case against Mr. Clinton" would be covered by Rule 6(e) if it were not for the fact that the New York Times article did not reveal any secret, for it was already common knowledge well before January 31, 1999, that a grand jury was investigating alleged perjury and obstruction of justice by the President. Once again, the President's appearance on national television confirmed as much. * * *

In light of our conclusion that the excerpt from the New York Times article does not constitute a prima facie violation of Rule 6(e), we reverse and remand with instructions to dismiss the Rule 6(e) contempt proceedings against OIC. * * *

D. ATTORNEY'S FEES FOR GOVERNMENT MISCONDUCT

The Supreme Court in *Bank of Nova Scotia* noted there were other means of remedying errors that did not have a prejudicial impact. They cited as illustrations of alternative remedies the punishment of a prosecutor's knowing violation of Rule 6 as contempt of court, requesting the bar or department of justice to initiate discipline proceedings, and the court "chastis[ing] the prosecutor in a published opinion." "Such remedies," it noted, "allow the court to focus on the culpable individual rather than granting a windfall to the unprejudiced defendant." Anne Poulin, *Supervision of the Grand Jury: Who Watches the Guardian?*, 68 WASH. U.L.Q. 885 (1990), is sharply critical of the Court's reliance upon such sanctions, noting that several factors limit their effectiveness. The "victim may have minimal incentive to invoke the sanction" since it will not address "the harm to the victim and the victim's reputation." Second, sanctions against the prosecutor "will only reach a narrow sub-group of abuses." As a practical matter, for various types of misconduct, such as leaks to the press, the victim will be unable to establish which government personnel engaged in the conduct. As to others, even if the abuser is identified, the victim will be unable to establish the element of bad faith that typically is a prerequisite to imposing the sanctions cited by the court. Finally, the "sanctions will have limited deterrent effect," as they are "unlikely to exert institutional pressure" beyond the individual sanctioned. The author suggests that, in the wake of *Bank of Nova Scotia* and *Mechanik*, "equitable intervention in the grand jury process may offer the only opportunity to address abusive grand jury practice." Would such intervention be permissible in light of *Williams*, apart from instances of violation of Rule 6 or statutory prohibitions? See Peter J. Henning, *Prosecutorial Misconduct in Grand Jury Investigations*, 51 S.C. L. REV. 1 (1999) ("The Supreme Court has eliminated direct judicial review of prosecutorial misconduct in the proceeding in which the misconduct occurred. If a grand jury indicts a defendant, the only means of seeking vindication is a trial in which a jury or a judge determines whether the government introduced proof beyond a reasonable doubt that the defendant committed a crime.").

In 1998, Congress adopted the Hyde Amendment, 18 U.S.C. § 3006A, to permit defendants subjected to improper federal prosecution to sue for attorneys fees after their exoneration. The statute permits a fee claim if the government's position was "vexatious, frivolous, or in bad faith." The statute does not define any of the three bases for an award of attorneys fees, and the legislative history sheds minimal light on the meaning of the terms. Therefore, the courts have been left to determine their meaning and apply them to claims of prosecutorial and investigatory misconduct in the wide variety of setting in which such misconduct arises including, *inter alia*, misconduct in obtaining a grand jury indictment.

UNITED STATES v. BRAUNSTEIN
281 F.3d 982 (9th Cir. 2002)

PREGERSON, Circuit Judge.

Appellant David T. Braunstein ("Braunstein") appeals the district court's order denying his motion for attorney's fees pursuant to the Hyde Amendment. Braunstein asserts that he incurred approximately $200,000 in attorney's fees defending against sixteen federal criminal charges of wire fraud, interstate transportation of goods obtained by fraud, and money laundering. He claims that under the Hyde Amendment, the government is required to pay his attorney's fees because the prosecution was "vexatious, frivolous, or in bad faith." * * *

Braunstein is a businessman who bought and sold computers, often through two companies he owned, Pacific Rim Technologies Corporation and Almacen. Braunstein maintained a computer distribution company in California and a computer retail store and refurbishing plant in Tijuana, Mexico. From September 1993 through April 1996, Braunstein bought computers from the Apple Latin America Company ("ALAC"). ALAC is a subdivision of Apple Computer, Inc. ("Apple"), an international computer manufacturer and sales company headquartered in the United States. ALAC is responsible for the sale of Apple products to Mexico, Central America, South America, and the Caribbean.

Braunstein's business relationship with ALAC consisted primarily of buying excess or obsolete Apple computers at greatly reduced prices. ALAC would ship the computers from Apple's warehouses in Chicago, California, and Canada to Braunstein's warehouse in San Diego. Although Braunstein was known as an ALAC distributor whose sales territory was Mexico, Braunstein sold most of his ALAC inventory within the United States, to an Arizona businessman named Alan Kaplan ("Kaplan"). Kaplan, in turn, sold the ALAC computers to other Apple resellers and wholesalers in the United States at prices substantially below Apple's listed wholesale price for such products. ALAC's former Sales Director referred to distributors like Braunstein and Kaplan as "the Marshalls or the T.J. Maxx of the computer industry."[1]

When purchasing Apple products, Braunstein dealt directly with Lopez and Carlos Valladeros ("Valladeros"), ALAC's regional sales representative

---

[1] The type of sales transacted between ALAC and Braunstein were alternately described as ALAC's method of "flushing" and "dumping" unwanted excess product.

for northern Latin America. In addition, Braunstein's business ventures with ALAC were overseen by Rubio.

Braunstein always paid ALAC up front, in cash. In exchange, he received an additional one percent discount. Lopez estimated that Braunstein's purchases brought ALAC "about a million dollars a month, which could be about five percent of the sales for Apple Latin America. It could have gone as high as 55 percent of the overall sales of Apple Latin America." Braunstein's dealings with ALAC were not, however, formalized by written contract; instead, the parties reached an oral understanding for each deal as to quantity and price. Lopez testified that it was unusual to conduct business with a distributor without a contract, but that "[i]t was done sometimes."

According to internal and external reports, ALAC "was under pressure to generate high sales volume," and deals such as the one with Braunstein facilitated that goal. Some of this pressure appears to stem from the fact that ALAC employees worked on commission. According to the postal inspector's report, if ALAC employees "made their gross margin, unit mix, and revenue, a bonus would be given." * * *

ALAC's deals with Braunstein benefitted ALAC in the short term by increasing the sales volume of products for which there were few, if any, other buyers. But the deals hurt Apple in the long-term by undercutting its ability to generate profitable sales in the United States. ALAC's business dealings effectively put ALAC's own distributors (whose sales area was limited to Latin America and the Carribean) into direct competition with Apple's United States distributors. Moreover, Braunstein and Kaplan were selling their Apple inventory within the United States at a much cheaper price than the other United States distributors were offering, which hurt the sales of those distributors and caused confusion and resentment in the market.

In August 1996, Apple's management became concerned about the systemic underselling of Apple's United States distributors by ALAC distributors. Specifically, Apple was concerned that ALAC distributors were engaging in "gray marketing," which involves the sale of Apple products outside the territory for which they are intended, and at a lower price than Apple would have authorized. Apple hired Kroll Associates ("Kroll"), an international private investigation firm, to look into ALAC's business practices.

Kroll issued its findings in a fifteen-page written report, on January 7, 1997. The report concluded that, "a potentially significant gray market problem existed" at ALAC and that "[t]here also appear to be a number of issues internal to ALAC which were contributing to the gray market problem." Kroll based this conclusion on its "preliminary findings, [which] consisted of specialized audits, interviewing selected persons, and reviewing pertinent documentation."

For reasons that are somewhat unclear from the record, the United States Attorney's Office in Arizona began investigating ALAC's business deals with Braunstein in the fall of 1997.[6] In August 1997, the Assistant United States Attorney ("AUSA") assigned to the ALAC case alerted Braunstein that he had become a target of a federal criminal investigation, and Braunstein retained Michael L. Lipman ("Lipman") as counsel.

In August, September, and October 1997, the AUSA conducted telephone interviews of several ALAC employees who had dealt directly with Braunstein, including Valladeros. The AUSA also interviewed Lopez. * * *

On September 23, 1997, Lipman wrote the AUSA a twenty-two page letter, in which he set forth in detail the legal and factual bases for his belief that Braunstein had done nothing illegal. * * * Lipman wrote:

> We believe that our client did not have a valid contract with Apple Latin America at any time during these transaction[s]; that Apple Latin America was aware that there were no legal restrictions on my client's resale of product; and that Apple Latin America knew, or should have known, that my client was selling the bulk of the product to a reseller in the U.S. Furthermore, Apple Latin America was more than happy to have these transactions occur because they created a material increase in their revenues.

Lipman continued, "To the degree that particular employees or former employees of Apple Latin America contend that they thought Mr. Braunstein was selling his product in Mexico, we submit that Apple's own financial documents will disprove these contentions." Lipman then detailed ALAC's financial woes and its efforts to "rebuild its distribution network," including its development of the "Alternate Channel Concept." He explained:

> [T]he "alternate channel" concept called for Apple Latin America to recruit United States distributors in the "border states" (primarily California, Texas and Florida). These distributors would be offered lower prices than U.S. distributors with the expectation that they could "recapture" the Latin American reseller market for ALAC.... This program was established so the U.S. distributors could not undercut the Latin American in-country distributors (and take away sales from the Apple Latin America division) and effectively "gray market" product into Latin America. Under the "alternate channel" concept, these distributors could sell to, among others, United States

[6] The most plausible reason for the investigation is that Apple alerted the United States Attorney's Office to the problem. The United States Attorney's Office in Arizona may have gotten involved because it was already investigating criminal fraud allegations against Kaplan. The Arizona United States Attorney's Office obtained an indictment against Kaplan in the fall of 1997 for conducting "a fraudulent rebate scheme involving Apple Powerbook 5300's." The government has never accused Braunstein of any involvement in that rebate scheme.

businesses with operations in Latin America. Thus, the program itself provided for sales of computers inside the United States. Additionally, it was anticipated by ALAC, and ALAC was willing to accept, that some "gray marketing" would occur into United States markets.

Lipman informed the AUSA that she could find confirmation of the alternative channel concept in "pricing studies performed by Apple Latin America," memos between ALAC and other Apple divisions, and internal documentation and memoranda within ALAC. Lipman also explained in detail Braunstein's relationship with ALAC and told the AUSA that internal ALAC documents would confirm that Braunstein was an alternate channel distributor who generated over $25 million in revenue for ALAC and that "ALAC had Braunstein existing entirely outside its normal distribution network for two years."

In a separate section of the letter, entitled "Apple's Knowledge Regarding Braunstein's Sales," Lipman listed "numerous sources of information and documentation" in Apple's possession that he believed would demonstrate that ALAC knew that Braunstein was selling its product in the United States. * * * Lipman concluded his letter by telling the AUSA: "You invited us to provide you evidence to support our theories; unfortunately, this documentation is at Apple, and *only you can gain access to it.*" (Emphasis added). [The court discussed other conversations and documents within the possession of the government.]

* * * The AUSA convened a grand jury in the District of Arizona to present her case against Braunstein. On August 21, 1997, the same day that the AUSA interviewed Valladeros by telephone, Valladeros appeared as a witness before the grand jury and testified about his business dealings with Braunstein. Valladeros testified that, as an ALAC sales representative, he sold computers to Braunstein from 1993 until Valladeros left the company in 1995. Responding to repeated questions from the AUSA as to whether Braunstein was told that he could only sell Apple products in Mexico, Valladeros stated that he did not recall. The AUSA then asked: "If [Braunstein] told you that the [Apple] product was going to stay in the United States and be shipped to Nebraska, for example, would you have sold him the product?" Valladeros replied: "No." Several transcript pages later, the following exchange occurred:

> AUSA: And did you explain to [Braunstein] he could not sell [Apple products] inside the United States?
>
> VALLADEROS: Again, when I explained to him the concept, I do not recall if I was explicit to him telling him that he could not sell in the United States.... And to be honest with you, having dealt in Latin America for eight, nine years, it never crossed my mind the fact that, you know, illegally selling product into the U.S., because it didn't make sense.

AUSA: So you assumed when you were negotiating with [Braunstein] that because you're Apple Latin America, this is all going to be exported to Latin America?
VALLADEROS: Correct.

The AUSA later asked Valladeros, "[D]o you know of anyone at Apple, either Apple Latin America or Apple America, who told Mr. Braunstein he could sell the product within the U.S. and not export it?" Valladeros replied, "Not to my knowledge."

This grand jury testimony by Valladeros flatly contradicted his answers to the AUSA's questions during the telephone conversation they had earlier *that same day*. In the telephone interview, Valladeros told the AUSA that "Braunstein could sell in his area of San Diego and sell to other U.S. companies who had dealings with Apple and exported products." Valladeros also told the AUSA that he and Braunstein "spoke extensively" about Braunstein's United States sales and that Valladeros "gave [a] report to Apple" about these conversations.

The AUSA also called Rubio and Lopez as grand jury witnesses. Both Lopez and Rubio testified that they were laid off by Apple in 1997 and that Braunstein was only authorized to sell Apple products within Latin America. On December 11, 1997, the grand jury returned an indictment charging Braunstein with multiple counts of wire fraud, in violation of 18 U.S.C. § 1343; interstate transportation of goods obtained by fraud, in violation of 18 U.S.C. § 2314; and money laundering, in violation of 18 U.S.C. § 1956. * * *

* * * On February 12, 1999, Philip H. Stillman, ("Stillman") who had replaced Lipman as Braunstein's counsel, subpoenaed various documents and records from Apple. Apple, represented by John J. Steele, ("Steele") moved to quash the subpoena as overly broad, and the government joined in the motion. On February 23, 1999, the district court granted the motion to quash and ordered Stillman to meet with Steele to "narrow down the number of areas of documents that you seek." The court also ordered Steele to "turn over the Kroll Report unredacted." * * * On March 8, 1999, the parties were back in court arguing over the subpoenas, and the district court was getting impatient with Apple * * *On March 12, 1999, Apple still had not turned over the Kroll report or any of the other subpoenaed documents. On March 22, Stillman moved for a continuance of the trial. On March 29, the court granted the motion and reset the trial date for May 11. On the same day, the court told Apple to turn over the subpoenaed documents "to the chambers of this court" no later than April 1. Apple did not comply with the order.

After joining in the first motion filed by Apple to quash the subpoena, the United States Attorney's Office was not involved in the discovery battle. Instead, as the AUSA later told the district court, "We remained silent."

On April 14, 1999, less than a month before the trial date, Apple turned over the subpoenaed documents to Braunstein. Among the documents that

Apple turned over were memos written by Lopez and Rubio in which they openly acknowledged the existence of gray market practices among ALAC's distributors. * * * On April 21, 1999, the AUSA moved for a continuance of the trial date. The court denied the motion. On May 3, 1999, the AUSA moved to dismiss the indictment without prejudice. The court granted the motion.

On July 2, 1999, Braunstein filed a motion for attorney's fees pursuant to the Hyde Amendment. The government filed an opposition, and a hearing was held on April 5, 2000. At the hearing, Stillman argued that the AUSA knew about the Lopez-Rubio memos detailing ALAC's knowledge of the gray market practices of its distributors. Specifically, Stillman pointed out that: (1) Lipman, told the AUSA about the Lopez-Rubio memos in his September 23, 1997 letter; (2) Lopez told the AUSA about the memos during their telephone interview on October 15, 1997; and (3) the Kroll report referred to the memos. Stillman stated:

> This was not a needle in a haystack. These documents came from Mr. Lopez's and Mr. Rubio's personnel files. There was a personnel file. It would have taken one phone call from [the AUSA]. [The AUSA] got stacks and stacks of documents, all sales invoices and so forth.... She could have made one phone call to Apple, who was cooperating with [the AUSA] for three years, providing logistic support, document support, and factual support, could have called them on the telephone and said, I want to see Lopez's personnel file.

The AUSA responded by stating that "the Government never alleged this as a gray market case. This is a fraud case ...." She continued:

> Now [the documents] may help the defendant put on his theory of the case which is that gray marketing was a problem at Apple. But they certainly do not constitute Brady material under the Government's theory of the case which is represented in the Indictment, and that is that the defendant engaged in fraudulent activity. He made misrepresentations to Apple repeatedly about where this product was going, and therein lie[s] the fraud.

The AUSA then stated that she received the documents that Stillman subpoenaed from Apple on April 14, 1999, the same day that Stillman did. She continued, "Did we know about a gray marketing issue? Well, obviously, we did, because we had the Kroll Report. But since gray marketing has nothing to do with wire fraud, mail fraud, interstate transportation of goods taken by fraud and money laundering, it's not exculpatory."

Stillman responded: "[T]he concept that gray marketing was not an issue in this case is simply gas. I mean it's–it's the core of the case. If Apple's condoning sales outside the territory, that's it. It's [the] end of [the] story."

On October 3, 2000, the district court entered its five-page order denying Braunstein's motion for attorney's fees. The court concluded that the government's case was not "contrary to established law on fraud ... [and] based on the facts as they evolved, was not frivolous." This appeal followed. * * *

The Hyde Amendment was enacted by Congress as part of a 1998 appropriations bill and is located in a statutory note to 18 U.S.C. § 3006A. It provides, in relevant part, that courts may award attorney's fees and other litigation expenses to prevailing criminal defendants "where the court finds that *the position of the United States was vexatious, frivolous, or in bad faith,* unless the court finds that special circumstances make the award unjust." Pub.L. No. 105-119,111 Stat. 2440, 2519 (1997) (reprinted in 18 U.S.C. § 3006A, historical and statutory notes) (emphasis added).[8] The defendant bears the burden of proof, "as well as establishing that he is otherwise qualified for the award under the law."[9] * * * The key terms of the Hyde Amendment, "vexatious, frivolous, or in bad faith," are not defined in the statute.

Because the district court based its ruling on a finding that the prosecution was not frivolous in instituting the criminal proceeding against Braunstein, our analysis will focus on that prong of the Hyde Amendment. United States v. Sherburne, 249 F.3d 1121 (9th Cir.2001), stated in a footnote that "frivolous" has only an objective component. No further guidance was given. Therefore, the Hyde Amendment's legislative history and out-of-circuit authority will be considered to provide helpful guidance in deciphering

---

[8] The full text of the Hyde Amendment provides: During fiscal year 1998 and in any fiscal year thereafter, the court, in any criminal case (other than the case in which the defendant is represented by assigned counsel paid for by the public) pending on or after the date of the enactment of this Act [Nov. 26, 1997], may award to a prevailing party, other than the United States, a reasonable attorney's fee and other litigation expenses, where the court finds that the position of the United States was vexatious, frivolous, or in bad faith, unless the court finds that special circumstances make such an award unjust. Such awards shall be granted pursuant to the procedures and limitations (but not the burden of proof) provided for an award under section 2412 of title 28, United States Code. To determine whether or not to award fees and costs under this section, the court, for good cause shown, may receive evidence ex parte and in camera ... and evidence or testimony so received shall be kept under seal. Fees and other expenses awarded under this provision to a party shall be paid by the agency over which the party prevails from any funds made available to the agency by appropriation. No new appropriations shall be made as a result of this provision.

[9] Specifically, as a threshold matter, the defendant must show that: (1) the case against him was pending on or after the enactment of the Hyde Amendment; (2) his net worth is less than $2 million; (3) he was the prevailing party in a criminal prosecution; (4) he was not represented by assigned counsel paid for by the public; (5) his attorney's fees were reasonable; and (6) no special circumstances exist to make the award unjust. United States v. Adkinson, 247 F.3d 1289, 1291 n.2 (11th Cir.2001).

the meaning of "frivolous." United States Representative Henry Hyde, who wrote the original version of the Amendment, explained that successful claimants under the Hyde Amendment must show that the prosecutors "are not just wrong, they are willfully wrong, they are frivolously wrong. They keep information from you that the law says they must disclose. They hide information. They do not disclose exculpatory information to which you are entitled." 143 Cong. Rec. H7786-04, HH7791 (Sept. 24, 1997) (statement of Rep. Hyde).[10] Thus, it is clear that, "[e]ven in its earliest form, the Hyde Amendment was targeted at prosecutorial misconduct, not prosecutorial mistake."

In [United States v.] Gilbert, the Eleventh Circuit interpreted "frivolous" using the "ordinary meaning" of the word as provided in Black's Law Dictionary. The court determined that "frivolous" means "groundless . . . with little prospect of success; often brought to embarrass or annoy the defendant." * * * Because the Eleventh's Circuit's approach to defining "frivolous" and "bad faith" is clear and well-reasoned, we [adopt] it.

To show that the criminal prosecution was "frivolous," Braunstein must demonstrate that the government's position was "foreclosed by binding precedent or so obviously wrong as to be frivolous."

The AUSA obtained an indictment against Braunstein for the federal crimes of wire fraud, interstate transportation of goods obtained by fraud, and money laundering. 18 U.S.C. §§ 1343, 2314, and 1956. * * *

To succeed in prosecuting Braunstein under any of the[se] statutes, * * * the government had to prove that Braunstein engaged in fraud; namely, that he obtained the computers from ALAC through false promises or representations. As the AUSA informed the district court during the argument on the Hyde Amendment motions, "this is a fraud case." Thus, the government's prosecution of Braunstein depended entirely on whether it could prove that he defrauded Apple.

The evidence in the record supports the conclusion that the government's position was so obviously wrong as to be frivolous. First, there was never an enforceable contract between Braunstein and ALAC. Thus, the AUSA's allegations of fraud were dependent on oral misrepresentations by Braunstein. Significantly, none of the grand jury witnesses testified that Braunstein made any such misrepresentations. More importantly, however,

---

[10] The legislation was motivated by Representative Hyde and his colleagues' outrage over the prosecution of former Labor Secretary Ray Donovan and former Congressman Joseph McDade. Both Donovan and McDade were subjected to lengthy federal criminal prosecutions and ultimately were acquitted. *Gilbert,* 198 F.3d at 1299-1300. The intent of the legislation was to ensure that innocent people would not bankrupt themselves defending against frivolous and bad faith prosecutions. *Id.* at 1300 (quoting Rep. Hyde as stating, "at least, if the Government tries to bankrupt someone because of attorney's fees, they ought to pay that").

the AUSA had reason to believe, based on information from four independent sources, that employees at ALAC knowingly sold computer products to distributors who resold the same products on the "gray market"; i.e., outside of Latin America, the intended territory.

First, there is the AUSA's interview with Valladeros. According to the AUSA's notes, Valladeros told her that "it was his understanding that Braunstein could sell in his area of San Diego and sell to other U.S. companies who had dealings with Apple." Valladeros made this statement to the AUSA on August 21, 1997, *over three months before the AUSA obtained the indictment against Braunstein.* [Emphasis in original] Second, the AUSA was aware that ALAC employees knew that their customers were selling Apple products in the United States through her interview with Lopez, Valladeros's supervisor. According to the AUSA's notes "there were pages and pages of hard copy documents sent between [Lopez] and Luis Rubio regarding this problem."

Third, the AUSA had in her possession the letter from Braunstein's attorney which detailed the defense to the fraud charges and directed her to sources within Apple and ALAC. Specifically, the letter stated that Apple had records of receiving registration records, warranty forms, and damage claims for the computers sold by Braunstein to United States distributors that were returned to Apple. The letter also described records of memoranda among its employees corroborating ALAC's participation in and dependence upon gray marketing. Fourth, the AUSA had the Kroll report, which supported the allegations that ALAC employees participated in gray market deals to boost their sales volume at the expense of long-term profits for Apple.

All of this information was in the AUSA's possession prior to her decision to seek a grand jury indictment against Braunstein. To the extent there was any confusion regarding the extent of gray market awareness on the part of ALAC employees, the AUSA could have clarified the matter by examining documents within the possession and control of Apple, described by the district court as a "complaining party."

ALAC's well-documented participation in gray marketing negated any well-founded prosecution based on fraud because ALAC could not be deceived about practices it actively endorsed. Accordingly, the government's case against Braunstein was frivolous. Braunstein is entitled to attorney's fees under the Hyde Amendment.

* * * We reverse the district court's denial of attorney's fees pursuant to the Hyde Amendment, finding that the court abused its discretion in denying Braunstein's motion. We hold that Braunstein, as the prevailing party in a criminal prosecution that was "frivolous" is entitled to an award of his attorney's fees.

NOTES AND QUESTIONS

1. ***"Vexatious" and "Bad Faith."*** *Braunstein* adopted the standard for whether the charges sought by the government were "frivolous." In United States v. Shaygan, 652 F.3d 1297 (11th Cir. 2011), the Eleventh Circuit explained the basis for analyzing a claim:

> The starting point for a potential award of attorney's fees and costs under the Hyde Amendment is an objectively wrongful prosecution: that is, a prosecution that either is baseless or exceeds constitutional constraints. If the prosecution is objectively reasonable, as was the case here, then a district court has no discretion to award a prevailing defendant attorney's fees and costs under the Hyde Amendment.

In United States v. Gilbert, 198 F.3d 1293 (11th Cir. 1999), the Eleventh Circuit defined "bad faith" as "not simply bad judgment or negligence, but rather it implies the conscious doing of a wrong because of dishonest purpose or moral obliquity; ... it contemplates a state of mind affirmatively operating with furtive design or ill will." Determining whether a prosecution was "vexatious" "has both a subjective and objective element: subjectively, the Government must have acted maliciously or with an intent to harass Appellants; objectively, the suit must be deficient or without merit. To prove vexatiousness, the defendant must show the Government had some 'ill intent.'" United States v. Manchester Farming Partnership, 315 F.3d 1176 (9th Cir. 2003).

Unlike a "frivolous" prosecution, a claim of vexatiousness and bad faith require proof of the individual prosecutor's subjective intent–"ill intent" or "conscious doing of a wrong." In United States v. Sherburne, 506 F.3d 1187 (9th Cir. 2007), the Ninth Circuit overturned a district court decision to award attorney's fees because the prosecutors did not understand their theory of the case. The appellate court noted that prosecutors lost much of their evidence of the defendant's involvement in the fraudulent scheme due to a suppression motion, and that "subjective intent to harass does not arise from merely factual mistakes or mistakes concerning the legal merit of the government's position."

While courts stress that each of the three elements of a Hyde Amendment claim define a separate type of prosecutorial misconduct, they are not easily distinguishable and claimants frequently allege violations under more than one prong of the statute. To prove the prosecutor's intent, to what extent should a court rely on circumstantial evidence? Can courts use the Hyde Amendment to police prosecutorial misconduct in a way that is denied under the Supreme Court's preclusion of the exercise of supervisory authority over the grand jury in *Williams*? Will an assessment of costs against a United States Attorney's Office have a deterrent effect on individual prosecutors?

2. ***Proving a Hyde Amendment Claim***. The Hyde Amendment provides that claims must be made "pursuant to the procedures and limitations (but not the burden of proof) provided for an award under section 2412 of title 28, United States Code," the Equal Access to Justice Act (EAJA). "[T]he Hyde Amendment has a more demanding burden of proof than the EAJA. Under the EAJA, a defendant will prevail unless the government can prove its position was substantially justified. However, recovering attorney fees and costs under the Hyde Amendment requires a stronger showing. Under the Hyde Amendment, the burden is on the defendant in the underlying case to prove the Government's position was vexatious, frivolous, or in bad faith." *Manchester Farming Partnership*. Similar to the EAJA, a "prevailing party" is one who has received at least some relief on the merits of the claim. Dismissal of charges after a defendant enters a diversion program and repays the government for its loss due to his conduct means the defendant was not a "prevailing party." United States v. Campbell, 291 F.3d 1169 (9th Cir. 2002).

CHAPTER TWELVE
SEARCHES

A. THE USE OF SEARCHES IN WHITE COLLAR CRIME INVESTIGATIONS

1. ***Current practice.*** Federal prosecutors, in the past 20 years, have increased dramatically their use of physical searches, authorized by warrants, as a tool of investigation in white collar cases. Some practitioners attribute the increased utilization of searches to their highly publicized and quite successful deployment during the late 1980s in the investigation of procurement fraud by defense contractors. Still others cite the Supreme Court's establishment in 1984 of an "objective good faith" exception to the exclusionary rule for searches conducted under a warrant. In large part, the searches in white collar cases are directed at seizing documents, although occasionally they may be aimed at obtaining other items (e.g., improperly acquired goods or equipment). The use of search warrants has been especially noticeable in investigations involving health care fraud and records stored on personal computers.[a] While subpoenas are the more common method for obtaining documents, especially from third-parties who are not involved in the underlying wrongdoing, the search warrant is readily available as an alternative, and sometimes superior, means of gathering records.

2. ***Costs.*** The search pursuant to a warrant has obvious costs and restrictions not applicable to the subpoena. First, the search is not as readily available to the prosecutor as the subpoena. To obtain a warrant authorizing a search for documents, a prosecutor must persuade a federal judicial officer that there is probable cause to believe that a crime has been committed and that specific documents which would constitute evidence of the crime can be found in a particular place (typically a business office or residence). This is a far more demanding grounding than the showing required when a subpoena is challenged.

Second, the affidavit presented to the magistrate to show probable cause is presumed to be open to the public (and press). See Baltimore Sun Co. v. Goetz 886 F.2d 60 (4th Cir. 1989). Upon a proper showing of need by the

---

[a] Under the Electronic Communications Privacy Act, 18 U.S.C. § 2703(a), the government must obtain a warrant if it seeks the contents of a wire or electronic communication from the provider of a remote computing service if it has been held in an electronic storage system for 180 days or less. See WAYNE R. LAFAVE, JEROLD H. ISRAEL, NANCY J. KING, & ORIN S. KERR, CRIMINAL PROCEDURE 3D § 4.8 (d)(2007).

prosecutor, the court may place the search warrant affidavit under seal. See In re Search Warrant for Secretarial Area Outside Office of Gunn, 855 F.2d 569 (8th Cir. 1988) (sealing must be justified by a "compelling government need"). Even if the sealing is ordered, however the subject of the search will eventually gain access to the affidavit in filing a Rule 41(g) motion challenging the search and asking that the seized property be returned.[b] This will give the subject far more information as to the scope and character of the government's investigation than would be obtained on a challenge to a subpoena. See *R. Enterprises*, p. 363.

Third, the remedy for conducting an unconstitutional search can be far more harsh than the remedy for issuing an illegal subpoena. If a subpoena is challenged and the court holds that it is overbroad or otherwise invalid, the subpoena is quashed, and the government can seek to fashion a new subpoena that meets the court's objections. If a search is conducted and a court subsequently holds that the search was invalid, the usual Fourth Amendment remedy is the "exclusionary rule" remedy. Under that remedy, the government is precluded from using the matter seized–and any other evidence obtained as a fruit of that illegal search (e.g., documents later discovered through information gleaned from the documents seized during the search)–in its case-in-chief in any subsequent prosecution against individuals or entities whose privacy was violated by the unconstitutional search.

Fourth, a search ordinarily entails considerably greater administrative costs than a subpoena duces tecum. With the subpoena, the recipient of the subpoena has the responsibility of collecting the documents identified in the subpoena and delivering them in accordance with the subpoena's directive. See chapter 15. With a search, the executing officers have the responsibility of finding and collecting the documents specified in the warrant. That can be a time consuming task where the search is conducted at a business that has voluminous records and many different documents are specified in the warrant. The search can also disrupt ongoing business activities on the premises being searched, antagonizing the employees as well as the employer.

---

[b] Fed. R. Crim. P. 41(g) provides:

(g) Motion to Return Property. A person aggrieved by an unlawful search and seizure of property or by the deprivation of property may move for the property's return. The motion must be filed in the district where the property was seized. The court must receive evidence on any factual issue necessary to decide the motion. If it grants the motion, the court must return the property to the movant, but may impose reasonable conditions to protect access to the property and its use in later proceedings.

In white collar cases, there often is a substantial time interval between a search and any subsequent indictment, so the challenge to the search is most likely to be first presented by a Rule 41(g) motion rather than a motion to suppress.

3. ***Advantages***. Offsetting the costs and limitations of utilizing a search are various attributes of the search that may be viewed as advantages–at least in some types of investigations. These include the following:

(a) Unlike the subpoena duces tecum, the search does not afford the party in possession of the documents the opportunity to destroy, conceal, or alter those documents. Of course, a "forthwith subpoena" can be used where destruction is a distinct possibility. However, the forthwith subpoena may be treated as a Fourth Amendment search if the agents themselves seize the documents, and if they do not, the subpoenaed party may not necessarily produce all the documents specified. Also, access may be delayed as the subpoenaed party may insist upon depositing the documents with the court and having them kept there until the party has the opportunity to present its challenge to the subpoena.

(b) A search gives the prosecutor immediate access to the documents seized. With a subpoena, the party in possession initially must be given sufficient time to produce the documents, and then may delay access further by obtaining an extension or challenging the subpoena.

(c) With a subpoena, specified documents are demanded and those documents are all that will be produced. With a search, there is the possibility of discovering and seizing documents beyond those specified in the warrant. That potential stems from the "plain view" doctrine. Under that doctrine, if an officer, in the course of the executing the search authorized by the warrant, should come across other matter in plain view and has probable cause to believe that matter constitutes evidence of a crime, the officer may seize that matter even though it is not among the items specified in the warrant.

(d) A person subpoenaed to produce documents may assert the self-incrimination privilege where the act of producing the documents is testimonial and potentially incriminatory. A search, however, does not compel the person in possession to produce anything; the documents are seized by the officers executing the search. Hence the Supreme Court held in Andresen v. Maryland, 427 U.S. 463 (1976), that the self-incrimination privilege was not a valid grounding for challenging a search. The same is not true, however, of other privileges, such as the lawyer-client privilege. Here the search warrant provides no advantage over the subpoena. However, such privileges are limited by exceptions, such as the crime-fraud exception under the lawyer-client privilege which often will render documentary evidence subject to seizure even though it would otherwise have been privileged.

(e) A search places investigators on the scene, where they can readily question employees. Such "on the spot" questioning often may be more productive than questioning pursuant to subpoena or prearranged interviews. The questioning comes without advance notice and usually before the employer has a chance to speak to the employees about the investigation and their rights, and to offer them the assistance of legal counsel. See United

States v. Hampton, 153 F.Supp. 2d 1262, 1265 (D. Kan. 2001) (rejecting defendant's claim that her interview with a government investigator while her company was being searched violated *Miranda* because it was a custodial interrogation when the agent twice told her she was free to leave and she consulted with her counsel during the interview; "Further, the mere fact that the defendants were the focus of an investigation does not indicate that they were in custody during the questioning.").

(f) The disruptive impact of a search can convey a special sense of urgency to those involved. The agents executing the warrant (often armed) will enter an office without previous warning, direct employees to immediately leave the room or stay off to the side, and proceed to go through desks and files. All of this may "throw a little scare" into employees and executives, leading to greater cooperation in subsequent requests for information, and possibly producing additional pressures on the subject to reach a swift settlement.

(g) The use of searches may be useful in conveying to the public the message that prosecutors are adopting a "tough, aggressive stance" in combating white collar crime. They are subjecting white collar suspects to the same intrusions on privacy as persons suspected of street crimes.

(h) The search warrant, the affidavit, and the evidence seized are not subject to the secrecy requirements that attach to a grand jury subpoena duces tecum. This can offer several additional advantages. At times, the prosecutor may desire to make an investigation, its grounding, and its current findings a matter of public record. That may put pressure on a target to reach a fast settlement and thereby minimize the impact of the bad publicity. Also, at times, the prosecutor may desire to share the product of the search with other agencies. In contrast to documents obtained by grand jury subpoena, documents obtained by an independently generated search may be shared without a Rule 6(e) order.

4. ***Mitigating the Effect of a Search.*** Recognizing that some of these advantages of a warrant can be limited (or even precluded) by certain action taken by the person in charge of the premises that are searched, counsel will advise clients of several steps they should take if agents suddenly appear on their property with a search warrant. These include: (1) immediate notification of counsel and hopefully delaying the search until counsel arrives; (2) sending employees home for the day (and thereby avoiding incidental questions in the course of the search); (3) demanding a copy of the warrant, and informing agents as to where the specified documents are located; (4) protesting any screening of other files where the documents are not located; (5) identifying files containing lawyer-client and other privileged material and demanding that they be sealed and not read until a court can determine their status; (6) monitoring the search, paying particular attention to the sequence of the search (e.g., did the officers first look in those places where the documents were most likely to be found, did they terminate the search upon finding the documents specified in the warrant); (7) keeping

track of all documents examined, whether or not seized; and (8) keeping a record of all matter seized and comparing it to the inventory that officers are required to leave with the person in charge of the premises under Rule 41(d).

5. ***Warrants Directed at Non-Suspects.*** In **Zurcher v. Stanford Daily**, 436 U.S. 547 (1978), the Supreme Court held that the Fourth Amendment does not prevent the government from seeking a warrant to search for evidence just because the owner or possessor of the place to be searched is not suspected of being involved in the underlying criminal conduct that is under investigation. In *Zurcher*, the police searched the offices of the *Stanford Daily*, a student newspaper, for photographs of those who had been involved in a protest in which officers were attacked. The district court held that because the newspaper was not suspected of any wrongdoing, the government was restricted to using a subpoena duces tecum to obtain the evidence rather than a search warrant. The Supreme Court, per Justice White writing for the majority, rejected the contention that the district court's reasoning found support in the broad underlying policy objectives of the Fourth Amendment:

> [W]e are unpersuaded that the District Court's new rule denying search warrants against third parties and insisting on subpoenas would substantially further privacy interests without seriously undermining law enforcement efforts. Because of the fundamental public interest in implementing the criminal law, the search warrant, a heretofore effective and constitutionally acceptable enforcement tool, should not be suppressed on the basis of surmise and without solid evidence supporting the change. As the District Court understands it, denying third-party search warrants would not have substantial adverse effects on criminal investigations because the nonsuspect third party, once served with a subpoena, will preserve the evidence and ultimately lawfully respond. The difficulty with this assumption is that search warrants are often employed early in an investigation, perhaps before the identity of any likely criminal and certainly before all the perpetrators are or could be known. The seemingly blameless third party in possession of the fruits or evidence may not be innocent at all; and if he is, he may nevertheless be so related to or so sympathetic with the culpable that he cannot be relied upon to retain and preserve the articles that may implicate his friends, or at least not to notify those who would be damaged by the evidence that the authorities are aware of its location. In any event, it is likely that the real culprits will have access to the property and the delay involved in employing the subpoena duces tecum, offering as it does the opportunity to litigate its validity, could easily result in the disappearance of the evidence, whatever the good faith of the third party.

B. FOURTH AMENDMENT PRINCIPLES

1. *The Fourth Amendment.*

> The right of the people to be secure in their persons, houses, papers, and effects, against unreasonable searches and seizures, shall not be violated, and no Warrants shall issue, but upon probable cause, supported by Oath or affirmation, and particularly describing the place to be searched, and the persons or things to be seized.

Only the second clause of the Amendment refers to warrants, and the Supreme Court has held that a variety of searches may be deemed reasonable under the first clause even though executed without a warrant. In general, conducting a search without first obtaining the "neutral and detached" probable-cause determination provided by the warrant process is justified either by "exigent circumstances," a "diminished expectation of privacy" in the area searched, or historical tradition. None of these justifications, however, bear upon the search of a business or residence to obtain documents believed to constitute evidence of a crime. Accordingly, such searches almost invariably are conducted pursuant to a warrant.

In United States v. Jones, 132 S. Ct. 945 (2012), the Supreme Court held that the installation of a global positioning system tracking device on an automobile constituted a search under the Fourth Amendment. Relying on that decision, the Court held in Grady v. North Carolina, 135 S. Ct. 1368 (2015), that a civil order requiring a defendant to wear a tracking device because of prior sex-offense convictions came within the Fourth Amendment. The Court noted that the constitutional protection from unreasonable searches and seizures "extends beyond the sphere of criminal investigations" to include civil cases. Many white collar crime investigations involve a substantial overlap between civil regulators and prosecutors, so the Fourth Amendment may be relevant cases involving civil subpoenas and other methods of gathering evidence.

Although the constitutional law governing the issuance and execution of search warrants has numerous elements, three stand out as having the greatest significance for the document searches utilized in white collar crime investigations. They are: (1) the requirement that the warrant be issued only upon a showing of probable cause before the magistrate; (2) the requirement that the warrant "particularly describ[e] * * * the * * * things to be seized"; and (3) the *Leon* exception to the remedy of exclusion of evidence obtained through a search that violates the Fourth Amendment.[a]

---

[a] Other elements of Fourth Amendment law relating to search warrants include: the requirement that the magistrate issuing the warrant be "neutral and detached"; the requirement that the warrant be supported by "oath or affirmation"; the requirement that the warrant "particularly describ[e] *** the place to be searched"; the requirement that the warrant be executed in a reasonable manner; and the

2. ***Probable Cause.*** **Illinois v. Gates**, 462 U.S. 213 (1983), involved the issuance of search warrant based upon a probable cause finding that relied in part upon a letter written to police by an anonymous informant. The Court majority said the following in the course of abandoning a previously adopted two-pronged standard for utilizing information from an informant:

> Perhaps the central teaching of our decisions bearing on the probable cause standard is that it is a "practical, nontechnical conception." Brinegar v. United States, 338 U.S. 160 (1949). 'In dealing with probable cause, * * * as the very name implies, we deal with probabilities. These are not technical; they are the factual and practical considerations of everyday life on which reasonable and prudent men, not legal technicians, act.' Our observation in United States v. Cortez, 449 U.S. 411 (1981), regarding "particularized suspicion," is also applicable to the probable cause standard:
>
>> The process does not deal with hard certainties, but with probabilities. Long before the law of probabilities was articulated as such, practical people formulated certain common-sense conclusions about human behavior; jurors as fact finders are permitted to do the same–and so are law enforcement officers. Finally, the evidence thus collected must be seen and weighed not in terms of library analysis by scholars, but as understood by those versed in the field of law enforcement.
>
>> As these comments illustrate, probable cause is a fluid concept–turning on the assessment of probabilities in particular factual contexts–not readily, or often usefully, reduced to a neat set of legal rules. Informants' tips doubtless come in many shapes and sizes from many different types of persons. * * * Rigid legal rules are ill-suited to an area of such diversity. "One simple rule will not cover every situation." * * *
>>
>>> * * * [W]e reaffirm the task of the issuing magistrate is simply to make a practical, common-sense decision whether, given all the circumstances set forth in the affidavit before him, including the "veracity" and "basis of knowledge" of persons supplying hearsay information, there is a fair probability that contraband or evidence of a crime will be

---

allowable seizure of items not named in the warrant under the "plain view" doctrine. See WAYNE R. LAFAVE, JEROLD H. ISRAEL, NANCY J. KING, & ORIN S. KERR, CRIMINAL PROCEDURE 3D § 3.4 (2007).

> found in a particular place.[b] And the duty of a reviewing court is simply to ensure that the magistrate had a "substantial basis for * * * conclud[ing]" that probable cause existed. Our earlier cases illustrate the limits beyond which a magistrate may not venture in issuing a warrant. A sworn statement of an affiant that "he has cause to suspect and does believe" that liquor illegally brought into the United States is located on certain premises will not do. Nathanson v. United States, 290 U.S. 41 (1933). An affidavit must provide the magistrate with a substantial basis for determining the existence of probable cause, and the wholly conclusory statement at issue in *Nathanson* failed to meet this requirement. * * * Sufficient information must be presented to the magistrate to allow that official to determine probable cause; his action cannot be a mere ratification of the bare conclusions of others. In order to ensure that such as abdication of the magistrate's duty does not occur, courts must continue to conscientiously review the sufficiency of affidavits on which warrants are issued. But when we move beyond the "bare bones" affidavits presented in cases such as *Nathanson* * * *, this area simply does not lend itself to a prescribed set of rules * * *."

3. ***Particularity of Description***. A significant issue for determining the validity of a search warrant in a white collar crime investigation is whether the warrant contains sufficient particularity regarding the place to be searched and the items that may be seized. In Marron v. United States, 275 U.S. 192 (1927), the Supreme Court stated, "The requirement that warrants shall particularly describe the things to be seized makes general searches under them impossible and prevents the seizure of one thing under a warrant describing another." To avoid the problem of general warrants, there are certain factors a court will consider in assessing the particularity of the description in the warrant:

Consider:

> [There] are certain general principles which may be distilled from the decided cases in this area. They are: (1) A greater degree of ambiguity will be tolerated when the police have done the best that could be expected under the circumstances, by acquiring all the descriptive facts which reasonable investigation of this type of crime

---

[b] In a later footnote, in the course of discussing the significance of police verification of details mentioned by the informant, even where those details deal with innocent activity, the *Gates* Court offered the following comment on this probability: "As discussed previously, probable cause requires only a probability or substantial chance of criminal activity, not an actual showing of such activity."

> could be expected to uncover and by ensuring that all of those facts were included in the warrant. (2) A more general type of description will be sufficient when the nature of the objects to be seized are such that they could not be expected to have more specific characteristics. (3) A less precise description is required of property which is, because of its particular character, contraband. (4) Failure to provide all of the available descriptive facts is not a basis for questioning the adequacy of the description when the omitted facts could not have been expected to be of assistance to the executing officer. (5) An error in the statement of certain descriptive facts is not a basis for questioning the adequacy of the description if the executing officer was nonetheless able to determine, from the other facts provided, that the object seized was that intended by the description. (6) Greater care in description is ordinarily called for when the type of property sought is generally in lawful use in substantial quantities. (7) A more particular description than otherwise might be necessary is required when other objects of the same general classification are likely to be found at the particular place to be searched. (8) The greatest care in description is required when the consequences of a seizure of innocent articles by mistake is most substantial, as when the objects to be seized are books or films or the papers of a newsgathering organization.

WAYNE R. LAFAVE, JEROLD H. ISRAEL, NANCY J. KING, & ORIN S. KERR, CRIMINAL PROCEDURE 3D §3.4(e)-(f) (2007).

4. ***The Exclusionary Rule and the* Leon *Exception*.** Because warrantless searches are comparatively rare in white collar crime cases, the focus is on searches pursuant to a warrant. The Supreme Court's decision in United States v. Leon, 468 U.S. 897 (1984), has a significant impact on the application of the exclusionary rule to searches in which the warrant that was not based on sufficient probable cause. In *Leon*, the Court stated that "[p]enalizing the officer for the magistrate's error, rather than his own, cannot logically contribute to the deterrence of Fourth Amendment violations." Therefore, application of the exclusionary rule to suppress evidence obtained pursuant to a warrant should be ordered "only in those unusual cases in which exclusion will further the purposes of the exclusionary rule." If officers act in good faith in executing a search warrant that appears facially valid, then the exclusionary rule does not apply.

Leon identified four circumstances in which a flaw in the warrant would still result in the application of the exclusionary rule: (1) where the officer presented knowing or reckless falsehoods to obtain the warrant; (2) "where the issuing magistrate wholly abandoned his judicial role"; (3) where the warrant was "so facially deficient – i.e., in failing to particularize the place to be searched or the things to be seized – that the executing officers cannot reasonably presume it to be valid"; and (4) where the affidavit supporting the warrant application was "so lacking in indicia of probable cause as to render official belief in its existence entirely unreasonable." *Leon* applies only to reasonable reliance on an invalid warrant, not when there are Fourth Amendment violations in the execution of the warrant unrelated to its validity or invalidity.

The issue in white collar cases is usually the lack of particularity in the warrant and supporting affidavit, and the following case illustrates the application of *Leon*.

UNITED STATES v. TRAVERS
233 F.3d 1327 (11th Cir. 2000)

HILL, Circuit Judge.

Joseph Travers was convicted on several counts of mail fraud, equity skimming, money laundering and bankruptcy fraud. * * *

Between 1991 and 1995, Joseph Travers obtained title to more than 97 houses by assuming Veterans Administration (VA) and Federal Housing Association (FHA) guaranteed home loans. He did so under a variety of false names and aliases. Travers collected the rents on these properties but never paid on any of the mortgages. He used a series of names on the deeds and filed successive bankruptcy petitions for each name in a successful attempt to forestall foreclosure during which time he would continue to collect the rents. Travers used a series of false identities and mail drops to hide his identity and avoid detection. During the two-year investigation of his activities, federal agents compiled a list of at least 40 VA and FHA mortgages that Travers had assumed, aliases he used in those transactions, mailboxes he had rented, and fraudulent bankruptcy proceedings that he had filed.

Agents arrested Travers on May 8, 1996. On the same day, they executed search warrants at his two properties on Bay Harbor Island, Florida. The agents seized voluminous boxes of documents detailing Travers' equity skimming operation.

Before trial, Travers filed a motion to suppress the evidence found during the searches of his residence and office on the grounds that the warrant authorizing the searches was unconstitutionally overbroad and the resulting searches general rather than limited. After an evidentiary hearing, the district court denied the motion, holding that, while the warrant was overly broad, "the agents acted in good faith in drafting and executing the warrant." * * *

The requirement that warrants particularly describe the place to be searched and the things to be seized makes general searches under them impossible. A warrant which fails to sufficiently particularize the place to be searched or the things to be seized is unconstitutionally over broad. The resulting general search is unconstitutional. In order to deter such warrants and searches, the Court has held that any evidence so seized must be excluded from the trial of the defendant. Stone v. Powell, 428 U.S. 465 (1976).

The exclusionary rule's deterrent effect is negated, however, where law enforcement officers act in the "objectively reasonable belief that their conduct does not violate the Fourth Amendment." United States v. Leon, 468 U.S. 897 (1984). When an officer has in good faith obtained a search warrant from a judge or magistrate and acted within its scope, "there is no police illegality and thus nothing to deter." In *Leon*, therefore, the Court carved out an exception to the exclusionary rule for evidence obtained in such a search.

* * * The United States does not contest the district court's holding that the warrant was overbroad. Therefore, the issue for our review is whether the good faith exception applies in this case to excuse the unconstitutionally over broad warrant. We conclude that it does.

The good faith exception may be applied to a search conducted pursuant to an overly broad warrant. The officers do not act in objective good faith, however, if the warrant is so overly broad on its face that the executing officers could not reasonably have presumed it to be valid.

The warrant in this case permitted the officers to search for all documents involving real estate, litigation, property, mailings, photographs and any other material reflecting identity, and anything reflecting potential fraud. Pursuant to the warrant, the executing officers seized copies of warranty deeds and other documents reflecting Travers' use of false identities to purchase properties; notary public seals for signatures that Travers forged on various deeds and other legal documents; passports, birth certificates, drivers licenses, and credit cards issued in various names; business cards for businesses in various names; letters to tenants written by Travers using both his names and aliases; copies of bankruptcy pleadings, letters to bankruptcy courts, and other filings reflecting Travers' attempts to delay foreclosures; and various other documents concerning Travers' use of aliases, mail drop boxes, and false addresses to avoid detection.

Although the district court ultimately held the warrant overly broad, it characterized its conclusion as a "close call." We agree. This case involves a complex scheme to commit financial fraud concerning real property. The charges include mail fraud, bankruptcy fraud, equity skimming, and money laundering. A wide variety of documents were relevant to prove this scheme-deeds, loan papers, legal pleadings, identity papers and cards, and mailing receipts and papers. Thus, the agents applied for and received a warrant which cut a wide swath through Travers' papers and documents. In [United States v. Accardo, 749 F.2d 1477 (11th Cir. 1985)], we recognized that cases involving "complex financial fraud . . . justify a more flexible reading of the fourth amendment particularity requirement." Thus, the warrant in this case, even if subsequently determined by the district court to be overly broad, was not "so facially deficient – i.e., failing to particularize the place to be searched or the things to be seized-that the executing officers could not have reasonably presumed it to be valid." The application of the good faith exception to the exclusionary rule, therefore, is not precluded in this case by a warrant that no reasonable officer could have relied upon.

Travers also contends that the district erred in finding that the agents obtained and executed the warrant in subjective good faith. He claims that the agents intentionally deceived the issuing magistrate by omitting details of their investigation thereby inducing him to grant an overly broad warrant. He also alleges that they deliberately exceeded the scope of their warrant in the items seized.

Whether the officers acted in subjective good faith in obtaining and executing the warrant is a mixed question of fact and law. While the ultimate conclusion of good faith is a legal one, findings of fact serve as the predicate for this conclusion. In order to hold that the officers acted in good faith in this case, the district court necessarily found as a matter of fact that the agents neither intentionally deceived the issuing magistrate by omitting details regarding the nature of their investigation, nor deliberately exceeded the scope of their warrant in the items seized during the searches. The agents testified unequivocally that they consulted with the United States Attorney in drafting the warrant application and included all information that they and she believed necessary to establish sufficient probable cause to support the warrant application. The supervising agent testified that he instructed the other agents regarding items to be seized according to his understanding of the warrant. The searching agents testified that there were documents strewn throughout Travers' residence and office with no apparent organization. In their effort to take only what was authorized by the warrant, they reviewed documents. The district court credited all this testimony. We find nothing in the record that would indicate that these factual findings that the officers obtained the warrant in cooperation with the United States Attorney who advised them on the requirements for showing probable cause and conducted their search in a conscious effort to stay within its limits are clearly erroneous. Nor do we disagree with the district court's legal conclusion that the officers, therefore, acted in good faith.

We hold that the district court did not err in holding that the good faith exception to the exclusionary rule applies to excuse the overly broad warrant at issue in this case. We find no merit in Travers' other allegations of error. Accordingly, Travers' conviction and sentence are due to be AFFIRMED.

C. SEARCH OF A BUSINESS

1. Standing and the Warrant Requirements

If a business or other organization directly engages in questionable activity, then the government will seek a wide range of documents that may ultimately involve nearly all the records of an organization. How specific does a warrant have to be in that type of situation? In United States v. Hickey, 16 F.Supp.2d 223 (E.D.N.Y. 1998), the District Court found that a warrant was overbroad in its description of the items to be seized:

> [T]he officers were simply furnished with warrants that directed the seizure of "all business records" of the four corporate defendants found at any one of the five search locations, absent any explicit or implicit reference points. That direction is followed by a list of items subject to seizure, many generic (e.g., "[b]ank records of any kind," "corporate resolutions," "ledgers," "invoices," "computer files," "computer software," and "correspondence files"), preceded by the troubling instruction that the searches were "not limited to" those items. In essence–given the format of the warrants–the officers were directed to search all of the business records of each of the defendant corporations and to seize any items that constituted evidence of any crime regardless of its nature or when it occurred.

The warrant also needs to identify the legal violation involving the business, and simply stating that the organization was involved in "violations of federal and state law" would not be sufficient. See United States v. Galpin, 720 F.3d 436 (2d Cir. 2013) ("[I]nsofar as the warrant generally authorized officers to search Galpin's physical property and electronic equipment for evidence of violations of 'NYS Penal Law and or Federal Statutes,' the warrant violated the Fourth Amendment's particularity requirement."

When a search warrant is executed at a business, it may result in the seizure of evidence that will be used against individual officers of the organization. To what extent can they challenge a warrant on the ground that it fails to meet the specificity requirement of the Fourth Amendment? Consider the following case:

UNITED STATES v. SDI FUTURE HEALTH, INC.

568 F.3d 684 (9th Cir. 2009)

O'SCANNLAIN, Circuit Judge:

We must decide whether corporate executives may challenge a police search of company premises not reserved for the executives' exclusive use.

After a nearly two-year investigation spearheaded by the Internal Revenue Service ("IRS") with the participation of four other federal and Nevada state agencies, investigators concluded that SDI Future Health, Inc. ("SDI"), a California corporation, had engaged in wide-ranging Medicare fraud. In addition, they believed that both SDI and Todd Stuart Kaplan, its president and part-owner, had committed extensive tax fraud. On January 28, 2002, based on the information obtained during the investigation, IRS Special Agent Julie Raftery applied for a warrant to search SDI's premises.

The warrant relied on an affidavit sworn by Raftery, which contained information she had learned from three former employees and two business associates of SDI. The affidavit alleged that SDI, Kaplan and Jack Brunk, also an officer and part-owner of SDI, participated in a conspiracy with physicians and cardiac diagnostic companies to defraud the Medicare program, the Federal Employees Health Benefit Program, and private healthcare insurance carriers by seeking payment for services that SDI never rendered. According to the affidavit, they sometimes billed twice for such services and made kickback payments to physicians who participated in the scheme. It alleged specifically that SDI employees who were placed in participating doctors' offices would induce patients to participate in a sleep study. While cardiac diagnostic companies affiliated with SDI would purport to complete a report of the results of each sleep study, officers of SDI would instead affix a signature stamp bearing the signatures of staff physicians on reports that other SDI employees had actually completed. Referring physicians were instructed to bill for time spent reviewing the reports, a task the physicians never actually performed. Frequently, SDI would then recommend that a patient participate in further studies, usually in cases where the patient's health insurer would pay for them.

The affidavit also revealed incidents of alleged tax fraud. It noted that Kaplan and his wife reported negative gross income and, consequently, paid no taxes in the years 1996, 1998 and 1999, and reported relatively low income in 1997 and 2000. During the same period, however, the couple purchased several expensive automobiles and watercraft and supported a home mortgage. This discrepancy, according to the affidavit, provided the probable cause to support the investigators' belief that Kaplan and his wife substantially underreported their gross income during those years. The government also alleged that SDI had violated federal tax laws by under-reporting its sales revenue and its income at least for the years 1996-2000.

The government submitted a proposed warrant with its affidavit. Appendix A of the warrant stated that the premises to be searched were SDI's corporate headquarters, principal business offices, and computers. Appendix B provided 24 categories of items to be seized and gave specific instructions concerning retrieving and handling of electronic data and other technical equipment.[2]

---

[2] The categories of items to be seized are as follows: 1. Documents relating to patient lists; 2. Documents relating to billing procedures, billing manuals, and billing materials; 3. Documents relating to lists of referring physicians both active and inactive; 4. Documents relating to billing records and records of payments received; 5. Documents relating to contracts or "purchase service agreements" with referring physicians; 6. Documents relating to contracts and agreements with cardiac diagnostic companies; 7. Documents relating to non-privileged correspondence with consultants; 8. Documents relating to correspondence with Medicare intermediaries and private insurance companies; 9. Documents relating to non-privileged internal memoranda and E-mail; 10. Documents relating to bank accounts, brokerage accounts, trusts; 11. Checking, savings, and money market account records including check registers, canceled checks, monthly statements, wire transfers, and cashier's checks; 12. Documents relating to personnel and payroll records; 13. Documents relating to accounting records; 14. Patient records including patient questionnaires,

* * * The day before the execution of the search warrant, Special Agent Raftery met with the forty-two agents who would make up the search team. She distributed copies of the affidavit and gave them time to read it. She then conducted a "verbal briefing," explaining the probable cause for the search warrant and "the items that [the search team was] searching for and the items to be seized." All members of the search team were to have the cellular phone number of Special Agent Raftery during the search.

The team executed the search early the following morning, on January 31, 2002. Upon arriving at the scene, Special Agent Raftery met with one of SDI's executive officers and delivered a copy of the search warrant, but not a copy of the affidavit because it had been sealed by the district court. The affidavit was, however, available to the members of the search team. Kaplan also received a copy of the warrant, and he consented to allow investigators to search an off-site storage warehouse used by SDI.

About three years after the search, a federal grand jury in the District of Nevada returned an indictment charging SDI, Kaplan and Brunk with one count of conspiracy, in violation of 18 U.S.C. § 371 – specifically conspiracy to commit health care fraud, in violation of 18 U.S.C. § 1347, and to provide illegal kickback payments, in violation of 42 U.S.C. § 1320a-7b(b); 124 counts of health care fraud, in violation of 18 U.S.C. § 1347; one count of illegal kickbacks, in violation of 42 U.S.C. § 1320a-7b(b); one count of conspiracy to commit money laundering, in violation of 18 U.S.C. §§ 1956(a)(1)(A)(i) and 1956(h); and three counts of attempting to evade or defeat taxes, in violation of 26 U.S.C. § 7201. Additionally, Kaplan and Brunk were each individually indicted for three and four counts, respectively, of attempting to evade or defeat taxes, in violation of 26 U.S.C. § 7201. * * *

On December 2, 2005, SDI, Kaplan and Brunk filed a motion to suppress evidence obtained from the search warrant, arguing that the warrant was

---

sleep study referrals, results of cardiac risk assessment tests, results of sleep studies, and sleep study reports; 15. Documents relating to raw sleep study data; 16. Documents relating to all state and federal income tax returns including personal, corporate, trust, estate, and partnership, and information relating to the preparation of those returns for the following: (a) Todd Stuart Kaplan, (b) Denise Kaplan, (c) SDI; 17. Signature stamps for Dr. Gavin Awerbuch, Dr. Susan Sprau, and any other physician signature stamps; 18. Computer zip discs containing sleep study data; 19. Documents relating to mailing or shipping records between physicians and SDI; 20. Documents relating to employee training materials regarding health service coordinator ("HSC") program, cardiac risk assessment program, and/or physician practice enhancement program; 21. Documents relating to presentations and/or training materials used to solicit patient referrals from physicians, and/or placement of HSCs in the physician's offices; 22. Holter monitor tapes containing cardiac monitor data; 23. Documents relating to material that provides instructions or examples concerning the operation of the computer system, computer software, and/or related device; and 24. Rolodexes, address books and calendars.

vague and overbroad in violation of the Fourth Amendment. On June 26, 2006, a magistrate judge entered a Findings and Recommendation, in which he recommended that the motion to suppress be granted in part.

On April 4, 2007, the district court adopted the magistrate judge's factual findings, but entered an order granting the defendants' motion to suppress in full rather than in part. The district court first held that Kaplan and Brunk had standing to challenge the search of SDI's business premises, because they "had significant ownership interests in SDI," "exercised a high level of authority over the operations of the company including the authority to set and control policy regarding access to SDI's business records and computer systems," "maintained offices at SDI's corporate headquarters and were present during the execution of the Search Warrant," and because SDI "maintained a level of security and confidentially [sic] practices regarding its premises and records that one would reasonably expect of a health care provider."

The district court concluded that items 7, 9-13, and 24 of the search warrant were overbroad and lacked sufficient particularity because "[t]he search warrant did not limit these general categories of business documents and financial records to the seizure of records relating to the criminal activity described in the affidavit," and because they lacked "any time restriction." Similarly, the district court noted that items 2, 4, 8, and 19, of the search warrant were "borderline in acceptability," but nevertheless violated the Fourth Amendment because "some additional description could and should have been provided regarding these categories." Lastly, the district court concluded that the "good faith exception" did not apply in this case based on its conclusion that the affidavit was not incorporated into the warrant. Without the affidavit, the court concluded, the agents' reliance on the warrant alone was not objectively reasonable, since it "did not contain any description of the alleged criminal activity relating to the listed categories of documents." * * *

The government first argues that Kaplan and Brunk lack standing to challenge the search and seizure of materials from SDI's premises.[3] According to the government, their mere ownership and management of SDI, and the steps SDI took to preserve the security of its business files, are inadequate to support the conclusion that Kaplan and Brunk personally had an expectation

---

[3] Wisely, the government does not argue that SDI itself lacks standing to challenge the underlying search and seizure. See United States v. Leary, 846 F.2d 592, 596 (10th Cir.1988) ("[A] corporate defendant has standing with respect to searches of corporate premises and seizure of corporate records." (internal citation and quotation marks omitted)). We therefore only consider the Fourth Amendment standing of Kaplan and Brunk. Insofar as they do indeed lack standing, all evidence is admissible as to charges against them. By contrast, insofar as we affirm the district court's suppression of some evidence, such evidence will be inadmissible against SDI. Standing, therefore, makes a difference in this case.

of privacy in the searched areas and seized materials. While "[i]t has long been settled that one has standing to object to a search of his office, as well as of his home," Mancusi v. DeForte, 392 U.S. 364 (1968), this case presents the novel issue of the extent to which a business employee may have standing to challenge a search of business premises generally.

The Fourth Amendment ensures that "[t]he right of the people to be secure in their persons, houses, papers, and effects, against unreasonable searches and seizures, shall not be violated, and no Warrants shall issue, but upon probable cause, supported by Oath or affirmation, and particularly describing the place to be searched, and the persons or things to be seized." U.S. Const. amend. IV. A person has standing to sue for a violation of this particular "right of the people" only if there has been a violation "as to him," personally. *Mancusi*. In other words, Fourth Amendment standing, unlike Article III standing, "is a matter of substantive [F]ourth [A]mendment law; to say that a party lacks [F]ourth [A]mendment standing is to say that his reasonable expectation of privacy has not been infringed." United States v. Taketa, 923 F.2d 665 (9th Cir.1991). This follows from the Supreme Court's famous observation that the Fourth Amendment "protects people, not places," Katz v. United States, 389 U.S. 347 (1967).

To show the government has violated his Fourth Amendment rights, an individual must have "a legitimate expectation of privacy in the invaded place," United States v. Crawford, 323 F.3d 700 (9th Cir.2003). Defendants must demonstrate "a subjective expectation of privacy in the area searched, and their expectation must be one that society would recognize as objectively reasonable." United States v. Sarkisian, 197 F.3d 966 (9th Cir.1999).

As a logical extension of this approach, "[p]roperty used for commercial purposes is treated differently for Fourth Amendment purposes from residential property." Minnesota v. Carter, 525 U.S. 83 (1998). Of course, individuals may still have a "reasonable expectation of privacy against intrusions by police" into their offices. O'Connor v. Ortega, 480 U.S. 709 (1987) ("Within the workplace context, . . . an expectation [of privacy] in one's place of work is based upon societal expectations that have deep roots in the history of the Amendment."). But, unlike the nearly absolute protection of a residence, the "great variety of work environments" requires analysis of reasonable expectations "on a case-by-case basis."

Our precedents provide numerous guideposts, however. For starters, it is crucial to Fourth Amendment standing that the place searched be "given over to [the defendant's] exclusive use." Schowengerdt v. General Dynamics Corp., 823 F.2d 1328 (9th Cir.1987). We have thus held that mere access to, and even use of, the office of a co-worker "does not lead us to find an objectively reasonable expectation of privacy." *Taketa*. By the same token, we have rejected managerial authority alone as sufficient for Fourth Amendment standing. In United States v. Cella, we held the corporate officer of a hospital, whom we described as the "de facto controlling force in [its] management," did not have standing to challenge the seizure of records from the hospital print shop. 568 F.2d 1266 (9th Cir.1977). Even though the defendant "had access to and control of the print shop operations, his rights did not include any expectation of privacy over documents which were kept at the print shop premises but over which [he] did not show an independent possessory or proprietary interest."

It thus appears that an employee of a corporation, whether worker or manager, does not, simply by virtue of his status as such, acquire Fourth Amendment standing with respect to company premises. Similarly, and notwithstanding the reference to "an independent . . . proprietary interest" in *Cella*, to be merely a shareholder of a corporation, without more, is also not enough.[5] As always, a reasonable expectation of privacy does not arise ex officio, but must be established with respect to the person in question.

We took this approach in *United States v. Gonzalez*, in which we held that the directors of a small, family-run corporation had standing to challenge a wiretap in one of the company's buildings. That holding relied on the facts of the case:

> [W]e simply hold that because the [defendants] were corporate officers and directors who not only had ownership of the [premises] but also exercised full access to the building as well as managerial control over its day-to-day operations, they had a reasonable expectation of privacy over calls made on the premises.

412 F.3d 1102 (9th Cir.2005). Thus, in *Gonzalez* we focused on the close control that the owner-operators exercised over their small business, which happened to be family-run.

Kaplan and Brunk argue that *Gonzalez* supports their claim of Fourth Amendment standing, but their argument rests on an overbroad reading of our opinion. We explicitly tied the defendants' standing to the "nature of the location." The defendants exercised in the context of "a small, family-run business housing only 25 employees at its peak," "managerial control over [the] day-to-day operations" of the office where the conversations the wiretap "seized" took place, they owned the building where the office was located, and they not only could access the office but actually "exercised full access tot he

[5] The Second Circuit summarized this point memorably in language quoted heavily by this and other circuits:

> When a man chooses to avail himself of the privilege of doing business as a corporation, even though he is its sole shareholder, he may not vicariously take on the privilege of the corporation under the Fourth Amendment; documents which he could have protected from seizure, if they had been his own, may be used against him, no matter how they were obtained from the corporation. Its wrongs are not his wrongs; its immunity is not his immunity.

Hill v. United States, 374 F.2d 871, 873 (9th Cir.1967).

building." In our detailed factual analysis, therefore, we made clear that it does not suffice for Fourth Amendment standing merely to own a business, to work in a building, or to manage an office.

The facts in this case place SDI in a gray area outside the particular facts of *Gonzalez*, because at most Kaplan and Brunk managed and worked in the office of a business of which they were, together, controlling shareholders. SDI's headquarters is twice the size of the office at issue in *Gonzalez*. The magistrate judge's findings of fact, which the district court adopted, emphasize primarily two aspects of the role Kaplan and Brunk played at SDI. First, the magistrate judge noted that Kaplan and Brunk owned and had authority to set policy at SDI. He also pointed out that, in their directorial capacities, they put in place significant security measures at SDI's headquarters. These facts show that SDI, through Kaplan and Brunk, took steps to protect the privacy of its headquarters. But the magistrate judge's findings do not show that Kaplan and Brunk personally managed the operation of the office on a daily basis, only that they set its general policy as officers of SDI. Because Kaplan and Brunk personally exercised less control over the premises in question than did the defendants in *Gonzalez*, that precedent does not control here. * * *

In United States v. Anderson, the Tenth Circuit laid out a test to deal with situations in which a corporate employee does not work on a regular basis in the area searched. See 154 F.3d 1225 (10th Cir.1998). Given our case law, *Anderson* suggests three factors a court should consider in cases where an employee has not established that the area searched is "given over to [his] exclusive use." The Tenth Circuit's *Anderson* test looks to "(1) the employee's relationship to the item seized; (2) whether the item was in the immediate control of the employee when it was seized; and (3) whether the employee took actions to maintain his privacy in the item."

Though phrased vaguely, the first factor really addresses whether the item seized was personal property without any relationship to work. In addition, we note that the third factor involves actions the employee takes on his own behalf, not as an agent of the corporation.

Reading *Anderson* alongside our own precedent, we conclude that, except in the case of a small, family-run business over which an individual exercises daily management and control, an individual challenging a search of workplace areas beyond his own internal office must generally show some personal connection to the places searched and the materials seized. To adapt *Anderson*, although all the circumstances remain relevant, we will specifically determine the strength of such personal connection with reference to the following factors: (1) whether the item seized is personal property or otherwise kept in a private place separate from other work-related material;[7] (2) whether the defendant had custody or immediate control of the item when officers seized it; and (3) whether the defendant took precautions on his own behalf to secure the place searched or things seized from any interference without his authorization.[8] Absent such a personal connection or exclusive use, a defendant cannot establish standing for Fourth Amendment purposes to challenge the search of a workplace beyond his internal office.

The district court relied on three facts in concluding that Kaplan and Brunk had Fourth Amendment standing: their ownership of SDI, their management of SDI from offices in the building searched, and the security measures SDI took to secure its business records. Our review of relevant precedent indicates that these facts are too broad and generalized to support the district court's conclusion. The security measures that SDI took to ensure the privacy of its business records are relevant only to the standing of the corporation itself, not of its officers. As for Kaplan and Brunk, their ownership and management do not necessarily show a legitimate expectation of privacy. Because neither claims to enjoy "exclusive use" of the places searched – that is, the entire SDI office – they each must show a personal connection, along the lines we have drawn out of *Anderson*, to justify an expectation of privacy.

Lacking precedent on what is admittedly a novel issue of law, the district court did not adequately develop the record. Therefore, the district court's grant of the motion to suppress must be reversed and the matter remanded for further fact-finding. It seems that none of the items seized were the personal property of Kaplan or Brunk, nor were they in the custody of either. Therefore, on remand, the district court should focus its inquiry on, but need not confine it to, whether either Kaplan or Brunk took measures, each on his or the pair's personal behalf, to keep the items private and segregated from other general business materials. Of course, Kaplan and Brunk do have standing to challenge the admission of any evidence obtained from their own personal, internal offices. * * *

---

[7] In light of the Supreme Court's opinion in *O'Connor,* it cannot suffice for Fourth Amendment standing to challenge the seizure of an item in the workplace that the item is the personal property of an individual. See 480 U.S. at 715-16 (noting that "[t]he workplace includes those areas and items that are related to work and are generally within the employer's control," such as "the hallways, cafeteria, offices, desks and file cabinets," "even if the employee has placed personal items in them, such as a photograph placed in a desk"). Therefore, though personal ownership is important, Supreme Court precedent precludes us from considering it sufficient by itself to confer standing in this context.

[8] We add that this list of factors is not exclusive, though it indicates what kind of factors are relevant. The law of Fourth Amendment standing in general, and of our cases on employee standing in particular, emphasize that a defendant must show a personal connection to the place searched and item seized; therefore we will only consider factors that relate to such inquiry.

[The court turned to SDI's challenge to the warrant.] Evaluating the warrant (including the affidavit) to determine whether it met the demands of the Fourth Amendment, we start with the relevant language, which, of course, provides that "no Warrants shall issue, but upon probable cause . . . and particularly describing the place to be searched, and the persons or things to be seized." U.S. Const. amend. IV. Our cases describe this requirement as one of "specificity" and we have distinguished its "two aspects": "particularity and breadth . . . . Particularity is the requirement that the warrant must clearly state what is sought. Breadth deals with the requirement that the scope of the warrant be limited by the probable cause on which the warrant is based." In re Grand Jury Subpoenas Dated Dec. 10, 1987, 926 F.2d 847 (9th Cir.1991).

Particularity means that "the warrant must make clear to the executing officer exactly what it is that he or she is authorized to search for and seize." Id. " 'The description must be specific enough to enable the person conducting the search reasonably to identify the things authorized to be seized.' " United States v. Smith, 424 F.3d 992 (9th Cir.2005). * * *

Particularity is not the problem with the warrant in this case. Even the most troubling items on the list, such as "[r]olodexes, address books and calendars," are particular in that they "enable the person conducting the search reasonably to identify the things authorized to be seized." *Smith*. The officers could tell from the warrant that, should they happen upon a rolodex, they should seize it. Because the warrant was not vague as to what it directed law enforcement officers to search for and to seize, we are satisfied that it did not lack particularity for Fourth Amendment purposes.

The district court only made one inquiry, which explicitly conflated particularity and overbreadth. The court found that the warrant "at issue here was unconstitutionally overbroad because the lack of particularity provided no guidance in limiting the search and no direction to government agents regarding the purpose of the search or what types of records were within its scope." This error is quite understandable, given that some of our own opinions have been unclear on the difference between particularity and overbreadth. However, we now insist that particularity and overbreadth remain two distinct parts of the evaluation of a warrant for Fourth Amendment purposes.

A warrant must not only give clear instructions to a search team, it must also give legal, that is, not overbroad, instructions. Under the Fourth Amendment, this means that "there [must] be probable cause to seize the particular thing[s] named in the warrant." In re Grand Jury Subpoenas. "[P]robable cause means a fair probability that contraband or evidence of a crime will be found in a particular place, based on the totality of circumstances." United States v. Diaz, 491 F.3d 1074 (9th Cir.2007). "The number of files that could be scrutinized . . . is not determinative. The search and seizure of large quantities of material is justified if the material is within the scope of the probable cause underlying the warrant." United States v. Hayes, 794 F.2d 1348 (9th Cir.1986).

We turn now to the specific items with respect to which the district court found the warrant invalid, keeping in mind the warrant's incorporation of the affidavit. First, the district court, adopting the findings and recommendations of the magistrate judge, pointed to four categories of materials that it concluded were "borderline in acceptability," but nevertheless invalid: "2. Documents relating to billing procedures, billing manuals, and billing materials. 4. Documents relating to billing records and records of payments received. 8. Documents relating to correspondence with Medicare intermediaries and private insurance companies. 19. Documents relating to mailing and shipping records between physicians and SDI."

The magistrate judge recognized that "SDI's entire business appears to have been the conducting of sleep studies, and the affidavit supported the conclusion that SDI's allegedly fraudulent conduct was routine."[12] All the same, he concluded that these categories were "overbroad and vague . . . and not adequately limited to seizure of documents relating to the fraudulent scheme under investigation."

In light of the warrant's incorporation of the affidavit, we reject this conclusion. According to the affidavit, SDI's entire business involved sleep studies, and billing for phony sleep studies lay at the core of its scheme. There was probable cause, therefore, to support Category 2, in that any and all documents related to billing practices would have information relevant to whether SDI trained its employees to commit fraud or otherwise engaged in fraudulent billing. The same applies to Category 8. While the magistrate judge faulted the government for failing to specify that it sought "billing and payments for sleep studies," such criticism relied on the nonincorporation of the affidavit into the warrant. Including the affidavit as part of the warrant moots this concern. The affidavit also alleged that SDI engaged in both tax fraud and Medicare fraud, providing probable cause to support the seizure of all documents within the purview of category 4. Finally, in light of the government's allegation that SDI was engaging in mail fraud and providing illegal kickback payments to referring physicians, we conclude that Category 19 adequately limited the search to documents related to the mailing and shipping records with physicians (i.e., as opposed to allowing the seizure of all mailing and shipping records). It did not have to be any more restrictive.

---

[12] The government does not expressly challenge the magistrate judge's conclusion that the "permeated with fraud" exception does not apply in this case, but it cites and applies cases setting forth such principle. To dispel any uncertainty, we confirm that the exception does not apply to this case. We have held that a generalized seizure of business documents may be justified if the government establishes probable cause to believe that the entire business is merely a scheme to defraud or that all of the business's records are likely to evidence criminal activity. However, in this case the affidavit did not allege that SDI's entire business was fraudulent, and therefore such exception is inapplicable.

The magistrate judge also pointed to seven categories that, he believed, more clearly violated the Fourth Amendment: "7. Documents relating to non-privileged correspondence with consultants. 9. Documents relating to non-privileged internal memoranda and E-mail. 10. Documents relating to bank accounts, brokerage accounts, trusts. 11. Checking, savings, and money market account records, including check registers, cancelled checks, monthly statements, wire transfers, and cashier's checks. 12. Documents relating to personnel and payroll records. 13. Documents relating to accounting records. 24. Rolodexes, address books and calendars."

Certainly, the district court had better justification finding these categories invalid under the Fourth Amendment. Indeed, we disagree with the district court only with respect to Categories 7 and 13.

Category 7 involves the "non-privileged correspondence of consultants." Consultants are contract counter-parties outside of a firm who assist it with one or another part of its business. Since, again, SDI's entire business involved sleep studies, it would have been difficult to specify beforehand which consultants were complicit in the fraudulent sleep studies.

Category 9, on the other hand, makes no attempt to limit the search team's reach to internal memoranda related to the sleep studies. Since internal documents typically cover a subject-matter far wider than do external communications, this failure constitutes an invitation to a general, "exploratory rummaging in a person's belongings." *United States v. Holzman*, 871 F.2d 1496 (9th Cir.1989). It is true that the affidavit stated that "SDI likely will have contracts, memoranda, Email and/or other documents explaining the relationship between SDI and [cardiac diagnostic companies] and the reasons for . . . payments." But even though we find the warrant incorporated the affidavit, this does not mean that every chance remark buried in its thirty-five pages can cure plain defects in the warrant.

Categories 10, 11, and 12 pose a similar problem. Companies keep documents relating to the bank and checking accounts or other financial information of most of their employees. In other words, by failing to describe the crimes and individuals under investigation, the warrant provided the search team with discretion to seize records wholly unrelated to the finances of SDI or Kaplan.

Although SDI's entire business revolved around sleep studies, that does not mean, and no one has suggested, that its entire business was a sham. As we noted above, the "permeated with fraud" exception to the specificity requirements of the warrant does not apply here. This makes Category 13 problematic. However, especially considering the allegations that SDI engaged in tax fraud by understating its earnings, it would be difficult to distinguish in the warrant between those records which would provide evidence of the alleged fraud and those that would not. Category 13, then, more closely resembles Category 4 rather than Categories 10-12. That is to say, the only accounting records companies typically keep are those of their business dealings; they do not keep accounting records of their employees' personal finances. Since SDI's entire business involved sleep studies, all of its accounting records could potentially reveal evidence of the alleged fraud.

Finally, Category 24 – SDI's rolodexes, address books, and calendars – amounts to the laziest of gestures in the direction of specificity. Again, this category practically begs the search team to find and to seize the contact information of every person who ever dealt with SDI. It would have been far more sensible, as well as constitutional, to limit the search to information relating to consultants, physicians, and health insurance companies, or some other group likely to turn up conspirators in the alleged fraud.

We therefore conclude that Categories 9, 10, 11, 12, and 24 were overbroad because probable cause did not exist to seize all items of those particular types.

[The court rejected the government's argument under *United States v. Leon*, 468 U.S. 897 (1984), that the good faith reliance exception to the exclusionary rule applied because the government failed to show that the officers executing the warrant actually relied on the affidavit. It upheld the suppression of the documents seized pursuant to the overbroad categories in the warrant.]

NOTE

Specificity of Time. When the government searches for records related to ongoing business transactions, how specific does the warrant have to be regarding the dates of the records? The government may argue that it needs records beyond just the time in which particular transactions under investigation occurred because the events can take place over a broader period. Courts have rejected warrants that cover an extensive period of time if there is no probable cause that improper activity took place during the entire period. In **United States v. Ford**, 184 F.3d 566 (6th Cir. 1999), the warrant included broad descriptions of financial records without any time limitation, and the officers seized "several file cabinets and eleven boxes of documents" in connection with an illegal bingo operation. The court found the warrant lacked the requisite specificity regarding the time period for the items to be seized:

> [The warrant] authorized a broader search than was reasonable given the facts in the affidavit supporting the warrant. The affidavit stated that the first of Ford's RVA posts was incorporated in December 1991, and there was no indication in the affidavit of criminal activity before that date. The affidavit described an investigation beginning on April 24, 1992. It also reported an interview with Clay Ballinger, who said he had operated the bingo himself but had "sold the Arcade Plaza Bingo back to Mr. Ford in 1991." However, the police seized promissory notes, deeds, and

> related papers dated between 1984 and 1988, which had no relation to the bingo operation. * * *
>
> The government argues that it was necessary to seize documents antedating the bingo operation to establish what money Ford had before the bingo business started. This would help the government to identify which of his present assets could be bingo proceeds. This argument would allow virtually unlimited seizure of a lifetime's worth of documentation, which is extremely intrusive. Moreover, the impracticability of tracing the origin of every dollar Ford owned to show whether it came from some enterprise other than bingo, casts doubt on whether the government really means to take on such a herculean task. At any rate, this rationale was not articulated in the affidavit, and therefore we need not decide whether it would have provided a justification for the warrant if it had been presented to the magistrate. * * *
>
> The government further argues that there was probable cause to seize all the documents at the RVA Hall because the business carried on there was "permeated with fraud." * * * The affidavit definitely contained evidence that Ford was abusing the form of charitable organizations in order to run bingo games for personal profit. However, the affidavit did not disclose any reason to believe that the scheme began before December 1991, the date given in the affidavit as the date when Ford reactivated his first RVA post. Even if one business carried on at a site is permeated with fraud, if other businesses run at the same site are separable and are not shown to be related to the suspected crime, a warrant permitting seizure of all documents at the site is not justified.[a]

2. Business Pervaded by Fraud

The Fourth Amendment requires that a warrant specify the place to be searched and the items to be seized. When the government executes a search for the records of a business, the documents and computers could be in a wide variety of locations within a business, and even at different offices in various parts of the country. Similarly, evidence of criminality will often consist of voluminous records of regularly conducted activities, so it will be difficult to specify at the outset exactly which records are related to the suspected criminal activity. If the operation of business is heavily tainted by suspected illegal activity–such as a boiler room operation selling worthless securities or an advanced-loan scheme operated out of a remote location–can the government simply seize all of the records of a business on the ground that every item is relevant to prove criminality? In **United States v. Bradley**,

---

[a] The government failed to argue that, under *Leon*, the agents' good faith reliance on the warrant should block application of the exclusionary rule.

644 F.3d 1213 (11th Cir. 2011), the Eleventh Circuit provided a description of the degree of pervasiveness required:

> "[P]ervasive fraud" does not refer to the percentage of a defendant's business that is fraudulent. In other words, the doctrine is not concerned with how deeply the fraud runs. Rather, the "pervasive fraud" doctrine addresses the extent to which fraud has permeated the scope of the defendant's business. That is, the doctrine is concerned with the breadth of the alleged fraud—whether evidence of fraud is likely to be found in records related to a wide range of company business.

Once the government seizes a large volume of records, the business may be crippled if it cannot get access to billing records, order forms, etc. There may be a substantial gap in time between when the government seizes records under a search warrant and when, if ever, it files criminal charges that would permit the defendant to challenge a search. Federal Rule of Criminal Procedure 41(g) provides an avenue to challenge the propriety of the government's seizure of documents and evidence, and motions brought under the Rule are only seen in cases involving white collar crimes and not illegal narcotics or other types or organized crime cases.

In re GRAND JURY INVESTIGATION CONCERNING SOLID STATE DEVICES, INC.

130 F.3d 853 (9th Cir. 1997)

D.W. NELSON, Circuit Judge.

Solid State Devices, Inc. and Unisem International (collectively "SSDI") appeal the district court's decision to deny their petition for return of property, filed pursuant to Federal Rule of Criminal Procedure 41(e). SSDI's property was seized in connection with a Department of Defense ("DoD") investigation of alleged fraudulent practices. SSDI challenges the legality of the seizure, arguing that the warrants executed against it were insufficiently specific.

SSDI supplies semiconductor devices to the DoD and to a number of DoD contractors. Because SSDI's semiconductors are used in sophisticated military, aerospace, and space programs, the Government requires that they be manufactured in conformity with exacting standards and tested to assure a high degree of reliability.

Since 1995, SSDI has been under investigation by agents of the Defense Criminal Investigative Service ("DCIS"), an investigative agency within the DoD. On May 17, 1995, Craig N. Wyckoff, a DCIS Special Agent, presented an affidavit to United States Magistrate Judge Virginia Phillips in support of the issuance of warrants to search SSDI. Based on interviews with two SSDI employees, SSDI clients, and government experts, Wyckoff alleged that

SSDI had acquired commercial-grade semiconductors that did not comply with the standards and specifications required under SSDI's government contracts. He alleged that SSDI then falsely labeled these parts as SSDI-manufactured components, falsified test results certifying that the parts had undergone the necessary quality inspections, and sold the parts to the government at "high reliability" component prices. Because Wyckoff's affidavit reveals sensitive information, including the identities of informants, Wyckoff filed it under seal and requested that its contents not be disclosed to SSDI.

On May 23, 1995, federal agents of the FBI, DCIS and NASA executed search warrants on the premises of SSDI. The warrants, the validity of which is at issue on this appeal, authorized the seizure of a broad array of documents and data storage equipment, including the following:

> a. Contracts, subcontracts, purchase orders, sales orders, invoices and correspondence, Certificates of Quality Conformance/Compliance (COQC), and memoranda relating to agreements between Solid State Devices, Inc., (SSDI), and any governmental or non-governmental entity regarding the manufacture, testing or inspection of semi-conductor devices supplied for U.S. Department of Defense (DoD) or other governmental programs from May 1, 1990 to the present.
>
> k. Electronic data processing and storage devices, computers and computer systems including central processing units; internal and peripheral storage devices such as fixed disks, floppy disk drives and diskettes, tape drives and tapes, optical storage devices or other memory storage devices; peripheral input/output devices such as keyboards, printers, video display monitors, optical readers, and related communications devices such as modems; together with system documentation, operating logs and documentation, software and instruction manuals, all passwords, test keys, encryption codes or similar codes that are necessary to access computer programs, data or other information or to otherwise render programs or data into a usable form.

The warrants made no reference either to any statutes allegedly violated or, with one minor exception,[1] to any illegal acts. Moreover, no one at SSDI has been permitted to see the affidavit on which the warrants were based.

---

[1] The warrants authorized the seizure of fourteen categories of materials. Only one of the categories specifically referred to illegal acts:

> j. Hewlett Packard computer utilized in the falsification of test results of the pre and post burn-in testing on Westinghouse semi-conductor parts.

Pursuant to the search warrants, the agents seized computers, computer storage media, and more than 2,000 file drawers and file boxes containing business records. SSDI claims that nearly ninety percent of all of the documents and items at SSDI dealing with contracts over a five-year period were seized. These items have been stored since their seizure in May 1995 at DCIS offices in El Toro, California. In March 1996, SSDI filed a petition for return of seized property pursuant to Federal Rule of Criminal Procedure 41(e). The district court denied the petition, and SSDI timely appeals.

Federal Rule of Criminal Procedure 41(e) provides, in part, "A person aggrieved by an unlawful search and seizure or by the deprivation of property may move the district court . . . for the return of the property on the ground that such person is entitled to lawful possession of the property."[a] A Rule 41(e) motion therefore should be granted either when the movant is aggrieved by an unlawful seizure or, if the seizure was lawful, when the movant is aggrieved by the government's continued possession of the seized property. On this appeal, SSDI confines itself to challenging the legality of the Government's seizure of its property.

The Fourth Amendment provides that "no Warrants shall issue, but upon probable cause, supported by Oath or affirmation, and particularly describing the place to be searched, and the persons or things to be seized." U.S. Const. amend. IV. * * * In assessing whether a warrant passes constitutional muster, a court therefore is obliged to make two inquiries: first, whether the scope of the search authorized by the warrant was justified by probable cause and, second, whether the warrant was sufficiently particular to limit the discretion of the officers executing it. Because we find that the scope of the search exceeded the Government's showing of probable cause, however, we do not reach the particularity analysis. * * *

The warrants executed against SSDI were exceptionally broad in scope. Indeed, the only limitations imposed by the warrants were that the records relate to the supply of semiconductors to government programs and that they date from 1990 to 1995. The Government acknowledges, however, that the vast majority of SSDI's business relates directly or indirectly to the supply of semiconductors for government programs. Moreover, the Government nowhere provides a rationale for the dates chosen. Under these circumstances, such limitations are not meaningful.

The Government does not dispute that the warrants served on SSDI were broad in scope. It simply contends that Wyckoff's affidavit indicates that SSDI was so pervaded by fraud that there was probable cause to seize the majority of its documents. Under the law of this circuit, it is well-settled that "[a] generalized seizure of business documents may be justified if the government establishes probable cause to believe that the entire business is merely a scheme to defraud or that all of the business's records are likely to

---

[a] Rule 41 was revised in 2002, and the applicable provision is now Rule 41(g).

evidence criminal activity." See generally United States v. Offices Known as 50 State Distrib. Co., 708 F.2d 1371 (9th Cir.1983) (finding breadth of warrant justified by breadth of probable cause in view of fact that affidavit evidenced "pervasively fraudulent operation").

SSDI, however, is substantially different from the types of businesses to which this Court has applied the "pervaded by fraud" exception in the past. This circuit first adopted the exception in *50 State,* relying on the First Circuit's decision in United States v. Brien, 617 F.2d 299 (1st Cir.1980). In both *50 State* and *Brien* the affidavits supporting the warrants at issue showed that the companies involved were little more than "boilershop" sales operations engaged only negligibly in legitimate business activities. Although Wyckoff's affidavit alleges that SSDI has routinely engaged in fraudulent practices, it does not provide cause to believe that the majority of SSDI's operations are fraudulent. To the contrary, the record indicates that SSDI has received an impressive array of awards and certificates from a variety of clients, commending its contributions to their projects. Where a business appears, as SSDI does here, to be engaged in some legitimate activity, this Court has required a more substantial showing of pervasive fraud than that provided by the Government in the instant case.

Thus, while Wyckoff's affidavit very likely would have provided probable cause for a narrower, more carefully-defined search, we find it to have been an insufficient basis for the broad scope of the warrants executed against SSDI.

For the foregoing reasons, we REVERSE the district court's order denying the plaintiffs' Rule 41(e) motion for return of property and REMAND with instructions to the district court to grant the plaintiffs' Rule 41(e) motion.

NOTES AND QUESTIONS

1. ***Effect on Future Use of the Evidence at Trial.*** Even if the court grants the Rule 41(g) motion, is the government precluded from offering the content of the records in evidence? While the seizure may be improper, requiring the return of the records, the government could still rely on *Leon* to argue that suppression is not the appropriate remedy. Would the "fruit of the poisonous tree" doctrine prohibit the government from obtaining the documents returned after the Rule 41(g) motion? Could the government just subpoena the same records it seized pursuant to the illegal warrant? Consider the Supreme Court's statement in **Silverthorne Lumber Co. v. United States**, 251 U.S. 385 (1920), in which federal officers unlawfully seized certain documents and, after a district court ordered their return, the grand jury issued subpoenas to the defendants to produce the very same documents:

> The essence of a provision forbidding the acquisition of evidence in a certain way is that not merely evidence so acquired shall not be

> used before the Court but that it shall not be used at all. Of course this does not mean that the facts thus obtained become sacred and inaccessible. If knowledge of them is gained from an independent source they may be proved like any others, but the knowledge gained by the Government's own wrong cannot be used by it in the way proposed.

If *Leon* would allow the use of derivative evidence notwithstanding the Rule 41(g) ruling, then why not give the government the means to reobtain the documents seized illegally? If the government in *Solid State* had shown that it intended to proceed with an indictment and the illegal search met the good faith standard of Leon, should that have precluded return of the property? Was *Solid State* assuming that the warrant there met the facially deficient exception of *Leon*? If *Leon* applies, then the target may not be able to get a Rule 41(g) "exception" by making a motion for return prior to indictment. The government can return copies of documents seized in a search to comply with an order to return property under Rule 41(g). In In re Search of Office of Tylman, 245 F.3d 978 (7th Cir. 2001), the circuit court noted that "the district court ordered the government to return copies of the seized documents. That was done. We have been given no compelling reason to think that this solution is not an adequate remedy for the appellants."

2. ***Pervasively Fraudulent Organization***. The Ninth Circuit asserted that a broad warrant permitting the seizure of all of an organization's documents might be permissible if the business were entirely criminal, although that was not the case in *Solid State*. In **United States v. Johnson**, 886 F.Supp. 1057 (W.D.N.Y. 1995), the District Court upheld a warrant for "any and all books and records * * * for the period 1982 to the present, including ledgers, journals, receipts, balance sheets, deeds, mortgages, contracts, invoices, bills, bank statements, financial statements, tax returns, stocks bonds and treasury notes" of four interrelated corporations involved in hazardous waste disposal. The court found that "although the search warrants at issue were broad, they were not unconstitutionally overbroad, as the businesses involved were shown to be sufficiently permeated with fraud to justify the wide scope of the warrant." In reviewing the warrant, the court noted that "[a]lthough a mere allegation of fraud is not enough to authorize the seizure of all business records, given the closely-connected nature of the Defendants' businesses here, it would not have been possible 'through a more particular description to segregate those business records that would be evidence of fraud from those that would not . . . .'"

3. ***Overbroad Warrants to Search a Business***. The Tenth Circuit rejected that position in **Voss v. Bergsgaard**, 774 F.2d 402 (10th Cir. 1985):

> To the extent that * * * cases can be read as allowing the seizure of all of an organization's records when there is probable cause to believe the organization is pervasively criminal, whether or not those records are relevant to an alleged crime, we decline to follow

> them. This is not to say that a search may never properly result in the seizure of all of an organization's records. Where a warrant authorizes the seizure of particularly described records relevant to a specific crime and all of an organization's records, in fact, fall into that category, they may all lawfully be seized. However, a warrant that simply authorizes the seizure of all files, whether or not relevant to a specified crime, is insufficiently particular.

Circuit Judge Logan, in a concurring opinion, stated:

> I do not accept the majority's disapproval of [cases that] * * * permitted an all records search. These cases hold that if an entire business enterprise is permeated with a scheme to defraud, and the government properly supports its probable cause determination, a warrant seeking all business records is not overbroad. In such a case the government's agents' discretion in the execution of the warrant is properly confined, and all of the organization's business records are likely to be relevant to the crime being investigated.

The scope of the organization's criminality does not create an exception to the Fourth Amendment so much as it makes it easier for the government to establish that the description is sufficient to meet the particularity requirement for a valid warrant. What level of proof is needed to establish that a business is pervaded by fraud? If a business successfully challenges that conclusion, should a court suppress the evidence because the warrant did not have the requisite specificity?

D. COMPUTER SEARCHES

A significant volume of the information that will assist the government in an investigation of any complex business transaction most likely was created and stored on a computer. Business records, memoranda, reports, spreadsheets, financial and tax records, and correspondence are just a few of the types of records that can be found on a computer. Of particular interest to investigators are the internal e-mail messages of corporate employees, which often give contain unguarded statements of the reasons for an action or decision, and they usually are contemporaneous with the transactions under investigation. "For prosecutors, [e-mail] has become the star witness–or perhaps an even better weapon than that. Think of e-mail as the corporate equivalent of DNA evidence . . . So ubiquitous has the smoking e-mail become that some lawyers have taken to calling it 'evidence mail.'" Nicholas Varchaver, *The Perils of E-Mail*, FORTUNE, Feb. 17, 2003, at 96. Individuals use Personal Digital Assistants and other portable electronic devices to store calendars, schedules, notes, documents, and e-mail, so that the amount of information held by an individual is much greater than when information was only in documentary form.

Businesses usually back-up computer data on a regular basis, so records may be available from multiple locations. Data stored on a computer is not easily destroyed, so that even a concerted effort to eliminate all documentary evidence of a transaction may not be completely effective. The government has focused its attention to a much greater degree obtaining evidence from internal corporate computer systems, and with much greater frequency seize individual computers and memory devices. The Department of Justice recognizes the importance of obtaining evidence from computers, and the Computer Crime and Intellectual Property Section of its Criminal Division published a detailed manual on issues related to computer searches. U.S. Dept. of Justice, SEARCHING AND SEIZING COMPUTERS AND OBTAINING ELECTRONIC EVIDENCE IN CRIMINAL INVESTIGATIONS (2009). The Department of Justice explains:

> Computers and the Internet have entered the mainstream of American life. Millions of Americans spend hours every day using computers and mobile devices to send and receive email, surf the Internet, maintain databases, and participate in countless other activities.
>
> Unfortunately, those who commit crimes have not missed the information revolution. Criminals use mobile phones, laptop computers, and network servers in the course of committing their crimes. In some cases, computers provide the means of committing crime. For example, the Internet can be used to deliver a death threat via email; to launch hacker attacks against a vulnerable computer network, to disseminate computer viruses, or to transmit images of child pornography. In other cases, computers merely serve as convenient storage devices for evidence of crime. For example, a drug dealer might keep a list of who owes him money in a file stored in his desktop computer at home, or a money laundering operation might retain false financial records in a file on a network server. Indeed, virtually every class of crime can involve some form of digital evidence.
>
> The dramatic increase in computer-related crime requires prosecutors and law enforcement agents to understand how to obtain electronic evidence stored in computers. Electronic records such as computer network logs, email, word processing files, and image files increasingly provide the government with important (and sometimes essential) evidence in criminal cases. The purpose of this publication is to provide Federal law enforcement agents and prosecutors with systematic guidance that can help them understand the legal issues that arise when they seek electronic evidence in criminal investigations.

SEARCHING AND SEIZING COMPUTERS, Introduction.

Searches of computers often raise thorny Fourth Amendment issues in the application of traditional doctrines to electronic devices, especially the particularity requirement for a valid warrant and the authority of a government agent under the "plain view" doctrine to look at materials stored on a computer or other electronic device to determine their relevance. In **United States v. Comprehensive Drug Testing, Inc.**, 621 F.3d 1162 (9th Cir. 2010) (en banc), the Ninth Circuit discussed the challenge of balancing the privacy interests of individuals with the government's need to search electronic media for evidence of a crime. The government had searched the computers at a company that conducted drug testing on behalf of Major League Baseball, and seized the results of a number of player tests that were not listed in the warrant. In discussing how to properly craft a warrant for computer files, the circuit court stated:

> Wrongdoers and their collaborators have obvious incentives to make data difficult to find, but parties involved in lawful activities may also encrypt or compress data for entirely legitimate reasons: protection of privacy, preservation of privileged communications, warding off industrial espionage or preventing general mischief such as identity theft. Law enforcement today thus has a far more difficult, exacting and sensitive task in pursuing evidence of criminal activities than even in the relatively recent past. The legitimate need to scoop up large quantities of data, and sift through it carefully for concealed or disguised pieces of evidence, is one we've often recognized.
>
> This pressing need of law enforcement for broad authorization to examine electronic records * * * creates a serious risk that every warrant for electronic information will become, in effect, a general warrant, rendering the Fourth Amendment irrelevant. The problem can be stated very simply: There is no way to be sure exactly what an electronic file contains without somehow examining its contents—either by opening it and looking, using specialized forensic software, keyword searching or some other such technique. But electronic files are generally found on media that also contain thousands or millions of other files among which the sought-after data may be stored or concealed. By necessity, government efforts to locate particular files will require examining a great many other files to exclude the possibility that the sought-after data are concealed there.
>
> Once a file is examined, however, the government may claim (as it did in this case) that its contents are in plain view and, if incriminating, the government can keep it. Authorization to search some computer files therefore automatically becomes authorization to search all files in the same sub-directory, and all files in an enveloping directory, a neighboring hard drive, a nearby computer or nearby storage media. Where computers are not near each other, but are connected electronically, the original search might justify

> examining files in computers many miles away, on a theory that incriminating electronic data could have been shuttled and concealed there.
>
> The advent of fast, cheap networking has made it possible to store information at remote third-party locations, where it is intermingled with that of other users. For example, many people no longer keep their email primarily on their personal computer, and instead use a web-based email provider, which stores their messages along with billions of messages from and to millions of other people. Similar services exist for photographs, slide shows, computer code and many other types of data. As a result, people now have personal data that are stored with that of innumerable strangers. Seizure of, for example, Google's email servers to look for a few incriminating messages could jeopardize the privacy of millions. * * *
>
> We recognize the reality that over-seizing is an inherent part of the electronic search process and proceed on the assumption that, when it comes to the seizure of electronic records, this will be far more common than in the days of paper records. This calls for greater vigilance on the part of judicial officers in striking the right balance between the government's interest in law enforcement and the right of individuals to be free from unreasonable searches and seizures. The process of segregating electronic data that is seizable from that which is not must not become a vehicle for the government to gain access to data which it has no probable cause to collect.

The case below presents the issue of how the government should handle files seized from a computer during the course of an evolving investigation. Federal Rule of Criminal Procedure 41(e)(2)(B) provides that "[u]nless otherwise specified, the warrant authorizes a later review of the media or information consistent with the warrant. The time for executing the warrant in Rule 41(e)(2)(A) and (f)(1)(A) refers to the seizure or on-site copying of the media or information, and not to any later off-site copying or review." It does not specify a time frame for the off-site review, and consider how the amount of time needed to pursue a white collar crime investigation makes it more difficult to deal with electronic information in a timely manner.

UNITED STATES v. GANIAS

755 F.3d 125 (2d Cir. 2014)

CHIN, Circuit Judge:

In the 1980s, after working for the Internal Revenue Service ("IRS") for some fourteen years, Ganias started his own accounting business in Wallingford, Connecticut. He provided tax and accounting services to individuals and small businesses. In 1998, he began providing services to James McCarthy and two of McCarthy's businesses, American Boiler and

Industrial Property Management ("IPM"). IPM had been hired by the Army to provide maintenance and security at a vacant Army facility in Stratford, Connecticut.

In August 2003, the Criminal Investigative Command of the Army received a tip from a confidential source that individuals affiliated with IPM were engaging in improper conduct, including stealing copper wire and other items from the Army facility and billing the Army for work that IPM employees performed for American Boiler. The source alleged that evidence of the wrongdoing could be found at the offices of American Boiler and IPM, as well as at the offices of "Steve Gainis [sic]," who "perform[ed] accounting work for IPM and American Boiler."

Based on this information, the Army commenced an investigation. Army investigators obtained several search warrants, including one to search the offices of Ganias's accounting business. The warrant, issued by the United States District Court for the District of Connecticut and dated November 17, 2003, authorized the seizure from Ganias's offices of: "All books, records, documents, materials, computer hardware and software and computer associated data relating to the business, financial and accounting operations of [IPM] and American Boiler . . . ."

The warrant was executed two days later. Army computer specialists accompanied investigators to Ganias's offices and helped gather the electronic evidence. The agents did not seize Ganias's computers; instead, the computer specialists made identical copies, or forensic mirror images, of the hard drives of all three of Ganias's computers. As a consequence, the investigators copied every file on all three computers—including files beyond the scope of the warrant, such as files containing Ganias's personal financial records. Ganias was present as the investigators collected the evidence, and he expressed concern about the scope of the seizure. In response, one agent "assured" Ganias that the Army was only looking for files "related to American Boiler and IPM." Everything else, the agent explained, "would be purged once they completed their search" for relevant files.

Back in their offices, the Army computer specialist copied the data taken from Ganias's computers (as well as data obtained from the searches of the offices of IPM and American Boiler) onto "two sets of 19 DVDs," which were "maintained as evidence." Some eight months later, the Army Criminal Investigation Lab finally began to review the files.

In the meantime, while reviewing the paper documents retrieved from Ganias's offices, the Army discovered suspicious payments made by IPM to an unregistered business, which was allegedly owned by an individual who had not reported any income from that business. Based on this evidence, in May 2004, the Army invited the IRS to "join the investigation" of IPM and American Boiler and gave copies of the imaged hard drives to the IRS so that it could conduct its own review and analysis. The Army and the IRS proceeded, separately, to search the imaged hard drives for files that appeared to be within the scope of the warrant and to extract them for further review.

By December 2004, some thirteen months after the seizure, the Army and IRS investigators had isolated and extracted the computer files that were relevant to IPM and American Boiler and thus covered by the search warrant. The investigators were aware that, because of the constraints of the warrant, they were not permitted to review any other computer records. Indeed, the investigators were careful, at least until later, to review only data covered by the November 2003 warrant.

They did not, however, purge or delete the non-responsive files. To the contrary, the investigators retained the files because they "viewed the data as the government's property, not Mr. Ganias's property." Their view was that while items seized from an owner will be returned after an investigation closes, all of the electronic data here were evidence that were to be protected and preserved. As one agent testified, "[W]e would not routinely go into DVDs to delete data, as we're altering the original data that was seized. And you never know what data you may need in the future.... I don't normally go into electronic data and start deleting evidence off of DVDs stored in my evidence room." The computer specialists were never asked to delete (or even to try to delete) those files that did not relate to IPM or American Boiler.

In late 2004, IRS investigators discovered accounting irregularities regarding transactions between IPM and American Boiler in the paper documents taken from Ganias's office. After subpoenaing and reviewing the relevant bank records in 2005, they began to suspect that Ganias was not properly reporting American Boiler's income. Accordingly, on July 28, 2005, some twenty months after the seizure of his computer files, the Government officially expanded its investigation to include possible tax violations by Ganias. Further investigation in 2005 and early 2006 indicated that Ganias had been improperly reporting income for both of his clients, leading the Government to suspect that he also might have been underreporting his own income.

At that point, the IRS case agent wanted to review Ganias's personal financial records and she knew, from her review of the seized computer records, that they were among the files in the DVDs copied from Ganias's hard drives. The case agent was aware, however, that Ganias's personal financial records were beyond the scope of the November 2003 warrant, and consequently she did not believe that she could review the non-responsive files, even though they were already in the Government's possession.

In February 2006, the Government asked Ganias and his counsel for permission to access certain of his personal files that were contained in the materials seized in November 2003. Ganias did not respond, and thus, on April 24, 2006, the Government obtained another warrant to search the preserved images of Ganias's personal financial records taken in 2003. At that point, the images had been in the Government's possession for almost two-and-a-half years. Because Ganias had altered the original files shortly after the Army executed the 2003 warrant, the evidence obtained in 2006 would not have existed but for the Government's retention of those images. * * * [Ganias was convicted after a jury trial on two counts of tax evasion for failure to pay personal income tax and sentenced to 24 months in prison.]

We must construe the Fourth Amendment "in light of what was deemed an unreasonable search and seizure when it was adopted, and in a manner which will conserve public interests as well as the interests and rights of individual citizens." Kyllo v. United States, 533 U.S. 27 (2001). Applying 18th Century notions about searches and seizures to modern technology, however, is easier said than done, as we are asked to measure Government actions taken in the "computer age" against Fourth Amendment frameworks crafted long before this technology existed. As we do so, we must keep in mind that "the ultimate touchstone of the Fourth Amendment is reasonableness." Missouri v. McNeely, 133 S.Ct. 1552 (2013) (Roberts, C.J., concurring in part and dissenting in part). Because the degree of privacy secured to citizens by the Fourth Amendment has been impacted by the advance of technology, the challenge is to adapt traditional Fourth Amendment concepts to the Government's modern, more sophisticated investigative tools.

"The chief evil that prompted the framing and adoption of the Fourth Amendment was the indiscriminate searches and seizures conducted by the British under the authority of general warrants." United States v. Galpin, 720 F.3d 436 (2d Cir.2013). General warrants were ones "not grounded upon a sworn oath of a specific infraction by a particular individual, and thus not limited in scope and application." Maryland v. King, 133 S.Ct. 1958 (2013). The British Crown had long used these questionable instruments to enter a political opponent's home and seize all his books and papers, hoping to find among them evidence of criminal activity. The Framers abhorred this practice, believing that "papers are often the dearest property a man can have" and that permitting the Government to "sweep away all papers whatsoever," without any legal justification, "would destroy all the comforts of society." Entick v. Carrington, 95 Eng. Rep. 807, 817–18 (C.P.1765). * * *

The Fourth Amendment guards against this practice by providing that a warrant will issue only if: (1) the Government establishes probable cause to believe the search will uncover evidence of a specific crime; and (2) the warrant states with particularity the areas to be searched and the items to be seized. * * *

These Fourth Amendment protections apply to modern computer files. Like 18th Century "papers," computer files may contain intimate details regarding an individual's thoughts, beliefs, and lifestyle, and they should be similarly guarded against unwarranted Government intrusion. If anything, even greater protection is warranted. * * *

Not surprisingly, the ability of computers to store massive volumes of information presents logistical problems in the execution of search warrants.

It is "comparatively" commonplace for files on a computer hard drive to be so intermingled that they cannot feasibly be sorted on site. As evidenced by this case, forensic analysis of electronic data may take months to complete. It would be impractical for agents to occupy an individual's home or office, or seize an individual's computer, for such long periods of time. It is now also unnecessary. Today, advancements in technology enable the Government to create a mirror image of an individual's hard drive, which can be searched as if it were the actual hard drive but without interfering with the individual's use of his home, computer, or files.

In light of the significant burdens on-site review would place on both the individual and the Government, the creation of mirror images for offsite review is constitutionally permissible in most instances, even if wholesale removal of tangible papers would not be. Indeed, the 2009 amendments to the Federal Rules of Criminal Procedure, which added Rule 41(e)(2)(B), clearly contemplated off-site review of computer hard drives in certain circumstances. Although Rule 41(e)(2)(B) was not in effect in 2003, when the warrant was executed with respect to Ganias's computers, case law both before and after the rule's adoption has recognized that off-site review of seized electronic files may be necessary and reasonable.

The off-site review of these mirror images, however, is still subject to the rule of reasonableness. The advisory committee's notes to the 2009 amendment of the Federal Rules of Criminal Procedure shed some light on what is "reasonable" in this context. Specifically, the committee rejected "a presumptive national or uniform time period within which any subsequent off-site copying or review of the media or electronically stored information would take place." The committee noted that several variables—storage capacity of media, difficulties created by encryption or electronic booby traps, and computer-lab workload—influence the duration of a forensic analysis and counsel against a "one size fits all" time period. Id. In combination, these factors might justify an off-site review lasting for a significant period of time. They do not, however, provide an "independent basis" for retaining any electronic data "other than [those] specified in the warrant." United States v. Comprehensive Drug Testing, Inc., 621 F.3d 1162, 1171 (9th Cir.2010) (en banc). * * *

[We consider the following issue]: whether the Fourth Amendment permits officials executing a warrant for the seizure of particular data on a computer to seize and indefinitely retain every file on that computer for use in future criminal investigations. We hold that it does not.

If the 2003 warrant authorized the Government to retain all the data on Ganias's computers on the off-chance the information would become relevant to a subsequent criminal investigation, it would be the equivalent of a general warrant. The Government's retention of copies of Ganias's personal computer records for two-and-a-half years deprived him of exclusive control over those files for an unreasonable amount of time. This combination of circumstances enabled the Government to possess indefinitely personal records of Ganias that were beyond the scope of the warrant while it looked for other evidence to give it probable cause to search the files. This was a meaningful interference with Ganias's possessory rights in those files and constituted a seizure within the meaning of the Fourth Amendment.

We conclude that the unauthorized seizure and retention of these documents was unreasonable. The Government had no warrant authorizing the seizure of Ganias's personal records in 2003. By December 2004, these documents had been separated from those relevant to the investigation of American Boiler and IPM. Nevertheless, the Government continued to retain them for another year-and-a-half until it finally developed probable cause to search and seize them in 2006. Without some independent basis for its retention of those documents in the interim, the Government clearly violated Ganias's Fourth Amendment rights by retaining the files for a prolonged period of time and then using them in a future criminal investigation.

The Government offers several arguments to justify its actions, but none provides any legal authorization for its continued and prolonged possession of the non-responsive files. First, it argues that it must be allowed to make the mirror image copies as a matter of practical necessity and, according to the Government's investigators, those mirror images were "the government's property." As explained above, practical considerations may well justify a reasonable accommodation in the manner of executing a search warrant, such as making mirror images of hard drives and permitting off-site review, but these considerations do not justify the indefinite retention of non-responsive documents. Without a warrant authorizing seizure of Ganias's personal financial records, the copies of those documents could not become ipso facto "the government's property" without running afoul of the Fourth Amendment.

Second, the Government asserts that by obtaining the 2006 search warrant, it cured any defect in its search of the wrongfully retained files. But this argument "reduces the Fourth Amendment to a form of words." Silverthorne Lumber Co. v. United States, 251 U.S. 385 (1920). In Silverthorne, the Government, "without a shadow of authority[,] went to the office of [the defendants'] company and made a clean sweep of all the books, papers and documents found there." The originals were eventually returned because they were unlawfully seized, but the prosecutor had made "[p]hotographs and copies of material papers" and used these to indict the defendants and obtain a subpoena for the original documents. Justice Holmes succinctly summarized the Government's argument supporting the constitutionality of its actions as follows:

> [A]lthough of course its seizure was an outrage which the Government now regrets, it may study the papers before it returns them, copy them, and then may use the knowledge that it has gained to call upon the owners in a more regular form to produce them; that the protection of the Constitution covers the physical possession but

> not any advantages that the Government can gain over the object of its pursuit by doing the forbidden act.

Unsurprisingly, the Supreme Court rejected that argument: "The essence of a provision forbidding the acquisition of evidence in a certain way is that not merely evidence so acquired shall not be used before the Court but that it shall not be used at all" unless some exception applies. The same rationale applies here. If the Government could seize and retain non-responsive electronic records indefinitely, so it could search them whenever it later developed probable cause, every warrant to search for particular electronic data would become, in essence, a general warrant.

Third, the Government argues that it must be permitted to search the mirror images in its possession because the evidence no longer existed on Ganias's computers. But the ends, however, do not justify the means. The loss of the personal records is irrelevant in this case because the Government concedes that it never considered performing a new search of Ganias's computers and did not know that the files no longer existed when it searched the mirror images in its possession. And even if it were relevant, the Fourth Amendment clearly embodies a judgment that some evidence of criminal activity may be lost for the sake of protecting property and privacy rights.

Fourth, the Government contends that returning or destroying the non-responsive files is "entirely impractical" because doing so would compromise the remaining data that was responsive to the warrant, making it impossible to authenticate or use it in a criminal prosecution. We are not convinced that there is no other way to preserve the evidentiary chain of custody. But even if we assumed it were necessary to maintain a complete copy of the hard drive solely to authenticate evidence responsive to the original warrant, that does not provide a basis for using the mirror image for any other purpose. * * *

Because the Government has demonstrated no legal basis for retaining the non-responsive documents, its retention and subsequent search of those documents were unconstitutional. The Fourth Amendment was intended to prevent the Government from entering individuals' homes and indiscriminately seizing all their papers in the hopes of discovering evidence about previously unknown crimes. Yet this is exactly what the Government claims it may do when it executes a warrant calling for the seizure of particular electronic data relevant to a different crime. Perhaps the "wholesale removal" of intermingled computer records is permissible where off-site sorting is necessary and reasonable, but this accommodation does not somehow authorize the Government to retain all non-responsive documents indefinitely, for possible use in future criminal investigations.

We turn now to the application of the exclusionary rule. * * * Suppression is required when (1) there is a widespread seizure of items not covered by the warrant and (2) agents do not act in good faith. There must also be a weighing of (3) the benefits of deterrence against (4) the costs of suppression.

First, as we set forth above, the Government effected a widespread seizure of files beyond the scope of the warrant-conduct that resembled an impermissible general search. For almost two-and-a-half years, the Government retained records that were beyond the scope of the 2003 warrant, in violation of Ganias's Fourth Amendment rights.

Second, the agents here did not act in good faith. Government agents act in good faith when they conduct searches in objectively reasonable reliance on binding appellate precedent. It is the Government's burden—not Ganias's—to demonstrate the objective reasonableness of the officers' good faith reliance. We are not persuaded that the agents in this case reasonably concluded that the 2003 warrant authorized their search of Ganias's personal records and their retention for more than two years. The agents acknowledged, at least initially, that the Government was obliged to "purge [ ]" the non-responsive data after they completed their search for relevant files. The record also makes clear that Government investigators "viewed the data as the government's property" and intentionally retained Ganias's records for future use. This clearly was not reasonable, and the agents could not have had a good-faith basis to believe the law permitted them to keep the nonresponsive files indefinitely.

Third, the benefits of deterrence in this case are great. With the Government's use of forensic mirror images becoming increasingly common, deterring its unconstitutional handling of non-responsive data has grown in importance. * * *

Finally, the costs of suppression are minimal here. This is not a case where a dangerous defendant is being set free. Even assuming Ganias committed tax evasion—a serious matter—this case does not involve drugs, guns, or contraband. Nor is this a case where police officers happened upon guns or drugs or other evidence they otherwise could not have found. Rather, early on, the evidence here was readily obtainable by subpoena or search warrant. Moreover, when guns or drugs are suppressed, that evidence is usually irreplaceable. The records here, however, conceivably are available elsewhere as hard copies or can be reconstructed from other records. As made clear by the Government's behavior, the costs of suppression that the Government has asserted are outweighed by the benefits of deterring future misconduct.

Accordingly, we reverse the denial of the motion to suppress and vacate the judgment of conviction.

PETER W. HALL, Circuit Judge, concurring in part and dissenting in part:

While I concur with my two colleagues that holding onto nonresponsive documents for an extended period of time without some independent basis for retention represents an unreasonable seizure for purposes of the Fourth Amendment, I respectfully dissent from that portion of the opinion which holds that in this case the evidence should be suppressed. * * *

In this case, I cannot agree with the majority's determination that the Government acted in bad faith. The documents were seized pursuant to a warrant and the non-responsive documents were culled and segregated. While testimony reveals that the Government mistakenly considered the mirror images it created of the non-responsive documents as its own property, there was little caselaw either at the time of the search or in the following years to indicate that the Government could not hold onto the non-responsive material in the way it did. Where caselaw existed, the Government complied with the guidelines for the seizure and offsite search of large amounts of documents. See United States v. Tamura, 694 F.2d 591 (9th Cir.1982) (noting that "[i]n the comparatively rare instances where documents are so intermingled that they cannot feasibly be sorted on site," the Government may seize items outside the scope of the warrant under certain conditions). What is more, the Government scrupulously avoided reviewing files that it was not entitled to review before obtaining the 2006 search warrant.

With respect to the balancing between deterrence and the cost of suppression, because the Government's actions did not violate established precedent at the time of the search, I do not perceive a need for deterrence. Additionally, as Ganias himself stated, the evidence to be suppressed in this case would not have existed but for the Government's retention of the non-responsive materials. The evidence to be suppressed is thus, contrary to the majority's conclusion, of the same irreplaceable nature as guns or drugs. Moreover, in light of the serious and nefarious effects of money fraud crimes on society, see, e.g., United States v. Madoff, I am loathe to conclude that guns, drugs and/or contraband are the only indicia of a dangerous defendant. Accordingly, while I agree that the Government violated the defendant's Fourth Amendment rights to be free from an unreasonable seizure because it held for a prolonged period of time mirror images of computer-generated records that were not responsive to the 2003 search warrant without returning them (or destroying them), I see no reason to suppress the evidence derived therefrom under the circumstances presented.

NOTES AND QUESTIONS

1. ***The Challenge of Electronic Searches - How Much Time?*** Was the concern of the Second Circuit in *Ganias* with the amount of time that it took the government to learn about the tax evasion (approximately 2 years)? Or was the problem that by seizing every file from the computer, including those that were clearly outside the scope of the warrant, the government had access to material it otherwise could not have seized if it were searching for physical

items, such as paper files at the defendant's accounting firm? If the investigators had learned about the tax evasion within a year of the search, would that have been too much time? Ninety days? If the concern is with access to evidence that the government should not have available to it, then the passage of time seems to be irrelevant, although it played a significant role in the Second Circuit's analysis.

Another issue in the case is the notion of separating out electronic files that fall outside the warrant and destroying them. When the government seizes a digital storage media, the possibility of separating out individual files may not be possible. For example, one cannot remove a piece of a physical hard drive, and if it that could be done, electronic data is not stored contiguously on the medium. And if the government were to purge files without first obtaining a defendant's consent, a claim could be made that exculpatory evidence was removed, or that the integrity of the electronic files had been compromised, which raises issues about the "chain of custody" for the evidence.

2. ***Computer Search Protocol.*** A warrant that authorizes the search of a computer or server cannot simply permit officers to view every file in search of evidence of a crime. In **United States v. Burgess**, 576 F.3d 1078 (10th Cir. 2009), the Tenth Circuit described the challenges facing investigators in crafting a warrant authorizing a search of a computer:

> It is unrealistic to expect a warrant to prospectively restrict the scope of a search by directory, filename or extension or to attempt to structure search methods—that process must remain dynamic. While file or directory names may sometimes alert one to the contents (e.g., "Russian Lolitas," "meth stuff," or "reagents"), illegal activity may not be advertised even in the privacy of one's personal computer—it could well be coded or otherwise disguised. The directory structure might give hints as to an effective search strategy, but could just as well be misleading and most often could not effectively, or even reasonably, be described or limited in a warrant. Keyword searches may be useful in locating suspect files, but not always. * * * On the other hand the path and/or filename may sometimes give an obscure hint as to the content. * * *
>
> In summary, it is folly for a search warrant to attempt to structure the mechanics of the search and a warrant imposing such limits would unduly restrict legitimate search objectives. One would not ordinarily expect a warrant to search filing cabinets for evidence of drug activity to prospectively restrict the search to "file cabinets in the basement" or to file folders labeled "Meth Lab" or "Customers." And there is no reason to so limit computer searches. But that is not to say methodology is irrelevant.
>
> A warrant may permit only the search of particularly described places and only particularly described things may be seized. As the

description of such places and things becomes more general, the method by which the search is executed become more important—the search method must be tailored to meet allowed ends. And those limits must be functional. For instance, unless specifically authorized by the warrant there would be little reason for officers searching for evidence of drug trafficking to look at tax returns (beyond verifying the folder labeled "2002 Tax Return" actually contains tax returns and not drug files or trophy pictures).

Respect for legitimate rights to privacy in papers and effects requires an officer executing a search warrant to first look in the most obvious places and as it becomes necessary to progressively move from the obvious to the obscure. That is the purpose of a search protocol which structures the search by requiring an analysis of the file structure, next looking for suspicious file folders, then looking for files and types of files most likely to contain the objects of the search by doing keyword searches. But in the end, there may be no practical substitute for actually looking in many (perhaps all) folders and sometimes at the documents contained within those folders, and that is true whether the search is of computer files or physical files. It is particularly true with image files.

Courts have taken a case-by-case approach in scrutinizing warrants to determine whether was probable cause to seize a computer and other types of digital storage devices, and then whether the actual search comported with the requirement to limit the search to those files that reasonably could contain evidence of the offenses described in the warrant. As the Sixth Circuit noted in United States v. Richards, 659 F.3d 527 (6th Cir. 2011), "Applying a reasonableness analysis on a case-by-case basis, the federal courts have rejected most particularity challenges to warrants authorizing the seizure and search of entire personal or business computers."

3. ***Plain View Doctrine***. While many of the exceptions to the warrant requirement, such as the automobile and border search exceptions, are irrelevant in white collar crime cases, the plain view doctrine can play a significant role when agents are executing a search warrant and review documents or computer files that may be relevant. In **Texas v. Brown**, 460 U.S. 730 (1983), the Supreme Court explained the requirements that allow the seizure of an item in plain view:

> First, the police officer must lawfully make an initial intrusion or otherwise properly be in a position from which he can view a particular area. Second, the officer must discover incriminating evidence inadvertently, which is to say, he may not know in advance the location of certain evidence and intend to seize it, relying on the plain view doctrine only as a pretext. Finally, it must be immediately apparent to the police that the items they observe may be evidence of a crime, contraband, or otherwise subject to seizure.

The prerequisite for application of the plain view doctrine to seize an item is that the officer be lawfully present when the observation occurs. In white collar cases, this usually occurs during the execution of a search warrant, when agents may review files to determine whether they come within the scope of the warrant. As *Brown* noted, "'Plain view' is perhaps better understood, therefore, not as an independent 'exception' to the warrant clause, but simply as an extension of whatever the prior justification for an officer's 'access to an object' may be."

In computer searches, the agents will often review all the files in the memory to determine which ones come within the warrant. There is some question whether viewing a file name or even the content of a file constitutes a "seizure" triggering the Fourth Amendment. In United States v. Stabile, 633 F.3d 219 (3d Cir. 2011), the Third Circuit stated, "Mere observation must be distinguished from seizure, a distinction that may become hazy in the digital environment. We do not believe that simply seeing the file names constitutes a seizure."

In **United States v. Gray**, 78 F.Supp. 2d 524 (E.D.Va. 1999), the district court rejected a defendant's challenge to the government's discovery of child pornography while agents were executing a warrant that allowed them to review his computer for files related to a computer intrusion at a government facility. The district court stated:

> The Fourth Amendment requires that a search warrant describe the things to be seized with sufficient particularity to prevent a general exploratory rummaging in a person's belongings. To prevent such rummaging, therefore, a "warrant must enable the executing officer to ascertain and identify with reasonable certainty those items that the magistrate has authorized him to seize." United States v. George, 975 F.2d 72 (2d Cir.1992). In some searches, however, it is not immediately apparent whether or not an object is within the scope of a search warrant; in such cases, an officer must examine the object simply to determine whether or not it is one that he is authorized to seize. Searches of records or documents present a variant of this principle, as documents, unlike illegal drugs or other contraband, may not appear incriminating on their face. As a result, in any search for records or documents, "innocuous records must be examined to determine whether they fall into the category of those papers covered by the search warrant." United States v. Kufrovich, 997 F.Supp. 246 (D.Conn.1997). Although care must be taken to minimize the intrusion, records searches require that many, and often all, documents in the targeted location be searched because "few people keep documents of their criminal transactions in a folder marked 'crime records.' " United States v. Hunter, 13 F.Supp.2d 574 (D.Vt.1998). Thus, agents authorized by warrant to search a home or office for documents containing certain specific information are entitled to examine all files located at the site to look for the specified information. So it is not surprising, then, that in the course

of conducting a lawful search pursuant to a search warrant, law enforcement agents often discover evidence of criminal activity other than that which is the subject of the warrant. If an agent sees, in plain view, evidence of criminal activity other than that for which she is searching, this does not constitute an unreasonable search under the Fourth Amendment, for "[v]iewing an article that is already in plain view does not involve an invasion of privacy." United States v. Jackson, 131 F.3d 1105 (4th Cir.1997). Further, such evidence may be seized under the "plain view" exception to the warrant requirement, provided that "(1) the officer is lawfully in a place from which the object may be plainly viewed; (2) the officer has a lawful right of access to the object itself; and (3) the object's incriminating character is immediately apparent." *Jackson*. These principles applied in the context of a document or record search means that, if an agent searching files pursuant to a search warrant discovers a document that contains evidence of another crime, that document can be seized under the "plain view" exception to the warrant requirement.

4. ***Reviewing Electronic Files.*** Federal Rule of Criminal Procedure 41(e)(2)(B), discussed in *Ganias*, provides that the timing for the execution of a warrant only relates to when the computer and other electronic media are seized, and not when the files are actually reviewed. The Rule provides that "[u]nless otherwise specified, the warrant authorizes a later review of the media or information consistent with the warrant." It is a standard practice for a computer specialist to create an electronic image of a computer hard drive and other storage devices and then return those items to the owner so that the search can be conducted later. How quickly must the government conduct the search of the files? In **United States v. Metter**, 860 F.Supp.2d 205 (E.D.N.Y. 2012), a district court concluded that the government acted unreasonably when it took no steps to review the files seized within a reasonable amount of time:

> The government seized 61 computer hard drives from Spongetech, four computer hard drives from Metter's home, and a snapshot of all of the activity that had occurred in Metter's personal email account. The government then promptly imaged the hard drives and returned them to their respective owners. Up to this point, there is nothing problematic with the manner in which the government executed the warrants. The point at which the government faltered is its delay in reviewing the imaged evidence to determine whether the evidence that the government seized and imaged fell within the scope of the categories of information sought in the search warrants.
>
> The Court recognizes that under current law there is no established upper limit as to when the government must review seized electronic data to determine whether the evidence seized falls within the scope of a warrant. However, the Fourth Amendment requires the government to complete its review, i.e., execute the warrant, within

> a "reasonable" period of time. Numerous cases hold that a delay of several months between the seizure of electronic evidence and the completion of the government's review of that evidence as to whether it falls within the scope of the warrant is reasonable.
>
> The parties have not provided the Court with any authority, nor has the Court found any, indicating that the government may seize and image electronic data and then retain that data with no plans whatsoever to begin review of that data to determine whether any irrelevant, personal information was improperly seized. The government's blatant disregard for its responsibility in this case is unacceptable and unreasonable. * * * The government's retention of all imaged electronic documents, including personal emails, without any review whatsoever to determine not only their relevance to this case, but also to determine whether any recognized legal privileges attached to them, is unreasonable and disturbing.

5. ***Warrantless Workplace Searches.*** "The rules for conducting warrantless searches and seizures in private-sector workplaces generally mirror the rules for conducting warrantless searches in homes and other personal residences. Private company employees generally retain a reasonable expectation of privacy in their workplaces. As a result, searches by law enforcement of a private workplace will usually require a warrant unless the agents can obtain the consent of an employer or a co-worker with common authority." SEARCHING AND SEIZING COMPUTERS § I.D.1. Public employer workplace searches, including computers, are much murkier. In **O'Connor v. Ortega**, 480 U.S. 709 (1987), Justice O'Connor's plurality decision offered a totality-of-the-circumstances test for determining when a public employer could search the office or workspace of a public employee. In *O'Connor*, the plaintiff, Dr. Ortega, filed a § 1983 suit against the public hospital where he worked because a search of his office violated his Fourth Amendment rights. The plurality analyzed whether a public employee has a reasonable expectation of privacy in the workplace in this way:

> [I]t is essential first to delineate the boundaries of the workplace context. The workplace includes those areas and items that are related to work and are generally within the employer's control. At a hospital, for example, the hallways, cafeteria, offices, desks, and file cabinets, among other areas, are all part of the workplace. These areas remain part of the workplace context even if the employee has placed personal items in them, such as a photograph placed in a desk or a letter posted on an employee bulletin board.
>
> Not everything that passes through the confines of the business address can be considered part of the workplace context, however. An employee may bring closed luggage to the office prior to leaving on a trip, or a handbag or briefcase each workday. While whatever expectation of privacy the employee has in the existence and the outward appearance of the luggage is affected by its presence in the

workplace, the employee's expectation of privacy in the *contents* of the luggage is not affected in the same way. The appropriate standard for a workplace search does not necessarily apply to a piece of closed personal luggage, a handbag or a briefcase that happens to be within the employer's business address.

Within the workplace context, this Court has recognized that employees may have a reasonable expectation of privacy against intrusions by police. * * *

[W]e reject the contention made by the Solicitor General and petitioners that public employees can never have a reasonable expectation of privacy in their place of work. Individuals do not lose Fourth Amendment rights merely because they work for the government instead of a private employer. The operational realities of the workplace, however, may make *some* employees' expectations of privacy unreasonable when an intrusion is by a supervisor rather than a law enforcement official. Public employees' expectations of privacy in their offices, desks, and file cabinets, like similar expectations of employees in the private sector, may be reduced by virtue of actual office practices and procedures, or by legitimate regulation. * * * The employee's expectation of privacy must be assessed in the context of the employment relation. An office is seldom a private enclave free from entry by supervisors, other employees, and business and personal invitees. Instead, in many cases offices are continually entered by fellow employees and other visitors during the workday for conferences, consultations, and other work-related visits. Simply put, it is the nature of government offices that others–such as fellow employees, supervisors, consensual visitors, and the general public–may have frequent access to an individual's office. We agree with Justice Scalia that "[c]onstitutional protection against *unreasonable* searches by the government does not disappear merely because the government has the right to make reasonable intrusions in its capacity as employer," but some government offices may be so open to fellow employees or the public that no expectation of privacy is reasonable. [The Court determined that Dr. Ortega had a reasonable expectation of privacy in his desk and file cabinets.] * * *

The legitimate privacy interests of public employees in the private objects they bring to the workplace may be substantial. Against these privacy interests, however, must be balanced the realities of the workplace, which strongly suggest that a warrant requirement would be unworkable. While police, and even administrative enforcement personnel, conduct searches for the primary purpose of obtaining evidence for use in criminal or other enforcement proceedings, employers most frequently need to enter the offices and desks of their employees for legitimate work-related reasons wholly unrelated to illegal conduct. Employers and supervisors are focused primarily on the need to complete the government agency's work in a prompt and efficient manner. An employer may have need for correspondence, or a file or report available only in an employee's office while the employee is away from the office. Or, as is alleged to have been the case here, employers may need to safeguard or identify state property or records in an office in connection with a pending investigation into suspected employee misfeasance.

In our view, requiring an employer to obtain a warrant whenever the employer wished to enter an employee's office, desk, or file cabinets for a work-related purpose would seriously disrupt the routine conduct of business and would be unduly burdensome. Imposing unwieldy warrant procedures in such cases upon supervisors, who would otherwise have no reason to be familiar with such procedures, is simply unreasonable. In contrast to other circumstances in which we have required warrants, supervisors in offices such as at the Hospital are hardly in the business of investigating the violation of criminal laws. Rather, work-related searches are merely incident to the primary business of the agency. Under these circumstances, the imposition of a warrant requirement would conflict with "the common-sense realization that government offices could not function if every employment decision became a constitutional matter." Connick v. Myers, 461 U.S. 138 (1983).***

As an initial matter, it is important to recognize the plethora of contexts in which employers will have an occasion to intrude to some extent on an employee's expectation of privacy. Because the parties in this case have alleged that the search was either a noninvestigatory work-related intrusion or an investigatory search for evidence of suspected work-related employee misfeasance, we undertake to determine the appropriate Fourth Amendment standard of reasonableness *only* for these two types of employer intrusions and leave for another day inquiry into other circumstances. * * *

In our view, therefore, a probable cause requirement for searches of the type at issue here would impose intolerable burdens on public employers. The delay in correcting the employee misconduct caused by the need for probable cause rather than reasonable suspicion will be translated into tangible and often irreparable damage to the agency's work, and ultimately to the public interest. * * * It is simply unrealistic to expect supervisors in most government agencies to learn the subtleties of the probable cause standard. * * *

In sum, we conclude that the "special needs, beyond the normal need for law enforcement make the . . . probable-cause requirement impracticable," for legitimate work-related, noninvestigatory intrusions as well as investigations of work-related misconduct. A standard of reasonableness will neither unduly burden the efforts of

> government employers to ensure the efficient and proper operation of the workplace, nor authorize arbitrary intrusions upon the privacy of public employees. We hold, therefore, that public employer intrusions on the constitutionally protected privacy interests of government employees for noninvestigatory, work-related purposes, as well as for investigations of work-related misconduct, should be judged by the standard of reasonableness under all the circumstances. Under this reasonableness standard, both the inception and the scope of the intrusion must be reasonable[.] * * *

Justice Scalia concurred in the judgment, but criticized the vagueness of the plurality's approach to determining whether a public employee has a legitimate expectation of privacy in the workplace and whether the search was reasonable:

> The plurality opinion instructs the lower courts that existence of Fourth Amendment protection for a public employee's business office is to be assessed "on a case-by-case basis," in light of whether the office is "so open to fellow employees or the public that no expectation of privacy is reasonable." No clue is provided as to how open "so open" must be; much less is it suggested how police officers are to gather the facts necessary for this refined inquiry. * * *
>
> Even if I did not disagree with the plurality as to what result the proper legal standard should produce in the case before us, I would object to the formulation of a standard so devoid of content that it produces rather than eliminates uncertainty in this field. * * *
>
> I cannot agree, moreover, with the plurality's view that the reasonableness of the expectation of privacy (and thus the existence of Fourth Amendment protection) changes "when an intrusion is by a supervisor rather than a law enforcement official." The identity of the searcher (police v. employer) is relevant not to whether Fourth Amendment protections apply, but only to whether the search of a protected area is reasonable.

Can a public employee ever have a reasonable expectation of privacy in files stored on a computer used in a public workplace, even if that person is the only one who uses the computer? What if the files were protected by a password known only to the employee, and did not include any material for use in the agency's public function? If the use of a public employer's computer for private purposes is prohibited–which is normally the case–then that misconduct would seem to permit a supervisor to access any files on the computer in an investigation of "work-related employee misfeasance" under the plurality's analysis in O'Connor v. Ortega.

E. LAW OFFICE SEARCHES

Attorneys may be involved in the crimes of their clients, either as direct participants or in advising them how to avoid detection. The issue of searching a law office for evidence is complex because of the presence of documents subject to protection from disclosure under the attorney-client privilege and the work product doctrine. The prospect of government agents rummaging through a law firm's files, searching for evidence of wrongdoing, is a particularly chilling thought.

The Department of Justice sought to balance the need to fully investigate wrongdoing by allowing searches of law offices with the need to be sensitive to confidentiality concerns not encompassed by the Fourth Amendment's warrant requirement. The *U.S. Attorney's Manual* § 9-13.420 requires that prosecutors and investigators follow procedures to limit the possibility that confidential documents and information that falls outside the scope of the search warrant will be reviewed by the government. Section 9-13.420 covers cases involving "a search warrant for the premises of an attorney who is a suspect, subject or target of a criminal investigation where information relating to the representation of clients is likely to be present and subject to search . . . [T]o avoid impinging on valid attorney-client relationships, prosecutors are expected to take the least intrusive approach consistent with vigorous and effective law enforcement when evidence is sought from an attorney actively engaged in the practice of law." Accordingly, consideration should be given to "alternatives to search warrants", such as "obtaining information from other sources or through the use of a subpoena." Where the prosecutor concludes that a warrant is needed, the Department of Justice requires that the application for the warrant be approved by "the United States Attorney or pertinent Assistant Attorney General." Ordinarily, authorization will be granted "only when there is a strong need for the information or material and less intrusive means have been considered and rejected."

In addition to the required authorization, prior consultation with the Criminal Division is required. The prosecutor is directed to submit to that office a form explaining why the search is desired, why alternatives means have been rejected, and what procedures are to be followed "to protect privilege and to ensure the prosecution is not tainted." The policy directive adds the following commentary on what is expected in conducting the search:

> **Safeguarding Procedures and Contents of the Affidavit.** Procedures should be designed to ensure that privileged materials are not improperly viewed, seized or retained during the course of the search. While the procedures to be followed should be tailored to the facts of each case and the requirements and judicial preferences and precedents of each district, in all cases a prosecutor must employ adequate precautions to ensure that the materials are

reviewed for privilege claims and that any privileged documents are returned to the attorney from whom they were seized.

Conducting the Search. The search warrant should be drawn as specifically as possible, consistent with the requirements of the investigation, to minimize the need to search and review privileged material to which no exception applies.

While every effort should be made to avoid viewing privileged material, the search may require limited review of arguably privileged material to ascertain whether the material is covered by the warrant. Therefore, to protect the attorney-client privilege and to ensure that the investigation is not compromised by exposure to privileged material relating to the investigation or to defense strategy, a "privilege team" should be designated, consisting of agents and lawyers not involved in the underlying investigation.

Instructions should be given and thoroughly discussed with the privilege team prior to the search. The instructions should set forth procedures designed to minimize the intrusion into privileged material, and should ensure that the privilege team does not disclose any information to the investigation/prosecution team unless and until so instructed by the attorney in charge of the privilege team. Privilege team lawyers should be available either on or off-site, to advise the agents during the course of the search, but should not participate in the search itself.

The affidavit in support of the search warrant may attach any written instructions or, at a minimum, should generally state the government's intention to employ procedures designed to ensure that attorney-client privileges are not violated.

If it is anticipated that computers will be searched or seized, prosecutors are expected to follow the procedures set forth in Federal Guidelines for Searching and Seizing Computers (July 1994), published by the Criminal Division Office of Professional Training and Development.

Review Procedures. The following review procedures should be discussed prior to approval of any warrant, consistent with the practice in your district, the circumstances of the investigation and the volume of materials seized.

- Who will conduct the review, i.e., a privilege team, a judicial officer, or a special master.
- Whether all documents will be submitted to a judicial officer or special master or only those which a privilege team has

determined to be arguably privileged or arguably subject to an exception to the privilege.

- Whether copies of all seized materials will be provided to the subject attorney (or a legal representative) in order that: a) disruption of the law firm's operation is minimized; and b) the subject is afforded an opportunity to participate in the process of submitting disputed documents to the court by raising specific claims of privilege. To the extent possible, providing copies of seized records is encouraged, where such disclosure will not impede or obstruct the investigation.

- Whether appropriate arrangements have been made for storage and handling of electronic evidence and procedures developed for searching computer data (i.e., procedures which recognize the universal nature of computer seizure and are designed to avoid review of materials implicating the privilege of innocent clients).

The use of a "privilege team" or "taint team" comprised of federal prosecutors has been criticized as not being fully protective of the attorney-client privilege. **In re Grand Jury Subpoenas**, 454 F.3d 511 (6th Cir. 2006), considered the use of a taint team in connection with a grand jury subpoena to a company as part of an investigation of its former owner, who claimed that certain materials at the company contained communications protected by the attorney-client privilege. In rejecting the government's suggestion that a taint team should review the subpoenaed materials to determine what was privileged, the court noted:

> Yet the taint team procedure would present a great risk to the appellants' continued enjoyment of privilege protections. In the first place, government taint teams seem to be used primarily in limited, exigent circumstances in which government officials have already obtained the physical control of potentially-privileged documents through the exercise of a search warrant. In such cases, the potentially-privileged documents are already in the government's possession, and so the use of the taint team to sift the wheat from the chaff constitutes an action respectful of, rather than injurious to, the protection of privilege. But the government does not actually possess the potentially-privileged materials here, so the exigency typically underlying the use of taint teams is not present.
>
> Furthermore, taint teams present inevitable, and reasonably foreseeable, risks to privilege, for they have been implicated in the past in leaks of confidential information to prosecutors. That is to say, the government taint team may have an interest in preserving privilege, but it also possesses a conflicting interest in pursuing the investigation, and, human nature being what it is, occasionally some taint-team attorneys will make mistakes or violate their ethical obligations. It is thus logical to suppose that taint teams pose a

> serious risk to holders of privilege, and this supposition is substantiated by past experience. In *United States v. Noriega*, 764 F.Supp. 1480 (S.D.Fla.1991), for instance, the government's taint team missed a document obviously protected by attorney-client privilege, by turning over tapes of attorney-client conversations to members of the investigating team. This Noriega incident points to an obvious flaw in the taint team procedure: the government's fox is left in charge of the appellants' henhouse, and may err by neglect or malice, as well as by honest differences of opinion.
>
> It is reasonable to presume that the government's taint team might have a more restrictive view of privilege than appellants' attorneys. But under the taint team procedure, appellants' attorneys would have an opportunity to assert privilege only over those documents which the taint team has identified as being clearly or possibly privileged. As such, we do not see any check in the proposed taint team review procedure against the possibility that the government's team might make some false negative conclusions, finding validly privileged documents to be otherwise; that is to say, we can find no check against Type II errors in the government's proposed procedure. On the other hand, under the appellants' proposal, which incidentally seems to follow a fairly conventional privilege review procedure employed by law firms in response to discovery requests, the government would still enjoy the opportunity to challenge any documents that appellants' attorneys misidentify (via the commission of Type I errors) as privileged. We thus find that, under these circumstances, the possible damage to the appellants' interest in protecting privilege exceeds the possible damage to the government's interest in grand jury secrecy and exigency in this case.

District courts have not been as hostile to this procedure as the Sixth Circuit and have authorized the government to use a "taint team" to review materials to determine initially whether they are subject to a valid claim of privilege. See In re Ingram, 915 F. Supp. 2d 761 (E.D. La. 2012) ("The Court finds that the government's proposed filter team protocol shows proper deference to any attorney-client or work product privileges while allowing the government's investigation to proceed."); United States v. Taylor, 764 F. Supp. 2d 230 (D. Me. 2011) ("The defendant does not contend that there has been any sharing of information between the filter agent and the case prosecutor or investigating agent and has not asked for an evidentiary hearing on this issue.").

NOTES

1. ***ALI Procedures***. The American Law Institute (ALI) adopted in 1975 a Model Code of Pre-Arraignment Procedure that includes a section entitled

"Execution and Return of Warrants for Documents" that provides procedures for seizing records, including those from a law office:

> (1) *Identification of Documents to Be Seized.* If the warrant authorizes documentary seizure *** the executing officer shall endeavor by all appropriate means to search for and identify the documents to be seized without examining the contents of documents not covered by the warrant. * * *
>
> (2) *Intermingled Documents.* If the documents to be seized cannot be searched for or identified without examining the contents of other documents, or if they constitute item or entries in account books, diaries, or other documents containing matter not specified in the warrant, the executing officer shall not examine the documents but shall either impound them under appropriate protection where found, or seal and remove them for safekeeping pending further proceedings pursuant to Subsection (3) of this Section.
>
> (3) *Return of intermingled Documents.* An executing officer who has impounded or removed documents pursuant to Subsection (2) of this Section shall, as promptly as practicable, report the fact and circumstances of the impounding or removal to the issuing official. As soon thereafter as the interests of justice permit, and upon due and reasonable notice to all interested persons, a hearing shall be held before the issuing official, *** at which the person from whose possession or control the documents were taken, and any other person asserting any right or interest in the document, may appear, in person or by counsel, and move (a) for the return of the documents, *** in whole or in part, or (b) for specification of such conditions and limitations on the further search for the documents to be seized as may be appropriate to prevent unnecessary or unreasonable invasion of privacy. * * * If the motion is not granted, the search shall proceed under such conditions and limitations as the order shall prescribe. * * *

In **United States v. Mittelman**, 999 F.2d 440 (9th Cir. 1992), an FBI agent assured the federal magistrate in seeking a warrant that the government would comply with the ALI procedures, but then failed to follow them as promised. The district court ordered that suppression of the evidence seized pursuant to the warrant under Franks v. Delaware because the agent knowingly or recklessly made false statements to the magistrate. The Ninth Circuit reversed, noting:

> [W]hile we agree that special care should be taken when conducting a search of law offices, separate legal rules are not necessary for remedying such searches when they exceed the scope of the warrant. [The exclusionary rule is] fully applicable to law office searches, [and] provide[s] ample protection and relief. *Tamura* is an instructive example in this regard. After suggesting the use of [the

> ALI] procedures designed to protect privacy interests during document searches, we nonetheless applied the traditional remedy for searches which exceed the scope of the warrant: we first examined whether the government had engaged in "indiscriminate fishing," and having determined it did not, we concluded that suppression was required of only that evidence seized outside the scope of the warrant. We vacate the suppression order and remand to allow the district court to determine first whether the search of Reeves's law office amounted to an "impermissible general search." If it did, suppressing all of the evidence seized during the search is appropriate. If the violations of the search warrant were not so extreme as to justify this extraordinary remedy, the district court should determine what evidence, if any, was seized in violation of the warrant and order the suppression of that evidence only.

2. ***Right to Practice Law.*** In **Conn v. Gabbert**, 526 U.S. 286 (1999), the Supreme Court unanimously rejected the Ninth Circuit's holding that a search warrant served on a lawyer, which was designed to interfere with his representation of a client currently testifying before a grand jury, violated the lawyer's Fourteenth Amendment right to practice his profession and therefore states a claim for damages under § 1983. The Court stated, "We hold that the Fourteenth Amendment right to practice one's calling is not violated by the execution of a search warrant, whether calculated to annoy or even to prevent consultation with a grand jury witness. In so holding, we thus of course pretermit the question whether such a right was 'clearly established' as of a given day."

CHAPTER THIRTEEN
SELF-INCRIMINATION PRIVILEGE

A. THE PRIVILEGE AGAINST SELF-INCRIMINATION

At trial, a criminal defendant exercises the Fifth Amendment privilege against self-incrimination by declining to testify. The prosecution may not call the defendant as a witness at the defendant's own trial and force the defendant to claim the privilege in response to each question asked by the prosecutor. While the Fifth Amendment also applies in the grand jury, federal courts have long held that the grand jury is not similarly prohibited from calling to testify a person that it expects to indict and thereby forcing that person to exercise the privilege as to individual questions.

The privilege against self-incrimination only applies if the testimony of the person claiming the privilege would be "incriminating." What standard determines whether testimony has that quality and who makes that determination? Both of these critical questions were largely resolved in **Hoffman v. United States**, 341 U.S. 479 (1951). In that case, a witness subpoenaed before a federal grand jury relied on the privilege in refusing to answer questions as to his current occupation and his contacts with a fugitive witness. The district court found that there was "no real and substantial danger of incrimination" and the privilege therefore was inapplicable. When the witness persisted in his claim, he was held in contempt. In reversing that conviction, the Supreme Court set forth the following guidelines for the district court:

> This provision of the [Fifth] Amendment must be accorded liberal construction in favor of the right it was intended to secure. The privilege afforded not only extends to answers that would in themselves support a conviction under a federal criminal statute but likewise embraces those which would furnish a link in the chain of evidence needed to prosecute the claimant for a federal crime. But this protection must be confined to instances where the witness has reasonable cause to apprehend danger from a direct answer. The witness is not exonerated from answering merely because he declares that in so doing he would incriminate himself–his say-so does not of itself establish the hazard of incrimination. It is for the court to say whether his silence is justified, and to require him to answer if 'it clearly appears to the court that he is mistaken.' However, if the witness, upon interposing his claim, were required to prove the hazard in the sense in which a claim is usually required to be established in court, he would be compelled to surrender the very protection which the privilege is designed to guarantee. To

> sustain the privilege, it need only be evident from the implications of the question, in the setting in which it is asked, that a responsive answer to the question or an explanation of why it cannot be answered might be dangerous because injurious disclosure could result.

Applying these guidelines, the Supreme Court concluded that the privilege clearly was available to the witness Hoffman. Since the district court was aware that the grand jury was investigating racketeering, it should have recognized that questions concerning Hoffman's current occupation might require answers relating to violations of federal gambling laws. It also should have recognized that the questions concerning Hoffman's contacts with the fugitive witness might relate to efforts to hide that witness.

Under the *Hoffman* guidelines it will be a rare case in which a court can properly reject a witness' assertion of the privilege. Is the case that follows such a situation?

In re MORGANROTH v. FITZSIMMONS

718 F.2d 161 (6th Cir. 1983)

KENNEDY, Circuit Judge.

Petitioner Morganroth seeks review of an order directing him to answer deposition questions to which he asserted his fifth amendment right to remain silent on the ground that his answers might tend to subject him to criminal liability. In 1975 the Central States, Southeast & Southwest Areas Pension Fund made a loan to Indico Corporation of $7,000,000. Morganroth was president of Indico Corporation at that time. Subsequently, Indico defaulted on the loan and as a result the Pension Fund suffered significant losses on its investment. Morganroth has since been involved in a number of lawsuits. He was indicted by a federal grand jury on conspiracy and mail and wire fraud charges arising out of this loan transaction with the Pension Fund. On October 20, 1979, subsequent to his indictment, Morganroth was deposed in a civil action * * * then pending in a Florida state court. This civil case was a foreclosure proceeding in connection with the same loan. At that deposition Morganroth appeared voluntarily and answered all questions put to him. Morganroth is himself an attorney. In March 1980, Morganroth was acquitted of the federal criminal charges. It appears that after his acquittal, Morganroth was subpoenaed to appear before a New York federal grand jury and was asked the same set of questions which he voluntarily answered in the Florida state foreclosure proceeding. Morganroth asserted his fifth amendment privilege to these same questions. Immunity was conferred upon Morganroth, his testimony given, and thereafter he was advised by one of the prosecutors that his testimony was in serious conflict with that of others appearing before the grand jury.

Subsequent to his acquittal and the immunized testimony before the New York federal grand jury, the Secretary of Labor subpoenaed Morganroth to appear for a deposition as a non-party witness in this civil action * * *. [T]he Secretary has alleged that defendants, who are former trustees and officials of the * * * Pension Fund, imprudently made, administered and monitored certain investments on behalf of the Fund in violation of their fiduciary obligations under the Employee Retirement Income Security Act. At the deposition, Morganroth was represented by counsel. He answered questions under oath. After providing information as to his name, address and occupation, Morganroth individually refused to answer each question propounded to him by counsel for the Secretary of Labor on the ground that each answer might tend to incriminate him, without elaborating further. The questions he refused to answer * * * covered the same aspects of the Indico loan transaction with the * * * Pension Fund about which he had previously given deposition answers voluntarily in the Florida state foreclosure proceeding * * * and pursuant to the grant of immunity in the New York federal grand jury proceeding. As a result, the Secretary of Labor moved the District Court * * * for an order pursuant to Fed.R.Civ.P. 37(a) compelling Morganroth to answer these questions on the grounds that he had waived any Fifth Amendment right he had with respect to these questions by answering virtually identical questions in the Florida state foreclosure proceeding and that he had no legitimate Fifth Amendment right to assert because there was no reasonable likelihood of criminal prosecution, given his acquittal in March 1980, that would flow from the answers requested. The District Court ordered Morganroth to testify [relying upon the waiver ground] * * *. The District Court did, however, confine the Secretary of Labor to asking only the identical questions asked at the prior deposition.

Morganroth then filed for certification under 28 U.S.C. § 1292(b) [and the] * * * District Court granted the motion and certified the [waiver] question * * *. In granting Morganroth's petition for leave to appeal, this Court stated that it may consider other issues raised in the order of the District Court even though they were not included in the certified question formulated by the District Court.* * *

In this appeal, Morganroth urges that this Court reject the "minority" rule [on waiver] adopted by the District Court, or its application of that rule, and adopt the "majority" rule that waiver of the privilege and voluntary testimony in response to specific questions or a particular subject matter in one proceeding does not constitute a waiver of the fifth amendment privilege with respect to identical questions or a particular subject matter in a second proceeding if the witness remains at risk for the same offense. * * * The policy behind the majority rule that the privilege is "proceeding specific" and not waived in a subsequent proceeding by waiver in an earlier one, rests on the thought that during the period between the successive proceedings conditions might have changed creating new grounds for apprehension, e.g., the passage of new criminal law, or that the witness might be subject to different interrogation for different purposes at a subsequent proceeding, or that repetition of testimony in an independent proceeding might itself be incriminating, even if it merely repeated or acknowledged the witness' earlier testimony, because it could constitute an independent source of evidence against him or her.

The Secretary of Labor urges that the District Court correctly adopted and applied the minority rule set forth in Ellis v. United States, 416 F.2d 791 (D.C.Cir.1969). In *Ellis*, the court held that a waiver of the assertion of a valid privilege in one proceeding, where a witness places himself or herself at risk of prosecution for a particular offense, constitutes a waiver of the privilege in all subsequent proceedings in response to the identical questions or the same general subject matter where the risk of prosecution for the identical offense remains the same. * * * The rationale behind the minority view of Ellis is that, absent intervening circumstances, a witness' repetition of the same information in a subsequent proceeding for which he originally placed himself at risk of prosecution in an earlier proceeding would not expose him to any real danger of legal harm to which he had not already exposed himself by virtue of his prior voluntary testimony. The rationale of the minority view of *Ellis* applies only where the witness faces the identical risk of prosecution in both proceedings in which he is called upon to testify. The *Ellis* court's exception recognizes this limitation.

We need not reach the issue of whether this Circuit should adopt the majority or minority view on waiver * * * because we find neither applicable to a factual situation where a fifth amendment privilege is asserted solely because the witness alleges he is apprehensive of providing incriminating evidence in regard to a possible perjury charge stemming from responses in an earlier proceeding under oath.[1] The District Court's adoption and application of the minority view is inappropriate in this case because the minority view presumes that the witness is facing identical risks in both proceedings. In contrast, as in this case, once a witness has testified under oath initially, the risk of prosecution which the witness faced in the earlier proceeding is not identical even though the questions may be the same in a subsequent proceeding or the same subject matter covered. Once a witness has testified under oath, he risks the possibility of perjury charges in addition to any risk he may face for prosecution for non-perjury offenses suggested by his testimony. * * * The risk of prosecution for which Morganroth has articulated a fear of prosecution in this case is that for perjury in his prior testimony. This possibility of prosecution exists independently of and is unaffected by his acquittal of federal conspiracy and mail and wire fraud charges. It is unclear whether he fears perjury charges stemming from his deposition testimony in the Florida state foreclosure proceeding or his New

[1] We also note that the Supreme Court's recent decision in Pillsbury Co. v. Conboy, 459 U.S. 248 (1983), raises doubt as to the continued validity of the *Ellis* Court's view. In *Conboy*, the Supreme Court emphasized that: "Questions do not incriminate; answers do." The Court reasoned that "answers to such questions 'are derived from the deponent's current, independent memory of events' and thus 'necessarily create a new source of evidence' that could incriminate a witness and could be used in a subsequent criminal prosecution against him."

York federal grand jury testimony. Either could provide a basis for a valid assertion of the privilege. * * * Therefore, because Morganroth alleges he is presently at risk for a different crime than those for which he initially faced a reasonable risk of prosecution, the question of whether the minority view should control the waiver issue is not properly raised by the facts.

We do, however, consider another issue raised by the order of the District Court even though not included in the certified question. At issue is what sort of showing must be made by a witness to justify the invocation of the fifth amendment privilege when the only possible risk of prosecution which might flow from testimony in a subsequent proceeding is for perjury.

We conclude that it is not enough that Morganroth answer each deposition question propounded by the Secretary of Labor with the conclusory statement: "I refuse to answer on the ground that the answer might tend to incriminate me." Morganroth must supply such additional statements under oath and other evidence to the District Court in response to each question propounded so as to enable the District Court to reasonably identify the nature of the criminal charge for which Morganroth fears prosecution, i.e., perjury and to discern a sound basis for the witness' reasonable fear of prosecution.

Before a witness, such as Morganroth, is entitled to remain silent, there must be a valid assertion of the fifth amendment privilege. It is for the court to decide whether a witness' silence is justified and to require him to answer if it clearly appears to the court that the witness asserting the privilege is mistaken as to its validity. *Hoffman.* A valid assertion of the fifth amendment privilege exists where a witness has reasonable cause to apprehend a real danger of incrimination. Id. A witness must, however, show a "real danger," and not a mere imaginary, remote or speculative possibility of prosecution. * * * While the privilege is to be accorded liberal application, the court may order a witness to answer if it clearly appears that he is mistaken as to the justification for the privilege in advancing his claim as a subterfuge. *Hoffman.* A blanket assertion of the privilege by a witness is not sufficient to meet the reasonable cause requirement and the privilege cannot be claimed in advance of the questions. The privilege must be asserted by a witness with respect to particular questions, and in each instance, the court must determine the propriety of the refusal to testify. See *Hoffman.*

A witness risks a real danger of prosecution if an answer to a question, on its face, calls for the admission of a crime or requires that the witness supply evidence of a necessary element of a crime or furnishes a link in the chain of evidence needed to prosecute. In *Hoffman*, the Supreme Court held that a real danger of prosecution also exists where questions, which appear on their face to call only for innocent answers, are dangerous in light of other facts already developed. In such a situation a witness bears no further burden of establishing a reasonable cause to fear prosecution beyond asserting the privilege and identifying the nature of the criminal charge or supplying sufficient facts so that a particular criminal charge can reasonably be identified by the court. The witness has met his burden and the court does not need to inquire further as to the validity of the assertion of the privilege, if it is evident from the implications of a question, in the setting in which it is asked, that a responsive answer might be dangerous to the witness because an injurious disclosure could result. * * *

The facts of this case make the *Hoffman* approach to a witness' burden of establishing a foundation for the reasonable cause determination, or rather lack of it, inapplicable. Morganroth is allegedly raising the specter of a perjury prosecution; i.e., his proposed truthful testimony might provide evidence that he had perjured himself in earlier proceedings under oath. Like *Hoffman*, the questions propounded to Morganroth appear on their face to be innocent. Unlike *Hoffman*, the present setting, in which the questions were propounded and representations made, sheds no light whatsoever on whether Morganroth's proposed truthful answers would constitute injurious disclosures in light of his previous testimony on the same subject matter in earlier proceedings.

The *Hoffman* guidelines for determining whether an assertion of the privilege against self-incrimination should be respected works well in cases in which an individual is at risk of prosecution on substantive charges or in which an individual expresses a concern of perjury prosecution stemming from statements made in earlier proceedings in which the trial judge has a personal familiarity. The *Hoffman* guidelines, however, are of little help in a case such as the one on appeal where the District Court making the privilege determination has no personal knowledge of the scope of content of prior proceedings and where the only possible prosecution for which the witness is at risk is perjury. This is due to the nature of the perjury offense in relation to the assertion of the privilege and the inability of the trial court, in this case and others like it, to draw upon its own knowledge of the case. In *Hoffman*, the Supreme Court stressed facts within the knowledge of the trial court. There the trial court was instructed that the privilege be "evident from the implications of the question in the setting in which it was asked," that the determination be governed "as much by his [trial judge's] personal perception of the particularities of the case as by the facts actually in evidence," and that it consider the "circumstances" of the case. *Hoffman*. *Hoffman* is typical of subsequent cases applying the *Hoffman* guidelines. As in *Hoffman*, those cases, in contrast to the one on appeal, reveal a superior knowledge by the trial court of the "setting in which it [the questions to which the privilege is sought] is asked." * * *

This case is in sharp contrast to *Hoffman* * * *. The trial court did not have any background familiarity with the setting in which the assertion was raised. The District Court had not participated in either the grand jury matter in New York or the Florida foreclosure proceeding. With respect to the New York grand jury statements, he did not even know the substance of those statements, the nature of the conflicting testimony by other witnesses or contradictory documentary evidence which might tend to show that Morganroth had perjured himself in that proceeding. Nor did Morganroth apprise the District Court that his testimony or deposition answers would differ from statements given in the earlier proceedings. The District Court in this case was merely informed by Morganroth's attorney that there was a possibility that material inconsistencies would exist between his proposed testimony, based on his current memory of the loan transactions, and prior testimony. This possibility, however, exists in every case in which a witness has given prior testimony. Thus, perjury prosecutions which are prospective and possible in nature present special problems in determining appropriate invocation of the fifth amendment right.

Whether a witness risks a "real danger" of prosecution from questions which appear on their face to call for only innocent answers and where the incriminating nature of the answer is not evident from the implications of the question in the setting in which it is asked, is a difficult question left unanswered by *Hoffman*. On one hand, while it is clear that a witness, upon interposing his claim of privilege, is not required to prove the hazard in the sense in which a claim is usually required to be established in court, it is equally clear that a witness' "say so" does not by itself establish the hazard of incrimination. *Hoffman*. Where there is nothing suggestive of incrimination about the setting in which a seemingly innocent question is asked, the burden of establishing a foundation for the assertion of the privilege should lie with the witness making it. We do not hold, however, that a witness has the burden of proof on this issue. A witness presents sufficient evidence to establish a foundation for the assertion of the privilege and shows a real danger of prosecution if it is not perfectly clear to the court "from a careful consideration of all of the circumstances in the case, that a witness is mistaken, and that the answer[s] cannot possibly have such a tendency to incriminate." *Hoffman*. Stated differently, sufficient evidence is presented by a witness if a court can, by the use of reasonable inference or judicial imagination, conceive a sound basis for a reasonable fear of prosecution. Short of uttering statements or supplying evidence that would be incriminating, a witness must supply personal statements under oath or provide evidence with respect to each question propounded to him to indicate the nature of the criminal charge which provides the basis for his fear of prosecution[2] and, if necessary to complement non-testimonial evidence,

---

[2] With respect to each question for which the privilege is asserted, it is important to the court's reasonable cause determination that Morganroth swear under oath or provide other evidence that the criminal charge for which he has reasonable cause to fear prosecution is perjury. Here he stated only that the issue would tend to incriminate him. This fear may have been based on the mistaken belief he could still be prosecuted for some statute of limitations barred offense. While no ritualistic formula or talismanic phrase is necessary to invoke the privilege, a court cannot be asked to scan all of the law for a possible connection between a question and a criminal offense. To impose such a duty on courts in response to a mere assertion of the privilege, without elaboration, in response to seemingly innocent questions devoid of a setting suggestive of producing injurious disclosures would result in a guessing game in which the witness is the final judge of the claim of privilege.

personal statements under oath to meet the standard for establishing reasonable cause to fear prosecution under this charge. Statements under oath, in person or by affidavit, are necessary because the present penalty of perjury may be the sole assurance against a spurious assertion of the privilege. Argument may be supplied by counsel but not the facts necessary for the court's determination.

Public policy also requires that a witness bear the burden of establishing the foundation of the privilege beyond his mere "say so." Unless something more is required in situations such as the one on appeal where seemingly innocent questions exist in a setting presently devoid of incriminating overtones, witnesses such as Morganroth will be the final arbiters of the validity of their asserted privileges. A litigant's right to information must be balanced against a witness' constitutional right to invoke the privilege. Only where there is some real danger can the loss of information to a litigant or to the judicial system be justified. In addition, unless some additional showing beyond the mere assertion of the privilege is required, no witness would ever have to testify twice regarding the same subject matter because the possibility of perjury would always exist in theory.

From the record on appeal, it appears that Morganroth has not met this burden of establishing a foundation necessary for the valid assertion of the privilege based on his alleged fear of a perjury prosecution. Accordingly, we remand this case to the District Court for further proceedings consistent with this opinion.

JONES, Circuit Judge, dissenting.

The majority reasons that the considerations that were before the Supreme Court in Pillsbury Co. v. Conboy, 459 U.S. 248 (1983), are not implicated in the instant case because of the particular offense for which appellant-Morganroth fears prosecution. The clear holding in *Conboy* is that a district court cannot compel a witness to answer deposition questions over a valid assertion of his Fifth Amendment right, absent a duly authorized grant of immunity at the time the testimony is sought. Thus, when a witness or deponent is accorded a grant of immunity for testimony that is given during one proceeding, a subsequent interrogation pertaining to the same subject matter must be accompanied by a new grant of immunity. The majority concludes that this rule is not applicable to the facts sub judice because the witness' attempt to invoke his Fifth Amendment privilege was based upon his fear of prosecution for perjury. * * * It is upon this basis that I enter my dissent.

My review of the proceedings below indicates that the appellant's response to the numerous questions that were propounded to him was "I refuse to answer on the ground it may incriminate me." During these proceedings, Morganroth's attorney advised the court that if the appellant testified, he ran the risk of possible prosecution for tax evasion. The majority apparently assumed that since the prosecutor informed the appellant that his answers during the grand jury proceeding contradicted the testimony of other witnesses, the appellant was invoking his right to remain silent in order that he would not perjure himself. However, the appellant declares that he invoked his Fifth Amendment privilege because of the possible threat of perjury and criminal tax evasion.* * *

B. THE PRIVILEGE IN THE GRAND JURY

1. ***Targets and Subjects of Grand Jury Investigations***. The United States Attorney's Manual (USAM) § 9-11.151 defines a target as "a person as to whom the prosecutor or the grand jury has substantial evidence linking him or her to the commission of a crime and who, in the judgment of the prosecutor, is a putative defendant." A "subject" of the grand jury investigation is "a person whose conduct is within the scope of the grand jury's investigation. USAM § 9-11.150 places internal restraints on federal prosecutors subpoenaing a target to testify. It provides:

> A grand jury may properly subpoena a subject or a target of the investigation and question the target about his or her involvement in the crime under investigation. However, in the context of particular cases such a subpoena may carry the appearance of unfairness. Because the potential for misunderstanding is great, before a known "target" (as defined in USAM 9-11.151) is subpoenaed to testify before the grand jury about his or her involvement in the crime under investigation, an effort should be made to secure the target's voluntary appearance. If a voluntary appearance cannot be obtained, the target should be subpoenaed only after the grand jury and the United States Attorney or the responsible Assistant Attorney General have approved the subpoena. In determining whether to approve a subpoena for a "target," careful attention will be paid to the following considerations:
>
> - The importance to the successful conduct of the grand jury's investigation of the testimony or other information sought;
>
> - Whether the substance of the testimony or other information sought could be provided by other witnesses; and
>
> - Whether the questions the prosecutor and the grand jurors intend to ask or the other information sought would be protected by a valid claim of privilege.

2. ***Inviting the Target to Testify***. USAM § 9-11.151 states that "[i]t is the policy of the Department of Justice to advise a grand jury witness of his or

her rights if such witness is a 'target' or 'subject' of a grand jury investigation." USAM § 9-11.153 provides:

> When a target is not called to testify pursuant to USAM 9-11.150, and does not request to testify on his or her own motion (*see* USAM 9-11.152), the prosecutor, in appropriate cases, is encouraged to notify such person a reasonable time before seeking an indictment in order to afford him or her an opportunity to testify before the grand jury, subject to the conditions set forth in USAM 9-11.152.

The USAM contains a "Sample Target Letter" that provides an invitation to a target of the grand jury investigation to testify, which is almost always declined:

> This letter is supplied to a witness scheduled to appear before the federal Grand Jury in order to provide helpful background information about the Grand Jury. The Grand Jury consists of from sixteen to twenty-three persons from the District of ___. It is their responsibility to inquire into federal crimes which may have been committed in this District.
>
> As a Grand Jury witness you will be asked to testify and answer questions, and to produce records and documents. Only the members of the Grand Jury, attorneys for the United States and a stenographer are permitted in the Grand Jury room while you testify.
>
> We advise you that the Grand Jury is conducting an investigation of possible violations of federal criminal laws involving, but not necessarily limited to * * *. You are advised that the destruction or alteration of any document required to be produced before the grand jury constitutes serious violation of federal law, including but not limited to Obstruction of Justice.
>
> You are advised that you are a target of the Grand Jury's investigation. You may refuse to answer any question if a truthful answer to the question would tend to incriminate you. Anything that you do or say may be used against you in a subsequent legal proceeding. If you have retained counsel, who represents you personally, the Grand Jury will permit you a reasonable opportunity to step outside the Grand Jury room and confer with counsel if you desire.

U.S. Department of Justice *Criminal Resource Manual* No. 160.

USAM 9-11.152 discusses the situation where a target asks to testify before the grand jury, and requests that the prosecutor all additional witnesses. As the Supreme Court made clear in *Williams*, there is no requirement that a prosecutor permit a target to testify or present exculpatory evidence, but the Department of Justice recognizes that in certain instances the prosecutor should afford a target the opportunity to present their side of the case:

> It is not altogether uncommon for subjects or targets of the grand jury's investigation, particularly in white-collar cases, to request or demand the opportunity to tell the grand jury their side of the story. While the prosecutor has no legal obligation to permit such witnesses to testify, a refusal to do so can create the appearance of unfairness. Accordingly, under normal circumstances, where no burden upon the grand jury or delay of its proceedings is involved, reasonable requests by a "subject" or "target" of an investigation, as defined above, to testify personally before the grand jury ordinarily should be given favorable consideration, provided that such witness explicitly waives his or her privilege against self-incrimination, on the record before the grand jury, and is represented by counsel or voluntarily and knowingly appears without counsel and consents to full examination under oath.

3. ***Advance Assertion of the Privilege.*** Upon receipt of a subpoena, a witness may inform the prosecutor that he or she will exercise the privilege as to all questions posed by the grand jury (apart from simple identification questions, e.g., name, address). While the grand jury may insist upon the appearance of such a witness, here again the internal guidelines of the Department of Justice suggest some restraint in exercising that authority. USAM § 9-11.154 provides, "If a 'target' of the investigation and his or her attorney state in a writing, signed by both, that the 'target' will refuse to testify on Fifth Amendment grounds, the witness ordinarily should be excused from testifying unless the grand jury and the United States Attorney agree to insist on the appearance."

4. ***Self-Incrimination Warnings.*** In **United States v. Mandujano**, 425 U.S. 564 (1976), the Court found it unnecessary to decide whether the Fifth Amendment required that a witness called before the grand jury initially be advised of the right to exercise the self-incrimination privilege, but there was considerable discussion of that issue by six of the Justices. The defendant Mandujano, known by the prosecutor to be a narcotics user, was called before the grand jury in the hope that he would furnish information about significant dealers. Instead, he steadfastly denied any involvement in the sale of narcotics and specifically disclaimed having sought within the year to make a purchase for a third-party for $650.00. The latter statement was a lie since (as the prosecutor already knew) Mandujano had recently tried to make such a purchase for a person who was actually an undercover agent. Subsequently prosecuted for perjury, Mandujano moved to suppress the grand jury testimony which was the basis of the charge. The trial court granted the motion on the ground that Mandujano had not been given full *Miranda* warnings prior to testifying. He had been informed of his privilege against self-incrimination and had been advised that he could have a retained lawyer located outside the grand jury room for the purpose of

consultation. However, he had not been told that a lawyer could be appointed at the government's expense even though he had informed the prosecutor that he could not afford to hire a lawyer. The Court unanimously rejected the lower court's ruling. All the Justices agreed that, even if adequate warnings had not been given, that failure could not constitute a defense to a perjury charge.

Speaking for himself and three other members of the Court, Chief Justice Burger also commented on the adequacy of the warnings given to Mandujano. The Chief Justice concluded that those warnings clearly were adequate under even the broadest reading of the Fifth Amendment. The *Miranda* warnings were prescribed in Miranda v. Arizona, 384 U.S. 436 (1966), for custodial police interrogation, and were designed specifically to negate the "compulsion" thought to be inherent in that setting. *Miranda* itself recognized "that many official investigations, such as grand jury questioning, take place in a setting wholly different from custodial police interrogation." To extend a standard devised to combat "police coercion" found in such practices as the "third degree" to "questioning before a grand jury inquiry into criminal activity under the guidance of a judge" would be "an extravagant expansion never remotely contemplated by this Court in *Miranda*." Justice Brennan, joined by Justice Marshall, responded to what he viewed as a "denigration of the privilege against self-incrimination" in the Chief Justice's opinion.

5. ***Warnings to Grand Jury Targets and Subjects.*** USAM § 9-11.151 directs federal prosecutors to advise a target or subject of the investigation of the following:

Advice of Rights

A. The grand jury is conducting an investigation of possible violations of federal criminal laws involving: (State here the general subject matter of inquiry, e.g., the conducting of an illegal gambling business in violation of 18 U.S.C. § 1955).

B. You may refuse to answer any question if a truthful answer to the question would tend to incriminate you.

C. Anything that you do say may be used against you by the grand jury or in a subsequent legal proceeding.

D. If you have retained counsel, the grand jury will permit you a reasonable opportunity to step outside the grand jury room to consult with counsel if you do so desire.

In **United States v. Washington**, 431 U.S. 181 (1977), the Court answered another question left open in *Mandujano*: whether a witness who is the target of a grand jury investigation constitutionally is entitled to notification of that status when called before the grand jury. Defendant Washington had been questioned by District of Columbia police officers regarding a stolen motorcycle found in his truck. He subsequently was questioned by a prosecuting attorney, who served him with a subpoena to testify before a grand jury. When Washington appeared before the grand jury, the prosecuting attorney did not tell him that he might be indicted on a stolen motorcycle charge (although he had been called to testify because the prosecutor and police were "more than a little skeptical" of his explanation of the presence of the motorcycle). The prosecutor did, however, give Washington a complete set of warnings, even going beyond the usual federal practice (Washington was told that a lawyer would be provided if he could not afford one). Washington stated that he understood his rights, and proceeded to testify, repeating the story he had told to the police and prosecutor. When subsequently indicted for the theft of the motorcycle, he argued that his testimony before the grand jury should be suppressed as he had been unable to intelligently waive his self-incrimination privilege due to the prosecutor's failure to advise him that he was a potential defendant. Rejecting that argument, the Supreme Court majority (per Burger, C.J.) reasoned:

> Even in the presumed psychologically coercive atmosphere of police custodial interrogation, *Miranda* does not require that any additional warnings be given simply because the suspect is a potential defendant; indeed, such suspects are potential defendants more often than not. Respondent points out that unlike one subject to custodial interrogation, whose arrest should inform him only too clearly that he is a potential criminal defendant, a grand jury witness may well be unaware that he is targeted for possible prosecution. While this may be so in some situations, it is an overdrawn generalization. * * * [E]vents here clearly put respondent on notice that he was a suspect in the motorcycle theft. * * * However, all of this is largely irrelevant, since we do not understand what constitutional disadvantage a failure to give potential defendant warnings could possibly inflict on a grand jury witness, whether or not he has received other warnings. * * * Because target witness status neither enlarges nor diminishes the constitutional protection against compelled self-incrimination, potential defendant warnings add nothing of value to protection of Fifth Amendment rights.

Although *Washington* does not require giving warnings to a grand jury witness, the Department of Justice's position is that

> [a]lthough the Court in *Washington* held that "targets" of the grand jury's investigation are entitled to no special warnings relative to their status as "potential defendant(s)," the Department of Justice continues its longstanding policy to advise witnesses who are known "targets" of the investigation that their conduct is being investigated for possible violation of Federal criminal law. This supplemental advice of status of the witness as a target should be repeated on the

record when the target witness is advised of the matters discussed in the preceding paragraphs.

U.S.A.M. § 9-11.151.

6. ***Subsequent Impeachment.*** **Grunewald v. United States**, 353 U.S. 391 (1957), held that where a defendant exercised his privilege during grand jury questioning and then testified at his trial, answering some of the same questions and offering explanations consistent with his innocence, the government should not have been allowed to bring out on cross-examination the fact that he had previously refused on the basis of the privilege to answer the same questions. This was so even though the trial judge had told the petit jury that the defendant's previous exercise of the privilege could be taken only as reflecting upon his credibility in answering the same questions at trial and that no inference as to guilt could be drawn therefrom. The Court reasoned:

> It is, of course, an elementary rule of evidence that prior statements may be used to impeach the credibility of a criminal defendant or an ordinary witness. But this can be done only if the judge is satisfied that the prior statements are in fact inconsistent. 3 Wigmore, Evidence, § 1040. And so the threshold question here is simply whether, in the circumstances of this case, the trial court erred in holding that [defendant] Halperin's plea of the Fifth Amendment privilege before the grand jury involved such inconsistency with any of his trial testimony as to permit its use against him for impeachment purposes. * * * [W]e deem it evident that Halperin's claim of the Fifth Amendment privilege before the Brooklyn grand jury in response to questions which he answered at the trial was wholly consistent with innocence. Had he answered the questions put to him before the grand jury in the same way he subsequently answered them at trial, this nevertheless would have provided the Government with incriminating evidence from his own mouth. For example, had he stated to the grand jury that he knew Grunewald, the admission would have constituted a link between him and a criminal conspiracy, and this would be true even though he was entirely innocent and even though his friendship with Grunewald was above reproach. There was, therefore, as we see it, no inconsistency between Halperin's statement to the grand jury that answering the question whether he knew Grunewald would tend to furnish incriminating evidence against him, and his subsequent testimony at trial that his acquaintance with Grunewald was free of criminal elements.

The *Grunewald* Court noted that a target of a grand jury investigation may have a very powerful reason for asserting the Fifth Amendment in the investigation even though the defendant maintains his innocence: "[M]any innocent men who know that they are about to be indicted will refuse to help create a case against themselves under circumstances where lack of counsel's assistance and lack of opportunity for cross-examination will prevent them from bringing out the exculpatory circumstances in the context of which superficially incriminating acts occurred." Does this analysis argue in favor of allowing defense counsel in the grand jury room to at least monitor the proceeding and provide some measure of assistance to the witness?

7. ***Sanctions for Asserting the Privilege in the Grand Jury***. Gardner v. Broderick, 392 U.S. 273 (1968), held that a state could not discharge a state employee because he exercised the privilege before a grand jury inquiring into possible criminality in the performance of his duties. In that case, involving a state grand jury proceeding under which witnesses received automatic immunity, the employee refused to waive that immunity, and was discharged under a statute making that refusal (or the exercise of the privilege) grounds for dismissal. The Court noted that, if the employee had been required as an obligation of his employment to "answer questions specifically, directly, and narrowly relating to performance of his official duties, without being required to waive his immunity with respect to the use of his answers or the fruits thereof in a criminal prosecution of him, * * * the privilege against self-incrimination would not have been a bar to dismissal." However, a dismissal based on his exercise of the privilege (or refusal to waive the immunity to which a witness was entitled under state law) imposed an impermissible burden on the exercise of a constitutional right. In Lefkowitz v. Turley, 414 U.S. 70 (1973), the Court similarly held that a state could not impose a penalty upon a contractor (here a five years disqualification from doing business with the state) based upon the contractor's exercise of the privilege (or refusal to waive automatic witness immunity) when called to testify before a grand jury.

C. WAIVER

ROGERS v. UNITED STATES

340 U.S. 367 (1951)

Chief Justice VINSON delivered the opinion of the Court.

This case arises out of an investigation by the regularly convened grand jury of the United States District Court for the District of Colorado. The books and records of the Communist Party of Denver were sought as necessary to that inquiry and were the subject of questioning by the grand jury. In September, 1948, petitioner, in response to a subpoena, appeared before the grand jury. She testified that she held the position of Treasurer of the Communist Party of Denver until January, 1948, and that, by virtue of her office, she had been in possession of membership lists and dues records of the Party. Petitioner denied having possession of the records and testified that she had turned them over to another. But she refused to identify the person to whom she had given the Party's books, stating to the court as her only reason: "I don't feel that I should subject a person or persons to the same thing that I'm going through.' The court thereupon committed petitioner to the custody of the marshal until ten o'clock the next morning, expressly advising petitioner of her right to consult with counsel.

The next day, counsel for petitioner informed the court that he had read the transcript of the prior day's proceedings and that, upon his advice, petitioner would answer the questions to purge herself of contempt. However, upon reappearing before the grand jury, petitioner again refused to answer the question. The following day she was again brought into court. Called before the district judge immediately after he had heard oral argument concerning the privilege against self-incrimination in another case, petitioner repeated her refusal to answer the question, asserting this time the privilege against self-incrimination. After ruling that her refusal was not privileged, the district judge imposed a sentence of four months for contempt. The Court of Appeals for the Tenth Circuit affirmed, and we granted certiorari.

* * * [T]he decisions of this Court are explicit in holding that the privilege against self-incrimination "is solely for the benefit of the witness," and "is purely a personal privilege of the witness." Petitioner expressly placed her original declination to answer on an untenable ground, since a refusal to answer cannot be justified by a desire to protect others from punishment, much less to protect another from interrogation by a grand jury. Petitioner's claim of the privilege against self-incrimination was pure afterthought. Although the claim was made at the time of her second refusal to answer in the presence of the court, it came only after she had voluntarily testified to her status as an officer of the Communist Party of Denver. To uphold a claim of privilege in this case would open the way to distortion of facts by permitting a witness to select any stopping place in the testimony.

The privilege against self-incrimination, even if claimed at the time the question as to the name of the person to whom petitioner turned over the Party records was asked, would not justify her refusal to answer. As a preliminary matter, we note that petitioner had no privilege with respect to the books of the Party, [which she kept] in "a representative rather than a personal capacity." United States v. White [p. 419]. Since petitioner's claim of privilege cannot be asserted in relation to the books and records sought by the grand jury, the only claim for reversal of her conviction rests on the ground that mere disclosure of the name of the recipient of the books tends to incriminate.

In Blau v. United States, 340 U.S. 159 (1950), we held that questions as to connections with the Communist Party are subject to the privilege against self-incrimination as calling for disclosure of facts tending to criminate under the Smith Act, 18 U.S.C. § 2386. But petitioner's conviction stands on an entirely different footing, for she had freely described her membership, activities and office in the Party. Since the privilege against self-incrimination presupposes a real danger of legal detriment arising from the disclosure, petitioner cannot invoke the privilege where response to the specific question in issue here would not further incriminate her. Disclosure of a fact waives the privilege as to details. As this Court stated in Brown v. Walker, 161 U.S. 591 (1896): "Thus, if the witness himself elects to waive his privilege, as he may doubtless do, since the privilege is for his protection and not for that of other parties, and discloses his criminal connections, he is not permitted to stop, but must go on and make a full disclosure."

* * * Requiring full disclosure of details after a witness freely testifies as to a criminating fact does not rest upon a further "waiver" of the privilege against self-incrimination. Admittedly, petitioner had already "waived" her privilege of silence when she freely answered criminating questions relating to her connection with the Communist Party. But when petitioner was asked to furnish the name of the person to whom she turned over Party records, the court was required to determine, as it must whenever the privilege is claimed, whether the question presented a reasonable danger of further crimination in light of all the circumstances, including any previous disclosures. As to each question to which a claim of privilege is directed, the court must determine whether the answer to that particular question would subject the witness to a 'real danger' of further crimination. After petitioner's admission that she held that office of Treasurer of the Communist Party of Denver, disclosure of acquaintance with her successor presents no more than a "mere imaginary possibility" of increasing the danger of prosecution.

Petitioner's contention in the Court of Appeals and in this Court has been that, conceding her prior voluntary crimination as to one element of proof of a Smith Act violation, disclosure of the name of the recipient of the Party records would tend to incriminate as to the different crime of conspiracy to violate the Smith Act. Our opinion in Blau v. United States, explicitly rejects petitioner's argument for reversal here in its holding that questions relating to activities in the Communist Party are criminating both as to "violation of (or conspiracy to violate) the Smith Act." Of course, at least two persons are required to constitute a conspiracy, but the identity of the other members of the conspiracy is not needed, inasmuch as one person can be convicted of conspiring with persons whose names are unknown. Affirmed.

Justice BLACK, with whom Mr. Justice FRANKFURTER and Justice DOUGLAS concur, dissenting.

* * * In the case of this petitioner, there is no evidence that she intended to give up her privilege of silence concerning the persons in possession of the Communist Party records. To the contrary, the record—as set out in the Court's opinion—shows she intended to avoid answering the question on whatever ground might be available and asserted the privilege against self-incrimination at the first moment she became aware of its existence. This fact and the cases which make it crucial are ignored in the decision today.

* * * Apparently, the Court's holding is that at some uncertain point in petitioner's testimony, regardless of her intention, admission of associations with the Communist Party automatically effected a 'waiver' of her constitutional protection as to all related questions. To adopt such a rule for

the privilege against self-incrimination, when other constitutional safeguards must be knowingly waived, relegates the Fifth Amendment's privilege to a second-rate position. Moreover, today's holding creates this dilemma for witnesses: On the one hand, they risk imprisonment for contempt by asserting the privilege prematurely; on the other, they might lose the privilege if they answer a single question. The Court's view makes the protection depend on timing so refined that lawyers, let alone laymen, will have difficulty in knowing when to claim it. In this very case, it never occurred to the trial judge that petitioner waived anything. And even if voluntary testimony can under some circumstances work a waiver, it did not do so here because what petitioner stated to the grand jury 'standing alone did not amount to an admission of guilt or furnish clear proof of crime * * *.' Arndstein v. McCarthy, 254 U.S. 71 (1920).

Furthermore, unlike the Court, I believe that the question which petitioner refused to answer did call for additional incriminating information. She was asked the names of the persons to whom she had turned over the Communist Party books and records. Her answer would not only have been relevant in any future prosecution of petitioner for violation of the Smith Act but also her conviction might depend on testimony of the witnesses she was thus asked to identify. For these reasons the question sought a disclosure which would have been incriminating to the highest degree. * * *

NOTES AND QUESTIONS

1. ***Scope of the Waiver.*** *Rogers* has led counsel to direct witnesses intending to invoke the privilege to provide the civilian counterpart of "name, rank, and serial number" and then turn to the privilege. Is that an appropriate employment of the privilege? Consider the analysis in Sara Sun Beale, William C. Bryson, James E. Felman, Michael J. Elston, & Katherine Earle Yanes, GRAND JURY LAW & PRACTICE § 6:10 (2d ed. 2013):

> The lower courts have tended to give the Rogers decision a fairly narrow interpretation, focusing on the rationale of the decision, not merely on whether the witness has already disclosed a "fact" and should be required to disclose the supporting details. Although there are lower court decisions denying the privilege on the basis of a finding that no further incrimination would result, many lower courts have taken a liberal approach toward identifying danger of further incrimination.
>
> If the witness is justified in claiming the privilege, the prosecutor has two options. If the witness's testimony is not critical, the prosecutor may excuse the witness after he has given any testimony that is not covered by the privilege. If the witness's testimony is vital, the prosecutor may wish to grant the witness immunity. * * *

If immunity is granted and the witness persists in his refusal to testify, the witness may be held in contempt.

As discussed in *Morganroth*, most federal courts take the position that giving testimony in one proceeding does not waive the claim in a later proceeding, even though the questioning relates to the same topic and the proceedings are related. The D.C. Court of Appeals, however, continues to adhere to its position in Ellis v. United States, 416 F.2d 791 (D.C.Cir.1969), that "a witness who voluntarily testifies before a grand jury without invoking the privilege against self-incrimination of which he has been advised, waives the privilege and may not thereafter claim it when he is called to testify as a witness on the indictment returned by the grand jury, where the witness is not the defendant or under indictment." United States v. Miller, 904 F.2d 65 (D.C. Cir. 1990). Note that the *Ellis* rule only applies to a witness, and not the defendant in the case. Of course, in a jurisdiction in which that position is rejected, the witness' exercise of the privilege at trial makes that person "unavailable," and while the witness' grand jury testimony was not subject to cross-examination, the prosecution may still seek to have it admitted under Federal Rule of Evidence 807 (residual hearsay exception allowing admission where prior statement of unavailable witness was made under circumstances guaranteeing trustworthiness, constitutes evidence more probative than other evidence, and admission serves interest of justice). See United States v. Barlow, 693 F.2d 954 (6th Cir. 1982).

2. Incrimination Under the Laws of Another Sovereign. For many years, American courts took the position that the privilege protected only against incrimination under the laws of the sovereign which was compelling the incriminating testimony. As applied to the state and the federal systems, the practical impact of this separate-sovereign doctrine related primarily to immunity. The overlap of federal and state criminal law is such that only rarely would a defendant's testimony not meet the Hoffman standard as to potential incrimination in one of those jurisdictions, yet meet that standard as to the other. That situation was only likely to exist where the testimony would not be incriminating in the jurisdiction compelling the response because it concerned an offense on which the witness had already been convicted or acquitted in that jurisdiction. Far more frequently the separate-sovereign doctrine came into play in the granting of witness immunity, as it allowed one jurisdiction to compel testimony by granting immunity only as to that jurisdiction, with no prohibition against the other jurisdiction using that testimony to prosecute the person under its law. This state of affairs was overturned in Murphy v. Waterfront Comm'n, 378 U.S. 52 (1964). The Supreme Court there rejected the separate-sovereign doctrine as applied to state and federal inquiries. Noting that a separate-sovereign limitation would permit a witness to be "whip-sawed into incriminating himself under both state and federal law," the Court concluded that the "policies and purposes" of the Fifth Amendment required that the privilege protect "a state witness against incrimination under federal as well as state law and a federal witness against incrimination under state as well as federal law."

Does it follow from *Murphy* that the privilege should be available where the witness' testimony would be incriminating only in a foreign country? In Zicarelli v. New Jersey Investigation Commission, 406 U.S. 472 (1972), the Supreme Court left that issue unresolved, noting that it would only be presented where a witness given immunity in this country could point to a "real" rather than a hypothetical risk of foreign prosecution. The Supreme Court resolved the issue in **United States v. Balsys**, 524 U.S. 666 (1998), when it held that "concern with foreign prosecution is beyond the scope of the Self-Incrimination Clause." The case involved an "administrative subpoena [issued by] the Office of Special Investigations of the Criminal Division of the United States Department of Justice (OSI) [that] sought testimony from the respondent, Aloyzas Balsys, about his wartime activities between 1940 and 1944 and his immigration to the United States in 1961. Balsys declined to answer such questions, claiming the Fifth Amendment privilege against self-incrimination, based on his fear of prosecution by a foreign nation." See Dianne Marie Amann, *A Whipsaw Cuts Both Ways: The Privilege Against Self-Incrimination In An International Court*, 45 U.C.L.A. L. REV. 1201 (1998) (international law arguments that still may remain available).

D. THE PRIVILEGE IN CIVIL AND ADMINISTRATIVE PROCEEDINGS

A person can invoke the Fifth Amendment privilege against self-incrimination in any proceeding so long as the statement might incriminate the person in a subsequent criminal prosecution. What is the effect of an invocation of the privilege in a non-criminal proceeding? Asserting the Fifth Amendment cannot, standing along, be a basis for depriving a person of a license or job. In Spevack v. Klein, 385 U.S. 511 (1967), the Court found that the disbarment of a lawyer because of his assertion of the privilege against self-incrimination in response to a subpoena issued in a disciplinary proceeding was impermissible because "[t]he threat of disbarment and the loss of professional standing, professional reputation, and of livelihood are powerful forms of compulsion to make a lawyer relinquish the privilege. That threat is indeed as powerful an instrument of compulsion as 'the use of legal process to force from the lips of the accused individual the evidence necessary to convict him * * *.'" Similarly, in the companion case of Garrity v. New Jersey, 385 U.S. 493 (1967), the Court overturned a state statute that required police officers to cooperate in an investigation or lose their jobs automatically because it violated the Fifth Amendment rights of the officers. The Court stated, "The choice given petitioners was either to forfeit their jobs or to incriminate themselves. The option to lose their means of livelihood or to pay the penalty of self-incrimination is the antithesis of free choice to speak out or to remain silent."

In Baxter v. Palmigiano, 425 U.S. 308 (1976), however, the Supreme Court considered a prison disciplinary policy under which "Palmigiano was advised that he was not required to testify at his disciplinary hearing and that he could remain silent but that his silence could be used against him." The Court held that "the prevailing rule [is] that the Fifth Amendment does not forbid adverse inferences against parties to civil actions when they refuse to testify in response to probative evidence offered against them: the Amendment 'does not preclude the inference where the privilege is claimed by a party to a Civil cause.' 8 J. Wigmore, Evidence 439 (McNaughton rev. 1961)."

When a person exercises the privilege in a civil or administrative proceeding, it may entail certain costs that would not arise in a criminal prosecution. For example, in People v. Jobi, 953 N.Y.S.2d 471 (N.Y. Sup. Ct. 2012), in which an attorney testified at a state bar proceeding, the New York Supreme Court (the state's trial level court) explained:

> [H]ad the defendant exercised her right to silence in the disciplinary proceeding, her silence could have been considered, along with other evidence, in determining whether she should be suspended from the practice of law. Had she done so, her assertion of that right could not, of course, have been offered in evidence against her in this trial. However, she chose instead to testify, and because that choice was voluntary and not compelled within the meaning of the Fifth Amendment, her testimony is admissible against her in this criminal case.

Similarly, in United States v. McKinney, 695 F. Supp. 2d 182, 186 (E.D. Pa. 2010), the district court rejected a doctor's motion to suppress testimony in the criminal case because he was forced to testify in a Drug Enforcement Administration administrative hearing, otherwise he would have lost his license to prescribe medicine that would have rendered him unable to treat his patients. The district court held that "Dr. McKinney, while fully represented by counsel at his DEA hearing, was able to choose whether or not he wanted to testify. Thus, Dr. McKinney was able to fully vindicate his Fifth Amendment rights."

While a court or administrative tribunal cannot directly punish a person for asserting the Fifth Amendment privilege, it can take steps to remedy the harm to an opposing party deprived of a useful source of information. For example, a party claiming the privilege may be precluded from offering evidence to support her side of the case, which may result in a grant of summary judgment. The finder of fact may be allowed to draw an adverse inference against the party asserting the privilege as to the withheld information, such as find that an answer not given would have been unfavorable to the party refusing to respond. When a non-party witness invokes the privilege, an adverse inference should not be drawn against either party unless the witness is so closely connected to a party that the person is within its control, such as the officers of a corporation who have particular knowledge of its activities.

What are the limits in a civil proceeding on the use of an individual's assertion of the Fifth Amendment as substantive proof that the person engaged in alleged misconduct? How much "compulsion" will a court permit?

UNITED STATES v. PALMQUIST

712 F.3d 640 (1st Cir. 2013)

WOODLOCK, District Judge.

Mark Palmquist is a Marine Corps veteran who worked as a civilian employee with the U.S. Department of Veterans Affairs from 2004 to 2010. He was convicted of fraud in connection with his own receipt of veterans benefits.

Adverting to Garrity v. New Jersey, 385 U.S. 493 (1967), Palmquist challenges his conviction on grounds that statements he made during an interview with a Veterans Administration investigator were coerced because they were induced by putting him to a choice between loss of his job or surrender of his right to remain silent under the Fifth Amendment and consequently should have been suppressed. * * *

On October 14, 2008, Palmquist filed a claim with the Veterans Administration for increased service-related disability benefits based on a back injury. He had filed six prior claims for back injury, all of which were denied because he could not establish that the injury was service-related. To support his October 2008 application, which was granted, Palmquist supplied a government memorandum purporting to establish that he sustained his injury in connection with military service in Panama in 1988. The memo, however, was a forgery, and no other evidence supported Palmquist's claim. Before the Veterans Administration uncovered the fraud, Palmquist received $37,440 in disability benefits to which he was not entitled. [Palmquist also failed to inform Veterans Affairs that he had divorced his wife, and continued to receive dependency benefits totaling $9,789 for 5 years.]

Palmquist was charged in a 27–count indictment with a variety of offenses involving misconduct in his receipt of benefits from the Veterans Administration. Pursuant to a plea bargain reserving the right to appeal the denial of his motion to suppress the statements he made to the Veterans Administration investigator, he pled guilty to two counts: knowingly submitting a false claim for Veterans Administration service-related benefits in violation of 18 U.S.C. § 287, and theft of Veterans Administration service-related benefits exceeding $1,000 in violation of 18 U.S.C. § 641. The district court sentenced Palmquist to 18 months of imprisonment, 3 years of supervised release, $47,228 in restitution, and $200 in special assessments.

Palmquist challenges the district court's refusal to suppress statements he made to Timothy Bond, a criminal investigator for the Veterans Administration Office of the Inspector General. The statements may be taken to indicate that his use of the forged memorandum was knowing and willful. * * *

On April 3, 2009, Bond interviewed Palmquist in Palmquist's office at the Togus Veterans Administration Hospital. Veterans Administration police officer Jeffrey Turner was also present for the interview. In keeping with Veterans Administration policy, Bond did not record the interview, but he did take notes.

Bond introduced himself to Palmquist as a member of the Office of the Inspector General's criminal investigation division, which he confirmed by showing Palmquist his badge. Bond explained that he had received allegations of fraud, specifically concerning Palmquist's dependency benefits. He also explained that the interview was voluntary, and that Palmquist could not be punished for refusing to answer questions. Before asking any questions, Bond presented Palmquist with a form that read:

> ADVISEMENT OF RIGHTS (FEDERAL EMPLOYEES—GARRITY)
>
> You are being contacted to solicit your cooperation in an official investigation regarding misconduct or improper performance of official duties. In accordance with the Privacy Act, you are advised that the authority to conduct this investigation is contained in the Inspector General Act of 1978, 5 U.S.C.App. 3.
>
> The matter under investigation could constitute a violation of law that could result in the criminal prosecution of the responsible individuals.
>
> This inquiry concerns __________
>
> You have the right to remain silent if your answers may tend to incriminate you. If you do decide to answer questions or make a statement, you may stop answering at any time.
>
> Anything you say may be used as evidence in both an administrative proceeding or any future criminal proceeding involving you.
>
> If you refuse to answer the questions posed to you on the grounds that the answers may tend to incriminate you, you cannot be removed (fired) solely for remaining silent; however, your silence can be considered in an administrative proceeding for any evidentiary value that is warranted by the facts surrounding your case.
>
> ACKNOWLEDGEMENT
> I understand the warnings and assurances stated above and I am willing to make a statement and answer questions voluntarily. No promises or threats have been made to me and no pressure or coercion of any kind has been used against me.

In the blank space following "This inquiry concerns," Bond wrote "VA compens[at]ion benefits for Mark Palmquist." The form was signed by Palmquist and by Turner, as a witness.

After summarizing the form for Palmquist, Bond gave Palmquist an opportunity to review the form and to ask questions. Palmquist looked only briefly at the form, but did not indicate any confusion about Bond's summary. Bond concluded that Palmquist was satisfied with his explanation, and observed that Palmquist showed no reluctance in signing the form.

During the interview, Palmquist seemed calm and cooperative. Early in the interview, Palmquist briefly discussed his medical problems—in addition to his back injury, Palmquist was being treated for PTSD—and asked a question about a civil employment discrimination suit he had pending against the Veterans Administration. Bond again reminded Palmquist that he was involved in a criminal investigation, but asked if Palmquist wanted his civil counsel present. Palmquist declined and agreed to continue the interview, which turned to the issue of benefits fraud. The entire interview lasted about 20 minutes, and ended cordially. * * *

In Garrity v. New Jersey, the Supreme Court prevented government entities from "us[ing] the threat of discharge to secure incriminatory evidence against an employee." When an employee faces the choice "between self-incrimination and job forfeiture," the Court ruled, his statements are deemed categorically coerced, involuntary, and inadmissible in subsequent criminal proceedings.

Not every possible threat of adverse employment action, however, triggers immunity under Garrity. As we have observed:

> In all of the cases flowing from Garrity, there are two common features: (1) the person being investigated is explicitly told that failure to waive his constitutional right against self-incrimination will result in his discharge from public employment (or a similarly severe sanction imposed in the case of private citizens); and (2) there is a statute or municipal ordinance mandating such procedure.

United States v. Indorato, 628 F.2d 711 (1st Cir.1980). Garrity immunity is contingent upon the degree of certainty that an employee's silence alone will subject the employee to severe employment sanctions. So, for example, potentially unfavorable inferences drawn from an employee's silence, which serve as one factor in adverse employment action against him, have been found "too conditional" a threat to trigger Garrity immunity. United States v. Stein, 233 F.3d 6 (1st Cir.2000) (distinguishing "the threat of automatic loss of one's livelihood and the threat of an inference that might lead to such a loss").

Nothing that Bond said or presented to Palmquist could have led Palmquist to believe that, if he remained silent, he would automatically lose his job or suffer similarly severe employment consequences solely for having remained silent. The magistrate judge credited Bond's testimony that he accurately summarized the Advisement of Rights. The Advisement, in turn, informed Palmquist that he could not be fired solely for refusing to participate in the interview, although his silence could be used as evidence in an administrative proceeding. Under Stein, the consequences of such a use of Palmquist's silence are too conditional to be deemed coercive.

Whatever Palmquist may have read or been told at the time, he argues he was also subject to coercion under the Veterans Administration Standards of Conduct, which provide:

> Employees will furnish information and testify freely and honestly in cases respecting employment and disciplinary matters. Refusal to testify, concealment of material facts, or willfully inaccurate testimony in connection with an investigation or hearing may be ground for disciplinary action. An employee, however, will not be required to give testimony against himself or herself in any matter in which there is indication that he or she may be or is involved in a violation of law wherein there is a possibility of self-incrimination.

38 C.F.R. § 0.735–12(b). This regulation is not inherently coercive, given that, read in full, it effectively precludes automatic disciplinary action for an employee's refusal to testify "in any matter in which there is indication that he or she may be or is involved in a violation of law wherein there is a possibility of self-incrimination." In such a case the employee "will not be required to give testimony." The regulation thus makes exactly the exception necessary to prevent the attachment of immunity under Garrity. * * *

Palmquist also argues that Bond and, alternatively, the Advisement of Rights misstated the law, thus rendering Palmquist's testimony involuntary. Bond's alleged misstatement was that Palmquist could not be punished for not answering questions. According to Palmquist, this misstated the extent to which his silence could be used against him in administrative proceedings. Bond was plainly referring to Palmquist's immunity from criminal punishment based on his silence; the statement is thus not inconsistent with Bond's later provision of an accurate summary of the Advisement of Rights, which discusses the potential evidentiary uses of silence. This alleged inconsistency, if inconsistency it was, does not give rise to any clear error such that we must reject the district court's determination that Bond summarized the Advisement of Rights form accurately.

Palmquist also complains that the warnings in the Advisement of Rights are inconsistent with model warnings provided by Department of Justice in its so-called "Wray Memorandum." Unlike the OIG Advisement of Rights, the Garrity warning suggested by the Wray Memorandum does not mention that an employee's silence may be used as evidence in an administrative or disciplinary proceeding. Putting aside that nothing requires the Veterans Administration to use the Department of Justice form, we have already observed that potential use of Palmquist's silence as evidence for what it is worth is too conditional to constitute coercion.

Palmquist makes no argument that his statements should have been suppressed on more conventional voluntariness grounds, and the record provides no such indication of coercion in any event. The interview was, by all accounts, calm and cordial. Having supportably determined that Palmquist's statements were not immunized under Garrity, the district court properly denied the motion to suppress.

E. IMMUNITY

Under 18 U.S.C § 6002, the United States can grant a witness immunity from prosecution and compel the person to testify. The immunity provided under the statute is called "use/fruits" immunity, and provides that at the request of the government, the court will issue an order that "the witness may not refuse to comply with the order on the basis of his privilege against self-incrimination; but no testimony or other information compelled under the order (or any information directly or indirectly derived from such testimony or other information) may be used against the witness in any criminal case, except a prosecution for perjury, giving a false statement, or otherwise failing to comply with the order." The other form of immunity that the government can offer is known as "transactional immunity," which grants the witness full immunity from any later prosecution for any crimes about which the witness testifies. For any number of reasons, prosecutors are reluctant to grant a witness transactional immunity because the person cannot be prosecuted at any point, while use/fruits immunity does not prevent a subsequent prosecution of the immunized witness. In Kastigar v. United States, 406 U.S. 441 (1972), the Court discussed the history of the immunity statute and the effect of an order of immunity on a subsequent prosecution of the witness.

> The power of government to compel persons to testify in court or before grand juries and other governmental agencies is firmly established in Anglo-American jurisprudence. * * * But the power to compel testimony is not absolute. There are a number of exemptions from the testimonial duty, the most important of which is the Fifth Amendment Privilege against compulsory self-incrimination. The privilege reflects a complex of our fundamental values and aspirations, Murphy v. Waterfront Comm'n, and marks an important advance in the development of our liberty. * * *
>
> Immunity statutes, which have historical roots deep in Anglo-American jurisprudence, are not incompatible with these values. Rather, they seek a rational accommodation between the imperatives of the privilege and the legitimate demands of

government to compel citizens to testify. The existence of these statutes reflects the importance of testimony, and the fact that many offenses are of such a character that the only persons capable of giving useful testimony are those implicated in the crime. Indeed, their origins were in the context of such offenses, and their primary use has been to investigate such offenses. Congress included immunity statutes in many of the regulatory measures adopted in the first half of this century. Indeed, prior to the enactment of the statute under consideration in this case, there were in force over 50 federal immunity statutes. In addition, every State in the Union, as well as the District of Columbia and Puerto Rico, has one or more such statutes. The commentators, and this Court on several occasions, have characterized immunity statutes as essential to the effective enforcement of various criminal statutes. * * *

The statute's explicit proscription of the use in any criminal case of "testimony or other information compelled under the order (or any information directly or indirectly derived from such testimony or other information)" is consonant with Fifth Amendment standards. We hold that such immunity from use and derivative use is coextensive with the scope of the privilege against self-incrimination, and therefore is sufficient to compel testimony over a claim of the privilege. While a grant of immunity must afford protection commensurate with that afforded by the privilege, it need not be broader. Transactional immunity, which accords full immunity from prosecution for the offense to which the compelled testimony relates, affords the witness considerably broader protection than does the Fifth Amendment privilege. The privilege has never been construed to mean that one who invokes it cannot subsequently be prosecuted. Its sole concern is to afford protection against being "forced to give testimony leading to the infliction of 'penalties affixed to * * * criminal acts.'" Immunity from the use of compelled testimony, as well as evidence derived directly and indirectly therefrom, affords this protection. It prohibits the prosecutorial authorities from using the compelled testimony in *any* respect, and it therefore insures that the testimony cannot lead to the infliction of criminal penalties on the witness. * * *

Although an analysis of prior decisions and the purpose of the Fifth Amendment privilege indicates that use and derivative-use immunity is coextensive with the privilege, we must consider additional arguments advanced by petitioners against the sufficiency of such immunity. * * * Petitioners argue that use and derivative-use immunity will not adequately protect a witness from various possible incriminating uses of the compelled testimony: for example, the prosecutor or other law enforcement officials may obtain leads, names of witnesses, or other information not otherwise available that might result in a prosecution. It will be difficult and perhaps impossible, the argument goes, to identify, by testimony or cross-examination, the subtle ways in which the compelled testimony may disadvantage a witness, especially in the jurisdiction granting the immunity.

This argument presupposes that the statute's prohibition will prove impossible to enforce. The Statute provides a sweeping proscription of any use, direct or indirect, of the compelled testimony and any information derived therefrom. * * * This total prohibition on use provides a comprehensive safeguard, barring the use of compelled testimony as an "investigatory lead," and also barring the use of any evidence obtained by focusing investigation on a witness as a result of his compelled disclosures. A person accorded this immunity under 18 U.S.C. § 6002, and subsequently prosecuted, is not dependent for the preservation of his rights upon the integrity and good faith of the prosecuting authorities. As stated in *Murphy* [*v. Waterfront Comm'n*, 378 U.S. 52 (1964)]:

> Once a defendant demonstrates that he has testified, under a state grant of immunity, to matters related to the federal prosecution, the federal authorities have the burden of showing that their evidence is not tainted by establishing that they had an independent, legitimate source for the disputed evidence.

This burden of proof, which we reaffirm as appropriate, is not limited to a negation of taint: rather, it imposes on the prosecution the affirmative duty to prove that the evidence it proposes to use is derived from a legitimate source wholly independent of the compelled testimony.

This is very substantial protection, commensurate with that resulting from invoking the privilege itself. The privilege assures that a citizen is not compelled to incriminate himself by his own testimony. It usually operates to allow a citizen to remain silent when asked a question requiring an incriminatory answer. This statute, which operates after a witness has given incriminatory testimony, affords the same protection by assuring that the compelled testimony can in no way lead to the infliction of criminal penalties. The statute, like the Fifth Amendment, grants neither pardon nor amnesty. Both the statute and the Fifth Amendment allow the Government to prosecute using evidence from legitimate independent sources.

NOTES AND QUESTIONS

1. Administrative Investigations. A decision whether to grant federal immunity is the prerogative of the Executive Branch, and as a general rule, only the Attorney General or a designated officer of Department of Justice

has authority to grant use immunity. Section 6004 also provides that an administrative agency may issue an immunity order to compel testimony in connection with agency proceedings "with the approval of the Attorney General." The statute requires that the agency seeking immunity determine that "(1) the testimony or other information from such individual may be necessary to the public interest; and (2) such individual has refused or is likely to refuse to testify or provide other information on the basis of his privilege against self-incrimination."

2. Prosecuting the Immunized Witness. While § 6002 immunity holds open the possibility of prosecuting an immunized witness for offenses that are the subject of the witness' testimony, the United States Attorney's Manual indicates that the prosecutorial decision to proceed on such a case involves considerations beyond the availability of independently obtained evidence that would sustain a conviction. It provides that the prosecutor must obtain express written authorization from the Attorney General, and "[t]he request to prosecute should indicate the circumstances justifying prosecution and the method by which the government will be able to establish that the evidence it will use against the witness will meet the government's burden under Kastigar v. United States." USAM § 9-23.400.

3. Prosecution's Burden. Lower courts have held that the prosecution's burden of establishing that its evidence was derived from an independent source, and not from the defendant's immunized testimony, is governed by a preponderance of the evidence standard (rather than a higher burden of persuasion, such as "clear and convincing"). The burden is placed at this level because the same standard is used in other settings that the courts view as analogous–the government's burden in establishing a Miranda waiver and proving the voluntariness of a confession. See United States v. Byrd, 765 F.2d 1524 (11th Cir. 1985); United States v. Abanatha, 999 F.2d 1246 (8th Cir. 1993). This burden is placed on the government only after the defendant meets the threshold requirement of establishing that he or she testified under immunity on matters that could conceivably relate to the current prosecution. As a practical matter, however, almost any immunized testimony, whether or not in the jurisdiction of prosecution, will serve that function.

4. The Kastigar Hearing. "[A] trial court may hold a Kastigar hearing pre-trial, post-trial, mid-trial (as evidence is offered) or it may employ some combinations of these methods." United States v. North, 910 F.2d 843 (D.C. Cir. 1990) (noting that the pre-trial hearing is the "most common choice"). Courts favoring the pretrial hearing argue that the defendant should not be forced to trial unless the government can first establish that it can meet the independent source burden. See United States v. Smith, 580 F.Supp. 1418 (D.N.J. 1984). Defendants commonly favor a pretrial hearing because, even if the government succeeds, the hearing will provide the defense with valuable discovery as the government identifies the evidence it intends to use and cites its independent source. But note United States v. Byrd, supra (government may be allowed to make a partial in camera showing as to independent sources where it has good cause, e.g., to protect grand jury

secrecy). Since the taint hearing will require a review of the immunized testimony, comparing it to the government's evidence, one disadvantage of a pretrial hearing is that it may make that testimony known to the government's trial prosecutors, who previously may have been shielded from the testimony by a wall. According to Sara Sun Beale, William C. Bryson, James E. Felman, Michael J. Elston, & Katherine Earle Yanes, GRAND JURY LAW & PRACTICE § 7:20 (2d ed. 2013):

> If a hearing is held prior to trial, and the prosecutor reads the immunized testimony in preparation for that hearing, the prosecutor's exposure to the immunized testimony at that time will ordinarily not be held to result in the kind of taint that requires dismissal of the indictment. On the other hand, the fact that the prosecutor will almost certainly be exposed to the immunized testimony or facts derived from the immunized testimony in preparation for and during the taint hearing provides a good reason for the court to postpone that hearing until after the trial.

If the Kastigar hearing is held after the trial, the court must assess whether all of the evidence used at trial was derived from an independent source, and not just the evidence to which the defendant objected. See United States v. Hill, 643 F.3d 807 (11th Cir. 2011).

5. “But For” Discovery. Is evidence "derived" from the immunized testimony if it would not have been discovered but for that testimony, no matter how attenuated the causal connection? Looking to Kastigar's reference to investigative leads, several lower courts have stated that a strict "but for" test applies. See e.g., In re Grand Jury Proceedings, 497 F.Supp. 979 (E.D. Pa. 1980). Illustrative is United States v. Kristel, 762 F.Supp. 1100 (S.D.N.Y. 1991), in which an F.B.I. agent investigating a padded billing scheme initially assumed the role of the defendant simply was that of a victim of extortion. However, he shifted the investigation to consider the possibility that defendant had used bribery to initiate the scheme (a shift that led to defendant's eventual prosecution for that bribery) when another agent, fortuitously overhearing a reference to defendant, commented that he had worked on another case in which defendant had cooperated (after being given immunity) and had acknowledged bribing a federal official. The district court concluded that "Mr. Kristel's immunized admissions in the [bribery of the federal official] assisted the Government in deciphering otherwise unintelligible or inconclusive information and evidence [relating to the padded commercial billings] and caused the Government to 'focus' its investigation in this matter as a bribe giver, in violation of the principles adopted by the Supreme Court in Kastigar."

In **United States v. Blau**, 159 F.3d 68 (2nd Cir. 1998), the Second Circuit again found the "but for" causation chain too attenuated to establish a *Kastigar* claim:

> Blau's "chain of taint" argument rests on the following logic: Blau's immunized testimony, by buttressing the case against Lupo, led to Lupo's decision to plead guilty. Lupo's guilty plea led to his decision to cooperate and to implicate Blau and Levin. This in turn led to the cooperation and testimony of Roger Levin against Blau. Blau's series of "but for" causation connections between his immunized proffer and his ultimate conviction is insufficient to make out a viable Kastigar claim. To make out a Fifth Amendment violation, Blau would have to demonstrate that Blau's proffer motivated Lupo and Levin to testify against him. We see no basis for disturbing the district court's finding that no such showing was made. The district court, relying on the record developed at trial and in Blau's post-trial motion, found that Lupo chose to plead guilty and then to cooperate and provide evidence against Blau for reasons unrelated to Blau's immunized proffer.

6. Nonevidentiary Use. Lower courts have divided over whether and how Kastigar applies to nonevidentiary uses–i.e., to prosecutorial consideration of immunized testimony in strategic decisions that do not deal directly with the production of evidence. Initially, there is a division as to whether the nonevidentiary category extends to such decisions as (1) deciding which witnesses to call, (2) planning cross-examination, and (3) interpreting previously discovered evidence. Compare United States v. McDaniel, 482 F.2d 305 (8th Cir. 1975) (characterizing such decisions as nonevidentiary). At least where decisions are uncontestably nonevidentiary (as in the case of the decision not to plea bargain), some courts suggest that Kastigar either does not apply or applies with, at most, a very limited impact. See United States v. Cozzi, 613 F.3d 725 (7th Cir. 2010); United States v. Byrd, 765 F.2d 1524 (11th Cir. 1985). In United States v. Slough, 641 F.3d 544 (D.C. Cir. 2011), the District of Columbia Circuit found that the defendants' proposed rule prohibiting the use of immunized testimony from having any impact on the decision to prosecute "clearly would entangle the court in what has hitherto normally been internal prosecutorial decision-making. And it would open a new field for courts' having to make complex causal judgments of the sort already required to assure clean evidence." While courts often do not flatly reject the possibility that a nonevidentiary use can violate Kastigar, they would at least shift the Kastigar burden and require the defense to show that a specific trial strategy was formed by reference to the immunized testimony and had a measurable bearing upon the strength of the case presented by the prosecution. See United States v. Mariani, 851 F.2d 595 (2d Cir. 1988).

Other courts conclude that neither the statute nor the reasoning of Kastigar permits a distinction to be drawn between evidentiary and nonevidentiary uses–i.e., both must be barred. See United States v. McDaniel, supra; United States v. Semkiw, 712 F.2d 891 (3d Cir. 1983). They note that the immunity statute refers to prohibiting use of "information" derived from immunized testimony, and that Kastigar spoke of that immunity as "prohibit[ing] the prosecutorial authorities from using the compelled testimony in any respect." They further note that "if the immunity protection is to be coextensive with the Fifth Amendment privilege," as Kastigar demanded, "then it must forbid all prosecutorial use of the testimony, not merely that which results in the presentation of evidence before the jury." United States v. McDaniel, supra.

7. Granting Immunity to Defense Witnesses. The Department of Justice has the sole authority to request immunity under § 6002, and courts generally will not grant immunity without government request. In some cases, a witness may have information favorable to a defendant, but refuses to testify unless the government grants immunity because of the person's fear of prosecution. Because the defense cannot grant immunity, and the government may be uninterested in helping a defendant, can a court order immunity under § 6002 despite the government's refusal to request immunity? Courts are quite reticent to do so, although in an extreme case in which the refusal to grant immunity will significantly hinder the ability to determine the truth a court can grant immunity to protect the defendant's due process rights. In United States v. Ebbers, 458 F.3d 110 (2d Cir. 2006), the Second Circuit set forth a test for evaluating a claim that the refusal to grant immunity impermissibly harmed the defense:

> In an extreme case, a court might hold that the absence of the non-immunized witness caused the government's evidence to fall short of proof beyond a reasonable doubt. In addition, a court may order the prosecution to choose between forgoing the testimony of an immunized government witness or granting use immunity to potential defense witnesses. To obtain such an order, a defendant must make a two-pronged showing.
>
> First, the defendant must show that the government has used immunity in a discriminatory way has forced a potential witness to invoke the Fifth Amendment through "overreaching" or has deliberately denied immunity for the purpose of withholding exculpatory evidence and gaining a tactical advantage through such manipulation.
>
> We have said that a discriminatory grant of immunity arguably may be no more than "a decision ... to confer immunity on some witnesses and not on others." [United States v. Dolah, 245 F.3d 98 (2d Cir. 2001)]. However, it may also be the case that the immunity decisions in question are so obviously based on legitimate law enforcement concerns-e.g., granting immunity to a witness who has pleaded guilty and has been sentenced to substantial jail time while denying it to a principal target of the ongoing criminal investigation-that it is clear that a court cannot intervene without substantially hampering the administration of justice.

> Prosecutorial "overreaching" can be shown through the use of "threats, harassment, or other forms of intimidation [which have] effectively forced the witness to invoke the Fifth Amendment." Blissett v. Lefevre, 924 F.2d 434 (2d Cir. 1991). The "manipulation" standard overlaps to a degree with the discrimination test but involves an express finding of a tactical purpose on the government's part.
>
> Second, the defendant must show that the evidence to be given by an immunized witness will be material, exculpatory and not cumulative and is not obtainable from any other source. In that regard, exculpatory evidence is material when it tends to show that the accused is not guilty. The bottom line at all times is whether the non-immunized witness's testimony would materially alter the total mix of evidence before the jury.

The Ninth Circuit stated a defendant "may prove that the prosecution acted with a certain purpose merely by demonstrating that the prosecution committed a set of acts (the selective denial of use immunity described) that had the effect of distorting the fact-finding process." United States v. Straub, 538 F.3d 1147 (9th Cir. 2008). In United States v. Quinn, 728 F.3d 243 (3d Cir. 2013), the Third Circuit set out a five-factor test for determining whether the government violated a defendant's due process right by refusing to immunize a defense witness: "[1] [I]mmunity must be properly sought in the district court; [2] the defense witness must be available to testify; [3] the proffered testimony must be clearly exculpatory; [4] the testimony must be essential; and [5] there must be no strong governmental interests which countervail against a grant of immunity."

8. ***Corporate Antitrust Immunity***. The Antitrust Division of the Department of Justice has a Corporate Leniency Policy that permits a company reporting its own misconduct to avoid being charged with a crime. Unlike individual immunity, in which the person can be compelled to testify, the company gains the benefit of not being prosecuted even though it has no Fifth Amendment privilege. The Policy provides:

> The Division has a policy of according leniency to corporations reporting their illegal antitrust activity at an early stage, if they meet certain conditions. "Leniency" means not charging such a firm criminally for the activity being reported. (The policy also is known as the corporate amnesty or corporate immunity policy.)
>
> A. Leniency Before an Investigation Has Begun
>
> Leniency will be granted to a corporation reporting illegal activity before an investigation has begun, if the following six conditions are met:

1. At the time the corporation comes forward to report the illegal activity, the Division has not received information about the illegal activity being reported from any other source;

2. The corporation, upon its discovery of the illegal activity being reported, took prompt and effective action to terminate its part in the activity;

3. The corporation reports the wrongdoing with candor and completeness and provides full, continuing and complete cooperation to the Division throughout the investigation;

4. The confession of wrongdoing is truly a corporate act, as opposed to isolated confessions of individual executives or officials;

5. Where possible, the corporation makes restitution to injured parties; and

6. The corporation did not coerce another party to participate in the illegal activity and clearly was not the leader in, or originator of, the activity.

If a corporation meets the requirements for the Policy, then "all directors, officers, and employees of the corporation who admit their involvement in the illegal antitrust activity as part of the corporate confession will receive leniency, in the form of not being charged criminally for the illegal activity, if they admit their wrongdoing with candor and completeness and continue to assist the Division throughout the investigation." In 2004, Congress adopted the Antitrust Criminal Penalty Enhancement and Reform Act, Pub.L. No. 108–237, § 213, 118 Stat. 665 (2004), to limit exposure to civil damages for an antitrust conspirator that has a "currently effective" leniency agreement with the Antitrust Division and who cooperates satisfactorily with the Department of Justice and with private litigants in related civil antitrust actions. The company is only liable for single damages, rather than the usual antitrust penalty of treble damages, and there is no "joint and several" liability with other conspirators.

The Antitrust Division informed Stolt-Nielsen, S.A., that it was revoking its immunity under the Corporate Leniency Policy because the company allegedly continued its illegal activity after entering into an agreement with the Department of Justice that required it to avoid future violations. After the indictment of the company and its executives in 2006, the District Court dismissed the charges in United States v. Stolt-Nielsen, S.A., 524 F.Supp.2d 609 (E.D.Pa. 2007). In finding that Stolt-Nielsen had not breached its agreement, the court discussed the standard of review for revocation of a corporate immunity agreement:

While non-prosecution agreements are binding contracts and their interpretation is guided by general principles of contract law, "such agreements are unique and are to be construed in light of 'special due process concerns.'" United States v. Baird, 218 F.3d 221 (3d Cir. 2000). Mindful of the fact that parties who enter into non-prosecution agreements frequently forego valuable constitutional rights, the Court must determine whether the Government's conduct comported with "what was reasonably understood by defendant when entering" the Agreement.

* * * The Division bears the burden of demonstrating that Stolt-Nielsen materially breached the Agreement. The Division urges the Court to apply a "preponderance of the evidence" standard, a standard applied by a number of courts evaluating alleged breaches of plea agreements. Defendants propose a "clear and convincing" standard of proof. The Court's findings of fact and conclusions of law would be unchanged regardless of which of the two standards is applied.

In determining whether a non-prosecution agreement has been breached, the Court must consider whether the non-breaching party received the benefit of the bargain, as well as the incriminating nature of the information provided by the defendant.

F. THE PROFFER AND LIMITED IMMUNITY

For many potential defendants, an immunity grant is the best for which one can hope. Very often, however, more than one potential defendant will have that same hope, and the prosecutor has no need to grant immunity to all of those persons. The government will need the testimony of an inside participant to make its case, and the inside participants will be competing with each other to see who will win the "immunity sweepstakes." How are the Department of Justice's guidelines helpful to the participant's counsel in suggesting those factors that should be emphasized in convincing the government's attorney to grant immunity to counsel's client? To what extent may the critical factor be which participant contacts the prosecutor first, especially in a situation where all participants up to that point have asserted the self-incrimination privilege (following the not always sound aphorism, "nobody talks, everybody walks")?

Obviously, the government attorney will be hesitant to grant immunity to a person without knowing a good deal about what kind of testimony that person can provide and the extent of the person's participation in the illegality. Thus, the prosecutor commonly will require that the individual's counsel make a "proffer" as to the individual's participation and the information that he/she can provide. One concern here is the possible waiver of the lawyer-client privilege, and counsel will often first obtain an agreement in writing that the proffer will not constitute such a waiver. Another concern is that the proffer will be used by the government as a lead to evidence which might then be used without granting the client immunity. Thus, where a proffer includes a reference to incriminating documents that the client can identify, it may give the government information about the existence and location of the documents that it would not otherwise have had, and thus allow the government to obtain those documents by subpoena.

In some instances the government attorney may want to interview the witness before deciding on an immunity grant. An interview often is desired to test the witness' credibility and to determine how he or she will perform in a courtroom setting. Federal Rule of Criminal Procedure 11(f) provides that "[t]he admissibility or inadmissibility of a plea, a plea discussion, and any related statement is governed by Federal Rule of Evidence 410." Rule 410 provides in turn that "any statement made in the course of plea discussions with an attorney for the prosecuting authority which do not result in a plea of guilty or which result in a plea of guilty later withdrawn" cannot be admitted in evidence against the person making the statement, with one exception being a perjury prosecution. Should the same rule apply to statements made in the course of negotiations for a grant of use/fruits immunity? Counsel commonly insist upon an agreement to that effect prior to allowing the client to be interviewed, often asking as well for a commitment that the statement made by the client similarly will not be used for civil purposes. The government may insist that the proffer at least be available to it for use to impeach the individual should he or she later be prosecuted and offer contrary testimony at trial.

In **United States v. Mezzanatto**, 513 U.S. 196 (1995), the Supreme Court considered the validity of a pre-indictment agreement reached as part of plea negotiations "that any statements he made during the meeting could be used to impeach any contradictory testimony he might give at trial if the case proceeded that far." The defendant then stated that he knew a package he tried to sell to an undercover officer contained methamphetamine, but attempted to minimize his role in a drug manufacturing operation. The government had evidence of more extensive involvement, and ultimately no plea agreement was reached. At trial, the defendant denied any involvement in selling drugs, and the prosecutor cross-examined him with the statements from the earlier meeting. The Court, per Thomas, J., upheld the validity of agreements waiving the protections of Rule 11(f) as a condition for negotiating a plea bargain, stating:

> Prosecutors may be especially reluctant to negotiate without a waiver agreement during the early stages of a criminal investigation, when prosecutors are searching for leads and suspects may be willing to offer information in exchange for some form of immunity or leniency in sentencing. In this "cooperation" context, prosecutors face "painfully delicate" choices as to "whether to proceed and prosecute those suspects against whom the already produced evidence makes a case or whether to extend leniency or

> full immunity to some suspects in order to procure testimony against other, more dangerous suspects against whom existing evidence is flimsy or nonexistent." Hughes, Agreements for Cooperation in Criminal Cases, 45 Vand.L.Rev. 1 (1992). Because prosecutors have limited resources and must be able to answer "sensitive questions about the credibility of the testimony" they receive before entering into any sort of cooperation agreement, prosecutors may condition cooperation discussions on an agreement that the testimony provided may be used for impeachment purposes. See Thompson & Sumner, Structuring Informal Immunity, 8 Crim.Just. 16 (spring 1993). If prosecutors were precluded from securing such agreements, they might well decline to enter into cooperation discussions in the first place and might never take this potential first step toward a plea bargain.
>
> Indeed, as a logical matter, it simply makes no sense to conclude that mutual settlement will be encouraged by precluding negotiation over an issue that may be particularly important to one of the parties to the transaction. A sounder way to encourage settlement is to permit the interested parties to enter into knowing and voluntary negotiations without any arbitrary limits on their bargaining chips. To use the Ninth Circuit's metaphor, if the prosecutor is interested in "buying" the reliability assurance that accompanies a waiver agreement, then precluding waiver can only stifle the market for plea bargains. A defendant can "maximize" what he has to "sell" only if he is permitted to offer what the prosecutor is most interested in buying. And while it is certainly true that prosecutors often need help from the small fish in a conspiracy in order to catch the big ones, that is no reason to preclude waiver altogether. If prosecutors decide that certain crucial information will be gained only by preserving the inadmissibility of plea statements, they will agree to leave intact the exclusionary provisions of the plea-statement Rules.
>
> In sum, there is no reason to believe that allowing negotiation as to waiver of the plea-statement Rules will bring plea bargaining to a grinding halt; it may well have the opposite effect. Respondent's unfounded policy argument thus provides no basis for concluding that Congress intended to prevent criminal defendants from offering to waive the plea-statement Rules during plea negotiation.

Justice Ginsburg concurred in Mezzanatto, but noted that "[i]t may be, however, that a waiver to use such statements in the case in chief would more severely undermine a defendant's incentive to negotiate, and thereby inhibit plea bargaining. As the Government has not sought such a waiver, we do not here explore this question." In United States v. Mitchell, 633 F.3d 997 (10th Cir. 2011), the Tenth Circuit rejected limiting the waiver of the protections of Rule 410 to just permitting use in rebuttal. The government introduced the defendant's statements from his guilty plea colloquy in which he acknowledge engaging in the crime and the plea agreement from which he later withdrew in its case-in-chief. The circuit court stated:

> Mitchell asks us to take the admonition of the Mezzanatto concurrence * * * to heart and bar the admissibility of the plea statements in the government's case-in-chief. This we cannot do. We see no analytical distinction between Rule 410's application to impeachment waivers and case-in-chief waivers. The same reasoning for the former compels the latter. Nor did Mitchell negotiate a narrower waiver in the first place.

For various reasons, a prosecutor may prefer to utilize a limited immunity to learn what the person can offer to assist the government's investigation and prosecution. This type of agreement–sometimes referred to as "Queen for a Day" immunity–grants the witness much less protection than a full grant of immunity. In United States v. Lauersen, 2000 WL 1693538 (S.D.N.Y. 2000), the district court described this form of immunity used in the Southern District of New York:

> A "Queen for a Day" agreement is a limited use immunity agreement where the suspect agrees to provide information in exchange for a promise from the Government that any statements made during the proffer will not be used against the profferor. Where plea negotiations break down or an immunity deal is rejected, the standard form Queen for a Day used in the Southern District of New York permits a prosecutor to use the proffered statements in a number of circumstances, including to pursue leads, to cross-examine the defendant if she testifies, and for purposes of rebuttal.

A grant of use/fruits immunity can be forced upon a witness who would prefer to exercise the privilege, but without a proffer the government may be granting immunity to a person it would not otherwise have entered into such an agreement with because of their involvement in criminal activity. A limited immunity agreement requires that the witness be willing to forego exercise of the privilege in return for what the agreement offers, thereby allowing the government to preview what the witness has to offer without fully committing to immunity or some type of plea bargain. Quite often, a person who can offer important assistance will be willing to enter into such an agreement. In some cases that may be because the person feels that he is gaining more than would be gained by an immunity grant. More often, the person is aware that he may be getting less, but that is the best he can expect to achieve (especially where there is a competition among various insiders to get the benefit of what the prosecutor might offer).

The government has become increasingly aggressive in offering fewer protections in these limited immunity agreements to individuals seeking to make a deal in exchange for cooperation. In Mezzanatto, the Supreme Court upheld an agreement that permitted the government to use the defendant's statements for impeachment if the defendant testified inconsistently. How far can the government go in limiting the protection afforded an individual? Consider the following case to see how the limited immunity agreement can permit the government to use the defendant's statements in its case-in-chief and not merely to impeach a defendant who testifies inconsistently with a prior statement.

UNITED STATES v. KRILICH

159 F.3d 1020 (7th Cir. 1999)

EASTERBROOK, Circuit Judge.

A golfer's dream came true for Andy Sarallo. On June 19, 1985, Andy lined up at the ninth tee at Country Lakes Country Club and struck the ball; an observer on the ninth green pulled Andy's ball out of the hole. Andy's foursome jumped up and down and shouted for joy. Because the ninth hole at Country Lakes was the subject of a hole-in-one contest that day, Andy had just won his choice of a 1931 Cadillac or a check for $40,000!

A hole-in-one is quite a thrill because it happens so infrequently–perhaps one chance in 40,000, rarer than a 300 game in bowling. But Andy's chances were close to 100%, because his father was mayor of Oakbrook Terrace, Illinois, and the mayor's support was needed for a bond offering to finance an apartment complex to be built by Robert Krilich–who sponsored the contest, pulled the ball out of the hole, and became the defendant in this criminal case. Krilich and Mayor Sarallo agreed to use the golf tournament as the vehicle for a payoff. Krilich palmed one of Andy's golf balls, put his hand into the cup, and displayed the ball. Delivering the bribe in this way enabled Krilich to shift the cost to the National Hole-In-One Association, which provided insurance. Thus fraud and bribery were coupled. Krilich admitted this scheme in a proffer to the United States Attorney, and he also conceded bribing the mayor to alter the zoning of some land and orchestrating the extraction of funds from municipal bond offerings. The bonds–Industrial Revenue Bonds, interest on which is not taxable to the investors–were sold to finance Krilich's developments. Because the bonds were limited to specific projects (tax exemption depended on that link), the funds were placed in trust, and the trustee banks were to release the money only to reimburse expenses associated with the projects. Preferring to use the money elsewhere, such as for payments on his yacht, Krilich instructed vendors to falsify their invoices and had those bogus invoices sent to the banks for payment out of the trust accounts.

Krilich was convicted of conspiracy to violate the Racketeer Influenced and Corrupt Organizations statute, 18 U.S.C § 1962(d) (RICO), and a fraud statute, 18 U.S.C. § 1014. Krilich maintains on appeal that the district court erred by permitting the prosecutor to use some of the proffer's contents at his trial. * * *

Statements made during plea negotiations are inadmissible, Fed.R.Evid. 410; Fed.R.Crim.P. 11(e)(6), but a defendant may waive the right to prevent their use. Mezzanatto. The agreement Krilich signed contains a conditional waiver:

> [S]hould [Krilich] subsequently testify contrary to the substance of the proffer or otherwise present a position inconsistent with the proffer, nothing shall prevent the government from using the substance of the proffer at sentencing for any purpose, at trial for impeachment or in rebuttal testimony, or in a prosecution for perjury.

By authorizing the prosecutor to use his statements if he should contradict himself, Krilich made his representations more credible and thus strengthened his hand in negotiations. A prosecutor may be reluctant to negotiate; what has the defendant to offer? A statement that shows how the defendant's aid could assist the prosecutor in other cases (or lead to the appropriate sentence in this one) may get negotiations under way and set the stage for a favorable bargain. But a prosecutor needs assurance that the defendant is being candid. A conditional waiver of the kind Krilich signed tends to keep the defendant honest, which makes the proffer device more useful to the both sides. For this strategy to work the conditional waiver must be enforceable; its effect depends on making deceit costly. We therefore reject the argument that waivers should be construed against prosecutors; that might help Krilich today but would hinder bargaining for other defendants tomorrow. We give this waiver neither a stingy reading nor a generous one, but a natural reading, which leaves the parties in control through their choice of language.

This agreement allowed the prosecutor to use the proffer as evidence if Krilich were to "testify contrary to the substance of the proffer or otherwise present a position inconsistent with the proffer." Introduction of the statements thus was proper if either his testimony, or evidence that he presented through the testimony of others, contradicted the proffer. Because Krilich did not testify, only the second clause is at issue. Krilich wants us to limit this clause to evidence presented through his own witnesses; evidence obtained by cross- examination of the prosecution's witnesses does not count, he insists. But that would be an unnatural reading of the language. Evidence is evidence, whether it comes out on direct or cross-examination. One can "otherwise present" a position through arguments of counsel alone, so it is easy to see how a position can be "presented" by evidence developed on cross-examination and elaborated by counsel. When the prosecution's witnesses are inclined to accommodate the defense, as many were in this case, developing one's position through cross-examination is especially attractive.

The prosecutor's position about the effect of the language is as unrealistic as Krilich's. According to the prosecutor, putting on any defense permits the United States to introduce the statements. A plea of not guilty followed by passivity at trial is about all the defense can do, the prosecutor contends–though, when pressed at oral argument, the prosecutor allowed that Krilich could have avoided introduction of the statements if he had limited his cross-examination to "the credibility, weight and sufficiency of the government's evidence in ways that were extrinsic to the facts of the case." On this understanding, asking a witness on cross-examination whether he had been convicted of perjury would be "extrinsic to the facts of the case," but asking the witness whether he had been in a position to see what happened at the ninth green on June 19 would open the door to the use of the proffer. Such a distinction makes sense of neither the language in the contract nor the reason why the waiver was conditional. The prosecutor wanted to give Krilich an incentive to tell the truth; Krilich wanted assurance that he could defend himself at trial if bargaining collapsed (for otherwise he was delivering himself into the prosecutor's hands); conditioning the use of the proffer statements on the presentation of a position "inconsistent with the proffer" does both of those things only if the judge must find genuine inconsistency before allowing use of the statements.

Impeachment of a witness need not be "contrary to" or "inconsistent with" a defendant's admission of guilt in a bargaining proffer. To take a simple example, the statements "I faked the hole-in-one on the ninth hole" (Krilich, in the proffer) and "I did not see Krilich palm a golf ball at the ninth hole on June 19" (a witness, on cross-examination) are not inconsistent. Investigation via cross-examination of witnesses' ability (or willingness) to observe and recount the facts they claim to have observed therefore could not have justified introduction of the proffer statements. Millions of people who live in Illinois did not see what happened at the ninth green on June 19; others who did see what happened may have had reasons to misrepresent what they saw; proof that a given person who took the stand at trial was in the set of non-observers (or liars) is not "inconsistent" with the proffer. Statements are inconsistent only if the truth of one implies the falsity of the other. The statements "Krilich pulled a palmed ball from the cup at the ninth hole" and "Krilich wasn't at the ninth hole when Andy hit his shot" are inconsistent because the former statement cannot be true if the latter is. This appeal turns on whether Krilich elicited such inconsistent testimony. The district judge concluded that he had, and that assessment is not clearly erroneous.

Several witnesses testified, in response to questions from Krilich's attorney, that the ninth hole at Country Lakes Country Club is close to the clubhouse and easily observed. Krilich wanted the jury to infer that no one would attempt to fake a hole-in-one there; that implication is inconsistent with the proffer. Defense counsel got two witnesses to say that they were at the ninth hole when Andy hit the shot but didn't think that Krilich was at the ninth hole then. This line of cross-examination was not designed to cast doubt on the witnesses' ability to see clearly or suggest that they are not trustworthy. Their testimony implied that Krilich did not fake the hole-in-one, contrary to what he admitted in his proffer. Similarly, in response to evidence that Krilich paid a bribe to obtain favorable zoning, his lawyer elicited testimony on cross-examination that no bribe was required because the city attorney thought the new zoning to be correct. Counsel likewise led witnesses to testify that the procedures followed for altering the zoning were not exceptional. Krilich's attorney also had the vice president of his company testify that he was not aware of any bribes paid to any public official in connection with any project. The implication was that if someone so close to Krilich (and the projects) was unaware of bribes, there must not have been any. These statements go well beyond casting doubt on the prosecutor's evidence; they advance a position inconsistent with the proffer—or so the trial judge sensibly could conclude.

Krilich insists that if the conditional waiver means what we think it means, then it is unenforceable because involuntary. Mezzanatto says that waivers of the plea-statement rules are unenforceable if given "unknowingly or involuntarily," but this is a far cry from saying that waivers mean whatever the defendants say they understood them to mean; no party to a contract has Humpty Dumpty's power over language either directly or through the gambit that unanticipated consequences render the agreement "involuntary." A waiver is voluntary in the absence of coercion, and is knowing if made "with a full awareness of both the nature of the right being abandoned and the consequences of the decision to abandon it." Krilich does not contend that his assent was coerced and offers no support for a conclusion that he didn't understand the rights that Rules 410 and 11(e)(6) confer. A defendant's understanding of the consequences of his waiver need not be perfect; it was Krilich's understanding of the rights being relinquished, not of all possible repercussions of relinquishing them, that made his waiver knowing. [The court affirmed the defendant's conviction.]

NOTES AND QUESTIONS

1. Inconsistent Positions. When has a defendant taken an "inconsistent" position that permits the government to introduce statements made at a proffer subject to the limited immunity agreement? The defendant's statements can have a devastating effect on any defense, especially if the government can use it in its case-in-chief to undermine the defendant's credibility even before the defense can mount its case. The scope of the waiver in the limited immunity agreement is the key, and prosecutors have been seeking ever broader waivers. In United States v. Barrow, 400 F.3d 109 (2d Cir. 2005), the Second Circuit considered whether defense counsel's opening statement and cross-examination of a prosecution witness allowed the government to introduce the defendant's statements made a proffer session. The agreement provided that the government could use the statements "as substantive evidence to rebut any evidence offered or elicited, or factual assertions made, by or on behalf of [defendant] at any stage of a

criminal prosecution (including but not limited to detention hearing, trial or sentencing)." This is broader than the waiver in Krilich, which was triggered if Krilich presented "a position inconsistent with the proffer." Analyzing the scope of the waiver, the court stated:

> The mere fact that a defendant pleads not guilty and stands trial is not a factual assertion that triggers the proffer agreement waiver, and the government certainly does not contend otherwise. See United States v. Krilich. Nor are defense arguments that attempt to demonstrate why the facts put in evidence by the prosecution are insufficient to permit the jury to find the elements of the crime proved. Thus, a defense argument that simply challenged the sufficiency of government proof on elements such as knowledge, intent, identity, etc., would not trigger the waiver here at issue. On the other hand, a statement of fact in a defense opening, such as the statement in this case unequivocally identifying Jamal Barrow as the real perpetrator of the charged crimes, does qualify as a factual assertion within the four corners of the waiver provision. Thus, we conclude that the waiver's "factual assertion" requirement was satisfied in this case.
>
> We note, however, that such a conclusion may not be reached so easily when counsel's arguments or questions assert facts implicitly rather than directly. For example, a cross-examination question challenging a witness's perception or recollection of an event does not necessarily imply that the event did not occur, only that the witness may not have seen or reported it accurately. On the other hand, a question accusing a witness of fabricating an event, such as counsel in this case put to Det. Campana with respect to the April 19, 2001 meeting with the confidential informant, does implicitly assert that no such meeting ever took place. Thus, when confronted with a government argument that a defense opening or cross-examination implicitly satisfies the factual assertion requirement for waiver, a district court may well have to consider carefully what fact, if any, has actually been implied to the jury before deciding whether proffer statements fairly rebut it.
>
> We further note that even when a district court is satisfied that a factual assertion triggering a Rule 410 waiver has been made, whether directly or implicitly, that conclusion does not mandate receipt of the proffer statements in evidence. A waiver agreement between the parties does not divest a district court of its considerable discretion to exclude relevant evidence that may inject "unfair prejudice" or "confusion" into the jury's resolution of the issues in dispute.

The Second Circuit shed further light on how far defense counsel can go in defending the case without triggering the government's use of statements made in plea negotiations in United States v. Oluwanisola, 605 F.3d 124 (2d

Cir. 2010). The agreement was identical to the one at issue in Barrow, and the district judge found that any questioning by defense counsel going to the veracity of a witness would permit the government to use the defendant's statements. The Second Circuit overturned the conviction, finding that the trial court's interpretation of what type of defense could be offered was too restrictive:

> In this case, the district court made a distinction between "generally tell[ing] the jury about the burden of proof and the necessity of the government proving all elements of the crime" and arguing that "specific elements of the crime [have] not be[en] met," ruling that while the former would not trigger the waiver provision, the latter would. Barrow did not make such a distinction and we can think of no rationale that would compel such a result. Under the district court's interpretation of Barrow, even if the government failed to introduce any evidence on a certain element, defense counsel would not be permitted to draw the jury's attention to the lack of evidence in his opening statement without triggering the waiver provision in the proffer agreement. Interpreting the waiver provision to permit such a result would leave the defendant, for all practical purposes, defenseless. As the record makes clear, Mr. Nobel was compelled by the court's ruling to limit his opening statement to generalized statements concerning the government's burden of proof and the jury's responsibilities. Under Barrow, however, Mr. Nobel should have been permitted during his opening statement to reference certain elements of the crime and argue that the government would be unable to sustain its burden of proof as to those elements. * * *
>
> It is true that in Barrow we stated that some cross examination questions, such as "a question accusing a witness of fabricating an event," could make an implicit factual assertion that would trigger the waiver provision. However, in Barrow we were faced with a situation in which defense counsel had affirmatively argued during his opening statement that the defendant had been mistaken for someone else and then asked a government witness during cross examination, "'You made up about meeting the [confidential informant] there that day, didn't you?'". In that situation one can easily infer that defense counsel was making the implicit factual assertion that no meeting took place because his theory of mistaken identity depended on that fact.
>
> But when the defendant has not directly or indirectly contradicted the facts he admitted in his proffer, the same inference does not apply. The defendant's admission in his proffer statement of the facts the witness testifies to having observed is not an admission that the witness observed those facts. There is no inconsistency or contradiction between a defendant's admission that he robbed the bank and his challenge to a witness's testimony that the witness saw the defendant rob the bank and recognizes the defendant. Indeed,

> there is no principled way of distinguishing between a cross-examination question that challenges a witness's perception of an event and a question that accuses the witness of fabricating an event. In both cases it is entirely possible that the event nevertheless occurred despite the inaccurate testimony. Moreover, both blatant accusations of fabrication and gentle inquiries into the witness's memory serve only one purpose—to question the credibility of the witness's testimony. A cross examination question that goes to the credibility of the government's witness, without a factual assertion contradicting the facts admitted in the proffer statement, is not sufficient to trigger the waiver provision here.

2. Other Uses. While the use of a defendant's prior proffer statement can be most damaging at trial, the agreement with the prosecutor may allow for other uses, even if they are not specifically addressed in the written terms. In United States v. Schwartz, 541 F.3d 1331 (11th Cir. 2008), an agent testified before the grand jury as to the substance of the proffer interviews with defendant Meyer. The relevant provision of the agreement provided: "The United States may make derivative use of the statements [Meyer] makes during the proffer and may pursue investigative leads therefrom, and would not be required to prove an independent source at any Kastigar or other hearing held thereon. By signing this agreement [Meyer] agrees to waive any right to a Kastigar hearing in the future." The Eleventh Circuit rejected the defendant's argument that the grand jury indictment should be dismissed because the government violated his rights under the proffer agreement:

> Although the agreement does not state explicitly that the Government may use Meyer's statement directly before the grand jury, we think it is nonetheless clear when read holistically. Meyer waived his right to a Kastigar hearing. Put differently, he waived his right to challenge the Government's use of his statements before the grand jury. We cannot conclude that he left himself vulnerable to what he characterizes as a Fifth Amendment violation but voluntarily waived his right to learn about and seek a remedy for that violation. The only reasonable inference is that Meyer intended to waive his Fifth Amendment privilege against use of his statements before the grand jury.
>
> That inference is strengthened by an application of the interpretive doctrine of noscitur a sociis, or a phrase is "known by its associates." In paragraph three of the agreement Meyer first voluntarily waives his Fifth Amendment privilege against derivative use of his statement against him at trial. In the next sentence he waives his right to a Kastigar hearing. We think the parties intended paragraph three to list ways the Government could use Meyer's statements notwithstanding the Fifth Amendment.

3. Knowing and Voluntary Waiver. In United States v. Plummer, 941 F.2d 799 (9th Cir. 1991), the Ninth Circuit applied "ordinary contract principles" in construing the limited immunity agreement, and found that the terms should be construed narrowly when the government drafted the agreement. Therefore, in determining the scope of immunity, the circuit court stated that "use immunity presumptively includes derivative use immunity, unless the government can demonstrate in a given case that, at the time the agreement was made, it expressly clarified that only direct use immunity was offered." In United States v. Aleman, 286 F.3d 86 (2d Cir. 2002), the circuit court noted that the contract interpretation also involved basic principles of fairness:

> Due process concerns color our interpretation of a contract involving defendant's constitutional rights. Due process not only requires that the government adhere to the terms of any plea bargain or immunity agreement it makes, but also requires us to construe agreements strictly against the government in recognition of its superior bargaining power and to presume that both parties to the agreement contemplated that all promises made were legal. Sometimes general fairness principles will require us to invalidate particular agreement terms.

4. Sixth Amendment. Can the government's demand for a waiver of the Rule 11(f) protections as a condition of negotiating a plea bargain violate the defendant's Sixth Amendment rights? In United States v. Duffy, 133 F.Supp.2d 213 (E.D.N.Y. 2001), District Judge Gershon ruled that a limited immunity agreement that permitted the government to use the defendant's statements "as substantive evidence to rebut any evidence offered or elicited, or factual assertions made, by or on behalf of [Duffy] at any stage of a criminal prosecution" violated the Sixth Amendment right to the effective assistance of counsel because it complete hamstrings any effort by counsel to represent the defendant. The Second Circuit rejected that position in United States v. Velez, 354 F.3d 190 (2d Cir. 2004). The defendant argued "that the waiver provision in the proffer agreement–which permits the Government to offer a proffer admission by the defendant in rebuttal to contradictory evidence or argument–violates defendant's constitutional rights to mount a defense, to the effective assistance of counsel, and to a fair trial." In rejecting this position, Circuit Judge Cabranes stated:

> In contending that the agreement is unenforceable, defendant relies principally on United States v. Duffy, 133 F.Supp.2d 213 (E.D.N.Y. 2001), in which the district court refused to enforce a waiver provision in a proffer agreement similar to the one we consider here. The Duffy ruling determined that the waiver provision "prevent[ed defense counsel] from making any sort of meaningful defense," and that it "exploit[ed]" a disparity of bargaining power between the Government and the defendant. The court stated: "After signing the standard proffer agreement, the terms of which are dictated by the government, the only thing that a defendant is guaranteed is the chance to convince the prosecutor to enter a deal. At the same time,

the defendant bears all of the risk." Concluding that the waiver provision effectively forfeited the defendant's fundamental rights to present a defense and to the effective assistance of counsel and, in doing so, implicated important public interests, the district court held the waiver provision unenforceable.

For the reasons that follow, we respectfully decline to adopt the position advanced in Duffy, and we note with approval the recent, contrasting opinion in United States v. Gomez, 210 F.Supp.2d 465 (S.D.N.Y. 2002), which found enforceable a proffer agreement containing a waiver provision identical to the one at issue in this case.

As the Gomez ruling points out, "fairness dictates that the agreement be enforced [. . .] If the proffer agreement is not enforced, a defendant will have less incentive to be truthful, for he will know that his proffer statements cannot be used against him at trial as long as he does not testify, even if he presents inconsistent evidence or arguments." See also United States v. Krilich (stating that, in proffer sessions, "a prosecutor needs assurance that the defendant is being candid" and that "[f]or this strategy to work the conditional waiver must be enforceable; its effect depends on making deceit costly ").

In addition, invalidating a waiver provision like the one before us would clearly interfere with plea bargaining and cooperation efforts–in direct contravention of the criminal justice system's legitimate goal of encouraging plea bargaining in appropriate circumstances. The Supreme Court has noted that, "[i]f prosecutors were precluded from securing [waiver] agreements, they might well decline to enter into cooperation discussions in the first place and might never take this potential first step toward a plea bargain." Mezzanatto; see also Gomez, ("Prosecutors will be reluctant to enter into cooperation agreements if they cannot obtain some assurance that the defendant will tell the truth.").

We do not lightly dismiss the observation in Duffy that the Government holds significant bargaining power in arranging proffer sessions and securing a waiver provision as a prerequisite for a defendant's participation. However, "[t]he mere potential for abuse of prosecutorial bargaining power is an insufficient basis for foreclosing negotiation altogether." * * * We thus reject the argument that defendant, relying on Duffy, makes in this case–that the asserted disparity of power between the Government and a defendant in proffers renders waiver provisions in proffer agreements unenforceable.

Finally, a defendant remains free to present evidence inconsistent with his proffer statements, with the fair consequence that, if he does, "the Government [is] then . . . permitted to present the defendant's own words in rebuttal." Gomez. With this avenue open to him, a defendant who has consented to a waiver provision like the one at issue here has not forfeited his constitutional right to present a defense, to the effective assistance of his counsel, or to a fair trial.

Accordingly, we reject defendant's claim that the waiver provision is unconstitutional, and we hold that, where a proffer agreement is entered into knowingly and voluntarily, a provision in which defendant waives his exclusionary privilege under Federal Rule of Evidence 410 by permitting the Government to introduce defendant's proffer statements to rebut contrary evidence or arguments presented by the defense, whether or not defendant testifies, is enforceable.

CHAPTER FOURTEEN
AGENCY INVESTIGATIONS AND THE PROBLEM OF PARALLEL PROCEEDINGS

The federal administrative agencies have developed enforcement staffs–comprised of both lawyers and investigators–with expertise in the intricacies of their particular fields. Unlike the United States Attorney's Offices, which deal with a broad range of cases from violent crime to sophisticated frauds, these enforcement officials are familiar with the inner workings of the industry they regulate and can ferret out wrongdoing that might not be apparent to the untrained eye. Quite often, federal prosecutors will rely on investigations by the administrative agencies to provide the details of the underlying misconduct, and agency lawyers may be appointed as "Special" Assistant United States Attorneys to assist in the presentation of a case to the grand jury and subsequent prosecution. 28 U.S.C. § 515.[a]

Of increasing importance in the field of administrative investigations are the Inspector Generals in now found in most federal agencies. The Inspector General Act, 5 U.S.C.App. 3 § 4(a)(1), created the office "to conduct, supervise, and coordinate audits and investigations relating to the programs and operations of the agency." The idea of an Inspector General who independently audits the work and conduct of an agency and its enforcement of the law was adopted by the Continental Congress during the Revolutionary War. The adoption of the Inspector General Act in 1978 came during an era in which the need for independent review of agency conduct was strong, and they are an important component in the law enforcement programs of many federal agencies, such as the Department of Health and Human Services, which is responsible for the oversight of programs with significant budgets, including Medicare and Medicaid. Professor Hartmus described the duties of the Inspector Generals:

> The Inspector General Act of 1978 charges IGs with five main duties. First, they are to conduct and supervise audits and investigations relating to the programs and operations of their agency. Second, they are to review existing and proposed legislation relating to their agencies, and to make recommendations regarding

[a] "The Attorney General or any other officer of the Department of Justice, or any attorney specially appointed by the Attorney General under law, may, when specifically directed by the Attorney General, conduct any kind of legal proceeding, civil or criminal, including grand jury proceedings and proceedings before committing magistrate judges, which United States attorneys are authorized by law to conduct, whether or not he is a resident of the district in which the proceeding is brought."

> the impact of such legislation on the economy and efficiency of the agency. Third, they are to recommend policies to promote economy, efficiency and effectiveness, and to provide leadership and coordination with other federal, state and local agencies. Fourth, they are to prevent and detect fraud and abuse in the programs and operations of their agencies. Fifth, they are to provide a means for keeping the head of the agency and the Congress informed about problems and deficiencies in the administration of their agencies' programs and operations, as well as the necessity for, and the progress of, corrective action.

Diane M. Hartmus, *Inspection and Oversight in the Federal Courts: Creating an Office of Inspector General*, 35 CALIF. WEST. L. REV. 243 (1999). The authority of the Inspector Generals includes investigations of misconduct by those outside the agency. In Adair v. Rose Law Firm, 867 F.Supp. 1111 (D.D.C. 1994), the District Court found that:

> the "relating to" language [in the Inspector General Act is] a broad grant of authority rather than a limitation. This language is expansive enough to extend the IG's authority beyond investigations of the agency itself to investigations of individuals and entities outside the agency involved with an agency's programs. Furthermore, other sections of the Inspector General Act clarify, if clarification is needed, that the IG's authority extends to conducting audits and investigations of programs that the agency finances, including investigations into alleged fraud, abuse and waste by government contractors and other recipients of government funds in connection with those programs. * * * It is obvious that the IG could not fulfill many of its responsibilities under * * * the Act * * * without investigating fraud, abuse and waste by both the agency administering and financing the program and the participants in the program.

In creating this broad administrative apparatus, Congress gave the regulatory authorities the power to compel the production of records and testimony that is, in many ways, similar to the investigative authority of the federal grand jury. As the Supreme Court discussed in **United States v. Morton Salt**, 338 U.S. 632 (1950):

> Because judicial power is reluctant if not unable to summon evidence until it is shown to be relevant to issues in litigation, it does not follow that an administrative agency charged with seeing that the laws are enforced may not have and exercise powers of original inquiry. It has a power of inquisition, if one chooses to call it that, which is not derived from the judicial function. It is more analogous to the Grand Jury, which does not depend on a case or controversy for power to get evidence but can investigate merely on suspicion that the law is being violated, or even just because it

> wants assurance that it is not. When investigative and accusatory duties are delegated by statute to an administrative body, it, too, may take steps to inform itself as to whether there is probable violation of the law.

The authority of an agency to conduct investigations and pursue administrative remedies is governed by particular statutes. Judicial oversight of administrative agencies will involve reviewing an agency's specific legislative authority, and also by reference to more general principles of fairness and due process. The Internal Revenue Service (IRS) is the most closely scrutinized federal agency because it deals with such highly sensitive information. Courts have been very careful in deciding whether to enforce the efforts of the IRS to gather information, and Congress has enacted detailed requirements for the agency to obtain information from a taxpayer and from third parties. The next section deals with the IRS investigations. The following sections treat other federal agencies, and consider the standards applied to those investigations and how courts have not scrutinized those agencies to the same degree as the IRS. This is especially notable in the area of concurrent civil and criminal investigations, and the use of a civil regulatory agency to gather information for use in a grand jury investigation. The Chapter reviews the administrative remedies available to an agency that finds a violation of the laws it is charged with administering, and concludes with consideration of the problems that can arise from parallel civil and criminal investigations.

A. INTERNAL REVENUE SERVICE INVESTIGATIONS

1. ***Civil and Criminal Investigations***. The Internal Revenue Service (IRS) is responsible for the collection of taxes and enforcement of the federal tax code, which reaches virtually every business and adult in the country. In **United States v. Peters**, 153 F.3d 445 (7th Cir. 1998), the Seventh Circuit explained how the IRS divides its investigatory authority into civil and criminal components:

> The IRS splits the responsibility for enforcing the nation's tax laws between its two investigative divisions. The Criminal Investigative Division ("CID") is charged with investigating criminal violations of the tax code and related federal statutes. CID investigators are called "special agents." Like many other criminal law enforcement agents, they carry firearms and badges. In addition, special agents must recite an administrative warning prior to soliciting information from taxpayers.
>
> On the other hand, the Examination Division of the IRS is responsible for conducting civil tax audits. Examination Division investigators are known as "revenue agents." In contrast to special agents, revenue agents do not carry firearms; nor are they required

to provide taxpayers with an administrative warning. Although an Examination Division audit typically concludes with some sort of civil settlement between the IRS and the taxpayer, such an audit may uncover evidence that causes the revenue agent to refer the case to the CID for criminal investigation. Under IRS regulations, a revenue agent who uncovers a "firm indication of fraud on the part of the taxpayer" must immediately suspend her audit and refer the case to the CID.

If the IRS uncovers evidence of what it believes is a criminal violation of the tax laws, then the case is referred to the Tax Division of the Department of Justice, which is responsible for the any resulting criminal prosecution of the case. The IRS remains involved in the criminal case because its CID agents assist in the investigation, in much the same way the FBI or Secret Service agents assist prosecutors in investigations.

The Internal Revenue Manual describes the process by which the agency determines whether to make a criminal referral in a matter under investigation:

> (1) This section discusses the fact that fraud case begins with the recognition of affirmative indications and acts of fraud by the taxpayer. Further development of these "indicators" assists the employee in establishing the firm indications necessary for a successful fraud case.
>
> (2) When initial indications of fraud are uncovered, the compliance employee should initiate a discussion with his/her group manager. A plan of action should be developed as early as possible to document firm indications of fraud. An integral part of the plan is establishing that sufficient affirmative acts exist which confirm fraud. * * *
>
> (3) When first alerted to the possibility of fraud, the compliance employee must know when to suspend action on the case and prepare a criminal referral. If the compliance employee stops too soon all the information necessary to document firm indications of fraud may not be developed sufficiently for the Criminal Investigation (Cl) function.
>
> (4) The minimum plan of development should include following up on all leads indicated as fraud indicators, securing copies of all relevant data relating to indicators of fraud and noting from whom and when obtained. Documents obtained from the taxpayer or other third parties should not be annotated with any comments by the compliance employee. It is critical for the employee to secure the taxpayer's explanations for any discrepancies.

> (5) An understatement of the tax liability alone is not fraud. In order to sustain the penalty or make a criminal referral, the compliance employee must establish the intent was to defraud.

Internal Revenue Manual Ch. 21.1.3.

Criminal tax prosecutions are comparatively rare, especially given the large number of tax returns filed every year by businesses and individuals, so the opportunities to avoid punishment for the evasion of taxes are significant. The IRS and the Tax Division of the Department of Justice have limited resources, and tax cases are considered among the most difficult to prosecute because of their complexity and perceived lack of jury appeal. Quite often, tax charges are brought as an adjunct to other substantive charges. For example, in McCormick v. United States [p. 119], the government charged the defendant with tax fraud for failing to report the payments from the foreign doctors that he asserted were campaign contributions, in addition to the Hobbs Act charge. For other tax prosecutions, the government targets its resources to achieve the greatest effect.

> As a practical matter the Service may be more likely to press a case involving a locally prominent taxpayer than a relatively obscure person. The basic reason for this is that the maximum deterrent, in the view of the Service, comes from prosecution of the otherwise reputable taxpayer. Similarly, in the case of celebrities or nationally prominent persons, indictment will be sought for their national publicity and deterrent value although the process of internal review is apparently more stringent in such instances.

Ray A. Knight & Lee G. Knight, *Criminal Tax Fraud: An Analytical Review*, 57 MO. L. REV. 175 (1992).

2. **The *Powell* Test.** The IRS has the authority to issue a summons to obtain information to determine whether a taxpayer has properly paid taxes. A summons is similar to a grand jury subpoena in that it compels the recipient to do any of the following:

> (1) To examine any books, papers, records, or other data which may be relevant or material to such inquiry;
>
> (2) to summon the person liable for tax or required to perform the act, or any officer or employee of such person, or any person having possession, custody, or care of books of account containing entries relating to the business of the person liable for tax or required to perform the act, or any other person the Secretary may deem proper, to appear before the Secretary at a time and place named in the summons and to produce such books, papers, records, or other data, and to give such testimony, under oath, as may be relevant or

material to such inquiry; and

(3) To take such testimony of the person concerned, under oath, as may be relevant or material to such inquiry.

26 U.S.C. § 7602(a). If the summons recipient refuses to comply, the IRS must apply to the court for an order compelling compliance with the summons. Unlike a proceeding to enforce a grand jury subpoena, a summons enforcement proceeding is treated as a separate civil proceeding, and an enforcement order is directly appealable by the taxpayer as a final decision under 28 U.S.C.A. § 1291. See Church of Scientology of California v. United States, 506 U.S. 9 (1992). The same is true for enforcement of subpoenas issued on behalf of other administrative agencies. Moreover, compliance with the enforcement order does not render moot a subsequent appeal, as the appellate court can order the return to the taxpayer of the subpoenaed material and destruction of all copies made by the agency. Church of Scientology of California v. United States.

In **United States v. Powell**, 379 U.S. 48 (1964), the Supreme Court established a four-part test to determine whether enforcement of an IRS summons is proper: "[The IRS] must show that the investigation will be conducted pursuant to a legitimate purpose, that the inquiry may be relevant to the purpose, that the information sought is not already within the Commissioner's possession, and that the administrative steps required by the Code have been followed." The *Powell* test has been further refined, as explained by the First Circuit in **United States v. Gertner,**[b] 65 F.3d 963 (1st Cir.1995):

---

[b] *Gertner* arose in the following context:

> At various times in 1991 and 1992, respondents Nancy Gertner and Jody Newman, then partners in a Boston law firm, filed forms reflecting four successive payments of hefty cash fees to the firm by a single client. Each of the forms was essentially complete except for the name of the client. The respondents advised the IRS that they were withholding the client's identity on the basis of ethical obligations, attorney-client privilege, and specified constitutional protections. * * *
>
> The parties remained deadlocked and the IRS issued summonses purporting to direct the respondents to furnish certain records and testimony anent the client's identity. The respondents declined to comply. The government then brought an enforcement action pursuant to I.R.C. §§ 7402(a) & 7604(a), claiming that it wanted the information in connection with an investigation of the law firm's tax liability.

The First Circuit noted the "remarkably thin prima facie case established by Agent Ameno's declaration provides a shallow foundation for a presumption in favor of the government."

* * * This court has constructed a three-tiered framework for [enforcement] determinations. To mount the first tier, the IRS must make a prima facie showing that it is acting in good faith and for a lawful purpose. * * * [That may be satisfied by] an affidavit of the investigating agent attesting to satisfaction of the four *Powell* elements * * *. Once this minimal showing surfaces, the burden shifts to the taxpayer to rebut the good-faith presumption that arises in consequence of the government's prima facie case. The taxpayer is not at this stage required to *disprove* the government's profession of good faith. She must, however, shoulder a significant burden of production: in order to advance past the first tier, the taxpayer must articulate specific allegations of bad faith and, if necessary, produce reasonably particularized evidence in support of those allegations. This showing does not demand that the taxpayer conclusively give the lie to the prima facie case, but only that she create a "substantial question in the court's mind regarding the validity of the government's purpose." To reach this goal, it is not absolutely essential that the taxpayer adduce additional or independent evidence; she may hoist her burden either by citing new facts or by bringing to light mortal weaknesses in the government's proffer. * * * If the taxpayer satisfies this burden of production, the third tier beckons. At this stage, the district court weighs the facts, draws inferences, and decides the issue. To do so, the court frequently will proceed to an evidentiary hearing, taking testimony and exhibits from both sides. But there is no hard-and-fast rule compelling an evidentiary hearing. A district court may, in appropriate circumstances, forgo such a hearing and decide the issues on the existing record.

A question lingers at the third tier as to the continuing viability of the original presumption in favor of the IRS. The case law seems to suggest that the presumption endures and serves at this stage to saddle the taxpayer with the burden of persuading the judge, *qua* factfinder, that at least one of the *Powell* elements is missing. * * * [The usual treatment of presumptions], codified in the Federal Rules of Evidence * * * [is that] "a presumption imposes on the party against whom it is directed the burden of going forward with evidence to rebut or meet the presumption, but does not shift to such party the burden of proof in the sense of the risk of nonpersuasion, which remains throughout the trial upon the party on whom it was originally cast." Fed. R. Evid. 301.* * * We are hard-pressed to fathom why IRS enforcement proceedings should diverge from this principle. It is the IRS, not the taxpayer, that seeks to invoke the processes of the court; and, in a related vein, the court is instructed to grant the requested relief only when "sufficient proof is made." § 7604(b). Though it certainly can be argued that "strong reasons of public policy" justify a burden-shifting scheme, it would seem that the IRS's legitimate interest in obtaining summary enforcement is satisfactorily addressed by the particularized burden of production

> imposed on the taxpayer, without going the whole hog. * * * [But] we defer a definitive decision on * * * [this question] to a different day. After all, the respondents concede that the district court tacitly required them to prove improper purpose by a preponderance of the evidence, and they accepted the burden of proof without any objection. * * *

The Ninth Circuit rejected the burden-shifting analysis advanced in *Gertner*, which it described as "*dicta*," and leaves the burden on the taxpayer once the IRS meets its initial "slight" burden of meeting the four-part *Powell* test. United States v. Crystal, 172 F.3d 1141 (9th Cir. 1999).

3. ***Challenging Good Faith.*** When a taxpayer believes that the IRS has not acted in good faith, the most common means to challenge that assertion under the *Powell* test is to seek the testimony of the agent responsible for the inquiry. The issue is what standard a court should apply to determining whether to permit questioning of the agent. In **United States v. Clark**, 134 S. Ct. 2361 (2014), the Supreme Court resolved a split in the circuits by adopting the following test for when a taxpayer challenges the good faith element:

> As part of the adversarial process concerning a summons's validity, the taxpayer is entitled to examine an IRS agent when he can point to specific facts or circumstances plausibly raising an inference of bad faith. Naked allegations of improper purpose are not enough: The taxpayer must offer some credible evidence supporting his charge. But circumstantial evidence can suffice to meet that burden; after all, direct evidence of another person's bad faith, at this threshold stage, will rarely if ever be available. And although bare assertion or conjecture is not enough, neither is a fleshed out case demanded: The taxpayer need only make a showing of facts that give rise to a plausible inference of improper motive. That standard will ensure inquiry where the facts and circumstances make inquiry appropriate, without turning every summons dispute into a fishing expedition for official wrongdoing.

4. ***Third-Party Summons.*** If the IRS issues a summons to a third-party to obtain information as part of an examination of a taxpayer, and the summons identifies the person whose information is the subject of the summons, then the IRS must provide a copy of the summons to the identified person. In addition, that person has a right to file a motion to quash the summons or intervene in a proceeding to enforce the summons. 26 U.S.C. § 7609(a).

The IRS can also issue what is known as a "John Doe Summons" in which the particular taxpayer who is the subject of the examination is not identified. Under 26 U.S.C. § 7609(f), the IRS must comply with the following procedures before the summons can be issued:

> Any summons * * * which does not identify the person with respect to whose liability the summons is issued may be served only after a court proceeding in which the Secretary establishes that--
>
> (1) the summons relates to the investigation of a particular person or ascertainable group or class of persons,
>
> (2) there is a reasonable basis for believing that such person or group or class of persons may fail or may have failed to comply with any provision of any internal revenue law, and
>
> (3) the information sought to be obtained from the examination of the records or testimony (and the identity of the person or persons with respect to whose liability the summons is issued) is not readily available from other sources.

5. ***Judicial Review of Internal IRS Decisions.*** In **United States v. Peters**, 153 F.3d 445 (7th Cir. 1998), the Seventh Circuit discussed the problem with the judicial role in determining whether the IRS agent had a "firm indication of fraud" such that the civil audit should have been terminated:

> [T]he "firm indications of fraud" standard is a difficult standard for federal courts to apply because it is inherently vague and depends, in large part, on the good faith and professional judgment of the revenue agents conducting the investigation at issue. When applying this standard, federal courts must navigate between two perils. On the one side, courts face the Scylla of judicial micromanagement of the inner functionings of an administrative agency, a peril recognized by many of the courts that have addressed this issue. Yet, on the other side, courts face the Charybdis of judicial abdication of their Article III duty to protect the constitutional rights of criminal defendants. As the district court recognized, this latter peril will be realized if the courts are forced to rely solely on the after-the-fact assessments of revenue agents who may have an incentive to use the discretionary nature of the "firm indications" rule to shield their actions from judicial scrutiny.
>
> In navigating the narrow course necessitated by these two perils, courts must remember that the "firm indications of fraud" rule is but a tool for courts to utilize in determining whether the revenue agents made an affirmative misrepresentation to a defendant or her representatives concerning the nature of their investigation.

6. ***Constitutional Protections in IRS Audits.*** The IRS Manual does not explicitly refer to any rights of a taxpayer in describing when a case should be referred for further criminal investigation and possible prosecution. In United States v. McKee, 192 F.3d 535 (6th Cir. 1999), the circuit court stated

that "an affirmative representation by an IRS agent that the investigation is routine when in fact it is a criminal investigation requires suppression of evidence." *McKee* referred to the Fourth and Fifth Amendment rights of the taxpayers, but those rights are not implicated in any traditional sense during an IRS civil audit. The Fifth Amendment right against self-incrimination only applies to compelled testimony or custodial interrogations, neither of which are present in a tax audit. Moreover, while the taxpayer may be compelled to produce records, the Fifth Amendment does not apply to pre-existing documents. Similarly, the Fourth Amendment applies to searches and seizures, but the IRS summons is equivalent to a grand jury subpoena and is not a search. Is the court's concern grounded more in the nature of the tax system, that taxpayers are expected to voluntarily report their income, so that instances of misleading conduct or misrepresentations by an IRS agent will have a detrimental effect on the operation of the tax system? See United States v. Grunewald, 987 F.2d 531 (8th Cir. 1993)("It would be a flagrant disregard of individuals' rights to deliberately deceive, or even lull, taxpayers into incriminating themselves during an audit when activities of an obviously criminal nature are under investigation."). The police are usually permitted to engage in deceptive actions to gather evidence, and in a voluntary interview, the government is not required to reveal whether a person is suspected of criminal behavior, so why would conduct by an IRS agent that "lulls" a taxpayer into revealing information be a constitutional violation?

7. ***Effect on Other Agencies.*** The solicitude of courts for the rights of taxpayers apparently springs from concern that the IRS may abuse its enormous authority in an area that touches virtually all citizens and involves some of the most intimate details of their lives. The restrictive approach to IRS civil audits does not translate to civil law enforcement investigations by other agencies of the federal government. See SEC v. Dresser Industries, 628 F.2d 1368 (D.C. Cir. 1980)(discussed in Note 4, p. 621).

B. CIVIL LAW ENFORCEMENT AGENCY INVESTIGATIONS

1. Distinguishing Between IRS and Other Agency Investigations

The subject of administrative investigations argued that the four-part *Powell* test required the Securities and Exchange Commission to notify the subject of its investigation that the agency issued a subpoena to a third party for records. The Supreme Court firmly rejected that position in **Securities and Exchange Commission v. Jerry T. O'Brien, Inc.**, 467 U.S. 735 (1984):

> There are several tenuous links in respondents' argument. Especially debatable are the proposition that a target has a substantive right to be investigated in a manner consistent with the

Powell standards and the assertion that a target may obtain a restraining order preventing voluntary compliance by a third party with an administrative subpoena. Certainly we have never before expressly so held. For the present, however, we may assume, *arguendo*, that a target enjoys each of the substantive and procedural rights identified by respondents. Nevertheless, we conclude that it would be inappropriate to elaborate upon those entitlements by mandating notification of targets whenever the Commission issues subpoenas.

Two considerations underlie our decision on this issue. First, administration of the notice requirement advocated by respondents would be highly burdensome for both the Commission and the courts. The most obvious difficulty would involve identification of the persons and organizations that should be considered "targets" of investigations. The SEC often undertakes investigations into suspicious securities transactions without any knowledge of which of the parties involved may have violated the law.[u] To notify all potential wrongdoers in such a situation of the issuance of each subpoena would be virtually impossible. The Commission would thus be obliged to determine the point at which enough evidence had been assembled to focus suspicion on a manageable subset of the participants in the transaction, thereby lending them the status of "targets" and entitling them to notice of the outstanding subpoenas directed at others. The complexity of that task is apparent. Even in cases in which the Commission could identify with reasonable ease the principal targets of its inquiry, another problem would arise. In such circumstances, a person not considered a target by the Commission could contend that he deserved that status and therefore should be given notice of subpoenas issued to others. To assess a claim of this sort, a district court would be obliged to conduct some kind of hearing to determine the scope and thrust of the ongoing investigation. Implementation of this new remedy would drain the resources of the judiciary as well as the Commission.

Second, the imposition of a notice requirement on the SEC would substantially increase the ability of persons who have something to hide to impede legitimate investigations by the Commission. A target given notice of every subpoena issued to third parties would be able to discourage the recipients from complying, and then further delay disclosure of damaging information by seeking

---

[u] So, for example, the Commission is sometimes called upon to investigate unusually active trading in the stock of a company during the period immediately preceding a tender offer for that stock. In such a case, the Commission may have no idea which (if any) of the thousands of purchasers had improper access to inside information.

> intervention in all enforcement actions brought by the Commission. More seriously, the understanding of the progress of an SEC inquiry that would flow from knowledge of which persons had received subpoenas would enable an unscrupulous target to destroy or alter documents, intimidate witnesses, or transfer securities or funds so that they could not be reached by the Government. Especially in the context of securities regulation, where speed in locating and halting violations of the law is so important, we would be loathe to place such potent weapons in the hands of persons with a desire to keep the Commission at bay.
>
> We acknowledge that our ruling may have the effect in practice of preventing some persons under investigation by the SEC from asserting objections to subpoenas issued by the Commission to third parties for improper reasons. However, to accept respondents' proposal "would unwarrantedly cast doubt upon and stultify the [Commission's] every investigatory move," *Donaldson v. United States*. Particularly in view of Congress' manifest disinclination to require the Commission to notify targets whenever it seeks information from others, we refuse so to curb the Commission's exercise of its statutory power.

2. Enforcement of Agency Subpoenas

In re ADMINISTRATIVE SUBPOENA JOHN DOE, D.P.M.

253 F.3d 256 (6th Cir. 2001)

MOORE, Circuit Judge.

Petitioner-Appellant John Doe ("Doe" or "petitioner") appeals the district court's order denying his motion to quash an administrative subpoena issued by the Department of Justice pursuant to a health care fraud investigation. Doe, a podiatrist, is under investigation for an alleged kickback arrangement with two medical testing laboratories. The administrative subpoena, issued pursuant to the Department of Justice's authority under § 248 of the Health Insurance Portability & Accountability Act ("HIPAA"), ordered Doe to turn over a number of documents, including:

> records relating to his professional education and ethical training; personal and business financial records; records evidencing any asset transfers by Doe to his children; and various patient files.

John Doe, D.P.M., a podiatrist operating a clinic in the Cleveland metropolitan area, is under investigation by the FBI and a federal grand jury for an alleged "kickback" arrangement with two medical testing laboratories. More specifically, it is alleged that Doe received payments from these labs for referring his patients to them for medically unnecessary vascular and electrodiagnostic tests. The government alleges that these kickbacks were disguised as rental payments that the labs made to Doe for the periodic use of one room in his clinic. The government has obtained documents through previous subpoenas evidencing lease agreements with the labs that show that, in less than three years, approximately $10,000 was paid to Doe for the use of a single room in his clinic for a few hours each month. By contrast, Doe himself only paid about $16,800 in rent for the entire office over that same period of time. The government claims that, based on information discovered thus far, Doe may have aided one of the laboratories in submitting false claims approximating $150,000 to various health care benefit programs. These programs paid approximately $57,000 on the claims.

The government also has evidence from independent medical experts stating that one of the labs to which Doe referred patients was performing a grossly excessive amount of electrodiagnostic testing. * * *

Pursuant to the DOJ's investigation, a series of subpoenas were issued to Doe requesting various documents. In the first subpoena, issued August 5, 1998, the DOJ requested lease agreements between Doe and the labs, any payments made to Doe by any medical service provider, including laboratories, and information on tests performed on patients by any medical service provider. The second subpoena, issued May 25, 1999, requested information on various patients. The third subpoena, an administrative subpoena and the subpoena at issue in this case, was ordered pursuant to the DOJ's authority under § 248 of the HIPAA, which allows the Attorney General or her designee to issue subpoenas requiring the production of records "which may be relevant to" a "Federal health care offense" investigation. 18 U.S.C. § 3486(a)(1)(A).[1]

The administrative subpoena ordered Doe's records custodian to turn over a number of documents by August 28, 2000.[a] * * * Doe did not turn over

---

[1] On December 19, 2000, several months after the subpoena was issued in this case, the Presidential Threat Protection Act of 2000, Pub.L. No. 106-544, 114 Stat. 2715, altered the precise statutory language authorizing the Attorney General to issue administrative subpoenas pursuant to federal health care investigations. Although we apply § 3486 as it existed at the time the subpoena was issued, we note that the changes made in the language of § 3486 would not alter the ultimate outcome in this case.

[a] Similar to the broad grand jury subpoenas duces tecum discussed in Chapter 9 supra., the administrative subpoena here sought voluminous documents from Doe, including five years of patient files if they were referred to a testing laboratory for certain tests:

1) all professional journals, magazines, and newsletters subscribed to or received by Doe from January 1990 through March 1998;
2) copies of recent bank and other financial records showing the current location, amount, and value of all Doe's personal and health care-related business assets, whether jointly or individually held;
3) copies of recent bank and other financial records showing the current

these documents. Instead, on August 29, 2000, Doe filed in the district court a motion to quash the subpoena, or, in the alternative, to issue a protective order. In this motion, Doe called the government's latest document request "unreasonably burdensome" and questioned its relevance.

* * * The district court denied the motion to quash because "the subpoena was issued within the authority of the U.S. Attorney General, the records sought [were] relevant to the government's health-care fraud investigation, the materials [were] not already in the possession of the Department of Justice, and [because the] Court's process would not be abused by enforcement of the subpoena." * * *

As noted in its heading, 18 U.S.C. § 3486 authorizes the Attorney General or her designee to issue "[a]dministrative subpoenas in [f]ederal health care investigations[.]" Doe claims that, by enforcing the DOJ's administrative subpoena in this case, his Fourth Amendment right to be free from unreasonable searches and seizures has been violated.

This circuit has noted that a district court plays only a limited role in the enforcement of an administrative subpoena. All the district court must do in deciding whether to enforce an administrative subpoena is 1) determine whether the administrative agency to which Congress has granted the subpoena power, in this case the DOJ, has satisfied the statutory prerequisites to issuing and enforcing the subpoena, and 2) determine whether the agency has satisfied the judicially created standards for enforcing administrative subpoenas. We first turn to the judicially created standards that must be met for an administrative subpoena to be enforced.

In Oklahoma Press Publishing Co. v. Walling, 327 U.S. 186 (1946), one of the Supreme Court's first major cases addressing the constitutionality of an administrative subpoena under the Fourth Amendment, the Court created

---

location, amount, and value of all Doe's children's assets insofar as those assets were provided or derived from the individual or jointly held assets of Doe;
4) all documents and patient files evidencing Doe's referral of patients for certain electrodiagnostic tests after April 2, 1998;
5) all documents and patient files after January 1, 1993 evidencing Doe's referral of patients to a specific medical testing laboratory for certain diagnostic ultrasound tests;
6) complete academic transcripts and records from medical or podiatric school, as well as any other post-graduate training;
7) all documents concerning the extent of Doe's continuing medical education, including a list and description of courses taken, credit hours earned, and any materials provided in those courses;
8) all documents concerning ethics, professional responsibility, and medical-billing issues in Doe's custody; and
9) retained copies of federal, state, and local tax returns both for Doe and any of his businesses from 1993 to the present.

standards for the enforcement of administrative subpoenas that are still used today. In *Oklahoma Press,* the Court held that a subpoena duces tecum for corporate records issued by the Department of Labor would comply with the Constitution so long as the demand for documents

> is authorized by Congress, is for a purpose Congress can order, and the documents sought are relevant to the inquiry. Beyond this the requirement of reasonableness, including particularity in describing the place to be searched, and the persons or things to be seized ... comes down to [whether] specification of the documents to be produced [is] adequate, but not excessive, for the purposes of the relevant inquiry. Necessarily, . . . this cannot be reduced to formula; for relevancy and adequacy or excess in the breadth of the subpoena are matters variable in relation to the nature, purposes and scope of the inquiry.

Put more succinctly in United States v. Morton Salt Co., 338 U.S. 632 (1950), another case involving a request for corporate documents, the Court stated that an agency's request for documents should be approved by the judiciary so long as it "is within the authority of the agency, the demand is not too indefinite and the information sought is reasonably relevant." In other words, the agency request must be reasonable.

It is from the last major Supreme Court case on the issue, United States v. Powell, 379 U.S. 48 (1964), that the basic language of the "reasonable relevance" test employed by this circuit emanates. * * *

The *Powell* Court was concerned that requiring the IRS to show probable cause that a tax fraud had been committed would seriously hinder the agency's ability to conduct these kinds of investigations. Thus, rather than probable cause, the Court held that all the IRS need show to obtain judicial enforcement of a summons is "that the investigation will be conducted pursuant to a legitimate purpose, that the inquiry may be relevant to the purpose, that the information sought is not already within the Commissioner's possession, and that the administrative steps required by the Code have been followed[.]" We still use this test today when examining administrative subpoenas. As this circuit has summarized, "[w]hile the court's function is neither minor nor ministerial" when deciding whether to enforce an administrative subpoena, "the scope of the issues which may be litigated in an enforcement proceeding must be narrow, because of the important governmental interest in the expeditious investigation of possible unlawful activity."

Following *Powell* and the precedent of this circuit, we hold that the DOJ need not make a showing of probable cause to issue an administrative subpoena under 18 U.S.C. § 3486, nor does petitioner argue for such a standard on appeal. In In re Subpoena Duces Tecum, 228 F.3d 341 (4th Cir.2000), the U.S. Court of Appeals for the Fourth Circuit was the first circuit court to address administrative subpoenas issued under § 3486. As the Fourth Circuit explained, whereas the Fourth Amendment mandates a showing of probable cause for the issuance of search warrants, subpoenas are analyzed only under the Fourth Amendment's general reasonableness standard. One primary reason for this distinction is that, unlike "the immediacy and intrusiveness of a search and seizure conducted pursuant to a warrant[,]" the reasonableness of an administrative subpoena's command can be contested in federal court before being enforced. * * *

We agree with the Fourth Circuit that the reasonable relevance test should apply to administrative subpoenas under § 3486. Both the Supreme Court and this circuit have long applied this test when reviewing administrative subpoena requests, and we see no convincing basis upon which to distinguish these binding precedents simply because this subpoena was issued pursuant to a criminal, as opposed to civil, investigation.

Following Supreme Court precedent on the enforcement of administrative subpoenas, this circuit has held that a subpoena is properly enforced if 1) it satisfies the terms of its authorizing statute, 2) the documents requested were relevant to the DOJ's investigation, 3) the information sought is not already in the DOJ's possession, and 4) enforcing the subpoena will not constitute an abuse of the court's process.

* * * [T]he administrative subpoena at issue in this case requested nine categories of documents [see footnote a supra]. Of these, two involve requests for the files of patients who were referred to outside labs for additional testing. Doe no longer disputes the reasonableness of the government's request for patient documents, however, and thus we will not address this aspect of the subpoena. Of the remaining categories, four encompass documents related to Doe's professional education and the extent of his ethical training, two involve Doe's personal and business financial records, and the final request seeks those bank and other financial records of Doe's children showing any assets that "were provided or derived from individual or jointly held assets of [John Doe.]"

We will now address whether the requirements for enforcing an administrative subpoena have been met in this case, focusing on each of the different categories of documents in turn. * * * Petitioner does not argue that this administrative subpoena fails to comply with the statutory requirements of § 3486. Indeed, to do so would be difficult given the broad subpoena power that the statute gives to the Attorney General and her designees. The provision states:

> In any investigation relating to any act or activity involving a Federal health care offense, . . . the Attorney General or the Attorney General's designee may issue in writing and cause to be served a subpoena . . . requiring the production of any records (including any books, papers, documents, electronic media, or other objects or tangible things), which may be relevant to an authorized

law enforcement inquiry, that a person or legal entity may possess or have care, custody, or control[.]

18 U.S.C. § 3486(a)(1)(A). The Code broadly defines a "Federal health care offense" as a violation of, or a conspiracy to violate, a number of health-care related offenses, including 18 U.S.C. § 1035 (false statements relating to health care matters) and 18 U.S.C. § 1347 (health care fraud). 18 U.S.C. § 24(a)(1). A federal health care offense also encompasses a variety of general criminal violations (*e.g.*, mail and wire fraud under 18 U.S.C. §§ 1341 and 1343), if those violations "relate[ ] to a health care benefit program." 18 U.S.C. § 24(a)(2).

Section 3486 also requires that any subpoena issued describe the objects to be produced and allow a reasonable period of time for the items to be assembled. 18 U.S.C. § 3486(a)(2). The subpoenaed party need not deliver any documents requested pursuant to § 3486 more than 500 miles from the place where it was served. 18 U.S.C. § 3486(a)(3).

There is no dispute that the investigation at issue in this case relates to a potential federal health care offense. While Doe does describe the subpoena as "overly burdensome[,]" he does not argue that the length of time given him to comply with the subpoena or the designated delivery location for the requested documents are beyond the scope of the authority granted in § 3486. Instead, the primary point of contention in this case is whether the documents requested are relevant to the DOJ's investigation of Doe. Because § 3486 authorizes subpoena requests for documents "which *may be relevant* to an authorized law enforcement inquiry," § 3486(a)(1)(A) (emphasis added), the question of the relevance of the documents requested is inherently a question of whether the DOJ had the statutory authority to issue this subpoena. Nevertheless, because the second element of our test for determining the enforceability of an administrative subpoena focuses on the relevance of the documents to the agency's investigation, we will address this issue under that heading. Thus, aside from the question of relevance, we are confident that the DOJ has satisfied § 3486's statutory requirements for issuing this administrative subpoena.

While we have no circuit precedent addressing the administrative subpoena relevance requirement as it relates to documents requested under § 3486, other administrative subpoena cases in this circuit, as well as Supreme Court precedent, hold that relevance should be construed broadly. First, we note that the language of § 3486 indicates that the question of an administrative subpoena's relevance is not a question of evidentiary relevance, but rather is simply a question of whether the documents requested pursuant to the subpoena are relevant to the health care fraud investigation being undertaken. 18 U.S.C. § 3486(a)(1)(A). Furthermore, in *Markwood,* while we did not have to engage in a discussion of the relevance of the documents requested through the administrative subpoena, we did note often the deference that courts must show to the statutory authority of the administrative agency, stating that subpoenas should be enforced when "'the evidence sought by the subpoena [is] not plainly incompetent or irrelevant to any lawful purpose of the [agency] in the discharge of [its] duties.'"

In EEOC v. Ford Motor Credit Co., 26 F.3d 44 (6th Cir.1994), this court discussed the relevance requirement as it related to administrative subpoenas issued by the EEOC. Following Supreme Court precedent, we explained that the term "relevant" in the statute authorizing the EEOC to issue administrative subpoenas had been construed broadly so as to allow "the Commission access to virtually any material that might cast light on the allegations against the employer." We noted that this broad interpretation of relevance was influenced by Congress's intent that the EEOC have the authority to demand documents that it deemed relevant to its investigation. We stated, however, that, while relevance should be viewed broadly, because the court was given the duty of reviewing the agency's decision to issue a subpoena, it did not simply have to accept the agency's opinion as to what is and is not relevant to agency investigations. Ultimately, we decided that, in reviewing whether an administrative subpoena should be enforced, we would "weigh the likely relevance of the requested material to the investigation against the burden . . . of producing the material."

As with the EEOC's subpoena power, it appears clear, both from the language of the statute and from Congress's intent in enacting HIPAA, that the DOJ's subpoena power in investigating federal health care offenses is meant to be broad. Section 3486 authorizes the Attorney General or her designee to subpoena any records "which *may be relevant*" to an authorized investigation, thus illustrating the substantial scope of the subpoena power Congress intended to give to the Attorney General. 18 U.S.C. § 3486(a)(1)(A) (emphasis added).

Aside from the statutory language, other evidence of Congress's intent to grant the Attorney General a broad subpoena power can be found in HIPAA's legislative history. One of the main legislative purposes of HIPAA was to prevent[ ] health care fraud and abuse. H.R.Rep. No. 104-496, at 67 (1996). As the House Ways and Means Committee Report stated in recommending that HIPAA be passed:

> In order to address the problem of health care cost inflation and make insurance more affordable, it is important to focus on key sources affecting levels of the underlying health care costs. Two key sources of excessive cost are medical fraud and abuse, and the current medical paperwork burden.
>
> According to the General Accounting Office (GAO), as much as 10 percent of total health care costs are lost to fraudulent or abusive practices by unscrupulous health care providers. The GAO reports that only a small fraction of the fraud and abuse committed in the health care system is identified and dealt with. Federal funding for prevention, detection, and prosecutions of the perpetrators of health

> care fraud and abuse has not kept pace with the problem. Coordination of the various law enforcement agencies at the federal and state levels has been insufficient, and law enforcement agencies agree that penalties for health care fraud and abuse should be increased.

H.R.Rep. No. 104-496. It is safe to assume that Congress, in passing HIPAA, recognized the serious problem that health care fraud had become, and that, through this legislation, Congress was intending to strike back at this problem. Accordingly, in light of both the statutory language and legislative history of § 3486, it appears that Congress intended to give the Attorney General broad authority to conduct health care fraud investigations, thus entailing a less restricted interpretation of what records may be subpoenaed under § 3486 because they are "relevant" to a health care investigation.

While the *Ford Motor* court's decision to weigh the likely relevance of requested material against the burden of producing that material came in the context of an EEOC administrative subpoena, we did not confine our reasoning only to that type of administrative subpoena, nor is there any basis for following a different course in this case. The administrative subpoena powers under both Title VII and HIPAA are broadly defined, and the *Ford Motor* court's approach of balancing the likely relevance of documents against the burden of their production clearly appears applicable in this case. With this background in mind, we now turn to an analysis of the relevance of the various materials requested in this subpoena.

As noted earlier, of the nine categories of documents subpoenaed by the DOJ, four categories request documents relating to Doe's professional education and training regarding ethical issues. * * *

The government claims that these documents are relevant to its investigation because they go to show Doe's intent. If it were to prosecute Doe for these alleged kickback agreements, the government states that it would have to prove that "[Doe] knew as a general matter that the concept of remuneration for referrals was somehow wrongful (whether illegal or unethical)[.]" The government further states that its request for documents relating to Doe's medical training will aid it in learning the extent to which Doe may have known that the tests to which he was subjecting his patients were medically unnecessary.

The government, through its proffered reasons for requesting documents relating to Doe's professional education and ethical training, has sufficiently shown how these documents are relevant to its underlying health care fraud investigation. The extent to which Doe knew that these tests were medically unnecessary and the extent to which he knew that kickback arrangements were illegal or unethical are not ancillary or unimportant issues in an investigation of possible health care fraud. Thus, this request falls within the broad concept of relevance intended by Congress in § 3486.

As this circuit has stated, however, this court must weigh against the relevance of the requested material the burden that would be placed on Doe in producing it. *Ford Motor.* The extent of Doe's argument regarding the burden imposed by this request is his statement that he "would have to literally put his life on hold and search for papers and documents which stretch *ten years* into the past[,][w]ell beyond any statute of limitations that the Government may apply to any alleged health care offenses." Of the four categories of documents currently under consideration, however, only one, the request for all professional journals, magazines, and newsletters subscribed to or received by Doe from January 1990 through March 1998, has the potential to pose any meaningful burden on Doe. Nevertheless, Doe has made no attempt to reach a reasonable accommodation with the government regarding this aspect of the subpoena, an effort the Supreme Court has suggested should be expected before a court is willing to hold an administrative subpoena overly burdensome. * * * Nor has Doe given us anything but a general and conclusory statement as to why this request constitutes an undue burden. Although Doe's arguments regarding the burden of this subpoena are rather general and conclusory, we do note that the government's investigation of Doe has gone on for more than two years, and that this is the third subpoena requesting documents from Doe issued over this time. While we do not believe that the length of the investigation or the number of subpoenas previously issued to Doe make any further request for documents unreasonable in this case, such factors may be taken into account when deciding whether an administrative subpoena is unduly burdensome.

In sum, we believe that the strong likelihood of the requested documents' relevance to the government's health care fraud investigation outweighs any burden imposed on Doe in producing these documents. Accordingly, this aspect of the government's administrative subpoena will be enforced so long as the final two elements of our administrative subpoena test are met.

The government's subpoena also requested "[c]opies of recent bank and other financial records sufficient to completely show current location, amount, and value of all assets for [John Doe], D.P.M., and/or his health care related businesses," as well as copies of Doe's business and personal tax returns from 1993 to the present. The government asserts that these documents are relevant because they go to show "[Doe]'s profit motive for alleged criminal activity, the degree to which [Doe] profited from illegal activity, and the assets that may be forfeitable as a result of criminal activity." Again, Doe offers no specific reason why the production of these documents would be overly burdensome.

Several courts have recognized that heightened privacy interests are at stake when dealing with personal, as opposed to corporate, financial records. Despite these heightened privacy concerns, the U.S. Courts of Appeals for the Second, Ninth, and District of Columbia Circuits have held that the same standard of reasonable relevance applied to corporate records when requested pursuant to the administrative subpoena power granted to the FDIC and the now-defunct Resolution Trust Corporation ("RTC") to investigate fraudulent asset transfers should also be applied to requests for the private financial records of corporate officials. * * *

We agree with the reasoning of these circuits applying the reasonable relevance standard to subpoenas requesting the personal financial documents of corporate officials, and believe that applying the reasonable relevance standard is particularly appropriate in light of the facts of this case. Doctors operating their own medical clinics or practices, as appears to be the case with Doe, can easily transfer assets from business accounts to personal accounts, arguably even more readily than the corporate officers whose personal financial documents were requested pursuant to the FDIC and RTC subpoenas. To apply a more stringent standard to Doe's personal financial records in this case, in light of the ease with which personal and corporate assets could be commingled and shuttled from one account to another, would be inconsistent with the Congressional mandate given the Attorney General in § 3486 to uncover information relevant to its health care fraud investigation.

Applying the reasonable relevance standard to the government's requests for Doe's personal and business financial records, we again hold that the likely relevance of these documents outweighs the burden imposed on Doe in producing them. Doe has not explained why producing documents related to this portion of the subpoena would burden him, nor has he proffered any argument to refute the government's explanation of the documents' relevance. So long as the remaining elements of the reasonable relevance test are met, we will enforce this aspect of the government's administrative subpoena.[5]

In addition to Doe's personal financial records, the DOJ's administrative subpoena also requested "[c]opies of recent bank and other financial records sufficient to show current location, amount, and value of all assets for any and all children of [John Doe], D.P.M., insofar as those assets were provided or derived from individual or jointly held assets of John Doe, D.P.M." The

---

[5] Even if we imposed a higher standard than reasonable relevance for the request of Doe's personal financial documents, we are confident that this standard would be met in this case. The most difficult standard for subpoenaing personal financial records announced by any court of appeals was that in the withdrawn First Circuit decision in *[United States v.] Parks,* in which the court held that an agency would have to show "a reasonable suspicion of wrongdoing[.]" *Parks,* 1995 WL 529629, at *8. In this case, the DOJ has articulated a reasonable suspicion of wrongdoing on the part of Doe. The government has evidence of medical testing laboratories making unusual rental payments to Doe, as well as evidence from independent medical experts stating that one of the labs to which Doe referred patients was performing excessive and unnecessary electrodiagnostic testing. Thus, even under a standard requiring a reasonable suspicion of wrongdoing before a subpoena can be enforced, the government has made a sufficient showing to request Doe's personal financial records.

government requests these documents for many of the same reasons it requested Doe's personal and business financial documents: to determine the degree to which Doe profited from this potentially illegal activity, and the assets that may be forfeitable as a result.

We are more troubled by the government's request for personal financial documents of the children of the target of a health care fraud investigation. Indeed, in other administrative subpoena cases, the U.S. Courts of Appeals for the Second and Ninth Circuits have recognized that family members of an investigation's target "have a greater reasonable expectation of privacy in their personal financial affairs than do those individuals who do participate in such matters."

Although we are more reluctant to enforce this aspect of the administrative subpoena, we believe that it is sufficiently narrowly-tailored to pass the reasonable relevance standard. The DOJ's request for Doe's children's financial documents explicitly limits its reach to only those records concerning assets "provided or derived from individual or jointly held assets of [John Doe], D.P.M." Further evidence of the government's efforts to confine the scope of this portion of the subpoena can be found in correspondence between the government and Doe's attorney following the issuance of the subpoena, in which the government stated that "the request concerning [Doe's] children's assets is limited to information relating to assets/moneys where [Doe] was the source, and where, presumably, the source of that money was his health-care business."

As his attorney acknowledged at oral argument, Doe's children are minors. Just as Doe could easily commingle assets between his personal and business financial accounts, so also could he transfer ill-gotten gains into the personal accounts of his unsuspecting minor children. Because the government has been careful to avoid a sweeping exploration of Doe's children's assets, we hold that the likely relevance of these documents to the government's health care fraud investigation outweighs the children's heightened privacy interests in guarding this information. Doe has made no other showing of why the production of these documents would be unduly burdensome, and, assuming the final elements of the reasonable relevance test are met, we will enforce the government's narrowly tailored request for specific personal financial documents belonging to Doe's children.

Having concluded our analysis of the relevance of the requested documents to the government's health care fraud investigation, we now proceed to the remaining elements of the reasonable relevance test. * * *

The Supreme Court has stated that a court's process is abused where the subpoena is "issued for an improper purpose, such as to harass the [investigation's target] or to put pressure on him to settle a collateral dispute, or for any other purpose reflecting on the good faith of the particular investigation." *Powell.* Furthermore, in *United States v. LaSalle,* the Court held that any bad faith asserted by a plaintiff may not be based on the improper motives of an individual agency employee, but instead must be founded upon evidence that the agency itself, in an institutional sense, acted in bad faith when it served the subpoena.

Doe asserts that, because this is the third subpoena served to him in two years, it constitutes harassment. While we are troubled by the fact that the government, after two years of investigation and two subpoenas, has now imposed yet another document request on Doe, Doe has proffered no evidence, nor is there any in the record, that would support a conclusion that the DOJ was motivated by an improper purpose when issuing this subpoena. Doe has not met his "heavy" burden of showing institutional bad faith in this case.

Thus, because all the requirements for enforcing an administrative subpoena have been met in this case, we AFFIRM the district court's decision enforcing the administrative subpoena.

NOTES AND QUESTIONS

1. ***Reviewing Subpoenas***. Note that the court relied on *Powell*'s four-part test, adopted to determine the propriety of an IRS summons, to review a subpoena issued by a different administrative agency operating under HIPPA's broader grant of authority. The *Powell* test provides courts with a meaningful, although deferential, standard to review the propriety of an agency subpoena, and the initial burden is on the government to meet show that the subpoena meets the requirements for enforcement. In *R. Enterprises* [p. 363], on the other hand, the Supreme Court largely precluded judicial review of a grand jury subpoena by stating that the subpoena is presumed to have been properly issued unless the recipient could demonstrate that it was unreasonable or oppressive. While *Powell* and its progeny place the initial burden on the government to justify its effort to gather documents, the heavy burden is on the recipient challenging a grand jury subpoena. Is the difference based on the source of the different tests for enforcement? The test for reviewing a grand jury subpoena is Rule 17(c)–"unreasonable or oppressive"–while the court in *John Doe* referred to the Fourth Amendment as the basis for imposing the *Powell* test for enforcement of an administrative subpoena. Is that a meaningful distinction, especially when the production of records pursuant to a subpoena is usually not considered a search subject to the requirements of the Fourth Amendment? Are courts concerned that civil investigations may be more intrusive because there is a much greater degree of regulation of businesses and individuals than there are criminal investigations and prosecutions? Are the privacy concerns expressed in *Boyd* [supra, p. 381] more applicable to a civil investigation than criminal proceedings, in which there are explicit constitutional protections for the accused?

2. ***Administrative Subpoenas for Personal Financial Information.*** Courts have adopted an even higher level of review for an administrative subpoena compelling an individual to produce their private financial information. The Second Circuit, in **In re McVane**, 44 F.3d 1127 (2d Cir. 1995), refused to enforce a Federal Deposit Insurance Corporation subpoena seeking personal financial records from family members of directors of a failed bank. The court stated:

> [W]e conclude that administrative subpoenas issued pursuant to an agency investigation into corporate wrongdoing, which seek personal records of persons who are not themselves targets of the investigation and whose connection to the investigation consists only of their family ties to corporate participants, must face more exacting scrutiny than similar subpoenas seeking records solely from corporate participants. With regard to subpoenas seeking such material * * * 'an administrative agency is not automatically entitled to obtain all material that may in come way be relevant to a proper investigation. Rather . . . the agency must make some showing of need for the material sought beyond its mere relevance to a proper investigation.' (Quoting FEC v. LaRouche Campaign, 817 F.2d 233 (2d Cir. 1987)).

A number of courts have applied *McVane*'s higher standard for subpoenas for financial records of parties who are not a subject of the administrative investigation. In FDIC v. Garner, 126 F.3d 1138 (9th Cir. 1997), the Ninth Circuit accepted *McVane*'s reasoning but still enforced the subpoena because there was information indicating that the family members received benefits from the failed bank and so the personal financial records were relevant to the investigation. In Resolution Trust Corporation v. Walde, 18 F.3d 943 (D.C. Cir. 1994), the District of Columbia Circuit refused to enforce a subpoena for personal financial records of former officers and directors of a failed savings bank, holding that "where the RTC has no articulable suspicion to believe that the former officer or director is liable to an S&L in its custody, the RTC may not subpoena his personal financial information for the purpose of assessing the cost-effectiveness of prospective litigation." The same court applied the "articulable suspicion" standard to a subpoena for personal financial records in In re Sealed Case (Administrative Subpoena), 42 F.3d 1412 (D.C. Cir. 1994), rejecting the agency's claim that the subpoena sought to uncover "other wrongdoing, as yet unknown" was sufficient to meet the standard for enforcement. In Lerman v. S.E.C., 928 F. Supp. 2d 798, (S.D.N.Y. 2013), the district court cited *McVane* in refusing to enforce a subpoena issued by the SEC for the financial records of the wife of one of the brokers being investigated for misappropriation of client assets. The district court noted that "the SEC has not put forward any evidence showing that the information it seeks cannot be obtained through a more narrowly drawn subpoena, or from the subpoena directed at Robert DePalo's bank statements."

3. ***Third-Party Subpoenas under the RFPA and ECPA***. The Right to Financial Privacy Act requires prior notice to the customer whose information is sought by an administrative subpoena, and that person can challenge the subpoena. 12 U.S.C. § 3410. Similarly, under the Electronic Communications Privacy Act, the government must provide notice to the person whose stored electronic communications it seeks to obtain by an administrative subpoena, and the person can challenge the subpoena. 18 U.S.C. § 2703.

4. ***Continuing the Civil Investigation After a Grand Jury Investigation Starts***. Unlike the limitation on the use of civil investigative authority by the IRS once a criminal referral has been made, other federal agencies may cooperate with the prosecutors and continue the civil investigation while also providing information to the criminal investigators. Recipients of agency subpoenas sought to extend the Supreme Court's decision in *LaSalle National Bank*–now codified in 26 U.S.C. § 7602(b)–that prohibits the IRS from continuing a civil audit once a criminal referral to the Department of Justice has been made, to block enforcement of subpoenas issued after the commencement of a criminal investigation. In **SEC v. Dresser Industries**, 628 F.2d 1368 (D.C. Cir. 1980), the District of Columbia Circuit rejected the argument that the court should deny enforcement of a Securities and Exchange Commission subpoena because the agency had forwarded information to the Department of Justice for use in a grand jury investigation of the same transactions:

> Dresser principally relies on an analogy to *United States v. LaSalle Nat'l Bank*, in which the Supreme Court said in dictum that the Internal Revenue Service (IRS) may not use its summons authority to investigate possible violations of the tax laws after it has referred those violations to Justice for criminal prosecution. Dresser argues that the SEC's transmittal of Dresser's file to Justice was equivalent to a "referral" under *LaSalle*, and thus that the SEC's power to enforce investigative subpoenas against Dresser in connection with that file lapsed at that time. Alternatively, Dresser suggests that, even if transmittal of the file was not analogous to a "referral" under *LaSalle*, initiation of the grand jury investigation precluded subsequent enforcement of SEC investigative subpoenas into the same matters.
>
> These two alternatives are vulnerable to the same objection: the *LaSalle* rule applies solely to the statutory scheme of the Internal Revenue Code, in which the IRS's civil authority ceases for all practical purposes upon referral of a taxpayer's case to Justice; it does not apply to the securities laws, in which the SEC's civil enforcement authority continues undiminished after Justice initiates a criminal investigation by the grand jury. * * *

Dresser asks this court to extend the reasoning of *LaSalle* to govern the conduct of the SEC under the securities laws. But IRS investigative and enforcement proceedings are not analogous to those of the SEC. The language of the securities laws and the nature of the SEC's civil enforcement responsibilities require that the SEC retain full powers of investigation and civil enforcement action, even after Justice has begun a criminal investigation into the same alleged violations.

The investigative provisions of the securities laws are far broader than Section 7602 of the Internal Revenue Code, as interpreted in *LaSalle*. SEC investigations are not confined to "four purposes only." Rather, the SEC may, "*in its discretion*, make such investigations as *it deems necessary* to determine whether any person has violated, is violating, or is about to violate any provision" of the '34 Act, Section 21(a)." Moreover, the SEC is "authorized *in its discretion* * * * to investigate *any* facts, conditions, practices, or matters which *it may deem necessary or proper* to aid in the enforcement of such provisions, in the prescribing of rules and regulations under this chapter, or in securing information to serve as a basis for recommending further legislation concerning matters to which this chapter relates." (emphasis added). Given this broad statutory mandate, there is virtually no possibility that in issuing this subpoena the SEC was acting *ultra vires*. The investigation of Dresser based as it was on the staff's conclusion that Dresser may have engaged in conduct seriously contravening the securities laws falls squarely within the Commission's explicit investigatory authority. Unlike the Internal Revenue Code as interpreted in *LaSalle*, the securities laws offer no suggestion that the scope of the SEC's investigative authority shrinks when a grand jury begins to investigate the same matters. Since the validity of summonses or subpoenas "depend(s) ultimately on whether they were among those authorized by Congress," *United States v. LaSalle Nat'l Bank*, we conclude that this subpoena is enforceable under the rule of that case.

Fulfillment of the SEC's civil enforcement responsibilities requires this conclusion. Unlike the IRS, which can postpone collection of taxes for the duration of parallel criminal proceedings without seriously injuring the public, the SEC must often act quickly, lest the false or incomplete statements of corporations mislead investors and infect the markets. Thus the Commission must be able to investigate possible securities infractions and undertake civil enforcement actions even after Justice has begun a criminal

> investigation. For the SEC to stay its hand might well defeat its purpose.[a]

5. ***Prosecutorial Use of Information***. An agency ordinarily faces no significant obstacles in sharing with the United States Attorney information it has obtained through its subpoena power, while the United States Attorney must obtain a court order based on a showing of "particularized need" to share "grand jury matter" with an agency. It therefore is not surprising that some United States Attorneys will encourage agencies to carry potential criminal investigations as far forward as possible, rather than have the investigation shifted earlier to the grand jury, so that the information obtained by compulsory process will be readily available to the agency as well as the federal prosecutors. Indeed, such an approach has at times been encouraged by the Department of Justice. Professor Hughes comments:

> Little appears to be left of the old incantation that pursuit of a criminal violation through civil process would be an illegitimate usurpation of the role of the grand jury. If the governing statute clearly bestows on a regulatory agency or on the investigative arm of government the power to investigate criminal violations, the statute will prevail, since courts have rightly acknowledged that no constitutional right is endangered. At the same time, as the cases discussed below demonstrate, the civil agency often may make its files and the fruit of its compulsory process fully available to a prosecutor, at least until an indictment has been returned. If civil process were more intrusive than grand jury investigation, a sensitive situation would arise, but since the grand jury is the most powerful inquisitorial engine in our system, no problem exists.

Graham Hughes, *Administrative Subpoenas and the Grand Jury: Converging Streams of Criminal and Civil Compulsory Process*, 47 VAND. L. REV. 573 (1994).

6. ***Coordinating Civil and Criminal Investigations***. In **United States v. Educational Development Network Corp.**, 884 F.2d 737 (3d Cir. 1989), the Third Circuit rejected a claim that such a maneuver, where designed to avoid the restrictions of grand jury secrecy, constituted an abuse of the

---

[a] Following *Jerry T. O'Brien, Inc.* and *Dresser*, federal courts have similarly rejected the applicability of IRS-type limitations on the exercise of subpoena power by various other governmental agencies. *See* United States v. Aero Mayflower Transit Co., 831 F.2d 1142 (D.C. Cir. 1987) (subpoena authority of Inspector General of Department of Defense); Donovon v. Spadea, 757 F.2d 74 (3d Cir. 1985) (Department of Labor Subpoenas); United States v. Merit Petroleum, 731 F.2d 901 (Temp.Emer.Ct.App. 1984) (Department of Energy subpoena); United States v. Gel Spice Co., 773 F.2d 427 (2d Cir. 1985) (F.D.A. inspections); In re Equal Opportunity Employment Commission, 709 F.2d 392 (5th Cir. 1983) (EEOC discovery); United States v. Medic House, Inc., 736 F.Supp. 1531 (W.D. Mo. 1989) (Department of Health and Human Services discovery).

agency's subpoena authority. The United States Attorney's office (USAO) had received sufficient information pointing to possible fraudulent practices by a defense contractor to open a grand jury file. The grand jury, however, did not proceed with the investigation. The office of the Inspector General (IG) of the Department of Defense was informed of the information received by the USAO, and the IG subsequently issued a subpoena demanding that the contractor produce various documents. The IG also obtained a search warrant allowing it to search the contractor's facilities and seize many of the same documents. The information obtained by the IG was shared with the USAO, which later presented it to the grand jury and obtained an indictment. The contractor then filed a "motion to compel discovery in aid of a suppression motion alleging that the USAO acted in 'bad faith' when it used IG subpoenas and a search warrant to gather evidence during a joint grand jury/criminal/civil/ administrative/military investigation." The district court held that the defendant had "failed to make out a prima facie case showing of grand jury abuse" and denied the motion (as well as a subsequent motion to suppress). Affirming that ruling, the Third Circuit noted:

> * * * The government candidly admits on appeal that the USAO and DOD agreed to conduct a joint investigation and to use DOD IG subpoenas so that the agencies could share the evidence obtained. * * * [But the appellants contend] that once the USAO's criminal division impaneled the grand jury and filed a notice of disclosure under Rule 6(e) [informing the district court that it intended to utilize certain investigative personnel, who would be bound by Rule 6(e) secrecy], the agency was not free to ignore the grand jury subpoena process and its secrecy requirements in favor of the IG subpoena process. * * *
>
> In presenting their argument appellants place great reliance on Federal Rule of Criminal Procedure 6(e)(2). However, we do not believe Rule 6(e) bars the USAO's criminal division from participating in other agencies' investigations before it actually begins presentation of evidence to the grand jury, and appellants refer us to no statutory or case law to the contrary. * * * In this case the USAO did not present any evidence to the grand jury until January 13, 1988. Therefore, the secrecy requirements of Rule 6(e) did not attach until that time, and the USAO was free to share information uncovered in the joint investigation with the DOD and the Army. What occurred here is the USAO's disclosure of information obtained by the DOD to the grand jury, not the USAO's disclosure of information obtained by the grand jury to the DOD. Therefore Rule 6(e), requiring grand jury secrecy, would seem to have no application. * * *
>
> Appellants also argue that the evidence must be suppressed because the USAO's criminal division obtained it pursuant to subpoenas and a search warrant it had caused to be issued in a bad faith attempt to do an end run around the constitutional requirement that

> indictments be secured only through a grand jury. EDN and Kress base this argument on the fact that the USAO was involved in the investigation and controlled, at least partially, the issuance of the IG subpoenas. We do not minimize the concerns appellants express about the USAO's criminal division's conceded express avoidance of the grand jury by choosing instead to use the Inspector General's civil investigative powers in the investigation of crime, but they fail to direct us to any statutory, regulatory, or case law that prevents the USAO from doing so. * * *
>
> In denying appellants' request for a hearing and suppression of the evidence, the district court relied on United States v. Aero Mayflower Transmit Co. In that case, the Antitrust Division of the Justice Department was investigating the moving and storage industry. In September 1985, the Department of Defense Inspector General began his own investigation of DOD contractors. The Antitrust Division and the FBI contacted the Inspector General and suggested a "cooperative investigation." The Inspector General then issued subpoenas to the appellants, who refused to comply. They argued that the Inspector General had "rubber stamped" the subpoenas and that the real investigator was the Justice Department which should have gotten its subpoenas from a grand jury. The Inspector General's subpoenas, they argued, were therefore issued for an improper purpose. * * * On appeal, the United States Court of Appeals for the District of Columbia Circuit made clear that the Justice Department was free to guide or influence the Inspector General and his subpoenas, "[s]o long as the Inspector General's subpoenas seek information relevant to the discharge of his duties." * * * It said that "no body of law, whether statutory or regulatory, explicitly or implicitly restricts the Inspector General's ability to cooperate with divisions of the Justice Department exercising criminal prosecutorial authority." * * *
>
> * * * Whatever our reservations regarding the USAO's use of IG subpoenas and its degree of involvement in the DOD and Army investigation, appellants' arguments are more properly addressed to the Congress than to a court. * * * Although the USAO's criminal division is traditionally restricted to conducting investigations before a grand jury, on this record we see no law or principle that would prevent it from presenting to the grand jury facts properly uncovered in the course of lawful investigations by another agency.

7. **Sharing Information Not Subject to Grand Jury Secrecy**. The grand jury secrecy obligation of Rule 6(e) applies only to "matter occurring before the grand jury." Recall *In re: Sealed Case No. 99-3091*, p. 477 supra, in which the District of Columbia Circuit discussed what constitutes information subject to the Rule, which was not construed literally as encompassing only events actually taking place before the grand jury. A Department of Justice publication, *Guide on Rule 6(e) After Sells and Baggot* 52-57 (1984), advised

government attorneys wishing to share information without obtaining a Rule 6(e)(3)(E)(i) order to gather information "independently" of the grand jury. [See p. 666] One suggested possibility was to encourage an administrative agency interested in the same events to obtain documents and testimony through its subpoena power. Another was the use of search warrants. Consider, however, **In re Grand Jury Subpoena (U.S. v. Under Seal)**, 920 F.2d 235 (4th Cir. 1990), where documents were obtained by IRS agents through a search warrant, prior to the service of grand jury subpoenas, that alone is not dispositive as the court could "easily visualize * * * circumstances where a government investigating agent may, in pursuing an investigation * * * became an agent of the grand jury," with "search warrants and subpoenas * * * used indiscriminately to obtain the targeted information"; here, however, the IRS investigation and the grand jury investigation were not "indiscriminately merged" and the search warrant was based on the "debriefing of informants and surveillance on the targeted residence * * * which was earlier than or apart from the grand jury proceedings".

C. COOPERATION AND DECEPTION

There is often a close collaboration between investigators for a civil agency and prosecutors from the Department of Justice. The administrative agency usually has far superior expertise in the subject matters it regulates, and so can provide valuable assistance to criminal investigators and prosecutors. The agency may have greater access to documents and other materials because of its authority to compel the disclosure of certain information from a regulated entity. The administrative agency may be less threatening to the companies it deals with on a regular basis, and a civil subpoena does not necessarily mean there is a criminal investigation, while a grand jury subpoena or execution of search warrant means a criminal investigation is under way. The targets and subjects of the criminal investigation likely will be much less forthcoming if they are aware of a criminal investigation, so it may be in the interests of prosecutors to use the civil investigation as a means to gather evidence that will be useful in a subsequent criminal prosecution. While some measure of deception on the government's part may be acceptable, questions have been raised when the government uses subterfuge to obtain information through an administrative agency that is misleading about the potential for criminal prosecution. **In S.E.C. v. ESM Government Securities, Inc.**, 645 F.2d 310 (5th Cir. 1981), the court discussed the need for the government to be honest in its dealings with those who it regulates and seeks information from:

> The key to both these cases, we believe, is the nature of the relationship between the government agent and the private citizen. We recognize that much law enforcement activity relies on the use of sanctions by the government. The police officer, the undercover agent, the FBI investigator, all threaten the potential miscreant with discovery and penalties. Thus people obey the law from fear of

> punishment. Many governments, indeed, depend exclusively on fear for their authority.
>
> In this country, while we have recognized the importance of sanctions, we have never been willing to rely on them exclusively. Inherent in our democracy is a belief that, since the government represents the will of the people, the people will accept its dictates voluntarily. There is a sense of trust between the government and the people. * * *
>
> We believe that a private person has the right to expect that the government, when acting in its own name, will behave honorably. When a government agent presents himself to a private individual, and seeks that individual's cooperation based on his status as a government agent, the individual should be able to rely on the agent's representations. We think it clearly improper for a government agent to gain access to records which would otherwise be unavailable to him by invoking the private individual's trust in his government, only to betray that trust. When that government agency then invokes the power of a court to gather the fruits of its deception, we hold that there is an abuse of process. * * *
>
> In holding that fraud, deceit or trickery is grounds for denying enforcement of an administrative subpoena, we exercise the well-established power of the courts to prevent abuse of process. * * * The Supreme Court's directives in *Powell* and *LaSalle* leave no doubt that this power may be properly invoked in cases involving the enforcement of administrative subpoenas. We note that this power is associated with our supervisory power which is distinct from the fourth amendment exclusionary rule, although the goals may sometimes overlap. * * * Consequently, the court should not invoke an automatic exclusionary rule. "The correct approach for determining whether to enforce a summons requires that court to evaluate the seriousness of the violation under all the circumstances, including the government's good faith and the degree of harm imposed by the unlawful conduct." United States v. Bank of Moulton, 614 F.2d 1063 (5th Cir. 1980). Each case must be examined on its facts.

While *E.S.M. Government Securities* spoke of the need to avoid "deceit, fraud, or trickery" when the government deals with a regulated entity, how much of a disclosure duty should the administrative agency have to warn a potential target of a criminal prosecution that an investigation is under way? In **United States v. Medic House, Inc.**, 736 F.Supp. 1531 (W.D. Mo. 1989), the recipient of an administrative subpoena alleged that the investigatory agent made "friendly overtures" to officers of the company and failed to disclose a pending formal criminal investigation when he met with the officers. The District Court found that the government did not engage in improper conduct, stating that "[s]ome kind of affirmative action (or inaction when there was a duty to act) is necessary before fraud, deceit or trickery can be found." At what point does the failure to disclose the fact that a criminal investigation has commenced become actively misleading to a cooperating individual or company? Should the recipient of an administrative subpoena always assume that a criminal investigation may be taking place? Consider the following case.

UNITED STATES v. STRINGER

535 F.3d 929 (9th Cir. 2008)

SCHROEDER, Circuit Judge:

The United States appeals from a final order of the district court dismissing criminal indictments against three individual defendants charging counts of criminal securities violations. The dismissal was premised on the district court's conclusion that the government had engaged in deceitful conduct, in violation of defendants' due process rights, by simultaneously pursuing civil and criminal investigations of defendants' alleged falsification of the financial records of their high-tech camera sales company. Foreseeing the possibility of an appeal, the district court held that the indictments must be dismissed, but ruled in the alternative that, should there be a criminal trial, all evidence provided by the individual defendants in response to Securities and Exchange Commission ("SEC") subpoenas should be suppressed. * * *

Accepting the district court's factual findings under the clear error standard, we hold that the government's conduct does not amount to a constitutional violation under either the Fourth or Fifth Amendments. We vacate the dismissal of the indictments because in a standard form it sent to the defendants, the government fully disclosed the possibility that information received in the course of the civil investigation could be used for criminal proceedings. There was no deceit; rather, at most, there was a government decision not to conduct the criminal investigation openly, a decision we hold the government was free to make. There is nothing improper about the government undertaking simultaneous criminal and civil investigations, and nothing in the government's actual conduct of those investigations amounted to deceit or an affirmative misrepresentation justifying the rare sanction of dismissal of criminal charges or suppression of evidence received in the course of the investigations. * * *

Background

Prior to the criminal action that forms the basis of this appeal, the SEC began investigating the defendants, J. Kenneth Stringer, III, J. Mark Samper, and William N. Martin, and their company for possible civil securities fraud violations. The company was FLIR Systems, Inc. ("FLIR"), an Oregon corporation headquartered in Portland that sells infrared and heat-sensing cameras for military and industrial use. The SEC began the investigation on June 8, 2000. About two weeks later, the SEC held the first of a series of meetings with the Oregon United States Attorney's Office ("USAO") to coordinate the ongoing SEC investigation with a possible criminal investigation. An SEC Assistant Director and an SEC Staff Attorney met with the supervisor of the white collar crime section of the USAO to discuss the possibility of opening a criminal investigation. The meeting apparently convinced the USAO supervisor to investigate. Within days, the USAO and the Federal Bureau of Investigation ("FBI") opened a criminal investigation.

Federal securities laws authorize the SEC to transmit evidence it has gathered to the USAO to facilitate a criminal investigation by the USAO. To gather evidence for its criminal investigation, the Oregon USAO in June of 2000 sent a letter to the SEC (the "Access Letter") requesting access to the SEC's non-public investigative files, and the SEC promptly granted access.

The civil and criminal investigations proceeded in tandem and the SEC continued to meet and communicate with the USAO and FBI. The SEC turned over documents the SEC collected through its civil investigation.

At the beginning of the criminal investigation, the USAO identified two of the three defendants, FLIR's former CEO, Stringer, and former CFO, Samper, as possible targets, and named them in the USAO's Access Letter to the SEC. A few months later, in October 2000, the Assistant United States Attorney ("AUSA") assigned to the case made a list of the subjects of the investigation and placed asterisks and the comment "knew what [was] going on" next to the entries for Samper and Stringer. A month later, the AUSA stated in his handwritten notes that Stringer had "lied [about] his role in" the company. In April 2001, an e-mail from the SEC Staff Attorney to the SEC Assistant Director stated the AUSA "define[d] [the] targets as Ken Stringer and Mark Samper."

The district court concluded that the third defendant, Martin, former VP of Sales, was also an early potential target of the criminal investigation. Martin appears on the AUSA's early list of the subjects of the investigation above the comment "knew pushing up sales." During a January 2001 meeting, the SEC advised the USAO and FBI that FLIR was blaming Stringer and Martin for the fraudulent conduct at the heart of the investigation.

Early in the criminal investigation, the USAO decided the investigation should remain confidential. At an October 2000 meeting between the SEC, USAO, and FBI, the AUSA advised that the evidence collected by the SEC might support criminal wire fraud charges. Nonetheless, an internal FBI memo issued in late October stated that the AUSA had concluded, based on the defendants' cooperation with the SEC at that point, that the SEC should investigate "without the assistance or inclusion of the FBI." At the January 2001 meeting between the SEC, FBI, and USAO, the SEC revealed that FLIR was cooperative and was providing evidence that was damaging to Stringer and Martin.

By June 2001, the USAO was not yet ready to convene a grand jury and issue indictments. The SEC and USAO believed that FLIR and defendant Samper would settle with the SEC so long as the U.S. Attorney was not directly involved. During a December 2001 phone conversation between the AUSA assigned to the case and the SEC Assistant Director, the AUSA continued to believe it was "premature [sic] to surface" and that the presence of an AUSA would "impede" a meeting between the SEC and defendants. During a December 2002 phone call, the SEC and USAO decided that the USAO would not "surface", i.e., convene a grand jury and issue indictments, until the "end of Jan/early Feb" 2003.

The SEC facilitated the criminal investigation in a number of ways. The SEC offered to conduct the interviews of defendants so as to create "the best record possible" in support of "false statement cases" against them, and the AUSA instructed the SEC Staff Attorney on how best to do that. The AUSA asked the relevant SEC office, located in Los Angeles, to take the depositions in Oregon so that the Portland Office of the USAO would have venue over any false statements case that might arise from the depositions, and the SEC did so. Both the SEC and USAO wanted the existence of the criminal investigation kept confidential. The SEC Staff Attorney, at one of the Portland depositions, made a note that she wanted to "make sure [the] court reporters won't tell [FLIR's Attorney]" that there was an AUSA assigned to the case.

The SEC, however, did not hide from the defendants the possibility – even likelihood – of such an investigation. The SEC sent each of the defendants subpoenas in the summer of 2001, and attached to each was Form 1662, a form sent to all witnesses subpoenaed to testify before the SEC. Under the header "Routine Uses of Information," the four-page form states that "[t]he Commission often makes its files available to other governmental agencies, particularly the United States Attorneys and state prosecutors. There is a likelihood that information supplied by you will be made available to such agencies where appropriate."

Form 1662 also advises witnesses of their Fifth Amendment rights. After the heading "Fifth Amendment and Voluntary Testimony," the form states that:

> Information you give may be used against you in any federal . . . civil or criminal proceeding brought by the Commission of any other agency. You may refuse, in accordance with the rights guaranteed to you by the Fifth Amendment of the Constitution of the United States, to give any information that may tend to incriminate you or subject you to fine, penalty, or forfeiture.

None of the defendants invoked his right against self-incrimination during his deposition, and all proceeded to testify in compliance with the subpoena. Each of the defendants was represented by counsel when he testified.

During the course of Stringer's deposition, taken in Portland in October 2001, Stringer's attorney actually questioned the SEC Staff Attorney about the involvement of the USAO. In response to those questions, the SEC Staff Attorney answered as follows:

> MR. MARTSON: My first question is whether Mr. Stringer is a target of any aspect of the investigation being conducted by the SEC.
>
> STAFF ATTORNEY: The SEC does not have targets in this investigation.
>
> MR. MARTSON: The other questions I have relate to whether or not, in connection with your investigation, the SEC is working in conjunction with any other department of the United States, such as the U.S. Attorney's Office in any jurisdiction, or the Department of Justice.
>
> STAFF ATTORNEY: As laid out in the 1662 form, in the "routine use of" section there are routine uses of our investigation, and it is the agency's policy not to respond to questions like that, but instead, to direct you to the other agencies you mentioned.
>
> MR. MARTSON: And which U.S. Attorney's Office might I inquire into?
>
> STAFF ATTORNEY: That would be a matter up to your discretion.

The record does not show the SEC did anything to impede an inquiry, nor does it disclose that any inquiry was made. The record reflects that the government never furnished defendants with any false information concerning the existence of a criminal investigation.

In September 2002, a year before the criminal indictments, defendants Samper and Martin entered into consent decrees in the civil action, agreeing to pay penalties, disgorgement, and pre-judgment interest. * * *

On September 17, 2003, a grand jury returned an indictment charging Stringer, Samper, and Martin with securities, mail, and wire fraud. Defendants filed motions to dismiss the indictments and to suppress statements they made to the SEC. The district court dismissed the indictments and suppressed the SEC statements because it concluded that the government, in violation of the due process clause, abused its authority to conduct parallel proceedings. The district court held that the government violated defendants' Fifth Amendment due process rights by using trickery and deceit to conceal the criminal investigation from defendants, and conducting a criminal investigation under the auspices of a civil investigation. * * *

Discussion

The Supreme Court has held that the government may conduct parallel civil and criminal investigations without violating the due process clause, so long as it does not act in bad faith. See United States v. Kordel, 397 U.S. 1 (1970). In *Kordel*, the Supreme Court held that the government did not violate the due process rights of corporate executives when it used evidence it obtained from an FDA civil investigation to convict them of criminal misbranding. The Court explained that the FDA did not act in bad faith when it made a request for information, which ultimately was used in the criminal investigation, for the agency made similar requests as a matter of course in 75% of its civil investigations. The Court suggested that the government may act in bad faith if it brings a civil action solely for the purpose of obtaining evidence in a criminal prosecution and does not advise the defendant of the planned use of evidence in a criminal proceeding. The Court thus distinguished the *Kordel* investigation from bad faith cases where

> the [g]overnment has brought a civil action solely to obtain evidence for its criminal prosecution or has failed to advise the defendant in its civil proceeding that it contemplates his criminal prosecution; . . . [or] any other special circumstances ... might suggest the unconstitutionality or even the impropriety of this criminal prosecution.

The Supreme Court has not had occasion to address such issues since Kordel, but lower courts have. In SEC v. Dresser Industries, Inc., the D.C. Circuit applied the principles laid down in *Kordel* to a case involving parallel SEC civil and Department of Justice criminal investigations. See 628 F.2d 1368, (D.C.Cir.1980) (en banc). The court emphatically upheld the propriety of such parallel investigations. "Effective enforcement of the securities laws requires that the SEC and Justice be able to investigate possible violations simultaneously." The court said it would refuse to bar such investigations absent unusual circumstances. Id. It said courts should refuse to "block parallel investigations by these agencies in the absence of 'special circumstances' in which the nature of the proceedings demonstrably prejudices substantial rights of the investigated party or of the government."

District courts have occasionally suppressed evidence or dismissed indictments on due process grounds where the government made affirmative misrepresentations or conducted a civil investigation solely for purposes of advancing a criminal case. See, e.g., United States v. Posada Carriles, 486 F.Supp.2d 599, 615 (W.D.Tex. 2007); United States v. Rand, 308 F.Supp. 1231, 1233 (N.D.Ohio 1970).

In this case, the district court concluded that the government should have told defendants of the criminal investigation and that it violated the standards laid down in *Kordel* when it failed to "advise defendants that it anticipated their criminal prosecution." It held that the government engaged in "trickery and deceit" when the SEC staff attorney instructed court reporters to refrain from mentioning the AUSA's involvement. When the SEC staff attorney responded to Stringer's attorney's question, during Stringer's deposition, by directing him to the U.S. Attorney, the district court concluded that the SEC attorney "evaded the question."

In its appeal, the government argues that it had no legal duty to make any further disclosure of the existence of the pending criminal investigation. It points to the warnings in Form 1662 in which the government disclosed the possibility of criminal prosecution, and it stresses that it did not make any affirmative misrepresentations. It maintains the SEC attorney's answer was appropriate and truthful.

The defendants argue that the district court properly held that the use of the evidence obtained by the SEC in a criminal prosecution would violate defendants' Fifth Amendment privilege against self-incrimination. The defendants were advised that the evidence could be used in a criminal investigation, but defendants did not invoke their Fifth Amendment privilege during the SEC investigation. The government on appeal correctly contends that defendants waived or forfeited their Fifth Amendment right against self-incrimination.

The privilege against self-incrimination protects an individual from being forced to provide information that might establish a direct link in a chain of evidence leading to his conviction. Hoffman v. United States, 341 U.S. 479, 486 (1951). It may be waived if it is not affirmatively invoked. In *Minnesota v. Murphy*, the Supreme Court stressed that the privilege is lost if not affirmatively invoked, even if the defendant did not make a knowing and intelligent waiver. 465 U.S. 420 (1984). * * *

The district court therefore erred in holding that defendants' waivers of the privilege were ineffective because they were not told of the U.S. Attorney's active involvement. The SEC Form 1662 used in this case alerts SEC investigative witnesses that the information can be used in a criminal proceeding. Defendants were on sufficient notice, and so were their attorneys. As one federal court has explained, all that was required was "sufficient notice . . . that any information could be used against [them] in a subsequent criminal proceeding." United States v. Teyibo, 877 F.Supp. 846 (S.D.N.Y.1995). That court emphasized that "SEC Form 1662 stated in no uncertain terms that the [g]overnment's request for information could be refused pursuant to the Fifth Amendment's protection against compelled self-incrimination." We agree.

The SEC here went even further, warning each defendant at the beginning of each deposition that "the facts developed in this investigation might constitute violations of . . . criminal laws." Nonetheless, defendants proceeded to testify and failed to invoke their privilege against self-incrimination. Defendants have forfeited any claims that the use of their testimony against them in the criminal proceedings violates the privilege against self-incrimination.

The defendants next contend that the district court properly concluded that the government used the civil investigation solely to obtain evidence for a subsequent criminal prosecution, in violation of due process. The Supreme Court in *Kordel* made it clear that dual investigations must meet the requirements of the Fifth Amendment Due Process Clause. While holding that "[i]t would stultify the enforcement of federal law" to curtail the government's discretion to conduct dual investigations strategically, the Court suggested that a defendant may be entitled to a remedy where "the [g]overnment has brought a civil action solely to obtain evidence for its criminal prosecution." In this case, the government argues that it did not violate defendants' due process rights because the civil investigation was not commenced solely to obtain evidence for a criminal prosecution.

It is significant to our analysis that the SEC began its civil investigation first and brought in the U.S. Attorney later. This tends to negate any likelihood that the government began the civil investigation in bad faith, as, for example, in order to obtain evidence for a criminal prosecution. In *United States v. Unruh*, 855 F.2d 1363 (9th Cir. 1987), we held that a defendant was not entitled to dismissal of his indictment when the U.S. Department of the Treasury instituted its investigation before any indictment and in order to file its own civil complaint.

United States v. Posada Carriles, 486 F.Supp.2d 599, 619-21 (W.D.Tex.2007), on the other hand, is a clear example of government bad faith. The district court dismissed an indictment because the U.S. Citizenship and Immigration Services ("USCIS") interviewed the defendant solely to collect evidence in support of a criminal case against him. The defendant, a Cuban national, filed an application for naturalization. Although USCIS had already determined that the defendant was not eligible for citizenship, the agency nonetheless invited him to a pre-citizenship interview in order to collect evidence for a crimina false statements case. The interview protocol was altered in so many ways to serve the needs of the criminal investigation that it became an interrogation. The court described the "interview" as follows:

> (1) it lasted eight hours over the course of two days as opposed to the usual maximum of thirty minutes, (2) it involved two interviewers, (3) the [g]overnment provided an interpreter, (4) there were a total of four attorneys present-two defense attorneys and two Government attorneys, and (5) it was both audio and videotaped.

Because the "entire interview was . . . a pretext for a criminal investigation," the district court dismissed the indictment.

Our case is not remotely similar to *Posada Carriles*. In this case the SEC's civil investigation was opened first, led to SEC sanctions and was conducted pursuant to the SEC's own civil enforcement jurisdiction. It was not a pretext for the USAO's criminal investigation of defendants. Congress has expressly authorized the SEC to share information with the Department of Justice to facilitate the investigation and prosecution of crimes. We must conclude the SEC interviewed the defendants in support of a bona fide civil investigation. There was no violation of due process.

Defendant appellees finally contend that the district court properly concluded that dismissal or, in the alternative, suppression, was warranted because the government lulled the defendants into turning over incriminating evidence by engaging in "trickery and deceit." It was dispositive for the district court that the SEC staff attorney instructed court reporters to refrain from mentioning the AUSA's involvement and that the SEC gave evasive answers to questions about the imminence of a dual investigation. We have previously applied the Fourth Amendment's bar to unreasonable searches and seizures in the context of dual investigations by the civil and criminal branches of the IRS, where review of documentary evidence is inherent in the investigation. We have thus held that a search is unreasonable, even if consensual, if the consent is obtained by trickery or deceit. While not every SEC and USAO dual investigation will necessarily involve a search and seizure, to the extent that the individual defendants may have been led through trickery or deceit to turn over documentary or physical evidence in their possession or to use their official authority to turn over evidence in the possession of the corporation, the defendants could state a claim under the Fourth Amendment.

Other circuits have agreed that Fourth Amendment and possible due process limitations may be implicated in a dual investigation. See United States v. Peters, 153 F.3d 445 (7th Cir. 1998) ("A consensual search is unreasonable under the Fourth Amendment or violative of due process under the Fifth Amendment if the consent was induced by fraud, deceit, trickery or misrepresentation."). Almost every other circuit has denied suppression, even when government agents did not disclose the possibility or existence of a criminal investigation, so long as they made no affirmative misrepresentations.

The district court in this case relied on the Eighth Circuit's opinion in [United States v. Grunewald, 987 F.2d 531 (8th Cir. 1993)], which said it would be a "flagrant disregard of individuals' rights" to "deliberately deceive, or even lull" a person into incriminating themselves in a criminal investigation being pursued under the guise of a civil one. The Eighth Circuit was referring to the criminal defendant's argument that he was the victim of a criminal investigation being pursued in the guise of a civil tax audit. The court rejected the argument and affirmed the district court's denial of suppression because there had been no deceit. * * *

In this case, the SEC made no affirmative misrepresentations. The SEC did advise defendants of the possibility of criminal prosecution. The SEC engaged in no tricks to deceive defendants into believing that the investigation was exclusively civil in nature. The SEC's Form 1662 explicitly warned defendants that the civil investigation could lead to criminal charges against them: "Information you give may be used against you in any federal . . . civil or criminal proceeding brought by the Commission or any other agency." Defendants were represented by counsel, and the government provided counsel, so far as this record reflects, with accurate information. The standard we laid down in Robson was not violated.

The defendant-appellees point to a number of collateral facts they argue demonstrate trickery or deliberate misleading. They argue the SEC Staff Attorney affirmatively misled Stringer's attorney when, in response to the attorney's question about other agency involvement, she directed him to the provision in Form 1662 that warned that the SEC would likely turn over to the USAO evidence it collected at the depositions. The Staff Attorney, during the deposition taken in Portland, declined to direct defense counsel to a specific U.S. Attorney's Office, which would have been the Portland Office, but there was nothing false or misleading in her response that it was up to the defendant to decide where to direct his inquiries.

The defendant-appellees also point to the Staff Attorney's request to the court reporters not to mention the AUSA in the presence of defendants' attorneys. While this indicates an intent to prevent disclosure to defendants of the actual criminal investigation, the possibility of criminal investigation should have been well known to both the defendants and their counsel. The request to the court reporters to, in effect, mind their own business did not mislead or misinform defendants about the existence of an investigation. Thus, to the extent that the Fourth Amendment may have been implicated by the dual investigation, the district court erred in concluding that the government's actions in this case constituted an unreasonable search or seizure. * * *

For the foregoing reasons, we conclude that there was no deception or affirmative misconduct on the part of the government in the course of the SEC and U.S. Attorney investigations that warranted dismissal of the indictment or suppression of any of the evidence in question. In addition, defendants' Fifth Amendment rights were not violated.

D. PARALLEL PROCEEDINGS

1. Types of Parallel Proceedings

White collar criminal offenses frequently involve common law torts or violations of statutes or administrative codes that can lead to sanctions, monetary penalties and civil damage actions. A substantial potential exists for simultaneous or seriatim criminal, civil, and administrative proceedings based upon essentially the same activities. Such "parallel proceedings" present a variety of legal questions, such as whether voluntarily providing information waives the attorney-client privilege (see Chapter 15), but the one that has attracted the most attention is the extent to which parallel proceedings can be utilized to develop information in one type of proceeding that will be available to litigants in another.

The "parallel proceedings" problem can arise in almost any type of litigation, in addition to administrative agency investigations. For example, evidence developed in private litigation involving securities fraud, *qui tam* actions for defrauding the government, and consumer fraud class actions is often used by the government in subsequent enforcement actions. In other cases, plaintiffs or defendants in civil actions will learn about a governmental investigation after the civil case commences, which will raise issues regarding whether to provide information that may be incriminating and whether civil discovery may be used to gain information related to a criminal investigation that might not otherwise be available. The problem is not limited to parties to litigation. Consider In re Grand Jury Subpoena, 836 F.2d 1468 (4th Cir. 1988), in which third-party deponents in one state refused to testify in a federal civil suit in another state until the court issued a protective order ostensibly prohibiting disclosure of their deposition transcripts. The Fourth Circuit held in that case that the grand jury in another state has a per se right to obtain evidence regardless of the protective order, which makes it even more likely that a witness will assert the Fifth Amendment rather than testify if there is any possibility that the information will be incriminating. The efficacy of protective orders in civil litigation is discussed in Chapter Nine, supra.

This Chapter considers information sharing as it relates to the civil case presented simultaneously with, or in advance of, a criminal investigation or prosecution, and the grand jury investigation that is followed by civil or administrative proceedings.

2. Use of Civil Discovery in a Criminal Prosecution

In **United States v. Kordel**, 397 U.S. 1 (1970), the Supreme Court rejected two constitutional challenges to parallel civil and criminal proceedings, which had been brought by the United States Attorney. Initially, the United States Attorney, following an investigation by the Food and Drug Administration, instituted a civil in rem action against two food products produced by the corporation of which Kordel and Feldten were president and vice president. The in rem action sought to seize and condemn the products on the ground that they were being distributed in violation of the Food, Drug, and Cosmetic Act. In connection with that suit, the United States Attorney served on the corporation, pursuant to Rule 33 of the Federal Rules of Civil Procedure, extensive interrogatories that had been prepared by FDA personnel. Shortly thereafter, the FDA served notice upon the corporation and its two officers informing them that the agency was contemplating recommending a criminal prosecution and that they had the opportunity to present their views in opposition. The corporation immediately moved to stay further proceedings in the civil action, or in the alternative to extend its time for answering the interrogatories until after the disposition of the anticipated criminal proceedings. The motion was denied, however, and the corporation was ordered to answer the interrogatories, which was done through Feldten. The civil case was subsequently settled, and Feldten and Kordel were thereafter prosecuted and convicted at a trial in which the government utilized Feldten's answers to the interrogatories to "provid[e] evidence or leads useful to the Government."

Finding no Fifth Amendment violation in the use of the civil discovery as evidence in the criminal prosecution, Justice Stewart's opinion for the Court stated:

> Feldten need not have answered the interrogatories. Without question he could have invoked his Fifth Amendment privilege against compulsory self-incrimination. Surely Feldten was not barred from asserting his privilege simply because the corporation had no privilege of its own, or because the proceeding in which the Government sought information was civil rather than criminal in character. To be sure, service of the interrogatories obliged the corporation to "appoint an agent who could, without fear of self-incrimination, furnish such requested information as was available to the corporation." The corporation could not satisfy its obligation under Rule 33 simply by pointing to an agent about to invoke his constitutional privilege. * * * Such a result would effectively permit the corporation to assert on its own behalf the personal privilege of its individual agents. * * * The respondents press upon us the situation where no one can answer the interrogatories addressed to the corporation without subjecting himself to a "real and appreciable" risk of self-incrimination. For present purposes we may assume that in such a case the appropriate remedy would be a protective order under Rule 30(b), postponing civil discovery until termination of the criminal action. But we need not decide this troublesome question. For the record before us makes clear that even though the respondents had the burden of showing that the Government's interrogatories were improper, they never even asserted, let alone demonstrated, that there was no authorized person who could answer the interrogatories without the possibility of compulsory self-incrimination. * * *

For a prospective criminal defendant, the perils of responding to civil discovery go beyond possibly providing leads to incriminatory information that could help the prosecution in building its criminal case-in-chief. Even where the privilege against self-incrimination would not be available legally because the information sought in the civil discovery presents no "real and appreciable" risk of providing a "link in the chain" of a prosecutor's proof of a crime, there remains the tactical disadvantage of exposing at this early point the basis of a defense that, in all likelihood, would not have to be revealed in the criminal prosecution until the trial itself. Where the opposing litigant is the government, however, the prospective defendant may find that disadvantage more than offset by the potential for using civil discovery to obtain information about the government's case that would not be available through pretrial criminal discovery. Federal Rule of Criminal Procedure 16 governs discovery in criminal cases, and it provides significantly less discovery than the Federal Rules of Civil Procedure.

3. *Qui Tam* Actions

Parallel civil actions brought by private parties take many forms. Of special concern to those entities selling goods or services to the federal government is a whistleblower's *qui tam* action. The *qui tam* action is authorized under the Civil False Claims Act, 31 U.S.C.A. § 3729, which creates civil and criminal liability for a broad range of "false claims" against the government (e.g., knowingly presenting false invoices or supporting documents, knowingly shorting the government in the delivery of property, and knowingly using false records to conceal or decrease an obligation owed to government). The *qui tam* action is a civil action for violation of the False Claims Act brought on behalf of the *qui tam* relator as an individual and on behalf of the government by the relator. The term "*qui tam*" derives from the Latin "*qui tam pro domino rege quam pro sic ipso in hoc parte sequitur*," meaning "who as well for the king as for himself sues in this manner." See Michelle D. Bernard, *Qui Tam Litigation Under the Civil and Criminal False Claims Act*, 1994 *Complex Crimes Journal* 193.

The filing of the *qui tam* action makes the *qui tam* relator and the government co-plaintiffs in the action. Upon filing, the relator must serve upon the government both the complaint and a "written disclosure of substantially all material evidence and information the person possesses." The government then has at least 60 days to decide whether to take over the action, and often seeks additional time to investigate whether to participate in the case. During that period, the complaint, which is filed *in camera*, must remain under seal. If the government chooses to intervene in the action, it has the primary responsibility for prosecuting the action and is not bound by an act of the *qui tam* relator. The relator has the right to continue as a party to the action, but the government may limit the relator's authority to call witnesses and cross-examine adverse witnesses, and may dismiss or settle the action without the relator's consent.

If the government declines to intervene, the relator has the right to conduct the action and no person other than the government may intervene or bring a related action based on the same underlying facts. The government may also take steps that, in effect, splinter the action. This is done when it files an amended complaint that includes some but not all of the claims contained in the relator's complaint. The unadopted claims, if the government does not move to dismiss them, can then be removed from under seal with the approval of the court, allowing the relator to proceed upon them. This leaves the defendant subject to two complaints, with one under the control of the government and the other under the control of the relator. But see Bernard, supra, at 209 (noting the Department of Justice's position that "relators are jurisdictionally barred under § 3730(e)(3) from separately continuing unadopted claims that arise out of the same facts and transactions as the claims adopted by the government").

Where the government decides to intervene, the *qui tam* relator will receive between 15-25% of the proceeds of any judgment or settlement, depending upon the "extent to which the relator substantially contributed to the prosecution of the action." § 3730(d)(1). If the government chooses not to participate the relator ordinarily receives "an amount which the court decides is reasonable for collecting the civil penalty or damages" which must be at least twenty-five percent but not more than thirty percent of the proceeds of the action or any settle. §3730(d)(2).[b]

4. Shareholder Derivative Suits

It is common for shareholders of a corporation to file a derivative action related to wrongdoing in the business alleging the directors and officers breached their fiduciary duties to the company. While the attorney-client privilege, which is discussed in greater detail in Chapter Fifteen, usually protects internal communications related to an internal investigation of the company, shareholders can seek to obtain otherwise privileged communications as part of the derivative litigation. There is a risk that the privileged information could be disclosed to prosecutors and civil

[b] Under certain circumstances, the relator's share may be reduced below these general ranges. If a case was based "primarily" (but not entirely) on specific information that had been publicly disclosed and the government has intervened, "the court may award such sums as it considers appropriate, but in no case more than ten percent of the proceeds, taking into account the significance of the information and the role of the person bringing the action in advancing the case to litigation." § 3730(d)(1). If the government has declined to intervene in such a case, there is no such limitation. Also, if the relator "planned and initiated" the fraudulent activity that is the subject of the case, the court may reduce the relator's award to the extent the court considers appropriate, "taking into account the role of that person in advancing the case to litigation and any relevant circumstances pertaining to the violation." If the relator is convicted of criminal conduct arising from his or her role in the violation, then no share of the proceeds can go to the relator. § 3730(d)(3).

investigative agencies. In describing whether the corporation can be compelled to disclose communications protected by the attorney-client privilege to shareholders, the Fifth Circuit in *Garner v. Wolfinbarger*, 430 F.2d 1093 (5th Cir.1970) stated:

> The attorney-client privilege still has viability for the corporate client. The corporation is not barred from asserting it merely because those demanding information enjoy the status of stockholders. But where the corporation is in suit against its stockholders on charges of acting inimically to stockholder interests, protection of those interests as well as those of the corporation and of the public require that the availability of the privilege be subject to the right of the stockholders to show cause why it should not be invoked in the particular instance.

E. DELAYING THE PARALLEL CIVIL ACTION

A party in a civil or administrative case who faces the possibility of a parallel criminal prosecution may seek to stay the civil proceeding pending the outcome of the criminal case. The general principles that guide a court's decision as to whether to grant such a stay are analyzed in a widely cited article by District Judge Milton Pollack:

> Generally, the courts have great discretion in regard to this question and, as you may expect, must balance the competing concerns of the private (or Government) plaintiff with the harm to the defendant by letting both proceedings go forward at once under special circumstances. In addition, a court should consider any prejudice which would be caused to both parties and non-parties if the civil suit is delayed and should consider the convenience to the courts as well. * * * In more practical terms, the courts generally treat four factors as significant, if not dispositive, weights which can tip the balance either in favor of or against a stay of the plaintiff's quest for discovery. These four factors are: (1) the commonality of transactions or issues, (2) the timing of the motion, (3) judicial efficiency, and (4) the public interest.
>
> *First.* The most important factor at the threshold is the degree to which the civil issues overlap with the criminal issues. Some civil issues are irrelevant to related criminal proceedings. For example, the issue of damages for wrongful death would not arise in most related criminal negligence prosecutions; in such a case, a stay of the civil proceedings on the issue of damages would rarely be appropriate.
>
> *Second.* The current stage of the parallel criminal proceeding will often substantially affect the net balance of equities. Is resolution nearby or remote in time? * * * The strongest case for a stay of

discovery in the civil case occurs during a criminal prosecution after an indictment is returned. * * * The potential for self-incrimination is greatest during this stage, and the potential harm to civil litigants arising from delaying them is reduced due to the promise of a fairly quick resolution of the criminal case under the Speedy Trial Act. See, e.g., *Dresser* [p. 621].

The chances of the defendant's procuring a stay are less favorable (but still possible) if the government is conducting an active parallel criminal *investigation* in which an indictment or information has not yet been filed. * * * If no indictment has been returned and no known investigation is underway, the case for a stay of discovery, no matter at whose instance, is "far weaker." * * * If criminal proceedings are over or there is no substantial criminal exposure, the courts are most likely to deny a delay of plaintiff's discovery or other pre-trial relief. The accused's trial tactics have already been exposed, and the likelihood of self-incrimination may be diminished, particularly if the defendant has testified at trial. And, the appeal process is an uncertain, potentially long-ranging, process. Only unusual circumstances would justify an order staying a post-conviction civil proceeding. * * *

Third. Judicial efficiency is also a factor in the balancing analysis. Resolution of the criminal case may increase prospects for settlement of the civil case. Due to differences in the standards of proof between civil suits and criminal prosecutions, the possibility always exists for a collateral estoppel or res judicata effect on some or all of the overlapping issues. Conviction of a defendant in a parallel criminal case may effectively dispose of all common issues in a subsequent civil action, although the reverse is not true. Thus, it was held that a district court did not abuse its discretion in deciding that judicial economy was best served by granting a stay of the civil case, where the proceedings involved substantial overlap of issues such that "resolution of the criminal case would moot, clarify, or otherwise affect various contentions in the civil case." United States v. Mellon Bank, N.A., 545 F.2d 869, 873 (3d Cir. 1976). This, however, might be thought to assume that the criminal proceedings will result in a conviction of the defendant, which as you know should not and cannot be predicted prematurely. And again, the degree to which the issues in the two proceedings overlap will greatly influence the extent to which such issues may later be precluded at all.

Fourth. The effect of a stay of the civil case upon the "public interest" is perhaps the most important factor in the equation, albeit the one hardest to define. As I noted before, both plaintiffs and defendants have an interest in a timely judgment. In civil securities actions, the public has an interest in the maintenance of and preservation of the integrity of the securities market. These interests can be

> substantially prejudiced by stays imposing significant delays upon the civil proceeding. To this end it would behoove both the litigants and the court to tailor a stay at the instance of the defendant (if one is to be granted) to minimize any delays upon the process.
>
> One additional, although relatively uncommon, factor which almost inevitably results in a denial of a motion for a stay is where the movant intentionally creates the impediment which he seeks to erect as a shield. Thus, where a criminal defendant pleads guilty to criminal charges and agrees to assist the government's prosecution of others while keeping such matters confidential, it is questionable whether at his insistence the civil proceedings against him should be held in abeyance because he purportedly cannot disclose confidential information in his answer to a civil complaint pursuant to his agreement with the Department of Justice and pursuant to the Fifth Amendment. See Arden Way Associates v. Boesky, 660 F.Supp. 1494 (S.D.N.Y. 1987). * * *

Judge Milton Pollack, *Parallel Civil Criminal Proceedings*, 129 F.R.D. 201 (1989). Consider how the court balanced the competing equities in the following opinion.

AFRO-LECON, INC. v. UNITED STATES

820 F.2d 1198 (Fed. Cir. 1987)

NICHOLS, Senior Circuit Judge.

Afro-Lecon, Inc. (Afro-Lecon) appeals the final decision of the General Services Administration Board of Contract Appeals (board), denying Afro-Lecon's motion to stay proceedings in its civil action relating to United States contract No. SB2-10-8(a)80C-045 until after the completion of related criminal proceedings against Afro-Lecon and dismissing the civil claim with prejudice. We vacate and remand.

The Small Business Administration awarded a subcontract to Afro-Lecon on February 29, 1980, to supply 18,298 filing cabinets for the General Services Administration (GSA). After disputes developed concerning the contract, the parties entered into a settlement agreement in October 1982 that terminated the contract without termination costs and preserved Afro-Lecon's right to assert claims concerning the delivered portion of the contract.

On June 8, 1983, Afro-Lecon submitted a certified claim, pursuant to this agreement, for costs through October 12, 1982. The basis of the claim was that the GSA delayed issuing purchase orders and bills of lading thereby increasing the company's costs. The contracting officer denied the claim on April 11, 1984, and Afro-Lecon appealed to the board.

The GSA, in preparation of its case before the board, requested discovery of the dates of the delay periods, the costs incurred during these periods, and the causal relationship between the government's actions and the claimed costs. Afro-Lecon did not respond to the satisfaction of the GSA. The GSA then issued a second set of interrogatories and a second document request. Afro-Lecon objected to the second discovery request and the agency then filed a motion to compel discovery, which the board granted on May 9, 1985. The responses provided by Afro-Lecon continued to be unacceptable to the GSA. On July 3, 1985, the board issued an order on accounting, which required Afro-Lecon to provide a detailed account of its claim with a response due by September 4, 1985.

In late July 1985, Afro-Lecon learned that it was the subject of a grand jury investigation regarding the civil claims before the board. On September 4, 1985, Afro-Lecon moved to suspend the civil proceedings because key witnesses such as officers, former employees, and consultants, were advised by counsel not to participate in the response to the order on accounting or in any portion of the civil litigation in order to avoid incrimination in the criminal proceedings. On October 17, 1985, the Assistant U.S. Attorney for the Western District of New York notified Afro-Lecon that the company and its president, Benjamin Okumabua, were potential defendants in a grand jury investigation into whether the company's claims were false, in violation of 18 U.S.C. §§ 641 and 1001.

On January 17, 1986, the board denied Afro-Lecon's September 4 motion for a stay of the civil appeal and required the company to respond to the order on accounting by February 18, 1986. In early February the grand jury, empaneled in the United States District Court for the Western District of New York, indicted Afro-Lecon and Okumabua for making false claims against the government. On February 15, 1986, Afro-Lecon renewed its motion to stay the civil proceedings in view of the indictment. The board denied the stay and dismissed the company's civil appeal on April 11, 1986. The board, in reaching this conclusion, noted that the refusal of crucial Afro-Lecon witnesses to testify made it impossible for Afro-Lecon to comply with the order on accounting. The board decided, however, that Afro-Lecon, as the party asserting the civil claim, could not use the fifth amendment as a basis to defer civil proceedings. * * *

The question in this case is whether the board properly denied Afro-Lecon's motion to stay the company's civil claim until completion of the criminal trial which concerned the same facts. This turns on whether the board has a right and duty to proceed in these circumstances and whether Afro-Lecon can maintain its civil suit and, at the same time, claim the fifth amendment privilege against self-incrimination. * * * We conclude that the board, in the exercise of its undoubted discretion, was mistaken in its analysis of the applicable legal standards in this case, and to Afro-Lecon's prejudice. * * *

Although the fifth amendment claims per se are not, as we shall show, the only consideration in the analysis of the propriety of parallel proceedings, we address the fifth amendment claims first in view of the emphasis placed on the fifth amendment claims by the parties and the board.

The fifth amendment provides that "[n]o person * * * shall be compelled in any criminal case to be a witness against himself * * * U.S. Const. amend. V. The board, citing United States v. Rylander, 460 U.S. 752 (1983) and Smith v. Black Panther Party, 458 U.S. 1118 (1982), concluded that in a civil suit, a party placing facts in issue may not rely upon the fifth amendment to avoid disclosure of such facts and still maintain the suit. [The court declined "to accept the interpretation of *Black Panther* as suggested by the board."]

* * * The second case relied on by the board, *Rylander,* did not concern the issue of parallel criminal and civil proceedings. The Court in *Rylander* considered the evidentiary effect of a fifth amendment claim and concluded that the fifth amendment does not excuse a claimant from meeting the appropriate burden of proof in his case. In the case at bar, Afro-Lecon recognizes that it is not possible to establish its civil case without producing the appropriate evidence and, therefore, requests only a stay of the civil proceedings. It does not ask to be excused from producing evidence before it can recover.

The board's scenario of the appellant waving its sword, the contract claim, over the government's head, while unfairly invoking the privilege against self- incrimination to deny the government access to evidence essential as its shield, is overstrained. In the first place, the government already has the evidence it improperly seized for the criminal trial. In the second place, the government has the money in dispute, which it retains while the stay, if granted, lasts. In the third place, a proceeding in a board of contract appeals is not precisely a combat arena. It is a mode of dispute resolution resorted to by election of the parties in a tribunal which is part of the government's own executive branch. The appellant is not necessarily waving the sword because the government may be seeking money from the appellant, not the other way around. If an appellant seeking money is willing to await the outcome of the criminal trial, the board does not point out how the government is prejudiced by delay. It is the government which wishes to deny the mode of dispute resolution it has contracted for, as a price for asserting a constitutional right.

We now consider the appropriate standards for determining whether a stay of the civil proceedings should have been granted in this case. The Constitution does not require a stay of civil proceedings pending the outcome of criminal proceedings. A court, however, has the discretion to stay civil proceedings, postpone civil discovery, or impose protective orders and conditions "when the interests of justice seem[ ] to require such action, sometimes at the request of the prosecution, * * * sometimes at the request of the defense[.]" United States v. Kordel, 397 U.S. 1 (1970).

* * * [T]he circumstances that weigh in favor of granting a stay include malicious prosecution, the absence of counsel for defendant during

depositions, agency bad faith, malicious government tactics, and "other special circumstances." * * *

The court in [SEC v. Dresser Industries, 628 F.2d 1368 (D.C. Cir. 1980, supra p. 621] outlined the circumstances of parallel proceedings in clear terms:

> Other than where there is specific evidence of agency bad faith or malicious governmental tactics, the strongest case for deferring civil proceedings until after completion of criminal proceedings is where a party under indictment for a serious offense is required to defend a civil or administrative action involving the same matter. The noncriminal proceeding, if not deferred, might undermine the party's Fifth Amendment privilege against self-incrimination, expand rights of criminal discovery beyond the limits of Federal Rule of Criminal Procedure 16(b), expose the basis of the defense to the prosecution in advance of criminal trial, or otherwise prejudice the case. If delay of the noncriminal proceeding would not seriously injure the public interest, a court may be justified in deferring it.

We agree with the court's assessment in *Dresser* that parallel proceedings may result in the abuse of discovery. We discuss, infra, the question of whether the position of the claimant, e.g., as plaintiff or defendant, is relevant. Although the government does not concede that discovery abuse is a concern in this case, it does admit on appeal that the evaluation of the motion to stay is multifaceted and not limited to the narrow issue of whether a corporation has a fifth amendment right.

The scope of civil discovery is broad and requires nearly total mutual disclosure of each party's evidence prior to trial. Hickman v. Taylor, 329 U.S. 495 (1947). Rule 26 broadly authorizes discovery of "any matter, not privileged, which is relevant to the subject matter involved in the pending action[.]" Fed.R.Civ.P. 26(b)(1). The information sought during discovery in a civil case need not be admissible at trial and need only be reasonably calculated to lead to discovery of admissible evidence.

Criminal "discovery" under the federal rules, in contrast, is highly restricted. For example, Rule 15 controls the deposition process and permits a party to an action to depose only its own witnesses and then only pursuant to a court order in "exceptional circumstances." Fed.R.Crim.P. 15(a). The civil rules, in contrast, allow depositions of all parties to the action and any other person necessary to obtain testimony relevant to the subject matter of the action. Fed.R.Civ.P. 26. Rule 15 also provides that the defendant cannot be deposed without his consent and that the scope of cross-examination must be the same as at trial. Fed.R.Crim.P. 15(d). Rule 16 also significantly restricts discovery in criminal cases by describing what is discoverable with specificity and detail.

The broad scope of civil discovery may present to both the prosecution, and at times the criminal defendant, an irresistible temptation to use that discovery to one's advantage in the criminal case. Such unconstitutional uses may begin with the surreptitious planting of criminal investigators in civil depositions, as in the case at bar, and end with passive abuses, such as when the civil party, who asserts fifth amendment rights, is compelled to refuse to answer questions individually, revealing his weak points to the criminal prosecutor. This point-by-point review of the civil case may lead to a "link in the chain of evidence" that unconstitutionally contributes to the defendant's conviction.

In Peden v. United States, 512 F.2d 1099 (Ct.Cl.1975), the court noted the dangers of parallel proceedings in a civil service action where the same circumstances were subject to both civil and criminal proceedings:

> [A] CSC [Civil Service Commission] hearing that is in the nature of a dress rehearsal for a criminal trial, in which all the Government witnesses testify and are cross-examined at length, but the defendant to be does not, is potentially a big lift to the criminal defense and could well be decisive in securing an acquittal, if anything could.

The court noted the remedy for the problem presented by this situation:

> [I]t has long been the practice to "freeze" civil proceedings when a criminal prosecution involving the same facts is warming up or under way. In the context of appeals from civil service adverse actions, we have repeatedly approved this practice.

The court in *Peden* suggested that postponement of civil proceedings is desirable not only for fifth amendment reasons, but also for the protection of the integrity of two separate processes:

> The "freeze" we think is not for the protection of the employee only, but also rises out of a sense that deferrable civil proceedings constitute improper interference with the criminal proceedings if they churn over the same evidentiary material.

* * * In the case at bar, the dangers of parallel proceedings have already been realized. Afro-Lecon's motion to suppress the fruits of the discovery abuses has been granted in part and denied in part. In this order, the court criticized the government:

> This Court is not approbatory of the prosecution's utilization of the ploy of having a criminal investigator "sit in" on and participate in a non-criminal conference or interview when criminal prosecution was, as here, eminently predictable and without advising the "target" of the investigator's role and purpose.

The district court concluded that, in regard to the documents involved, there was no harm to the defendants because their existence was known prior to the conference and would have properly become available through a *subpoena duces tecum*. Verbal statements, however, made by the defendants, the court noted, could not be used against the defendants because of the improper tactics employed by the prosecution. The district court noted:

> Suppression * * * is merited not only by equity and good conscience but also by the salutary aspect of impressing upon the prosecution that such overreaching is not compatible with evenhanded justice which, rather than achieving convictions, should be a prosecutor's goal.

The abuse of civil discovery sanctioned by the district court is now fait accompli. On remand, we ask the board to evaluate in view of the precedent cited whether there is any additional danger of abuse of discovery or whether there is any likelihood that the civil case, if proceeded with, will interfere with the administration of the criminal proceedings.

As Judge Friedman noted in Zenith Radio Corporation v. United States, 764 F.2d 1577 (Fed. Cir. 1985), there are three schools of thought in treating privileges asserted by plaintiffs. The first approach considers that the party automatically waives his privilege by pursuing judicial relief. The second approach balances the need for discovery against the need for secrecy. The third theory denies a plaintiff the privilege if he places the matter subject to the privilege in issue and the information is vital to the defendant's case.

The board adopted the "automatic waiver" theory. We believe that this approach is too rigid and choose instead the balancing approach * * *. This is particularly appropriate where the civil case is not in court but in a tribunal provided by defendant itself for dispute resolution. We conclude that there may be greater reasons to postpone civil proceedings when even an appellant requests it where there is a parallel criminal suit.

In *Kordel* the Court noted the strong policy interest in allowing both the civil and criminal cases brought by the *government* to go forward:

> It would stultify enforcement of federal law to require a governmental agency such as the FDA invariably to choose either to forgo recommendation of a criminal prosecution once it seeks civil relief, or to defer civil proceedings pending the ultimate outcome of a criminal trial.

This important government interest is absent when the civil case is not initiated by the government. Although there are other interests of possible harm to the civil defendant, which we will address *infra,* the harm discussed in *Kordel* is not at issue at present.

Essentially, the board concludes that one may not bring a suit, "wave the sword" of the fifth amendment, and then maintain the suit. We agree that a party may not claim a fifth amendment privilege and *proceed* with his suit. Afro-Lecon, however, asks for a *stay* of civil proceedings and, as a result, does not raise the problem of placing the defendant in the position of maintaining a defense without necessary discovery.

In Wehling v. Columbia Broadcasting System, 608 F.2d 1084 (5th Cir. 1979), the [Fifth Circuit] considered circumstances very much like those at issue in the case at hand. In *Wehling,* the plaintiff appealed the dismissal of his libel action against CBS where his refusal to testify deprived CBS of information essential to its defense. Wehling was required to appear before a grand jury and believed that he was the subject of their investigation.

The court in *Wehling* concluded that the federal rules do not permit a court to punish a party who resists discovery by asserting a valid claim of privilege and that dismissing a plaintiff's action with prejudice solely because he exercises his privilege against self-incrimination is constitutionally impermissible. The basis of this decision was the principle articulated by the Court in Simmons v. United States, 390 U.S. 377 (1968), and elsewhere, that procedures should not require a party to surrender one constitutional right in order to assert another one. * * *

In *Wehling,* CBS advocated, as does the government here, agreed with by the board, that one who brings suit and then claims fifth amendment privileges is akin to the spoiled child who wants the cake and the right to consume it as well. In *Wehling,* the court properly addressed this misguided idea:

> It is true that, as a voluntary litigant, the civil plaintiff has created the situation which requires him to choose between his silence and his lawsuit. In most cases, however, a party "voluntarily" becomes a plaintiff only because there is no other means of protecting legal rights. As one commentator has observed, although the plaintiff-defendant "distinction is superficially appealing, * * * civil plaintiffs seldom voluntarily seek situations requiring litigation."

* * * We agree with the Fifth Circuit and decline to accept the wooden plaintiff-defendant distinction.

We now address the appropriate analysis for parallel proceedings. Neither the court in *Wehling* nor this court concludes that there is a per se right to postponement of civil proceedings under the circumstances of these two cases. Rather, a balancing must occur of the interest of the appellant in postponement, which is strong, against the possible prejudice to the appellee by way of important evidence that will be lost over time. The court in *Wehling* found that the district court abused its discretion by not granting the stay, yet noted that the district court could dismiss the plaintiff's case at any future point if crucial avenues of discovery were shown to be closing during the three-year period of the stay. We remand to the board to assess the sources of evidence for the order on accounting and to find whether the requested postponement will create an appreciable prejudice to the defendant's case. * * *

NIES, Circuit Judge, concurring.

I concur because I see the issue somewhat differently. Appellant sought a stay of board proceedings on the ground that at the time its response was due to the board's Order on Accounting, it was impossible to respond because the persons who could provide the explanation for its claim were potential defendants in a criminal case and allegedly refused, on advice of counsel, to cooperate. The board accepted that explanation stating, "The immediate effect of their refusal to cooperate is the inability of appellant to satisfactorily comply with the Board's Order on Accounting." Under such circumstances, appellant is guilty of no willful disobedience or even gross negligence in failing to respond to the board's order. A dismissal of its claim with prejudice would have been an abuse of discretion in my view. Notably, however, the board did not dismiss the claim as a matter of *discretion*. The board held, as a matter of *law,* "that in a civil suit a party placing facts in issue may not rely upon the fifth amendment to avoid disclosure of such facts and still maintain his suit." From that legal premise, the board concluded that appellant was not entitled to a stay.

The board's premise, i.e., that a party may not maintain its claim and at the same time assert the fifth amendment, even if correct, does not apply here. Appellant sought a stay of the order because of an impossibility in complying, not because of its assertion of a fifth amendment privilege. Indeed, as far as the record here is concerned, no one has asserted fifth amendment rights *in this proceeding.* Such rights have merely been alluded to by appellant's counsel as the explanation for the appellant's failure to respond. The board, nevertheless, treated counsel's statements as sufficient to establish that it was impossible for appellant to comply with its order. At this moment in these proceedings, that is its ruling.

Thus, I agree that the board's order must be vacated and the matter remanded. Having found impossibility of compliance with its order, the board should not have dismissed but, rather, should have granted a stay for a reasonable period. The government would be, of course, free at any time to seek to have the stay lifted if the impossibility is removed in the interim. At the end of the stay appellant would be required to proceed or to put forth satisfactory grounds for a continuance, at which time the matter would be re-evaluated in light of subsequent developments and the prejudice to the government caused by further delay.

NOTES AND QUESTIONS

1. ***Granting a Stay.*** The decision to stay is not simply an issue for trial courts. As *Afro-Lecon* shows, administrative bodies will have to determine

whether to halt their proceedings until the criminal action is complete. Note that this may involve cases in different jurisdictions, such as a state license boards and federal grand jury investigations. See J. Cal McCastlain and Steven Schooner, *To Stay or Not To Stay: Difficult Decisions For Boards of Contract Appeals Confronted With Parallel Proceedings*, 16 PUB. CONT. L.J. 418 (1987).

2. ***Effect of Denying a Stay***. If a party fails to obtain a stay in a civil suit, what is the effect on discovery in that action if the party asserts the Fifth Amendment? Consider the analysis of the Fourth Circuit in **In re Grand Jury Subpoena**, 836 F.2d 1468 (4th Cir. 1988):

> In many civil cases the burden placed on a person's silence may be unavoidable. Where a plaintiff has gathered sufficient evidence to establish a claim prior to discovery, a defendant who risks incrimination by speaking will inevitably face the choice of forsaking silence or losing a civil judgment, even if the defendant's silence is not used against him. See 8 Wright & Miller, Federal Practice & Procedure §2018 & n. 49 (1970) [noting that where there is no evidence to support the defendant's case, by virtue of the claim of the privilege, a "directed verdict or grant of summary judgment will be proper"]. A plaintiff whose claim requires incriminating testimony will likewise always face the choice of speaking or forsaking his prayer for redress. In either case, a district court may reduce the risk of a party's silence by not dismissing an action for failing to cooperate with discovery, but the party will nonetheless face the inevitable judgment of the trier of fact who must make a decision based on an imbalanced presentation of the evidence.

For a discussion of how an assertion of the Fifth Amendment can be used in an attorney disciplinary proceeding, see Chapter 17.

3. ***The Government's Tactical Advantage***. Courts have expressed concerns about whether to grant a stay just to preserve the advantage of limited discovery granted under the criminal rules when there is a parallel civil or administrative proceeding that would allow the criminal defendant the opportunity to obtain evidence, especially witness testimony, not otherwise available. In **United States v. Fin. Indus. Regulatory Auth. (FINRA)**, 607 F. Supp. 2d 391 (E.D.N.Y. 2009), the district court considered the prosecutor's request to stay a private arbitration involving the same underlying transactions as those in a criminal case:

> The U.S. Attorney asserts that allowing the arbitration to go forward will compromise the criminal case because it will "permit the Criminal Defendants to gain access to witness statements that they would not otherwise be entitled to under the Federal Rules of Criminal Procedure and would therefore frustrate the clear purpose of the Federal Rules and prejudice the public's interest in the criminal justice process." This argument proceeds from the premise

that by limiting discovery, the Federal Rules of Criminal Procedure are intended to enshrine a tactical advantage in favor of the government. But as the Court observed in connection with the U.S. Attorney's motion to stay discovery in the civil enforcement proceeding by the Securities and Exchange Commission ("SEC") against the criminal defendants, "the limits on criminal discovery do not exist for their own sake,"; rather, they are intended to guard against specific concerns: (1) the broad disclosure of the essentials of the prosecution's case may lead to perjury and manufactured evidence; (2) the revelation of the identity of prospective witnesses may create the opportunity for intimidation; and (3) the criminal defendants may unfairly surprise the prosecution at trial with information developed through discovery, while the self-incrimination privilege would effectively block any attempts by the Government to discover relevant evidence from the defendants.

With regard to the first concern, the U.S. Attorney does not argue that allowing the arbitration to go forward increases the risk of false evidence. Instead, he rephrases the concern as preventing the criminal defendants from having "an opportunity to build a defense tailored to the Government's case." By "tailoring a defense," he apparently means that the criminal defendants will have more information with which to highlight potential weaknesses in the government's case. But the criminal defendants have every right to meet the allegations and evidence against them. One of the most frequent — if not the most frequent — means of doing so is pointing out inconsistencies in a witness's testimony.

If there is any concern about "tailoring" here, it is the government's concern with what its witnesses may say at the arbitration. Absent any indication to the contrary, however, the Court must assume that the arbitration witnesses will accurately and honestly report the material facts within their knowledge. Unlike perjury and manufactured evidence, any inconsistencies between the testimony adduced at the arbitration and that adduced at the criminal trial are legitimate fodder for the defense.

With respect to the second concern, the U.S. Attorney argues that early disclosure of the identity of the government's witnesses increases, not the risk of witness intimidation, but of "subordination [sic] of perjury." Whether the concern is with witness intimidation or subornation of perjury, however, it is not present here. The identities of the witnesses who will testify at the arbitration have already been disclosed and, indeed, are listed in the U.S. Attorney's memorandum of law, along with the statement that "[a]part from the Criminal Defendants, these same witnesses are all likely to testify at the criminal trial." Thus, whatever the risk is that those witnesses will be intimidated or asked to testify falsely, allowing the arbitration to go forward will not increase it.

> The third concern — the risk of unfair surprise flowing from the privilege against self-incrimination—is also not present. The testimony that will be adduced at the arbitration is equally available to both the government and the defendants.
>
> In sum, the only "prejudice" the Court can discern is that allowing the arbitration to go forward will result in the criminal defendants having more information than they would otherwise be entitled to at this stage under the Federal Rules of Criminal Procedure. This loss of the government's usual tactical advantage is insufficient to justify enjoining the arbitration.

4. ***Prosecutorial Request for Stay During Grand Jury Investigation***. Although many requests for a stay are brought by individuals seeking to avoid discovery, the government may request that a civil action–including those brought by federal administrative agencies–be stayed pending completion of the criminal investigation. The reason given is that the defendant in the civil case will obtain discovery of materials otherwise unavailable in a criminal investigation. A defendant in a civil enforcement action can use the discovery tools afforded by the Federal Rules of Civil Procedure to take the deposition of witnesses–especially those who may be cooperating with the criminal investigators–to learn what has been revealed to the criminal investigators. In **Securities & Exchange Commission v. HealthSouth Corp.**, 261 F.Supp.2d 1298 (N.D. Ala. 2003), the SEC sought a freeze on the assets of a corporation's former CEO, Richard Scrushy, pending resolution of a civil securities fraud action while the criminal investigation proceeded. The SEC sought to use the plea agreements of 11 former company officers as evidence of Scrushy's involvement in the underlying fraud, but the former officers asserted the Fifth Amendment in response to questions from defense counsel. In response to efforts by Scrushy to obtain information about the criminal investigation, the United States Attorney and the Department of Justice sought a 60 day stay in the proceeding "as alternative relief for the purpose of 'permitting the grand jury to complete its investigation and the Government to properly pursue its criminal prosecution.'" The SEC, however, pressed forward with its request for the asset freeze, which the district court denied. In granting a stay, the district court emphasized the impact of the ongoing criminal investigation on the civil suit:

> The government having repeatedly asked the court to stay this matter raised the very question with which this court is now confronted, that being defendant Scrushy's inherent inability to present evidence in his defense due to the ongoing criminal investigation. Although the SEC repeatedly represented that it was not offering the plea colloquies for the truth of the matters asserted therein, counsel's statements in closing argument contradict that representation. Because the individual witnesses who had already entered pleas, or already arranged to enter pleas, when called by defendant Scrushy to testify, stated only that they invoked their

Fifth Amendment privilege against self-incrimination, defendant Scrushy was effectively denied his right to cross examine these witnesses. Additionally, defendant Scrushy was denied the right to explore these witnesses' motives or reasons for entering guilty plea agreements. Because the SEC then represented to the court in its closing argument that these plea colloquies implicate the defendant, cross examination was critical to the defendant's right to a fair hearing. Further adding to this inability to engage in cross examination was [U.S. Department of Justice attorney] Mr. Richard Smith's representation to the court that should Bill Owens be called to the stand, he would be forced to file another motion to intervene to object to the defendant "attempting to put on a witness in a criminal case in a civil proceeding." He made similar motions with regard to every individual who was called to testify by defendant Scrushy who had already entered into a plea bargain arrangement with the U.S. Attorney's Office.

* * * As long as a criminal investigation is ongoing and the individuals who have pled guilty have not yet been sentenced, the key witnesses to defendant Scrushy's involvement or lack thereof will refuse to answer the very questions that would either support or rebut the SEC's allegations. Yet these are the same witnesses upon which the SEC relies to keep the asset freeze in place. This court has no way to predict when the criminal case may be resolved so that this case may proceed without these crucial witnesses who are taking the Fifth Amendment.

Because of the ongoing criminal investigation, defendant Scrushy has been placed in the precarious position of either waiving his Fifth Amendment rights and defending himself in the matter before this court, or asserting the privilege and probably losing this civil proceeding. While such a choice may not be unconstitutional, this court may still exercise its discretion to stay this case in the interest of justice.

* * * [T]he SEC's other evidence of an alleged fraud on the part of defendant Scrushy was obtained from both FBI and from the parallel criminal investigation. Although the SEC, since the conclusion of the hearing on whether or not the asset freeze should remain in full force and effect, has filed a "motion to supplement the record with the guilty pleas of Michael Martin and Malcom McVay," such motion further supports defendant's argument that the SEC's investigation into this civil matter is in fact a precursor for a setup to the criminal indictment and this court's conclusion that the SEC has no evidence other than what stems from the parallel criminal investigation. Allowing those pleas as evidence of defendant Scrushy's involvement in the alleged securities fraud, without allowing defense counsel to cross-examine these witnesses, is just another reason to support the court's conclusion that this matter

should be stayed pending completion of the criminal investigation or until such witnesses have been sentenced and can no longer invoke their privilege pursuant to Fifth Amendment of the United States Constitution.

* * * The court finds the criminal and civil cases overlap completely. The issues in both are identical. Although defendant Scrushy has not yet been indicted, no one has represented to the court that such indictment is anything but an eventuality. During this court's hearing, the U.S. Attorney's Office intervened repeatedly in an attempt to prevent defendant Scrushy from obtaining any evidence in this civil proceeding that he would not be entitled to in a criminal proceeding. Although the plaintiff does have an interest in the expeditious resolution of this case, the court finds the harm to defendant Scrushy from blindly pushing ahead with this matter to greatly outweigh the prejudice to the SEC from a stay of this civil proceeding. Given that the evidence presented by the SEC was that obtained from the FBI pursuant to the criminal investigation, and the guilty pleas already entered, the court actually finds the SEC may actually benefit from a stay to allow the FBI to continue gathering evidence. The court finds, in the same vein, that both the SEC and defendant Scrushy would benefit from a stay of this case until all those who pled guilty have been sentenced, so that testimony may be obtained from them at the final hearing in this case, rather than repeated insistence by these individuals on their Fifth Amendment rights. This is especially true given the U.S. Attorney's Office's great efforts to prevent the testimony of "Owens, Livesay, Smith, Harris, or Morgan, or any other witness with knowledge about matters being criminally investigated . . ." Additionally, the plaintiff here is not an individual who has been wronged, but the SEC, which is a governmental body.

While a stay in a civil proceeding when no indictment has yet issued in the criminal proceeding is rare, issuing such a stay is within this court's inherent powers.

* * * The court's role in a civil proceeding such as that before it is to ensure that fairness permeates the proceeding and to try to ascertain the truth.[48] The court is unable to accomplish either of

[48] The Ninth Circuit Court of Appeals has wisely noted that "[i]n highly publicized cases, such as the one at hand, judicial . . . decisionmakers need to be especially careful that undue consideration is not given a proceeding's impact on the public. Governmental entities are frequently aware of the need to reassure the public that they are taking prompt action in response to a crisis. In such high visibility situations, it is especially necessary to guard the rights of defendants, and concern for the public deterrence value of an enforcement proceeding must not be allowed to override the individual defendant's due process rights." Keating v. Office of Thrift Supervision, 45 F.3d 322 (9th Cir.1994).

these purposes here, as the witnesses who could testify as to the allegations in the SEC's complaint have refused to do so, by invoking their Fifth Amendment rights. Although the court may draw inferences from such use of the Fifth Amendment in a civil proceeding, the inferences here are too speculative to draw.[50] These problems are further compounded by the U.S. Attorney's Office and Department of Justice's efforts to prevent defendant Scrushy from obtaining any discovery. These entities argued that "to permit any depositions to be conducted by the defendants in this civil action would result in disclosure of sensitive information critical to the criminal investigation and to an anticipated trial. For these reasons, the Government requests that it be permitted to intervene and that this Court either quash any and all subpoenas issued by Defendant Scrushy to the above-named specific individuals and to any and all witnesses who may be called who have knowledge about the criminal investigation in this case, and prohibit their compelled testimony, or in the alternative, that these civil proceedings be stayed in their entirety."

* * * This case is stayed pending the resolution of any criminal charges against defendant Scrushy, or notification by either party that such charges will not be forthcoming.

5. ***Prosecutorial Request for Stay After Indictment***. When the government indicts a defendant who is also the subject of a civil enforcement action, the defendant may try to take advantage of the more liberal civil discovery rules to gather information about the criminal case that would not be as readily available through the criminal discovery rules. Is the prosecutor's interests in preventing discovery of the criminal case sufficient to warrant a stay? Consider the analysis in **Securities & Exchange Comm'n v. Doody**, 186 F.Supp.2d 379 (S.D.N.Y. 2002), in which only one defendant in an SEC civil suit was charged in the criminal case, and the

---

[50] Each of the witnesses in this case who have entered guilty pleas have entered plea bargains with the government. Each has agreed to provide "substantial assistance" to the U.S. Attorney's office in its ongoing investigation in exchange for a downward departure upon sentencing. Each has taken the Fifth in response to questions about his or her, or defendant Scrushy's role in the allegations. The court has considered what motivations a witness, who has already entered a plea, but not yet been sentenced, may have to invoke the Fifth Amendment in response to information stated by him or her in open court upon entering a plea of guilty. The court has considered perhaps the prosecutor's desire to not reveal its hand during this civil proceeding, evidence of additional, uncharged crimes, and even possible future perjury charges as motivating factors. Given these uncertainties, the court is unable to draw any inferences adverse to defendant Scrushy from such testimony. The court notes issues such as this should resolve themselves upon these witnesses giving their testimony during the criminal proceeding and being sentenced. At least then, defendant Scrushy will have some factual basis to determine how best to defend himself, or whether to defend himself at all.

prosecutor sought a stay of discovery in the civil case pending completion of the criminal matter:

> On November 8, 2001, a grand jury sitting in this district returned an indictment charging Joseph F. Doody, IV, with securities fraud. The charge, in substance, is that Doody traded on material inside information regarding an impending merger between BetzDearborn, Inc. and Hercules Incorporated which he obtained from his girlfriend, Diane Neiley.
>
> On the same date, the SEC brought this civil action against Doody, his father, Joseph F. Doody ("Doody Sr."), and Neilly charging the same insider trading scheme. Doody is alleged to have tipped Doody Sr. on the basis of the tips he received from Neilly, and Doody Sr. is alleged to have traded on that information as well. The SEC seeks an injunction and other relief.
>
> The trial of the criminal case now is set * * *. In the meantime, Doody Sr. has commenced an ambitious discovery program in this action, seeking answers to interrogatories from and production of documents by the SEC which, the government says, would result in premature disclosure of the evidence upon which it hopes to rely in the criminal case. In addition, Doody Sr. has noticed Neilly's deposition, and the government apprehends that he will seek to depose individuals who are likely to be witnesses in the criminal trial, thus further tipping the government's hand and, in effect, giving Doody an extra opportunity to cross-examine the government's witnesses.
>
> The government has made a persuasive case that its interest in protecting its criminal case justifies its intervention here, and Doody makes no serious argument to the contrary. Accordingly, the government will be permitted to intervene for the purpose of seeking relief against discovery in this case pending the completion of the criminal trial. The question is whether it is entitled to that relief.
>
> Once an indictment has been returned, the government often moves for and frequently obtains relief preventing a criminal defendant from using parallel civil proceedings to gain premature access to evidence and information pertinent to the criminal case. In granting such relief, courts must weigh competing interests, including "the interests of the defendants, the interests of the plaintiffs in proceeding with the litigation, the public interest, and the interests of the courts and of third parties."
>
> Doody Sr. argues that the abundance of authority is not controlling or, arguably, even pertinent here because he is not a defendant in the criminal case and, moreover, has a compelling need to proceed expeditiously in the civil case. The need is said to stem from the fact

that he is employed by Enron, is likely soon to be out of a job and, absent speedy disposition of the civil case, would have difficulty finding employment with the stigma from the SEC's charges against him hanging over his head.

To be sure, most cases involving stays of civil actions pending the completion of parallel criminal proceedings have involved common defendants. This case therefore is different to the extent that it is Doody Sr. who is leading the charge toward discovery in this civil case. But the Court would have to be unimaginably naive to suppose that Doody Sr. is not a stalking horse for Doody himself. Whether Doody Sr. discovers the government's case against his son or his son's attorneys do it by exercising their right, as counsel to a co-defendant in the civil case, to participate in discovery here is immaterial. The fact is that discovery here that would afford Doody access to information to which he would not be entitled in his defense of the criminal case almost surely would occur absent some relief.

Doody Sr. is at least arguably right also in saying that this case is unusual in that he would be subjected to some prejudice by a delay of civil discovery different than anything that might be claimed by one who is a defendant in both cases. But he has failed to demonstrate that he will suffer prejudice that outweighs the government's interest in obtaining a stay. Perhaps he will lose his job, and perhaps he will have some difficulty finding new employment while this action is pending. But the fact is that he has not lost it yet and may not lose it. Even if he does, the criminal case is scheduled for trial in approximately four weeks. Doody Sr. has provided no information concerning his financial situation, so there is no basis whatever to suppose that a delay of discovery in this case for, say, six weeks would mean the difference between his putting food on the table and starvation. Thus, Doody Sr.'s position is based on unfounded assumptions and inappropriate exaggerations. But he is not alone in having overstated his case.

The relief the government seeks is virtually a blanket stay of all disclosure in this case. Perhaps no discovery could be provided here without implicating its legitimate concerns in the criminal case, but that is not self evident. In consequence, the Court is left guessing as to just what protection the government legitimately requires. After having weighed the competing interests of the various parties, it therefore must make the best judgments it can in the circumstances.

* * * The following discovery is stayed until the earliest of (i) the entry of a plea of guilty, (ii) the completion of the trial of the criminal case, and (iii) March 20, 2002:

(1) Rule 26(a)(i)(A) discovery.

(2) Production of transcripts of SEC testimony and notes of interviews of any person whom the United States Attorney's office certifies may be called as a witness in the criminal case.

(3) Depositions of any person whom the United States Attorney's office certifies may be called as a witness in the criminal case.

F. ADMINISTRATIVE SANCTIONS

In addition to the authority to investigate possible violations, the civil law enforcement agencies can impose various sanctions for violations. These penalties may be imposed after a administrative hearing or be ordered by a federal court after a judicial determination that a violation has occurred. The sanctions may be imposed after the completion of a criminal prosecution, although a conviction is not a prerequisite to the administrative agency pursuing its own remedies. Quite often, an individual or company will settle the agency action and accept a civil penalty as part of a global settlement of a parallel criminal investigation that may result in a guilty plea or, for a corporation, a deferred or non-prosecution agreement. The penalties an agency can impose are established by statute, and can include monetary penalties, suspension or revocation of a license, forfeiture of goods or money, and prohibition on future participation in government programs or contracts.

At one point, the imposition of civil penalties raised potential problems in parallel criminal cases under the Double Jeopardy Clause of the Fifth Amendment. In **United States v. Halper**, 490 U.S. 435 (1989), the Supreme Court held that a fixed civil penalty imposed after the defendant's criminal conviction arising from the same underlying conduct violated the multiple punishment prong of the prohibition on double jeopardy because the civil penalty was punitive and not remedial. The Court overruled *Halper* in **Hudson v. United States**, 522 U.S. 93 (1997), stating that "*Halper*'s deviation from longstanding double jeopardy principles was ill considered." After *Hudson*, the test for determining whether the Double Jeopardy Clause applies is whether the statute is civil or criminal, based on whether Congress designated the provision as criminal or civil, or whether it intended a criminal provision. The Eighth Amendment's proscription on excessive fines applies to both civil and criminal penalties, and in **United States v. Bajakajian**, 524 U.S. 321 (1998), the Court found the civil forfeiture of $357, 144 of undeclared currency to be excessive and in violation of the Eighth Amendment.

When an administrative agency imposes sanctions for a violation, what standard applies to judicial enforcement of that determination?

BURKE v. ENVIRONMENTAL PROTECTION AGENCY

127 F.Supp.2d 235 (D.D.C. 2001)

KENNEDY, District Judge.

* * * Plaintiff Paul M. Burke ("Burke") challenges the decision of the United States Environmental Protection Agency ("EPA" or "the agency") to debar him from contracting with the federal government and from participating in federal assistance, loans, and benefit programs for a period of five (5) years. Burke claims that EPA's debarment decision was arbitrary and capricious, an abuse of discretion, and not in accordance with law, all of which EPA denies. * * *

From 1989 to 1998, Burke was the president and sole shareholder of ACMAR Regional Landfill, Inc. ("ACMAR"), and the majority shareholder of Acmar Landfill, a Partnership ("the Partnership"). ACMAR and the Partnership owned and operated the ACMAR Regional Landfill ("the Landfill") located in Moody, Alabama. The Landfill accepted residential and industrial waste and bordered on the Big Black Creek, which flows into the Cahaba River, a source of drinking water for the residents of Birmingham, Alabama. In March 1990, the Alabama Department of Environmental Management ("ADEM") issued a permit to ACMAR for the disposal of solid waste within a fifty-acre, cigar-shaped parcel of land, referred to as the "cigar parcel." ADEM also issued to ACMAR a National Pollution Discharge Elimination System ("NPDES") permit, which authorized the release of storm water runoff that does not contain leachate[1] into the Big Black Creek.

On February 24, 1998, an information was filed in the United States District Court for the Northern District of Alabama, Middle Division, charging Burke with violating the Clean Water Act ("CWA"), 33 U.S.C. § 1319(c)(1)(A), for the negligent discharge of leachate into the Big Black Creek. The discharge occurred almost five years earlier on March 30, 1993. Burke pled guilty to violating the CWA, was fined $10,000, and was sentenced to eight months in prison, four months at a halfway house, and one year supervised release if he continued to own or work for ACMAR or the Partnership at the time of his release from custody. In addition, ACMAR pled guilty to conspiring to defraud the United States through the illegal expansion of the Landfill, the disposal of solid waste in an unpermitted area, and the defrauding of landfill clients. ACMAR was fined $1.8 million and was ordered to develop an effective environmental compliance plan. Pursuant to his plea agreement, Burke sold ACMAR to Superior Star Ridge in March 1998.

---

[1] Leachate is a liquid by-product produced in landfills when either precipitation or other fluid mixes with contaminants found in the waste, thereby creating a biological reaction. Depending on the amount of decomposition or available oxygen, the leachate leads to the production of additional contaminants in downward moving water. Leachate also stains the ground as it seeps back into the soil.

On July 16, 1998, the EPA Suspension and Debarment Division ("SDD") requested, through an Action Referral Memorandum ("ARM"), that Burke be suspended immediately, pending a proposed five-year debarment based on his conviction for violating the Clean Water Act. Robert F. Meunier, EPA Debarring Official, issued the notice of suspension on August 4, 1998[.] Burke timely contested the notice and requested an oral hearing, which was held on April 27, and 28, 1999.

On August 30, 1999, Meunier officially debarred Burke from participating in federal assistance, loans, and benefit programs and from contracting with the federal government for a five-year period, measured from the date of his suspension. In the Decision, EPA concluded that Burke's criminal conviction provided cause for debarment and that Burke did not demonstrate sufficient mitigating factors or remedial measures showing that debarment was unnecessary. EPA also found that a five-year, as opposed to a three-year, period of debarment was warranted under the circumstances. This action followed. * * *

Judicial review of EPA's Decision is available pursuant to the Administrative Procedure Act ("APA"), 5 U.S.C. § 701 *et seq.* The APA provides that the reviewing court shall hold unlawful an agency action that is "arbitrary, capricious, an abuse of discretion, or otherwise not in accordance with law." 5 U.S.C. § 706(2)(A). * * * The arbitrary and capricious standard is highly deferential and presumes the agency action to be valid. It is also well established that when reviewing matters under this standard, the court may not substitute its judgment for that of the agency officials. Rather, the court's inquiry is limited to determining whether the agency examined the case facts and articulated a satisfactory explanation for its decision, including a "rational connection between the facts found and the choice made." * * *

Debarment is a discretionary measure taken to protect the public interest and to promote an agency's policy of conducting business only with responsible persons. Debarment cannot be used to punish an individual; rather, it serves a remedial purpose of protecting the federal government from the business risk of dealing with an individual who lacks "business integrity or business honesty." The initiation of a debarment proceeding requires the existence of past misconduct; however, the final decision to debar an individual must focus on that individual's present business responsibility. In addition, the debarring official must determine whether any mitigating factors show that the business risk to the government has been eliminated to the extent that debarment would be unnecessary.

EPA found that Burke's criminal conviction for a negligent violation of the Clean Water Act established cause for debarment under 40 C.F.R. §

32.305(a)(4)[4] because the offense indicates a lack of business integrity that directly affects Burke's present responsibility. The agency also found an alternative cause for debarment under 40 C.F.R. § 32.305(d)[5] because the "factual misconduct" providing the basis for Burke's conviction "shows a serious lack of business responsibility."

Burke offers several arguments in support of his claim that EPA's determination was "arbitrary, capricious, an abuse of discretion, or otherwise not in accordance with law." First, Burke argues that the Decision erred as a matter of law by concluding that his criminal conviction established an offense-based cause for debarment. Burke contends that his conviction for the negligent discharge of leachate is neither one of the specified offenses listed in 40 C.F.R. § 32.305(a)(1-3) nor within the "nature and character" of offenses generally described in 40 C.F.R. § 32.305(a)(4). EPA responds by pointing out that it interprets 40 C.F.R. § 32.305(a)(4) to include environmental crimes where there is a reasonable connection between the participant's misconduct and his business integrity. Burke does not challenge EPA's interpretation of Section 32.305; rather, he contends that his case does not fall within the parameters of that interpretation.

* * * [T]here is no basis for concluding that EPA's interpretation of the parameters of Section 32.305 is wrong. EPA evaluated the relevant case facts and discerned a reasonable connection between Burke's misconduct and his business integrity:

> Operation of landfills in an environmentally compliant manner protects the environment and human health and safety. The negligent discharge of leachate, in the course of Mr. Burke's commercial operation of Acmar, raises serious questions about his business integrity.

Moreover, the administrative record contains substantial evidence to support EPA's finding that a nexus exists between Burke's criminal conviction and his business integrity. As a result of his guilty plea, Burke was fined $10,000 and sentenced to eight months in prison, four months in a

---

[4] 40 C.F.R. § 32.305(a) states: "Debarment may be imposed in accordance with the provisions of §§ 32.300 through 32.314 for (a) Conviction of or civil judgment for: (1) Commission of fraud or a criminal offense in connection with obtaining, attempting to obtain, or performing a public or private agreement or transaction; (2) Violation of Federal or State antitrust statutes, including those proscribing price fixing between competitors, allocation of customers between competitors, and bid rigging; (3) Commission of embezzlement, theft, forgery, bribery, falsification or destruction of records, making false statements, receiving stolen property, making false claims, or obstruction of justice; or (4) *Commission of any other offense indicating a lack of business integrity or business honesty that seriously and directly affects the present responsibility of a person.*" (emphasis added).

[5] 40 C.F.R. § 32.305(d) provides for debarment for "[a]ny other cause of so serious or compelling a nature that it affects the present responsibility of a person." Id.

halfway house, and twelve months supervised release if he continued his relationship with ACMAR. The details of the plea agreement, along with the fact that Burke was essentially compelled to discontinue his relationship with ACMAR, adequately support EPA's conclusion that Burke's criminal conviction reflected, to a significant degree, on his business integrity.

In addition, EPA properly evaluated Burke's criminal offense in light of ACMAR's fraud and deceit. Here the totality of the circumstances–especially the fact that Burke was the president and sole owner of ACMAR, which pled guilty to criminal conspiracy and was fined $1.8 million–gives rise to adverse inferences regarding Burke's business practices. The administrative record also confirms that Burke's guilty plea and fine were considered as part of the overall plea agreement with ACMAR. Even though Burke's individual conviction *alone* provides sufficient cause for debarment, it was hardly arbitrary and capricious for EPA to consider Burke's criminal offense in light of his company's related criminal fraud.

Before imposing a debarment, EPA must ascertain whether any mitigating factors or remedial measures show that the business risk of dealing with the individual has been eliminated to the extent that debarment is unnecessary. Federal Acquisition Regulations ("FARs") set forth relevant mitigating factors the agency should consider. The respondent has the burden of demonstrating–to the satisfaction of the debarring official–that sufficient mitigating factors make debarment unnecessary, however. Burke argues that EPA failed to consider substantial mitigating evidence in concluding that he should be debarred and failed to evaluate properly the seriousness of his conduct.

Burke first points to testimony in the administrative record indicating that the leachate violations were eliminated before the government informed Burke or ACMAR of the problem. Burke also contends that the off-site disposal was the result of a mere "misunderstanding" with the state regulatory agency. According to Burke, the circumstances of the off-site disposal prove that his conduct was "hardly serious enough to warrant debarment." Burke next asserts that he did not have a high degree of relative culpability, as EPA claimed, because he tried to make sure that the leachate problem was addressed and because other staff members were more responsible for the day-to-day activities at the Landfill. Finally, Burke claims that his overall character, the time period since his violation, and his compliance with court-ordered sanctions all demonstrate that debarment is unnecessary.

It is apparent that Burke seeks to expand the court's limited standard of review. However, we can neither perform a de novo review of the record, nor substitute our judgment for that of agency officials. Based on our evaluation of the administrative record and EPA's Decision, the court cannot conclude that the agency was arbitrary and capricious in considering the relevant mitigating factors. The Decision clearly indicates that EPA evaluated each mitigating factor Burke raised. Moreover, there is substantial evidence in the record to support EPA's assessment of each factor and the relative *weight* assigned to each factor. While there are some aspects of the record that support Burke's position, EPA's determination that such evidence is outweighed by other evidence in the record is reasonable and must be upheld under the applicable standard of review.

Burke argues that the administrative record does not support EPA's conclusion that a five-year, as opposed to three-year, debarment is warranted. Federal regulations provide that debarment shall be for a period of time commensurate with the seriousness of the cause and in consideration of any mitigating factors. Debarment is generally imposed for a three-year period, though a longer time frame is permitted "[w]here circumstances warrant." Here EPA determined that the seriousness of Burke's misconduct, "based on the fact that Mr. Burke was the sole shareholder and president of Acmar; that he knew that Acmar was not acting in accordance with their permit; and that he misrepresented to customers that solid waste would be disposed of in accordance with state and federal regulations," warrants a five year debarment period. EPA also imposed the five-year debarment because "[o]nly when Mr. Burke was forced into a position of compliance by ADEM did he begin to implement actions that should have been a part of the daily operation of Acmar . . . [and because] Mr. Burke has not presented persuasive evidence of altered personal business conduct which demonstrates that he now does not pose a risk to the government."

Burke challenges the length of his debarment on several grounds. First, he argues that EPA misstated the facts when it claimed that he implemented remedial actions only after the ADEM forced him into compliance. Second, Burke contends that his criminal conviction resulted from a one-day violation, rather than multiple violations extending over several years, as EPA implies. Third, Burke again claims that the agency failed to consider evidence that he undertook voluntary compliance efforts "more and more seriously, and more and more proactively, over time."

EPA responds that it properly weighed the circumstances surrounding Burke's conviction and any relevant mitigating factors. Though EPA acknowledges that its Decision misstated certain aspects of Burke's offense, this mistake was not a "grossly erroneous mischaracterization" that warrants reversal, as Burke contends. In fact, in the Decision's very next paragraph, EPA correctly notes that "Mr. Burke pled guilty to a *one* count violation of the CWA."

EPA has discretion to impose debarment periods consistent with the case circumstances and mitigating factors. This court's only responsibility then is to ensure that such discretion was exercised non-arbitrarily and that EPA's Decision was supported by the administrative record. Even if the Decision was "of less than ideal clarity," the court must nonetheless uphold it "if the agency's path may reasonably be discerned." This is the case here.

EPA provided several valid reasons in support of its determination that a five-year, as opposed to three-year, debarment was appropriate. The seriousness of Burke's criminal conviction, his failure to take personal responsibility for his offense, and his direct control of and involvement with ACMAR and the Landfill[9] each provided an independent basis for EPA's conclusion. In addition, EPA adequately demonstrated that it considered–though found unpersuasive–Burke's arguments concerning his past "misunderstandings" with environmental regulators. EPA also properly entertained Burke's alternative argument that other EPA debarment decisions suggest that a longer debarment period is unwarranted. Because there is no clear error of judgment or failure to consider relevant factors, this court concludes that EPA's imposition of a five-year, as opposed to a three-year, debarment was not arbitrary and capricious.

After reviewing the EPA Decision and administrative record, the court cannot conclude that the agency's five-year debarment of Burke was arbitrary, capricious, an abuse of discretion, or otherwise not in accordance with the law. There was substantial evidence to support Burke's debarment, and EPA articulated a rational connection between the facts found and the decision made. Also, there was no clear error of judgment. The court, therefore, denies Burke's motion for summary judgment and enters judgment on all counts in favor of EPA. An appropriate order accompanies this memorandum.

NOTES AND QUESTIONS

1. ***Debarment and Suspension***. Suspension and debarment are administrative actions that prohibit or limit an individual or business from doing future business with the federal government. Designed to protect the government by ensuring that it contracts only with "presently responsible" contractors, these sanctions may be imposed on those who engaged in wrongful conduct, including a criminal conviction, or who violated the requirements of a contract or program. Debarment means the person or business is prohibited from doing business with the government for a defined period, with three years being the usual maximum. A suspension is a temporary exclusion imposed upon a suspected wrongdoer pending the outcome of an investigation and any ensuing judicial or administrative proceedings. 48 C.F.R. § 9.406.

---

[9] Burke strongly argues that his business conduct should not be evaluated in the context of ACMAR, a company Burke controlled and directed. But as the agency rightly points out, Burke tries to have it both ways: he takes credit for the positive attributes at ACMAR (its "state-of-the-art facilities"), while distancing himself from its negative history (its guilty plea to criminal conspiracy and $1.8 million fine). Burke also takes an extremely narrow view of his conviction and fails to recognize that his punishment was considered as part of the overall plea agreement with ACMAR. Moreover, the record includes substantial evidence that Burke was intimately involved with ACMAR and that he directly benefitted from the company's criminal conspiracy.

Federal procurement regulations provide that a contractor can be debarred based on a conviction or civil judgment for:

> (1) Commission of fraud or a criminal offense in connection with (i) obtaining, (ii) attempting to obtain, or (iii) performing a public contract or subcontract;
>
> (2) Violation of Federal or State antitrust statutes relating to the submission of offers;
>
> (3) Commission of embezzlement, theft, forgery, bribery, falsification or destruction of records, making false statements, tax evasion, or receiving stolen property;
>
> (4) Intentionally affixing a label bearing a "Made in America" inscription (or any inscription having the same meaning) to a product sold in or shipped to the United States or its outlying areas, when the product was not made in the United States or its outlying areas (see Section 202 of the Defense Production Act (Public Law 102-558)); or
>
> (5) Commission of any other offense indicating a lack of business integrity or business honesty that seriously and directly affects the present responsibility of a Government contractor or subcontractor.

48 C.F.R. § 9.406.2(a). Other types of conduct that can lead to debarment include willful failure to perform a contract, drug violations by the contractor, a failure to comply with the Immigration and Nationality Act employment provisions, and unfair trade practices under the Defense Production Act. There is also a general catch-all provision that authorizes debarment "based on any other cause of so serious or compelling a nature that it affects the present responsibility of the contractor or subcontractor." 48 C.F.R. § 9.406.2(b)-(c)). Just the threat of debarment or suspension "often causes a much greater concern than either a criminal prosecution or civil action, because a contractor or participant might be disqualified immediately from dealing with the government, even before the criminal or civil matter is resolved." *ABA Practitioner's Guide to Suspension and Debarment* 6 (1994).

2. ***"Arbitrary and Capricious".*** The standard of review of an agency's decision to debar or suspend an individual from a government program is a forgiving one, requiring that the decision be upheld unless it can be shown the agency acted in a manner that was "arbitrary and capricious." In **Friedman v. Sebelius**, 686 F.3d 813 (D.C. Cir. 2012), three executives of a pharmaceutical company pleaded guilty under the "responsible corporate officer" doctrine to the misdemeanor of misbranding a drug. Based on the convictions, the Department of Health and Human Services excluded them from participation in Federal health care programs for 12 years, pursuant to 42 U.S.C. § 1320a–7(b). The District of Columbia Circuit upheld the Department's power to impose a discretionary suspension on individuals even

though their conviction for a misdemeanor did not involve proof that they directly engaged in the prohibited conduct, but reversed the lengthy suspensions as arbitrary and capricious. The circuit court stated:

> The Appellants may overstate their case by claiming their 12–year exclusion is "unprecedented"; the [Departmental Appeals Board ("DAB")] cited a number of prior decisions in which it had excluded individuals for more than 10 years. The DAB's mere citation of these cases, however, does not stand as a reasoned explanation if, as the Appellants argue, those cases are materially different. And so it seems they are: As the Appellants point out, every one of the cases cited by the DAB involved a mandatory exclusion with a presumptive baseline of five years, not a discretionary exclusion with a presumptive baseline of three years; in addition, every cited case involved either a felony conviction or a conviction for Medicare fraud for which the defendant was incarcerated, none of which factors is present in this case. In fact, none of the cases cited by the DAB even concerned an exclusion under section 1320a–7(b)(1); it appears the Secretary has never excluded anyone for more than ten years under that provision of the statute. Research reveals the longest period of exclusion the DAB had ever approved under section 1320a–7(b)(1) was four years. When the DAB affirmed the Appellants' 12–year exclusion the agency had never excluded anyone fr more than ten years based upon a misdemeanor – a departure the agency does not even acknowledge, much less explain.
>
> We do not suggest the Appellant's exclusion for 12 years based upon a conviction for misdemeanor misbranding might not be justifiable; we express no opinion on that question. Our concern here is that the DAB did not justify it in the decision under review. Simply pointing to prior cases with the same bottom line but arising under a different law and involving materially different facts does not provide a reasoned explanation for the agency's apparent departure from precedent. Therefore we hold the decision of the DAB was arbitrary and capricious with respect to the length of the Appellants' exclusion.

3. ***Professional Practice Exclusion***. The Securities and Exchange Commission adopted Rule 102(e), 17 C.F.R. 201.102(e), permitting it to exclude an accountant or lawyer from practicing before it if the person acts improperly. The Rule provides:

> e) Suspension and disbarment.
>
> > (1) Generally. The Commission may censure a person or deny, temporarily or permanently, the privilege of appearing or practicing before it in any way to any person who is found by the Commission after notice and opportunity for hearing in the matter:

(i) Not to possess the requisite qualifications to represent others; or

(ii) To be lacking in character or integrity or to have engaged in unethical or improper professional conduct; or

(iii) To have willfully violated, or willfully aided and abetted the violation of any provision of the Federal securities laws or the rules and regulations thereunder.

(iv) With respect to persons licensed to practice as accountants, "improper professional conduct" under § 201.102(e)(1)(ii) means:

(A) Intentional or knowing conduct, including reckless conduct, that results in a violation of applicable professional standards; or

(B) Either of the following two types of negligent conduct:

(1) A single instance of highly unreasonable conduct that results in a violation of applicable professional standards in circumstances in which an accountant knows, or should know, that heightened scrutiny is warranted.

(2) Repeated instances of unreasonable conduct, each resulting in a violation of applicable professional standards, that indicate a lack of competence to practice before the Commission.

17 C.F.R. § 201.102(e). In **Altman v. S.E.C.**, 666 F.3d 1322 (D.C. Cir. 2011), a lawyer challenged a bar to practicing before the Commission imposed by the SEC for unethical conduct when there was no finding by the state bar that he violated one of its rules. The SEC determined that he offered to have his client refuse to cooperate in exchange for having her name removed from auto leases and a severance payment from her former employer that was the subject of the investigation. His conversations with the company's counsel were recorded and later provided to the SEC, which imposed a permanent bar against the attorney. The District of Columbia Circuit rejected the lawyer's challenge to the SEC's authority to impose discipline:

> Altman's challenge to the Commission's authority to sanction him based on violations of the New York Bar disciplinary rules fails. Section 4C of the [Securities Exchange] Act provides: "The Commission may censure any person, or deny, temporarily or permanently, to any person the privilege of appearing or practicing before the Commission in any way, if that person is found by the Commission, after notice and opportunity for hearing in the matter

. . . to be lacking in character or integrity, or to have engaged in unethical or improper professional conduct."15 U.S.C. § 78d–3(a)(2). By its plain terms Section 4C authorizes the Commission to deny the privilege of appearance upon finding improper professional conduct. Because it does not unambiguously define "unethical or improper professional conduct," the question is whether the Commission's interpretation of the statute to allow it to apply State Bar disciplinary rules to define the proscribed conduct is permissible. ***

[T]he Commission was entitled to rely on Altman's knowledge of and duty to conform to the New York Bar disciplinary rules. Contrary to Altman's position, the Commission did not lack authority to act because of previous pronouncements that it would generally not do so without prior judicial or administrative findings of misconduct. Altman points to the Commission's statements of its general policy. Nothing in these statements suggested the Commission would not act in the appropriate circumstances. To the extent the Commission has for nearly 20-years stayed its hand on attorney discipline, the Commission's powers are not lost by being allowed to lie dormant.

Neither, as Altman contends, does the Commission's exercise of authority absent prior disciplinary proceedings against him by New York State implicate separation of powers or federalism concerns. The sanction imposed on Altman is limited to appearances before the Commission and has no effect either on his ability to practice law in New York State and to appear before any court, or on New York State's authority to discipline him.

CHAPTER FIFTEEN
ATTORNEY-CLIENT PRIVILEGE AND WORK PRODUCT DOCTRINE

A. *SCOPE OF LAWYER-CLIENT PRIVILEGE AND WORK PRODUCT DOCTRINE*

1. Upjohn v. United States

While corporations can be charged with crimes under the Due Process Clause, and are protected by the Fourth Amendment from unreasonable searches, a collective entity cannot assert the Fifth Amendment privilege to avoid producing its business records. Outside of the constitutional protections, can a corporation assert the attorney-client privilege? The answer is "yes," but the issue is complicated by the fact that the actual communications between the corporate client and its attorneys take place with individual officers and employees who are usually not the client. Unlike the classic lawyer-client relationship, which involves two individuals meeting alone, a corporation can have thousands of employees, each of whom may bind the corporation and subject it to criminal liability. Does the attorney-client privilege extend to every communication between a lawyer and a corporate employee or agent? The Supreme Court dealt with this question in the following case.

UPJOHN CO. v. UNITED STATES
449 U.S. 383, 101 S.Ct. 677, 66 L.Ed.2d 584 (1981)

Justice REHNQUIST delivered the opinion of the Court.

[The Upjohn Company conducted an internal investigation into potentially illegal payments made to third parties by employees of the company's foreign subsidiaries. As described by the Court, "As part of this investigation the attorneys prepared a letter containing a questionnaire which was sent to 'All Foreign General and Area Managers' over the Chairman's signature. The letter began by noting recent disclosures that several American companies made 'possibly illegal' payments to foreign government officials and emphasized that the management needed full information concerning any such payments made by Upjohn. The letter indicated that the Chairman had asked Thomas, identified as 'the company's General Counsel,' 'to conduct an investigation for the purpose of determining the nature and magnitude of any payments made by the Upjohn Company or any of its subsidiaries to any employee or official of a foreign government.'"

After completing its investigation, the company submitted its findings of possible illegal conduct to the SEC and IRS. The IRS then issued a summons requiring Upjohn to produce the documents generated in its internal investigation.

The company objected on the grounds that the documents were protected by the attorney-client privilege and the work product doctrine. The government argued that communications with lower-level employees who were not part of the company's "control group" fell outside the privilege and the protection afforded attorney work product. The opinion for a unanimous Court, by then-Justice Rehnquist, rejected the control group test and presented a flexible analysis of how far the privilege can extend].

Federal Rule of Evidence 501 provides that "the privilege of a witness . . . shall be governed by the principles of the common law as they may be interpreted by the courts of the United States in light of reason and experience." The attorney-client privilege is the oldest of the privileges for confidential communications known to the common law. 8 J. Wigmore, Evidence § 2290 (McNaughton rev. 1961). Its purpose is to encourage full and frank communication between attorneys and their clients and thereby promote broader public interests in the observance of law and administration of justice. The privilege recognizes that sound legal advice or advocacy serves public ends and that such advice or advocacy depends upon the lawyer's being fully informed by the client. * * * Admittedly complications in the application of the privilege arise when the client is a corporation, which in theory is an artificial creature of the law, and not an individual; but this Court has assumed that the privilege applies when the client is a corporation, and the Government does not contest the general proposition. * * *

The Court of Appeals, however, considered the application of the privilege in the corporate context to present a "different problem," since the client was an inanimate entity and "only the senior management, guiding and integrating the several operations, . . . can be said to possess an identity analogous to the corporation as a whole." * * * Such a view, we think, overlooks the fact that the privilege exists to protect not only the giving of professional advice to those who can act on it but also the giving of information to the lawyer to enable him to give sound and informed advice. * * *

In the case of the individual client the provider of information and the person who acts on the lawyer's advice are one and the same. In the corporate context, however, it will frequently be employees beyond the control group * * *. Middle-level—and indeed lower-level—employees can, by actions within the scope of their employment, embroil the corporation in serious legal difficulties, and it is only natural that these employees would have the relevant information needed by corporate counsel if he is adequately to advise the client with respect to such actual or potential difficulties. * * *

The control group test adopted by the court below thus frustrates the very purpose of the privilege by discouraging the communication of relevant information by employees of the client to attorneys seeking to render legal advice to the client corporation. The attorney's advice will also frequently be more significant to noncontrol group members than to those who officially sanction the advice, and the control group test makes it more difficult to convey full and frank legal advice to the employees who will put into effect the client corporation's policy. * * * The communications at issue were made by Upjohn employees[3] to counsel for Upjohn acting as such, at the direction of corporate superiors in order to secure legal advice from counsel. * * *

Application of the attorney-client privilege to communications such as those involved here, however, puts the adversary in no worse position than if the communications had never taken place. The privilege only protects disclosure of communications; it does not protect disclosure of the underlying facts by those who communicated with the attorney:

> [T]he protection of the privilege extends only to *communications* and not to facts. A fact is one thing and a communication concerning that fact is an entirely different thing. The client cannot be compelled to answer the question, "What did you say or write to the attorney?" but may not refuse to disclose any relevant fact within his knowledge merely because he incorporated a statement of such fact into his communication to his attorney. Philadelphia v. Westinghouse Electric Corp., 205 F. Supp. 830, 831.

* * * Here the Government was free to question the employees who communicated with Thomas and outside counsel. Upjohn has provided the IRS with a list of such employees, and the IRS has already interviewed some 25 of them. While it would probably be more convenient for the Government to secure the results of petitioner's internal investigation by simply subpoenaing the questionnaires and notes taken by petitioner's attorneys, such considerations of convenience do not overcome the policies served by the attorney-client privilege. * * *

Needless to say, we decide only the case before us, and do not undertake to draft a set of rules which should govern challenges to investigatory subpoenas. * * * While such a "case-by-case" basis may to some slight extent undermine desirable certainty in the boundaries of the attorney-client privilege, it obeys the spirit of the Rules. * * *

---

[3] Seven of the eighty-six employees interviewed by counsel had terminated their employment with Upjohn at the time of the interview. Petitioners argue that the privilege should nonetheless apply to communications by these former employees concerning activities during their period of employment. Neither the District Court nor the Court of Appeals had occasion to address this issue, and we decline to decide it without the benefit of treatment below.

NOTES

1. ***Scope of* Upjohn.** The Supreme Court notes a number of factors in support of extending the privilege to the communications between the company employees and corporate counsel: (1) communications were made and sought by counsel in connection with rendering legal advice; (2) corporate superiors directed employees to provide information to counsel; (3) employees were "sufficiently aware that they were being questioned in order that the corporation could obtain legal advice"; (4) "the communications concerned matters within the scope of the employees' corporate duties"; (5) the information provided was "not available from upper echelon management" and "was needed to supply a basis for legal advice"; and (6) the company informed employees that the communications were "highly confidential" and were subsequently "kept confidential by the company." It is not clear whether the application of the privilege requires all of the factors, or whether some are more important than others.

2. ***Former Employees.*** In footnote 3 in *Upjohn*, the Supreme Court did not rule on whether the corporation's attorney-client privilege extended to communications with former employees. When the attorney's communications with the former employee concern matters that arose while the person was an employee, courts generally view the discussions as coming within the privilege. In In re Allen, 106 F.3d 582 (4th Cir. 1997), the Fourth Circuit stated:

> The Supreme Court has explained that the attorney-client privilege "rests on the need for the advocate and counselor to know all that relates to the client's reasons for seeking representation if the professional mission is to be carried out." Trammel v. United States, 445 U.S. 40 (1980). The Court reiterated this "need to know" focus in *Upjohn*: "the privilege exists to protect not only the giving of professional advice to those who can act on it but also the giving of information to the lawyer to enable him to give sound and informed advice." In rejecting the "control group" test for determining which employees are within the scope of a corporation's attorney-client privilege, the Upjohn Court recognized that "it will frequently be employees beyond the control group . . . who will possess the information needed by the corporation's lawyers." Accordingly, we hold that the analysis applied by the Supreme Court in *Upjohn* to determine which employees fall within the scope of the privilege applies equally to former employees.

When the communication does not relate to actions while the person was an employee, but only after the employment relationship has ended, then it is much less likely to be protected by the corporation's attorney-client privilege and instead viewed as a communication with a third party absent special circumstances. See, e.g., Infosystems, Inc. v. Ceridian Corp., 197 F.R.D. 303 (E.D. Mich. 2000)) ("there may be situations where the former employee retains a present connection or agency relationship with the client corporation, or where the present-day communication concerns a confidential matter that was uniquely within the knowledge of the former employee when he worked for the client corporation, such that counsel's communications with this former employee must be cloaked with the privilege in order for meaningful fact-gathering to occur. ").

2. Attorney-Client Privilege – Internal Investigations

Internal investigations have become standard in corporate criminal investigations. The Department of Justice and the regulatory agencies frequently rely on the company's investigation as the starting point for a determination whether to pursue criminal charges and how to resolve a case. This is especially true when foreign conduct is involved because corporate counsel will often have greater access to documents and employees involved in the transactions than a prosecutor or government investigator. Major law firms that once shunned criminal work now embrace corporate investigations as a major source of revenue. The cost of an internal investigation involving a global corporation can be significant. Siemens A.G. spent over $1 billion investigating bribery by employees in a number of nations to win contracts, an amount greater than the $850 million it had to pay in disgorgement, fines and civil penalties. The reason for using lawyers to conduct the investigation is clear from the decision of the district court in the following decision finding that the attorney-client privilege does not apply when it was conducted by a non-lawyer:

UNITED STATES v. ISS MARINE SERVS., INC.

905 F. Supp. 2d 121 (D.D.C. 2012)

BERYL A. HOWELL, District Judge.

The petitioners * * * bring this Petition against the respondent ISS Marine Services, Inc. to enforce the respondent's compliance with an administrative subpoena *duces tecum* issued by the Inspector General of the U.S. Department of Defense on March 28, 2011. In particular, the petitioners ask the Court to require the respondent to produce the contents of a March 2008 internal audit report. The primary question presented by the Government's Petition is whether the Audit Report enjoys the protection of either the attorney-client privilege or the work-product doctrine.

ISS Marine is a United States affiliate of Inchcape Shipping Services Holdings, Ltd., which is a company incorporated in the United Kingdom. ISS Marine contracts with the Department of Defense, through the U.S. Navy, to provide ship husbanding and other port services and goods to the Navy, Coast Guard, and other Government-owned ships. * * *

One of the places where Inchcape contracted to provide husbanding services to the U.S. Government was in the Middle East. In December 2007, two Inchcape employees traveled to Dubai and Bahrain to attend a corporate workshop and to inspect Inchcape facilities. During this trip, the Inchcape employees reported a variety of practices that Inchcape was engaging in that raised concern about potential liability for fraudulent conduct. In response, Larry Cosgriff, who was then Senior Vice-President of Government Services for Inchcape, brought the allegations to the attention of a partner at the Washington, D.C. law firm Arnold & Porter, LLC ("A & P"), with whom Inchcape regularly consulted.

The A & P partner subsequently spoke directly to the two employees who reported on the questionable Inchcape practices, and to the CEO of Inchcape, Claus Hyldager. On January 21, 2008, A & P sent a draft engagement letter to Cosgriff and Hyldager, proposing the retention of A & P to conduct an internal investigation. Thereafter, Cosgriff, Hyldager, and Simon Tory, the Group Company Secretary for Inchcape's subsidiary ISS Group Holdings Limited, met to discuss the draft engagement letter. According to Cosgriff, Hyldager "expressed dismay, both orally and in writing, that [Cosgriff] had involved counsel in th[e] matter," and both Hyldager and Tory "rejected [Cosgriff's] recommendation that [Inchcape] retain A & P to conduct an investigation." Instead, Cosgriff states that Hyldager informed him "that [Hyldager], Mr. Tory and the Inchcape Board of Directors had decided that Mr. Tory would institute an internal audit of Inchcape's billing and accounting practices" and that "Inchcape's Board of Directors would utilize the audit findings to determine how it would proceed in addressing the matter." Since the internal audit would be carried out by Inchcape internal auditor Bharat Khadalia, under the direction of Mr. Tory, Cosgriff states that he cautioned Hyldager and Tory that "the investigation itself and its findings would not be protected by attorney client privilege," and he asserts "[b]oth men stated that they understood that fact." According to Cosgriff, A & P sent a second draft engagement letter to Hyldager on January 29, 2008, which "stated that A & P would support the investigation for purposes of advising Inchcape of its legal obligations, [but] the engagement letter did not provide for any role by A & P in the conduct of the investigation." Ultimately, it was Cosgriff's understanding that "Messrs. Hyldager and Tory undertook this internal audit to obtain information to enable Messrs. Hyldager and Tory, the Inchcape audit committee and the Inchcape Board of Directors to make a business decision as to what further action, if any, Inchcape would take to address" the allegations raised by the two Inchcape employees.

The internal investigation was conducted over the next few weeks by Bharat Khadalia, an internal auditor at Inchcape, who prepared a draft report of his findings that was completed on March 5, 2008. The Audit Report was marked "Confidential," but was not marked as privileged. After the draft of the Audit Report was complete, Khadalia sent it to Hyldager and Tory. After reviewing the draft report, Hyldager decided to follow up directly with some of the witnesses to ensure that the information provided to A & P was complete, which took approximately two additional months. * * *

Sometime after the Audit Report was completed, the Government began investigating whether Inchcape charged the Navy more than the amounts permissible under its contracts and whether Inchcape failed to make required reconciliation payments to the Navy for amounts overbilled on an interim basis. [The Inspector General's Office filed a petition to enforce the administrative subpoena for the internal audit report.]

[T]he Government argues that the Audit Report was not created for the purpose of seeking legal advice. The Government posits that "nothing about the March 2008 Audit Report indicates that it was part of a request for legal advice," the Report was "not directed to any attorney or a person employed by an attorney," it "does not contain any legends indicating that it is privileged," and "Inchcape's CEO waited nearly two months after it was completed to forward the Audit Report to its outside counsel." In support of this argument, the Government offers the sworn declaration of Larry Cosgriff, who served as the Senior Vice–President of Inchcape Government Services during the relevant time period. * * * Cosgriff states that it was his understanding that Hyldager and Tory "undertook this internal audit to obtain information to enable Messrs. Hyldager and Tory, the Inchcape audit committee and the Inchcape Board of Directors to make a business decision as to what further action, if any, Inchcape would take to address" the allegations raised by the two Inchcape employees.

ISS Marine responds, however, that the Audit Report "was specifically prepared to be sent, and was in fact sent, under the explicit legend 'Attorney-Client Privileged,' to outside counsel for the purpose of obtaining legal advice." ISS Marine maintains that, although the Audit Report was prepared by a non-attorney (Khadalia) and was initially transmitted to non-attorneys (Hyldiger, Cosgriff, and Tory) before being sent to outside counsel, the Audit Report was "part of an on-going attorney-client communication for the purpose of obtaining legal advice about concerns over potentially serious misconduct and exposure to criminal and civil liability." ISS Marine argues, relying on Tory's sworn declaration, that the Audit Report was created and transmitted for the purpose of seeking legal advice because A & P "framed the issues, identified information to collect and outlined the legal framework" for the investigation.

The respondent has failed, however, in light of the Cosgriff Declaration, to put forth evidence "sufficient to establish the privilege with reasonable certainty." At bottom, the respondent's claim to privilege appears to be premised on a gimmick: exclude counsel from conducting the internal investigation but retain them in a watered-down capacity to "consult" on the investigation in order to cloak the investigation with privilege. Unfortunately for the respondent, this sort of "consultation lite" does not qualify the Audit Report for the protections of the attorney-client privilege. First and foremost, the fact that Inchcape purposefully eschewed the involvement of outside counsel—or any attorneys whatsoever—in the internal investigation and audit militates strongly against applying the attorney-client privilege. When a company fails to involve lawyers directly in an internal investigation, the company faces a higher burden to demonstrate that the attorney-client privilege applies to the results of that investigation. The Tory Declaration indicates that, at most, A & P generically "recommended initiating an internal investigation" and drafted a memorandum that "framed" the issues relating to "potential criminal and civil liability implicated by the activities as reported." The Tory Declaration also states that A & P "prepared a list of documents necessary to more fully assess the issues identified," though Tory notably does not specify that A & P would be the ones "more fully assess[ing] the issues identified." Although Tory states that he pursued the internal investigation "in consultation with outside counsel," the record is devoid of any evidence to suggest that A & P provided any consultation to ISS Marine while the investigation was actually being conducted. A & P's framing of the issues related to potential liability and its guidance about the types of documents that would be helpful all took place before the investigation began. As Cosgriff explains: "A & P did not participate in the interview process or the review of documentary evidence." Even when Inchcape took steps to verify the information in the Audit Report, Tory indicates that Hyldager performed this "follow up," rather than an attorney.

This sort of arms-length coaching by counsel, as opposed to the direct involvement of an attorney, undercuts the purposes of the attorney-client privilege in the context of an internal investigation. Clearly, when an attorney is absent from the information-gathering process, "the original communicator has no intention that the information be provided a lawyer for the purposes of legal representation." *Nesse v. Shaw Pittman*, 206 F.R.D. 325 (D.D.C. 2002). "At that point, the interest in advancing client candor has become so attenuated, if it exists at all, that [it] is trumped by the law's interest in ascertaining the truth." This principle discussed in *Nesse* is consistent with the Supreme Court's teaching in *Upjohn*, where the Court emphasized that the privilege attached to internal investigation materials because "the employees themselves were sufficiently aware that they were being questioned in order that the corporation could obtain legal advice," and the questions presented to the employees, at times directly by counsel, "clearly indicated the legal implications of the investigation."

The respondent has offered no evidence to demonstrate that the employees who were interviewed had any idea that their responses were going to be conveyed to an attorney for the purpose of obtaining legal advice. Indeed, it appears that Inchcape affirmatively did not want its employees to know that the investigation related to legal concerns, see Cosgriff Decl. ¶ 10 (stating that Hyldager "did not want to alarm Inchcape Middle East employees and deflate their morale by having an outside law firm making inquiries"). The top management also fully understood that the failure to involve attorneys in the investigation was likely to forfeit the protections of the attorney-client privilege. The employees certainly would not have been able to infer the legal nature of the inquiry by virtue of the interviewer, who was a non-attorney.

Upjohn makes clear that the privilege applies as long as "[t]he communications at issue were made by [company] employees to counsel for [the company] acting as such." Here, the employees were communicating to a non-attorney who was not accompanied or assisted by attorneys, and the communicators did not know that the information they were conveying would be transmitted to counsel for the purpose of seeking legal advice. What is more, Tory does not state that he even informed Khadalia – the person conducting the investigation – that the investigation was for the purpose of seeking legal advice. Tory only told Khadalia that "the review was to be conducted immediately," that the investigation was supposed "to address the issues as framed by counsel," and that he was "to keep the information confidential." Thus, the Audit Report memorializing the contents of the documents and information gathered from this investigation and audit does not justify the protection of the attorney-client privilege. For the results of an internal investigation to enjoy the attorney-client privilege, the company must clearly structure the investigation as one seeking legal advice and must ensure that attorneys themselves conduct or supervise the inquiries and, at the very least, the company must make clear to the communicating employees that the information they provide will be transmitted to attorneys for the purpose of obtaining legal advice. Only then do the candor-promoting purposes of the privilege outweigh the public's and the adversary system's longstanding and important interest in scrutinizing "every man's evidence."

[The district court also found that the internal audit report was not protected by the work product doctrine, and even if it was the government established a substantial need for it.]

3. Attorney-Client Privilege – Legal Advice

The decision in *ISS Marine* makes it clear that lawyers are retained to conduct a internal investigation because the protections afforded by the attorney-client privilege, along with the work product doctrine, can be applied to resist disclosure of the information gathered by counsel, at least until the company decides to reveal the results of its inquiry. Even when conducted by an attorney, however, it must be clear that the purpose of the internal investigation must be to provide legal advice to the client, and not just for a business purpose. But that need not be the sole reason for the internal investigation, which frequently also helps the company conduct its business in compliance with applicable rules and regulations. In **In re Kellogg, Brown & Root, Inc.**, 756 F.3d 754 (D.C. Cir. 2014), the District of Columbia Circuit explained the scope of the attorney-client privilege in relation to an internal investigation:

> Under the District Court's approach, the attorney-client privilege apparently would not apply unless the sole purpose of the communication was to obtain or provide legal advice. That is not the law. We are aware of no Supreme Court or court of appeals decision that has adopted a test of this kind in this context. The District

> Court's novel approach to the attorney-client privilege would eliminate the attorney-client privilege for numerous communications that are made for both legal and business purposes and that heretofore have been covered by the attorney-client privilege. And the District Court's novel approach would eradicate the attorney-client privilege for internal investigations conducted by businesses that are required by law to maintain compliance programs, which is now the case in a significant swath of American industry. In turn, businesses would be less likely to disclose facts to their attorneys and to seek legal advice, which would "limit the valuable efforts of corporate counsel to ensure their client's compliance with the law." *Upjohn*. We reject the District Court's but-for test as inconsistent with the principle of *Upjohn* and longstanding attorney-client privilege law.
>
> Given the evident confusion in some cases, we also think it important to underscore that the primary purpose test, sensibly and properly applied, cannot and does not draw a rigid distinction between a legal purpose on the one hand and a business purpose on the other. After all, trying to find the one primary purpose for a communication motivated by two sometimes overlapping purposes (one legal and one business, for example) can be an inherently impossible task. It is often not useful or even feasible to try to determine whether the purpose was A or B when the purpose was A and B. It is thus not correct for a court to presume that a communication can have only one primary purpose. It is likewise not correct for a court to try to find the one primary purpose in cases where a given communication plainly has multiple purposes. Rather, it is clearer, more precise, and more predictable to articulate the test as follows: Was obtaining or providing legal advice a primary purpose of the communication, meaning one of the significant purposes of the communication? * * * Sensibly and properly applied, the test boils down to whether obtaining or providing legal advice was one of the significant purposes of the attorney-client communication.

If a district court orders the disclosure of material believed to be protected by the attorney-client privilege, can that decision be immediately appealed? In **Mohawk Industries, Inc. v. Carpenter**, 558 U.S. 100 (2009), the Supreme Court answered that question "no" by finding that the issue did not qualify for an interlocutory appeal under the "collateral order" doctrine, much like the denial of a pretrial motion to dismiss an indictment for prosecutorial misconduct. The Court found that "postjudgment appeals generally suffice to protect the rights of litigants and ensure the vitality of the attorney-client privilege. Appellate courts can remedy the improper disclosure of privileged material in the same way they remedy a host of other erroneous evidentiary rulings: by vacating an adverse judgment and remanding for a new trial in which the protected material and its fruits are excluded from evidence." In *Kellogg, Brown & Root*, however, the District of Columbia Circuit found that the requirements for issuing a writ of mandamus had been satisfied, reaching the merits of the issue of whether the attorney-client privilege applied to the results of an internal investigation.

White collar crime practitioners – whether in the Department of Justice or private practice – are primarily trial lawyers, and do not have expertise in specialized areas that may come up in a wide range of cases, such as medical procedures, accounting principles, or the valuation of complex securities. They will frequently retain outside experts to advise them on the technical issues that may arise in a case, and in some instances use the expert to testify at trial. In **United States v. Kovel**, 296 F.2d 918 (2d Cir. 1961), the Second Circuit held that the attorney-client privilege extended to counsel's consultations with an accountant retained to assist the attorney in understanding the client's financial transactions. Comparing an outside expert to an interpreter who can translate foreign documents, the Second Circuit stated, "Accounting concepts are a foreign language to some lawyers in almost all cases, and to almost all lawyers in some cases. Hence the presence of an accountant, whether hired by the lawyer or by the client, while the client is relating a complicated tax story to the lawyer, ought not destroy the privilege, any more than would that of the linguist in the second or third variations of the foreign language theme discussed above; the presence of the accountant is necessary, or at least highly useful, for the effective consultation between the client and the lawyer which the privilege is designed to permit."

The practice of including outside experts to an internal investigation to ensure that communications with them come within the protections of the attorney-client privilege, is sometimes referred to as "*Kovelling*" the expert. The use of an outside expert by an attorney is not automatically protected by the attorney-client privilege, however, as the Second Circuit noted in United States v. Ackert, 169 F.3d 136 (2d Cir. 1999): "[A] communication between an attorney and a third party does not become shielded by the attorney-client privilege solely because the communication proves important to the attorney's ability to represent the client." Similarly, in Cavallaro v. United States, 284 F.3d 236, 240 (1st Cir. 2002), the First Circuit held that because the hiring of the Ernst & Young accounting firm was not related to any effective consultation between the client and the lawyer, the attorney-client privilege did not extend to the documents in question. The Court did "not decide whether, in all instances, the attorney or client (as opposed to some third party) must hire the accountant in order to sustain a privilege * * *." The Court further noted that "an attorney, merely by placing an accountant on her payroll, does not, by this action alone, render communications between the attorney's client and the accountant privileged."

In **In re Grand Jury Subpoena Dated March 24, 2003**, 265 F. Supp.2d 321 (S.D.N.Y. 2003), the district court applying *Kovel* held that both the attorney-client privilege and the work product protection reached communications between a prospective defendant in a criminal case, her lawyers, and a public relations firm hired by the lawyers to aid in avoiding an indictment. The P.R. firm's activities included not just advising the target and her lawyers, but also spoke to members of the media on behalf of the attorney. The district court focused on "the effective operation of the attorney-client privilege of a client and lawyer under conditions where the lawyer needs outside help." The district court noted that the communications between the target and the P.R. firm would not have been privileged if she had simply gone out and hired public relations counsel; in this case the attorneys hired the P.R. firm. The district court resolved in favor of the target, the "ultimate issue" – "whether attorney efforts to influence public opinion in order to advance the client's legal position– in this case by neutralizing what the attorneys perceived as a climate of opinion pressing prosecutors and regulators to act in ways adverse to Target's interests–are services, the rendition of which also should be facilitated by applying the privilege to relevant communications which have this as their object." The Court applied the protections not just to Target's communications with the P.R. firm that took place in the presence of lawyers, but also to those between the Target and the firm, provided they were directed at giving or obtaining legal advice. Finally, the court noted that the presence of the Target's spouse during some of the conversations did not destroy any applicable privilege, because disclosure of communications protected by the attorney-client privilege in the context of another privilege (spouse) does not constitute waiver of the attorney-client privilege. In different circumstances, however, communications with a public relations firm will not be protected. See Egiazaryan v. Zalmayev, 290 F.R.D. 421 (S.D.N.Y. 2013) (The consultant "was not called upon to perform a specific litigation task that the attorneys needed to accomplish in order to advance their litigation goals—let alone a task that could be characterized as relating to the 'administration of justice.' Rather, it was involved in a wide variety of public relations activities aimed at burnishing Egiazaryan's image.").

4. Work Product

The protection afforded the work product of an attorney is distinct from, and in some cases broader than, the privilege for communications between a lawyer and client.

> Privileged information is immune totally from discovery, no matter how compelling the need for the information seems to be. Information that is collected in anticipation of litigation or trial is protected from discovery, but that protection may yield to a showing of need on the part of the requesting party. Mental impressions of the attorney enjoy the highest level of protection under the work product doctrine, but * * * even they may be revealed, at least in part, upon a sufficient showing. Thus, the application of the work product rule often requires a balancing of the competing needs of the parties, as well as an inquiry into whether the material involved properly falls within the concerns that originally produced this discovery exception.

JACK H. FRIEDENTHAL, MARY KAY KANE, & ARTHUR R. MILLER, CIVIL PROCEDURE § 7.5 (4th ed. 2005). The Supreme Court in *Upjohn* discussed the scope of the work product protection:

> Our decision that the communications by Upjohn employees to counsel are covered by the attorney-client privilege disposes of the case so far as the responses to the questionnaires and any notes reflecting responses to interview questions are concerned. The summons reaches further, however, and Thomas has testified that his notes and memoranda of interviews go beyond recording responses to his questions. To the extent that the material subject to the summons is not protected by the attorney-client privilege as disclosing communications between an employee and counsel, we must reach the ruling by the Court of Appeals that the work-product doctrine does not apply to summonses issued under 26 U.S.C. § 7602.
>
> The Government concedes, wisely, that the Court of Appeals erred and that the work-product doctrine does apply to IRS summonses. This doctrine was announced by the Court over 30 years ago in Hickman v. Taylor, 329 U.S. 495 (1947). In that case the Court rejected "an attempt, without purported necessity or justification, to secure written statements, private memoranda and personal recollections prepared or formed by an adverse party's counsel in the course of his legal duties." The Court noted that "it is essential that a lawyer work with a certain degree of privacy" and reasoned that if discovery of the material sought were permitted much of what is now put down in writing would remain unwritten. An attorney's thoughts, heretofore inviolate, would not be his own. Inefficiency, unfairness and sharp practices would inevitably develop in the giving of legal advice and in the preparation of cases for trial. The effect on the legal profession would be demoralizing. And the interests of the clients and the cause of justice would be poorly served. [Hickman v. Taylor].
>
> The "strong public policy" underlying the work-product doctrine was reaffirmed recently in United States v. Nobles, 422 U.S, 225 (1975) and has been substantially incorporated in Federal Rule of Civil Procedure 26(b)(3).
>
> As we stated last Term, the obligation imposed by a tax summons remains "subject to the traditional privileges and limitations." United States v. Euge, 444 U.S. 707 (1980). Nothing in the language of the IRS summons provisions or their legislative history suggests an intent on the part of Congress to preclude application of the work-product doctrine. Rule 26(b)(3) codifies the work-product doctrine, and the Federal Rules of Civil Procedure are made applicable to summons enforcement proceedings by Rule 81(a)(3). While conceding the applicability of the work-product doctrine, the

Government asserts that it has made a sufficient showing of necessity to overcome its protections. * * *

Rule 26 accords special protection to work product revealing the attorney's mental processes. The Rule permits disclosure of documents and tangible things constituting attorney work product upon a showing of substantial need and inability to obtain the equivalent without undue hardship. * * * Rule 26 goes on, however, to state that "[i]n ordering discovery of such materials when the required showing has been made, the court shall protect against disclosure of the mental impressions, conclusions, opinions or legal theories of an attorney or other representative of a party concerning the litigation." Although this language does not specifically refer to memoranda based on oral statements of witnesses, the *Hickman* court stressed the danger that compelled disclosure of such memoranda would reveal the attorney's mental processes. It is clear that this is the sort of material the draftsmen of the Rule had in mind as deserving special protection. * * *

Based on the foregoing, some courts have concluded that no showing of necessity can overcome protection of work product which is based on oral statements from witnesses. * * * Those courts declining to adopt an absolute rule have nonetheless recognized that such material is entitled to special protection. * * *

We do not decide the issue at this time. It is clear that the Magistrate applied the wrong standard when he concluded that the Government had made a sufficient showing of necessity to overcome the protections of the work-product doctrine. The Magistrate applied the "substantial need" and "without undue hardship" standard articulated in the first part of Rule 26(b)(3). The notes and memoranda sought by the Government here, however, are work product based on oral statements. If they reveal communications, they are, in this case, protected by the attorney-client privilege. To the extent they do not reveal communications, they reveal the attorneys' mental processes in evaluating the communications. As Rule 26 and *Hickman* make clear, such work product cannot be disclosed simply on a showing of substantial need and inability to obtain the equivalent without undue hardship.

While we are not prepared at this juncture to say that such material is always protected by the work-product rule, we think a far stronger showing of necessity and unavailability by other means than was made by the Government or applied by the Magistrate in this case would be necessary to compel disclosure. Since the Court of Appeals thought that the work-product protection was never applicable in an enforcement proceeding such as this, and since the Magistrate whose recommendations the District Court adopted applied too lenient a standard of protection, we think the best procedure with respect to this aspect of the case would be to reverse the judgment of the Court of Appeals for the Sixth Circuit and remand the case to it for such further proceedings in connection with the work-product claim as are consistent with this opinion. * * *

The work product doctrine is codified in part in Federal Rule of Civil Procedure 26(b)(3). In In re Grand Jury Subpoena, 220 F.R.D. 130, 141 (D. Mass. 2004), the court noted:

> There are important differences between the doctrine articulated in *Hickman* [v. Taylor, 329 U.S. 495 (1947)] and the text of Rule 26(b)(3) . . . . for example, unlike Hickman, Rule 26(b)(3) does not reach "intangible" work product, but Rule 26(b)(3) more clearly protects non-attorney work product than Hickman does.

5. Work Product – "In Anticipation of Litigation"

In **In re Grand Jury Subpoenas Dated March 9, 2001**, 179 F.Supp.2d 270 (S.D.N.Y. 2001), the district court enforced subpoenas to five attorneys for two men, Marc Rich and Pincus Green, who had obtained a pardon from President Clinton on his last day in office. The pardons were "highly controversial and generated much public outcry" because the defendants had fled the United States after their indictment and could not be extradited to stand trial. The attorneys argued that they did not have to comply with the subpoenas, *inter alia*, because the documents constituted work product. The district court rejected that argument, stating that the "reliance on the work product doctrine is misplaced because the process by which Rich and Green sought their pardons here was not an adversarial one; rather, it was an *ex parte* process that did not anticipate further litigation because it was clear that Rich and Green were never going to return to face the charges." Rich and Green avoided dealing directly with the Department of Justice–*i.e.* litigation–and concentrated their efforts on the White House–*i.e.* Executive authority.

How likely does the litigation have to be to invoke the protection of the work product doctrine? Consider the following case involving advice from a lawyer that involved a pending business decision and potential related litigation.

UNITED STATES v. ADLMAN

134 F.3d 1194 (2nd Cir. 1998)

LEVAL, Circuit Judge:

This appeal concerns the proper interpretation of Federal Rule of Civil Procedure 26(b)(3) ("the Rule"), which grants limited protection against discovery to documents and materials prepared "in anticipation of litigation."

Specifically, we must address whether a study prepared for an attorney assessing the likely result of an expected litigation is ineligible for protection under the Rule if the primary or ultimate purpose of making the study was to assess the desirability of a business transaction, which, if undertaken, would give rise to the litigation. We hold that a document created because of anticipated litigation, which tends to reveal mental impressions, conclusions, opinions or theories concerning the litigation, does not lose work-product protection merely because it is intended to assist in the making of a business decision influenced by the likely outcome of the anticipated litigation. Where a document was created because of anticipated litigation, and would not have been prepared in substantially similar form but for the prospect of that litigation, it falls within Rule 26(b)(3).

The district court ruled that the document sought by the IRS in this case did not fall within the scope of Rule 26(b)(3) and ordered its production. Because we cannot determine whether the district court used the correct standard in reaching its decision, we vacate the judgment and remand for reconsideration. * * *

Sequa Corporation is an aerospace manufacturer with annual revenues of nearly $2 billion. Prior to 1989, Atlantic Research Corporation ("ARC") and Chromalloy Gas Turbine Corporation ("Chromalloy") were wholly-owned Sequa subsidiaries. Appellant Monroe Adlman is an attorney and Vice President for Taxes at Sequa.

In the spring of 1989, Sequa contemplated merging Chromalloy and ARC. The contemplated merger was expected to produce an enormous loss and tax refund, which Adlman expected would be challenged by the IRS and would result in litigation. Adlman asked Paul Sheahen, an accountant and lawyer at Arthur Andersen & Co. ("Arthur Andersen"), to evaluate the tax implications of the proposed restructuring. Sheahen did so and set forth his study in a memorandum (the "Memorandum"). He submitted the Memorandum in draft form to Adlman in August 1989. After further consultation, on September 5, 1989, Sheahen sent Adlman the final version. The Memorandum was a 58-page detailed legal analysis of likely IRS challenges to the reorganization and the resulting tax refund claim; it contained discussion of statutory provisions, IRS regulations, legislative history, and prior judicial and IRS rulings relevant to the claim. It proposed possible legal theories or strategies for Sequa to adopt in response, recommended preferred methods of structuring the transaction, and made predictions about the likely outcome of litigation.

Sequa decided to go ahead with the restructuring, which was completed in December 1989 in essentially the form recommended by Arthur Andersen. Sequa sold 93% of its stock in ARC to Chromalloy for $167.4 million, and the remaining 7% to Bankers Trust for $12.6 million. The reorganization resulted in a $289 million loss. Sequa claimed the loss on its 1989 return and carried it back to offset 1986 capital gains, thereby generating a claim for a refund of $35 million.

In an ensuing audit of Sequa's 1986-1989 tax returns, the IRS requested a number of documents concerning the restructuring transaction. Sequa acknowledged the existence of the Memorandum, but cited work-product privilege as grounds for declining to produce it. On September 23, 1993, the IRS served a summons on Adlman for production of the Memorandum.

When Adlman declined to comply, the IRS instituted an action in the United States District Court for the Southern District of New York to enforce the subpoena. Adlman defended on the grounds that the Memorandum was protected by both the attorney-client and work-product privileges. The district court (Knapp, J.) in its first decision rejected Adlman's claim that the Memorandum was protected by attorney-client privilege, finding that Adlman had not consulted Arthur Andersen in order to obtain assistance in furnishing legal advice to Sequa. * * * It rejected Adlman's claim of work-product privilege because the Memorandum was prepared for litigation based on actions or events that had not yet occurred at the time of its creation. The court granted the IRS's petition to enforce the summons.

On appeal, we affirmed denial of Adlman's claim of attorney-client privilege. United States v. Adlman, 68 F.3d 1495 (2d Cir.1995). We vacated the district court's enforcement order, however, because the district court had evaluated Adlman's claim of work-product privilege under the wrong standard. Although the non-occurrence of events giving rise to litigation prior to preparation of the documents is a factor to be considered, we explained, it does not necessarily preclude application of work-product privilege. * * *

On remand, Adlman argued that the Memorandum was protected by Rule 26(b)(3) because it included legal opinions prepared in reasonable anticipation of litigation. * * * The district court again rejected the claim of work-product privilege, concluding that the Memorandum was not prepared in anticipation of litigation. * * * Adlman appeals.

* * * The work-product doctrine, codified for the federal courts in Fed.R.Civ.P. 26(b)(3), is intended to preserve a zone of privacy in which a lawyer can prepare and develop legal theories and strategy "with an eye toward litigation," free from unnecessary intrusion by his adversaries. Hickman v. Taylor, 329 U.S. 495 (1947). Analysis of one's case "in anticipation of litigation" is a classic example of work product, * * * and receives heightened protection under Fed.R.Civ.P. 26(b)(3).

This case involves a question of first impression in this circuit: whether Rule 26(b)(3) is inapplicable to a litigation analysis prepared by a party or its representative in order to inform a business decision which turns on the party's assessment of the likely outcome of litigation expected to result from the transaction. Answering that question requires that we determine the proper interpretation of Rule 26(b)(3)'s requirement that documents be prepared "in anticipation of litigation" in order to qualify for work-product protection. * * *

The first problem we face is to determine the meaning of the phrase prepared "in anticipation of litigation." The phrase has never been interpreted by our circuit; furthermore, courts and commentators have expressed a range of views as to its meaning. It is universally agreed that a document whose purpose is to assist in preparation for litigation is within the scope of the Rule and thus eligible to receive protection if the other conditions of protection prescribed by the Rule are met. The issue is less clear, however, as to documents which, although prepared because of expected litigation, are intended to inform a business decision influenced by the prospects of the litigation. The formulation applied by some courts in determining whether documents are protected by work-product privilege is whether they are prepared "primarily or exclusively to assist in litigation"–a formulation that would potentially exclude documents containing analysis of expected litigation, if their primary, ultimate, or exclusive purpose is to assist in making the business decision. Others ask whether the documents were prepared "because of" existing or expected litigation–a formulation that would include such documents, despite the fact that their purpose is not to "assist in" litigation. Because we believe that protection of documents of this type is more consistent with both the literal terms and the purposes of the Rule, we adopt the latter formulation. * * *

We believe that a requirement that documents be produced primarily or exclusively to assist in litigation in order to be protected is at odds with the text and the policies of the Rule. Nowhere does Rule 26(b)(3) state that a document must have been prepared to aid in the conduct of litigation in order to constitute work product, much less primarily or exclusively to aid in litigation. Preparing a document "in anticipation of litigation" is sufficient.

The text of Rule 26(b)(3) does not limit its protection to materials prepared to assist at trial. To the contrary, the text of the Rule clearly sweeps more broadly. It expressly states that work-product privilege applies not only to documents "prepared . . . for trial" but also to those prepared "in anticipation of litigation." If the drafters of the Rule intended to limit its protection to documents made to assist in preparation for litigation, this would have been adequately conveyed by the phrase "prepared . . . for trial." The fact that documents prepared "in anticipation of litigation" were also included confirms that the drafters considered this to be a different, and broader category. Nothing in the Rule states or suggests that documents prepared "in anticipation of litigation" with the purpose of assisting in the making of a business decision do not fall within its scope.

In addition, the Rule takes pains to grant special protection to the type of materials at issue in this case–documents setting forth legal analysis. While the Rule generally withholds protection for documents prepared in anticipation of litigation if the adverse party shows "substantial need" for their disclosure and inability to obtain their equivalent by other means, even where the party seeking disclosure has made such a showing the Rule directs that "the court shall protect against disclosure of the mental impressions, conclusions, opinions, or legal theories of . . . [a party or its representative] concerning the litigation." Fed.R.Civ.P. 26(b)(3) (emphasis added). As the Advisory Committee notes indicate, Rule 26(b)(3) is intended to ratify the principles that "each side's informal evaluation of its case should be protected, that each side should be encouraged to prepare independently, and that one side should not automatically have the benefit of the detailed preparatory work of the other side." Where the Rule has explicitly established a special level of protection against disclosure for documents revealing an attorney's (or other representative's) opinions and legal theories concerning litigation, it would oddly undermine its purposes if such documents were excluded from protection merely because they were prepared to assist in the making of a business decision expected to result in the litigation.

Admittedly, there are fragmentary references in the caption to the Rule and in its commentary that can be read to lend support to a contrary interpretation. The caption, for example, refers to "Trial Preparation," and the Advisory Committee Notes make occasional reference to "trial preparation materials." We attach small importance to those references. Given that the text of the Rule (and of the commentary) expressly goes beyond documents "prepared . . . for trial" to encompass also those documents "prepared in anticipation of litigation," we cannot read the references in the caption and commentary as overriding the text of the Rule. * * *

In addition to the plain language of the Rule, the policies underlying the work-product doctrine suggest strongly that work-product protection should not be denied to a document that analyzes expected litigation merely because it is prepared to assist in a business decision. Framing the inquiry as whether the primary or exclusive purpose of the document was to assist in litigation threatens to deny protection to documents that implicate key concerns underlying the work-product doctrine. * * *

* * * The formulation of the work-product rule used by the Wright & Miller treatise, and cited by the Third, Fourth, Seventh, Eighth and D.C. Circuits, is that documents should be deemed prepared "in anticipation of litigation," and thus within the scope of the Rule, if "in light of the nature of the document and the factual situation in the particular case, the document can fairly be said to have been prepared or obtained because of the prospect of litigation." * * *

* * * [W]e find that the Wright & Miller "because of" test appropriately focuses on both what should be eligible for the Rule's protection and what should not. We believe this is the proper test to determine whether a document was prepared "in anticipation of litigation" and is thus eligible for protection depending on the further findings required by the Rule. * * * We cannot determine from the district court's opinion what test it followed in concluding that the Memorandum was ineligible for protection.

There are indications that the district court may have followed the "primarily to assist in litigation" test, which we here reject. * * * On the other hand, the tenor of the discussion in the court's opinion suggests it may have focused properly on the question whether the Memorandum studying the tax implications of the contemplated restructuring would have been prepared in substantially similar form regardless whether litigation was contemplated, and thus was not prepared "because of" the expected litigation.

We remand with instructions to the district court to reconsider the issue under the Wright & Miller test of whether "the document can fairly be said to have been prepared . . . because of the prospect of litigation." There is little doubt under the evidence that Sequa had the prospect of litigation in mind when it directed the preparation of the Memorandum by Arthur Andersen. Whether it can fairly be said that the Memorandum was prepared because of that expected litigation really turns on whether it would have been prepared irrespective of the expected litigation with the IRS.

If the district court concludes that substantially the same Memorandum would have been prepared in any event–as part of the ordinary course of business of undertaking the restructuring–then the court should conclude the Memorandum was not prepared because of the expected litigation and should adhere to its prior ruling denying the protection of the Rule.

On the other hand, if the court finds the Memorandum would not have been prepared but for Sequa's anticipation of litigation with the IRS over the losses generated by the restructuring, then judgment should be entered in favor of Sequa. * * *

KEARSE, Circuit Judge, dissenting.

I respectfully dissent. It does not appear to me that the district court applied an erroneous standard in this case. Accordingly, I would affirm. * * * I disagree with the majority's expansion of the work-product privilege to afford protection to documents not prepared in anticipation of litigation but instead prepared in order to permit the client to determine whether to undertake a business transaction, where there will be no anticipation of litigation unless the transaction is undertaken.

6. Work-Product - Disclosure to Auditors

The Supreme Court refused to recognize an accountant work product protection related to tax accrual workpapers in **United States v. Arthur Young & Co.**, 465 U.S. 805 (1984). The Court stated:

> Nor do we find persuasive the argument that a work-product immunity for accountants' tax accrual workpapers is a fitting analogue to the attorney work-product doctrine established in Hickman v. Taylor, supra. The *Hickman* work-product doctrine was

> founded upon the private attorney's role as the client's confidential advisor and advocate, a loyal representative whose duty it is to present the client's case in the most favorable possible light. An independent certified public accountant performs a different role. By certifying the public reports that collectively depict a corporation's financial status, the independent auditor assumes a public responsibility transcending any employment relationship with the client. The independent public accountant performing this special function owes ultimate allegiance to the corporation's creditors and stockholders, as well as to investing public. This "public watchdog" function demands that the accountant maintain total independence from the client at all times and requires complete fidelity to the public trust. To insulate from disclosure a certified public accountant's interpretations of the client's financial statements would be to ignore the significance of the accountant's role as a disinterested analyst charged with public obligations.

Disclosure by an attorney to an outside auditor, however, does not necessarily waive the protections of the work product doctrine. Accountants routinely meet with corporate counsel to assess pending and potential litigation as part of the annual review of a company's books. These meetings frequently include disclosure about the attorney's views of the potential for a damage award and legal strategies the company employs to defend cases. In **United States v. Deloitte LLP**, 610 F.3d 129 (D.C. Cir. 2010), as part of a tax investigation of Dow Chemical, the IRS sought the production of a memorandum prepared by a company's outside auditor, Deloitte, that summarized a meeting between Dow employees, Dow's outside counsel, and Deloitte employees about the possibility of litigation over a partnership and the necessity of accounting for such a possibility in an ongoing audit. The District of Columbia Circuit rejected the argument that a document created by an outside auditor cannot constitute attorney work product:

> The government focuses on Deloitte's role in creating the document and on its relationship to Dow. Under *Hickman*, however, the question is not who created the document or how they are related to the party asserting work-product protection, but whether the document contains work product—the thoughts and opinions of counsel developed in anticipation of litigation. The district court found that the memorandum records those thoughts, even though Deloitte and not Dow or its attorney committed them to paper. The work product privilege does not depend on whether the thoughts and opinions were communicated orally or in writing, but on whether they were prepared in anticipation of litigation. Thus Deloitte's preparation of the document does not exclude the possibility that it contains Dow's work product.

7. Work Product – Dual Purpose Documents

The Second Circuit's adoption of the Wright & Miller "because of" test in *Adlman* requires courts to determine the purpose for the document's creation, which may be difficult to ascertain. The attorney asserting the work product protection will emphasize its relationship to litigation while the opposing party–often the grand jury seeking to obtain the record–will focus on its use for a company's business. What happens when the company operates in a heavily regulated area, and the document was created in response to the settlement of an action with the regulator that requires the company to gather information about its operation to assure future compliance with the law? Is that document created "for or because of" future litigation against the company, or is it merely the record of a company that is required to create such information in order to conduct its business?

In re GRAND JURY SUBPOENA (TORF)
357 F.3d 900 (9th Cir. 2004)

DAVID R. THOMPSON, Senior Circuit Judge.

[Ponderosa Paint Manufacturing, Inc., hired an attorney, McCreedy, to represent it in connection with an investigation by the Environmental Protection Agency about disposal of waste material at one of its plants. McCreedy then hired Torf to investigate possible violations and provide a report to assist McCreedy in representing the company in the investigation. To avoid litigation with the EPA, Ponderosa later entered into an Information Request and Consent Order that required it to "preserve all documents and information related to work performed under this Order or relating to hazardous substances found on or released from this Site." McCreedy continued to advise the company on its compliance, and he used Torf to assist him. Believing the company may have continued violating the law, a grand jury subpoenaed Torf for all records related to "disposal of waste material" by Ponderosa, including documents created after entry of the Consent Order. Ponderosa asserted a work product claim to prevent disclosure of Torf's reports prepared for McCreedy.]

The "because of" standard does not consider whether litigation was a primary or secondary motive behind the creation of a document. Rather, it considers the totality of the circumstances and affords protection when it can fairly be said that the "document was created because of anticipated litigation, and would not have been created in substantially similar form but for the prospect of that litigation[.]" *Adlman*. Here, there is no question that all of the documents were produced in anticipation of litigation. McCreedy hired Torf because of Ponderosa's impending litigation and Torf conducted his investigations because of that threat. The threat animated every document Torf prepared, including the documents prepared to comply with the Information Request and Consent Order, and to consult regarding the cleanup.

The government argues, however, that the withheld documents would have been created in substantially similar form in any event to comply with the Information Request and the Consent Order, and therefore are not protected by the work product doctrine. The government relies on language in Adlman which states: "the 'because of' formulation . . . withholds protection from documents . . . that would have been created in essentially similar form irrespective of the litigation." We do not view this language as eviscerating work product protection for the documents withheld in this case.

The question of entitlement to work product protection cannot be decided simply by looking at one motive that contributed to a document's preparation. The circumstances surrounding the document's preparation must also be considered. In the "because of" Wright & Miller formulation, "the nature of the document and the factual situation of the particular case" are key to a determination of whether work product protection applies. When there is a true independent purpose for creating a document, work product protection is less likely, but when two purposes are profoundly interconnected, the analysis is more complicated.

Here, Ponderosa's response to the Information Request and its accession to the Consent Order were done under the direction of an attorney in anticipation of litigation. By cooperating with the EPA, Ponderosa sought to avoid litigation with the government. Having chosen to pursue a criminal investigation, the government now seeks to capitalize on Ponderosa's earlier cooperation and obtain all of Torf's documents pertaining to the disposal of Ponderosa's waste material. The withheld documents, however, just like the others, were prepared by Torf, at least in part, to help McCreedy advise and defend Ponderosa in anticipated litigation with the government. Thus, the withheld documents fall within the broad category of documents that were prepared for the overall purpose of anticipated litigation.

To the extent that *Adlman* suggests there is no work product protection when, viewed in isolation of the facts of the case, a document can be said to have been created for a nonlitigation purpose, we believe the better view is set forth in two Seventh Circuit cases. In the first, In re Special September 1978 Grand Jury, 640 F.2d 49 (7th Cir. 1980) ("*Special September*"), the court extended work product protection to materials that were produced both in anticipation of litigation and for the filing of Board of Elections reports required under state law. Work product protection was proper because, by the time the law firm's client received the Board's request for the required reports, the client had already received a subpoena from a federal grand jury. The so-called "independent" purpose of complying with the Board's request was grounded in the same set of facts that created the anticipation of litigation, and it was the anticipation of litigation that prompted the law firm's work in the first place.

In the later case, United States v. Frederick, 182 F.3d 496 (7th Cir. 1999), the Seventh Circuit held that "a dual-purpose document–a document prepared for use in preparing tax returns and for use in litigation–is not privileged; otherwise, people in or contemplating litigation would be able to invoke, in effect, an accountant's privilege, provided that they used their lawyer to fill out their tax returns."

Frederick does not discuss or distinguish *Special September*, but the two cases can be reconciled by the extent to which the so-called independent purpose is truly separable from the anticipation of litigation. In Frederick, at issue were accountants' worksheets, albeit prepared by a lawyer, in preparation of his clients' tax returns. Although his clients were under investigation (which the court acknowledged was a "complicating factor"), work product protection was ultimately inappropriate because tax return preparation is a readily separable purpose from litigation preparation and "using a lawyer in lieu of another form of tax preparer" does nothing to blur that distinction. In Special September, on the other hand, the materials used to prepare the Board of Elections reports were compiled by lawyers and were necessarily created in the first place because of impending litigation.

Similarly here, by hiring McCreedy who in turn hired Torf, Ponderosa was not assigning an attorney a task that could just as well have been performed by a non-lawyer. The company hired McCreedy only after learning that the federal government was investigating it for criminal wrongdoing; a circumstance virtually necessitating legal representation. Torf assisted McCreedy in preparing Ponderosa's defense. He also acted as an environmental consultant on the cleanup. Although in that capacity he could have been retained by Ponderosa directly, this circumstance does not preclude the application of the work-product privilege to documents produced in that capacity, if the documents were also produced "because of" litigation. The challenged documents were prepared under the direction of McCreedy, who was providing legal advice to Ponderosa in anticipation of the impending litigation.

We conclude that the withheld documents, notwithstanding their dual purpose character, fall within the ambit of the work product doctrine. The documents are entitled to work product protection because, taking into account the facts surrounding their creation, their litigation purpose so permeates any non-litigation purpose that the two purposes cannot be discretely separated from the factual nexus as a whole.

8. Work Product – Preexisting Documents

Many categories of documents are easily assigned the label "Work Product," such as drafts of memoranda, notes of meetings, and internal communications. Are documents obtained by an attorney in the course of legal representation that were not created for the purpose of the attorney-client relationship also work product? If so, are they "fact" or "opinion" work product?

In re GRAND JURY SUBPOENAS DATED MARCH 19, 2002 AND AUGUST 2, 2002 (THE MERCATOR CORPORATION)

318 F.3d 379 (2d Cir. 2003)

RAGGI, Circuit Judge.

Appellants, The Mercator Corporation, its chairman James H. Giffen, and their attorneys, the law firm of Akin, Gump, Strauss, Hauer & Feld, L.L.P. ("Akin Gump"), appeal from the September 9, 2002 order of the District Court for the Southern District of New York (Denny Chin, Judge), granting the United States' motion to compel Akin Gump to produce bank records for thirty specific accounts at four Swiss banks called for in grand jury subpoenas. * * *

[The Department of of Justice was investigating possible violations of the Foreign Corrupt Pracitces Act, and filed a Mutual Legal Assistance Treaty ("MLAT") request with Swiss authorities seeking bank records relating to specific accounts held by a foreign country or its officials that were suspected of taking bribes from American corporations. The response received from Switzerland was incomplete or unsatisfactory in several respects. Grand jury subpoenas were served on Akin Gump requiring the production of bank records for thirty accounts that were also sought in the MLAT request, and Akin Gump refused to compy by asserting the work product doctrine. The district court found that the work product doctrine did not apply to third-party documents.]

Appellants submit that an exception to this third-party documents rule applies when an attorney has so specifically selected and compiled such documents in anticipation of litigation that production would necessarily reveal the attorney's developing strategy. This argument relies largely on decisions in two civil cases from outside this circuit: Sporck v. Peil, 759 F.2d 312 (3d Cir.1985); and Shelton v. American Motors Corp., 805 F.2d 1323 (8th Cir.1986). In both cases, the issue was not so much whether the work product doctrine shielded counsel from producing certain documents, for it appears they had been produced in the course of discovery; rather, the issue was whether counsel was obliged to identify from voluminous discovery materials those discrete documents that the attorney had selected for review with his client in advance of deposition, see *Sporck v. Peil*, or that an attorney specifically recalled as existing in her client's files, see *Shelton v. American Motors Corp.* The courts ruled that such narrowly focused inquiries constituted impermissible intrusions into attorneys' thought processes in preparing their clients' defenses.

Citing *Sporck*, we too have observed that "where a request is made for documents already in the possession of the requesting party, with the precise goal of learning what the opposing attorney's thinking or strategy may be, even third-party documents may be protected." *In re Grand Jury Subpoenas (Paul Weiss)* (distinguishing *Sporck* by noting, *inter alia*, that the subpoenaed telephone records appeared to be unavailable to the grand jury except from the law firm). That, however, is clearly not this case. The grand jury does not already possess the bank records subpoenaed from Akin Gump, at least not all of them. Further, the challenged subpoenas, in demanding any and all records for thirty specific Swiss bank accounts, are designed not to "glean what [bank records Akin Gump] deems relevant" but to mirror [Mutual Legal Assistance Treaty] requests that the government has pursued without success for more than two years. Indeed, at oral argument, prosecutors represented that they will not attempt to authenticate the subpoenaed bank records through a member of the Akin Gump firm.

Appellants submit that work product protection for an attorney's "selection and compilation" of third-party documents should not depend on the subjective intent of the prosecutors, but rather on an objective consideration of whether the disclosure of the documents will necessarily reveal the attorney's thought processes in anticipation of litigation. We agree that subjective intent is only one among many factors to be weighed in making an objective determination of whether documents constitute work product. But that conclusion hardly benefits appellants.

Not every selection and compilation of third-party documents by counsel transforms that material into attorney work product. To fit within what we have repeatedly characterized as a "narrow exception" to the general rule that third-party documents in the possession of an attorney do not merit work product protection, the party asserting the privilege must show "a real, rather than speculative, concern" that counsel's thought processes "in relation to pending or anticipated litigation" will be exposed through disclosure of the compiled documents. This burden of objective proof cannot be met through conclusory ex parte affidavits, such as those filed by appellants with the district court in this case, which simply assert that Akin Gump possesses only a subset of the materials subpoenaed and that this subset was created pursuant to a carefully orchestrated defense strategy. Akin Gump's failure to disclose that strategy ex parte to the district court made it impossible for Judge Chin to determine–and makes it impossible for us to review–whether the responsive subset indeed reflects Akin Gump's discriminating selection, or, instead, whether the subset is simply the product of document maintenance practices by the various banks, a lack of cooperation from some of the account holders, or some combination of these and other factors. Without such disclosure, no court can decide if Akin Gump's work product concern is real, or only speculative. Similarly troubling is the firm's failure to identify or submit the responsive documents for in camera review, a practice both long-standing and routine in cases involving claims of privilege. Without reviewing the documents, the district court could not ascertain whether Akin Gump's collection was missing only a few bank records out of a voluminous mass, or whether the subset consisted of so few records focused on such discrete transactions that counsel's strategic thinking was apparent, or something in between the two. Moreover, without the documents, the district court could not consider the possibility of issuing a protective order that disclosed some, if not all, of the account records in Akin Gump's possession to the grand jury, thereby confounding any conclusions that might be drawn about counsel's selection strategy.

B. SCOPE OF THE ATTORNEY-CLIENT PRIVILEGE AND WORK PRODUCT DOCTRINE

1. "Advice of Counsel" Defense

Does presentation of an attorney's testimony to show a "good faith" compliance with the law waive the attorney-client privilege as to other communications with the attorney? Consider the court's analysis in **United States v. Bilzerian**, 926 F.2d 1285 (2d Cir. 1991):

> [Bilzerian] was convicted of nine counts of an indictment charging violations of securities fraud, making false statements to the Securities and Exchange Commission (SEC), and conspiracy to commit specific offenses, and to defraud the SEC and the Internal Revenue Service (IRS). * * *
>
> At trial, defendant argued that he did not intend to violate the securities laws, but believed the financing structure of the transactions, utilizing trusts to borrow funds, would allow him legally to avoid disclosure regarding other investors, and that describing the source of his funds as "personal" was lawful. A motion was made *in limine* seeking a ruling permitting him to testify regarding his belief in the lawfulness of describing the source of his funds as "personal" without being subjected to cross-examination on communications he had with his attorney on this subject, discussions ordinarily protected by the attorney-client privilege. * * *
>
> Defendant contends the testimony he sought to introduce regarding his good faith attempt to comply with the securities laws would not have disclosed the content or even the existence of any privileged communications or asserted a reliance on counsel defense. As such, he continues, the attorney-client privilege would not be waived by his testimony and, therefore, the trial court committed reversible error when it denied his motion *in limine* seeking to protect the privilege. He alleges that this ruling, together with similar rulings made during the course of the trial, prevented him from refuting the charge that he acted with criminal intent—a central element of the government's case–and that his constitutional right to "the fullest opportunity to meet the accusation against him . . . [and] to deny all the elements of the case against him," was thereby encroached upon. * * *

> [T]he attorney-client privilege cannot at once be used as a shield and a sword. * * * A defendant may not use the privilege to prejudice his opponent's case or to disclose some selected communications for self-serving purposes. Thus, the privilege may implicitly be waived when defendant asserts a claim that in fairness requires examination of protected communications. This waiver principle is applicable here for Bilzerian's testimony that he thought his actions were legal would have put his knowledge of the law and the basis for his understanding of what the law required in issue. His conversations with counsel regarding the legality of his schemes would have been directly relevant in determining the extent of his knowledge and, as a result, his intent.
>
> * * * The district court took great pains to point out that application of the privilege would hinge on the testimony elicited on direct examination. In response to defense counsel's statement that "[t]he government presumably then would be able to call the attorney because the privilege is gone," the court stated:
>
> > I am not going to go to that point. It may be that the government would be bound by the answer of the witness but I am not going to get to that point because I don't think I have to at this juncture. I don't know how this is going to play out. Until I do, I think it is inappropriate for me to give any advisory opinion.
>
> In effect, defendant was seeking an advisory ruling in advance, assuring that the attorney-client privilege would not be waived regardless of what developed in his direct testimony. In order for the privilege to operate effectively defendants must be able to rely on its protection, but courts cannot sanction the use of the privilege to prevent effective cross-examination on matters reasonably related to those introduced in direct examination.

2. Corporate Counsel and Individual Officers

A client can waive the attorney-client privilege, while the protections afforded by the work product doctrine can be asserted in some cases even if the client is willing to waive the privilege. As demonstrated by *Upjohn*, a corporation can assert the privilege to the same extent as an individual, and given the resources of a large organization, the privilege will likely cover a much greater volume of communications than those by one person meeting with a lawyer. Who can waive the corporation's privilege? Usually, the issue is not difficult because the company's board of directors or chief executive has the authority to act on behalf of the corporation. In CFTC v. Weintraub, 471 U.S. 343 (1985), the Supreme Court held that a trustee in bankruptcy appointed to conduct the affairs of a bankrupt corporation had the authority to waive the attorney-client privilege. The corporation's waiver of its privilege can result in communications from senior officers to the company's attorney being used as proof of their knowledge or criminal intent.

A key issue is whether the company's lawyer also represented the officer individually, which means each must agree to waive the attorney-client privilege to allow for disclosure. Model Rule of Professional Conduct 1.13(a) provides that "[a] lawyer employed or retained by an organization represents the organization acting through its duly authorized constituents." It may not be immediately apparent to an employee that the lawyer's client is the company and not the individual. Rule 1.13(f) states, "In dealing with an organization's directors, officers, employees, members, shareholders or other constituents, a lawyer shall explain the identity of the client when the lawyer knows or reasonably should know that the organization's interests are adverse to those of the constituents with whom the lawyer is dealing." Sometimes referred to as "corporate *Miranda*," the lawyer should make it clear that the attorney-client privilege and protection afforded work product is within the control of the company, not the individual, and that the person should seek counsel's advice. Of course, this might discourage an employee from talking with the corporate lawyer, so there can be an incentive not to provide this warning, or to make only a cursory statement.

In the corporate context, especially when dealing with senior management, the issue of who corporate counsel represents can become blurred quickly, especially when there are parallel proceedings involving the company and individuals officers along with a criminal investigation. Consider how the issue of who controls the attorney-client privilege played out in the following case, and consider what the officer should have done to protect himself.

UNITED STATES v. RUEHLE

583 F.3d 600 (9th Cir. 2009)

TALLMAN, Circuit Judge:

We here explore the treacherous path which corporate counsel must tread under the attorney-client privilege when conducting an internal investigation to advise a publicly traded company on its financial disclosure obligations. Defendant-Appellee William J. Ruehle is the former Chief Financial Officer of Broadcom Corporation, a California-based, publicly traded semiconductor supplier that came under intense scrutiny for its suspected backdating of company stock options. Following a government investigation, Ruehle was criminally indicted for his involvement in an alleged backdating scheme that ultimately resulted in Broadcom's restatement of its earnings to account for approximately $2.2 billion in additional stock-based compensation expenses. The district court held an evidentiary hearing and, after evaluating the extensive briefing and evidence presented, issued an order suppressing all evidence reflecting Ruehle's statements to attorneys from Irell & Manella LLP (Irell), Broadcom's outside counsel, regarding the stock option granting practices at Broadcom. The court found that at the initial stages of the inquiry by Irell (called the "Equity Review") an attorney-client relationship also existed with the CFO individually, and not just with Broadcom, and that the lawyers breached their ethical duties to their client Ruehle in disclosing what he had told them in a preliminary interview.

I

In March 2006, the Wall Street Journal published the first of a series of articles called "The Perfect Payday," which suggested that a number of public companies were backdating stock options granted to their employees.[1] Shortly thereafter, in mid-May 2006, an investor rights group publicly identified Broadcom as one of the corporations that appeared to have engaged in backdating. As a result of the media attention and in anticipation of an inquiry from the Securities and Exchange Commission ("SEC"), Broadcom's Board of Directors and company management decided to bring in outside counsel to commence an internal review of the company's current and past stock option granting practices. Ruehle, as Broadcom's CFO, was among those intimately involved in that decision from the outset. On May 18, 2006, Broadcom's Audit Committee engaged Irell, a private law firm with which it had longstanding ties, to conduct the Equity Review by investigating the propriety of the measurement dates utilized by Broadcom in its option granting process and identifying those grants which failed to meet the

[1] Stock options give individuals the right to buy shares of stock on a future date at a set price, commonly known as the "exercise" or "strike" price. Typically, as was the practice at Broadcom, stock options granted to employees could not be exercised until the end of a fixed vesting period. Once an option vested, the holder could exercise it and purchase stock from the company at the strike price. Thus, options that have a strike price below the current trading price in the stock market are commonly referred to as being "in the money," whereas options with a strike price above the current trading price are considered "underwater."

The strike price is typically equal to the market price on the date that the option is granted. "Backdating" refers to the practice of recording an option's grant date and strike price retrospectively. See United States v. Reyes, 577 F.3d 1069 (9th Cir. 2009). The ability to manipulate the strike price maximizes the benefit to the option holders. Selection of an initial grant date when the share price, and thus the strike price, is at its lowest during a given period will increase the amount an option is "in the money" or, in some cases, may determine whether an option is "in the money" at all, rather than "underwater." In either case, the employee may immediately exercise the options to buy shares at the optimally low strike price, sell the stock at the current market price, and pocket any gain. "Backdating is not itself illegal, provided that the benefit to the employees is recorded on the corporate books as a non-cash compensation expense to the corporation, in accordance with an accounting convention promulgated in 1972 referred to as Accounting Principles Board Opinion No. 25." *Reyes*.

measurement date requirements of generally accepted accounting principles.[2] Irell immediately commenced its review, which entailed collecting corporate documents and records and conducting interviews with past and current Broadcom employees.

Broadcom representatives, including Ruehle, met with Irell lawyers on May 24 and 25, 2006, to discuss the scope of the Equity Review. It was agreed that Irell would report the results of its inquiries to the Audit Committee. It was also decided that the Board would not appoint a panel of independent, outside directors to oversee the Equity Review. On May 26, 2006, a formal meeting of the Audit Committee was convened. Ruehle and other senior Broadcom executives, several members of the Board, and Irell lawyers were among those present. During the hour-long meeting, Irell partner David Siegel explained the nature of typical "backdating" investigations and discussed the status of Irell's internal review, including the necessary involvement of Broadcom's outside independent auditors, Ernst & Young LLP, who would have to review and opine on the accuracy of the company's audited financial statements and regulatory filings. Siegel also cautioned "that Irell can handle issues related to the proper accounting for option grants but that if an issue of self-dealing or management or Board integrity arose, a special committee of independent directors would need to be appointed and special independent counsel engaged to conduct that inquiry." The Audit Committee and other representatives of Broadcom made clear that the intent was to turn over the information obtained through the Equity Review to the auditors, to fully cooperate with government regulators, and, if necessary, to self-report any problems with Broadcom's financial statements.

As many within Broadcom had anticipated, civil lawsuits soon followed the media reports about the company's back-dating of stock options. On May 25, 2006, a shareholder derivative suit captioned *Murphy v. McGregor* was filed in California federal court. The following day, on May 26, the plaintiffs in the ongoing securities class action in California state superior court, *Jin v. Broadcom Corp.*, filed an amended complaint. Both the *Murphy* action and the *Jin* amended class action now alleged wrongdoing in relation to

---

[2] The relationship between Broadcom and Irell runs deep, as Ruehle contends, and dates back to before 1998 when Irell assisted Broadcom in its initial public offering of stock ("IPO"), which led to its becoming an investor-owned public company. Irell itself acquired stock during the IPO and its partners profited handsomely when the stock price rose. Since then, Irell has represented Broadcom in relation to numerous acquisitions and the firm has handled several litigation matters for Broadcom and its officers and directors. At the time it was engaged to conduct the Equity Review, the firm was counsel of record for Broadcom and its management employees named as individual defendants in a then-unrelated securities class action, Jin v. Broadcom Corp., pending in California state superior court. Moreover, Irell had recently represented Broadcom, as well as several of its officers and directors, including Ruehle, in an unrelated securities action referred to as the "warrants litigation." The warrants litigation settled several months prior, in December 2005.

Broadcom's stock option granting practices; both suits named Broadcom and also personally named Ruehle, among other Broadcom officers and directors, as an individual defendant.

On May 30, 2006, Broadcom's in-house General Counsel David Dull sent an e-mail to various Broadcom employees, including Ruehle, notifying them of the *Murphy* action and of the amended complaint filed in the *Jin* securities class action. Dull invited anyone with concerns to contact either him or Irell attorneys Siegel, Kenneth Heitz, or Dan Lefler. Shortly after receiving Dull's message, Ruehle received a separate e-mail from Heitz, one of the Irell partners with whom Ruehle had already conferred as part of the Equity Review. Heitz's e-mail updated Ruehle concerning the scheduling of interviews of three current or former Broadcom employees and, finally, inquired, "if you have open time on Thursday Dan Lefler and I would like to spend an hour or so with you . . . ."

As arranged, Heitz and Lefler met with Ruehle in his office on Thursday, June 1, 2006, to discuss Broadcom's stock option granting practices and his role as the company's CFO.

Ruehle had subsequent, brief discussions with the Irell lawyers as the Equity Review continued and the lawyers reported back to the CFO their progress in unearthing the facts. At no point did the topic of the civil securities lawsuits arise as it might relate to Ruehle personally. Nor did Ruehle ever indicate to the lawyers that he was seeking legal advice in his individual capacity. It is the substance of these June 2006 interactions that lies at the center of the present dispute.

In late June 2006, Irell advised Ruehle to secure independent counsel with respect to the investigations and the pending civil suits. Ruehle retained the law firm Wilson Sonsini Goodrich & Rosati to represent him individually. Nevertheless, Ruehle remained heavily involved in the company's internal review and he was privy to Irell's reports to the Audit Committee of its findings and ultimately the disclosures of the information gathered by Irell to Ernst & Young.

In August 2006, at Broadcom's direction, Irell fully disclosed the information obtained from the Equity Review to the Ernst & Young auditors. Irell had a series of meetings with Ernst & Young in which the lawyers reported what they had found, which necessarily included the substance of Ruehle's June 1, 2006, interview with Heitz and Lefler. Ruehle was present for at least some of these meetings between Irell and the Ernst & Young auditors. There is no dispute that the Irell lawyers regularly updated Ruehle and others in senior management about the progress of the Equity Review and their meetings and contacts with the auditors.

The Equity Review revealed several accounting irregularities with respect to certain stock option grants. In January 2007, on the advice of its outside counsel and auditors, Broadcom restated its earnings as reported in its financial disclosure statements to include a total of $2.2 billion in previously undisclosed compensation expenses.

The SEC and the United States Attorney's Office commenced formal enforcement and grand jury investigations of several company executives in relation to Broadcom's stock option granting practices. In May and June 2007, with Broadcom's authorization, government investigators interviewed Irell attorneys Heitz and Lefler by telephone regarding their conversations with Ruehle in June 2006. The information they provided was summarized in FBI Form FD-302 reports of investigation, which are part of the sealed record. When he learned that the government intended to use this information against him in connection with possible criminal charges, Ruehle objected and claimed that any statements to the Irell attorneys were protected by his attorney-client privilege. Ruehle also insisted, after the fact, that whatever he said to Irell could not be disclosed without his prior written consent.

On June 4, 2008, a grand jury in the Central District of California indicted Ruehle and Henry T. Nicholas III – Broadcom's founder, and former President and Chief Executive Officer – on charges of conspiracy, securities and wire fraud, and various other violations of Title 15 of the United States Code. The indictment alleges that beginning in or around 1999 and continuing until at least in or around 2005, Nicholas and Ruehle, among others, engaged in a fraudulent scheme and conspiracy to disguise, conceal, understate, and mischaracterize compensation expenses Broadcom was required to recognize in connection with granting its stock options to various employees. Among the allegations of wrongdoing, the indictment claims that as part of the backdating scheme the defendants paid a former employee who threatened to expose the scheme, concealed the payoff from Broadcom's Board and its independent auditors, and took various steps to create plausible deniability as to Broadcom's option backdating practices.

On January 12, 2009, the government moved *ex parte* for a hearing to resolve whether the statements Ruehle made to Irell lawyers in June 2006 were privileged communications. Ruehle argued that he had an individual attorney-client relationship with Irell arising from the securities lawsuits, in which he was a named defendant. Beginning on February 23, 2009, the district court held a three-day evidentiary hearing at which Ruehle and Irell attorneys Heitz and Lefler testified. At Ruehle's request, a substantial portion of the testimony and evidence was received in camera outside the presence of the federal prosecutors. Both Irell attorneys insisted that Irell's individual representation of Ruehle in relation to the civil securities lawsuits did not commence until after the June 1, 2006, interview. Among other things, the attorneys testified that they began the June 2006 meeting with a so-called *Upjohn* or corporate *Miranda* warning, which included notice that the Irell attorneys were acting as representatives of Broadcom – specifically, the Audit Committee – and that the privilege therefore rested only with the company. Ruehle, however, denied any recollection of receiving such cautionary warnings at the June 1, 2006, interview. Ruehle testified that at the time he spoke with Heitz and Lefler he believed Irell represented everyone named in the civil suits, including him, and that Heitz and Lefler were acting at least in part as his personal attorneys during the interview.

At the conclusion of the hearing, the district court rendered its oral ruling which strongly condemned the Irell attorneys' behavior with respect to the firm's handling of the Equity Review. The court then found that Ruehle "had a reasonable belief that Irell and Manella were his lawyers prior to the June 1, 2006 interrogation by Irell, and that he never gave informed written consent, either to the dual representation by Irell or the disclosure of privileged information to third parties, including Ernst & Young and the government." Based on this reasoning, the court ordered suppression. The district court subsequently issued a written order, which included an additional finding that Ruehle intended his statements to Heitz and Lefler to be confidential. * * * The court also referred Irell to the California State Bar for possible discipline in light of numerous perceived violations of state rules of professional conduct. * * *

III

The government raises several arguments challenging the district court's order excluding Ruehle's statements to Irell attorneys. We begin with some basic premises. First, there is no dispute that Broadcom had an existing attorney-client relationship with Irell and, by electing to reveal the information gathered to Ernst & Young (and later to various agencies of the United States), deliberately waived any corporate attorney-client privilege it held with respect to all matters at issue. Second, the Equity Review and the civil securities suits, to which Ruehle was a party, both concerned the same general subject matter as of June 1, 2006 – i.e., the stock option granting practices of Broadcom. Finally, the district court concluded as a fact that Ruehle reasonably believed that Irell represented him individually with respect to the ongoing civil lawsuits when the June 1, 2006, meeting took place. Because this factual finding is not clearly erroneous, we approach the parties' arguments from the perspective that Irell had attorney-client relationships with both Broadcom and Ruehle individually.

We, however, must inquire further. After all, a party asserting the attorney-client privilege has the burden of establishing the relationship and the privileged nature of the communication. [See] In re Grand Jury Subpoenas, 144 F.3d 653 (10th Cir. 1998) ("In certain circumstances, reasonable belief may be enough to create an attorney-client relationship, but it is not sufficient here to create a personal attorney-client privilege."). We must determine whether Ruehle's communications to the Irell attorneys regarding Broadcom's stock option granting practices are protected by a personal attorney-client privilege belonging to Ruehle.

"The attorney-client privilege protects confidential disclosures made by a client to an attorney in order to obtain legal advice, . . . as well as an attorney's advice in response to such disclosures." United States v. Chen, 99

F.3d 1495 (9th Cir. 1996). "The fact that a person is a lawyer does not make all communications with that person privileged." * * * Because it impedes full and free discovery of the truth, the attorney-client privilege is strictly construed. Typically, an eight-part test determines whether information is covered by the attorney-client privilege:

> (1) Where legal advice of any kind is sought (2) from a professional legal adviser in his capacity as such, (3) the communications relating to that purpose, (4) made in confidence (5) by the client, (6) are at his instance permanently protected (7) from disclosure by himself or by the legal adviser, (8) unless the protection be waived.

In re Grand Jury Investigation, 974 F.2d 1068 (9th Cir. 1992).[7] The party asserting the privilege bears the burden of proving each essential element.

At the outset we note a fundamental flaw in the district court's analysis. "Issues concerning application of the attorney-client privilege in the adjudication of federal law are governed by federal common law." Clarke v. Am. Commerce Nat. Bank, 974 F.2d 127 (9th Cir. 1992). The district court, however, applied a "reasonable belief" standard without ever referencing the well-established eight-part test. Rather, in reaching its holding, the court relied almost exclusively upon California state law to define both the attorney-client relationship and the attorney-client privilege. Most significantly, the court cited California Evidence Code section 917(a) for the proposition that all "communications made in the course of an attorney-client relationship are presumed confidential."

This legal error is critical in this case. The district court applied a liberal view of the privilege that conflicts with the strict view applied under federal common law, which governs here. * * *

---

[7] The government urges that the special problems presented by joint representation of a corporation and its individual officers counsel adoption of particularized requirements before the individual officer could assert an attorney-client privilege. The Third Circuit in In re Bevill, Bresler & Schulman Asset Mgmt. Corp., 805 F.2d 120 (3d Cir. 1986), adopted a five-factor test intended to clarify that "any privilege that exists as to a corporate officer's role and functions within a corporation belongs to the corporation, not the officer." Several other circuits have adopted some form of tailored test for joint-representation scenarios. We do not decide the propriety of adopting the specialized test of *Bevill* because, given Irell's longstanding representation of Ruehle as an individual before the instant case arose and in light of the planned disclosure of facts gained in the Equity Review investigation to the third-party independent auditor, this case can be resolved using our usual eight-part test. Accordingly, we leave for another day consideration of the extraordinary requirements of the *Bevill* five-prong test for establishing attorney-client privilege in a situation where both the executive and the corporation assert that they are dually represented. * * *

As the party asserting the privilege, Ruehle was obliged by federal law to establish the privileged nature of the communications and, if necessary, to segregate the privileged information from the non-privileged information. With respect to the latter obligation, Ruehle has made no effort to identify with particularity which of his communications to the Irell attorneys are within his claim of privilege, in either his public or sealed filings before us. Under federal law, the attorney-client privilege is strictly construed. Ruehle's failure to define the scope of his claim of privilege weighs in favor of disclosure; in any event, his claim cannot support the overly broad, blanket suppression order entered here.

With the burden properly on Ruehle, and after carefully reviewing and evaluating the record, we hold that Ruehle fails the fourth element of the traditional eight-part privilege test. Ruehle's statements to the Irell attorneys were not "made in confidence" but rather for the purpose of disclosure to the outside auditors. That he might regret those statements after later learning of the subsequent corporate disclosure to law enforcement officials is not material to the privilege determination as of June 2006.

* * * The notion that Ruehle spoke with Irell attorneys Heitz and Lefler with the reasonable belief that his statements were confidential is unsupported by the record. * * * He frankly admitted that he understood the fruits of Irell's searching inquiries would be disclosed to Ernst & Young in order to convince the independent auditors of the integrity of Broadcom's financial statements to the public, or to take appropriate accounting measures to rectify any misleading reports. We reject the district court's contrary finding that an expectation of confidentiality was established because, upon review of the record, we are left with the "definite and firm conviction that a mistake has been committed" and thus we determine that this factual finding was clearly erroneous. United States v. Overton, 573 F.3d 679 (9th Cir. 2009).

Ruehle was no ordinary Broadcom employee. He served as the public company's CFO – the senior corporate executive charged with primary responsibility for Broadcom's financial affairs. * * * Ruehle cannot now credibly claim ignorance of the general disclosure requirements imposed on a publicly traded company with respect to its outside auditors or the need to truthfully report corporate information to the SEC.

Ruehle was also intimately involved in all aspects of the Equity Review, including the planning, investigatory, and disclosure stages. * * *

In his testimony at the evidentiary hearing, Ruehle acknowledged the broad nature of the planned third-party disclosure, noting that Irell was directed, to his knowledge, to freely share "all factual information" gleaned through the Equity Review – whether "good, bad, or ugly." * * *

Indeed, Ruehle confirmed over and over again his awareness that the substance of his June 2006 interviews with the Irell lawyers was not to be held in confidence:

> Q: You understood that Irell was going to be sharing the factual information they gathered to third parties?
>
> A: That's correct.
>
> Q: And fair to say you understood that Irell was there, among other things, to gather facts; correct?
>
> A: Correct.

To dispel any doubt, Ruehle also confirmed that the information he provided to Heitz and Lefler was largely factual in nature – the type of information he understood would be disclosed to third parties.

> Q: To be clear, the information you provided to Irell was factual information; correct?
>
> A: It was a combination of factual information and some assumptions and some recollections.* * *
>
> Q: And you understood that Ernst & Young was going to be looking to you, among other people, to help them understand what had happened as part of Broadcom's historical options review; correct?
>
> A: That's correct. * * *

On appeal, Ruehle tries to minimize the damning evidence confirming his awareness that his interactions with Irell would not be held in confidence. He places much weight on the assertion that he only learned of the details of Irell's disclosures to Ernst & Young and the government in 2008 and that he was "shocked." Ruehle contends that, notwithstanding his obligation to fully cooperate in Broadcom's internal review, he would not have provided information as part of the Equity Review had he known it could be used in support of a criminal investigation or an SEC enforcement action. * * *

Ruehle attempts to raise an exception to the full disclosure of all factual information, insisting that he anticipated the disclosure of only factual information "that was not otherwise privileged information." In other words, Ruehle now asserts an expectation of confidentiality only over statements that he claims were really given in confidence. He does not distinguish what those statements might be in his blanket invocation of the privilege. This circular reasoning is, analytically speaking, unpersuasive and cannot overcome the concrete evidence in the record before us. Even supposing he subjectively believed that some of the information he conveyed to the Irell lawyers was confidential, upon asserting the attorney-client privilege Ruehle was obliged to distinguish which particular statements should be afforded the privilege. * * *

Moreover, Ruehle's argument runs squarely into the settled rule that any voluntary disclosure of information to a third party waives the attorney-client privilege, regardless of whether such disclosure later turns out to be harmful. * * *

In sum, the overwhelming evidence demonstrates that Ruehle's statements to Heitz and Lefler were not "made in confidence" but rather for the purpose of outside disclosure. Accordingly, we hold that Ruehle has failed to meet his burden of establishing the existence of an individual attorney-client privilege with respect to the information provided to the Irell attorneys in the June 2006 time frame. * * *

V

* * * The district court's order suppressing the Irell evidence is reversed and the matter is remanded for trial.

NOTES AND QUESTIONS

1. ***Applying Bevill.*** In **United States v. Norris**, 722 F. Supp.2d 632 (E.D. Pa. 2010), the court applied the factors from the *Bevill* test [p. 704 n.7], denying the defendant's argument that he had been individually represented by the corporate attorney. The court found that the defendant was unable to demonstrate that he "sought legal advice or representation from the Law Firm in general or from" the attorney representing the corporation. But see Bruce A. Green & Ellen S. Podgor, *Unregulated Internal Investigations: Achieving Fairness for Corporate Constituents*, 54 B.C. L. REV. 73 (2013)(expressing the need to readjust the interpretation of the attorney-client privilege in internal investigations to achieve fairness for corporate constituents).

2. ***Public v. Private Sector.*** Should a different standard apply when a state government or agency is asserting the privilege? Who is the client–the employees of the agency or the citizens being represented? In In re Thirty-Third Statewide Investigating Grand Jury, 86 A.3d 204 (Pa. 2014 WL 619901), the Supreme Court of Pennsylvania examined federal circuit decisions in holding that the attorney-client privilege would not apply "where the 'client' is actually the state government or its agency."

3. Demanding Waiver from Corporations

In 1999, the Department of Justice issued a memorandum called "Federal Prosecution of Corporations" – called the Holder Memo after then-

Deputy Attorney General Eric Holder – that discussed the general policy of federal prosecutors in deciding whether th charge a corporation with a crime. One of the principles that informed the decision was a "corporation's timely and voluntary disclosure of wrongdoing and its willingness to cooperate in the investigation of its agents, including, if necessary, the waiver of the corporate attorney-client and work-product privileges." The policy has been refined several times since then, and in August 2008 the Department issued newly revised *Principles of Federal Prosecution of Business Organizations* that can be found in the United States Attorney's Manual. The current policy was adopted in response to significant criticism of earlier statements that encouraged prosecutors to seek waivers of the attorney-client privilege and work product protection by corporations being investigated, often at a very early stage before the company had even completed its internal investigation. The Department's policy now actively discourages federal prosecutors from seeking such waivers from a company under investigation, emphasizing instead the need for corporate disclosure of facts that are generated in an internal investigation:

> The attorney-client privilege and the attorney work product protection serve an extremely important function in the American legal system. The attorney-client privilege is one of the oldest and most sacrosanct privileges under the law. See *Upjohn v. United States*, [p. 670]. As the Supreme Court has stated, "[i]ts purpose is to encourage full and frank communication between attorneys and their clients and thereby promote broader public interests in the observance of law and administration of justice." Id. The value of promoting a corporation's ability to seek frank and comprehensive legal advice is particularly important in the contemporary global business environment, where corporations often face complex and dynamic legal and regulatory obligations imposed by the federal government and also by states and foreign governments. The work product doctrine serves similarly important goals.
>
> For these reasons, waiving the attorney-client and work product protections has never been a prerequisite under the Department's prosecution guidelines for a corporation to be viewed as cooperative. Nonetheless, a wide range of commentators and members of the American legal community and criminal justice system have asserted that the Department's policies have been used, either wittingly or unwittingly, to coerce business entities into waiving attorney-client privilege and work-product protection. Everyone agrees that a corporation may freely waive its own privileges if it chooses to do so; indeed, such waivers occur routinely when corporations are victimized by their employees or others, conduct an internal investigation, and then disclose the details of the investigation to law enforcement officials in an effort to seek prosecution of the offenders. However, the contention, from a broad array of voices, is that the Department's position on attorney-client privilege and work product protection waivers has promoted an

> environment in which those protections are being unfairly eroded to the detriment of all.
>
> The Department understands that the attorney-client privilege and attorney work product protection are essential and long- recognized components of the American legal system. What the government seeks and needs to advance its legitimate (indeed, essential) law enforcement mission is not waiver of those protections, but rather the facts known to the corporation about the putative criminal misconduct under review. In addition, while a corporation remains free to convey non-factual or "core" attorney-client communications or work product—if and only if the corporation voluntarily chooses to do so—prosecutors should not ask for such waivers and are directed not to do so. The critical factor is whether the corporation has provided the facts about the events, as explained further herein.
>
> Eligibility for cooperation credit is not predicated upon the waiver of attorney-client privilege or work product protection. Instead, the sort of cooperation that is most valuable to resolving allegations of misconduct by a corporation and its officers, directors, employees, or agents is disclosure of the relevant facts concerning such misconduct. In this regard, the analysis parallels that for a non-corporate defendant, where cooperation typically requires disclosure of relevant factual knowledge and not of discussions between an individual and his attorneys.
>
> Thus, when the government investigates potential corporate wrongdoing, it seeks the relevant facts. For example, how and when did the alleged misconduct occur? Who promoted or approved it? Who was responsible for committing it? In this respect, the investigation of a corporation differs little from the investigation of an individual. In both cases, the government needs to know the facts to achieve a just and fair outcome. The party under investigation may choose to cooperate by disclosing the facts, and the government may give credit for the party's disclosures. If a corporation wishes to receive credit for such cooperation, which then can be considered with all other cooperative efforts and circumstances in evaluating how fairly to proceed, then the corporation, like any person, must disclose the relevant facts of which it has knowledge.

U.S.A.M. § 9-28.710-720.

4. Voluntary Disclosure as Waiver

Will turning over documents to the government as part of an entity's effort to cooperate with a government investigation serve as a waiver of the work product doctrine? What effect will the disclosure of documents have on subsequent civil actions?

UNITED STATES v. MASSACHUSETTS INSTITUTE OF TECHNOLOGY

129 F.3d 681 (1st Cir. 1997)

BOUDIN, Circuit Judge.

This case concerns an attempt by the Massachusetts Institute of Technology to assert the attorney-client privilege and work-product doctrine in response to a document request by the Internal Revenue Service. The most important issue presented is whether MIT's disclosure of certain of the documents to another government agency caused it to lose the privilege. The background facts are essentially undisputed.

MIT is a famous university with tax-exempt status under 26 U.S.C. § 501(c)(3). In 1993, the IRS conducted an examination of MIT's records to determine whether MIT still qualified for exempt status and to determine whether it was complying with provisions relating to employment taxes and the reporting of unrelated business income. In aid of this examination, the IRS requested from MIT copies of the billing statements of law firms that had represented MIT and minutes of the MIT Corporation and its executive and auditing committees.

In response, MIT supplied the documents requested but redacted information claimed to be covered by the attorney-client privilege or the work-product doctrine or both. In mid-1994 the IRS requested that the redacted information be supplied, and MIT declined. At this point the IRS sought to obtain the same documents in unredacted form from the Defense Contract Audit Agency ("the audit agency"), the auditing arm of the Department of Defense.

It appears that the same billing statements and possibly some or all of the minutes sought by the IRS had earlier been provided to the audit agency pursuant to contracts between MIT and components of the Department of Defense. The audit agency helps entities in the Department of Defense review contract performance to be sure that the government is not overcharged for services. Not surprisingly, the audit agency often reviews the private contractor's books and records.

In November 1994, the audit agency advised the IRS that it would not turn over the documents provided to it by MIT without the latter's consent, which MIT declines to give. The audit agency had made no unconditional promise to keep the documents secret, but its regulations and practices offered MIT some reason to think that indiscriminate disclosure was unlikely. The IRS then served an administrative summons on MIT in December 1994 seeking specific unredacted minutes of nine meetings of the MIT Corporation and auditing and executive committees in 1990 and 1991, and attorneys' billing statements for almost all legal expenses paid or incurred by MIT from July 1, 1990, through June 30, 1991.

When MIT declined to comply, the IRS in early 1996 petitioned the district court to enforce the summons. * * * In January 1997, the district court issued a memorandum and order enforcing the IRS administrative summons as to the unredacted legal bills and the unredacted versions of most of the minutes sought by the IRS. * * *

We begin with the attorney-client privilege. That privilege has been familiarly summed up by Wigmore in a formula that federal courts have often repeated:

> (1) Where legal advice of any kind is sought (2) from a professional legal adviser in his capacity as such, (3) the communications relating to that purpose, (4) made in confidence (5) by the client, (6) are at his instance permanently protected (7) from disclosure by himself or by the legal adviser, (8) except the protection be waived.

8 J. Wigmore, Evidence § 2292, at 554 (McNaughton rev.1961). The government argues, and the district court agreed, that by its disclosure to the audit agency, MIT waived the privilege to whatever extent that it might otherwise have protected the billing statements and various of the minutes.

The attorney-client privilege is well-established and its present rationale straightforward: by safeguarding communications between lawyer and client, it encourages disclosures by client to lawyer that better enable the client to conform his conduct to the requirements of the law and to present legitimate claims or defenses when litigation arises. Waiver issues aside, the contours of the privilege are reasonably stable.

Quite a different scene presents itself when one turns to the problem of "waiver," a loose and misleading label for what is in fact a collection of different rules addressed to different problems. Cases under this "waiver" heading include situations as divergent as an express and voluntary surrender of the privilege, partial disclosure of a privileged document, selective disclosure to some outsiders but not all, and inadvertent overhearings or disclosures.

Even where the cases are limited to those involving a deliberate and voluntary disclosure of a privileged communication to someone other than the attorney or client, the case law is far from settled. But decisions do tend to mark out, although not with perfect consistency, a small circle of "others" with whom information may be shared without loss of the privilege (e.g., secretaries, interpreters, counsel for a cooperating co-defendant, a parent present when a child consults a lawyer).

Although the decisions often describe such situations as ones in which the client "intended" the disclosure to remain confidential, the underlying concern is functional: that the lawyer be able to consult with others needed in the representation and that the client be allowed to bring closely related persons who are appropriate, even if not vital, to a consultation. Cf. Westinghouse Elec. Corp. v. Republic of the Philippines, 951 F.2d 1414 (3d Cir.1991). An intent to maintain confidentiality is ordinarily necessary to continued protection, but it is not sufficient.

On the contrary, where the client chooses to share communications outside this magic circle, the courts have usually refused to extend the privilege. The familiar platitude is that the privilege is narrowly confined because it hinders the courts in the search for truth. Fairness is also a concern where a client is permitted to choose to disclose materials to one outsider while withholding them from another.

Should this inclination not to protect a document disclosed outside the circle apply where, as here, the initial disclosure was to and at the request of a government agency? This problem has presented itself to six circuits. The most common cases have been disclosures of otherwise privileged attorney-client communications to the Securities and Exchange Commission by corporations during voluntary internal investigations or in response to SEC subpoenas. The Eighth Circuit, *en banc* but without more than a paragraph of analysis, treated this kind of disclosure as not comprising a total waiver of the privilege. *See* Diversified Indus., Inc. v. Meredith, 572 F.2d 596 (8th Cir.1978). Subsequently, the Second, Third, Fourth, Federal and D.C. Circuits took the opposite view and ruled that such limited disclosures do destroy the privilege.

The primary argument in favor of the Eighth Circuit position is that loss of the privilege may discourage the frank exchange between attorney and client in future cases, wherever the client anticipates making a disclosure to at least one government agency. We put to one side the interest of the government agency in obtaining voluntary disclosures; such agencies usually have means to secure the information they need and, if not, can seek legislation from Congress. By contrast, the safeguarding of the attorney-client relationship has largely been left to the courts, which have a comparative advantage in assessing consequences in this sphere.

But MIT, like any client, continues to control both the nature of its communications with counsel and the ultimate decision whether to disclose such communications to third parties. The only constraint imposed by the traditional rule here invoked by the government–that disclosure to a third party waives the privilege–is to limit *selective* disclosure, that is, the provision of otherwise privileged communications to one outsider while withholding them from another. MIT has provided no evidence that respecting this constraint will prevent it or anyone else from getting adequate legal advice.

Admittedly, the arguments on the other side are far from overwhelming. The IRS' search for truth will not be much advanced if MIT simply limits or recasts its disclosures to the audit agency. But the general principle that disclosure normally negates the privilege is worth maintaining. To maintain it here makes the law more predictable and certainly eases its administration. Following the Eighth Circuit's approach would require, at the very least, a new set of difficult line-drawing exercises that would consume time and increase uncertainty.

MIT says that even if we are not prepared to follow the Eighth Circuit onto new ground, MIT's disclosure to the audit agency should be regarded as akin to the disclosure by a client's lawyer to another lawyer representing another client engaged in a common defense. Invoking the concept of "common interest," MIT seeks to compare its situation to cases where disclosure has been allowed, without forfeiting the privilege, among separate parties similarly aligned in a case or consultation (e.g., codefendants, insurer and insured, patentee and licensee).

In a rather abstract sense, MIT and the audit agency do have a "common interest" in the proper performance of MIT's defense contracts and the proper auditing and payment of MIT's bills. But this is not the kind of common interest to which the cases refer in recognizing that allied lawyers and clients–who are working together in prosecuting or defending a lawsuit or in certain other legal transactions–can exchange information among themselves without loss of the privilege. To extend the notion to MIT's relationship with the audit agency, which on another level is easily characterized as adversarial, would be to dissolve the boundary almost entirely.

MIT further argues that the disclosure to the audit agency was not "voluntary" because of the practical pressures and the legal constraints to which it was subject as a government contractor. The extent of those pressures and constraints is far from clear, but assuming *arguendo* that they existed, MIT chose to place itself in this position by becoming a government contractor. In short, MIT's disclosure to the audit agency resulted from its own voluntary choice, even if that choice was made at the time it became a defense contractor and subjected itself to the alleged obligation of disclosure.

Anyone who chooses to disclose a privileged document to a third party, or does so pursuant to a prior agreement or understanding, has an incentive to do so, whether for gain or to avoid disadvantage. It would be perfectly possible to carve out some of those disclosures and say that, although the disclosure itself is not necessary to foster attorney-client communications, neither does it forfeit the privilege. With rare exceptions, courts have been unwilling to start down this path–which has no logical terminus–and we join in this reluctance.

We add, finally, a word about reliance and fair warning. MIT may have had some reason to think that the audit agency would not disclose the documents to the IRS (and the agency did not do so). But MIT had far less reason to think that it could disclose documents to the audit agency and still maintain the privilege when IRS then sought the same documents. The choice to disclose may have been reasonable but it was still a foreseeable gamble.

We turn now to the government's cross-appeal. Here, the IRS challenges the district court's refusal to require MIT to produce three specific minutes. The refusal reflected the district court's view that the documents contained privileged material, and that there was no waiver because MIT had not been shown to have disclosed those minutes to the audit agency. On the latter point, MIT effectively concedes error, and properly so.

Where privilege is claimed and the opponent alleges a specific disclosure, the burden of proof is upon the claimant to show nondisclosure wherever that is material to the disposition of the claim. Here, MIT concedes that it cannot prove that the minutes in question were withheld from the audit agency. Instead, it proffers alternative grounds for sustaining the district court's judgment as to these minutes, namely, that the minutes were protected under the attorney-client privilege and the work product doctrine and that these protections were not waived even though the minutes were turned over to the audit agency.

A party may defend a judgment in its favor on any legitimate ground without appealing from the judgment on that issue. Our discussion of the billing statements disposes of MIT's argument that the protection of the attorney-client privilege survived disclosure to the audit agency. We therefore turn to the work product doctrine. * * *

The district court assumed that work product protection did not apply because the minutes were not prepared "in anticipation of litigation," as required by Fed.R.Civ.P. 26(b)(3). MIT argues that the minutes contained substantive information that did represent attorney work product even if the minutes had a more general function. There is little law in this area–partly, one suspects, because work product usually remains embodied in documents unquestionably prepared for litigation or, if given to the client, in documents independently protected by the attorney client privilege.

The government has chosen in its brief to assume that, to the extent that the minutes contained "the mental impressions, conclusions, opinions, or legal theories" of MIT's attorneys, Fed.R.Civ.P. 26(b)(3), the district court erred in concluding that work product lost its protection when repeated in another confidential document not prepared in anticipation of litigation. A Third Circuit precedent supports this assumption, which MIT presses and the government does not resist. See In re Ford Motor Co., 110 F.3d 954 (3d Cir.1997). In view of the government's concession, we will take the point as settled for this case.

Nevertheless, the government claims that any such protection was lost when the minutes were turned over to the audit agency, MIT having conceded that it cannot prove that the minutes were not so disclosed. One might wonder why the standard of waiver for the attorney-client privilege–that any voluntary disclosure outside the magic circle constitutes waiver–would not also apply to the work product doctrine. Equivalent waiver standards would make easier the resolution of evidentiary disputes where, as often happens, the two objections are raised together.

Nonetheless, the cases approach uniformity in implying that work-product protection is not as easily waived as the attorney-client privilege. The privilege, it is said, is designed to protect confidentiality, so that any disclosure outside the magic circle is inconsistent with the privilege; by contrast, work product protection is provided against "adversaries," so only disclosing material in a way inconsistent with keeping it from an adversary waives work product protection. At least five circuits have adopted this rule in some form.

Perhaps such formulations simply beg the question. If one wanted to explain the discrepant outcomes, it might be more persuasive to say that the privilege is strictly confined because it is absolute; on the other hand, work product protection (with certain qualifications) can be overcome by a sufficient showing of need. In all events, it would take better reason than we have to depart from the prevailing rule that disclosure to an adversary, real or potential, forfeits work product protection.

MIT's disclosure to the audit agency was a disclosure to a potential adversary. The disclosures did not take place in the context of a joint litigation where the parties shared a common legal interest. The audit agency was reviewing MIT's expense submissions. MIT doubtless hoped that there would be no actual controversy between it and the Department of Defense, but the potential for dispute and even litigation was certainly there. The cases treat this situation as one in which the work product protection is deemed forfeit.

In closing, it may be helpful to stress that–with regard to both the attorney-client privilege and the work product doctrine–we are concerned only with loss of protection as to the very documents already disclosed to the audit agency. Nothing in this opinion is intended to be directed to the different and difficult question when disclosure of one document warrants forfeiture of protection for a different but related document.

Similarly, even where work product can be discovered, the governing rule directs that "the court shall protect against disclosure of the mental impressions, conclusions, opinions, or legal theories of an attorney or other representative of a party concerning the litigation." Fed.R.Civ.P. 26(b)(3). Conceivably, the strong policy underlying this reservation might serve to protect such materials, even if protection of ordinary work product materials were deemed waived because of selective disclosure. This possibility has not been briefed or argued to us; it may or may not be pertinent in this case; and we mention it only to stress that we are not deciding the issue.

Accordingly, on MIT's appeal, the judgment of the district court is affirmed. On the government's cross-appeal, the judgment of the district court refusing to order production of three specified minutes is vacated, and the matter is remanded to the district court for further proceedings consistent with this opinion.

5. Federal Rule of Evidence 502(d) and Waiver

Does the voluntary disclosure of information to the government always waive the attorney-client privilege and work product protection? Federal Rule of Evidence 502(d) may provide a means for parties to protect confidential information by obtaining a court order. Rule 502(d) provides, "A federal court may order that the privilege or protection is not waived by disclosure connected with the litigation pending before the court — in which event the disclosure is also not a waiver in any other federal or state proceeding." The rule is especially important as electronic discovery has become the primary means of obtaining information in civil cases, and it increasingly seen in white collar crime prosecutions in which large volumes of digital information is sought by the government. Rule 502(b) also provides protection in the case of inadvertent disclosure of communications protected by the attorney-client privilege and materials subject to the work product doctrine. The rule provides that such disclosure does not constitute a waiver so long as "(1) the disclosure is inadvertent; (2) the holder of the privilege or protection took reasonable steps to prevent disclosure; and (3) the holder promptly took reasonable steps to rectify the error, including (if applicable) following Federal Rule of Civil Procedure 26 (b)(5)(B)."

6. Waiving Work Product Protection

Work product is treated differently from privileged communications because the doctrine protects the attorney's thought process and not just client communications. Courts are generally much less willing to find waiver of work product even when the work product is provided to a non-client, so long as the person receiving it is not viewed as an adversary or with interests inimical to the client. The prosecution of Martha Stewart for conspiracy, obstruction of justice, and making false statements raised this issue regarding whether the forwarding of an e-mail from Stewart to her daughter undermined the protection of the work product doctrine for the content of the e-mail. **United States v. Stewart**, 287 F.Supp.2d 461 (S.D.N.Y. 2003).

During the course of the government's investigation, and prior to her indictment, Stewart composed and sent an e-mail to one of her attorneys recounting her recollection regarding the sale of Imclone stock, the subject of the government's investigation. The following day, she forwarded the e-mail to her daughter, Alexis. Stewart prepared and sent the e-mail from her computer at Martha Stewart Living Omnimedia, Inc. (MSLO), and a copy of it was retained on the company's computer server. During the investigation, the government subpoenaed MSLO for documents, including "[a]ll desktop and laptop computers used by Martha Stewart" and certain files located on the company's server. The company submitted the records, withholding the e-mail Stewart sent to her attorney on the ground that it was attorney work product but mistakenly submitted the forwarded e-mail sent the following day to Alexis. After the indictment, the government informed Stewart's attorneys that it had the e-mail and asked whether she asserted that it was protected by the work product doctrine, which she did. In response to the government's argument that forwarding the e-mail to her daughter waived any work product claim, the district court stated:

> By forwarding the e-mail to a family member, Stewart did not substantially increase the risk that the Government would gain access to materials prepared in anticipation of litigation. Martha Stewart stated in her affidavit that "Alexis is the closest person in the world to me. She is a valued confidante and counselor to me. In sharing the e-mail with her, I knew that she would keep its content strictly confidential." Martha Stewart Aff. ¶ 6. Alexis Stewart stated that while she did not recall receiving the June 24 e-mail, she "never would have disclosed its contents." Alexis Stewart Aff. ¶ 2. The disclosure affected neither side's interests in this litigation: it did not evince an intent on Stewart's part to relinquish work product immunity for the document, and it did not prejudice the Government by offering Stewart some litigation-based advantage. Accordingly, I hold that Stewart did not waive work product protection over the June 23 and 24 e-mails.

In **United States v. Ghavami**, 882 F. Supp. 2d 532 (S.D.N.Y. 2012), a magistrate judge found that the attorney-client privilege had been waived but not the work product protection when two targets of an investigation spoke with another person involved in the underlying conduct who they did not know had secretly started cooperating with the government. During the conversations, they recounted legal advice provided by their attorney. The magistrate judge found:

> Work product protection, however, remains intact for the communications at issue. These communications were made in anticipation of litigation. And, while they were revealed to Government Cooperator 1, this did not effect a forfeiture of the protection. Work product protection is waived only if disclosure to a third party substantially increases the risk that it will be obtained by an adversary, in this case the government. This risk must be evaluated from the viewpoint of the party seeking to take advantage of the doctrine. As far as Privilege Claimants 1 and 2 knew, they were disclosing work product not to a government agent, but to a friend who was similarly positioned in relation to the government's investigation and who had seemingly shared his own privileged information with them. To be sure, there is always some danger that

the recipient of work product is, or will later become, an informant. But that cannot constitute a "substantial risk" that the work product would be disclosed to the adversary. If it did, the exception would swallow the rule, and the distinction between waiver of the attorney-client privilege and waiver of work product would be rendered a nullity, at least in the criminal context.

C. CRIME-FRAUD EXCEPTION

1. The Prima Facie Case

A frequently used means for prosecutors to avoid an assertion of the attorney-client privilege and work product doctrine is to argue that the communications were in furtherance of a current or future crime or fraud. The "crime-fraud exception" removes the confidentiality the normally attaches to attorney-client communications and attorney work product. To establish the exception, the traditional rule is that the party seeking to undermine the confidentiality the normally attaches to the communication or work product must establish a prima facie case that the client sought the assistance of the attorney for a present or future crime or fraud, but not a past crime. The attorney need not be a party to the misconduct, but the legal services must be related to the client's wrongdoing. The requirements for establishing a prima facie case that the consultation was in connection with a future crime or fraud are discussed in the following decision.

In re: GRAND JURY INVESTIGATION
445 F.3d 266 (3d Cir. 2006)

SLOVITER, Circuit Judge.

* * * In late 2003, a grand jury began investigating the financial arrangements and business dealings of the individual who we believe may be the Primary Target. Some of his business dealings have apparently been carried out by an entity we call, for want of a better designation, the Organization. The grand jury investigation led to inquiry of Jane Doe, the Executive Director of the Organization, who had, and has, intimate knowledge of and access to the papers and other material of both the Primary Target and the Organization. It appears that Jane Doe is also a target of the grand jury investigation. If she was not at the outset, she certainly has become a target in light of the events with which we are concerned. The Organization, through its counsel ("Attorney"), has entered into a joint-defense agreement with Jane Doe and her counsel in response to the investigation.

On April 27, 2004, the Government issued a grand jury subpoena to the Organization. It requested all documents, including email, from January 1, 1996 to the present, concerning, inter alia: the Organization's document retention and destruction policy; the payment of certain expenses, contributions, or donations to the Primary Target; and all grants, contributions, or donations to the Primary Target. * * *

The Government was unsatisfied with the document production, particularly with respect to what it perceived as the Organization's failure to search for and produce email stored on the Organization's computer hard drives. On January 18, 2005, the Government issued a second subpoena to the Organization, requesting essentially the same documents as in its previous subpoena. In a letter dated January 19, 2005, the Government notified Attorney that it wished to have FBI and IRS experts perform a scan of the Organization's computers to recover stored information, including deleted email files.

On February 10, 2005, pursuant to an agreement among the parties, an FBI computer technician went to the Organization's place of business and "imaged" the hard drive on Jane Doe's computer. The Government thus made an exact copy of the contents of the hard drive, including deleted email files. It uncovered numerous stored messages which could be construed to show a conscious effort by the Organization's staff to destroy emails.

Concerned about the potential obstruction of justice by Jane Doe and others at the Organization, the Government issued a subpoena duces tecum to Attorney on March 1, 2005. It sought to compel grand jury testimony regarding his discussions with Jane Doe as to her compliance (or apparent non-compliance) with the prior subpoenas for production of the Organization's email. The Government also sought production of Attorney's notes concerning his conversation with Jane Doe regarding the Organization's compliance with the two grand jury subpoenas and the January 19, 2005, letter. On March 10, 2005, the Government issued a separate subpoena for production of documents to the custodian of records at Attorney's law firm.

The Government, Attorney and Jane Doe then sought to reach an agreement that would limit the scope of Attorney's testimony before the grand jury. The Government proposed that Attorney testify on five subjects: (1) that he represents the Organization in connection with the April 27, 2004, and January 18, 2005, subpoenas; (2) that he received the January 18, 2005, subpoena and January 19 letter from the Government; (3) that he informed Jane Doe by telephone on January 20, 2005, of his receipt of the January 18 subpoena; (4) that he faxed a cover letter to Jane Doe enclosing the cover letter and subpoena from the Government; and (5) that he advised Jane Doe on January 20 regarding how to comply with the subpoena. Jane Doe voiced no objection to subjects (1)-(4), but she challenged number (5), claiming that Attorney's advice regarding compliance with the subpoena is privileged.

On January 4, 2006, the Government filed a motion to enforce the subpoena and to compel Attorney's testimony. Attorney and Jane Doe were permitted to intervene with regard to the motion, and they filed a motion to quash or to modify the subpoena to the extent that it required disclosure of privileged information.

On January 17, 2006, the District Court held a closed-court hearing on the motions. The Government argued that the crime-fraud exception should overcome the claim of privilege. In support of its position, it submitted an ex parte affidavit from an FBI agent with knowledge of the evidence gathered in the investigation. The District Court also heard testimony from Attorney and from Jane Doe's Attorney (hereinafter "Doe's Attorney"). With the Government absent from the courtroom, the two Attorneys testified essentially to their recollection of the conversations with Jane Doe on January 20, 2005, after receipt of the second subpoena and the Government's cover letter.

The dispute before the District Court was limited to whether Attorney should be compelled to reveal the substance of his January 20, 2005, telephone conversation with Jane Doe and to produce his handwritten notes concerning that conversation. On February 1, 2006, the District Court granted the Government's motion to enforce its subpoena. The Court concluded that although Attorney's advice regarding the subpoena is protected by the attorney-client privilege, and his notes are covered by the work-product doctrine, disclosure was appropriate in light of the crime-fraud exception. Based on its review of the Government's ex parte affidavit, the District Court found sufficient evidence that Jane Doe was in the process of committing obstruction of justice at the time of her January 20 conversation with Attorney, and used the information provided by Attorney in furtherance of the crime.

The Government promptly scheduled Attorney's appearance before the grand jury. The District Court denied a stay pending appeal. Jane Doe timely appealed, and this court also denied a stay. On February 7, 2006, Attorney provided the requested documents and testified before the grand jury.

* * * [Jane Doe] argues that the District Court's order enforcing and refusing to quash the subpoena to Attorney undermines the attorney-client privilege because the subpoena seeks to ascertain the contents of her conversation with Attorney on January 20, 2005. Although Jane Doe retained a personal lawyer, her lawyer and Attorney (who represents the Organization) entered into a joint defense agreement, and therefore the attorney-client privilege is applicable. In any event, the Supreme Court has held that communication between a corporation's counsel and the employees of the corporation are covered by the attorney-client privilege. Upjohn Co. v. United States, 449 U.S. 383 (1981).

The Court stated that the attorney-client privilege is the "oldest of the privileges for confidential communications known." "[C]ourts long have viewed [the privilege's] central concern as one 'to encourage full and frank communication between attorneys and their clients and thereby promote broader public interests in the observance of law and administration of justice.'" United States v. Zolin, 491 U.S. 554 (1989) (quoting *Upjohn*).

Despite the importance of the attorney-client privilege in the administration of justice, the Supreme Court in *Zolin* commented on the costs of the privilege in that it "has the effect of withholding relevant information from the factfinder." Therefore, the privilege can be overridden if the client used the lawyer's services to further a continuing or future crime or fraud.

Jane Doe argues that the crime-fraud exception is inapplicable in this case because she did not initiate the communication with Attorney or solicit any advice. She relies on the language in Doe, where this court stated, "[o]nly when a client knowingly seeks legal counsel to further a continuing or future crime does the crime-fraud exception apply." United States v. Doe, 429 F.3d 450 (3d Cir. 2005).

That sentence in the *Doe* opinion reflects the facts in that case, i.e., the client, a law enforcement officer, initiated the communication with the attorney and sought his advice as to how to circumvent the prohibition against investing in a witness's business. Nothing in that opinion, or in any opinion, suggests that the crime-fraud exception applies only if the client initiates the conversation.

To the contrary, the crime-fraud exception is equally applicable in situations where there has been a prior attorney-client relationship and the communication at issue was made in the context of that relationship. There would be no reason to limit the applicability of the crime-fraud exception to client-initiated contact, as the exception's purpose is to further frank and open exchanges between the client and his or her attorney, whether newly retained for purposes of the investigation or otherwise.

The burden to make the necessary showing for the crime-fraud exception falls on the party who seeks application of the exception. In criminal cases, it is the Government that seeks to invoke the crime-fraud exception to counter a defendant's effort to prevent disclosure of certain testimony or documents on the ground of the attorney-client privilege. Therefore, it is the Government that must bear the initial burden. We have described the showing that must be made as follows:

> [T]he government must make a prima facie showing that (1) the client was committing or intending to commit a fraud or crime, and (2) the attorney-client communications were in furtherance of that alleged crime or fraud. A "prima facie showing" requires presentation of "evidence which, if believed by the fact-finder, would be sufficient to support a finding that the elements of the crime-fraud exception were met."

In re Grand Jury Subpoena, 223 F.3d 213 (3d Cir. 2000).[a]

In Clark v. United States, 289 U.S. 1 (1933), the Supreme Court, in describing the evidentiary standard for the application of the crime-fraud exception, stated:

> There must be a showing of a prima facie case sufficient to satisfy the judge that the light should be let in . . To drive the [attorney-client] privilege away, there must be "something to give colour to the charge"; there must be "prima facie evidence that it has some foundation in fact." When that evidence is supplied, the seal of secrecy is broken.

The burden is not a particularly heavy one. As the Court of Appeals for the Seventh Circuit stated, prima facie evidence cannot mean "enough to support a verdict in favor of the person making the claim." In re Feldberg, 862 F.2d 622 (7th Cir. 1988).

In this case, the District Court found that at the time of Jane Doe's January 20, 2005 conversation with Attorney, Jane Doe was committing the crime of obstruction of justice. The Court's finding that the Government met its burden of presenting evidence demonstrating a reasonable basis to suspect the perpetration of a crime, if based on adequate evidence, satisfies the first prong of the crime-fraud exception.

The District Court based its finding on the evidence before it, which included the ex parte affidavit provided by the Government. The Supreme Court has made clear that the district courts may use ex parte evidence supplied by the Government in order to make the required findings. *Zolin*

In *Zolin*, the IRS sought to use two tape recordings produced in an earlier case to make the required showing that the crime-fraud exception overcame the claimed attorney-client privilege. The Court of Appeals for the Ninth Circuit had opined that the determination of the applicability of the crime-fraud exception must be based on "sources independent of the attorney-client communications recorded on the tapes." In holding that was error, the Supreme Court stated that "a rigid independent evidence requirement does not comport with 'reason and experience,'. . . that in camera review may be used to determine whether allegedly privileged attorney-client

---

[a] Some circuits appear to apply a lower threshold for establishing the crime or fraud to vitiate the privilege. For example, the First Circuit stated that "it is enough to overcome the privilege that there is a reasonable basis to believe that the lawyer's services were used by the client to foster a crime or fraud." In re Grand Jury Proceedings, 417 F.3d 18 (1st Cir. 2005). The Ninth Circuit stated that a prima facie case is established when "[r]easonable cause existed to believe that the attorney was used in furtherance of an ongoing scheme." In re Grand Jury Proceedings, 87 F.3d 377 (9th Cir. 1996).

communications fall within the crime-fraud exception," and that the party opposing the privilege "must present evidence sufficient to support a reasonable belief that in camera review may yield evidence that establishes the exception's applicability."

In accordance with *Zolin*, the District Court here used the affidavit of the FBI agent to support its finding that at the time of Jane Doe's January 20, 2005 conversation with Attorney, Jane Doe was committing the crime of obstruction of justice by participating in a scheme to delete emails on the computers of the Organization, its officers, and staff. That this was the crime on which the Government hinged its arguments with respect to the crime-fraud exception was made clear in the Assistant U.S. Attorney's arguments before this court.

In conducting our review of the District Court's finding, we too must base our decision on the evidence submitted to the District Court ex parte. We are hampered in articulating the basis for our conclusion by the need to keep the evidentiary support confidential because much of the relevant information that was before the District Court is sealed as it pertains to the ongoing investigation of the grand jury. Moreover, the parties' briefs have been sealed. We are therefore comfortable to discuss only such facts as the Assistant U.S. Attorney disclosed in his argument in open court before us.

Based on our review, we agree that there was sufficient evidence to support the District Court's finding that Jane Doe could be found to have engaged in the ongoing crime of obstruction of justice. That does not mean we believe there is sufficient evidence to support a jury verdict to that effect beyond a reasonable doubt. However, there is enough evidence to meet the first prong of the crime-fraud standard.

* * * This court's precedential opinions have repeatedly set forth the crime-fraud test as requiring that the communication have been "in furtherance" of the crime, not only in In re Grand Jury Subpoena, but more recently in Doe. * * * Of significance, despite the District Court's articulation of the more relaxed "related to" standard, in fact the District Court made the requisite finding under the "in furtherance of the crime" standard.

When questioned by this court at the oral argument as to how the Attorney-Jane Doe conversation furthered the crime of obstruction of justice, the Assistant U.S. Attorney used as an example a baseball player who seeks information about a grand jury investigation of the illegal use of steroids. He posited a player who "receive[d] a subpoena that directly asks for documents related to his potential criminal use of illegal drugs. And in the course of that he does, takes certain steps to prevent the documents from being turned over, for example, by destroying them." One may infer from his use of that example that the obstruction of justice that the Government is investigating is the deletion of potentially relevant email files with knowledge of their relevance to the grand jury's investigation.

In this era, when communications between leaders of business organizations are transmitted to their employees by email rather than by phone or mail, examination of those emails is the method most commonly used by government investigators. That is evident to those engaged in the criminal or fraudulent activity that is the subject of the investigation. It should therefore come as no surprise that efforts to forestall such investigations frequently take the form of deletion of past emails. See, e.g., Arthur Andersen LLP v. United States, 544 U.S. 696 (2005).

* * * Concededly, there are no opinions of which we are aware that apply the crime-fraud exception in precisely these circumstances. However, we see no reason why it does not apply. The Assistant U.S. Attorney stated, or it can be inferred from his statements at oral argument, that in the course of the communication between Jane Doe and Attorney, Attorney advised Jane Doe of the contents of the most recent subpoena and of the Government's interest in retrieving from Organization's computers emails to or from certain persons, including Jane Doe, who were or are connected with the Organization. Apparently, the ongoing deletion of email included information stored on the hard drive of Jane Doe's own computer. There is no suggestion that Attorney did anything improper in transmitting this communication to Jane Doe and providing legal advice on how to respond. Nor is there any suggestion that Attorney was aware of either past wrongdoing or potential future wrongdoing.

If, with knowledge of the Government's interest in retrieving any remaining emails, Jane Doe continued to receive emails that were arguably responsive to the subpoena and failed to use her position as an executive of the Organization to direct that all email deletions stop immediately, she may be viewed as furthering the obstruction of the grand jury's investigation or the obstruction of justice. Certainly, the temporal proximity of the ongoing deletion of emails after January 20 could be viewed as an additional indication that Jane Doe intended to use the information she gathered from the January 20 communication to further the scheme to obstruct. In any event, if Jane Doe learned of the Government's interest in certain documents from her conversation with Attorney on January 20, 2005 and subsequently acquiesced in the deletion or destruction of those documents, the second prong of the crime-fraud exception would be satisfied.

According to the Assistant U.S. Attorney's statements at the oral argument, Jane Doe's communication with Attorney on January 20 made it clear what the Government wanted and what was called for in response to the subpoenas. As we previously noted, the Government does not bear a heavy burden in showing that Jane Doe misused her communication with Attorney in furtherance of an improper purpose. As one court has observed, "The government does not have to show that the intended crime or fraud was accomplished, only that the lawyer's advice or other services were misused. Typically that can be shown by evidence of some activity following the improper consultation, on the part of either the client or the lawyer, to advance the intended crime or fraud." In re Public Defender Serv., 831 A.2d 890 (D.C. 2003).

* * * The District Court here was required to, and did, closely scrutinize the Government's evidence, and it also received in camera evidence proffered by Attorney and Doe's Attorney regarding the substance of the January 20 communication. Although the District Court was compelled by the secrecy of the grand jury proceeding to redact its substantive analysis from the version of its Opinion that it released to the parties, an unredacted version of its Opinion has been provided to this court. Based on our review of the same evidentiary record and the District Court's thoughtful analysis, we see no abuse of discretion in the District Court's decision to enforce the subpoena to Attorney.

2. Attorney Complicity

While the crime-fraud exception is usually raised to obtain otherwise privileged communications, it can also be used to overcome a claim that materials are protected by the work product doctrine. The question in that situation is whether the client's crime or fraud should vitiate the protections afforded to the attorney's work product, especially opinion work product. An issue in some crime-fraud exception cases is the extent of a lawyer's complicity in the client's misconduct. This issue is particularly important for obtaining attorney work product because the lawyer has a separate basis to claim the protection apart from the client. At what point does a lawyer's legal advice make that person part of the client's underlying crime or fraud? Consider how the Eighth Circuit analyzed the issue in the following case:

IN RE GRAND JURY PROCEEDINGS, G.S., F.S.,
609 F.3d 909 (8th Cir. 2010)

This case involves a grand jury investigation for bankruptcy fraud. In order to observe the requirements of grand jury secrecy, we provide only a limited recitation of the facts. Clients G.S. and F.S. are Iowa residents who owned several businesses that started experiencing financial difficulty around 2001. Recognizing that they would likely be unable to meet all of their financial obligations, G.S. and F.S. began planning to file for bankruptcy protection. In late 2001 they sought legal advice from attorney J.P., who had substantial experience in the area of bankruptcy law. G.S. and F.S. subsequently changed their residence from Iowa to Florida, a state which allows debtors to exempt more of their assets from the bankruptcy estate.

When G.S. and F.S. first met with J.P., they had a number of non-exempt assets that would have potentially been subject to liquidation by the bankruptcy trustee to pay their creditors, including thousands of dollars worth of household furniture, jewelry, various stock holdings, and a contract from the sale of a business that entitled them to payments of approximately

$300,000 over seven years. G.S. and F.S. sought J.P.'s advice in divesting themselves of these assets and converting the proceeds into assets that would be exempt from the bankruptcy estate. In documents that we have reviewed *in camera*, J.P. warned his clients about avoiding bankruptcy fraud, counseling them concerning the dangers of engaging in insider transactions with close relatives and recovering assets post-bankruptcy. J.P. advised G.S. and F.S., for example, that they should not sell their furniture to G.S.'s father and keep it in their home, as the circumstances would suggest a sham transaction that bore badges of fraud. J.P. also cautioned against involving G.S.'s father in a transaction in which non-exempt stock would be pledged as collateral for a loan, telling G.S. that "I strongly advised your father to have nothing to do with this transaction."

Notwithstanding this advice, G.S. and F.S. divested themselves of nearly all of their non-exempt assets by selling or loaning them to close family members. The furniture, jewelry, business contract, and some of the stock holdings were sold to G.S.'s parents. The remaining stock was pledged to another relative, H.B., in exchange for a $52,000 loan. Because H.B. did not have money to make the loan, however, G.S.'s father gave her $52,000 to give to G.S., and attorney J.P. assisted with the transaction. G.S. and F.S. deposited the proceeds from these various transactions into life insurance policies that were exempt from the bankruptcy estate. In March 2003, a little over a year after the transactions had been completed, G.S. and F.S. began bankruptcy proceedings in Florida.

After the bankruptcy was complete, G.S. and F.S. returned to Iowa and recovered their original assets, repurchasing them from their relatives for the prices at which the assets had been sold. The Federal Bureau of Investigation subsequently began investigating G.S. and F.S. for bankruptcy fraud. In connection with the investigation, the government sought to compel the production of documents and testimony relating to J.P.'s representation of G.S. and F.S. prior to their bankruptcy proceedings. Attorney J.P. invoked the attorney-client and work product privileges and refused to testify or surrender documents to the government. G.S. and F.S. moved to intervene. After an *in camera* review of the relevant testimony and documents, the district court concluded that the subpoenaed evidence fell within the crime-fraud exception to the asserted privileges and ordered J.P. to appear before the grand jury. * * *

The ability of an attorney to resist discovery of his or her own work product involves a somewhat different analysis [from the attorney-client privilege], because it is based on the attorney's interest in protecting his opinions and thought processes from disclosure. In analyzing the extent of an attorney's own work product privilege, we distinguish between two types of work product. Non-opinion work product is generally discoverable upon a showing of substantial need and an inability to secure the substantial equivalent of the materials by alternate means without undue hardship. Opinion work product–which encompasses a lawyer's opinions, conclusions, mental impressions, and legal theories–is afforded substantially more protection. An attorney who is not complicit in his client's wrongdoing may assert the work product privilege with respect to his opinion work product. Thus, even when an attorney's clients have used the attorney's services to commit a crime or fraud, the government cannot compel production of an attorney's opinion work product if the attorney was unaware of his client's wrongful activities. * * *

[The appeals court upheld the district judge's finding that there was sufficient evidence to establish a prima facie case of a crime or fraud perpetrated as part of the bankruptcy.] Even if certain individual transactions might have been permissible standing alone, as the appellants argue, when taken together these activities evince a pattern of conduct that may have gone beyond legitimate pre-bankruptcy exemption planning. Further, some of the transfers appeared to be specifically designed to conceal the true nature of the underlying transactions, as when G.S.'s father gave another relative, H.B., $52,000 so that she could loan the money to G.S., with his nonexempt stock holdings serving as collateral. The circumstances suggest that G.S. and F.S. may have avoided a more direct transaction with G.S.'s father because they feared that an intra-familial loan would arouse the suspicion of the bankruptcy trustee.

Attorney J.P. separately resists the government's discovery of his work product related to representation of G.S. and F.S. In light of our holding regarding the possible misconduct of J.P.'s clients in close connection with J.P.'s legal advice, we conclude that the government has shown a substantial need for J.P.'s non-opinion work product. That evidence may contain information critical to the government's case should this matter proceed to a criminal trial, for the government would likely need to prove both the exact nature of the transactions and the clients' intent at the time that they were undertaken. Because the appellants do not contend that the government can obtain the materials through any other means, we also conclude that the district court did not err in compelling production of non-opinion work product.

The district court determined that J.P.'s opinion work product was discoverable because there was probable cause to believe J.P. was complicit in his clients' unlawful activity. We conclude that the district court did not abuse its discretion in making this finding. J.P.'s prior experience in the area of bankruptcy law should have made obvious to him the distinction between legitimate exemption planning and bankruptcy fraud. As noted previously, in documents that we have reviewed in camera, J.P. expressed concern to his clients about the legality of transferring assets to close relatives and retrieving the transferred assets post-bankruptcy.[4] Although J.P. warned his

[4] J.P.'s experience arguably should have also apprised him of the fact that a bankruptcy court could find fraud in his clients' attempt to shield virtually all of their assets from creditors while seeking the bankruptcy court's help in discharging a substantial amount of debt.

clients that G.S.'s father should not be involved in the stock transfer in which some of G.S.'s non-exempt stock was pledged as collateral for a loan, J.P. later apparently ignored his own advice and helped facilitate the questionable transaction.

There is also a reasonable likelihood that J.P. either knew or was willfully blind to the fact that his clients were entering sham transactions with relatives so that they could later retrieve their original assets after discharging their debts. The appellants contend that J.P. had no knowledge of his clients' plans once the bankruptcy proceedings were complete. The documents that we have reviewed, however, suggest that J.P. was aware that G.S. and F.S. were contemplating strategies for reacquiring at least some of their assets at a later time. In spite of his apparent knowledge that this scheme could be illegal, J.P. continued to assist G.S. and F.S. in parking their assets with close family. Giving the district court's determination the deference to which it is entitled, we hold that the court did not abuse its discretion in finding that there was probable cause to believe that J.P. was complicit in his clients' crime or fraud. Accordingly, the district court properly held that J.P. could not assert the work product privilege with regard to his representation of G.S. and F.S. in matters related to their bankruptcy.

BYE, Circuit Judge, concurring in part and dissenting in part.

I join in the Court's decision * * * affirming the district court's application of the crime-fraud exception to the attorney-client privilege. However, I would conclude the district court erred in its application of the crime-fraud exception to J.P.'s assertion of the work product privilege because of the great protection afforded opinion work product. * * *

Historically, a lawyer's mental impressions, conclusions, opinions, and legal theories have been afforded substantial protection in order to secure the lawyer's effective advocacy and representation of his or her clients' interests. * * *

I do not believe the instant matter presents the "rare and extraordinary" case where J.P.'s opinion work product may be discovered because there has not been a compelling showing justifying such a demanding intrusion. Even if the government established a prima facie case that G.S. and F.S. were engaged in criminal activity, and they used J.P.'s advice in furtherance of that activity, the government failed to establish J.P. himself knowingly participated in any criminal activity.

Notably, the district court relies on J.P.'s knowledge of the $52,000 stock transfer from G.S. to H.B. in support of its determination to compel production of J.P.'s opinion work product. However, contrary to the government's assertion, it appears this transaction was merely a loan whereby the stock was pledged as collateral in order for G.S. to maintain his lifetime healthcare coverage associated with the stock. The stock remained an asset of G.S., and therefore an asset of the bankruptcy estate, which was explicitly disclosed on both the personal property and secured creditor schedules attached to G. S.'s bankruptcy filing. Moreover, a review *in camera*, at best, demonstrates J.P. helped G.S. effectuate the loan; it does not establish J.P. assisted G.S. or F.S. in wrongly reacquiring the stock, or any other assets, post-bankruptcy. J.P. testified he was not aware G.S. reacquired the stock until the day of his grand jury testimony. Indeed, there is no dispute J.P.'s representation ceased prior to G.S. and F.S. filing for bankruptcy, a task which was accomplished for them utilizing another lawyer.

The above circumstances demonstrate J.P.'s conduct appears more aligned with legitimate exemption planning than fraudulent activity. It is well settled that the mere conversion of non-exempt assets to exempt assets is not in itself fraudulent. Given the near absolute immunity afforded opinion work product, I believe the government failed to present a compelling showing that J.P. was knowingly complicit in any criminal activity. In cases such as this, I believe the freedom from intrusion lawyers enjoy and require for their opinion work product must be protected in order to best serve their clients' interests and maintain the integrity of our legal system. Accordingly, I would conclude the district court erred by applying the crime-fraud exception.

3. Ex Parte and In Camera Submissions

In **Zolin v. United States**, 491 U.S. 554 (1989), the Supreme Court explained that a court considering a crime-fraud claim may review the purported communication to determine whether it was made in connection with an ongoing or future crime or fraud. Disclosure to the judge would not eviscerate the privilege because only the court reviews it, thus maintaining the confidentiality of the communication. The Court explained the standard under which a court can compel the ex parte and in camera submission of the privilege communication:

> Before engaging in in camera review to determine the applicability of the crime-fraud exception, "the judge should require a showing of a factual basis adequate to support a good faith belief by a reasonable person," Caldwell v. District Court, 644 P.2d 26, 33 (Colo.1982), that in camera review of the materials may reveal evidence to establish the claim that the crime-fraud exception applies.

In criminal cases, the crime-fraud exception will often involve information gathered by a grand jury, which is subject to the secrecy requirement of Federal Rule of Criminal Procedure 6(e) that prohibits disclosure of matters occurring before the grand jury. Prosecutors often make their own ex parte and in camera submissions of such material to establish the prima facie case for the crime-fraud exception, or to show the factual basis to support a good faith belief under Zolin. Defendants object because they are not appraised of the information and so cannot respond to assertions about which they are kept in the dark. Courts do not require disclosure, however, as explained in **In re Vargas**, 723 F.2d 1461(C.A. 10th 1983):

> The petitioner claims that the trial court usurped its power by finding that the attorney-client privilege was not applicable. The privilege does not apply where the client consults an attorney to further a crime or fraud. Petitioner correctly argues that the government must do more than allege that an attorney is a target of a grand jury investigation to vitiate the privilege. Before the privilege is lost there must be prima facie evidence that the allegation of attorney participation in a crime or fraud has some foundation in fact. Petitioner, however, argues that certain procedures must be followed, including an opportunity for the attorney and client to rebut the prima facie evidence and to be present at any hearing which is intended to establish such a prima facie foundation. Petitioner misconstrues the law in this circuit. As this court held in its opinion In re September 1975 Grand Jury Term, 532 F.2d 734 (10th Cir.1976), "[t]he determination of whether the government shows a prima facie foundation in fact for the charge which results in the subpoena lies in the sound discretion of the trial court." In particular, that determination can be made ex-parte and a "preliminary minitrial" is not necessary. Furthermore, the prima facie foundation may be made by documentary evidence or good faith statements by the prosecutor as to testimony already received by the grand jury. * * * [I]t is clear that there was no abuse of discretion.

4. Rebutting the Prima Facie Case

As discussed in *In re Grand Jury Subpoenas*, a significant problem for defense counsel in rebutting a crime-fraud claim in a grand jury investigation is the secrecy rule of Federal Rule of Criminal Procedure 6(e). The government frequently invokes the Rule to limit the material disclosed to the subpoena recipient in its filings arguing that there is a prima facie case of a crime or fraud. Defense counsel may be in the dark as to exactly what crime or fraud is alleged to have occurred, and when it took place. Courts have been unwilling to require disclosure to the subpoena recipients of the government's information that relates to its grand jury investigation, as discussed in **In re Grand Jury Subpoena**, 223 F.3d 213 (3d Cir. 2000).

> The attorney who was subpoenaed has represented the target for more than a year in connection with the criminal investigation. The government subpoenaed the attorney "as a witness in the investigation" of his client. The attorney moved to quash the grand

jury subpoena, asserting that testimony and production of documents concerning the subject matter specified in the subpoena would result in disclosure of privileged attorney-client communications and work product material * * *.

Given the acknowledged need for secrecy in grand jury proceedings, we reject Appellant's argument that the 'unique facts and circumstances in this case,' including the length of time the investigation has been pending and the fact that the nature of the investigation has already been made public in several contexts, required the District Court to order disclosure of the government's ex parte affidavit. As we have stated, the ex parte affidavit includes excerpts of witness testimony and documents obtained during the investigation, which is ongoing. We conclude that the District Court did not abuse its discretion in denying Appellant and/or his attorney access to this information to protect grand jury secrecy.

Our decision is in accord with those of the other federal courts of appeal that have already addressed this precise issue and rejected due process claims made under virtually identical facts. For example, in In re Grand Jury Subpoenas, 144 F.3d 653 (10th Cir.1998), the former president and chief executive officer of a hospital who was among various targets of a grand jury investigation appealed the order denying his motion to quash a grand jury subpoena directed to the hospital's counsel, with whom he had a personal attorney-client relationship. The Court of Appeals held there was no abuse of discretion or due process violation by the district court's refusal to disclose the ex parte government affidavit from which it determined that the crime-fraud exception applied.

Similarly, when faced with the argument by grand jury targets that their due process rights were violated by their inability to inspect and rebut the ex parte affidavit submitted by the government in support of its invocation of the crime-fraud exception to the attorney-client privilege, the Second Circuit held that they were properly denied access. In re John Doe, Inc., 13 F.3d 633 (2d Cir.1994). The court also stated that "[i]n light of the district court's legitimate concern that the secrecy of the grand jury be preserved, its in camera examination of the attorney was the most effective method of determining that the crime-fraud exception had been established." See also In re Grand Jury Subpoena as to C97-216, 187 F.3d 996 (8th Cir.1999) (court of appeals found no error and rejected argument that due process was violated by district court's reliance on ex parte affidavit to decide government made a threshold showing sufficient to justify an in camera hearing to determine whether the crime-fraud exception applied); In re Grand Jury Proceedings, Thursday Special Grand Jury September Term, 1991, 33 F.3d 342 (4th Cir.1994) (same general holding); In re Grand Jury Proceedings, 867 F.2d 539 (9th Cir.1989) (same); In re Special

> September 1978 Grand Jury (II), 640 F.2d 49, 57 (7th Cir.1980) (same).
>
> We today join the ranks of our sister circuits in holding that it is within the district courts' discretion, and not violative of due process, to rely on an ex parte government affidavit to determine that the crime-fraud exception applies and thus compel a target-client's subpoenaed attorney to testify before the grand jury.
>
> We do so confident that the district courts will vigorously test the factual and legal bases for any subpoena, and a court which questions the sufficiency of the affidavits has available various avenues of inquiry, among them discovery, in camera inspection, additional affidavits and a hearing. In the last analysis, however, we must rely on the district courts' discretion and appellate review of the exercise of that discretion to ensure that the power of the grand jury is not abused while preserving the secrecy that is a necessary element of the grand jury process.

D. JOINT DEFENSE AGREEMENTS

In United States v. Moss, 9 F.3d 543 (6th Cir. 1993), the court noted that "[a] joint defense extension of the attorney client privilege has been applied to confidential communications shared between co-defendants which are part of an on-going and joint effort to set up a common defense strategy. The burden to establish the applicability of the privilege is upon the defendants." The court described the purpose of the application of the privilege in this context in John Morrell & Co. v. Local Union 304A, 913 F.2d 544 (8th Cir. 1989):

> [W]hen information is exchanged between various co-defendants and their attorneys [,] . . . this exchange is not made for the purpose of allowing unlimited publication and use, but rather, the exchange is made for the limited purpose of assisting in their common cause. It is fundamental that the joint defense privilege cannot be waived without the consent of all parties to the defense.

The Joint Defense Privilege is an extension of the attorney-client privilege to a special situation where multiple parties can achieve significant benefits by pooling their resources, including the representation of counsel. Although the privilege claim is often based on a written agreement among the parties, that is not a necessary condition for a court to recognize that communications are privileged. A significant issue can be when the common interest among the parties arose.

In re: SANTA FE INTERNATIONAL CORPORATION

272 F.3d 705 (5th Cir. 2001)

DENNIS, Circuit Judge.

* * * Plaintiffs, who are present and former offshore drilling workers for Santa Fe and some twenty-one other offshore drilling corporations, filed this action on August 14, 2000, naming those companies as defendants. The complaint alleges that the defendants secretly met over the past ten years to set, stabilize, maintain, or limit the wages and benefits paid to offshore drilling employees. The plaintiffs seek certification of a class of such employees, damages for defendants' alleged antitrust violations, and a permanent injunction to prevent such conduct in the future. * * *

Turning our attention directly to Santa Fe's claim for protection under the "common legal interest" extension of the attorney-client privilege ("CLI privilege"), we conclude that it has no merit. * * *

According to our circuit precedents, the two types of communications protected under the CLI privilege are: (1) communications between co-defendants in actual litigation and their counsel; and (2) communications between *potential* co-defendants and their counsel. With respect to the latter category, the term "potential" has not been clearly defined. However, because the privilege is "an obstacle to truthseeking," it must "be construed narrowly to effectuate necessary consultation between legal advisers and clients." In re LTV Sec. Litig., 89 F.R.D. 595 (N.D.Tex.1981).

Considering that caveat, and in looking at other cases discussing the CLI privilege in this circuit, it appears that there must be a palpable threat of litigation at the time of the communication, rather than a mere awareness that one's questionable conduct might some day result in litigation, before communications between one possible future co-defendant and another, such as the ones here made between one horizontal competitor and another, could qualify for protection. * * *

In the present case, Santa Fe admits in the motion for reconsideration it filed in the district court that the communications it claims are protected by the privilege were not made in anticipation of future litigation. Instead, the documents were "circulated for the purpose of ensuring compliance with the antitrust laws and minimizing any potential risk associated with the exchange of wage and benefit information." In sharing the communications, therefore, they sought to avoid conduct that might lead to litigation. They were not preparing for future litigation. Furthermore, Santa Fe denied, in its responses to the plaintiffs' requests for admissions, that it anticipated or perceived a threat of antitrust litigation against it in May of 1991, when Santa Fe's senior counsel prepared the memorandum that was distributed to the company's competitors. Considering that the original complaint in this case was not filed until August 14, 2000, we cannot say that the district court clearly erred in its implicit finding of fact that Santa Fe's disclosures to third persons of the 1991 memorandum were not made for the purpose of preparing a joint defense to lawsuits based on pre-1991 antitrust law violations. * * *

Here, the lack of any temporal connection to actual or threatened litigation is striking. Had these Defendants been jointly defending a suit, as opposed to merely discussing concerns, the long elapse of time would not bear so heavily on the Court's inquiry. But, when the threat of litigation is merely a thought rather than a palpable reality, the joint discussion is more properly characterized as a common business undertaking, which is unprivileged, and certainly not a common legal interest. There is no justification within the reasonable bounds of the attorney-client privilege for horizontal competitors to exchange legal information, which allegedly contains confidences, in the absence of an actual, or imminent, or at least directly foreseeable, lawsuit.

As the district court's reasons suggest, the record in this case is neither clear nor indisputable with respect to Santa Fe's motive for sending its in-house counsel's memorandum to its horizontal offshore drilling competitors. It is possible that the disclosures were made to facilitate future price fixing in violation of the antitrust laws, as the plaintiffs contend.[9] Alternatively, the disclosures were perhaps made in the sole interest of preventing future antitrust violations, as the defendants argue in their motion for reconsideration, in which case they hardly could be seen as the commencement of an allied litigation effort. Furthermore, it is difficult to find that the disclosures were made for the purpose of forming a common defense against alleged prior violations of the antitrust laws, in view of Santa Fe's stout denials that in 1991 it anticipated or perceived a threat of future antitrust litigation.

The ambiguity of the record and the cloudiness of the crucial legal concept involved strongly militate in favor of the conclusion that, if the district court erred at all, it certainly was not clearly and indisputably wrong in finding that Santa Fe's disclosures of its in-house counsel's memorandum to its horizontal competitors were not communications protected under any attorney-client privilege to which Santa Fe was entitled.

SMITH, Circuit Judge, dissenting.

[Judge Smith dissented on a number of grounds. On the issue of the Joint Defense Privilege, he stated:] As long as Santa Fe shows that the documents were given in confidence and that the communication regarded a common legal interest with respect to the subject matter of the communication–both assertions that Santa Fe says it can satisfy–the district court should not order production. * * *

---

[9] If so, they would fall outside the scope of any attorney-client privilege as communications made for criminal or fraudulent purposes.

Neither we nor the district court knows whether the documents are privileged. Neither the district court nor this court has viewed the documents. It may be that some are privileged and some are not. All that is recorded in the transcript of March 9 is Santa Fe's statement that they are privileged and the district court's decree that they are not.

More analysis is needed before any such documents should be ordered produced. Instead, however, the district court ordered all the documents, from all the defendants, to be turned over at once.

NOTES AND QUESTIONS

1. ***Joint Knowledge.*** One potential danger of using a joint defense agreement is that the government can try to defend its failure to produce *Brady* materials to all of the parties on the ground that since one of the participants was aware of the witness about whom the materials related, the entire defense team should be deemed to have been made aware. Thus, the burden is put on other defense counsel to exercise due diligence to find the materials the government failed to provide to each individually.

2. ***Nature of the Agreement.*** In most cases, the parties have a writer or express verbal agreement to conduct a joint defense. Careful defense counsel will want the terms of the agreement spelled out in order to protect the client in case one member of the joint defense decides to cooperate with the government. But an agreement can be implied from the conduct of parties, as the Ninth Circuit found in United States v. Gonzalez, 669 F.3d 974 (9th Cir. 2012). The circuit court noted that "the existence of a JDA is not necessarily an all-or-nothing proposition, and may be created (and ended) by conduct as well as express agreement. The timeline of events and the facts of this case could suggest that a JDA existed at the outset between the parties and their counsel, but that it had ended at least by the time Gonzalez decided to pursue his own defense and blame Paiz for the crime (thus ending their common legal interests)."

3. ***Pre-Agreement Communications.*** In United States v. Weissman, 195 F.3d 96 (2nd Cir. 1999), a corporate officer made "damaging admissions regarding his own conduct" to corporate counsel, under the belief that the statements were protected by the privilege because there was a Joint Defense Agreement. The Second Circuit upheld the district court's finding that the statements were not protected because the parties had not yet entered into the Joint Defense Agreement, crediting the testimony of corporate counsel that they had not yet reached an agreement over the recollection of the witness' counsel that such an agreement had been reached.

The key issue in *Santa Fe Corporation* was the timing of the communication. As the litigation gets closer, does the attorney-client privilege extend to communications made to an attorney at a pre-representation meeting? What if individuals with common defenses approach the attorney together? In **In re Grand Jury Proceedings Jean Auclair**, 961 F.2d 65 (5th Cir. 1992), the court stated:

> * * * The Model Rules of Professional Conduct, which replaced the earlier Code of Professional Responsibility, require an attorney to evaluate the relevant facts, circumstances, and parties to determine the appropriateness and propriety of assent to representation. "A lawyer should not accept representation in a matter unless it can be performed . . . without improper conflict of interest." Of critical importance to a meaningful pre-representation interview is the availability of the attorney-client privilege from the initial salutation and greeting on. The existence of the privilege is an essential ingredient to a full and free exchange of information needed by the attorney for an intelligent assessment of the representation invitation. The early declining of representation is in the mutual best interests of both the attorney and the prospective client. For the attorney there is the obvious savings of time and the avoidance of possible future conflicts. For the prospective client the threshold declining of potentially problematic representation permits the timely seeking of other counsel, thus minimizing the possible losses and difficulties experienced if the attorney must later withdraw from an improvidently undertaken representation.
>
> It necessarily follows that when more than one person seeks consultation with an attorney on a matter of common interest, the parties and the attorney may reasonably presume that the parties are seeking representation of a common or joint matter. * * * Neither the fact that the joint representation ultimately proved impracticable nor the subsequent waiver by either or both * * * can effect a retroactive recharacterization of the attorney-client relationship as it existed during the pre-representation meeting so as to defeat the protection the privilege affords * * *.

4. ***Disqualification***. By receiving confidential information from a member of the joint defense group, the attorney has a duty to maintain the confidentiality of those communications and not use them to the detriment of the person making the privilege communication. A significant problem can arise if a member of the joint defense group decides to cooperate with the government. Can defense counsel who may have received confidential information from the now-cooperating witness continue to represent other members of the group? This may be grounds for disqualifying counsel for the remaining members of the joint defense group because of the conflict, as discussed in Chapter 16.

5. ***Waiver and the Joint Defense Agreement***. An important issue that arises with some regularity in joint defense situations is whether one party can withdraw from the agreement and provide the government with

protected communications. While an individual can always choose to waive the privilege with regard to communications with his or her own attorney, it is less clear whether a member of a joint defense agreement can disclose communications with other members of the joint defense team. The agreement governs the issue, and defense counsel should be careful to address this issue at the inception of the joint undertaking rather than waiting until a problem arises. As with any contract, the parties can modify their agreement, as discussed in **United States v. LeCroy**, 348 F.Supp.2d 375 (E.D. Pa. 2004). The defendants, LeCroy and Snell, were employees of J.P. Morgan Chase Bank (JPMC), and entered into an oral joint defense agreement related to a grand jury investigation into their conduct on behalf of the bank that resulted in their indictment for wire fraud. During the investigation, JPMC informed counsel for the defendants that the bank planned to cooperate with the government and would turn over all materials from its internal investigation, including privileged information. Nevertheless, counsel allowed LeCroy and Snell to engage in further interviews with JPMC's counsel. The district court explained why JPMC did not violate the joint defense agreement by turning over notes of the interviews to prosecutors:

> There were good and abundant reasons why LeCroy and Snell, with the advice of their counsel, rationally, intelligently and knowingly decided to allow JPMC and its counsel to interview them, knowing that the notes of the interviews may be turned over to the government, but also knowing the JDA would continue, as modified. Under the JDA, the parties could continue to share information, documents, and access to witnesses without fear that any party continuing with the JDA would divulge that information. The only change in the terms of the JDA was that the notes of the interviews of LeCroy and Snell by JPMC could be turned over to the government. Assuming LeCroy and Snell were telling JPMC counsel the truth, their counsel wisely advised them to proceed with the interview even though the notes may be turned over to the government. This may have been the best possible strategy to avoid indictment. This Court intends to uphold the JDA to the extent that it was not modified. However, it is clear that JPMC initiated a modification of the JDA, or a partial withdrawal from it, and that LeCroy and Snell, with their counsel's advice, by agreeing to be interviewed by JPMC's counsel, and knowing that the notes and memoranda of such interviews may be turned over to the government, knowingly and intelligently agreed to the modification and thus waived the protections of the JDA as to those notes and memoranda on a prospective basis.
>
> The provisions in the prior 2000 written agreement between Recker and Dodds [counsel for LeCroy and Snell] regarding withdrawal were quoted above because it is clear to this Court that, notwithstanding and not necessarily inconsistent with the terms of the JDA – and the understanding of the lawyers who entered into it

> – there was indisputably, in January 2004, a partial withdrawal, or a modification, or a partial waiver by LeCroy and Snell, of the protections of the JDA to the extent that JPMC could turn over the notes of its counsel's interviews with LeCroy and Snell to the grand jury pursuant to the grand jury subpoena.
>
> Modification took place by JPMC insisting that it would have to have the right to turn over the notes of its interviews of LeCroy and Snell to the government pursuant to the grand jury subpoena. By Dodds [counsel for JPMC] communicating this to counsel for LeCroy and Snell prior to the interviews, and counsel repeating this to their clients, and all parties proceeding with the interviews, there was an acknowledgment by all parties that the JDA had been modified to allow JPMC to produce the notes to the government. Notwithstanding Recker's and Suddath's dispute with Dodds as to whether JPMC had the right to do this, by the conduct of LeCroy and Snell (with their counsel's advice) of going to New York and submitting themselves to interviews with the knowledge that the notes of the interviews may be turned over to the government, the Court finds that this constituted a modification by their explicit conduct, done on a knowing and voluntary basis. LeCroy and Snell were not obliged to submit to the JPMC interviews. They could have refused to do so; what the consequences of their refusal may have been are undetermined but irrelevant.

6. ***Payment of Legal Fees.*** It is common in investigations of corporate misconduct that the company will provide representation to individual employees, officers, and directors who are called before the grand jury or who may be targets of the investigation. Many corporations have indemnification agreements–either in individual employment contracts or in the company's by-laws or charter–that require the corporation to pay for legal counsel in an investigation. That arrangement can raise sensitive issues regarding conflicts of interest among the various defense counsel. ABA Model Rule of Professional Conduct 1.8(f) specifically deals with the issue of third-party payment of legal fees:

> A lawyer shall not accept compensation for representing a client from one other than the client unless:
>
> (1) the client gives informed consent;
>
> (2) there is no interference with the lawyer's independence of professional judgment or with the client-lawyer relationship; and
>
> (3) information relating to representation of a client is protected as required by Rule 1.6.

Corporations, particularly those whose shares are publicly-traded, often obligate themselves to pay the attorney's fees of employees, officers, and directors through individual employment agreements or in corporate by-laws.

Delaware law, which governs many larger corporations, provides:

> A corporation shall have power to indemnify any person who was or is a party or is threatened to be made a party to any threatened, pending or completed action, suit or proceeding, whether civil, criminal, administrative or investigative (other than an action by or in the right of the corporation) by reason of the fact that the person is or was a director, officer, employee or agent of the corporation, or is or was serving at the request of the corporation as a director, officer, employee or agent of another corporation, partnership, joint venture, trust or other enterprise, against expenses (including attorneys' fees), judgments, fines and amounts paid in settlement actually and reasonably incurred by the person in connection with such action, suit or proceeding if the person acted in good faith and in a manner the person reasonably believed to be in or not opposed to the best interests of the corporation, and, with respect to any criminal action or proceeding, had no reasonable cause to believe the person's conduct was unlawful.

8 Del. G.C.L. § 145(a).

In addition, state corporate codes authorize a company to agree to mandatory advancement of attorney's fees, often conditioned on the recipient's agreement to repay the fees if it turns out the person was not eligible to receive them. In **Westar Energy, Inc. v. Lake**, 552 F.3d 1215 (10th Cir. 2009), the Tenth Circuit considered a lower court's order directing a corporation to advance the legal fees of a former officer and director facing charges arising from his tenure at the company. The court explained the importance of advancement of attorney's fees:

> Lake's right to advancement is a contractual right originating in Westar's Articles of Incorporation. Advancement is a distinct right complementary to the right to indemnification. Indemnification and advancement work in tandem to encourage talented individuals to serve as corporate officers. Corporate service entails the risk of civil and criminal liability, and corporations may be willing to assume the expenses of defending such suits to attract talented employees. The right to indemnity, however, is often impossible to determine until the legal proceedings are finished. Absent advances, the officer himself must front the cost of defending the legal proceeding, significantly diminishing the attractiveness of indemnity. Advancement addresses this problem by providing timely relief in the midst of litigation. If a corporation withholds advances, the right will be irretrievably lost at the conclusion of the litigation, because at that point the officer will only be entitled to indemnity.

> In this case, Lake faces the possibility of a prison term if he is convicted in his third criminal trial. He is relying on advances to fund his legal defense. The district court's prospective remedy protects Lake's right to advances, and is thus crucial to Lake's defense of his liberty. Lake therefore meets the requirement of showing irreparable injury in the absence of the prospective relief granted by the district court.

Companies usually buy insurance to cover the cost of defending their directors, officers, and employees who retain counsel during an investigation. The language of the policy is crucial in determining the insurer's duty to pay a claim for reimbursement. In Office Depot, Inc. v. Nat'l Union Fire Ins. Co. of Pittsburgh, Pa., 734 F. Supp. 2d 1304 (S.D. Fla. 2010), the district court found that the insurance policy did not cover the legal costs of a preliminary SEC investigation in which the company and its employees voluntarily cooperated. The policy defined a "Securities Claim" to mean "a Claim, other than an administrative or regulatory proceeding against, or investigation of an Organization, made against any insured . . . ." Finding the language clear, the court held that responding to the agency's request for information without a subpoena being served took the case outside the coverage under the policy.

E. OTHER PRIVILEGES

1. Tax Advice Privilege

In 1998, Congress adopted the Internal Revenue Service Restructuring and Reform Act of 1998, which, *inter alia*, created a limited privilege in federal actions involving tax advice. The privilege, codified at 26 U.S.C. § 7525(a)(1), provides: "With respect to tax advice, the same common law protections of confidentiality which apply to a communication between a taxpayer and an attorney shall also apply to a communication between a taxpayer and any federally authorized tax practitioner to the extent the communication would be considered a privileged communication if it were between a taxpayer and an attorney." A "federally authorized tax practitioner" includes certified public accountants and "enrolled agents" who are authorized to file tax returns with the IRS. The new privilege is not as extensive as the attorney-client privilege, covering only tax advice and subject to two important limitations: the privilege "may only be asserted in–(A) any noncriminal tax matter before the Internal Revenue Service; and (B) any noncriminal tax proceeding in Federal court brought by or against the United States." 26 U.S.C. § 7525(a)(2). In addition to the federal privilege under § 7525, some states recognize an accountant-client privilege. See Francis M. Dougherty, *Privileged Communications Between Accountant and Client*, 33 A.L.R. 4th 539. Section 7525 does not, however, extend the protection of the work product doctrine to tax advice provided by an accountant automatically, so that the usual requirements to qualify for the work product doctrine must be met. See Long-Term Capital Holdings v. United States, 2002 WL 31934139 (D. Conn. Oct. 30, 2002).

The scope of the accountant-client privilege under § 7525 is discussed the following case related to a broad IRS investigation of abusive tax shelters.

UNITED STATES v. BDO SEIDMAN

337 F.3d 802 (7th Cir. 2003)

RIPPLE, Circuit Judge.

Several unnamed clients of BDO Seidman, LLP ("BDO"), a public accounting and consulting firm, appeal from the district court's denial of their motions to intervene in an Internal Revenue Service ("IRS") enforcement action against BDO.

The IRS had issued twenty summonses to BDO as part of its investigation of BDO's compliance with Internal Revenue Code registration and list-keeping requirements for organizers and sellers of potentially abusive tax shelters. See 26 U.S.C. §§ 6111, 6112. The clients sought to intervene to assert a confidentiality privilege regarding certain documents that BDO intended to produce in response to those summonses. The clients argued that, because these documents reveal their identities as BDO clients who sought advice regarding tax shelters and who subsequently invested in those shelters, disclosure inevitably would violate the statutory privilege protecting confidential communications between a taxpayer and any federally authorized tax practitioner giving tax advice. See 26 U.S.C. § 7525. For the reasons that follow, we affirm the district court's denial of the clients' motions to intervene.

In September 2000, the IRS received information suggesting that BDO was promoting potentially abusive tax shelters without complying with the registration and listing requirements for organizers and sellers of tax shelters. Section 6111(a) of the Internal Revenue Code requires organizers of tax shelters to register the tax shelter with the IRS. Any tax shelter required to be registered under § 6111, as well as any "arrangement which is of a type which the Secretary determines by regulations as having a potential for tax avoidance or evasion," is considered to be "potentially abusive." 26 U.S.C. § 6112(b). Accordingly, the organizers and sellers of such tax shelters must keep a list identifying each person to whom an interest of the tax shelter was sold. See 26 U.S.C. § 6112(a). Failure to comply with the registration and listing requirements of § 6111 and § 6112 can lead to the imposition of penalties. Because the IRS suspected that BDO had violated these statutory provisions by organizing and selling interests in potentially abusive tax shelters without complying with the registration and list-keeping requirements, it issued a series of summonses to BDO, identifying twenty types of tax shelter transactions in which it suspected that BDO's clients had invested.

The summonses command production of documents and testimony relating to the identified transactions, as well as information about BDO clients who invested in the identified tax shelters. For example, the summonses demand documents identifying the investors in the transactions, the date on which those investors acquired an interest, and all tax shelter registrations filed and investor lists prepared with respect to the transactions.

In July 2002, when BDO failed to produce documents as required by the summonses, the IRS petitioned the district court for enforcement. BDO opposed enforcement. It argued that the investigation did not have a legitimate purpose, that the summonses were overbroad and issued in bad faith, and that the information sought was already in the possession of the IRS and was not relevant to the investigation. BDO also claimed that some of the summoned information was protected from disclosure by the attorney-client privilege, the work product doctrine, and the confidentiality privilege of § 7525 of the Internal Revenue Code. In October 2002, the district court ruled that the IRS had met its burden of showing that it issued the summonses in good faith, and that BDO had failed to show that enforcement of the summonses would constitute an abuse of process. * * *

Among the responsive documents not previously submitted for the court's in camera inspection were records that reveal the identities of the BDO clients who invested in at least one of the 20 types of tax shelters identified in the summonses. BDO informed its clients that it intended to produce these documents to the IRS. In response, two sets of unidentified taxpayers–the John and Jane Does and the Richard and Mary Roes (hereinafter referred to collectively as "the Does")–filed emergency motions to intervene in the enforcement proceedings pursuant to Federal Rule of Civil Procedure 24(a)(2). The Does, asserting that they are BDO clients who sought BDO's confidential advice regarding the potential tax effects of certain proposed financial transactions, argued that the documents revealing their identities are privileged under 26 U.S.C. § 7525, and that BDO was not adequately representing their interest in keeping that information confidential. The Does conceded that, aside from the fact that the documents reveal their identities as BDO clients who invested in at least one of the 20 types of tax shelters described in the summonses, the documents themselves do not contain any otherwise privileged communication. After a hearing, the district court denied the Does' emergency motions to intervene. * * *

The primary issue before us is whether the district court erred when it denied the Does' motions to intervene because it believed that they had failed to establish a colorable claim of privilege under § 7525. Unless the Does can establish that the § 7525 privilege can protect a taxpayer's identity from disclosure in the IRS enforcement action, the Does will not prevail on appeal. * * *

We first consider the regulatory context in which the Does' claim of privilege arises. The Does sought to intervene in proceedings involving the

IRS investigation of BDO for potential violations of the tax code, including the provisions requiring organizers of tax shelters to register tax shelters with the IRS, 26 U.S.C. § 6111, and organizers and sellers of such shelters to keep lists of the investors, 26 U.S.C. § 6112. These provisions were enacted by Congress as part of the Deficit Reduction Act of 1984, for the purpose of providing the IRS with means to better monitor tax shelters, and, consequently, to deter abusive tax shelters that can adversely impact public revenues. Before 1984, no systematic information was available to assist the IRS in identifying the shelters that should be investigated. The IRS could audit individual taxpayers, but such a process only randomly identified participants in potentially abusive tax shelters. The statutory registration and list-keeping provisions allow the IRS to identify more easily those transactions that it deems to be abusive and "to identify quickly all of the participants in related tax-shelter investments." These provisions also enable the IRS to examine every purchaser of a given type of tax shelter investment and to treat those taxpayers in a more uniform manner. * * *

Having described the general framework of this regulatory authority, we now turn to the specific context of the Does' claim. The Does seek to intervene to prevent the disclosure, through IRS summonses, of documents that the Does contend are privileged. The Does' privilege claim rests entirely on § 7525, a statute enacted on July 22, 1998, to provide a confidentiality privilege for communications between a taxpayer and a tax practitioner. This limited privilege applies only to communications occurring after the date of the statute's enactment. Section 7525, provides in pertinent part:

With respect to tax advice, the same common law protections of confidentiality which apply to a communication between a taxpayer and an attorney shall also apply to a communication between a taxpayer and any federally authorized tax practitioner to the extent the communication would be considered a privileged communication if it were between a taxpayer and an attorney.

Thus the § 7525 privilege is no broader than that of the attorney-client privilege * * *. Because the scope of the tax practitioner-client privilege depends on the scope of the common law protections of confidential attorney-client communications, we must look to the body of common law interpreting the attorney-client privilege to interpret the § 7525 privilege.

The attorney-client privilege is "one of the oldest recognized privileges for confidential communications" known to the common law. Swidler & Berlin v. United States, 524 U.S. 399 (1998). The purpose of the privilege is to encourage full disclosure and to facilitate open communication between attorneys and their clients. However, because "the privilege has the effect of withholding relevant information," courts construe the privilege to apply only where necessary to achieve its purpose. Fisher v. United States, 425 U.S. 391 (1976). The mere assertion of a privilege is not enough; instead, a party that seeks to invoke the attorney-client privilege has the burden of establishing all of its essential elements.

A party that seeks to assert a § 7525 privilege bears the same burden. Among the essential elements of the attorney-client privilege are the requirements that the communication be made to the attorney in confidence, and that the confidences constitute information that is not intended to be disclosed by the attorney. Furthermore, the party asserting a privilege must show that the attorney-client communication was made for the purpose of obtaining legal advice, or, more precisely in the case of the § 7525 privilege, tax advice.

The attorney-client privilege protects confidential communications made by a client to his lawyer, and so ordinarily the identity of a client does not come within the scope of the privilege. However, over the years, a limited exception to this general rule has developed; the identity of a client may be privileged in the rare circumstance when so much of an actual confidential communication has been disclosed already that merely identifying the client will effectively disclose that communication.

In their discussion of this narrow exception, the parties primarily focus on two cases in which we held that attorney-client privilege could prevent the disclosure of a client's identity. In Tillotson [v. Boughner, 350 F.2d 663 (7th Cir. 1965)], an unidentified taxpayer had determined that he understated his tax liability on previously filed returns and retained an attorney to deliver a cashier's check in the amount of $215,499.95 to the IRS. The IRS sought to enforce a summons it had served on the attorney, demanding that he testify about his client. The attorney asserted the attorney-client privilege and refused to disclose his client's identity. We upheld the invocation of the privilege because "under the peculiar facts of this case, the attorney-client privilege includes, within its scope, the identity of the client." We reasoned that the IRS had become aware of the substantive content of the confidential communication between the unknown taxpayer and his attorney-namely, the taxpayer's tax liability–the moment the cashier's check was delivered. Because revealing the taxpayer's identity would also reveal the content of the confidential communication, the privilege attached. Similarly, in [In re Grand Jury Proceeding (Cherney), 898 F.2d 565 (7th Cir. 1990)], we held that the privilege encompasses the identity of a client when the Government knows that the unidentified client paid fees for a criminal defendant out of concern about his own involvement in the charged drug conspiracy. In that case, we explained, the client's identity was privileged "because its disclosure would be tantamount to revealing the premise of a confidential communication: the very substantive reason that the client sought legal advice in the first place." In other words, "the privilege protects an unknown client's identity where its disclosure would reveal a client's motive for seeking legal advice."

Relying on these cases, the Does submit that the IRS' summonses set forth such detailed descriptions about suspect types of tax shelters under investigation that any document produced in response that also reveals a client's identity will inevitably reveal that client's motivation for seeking tax advice from BDO. The Does define their "motive" for retaining BDO's services as the "desire to engage in financial transactions which the government might later decide to be questionable, or . . . 'potentially abusive.'" Because a client's "motive" for seeking legal advice is considered a confidential communication, the Does contend that the § 7525 privilege should protect against the disclosure of their motive for seeking tax advice, a motive that would be known if their identities are revealed.

The Does have not established that a confidential communication will be disclosed if their identities are revealed in response to the summonses. Disclosure of the identities of the Does will disclose to the IRS that the Does participated in one of the 20 types of tax shelters described in its summonses. It is less than clear, however, as to what motive, or other confidential communication of tax advice, can be inferred from that information alone. Compared to the situations in the Tillotson and Cherney cases, where the Government already knew much about the substance of the communications between the attorney and his unidentified client, in this case the IRS knows relatively little about the interactions between BDO and the Does, the nature of their relationship, or the substance of their conversations. Moreover, the Does concede that the documents that BDO intends to produce in response to the summonses are not subject to any other independent claim of privilege beyond the Does' assertion of privilege as to identity.

More fundamentally, the Does' participation in potentially abusive tax shelters is information ordinarily subject to full disclosure under the federal tax law. See 26 U.S.C §§ 6111, 6112. Congress has determined that tax shelters are subject to special scrutiny, and anyone who organizes or sells an interest in tax shelters is required, pursuant to I.R.C. § 6112, to maintain a list identifying each person to whom such an interest was sold. This list-keeping provision precludes the Does from establishing an expectation of confidentiality in their communications with BDO, an essential element of the attorney-client privilege and, by extension, the § 7525 privilege. At the time that the Does communicated their interest in participating in tax shelters that BDO organized or sold, the Does should have known that BDO was obligated to disclose the identity of clients engaging in such financial transactions. Because the Does cannot credibly argue that they expected that their participation in such transactions would not be disclosed, they cannot now establish that the documents responsive to the summonses, which do not contain any tax advice, reveal a confidential communication.

BDO's affirmative duty to disclose its clients' participation in potentially abusive tax shelters renders the Does' situation easily distinguishable from the limited circumstances in which we have determined that a client's identity was information subject to the attorney-client privilege. The district court committed no error when it concluded that the Does failed to establish a colorable claim of privilege under § 7525.

Because the Does cannot demonstrate a colorable claim of privilege, they have failed to establish a legally protectable interest in preventing the disclosure of the documents revealing their identities as individuals who participated in tax shelters promoted by BDO. For the reasons stated above, the district court's judgments denying the Does' motions for intervention are affirmed.

NOTE

In a subsequent decision in the same investigation of BDO, the Seventh Circuit determined that the burden of establishing the tax shelter exception to the accountant-client privilege rested with the party seeking to obtain the communication. The court stated, "Thus, based on the text, structure and purpose of subsection (b), it is clear that the tax shelter 'exception' is a true exception to the tax practitioner privilege. As with any other exception to a claimed privilege, the burden rests on the opponent of the privilege to prove preliminary facts that would support a finding that the claimed privilege falls within an exception. As with the crime-fraud exception, the opponent meets this burden by bringing forth enough evidence to show 'some foundation in fact' that the exception applies." United States v. BDO Seidman, LLP, 492 F.3d 806 (7th Cir. 2007).

2. Self Evaluation/Self-Criticism Privilege

Another privilege, thus far available with only very limited application, is the corporate "self-evaluation" or self-criticism privilege.

> In general, the party asserting the privilege must demonstrate that the material to be protected satisfies at least three criteria: (1) the information must result from a critical self-analysis undertaken by the party seeking protection; (2) the public must have a strong interest in preserving the free flow of the type of information sought; and (3) the information must be of the type whose flow would be curtailed if discovery were allowed. In addition to these basic requirements, self-evaluative material must have been prepared with the expectation that it would be kept confidential and it must, in fact, have been confidential.

Thomas R. Mulroy & Eric J. Munoz, *The Internal Corporate Investigation*, 1 DEPAUL BUS. & COM. L.J. 49 (2002). In **Reichhold Chemicals v. Textron**, 157 F.R.D. 522 (N.D. Fla. 1994), the district court stated:

> The self-critical analysis privilege has been recognized as a qualified privilege which protects from discovery certain critical self-appraisals. It allows individuals or businesses to candidly assess their compliance with regulatory and legal requirements without creating evidence that may be used against them by their opponents in future litigation. The rationale for the doctrine is that such critical self-evaluation fosters the compelling public interest in

> observance of the law. See, e.g., Granger v. National R.R. Passenger Corp., 116 F.R.D. 507 (E.D. Pa. 1987) * * * The self-critical analysis privilege is analogous to, and based on the same public policy considerations as Rule 407, Federal Rules of Evidence, which excludes evidence of subsequent remedial measures.

Areas where some courts have recognized a self-evaluation or self-criticism privilege are medical peer review, securities audits, academic peer reviews, product safety assessments, equal employment compliance, accounting records, prior accident investigations, and environmental audits.

Among the other types of communications that may be covered by this privilege are:

(a) communications with an organization's ombudsman. Kientzy v. McDonnell Douglas Corp., 133 F.R.D. 570 (E.D. Mo. 1991); *disagreed with by* Carman v. McDonnell Douglas Corp., 114 F.3d 790 (8th Cir. 1997) ("We do not find the reasoning of [*Kientzy*] convincing.").

(b) self-critical portions of affirmative action plans, O'Connor v. Chrysler Corp., 86 F.R.D. 211 (D. Mass. 1980); Banks v. Lockheed Georgia Co., 53 F.R.D. 283 (N.D. Ga. 1971). See Webb v. Westinghouse Elec., 81 F.R.D. 431 (E.D. Pa. 1978); Contra Martin v. Potomac Electric Power Co., CA # 86-0603 (D.D.C. 5-25-90); 58 Fair Empl. Prac. Cas. (BNA) 355.

(c) hospital's evaluation of its staff procedures concerning a patient's death, Bredice v. Doctor's Hospital, 50 F.R.D. 249 (D.D.C. 1970). Most courts have not recognized such a privilege, or reject its application in a particular context without rejecting it completely. See In re Kaiser Aluminum & Chemical Co., 214 F.3d 586 (5th Cir. 2000); In re Continental Illinois Securities Litigation, 732 F.2d 1302 (7th Cir. 1984); FTC v. TRW, 628 F.2d 207 (D.C. Cir. 1980); Wei v. Bodner, 127 F.R.D. 91 (D.N.J. 1989); Dowling v. American Hawaii Cruises, 971 F.2d 423 (9th Cir. 1992).

3. Other Privileges

Another privilege that may arise as part of, or collateral to, a white collar case is the "deliberative process privilege" which "protects documents reflecting advisory opinions, recommendations, and deliberations comprising an agency's decisionmaking process." United Western Bank v. Office of Thrift Supervision, 853 F. Supp. 2d 12 (D.C. D.C. 2012)(citing First Eastern Corp. V. Mainwaring, 21 F.3d 465 (D.C. Cir. 1994). Likewise, the "bank examination privilege" "is a qualified privilege protecting bank examiners' reports and related information." *United Western*.

CHAPTER SIXTEEN
THE ROLE OF COUNSEL

A. PROTECTING CLIENT INFORMATION

1. Client Identity

Does the attorney-client privilege permit an attorney to withhold the name of a client or the fees paid for legal services? As the court noted in Lefcourt v. United States, 125 F.3d 79 (2d Cir. 1997), "[a]s a general rule, a client's identity and fee information are not privileged." Nevertheless, occasionally an attorney can assert the privilege successfully for this type of information, if "special circumstances" can be shown, as discussed in the following case.

In re: SUBPOENAED GRAND JURY WITNESS
171 F.3d 511 (7th Cir. 1999)

EVANS, Circuit Judge.

A federal grand jury sitting in Chicago issued a subpoena to an unnamed Illinois lawyer (we'll give him a fake name–Tom Hagen–in this opinion). The subpoena ordered Hagen to testify and produce documents and records identifying all "individuals, companies, corporations or any other entities (including, but not limited to, All Games Amusement, OK Amusement, Universal Amusement, Nicholas J. "Buddy" Ciotti, Rocco Circelli, and Robert Cechini and their agents or representatives) who paid legal fees, including the amounts and dates of payments," to him in connection with his representation of 21 specifically named defendants in various state court gambling cases. Hagen received a similar directive for fees paid by certain third parties to persons other than the 21 named state court defendants.

At a closed hearing in the district court to quash the subpoena Hagen argued that "any testimony concerning payment of fees will provide the government with the 'last link' and will identify a client and subject him to prosecution for the very investigation for which the government intends to prosecute," and that "[a]s in the *Cherney* [Matter of Grand Jury Proceeding (Cherney), 898 F.2d 565 (7th Cir.1990)] case, [his] testimony . . . will give rise to an identification of an individual who has sought [Hagen's] legal advice and in disclosing these confidential communications and the fee arrangement structure, etc., [Hagen] will be compelled to testify against his own client as to attorney/client privileged communications." Hagen's "last link" comment referred to a theory embraced by two other circuit courts of appeals that could support withholding the requested information. See In re Grand Jury Proceedings 88-9 (MIA) Newton, 899 F.2d 1039 (11th Cir.1990); In re Grand Jury Proceedings (Pavlick), 680 F.2d 1026 (5th Cir.1982). The district court concluded that the "last link" exception did not apply and that the subpoenaed material was not protected by the attorney-client privilege.* * *

But we backpedaled on this bright-line principle in *Cherney*, the case Hagen says is "directly on point" and compels reversal of the district court's ruling. In that case, Attorney David Cherney represented a chap named Hrvatin in a drug conspiracy trial. Hrvatin's legal fees were paid by an unknown person who was also, apparently, involved in the same conspiracy. That person, the government conceded, consulted Cherney for legal advice regarding the same conspiracy. Following Hrvatin's conviction, Cherney was served with a subpoena directing him to identify the person who paid Hrvatin's bill. Cherney's motion to quash the subpoena was granted by the district court, and we affirmed that decision on appeal.

Hagen argues that his situation is "strikingly similar" to that of the attorney in *Cherney*. In his case, Hagen represented 21 defendants (and perhaps others) in state gambling cases involving the use of video machines and other electronic devices. Hagen asserts that the 21 listed persons, all previously charged and tried in state gambling cases, are likely to be indicted or named as unindicted coconspirators arising out of the current federal grand jury proceeding to which he has been subpoenaed. The government has also set its sights on the third-party payor (or payors) of Hagen's bills, and Hagen says his testimony–linking the third-party fee payor(s) to the gamblers–will give the government the ammunition it needs to secure an indictment.

So our issue boils down to a simple proposition, i.e., whether Hagen can avoid the subpoena under the cover of *Cherney*. The answer to that simple question is, unfortunately, a bit elusive. Addressing a similar issue in Vingelli v. United States, 992 F.2d 449 (1993), the Second Circuit wrote:

> Recognizing that client identity and fee information are not presently sheltered under the privilege, defense counsel urges that the information sought falls into one of the special exceptions to that rule. What those "special circumstances" are that would protect this information has not been precisely defined. What they are remains as enigmatic as the smile that Leonardo Da Vinci left us on the face of the Mona Lisa.

We agree. While a bright-line rule would be easy to understand and enforce, *Cherney* requires that we read the nuance in Mona Lisa's smile. *Cherney* protects from disclosure certain, and limited, client identity and third-party fee payor information.

So, does Hagen's situation, as described in his four-page affidavit, sealed and a part of the record on this appeal, move him into one of the "special exceptions" that allows him to pass on the government's request for disclosure? We have examined the affidavit and, reviewing it *de novo* which we are required to do, we believe Hagen slides through the crack left open by *Cherney*. We think it is clear, based on Hagen's affidavit, that he would be forced to violate the attorney-client privilege if he were made to say who paid the fees in question. We will not go into detail as to why we make this finding–that would be showing the hand to the government–but we are sure that disclosure of this information would identify a client of Hagen's who is potentially involved in targeted criminal activity which, on this record, would lead to revealing that client's motive to pay the legal bills for some of Hagen's other clients. And motive, we think, is protected by the attorney-client privilege. For as we observed in *Cherney*, "A client's motive for seeking legal advice is undeniably a confidential communication. Accordingly, the privilege protects an unknown client's identity where its disclosure would reveal a client's motive for seeking legal advice." This case, as Hagen suggests, is in fact on all fours with *Cherney*, and the government can only prevail if we are prepared to walk away from that opinion. And that's a trip we decline to take. This conclusion also makes it unnecessary for us to consider Hagen's alternative argument regarding the "last link" exception. With that, the order denying the motion to quash the subpoena is REVERSED. The subpoena is quashed.

2. Providing Payment Information

UNITED STATES v. SINDEL

53 F.3d 874 (8th Cir. 1995)

MORRIS SHEPPARD ARNOLD, Circuit Judge.

Attorney Richard Sindel of Sindel & Sindel, P.C., appeals a district court order requiring him to disclose information about two clients, intervenors John Doe and Jane Doe, on Internal Revenue Service Form 8300. These forms, which are used to report cash transactions in excess of $10,000 pursuant to 26 U.S.C. § 6050I, request the name, address, tax identification number, and other information about each payor and each person on whose behalf payment is made. Sindel argues that completion of the forms would violate his own ethical duties and the First, Fifth, and Sixth Amendment rights of his clients. After considering the circumstances surrounding each client, we affirm the district court order with respect to John Doe and reverse it with respect to Jane Doe.

During 1990 and 1991, Sindel received a cash payment of $53,160 for John Doe and two cash payments of $10,000 each for Jane Doe for legal services rendered. Sindel reported each of these transactions using the August, 1988, version of IRS Form 8300, but omitted any identifying information regarding the payers or the persons on whose behalf payments were made. In an attachment to each form, Sindel claimed that disclosure would "violate ethical duties owed said client, and constitutional and/or attorney-client privileges that the reporting attorney is entitled or required to invoke," and that the client had not authorized release of the information. At the request of the IRS, Sindel later withdrew the two forms reporting payments on behalf of Jane Doe and consolidated them using the January, 1990, version of Form 8300, again omitting any identifying information. This later version of Form 8300 asks the reporting party to check a box if the payment is a "suspicious transaction." The instructions accompanying the January, 1990, version of Form 8300 define a suspicious transaction as "[a] transaction in which it appears that a person is attempting to cause this report not to be filed or a false or incomplete report to be filed; or where there is an indication of possible illegal activity." Sindel left the box blank.

After filing these forms, Sindel was served with an IRS summons requesting the missing information. The government then brought an enforcement action, and the district court ordered Sindel to show cause why the summons should not be enforced. The district court divided the ensuing proceedings into two parts, one held in open court and the other an ex-parte hearing held in camera. During the in-camera portion of the proceedings, Sindel presented evidence regarding his clients' special circumstances. The district court ordered enforcement of the summons, but stayed its order pending this appeal.

* * * Although the federal common law of attorney-client privilege protects confidential disclosures made by a client to an attorney in order to obtain legal representation, it ordinarily does not apply to client identity and fee information. The various Circuit Courts have, however, identified certain circumstances under which the privilege protects even client identity and fee information. One court has categorized these overlapping "special-circumstance" exceptions as the legal advice exception, the last link exception, and the confidential communications exception. [In re Grand Jury Subpoenas (Anderson), 906 F.2d 1485 (10th Cir. 1990)]. The legal advice exception protects client identity and fee information when "there is a strong probability that disclosure would implicate the client in the very criminal activity for which legal advice was sought." The last link exception, as its name implies, prevents disclosure of client identity and fee information when it would incriminate the client by providing the last link in an existing chain of evidence. The confidential communications exception, which we have recognized on another occasion, protects client identity and fee information "if, by revealing the information, the attorney would necessarily disclose confidential communications." * * * After examining Sindel's in-camera testimony about his clients' special circumstances, we conclude that he could not release information about the payments on behalf of Jane Doe without revealing the substance of a confidential communication. We do not find any similar constraints upon the disclosure of information about the payments on behalf of John Doe.

[The court ruled that the Missouri Rules of Professional Conduct[a] did not "expand the scope of the exemption beyond what is established by the federal common law of attorney-client privilege."]

As we do not believe that the information regarding payments on behalf of John Doe is protected from disclosure to the IRS by the federal common law of attorney-client privilege or the Missouri Rules of Professional Conduct, we necessarily undertake a consideration of Sindel's constitutional claims.

Sindel first argues that application of 26 U.S.C. § 6050I to an attorney violates the client's Sixth Amendment right to counsel by inhibiting the ability to retain counsel, discouraging communication between attorney and client, forcing the attorney to act as an agent for the government, and disqualifying counsel of choice. As the Second Circuit accurately points out in United States v. Goldberger & Dubin, 935 F.2d 501 (2d Cir. 1991), the statutory reporting requirements do not prevent a would-be client from hiring counsel. Not only are cash payments not automatically forfeit, but a client is also free to pay counsel in some other manner to avoid being reported to the IRS. * * * Similarly, a client is not prevented from communicating with an attorney at will merely because the attorney must report large cash transactions. By contrast, we recognize the serious Sixth Amendment implications of Sindel's claim that an attorney becomes a de facto agent for the government when compelled to offer an opinion as to whether a particular cash payment was a "suspicious transaction," a question added to the January, 1990, version of Form 8300. Sindel used this later version of Form 8300 to consolidate his reporting of the payments made on behalf of Jane Doe. Because we have already determined that the federal common law of attorney-client privilege excuses Sindel from reporting any additional information regarding the Jane Doe payments, however, the constitutionality of the January, 1990, version of Form 8300 is not at issue in this case. Sindel's speculative claim that the reporting requirements of 26 U.S.C. § 6050I would disqualify counsel by allowing prosecutors to subpoena a reporting attorney to testify against a client is likewise not ripe for adjudication. There is thus no Sixth Amendment bar to enforcement of the IRS summons against Sindel.

Sindel next claims that requiring him to complete the Forms 8300 would violate his clients' Fifth Amendment privilege against self-incrimination. This guarantee, however, applies only to compulsion of the individual holding the privilege, not to other methods of obtaining potentially incriminating information. As compliance with the IRS summons would merely require disclosure of information which Sindel's clients have already given to him, their Fifth Amendment privilege is not implicated. * * *

---

[a] Rule 1.6 of the Missouri Rules of Professional Conduct differed from the ABA Model Rules of Professional Conduct existing at the time of this case.

Sindel's final constitutional claim is that completion of Form 8300 constitutes "compelled speech" and thus violates both his own and his clients' First Amendment rights. * * * A First Amendment protection against compelled speech, however, has been found only in the context of governmental compulsion to disseminate a particular political or ideological message. * * * The IRS summons requires Sindel only to provide the government with information which his clients have given him voluntarily, not to disseminate publicly a message with which he disagrees. Therefore, the First Amendment protection against compelled speech does not prevent enforcement of the summons. * * * For the foregoing reasons, we vacate the district court's order with respect to Jane Doe and affirm the order with respect to John Doe.

NOTES AND QUESTIONS

1. ***Special Circumstances.*** Courts have held that "absent special circumstances" attorneys are required to provide the information requested by Form 8300. Does the court in *Sindel* provide a clear definition of what constitutes "special circumstances?" A failure to comply with the obligations of § 6050I can result in fines and criminal charges to the attorney. For example, in United States v. Lefcourt, 125 F.3d 79 (2d Cir. 1997), the attorney filed Form 8300 omitting the taxpayer's name. After paying the fine assessed against him, Lefcourt unsuccessfully sued the Internal Revenue Service for return of the funds. The court, in finding " no reasonable basis for failing to provide the information required by § 6050I, stated that "[a]lthough the contours of the special circumstance exception have not been exhaustively developed, no doubt due to the fact special circumstances are seldom found to exist, it is clear that there is no special circumstance in this circuit simply because the provision of client-identifying information could prejudice the client in the case for which legal fees are paid."

2. ***Implications to Defense Counsel.*** What effect does the government's proceeding against criminal defense attorneys have on the adversary process? Consider the following comments by Bennett L. Gershman, *The New Prosecutors*, 53 U. PITT. L. REV. 393, 401-03 (1992):

> Added to these new developments is an even more ominous threat to the adversary system: the unprecedented use by prosecutors of the grand jury and other means to attack and cripple the criminal defense bar. One of the most alarming events during the last decade has been the prosecutor's attempt to compel criminal defense attorneys to give testimony and produce documents that might incriminate their clients. The testimony is usually sought in connection with fees, a subject that most courts have held is not covered by the attorney-client privilege. Recent statistics show that prosecutors in the United States issue subpoenas to defense attorneys at the rate of 645 per year. Further, most courts do not

require any special evidentiary showing before a subpoena can be enforced against a lawyer. Attorneys have been jailed for refusing to cooperate with the prosecutor. As with grand jury subpoenas, prosecutors also have begun to use the statutory summoning power of the Internal Revenue Service to force criminal defense attorneys to disclose the identities of clients or third parties who pay fees in excess of $10,000 cash. * * *

3. SEC Disclosure Rules

In the wake of the various accounting problems that engulfed a number of large corporations, Congress enacted the Sarbanes-Oxley Act of 2002. "Section 307 of the * * * Act (15 U.S.C. § 7245) mandates that the [Securities & Exchange] Commission issue rules prescribing minimum standards of professional conduct for attorneys appearing and practicing before it in any way in the representation of issuers, including at a minimum a rule requiring an attorney to report evidence of a material violation of securities laws or breach of fiduciary duty or similar violation by the issuer or any agent thereof to appropriate officers within the issuer and, thereafter, to the highest authority within the issuer, if the initial report does not result in an appropriate response." *Implementation of Standards of Professional Conduct for Attorneys*, SEC Rel. No. 34-47276 (2003). In addition to the internal reporting requirements, the SEC rule permits disclosure to the Commission in the following circumstances:

> (2) An attorney appearing and practicing before the Commission in the representation of an issuer may reveal to the Commission, without the issuer's consent, confidential information related to the representation to the extent the attorney reasonably believes necessary:
>
> > (i) To prevent the issuer from committing a material violation that is likely to cause substantial injury to the financial interest or property of the issuer or investors;
> >
> > (ii) To prevent the issuer, in a Commission investigation or administrative proceeding from committing perjury, proscribed in 18 U.S.C. 1621; suborning perjury, proscribed in 18 U.S.C. 1622; or committing any act proscribed in 18 U.S.C. 1001 that is likely to perpetrate a fraud upon the Commission; or
> >
> > (iii) To rectify the consequences of a material violation by the issuer that caused, or may cause, substantial injury to the financial interest or property of the issuer or investors in the furtherance of which the attorney's services were used.

17 C.F.R. 205.3(d)(2) (2012). This rule is permissive, not mandatory, and the ethics rules of the state in which an attorney is admitted to practice may prohibit any disclosure of client wrongdoing except for a future crime of violence. See ABA Model Rule of Professional Conduct 1.6(b) (lawyer may reveal confidential client information "to prevent reasonably certain death or substantial bodily harm" and "to prevent the client from committing a crime or fraud that is reasonably certain to result in substantial injury to the financial interests or property of another and in furtherance of which the client has used or is using the lawyer's services").

B. SUBPOENA OF ATTORNEYS

The attorney for a target of a grand jury investigation may be able to provide highly incriminating information about the client. The attorney-client relationship is a cornerstone of the criminal justice system, and attempts to interfere with that relationship are viewed with great suspicion. Nevertheless, the government increasingly seeks to obtain information from attorneys about their clients because it is so valuable, and is often reliable evidence to evaluate the intent of a target. Put simply, clients trust their attorneys and are as likely to be honest with them as with anyone else. The Department of Justice permits federal prosecutors to subpoena attorneys for information about their clients, but exercises "close control" over such subpoenas by requiring prior approval of the Assistant Attorney General for the Criminal Division. USAM 9-13.410 provides the following guidelines for determining whether the subpoena is appropriate:

> When determining whether to issue a subpoena to an attorney for information relating to the attorney's representation of a client, the Assistant United States Attorney must strike a balance between an individual's right to the effective assistance of counsel and the public's interest in the fair administration of justice and effective law enforcement. To that end, all reasonable attempts shall be made to obtain the information from alternative sources before issuing the subpoena to the attorney, unless such efforts would compromise the investigation or case. These attempts shall include reasonable efforts to first obtain the information voluntarily from the attorney, unless such efforts would compromise the investigation or case, or would impair the ability to subpoena the information from the attorney in the event that the attempt to obtain the information voluntarily proves unsuccessful.

Chapter 15 reviewed issues related to the attorney-client privilege and work product doctrine, and exceptions to the privilege that permit the government to compel the attorney to provide information about a client. If an attorney is called before a grand jury, can the subpoena be challenged as unreasonable under Rule 17(c) if it infringes on the attorney-client relationship but does not seek otherwise privileged information? Should courts require a special showing of need when an attorney is the recipient of the subpoena that seeks information related to a client?

In re IMPOUNDED

241 F.3d 308 (3d Cir. 2001)

SCIRICA, Circuit Judge.

In this grand jury proceeding, the issue on appeal is whether, on the facts presented, the crime-fraud exception overrides the attorney-client privilege. In the proceedings below, the District Court declined to enforce a grand jury subpoena issued to an attorney. Citing the crime-fraud exception, the government has appealed.

Over four years ago in April 1996, a federal grand jury commenced investigating the target's business transactions and issued several subpoenas to the target's affiliated businesses. The target's attorney assumed responsibility in responding to the United States Attorney's office. The government's first subpoena sought,

> all records . . . relating to work performed [by the target]. . . . These records should include but are not limited to: All business checks, check registers, cash receipt and disbursement records. These records should also include contracts, invoices, billing documents, bid documents and correspondence specifically relating to [the target's activities] for the [relevant] period.

The attorney produced several documents. But believing them inadequate, the government requested fuller document production. The attorney responded that certain categories of requested documents did not exist.

In May 1996, the government again requested the documents under its initial subpoena and advised the attorney that "the grand jury will also request that the target appear before it with regard to the production of the documents in question." The attorney provided some additional documents including check ledgers and canceled checks. The target was not summoned to appear before the grand jury.

In September 1996, the government issued a second subpoena requesting additional documents including: general ledgers, cash disbursement journals, cash receipts, sales and accounts payable journals, as well as calendars, diaries and appointment books for all of the target's business officers and employees. The attorney again responded that most of the requested documents did not exist. On January 10, 1997 the government advised the attorney that it was subpoenaing "the custodian of records [of one of] the target business[es] to produce all responsive *original* records before the Grand Jury next Thursday [January 16]." The government also subpoenaed an officer of the target business to testify before the grand jury (also on January 16) about her knowledge of the existence of the subpoenaed documents. The government never enforced its subpoenas.

In April 1997, November 1998, and March 1999 the government subpoenaed more records from the target business. The attorney produced some of the requested documents but again represented that certain categories of documents did not exist. On March 8, 1999, the Federal Bureau of Investigation executed search warrants on the target's home and also on the target's business offices. The FBI uncovered and seized many records and documents the attorney had represented did not exist. On April 30, 1999, the government subpoenaed the attorney to testify before the grand jury about the "source[s] of information for [his] . . . factual assertions . . . and basis for failing to produces [sic] certain categories of records."

After the attorney invoked the attorney-client privilege, the government filed a motion to compel his testimony. Claiming the crime-fraud exception invalidated the attorney-client privilege, the government argued the target used the attorney to obstruct justice in violation of 18 U.S.C. § 1503 [Obstruction of Justice]. Holding it was "fundamentally unfair" to compel the attorney's testimony, the District Court declined to assess the applicability of the crime-fraud exception.

The government appeals contending the District Court erred in failing to decide whether the crime-fraud exception applied. It also contends the District Court exceeded its authority in quashing the subpoena because of "fundamental unfairness." * * *

Despite these broad investigatory powers, there are some limitations on the grand jury's authority to subpoena evidence. * * * The Supreme Court has stated, "grand juries are not licensed to engage in arbitrary fishing expeditions, nor may they select targets of investigation out of malice or an intent to harass." *R. Enterprises.* * * *

As a safeguard against potential abuse of the grand jury's broad investigative power, the Federal Rules of Evidence and the Federal Rules of Criminal Procedure grant limited authority for courts to review grand jury subpoenas. In this case, the two principal mechanisms for judicial review are Fed.R.Evid. 501, recognizing the attorney-client privilege which protects confidential communications between an attorney and his client from disclosure, and Fed.R.Crim.P. 17(c), providing that "[t]he court on motion made promptly may quash or modify the subpoena if compliance would be unreasonable or oppressive."

The District Court did not refer to Fed.R.Crim.P. 17(c) nor to the attorney-client privilege when it declined to compel the attorney's testimony. It stated,

> The Court will assume for purposes of its analysis that [the attorney] is innocent of any wrongdoing and has been used merely as a conduit for wrongdoing, i.e., the obstruction of justice. Nevertheless it is fundamentally unfair for the U.S. Attorney's Office to seek [the attorney's] testimony in this case.

Reasoning that to obtain the desired information, the government could have pursued avenues less harmful to the attorney-client privilege, including enforcing its subpoenas on the target and the records custodian, the District Court stated

> The award for neither appointing nor insisting upon a custodian of records cannot be securing the testimony of the subject's attorney. Instead the U.S. Attorney's Office should have acted upon the subpoenas it procured and not assume that it could fall back on the subject's attorney.

Compelling the lawyer's testimony, the court said, "goes against the core of the adversarial system and would unnecessarily 'drive a wedge' between a client and his attorney, thereby 'chilling' communications."[4]

Because the District Court relied on neither Fed.R.Crim.P. 17 nor an analysis of the crime-fraud exception, the government contends the Court exceeded its authority in quashing the subpoena. * * * It is well established that courts may not impose substantive limitations on the power of the grand jury to issue subpoenas nor place the initial burden on the government to prove the validity of its subpoenas. * * * The Supreme Court stated,

> Any power federal courts have to fashion, on their own initiative, rules of grand jury procedure is a very limited one, not remotely comparable to the power they maintain over their own proceedings. It certainly would not permit judicial reshaping of the grand jury institution, substantially altering the traditional relationships between the prosecution, the constituting court, and the grand jury itself. (citation omitted).

* * * One form of restraint, however, may be found in Fed.R.Crim.P. 17(c). But as noted, the District Court never applied Fed.R.Crim.P. 17(c).

---

[4] In discussing the impact of this subpoena on criminal practice, the District Court stated it is common for criminal defense attorneys and the government to informally negotiate the production of materials for grand jury investigations. By forcing attorneys to testify against their clients, the court feared many criminal defense attorneys would be "unwilling to informally satisfy the subpoena for fear of the consequences."

Instead, it held that the government must demonstrate the evidence sought could not be obtained by other means. The District Court's prescribed course of action may be salutary and efficacious to safeguard the attorney-client privilege. Under appropriate circumstances, it may well constitute the better practice. But we see no authority for it in the rules or the case law. Generally, the government does not bear the initial burden to justify its grand jury subpoena.

The institutional independence and secrecy of the grand jury has been a hallmark of criminal indictments for over three centuries. Any deviation from the established practices governing court involvement should not be taken lightly. We recognize the District Court was concerned with the effect of this subpoena on the attorney-client relationship. But the proper course under Fed.R.Crim.P. 17(c) was to rule on whether the lawyer's testimony was protected under the attorney-client privilege. By employing "a different analysis" based on "fundamental fairness" the District Court deviated from the established procedures which ensure the institutional independence of the grand jury. Therefore, the District Court abused its discretion. * * *

The grand jury may not "itself violate a valid privilege, whether established by the Constitution, statutes, or the common Law." For this reason, courts may quash an otherwise valid grand jury subpoena for an attorney's testimony under the attorney-client privilege. When legal advice is sought in furtherance of a crime or fraud, however, the attorney-client privilege is waived and a grand jury may compel a lawyer's testimony.

* * * Here, the government asserts the target business obstructed justice by failing to disclose documents subpoenaed by the grand jury. * * * Challenging this assessment, the attorney contends the government presented insufficient evidence that the target and the target business corruptly intended to obstruct justice.

The District Court declined to decide whether the government submitted sufficient prima facie evidence of intent to obstruct justice. * * * We believe this was error. * * * The District Court must decide whether the government has submitted sufficient evidence of the intent to obstruct justice and determine whether this evidence supports a waiver of the attorney-client privilege. * * *

NYGAARD, Circuit Judge, dissenting.

Because I disagree with the Majority's conclusion that "the District Court never applied Fed.R.Crim.P. 17(c) [and instead] held that the government must demonstrate the evidence sought could not be obtained by other means," I respectfully dissent. I believe that the District Court validly exercised its discretion under Rule 17(c) and did *not* impose a broad "no-alternative-means" test. Therefore, I would affirm.

The Government claims that the District Court applied a broad-reaching "no-alternative-means test" to determine whether the attorney's subpoena was fair and therefore enforceable. Apparently, the Majority agrees. It holds that the court employed an analysis "based on 'fundamental fairness' [that] deviated from the established procedures which ensure the institutional independence of the grand jury." I agree that such a blanket rule, *if* it were imposed, would improperly place a substantive limitation upon the grand jury, is outside the District Court's supervisory powers, and has been implicitly rejected by this Court. * * *

However, I disagree with the Majority's characterization of the District Court's holding. The District Court did not impose a new substantive limitation upon the grand jury. * * * The Majority recognizes Rule 17(c) as a valid "form of restraint" upon the grand jury, but nonetheless holds that the District Court failed to apply it. I concede that the District Court never *explicitly* invoked Fed.R.Crim.P. 17(c), but such an omission is *not* fatal as long as what the court did is clear. * * *

The District Court in his case considered the specific facts and circumstances before it and found that it was "fundamentally unfair for the U.S. Attorney's Office to seek [the attorney's] testimony."[3] Rule 17(c) empowers a court to quash a subpoena if it is "unreasonable or oppressive." Presumably, the Majority believes that a finding of "fundamental unfairness" is insufficient to satisfy this standard. In contrast, I fail to see a difference. A subpoena described as "fundamentally unfair" could just as easily be described as "unreasonable and oppressive." Therefore, I believe that the District Court sufficiently invoked the authority of Rule 17(c). Unlike the Majority, I would not reverse based entirely upon an unimportant semantic distinction.[4]

* * * There is nothing in the record to suggest that the District Court's decision to quash the Government's subpoena *under these specific facts* constituted an abuse of discretion. The court was concerned that enforcing the Government's subpoena would put attorneys in a "very precarious position," subjecting them to grand jury subpoena any time they made representations pertaining to the existence of subpoenaed records. * * * This

---

[3] The court cited numerous avenues that the Government could have pursued to obtain the same information, "which are far less offensive [than] seeking to pierce the attorney-client privilege." These included subpoenas that the U.S. Attorney's Office choose not to enforce and the Government's failure to insist that a custodian of records confirm the attorney's assertions. The court also noted that compelling his testimony could "unnecessarily 'drive a wedge' between a client and his attorney, thereby 'chilling' communications."

[4] It is beyond dispute that "unfair," "unreasonable," and "oppressive" are often used synonymously. A Westlaw searched revealed 1710 federal decisions, 40 of which were Supreme Court decisions, where "unfair" appeared within five words of "unreasonable" or "oppressive." * * *

threat would certainly chill communication between attorney and client. Both the government and the Majority seem to believe, however, that the attorney-client privilege is the *only* means by which a district court can protect that relationship. I do not read a district court's discretion so narrowly. American jurisprudence has long recognized the central importance of the attorney-client relationship. The privilege is the most common means of protecting the relationship, but it is not the only one. In appropriate factual situations, such as the present case, a district court can, within its discretion, conclude that a subpoena is unreasonable and oppressive because it harms the attorney-client relationship, even if the privilege does not apply.

A constant threat of subpoena would also affect the ability of lawyers to cooperate with the government. The Government contends that "[t]he duty to safeguard 'the healthy relationship between the criminal defense bar and the U.S. Attorney's Office' lies squarely with the parties to that relationship itself, not the district court." It appears that the Government misunderstands the court's concern. If a court were to enforce a grand jury subpoena against an attorney in a case such as this, where there were numerous alternative avenues of gathering the desired information, it would impose the threat of subpoena over all representations made by counsel. It does not escape my attention that this would grant the U.S. Attorney's Office tremendous leverage–so much in fact that any competent counsel would produce a custodian rather than respond to inquires. This would severely hamper the efficient administration of justice, a matter of paramount concern to this Court.

These consequences might be acceptable (and reasonable) if the Government had no other means of obtaining the desired information. In this case, however, the U.S. Attorney's Office repeatedly served subpoenas that were never enforced, and it failed to insist upon authentication from a custodian of records. As a result, the District Court found that the burden upon the attorney was unreasonable, and I cannot disagree.

NOTE

Supervisory Power to Quash. While refusing to impose a special showing of need, several circuits have recognized a supervisory authority in the district court sufficiently broad to justify quashing a subpoena to an attorney in an exceptional case. The First Circuit upheld the quashing of subpoenas to attorneys who were currently serving as defense counsel in a state criminal prosecution where the district court concluded that the "forced disclosures would jeopardize the attorney-client relationship at a crucial point in the defense preparations" and constituted "harassment". In re Grand Jury Matters, 751 F.2d 131 (1st Cir. 1984) (also noting that the government had not shown an "urgent need" for obtaining at this time the information being sought from the attorney).

In **In re Grand Jury Subpoena for Attorney Representing Criminal Defendant (Reyes-Requena)**, 913 F.2d 1118 (5th Cir. 1990), the Fifth Circuit found that a district court correctly found a subpoena "oppressive" under Rule 17(c), discussed in Chapter 9, in quashing a subpoena to an attorney, DeGeurin, for fee information related to his current representation of Reyes-Requena. The government issued the subpoena to DeGeurin the same day that he represented Reyes-Requena at a bond hearing related to a cocaine possession charge. The grand jury subpoena required DeGeurin to testify about the identity of any party paying his fee for representing Reyes-Requena and the amount of the payment. The district court quashed the subpoena on various grounds, including a finding that the subpoena was oppressive because the "timing of the subpoena impinged upon the attorney-client relationship and severely hindered the effectiveness of DeGeurin's representation. The Fifth Circuit stated:

> In this case, the district court's exercise of its discretion to quash the subpoena because it created a serious interference with Reyes-Requena's relationship with his attorney is justified for several reasons. Reyes-Requena's Sixth Amendment rights had attached. The prosecution against him was moving swiftly–an indictment issued within three weeks of Reyes-Requena's detention hearing. DeGeurin's representation of Reyes-Requena was effectively stalled during the two-to-three-week interval that he contested the subpoena. The government made no effort to explain, even rhetorically, why it was necessary to subpoena DeGeurin during that critical juncture in his representation of the defendant. The government made not a single argument in the district court or before this court to suggest that a brief delay in the process, until a lull in the Reyes-Requena prosecution or until after his conviction, would have been imprudent.[15] Thus, when the district court quashed the subpoena to DeGeurin, solely because of its oppressive timing, we do not believe that the court abused its discretion. Alternatively, the court could have modified the subpoena, continuing it to a future date that would not have interfered so starkly with DeGeurin's representation of his client. As the government did not suggest a modification, the district court can be excused for not exercising its discretion to grant one.[a]

---

[15] We do not imply that the government was required to justify its subpoena of DeGeurin substantively beyond the usual minimum requirements of relevance, specificity, and timeliness. The government could, however, have furnished some factual basis, if one existed, for the exigency of enforcing a subpoena at this particularly onerous time.

[a] The Fifth Circuit ultimately reversed the district court because Reyes-Requena was convicted before the government's appeal could be decided, and the court found that the exigency supporting the finding of oppression had dissipated.

C. RIGHT TO COUNSEL

UNITED STATES v. STEIN

541 F.3d 130 (2d Cir. 2008)

DENNIS JACOBS, Chief Judge:

The United States appeals from an order of the United States District Court for the Southern District of New York (Kaplan, J.), dismissing an indictment against thirteen former partners and employees of the accounting firm KPMG, LLP. Judge Kaplan found that, absent pressure from the government, KPMG would have paid defendants' legal fees and expenses without regard to cost. Based on this and other findings of fact, Judge Kaplan ruled that the government deprived defendants of their right to counsel under the Sixth Amendment by causing KPMG to impose conditions on the advancement of legal fees to defendants, to cap the fees, and ultimately to end payment. See United States v. Stein, 435 F.Supp.2d 330, 367-73 (S.D.N.Y.2006) ("Stein I"). Judge Kaplan also ruled that the government deprived defendants of their right to substantive due process under the Fifth Amendment.

We hold that KPMG's adoption and enforcement of a policy under which it conditioned, capped and ultimately ceased advancing legal fees to defendants followed as a direct consequence of the government's overwhelming influence, and that KPMG's conduct therefore amounted to state action. We further hold that the government thus unjustifiably interfered with defendants' relationship with counsel and their ability to mount a defense, in violation of the Sixth Amendment, and that the government did not cure the violation. Because no other remedy will return defendants to the status quo ante, we affirm the dismissal of the indictment as to all thirteen defendants In light of this disposition, we do not reach the district court's Fifth Amendment ruling.

BACKGROUND

The Thompson Memorandum

In January 2003, then-United States Deputy Attorney General Larry D. Thompson promulgated a policy statement, Principles of Federal Prosecution of Business Organizations (the "Thompson Memorandum"), which articulated "principles" to govern the Department's discretion in bringing prosecutions against business organizations. [See Chapter 3] The Thompson Memorandum was closely based on a predecessor document issued in 1999 by then-U.S. Deputy Attorney General Eric Holder, Federal Prosecution of Corporations. Along with the familiar factors governing charging decisions, the Thompson Memorandum identifies nine additional considerations, including the company's "timely and voluntary disclosure of wrongdoing and its willingness to cooperate in the investigation of its agents." The Memorandum explains that prosecutors should inquire

> whether the corporation appears to be protecting its culpable employees and agents [and that] a corporation's promise of support to culpable employees and agents, either *through the advancing of attorneys fees*, through retaining the employees without sanction for their misconduct, or through providing information to the employees about the government's investigation pursuant to a joint defense agreement, may be considered by the prosecutor in weighing the extent and value of a corporation's cooperation.

A footnote appended to the highlighted phrase explains that because certain states require companies to advance legal fees for their officers, "a corporation's compliance with governing law should not be considered a failure to cooperate." In December 2006–after the events in this prosecution had transpired–the Department of Justice replaced the Thompson Memorandum with the McNulty Memorandum, under which prosecutors may consider a company's fee advancement policy only where the circumstances indicate that it is "intended to impede a criminal investigation," and even then only with the approval of the Deputy Attorney General.

Commencement of the Federal Investigation

After Senate subcommittee hearings in 2002 concerning KPMG's possible involvement in creating and marketing fraudulent tax shelters, KPMG retained Robert S. Bennett of the law firm Skadden, Arps, Slate, Meagher & Flom LLP ("Skadden") to formulate a "cooperative approach" for KPMG to use in dealing with federal authorities. Bennett's strategy included "a decision to 'clean house'–a determination to ask Jeffrey Stein, Richard Smith, and Jeffrey Eischeid, all senior KPMG partners who had testified before the Senate and all now [Defendants-Appellees] here–to leave their positions as deputy chair and chief operating officer of the firm, vice chair-tax services, and a partner in personal financial planning, respectively." Smith was transferred and Eischeid was put on administrative leave. Stein resigned with arrangements for a three-year $100,000-per-month consultancy, and an agreement that KPMG would pay for Stein's representation in any actions brought against Stein arising from his activities at the firm. KPMG negotiated a contract with Smith that included a similar clause; but that agreement was never executed.

In February 2004, KPMG officials learned that the firm and 20 to 30 of its top partners and employees were subjects of a grand jury investigation of fraudulent tax shelters. On February 18, 2004, KPMG's CEO announced to all partners that the firm was aware of the United States Attorney's Office's ("USAO") investigation and that "[a]ny present or former members of the firm asked to appear will be represented by competent coun[sel] at the firm's expense."

The February 25, 2004 Meeting

In preparation for a meeting with Skadden on February 25, 2004, the prosecutors–including Assistant United States Attorneys ("AUSAs") Shirah Neiman and Justin Weddle–decided to ask whether KPMG would advance legal fees to employees under investigation. Bennett started the meeting by announcing that KPMG had resolved to "clean house," that KPMG "would cooperate fully with the government's investigation," and that its goal was not to protect individual employees but rather to save the firm from being indicted. AUSA Weddle inquired about the firm's plans for advancing fees and about any legal obligation to do so. Later on, AUSA Neiman added that the government would "take into account" the firm's legal obligations to advance fees, but that "the Thompson Memorandum [w]as a point that had to be considered." Bennett then advised that although KPMG was still investigating its legal obligations to advance fees, its "common practice" was to do so. However, Bennett explained, KPMG would not pay legal fees for any partner who refused to cooperate or "took the Fifth," so long as KPMG had the legal authority to do so.

Later in the meeting, AUSA Weddle asked Bennett to ascertain KPMG's legal obligations to advance attorneys' fees. AUSA Neiman added that "misconduct" should not or cannot "be rewarded" under "federal guidelines." One Skadden attorney's notes attributed to AUSA Weddle the prediction that, if KPMG had discretion regarding fees, the government would "look at that under a microscope."

Skadden then reported back to KPMG. In notes of the meeting, a KPMG executive wrote the words "[p]aying legal fees" and "[s]everance" next to "not a sign of cooperation."

Communications Between the Prosecutors and KPMG

On March 2, 2004, Bennett told AUSA Weddle that although KPMG believed it had no legal obligation to advance fees, "it would be a big problem" for the firm not to do so given its partnership structure. But Bennett disclosed KPMG's tentative decision to limit the amount of fees and condition them on employees' cooperation with prosecutors.

Two days later, a Skadden lawyer advised counsel for Defendant-Appellee Carol G. Warley (a former KPMG tax partner) that KPMG would advance legal fees if Warley cooperated with the government and declined to invoke her Fifth Amendment privilege against self-incrimination.

On a March 11 conference call with Skadden, AUSA Weddle recommended that KPMG tell employees that they should be "totally open" with the USAO, "even if that [meant admitting] criminal wrongdoing," explaining that this would give him good material for cross-examination. That same day, Skadden wrote to counsel for the KPMG employees who had been identified as subjects of the investigation. The letter set forth KPMG's new fees policy ("Fees Policy"), pursuant to which advancement of fees and expenses would be

> [i] capped at $400,000 per employee;
>
> [ii] conditioned on the employee's cooperation with the government; and
>
> [iii] terminated when an employee was indicted.

The government was copied on this correspondence.

On March 12, KPMG sent a memorandum to certain other employees who had not been identified as subjects, urging them to cooperate with the government, advising them that it might be advantageous for them to exercise their right to counsel, and advising that KPMG would cover employees' "reasonable fees."

The prosecutors expressed by letter their "disappoint[ment] with [the] tone" of this memorandum and its "one-sided presentation of potential issues," and "demanded that KPMG send out a supplemental memorandum in a form they proposed." The government's alternative language, premised on the "assum[ption] that KPMG truly is committed to fully cooperating with the Government's investigation," Letter of David N. Kelley, United States Attorney, Southern District of New York, March 17, 2004, advised employees that they could "meet with investigators without the assistance of counsel." KPMG complied, and circulated a memo advising that employees "may deal directly with government representatives without counsel."

At a meeting in late March, Skadden asked the prosecutors to notify Skadden in the event any KPMG employee refused to cooperate. Over the following year, the prosecutors regularly informed Skadden whenever a KPMG employee refused to cooperate fully, such as by refusing to proffer or by proffering incompletely (in the government's view). Skadden, in turn, informed the employees' lawyers that fee advancement would cease unless the employees cooperated. The employees either knuckled under and submitted to interviews, or they were fired and KPMG ceased advancing their fees. For example, Watson and Smith attended proffer sessions after receiving KPMG's March 11 letter announcing the Fees Policy, and after Skadden reiterated to them that fees would be terminated absent cooperation. They did so because (they said, and the district court found) they feared that KPMG would stop advancing attorneys fees–although Watson concedes he attended a first session voluntarily. As Bennett later assured AUSA Weddle: "Whenever your Office has notified us that individuals have not . . . cooperat [ed], KPMG has promptly and without question encouraged them to cooperate and threatened to cease payment of their attorney fees and . . . to take personnel action, including termination." Letter of Robert Bennett to United States Attorney's Office, November 2, 2004.

KPMG Avoids Indictment

In an early-March 2005 meeting, then-U.S. Attorney David Kelley told Skadden and top KPMG executives that a non-prosecution agreement was unlikely and that he had reservations about KPMG's level of cooperation: "I've seen a lot better from big companies." Bennett reminded Kelley how KPMG had capped and conditioned its advancement of legal fees. Kelley remained unconvinced.

KPMG moved up the Justice Department's chain of command. At a June 13, 2005 meeting with U.S. Deputy Attorney General James Comey, Bennett stressed KPMG's pressure on employees to cooperate by conditioning legal fees on cooperation; it was, he said, "precedent[ ]setting." KPMG's entreaties were ultimately successful: on August 29, 2005, the firm entered into a deferred prosecution agreement (the "DPA") under which KPMG admitted extensive wrongdoing, paid a $456 million fine, and committed itself to cooperation in any future government investigation or prosecution.

Indictment of Individual Employees

On August 29, 2005–the same day KPMG executed the DPA–the government indicted six of the Defendants–Appellees (along with three other KPMG employees): Jeffrey Stein; Richard Smith; Jeffrey Eischeid; John Lanning, Vice Chairman of Tax Services; Philip Wiesner, a former tax partner; and Mark Watson, a tax partner. A superseding indictment filed on October 17, 2005 named ten additional employees, including seven of the Defendants-Appellees: Larry DeLap, a former tax partner in charge of professional practice; Steven Gremminger, a former partner and associate general counsel; former tax partners Gregg Ritchie, Randy Bickham and Carl Hasting; Carol G. Warley; and Richard Rosenthal, a former tax partner and Chief Financial Officer of KPMG. Pursuant to the Fees Policy, KPMG promptly stopped advancing legal fees to the indicted employees who were still receiving them.

Procedural History

On January 12, 2006, the thirteen defendants (among others) moved to dismiss the indictment based on the government's interference with KPMG's advancement of fees. In a submission to the district court, KPMG represented that

> the Thompson memorandum in conjunction with the government's statements relating to payment of legal fees affected KPMG's determination(s) with respect to the advancement of legal fees and

> other defense costs to present or former partners and employees . . . . In fact, KPMG is prepared to state that the Thompson memorandum substantially influenced KPMG's decisions with respect to legal fees . . . .

At a hearing on March 30, 2006, Judge Kaplan asked the government whether it was "prepared at this point to commit that [it] has no objection whatsoever to KPMG exercising its free and independent business judgment as to whether to advance defense costs to these defendants and that if it were to elect to do so the government would not in any way consider that in determining whether it had complied with the DPA?" The AUSA responded: "That's always been the case, your Honor. That's fine. We have no objection to that . . . . They can always exercise their business judgment. As you described it, your Honor, that's always been the case. It's the case today, your Honor." * * *

[After holding three days of hearings on the defendants' motion to dismiss the indictment,] Judge Kaplan arrived at the following ultimate findings of fact, all of which the government contests on appeal:

> [1] "the Thompson Memorandum caused KPMG to consider departing from its long-standing policy of paying legal fees and expenses of its personnel in all cases and investigations even before it first met with the USAO" and induced KPMG to seek "an indication from the USAO that payment of fees in accordance with its settled practice would not be held against it";
>
> [2] the government made repeated references to the Thompson Memo in an effort to "reinforce[ ] the threat inherent in the Thompson Memorandum";
>
> [3] "the government conducted itself in a manner that evidenced a desire to minimize the involvement of defense attorneys"; and
>
> [4] but for the Thompson Memorandum and the prosecutors' conduct, KPMG would have paid defendants' legal fees and expenses without consideration of cost.

Against that background, Judge Kaplan ruled that a defendant has a fundamental right under the Fifth Amendment to fairness in the criminal process, including the ability to get and deploy in defense all "resources lawfully available to him or her, free of knowing or reckless government interference," and that the government's reasons for infringing that right in this case could not withstand strict scrutiny. Judge Kaplan also ruled that the same conduct deprived each defendant of the Sixth Amendment right "to choose the lawyer or lawyers he or she desires and to use one's own funds to mount the defense that one wishes to present." He reasoned that "the government's law enforcement interests in taking the specific actions in question [do not] sufficiently outweigh the interests of the KPMG Defendants in having the resources needed to defend as they think proper against these charges." "[T]he fact that advancement of legal fees occasionally might be part of an obstruction scheme or indicate a lack of full cooperation by a prospective defendant is insufficient to justify the government's interference with the right of individual criminal defendants to obtain resources lawfully available to them in order to defend themselves . . . ." * * *

Judge Kaplan dismissed the indictment against the thirteen defendants on July 16, 2007. * * * Judge Kaplan concluded that no remedy other than dismissal of the indictment would put defendants in the position they would have occupied absent the government's misconduct. * * *

We review first [I] the government's challenges to the district court's factual findings, including its finding that but for the Thompson Memorandum and the prosecutors' conduct KPMG would have paid employees' legal fees-pre-indictment and post-indictment-without regard to cost. Next, because we are hesitant to resolve constitutional questions unnecessarily, [II] we inquire whether the government cured the purported Sixth Amendment violation by the AUSA's in-court statement on March 30, 2006 that KPMG was free to decide whether to advance fees. Since we conclude that this statement did not return defendants to the status quo ante, [III] we decide whether the promulgation and enforcement of KPMG's Fees Policy amounted to state action under the Constitution and [IV] whether the government deprived defendants of their Sixth Amendment right to counsel.

The government challenges certain factual findings of the district court. * * *

The government points out that the Thompson Memorandum lists "fees advancement" as just one of many considerations in a complex charging decision, and thus argues that Judge Kaplan overread the Thompson Memorandum as a threat that KPMG would be indicted unless it ceased advancing legal fees to its employees.

Judge Kaplan's finding withstands scrutiny. KPMG was faced with the fatal prospect of indictment; it could be expected to do all it could, assisted by sophisticated counsel, to placate and appease the government. As Judge Kaplan noted, KPMG's chief legal officer, Sven Erik Holmes, testified that he considered it crucial "to be able to say at the right time with the right audience, we're in full compliance with the Thompson Memorandum." Moreover, KPMG's management and counsel had reason to consider the impact of the firm's indictment on the interests of the firm's partners, employees, clients, creditors and retirees.

The government reads the Thompson Memorandum to say that fees advancement is to be considered as a negative factor only when it is part of a campaign to "circle the wagons," *i.e.*, to protect culpable employees and obstruct investigators. And it is true that the Thompson Memorandum instructs a prosecutor to ask "whether the corporation appears to be protecting its culpable employees and agents." But even if the government's reading is plausible, the wording nevertheless empowers prosecutors to determine which employees will be deprived of company-sponsored counsel: prosecutors may reasonably foresee that employees they identify as "culpable" will be cut off from fees.

The government also takes issue with Judge Kaplan's finding that the prosecutors (acting under DOJ policy) deliberately reinforced the threat inherent in the Thompson Memorandum. It protests that KPMG considered conditioning legal fees on cooperation even before the February 25, 2004 meeting and that KPMG adopted its Fees Policy free from government influence. However, Judge Kaplan's interpretation of the meeting is supported by the following record evidence. Because withholding of fees would be problematic for a partnership like KPMG, Bennett began by attempting to "sound out" the government's position on the issue. The prosecutors declined to sign off on KPMG's prior arrangement. Instead they asked KPMG to ascertain whether it had a legal obligation to advance fees. KPMG responded with its fallback position: conditioning fees on cooperation. In Judge Kaplan's view, this was not an official policy announcement, but rather a proposal: Skadden lawyers repeatedly emphasized to the prosecutors that no final decision had been made. One available inference from all this is that the prosecutors' inquiry about KPMG's legal obligations was a routine check for conflicts of interest; but on this record, Judge Kaplan was entitled to see things differently.

Nor can we disturb Judge Kaplan's finding that "the government conducted itself in a manner that evidenced a desire to minimize the involvement of defense attorneys." During the March 11 phone call between the prosecutors and Skadden, AUSA Weddle demanded that KPMG tell its employees to be "totally open" with the USAO, "even if that [meant admitting] criminal wrongdoing," so that he could gather material for cross-examination. On March 12, the prosecutors prevailed upon KPMG to supplement its first advisory letter with another, which clarified that employees could meet with the government without counsel. In addition, prosecutors repeatedly used Skadden to threaten to withhold legal fees from employees who refused to proffer-even if defense counsel had recommended that an employee invoke the Fifth Amendment privilege. Judge Kaplan could reasonably reject the government's version of these events.

Finally, we cannot say that the district court's ultimate finding of fact–that absent the Thompson Memorandum and the prosecutors' conduct KPMG would have advanced fees without condition or cap–was clearly erroneous. The government itself stipulated in *Stein I* that KPMG had a "longstanding voluntary practice" of advancing and paying employees' legal fees "without regard to economic costs or considerations" and "without a preset cap or condition of cooperation with the government . . . in any civil, criminal or regulatory proceeding" arising from activities within the scope of employment. Although it "is far from certain" that KPMG is legally obligated to advance defendants' legal fees, a firm may have potent incentives to advance fees, such as the ability to recruit and retain skilled professionals in a profession fraught with legal risk. Also, there is evidence that, before the prosecutors' intervention, KPMG executed an agreement under which it would advance Stein's legal fees without cap or condition (and negotiated toward an identical agreement with Smith). And while the government maintains that the civil, criminal and regulatory investigations confronting KPMG constituted an unprecedented state of affairs that might have caused KPMG to adopt new and different policies, Judge Kaplan was not required to agree. Indeed, KPMG itself represented to the court that the Thompson Memorandum and the prosecutors' conduct "substantially influenced [its] determination(s) with respect to the advancement of legal fees."

For the foregoing reasons, we cannot disturb Judge Kaplan's factual findings, including his finding that, but for the Thompson Memorandum and the prosecutors' conduct, KPMG would have advanced legal fees without condition or cap. * * *

[The Second Circuit determined that the government had not cured any violation of the defendants' right to counsel by the later statement that KPMG was free to pay the attorney's fees. The court concluded:]

The appropriate remedy for a constitutional violation is one that as much as possible restores the defendant to the circumstances that would have existed had there been no constitutional error. Since it has been found that, absent governmental interference, KPMG would have advanced unlimited legal fees unconditionally, only the unconditional, unlimited advancement of legal fees would restore defendants to the status quo ante. The government's in-court statement and the ensuing 16-month delay were not enough. If there was a Sixth Amendment violation, dismissal of the indictment is required. * * *

Judge Kaplan found that "KPMG's decision to cut off all payments of legal fees and expenses to anyone who was indicted and to limit and to condition such payments prior to indictment upon cooperation with the government was the direct consequence of the pressure applied by the Thompson Memorandum and the USAO." The government protests that KPMG's adoption and enforcement of its Fees Policy was private action, outside the ambit of the Sixth Amendment. * * *

Actions of a private entity are attributable to the State if "there is a sufficiently close nexus between the State and the challenged action of the ... entity so that the action of the latter may be fairly treated as that of the State itself." Jackson v. Metro. Edison Co., 419 U.S. 345 (1974). The "close nexus" test is not satisfied when the state "[m]ere[ly] approv[es] of or acquiesce[s] in the initiatives" of the private entity, S.F. Arts & Athletics, Inc. v. U.S. Olympic Comm., 483 U.S. 522, 547 (1987), or when an entity is merely subject to governmental regulation, see Jackson. "The purpose of the [close-nexus requirement] is to assure that constitutional standards are invoked only when it can be said that the State is responsible for the specific conduct of which the plaintiff complains." Blum v. Yaretsky, 457 U.S. 991 (1982). Such responsibility is normally found when the State "has exercised coercive power or has provided such significant encouragement, either overt or covert, that the choice must in law be deemed to be that of the State." * * *

The government argues: KPMG simply took actions in the shadow of an internal DOJ advisory document (the Thompson Memorandum) containing multiple factors and caveats; the government's approval of KPMG's Fees Policy did not render the government responsible for KPMG's actions enforcing it; even if the government had specifically required KPMG to adopt a policy that penalized non-cooperation, state action would still have been lacking because KPMG would have retained the power to apply the policy; and although the prosecutors repeatedly informed KPMG when employees were not cooperating, they did so at KPMG's behest, without knowing how KPMG would react. We disagree.

KPMG's adoption and enforcement of the Fees Policy amounted to "state action" because KPMG "operate[d] as a willful participant in joint activity" with the government, and because the USAO "significant[ly] encourage[d]" KPMG to withhold legal fees from defendants upon indictment. The government brought home to KPMG that its survival depended on its role in a joint project with the government to advance government prosecutions. The government is therefore legally "responsible for the specific conduct of which the [criminal defendants] complain[ ]."

The government argues that "KPMG's decision to condition legal fee payments on cooperation, while undoubtedly influenced by the Thompson Memorandum, was not coerced or directed by the Government." But that argument runs up against the district court's factual finding (which we do not disturb) that the fees decision "was the direct consequence" of the Memorandum and the prosecutors' conduct. Nevertheless, it remains a question of law whether the facts as found by the district court establish state action.

State action is established here as a matter of law because the government forced KPMG to adopt its constricted Fees Policy. The Thompson Memorandum itself-which prosecutors stated would be considered in deciding whether to indict KPMG-emphasizes that cooperation will be assessed in part based upon whether, in advancing counsel fees, "the corporation appears to be protecting its culpable employees and agents." Since defense counsel's objective in a criminal investigation will virtually always be to protect the client, KPMG's risk was that fees for defense counsel would be advanced to someone the government considered culpable. So the only safe course was to allow the government to become (in effect) paymaster.

The prosecutors reinforced this message by inquiring into KPMG's fees obligations, referring to the Thompson Memorandum as "a point that had to be considered," and warning that "misconduct" should not or cannot "be rewarded" under "federal guidelines." The government had KPMG's full attention. It is hardly surprising, then, that KPMG decided to condition payment of fees on employees' cooperation with the government and to terminate fees upon indictment: only that policy would allow KPMG to continue advancing fees while minimizing the risk that prosecutors would view such advancement as obstructive.

To ensure that KPMG's new Fees Policy was enforced, prosecutors became "entwined in the . . . control" of KPMG. They intervened in KPMG's decisionmaking, expressing their "disappoint[ment] with [the] tone" of KPMG's first advisory memorandum, and declaring that "[t]hese problems must be remedied" by a proposed supplemental memorandum specifying that employees could meet with the government without being burdened by counsel. Prosecutors also "made plain" their "strong preference" as to what the firm should do, and their "desire to share the fruits of such intrusions." They did so by regularly "reporting to KPMG the identities of employees who refused to make statements in circumstances in which the USAO knew full well that KPMG would pressure them to talk to prosecutors." The government's argument that it could not have known how KPMG would react when informed that certain employees were not cooperating is at best plausible only vis-à-vis the first few employees. The prosecutors thus steered KPMG toward their preferred fee advancement policy and then supervised its application in individual cases. Such “overt” and "significant encouragement" supports the conclusion that KPMG's conduct is properly attributed to the State.

In *Blum* and *Albert*, it was decisive that [1] actions of the private entity were based on independent criteria (the medical standards; the college rules of conduct), and that [2] the government was not dictating the outcomes of particular cases. * * *

Here * * *, [1] KPMG was never "free to define" cooperation independently: AUSA Weddle told Bennett that he had "had a bad experience in the past with a company conditioning payments on a person's cooperation, where the company did not define cooperation as 'tell the truth' the[ ] way we [the prosecutors] define it." KPMG's fees advancement decisions in individual cases thus depended largely on state-influenced standards. In addition, [2] the prosecution designated particular employees for deprivation of fees (and, in some cases, termination of employment) by demanding that KPMG threaten and penalize those employees for non-cooperation. As Bennett later reported to the Deputy Attorney General, "[w]henever your Office has notified us that individuals have not . . . cooperat[ed], KPMG has promptly and without question encouraged them to cooperate and threatened to cease payment of their attorneys fees and . . . to take personnel action, including termination." Furthermore, by indicting the thirteen defendants after inspiring and shaping KPMG's Fees Policy and after exacting KPMG's compliance with it, prosecutors effectively selected which employees would be deprived of attorneys' fees. Having forced the constriction of KPMG's longstanding policy of advancing fees, the government then compelled KPMG to apply the Fees Policy to particular employees both pre- and post-indictment. This conduct finds no protection in *Blum* and *Albert.*

The government also directs us to another line of state action cases: D.L. Cromwell Investments, Inc. v. NASD Regulation, Inc., 279 F.3d 155 (2d Cir.2002), and United States v. Solomon, 509 F.2d 863 (2d Cir.1975). These cases involved parallel, cooperative investigations by private regulatory entities and government investigators. * * *

In both cases, we held that there was no state action because the private actors had independent regulatory interests and motives for making their inquiries and for cooperating with parallel investigations being conducted by the government. In *D.L. Cromwell*, the NASD had a preexisting "regulatory duty to investigate questionable securities transactions,"–that is, it would have requested interviews regardless of governmental pressure. And in *Solomon*, the NYSE's efforts were "in pursuance of its own interests and obligations, not as an agent of the [government],"–absent SEC involvement, the NYSE would have investigated anyway. Because the NASD and the NYSE had preexisting and independent investigatory missions, their cooperation with the government was not state action. By contrast (as the district court found), absent the prosecutors' involvement and the Thompson Memorandum, KPMG would not have changed its longstanding fee advancement policy or withheld legal fees from defendants upon indictment.

The government responds: Solomon declined to find state action even though it involved a private entity compelling interviews with one of its members, backed by the explicit threat of expulsion, in the context of continuous coordination between the NYSE and the SEC on the same side. So how can KPMG, an adversary of the government, also be its partner? See Brentwood Acad. v. Tenn. Secondary Sch. Athletic Ass'n, 531 U.S. 288 (2001) ("The state-action doctrine does not convert opponents into virtual agents.").

An adversarial relationship does not normally bespeak partnership. But KPMG faced ruin by indictment and reasonably believed it must do everything in its power to avoid it. The government's threat of indictment was easily sufficient to convert its adversary into its agent. KPMG was not in a position to consider coolly the risk of indictment, weigh the potential significance of the other enumerated factors in the Thompson Memorandum, and decide for itself how to proceed.

We therefore conclude that KPMG's adoption and enforcement of the Fees Policy (both before and upon defendants' indictment) amounted to state action. The government may properly be held "responsible for the specific conduct of which the [criminal defendants] complain[ ]," *Blum*, *i.e.*, the deprivation of their Sixth Amendment right to counsel, if the violation is established.

* * * Most of the state action relevant here–the promulgation of the Thompson Memorandum, the prosecutors' communications with KPMG regarding the advancement of fees, KPMG's adoption of a Fees Policy with caps and conditions, and KPMG's repeated threats to employees identified by prosecutors as being uncooperative–pre-dated the indictments of August and October 2005. So we must determine how this pre-indictment conduct may bear on defendants' Sixth Amendment claim.

"The Sixth Amendment right of the 'accused' to assistance of counsel in 'all criminal prosecutions' is limited by its terms: it does not attach until a prosecution is commenced." Rothgery v. Gillespie County, 128 S.Ct. 2578 (2008). "Attachment" refers to "when the [Sixth Amendment] right may be asserted"; it does not concern the separate question of "what the right guarantees," i.e., "what the substantive guarantee of the Sixth Amendment" is at that stage of the prosecution. The Supreme Court has "pegged commencement [of a prosecution] to the initiation of adversary judicial criminal proceedings–whether by way of formal charge, preliminary hearing, indictment, information, or arraignment. The rule is not 'mere formalism,' but a recognition of the point at which the government has committed itself to prosecute, the adverse positions of government and defendant have solidified, and the accused finds himself faced with the prosecutorial forces of organized society, and immersed in the intricacies of substantive and procedural criminal law." * * *

[Judge Kaplan determined that the government's conduct before the indictment violated the Sixth Amendment for the following reasons:]

> * * * It is true, of course, that the Sixth Amendment right to counsel typically attaches at the initiation of adversarial proceedings–at an arraignment, indictment, preliminary hearing, and so on. But the analysis can not end there. The Thompson Memorandum on its face and the USAO's actions were parts of an effort to limit defendants' access to funds for their defense. Even if this was not among the conscious motives, the Memorandum was adopted and the USAO acted in circumstances in which that result was known to be exceptionally likely. The fact that events were set in motion prior to indictment with the object of having, or with knowledge that they were likely to have, an unconstitutional effect upon indictment cannot save the government. This conduct, unless justified, violated the Sixth Amendment.

In other words, the government's pre-indictment conduct was of a kind that would have post-indictment effects of Sixth Amendment significance, and did.

We endorse this analysis. Although defendants' Sixth Amendment rights attached only upon indictment, the district court properly considered pre-indictment state action that affected defendants post-indictment. When the government acts prior to indictment so as to impair the suspect's relationship with counsel post-indictment, the pre-indictment actions ripen into cognizable Sixth Amendment deprivations upon indictment. As Judge Ellis explained in United States v. Rosen, 487 F.Supp.2d 721 (E.D.Va.2007), "it is entirely plausible that pernicious effects of the pre-indictment interference continued into the post-indictment period, effectively hobbling defendants' Sixth Amendment rights to retain counsel of choice with funds to which they had a right . . . . [I]f, as alleged, the government coerced [the employer] into halting fee advances on defendants' behalf and the government did so for the purpose of undermining defendants' relationship with counsel once the indictment issued, the government violated defendants' right to expend their own resources towards counsel once the right attached."

Since the government forced KPMG to adopt the constricted Fees Policy–including the provision for terminating fee advancement upon indictment–and then compelled KPMG to enforce it, it was virtually certain that KPMG would terminate defendants' fees upon indictment. We therefore reject the government's argument that its actions (virtually all pre-indictment) are immune from scrutiny under the Sixth Amendment.***

The Sixth Amendment ensures that "[i]n all criminal prosecutions, the accused shall enjoy the right . . . to have the Assistance of Counsel for his defence." U.S. Const. amend. VI. Thus "the Sixth Amendment guarantees the defendant the right to be represented by an otherwise qualified attorney whom that defendant can afford to hire, or who is willing to represent the defendant even though he is without funds." Caplin & Drysdale, Chartered v. United States, 491 U.S. 617, (1989). "[A]n element of this right is the right of a defendant who does not require appointed counsel to choose who will represent him." United States v. Gonzalez-Lopez, 548 U.S. 140 (2006).

The government must "honor" a defendant's Sixth Amendment right to counsel:

> This means more than simply that the State cannot prevent the accused from obtaining the assistance of counsel. The Sixth Amendment also imposes on the State an affirmative obligation to respect and preserve the accused's choice to seek this assistance . . . . [A]t the very least, the prosecutor and police have an affirmative obligation not to act in a manner that circumvents and thereby dilutes the protection afforded by the right to counsel.

Maine v. Moulton, 474 U.S. 159 (1985). This is intuitive: the right to counsel in an adversarial legal system would mean little if defense counsel could be controlled by the government or vetoed without good reason. * * *

It is axiomatic that if defendants had already received fee advances from KPMG, the government could not (absent justification) deliberately interfere with the use of that money to fuel their defenses. And the government concedes that it could not prevent a lawyer from furnishing a defense gratis.

Presumably, such a lawyer could pay another lawyer to represent the defendant (subject, of course, to ethical rules governing third-party payments to counsel). And if the Sixth Amendment prohibits the government from interfering with such arrangements, then surely it also prohibits the government from interfering with financial donations by others, such as family members and neighbors-and employers. In a nutshell, the Sixth Amendment protects against unjustified governmental interference with the right to defend oneself using whatever assets one has or might reasonably and lawfully obtain.

* * * It is also urged that a company may pretend cooperation while "circling the wagons," that payment of legal fees can advance such a strategy, and that the government has a legitimate interest in being able to assess cooperation using the payment of fees as one factor. Even if that can be a legitimate justification, it would not be in play here: prosecutors testified before the district court that they were never concerned that KPMG was "circling the wagons." Moreover, it is unclear how the circling of wagons is much different from the legitimate melding of a joint defense.

The government conceded at oral argument that it is in the government's interest that every defendant receive the best possible representation he or she can obtain. A company that advances legal fees to employees may stymie prosecutors by affording culpable employees with high-quality representation. But if it is in the government's interest that every defendant receive the best possible representation, it cannot also be in the government's interest to leave defendants naked to their enemies.

* * *A defendant who is deprived of counsel of choice (without justification) need not show how his or her defense was impacted; such errors are structural and are not subject to harmless-error review. See *Gonzalez-Lopez* ("[T]he right at stake here is the right to counsel of choice, . . . and that right was violated because the deprivation of counsel was erroneous. No additional showing of prejudice is required to make the violation 'complete.'"). Of course, a completed constitutional violation may still be remediable. However, * * * the government has failed to cure this Sixth Amendment violation. Therefore, the government deprived defendants Gremminger, Hasting, Ritchie and Watson of their Sixth Amendment right to counsel of choice.

The remaining defendants–Bickham, DeLap, Eischeid, Lanning, Rosenthal, Smith, Stein, Warley, and Wiesner–do not claim they were deprived of their chosen counsel. Rather, they assert that the government unjustifiably interfered with their relationship with counsel and their ability to defend themselves. In the district court, the government conceded that these defendants are also entitled to dismissal of the indictment, assuming the correctness of *Stein I*. We agree: these defendants can easily demonstrate interference in their relationships with counsel and impairment of their ability to mount a defense based on Judge Kaplan's non-erroneous findings that the post-indictment termination of fees "caused them to restrict the activities of their counsel," and thus to limit the scope of their pre-trial investigation and preparation. Defendants were indicted based on a fairly novel theory of criminal liability; they faced substantial penalties; the relevant facts are scattered throughout over 22 million documents regarding the doings of scores of people; the subject matter is "extremely complex"; technical expertise is needed to figure out and explain what happened; and trial was expected to last between six and eight months. As Judge Kaplan found, these defendants "have been forced to limit their defenses . . . for economic reasons and . . . they would not have been so constrained if KPMG paid their expenses." We therefore hold that these defendants were also deprived of their right to counsel under the Sixth Amendment.[15]

NOTES AND QUESTIONS

1. **Principles of Federal Prosecution of Business Organizations.** *Stein* discussed the McNulty Memo that modified the Thompson Memo by limiting the Department of Justice's policy on considering payment of attorney's fees for employees suspected of being involved in wrongdoing. In August 2008, the Department issued the *Principles of Federal Prosecution of Business Organizations* [see Chapter 15] that rejects completely any consideration of the payment of attorney's fees in deciding whether a company has cooperated: "In evaluating cooperation, however, prosecutors should not take into account whether a corporation is advancing or reimbursing attorneys' fees or providing counsel to employees, officers, or directors under investigation or indictment. Likewise, prosecutors may not request that a corporation refrain from taking such action." *U.S. Attorney's Manual* § 9-28.730. Assuming federal prosecutors adhere to the *Principles* and do not take into consideration a company's payment of attorney's fees for its employees and officers, then the situation that arose in *Stein* is unlikely to occur again.

2. **What's Wrong with Attorney's Fees?** Unlike the Thompson Memo, which encouraged prosecutors to view the payment of attorney's fees as a sign of a lack of cooperation, the current policy does not view it as a negative sign. Why would the Department of Justice view the payment of attorney's fees as indicating a lack of cooperation? Consider the following:

> The payment of attorney's fees by a corporation is not a failure of cooperation unless one views the presence of a lawyer for a corporate

[15]This case does not raise, and therefore we have no occasion to consider, the application of our holding to the following scenario: A defendant moves unsuccessfully in the district court to dismiss the indictment on the same Sixth Amendment theory. The defendant proceeds to trial with his or her chosen attorney, and the attorney is forced to limit the scope of his or her efforts due to the defendant's financial constraints. The defendant is convicted based on overwhelming evidence of his or her guilt.

> officer as an impediment to an investigation. A lawyer is unlikely to recommend that a client, who is the target of an investigation, cooperate with the government, or at least, not without the protection of an immunity agreement or plea bargain. This does not mean the lawyer's advice is wrongful or designed to obstruct justice.

Peter J. Henning, *Targeting Legal Advice*, 54 AM. U. L. REV. 669 (2005).

3. **State Action**. The key to the Second Circuit's application of the Sixth Amendment was the finding that KPMG was acting on behalf of the government in denying the attorney's fees. Companies often pledge their cooperation when a government investigation commences, and often interview employees as part of an internal investigation while keeping prosecutors informed of their progress. It is not unknown that prosecutors will ask that a certain employee be interviewed or that a specified set of questions be asked during the investigation. If the company agrees to follow the prosecutor's suggestions, is that state action so that various constitutional protections apply, such as *Miranda*'s right to counsel in a custodial interrogation?

D. ETHICAL REGULATIONS

1. ABA Model Rule of Professional Conduct 3.8(e)

ABA Model Rule of Professional Conduct 3.8(e) (2002) provides:

> The prosecutor in a criminal case shall: * * * (e) not subpoena a lawyer in a grand jury or other criminal proceeding to present evidence about a past or present client unless the prosecutor reasonably believes: (1) the information sought is not protected from disclosure by any applicable privilege; (2) the evidence sought is essential to the successful completion of an ongoing investigation or prosecution; and (3) there is no other feasible alternative to obtain the information; * * *

Most states follow Model Rule 3.8(e), and it appears to require a federal prosecutor to meet the same criteria for issuance of a subpoena to an attorney as the Department of Justice rules. An earlier version of Model Rule 3.8(e) also required prosecutors to seek prior judicial approval before issuing a subpoena to an attorney, but the ABA later dropped that requirement. The ethical rules do not create additional rights for an opposing litigant. Preamble ¶ 20 ("Violation of a Rule should not itself give rise to a cause of action against a lawyer nor should it create any presumption in such a case that a legal duty has been breached."). See United States v. Parker, 165 F.Supp.2d 431 (W.D.N.Y. 2001) ("even if the alleged misconduct, attributed by Defendants to the Government attorneys in this case, were deemed an ethical violation, and the relevant disciplinary rule were applicable to the instant facts, such does not warrant use of the exclusionary rule as a remedy for such violation.").

2. McDade Act (28 U.S.C. § 530B)

Ethical regulation of federal prosecutors has largely been through internal enforcement by the Department of Justice's Office of Professional Responsibility. In 1998, however, Congress adopted 28 U.S.C. § 530B, entitled "Ethical standards for attorneys for the government" that provides: "An attorney for the Government shall be subject to State laws and rules, and local Federal court rules, governing attorneys in each State where such attorney engages in that attorney's duties, to the same extent and in the same manner as other attorneys in that State." The statute is named for former Representative Joseph McDade, who was acquitted of federal charges involving misuse of campaign funds. Although the statute was opposed by the Department of Justice, prior to taking the position of deputy attorney general, Larry Thompson wrote that the "McDade law is good for the profession." Larry D. Thompson, *The McDade Law: Necessary for Justice or a Burden for Federal Attorneys?*, 48 FED. LAW. 20 (2001). The original proposal called for the creation of a Misconduct Review Board and listed a number of actions that would subject a federal prosecutor to discipline. Those provisions were stripped out of the bill, and Congress ultimately passed it as part of a broader appropriations bill.

The McDade Act was in part a reaction to efforts by the Department of Justice to exempt its attorneys from state ethics rules governing contacts with persons who were represented by attorneys. The McDade Act thwarted that effort by requiring federal prosecutors to adhere to state ethics codes. The law also requires the Department of Justice to adopt rules to implement the statute. The Department of Justice's interpretation of "State laws and rules" does not include "Any statute, rule, or regulation which does not govern ethical conduct, such as rules of procedure, evidence, or substantive law, whether or not such rule is included in a code of professional responsibility for attorneys." 28 C.F.R. § 77.2(h). For a discussion of the ethical regulation of federal prosecutors, see Bruce A. Green & Fred C. Zacharias, *Regulating Federal Prosecutors' Ethics*, 55 VAND. L. REV. 381 (2002).

Federal district courts commonly incorporate a state's rules of professional responsibility as the standards applicable in their courts. In Baylson v. Disciplinary Board of the Supreme Court, 975 F.2d 102 (3d Cir. 1992), the Third Circuit concluded that a district court could not incorporate a Pennsylvania disciplinary rule modeled after the earlier version of Model Rule 3.8(e), that required prosecutors to obtain prior judicial approval before issuing a grand jury subpoena to an attorney. The court held that the state rule was "not compatible with the Federal Rules of Criminal Procedure or well-settled grand jury practice" and therefore the local courts did not have the authority to adopt such a rule.

In United States v. Colorado Supreme Court, 189 F.3d 1281 (10th Cir. 1999), the Tenth Circuit found that a Colorado ethics rule almost identical to the Model Rule 3.8(e) could be enforced under the McDade Act to require prior judicial approval of a subpoena to an attorney issued by federal prosecutors. The court stated:

> [A] prosecutor violating Rule 3.8 has violated the generally accepted principle that the attorney-client relationship should not be disturbed without cause. To do so would constitute essentially 'unethical' attorney conduct unbecoming any member of the bar, including prosecutors. Because of the characteristics of Rule 3.8, we conclude that the rule in its current incarnation is a rule of ethics applicable to federal prosecutors by the McDade Act.

In Whitehouse v. United States District, 53 F.3d 1349 (1st Cir. 1995), the court disagreed with *Baylson* and upheld a Rhode Island local district court rule, based on the earlier version of Model Rule 3.8(e) that was strikingly similar to the Pennsylvania rule. The First Circuit concluded that the rule in question was "not aimed at grand jury action," did not preclude "an *ex parte, in camera* [judicial] hearing," and operated "merely [to] change * * * the timing with respect to motions to quash in recognition of the fact that service itself of an attorney-subpoena seeking to compel evidence concerning a client may cause irreparable damage to the attorney-client relationship."

Five years later, in Stern v. United States District Court, 214 F.3d 4 (1st Cir. 2000), the same court *rejected* a new Massachusetts rule that was again modeled after the earlier version of Model Rule 3.8(e). The court distinguished *Whitehouse* on the ground that the Rhode Island rule only contained the three criteria listed in Rule 3.8(e) in the comments, and therefore those requirements were not mandatory but only precatory. The Massachusetts rule, on the other hand, "differs significantly in that it imposes new substantive requirements for judicial preapproval of grand jury subpoenas. In so doing, the rule alters the grand jury's historic role, place it under overly intrusive court supervision, curbs its broad investigative powers, reverses the presumption of validity accorded to its subpoenas, undermines the secrecy of its proceedings, and creates procedural detours and delays. It therefore impermissibly interferes with grand jury proceedings."

In United States v. Lowery, 166 F.3d 1119 (11th Cir. 1999), the Eleventh Circuit overturned a lower court decision suppressing evidence that the court determined had been obtained in violation of a state ethical rule, stating that the McDade Act does not alter the status of state ethics rules because such rules "cannot provide an adequate basis for a federal court to suppress evidence that is otherwise admissible. Federal law, not state law, determine the admissibility of evidence in federal court. * * * State rules of professional conduct, or state rules on any subject, cannot trump the Federal Rules of Evidence."

3. Lawyer Involvement in Client Misconduct

Counsel's representation of a client can trigger an accusation that the lawyer engaged in criminal conduct. Do the ethical rules of the profession provide guidance regarding whether a lawyer's conduct constituted a criminal act? In **United States v. Kellington**, 217 F.3d 1084 (9th Cir. 2000), the court considered whether the trial judge's limiting instruction to the jury on the role of the legal ethics rules in assessing the defendant's intent was proper in a prosecution for obstruction of justice (see supra Chapter 8).

> It is well settled that in the prosecution of a lawyer for conduct stemming from his or her representation of a client, expert testimony on the lawyer's ethical obligations is relevant to establish the lawyer's intent and state of mind. * * * [C]ounsel for Kellington was unable to frame and give content to the core of his defense–that Kellington was attempting (however imprudently in hindsight) to provide his client with bona fide legal representation, and that much of the conduct from which the government would have the jury infer criminal intent can be explained by his ethical obligations to McFarlane, his background and experience, and the nature of the attorney-client relationship. Combined with the court's instruction to the jury that the ethics testimony was merely background information, we can have no confidence that the jury gave due regard to the ethics evidence in assessing the government's largely circumstantial case against Kellington on the question of criminal intent. Accordingly, we affirm the district court's considered judgment that, "the evidence convicting Kellington of a violation of 18 U.S.C. § 1512(b)(2)(B) in conjunction with the court's restrictions on closing argument preponderates sufficiently heavily against the verdict that a serious miscarriage of justice may have occurred."

Investigating potential lawyer misconduct during a pending criminal investigation or trial raises significant issues regarding the Sixth Amendment right of the client, which can be substantially harmed if the government seeks information about the ongoing representation. In **United States v. Simels**, 654 F.3d 161, 166-67 (2d Cir. 2011), the Second Circuit explained:

> The possibility that an attorney is attempting to obstruct justice in the course of representing a client presents Government investigators with a sensitive choice. If they act precipitously to determine whether obstruction is being attempted, they risk an unwarranted intrusion into the attorney-client relationship, an

intrusion that may well jeopardize their case against the client. On the other hand, if they unduly delay an inquiry, they risk serious harm to witnesses. Whether or not investigators facing this choice are constitutionally required to have a reasonable basis for their suspicion of possible obstruction before sending an informant to contact the lawyer, the existence of such a basis adequately allays any concern that the attorney-client relationship has been improperly invaded.

E. CONTACT WITH REPRESENTED PERSONS

ABA Model Rule of Professional Conduct 4.2 (2002) states: "In representing a client, a lawyer shall not communicate about the subject of the representation with a person the lawyer knows to be represented by another lawyer in the matter, unless the lawyer has the consent of the other lawyer or is authorized by law to do so." The ABA amended the Rule in 1995 by substituting "person" for "party" so that the scope of the Rule was not limited to those who are adversaries in litigation. Even after the change, does the Rule limit the ability of the government to conduct undercover investigations that involve contact with individuals who the government knows has retained counsel?

In 1990, the Department of Justice issues a memorandum to its attorneys–known as the "Thornburgh Memorandum," named for then-Attorney General Dick Thornburgh–that purported to exempt federal prosecutors from state ethics rules, specifically Rule 4.2, that could interfere with federal criminal investigations. The Thornburgh Memorandum caused significant controversy and was one of the principal contributing factors to congressional adoption of the McDade Act, which now requires all federal attorneys to comply with applicable state ethics rules. Most courts read the state counterparts to Model Rule 4.2 in a limited way that does not restrict the government's ability to have contacts with the targets of its investigation, regardless of whether they are represented by counsel. Consider the district court's analysis of the issue in the following case.

UNITED STATES v. GRASS

239 F.Supp.2d 535 (M.D. Pa. 2003)

RAMBO, District Judge.

On June 21, 2002, a federal grand jury sitting in Harrisburg, Pennsylvania issued a thirty-seven count indictment against Defendants Grass and Brown, former officers and directors for the Rite Aid Corporation. The indictment alleges that Defendants engaged in a conspiracy intended to enrich themselves by defrauding Rite Aid and its stockholders, creditors, and vendors. This conspiracy allegedly lasted the duration of Defendant Grass's tenure as Rite Aid's Chief Executive Officer ("CEO"). The indictment also alleges that Defendants Grass and Brown engaged in a conspiracy to obstruct justice by impeding investigations by the United States Securities and Exchange Commission ("SEC"), the Federal Bureau of Investigation ("FBI"), the United States Attorney's Office for the Middle District of Pennsylvania, and the Grand Jury.

On September 4, 2002, Defendants Grass and Brown filed a motion to suppress tapes of conversations that they had with Timothy Noonan, Rite Aid's former President. Defendants contend that Assistant United States Attorney Kim Douglas Daniel obtained the recorded conversations in violation of Rules 4.2 and 8.4(a) of the Pennsylvania Rules of Professional Conduct. * * *

Most of the facts pertinent to this motion are not in dispute. Defendant Grass resigned as Rite Aid's CEO on October 18, 1999. * * * Around that same time, the FBI's field office in Harrisburg, Pennsylvania began an investigation in conjunction with the United States Attorney's Office for the Middle District of Pennsylvania. The Government assigned FBI Agent George Delaney and Assistant United States Attorney ("AUSA") Kim Douglas Daniel to lead its criminal investigation.

At the suppression hearing, Noonan testified that between October of 1999 and July of 2000 he met with Defendant Brown several times. During those meetings, the two men discussed what each would tell Rite Aid's internal investigators regarding the fraud allegations. Both men were aware, during this period, that both civil and criminal investigations were pending as well.

On February 12, 2001, AUSA Daniel phoned Defendant Brown's counsel at the time, Herbert Stern. During that conversation, the two agreed that the Government would interview Defendant Brown on April 4, 2001. Mister Stern, however, requested that the Government provide, in advance of the interview, an agenda listing the topics that would be discussed. On March 28, 2001, AUSA Daniel faxed Mr. Stern an agenda letter setting forth the topics that the parties would discuss during the interview. No later than March 30, 2001, Mr. Stern informed AUSA Daniel that Defendant Brown had changed his mind and would not consent to an interview.

Previously, on March 9, 2001, Noonan met with AUSA Daniel and Agent Delaney at the United States Attorney's Office in Philadelphia, Pennsylvania. During that meeting, the parties discussed the fraud allegations and any contact that Noonan may have had with Defendants Grass and Brown subsequent to Noonan's departure from Rite Aid in December of 1999. The following day, Defendant Brown called Noonan at his home requesting that the two meet. Noonan deferred the meeting until March 13, 2001. In the meantime–on either March 11 or March 12, 2001–Noonan contacted Agent Delaney and informed him of Brown's phone call. * * *

[Noonan agreed with Agent Delaney to wear a secret recording device to his meeting with Brown. At the meeting,] Defendant Brown informed Noonan that he would be meeting with the Government in early April. Defendant Brown also told Noonan that Defendant Grass had retained Attorney William Jeffress to represent him in any criminal proceedings that might occur. * * *

[Noonan agreed to cooperate in the government's investigation in March 2001, and arranged another meeting with Brown. Before the meeting,] Agent Delaney also gave Noonan a fake letter signed by AUSA Daniel and addressed to Attorney David Howard, Noonan's retained counsel. That document was similar in content to the agenda letter that AUSA Daniel had already sent to Mr. Stern regarding Defendant Brown's proposed interview. Agent Delaney instructed Noonan to use the letter as a prop to guide his conversation with Brown to the topics listed in the letter. However, Agent Delaney warned Noonan to avoid talking about Defendant Brown's conversations with his attorney. "[Agent Delaney] did say that if Franklin brought up or said he had this discussion with his attorney or that discussion or that these were topics that his attorney said, don't get into those conversations." [Noonan recorded his next meeting with Brown.]

* * * On either April 16 or April 18, 2001, Noonan, at Agent Delaney's behest, traveled to Defendant Grass's office in Lemoyne, Pennsylvania to attempt to record a conversation with Grass regarding the fraud allegations.[3] Defendant Grass, however, was not in his office.

Following this attempted meeting, Noonan met once again with Agent Delaney in Philadelphia. During this meeting, Delaney instructed Noonan to meet with Defendant Brown again to arrange for a meeting with both Defendants Brown and Grass. On April 27, 2001, Noonan and Defendant Brown met at the Hampden Center Shopping Mall in Mechanicsburg, Pennsylvania. As before, Noonan recorded the conversation. During the course of the meeting, Noonan, as instructed, requested an audience with Defendant Grass. Defendant Brown indicated that Defendant Grass would probably be amenable to such a meeting.

On May 1, 2001, Noonan met with Agent Delaney, another unidentified FBI agent, AUSA Daniel, and AUSA George Rocktashel at the Federal Building in Harrisburg. Although AUSA Daniel was aware of Noonan's cooperation, this marked the first time he and Noonan had spoken since Noonan's initial interview on March 9 in Philadelphia. Their conversation covered a wide variety of subjects relating to the Government's investigation of fraud at Rite Aid and what Noonan's conversations with Brown had

[3] As he did before Noonan's meeting with Defendant Brown, Agent Delaney instructed Noonan to stay clear of the substance of Defendant Grass's conversations with his attorney. "[Agent Delaney] said if they start talking about their lawyers or conversations with their lawyers, I don't want you to get into any conversation. He said that to me."

unveiled. Noonan also informed AUSA Daniel that he would soon be meeting with both Defendants Grass and Brown. AUSA Daniel then delineated the topics that he wished to have Noonan raise during that meeting. Following his two to three hour meeting with the Government officials, Noonan jotted down on a sheet of paper notes regarding what topics AUSA Daniel wanted Noonan to discuss with Defendants Brown and Grass.

The following day, May 2, 2001, Noonan met with Defendants Grass and Brown at Grass's office. Once again, the Government recorded the conversations through a hidden microphone worn by Noonan. During the course of this meeting, Noonan removed his notes from his pocket and used them to guide the conversation. Noonan told Defendants Grass and Brown that the notes were taken during Noonan's meeting with the Government in Philadelphia in March of 2001. Following the meeting with Grass and Brown, Noonan met with AUSA Daniel. Noonan subsequently threw the notes away.

After the May 2, 2001 meeting, Defendant Brown called Noonan and stated: "That he would like to get together." Noonan and Brown met for the last time on May 21, 2001. As with the other conversations, the Government surreptitiously recorded this conversation through a wire that Noonan was wearing.

Although AUSA Daniel only met with Noonan twice, he approved the recording of each conversation. It is undisputed that at the times he authorized these recordings, AUSA Daniel knew that Defendants Grass and Brown were both represented by counsel. Additionally, it is likewise beyond dispute that, at least with respect to five of the six conversations, AUSA Daniel knew that Defendant Brown had refused to consent to an interview with the Government. Finally, it is also undisputed that neither Defendant was under indictment at the time Noonan recorded their conversations. As stated at the outset of this memorandum, the indictment in this case did not issue until June 21, 2002.

In the instant motion, Defendants argue that AUSA Daniel violated Rules 4.2 and 8.4(a) of the Pennsylvania Rules of Professional Conduct by using a surrogate to communicate with parties whom he knew to be represented by counsel. Thus, according to Defendants, the tapes of these conversations should be suppressed pursuant to the court's inherent supervisory power. For the following reasons, the court will deny Defendants' motion: (1) AUSA Daniel did not violate the Rules of Professional Conduct; and (2) even if he did violate those rules, suppression of the evidence is not an appropriate remedy under the facts in this case.

Rule 4.2 of the Pennsylvania Rules of Professional Conduct, also known as the "no-contact rule," prohibits an attorney from communicating "about the subject of the representation with a party the lawyer knows to be represented by another lawyer in the matter, unless the lawyer has the consent of the other lawyer or is authorized by law to do so." Rule 8.4(a) states that it is professional misconduct for an attorney to knowingly assist another in violating the rules of professional conduct. Defendants argue that the tapes of the conversations between Noonan and Defendants must be suppressed because AUSA Daniel violated Rule 4.2. According to Defendants, AUSA Daniel employed Noonan as his surrogate to communicate with Defendants after AUSA Daniel knew that Defendants had retained counsel; thus, violating Rule 8.4(a).

In order to prevail on this motion, Defendants must demonstrate the following. First, AUSA Daniel violated Rule 4.2. Second, Defendants were represented by counsel at the time the statements were elicited. Third, suppression is an appropriate remedy for violation of the Rule.

In the past, significant debate surrounded the issue of whether state rules of professional responsibility apply at all to federal prosecutors. However, in 1998, Congress eliminated all doubt regarding this issue by enacting what is commonly referred to as the McDade Amendment. The McDade Amendment states, in relevant part: "An attorney for the [Federal] Government shall be subject to State laws and rules . . . governing attorneys in each State where such attorney engages in that attorney's duties, to the extent and in the same manner as other attorneys in that State." [28 U.S.C.] § 530B(a).

Therefore, it is beyond doubt that AUSA Daniel was bound by the Pennsylvania Rules of Professional Conduct at all times relevant to the instant motion. Furthermore, based on Rule 8.4(a) of the Rules of Professional Conduct, AUSA Daniel could not avoid the dictates of Rule 4.2 by employing Noonan as his surrogate to accomplish what he himself could not do without violating the Rules of Professional Conduct. However, it remains to be seen whether AUSA Daniel's conduct in this case violated Rule 4.2. Although the McDade Amendment makes clear that state rules of professional conduct apply to Government attorneys, that legislation does not define what those standards are, when they attach, or what is an appropriate remedy to impose if Government lawyers breach those rules. Instead, it is completely silent as to these matters.

The Government argues that AUSA Daniel did not violate Rule 4.2 because (1) neither Defendants Grass, nor Brown, were a "party," as no indictment had issued at the time Noonan recorded the conversations, and (2) even if either Defendant Grass or Brown were a "party," the communications were "authorized by law," as that term is used in the no-contact rule. Pa. R. Prof'l Conduct 4.2. In support, the Government cites the Third Circuit's decision in United States v. Balter, 91 F.3d 427 (3d Cir.1996). In this pre-McDade Amendment case, the Third Circuit affirmed the District Court's refusal to suppress recordings of non-custodial conversations between a Government agent and the defendant made after the Government learned that the defendant was represented by counsel.

The Circuit Court's holding in that case was based on the identical two-prong argument that the Government proffers in opposition to the instant motion. That is, first, the court held that the Government did not violate the no-contact rule because the agent recorded the conversations prior to the defendant's indictment. Therefore, at that time, the defendant was not a party. Second, even if the defendant were a party, the court held that the communications fell within Rule 4.2's "authorized by law" exception.

It is important to note that, in *Balter,* the court addressed whether the Government violated the no-contact rule as that rule appears in the New Jersey Rules of Professional Conduct. Crucial to the court's holding that the defendant was not a "party," as that term is used in the rule, was the fact that courts interpreting the New Jersey no-contact rule had concluded that it does not attach until after initiation of formal legal or adversarial proceedings. This portion of the *Balter* holding is, therefore, inapplicable to the instant case. Although the Pennsylvania and New Jersey no-contact rules employ virtually identical language, there is no caselaw limiting application of the Pennsylvania no-contact rule to post-indictment contacts. In fact, the commentary to Pennsylvania Rule 4.2 states the contrary: "This Rule covers any person, whether or not a party to a formal proceeding, who is represented by counsel concerning the matter in question." Therefore, it is clear that, at the time of the recorded conversations, Defendants Grass and Brown were parties as that term is contemplated in Rule 4.2 of the Pennsylvania Rules of Professional Responsibility.

However, this does not, as Defendants contend, automatically lead to the conclusion that AUSA Daniel violated the no-contact rule by employing Noonan as his alter ego to communicate with Defendants. Rule 4.2 does not prohibit all contact between attorneys and parties represented by counsel. Rather, that rule specifically makes an exception for those contacts which are "authorized by law." In fact, the *Balter* court specifically held that the person-party distinction under the New Jersey no-contact rule was irrelevant to its holding that the Government did not violate the rule because "even if a criminal suspect were a 'party' within the meaning of the rule, pre-indictment investigation by prosecutors is precisely the type of contact exempted from the Rule as 'authorized by law.' " Therefore, *Balter* makes clear that pre-indictment non-custodial interrogations by Government agents do not violate the no-contact rule because such contacts are authorized by law.

With the exception of the Second Circuit, every other court of appeals that has considered the issue has similarly held that the no-contact rule does not prevent non-custodial pre-indictment communications by undercover agents with represented parties which occur in the course of legitimate criminal investigations. * * *

Moreover, such a reading is consistent with the intentions of the authors of the original no-contact rule. The commentary to American Bar Association Model Rule of Professional [Conduct] 4.2 states the following:

> Communications authorized by law also include constitutionally permissible investigative activities of lawyers representing

> governmental entities, directly or through investigative agents, prior to the commencement of criminal or civil enforcement proceedings, when there is an applicable judicial precedent that either has found the activity permissible under this Rule or has found this Rule inapplicable. However, the Rule imposes ethical restrictions that go beyond those imposed by constitutional provisions.

Because there is caselaw indicating that AUSA Daniel's pre-indictment investigation was permitted pursuant to the no-contact rule, according to the commentary to the Model Rule, his conduct was "authorized by law" so long as it was constitutionally permissible. Defendants do not contend that the Government's actions here violated their Fifth or Sixth Amendment rights to have counsel present. Nor could they present a credible argument regarding either. Noonan's interrogation, if any, did not take place in a custodial setting nor were Defendants compelled to speak to Noonan. Thus, Defendants' Fifth Amendment right to counsel was not implicated. Additionally, Noonan recorded the conversations with Defendants before the initiation of adversarial proceedings; placing those contacts outside the scope of the Sixth Amendment right to counsel. Nor is there any allegation that AUSA Daniel authorized Noonan to engage in more egregious conduct which might constitute a due process violation. Thus, because AUSA Daniel's conduct did not violate Defendants' constitutional rights, in addition to the fact that there is a significant body of caselaw indicating that such conduct is not prohibited by the no-contact rule, it must be that his conduct was "authorized by law."

In support of their contention that AUSA Daniel violated Rule 4.2, Defendants rely primarily on the Second Circuit's decision in United States v. Hammad, 858 F.2d 834 (2d Cir.1988). In that case–on facts somewhat similar to those in the instant matter–the court initially rejected the Government's contention that the no-contact rule only applied to the same extent as the Sixth Amendment right to counsel; *i.e.* only upon the initiation of formal legal proceedings. * * * Having determined that the no-contact rule applied to the Government attorney's pre-indictment conduct, the court went on to hold that, normally, the no-contact rule would not serve to prevent the Government from using confidential informants to elicit incriminating statements from parties that the Government knows to be represented by counsel. The court, however, went on to state the following:

> Notwithstanding this holding, however, we recognized that in some instances a government prosecutor may overstep the already broad powers of his office, and in doing so, violate the ethical precepts of [the no-contact rule]. In the present case, for example, the prosecutor's use of a counterfeit grand jury subpoena, bearing the purported seal of the district court and the false signature of the Clerk, was an improper and illegitimate stratagem. We will not countenance such a misuse of the name and power of the court. The employment of a specious and contrived subpoena is the sort of egregious misconduct that, even before the 6th amendment protections attach, violates [the no-contact rule] . . . .

> Notwithstanding requests for a bright-line rule, we decline to list all possible situations that may violate [the no-contact rule] . . . . As our holding above makes clear, however, use of informants by government prosecutors in a pre-indictment, non-custodial situation, *absent the type of egregious misconduct that occurred in this case,* will generally fall within the "authorized by law" exception to [the no-contact rule] and therefore will not be subject to sanctions. (emphasis added)

Thus, it appears that the court, in *Hammad,* was more concerned with curbing prosecutorial skullduggeries than it was with preventing the use of government informants to obtain incriminating statements from parties represented by counsel in the pre-indictment non-custodial setting.

Defendants, however, argue that the no-contact rule bars the introduction of the Noonan tapes because "[t]he facts in *Hammad* almost precisely parallel the facts of this case." Like the Government attorney in *Hammad,* AUSA Daniel used fake documents and had his informant falsely indicate to the targets of the investigation that the informant himself was still under investigation. Thus, according to Defendants, "Daniel's actions are clear cut violations of Rules 4.2 and 8.4(a)."

The court disagrees both with Defendants' interpretation of the facts in this case and the weight it gives to the *Hammad* decision. Although the Second Circuit, in *Hammad,* held that the use of fake documents places a prosecutor's conduct outside of the authorized by law exception to the no-contact rule, that portion of the *Hammad* decision is inapplicable in the instant matter. First, AUSA Daniel did not employ a counterfeit grand jury subpoena bearing the forged signature of the Clerk of Court as the Government prosecutor in *Hammad* did. Instead, AUSA Daniel simply drew up a fake agenda letter addressed to Noonan's attorney and signed by AUSA Daniel himself. This document was fake only insofar as there was no pending interview between the Government and Noonan scheduled for April of 2001, as indicated in the letter. By the time AUSA Daniel had written this letter, Noonan was already cooperating with the Government. At the hearing, Noonan testified that the Government fabricated the letter for Noonan to use during his meeting with Defendant Brown. Although preparing and presenting such a letter to an unwitting criminal suspect involves a certain level of dishonesty, it certainly does not rise to the level of employing a sham grand jury subpoena. Second, even if the court were to find that this practice was equivalent to the prosecutor's actions in *Hammad,* the Third Circuit has long held that the use of a fabricated grand jury subpoena "to protect a cover in an ongoing undercover investigation" does not constitute prosecutorial misconduct. United States v. Martino, 825 F.2d 754 (3d Cir.1987). Given that the holding in *Hammad* explicitly relied on the finding of prosecutorial misconduct, the court finds its applicability to the instant matter limited based on the fact that no prosecutorial misconduct occurred here.

Defendants also argue that a finding that AUSA Daniel's conduct in this case is "authorized by law" would allow the exception to swallow Rule 4.2's prohibition against contact with represented parties. Moreover, according to Defendants, such a ruling would eviscerate the purpose of the McDade amendments; that is, making the no-contact rule explicitly applicable to the conduct of Government attorneys. In support of their position, Defendants cite the following passage from United States v. Lopez, 765 F.Supp. 1433 (N.D.Cal.1991):

> Were this court to accept the Department's argument in this regard, it is not clear that there would *any* conduct the prosecutor could not undertake, as long as it was pursuant to his or her responsibility to investigate and prosecute crimes. [Department of Justice] attorneys would be exempt from rules adopted by federal courts to govern ethical conduct of attorneys practicing before them. This, quite simply, is an unacceptable result.

Lopez, however, is readily distinguishable from the facts in this case. That case involved multiple defendants who had already been indicted on various drug charges. Apparently, an attorney for one of Lopez's co-defendants contacted Lopez and encouraged him to engage in plea negotiations with the Government without having his attorney present. Once these protracted negotiations broke down and the Government's conduct came to light, Lopez's attorney withdrew from the case. Lopez subsequently moved to have the indictment dismissed because, he alleged, the Government attorney violated the no-contact rule. The District Court agreed and granted the motion. In doing so, it made two specific holdings. First, attorneys representing the Federal Government are not exempt from state rules of professional responsibility. Second, post-indictment contacts by Government attorneys are not "authorized by law." The first of these holdings is unexceptional after the enactment of the McDade Amendment. The second is irrelevant to the instant matter because it is beyond dispute that Defendants were not indicted until well over a year after Noonan's last recording took place. Therefore, to the extent Defendants rely on *Lopez* for the proposition that it would impermissibly stretch the no-contact rule to hold that the Government's conduct in this case was authorized by law, the court finds that *Lopez* is neither instructive, nor relevant to that point.

The McDade Amendment's lone function was to make state rules of professional responsibility applicable to the conduct of Government attorneys. That legislation did not state what those rules were, nor did it amend the well-established contours of those rules. Therefore, as it applies in this case, the McDade Amendment makes it clear only that Rules 4.2 and 8.4(a) applied to AUSA Daniel's conduct. Those rules prohibit attorneys, or their agents, from contacting parties that are represented by counsel unless such contact is authorized by law. As previously stated, AUSA Daniel's conduct was authorized by law and, thus, did not violate the Pennsylvania Rules of Professional Conduct. Defendants, however, contend that such a reading would allow the exception to swallow the rule, thus weakening the purpose behind the McDade Amendment. However, Defendants fail to recognize that the exception is part and parcel of Rule 4.2. Therefore, the McDade Amendment made the entire Rule 4.2, including the authorized by law exception, applicable to the conduct of Government attorneys. To adopt Defendants' argument would be tantamount to reading the McDade Amendment as amending all fifty states' rules of professional responsibility as they apply to Government attorneys. Absent a clear indication from Congress that it intended to do so, the court will not read such an awesome power into the McDade Amendment's humble command that attorneys for the Government "shall be subject to State laws and rules ... governing attorneys in each State . . . to the extent and in the same manner as other attorneys in that State." 28 U.S.C. § 530B(a).

Moreover, reading the McDade Amendment according to Defendants' interpretation raises serious public policy concerns regarding the fairness of the judicial system. It is axiomatic that criminal defendants' trial rights should not depend on the extent of their financial resources. Yet, adopting a rule that the McDade Amendment prohibits the Government from contacting any person known to be represented by counsel in any way whatsoever, will insulate from undercover investigation any defendant with enough financial resources to permanently obtain private counsel. Such a rule would dramatically impugn the integrity of the judiciary; not to mention the crippling effect it would have on the Government's ability to investigate on-going criminal activity. Although Defendants argue that such a contention is irrelevant, it would ignore reality to deny the very real consequences that Defendants' interpretation would have on the day-to-day administration of justice.

[The District Court concluded that "[e]ven assuming that the court were to find that AUSA Daniel violated Rule 4.2 of the Pennsylvania Rules of Professional Conduct, the court doubts that suppression of the Noonan tapes is a proper remedy for such a violation."]

NOTE

When a corporation is the target of an investigation, can its counsel represent both the organization and the individual employees, at least during the investigation? While there may be a conflict of interest in a joint representation after an indictment, discussed in the next section, the company has a strong interest in having its counsel present for any contacts with the government because the employees' statements can be used to establish the company's criminal liability. In In re Criminal Investigation of John Doe, Inc., 194 F.R.D. 375 (D. Mass. 2000), the district court granted the government's ex parte motion for an order permitting it to contact three employees of a corporation that was represented by counsel. The court noted that "[i]n such an unsettled legal wilderness, government counsel should not be placed in a position of being handcuffed in pursuing a valid criminal investigation for fear of being personally at risk." The court did require the prosecutor to avoid speaking with the employees about privileged information and to inform them that they can elect to have a personal attorney or the corporation's counsel present during an interview.

In **United States v. Taleo**, 222 F.3d 1133 (9th Cir. 2000), the government subpoenaed a corporation's bookkeeper, Ferrer, to testify about wrongdoing by the corporation and its controlling shareholders. The corporation's attorney informed the government that he represented the corporation and all of its employees, and met with Ferrer prior to her testimony. In addition, the controlling shareholders allegedly told Ferrer to "stick with the story" in her grand jury testimony. On the date of her grand jury testimony, Ferrer initiated contact with the Assistant U.S. Attorney and said that she did not want the corporation's attorney to represent her and that "she did not believe she could" tell the truth if the attorney were present. After being interviewed by the prosecutor, she testified before the grand jury. After the indictment of the corporation and its controlling shareholders, the district court refused to dismiss the indictment because of the prosecutor's conduct, but did find that prosecutor violated the California Rule 2-100, which is the counterpart of Rule 4.2. On the issue of the district court's finding that the prosecutor acted unethically in meeting with a "represented party," the Ninth Circuit stated:

> Under the circumstances of this case, we conclude that Rule 2-100 did not prohibit Harris's conduct. Despite the apparent conundrum created by Ferrer's dual role as employee/party and witness, the interests in the internal integrity of and public confidence in the judicial system weigh heavily in favor of the conclusion that Harris' conduct was at all times ethical. We deem manifest that when an employee/party of a defendant corporation initiates communications with an attorney for the government for the purpose of disclosing that corporate officers are attempting to suborn perjury and obstruct justice, Rule 2-100 does not bar discussions between the employee and the attorney. Indeed, under these circumstances, an automatic, uncritical application of Rule 2-100 would effectively defeat its goal of protecting the administration of justice. It decidedly would not add meaningfully to the protection of the attorney-client relationship if subornation of perjury, or the attempt thereof, is imminent or probable.
>
> Few, if any, unethical acts by counsel are more heinous than subornation of perjury. It would be an anomaly to allow the subornation of perjury to be cloaked by an ethical rule, particularly one manifestly concerned with the administration of justice. As commentators have noted with regard to the crime-fraud exception to the attorney-client privilege, "[s]ince the policy of the privilege is that of promoting the administration of justice, it would be a perversion of the privilege to extend it to the client who seeks advice to aid him in carrying out the illegal or fraudulent scheme." In a

> similar vein, it would be a perversion of the rule against ex parte contacts to extend it to protect corporate officers who would suborn perjury by their employees.
>
> Appellees maintain that application of Rule 2-100 is necessary here in order to protect the attorney-client relationship between the corporation and its counsel. We are keenly aware that assuring the proper functioning of the attorney-client relationship is an important rationale behind the rule. Again, however, like the attorney-client privilege, the prohibition against ex parte contacts protects that relationship at the expense of "the full and free discovery of the truth." For that reason, the attorney-client privilege "applies only where necessary to achieve its purpose." When a corporate employee/witness comes forward to disclose attempts by the corporation's officers to coerce her to give false testimony, the prohibition against ex parte contacts does little to support an appropriate attorney-client relationship. Once the employee makes known her desire to give truthful information about potential criminal activity she has witnessed, a clear conflict of interest exists between the employee and the corporation. Under these circumstances, corporate counsel cannot continue to represent both the employee and the corporation.

In United States v. Carona, 660 F.3d 360 (9th Cir. 2011), the Ninth Circuit applied *Taleo*'s case-by-case approach to consider whether providing false subpoena attachments to an undercover informant but not a fake subpoena should have resulted in suppression of the evidence gained from the contact with a represented person. The circuit court held, "[w]e have not previously needed to consider the question of whether providing fake court papers to an informant to use during a conversation with a represented party is conduct that violates Rule 2–100. Under the facts presented here, we conclude that it does not."

Contact with an employee who is represented by corporate counsel can result in a violation of Rule 4.2 when investigators approach the person directly for an interview rather than making contact by means of an undercover informant or agent. In **United States v. Koerber**, 966 F. Supp. 2d 1207, 1232 (D. Utah 2013), appeal dismissed (Feb. 10, 2014), the district court ordered suppression of a defendant's statements for a violation of the "no contact" rule after two interviews with government agents when the prosecutor was aware that the person was represented by counsel. In rejecting the government's argument that the contact was "authorized by law," as provided in Rule 4.2, the district court stated:

> But the 'well-established investigatory technique' of making noncustodial, pre-indictment covert or undercover contact (such as through an informant) with a target known to be represented is not at issue here. The court does not accept that it is a 'well-established investigatory technique' for the IRS and FBI to jointly interview a

> target known to be represented by counsel at the instruction of prosecutors who have previously attempted to subpoena the target to testify before a grand jury as the documents custodian for his companies (and were rebuffed by his counsel on the matter in the attempt). To the contrary, the court finds that this technique is off limits, both by operation of Utah's no-contact rule and as a result of the internal policies of all the agencies/offices involved in the investigation and prosecution of Defendant . . . .

F. CONFLICTS OF INTEREST

1. Concurrent Representation

Federal Rule of Criminal Procedure 44(c) requires a court to promptly inquire about the propriety of joint representation of defendants in the same criminal case to insure each defendant's right to effective assistance of counsel is protected. The Rule presumes the likelihood of a conflict of interest arising from a joint representation by providing that "[u]nless there is good cause to believe that no conflict of interest is likely to arise, the court must take appropriate measures to protect each defendant's right to counsel." In **Mickens v. Taylor**, 535 U.S. 162 (2002), the Supreme Court noted the distinction between Rule 44's application to conflicts arising from concurrent and prior representation:

> Thus, the Federal Rules of Criminal Procedure treat concurrent representation and prior representation differently, requiring a trial court to inquire into the likelihood of conflict whenever jointly charged defendants are represented by a single attorney (Rule 44(c)), but not when counsel previously represented another defendant in a substantially related matter, even where the trial court is aware of the prior representation.

2. Waiver

To what extent is a court required to accept a defendant's waiver of a conflict of interest, especially a concurrent conflict? In **Wheat v. United States**, 486 U.S. 153 (1988), the defendant selected counsel who also represented two other members of a large drug importation conspiracy. The government sought to disqualify counsel–who happened to have won an acquittal of the alleged kingpin in an earlier trial–on the ground that there was a potentially serious conflict of interest because the government planned to call one of the other clients to testify against the defendant. Although all three clients of the attorney were willing to waive any conflict of interest, the Supreme Court held even an apparently intelligent and knowing waiver does not preclude ordering disqualification where a serious potential for conflict exists. The Supreme Court noted that while a defendant usually has a right to the counsel of choice, that right does not overcome the government's interest in the trial untainted by a conflict of interest. The Court stated:

> Petitioner insists that the provision of waivers by all affected defendants cures any problems created by the multiple representation. But no such flat rule can be deduced from the Sixth Amendment presumption in favor of counsel of choice. Federal courts have an independent interest in ensuring that criminal trials are conducted within the ethical standards of the profession and that legal proceedings appear fair to all who observe them.

The *Wheat* Court also cited the difficulties presented in obtaining a truly knowledgeable waiver at a pretrial stage. The Court then concluded:

> For these reasons we think the District Court must be allowed substantial latitude in refusing waivers of conflicts of interest not only in those rare cases where an actual conflict may be demonstrated before trial, but in the more common cases where a potential for conflict exists which may or may not burgeon into an actual conflict as the trial progresses.

Wheat, of course, was dealing with waivers by persons already charged. Should a waiver be given more, less, or the same weight where the persons seeking to waive simply are grand jury witnesses or targets?

UNITED STATES v. MALPIEDI

62 F.3d 465 (2nd Cir. 1995)

WINTER, Circuit Judge.

Stephen Delli Bovi appeals from his convictions by a jury * * * for fraud and obstruction of justice. He argues that his trial counsel rendered constitutionally ineffective assistance due to a conflict of interest arising from counsel's previous representation of an important government witness.

Delli Bovi was convicted of two counts of wire fraud in violation of 18 U.S.C. § 1343, five counts of interstate transportation of checks taken by fraud in violation of 18 U.S.C. § 2314, and one count of obstruction of justice in violation of 18 U.S.C. § 1503. The fraud charges arose out of an alleged kickback scheme in which Delli Bovi, an outside contractor, submitted inflated invoices to the Twenty-First Century Corporation and shared the illicit profits with certain executives of that company. The obstruction of justice charge concerned certain checking records that had been subpoenaed by a grand jury from one of Delli Bovi's companies. A number of cancelled checks did not match copies retained by the bank when the checks were cashed, allegedly because they had been altered before being turned over to the grand jury.

At trial, Susan Goldfine, Delli Bovi's sister-in-law and part-time secretary and the daughter of two co-defendants, was an important government witness. Goldfine testified that she saw Delli Bovi alter check stubs when she assisted him in gathering documents in response to the grand jury subpoena. This testimony was direct evidence of Delli Bovi's obstruction of justice and of his consciousness of guilt of the other charges.

In an appearance before the grand jury, Goldfine had testified as a custodian of records to authenticate the subpoenaed documents, including the altered checking records. Prior to testifying, Goldfine had reviewed copies of the documents in the office of Delli Bovi's attorney, John Kelly. Kelly then accompanied Goldfine to the grand jury, waiting outside the grand jury room until her appearance had been completed. Goldfine considered Kelly to be her lawyer. She later stated that she had asked Kelly questions about the grand jury proceedings and that he answered those questions.

In her testimony before the grand jury, Goldfine falsely claimed not to recognize Delli Bovi's handwriting. She also gave testimony regarding the collection of documents in response to the grand jury subpoena. This testimony failed to disclose any tampering with the documents by Delli Bovi.

More than a year later and after being granted immunity, Goldfine made a second grand jury appearance in which Kelly did not represent her. On this occasion, she testified that she did not know what the initials "BG" stood for when they were in fact a reference to her father, who was then under indictment in connection with the kickback scheme. She again failed to mention Delli Bovi's tampering with the documents, although a direct question on that subject was not asked.

The government decided to call Goldfine as a witness in Delli Bovi's trial to testify as to routine custodial matters. After this decision was made and some weeks before trial, Goldfine disclosed to the government that she had seen Delli Bovi alter the documents. Her importance as a government witness was thus greatly enhanced. Nevertheless, the government failed to alert the district judge to Kelly's role in Goldfine's first grand jury appearance until the morning that Goldfine was to testify. At that point, the government informed the court that Goldfine would give "some fairly powerful testimony against [Delli Bovi]" and that "Mr. Kelly had represented her in the past." The delay in informing Judge Raggi appears not to have been an oversight but the result of the government's desire to use Kelly's prior representation of Goldfine to its advantage.[1] The government thus informed the district court that it would elicit from Goldfine testimony that Kelly had represented her at the first grand jury appearance. It hoped that evidence of her close

[1] At oral argument, the government took the position that it delayed bringing Kelly's conflict to Judge Raggi's attention because it believed Kelly's assertion that he had not represented Goldfine. However, the prosecutor's statement to Judge Raggi indicated in the clearest fashion the government's understanding that Kelly had represented Goldfine.

association with Kelly and Delli Bovi would "bolster her testimony and lend credence to it."

Kelly claimed he did not raise the matter earlier because he believed that he had no attorney-client relationship with Goldfine and that she was therefore "fair game" for cross-examination. Judge Raggi was understandably displeased that she had not been informed of this problem earlier.

Before Goldfine testified, the government and the defense agreed that Kelly would question Goldfine only about whether she was alone with the documents in a conference room while preparing for the first grand jury appearance and that the government would elicit from her only that Kelly had accompanied her to that proceeding. Nevertheless, Kelly's cross-examination of Goldfine strayed into detailed questions concerning the first grand jury appearance. Judge Raggi interrupted Kelly's cross-examination and, outside the presence of the jury, conducted an inquiry into the nature of Kelly's representation of Goldfine. Kelly stated that "in [his] mind," he was never Goldfine's lawyer. However, Goldfine stated that Kelly had answered her questions about the grand jury proceeding and that she had believed that Kelly was her lawyer.

Judge Raggi then chastised Kelly for not recognizing that he had "an ethical problem." In response, Kelly stated, "Judge, I will certainly move away from that at this point," apparently a reference to the line of questioning about Goldfine's first grand jury appearance.

Goldfine, through another lawyer, thereafter invoked the attorney-client privilege. Judge Raggi prohibited Kelly from making arguments about Goldfine's testimony in the first grand jury proceeding, forbidding him from using "any of the evidence that was developed because Mr. Kelly represented Ms. Goldfine in any way to suggest wrongdoing on her part. He owes her... the loyalty of an attorney representing a client during that period of time." Kelly agreed to limit his argument, but stated:

> But there–the one thing I'd–I keep getting into hot water–that I wanted to touch upon now is, I was intending, and I guess I'm asking for guidance on this, to use her first grand jury testimony for impeachment purposes in terms of her being asked about–there were a couple of questions about her collecting the records and her being with Stephen Delli Bovi and what they did at that time. There is no mention certainly of records being changed or her observing anything Mr. Delli Bovi did.

After further discussion with the court and Goldfine's counsel, Kelly agreed not to cross-examine Goldfine about her first grand jury appearance and stated that cross-examination about the second grand jury appearance would suffice.

During the proceedings described above, the district court and the parties focused exclusively on Goldfine's attorney-client privilege. Delli Bovi's right to conflict-free counsel was not raised until the end of the trial day when Judge Raggi inquired whether Delli Bovi was satisfied with Kelly's cross-examination of Goldfine. Although Delli Bovi responded that he was satisfied, it is undisputed that this was not a valid waiver under United States v. Curcio, 680 F.2d 881 (2d Cir.1982).[2]

After his conviction, Delli Bovi, represented by new counsel, informed the district court that he would appeal on the ground that Kelly's conflict of interest deprived Delli Bovi of effective assistance of counsel. Judge Raggi suggested that Delli Bovi pursue this claim first as a motion for a new trial, so that a record could be developed in the district court. The parties agreed to this suggestion, and the district court conducted an evidentiary hearing at which Kelly testified.

After the hearing, Judge Raggi read her findings into the record. The district court found Kelly to be a "totally credible" witness at the hearing and credited his testimony that he had made a strategic decision not to cross-examine Goldfine about the first grand jury appearance. The district court determined that Kelly's representation of Delli Bovi was not adversely affected by the conflict because (i) Kelly's cross-examination of Goldfine was, over all, very effective, (ii) Kelly was able to "indirectly" establish that Goldfine's grand jury testimony was inconsistent with her testimony at trial, (iii) Kelly effectively impeached Goldfine with other evidence that was stronger than the grand jury testimony, and (iv) Kelly established that Goldfine had lied in the second grand jury proceeding, rendering her lies in the first proceeding cumulative for the purposes of impeaching her credibility. Accordingly, the district court denied Delli Bovi's motion for a new trial. This appeal followed.

The principles to be applied are familiar ones. Every defendant is entitled to "representation that is free from conflicts of interest." Wood v. Georgia, 450 U.S. 261 (1981). An actual, as opposed to a potential, conflict of

---

[2] In United States v. Levy, 25 F.3d 146 (2nd Cir.1994), we stated that once a district court is apprised of even a possible conflict of interest, it is obligated to investigate the conflict. If the court determines that an actual or potential conflict exists, it must either (i) disqualify the defense attorney if the conflict is so severe that no rational defendant could knowingly and intelligently desire that lawyer's representation, or (ii) secure a valid waiver under *Curcio*. Here, the district court fulfilled its inquiry obligation by questioning Kelly and Goldfine about the nature of their previous relationship. However, there was no *Curcio* hearing. In United States v. Iorizzo, 786 F.2d 52 (2nd Cir.1986), we summarized the requirements of *Curcio* as applicable in the context of the present case. *Curcio* requires the district court to (i) advise the defendant of the dangers arising from the particular conflict and ascertain that he or she understands the risks involved, (ii) encourage the defendant to seek advice from independent counsel and provide time to digest and contemplate the risks, and (iii) secure a knowing waiver of the right to conflict-free counsel before proceeding.

interest exists "when, during the course of the representation, the attorney's and defendant's interests 'diverge with respect to a material factual or legal issue or to a course of action.'" Winkler v. Keane, 7 F.3d 304 (2d Cir.1993) (*quoting* Cuyler v. Sullivan, 446 U.S. 335 (1980)).

In the instant matter, Kelly had an actual conflict of interest because his duty to Goldfine conflicted with Delli Bovi's interest in a full and effective cross-examination of Goldfine. Goldfine was a key government witness. Her testimony as to document tampering was direct evidence of obstruction of justice and also demonstrated Delli Bovi's consciousness of guilt of the other charges. It was therefore in Delli Bovi's interest to have his attorney conduct a thorough, no-holds-barred cross-examination of Goldfine. Kelly was unable to cross-examine Goldfine on her testimony during her first grand jury appearance because of his obligations as her prior attorney and her invocation of the attorney-client privilege.

Although a defendant generally is required to demonstrate prejudice to prevail on a claim of ineffective assistance of counsel, prejudice is presumed when counsel is burdened by an actual conflict of interest.[c] This presumption is "fairly rigid." Moreover, "once the defendant establishes that there was an actual conflict, he need not prove prejudice, but simply that a 'lapse in representation' resulted from the conflict." *Iorizzo*. To prove a lapse in representation, a defendant must "demonstrate that some 'plausible alternative defense strategy or tactic might have been pursued,' and that the 'alternative defense was inherently in conflict with or not undertaken due to the attorney's other loyalties or interests.'" *Levy*.

This is not a test that requires a defendant to show that the alternative strategy or tactic not adopted by a conflicted counsel was reasonable, that the lapse in representation affected the outcome of the trial, or even that, but for the conflict, counsel's conduct of the trial would have been different. Rather, it is enough to show that a conflict existed that "was inherently in conflict with" a plausible line of defense or attack on the prosecution's case. *Levy*. Once such a showing is made, [the] "fairly rigid" presumption of prejudice applies.

The test is a strict one because a defendant has a right to an attorney who can make strategic and tactical choices free from any conflict of interest. An attorney who is prevented from pursuing a strategy or tactic because of the canons of ethics is hardly an objective judge of whether that strategy or tactic is sound trial practice. Counsel's inability to make such a conflict- free decision is itself a lapse in representation.

---

[c] In Mickens v. Taylor, 535 U.S. 162 (2002), the Supreme Court noted that the presumption of prejudice may not apply to a successive conflict of interest rather than an actual, concurrent conflict of the type that occurred in *Malpiedi*. See WAYNE R. LAFAVE, JEROLD H. ISRAEL, NANCY J. KING, & ORIN S. KERR, CRIMINAL PROCEDURE 3D § 11.9(d)(2007).

We do not exclude, of course, the possibility that a foregone strategy or tactic may be so insubstantial that even the most ardent and talented, conflict-free advocate would likely have avoided it. Nor do we exclude the possibility that the foregone strategy or tactic might be so clearly against the defendant's interest that unconflicted counsel would never pursue it. Under such circumstances, we would conclude that no lapse of representation occurred.

Moreover, we emphasize that the government can protect itself by informing the district judge of potential conflicts at the earliest possible moment. The court can then secure a waiver under *Curcio* or disqualify defense counsel under *Levy*. The government can itself seek to disqualify defense counsel because of a conflict. Indeed, it frequently does so.

Cross-examination of Goldfine about testimony at her first grand jury appearance was a tactic that was entirely plausible but barred by Kelly's conflict of interest. The record clearly shows that Kelly began this line of cross-examination, and the district court quite properly interrupted him. Kelly stated that he wished to impeach Goldfine's testimony with her testimony before the first grand jury but needed guidance from the court. When the court's reaction was decidedly negative, Kelly retreated. The foregone opportunity involved cross-examination regarding not only Goldfine's failure to give the grand jury the damaging testimony she offered at trial, but also her perjury regarding Delli Bovi's handwriting.

Even if we accept Kelly's testimony that he had strategic reasons for not cross-examining Goldfine about her first grand jury appearance–an assertion not entirely reconcilable with his seeking a ruling from the court on the matter–Delli Bovi had a right to a lawyer who could make strategic and tactical decisions free from any conflict of interest. Kelly was clearly in no position to make an objective, professional decision regarding cross-examination as to Goldfine's first grand jury testimony. Indeed, that option was not his to exercise.[d]

We give no weight to the post-trial hearing or findings regarding the need for cross-examination on Goldfine's first grand jury appearance or Kelly's thought processes in that regard. First, the applicable standard requires only the demonstration of a conflict inconsistent with a plausible trial strategy or tactic. Cross-examination regarding Goldfine's failure to mention document tampering and her perjury as to Delli Bovi's handwriting, even if not mandatory, was certainly a plausible strategy. Second, after-the-

[d] The events here were largely a replay of *Iorizzo* by both the defense and the government. We trust that it will not take yet another decision of this court to induce counsel for a potential defendant to refrain from assisting or accompanying a witness who testifies before an investigatory tribunal looking into the client's conduct. We also trust that it will not take another decision to induce the government to bring any conflict of interest to the district court's attention, rather than remaining silent in order to gain a tactical advantage from that conflict.

fact testimony by a lawyer who was precluded by a conflict of interest from pursuing a strategy or tactic is not helpful. Even the most candid persons may be able to convince themselves that they actually would not have used that strategy or tactic anyway, when the alternative is a confession of ineffective assistance resulting from ethical limitations. * * * We therefore vacate the judgment of conviction and remand for further proceedings.

3. Strategic Removal of Defense Counsel

In *Wheat*, the Supreme Court took note of the possibility that the government "may seek to 'manufacture' a conflict in order to prevent a defendant from having a particularly able defense counsel", stating that this was a factor "to be taken into consideration along with all other factors which inform this sort of decision." Should the government be seen as "manufacturing" a conflict when counsel is representing two targets and the government offers one leniency if that person will testify against the other? Can such a situation be handled without full disqualification, by having the witness seek the advice of a different attorney as to acceptance of the offer, and then allowing the original counsel to resume representation if the offer is rejected?

On occasion, prosecutors have maintained that courts may bar multiple representation where counsel has represented a large group of grand jury witnesses and has led them to take a united position of refusing to testify on self-incrimination grounds. See, e.g., Pirillo v. Takiff, 341 A.2d 896 (Pa. 1975) (disqualifying an attorney, paid by the policeman's fraternal order, who represented all 12 police officers subpoenaed to testify before grand jury investigating police corruption, where all 12 relied upon the privilege). The argument here is that though witnesses are free to choose independently to subscribe to a joint "stonewalling" strategy, that strategy, because it threatens the effectiveness of the grand jury's investigation, should not be facilitated by multiple representation, which naturally leads the lawyer to treat the clients as a group and to insist upon a group strategy. The few federal courts that have considered disqualification motions in such "stonewalling cases" have frowned upon this argument, and have refused to disqualify in the absence of a specific showing of conflicting interests among the clients. See, e.g., In re Investigation Before April 1975 Grand Jury, 531 F.2d 600 (D.C.Cir. 1976); Matter of Abrams, 465 N.E.2d 1 (N.Y. 1984) ("disqualification of an attorney representing multiple witnesses * * * may never be ordered if the sole reason for the request is to allow the prosecutor * * * to pit the witnesses against each other so the maximum amount of testimony can be obtained while granting the least amount of immunity"). In In re Grand Jury Investigation, 182 F.3d 668 (9th Cir. 1999), the district court disqualified an attorney who represented multiple witnesses in a grand jury investigation after the government designated certain of them as "targets." The Ninth Circuit refused to consider the appeal of the disqualification order because it was a "collateral order" and therefore unappealable until there was a final judgment in the case.

There is a danger in seeking to disqualify defense counsel if an appellate court determines that the removal violated the defendant's counsel of choice. The Supreme Court explained in **United States v. Gonzalez-Lopez**, 548 U.S. 140 (2006), that the Sixth Amendment's guarantee of the right to counsel of choice is not simply to ensure that a defendant receives a fair trial. In *Gonzalez-Lopez*, the district court erroneously refused to permit defendant's retained counsel to appear at trial pro hac vice, thus requiring him to retain a local attorney. Although new counsel was not found to be ineffective at the trial, the defendant asserted that the judge's improper refusal to permit his chosen attorney to represent him was a constitutional violation regardless of whether he was prejudiced by the decision. The Court stated:

> [The Sixth Amendment] commands, not that a trial be fair, but that a particular guarantee of fairness be provided–to wit, that the accused be defended by the counsel he believes to be best. "The Constitution guarantees a fair trial through the Due Process Clauses, but it defines the basic elements of a fair trial largely through the several provisions of the Sixth Amendment, including the Counsel Clause." Strickland [v. Washington, 466 U.S. 668 (1984)]. In sum, the right at stake here is the right to counsel of choice, not the right to a fair trial; and that right was violated because the deprivation of counsel was erroneous. No additional showing of prejudice is required to make the violation "complete." * * *
>
> The right to select counsel of one's choice, by contrast, has never been derived from the Sixth Amendment's purpose of ensuring a fair trial. It has been regarded as the root meaning of the constitutional guarantee. See Wheat. Where the right to be assisted by counsel of one's choice is wrongly denied, therefore, it is unnecessary to conduct an ineffectiveness or prejudice inquiry to establish a Sixth Amendment violation. Deprivation of the right is "complete" when the defendant is erroneously prevented from being represented by the lawyer he wants, regardless of the quality of the representation he received. To argue otherwise is to confuse the right to counsel of choice–which is the right to a particular lawyer regardless of comparative effectiveness–with the right to effective counsel–which imposes a baseline requirement of competence on whatever lawyer is chosen or appointed.

The remedy for a violation of the right to counsel is automatic reversal of the conviction, and the defendant need not show prejudice from the removal of the counsel of choice. At the same time, the majority noted that the decision did not limit "previous holdings that limit the right to counsel of choice and recognize the authority of trial courts to establish criteria for admitting lawyers to argue before them." The right to counsel of choice does not extend to defendants who require appointed counsel, and a defendant cannot "insist on representation by a person who is not a member of the bar, or demand that a counsel honor his waiver of conflict free representation." *Gonzalez-Lopez* was not "about a court's powers to enforce rules or adhere to practices that determine which attorneys may appear before it, or to make schedule and other decisions that effectively exclude a defendant's first choice of counsel."

4. Attorney Participation in the Conduct

If there is a possibility that the attorney participated in the misconduct under investigation or the subject of an indictment, then counsel likely has a conflict of interest because the range of defenses that can be raised at trial would be limited if any of them implicated the attorney. See United States v. Hanna, 207 F.Supp.2d 45 (E.D.N.Y. 2002) (disqualifying counsel in a securities fraud prosecution when the law firm had advised the brokerage firm controlled by the defendants on their compliance with the securities laws, and the lawyer had "a strong personal interest in avoiding criminal prosecution, civil lawsuits, professional sanctions and harm to reputation arising from" his representation of the broker). In United States v. Matta-Timmins, 81 F.Supp.2d 193 (D. Mass. 2000), the district court denied the government's motion to disqualify counsel because the potential conflict was "too remote" when counsel received funds from the defendant that might be subject to forfeiture if the defendant were convicted. The court also found that the defendant's waiver of any conflict was effective at the pre-trial stage, but noted that an actual conflict "might arise if Matta-Timmins decided to plead guilty to money laundering counts, thereby subjecting [attorney] Thornton's attorney's fee to civil or criminal forfeiture."

5. Conflicts From Joint Defense Agreements

As discussed in Chapter 15, a group of defendants in an investigation may enter into a joint defense agreement under which the communications by any one member with any attorney will be privileged. The issue raises significant conflict of interest questions, especially if the attorney must maintain the confidentiality of the information and cannot use it to cross-examine the cooperating witness. ABA Model Rule of Professional Conduct 1.9(a) provides, "A lawyer who has formerly represented a client in a matter shall not thereafter represent another person in the same or a substantially related matter in which that person's interests are materially adverse to the interests of the former client unless the former client gives informed consent, confirmed in writing." Could the government make it a condition of a cooperation agreement that the former member of the joint defense refuse to give the consent required by Rule 1.9(a)? Would that constitute the type of strategic conduct manufacturing a conflict that the Supreme Court said in *Wheat* that a court should consider in disqualifying an attorney? Would the agreement show that the government acted in bad faith?

For a detailed discussion of the prosecution and defense views on conflicts created by joint defense agreements see Ronald J. Nessim & Paul L. Seave, *Conflicts and Confidences: Does Conflict of Interest Kill the Joint Defense Privilege?* 7 Crim. Justice 6 (1992). Ronald J. Nessim, representing the defense view, states, "[e]ven if there is a conflict when a defendant's attorney examines a witness from whom he or she received confidential joint defense communications, withdrawal or disqualification of the attorney should never be the remedy." In contrast, Paul L. Seave, taking the prosecution view, argues for use of conflict of interest rules concerning confidential information. He states that when inconsistent theories develop between the parties to a joint defense agreement, "[t]he conflict of interest rules * * * require that the attorneys for defendants demonstrate that they were not privy to the confidences (if any) previously communicated by the parties who now stand ready to testify for the government." Consider the court's resolution of the issue in the following.

UNITED STATES v. HENKE

222 F.3d 633 (9th Cir. 2000)

PER CURIAM.

Chan Desaigoudar and Steven Henke, former executives of California Micro Devices, Inc. ("Cal Micro"), appeal their convictions for conspiracy to make false statements to the Securities Exchange Commission, making false statements, securities fraud, and insider trading. * * *

The defendants claim that their convictions must be set aside because a conflict of interest prevented their counsel from cross-examining a key government witness and because there was insufficient evidence to support their insider trading convictions. * * * We agree with the defendants that a new trial is necessary because their lawyers' ability to conduct their defense was impaired by a conflict of interest.

This case arises from a false revenue reporting conspiracy carried out by Cal Micro executives in order to preserve the appearance that the company was a good investment option when in fact it was struggling financially. Cal Micro designs, manufactures, and markets electronic components and semiconductor products for the defense and electronics industries. The company was purchased in 1980 by Desaigoudar, who turned it into a multi-million dollar company during the 1980s. In addition to being Cal Micro's largest shareholder, Desaigoudar served as its Chief Executive Officer and Chairman of the Board until he was removed in 1994. * * *

Unable to close the widening gap between revenue targets and actual sales, some Cal Micro executives devised a plan to make it appear on paper that the company was meeting its financial goals. Under Cal Micro's stated revenue recognition policy, revenue was recognized when an order was shipped. These Cal Micro executives began to deviate from this practice in several ways. They started: (1) recognizing revenue when some orders were received, rather than when shipped; (2) shipping orders earlier than requested in order to recognize the revenue during a certain fiscal period; (3) sending unwanted shipments; (4) creating false orders; and (5) executing "title transfers" falsely reflecting that products stored at Cal Micro had been purchased by a client. * * *

Things then took a turn for the worse. Those involved began to worry about the implications of the revenue scheme. Moreover, the company's plan to write off several million dollars in "bad debts" caused Cal Micro's investment bankers to balk at a second public offering. The Board eventually instituted an investigation and ultimately ousted Desaigoudar.

Desaigoudar and Henke, a former Chief Financial Officer, Vice President, and Treasurer of Cal Micro, were indicted on charges of conspiracy, making false statements, securities fraud, and insider trading. Surendra Gupta, Cal Micro's President during the revenue reporting scheme, was also indicted, but reached a plea agreement with the government shortly before trial was to begin. The central issue at trial was whether the defendants had early knowledge of the false revenue reporting scheme and whether they traded their stock because of this inside information. Several of Cal Micro's executive officers, including former co-defendant Gupta, testified that the defendants did have such early knowledge. The jury believed the government's witnesses and convicted the defendants.

The defendants' principal claim is that they are entitled to a new trial because their attorneys worked under an actual conflict of interest that prohibited them from cross-examining one of the government's key witnesses, Gupta.

Before trial, Desaigoudar, Henke, and Gupta participated in joint defense meetings during which confidential information was discussed. Communications made during these pre-trial meetings were protected by the lawyers' duty of confidentiality imposed by a joint defense privilege agreement. Before trial was to begin, Gupta accepted a plea agreement and promised to testify for the government.

Desaigoudar's attorney then moved for a mistrial and to withdraw because his duty of confidentiality to Gupta under the joint defense agreement prevented him from cross-examining Gupta on matters involving information he learned as a result of the privileged pre-trial meetings. Henke's lawyer was also present at the joint defense meetings and felt that his duty to Gupta impaired his ability to adequately represent Henke.

The district court denied the motion to withdraw. It reasoned that any privileged impeaching information counsel learned about Gupta would not be known to new counsel and the defendants were therefore no worse off for being represented by their original attorneys. The court granted the motion for a mistrial to allow defense counsel to regroup after Gupta's plea.

Once the new trial began, Gupta testified for the government. Defense counsel conducted no cross-examination for fear that the examination would lead to inquiries into material covered by the joint defense privilege.

The issue for our decision is whether the government's use of a former defendant, with whom both Henke's and Desaigoudar's attorneys had an attorney-client relationship arising from a joint defense agreement, as a key witness at trial created a conflict of interest that impaired defense counsel's ability to defend their clients.

The joint defense privilege is an extension of the attorney-client privilege. It has been recognized by this Circuit since at least 1964. A joint defense agreement establishes an implied attorney-client relationship with the co-defendant, here between Henke's and Desaigoudar's attorneys and Gupta. *See* Wilson P. Abraham Constr. Corp. v. Armco Steel Corp., 559 F.2d 250 (5th Cir.1977). The government concedes in its brief the existence of this privilege in this case.

This privilege can also create a disqualifying conflict where information gained in confidence by an attorney becomes an issue, as it did in this case. As the court said in *Abraham Construction,*

> Just as an attorney would not be allowed to proceed against his former client in a cause of action substantially related to the matters in which he previously represented that client, an attorney should also not be allowed to proceed against a co-defendant of a former client wherein the subject matter of the present controversy is substantially related to the matters in which the attorney was previously involved, and wherein confidential exchanges of information took place between the various co-defendants in preparation of a joint defense.

Here, what Gupta allegedly said in confidence during pre-trial joint defense meetings about the defendants' presence at a critical meeting of Cal Micro executives was claimed to be at odds with his trial testimony for the government. This evidence put the two defense attorneys in a difficult position. Had they pursued the material discrepancy in some other way, a discrepancy they learned about in confidence, they could have been charged with using it against their one-time client Gupta. In fact, Gupta's lawyers had threatened Henke's and Desaigoudar's attorneys with legal action if they failed to protect Gupta's confidences. Here is the text of the letter received by defense counsel:

June 26, 1998

> Re: U.S. v. Desaigoudar and Henke
>
> Dear [attorneys for defendants Desaigoudar and Henke]:
> It has come to our attention you may be contemplating filing an ex parte in camera submission to Judge Walker outlining what you

contend are the contradictory statements made by Mr. Gupta in what you have conceded was a joint defense privileged meeting.

Please be advised that we do not, waive, and at no point ever have waived the joint defense privilege. Please be further advised that we are aware of no legal basis upon which you have any right to breach the privilege and that we reserve Mr. Gupta's right to pursue any and all appropriate legal remedies for any unauthorized breach of the privilege.

Please consider this letter as a formal objection to any ex parte in camera submissions to Judge Walker of any joint defense privileged information.

Yours very truly,
[Signed]
Attorneys for Suren Gupta

Under these circumstances, the district court erred in not fully acknowledging the conflict and then acting on its implications.

Nothing in our holding today is intended to suggest, however, that joint defense meetings are in and of themselves disqualifying. We stress that it was defense counsel in this case that timely moved for disqualification. As the Supreme Court said in Holloway v. Arkansas, the attorney "is in the best position professionally and ethically to determine when a conflict of interest exists or will probably develop in the course of a trial." 435 U.S. 475 (1978). There may be cases in which defense counsel's possession of information about a former co-defendant/government witness learned through joint defense meetings will not impair defense counsel's ability to represent the defendant or breach the duty of confidentiality to the former co-defendant. Here, however, counsel told the district court that this was not a situation where they could avoid reliance on the privileged information and still fully uphold their ethical duty to represent their clients. There is nothing in this record to suggest that the attorneys were doing anything other than attempting to adhere to their ethical duties as lawyers.

Few aspects of our criminal justice system are more vital to the assurance of fairness than the right to be defended by counsel, and this means counsel not burdened by a conflict of interest. Here, because of that conflict, the appellants' lawyers were constrained to impair yet another primary right of their clients: the right to cross-examine a witness who testified against them. By choosing to convert Gupta into a prospective witness shortly before the trial was scheduled to start, the government–which may not have anticipated this complication when it made a deal with Gupta–caused this problem, and should not now be heard to complain.

6. Limiting Joint Defense Agreement Conflicts

If a joint defense agreement creates a confidential relationship among the various defendants and their defense counsel, then there is a risk in every case that involves such an agreement that a large number of defense counsel will be disqualified if one member cooperates with the government. Can a court limit the scope of such agreements by requiring that a defendant participating in such agreements prospectively waive the right to confidentiality from counsel for other defendants?

In **United States v. Executive Recycling, Inc.**, 908 F. Supp. 2d 1156 (D. Colo. 2012), a company and two executives, Richter and Olson, were charged with environmental violations, wire fraud, and obstruction of justice. One lawyer, Mackey, represented both Richter and Executive Recycling, and another attorney represented Olson; they were all participants in a joint defense agreement. During trial, it came to light that corporate accounting records may have been improperly altered. Mackey moved to withdraw because of her concern over the possibility that each defendant would blame the other for the change in the records, and that the joint defense agreement would limit her ability to cross-examine Olson if he chose to testify. The district court found the conflict insufficient to justify allowing withdrawal, which would result in a mistrial. It held:

> The Court finds that the severity of the alleged conflict at issue here is much less significant than the conflict in *Henke*. There, the conflict (coupled with the cooperating defendant's counsel's threatening letter) caused counsel for the remaining defendants to decline to conduct any cross-examination of the testifying co-defendant. As the cooperating defendant was a key witness in the government's case, the failure to cross-examine such witness caused the remaining defendants significant prejudice. In this case, should Mr. Olson choose to testify, he will be testifying on his own behalf and not on behalf of the Government. Aside from the obstruction of justice count, there has been no indication that Defendants' interests are adverse to each other. Therefore, the extent to which Mr. Olson's testimony will be adverse to Mr. Richter or Executive Recycling is far less significant than the cooperating defendant in *Henke*. Moreover, given the limited nature of the conflict alleged here, the Court has a hard time believing that Ms. Mackey will be wholly unable to examine Mr. Olson, should he choose to take the stand. Thus, the Court finds that the conflict alleged here is not so significant that it warrants allowing counsel to withdraw.
>
> Rather than lead the Court to conclude that the Motion to Withdraw should be granted, the Court finds that *Henke* actually suggests that the Motion should be denied. The Ninth Circuit stated: "There may be cases in which defense counsel's possession of information about a former co-defendant/government witness learned through joint

> defense meetings will not impair defense counsel's ability to represent the defendant or breach the duty of confidentiality to the former co-defendant." The Court finds that, to the extent there is any actual conflict of interest, it is so minimal that it will not affect Counsel's ability to adequately represent her clients' interests.

In **United States v. Stepney**, 246 F.Supp.2d 1069 (N.D. Cal. 2003), the district court required such a waiver as a condition to permitting them to participate in a joint defense agreement in a complex, multi-defendant case. The court relied on its supervisory power and the requirement of Federal Rule of Criminal Procedure 44(c) that a court protect against conflicts of interest arising from concurrent representation, to require defendants to prospectively waive any confidentiality claim against an attorney other than their own, explaining:

> The conditional waiver of confidentiality also provides notice to defendants that their confidences may be used in cross-examination, so that each defendant can choose with suitable caution what to reveal to the joint defense group. Although a limitation on confidentiality between a defendant and his own attorney would pose a severe threat to the true attorney-client relationship, making each defendant somewhat more guarded about the disclosures he makes to the joint defense effort does not significantly intrude on the function of joint defense agreements. The attorney-client privilege protects "full and frank" communication because the attorney serves as the client's liaison to the legal system. Without a skilled attorney, fully apprised of her client's situation, our adversarial system could not function. Any secret a client keeps from his own counsel compromises his counsel's ability to represent him effectively and undermines the purpose of the attorney-client privilege.
>
> Joint defense agreements, however, serve a different purpose. Each defendant entering a joint defense agreement already has a representative, fully and confidentially informed of the client's situation. The joint defense privilege allows defendants to share information so as to avoid unnecessarily inconsistent defenses that undermine the credibility of the defense as a whole. In criminal cases where discovery is limited, such collaboration is necessary to assure a fair trial in the face of the prosecution's informational advantage gained through the power to gather evidence by searches and seizures. Co-defendants may eliminate inconsistent defenses without the same degree of disclosure that would be required for an attorney to adequately represent her client. The legitimate value of joint defense agreements will not be significantly diminished by including a limited waiver of confidentiality by testifying defendants for purposes of cross-examination only.

> For the foregoing reasons, the Court rules as follows:
>
> (1) Any joint defense agreement entered into by defendants must be committed to writing, signed by defendants and their attorneys, and submitted in camera to the court for review prior to going into effect.
>
> (2) Each joint defense agreement submitted must explicitly state that it does not create an attorney-client relationship between an attorney and any defendant other than the client of that attorney. No joint defense agreement may purport to create a duty of loyalty.
>
> (3) Each joint defense agreement must contain provisions conditionally waiving confidentiality by providing that a signatory attorney cross-examining any defendant who testifies at any proceeding, whether under a grant of immunity or otherwise, may use any material or other information contributed by such client during the joint defense.
>
> (4) Each joint defense agreement must explicitly allow withdrawal upon notice to the other defendants.

The Eleventh Circuit adopted a waiver approach to the question of whether a joint defense agreement prevents a counsel for a defendant from cross-examining a former member of the joint defense team about otherwise confidential communications. In **United States v. Almeida**, 341 F.3d 1318 (11th Cir. 2003), the district court precluded counsel for the defendant from utilizing statements made by a cooperating witness when the witness was a participant in a joint defense agreement. The Eleventh Circuit reversed the conviction and found that the cooperating witness's decision to leave the joint defense agreement operated as an implied waiver of any privilege with counsel for other defendants:

> While the privilege may be waived by the client, it is generally held that he does not do so merely by becoming a witness and testifying in his own behalf. But when one jointly indicted with others turns state's evidence, and attempts to convict others by testimony which also convicts himself, the rule must be different, and he has no right to claim any privilege concerning any of the facts pertinent to the issue, nor any exemption from the broadest latitude of cross-examination. He thereby waives all privilege against criminating himself, and against disclosing communications between himself and his counsel touching the offense charged. Both client and counsel may, in such case, be compelled to disclose such communications.
>
> Both exceptions to the attorney-client privilege are open to criticism. By finding implied waivers, courts risk eroding the public's confidence that their communications will remain confidential so

long as communicated to a lawyer. For this reason, we do not hold that accomplices always waive the privilege when they testify on behalf of the government; nor do we hold that persons represented by the same attorney always waive the privilege in the event that one of them becomes a government witness against the other. In the joint defense agreement context, however, the policy rationales behind the two exceptions outweigh the minimal benefit of the attorney-client privilege. As one court recently explained:

> We hold that when each party to a joint defense agreement is represented by his own attorney, and when communications by one co-defendant are made to the attorneys of other co-defendants, such communications do not get the benefit of the attorney-client privilege in the event that the co-defendant decides to testify on behalf of the government in exchange for a reduced sentence.

7. Conflicts with the Trial Judge

In addition to conflicts an attorney may have with different clients, counsel can have a relationship with the trial judge that would affect the judge's ability to hear the case. Can a defendant attempt to disqualify a judge by hiring a lawyer whose relationship with the judge would trigger a successful request for recusal? In United States v. Casey, 480 F.2d 151 (5th Cir. 1973), the Fifth Circuit pointed out that "[t]he freedom to choose one's counsel may not be used as a device to manipulate or subvert the orderly procedure of the courts or the fair administration of justice." In **McCuin v. Texas Power & Light Co.**, 714 F.2d 1255 (5th Cir. 1983), the Fifth Circuit held that counsel can be disqualified if the party employs the lawyer for the purpose of seeking recusal of the judge to whom the case is assigned:

> A lawyer's acceptance of employment solely or primarily for the purpose of disqualifying a judge creates the impression that, for a fee, the lawyer is available for sheer manipulation of the judicial system. It thus creates the appearance of professional impropriety. Moreover, sanctioning such conduct brings the judicial system itself into disrepute. To tolerate such gamesmanship would tarnish the concept of impartial justice. To permit a litigant to blackball a judge merely by invoking a talismanic "right to counsel of my choice" would contribute to skepticism about and mistrust of our judicial system.

CHAPTER SEVENTEEN
SENTENCING

A. INTRODUCTION

1. The United States Sentencing Commission

Federal Guideline Sentencing was established by the Sentencing Reform Act of 1984. The Act, which became effective in 1987, created determinate sentencing, eliminated parole, and limited "good time" reductions to fifty-four days a year after the first year of incarceration. Congress' intention in enacting the Guidelines was to ensure truth in sentencing: that a defendant would serve close to the total sentence imposed.

Congress established the United States Sentencing Commission as an independent entity in the judicial branch (28 U.S.C. § 991(a)). The Commission is composed of seven voting members–including no more than three federal judges–appointed by the President with the advice and consent of the Senate, and two non-voting ex-officio members – the Attorney General and the Chief of the Parole Commission. The Sentencing Commission drafted the original Guidelines, and after referral to Congress, they became law when Congress did not chose to exercise its authority to veto or change them. This same procedure applies to subsequent amendments to the Guidelines proposed by the Commission. Congress, of course, is free to legislate amendments sua sponte to the Guidelines, as it did in the Prosecutorial Remedies and Tools Against the Exploitation of Children Today [PROTECT] Act of 2003. See infra p. 828.

A major impetus for guideline sentencing was to level the playing field between white collar offenders and street offenders. Senator Edward M. Kennedy, co-sponsor of the Act with Senator Strom Thurmond, stated: "One important goal of the 1984 Act was to eliminate the two-tier system of justice in which white collar criminals received lenient treatment for acts of theft and fraud that would merit lengthy prison terms if committed on the street." *Address of Senator Kennedy before the U.S. Sentencing Commission Symposium on Corporate Crime*, September 12, 1995.

2. Basic Statutory Structure

The Sentencing Reform Act directed the sentencing court to impose one or more of four types of punishment in every case: probation, fine, imprisonment, and supervised release. In choosing among these punishments, courts were directed to consider a broad variety of purposes and factors, including "guidelines" and "policy statements" promulgated by the Sentencing Commission. 18 U.S.C. § 3553(a)(4)(A), (a)(5); see also 28 U.S.C. § 994(a)(1), (a)(2). But while the Act provided for a broad range of sentencing considerations, it did not allow an equally broad range of sentencing discretion. Instead, it cabined the court's discretion within a fixed set of sentencing ranges specified by the guidelines, ranges that were mandatory absent a valid ground for departure. See 18 U.S.C. § 3553(b)(1), (b)(2) (2004). A departure from the applicable range was authorized only when the court found "an aggravating or mitigating circumstance of a kind, or to a degree," not adequately taken to the Commission's sentencing guidelines, policy statements, and official commentary. § 3553(b)(1). In determining whether a circumstance was adequately considered, the court's review was restricted to the Commission's sentencing guidelines, policy statements, and official commentary. § 3553(b)(1).

The Supreme Court's decision in [United States v. Booker, 543 U.S. 220 (2005),] fundamentally changed 18 U.S.C. § 3553. Applying a line of recent constitutional decisions, *Booker* held that the mandatory guidelines system created by § 3553(b)(1) triggered the Sixth Amendment right to jury trial with respect to sentencing determinations. Rather than require jury findings, however, the Court excised § 3553(b)(1). The result was a truly advisory guidelines system.

After *Booker*, the sentencing court must consider the Commission's guidelines and policy statements, but it need not follow them. They are just one of the many sentencing factors to be considered under § 3553(a), along with the nature and circumstances of the offense, the history and characteristics of the defendant, the kinds of sentences available, the need to avoid unwarranted sentencing disparities and provide restitution, and others. The only restriction § 3553(a) places on the sentencing court is the "parsimony" provision, which requires the court to "impose a sentence sufficient, but not greater than necessary," to achieve a specific set of sentencing purposes:

- to reflect the seriousness of the offense, to promote respect for the law, and to provide just punishment for the offense;

- to afford adequate deterrence to criminal conduct;

- to protect the public from further crimes of the defendant; and

- to provide the defendant with needed education or vocational training, medical care, or other correctional treatment in the most effective manner.

> § 3553(a)(2). Beyond this requirement, and the procedural requirement that the court give reasons for the sentence it selects, § 3553(c), the Sentencing Reform Act as modified by *Booker* places few restrictions on the sentence the court may impose within the limits of the statute of conviction. And the sentence the court chooses is subject to appellate review only for "unreasonableness."

Henry J. Bemporad, *An Introduction to Guideline Sentencing* 2-3 (13th ed. 2011).

B. THE GUIDELINES

1. Computing the Sentence

> The Guidelines Manual comprises eight chapters and three appendices. It contains the Sentencing Commission guidelines, policy statements, and commentary that the court considers when it imposes sentence in a federal case. See 18 U.S.C. § 3553(a)(4)(A) (court must consider guidelines); § 3553(a)(5) (court must consider policy statements). The Manual establishes two numerical values for each guidelines case: an offense level and a criminal history category. The two values correspond to the axes of a grid, called the sentencing table; together, they specify a sentencing range for each case. (The sentencing table is appended to this paper.) The Manual provides rules for sentencing within the range, and for departures outside of it. It also states the Commission's views on *Booker*.
>
> While *Booker* returned a large measure of sentencing discretion to the court, it did not diminish the importance of understanding the guidelines' application in a particular case. This is not just because the guidelines remain the "starting point and the initial benchmark" for the sentencing decision. Statistics show that, while the percentage of guideline sentences has steadily decreased since Booker, courts still follow the guidelines' recommendation more often than not.

Henry J. Bemporad, *An Introduction to Guideline Sentencing* 9 (13th ed. 2011).

The offense level is determined by establishing the base offense level for the crime(s) of conviction and, as applicable, the specific offense characteristics and adjustments. In addition to setting a "base level," each offense-conduct category lists specific offense characteristics which may or may not be applicable, depending on the circumstances of the particular case. Where specific offense characteristics are applicable, they generally increase the offense level and, accordingly, the sentence. Specific offense characteristics include: (1) more than minimal planning; (2) amount of loss involved; and, (3) infliction of bodily injury.

In applying the specific offense characteristics, the court looks to both the crime of conviction and any other conduct deemed "relevant" under U.S.S.G. § 1B1.3. Relevant conduct includes a wide range of conduct beyond the specific crime of conviction. Relevant conduct includes "all acts and omissions" of the defendant (and of accomplices for which the defendant is legally accountable) which occurred "during the commission of the offense of conviction, in preparation for that offense, or in the course of attempting to avoid detection or responsibility for that offense." Section 1B1.3(a)(1) . These acts or omissions need not have been charged in the offense of commission. Indeed, they can constitute separate offenses that were (1) uncharged, (2) charged and dismissed, or (3) charged and resulted in acquittal. For sentencing purposes, proof beyond a reasonable doubt is not needed to hold defendant responsible for an act that increases the base offense level as a specific offense characteristic; a preponderance proof level is sufficient. Illustrative is an obstruction of justice by the defendant in an attempt to avoid detection on the charged crime. The prosecution need not charge obstruction as a separate offense to increase a sentence based on the conduct.

Section 1B1.3(a)(2) adds still more relevant conduct that is not part of the offense of conviction. It includes, with respect to separate offenses of "a character for which §3D1.2(d) would require grouping of multiple counts," all acts and omissions "that were part of the same course of conduct or common scheme or plan as the offense of conviction." Here too, the provision adds offenses that were uncharged, charged and dismissed, or charged and producing an acquittal. In one sense, the range is broader than under §1B1.3(a)(1), as it extends to all offenses that were part of "a common scheme," even though they did not occur during the commission, preparation, or detection-avoidance phases of the offense of conviction. However, to be included, the offenses must be of a character that would have required their grouping for a single sentence if they had been charged and had produced multiple counts of conviction.

Consider, as an illustration, a case in which a defendant used a common scheme to swindle a series of victims, but is prosecuted and convicted for the fraud as to one victim (A). The additional criminal conduct as to the other victims will be used in calculating the specific offense characteristics of the single count of conviction. This means that all harm flowing from the additional uncharged conduct and all the specific offense characteristics of that conduct will be added to the offense of conviction. Thus, the harm would be measured by reference to the total loss caused by all of the frauds and consideration would be given to aggravating factors – e.g., the use of foreign bank accounts to conceal transactions – involved in the uncharged fraud, as well as in the fraud against A.

2. Relevant Conduct

Establishing the nature and extent of a defendant's involvement in the offense can be important for determining the sentence because the Guidelines use what is termed a "modified real offense" system that considers the circumstances of the crime in imposing the sentence. The first step in the Guidelines sentencing process is ascertaining the defendant's "relevant conduct" for purposes of applying the offense level.

In **United States v. Williams**, 216 F.3d 1099 (D.C. Cir. 1999), the District of Columbia Circuit remanded to the trial court for more complete development of the record concerning the scope of one defendant's involvement in a scheme to accept bribes in exchange for automobile inspection stickers issued by the District of Columbia government. The court stated:

> Defendants Ellis Williams and Leon Depp challenge the district court's calculation of the relevant conduct attributable to them for their roles in the bribery scheme. They complain that the court failed to make specific findings concerning when they joined the conspiracy and attributed bribe amounts to them that were not reasonably foreseeable in furtherance of jointly undertaken criminal activity. The district court held, and the government now argues, that Depp and Williams are responsible for all bribes taken after they began working at the inspection station, in 1991 and 1992 respectively.
>
> Under the Sentencing Guidelines [§2C1.1], bribery of a public official carries a base offense level of ten, which is increased when the offense involves multiple bribes or amounts more than $2,000. When calculating the number and amount of bribes involved, the sentencing court may consider all relevant conduct attributable to the defendant. In the case of a jointly undertaken criminal activity, this includes any acts and omissions of others in furtherance of the jointly undertaken criminal activity that were reasonably foreseeable to the defendant. Applying this standard, the district court held that Depp and Williams were accountable for the bribes taken by the other inspectors because those actions were both in furtherance of jointly undertaken activity and reasonably foreseeable to them. Accordingly, the court held Williams responsible for payments totaling between $40,000 to $70,000 and Depp for payments between $70,000 to $120,000.
>
> The court based its determination * * * on the assumption that Depp and Williams began participating in the bribery scheme as soon as they began working at the inspection station. Instead of identifying specific facts to establish that their involvement began at that time, the court relied on the fact that the "conspiracy . . . started back in the '80s" and required the cooperation of other inspectors to make it

work. With respect to Depp, the court found it significant that "there was never any indication that he was not involved from the beginning." From this, the court inferred–unreasonably, we think–that both must have joined the scheme quite soon after starting work at the station. That inference is without an evidentiary basis. For one thing, the record shows that not all of the inspectors at the inspection station were involved in the conspiracy. It is possible that Williams and Depp waited some time before opting to join in. The district court's conclusion was thus improper in the absence of particularized findings demonstrating that Williams and Depp joined the conspiracy soon after their employment began.

Nevertheless, as applied to Williams, the district court's erroneous determination is harmless. The court held Williams responsible for bribes taken as of 1992. Williams maintains the evidence established his involvement began no earlier than 1994. Even if Williams is correct, and we subtract the bribe amounts from 1992 to 1994, Williams is still accountable for more than $40,000. The district court relied on figures submitted by the probation officer and the government, both of whom put the total amount at more than $49,000. Eliminating bribes taken before 1994 only reduces the total amount by about $4,700. Had the district court included only bribes taken after Williams is known to have joined the scheme, the total would still have been more than $44,000. Because the district court's error made no difference to its relevant conduct determination, resentencing of Williams is unwarranted.

As to Depp, the error is not inconsequential. The district court used a conspiracy period from 1991 through the indictment in 1998. At the sentencing hearing, Depp disputed the length of this period, contending the evidence establishes his involvement only as of February 1996. Refusing to shorten the conspiracy period, the court held Depp responsible for bribes valued at the low end of the $70,000 to $120,000 range–calculating the total as $70,065 but conceding that the government's figure of $86,325 was largely credible. If we recalculate the amount without bribes taken from 1991 through 1995 the total figure is significantly reduced. The reduction for bribes provided by just one individual (Otoo) to Johnson alone, even crediting Depp's objections, amounts to at least $24,500. Given the potential for such a substantial reduction, a remand for a new assessment of Depp's relative conduct is necessary. In making that reassessment, the district court may rely on either of the two methods the government presented for calculating relevant conduct–the testimony of the inspectors' customers or the extrapolation from a sampling of illegal stickers. It may not, however, decide that Depp's participation in the scheme began at the same time as his employment without the support of particularized findings.

3. Sentencing the White Collar Offender

UNITED STATES v. PARRIS
573 F.Supp. 2d 744 (E.D. N.Y. 2008)

MEMORANDUM AND STATEMENT OF REASONS

BLOCK, Senior District Judge:

I have sentenced Lennox and Lester Parris today to a term of incarceration of 60 months in the face of an advisory guidelines range of 360 to life. This case represents another example where the guidelines in a securities-fraud prosecution "have so run amok that they are patently absurd on their face," United States v. Adelson, 441 F.Supp.2d 506, 515 (S.D.N.Y.2006), due to the "kind of 'piling-on' of points for which the guidelines have frequently been criticized." * * *

Although I do not consider my sentence to be unusually lenient, I am nonetheless mindful that a departure of 300 months from the low end of the advisory guidelines range is a major one and "should be supported by a more significant justification than a minor one," Gall v. United States, 552 U.S. 38 (2007); moreover, since I am of the view that the guidelines range "fails properly to reflect § 3553(a) considerations," Kimbrough v. United States, 552 U.S. 85 (2007), "a closer review may be in order" in the event of an appeal by the government. United States v. Cutler, 520 F.3d 136, 156 (2d Cir.2008) (quoting *Kimbrough*). For these two reasons, I believe a fuller exposition of how I arrived at my sentence is warranted than normally would be set forth in the space provided in the Statement of Reasons section of the judgment; hence, I am attaching this document to the judgment as the requisite written statement of reasons for the sentences I have imposed. See18 U.S.C. § 3553(c)(2). As the Second Circuit has made clear, § 3553(c)(2) remains obligatory despite the now-advisory nature of the Guidelines. See United States v. Rattoballi, 452 F.3d 127, 138 (2d Cir.2006). * * *

Although the jury found each defendant guilty of conspiracy to commit securities fraud, six counts of securities fraud, one count of conspiracy to commit witness tampering and one count of witness tampering, the nature of their crimes-while clearly deserving of the punishment which I have meted out-is simply not of the same character and magnitude as the securities-fraud prosecutions of those who have been responsible for wreaking unimaginable losses on major corporations and, in particular, on their companies' employees and stockholders, many of whom lost their pensions and were financially ruined. Yet the sentences entailed in those cases, such as Enron, WorldCom and Computer Associates, were each less, and in some cases markedly less, than the lowest end of the guidelines range in this case.

Here, the Parris brothers were engaged in a rather typical "pump and dump" scheme in the world of the high-risk penny-stock investor. At trial, the

Government established that, in January and February of 2004, they issued several press releases falsely representing the business prospects and financial condition of Queénch, Inc. ("Queénch"), a fledgling publicly traded company based in Jericho, New York. As a result, shares of Queénch-which had traded at around $0.18/share immediately before the first press release was issued-began trading at artificially inflated prices; the share price peaked at $0.32 on January 29th, following the issuance of the third press release. The increased demand was also reflected in a dramatic surge in Queénch's trading volume, which had hovered at around 30,000 shares per day; during the period of the fraud, the volume of shares traded regularly reached into the millions.

"Queénch" was also the name the Parrises gave their company's product, a new breed of bottled water which they wanted to pitch to minorities. They were the sole directors and their criminal misdeeds centered around their efforts to establish a market for their new product; by and large, their press releases contained some degree of truthfulness about Queénch's business prospects, but they clearly went beyond mere puffing and the jury was entitled to view them as material misrepresentations.

More telling, perhaps, was the means by which the Parrises personally capitalized on these misrepresentations. Between January and March of 2004, Queénch issued a total of 28.6 million new, unregistered shares to two Florida stock-promotion companies, Sprout Investments LLC and Alpine Equity LLC; the corporate resolutions authorizing Queénch's transfer agent to execute the issues were signed by both defendants as principals for the company.

In late February, Queénch's transfer agent, Richard Day of American Registrar, began questioning the issues of stock to Sprout and Alpine. The defendants provided a legal opinion supporting the transfers, but Day rejected it as inadequate. The defendants thereupon switched to a different transfer agent.

Sprout and Alpine sold the newly issued Queénch shares to the investing public for a total of approximately $4.9 million. At the same time, the companies made wire transfers totaling $2.56 million to Parris Global Sports Network, LLC, whose bank account was controlled by Lester Parris. The money ultimately made its way to both defendants.

The Securities Exchange Commission ("SEC") launched an investigation. During the investigation, Lennox asked his then-girlfriend, Terry Dussek ("Dussek"), to sign a back-dated statement that she had sold 4 million Queénch shares to Sprout and lent Parris Global Sports Network $300,000. Although Dussek refused, Lester nevertheless submitted the statement to the SEC with her forged signature. Both defendants later told Dussek to tell investigators that she had authorized them to sign her name.

The investigation was made public on March 19, 2004, when the SEC suspended trading of Queénch's stock, which was then trading at $0.13/share. When trading resumed on April 2nd, the share price was $0.12; it steadily fell to between $0.01 and $0.02 by the beginning of 2005. As of September 2005, Queénch shares traded at $0.0005-1/20th of a cent-per share. * * *

As explained during the sentencing, under the strictures of the Guidelines, the Presentence Report ("PSR") correctly added up the applicable guidelines points to be 42 for each defendant because, pursuant to Guidelines § 2B1.1(a)(1), the base offense levels were 7 and the following upward adjustments were applicable:

(1) 18 levels because the securities frauds caused more than $2,500,000 in loss, *see* Guidelines § 2B1.1(b)(1);

(2) 6 levels because the securities frauds involved 250 or more victims, *see id.*§ 2B1.1(b)(2)(C);

(3) 2 levels because the securities frauds involved "sophisticated means," *id.*§ 2B1.1(b)(9)(C);

(4) 4 levels because the defendants were officers or directors of a publicly traded company, *see id.*§ 2B1.1(b)(15)(A);

(5) 3 levels because the defendants were managers or supervisors of criminal activity involving 5 or more participants, *see id.*§ 3B1.1(b); and

(6) 2 levels because the defendants obstructed justice by tampering with a witness and providing forged documents and false testimony to the SEC, *see id.*§ 3C1.1.

1. Amount of Loss

The Government and the PSRs relied on Application Note 3 of Guidelines § 2B1.1, permitting the court to "use the gain that resulted from the offense as an alternative measure of loss" if actual loss "reasonably cannot be determined," and I agreed that the difficulties inherent in calculating loss to the market in this case made its use appropriate. * * * There were two potential bases for calculating the gain: the $4.9 million that Sprout and Alpine received from the sale of Queénch shares, and the $2.56 million that found its way back to the defendants. The issue was academic insofar as both equated to an 18-level enhancement under § 2B1.1(b)(1).

I also determined that the gain was traceable to the defendants' frauds. Although Queénch's stock had pre-fraud value, injecting a total of 28.6 million new shares into the market over a period of only two months would have exerted an immense downward pressure on Queénch's share price, as the value of each share became increasingly diluted. I concluded, therefore, that there would have been no significant market for the new shares-and little to be gained from their sale-without the artificially inflated demand created by the false press releases. Although it was impossible to determine with precision, I was satisfied that the frauds generated enough of the $4.9 million realized by Sprout and Alpine to account for the $2.56 million that was kicked back to the Parrises. * * *

2. Number of Victims

An analysis of the trading data for Queénch shares proffered by the Government, without objection from the defendants, revealed "over 500 individuals who purchased Queénch stock after January 15, the date of the first false press release, and before February 5, 2004 (the date of the final charged press release), and who had not yet sold the stock by March 19, 2004, the date the SEC halted trading in Queénch stock and the fraud was revealed." Letter from Taryn A. Merkl & Jonathan E. Green (Jan. 8, 2008), at 6. Because the number of identifiable victims exceeded 250, a 6-level enhancement was required under Guidelines § 2B1.1(b)(2)(C).

3. "Sophisticated Means"

On a prior occasion, I had stated that I was not inclined to impose a 2-level enhancement for sophisticated means because there was nothing particularly complex about issuing false press releases. * * * In response, the Government persuasively argued that the defendants' fraudulent scheme also involved concealing their involvement by issuing the press releases under a pseudonym, by using Sprout and Alpine to sell the newly-issued shares (which defendants would have been unable to do directly), and by channeling the "kickbacks" from Sprout and Alpine through Parris Global Sports Network. I was satisfied, therefore, that defendants' conduct, taken as a whole, was sufficiently sophisticated to warrant this enhancement.

4. Officers/Directors

There was no dispute that Lennox was a director of Queénch during the period of the fraud. Lester, on the other hand, argued that he had resigned from the board of directors before the press releases were issued; however, he did not offer any corporate minutes or other evidence attesting to this claimed resignation. Tellingly, both Lester and Lennox continued to sign documents as directors as late as March 5, 2004, when the company entered into a memorandum of understanding to promote its product in the Caribbean and Europe. Based on this evidence, the 4-level enhancement under Guidelines § 2B1.1(b)(15)(A) was required.

5. Role in the Offense

The evidence at trial established that the defendants directed Dussek to proofread the fraudulent press releases and directed Jonathan Sinclair and Herbert Haft to disseminate them on the Internet and elsewhere. In addition, the defendants directed two transfer agents to issue Queénch stock to Sprout and Alpine. Thus, the defendants satisfied the criteria for a 3-level "manager or supervisor" enhancement under Guidelines § 3B1.3.

6. Obstruction of Justice

The defendants' conduct during the SEC investigation fell squarely within the ambit of Guidelines § 3C1.1. *See* Application Note 4(a) ("threatening, intimidating, or otherwise unlawfully influencing a co-defendant, witness, or juror, directly or indirectly, or attempting to do so"), 4(c) ("producing or attempting to produce a false, altered, or counterfeit document or record during an official investigation or judicial proceeding"). The two-level enhancement for obstruction of justice was, therefore, justified. * * *

The defendants have no prior criminal record; therefore, with a Criminal History Category of I and total offense levels of 42, I could not have sentenced them to less than 30 years if not for *Booker* and its progeny because there was no basis that I could perceive, and none advanced by the defendants, for any downward departure. Indeed, neither defendant presented any particular health concerns or unique family responsibilities. * * *

In sum, if not for the wisdom of the Supreme Court in recognizing the need to free district courts from the shackles of the mandatory guidelines regime, I would have been confronted with the prospect of having to impose what I believe any rational jurist would consider to be a draconian sentence. * * *

Although I began the sentencing proceeding "by correctly calculating the applicable Guidelines range,"*Gall,* * * *, and recognized that "the Guidelines should be the starting point and the initial benchmark," it is difficult for a sentencing judge to place much stock in a guidelines range that does not provide realistic guidance. My search for more relevant guidance, therefore, had to proceed in other directions, although I would have much preferred a sensible guidelines range to give me some semblance of real guidance. Accordingly, I reached out to the parties for their thoughts.

To its credit, the Government shared my angst, recognizing that "your Honor is in a difficult position where you have an enormous guideline range," and conceding that "many reasonable sentences would fall outside that range." * * * In the admirable discharge of the higher duty of Government lawyers "to seek justice, and not merely to convict," * * *, AUSA Green commendably stated that "the Government is not advocating for a sentence under the Guidelines," and understood that a reasonable sentence "may well be one less, perhaps significantly less, than the guidelines range." * * * Consequently, the Government joined me and defense counsel in a collaborative effort to search for an effective means to avoid what Judge Rakoff has appropriately described as "the utter travesty of justice that sometimes results from the guidelines' fetish with absolute arithmetic, as well as the harm that guideline calculations can visit on human beings if not cabined by common sense." *Adelson.*

We first explored whether the Second Circuit's recent decision in United States v. Wills, 476 F.3d 103 (2007), might have some relevance. There, the circuit court recognized that the "primary purpose" of § 3553(a)(6)–calling for "the need to avoid unwarranted sentence disparities among defendants with similar records who have been found guilty of similar crimes"–was "to reduce unwarranted sentence disparities *nationwide.*" * * *

In light of *Wills,* I asked counsel to search for nationwide similarities in securities-fraud cases. * * * It shows, in contrast to the 360-to-life guidelines range for the Parrises' crimes, the mean terms of imprisonment, in months, imposed by district courts nationwide for just about all crimes other than securities fraud, including murder (253.1), manslaughter (46.7), sexual abuse (103.5), robbery (91.5), drug trafficking (84.4), firearms (82.1), racketeering/extortion (95.6), pornography/prostitution (98.6), and general fraud (26.2).

After reviewing all of these data, I concluded that the holding in *Wills* was essentially conceptual since the data showed, as one might suspect, marked dissimilarities from case to case, causing me to surmise that it was realistically impossible "to line up similarly situated defendants on a national scale." * * *

The Government and I were in agreement, therefore, that even if there were dissimilarities in the array of national securities-fraud sentences precluding the applicability of § 3553(a)(6) under *Wills,* they nonetheless bore upon the relative seriousness of the nature of the defendants' crimes under § 3553(a)(1). Thus, although the sentences in the Government's compendium obviously were impacted by many variables, such as whether they were imposed before or after the passage of the Sarbanes-Oxley Act, or whether the defendant pleaded guilty or was a cooperator, it was perfectly clear that there was a correlation between the losses in those cases and the periods of incarceration: Those who were not cooperators and were responsible for enormous losses were sentenced to double-digit terms of imprisonment (in years); those whose losses were less than $100 million were generally sentenced to single-digit terms.

Thus, on the double-digit side, amongst the non-cooperators, there are, as representative, the following:

Name	Amount of Loss	Sentence
Bennett	$100 million	14 years
Ebbers	over $100 million[8]	25 years
Rigas (John)	over $200 million	15 years
Rigas (Timothy)	over $200 million	20 years
Skilling	over $1 billion	24 years
Forbes	approx. $14 billion	10 years
Kumar	$2.2 billion	12 years
Ferrarini	$25 million	145 months

And on the single-digit, non-cooperator side of the Government's compendium, there are:

Name	Amount of Loss	Sentence
Hotte	$67 million	108 months
Formisano	$9.8 million	78 months
Smirlock	$12.6 million	48 months
Adelson	$50-$100 million (intended)	42 months
Betts	$1.3 million	366 days
Chavrat	$1.1 million	6 months
Tursi	$1.1 million	41 months
Scuteri	$2.5 million	21 months
Kearney	$1.3 million	51 months
Rutkoske	$12 million	108 months
Cushing	$24 million	97 months

* * * To be sure, there were undoubtedly a host of factors that entered into these sentences, and there were others that seem on the surface to defy this pattern— * * * but I simply could not dismiss, in assessing the nature and seriousness of the Parrises' crimes under § 3553(a)(1), the overall relationship of the amount of losses in those cases to the sentences imposed; fairness in sentencing required that I recognize that, although the Parrises' criminal conduct was reprehensible, they were simply not in the same league as the likes of the Enron, WorldCom and Computer Associates defendants. * * *

There were other concerns that I had in evaluating the nature and seriousness of the Parrises' crimes under § 3553(a)(1). Initially, I was cognizant of how the changes in the Sentencing Guidelines over the past several years reflected Congress' appropriate disdain for the current crop of

[8] Although Appendix A simply states the loss as over $100 million, presumably because any loss over this sum represented the outer limit for the loss enhancement under the applicable guidelines at that time, the loss occasioned by Ebbers, as CEO of WorldCom, with 2.9 billion shares of stock outstanding, was $2.2 billion. *See* United States v. Ebbers, 458 F.3d 110 (2d Cir.2006).

corporate predators: If the Parrises had been sentenced under the pre-November 1, 2001 guidelines, their sentencing ranges would have been 78 to 97 months. Between then and January 25, 2003-when the Guidelines were amended pursuant to the directives of Sarbanes-Oxley, seeU.S.S.G., app. C, amend. 647-the ranges would have risen to 168 to 210 months; the differences were occasioned by an increase in the loss calculation from 13 to 18 points and an additional two points for more than 250 victims. The spike in the current, post-Sarbanes-Oxley Guidelines applicable to the Parrises reflects an increase of one point to the base offense level, two more points for 250 or more victims, and the advent of a four-point uptick for the previously unaccounted-for category covering officers or directors of publicly traded companies.

As a consequence, we now have an advisory guidelines regime where, as reflected by this case, any officer or director of virtually any public corporation who has committed securities fraud will be confronted with a guidelines calculation either calling for or approaching lifetime imprisonment. Indeed, in *Ebbers,* the circuit court recognized that "[u]nder the Guidelines, it may well be that all but the most trivial frauds in publicly traded companies may trigger sentences amounting to life imprisonment." * * * While I acknowledge that the Guidelines "reflect Congress' judgment as to the appropriate national policy for such crimes," * * * this does not mean that the Sentencing Guidelines for white-collar crimes should be a black stain on common sense.

Fortunately, thanks to the Supreme Court, district courts are now "allowed to impose a sentence that varies from the Guidelines based solely on ... disagreements with the Guidelines," as long as they "state the basis for [their] disagreement along with 'sufficient justifications' for 'the extent of any departure.'" * * * While it may well be that the 25-year sentence for someone like Ebbers–who, as CEO of a major multinational corporation with 2.9 billion shares of outstanding stock, was responsible for a $2.2 billion loss to hundreds of thousands of investors–was "harsh but not unreasonable," * * * , any comparable sentence meted out to the Parrises, would, in contrast, be unreasonable as a matter of law.

My disagreement with the advisory guidelines range was not only driven by the double-digit/single-digit sentencing comparators * * * , but also by the guidelines' "one-shoe-fits-all" approach for its number of victims, officer/director and manager/supervisor enhancements. Thus, in all securities-fraud cases, once the threshold of 250 victims is met, the same 6 points applies for the victim enhancement, whether the number of victims be in the neighborhood of 500, as apparently in this case, or in the hundreds of thousands, as in WorldCom. The three-point leadership role enhancement attaches regardless, for example, of whether the requisite minimum of five, as here, were supervised, or 500. As for the four-level enhancement for officers and directors, there is simply no accounting for the differences their decisions may have had on destroying a major corporation affecting the lives of hundreds of thousands, compared to decisions-although inexcusable-of those jeopardizing the investments of several hundred investors in speculative penny stocks.

All of these thoughts impacted my assessment of the nature of the defendants' securities-fraud convictions under the first subparagraph of § 3553(a). I also considered, of course, the fact that the defendants were also convicted of obstructing justice; if not for that, their guidelines ranges would have been between 292 and 365 months, and the sentences somewhat lower. I also assessed each defendant's personal history and characteristics, as put forth in their attorneys' submissions, as also required under § 3553(a)(1), as well as all the other § 3553(a) factors. * * *

NOTES AND QUESTIONS

1. ***Loss.*** Should "loss" be a significant and controlling factor in determining a white-collar sentence? The main Guideline provision for fraud and theft offenses is § 2B1.1, which increases the base offense level depending on the amount of the loss caused by the defendant's conduct. The Sentencing Commission substantially revised the Guideline's definition of loss to clarify that crucial determination. The Guideline now defines loss to include both "actual loss" and "intended loss." Actual loss is "the reasonably foreseeable pecuniary harm that resulted from the offense," while intended loss is "the pecuniary harm that was intended to result from the offense; and * * * includes intended pecuniary harm that would have been impossible or unlikely to occur (e.g., as in a government sting operation, or an insurance fraud in which the claim exceeded the insured value)." The Guideline in turn defines "pecuniary harm" as "harm that is monetary or that otherwise is readily measurable in money. Accordingly, pecuniary harm does not include emotional distress, harm to reputation, or other non-economic harm," and "reasonably foreseeable pecuniary harm" as "pecuniary harm that the defendant knew or, under the circumstances, reasonably should have known, was a potential result of the offense." The Guideline further notes that "[t]he court need only make a reasonable estimate of the loss. The sentencing judge is in a unique position to assess the evidence and estimate the loss based upon that evidence. For this reason, the court's loss determination is entitled to appropriate deference." Not all fraudulent schemes result in a direct loss by the victims, even though the defendant realizes a gain from the offense conduct. Therefore, the Guideline also provides that a "court shall use the gain that resulted from the offense as an alternative measure of loss only if there is a loss only if there is a loss but it reasonably cannot be determined."

2. ***Economic Crimes Guideline Reform.*** One of the Sentencing Commission's key policy priorities for 2014-15 was the review of the current fraud guidelines. Available at: http://www.ussc.gov/sites/default/files/pdf/news/press-releases-and-news-advisories/press-releases/20140814_Press_Release.pdf. Many criticized the economic crime guidelines as being too harsh, most vocally concerning the use of financial loss as a key component in computing a sentence. Recently, some modifications were made to address

some of these problems. See Keynote Address, Chief Judge Patti B. Saris, Chair, United States Sentencing Commission, The 2015 Economic Crime Amendments (April 14, 2015). The American Bar Association, Criminal Justice Section Task Force on the Reform of Federal Sentencing for Economic Crimes has also offered a proposal to address weaknesses in the current sentencing of economic crimes. See http://www.americanbar.org/groups /criminal_justice/economic_crimes_taskforce.html. In some cases, defense counsel have argued for the court to use the ABA Proposal in sentencing their client. See Criminal Sentencing Materials Citing ABA Proposal. Available at http://www.nacdl.org /criminaldefense.aspx?id=34256%20.

3. ***Acceptance of Responsibility.*** A defendant who manifests acceptance of responsibility for the crime can receive a two- or three-level reduction in the offense level. The judge determines whether to grant the two-level reduction. Under the PROTECT Act, effective April 30, 2003, for a defendant to be eligible for an additional one-level reduction, the government must make a motion indicating that the defendant has "timely notif[ied] authorities of his intention to enter a plea of guilty, thereby permitting the government to avoid preparing for trial and permitting the government and the court to allocate their resources efficiently . . . ." U.S.S.G. § 3E1.1(b). Often, the two- or three-level reduction can have a significant impact on the length of the sentence or even the possibility of home confinement as a substitute for incarceration. After Booker, the trial court has significant discretion in determining the final sentence, but the Guidelines calculation continues to play a significant role in the final sentence. Can a defendant go to trial and still receive the two-level acceptance of responsibility reduction at sentencing? Consider the in in the Ninth Circuit's analysis in **United States v. Ramos-Medina**, 706 F.3d 932, 940-42 (9th Cir. 2013):

> The Sentencing Guidelines allow district courts to grant a two-level downward adjustment to a defendant who "clearly demonstrates acceptance of responsibility for his offense." U.S.S.G. § 3E1.1(a). The defendant bears the burden of showing that he has accepted responsibility for his actions.
>
> Ramos argues that the district court erroneously interpreted the Sentencing Guidelines to forbid a downward adjustment for acceptance of responsibility when a defendant pleads not guilty and goes to trial. We disagree with Ramos's characterization of the district court's decision. The district court did not base its denial of the adjustment on Ramos's decision to put the government to its proof alone, but searched Ramos's conduct as a whole to determine whether he nevertheless accepted responsibility. * * *
>
> A guilty plea is one way a defendant can demonstrate acceptance of responsibility, but it is not the only way. A defendant's right to contest his guilt before a jury is protected by the Constitution, and his decision to do so cannot be held against him. Accordingly, a defendant who puts the government to its proof may still be eligible

> for a downward adjustment if, and only if, he has otherwise demonstrated sincere contrition. * * *
>
> In this case, the district court * * * noted the fact that "this case went to a full blown jury trial," but it based its final decision on "the facts of this case and on this particular record" as a whole. This was the correct analytical approach. The district court's ultimate decision that Petitioner had not adequately accepted responsibility was not clearly erroneous. "[A] defendant who . . . frivolously contests[ ] relevant conduct that the court determines to be true has acted in a manner inconsistent with acceptance of responsibility." U.S.S.G. § 3E1.1 cmt. n. 1(A). Ramos contested the fact and validity of his deportation at trial. The district court asked Ramos's counsel not to pursue this line of argument any further because it "r[an] afoul of the *in-limine* motion order with respect to the deportation order" and was not supported by any "offer of proof." In addition, Ramos disputed during trial and in a motion for judgment of acquittal that he ever reentered the United States. The court denied the motion, holding that "[t]he evidence is rather overwhelming that . . . the defendant was detected and detained" in the United States. On this record, the district court did not clearly err in finding that Ramos's actions were inconsistent with acceptance of responsibility. Accordingly, we affirm Ramos's sentence.

4. ***Sophisticated Means***. The Guidelines provide a two-level enhancement for using "sophisticated means" to accomplish fraud and tax offenses that involve "especially complex or especially intricate offense conduct pertaining to the execution or concealment of an offense." In **United States v. Kontny**, 238 F.3d 815 (7th Cir. 2001), in which the defendants were convicted for failing to pay federal payroll withholding taxes, Circuit Judge Posner described the type of "sophisticated" conduct that the Guidelines recognize as the basis for increased punishment:

> Moving to the sentencing issue, we confront the argument that the efforts the Kontnys made to conceal their scheme of tax evasion did not amount to the "sophisticated concealment"[i] that requires a two-level sentencing bonus under U.S.S.G. § 2T1.4(b)(2). That they did make such efforts is not in question. They wrote separate checks to the employees, one for regular wages and one for overtime, and sometimes the overtime checks would include reimbursement for expense items to disguise the fact that the checks were for wages. The Kontnys programmed their computer so that the amount of the overtime checks was classified in nonwage expense categories. The

[i] The Guidelines were amended in November, 2001, by changing "sophisticated concealment" to "sophisticated means" for the tax-related provisions. There was no substantive change in the scope of the enhancement.

stubs for the overtime checks, which they gave their accountant, likewise placed the expense in nonwage categories.

But did these efforts amount to "sophisticated concealment"? They were not very sophisticated in the lay sense of the word, especially in context. By creating a fraud that involved the knowing participation of more than two dozen employees, they not only armed the employees to blackmail them but greatly increased the risk of eventual detection, though it is true that the fraud persisted for at least a decade before the inevitable occurred. The Kontnys' efforts at concealment were sophisticated in relation to a case in which the owner of a shop evades taxes by emptying the drawer of the cash register before counting the day's cash receipts and puts the cash thus skimmed into a shoebox and slides it under his bed, but unsophisticated in relation to a scheme of evasion that does not depend on the continuing goodwill of one's entire workforce and that creates a paper trail that is more difficult to follow to its guilty conclusion than the one the Kontnys created. * * *

The more sophisticated the efforts that an offender employs to conceal his offense, the less likely he is to be detected, and so he should be given a heavier sentence to maintain the same expected punishment, and hence the same deterrence, that confronts the average offender. Implementation of this rule requires both determining how much the average offense is concealed and relating the guideline concept of "sophistication" to deterrent needs. The complication in the first half of this inquiry is that fraud is by nature self-concealing–its success depends on its being hidden from the victim. The average criminal tax fraud thus involves some concealment; "sophisticated" tax fraud must require more. A parallel distinction has arisen in determining when statutes of limitations in fraud cases are tolled. If concealment were enough to toll such a statute of limitations, the statute would be tolled in almost every case, because fraud is inherently covert. So the courts distinguish between the initial fraud and any distinct efforts at cover up ("fraudulent concealment") and toll the statute only when the defendant has resorted to such efforts. Likewise the concealment that is inherent in criminal tax fraud, as in our shoebox example, must be distinguished from efforts over and above that concealment to prevent detection. Only the latter permit the sentencing enhancement.

In light of its purpose and context, we think "sophistication" must refer not to the elegance, the "class," the "style" of the defrauder–the degree to which he approximates Cary Grant–but to the presence of efforts at concealment that go beyond (not necessarily far beyond, for it is only a two-level enhancement that is at issue, which in this case added roughly six months to the defendants' sentences) the concealment inherent in tax fraud. It is true that the guideline

> commentary illustrates with examples suggesting a higher level of financial sophistication: "'sophisticated concealment' means especially complex or especially intricate offense conduct in which deliberate steps are taken to make the offense, or its extent, difficult to detect. Conduct such as hiding assets or transactions, or both, through the use of fictitious entities, corporate shells, or offshore bank accounts ordinarily indicates sophisticated concealment." U.S.S.G. § 2T1.4, Application Note 3. But these are offered as examples * * * the essence of the definition is merely "deliberate steps taken to make the offense ... difficult to detect." When the term "sophisticated" is defined so, it becomes apparent that the district judge did not commit a clear error in enhancing the defendants' sentences.

5. ***Abuse of Position of Trust***. Individuals in white collar cases may sometimes be subject to a sentence enhancement for occupying a "position of trust." What constitutes a "position of trust" for purposes of sentencing? In **United States v. Brogan**, 238 F.3d 780, 783-84 (6th Cir. 2001), the court noted that one looks at "the inherent nature of the work" as opposed to what "in fact happened" in the case:

> A position of trust under the guidelines is one "characterized by professional or managerial discretion." USSG § 3B1.3, comment. (n. 1). The guidelines continue by explaining that "[p]ersons holding such positions ordinarily are subject to significantly less supervision than employees whose responsibilities are primarily non-discretionary in nature." Although a number of cases on this issue look to how well the individual in fact was supervised, we have recently reaffirmed that "the level of discretion accorded an employee is to be the decisive factor in determining whether his position was one that can be characterized as a trust position." * * * The "position" must be one "characterized by substantial discretionary judgment that is ordinarily given considerable deference."
>
> * * *The trust relationship arises when a person or organization intentionally makes himself or itself vulnerable to someone in a particular position, ceding to the other's presumed better judgment some control over their affairs. Indeed, the guideline examples of where the enhancement is appropriate correspond to the types of relationships where fiduciary duties are often implied: physician-patient, lawyer-client, officer- organization. By contrast, basic employment positions such as an "ordinary bank teller" or "hotel clerk" are mentioned as inappropriate. * * *

In **United States v. Miell**, 661 F.3d 995, 997 (8th Cir. 2011), the Eighth Circuit upheld a district court's determination that a landlord occupied a position of trust vis-à-vis tenants in mail fraud prosecution for retaining their damage deposits after inflating the costs of repairs on tenants' "Summary of

Move-Out Work" forms and demanding additional alleged repair costs. The circuit court explained how an ordinary business relationship rose to the level of a trust:

> Miell was required by Iowa law to hold his tenants' deposits in a federally insured bank account or trust account separate from his personal funds and to return each rental deposit minus legitimate costs within thirty days after termination of each tenancy. He retained substantial discretionary judgment while occupying the highest management position in his companies, a position that afforded him the opportunity to access tenants' apartments and money, exercise control over damage deposits and documentation regarding alleged damages, and choose the means of repairs. The tenants were incapable of monitoring Miell in these undertakings, and traditional paths of legal recourse were relatively fruitless considering the costs of litigation. Moreover, the deposits were a prerequisite to housing for the tenants, who often were economically vulnerable, unsophisticated, and thus – unlike large commercial tenants – unable to negotiate a better deal.
>
> Miell also used his essentially unreviewable position of authority to facilitate and conceal his fraud, as his possession of the deposits put him in a position of power relative to tenants. His possession of tenants' rental units following tenants' departures, along with control of paperwork itemizing the costs of repairs, enabled him to commit and conceal the fraud by inflating repair costs and doctoring or destroying the applicable records. Because tenants did not repair the rental units, they lacked first-hand knowledge about the actual costs of such repairs and had to rely to an extent on Miell's representations regarding repairs and costs. Those representations ordinarily are given considerable deference: Miell, the fourth-largest property owner in Linn County, Iowa, controlled the property and records, and the tenants—many of whom, as noted above, were unsophisticated and economically disadvantaged—faced significant costs and barriers to challenging Miell's representations concerning the damage deposits.
>
> Miell further argues that the district court erred by finding that he held a position of trust because his tenants did not in fact trust him. Whether a defendant holds a position of trust with respect to a victim, however, turns on the nature of the defendant's position and amount of discretion and control relative to the victim, not whether the victim subjectively trusted the defendant.

6. ***Departures.*** Consider the departure in the *Parris* case above. Congress authorized judges to depart upward or downward if "there exists an aggravating or mitigating circumstance of a kind, or to a degree, not adequately taken into consideration by the Sentencing Commission in formulating the guidelines that should result in a sentence different from

that described." 18 U.S.C. § 3553(b). When is a departure appropriate in a post-*Booker* world?

> Before *Booker* excised § 3553(b)(1) from the Sentencing Reform Act, these parts strictly limited the district court's authority to sentence outside the guideline range; departures were available only when a case presented an aggravating or mitigating circumstance "of a kind, or to a degree, not adequately taken into consideration by the Sentencing Commission in formulating the guidelines." *See* §5K2.0(a), (b), p.s. Now, with the exception of special government-sponsored downward departures, courts more often sentence below the guideline range based on § 3553(a) factors than on the departure grounds listed in Chapter Five. Despite the increase in non-guideline sentences, however, the Commission's Chapter Five policy statements on departures can have a profound effect on the sentence in an individual case.
>
> Part H states the Commission's policy that many important offender characteristics, including education and vocational skills, employment record, family ties and responsibilities, and community ties, are "not ordinarily relevant" in determining the propriety of a departure. USSG Ch.5, Pt.H, intro. comment. Other characteristics—age, mental and emotional conditions, physical condition, and military service—may be grounds for departure if "individually or in combination with other [offender] characteristics" they are "present to an unusual degree and distinguish[ ] the case from the typical cases covered by the guidelines." Id. The operative words in these policy statements are "ordinarily" and "typical" – in exceptional or atypical cases, one or more of the identified characteristics may support a departure. Even in the typical case, these characteristics may be relevant for courts deciding where to sentence within the guideline range, or whether to impose a sentence outside the range under *Booker* and § 3553(a).

Henry J. Bemporad, *An Introduction to Guideline Sentencing* 17 (13th ed. 2011).

7. ***Cooperation.*** In *Parris*, the court compares sentences of non-cooperators. Should the sentences of those who cooperate with the government also be considered? For example, Andrew Fastow, former Chief Financial Officer (CFO) of Enron, received a sentence of six years after a guilty plea and cooperation with the government. His plea agreement had called for a maximum sentence of ten years. In contrast, CEO of Enron Corporation, Jeffrey Skilling, received an initial sentence of twenty-four years after a trial by jury. He later agreed to a reduction to 14 years in exchange for dropping any further appeals in his case after the Supreme Court's decision in 2010. See p.169. A study of insider trading sentences showed that cooperating defendants usually did not receive a prison sentence, or if they did it was well below that punishment recommended by the Guidelines. For non-cooperating

defendants "who entered into a plea bargain received sentences equal to 70% of the minimum recommended Guidelines range, and defendants who went to trial received average sentences equal to 64% of the minimum Guidelines range." Morrison & Foerster, *Insider Trading Annual Review 2013*. Should a defendant receive a substantial benefit for his or her cooperation with the government? If so, how much should that benefit be in terms of time to be served in prison? Should the amount of cooperation provided make a difference in the sentence received? What if a defendant has nothing to offer in cooperation?

8. ***Substantial Assistance.*** The Sentencing Guidelines authorize the government to file a motion requesting that the sentencing judge depart downward from the sentence range prescribed by the Guidelines if the defendant provides "substantial assistance" to the prosecutor. The Guidelines provide in § 5K1.1:

> Upon motion of the government stating that the defendant has provided substantial assistance in the investigation or prosecution of another person who has committed an offense, the court may depart from the guidelines.
>
> (a) The appropriate reduction shall be determined by the court for reasons stated that may include, but are not limited to, consideration of the following:
>
>> (1) the court's evaluation of the significance and usefulness of the defendant's assistance, taking into consideration the government's evaluation of the assistance rendered;
>>
>> (2) the truthfulness, completeness, and reliability of any information or testimony provided by the defendant;
>>
>> (3) the nature and extent of the defendant's assistance;
>>
>> (4) any injury suffered, or any danger or risk of injury to the defendant or his family resulting from his assistance;
>>
>> (5) the timeliness of the defendant's assistance.

In Wade v. United States, 504 U.S. 181 (1992), the Court found that § 5K1.1 gives "the Government a power, not a duty, to file a motion when a defendant has substantially assisted," and therefore a defendant cannot challenge the government's refusal to file by claiming that the defendant did, in fact, provide substantial assistance. The Court noted, however, that "a defendant would be entitled to relief if a prosecutor refused to file a substantial-assistance motion, say, because of the defendant's race or religion." In United States v. Jones, 58 F.3d 688 (D.C. Cir. 1995), the court, although affirming a judgment of the district court denying defendant's motion to compel the government to file a § 5K1.1 motion, expressed concern "that prosecutors might dangle the suggestion of a § 5K1.1 motion in front of defendants to lure them into plea agreements, all the while knowing that the defendant's cooperation could not possibly constitute assistance valuable enough for the * * * [government] to find it 'substantial.' " In **United States v. Moore**, 225 F.3d 637 (6th Cir. 2000), however, the Sixth Circuit stated:

> [T]his Circuit has expressly ruled that when a plea agreement allocates complete discretion to the government to consider whether a substantial assistance motion should be filed, we may only review the government's decision for unconstitutional motives. On the other hand, when the government bargains away its discretion and agrees to a plea agreement in which it promises to file a substantial assistance motion, we may ascertain whether the government complied with the terms of the agreement.

9. ***Collateral Consequences.*** White collar offenders often have collateral consequences as a result of a conviction. Although all offenders face the collateral consequences of a felony conviction, such as the right to vote, unique to the white collar offender can be consequences such as a loss of a license to practice law, or to practice before the Securities Exchange Commission. See p. 659. See also *Internal Exile: Collateral Consequences of Conviction in Federal Law and Regulations*, available at http://www.abanet.org/cecs/internalexile.pdf.

10. ***Special Skills.*** A sentencing issue that can arise in a white collar crime case is whether the defendant should have his or her sentence increased because of a "special skill." Being an attorney or accountant can be considered a special skill when the defendant's crime related to those skills. But how far should a court go in determining whether something is a "special skill?" The court considered this question in the following case:

UNITED STATES v. LIANG

362 F.3d 1200 (9th Cir. 2004)

O'SCANNLAIN, Circuit Judge.

We must decide whether extraordinary eyesight may be considered a "special skill" supporting an enhanced sentence in a casino card cheating scheme.

Jing Bing Liang had long gambled at cards when he met a group of players sharing a mutual dissatisfaction with the odds imposed upon them by casinos. They decided to get together and remedy the situation, so they began to cheat. It started with the game of baccarat, and the revelation that by turning the shoe[1] in a particular way, they could see the next card to be dealt. Although this could not guarantee a win, it significantly increased the chances of a payout and, when employed over the course of an evening, apparently proved quite remunerative. For example, in November 1994 at a casino in Las Vegas, Liang and four others won $1,500,000 by peeking at the shoe.

This proved enticing, so the scale and sophistication of the group steadily increased. Members began to differentiate their roles: aside from the overall ringleaders, there were those who organized particular cheats at varying casinos and those that were lookouts; some would distract the dealers, while still others did the actual cheating. Liang's expertise was as a cheater. He perfected his ability not only to peek, but to mark cards by "crimping" or "daubing" them,[2] and then utilized these methods in baccarat, its mini- and midi-variations, and blackjack. All told, Liang participated in at least six cheats from 1994 through 1999 at casinos in Las Vegas, Lake Tahoe, and Atlantic City.

Federal authorities eventually caught wind of the scheme, and on October 17, 2000, Liang and his co-conspirators were indicted on charges of conspiracy to participate in an enterprise through a pattern of racketeering by cheating. See 18 U.S.C. § 1962(d). Liang pleaded guilty on May 9, 2002.

After some wrangling at his sentencing hearing, all parties eventually agreed that at least a guideline offense level of 16 applied which, in conjunction with criminal history category I, specified a 21 to 27-month term of incarceration. The government then orally moved for a two-level sentence enhancement for the use of "special skills," pursuant to United States Sentencing Guidelines Manual § 3B1.3 (2001) ("U.S.S.G."). It argued that Liang had "extraordinary eyesight" allowing him to peek at the cards in the shoe, and that he had become specially trained in the art of cheating at cards. Liang objected, but the district court agreed with the government:

> The fact that very few members of the public have the skill [of card cheating and extraordinary eyesight] suggests that it is not quite that easy to become proficient and successful at it. [A special skills enhancement] usually requires substantial education, training, or licensing. It's the core the Court takes note of. Obviously there are a lot of special skills that are not licensed. There are a lot of special skills that are not formally obtained by formal education. It says

---

[1] A "shoe" is a device casinos use to dispense playing cards from a reservoir containing a large number of shuffled decks.

[2] Certain cards can be marked for future detection either by slightly folding them ("crimping") or by smearing on a small bit of petroleum jelly or similar substance that subtly can be identified by touch ("daubing"). These cards later can be identified without seeing their faces, which can thereby substantially increase the odds of winning a particular hand.

> substantial education. I don't think it's formal education, and obviously there was some training done to do this as efficiently and successfully as they have done it. Accordingly, the Court will [grant] the motion . . . .

As a result, Liang's offense level increased to 18 (27 to 33 months), and the district court entered a judgment sentencing him to 27 months imprisonment on October 24, 2002. * * *

Section 3B1.3 provides for a two-level sentence enhancement "if the defendant abused a position of public or private trust, or used a special skill, in a manner that significantly facilitated the commission or concealment of the offense." The application note defines a "special skill" as "a skill not possessed by members of the general public and usually requiring substantial education, training or licensing. Examples would include pilots, lawyers, doctors, accountants, chemists, and demolition experts." * * * When read in conjunction with the abuse of a "position of public or private trust" provision, it is clear that a § 3B1.3 "special skill" involves legitimate, socially valuable expertise that a criminal has perverted to uncivilized and illegal ends.

Indeed, each of the guidelines's own illustrating examples–"pilots, lawyers, doctors, accountants, chemists, and demolitions experts"–involve legitimate and important skills that only have the potential to be abused. Conversely, the ability to kidnap, to rob, or to smuggle is inherently illegitimate, creating little or no potential for gainful employment, and thus would not belong in this class even if arguably classified as a "skill." * * *

Liang's ability to cheat at cards cannot be understood as legitimate: It was basically useless outside the criminal context, no matter how good he got. And unlike a doctor or lawyer gone bad, Liang abused no societal trust by appropriating an otherwise positive educational investment for illegal personal gain. * * * Rather, he only developed his criminal expertise, a course of conduct we do not condone, but which cannot form the legal basis for a § 3B1.3 enhancement.

Moreover, a skill is only "special" for purposes of § 3B1.3 if a district court determines "not just whether the skill is 'not possessed by members of the general public,' but also, as a sine qua non, whether it is a skill 'usually requiring substantial education, training, or licensing.' " United States v. Lee, 296 F.3d 792 (9th Cir.2002). Perhaps most of us are unable to mark or to peek at cards. Nevertheless, the district court made no findings with respect to the extent of Liang's training or sophistication at card cheating, and whether it required "substantial" effort to obtain.

Liang suggests that peeking, crimping, or daubing is relatively simple, and that anyone could learn to do it in a short amount of time. In any event, without additional findings by the district court, it certainly seems no more sophisticated than many skills that have been insufficient to trigger § 3B1.3.

In light of the district court's limited findings on the matter, the enhancement cannot stand.

For these reasons, the district court erred by applying a "special skills" enhancement based on Liang's ability to cheat at cards.

The government also argues that the district court correctly based the application of § 3B1.3 on Liang's "extraordinary eyesight." Whether an underlying physical characteristic may form the basis for a "special skills" enhancement appears to be a question of first impression. It is not unusual to describe certain well-developed physical capabilities as "skills." Indeed, in some instances, formalized physical training might result in "special skills" that could be abused for illegal gain. For example, an ex-soldier theoretically might apply armed combat skills, acquired in the military, in order to facilitate a murder or a bank robbery.

Still, the fact that a skill can involve physical ability does not mean that a physical characteristic, standing alone, can also be described as a skill. While the ability to use one's hands in a certain way might be deemed a skill, the power to use them in the first place cannot. Intrinsic physical attributes are not skills–no matter how impressive they may be–because skills involve proficiency with respect to a discrete task or set of tasks. See Webster's New International Dictionary Unabridged 2133 (3d ed.1986) (defining "skill" as "knowledge of the means or methods of accomplishing a task"). Physical characteristics, on the other hand, are not knowledge nor acquired know-how: one cannot be skilled at "stamina" no matter how much he or she jogs. Likewise, it makes little sense to describe Liang as possessing the "skill of good eyesight." No matter how much it contributed to his ability to peek at cards, Liang's extraordinarily acute vision cannot be described as a skill. And because substantial training or education is what makes a skill "special" for purposes of § 3B1.3, Liang's visual acuity is simply irrelevant to the question of whether he should be subject to the enhancement.

Accordingly, the district court also erred by considering this factor.

C. APPELLATE REVIEW

UNITED STATES v. TOMKO

562 F.3d 558 (3rd Cir. 2009)

SMITH, Circuit Judge, with whom McKEE, BARRY, AMBRO, FUENTES, CHAGARES, JORDAN, and HARDIMAN, Circuit Judges, join.

The Government appeals the reasonableness of William Tomko's below-Guidelines sentence of probation, community service, restitution, and fine for his tax evasion conviction. If any one of a significant number of the members of this Court–including some in today's majority–had been sitting as the District Judge, Tomko would have been sentenced to some time in prison. But "[t]he fact that the appellate court might reasonably have concluded that a different sentence was appropriate is insufficient to justify reversal of the district court." Gall v. United States, 552 U.S. 38 (2007). *Gall* reminds us that "[t]he sentencing judge is in a superior position to find facts and judge their import under § 3553(a) in the individual case. The judge sees and hears the evidence, makes credibility determinations, has full knowledge of the facts and gains insights not conveyed by the record." This reality is why, post-*Booker*, "the familiar abuse-of-discretion standard of review now applies to appellate review of sentencing decisions." Where, as here, a district court decides to vary from the Guidelines' recommendations, we "must give due deference to the district court's decision that the § 3553(a) factors, on a whole, justify the extent of the variance." These principles require us to affirm Tomko's sentence.

On May 11, 2004, Tomko pleaded guilty to a one-count information charging him with tax evasion in violation of 26 U.S.C. § 7201. Tomko was the owner and Chief Executive Officer of W.G. Tomko & Son, Inc. ("Tomko, Inc."), a plumbing contractor. From 1995 to 1998, Tomko directed numerous subcontractors, who were building his multimillion dollar home in Washington County, Pennsylvania, to falsify information on billing invoices so that the invoices would show work being done at one of Tomko, Inc.'s many job sites instead of at Tomko's home. As a result, Tomko, Inc. paid for the construction of Tomko's home and illegally deducted those payments as business expenses. Tomko also did not properly report those payments as income on his personal tax return. All told, Tomko's tax evasion scheme involved twelve different subcontractors and his general contractor, and resulted in a tax deficiency of $228,557.

The United States District Court for the Western District of Pennsylvania conducted Tomko's sentencing hearing on September 30, 2005. Using the 1997 edition of the United States Sentencing Guidelines Manual, the District Court calculated Tomko's total offense level to be thirteen and his criminal history category to be I. Based on these calculations, the Guidelines recommended a range of imprisonment between twelve and eighteen months and a fine between $3,000 and $30,000.

Tomko, however, proposed that in light of the then-recent Hurricane Katrina catastrophe and his construction expertise, the Court should sentence him to probation and home detention, and require him to work for Habitat for Humanity. The Executive Director for Habitat for Humanity's Pittsburgh affiliate testified that the organization would appreciate Tomko's help in its efforts to rebuild the Gulf Coast and that Tomko had performed well in past projects, including providing onsite assistance and advice.

Tomko also proffered testimony from Tomko, Inc.'s Chief Financial Officer that the company was in danger of losing its line of credit if he were imprisoned. If this happened, Tomko, Inc. would be in dire straits financially and the jobs of its 300-plus employees would be threatened.

Finally, Tomko submitted a Motion for Downward Departure. The motion argued that Tomko should be sentenced below his Guidelines range because 1) his incarceration could cause Tomko, Inc.'s innocent employees to lose their jobs; 2) he has performed exceptional charitable acts and good works; 3) he has demonstrated an extraordinary degree of acceptance of responsibility; and 4) a combination of these three factors. As exhibits, Tomko attached over fifty letters from family, friends, community leaders, and others attesting to his pre-indictment charitable activities and other good works. * * *

[After reviewing the sentencing factors in § 3353(a), the district court stated: * * * "I recognize the need for consistent sentencing; however, in this case, given the Defendant's lack of any significant criminal history, his involvement in exceptional charitable work and community activity, and his acceptance of responsibility, we find that a sentence that is mitigated by the factors of 3553 [is] warranted.]

In response, the Government insisted that the Court impose a sentence that included a term of imprisonment. The Government did not challenge Tomko's factual assertions or submissions. Instead, it juxtaposed his criminal conduct with the patriotism of American soldiers fighting wars abroad and argued that greed, not community service and philanthropy, defined Tomko's character. It focused on the fact that Tomko coerced his subcontractors to file false documentation, and highlighted the "gilded cage" nature of a sentence of home detention. The Government claimed that it would be "absurd" to sentence Tomko to live in the same multimillion dollar mansion that the illegally obtained tax monies helped fund. * * *

Despite the Government's arguments, the District Court did not sentence Tomko to a term of imprisonment. Instead, the Court sentenced Tomko to three years of probation (the first of which would be served as home detention), participation in an alcohol treatment program, 250 hours of community service, full restitution, and the statutory maximum fine of $250,000. * * *

Two basic principles underlie the application of the abuse-of-discretion standard. First, "deferential review is used when the matter under review was decided by someone who is thought to have a better vantage point than we on the Court of Appeals to assess the matter." * * * Accordingly, the Supreme Court has applied the abuse-of-discretion standard where it "noted that deference was owed to the 'judicial actor . . . better positioned than another to decide the issue in question.'" Koon v. United States, 518 U.S. 81 (1996) (quoting Pierce v. Underwood, 487 U.S. 552 (1988)). As one leading commentator has put it, "[i]n the dialogue between the appellate judges and the trial judge, the former often would seem to be saying: 'You were there. We do not think we would have done what you did, but we were not present and we may be unaware of significant matters, for the record does not adequately convey to us all that went on at the trial. Therefore, we defer to you.'" * * *

Second, courts of appeals apply the abuse-of-discretion standard to fact-bound issues that are ill-suited for appellate rule-making. * * *

Post-*Booker*, the sentencing court's superior vantage point has been the oft-cited reason for applying the abuse-of-discretion standard to sentencing review. In *Gall*, the Court emphasized that "[t]he sentencing judge is in a superior position to find facts and judge their import under § 3553(a) in the individual case. The judge sees and hears the evidence, makes credibility determinations, has full knowledge of the facts and gains insights not conveyed by the record." This means that "[t]he sentencing judge has access to, and greater familiarity with, the individual case and the individual defendant before him than the [Sentencing] Commission or the appeals court." * * * Additionally, "district courts have an institutional advantage over appellate courts in making these sorts of determinations, especially as they see so many more Guidelines sentences than appellate courts do." * * *

Our appellate review proceeds in two stages. It begins by "ensur[ing] that the district court committed no significant procedural error, such as failing to calculate (or improperly calculating) the Guidelines range, treating the Guidelines as mandatory, failing to consider the § 3553(a) factors, selecting a sentence based on clearly erroneous facts, or failing to adequately explain the chosen sentence-including an explanation for any deviation from the Guidelines range." *Gall*. We do not presume that a district court considered the factors solely because the sentence falls within the Guidelines range. If a district court's procedure passes muster, "we then, at stage two, consider its substantive reasonableness." *Levinson*. Our substantive review requires us not to focus on one or two factors, but on the totality of the circumstances. Indeed, we cannot presume that a sentence is unreasonable simply because it falls outside the advisory Guidelines range. At both stages of our review, the party challenging the sentence has the burden of demonstrating unreasonableness.

The abuse-of-discretion standard applies to both our procedural and substantive reasonableness inquiries. For example, an abuse of discretion has occurred if a district court based its decision on a clearly erroneous factual conclusion or an erroneous legal conclusion. This also means that, absent any significant procedural error, we must "give due deference to the district court's determination that the § 3553(a) factors, on a whole," justify the sentence. *Gall*. In other words, if the district court's sentence is procedurally sound, we will affirm it unless no reasonable sentencing court would have imposed the same sentence on that particular defendant for the reasons the district court provided.

Ultimately, "[t]he touchstone of 'reasonableness' is whether the record as a whole reflects rational and meaningful consideration of the factors enumerated in 18 U.S.C. § 3553(a)." United States v. Grier, 475 F.3d 556 (3d Cir.2007) (en banc). "An estimation of the outer bounds of what is 'reasonable' under a given set of circumstances may not always be beyond debate, but the abuse-of-discretion standard by which that estimation must be judged limits the debate and gives district courts broad latitude in sentencing."

The Government makes only one claim of procedural error: it argues that the District Court failed to meaningfully consider general deterrence. Based on our review of the record, we cannot agree. A sentencing court does not have to "discuss and make findings as to each of the § 3553(a) factors if the record makes clear the court took the factors into account in sentencing." Here, "[t]he record makes clear that the sentencing judge listened to each argument," *Rita*, and rejected the ones the Government made concerning general deterrence. * * *

* * * The District Judge noted that he viewed Tomko's sentence as "address[ing] the sentencing goals of punishment, *deterrence* and rehabilitation." (Emphasis added.) This demonstrates that the District Court heard the Government's impassioned plea, considered general deterrence, and handed down Tomko's sentence. Therefore, we conclude that the District Court did not commit any procedural error at Tomko's sentencing.

The crux of the Government's appeal is its claim that Tomko's sentence is substantively unreasonable. * * * In essence, the Government is asking this Court to apply the already-rejected "proportionality test" by a different name. The Government's appeal boils down to a claim that Tomko's criminal history, employment record, community ties, and charitable works do not differentiate him enough from the "mine-run" tax evasion case to justify his below-Guidelines sentence. Similarly, a "proportionality test" rests on "the proposition that the strength of the justification needed to sustain an outside-Guidelines sentence varies in proportion to the degree of the variance." *Rita*. As applied by some courts of appeals, this meant that "a sentence that constitute [d] a substantial variance from the Guidelines [had to] be justified by extraordinary circumstances." *Gall*. In *Gall*, the Supreme Court explicitly barred the application of such an approach because it necessarily applies a "heightened standard of review to sentences outside the Guidelines range." That, of course, is "inconsistent with the rule that the abuse-of-discretion standard of review applies to appellate review of all sentencing decisions–whether inside or outside the Guidelines range." * * *

Based on our review of the record, we conclude that the District Court did not abuse its discretion here. At Tomko's sentencing hearing, the District Court explicitly examined subsections (a)(1), (a)(2)(A), (a)(2)(B), (a)(2)(C), (a)(2)(D), (a)(3), (a)(4), and (a)(6) of § 3553. The District Court also ordered full restitution. After hearing argument from the Government concerning the need for a term of imprisonment, the Court reiterated its reasons for imposing a sentence without one. The District Court gave specific reasons for why Tomko's sentence varies from the Guidelines range. This variance took into account his negligible criminal history, his employment record, his community ties, and his extensive charitable works as reasons for not incarcerating Tomko, while also factoring in his substantial wealth as a reason for imposing a fine far above the Guidelines range. Indeed, the

District Court provided more than just a boilerplate recitation of the § 3553(a) factors; it detailed, step-by-step, its individualized assessment of the sentence that it believed appropriate in this particular case. * * *

It bears mentioning that the District Court's variance here was not substantial. The difference between Tomko's actual sentence and the lower end of his Guidelines range is twelve months. * * * We cannot say that, in absolute terms, the variance here was so large that it was per se unreasonable. In *Gall*, the Supreme Court affirmed a district court's probationary sentence where the advisory Guidelines range was thirty to thirty-seven months of imprisonment. Similarly, post-*Gall*, a number of courts of appeals, including our own, have affirmed sentences that involved greater variances or departures than the one here. "It will be a rare case when it is clear that no acceptable reasoning can justify a given sentence." * * * This is not one of them.

If abuse-of-discretion review cannot strike such a balance, it is not our role as appellate judges to adjust the scales. * * * The risk of affirming an unwarranted sentencing disparity in this case is one we must accept while following the Supreme Court's "pellucidly clear" command that we apply the abuse-of-discretion standard of review. *Gall*.

Our decision today should not suggest that variances of the size and character of Tomko's will always be substantively reasonable. District courts must make sentencing determinations on an individualized basis. Accordingly, the substantive reasonableness of each sentence must be evaluated on its own terms, based on the reasons that the district court provided, in light of the particular facts and circumstances of that case.* * *

* * * Here, the record demonstrates the District Court's thoughtful attempt to tailor the off-the-rack Guidelines recommendations into a sentence that fits Tomko personally. Where it believed the Guidelines recommendations too large or too small-for example, in the advisory ranges for imprisonment and fine–the Court took care to explain why this was the case before making the adjustments it felt necessary. This is precisely the type of individualized assessment that *Gall* demands, and to which we must defer. Accordingly, we will affirm the sentence that the District Court imposed.

FISHER, Circuit Judge, dissenting, with whom Chief Judge SCIRICA, Judge SLOVITER, Judge RENDELL and Judge COWEN join.

As the procedural history of this appeal clearly shows, this Court has wrestled with the decision in this case for close to two and one half years, during which time the judges on this Court have tried to determine whether the sentence given for this crime was substantively reasonable. The offense we encounter in this case is no garden variety tax evasion. The conduct underlying the offense involved an intricate scheme spanning several years and involved the coercion and coordination of numerous other individuals, all for the personal gain of one man, William G. Tomko, Jr., a successful business owner with the means to easily pay the taxes he owed to the Government.

* * * This case presents the opportunity for us to examine the implications of the Supreme Court's directive in *Gall* that in reviewing for reasonableness, appellate courts are to conduct a substantive inquiry as well as a procedural one.

* * * If the substance of a sentence is not "logical and consistent" with the § 3553(a) factors or fails to "reasonably appl[y]" them to "the circumstances of the case," United States v. Cooper, 437 F.3d 324 (3d Cir.2006), the sentence is not substantively reasonable and does not survive abuse-of-discretion review. * * *

[The dissenting judges agreed with the majority that the district judge properly addressed the question of general deterrence in the sentencing.]

Viewed cumulatively, out of the three reasons offered by the District Court for mitigating Tomko's sentence, only one – community support based on charitable work – even begins to justify a downward variance in this case. Thus, these considerations fall short of placing the sentence imposed within the albeit broad range of permissible choices, even when we add them together. Moreover, the "mitigating" circumstances relied upon by the District Court only address one of the § 3553(a) factors, namely "the history and characteristics of the defendant" under § 3553(a)(1), and therefore do not reflect the "totality of the circumstances" and the "§ 3553(a) factors, on a whole." *Gall*, 128 S.Ct. at 597. As a number of our sister courts of appeals have recognized, excessive reliance on a single § 3553(a) factor is indicative of an unreasonable sentence. As the remainder of our analysis reveals, the District Court's over-reliance on § 3553(a)(1) as justification for the significant qualitative and quantitative variance it granted pales in comparison to the numerous § 3553(a) factors which suggest that a term of imprisonment is warranted in a case of tax evasion as willful and brazen as Tomko's.

Viewed cumulatively, we conclude that the relevant § 3553(a) factors advocate in the strongest possible terms for a sentence including a term of imprisonment. Beginning with § 3553(a)(1), district courts are instructed to consider not only a defendant's "history and characteristics," but also "the nature and circumstances of the offense," which the District Court did not emphasize. In this respect, Tomko did much more than fail to report income on a form; he conceived of a sophisticated plan to evade taxation and compelled multiple individuals to aid him in the scheme. This scheme spanned several years, involved the planning, coordination, and coercion of numerous subcontractors, required a complicated system of concealment through fraudulent billing, and resulted in a stipulated tax loss of over $225,000. Thus, while the District Court's stated justifications for mitigating Tomko's sentence fail to differentiate him from other tax evaders, the severity of his offense and the extent of his culpability, as evidenced by the willful and brazen nature of his conduct, remove Tomko's tax evasion from the garden variety type. As such, even assuming "the history and characteristics of the defendant" point in the direction of a lenient sentence, "the nature and circumstances of the offense" certainly do not. * * *

D. RESTITUTION, CRIMINAL FORFEITURE AND DISGORGEMENT

The federal courts do not have the inherent authority to order a defendant to pay restitution. Congress provided that authority in the Mandatory Victims Restitution Act of 1996 (MVRA), 18 U.S.C. § 3662 et seq. A Senate report on the statute stated that the law was designed "to ensure that the loss to crime victims is recognized, and that they receive the restitution that they are due . . . to ensure that the offender realizes the damage caused by the offense and pays the debt owed to the victim as well as to society." S. Rep. No. 104-179 (1995). A defendant must pay "the full amount of each victim's losses as determined by the court and without consideration of the economic circumstances of the defendant," 18 U.S.C.A. § 3664(f)(1)(A).

The MVRA gives victims a recovery that could have been obtained in a private civil action by making it part of the criminal process. A restitution order covers direct losses resulting from specified crimes, including most white collar offenses, but does not authorize recovery of consequential damages. A defendant need not have benefitted personally from the loss to the victim to be held responsible for restitution under the MVRA. In United States v. Moten, 551 F.3d 763 (8th Cir. 2008), the court held that a defendant convicted of aiding and abetting the theft of government funds could be held jointly and severally liable for the losses, including for funds that went to other co-defendants. Unlike the Sentencing Guidelines that focus on "relevant conduct" to determine the scope of the misconduct, the MVRA adopts a victim-oriented approach that measures the harm based on the offense of conviction to determine the amounts subject to an order of restitution.

The MVRA requires that defendants "make restitution to the victim of the offense" or to persons who are not victims if agreed to pursuant to a plea agreement. A "victim" is defined as a person or organization "directly and proximately harmed as a result of the commission of an offense." In addition, in the case of an offense that involves as an element a scheme, conspiracy, or pattern of criminal activity, any person directly harmed by the defendant's criminal conduct in the course of the scheme, conspiracy, or pattern. 18 U.S.C.A. § 3663A(a)(2). The harm to the victims can be either physical injuries or pecuniary losses as a result of certain criminal offenses, which can include reimbursement for lost investment earnings. In addition, a defendant can be required to pay restitution for "lost income and necessary child care, transportation, and other expenses incurred during participation in the investigation or prosecution of the offense or attendance at proceedings related to the offense." 18 U.S.C. § 3663A(b)(4). In United States v. Amato, 540 F.3d 153 (2d Cir. 2008), the defendants were convicted of fraud and conspiracy for deceiving their employer. The court ordered them to pay the employer $3,088,466 of its attorney fees and accounting costs related to the government's investigation that led to their convictions as "other expenses." The Second Circuit rejected the argument that only costs similar to child care and transportation were covered, and found that "this fraud would force the corporation to expend large sums of money on its own internal investigation as well as its participation in the government's investigation and prosecution of defendants' offenses is not surprising. There is no doubt that [the company's] attorney fees and auditing costs were a direct and foreseeable result of defendants' offenses."

The MVRA provides that restitution will not be ordered in only two circumstances: when there are so many victims that restitution is impracticable, or when "determining complex issues of fact related to the cause or amount of the victim's losses would complicate or prolong the sentencing process to a degree that the need to provide restitution to any victim is outweighed by the burden on the sentencing process." 18 U.S.C. § 3663A(c)(3)(B).

Criminal asset forfeiture is part of the sentence imposed on a defendant in a criminal case. Pursuant to Federal Rule of Criminal Procedure 32.2(a), a court "must not enter a judgment of forfeiture in a criminal proceeding unless the indictment or information contains notice to the defendant that the government will seek the forfeiture of property as part of any sentence." The indictment or criminal information will contain a forfeiture count, usually the last one in the document, but the forfeiture allegation need not specify precisely what interest the defendant has in the property or the exact amount the government will seek to forfeit. The amount of the forfeiture, and what property is subject to forfeiture, is determined after a conviction in a separate proceeding. The standard of proof for forfeiture is by a preponderance of the evidence, not beyond a reasonable doubt, because it is part of the sentencing and not an element of the offense. In a criminal case, the government can also seek the forfeiture of "substitute assets," what are assets under the defendant's control that were not the proceeds of unlawful activity. So long as the Government can prove that assets directly connected to the illegal activity cannot be located, or do not satisfy the amount of the forfeiture judgment, then substitute assets may be taken to pay off what is owed.

The power of the criminal asset forfeiture laws is shown by the pretrial restraint of assets, which can include funds or property the defendant intended to use to pay the cost of the legal defense. Once an indictment is returned in a criminal case, the Government is able to move ex parte for a pre-trial restraining order to preserve forfeitable property pending trial. The order usually prohibits a defendant from alienating, encumbering, dissipating or destroying property subject to forfeiture before the conclusion of the trial.

Although there is some controversy over this point, most federal courts do not permit the pretrial restraint of substitute assets, i.e. assets that are not traceable to the criminal activity. The majority rule is that a defendant can be ordered to pay both forfeiture and restitution, the the court will not reduce the amount of the forfeiture by any money paid as restitution.

For large scale frauds, the amount of forfeiture ordered can be enormous, far beyond what any individual could ever hope to pay. Thomas Petters, who was convicted of conducting a Ponzi scheme that involved a number of different company, was ordered to forfeit over $3.5 billion. The forfeiture order entered for Bernie Madoff, perpetrator of the largest Ponzi scheme in history, included a money judgment of over $170 billion, an amount greater than the gross national product of a number of countries, including New Zealand and Slovakia. Although there is no possibility these amounts could ever be paid, the forfeiture order allows the government to seek every possible asset connected to the defendant, including anything acquired after the conviction by identifying it as a substitute asset.

Disgorgement of profits earned from a course of illegal conduct is an equitable remedy available in civil enforcement actions as part of the relief a court grants for a violation. The Securities and Exchange Commission makes disgorgement a key feature of in cases in which it seeks to reclaim the profits from insider trading or compensation and bonuses from manipulation of corporate revenue and profits. Typically, the SEC uses any disgorged funds to repay investors harmed by the violation. In addition to the equitable remedy, Congress expressly authorized the SEC to seek disgorgement for certain violations of the federal securities laws. For example, the Sarbanes-Oxley Act authorizes the SEC to recoup "any bonus or other incentive-based or equity-based compensation" received by a chief executive or chief financial officer if the company issues a restatement of its books and records due to material noncompliance with the accounting rules. 15 U.S.C.A. § 7243. The Dodd-Frank Act in 2010 expanded the SEC's authority by allowing it to order disgorgement in an administrative proceeding for any violation of the federal securities laws, which means a federal court's authority need not be invoked for what is putatively an equitable remedy. 15 U.S.C.A. § 78u-2(e).

There is an overlap between forfeiture, which seeks to recover the proceeds of criminal activity, restitution, which focuses on restoring any losses to the victim, and disgorgement, which looks at the gains derived by the defendant from illegal conduct. But the two remedies are not identical. When the government pursues parallel criminal and civil cases, a defendant may be responsible to pay disgorgement in the civil case that is more than what the asset forfeiture laws and the MVRA would require in the criminal case, as the following case illustrates.

SECURITIES & EXCHANGE COMMISSION v. CONTORINIS

743 F.3d 296 (2d Cir. 2014)

GERARD E. LYNCH, Circuit Judge:

Defendant-appellant Joseph Contorinis, a Managing Director at Jeffries & Company, Inc., executed several illegal insider trades involving the stock of the supermarket chain Albertson's, Inc., using material nonpublic information received from Nicos Stephanou, an employee of UBS Investment Bank. The offense had its origins in September 2005, when Stephanou informed Contorinis that UBS would be advising on a major financial acquisition involving Albertson's. As a UBS employee involved in the transaction, Stephanou was privy to confidential material information regarding the acquisition, and Contorinis asked Stephanou to keep him apprised of developments.

In January 2006, as negotiations involving the acquisition of Albertson's unfolded, Stephanou on several occasions disclosed material inside information regarding the acquisition to Contorinis before the information became public. Relying on that information, Contorinis made several opportune trades in Albertson's stock. Contorinis did not execute these trades with his personal assets, but rather did so on behalf of the Jeffries Paragon Fund, of which Contorinis was a co-manager and over which he had investment control. As a result of these insider trades the Paragon Fund realized profits of $7,304,738, and avoided losses of $5,345,700.

In February 2009, Contorinis was indicted on one count of conspiracy to commit securities fraud and nine counts of securities fraud. A jury found him guilty of the conspiracy and of seven counts of securities fraud, and on October 6, 2010, he was sentenced to six years of imprisonment and ordered to pay $12,650,438 (the combined value of the Paragon Fund's realized profits and avoided losses) in criminal forfeiture penalties.

On appeal, this Court affirmed Contorinis's conviction but vacated the forfeiture order, remanding to the district court to redetermine the proper amount. United States v. Contorinis, 692 F.3d 136 (2d Cir. 2012). We observed that neither the language of the criminal forfeiture statute nor Circuit case law supported the proposition that a defendant must forfeit proceeds that "go directly to an innocent third party and are never possessed by the defendant." Rather, criminal forfeiture penalties are "usually based on the defendant's actual gain." The district court's initial forfeiture calculation reflected the total benefit to the Paragon Fund, not the gains accruing to Contorinis himself. On remand, the district court found that Contorinis's personal profit, in the form of linked compensation from the trades, amounted to $427,875, and ordered forfeiture of that amount.

Following the filing of the criminal indictment, the Securities and Exchange Commission brought this civil action against Contorinis in the United States District Court for the Southern District of New York, seeking disgorgement of $7,260,604 in unlawful profits obtained by the Paragon Fund (equivalent to the total profit from insider trading less trading commission costs), as well as additional civil monetary penalties and an injunction against future securities law violations. After Contorinis was convicted at his criminal trial, the SEC moved for summary judgment, and Contorinis, without admitting to the underlying offense, acknowledged that the jury verdict had a preclusive effect requiring a finding of civil liability. On February 3, 2012, the district court granted the SEC's summary judgment motion against Contorinis and granted relief in the forms requested by the SEC, permanently enjoining Contorinis from violating the securities laws in the future, ordering Contorinis to disgorge $7,260,604 (less any amount paid pursuant to the criminal forfeiture), and imposing a civil penalty of $1,000,000. * * *

Contorinis timely brought this appeal, challenging the judgment insofar as it required him to disgorge the entire amount obtained by the Paragon Fund through insider trading * * *.

Disgorgement serves to remedy securities law violations by depriving violators of the fruits of their illegal conduct. Disgorgement is an equitable remedy, imposed to "forc[e] a defendant to give up the amount by which he was unjustly enriched." FTC v. Bronson Partners, 654 F.3d 359 (2d Cir. 2011). By forcing wrongdoers to give back the fruits of their illegal conduct, disgorgement also "has the effect of deterring subsequent fraud." SEC v. Cavanagh, 445 F.3d 105, 117 (2d Cir. 2006). Because disgorgement does not serve a punitive function, the disgorgement amount may not exceed the amount obtained through the wrongdoing. At the same time, however, as it operates to make the illicit action unprofitable for the wrongdoer, disgorgement need not serve to compensate the victims of the wrongdoing. Because disgorgement is not compensatory, it forces a defendant to account for all profits reaped through his securities law violations and to transfer all such money to the court, even if it exceeds actual damages to the victim. Because disgorgement's underlying purpose is to make lawbreaking unprofitable for the law-breaker, it satisfies its design when the lawbreaker returns the fruits of his misdeeds, regardless of any other ends it may or may not accomplish. * * *

Contorinis argues that because he never personally controlled the profits that accrued to the Paragon Fund – although he could make investment decisions, he did not control disbursement of the proceeds – ordering him to disgorge the entire amount gained through his insider trading is a misapplication of the disgorgement principle. The argument identifies an ambiguity in the concept of disgorgement. Disgorgement instantiates the equitable principle that wrongdoers should not benefit from their misdeeds, and thus should relinquish any profits obtained from them. On the one hand, Contorinis argues that because he illegally traded not for his own account with his own funds, but rather on behalf of an investment fund that he managed and whose assets belonged to third-party investors, he did not personally enjoy the proceeds of the resulting gain (beyond the increase in his compensation linked to the performance of the Paragon Fund). On the other hand, although Contorinis did not pocket the profits from his trades, it was he who utilized the inside information, executed the trades, and secured the resulting profit for the benefit of his clients. The question is thus posed whether an insider trader can be required to disgorge not only the profit that he personally enjoyed from his exploitation of inside information, but also the profits of such exploitation that he channeled to friends, family, or clients. Contorinis argues, in effect, that one can only "disgorge" what one has personally "swallowed"; the SEC argues that a fraudster should be compelled to return not only those profits from the fraud that he has reserved for his own use, but also those that he has bestowed on others.

In resolving this dispute, we do not write on a clean slate. Our prior cases indicate that an insider trader may be ordered to disgorge not only the unlawful gains that accrue to the wrongdoer directly, but also the benefit that accrues to third parties whose gains can be attributed to the wrongdoer's conduct. We have long applied that principle in the tipper-tippee context. Thus, in SEC v. Warde we held that, in the determination of a disgorgement amount, "[a] tippee's gains are attributable to the tipper, regardless whether benefit accrues to the tipper." 151 F.3d 42 (2d Cir. 1998). That principle has deep roots in parallel civil remedial structures. For example, in Elkind v. Liggett & Myers, Inc., 635 F.2d 156 (2d Cir. 1980), we concluded that "[t]rades by tippees are attributed to the tipper" in determining liability for damages, and in SEC v. Texas Gulf Sulphur Co., 446 F.2d 1301 (2d Cir. 1971), the foundational case for insider trading liability, we required a tipper to make common-law civil restitution "for the profits derived by his tippees."

That rule makes perfect sense. A potential tipper in possession of inside information who seeks to confer a benefit on a friend or to curry favor with someone who can confer reciprocal benefits in the future can do so either by trading on this information himself and passing the profit on to the intended beneficiary, or by passing the information to the beneficiary and thus allowing the tippee to realize the profit himself. In the former case, the insider would unquestionably be liable to disgorge the profit; disgorgement is required whether the insider trader has put his profits into a bank account, dissipated them on transient pleasures, or given them away to others. It would make little sense to allow the insider to escape disgorgement when he gives away not the proceeds of a trade predicated on his insider knowledge, but rather the knowledge itself to others who he knows will spin the information into gold by trading on it themselves.

But if that is so, and our precedents confirm that it is, it must follow that the insider who, rather than passing the tip along to another, directly trades for that other's account must equally disgorge the benefit he obtains for his favored beneficiary. Indeed, that was the actual situation in *Warde*, in which the defendant utilized an account belonging to his wife, over which he had control, to make trades based on material nonpublic information. Whether he traded on his own account and gave the profit to his wife, gave the information to his wife to enable her to trade on it, or executed the trades on his own authority using his wife's account such that the proceeds accrued to her, the wrong committed by the defendant would be the same, as would the economic result. Whether the defendant's motive is direct economic profit, self-aggrandizement, psychic satisfaction from benefitting a loved one, or future profits by enhancing one's reputation as a successful fund manager, the insider trader who trades for another's account has engaged in a fraud, secured a benefit thereby, and directed the profits of the fraud where he has chosen them to go.

Thus, given our precedent establishing that tippers may be held liable to disgorge the gains of their tippees, it would be inconsistent to deny the district court the discretion to impose equivalent liability for conduct such as Contorinis's. Indeed, to the extent that this case can be distinguished from the tipper-tippee situation, the case for disgorgement is stronger here. The tipper in possession of material nonpublic information who passes that inside information to another, even with full knowledge that the tippee will use the information to trade, has no control over, and likely no knowledge of, the extent to which the tippee will trade. The tippee may make a modest wager or take a deep plunge; she may act at the ideal moment, or sacrifice some potential profit by trading prematurely or delaying too long. The tipper is liable for the tippee's gains, whatever they may be.

In contrast, Contorinis had greater control over the Paragon Fund's illegal profits than a tipper does over a tippee. Contorinis both obtained the inside information that facilitated the illegal trade and executed the trade on behalf of the Paragon Fund. He controlled the size and timing of the trades, and was then entirely responsible for the size of the Paragon Fund's gains. Moreover, it was Contorinis's business to make trades on behalf of the Paragon Fund. Not only did he profit directly from the additional incentive compensation he received based on his successful (but corrupt) trades, but by making profitable trades on behalf of his clients he enhanced his reputation and increased the likelihood of his receiving future benefits as a fund manager. In this way, Contorinis's case is even closer than a tipper's to the bedrock disgorgement case of the insider who executes illegal trades using his own money, and donates the profit to a third party. There is no injustice, therefore, in making him responsible for the profits he made for others, as well as for himself, through his fraudulent insider trades.

It thus necessarily follows from existing Circuit precedent, and from the logic of the disgorgement remedy, that Contorinis may be held responsible for disgorgement of the Paragon Fund's illegal profits. To conclude otherwise would permit greater liability in a relationship (tipper-tippee) which is, in all material respects, more tenuous than the relationship here (controlling manager-financial vehicle). Our conclusion is required to maintain consistency in the remediation of securities law violations. * * *

We do not conclude that district courts must impose disgorgement liability for insider trading upon wrongdoers when the gains accrue to innocent third parties, but rather that the district courts may elect to do so in appropriate circumstances. It is well established that district courts have broad discretion to impose disgorgement liability, and that liability should fall upon the wrongdoer in cases of uncertainty.

Contorinis's argument that he should be forced to disgorge only the amounts that he directly obtained as personal pecuniary benefit seeks to undermine this discretion by conflating a central, well-established principle in disgorgement law – that "the court may only exercise its equitable power only over property causally related to the wrongdoing," SEC v. First City Fin. Corp., 890 F.2d 1215 (D.C. Cir. 1989) – with the proposition, unsupported in our case law, that the wrongdoer need disgorge only the financial benefit that accrues to him personally. Yet as our consideration of the tipper-tippee context demonstrates, that proposition is without foundation. The amount a court may order a wrongdoer to disgorge may not exceed the total amount of gain from the illegal action, but that does not entail that the gain must personally accrue to the wrongdoer. As our consideration of the tipper context demonstrates, to so limit the power of courts to order disgorgement would permit evasion of the prohibition on insider trading by allowing the direction of benefits to acquaintances. * * *

Contorinis further argues that our recent decision in his criminal appeal limiting the extent of the criminal forfeiture to his personal gain, should be applied in the civil disgorgement context. That argument is unavailing. As we noted in deciding Contorinis's criminal appeal, criminal forfeiture "serves no remedial purpose, is designed to punish the offender, and cannot be imposed upon innocent owners." Disgorgement, in contrast, is a civil remedy which serves the remedial purpose of preventing unjust enrichment.

Thus, while both criminal forfeiture and disgorgement serve to deprive wrongdoers of their illicit gain, the two remedies reflect different characteristics and purposes—disgorgement is an equitable remedy that prevents unjust enrichment, and criminal forfeiture a statutory legal penalty imposed as punishment. One ramification in particular of this qualitative divergence between disgorgement and criminal forfeiture nullifies Contorinis's argument. As disgorgement is designed to equitably deprive those who have obtained ill-gotten gains of enrichment, it may be imposed upon innocent third parties who have received such ill-gotten funds and have no legitimate claim to them. That is consistent with disgorgement's remedial purpose – disgorgement is imposed not to punish, but to ensure illegal actions do not yield unwarranted enrichment even to innocent parties.

However, unjust enrichment may also be prevented by requiring the violator to disgorge the unjust enrichment he has procured for the third party. As our case law has indicated (and as our opinion here confirms), when third parties have benefitted from illegal activity, it is possible to seek disgorgement from the violator, even if that violator never controlled the funds. The logic of this, as more fully articulated [above], is that to fail to impose disgorgement on such violators would allow them to unjustly enrich their affiliates. Thus, ordering a violator to disgorge gain the violator never possessed does not operate to magnify penalties or offer an alternative to fines, but serves disgorgement's core remedial function of preventing unjust enrichment. District courts possess the equitable discretion to determine whether disgorgement liability should fall upon third parties or violators, a responsibility concordant with the district courts' broad discretion to assay disgorgement more generally.

Moreover, unlike disgorgement, which is a discretionary, equitable remedy, criminal forfeiture is mandatory, and a creature of statute. Thus, unlike the criminal forfeiture case, the district court's discretion in determining disgorgement is not confined by precise contours of statutory language, but rather serves the broader purposes of equity. There is nothing inequitable about requiring a person who created an unjust gain by fraudulently trading on material nonpublic information, and allocated that gain, for reasons of his own, to beneficiaries that he chose, to return that gain to the public by disgorging the illegal benefits he obtained and directed.

Therefore, the substantive distinctions between the liability imposed by the disgorgement remedy and the criminal forfeiture penalty, and the subsequently differing impacts on violators, reflect the diversity of corrective action necessary to enforce the securities regime. As forfeiture is punitive in nature, it would be irrational to impose it upon innocent third parties, whereas disgorgement's purpose – the prevention of unjust enrichment – would be thwarted if securities law violators were able to pass their illicit gains off to affiliates. To expect the same outcomes from legal concepts with such different characteristics is unrealistic, and Contorinis's efforts to analogize his criminal forfeiture penalty and disgorgement remedy are unavailing.

We therefore conclude that the district court did not abuse its discretion in requiring Contorinis to disgorge profits of $7,260,604 obtained by the Paragon Fund through his illegal insider trading.

DENNY CHIN, Circuit Judge, Dissenting:

In this case, the district court ordered defendant-appellant Joseph Contorinis to "disgorge" $7.2 million in "profits." The profits were not his, however, and the monies were never in his possession or control. Instead they were earned by the fund by which he was employed. The majority nonetheless affirms. I respectfully dissent, for the district court's order is, in my view, inconsistent with both the nature and purpose of disgorgement as well as our decision in the related criminal case, United States v. Contorinis, 692 F.3d 136 (2d Cir. 2012). * * *

Here, the district court ordered Contorinis to pay an amount substantially above what he acquired through his wrongdoing. The district court ordered him to disgorge funds he never had and to pay back profits he never received. Instead of returning Contorinis to his status quo prior to his wrongdoing, the district court's disgorgement order penalized him by requiring him to pay an amount equal to the $7.2 million in profits earned by the Fund and an additional $2.5 million in prejudgment interest.

Disgorgement, however, is not intended to be punitive; it is remedial in nature. As the district court's order had the effect of punishing Contorinis for his wrongdoing, it went beyond the permissible scope of disgorgement. While Contorinis undeniably deserved to be punished, disgorgement was not the proper mechanism to be used to impose that punishment.

The district court's disgorgement order is also inconsistent with our decision in the related criminal case. There, we held that Contorinis could not be required to forfeit profits that the Fund earned from his illegal use of inside information. Our holding rested on the principle that a defendant can be ordered to forfeit only the proceeds that he actually received or controlled. Because Contorinis never received or controlled the proceeds sought by the government, we concluded that Contorinis could not be ordered to forfeit those proceeds. Now, in this civil proceeding involving the same defendant, the same investment fund, and the same proceeds, the majority reaches the opposite result, holding that Contorinis must "disgorge" the Fund's profits and forfeit millions of dollars that he never received.

To be sure, as the majority discusses, there are differences between criminal forfeiture and civil disgorgement. But conceptually they are largely the same. We even used the terms together in *Contorinis* as we explained that: "Criminal forfeiture focuses on the disgorgement by a defendant of his ill-gotten gains." Both forfeiture and disgorgement seek to force a defendant to give up – that is, to forfeit or to disgorge – what he has wrongfully gained. Thus, we held that the district court had erred in ordering Contorinis "to forfeit funds that were never possessed or controlled by himself or others acting in concert with him."

Contorinis is also instructive with respect to the majority's reliance on the tipper-tippee cases that hold that "[a] tippee's gains are attributable to the tipper, regardless whether benefit accrues to the tipper." SEC v. Warde, 151 F.3d 42 (2d Cir.1998). We acknowledged in *Contorinis* that "a court may order a defendant to forfeit proceeds received by others who participated jointly in the crime, provided the actions generating those proceeds were reasonably foreseeable to the defendant." We observed that "[t]he extension of forfeiture to proceeds received by actors in concert with a defendant may be deemed to be based on the view that the proceeds of a crime jointly committed are within the possessory rights of each concerted actor." We concluded, however, that "[t]his view does not support an extension to a situation where the proceeds go directly to an innocent third party and are never possessed by the defendant." This reasoning applies with equal force here.

In the tipper-tippee situation, the tipper and tippee are concerted actors, jointly engaging in fraudulent activity – the tipper breaches a fiduciary duty by disclosing inside information; the tippee trades on that information, knowing of the breach and without disclosing what he knows; and the tipper obtains a direct or indirect personal benefit from the disclosure, such as a pecuniary gain or a reputational benefit that will translate into future earnings. A tipper can be held responsible for the tippee's profits because both joint actors are deemed to be in possession or control of the proceeds of their concerted activity.

We do not have a tipper-tippee relationship here. Contorinis was not a tipper. Nor is there any evidence that the Fund knew that Contorinis breached any duty when he made his investment decisions. As we concluded in the criminal case, the Fund did not act in concert with Contorinis in his criminal venture, and he never possessed or controlled its profits. Hence, the Fund's gains were not properly included in the disgorgement calculation.

NOTE

In **United States v. Bengis**, 783 F.3d 407 (2d Cir. 2015), the Second Circuit considered a restitution order following defendants' pleading guilty for activities related to illegally harvesting lobsters in South African waters that would be exported to United States. The defendants appealed the district court restitution order requiring them to pay $22,446,720 to South Africa. One of their arguments was that the "restitution order violated their Sixth Amendment rights." The Second Circuit held, "[r]estitution under the MVRA and VWPA has only one valuation—the amount of the victim's loss. There is no alternative maximum penalty. In sum, where, as here, there is no determinate statutory maximum that a district court can exceed, there is no range prescribed by statute and thus there can be no *Apprendi* violation." In affirming the judgment, the court found that "judicial factfinding to determine the appropriate amount of restitution under a statute that does not prescribe a maximum does not implicate a defendant's Sixth Amendment rights."

E. SENTENCING CORPORATIONS

1. Development of the Organizational Guidelines

Like an individual, an organization–such as Arthur Andersen–can be charged and convicted for violating the law. See supra Chapter 3. Chapter 8 of the Guidelines, effective November 1, 1991, covers Sentencing of Organizations. This Chapter reflects the view that organizations must be dealt with, in addition to their agents who can be prosecuted separately, to reach the goal of "just punishment, adequate deterrence, and incentives for organizations to maintain internal mechanisms for preventing, detecting, and reporting criminal conduct." Ch. 8, Introductory Commentary.

The Commission endorsed the following principles in establishing the Guidelines for organizational punishment:

a. Remedy any harm caused by the offense.

b. "If the organization operated primarily for a criminal purpose or primarily by criminal means, the fine should be set sufficiently high to divest the organization of all its assets."

c. Base the fine on the seriousness of the offense and the culpability of the organization. In determining organizational culpability, the Commission emphasized the importance of preventive steps taken by the organization to prevent misconduct: "Culpability generally will be determined by the steps taken by the organization prior to the offense to prevent and detect criminal conduct, the level and extent of involvement in or tolerance of the offense by certain personal, and the organization's actions after an offense has been committed."

d. Impose a probationary sentence on the organizational defendant when necessary to "ensure that another sanction will be fully implemented, or to ensure that steps will be taken within the organization to reduce the likelihood of future criminal conduct."

These principles lay out a very clear roadmap for an organization to follow *before* any criminal charges are even brought, to wit, implement a plan to prevent and detect criminal conduct.

Chapter 8 applies to felony and Class A misdemeanor offenses. The Commission sets forth General Application Principles and Remedies. The latter include restitution, remedial orders, community service, and notice to victims. The organizational Guidelines also provide directions for the sentencing judge to utilize in determining an appropriate fine. Significant factors for the court's utilization include the organization's culpability, prior history, violation of an order, obstruction of justice, whether it had an effective program to prevent and detect violations of law, and whether it engaged in self-reporting, cooperation, and acceptance of responsibility. Further, the Guidelines in §8C2.6 provide for "multipliers" to be applied to fines based on the organization's culpability.

As with the Guidelines applicable to individual defendants, Chapter 8 provides for "Departures [upward and downward] from the Guideline Fine Range" for:

a. Substantial assistance

b. Creating a Risk of Death or Bodily Injury

c. Threat to National Security

d. Threat to the Environment

e. Threat to a Market

f. Official corruption–payment to a public official

g. Whether or not the organization is a public entity

h. If members or beneficiaries of the organization, other than shareholders, are direct victims of the offense

i. If the remedial costs paid by the organization greatly exceed the organization's gain

j. If there is Exceptional Organizational Culpability

Finally, Chapter 8 deals with the circumstances under which a probationary sentence is required. A probationary sentence can include:

a. Making periodic submissions to the court;

b. Submitting to regular unannounced examinations of books or interrogations of individuals; and

c. Developing a program to prevent and detect further violations of law.

If probation is violated, the corporation could have more restrictive conditions imposed, or even have probation revoked and be resentenced.

2. "Encouraging" Cooperation

Can a corporation resist cooperating with the government when the guidelines provide concrete benefits by lowering the fines that will be imposed? Recall the Department of Justice's policy regarding charging corporations discussed in Chapter 3, supra, and the premium placed on cooperation in deciding whether to even charge a corporation with a criminal offense. Also consider the role of the corporate directors in deciding whether cooperation would be in the best interests of the corporation. See p. 86. In **In re Caremark International Inc. Derivative Litigation**, 698 A.2d 959 (Del. Ch. 1996), a Delaware Chancery Court Judge considered whether a corporations board of directors could fulfill their fiduciary duty to the corporation by not informing themselves about actual or potential corporate wrongdoing and then cooperate with the government if such misconduct occurred. The court stated:

> Can it be said today that, absent some ground giving rise to suspicion of violation of law, that corporate directors have no duty to assure that a corporate information gathering and reporting systems exists which represents a good faith attempt to provide senior management and the Board with information respecting

> material acts, events or conditions within the corporation, including compliance with applicable statutes and regulations? I certainly do not believe so. I doubt that such a broad generalization of the *Graham* [*v. Allis-Chalmers*] holding would have been accepted by the Supreme Court in 1963. The case can be more narrowly interpreted as standing for the proposition that, absent grounds to suspect deception, neither corporate boards nor senior officers can be charged with wrongdoing simply for assuming the integrity of employees and the honesty of their dealings on the company's behalf. A broader interpretation of Graham v. Allis-Chalmers–that it means that a corporate board has no responsibility to assure that appropriate information and reporting systems are established by management–would not, in any event, be accepted by the Delaware Supreme Court in 1996, in my opinion. In stating the basis for this view, I start with the recognition that in recent years the Delaware Supreme Court has made it clear–especially in its jurisprudence concerning takeovers * * * . Secondly, I note the elementary fact that relevant and timely information is an essential predicate for satisfaction of the board's supervisory and monitoring role under Section 141 of the Delaware General Corporation Law. Thirdly, I note the potential impact of the federal organizational sentencing guidelines on any business organization. Any rational person attempting in good faith to meet an organizational governance responsibility would be bound to take into account this development and the enhanced penalties and the opportunities for reduced sanctions that it offers.

Consider Professor William S. Laufer's analysis of the pressure on corporations to cooperate with the government's investigation in his article *Corporate Prosecution, Cooperation, and the Trading of Favors*, 87 Iowa L. Rev. 643 (2002):

> Congress approved the Sentencing Guidelines at a time of increasing dissatisfaction with the command and control strategies of corporate regulation. Theories of cooperative regulation, co-regulation, enforced self-regulation, and negotiated compliance had developed, and the Commission and regulators were ready to implement mixed regulatory strategies. Drafters of the Sentencing Guidelines wanted corporations to face the threat of significant punishment and, at the same time, the possibility of mitigation, leniency, and amnesty. In the ideal, the objective was to construct regulatory strategy at once both provokable and forgiving.
>
> The Sentencing Guidelines became * * * the centerpiece of a dynamic enforcement game backed by a "tall enforcement pyramid." Voluntary corporate compliance under the Sentencing Guidelines is achieved through the old carrot and stick trope. Understandably, this approach earned praise for encouraging businesses to join the government in the battle against corporate crime. Good corporate

citizenship that institutionalizes ethics and sound compliance practices minimizes corporate deviance. When wayward employees are identified, the Sentencing Guidelines reward post-offense corporate cooperation, strong internal disciplinary action, and the organization's acceptance of responsibility. Recently released prosecutorial guidelines for corporations ("Prosecutorial Guidelines") extend this valuable partnership to charging decisions and plea negotiations and address concerns that the Sentencing Guidelines shift discretion from judges to prosecutors.

Both Guidelines translate into reciprocal promises–organizational cooperation and acceptance of responsibility in exchange for mitigation, exculpation, or absolution. This bargained-for exchange, or trading of favors, with an arsenal of sanctions in the background, is a decision template for prosecutors and judges in cases of corporate crime. With the threat of significant Guideline-prescribed fines, corporations have little choice but to trade favors with authorities. The importance of and need for these reciprocal promises is rarely challenged. Given extremely limited resources, the complex nature of the corporate form, and the accompanying evidentiary challenges facing prosecutors, it is little wonder that the government often exchanges leniency for conciliatory post-offense behavior. Strict enforcement, sanctioning, or deterrent styles of regulation focusing on criminalization and prosecution have long been recognized as significantly inhibiting corporate cooperation by keeping control of information and incriminating evidence in the hands of the regulated rather than the regulator. If anything, this promotes gaming by organizations and, according to some commentators, encourages law evasion and deviance.

To free the hand of regulators and prosecutors and minimize the costs of compliance, reciprocity and negotiated forbearance are now preferred strategies. Substantial assistance departures and mitigation credits, as well as voluntary disclosure, leniency, and amnesty programs, dot the enforcement and regulatory landscape. In theory, the substantive corporate criminal law is ruled by principles of vicarious liability that stretch back to rules articulated in *New York Central & Hudson River Railroad Co. v. United States*. [p. 51]. In practice, cases of corporate crime are adjudicated by a brand of negotiated compliance. Corporate cooperation that facilitates the flow of evidence to authorities is the critical feature of this regulatory strategy.

3. Corporate Compliance Programs

A key issue in cases involving corporate criminal liability is whether the company had a compliance program in place that could reasonably be expected to detect violations. While no such program is perfect, the government looks at the company's commitment to its compliance measures in assessing whether to file charges and what potential penalty might be assessed, if any, for a violation. A key issue is whether the company came forward to report itself, and the extent of its cooperation. The evaluation of a compliance program is discussed in a publication of the Department of Justice and the Securities and Exchange Commission, *A Resource Guide to the U.S. Foreign Corrupt Practices Act*:

> In a global marketplace, an effective compliance program is a critical component of a company's internal controls and is essential to detecting and preventing FCPA violations. Effective compliance programs are tailored to the company's specific business and to the risks associated with that business. They are dynamic and evolve as the business and the markets change.
>
> An effective compliance program promotes "an organizational culture that encourages ethical conduct and a commitment to compliance with the law." Such a program protects a company's reputation, ensures investor value and confidence, reduces uncertainty in business transactions, and secures a company's assets. A well-constructed, thoughtfully implemented, and consistently enforced compliance and ethics program helps prevent, detect, remediate, and report misconduct, including FCPA violations.
>
> In addition to considering whether a company has self-reported, cooperated, and taken appropriate remedial actions, DOJ and SEC also consider the adequacy of a company's compliance program when deciding what, if any, action to take. The program may influence whether or not charges should be resolved through a deferred prosecution agreement (DPA) or non-prosecution agreement (NPA), as well as the appropriate length of any DPA or NPA, or the term of corporate probation. It will often affect the penalty amount and the need for a monitor or self-reporting. [The] SEC's Seaboard Report focuses, among other things, on a company's self-policing prior to the discovery of the misconduct, including whether it had established effective compliance procedures. Likewise, three of the nine factors set forth in DOJ's Principles of Federal Prosecution of Business Organizations relate, either directly or indirectly, to a compliance program's design and implementation, including the pervasiveness of wrongdoing within the company, the existence and effectiveness of the company's pre-existing compliance program, and the company's remedial actions. DOJ also considers the U.S. Sentencing Guidelines' elements of an effective compliance program, as set forth in § 8B2.1 of the Guidelines.
>
> These considerations reflect the recognition that a company's failure to prevent every single violation does not necessarily mean that a particular company's compliance program was not generally effective. DOJ and SEC understand that "no compliance program can

> ever prevent all criminal activity by a corporation's employees," and they do not hold companies to a standard of perfection. An assessment of a company's compliance program, including its design and good faith implementation and enforcement, is an important part of the government's assessment of whether a violation occurred, and if so, what action should be taken. In appropriate circumstances, DOJ and SEC may decline to pursue charges against a company based on the company's effective compliance program, or may otherwise seek to reward a company for its program, even when that program did not prevent the particular underlying FCPA violation that gave rise to the investigation.
>
> DOJ and SEC have no formulaic requirements regarding compliance programs. Rather, they employ a common-sense and pragmatic approach to evaluating compliance programs, making inquiries related to three basic questions:
>
> - Is the company's compliance program well designed?
> - Is it being applied in good faith?
> - Does it work?

4. Determining the Fine

Organizations convicted of an offense are subject to a fine and probation, but cannot be sentenced to a term of imprisonment. The Sentencing Guidelines adopted a system for determining the applicable range for a fine that may be imposed on an organization that is similar to the sentencing for an individual. The starting point is the determination of the base offense level, and then consideration of the size of the organization, the level of involvement of senior officers, and the cooperation of the organization in the government's investigation. The results in a "Culpability Score," which provides a multiplier for the fine that may be imposed. The multiplier ranges from .05 to 2.0, depending on the Culpability Score, as explained by Professor Michael A. Simons in his article, *Vicarious Snitching: Crime, Cooperation, and "Good Corporate Citizenship,"* 76 ST. JOHN'S L. REV. 979 (2002):

> Under the Organizational Sentencing Guidelines, a corporation's sentence–like an individual's sentence–is "based on the seriousness of the offense and the culpability of the organization." The seriousness of the offense is typically determined either by the economic impact of the crime (i.e., the loss to the victim or the gain to the offender) or by reference to the "offense levels" in the individual sentencing guidelines.
>
> This calculation will yield the corporation's "base fine," which is then adjusted up or down based upon the corporation's "culpability score."

The culpability score is determined by a mathematical calculation based on the following factors: (1) whether the organization's top management "participated in, condoned, or was willfully ignorant of the offense"; (2) whether "tolerance" of the offense by middle management was "pervasive throughout the organization"; (3) whether the organization has a history of criminal convictions or regulatory violations; (4) whether the organization obstructed justice or violated specific court orders; (5) whether the organization had in place "an effective program to prevent and detect violations of law"; (6) whether the organization reported the offense prior to any imminent threat of disclosure or government investigation; (7) whether the organization "fully cooperated in the investigation"; and (8) whether the organization "demonstrated recognition and affirmative acceptance of responsibility for its criminal conduct." A corporation with a high culpability score could see its fine increased by up to 400%, while a corporation with a low culpability score could see its fine cut by up to 95%.

NOTE

Ability to Pay Fine. Issues regarding the ability to pay the fine, and the terms of its payment, can be contested in the sentencing of a corporation. In **United States v. Electrodyne Systems Corp.**, 147 F.3d 250 (3d Cir. 1998), the court considered a company's ability to pay a fine and vacated and remanded the district court's ruling "with instructions to make factual findings on both the ability to pay a fine and the time within which the fine can be paid." Senior District Judge Schwartz stated:

> We do not believe the district judge must be a puppet dancing to whatever financial disclosure strings a defendant corporation wishes to pull. We can think of no reason why the district judge does not have the power to require production of necessary financial documents so as to have a basis in fact for any fine which is to be imposed. Should the defendant corporation fail to produce financial documentation requested by the probation office and/or the court, the necessity for the district judge to have a basis in fact for establishing the amount of fine is reduced. Similarly, the sentencing judge is not controlled by, but may accept, a fine amount negotiated by the corporate defendant and the government. If the judge accepts the negotiated fine, no detailed finding of ability to pay is necessary because the defendant has implicitly acknowledged its ability by virtue of the agreement.
>
> Section 3572(a)(1) of Title 18 of the United States Code mandates that when a court imposes a fine and determines "the amount, time for payment and method of payment," the court must consider, inter alia, "the defendant's income, ensuring capacity and financial resources." Further, it is well settled in this circuit that "[t]he district court must make findings regarding a defendant's ability to

> pay a fine." United States v. Seale, 20 F.3d 1279 (3d Cir. 1994). "Where the court has created enough of a factual record that it is clear that it considered a defendant's ability to pay, its findings may be deemed adequate." Here the district judge failed to make any findings pertaining to imposition of a fine without factual findings there can be no meaningful appellate review. * * *

Criminal fines may still be required even if the company goes into bankruptcy, dissolves, or transfers the company to new owners. See p. 66.

5. Corporate and Individual Liability

To what extent should the potential liability of individual agents and officers affect the court's decision to accept a plea bargain by the organization? Should corporate liability be a substitute for prosecuting individuals? Should penalties imposed on the company mitigate whether there are any individual officer's liability?

UNITED STATES v. PURDUE FEDERICK CO., INC.

495 F.Supp. 2d 569 (W.D. Va. 2007)

JONES, Chief Judge.

The issue before the court is whether or not to accept the plea agreements in this case.

The Purdue Frederick Company, Inc. has pleaded guilty to misbranding OxyContin, a prescription opiod pain medication, with the intent to defraud or mislead, a felony under the federal Food, Drug, and Cosmetic Act. 21 U.S.C.A. §§ 331(a), 333(a)(2). The individual defendants, Michael Friedman, Howard R. Udell, and Paul D. Goldenheim, have pleaded guilty to the misdemeanor charge of misbranding, solely as responsible corporate officers. [Friedman is the former president and CEO of Purdue, Udell is the executive vice president and chief legal officer, and Goldenheim is the former chief scientific officer.] The individual defendants are not charged with personal knowledge of the misbranding or with any personal intent to defraud.

The Information in this case charges, among other things, that

> [b]eginning on or about December 12, 1995, and continuing until on or about June 30, 2001, certain PURDUE supervisors and employees, with the intent to defraud or mislead, marketed and promoted OxyContin as less addictive, less subject to abuse and diversion, and less likely to cause tolerance and withdrawal than other pain medications as follows:

a. Trained PURDUE sales representatives and told some health care providers that it was more difficult to extract the oxycodone from an OxyContin tablet for the purpose of intravenous abuse, although PURDUE's own study showed that a drug abuser could extract approximately 68% of the oxycodone from a single 10mg OxyContin tablet by crushing the tablet, stirring it in water, and drawing the solution through cotton into a syringe;

b. Told PURDUE sales representatives they could tell health care providers that OxyContin potentially creates less chance for addiction than immediate-release opioids;

c. Sponsored training that taught PURDUE sales supervisors that OxyContin had fewer "peak and trough" blood level effects than immediate-release opioids resulting in less euphoria and less potential for abuse than short-acting opioids;

d. Told certain health care providers that patients could stop therapy abruptly without experiencing withdrawal symptoms and that patients who took OxyContin would not develop tolerance to the drug; and

e. Told certain health care providers that OxyContin did not cause a "buzz" or euphoria, caused less euphoria, had less addiction potential, had less abuse potential, was less likely to be diverted than immediate-release opioids, and could be used to "weed out" addicts and drug seekers.

Purdue has agreed that these facts are true, and the individual defendants, while they do not agree that they had knowledge of these things, have agreed that the court may accept these facts in support of their guilty pleas.

The plea agreements have been submitted pursuant to Federal Rule of Criminal Procedure 11(c)(1)(C), which allows the parties to agree to a specific sentence to be imposed. The court is not bound by the plea agreements, and may reject them. If a plea agreement is rejected, that defendant must be given an opportunity to withdraw the guilty plea. Fed.R.Crim.P. 11(c)(5)(B). The government has agreed in this case that if the court rejects any of the plea agreements, the government will dismiss the Information filed in the case, without prejudice to the government's right to later indict the defendants or any other entity or individual on any charge. Accordingly, if the court rejects any of the plea agreements, the present case may end, and it will be up to the government to decide whether to re-prosecute the defendants, or any of them. * * *

Rule 11 explicitly states that a court cannot accept a plea if it is not supported by the factual record or if the court believes that that the plea is not voluntary. But Rule 11 also allows a district judge to reject a plea agreement if it is too lenient or too harsh.

In determining the proper criminal sentence, the court must consider certain factors set forth by statute. I must consider "the nature and circumstances of the offense and the history and characteristics of the defendant," as well as

> the need for the sentence imposed (A) to reflect the seriousness of the offense, to promote respect for the law, and to provide just punishment for the offense; (B) to afford adequate deterrence to criminal conduct; (C) to protect the public from further crimes of the defendant; and (D) to provide the defendant with needed educational or vocational training, medical care, or other correctional treatment in the most effective manner.

18 U.S.C.A. § 3553(a). The court's obligation is to impose "a sentence sufficient, but not greater than necessary, to comply with" these purposes.

Under the law, Purdue is subject to a penalty of five years probation and a fine of up to $500,000. In its plea agreement, Purdue has agreed to substantial additional monetary sanctions totaling $600 million, reported to be one of the largest in the history of the pharmaceutical industry. The amount includes the following:

1. $100,615,797.25 payable to federal government health care agencies under a Civil Settlement Agreement;

2. $59,384,202.75 in escrow for those states that elect to settle their claims against Purdue. These civil settlements to the federal and state government total $160 million, of which the federal government is receiving sixty percent;

3. $3,471,220.68 to Medicaid programs for improperly calculated rebates;

4. $500,000 fine to the United States;

5. $20 million in trust to the Commonwealth of Virginia for operating the Virginia Prescription Monitoring Program;

6. $5.3 million to the Virginia Medicaid Fraud Control Unit's Program Income Fund;

7. $276.1 million forfeiture to the United States;

8. $130 million to settle private civil claims related to OxyContin; and

9. $4,628,779.32 to be expended by Purdue for monitoring costs in connection with a Corporate Integrity Agreement with the U.S. Department of Health and Human Services.

The individual defendants are subject to a punishment of twelve months imprisonment and a fine of up to $100,000. In their plea agreements, they have agreed to pay a total of $34.5 million to the Virginia Medicaid Fraud Unit's Program Income Fund. [Defendant Friedman has agreed to pay $19 million, whereas defendants Udell and Goldenheim have agreed to pay $8 million and $7.5 million, respectively.] In return, the government has agreed to sentences for them without any imprisonment.

There have been several reasons suggested why the court should reject the plea agreements.

Lack of Restitution. The plea agreements preclude restitution other than as set forth in the agreements and a number of alleged victims object to this provision, contending that the amounts allocated to private parties are insufficient, compared to the recovery by governmental victims. BlueCross BlueShield of Tennessee has filed a Request for Notice, an Opportunity to be Heard at Sentencing, and an Order of Restitution. Other third-party health care payors have joined in this motion. In addition, an individual who considers herself a victim because of her addiction to OxyContin has objected to the plea agreements and has filed a formal Motion to Assert Victim's Rights, in which she complains about restitution, as well as other matters.

These parties have received notice of this present proceedings and the court has allow them an opportunity to speak.

The government and the defendants, in agreeing to preclude other restitution, rely on the Victim and Witness Protection Act of 1982, which states in relevant part as follows:

> To the extent that the court determines that the complication and prolongation of the sentencing process resulting from the fashioning of an order of restitution under this section outweighs the need to provide restitution to any victims, the court may decline to make such an order.

18 U.S.C.A. § 3663(a)(1)(B)(ii).

In order to award an alleged victim restitution under either the VWPA or the MVRA, the court would have to determine whether that person was "directly and proximately" harmed by the misbranding offense that was the subject of the plea agreements. The Fourth Circuit has held that to be considered "directly and proximately harmed" under either the VWPA or the MVRA, a person must show that the harm resulted from "conduct underlying an element of the offense of conviction." United States v. Blake, 81 F.3d 498 (4th Cir.1996).

Purdue argues that third-party payors cannot show that they were directly and proximately harmed by Purdue's misbranding, unless they can prove the following:

> 1. That a Purdue sales representative misstated to a specific prescribing physician that OxyContin was less addictive, less subject to abuse and diversion, or less likely to cause tolerance or withdrawal than other pain medications;
>
> 2. That specific prescribing physician relied upon that misstatement by that Purdue sales representative and, in reliance on that misstatement, prescribed OxyContin rather than an alternative pain medication (e.g. Percocet) for one of the private third-party payor's insured individuals;
>
> 3. That the physician prescribed OxyContin for the insured because of the misstatement and not because of the other attributes of OxyContin (e.g., twelve-hour dosing or the absence of acetaminophen, which risks liver toxicity);
>
> 4. That the private third-party payor paid for that prescription of OxyContin; and
>
> 5. That the private third-party payor paid more for the OxyContin prescription than the particular alternative pain medication that the prescribing physician would have prescribed if he or she had not relied on the misstatement and prescribed OxyContin.

Purdue further argues that the chain of causation between the harm alleged and the misbranding offense could have been broken by any intervening act on behalf of the insured patient or the prescribing health care professional. For example, if patients obtained OxyContin improperly by deceiving their physicians or by altering an otherwise proper prescription, the third-party payors would not be entitled to restitution for those prescriptions since the misbranding did not directly and proximately caused any financial loss to the third-party payor. Or if a physician negligently prescribed OxyContin, the third-party payor that paid for that prescription is also not entitled to restitution because the misbranding once again did not directly and proximately cause the third-party payor's financial loss.

Even if third-party payors can show that they were directly harmed by Purdue's misbranding, Purdue claims that each payor would have to present to this court the facts of every instance of overpayment in order for the Court to determine the proper amount of restitution for each third-party payor.

As to any individuals injured by the use of OxyContin, the difficulties of establishing causation are demonstrated by the numerous civil suits that have been filed by such persons against Purdue, including two before this court. Courts have consistently found that despite extensive discovery, plaintiffs were unable to show that Purdue's misbranding proximately caused their injuries.

It is argued that restitution might be handled in this case as with a civil class action claim, but class certification has been generally denied in OxyContin claims because of the variety of causation issues.

It is true that the governmental health care providers have been allotted a portion of Purdue's payment in settlement of their civil claims for the misbranding of OxyContin ($160 million) that is greater than the portion to be used by Purdue to settle private claims ($130 million). However, Purdue's liability for private claims is not capped by the plea agreements. Purdue agrees to pay at least $130 million to settle private claims, but no maximum limit is imposed. I do not find that the plea agreements are inherently unfair in this regard.

Accordingly, in spite of the arguments by putative victims, I agree that the restitution process would unduly complicate and prolong the sentencing process. In order to prove causation, litigation over many months, if not years, would be required before final judgment in this case could be entered. Such delay would be contrary to the basic principles of our criminal justice system.

I would have preferred that the plea agreements had allocated some amount of the money for the education of those at risk from the improper use of prescription drugs, and the treatment of those who have succumbed to such use. Prescription drug abuse is rampant in all areas of our country, particularly among young people, causing untold misery and harm. The White House drug policy office estimates that such abuse rose seventeen percent from 2001 to 2005. That office reports that currently there are more new abusers of prescription drugs than new users of any illicit drugs. As recently reported, "Young people mistakenly believe prescription drugs are safer than street drugs ... but accidental prescription drug deaths are rising and students who abuse pills are more likely to drive fast, binge-drink and engage in other dangerous behaviors." Carla K. Johnson, Arrest Puts Spotlight on Prescription Drug Abuse, The Roanoke Times, July 6, 2007, at 4A. It has been estimated that there are more than 6.4 million prescription drug abusers in the United States.

On the other hand, I am forbidden by law to participate in plea discussions, Fed.R.Crim.P. 11(c)(1), and I will not reject these agreements simply because they do not contain provisions that I would have preferred. The government has represented that it did not demand inclusion of a treatment provision in the plea agreements because national drug policy has been placed by Congress in the Substance Abuse and Mental Health Service Administration, an agency of the U.S. Department of Health and Human Services. The government prosecutors were reluctant to direct treatment funds in a manner beyond their expertise and possibly contrary to national policy. I will not second-guess their decision in this regard.

Political Interference. It has been suggested that Purdue may have received a favorable deal from the government solely because of politics.

I completely reject this claim. I have had long experience with the United States Attorney for this district, and I am convinced that neither he nor the career prosecutors who handled this case would have permitted any political interference. In fact, I am sure that they would have refused to accept a plea agreement that they did not sincerely feel was in the best interests of justice.

Lack of Incarceration. The plea agreements provide for no incarceration for the individual defendants. The government points out that a sentence of incarceration under the federal sentencing guidelines would be unusual based on the facts of the case. The government is also convinced that the nature of the convictions of the individual defendants-based on strict liability for misbranding-will send a strong deterrent message to the pharmaceutical industry. The defendants point to their lack of prior criminal record, their strong commitment to civic and charitable endeavors, as well as their other positive personal attributes. On the other hand, the potential damage by the misbranding disclosed in this case was substantial and I do not minimize the danger to the public from this crime. The defendants voluntarily accepted responsibility over this business enterprise, for which they were generously rewarded. However, while the question is a close one, I find that in the absence of government proof of knowledge by the individual defendants of the wrongdoing, prison sentences are not appropriate.

Summary. In summary, I find that the plea agreements are supported by the facts and the law and impose adequate punishment on the defendants and I accept them.

NOTE AND QUESTIONS

Deferred Prosecution Agreements. Corporations routinely enter into deferred prosecution agreements (DPA) with the government that allow for the corporation to continue its business. Many of these agreements require the corporation to provide information to the government concerning culpable individuals in the company. Deferred and non-prosecution agreements frequently include a provision on fines, civil penalties, and restitution. When the agreement is a non-prosecution agreement (NPA), there is no judicial oversight unless there is a later breach of the agreement. Thus the determination of the amount of the fine is negotiated between the company and the Department of Justice and the parties do not present the agreement to the court. See Chapter 3, part 5. When the agreement is a deferred prosecution agreement (DPA), however, the agreement is presented to the court. Recently, some courts have questioned whether the fine is sufficient and in the process rejected a DPA agreed upon by the parties. For example, in **United States v. Fokker Services B.V.**, 2015 WL 729291 (D.C. D.C. 2015), appeal pending, the district court rejected a deferred prosecution agreement stating:

> * * * Fokker Services is charged with a five-year conspiracy to violate and evade United States export laws for the benefit, largely, of Iran and its military during the post- 9/11 world when we were engaged in a two-front War against terror in the Middle East. These voluminous violations during that period were knowing and willful, and were orchestrated at the highest levels of the company. The company brought in $21 million in revenue from these illegal transactions of parts that were being excluded from sale to these particular countries for national security and anti-terrorism reasons. Indeed, the majority of Fokker Services' illegal conduct involved sales of aviation and avionic parts to Iran.
>
> Notwithstanding this egregious conduct over a sustained period of time, the Government has agreed to dismiss the Information if Fokker Services pays a fine of $10.5 million, cooperates with the Government, implements its compliance program, and complies with U.S. export laws for only eighteen months. As such, even when combined with penalties it must pay to other U.S. regulatory agencies as part of a global settlement on these issues, the Government is not requiring Fokker Services to pay as its fine a penny more than the $21 million in revenue it collected from its illegal transactions. * * *
>
> While I do not discount Fokker Services' cooperation and voluntary disclosure or, for that matter, its precarious financial situation, after looking at the DPA in its totality, I cannot help but conclude that the DPA presented here is grossly disproportionate to the gravity of Fokker Services' conduct in a post-9/11 world. In my judgment, it would undermine the public's confidence in the administration of justice and promote disrespect for the law for it to see a defendant prosecuted so anemically for engaging in such egregious conduct for such a sustained period of time and for the benefit of one of our country's worst enemies. Surely one would expect, at a minimum, a fine that exceeded the amount of revenue generated, a probationary period longer than 18 months, and a monitor trusted by the Court to verify for it and the Government both that this rogue company truly is on the path to complete compliance. As such, the Court concludes that this agreement does not constitute an appropriate exercise of prosecutorial discretion and I cannot approve it in its current form.

Should courts scrutinize government agreements with corporations? How much weight should be given for having a strong compliance program, cooperation, the financial stability of the company, or the importance of the company to national security?

INDEX

References are to Pages